Decision Applications	Companies in Assignments
You Make the Call: You are a Product Manager **You Make the Call:** You are a Financial Analyst **You Make the Call:** You are a Shareholder **You Make the Call:** You are a Chief Financial Officer **You Make the Call:** You are a CEO **You Make the Call:** You are a Member of the Board of Directors	Abercrombie & Fitch, Berkshire Hathaway, Briggs & Stratton, Cisco, Colgate-Palmolive, Dell, DuPont, Enron, Ford, General Mills, General Motor, Ford, Hewlett-Packard, Intel, JetBlue, Kimberly-Clark, Kraft, McDonald's, Merck, Motorola, Nokia, Nordstrom, Procter & Gamble, Wal-Mart, Walt Disney, Winn-Dixie
You Make the Call: You are an Operations Manager **You Make the Call:** You are an Analyst	Abercrombie & Fitch, Albertsons, Briggs & Stratton, Harley-Davidson, Johnson & Johnson, Kimberly-Clark, Microsoft, Nike, Nordstrom, Procter & Gamble, Starbucks, Target, 3M, World Wrestling Entertainment, YUM! Brands
You Make the Call: You are the Chief Accountant **You Make the Call:** You are the Bank Loan Officer **You Make the Call:** You are the Auditor	Barnes & Noble, Dick's Sporting Goods, Eli Lilly, Ethan Allen, Hartford Insurance, J. Jill Group, Kimberly-Clark, Pacific Sunwear, Pfizer, Walgreen, Winnebago, Zale
You Make the Call: You are a Business Consultant **You Make the Call:** You are the Securities Analyst **You Make the Call:** You are the Chief Accountant	Acushnet, Aldila, Amgen, Borders, Callaway, Campbell Soup, Columbia Sportswear, Dole, Ethan Allen, Lowe's, Nordstrom, Oakley, Pacific Sunwear, Ping, Robert Mondavi, Staples, Target, TaylorMade
You Make the Call: You are a Business Reporter **You Make the Call:** You are the Entrepreneur	Abercrombie & Fitch, Albertsons, Alcoa, Caterpillar, Coca-Cola, Colgate-Palmolive, CVS, The Gap, Harley-Davidson, Home Depot, Kroger, McDonald's, Merck, Nike, PepsiCo, Procter & Gamble, Reebok, SBC Communications, Southwest Airlines, Target, Toys-R-Us, Wal-Mart, Walt Disney, Walgreen
You Make the Call: You are the Bank Loan Officer	Abbott Laboratories, Colgate-Palmolive, Ford, General Motors, Gibson Greetings, Gillette, Hon Industries, Merck, Pfizer, Procter & Gamble, Toys-R-Us, Verizon, Viacom, Wal-Mart, Walt Disney
You Make the Call: You are the Controller **You Make the Call:** You are a Financial Analyst	Abbott Laboratories, Abercrombie & Fitch, Agilent Technologies, Albertsons, Altria, Amazon.com, AOL Time-Warner, Bank of America, BannerAd Corporation, Boeing, Dell, Dow Chemical, eBay, Ethen Allen, FedEx, The Gap, General Electric, Harley-Davidson, Hewlett-Packard, Honeywell International, Intuit, John Deere, Johnson Controls, The Limited, Miller Brewing, Merck, MTV, Nike, Oracle, PepsiCo, Pfizer, Real Money.Com, The Street.Com, 3M, Time-Warner, Viacom, Xerox
You Make the Call: You are the Receivables Manager **You Make the Call:** You are the Plant Manager **You Make the Call:** You are the Division Manager	Abbott Laboratories, AOL Time-Warner, Best Buy, Carnival, Caterpillar, Colgate-Palmolive, Deere & Company, Ethan Allen, General Electric, Harley-Davidson, Hewlett-Packard, Hormel Foods, Intel, Kaiser Aluminum, Kmart, Kraft Foods, Microsoft, Oakley, Oracle, Procter & Gamble, Rohm & Haas, Sears, Sharper Image, Stride Rite, 3M, Texas Instruments, Whole Foods Market, WW Grainger
You Make the Call: You are the Company Lawyer **You Make the Call:** You are the Division Manager **You Make the Call:** You are a Financial Analyst	Abbott Laboratories, Abercrombie & Fitch, Addams Golf, Advanced Medical Optics, Agilent, American Express, Apple, Baxter International, Best Buy, Callaway Golf, Deere & Company, Dell, Dow Chemical, FedEx, General Motors, Hewlett-Packard, Intel, Merck, Motorola, Nordstrom, Pfizer, Robert Mondavi, Rohm & Haas, Southwest Airlines, Staples, Target, 3M, Texas Instruments, Williams-Sonoma
You Make the Call: You are the Analyst **You Make the Call:** You are the Vice President of Finance	Abbott Laboratories, AT&T, Boston Scientific, Bristol-Myers Squibb, Comcast, CVS, Fitch Ratings LTD, General Mills, International Paper, Lockheed Martin, Southwest Airlines
You Make the Call: You are the Chief Financial Officer **You Make the Call:** You are the CEO	Abercrombie & Fitch, Altria, AT&T, Bristol-Myers Squibb, Caterpillar, Cisco Systems, IMS Health, JetBlue Airways, Lucent, Merck, Procter & Gamble, 3M, Viacom
You Make the Call: You are the Chief Financial Officer	Abbott Laboratories, American Express, Amgen, Berkshire Hathaway, Caterpillar, General Mills, Gillette, Shin Caterpillar Mitsu
You Make the Call: You are the Division President	Abercrombie & Fitch, Stratton, Dow Chemi, Oakley, Outback Stea, Staples, Target, Verizon, Xerox,

Financial Accounting

THOMAS R. DYCKMAN
Cornell University

PETER D. EASTON
University of Notre Dame

GLENN M. PFEIFFER
Chapman University

Cambridge
BUSINESS PUBLISHERS

To my wife, Ann, and children, Daniel, James, Linda, and David; and to
Pete Dukes, a friend who is always there.
　　—TRD

To my daughters, Joanne and Stacey
　　—PDE

To my wife, Kathie, and my daughter, Jaclyn
　　—GMP

Cambridge Business Publishers

FINANCIAL ACCOUNTING, First Edition, by Thomas R. Dyckman,
Peter D. Easton, and Glenn M. Pfeiffer.

ISBN 0-9759701-8-6

To order this book, contact the company via email **customerservice@cambridgepub.com**
or call 800-619-6473.

For permission to use material from this text, contact the company via email
permissions@cambridgepub.com.

Printed in the United States of America
10 9 8 7 6 5 4 3 2 1

T he combined skills and expertise of Dyckman, Easton, and Pfeiffer create the ideal team to author this exciting, new financial accounting textbook. Their combined experience in award-winning teaching, consulting, and research in the area of financial accounting and analysis provides a powerful foundation for this pioneering textbook.

Thomas R. Dyckman is Ann Whitney Olin Professor of Accounting and Quantitative Analysis and Associate Dean for Academic Affairs at Cornell University's Johnson Graduate School of Management. In addition to teaching accounting and quantitative analysis, he has taught in Cornell's Executive Development Program. He earned his doctorate degree from the University of Michigan. He is a former member of the Financial Accounting Standards Board Advisory Committee and the Financial Accounting Foundation, which oversees the FASB. He was president of the American Accounting Association in 1982 and received the association's *Outstanding Educator* Award for the year 1987. He also received the AICPA's *Notable Contributions to Accounting Literature Award* in 1966 and 1977.

Professor Dyckman has extensive industrial experience that includes work with the U.S. Navy and IBM. He has conducted seminars for Cornell Executive Development Program and Managing the Next Generation of Technology, as well as for Ocean Spray, Goodyear, Morgan Guaranty, GTE, Southern New England Telephone, and Goulds Pumps.

Professor Dyckman has coauthored eleven books and written over 50 journal articles on topics from financial markets to the application of quantitative and behavioral theory to administrative decision making. He has been a member of the editorial boards of *The Accounting Review, The Journal of Finance and Quantitative Analysis, The Journal of Accounting and Economics, The Journal of Management Accounting Research,* and *The Journal of Accounting Education.*

Peter D. Easton is an expert in accounting and valuation and holds the Notre Dame Alumni Chair in Accountancy in the Mendoza College of Business. Professor Easton's expertise is widely recognized by the academic research community and by the legal community. Professor Easton has been qualified as an expert witness in the Delaware Chancery Court and he has consulted on valuation issues for investment firms and accounting firms in Australia, the UK, and the USA.

Professor Easton holds undergraduate degrees from the University of Adelaide and the University of South Australia. He holds a graduate degree from the University of New England and a PhD in Business Administration (majoring in accounting and finance) from the University of California, Berkeley.

Professor Easton's research on corporate valuation has been published in the *Journal of Accounting and Economics, Journal of Accounting Research, The Accounting Review, Contemporary Accounting Research, Review of Accounting Studies, and Journal of Business Finance* and *Accounting.* Professor Easton has served as an associate editor for 11 leading accounting journals and he is currently an associate editor for the *Journal of Accounting Research, Contemporary Accounting Research, Journal of Business Finance and Accounting,* and *Journal of Accounting, Auditing, and Finance.* He is an editor of the *Review of Accounting Studies.*

Professor Easton has held appointments at the University of Chicago, the University of California at Berkeley, Ohio State University, Macquarie University, the Australian Graduate School of Management, the University of Melbourne, and Nyenrode University. He is the recipient of numerous awards for excellence in teaching and in research. Professor Easton regularly teaches accounting analysis and security valuation. In addition, Professor Easton has taught managerial accounting at the graduate level.

Glenn M. Pfeiffer is Professor of Accounting at the George L. Argyros School of Business and Economics at Chapman University. He received his M.S. and Ph.D. from Cornell University after he earned a bachelors degree from Hope College. Prior to joining the faculty at the Argyros School, he held appointments at the University of Washington, Cornell University, the University of Chicago, the University of Arizona, and San Diego State University.

Professor Pfeiffer's research focuses on financial reporting and capital markets. He has investigated issues relating to lease accounting, LIFO inventory liquidation, earnings per share, employee stock options, corporate reorganization, and technology investments. He has published articles in *The Accounting Review*, the *Financial Analysts Journal*, the *International Journal of Accounting Information Systems*, the *Journal of Applied Business Research*, the *Journal of High Technology Management Research*, the *Journal of Accounting Education*, and several other academic journals. In addition, he has published numerous case studies in financial accounting and reporting.

Professor Pfeiffer teaches financial accounting and financial analysis to undergraduate, MBA, and Executive students. He has also taught managerial accounting for MBAs. He has won several teaching awards at both the undergraduate and graduate levels.

PREFACE

W elcome to *Financial Accounting*! We wrote this book for **today's** business students. It reflects our combined experience in teaching financial accounting to college students at all levels. For anyone who pursues a career in business, the ability to read, analyze and interpret published financial reports is an essential skill in today's business environment. *Financial Accounting* is written for future business leaders who want to understand how financial statements are prepared and how the information in published financial reports is used by investors, creditors, financial analysts, and managers. Our goal is to provide the most up-to-date, engaging, accessible, and user-oriented textbook available.

> "This book is very well laid out and addresses topics that have high appeal to audiences beyond accounting majors (I think that this is important for an intro text)."
> —**Matt Anderson**, *Michigan State University*

> "Clear, complete and with great end-of-chapter materials."
> —**Susan Parker**, *Santa Clara University*

TARGET AUDIENCE

Financial Accounting is intended for use in the first financial accounting course at either the undergraduate or graduate level; one in which decision making and analysis are emphasized. This book easily accommodates mini-courses lasting only several days as well as extended courses lasting a full semester.

> "It is very well-written and presents the material in an engaging tone that uses current, substantive real-world examples."
> —**Elliott Levy**, *Bentley College*

INNOVATIVE APPROACH

Financial Accounting is real-world oriented and focuses on the most salient aspects of accounting. It teaches students how to read, analyze, and interpret financial accounting data to make informed business decisions. This textbook makes financial accounting **engaging**, **relevant**, and **contemporary**. To that end, it consistently incorporates **real company data**, both in the body of each chapter and throughout assignment material.

> The book does an outstanding job of integrating real-world companies both in the text and in the homework, which provides students with an opportunity to use the accounting concepts they have learned in class in practical situations.
> —**Rada Brooks**, *University of California-Berkeley*

BALANCED APPROACH

As instructors of introductory financial accounting, we recognize that the first financial accounting course serves the general business students as well as potential accounting majors. *Financial Accounting* embraces this reality. This book **balances financial reporting, analysis, interpretation**, and **decision making** with the more standard aspects of accountings such as **journal entries**, **T-accounts**, and the **preparation of financial statements**. We incorporate the following **financial statement effects template** and link the template to the related **journal entries** and **T-accounts** to illustrate the impact of various transactions on the financial statements. This analytical tool is a great resource for students in learning accounting and applying it to their future courses and careers.

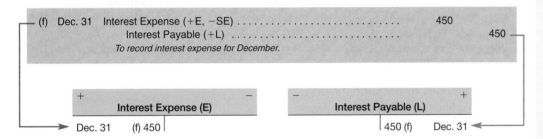

	Balance Sheet						Income Statement		
Transaction	Cash Asset	+ Noncash Assets	= Liabil-ities	+ Contrib. Capital	+ Retained Earnings		Revenues	– Expenses	= Net Income
(f) Adjusting entry to record interest owed but not yet paid			= +450 Interest Payable		–450 Retained Earnings			–450 Interest Expense	= –450

```
(f)  Dec. 31   Interest Expense (+E, –SE) ...........................          450
                    Interest Payable (+L) ...........................                    450
                    To record interest expense for December.
```

+ Interest Expense (E) –	– Interest Payable (L) +
Dec. 31 (f) 450	450 (f) Dec. 31

> "An excellent, conceptually complete text. Meets our need for the user approach, as well as providing the preparer focus needed for accounting majors."
> —**Marianne James**, *California State University – Los Angeles*

Today's business students must be skilled in using financial statements to make business decisions. These skills often require application of ratio analyses, benchmarking, forecasting, valuation, and other aspects of financial statement analysis to decision making. Furthermore, today's business students must have the skills to go beyond basic financial statements to interpret and apply nonfinancial statement disclosures, such as footnotes and supplementary reports.

This book, therefore, emphasizes **real company data**, including detailed **footnote and other management disclosures**, and shows how to use this information to make managerial inferences and decisions. This approach makes financial accounting interesting and relevant for all students.

INNOVATIVE PEDAGOGY

Financial Accounting includes special features specifically designed for the student.

Focus Companies for Each Chapter

Each chapter's content is explained through the accounting and reporting activities of real companies. To that end, each chapter incorporates a "focus company" for special emphasis and demonstration. The enhanced instructional value of focus companies comes from the way they engage students in real analysis and interpretation. Focus companies were selected based on the industries that students typically enter upon graduation.

Real Company Data Throughout

We have gone to great lengths to incorporate real company data throughout each chapter to reinforce important concepts and engage students. We engage nonaccounting students specializing in **finance, marketing, management, real estate, operations**, and so forth, with companies and scenarios that are relevant to them.

Decision Making Orientation

One primary goal of a financial accounting course is to teach students the skills needed to apply their accounting knowledge to solving real business problems and making informed business decisions. With that goal in mind, **You Make the Call** boxes in each chapter encourage students to apply the material presented to solving actual business scenarios.

> "You make the call" (is) good for making the students think about consequences of decision making. "
> —**Vic Stanton,** *University of California—Berkeley*

Mid-Chapter and Chapter-End Reviews

Financial accounting can be challenging—especially for students lacking business experience or previous exposure to business courses. To reinforce concepts presented in each chapter and to ensure student comprehension, we include mid-chapter and chapter-end reviews that require students to recall and apply the financial accounting techniques and concepts described in each chapter.

> "The mid-chapter review exercises and problems are excellent."
> —**Hank Adler,** *Chapman University*

Research Insights for Business Students

Academic research plays an important role in the way business is conducted, accounting is performed, and students are taught. It is important for students to recognize how modern research and modern business practice interact. Therefore, we periodically incorporate relevant research to help students understand the important relation between research and modern business.

Excellent, Class-Tested Assignment Materials

Excellent assignment material is a must-have component of any successful textbook (and class). We went to great lengths to create the best assignments possible. In keeping with the rest of the book, we used real company data extensively. We also ensured that assignments reflect our belief that students should be trained in analyzing accounting information to make business decisions as well as interpreting and preparing financial reports. The assignments encourage students to analyze accounting information, interpret it, and apply the knowledge gained to a business decision. There are six categories of assignments: **Multiple Choice Questions**, **Discussion Questions**, **Mini Exercises**, **Exercises**, **Problems**, and **Cases & Projects**.

> "The diversity and availability of problems and exercises at the end of the chapter continues to be one strong point of this textbook."
> —Sean Chen, *Loyola Marymount*

KEY FEATURES

- **Analysis and decision making**: This book considers accounting from an analysis and decision usefulness perspective because today's students must understand, analyze, and interpret financial reports to make business decisions.

- **Accounting mechanics**: Transactions are explained with a combination of journal entries, T-accounts, and the authors' unique Financial Statement Effects Template.

- **Financial Statement Effects Template**: Introduced in Chapter 2 and used throughout the book, this template shows the impact of transactions on the balance sheet, income statement, and statement of cash flows.

- **Early introduction to cash flows**: The statement of cash flows is described precisely and simply in Chapter 4. This chapter was written to give instructors maximum flexibility and, as a result, can be covered at any point after Chapter 3.

- **Profitability analysis**: Contemporary coverage of profitability analysis sets this book apart from the pack. It goes beyond traditional ratio analysis to show how return on equity (ROE) and its components reveal company profitability drivers.

- **Real data, including assignments**: To prepare students for the real world, the book draws on real company data throughout, including the assignments. Excerpts from annual reports and footnotes are used generously, as are company comparisons both within and across industries.

- **Focus companies**: Each chapter is launched with the accounting practices of a real company. That focus company is then continually referenced for chapter illustrations. Examples include Berkshire Hathaway, Cisco Systems, Walt Disney, Starbucks, Verizon, 3M, Hewlett-Packard, FedEx, Midwest Airlines, Kimberly-Clark, Gillette, Procter & Gamble, and Pfizer.

SUPPLEMENT PACKAGE

For Instructors

Electronic Solutions Manual: Created by the authors, the *Instructor's Manual with Solutions* contains teaching outlines and complete solutions to all the assignment material in the text.

PowerPoint: The PowerPoint slides outline key elements of each chapter.

Electronic Test Bank: The test bank includes multiple-choice items, matching questions, short essay questions, and problems.

Website: All instructor materials are accessible via the book's website (password protected) along with other useful links and marketing information. www.cambridgepub.com

Online Course Management Systems: A full complement of online material is available for incorporation with your school's course management system (Blackboard and other platforms).

For Students

Student Solutions Manual: Created by the authors, the student solutions manual contains all solutions to the assignment materials in the textbook. This is a restricted item that is only available to students after their instructor has authorized its purchase.

Website: Practice quizzes and other useful links are available to students free of charge on the book's Website. www.cambridgepub.com

ACKNOWLEDGMENTS

This book benefited greatly from the invaluable feedback of focus group attendees, reviewers, students, and colleagues. We are extremely grateful to them for their help in making this project a success.

Hank Adler, *Chapman University*

Matthew Anderson, *Michigan State University*

Eli Bartov, *New York University*

Rada Brooks, *University of California-Berkeley*

Helen Brubeck, *San Jose State University*

Richard Campbell, *University of Rio Grande*

Sean Chen, *Loyola Marymount University*

Bruce Dehning, *Chapman University*

Douglas DeJong, *University of Iowa*

Norris Dorsey, *California State University-Northridge*

Allan Drebin, *Northwestern University*

James Emig, *Villanova University*

Lisa Gillespie, *Loyola University*

Rajul Gokarn, *Clark Atlanta University*

Karl Hackenbrack, *Vanderbilt University*

Al Hartgraves, *Emory University*

Rayford Harwell, *California State University-East Bay*

Susan Hass, *Simmons College*

Haihong He, *California State University-Los Angeles*

Marsha Huber, *Otterbein College*

Richard Hurley, *University of Connecticut*

Robert Hurt, *California State University-Pomona*

Marianne James, *California State University-Los Angeles*

Rick Johnston, *Ohio State University*

William Kross, *Purdue University*

Elliot Levy, *Bentley College*

Francine Lipman, *Chapman University*

Ariel Markelevich, *Long Island University*

John McCauley, *San Diego State University*

Susan Parker, *Santa Clara University*

S.E.C. Purvis, *California State University*

Edward Riedl, *Harvard University*

Anwar Salimi, *California State University-Pomona*

Robert Scharlach, *University of Southern California*

Chandra Seethamraju, *Washington University*

Devin Shanthikumar, *Harvard University*

Carole Shook, *University of Arkansas*

Praveen Sinha, *Chapman University*

Vic Stanton, *University of California-Berkeley*

Phillip Stocken, *Dartmouth College*

Robin Tarpley, *George Washington University*

Wayne Thomas, *University of Oklahoma*

Mark Vargus, *University of Texas-Dallas*

Joseph Weintrop, *City University of New York*

James Williamson, *San Diego State University*

In addition, we are extremely grateful to George Werthman, Helena Zielinski, Jack McKenzie, Debbie Golden, Debbie Berman, Julie Searls, and the entire team at Cambridge Business Publishers for their encouragement, enthusiasm, and guidance. Their market research and editorial development are without peer. We have had a very positive textbook authoring experience thanks, in large part, to our publisher.

Thomas R. Dyckman
Peter D. Easton
Glenn M. Pfeiffer

March 2006

BRIEF CONTENTS

CONTENTS

Chapter 3

Adjusting Accounts for Financial Statements   86

Chapter 4

Reporting of Cash Flows   142

Chapter 5

Financial Statements and Profitability Analysis   192

Chapter 6

Financial Statements, Liquidity and Solvency Analysis   236

Chapter 7

Reporting Operating Income   278

Chapter 8

Reporting Short-Term Operating Assets   320

Chapter 11

Reporting Owner Financing   466

Chapter 12

Reporting Intercorporate Investments   516

Introducing Financial Accounting

LEARNING OBJECTIVES

After completing the chapter, you should be able to:

LO1 Describe how companies report their business activities and how this fits with the accounting equation. (p. 4)

LO2 Identify the users (and suppliers) of financial information. (p. 10)

LO3 Introduce the four basic financial statements including the balance sheet, the income statement, the statement of stockholders' equity, and the statement of cash flows. (p. 13)

LO4 Explain the importance and basics of analyzing profitability. (p. 20)

LO5 Discuss the need to interpret accounting information within the broader business environment. (p. 22)

BERKSHIRE HATHAWAY

D o you recognize the two people in the picture above? Many of you will probably recognize Arnold Schwarzenegger as a celebrity who began his career in body building and later became a movie star in action films such as *Collateral Damage, Predator,* and *Terminator* (1, 2, and 3). More recently, Mr. Schwarzenegger became Governor of the state of California. But, how many of you recognize the person next to Arnold Schwarzenegger? Would it surprise you to know that he is also quite famous? His name is Warren Buffett, and he isn't a movie star or a politician. He is a CEO (Chief Executive Officer), and his fame stems from his success managing Berkshire Hathaway. Buffett's business success is so widely admired that Governor Schwarzenegger asked Buffett to be his economic advisor for the state of California, which Buffett agreed to be.

To understand why Warren Buffett is famous, we need to consider the performance of Berkshire Hathaway. One way to gauge a company's success is to consider the increase (or decrease) in the value of its stock. According to its 2004 Annual Report, a single share of Berkshire Hathaway's stock purchased for $19 in 1964, is now worth an eye-popping $55, 824. The increase in Berkshire Hathaway's stock price between 1964 and 2004 equates to a 21.9% average annual gain. As a point of reference, let's consider the performance of the S&P 500 (a commonly used benchmark for stock returns) during the same period of time. From 1964 to 2004, the annual rate of return for the S&P 500 was 10.4%. That means that the average annual return on shares of Berkshire Hathaway stock more than doubled the average annual return of the S&P 500 during the same period. For over forty years, Berkshire Hathaway has significantly and consistently outperformed other companies, and Warren Buffett is credited with much of this achievement.

Buffett's success is not accidental. His understanding and use of financial accounting information are central to his ability to manage Berkshire Hathaway. He provides some especially useful guidance about accounting information in his Chairman's letter from the Berkshire Hathaway 2002 annual report:

Three suggestions for investors:

First, beware of companies displaying weak accounting. If a company still does not expense options, or if its pension assumptions are fanciful, watch out. When managements take the low road in aspects that are visible, it is likely they are following a similar path behind the scenes. There is seldom just one cockroach in the kitchen.

Second, unintelligible footnotes usually indicate untrustworthy management. If you can't understand a footnote or other managerial explanation, it's usually because the CEO doesn't want you to. Enron's descriptions of certain transactions still baffle me.

(Continued on next page)

(Continued from previous page)

Finally, be suspicious of companies that trumpet earnings projections and growth expectations. Businesses seldom operate in a tranquil, no-surprise environment, and earnings simply don't advance smoothly.

This book explains Buffett's references to "weak accounting" (for stock option accounting and pension assumptions) as well as a host of other accounting issues that affect the interpretation and valuation of company financial performance. We will analyze and interpret the footnotes, which Buffett views as crucial to successful analysis. Our philosophy is simple: we must understand the intricacies of financial reporting to become critical readers and users of financial reports for company analysis and valuation. Financial statements tell a story—a business story. The task is to understand that story, analyze and interpret it in the context of competing stories, and apply the knowledge gleaned to business decisions.

Sources: Berkshire Hathaway 2004 10-K Report, Berkshire Hathaway 2004, 2003, 2002, and 2001 Annual Reports.

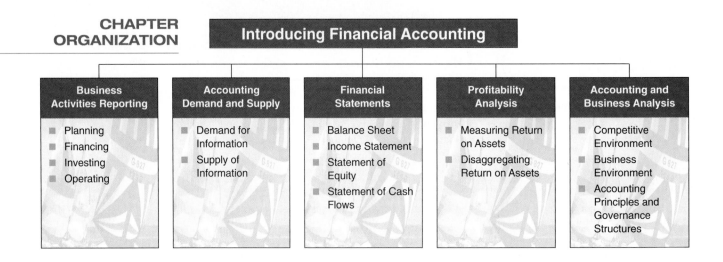

CHAPTER ORGANIZATION

Introducing Financial Accounting

Business Activities Reporting	Accounting Demand and Supply	Financial Statements	Profitability Analysis	Accounting and Business Analysis
■ Planning ■ Financing ■ Investing ■ Operating	■ Demand for Information ■ Supply of Information	■ Balance Sheet ■ Income Statement ■ Statement of Equity ■ Statement of Cash Flows	■ Measuring Return on Assets ■ Disaggregating Return on Assets	■ Competitive Environment ■ Business Environment ■ Accounting Principles and Governance Structures

REPORTING ON BUSINESS ACTIVITIES

LO1 Describe how companies report their business activities and how this fits with the accounting equation.

To effectively manage a company or infer whether it is well managed, we must understand business activities. The information system called *financial accounting* contributes to our understanding of these business activities. This system reports on a company's performance and financial condition, and conveys privileged information and insights into management's decisions.

Financial accounting information helps us, as managers, to evaluate potential future strategies and ascertain the effectiveness of present and past strategies. It improves the soundness of our investment decisions, including how to allocate scarce resources across alternative investment projects and whether to invest additional resources in existing product lines or divisions. Financial accounting information is essential for preparing client proposals, analyzing the effectiveness of production processes, and evaluating the performance of management teams.

Information that flows from the financial accounting system also helps us, as investors, select the company in whose securities we invest. Yet before this accounting information is used to make decisions, it must be scrutinized and sometimes adjusted. This task is accomplished in part by analyzing information contained in footnotes to companies' financial reports to determine the quality of reported figures and any necessary adjustments.

More generally, financial accounting satisfies the needs of different groups of users. Within firms, the *functioning* of this information system involves the application of accounting standards to produce financial reports. Effectively *using* this information system involves making judgments, assumptions, and estimates based on data contained in the financial reports. The greatest value we derive from this system as users of financial information is the insights we gain into business activities.

To effectively analyze and use accounting information, we must consider the business context in which it is created—see Exhibit 1.1. Without exception, all companies *plan* business activities, *finance* those activities, *invest* in those activities, and then engage in *operating* activities. Firms conduct all these activities while confronting *business forces,* including market constraints and competitive pressures. Examining each of these business activities helps us better understand the context of financial accounting and its proper application and interpretation.

Reporting Planning Activities

The goals and objectives of a company are the outputs of its planning activities. Berkshire Hathaway, for example, strives to own and manage a diversified set of businesses to obtain a long-run return that exceeds the Standard & Poor's (S&P) index. As Buffett comments in his 2004 annual report:

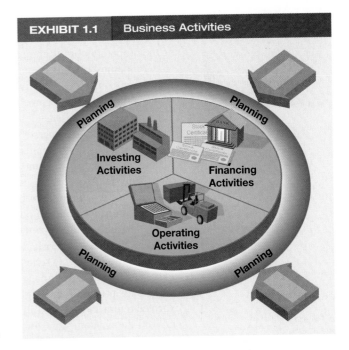

EXHIBIT 1.1   Business Activities

> Berkshire's long-term performance versus the S&P remains all-important. Our shareholders can buy the S&P through an index fund at very low cost. Unless we achieve gains in per-share intrinsic value in the future that outdo the S&P's performance, Charlie and I will be adding nothing to what you can accomplish on your own.

A company's *strategic* (or *business*) *plan* describes how it plans to achieve its goals and objectives. The plan's success depends on an effective review of market demand and supply. Specifically, the company must assess both the demand for its products and services, and the supply of its inputs (both labor and capital). The plan must also include competitive analyses, opportunity assessments, and consideration of business threats. The strategic plan specifies both broad management designs that generate company value and tactical actions to achieve those designs. Tactical actions involve production, marketing, human resources, operations, and supply-chain management.

Most information in a strategic plan is proprietary and guarded closely by management. However, outsiders can gain insight into planning activities through various channels. Less formal channels include newspapers, magazines, and company publications. More formal channels include management's Letter to Shareholders and its Management Discussion and Analysis (MD&A) report. Understanding a company's planning activities helps focus accounting analysis and place it in context.

> NOTE
> Corporations are businesses separate from their owners (called stockholders). Public corporations are those with their stock traded on exchanges.

BUSINESS INSIGHT

Warren Buffett on MD&A   "When Charlie and I read reports, we have no interest in pictures of personnel, plants or products. References to EBITDA [earnings before interest, taxes, depreciation and amortization] make us shudder—does management think the tooth fairy pays for capital expenditures? We're very suspicious of accounting methodology that is vague or unclear, since too often that means management wishes to hide something. And we don't want to read messages that a public relations department or consultant has turned out. Instead, we expect a company's CEO to explain in his or her own words what's happening."
—Berkshire Hathaway annual report

Reporting Financing Activities

A company's strategic plan guides management with its decisions on what resources to acquire. These resources include, for example, raw materials for product manufacturing, machinery to produce and support production, land and buildings to support operations, and sales outlets for products and services. Resource investments also include those in employees, marketing, and research and development.

NOTE
Creditors are those to whom a company owes money.

Investments in resources require funding. **Financing activities** refer to methods that companies use to fund those resources. *Financial management* is the planning of resource needs, including the proper mix of different financing sources.

Companies obtain financing from two sources: equity (owner) financing and creditor (nonowner) financing. *Equity financing* is the resources contributed to the company by its owners along with any income retained by the company. One form of equity financing is the cash raised from the sale (issuance) of stock by a company. *Creditor* (or debt) *financing* is resources contributed from nonowners. One example of creditor financing is a loan from a bank. We draw this distinction between financing sources for an important reason: creditor financing entails a legal obligation to repay amounts borrowed, usually with interest, and failure to repay amounts borrowed can yield severe consequences to the borrower. Equity financing entails no such legal obligation for repayment. For instance, if you own shares of stock of a company that goes bankrupt, the company is under no legal obligation to pay you back for your loss. All companies use both equity and creditor financing. An important goal is to employ these financing sources at the lowest possible cost and risk.

Berkshire Hathaway relies on both owner and nonowner financing. In 2004 its owners provided $86,658 million in financing (46%), while its nonowners provided $102,216 million (54%). Both groups provide financing in a desire for a return on their investment, after considering both expected return and risk. Exhibit 1.2 gives a sense of differences in financing proportions for several well-known companies in 2003.

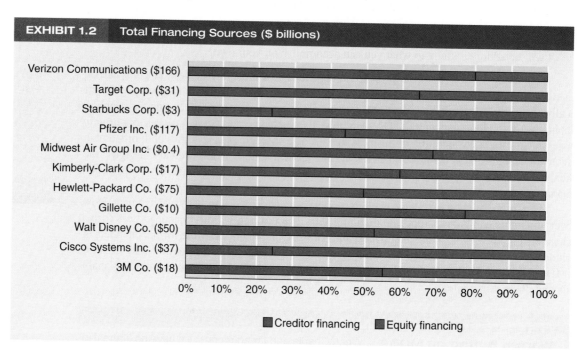

EXHIBIT 1.2   Total Financing Sources ($ billions)

NOTE
An important distinction for analysis is to separate owner from nonowner financing.

These companies are financed with different proportions of creditor and equity financing. Companies like **Cisco Systems**, **Starbucks**, and **Pfizer** utilize a greater proportion of equity financing than do **Verizon**, **Gillette**, and **Midwest Air**. This variation is not by chance. Each industry, over time, reaches its own optimum proportion of creditor and equity financing.

We can further separate creditor (nonowner) financing into two sources:

1. Investing creditors—those who primarily fund the overall business (such as bank lenders).

2. Operating creditors—those who primarily fund the production of products and services by providing raw materials or other items of value (such as suppliers).

Investing creditors are lenders that are party to financing agreements that support the overall business. These agreements are often in the form of multiyear notes and bonds. Such agreements specify repayment terms, interest, and any mortgage and covenants. *Operating creditors* are lenders that are also party to financing agreements that fund the production of products and services by providing raw materials or other items of value. These agreements typically involve suppliers, employees, utilities, and government agencies.

The distinction between these two types of creditors is important. Obligations to investing creditors are generally interest bearing and are subject to legal agreements that can place constraints upon a company's operating activities. Obligations to operating creditors are generally non-interest bearing and represent an important source of funding for the company. Also, the ability of operating creditors to provide needed supplies of acceptable quality and at the appropriate time is crucial to company success.

Berkshire Hathaway reports total nonowner financing of $102,216 million, which consists of $23,858 million from investing creditors and $78,358 million from operating creditors. Exhibit 1.3 highlights differences in these sources of financing in 2003 for the same set of companies described above.

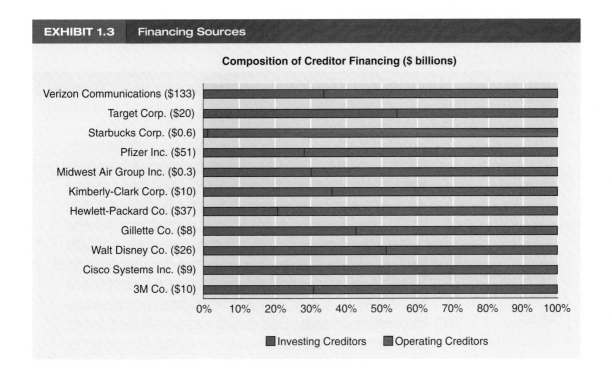

EXHIBIT 1.3   Financing Sources

Composition of Creditor Financing ($ billions)

For most of these companies, operating creditors make up a larger proportion of creditor financing. This is a desired result as operating credit is typically interest-free and, therefore, costs less. Moreover, investing creditors usually require loan agreements or bond indentures (also called covenants) that place restrictions on a company's activities and, thereby, limit its operating flexibility.

YOU MAKE THE CALL

You are a Product Manager   There is often a friction between investor need for information and a company's desire to safeguard competitive advantages. Assume that you are the product manager for a key department at your company and you are asked for advice on the extent of information to disclose in the MD&A section of your annual report on a potentially very lucrative new product that your department has test marketed and plans to further finance. What advice do you provide and why? [Answers on page 30]

Reporting Investing Activities

Investing activities are the acquisition and disposition of resources, called *assets,* that a company uses to produce and sell its products and services. Companies differ on the amount and mix of investing resources. Some require buildings and inventories to operate. Others need only people. *Asset management* is the task of selecting the proper asset composition.

NOTE
Distinguishing between operating and nonoperating assets is critical in analyzing performance.

Investing resources are of two types:

1. Operating assets—resources devoted to production of the company's products and services.
2. Nonoperating (financial) assets—resources devoted to those activities that are not related to the production of the company's products and services.

Operating assets refer to resources devoted to executing a company's primary business activities. *Nonoperating* (or *financial*) *assets* consist of excess (nonoperating) resources such as those held for future expansion or unexpected needs. Such assets are often invested in other companies' stocks and in corporate or government bonds. The distinction between operating and nonoperating assets is important and impacts the analysis of financial performance described later in this and other chapters. This is because companies concentrate most of their efforts in and create most of their market value from operating activities.

Exhibit 1.4 illustrates the breakdown between operating and nonoperating assets for several companies in 2003.

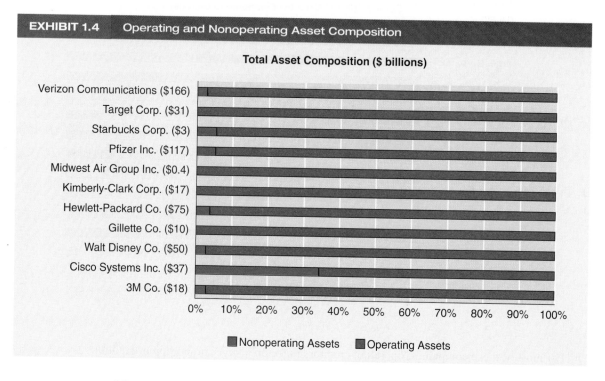

EXHIBIT 1.4 Operating and Nonoperating Asset Composition

Most companies do not carry large amounts of nonoperating assets (such as investments). An exception is **Cisco Systems**, where its investments provide it with financial flexibility in a rapidly changing industry. Other companies such as **Microsoft**, however, have come under pressure from their owners (shareholders) to pay out a portion of such assets to their shareholders.

The total of a company's resources is referred to as its *assets*. Company financing, which consists of owner and nonowner financing, reflects claims on those assets. Owner claims on assets are referred to as *equity* and nonowner claims are referred to as *liabilities* (or debt). Because all financing must be invested in something, we obtain the following basic relation: *investing equals financing*. This equality is called the **accounting equation**, which is expressed as:

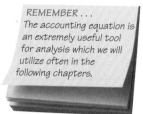

REMEMBER . . . The accounting equation is an extremely useful tool for analysis which we will utilize often in the following chapters.

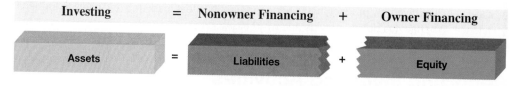

At December 31, 2004, the accounting equation for Berkshire Hathaway follows ($ millions):

$$\$188,874 = \$102,216 + \$86,658$$

The accounting equation works for all companies at all times.

RESEARCH INSIGHT

Return and Risk   Return, also called *yield,* is the amount earned from an investment. Return is often expressed as the income from the investment divided by the amount invested. U.S. government bonds, for example, express return in the form of an interest rate such as 5%. **Risk** is the uncertainty of expected return. Each investment has risk, and some investments carry more risk than others. The trade-off between return and risk impacts investment decisions. The greater the investment risk, the greater is its expected return, and vice-versa. Government bonds earn a low return because they carry little risk of loss. We expect a greater return from a share of Berkshire Hathaway. Yet, that greater return carries greater risk, including risk of loss.

The following chart shows that return is higher for higher-risk bonds and for bonds with more distant maturity dates. Specifically, return increases (shifts upward) as bond quality moves from U.S. Treasury, which is the lowest-risk bond, to BBB, which is a higher risk bond. This difference is substantial. For example, for a 10-year bond, the government bond yield is 4.71%, the AAA bond yield is 0.60% higher (at 5.31%), and the BBB bond yield is 1.41% higher (at 6.12%). Also, as maturity terms lengthen, uncertainty (risk) increases, and return increases.

REMEMBER . . . Return cannot be evaluated without considering risk. The larger the business risk of any decision, the larger the expected return should be.

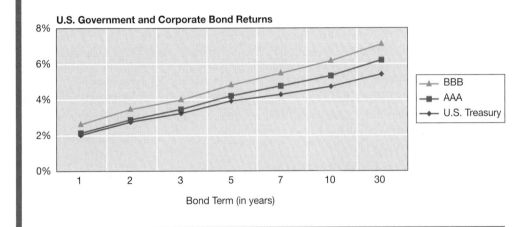

U.S. Government and Corporate Bond Returns

Reporting Operating Activities

Operating activities are the use of company resources to produce, promote, and sell its products and services. These activities extend from input markets involving suppliers of materials and labor to a company's output markets involving customers of products and services. Input markets generate most *operating expenses* (or *costs*) such as inventory, salaries, materials, and logistics. Output markets generate *operating revenues* (or *sales*) to customers. Output markets also generate some operating expenses such as marketing and distributing products and services to customers. *Operating income,* also called *operating profit* or *operating earnings,* arises when operating revenues exceed operating expenses. An operating loss occurs when operating expenses exceed operating revenues. Selecting the proper mix of operating activities is known as *strategic management.*

NOTE Financial accounting is molded by generally accepted accounting principles (GAAP) and other important factors in the business environment. Appendix 1A to this chapter describes GAAP and the environment.

Management performance with operating activities is assessed using various benchmarks. For example, **Harley-Davidson** earned $580 million in a recent year. This number by itself is not very meaningful. Instead, we can better assess income performance relative to the level of investment used to generate that income. Specifically, Harley's return on its average asset level of $3,490 million is 16.6%. The same $3,490 million invested in a savings account earning 2% would yield earnings of only $70 million.

Defining Company Value

Business activities are set within a mix of business forces. These forces include key stakeholders, who are individuals with vested interests in a company's performance and condition. Many of these stakeholders participate in **capital markets**, which refer to financing sources. Capital markets often involve a company's issuance of securities (stocks, bonds, and notes) that are traded on organized exchanges such as the New York Stock Exchange (NYSE) and NASDAQ. They also include capital raised from family members, friends, venture capitalists, and local banks.

Most owners and nonowners formalize their claims on a company in the form of a *contract* or a *security*. A typical owner security is stock, and typical nonowner securities are bonds and notes. A security can often be traded in capital markets. For example, the original owners can sell those claims in capital markets if they wish to liquidate their securities. All subsequent owners are called *secondary holders* of such securities.

The value of the company's total resources is the value of all owner and nonowner claims.

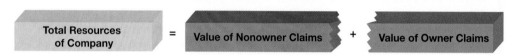

Total Resources of Company = Value of Nonowner Claims + Value of Owner Claims

Business activities are the *drivers* of company value.

DEMAND FOR AND SUPPLY OF INFORMATION

LO2 Identify the users (and suppliers) of financial information.

Financial accounting information facilitates economic transactions and promotes efficient resource allocations. Decision makers demand information on a company's past and prospective returns and risks. Companies are encouraged to supply such information to lower their costs of financing and some less obvious costs such as political, contracting, and labor costs.

As with all goods, the supply of information depends on companies weighing the costs of disclosure against the benefits of disclosure. Regulatory agencies intervene in this process with various disclosure requirements that establish a minimum supply of information.

Demand for Information

Demand for financial accounting information extends to numerous users including:

- Managers and employees
- Creditors and suppliers
- Shareholders and directors
- Customers and sales staff
- Regulators and tax agencies
- Voters and their representatives
- Financial analysts
- Labor unions

Managers and Employees

For their own well-being and future earnings potential, managers and employees demand accounting information on the financial condition, profitability, and prospects of their companies. Managers and employees also demand comparative financial information on competing companies and other business opportunities. This permits them to conduct comparative analyses to benchmark company performance and condition.

Managers and employees also demand financial accounting information for use in compensation and bonus contracts that are tied to such numbers. The popularity of employee profit sharing and stock ownership plans has further increased demand for financial information. Other sources of demand include union contracts that link wage negotiations to accounting numbers and for pension and benefit plans whose solvency depends on company performance.

Creditors and Suppliers

Creditors such as banks and other lenders demand financial accounting information to help determine loan terms, loan amounts, interest rates, and collateral. Creditors' loans often include contractual requirements, called **covenants**, for the loan recipient to maintain minimum levels of capital to safeguard lenders. Covenant violations can yield technical default, enabling the creditor to demand early payment or other compensation.

Suppliers similarly demand financial information to establish credit sales terms and to determine their long-term commitment to supply-chain relations. Both creditors and suppliers use financial information to monitor and adjust their contracts and commitments with a debtor company.

Shareholders and Directors

Shareholders and directors demand financial accounting information to assess the profitability and risks of companies. Shareholders and others (including investment analysts, brokers, potential investors, etc.) look for information useful in their investment decisions. **Fundamental analysis** uses financial information to estimate company value and, hence, buy-sell stock strategies.

Both directors and shareholders use accounting information to evaluate manager performance. Managers similarly use such information to request further compensation and managerial power from directors. Outside directors are crucial to determining who runs the company, and these directors use accounting information to help make this assessment.

Customers and Sales Staff

Customers and sales staffs demand accounting information to assess the ability of a company to provide products or services as agreed and to assess the company's staying power and reliability. Customers and sales staffs also wish to estimate the company's profitability to assess fairness of returns on mutual transactions.

RESEARCH INSIGHT

Degrees of Market Efficiency   Capital markets are efficient if, at any given time, current stock prices reflect information that determines those prices. That is, the market is efficient if disclosure of some information does not alter stock prices. This implies that excess stock returns cannot be earned from analysis of that information in predicting stock prices. Three degrees of market efficiency are defined with respect to the information set:

- Weak-form efficiency: The information set includes only the history of stock prices.
- Semistrong-form efficiency: The information set includes all information known to market participants, but is limited to public information.
- Strong-form efficiency: The information set includes all information known to market participants, including private information.

Strong-form efficiency is dismissed. Further, research has revealed stock pricing anomalies that cast doubt on semistrong-form efficiency. For example, investor over- and under-reaction to income announcements, the size effect (smaller firms yield higher returns), the book-to-market effect (firms with a higher book value-to-market value ratio earn higher returns), and others reject semistrong-form efficiency. There is also evidence that the degree of efficiency varies with the information environment such as the quality and quantity of disclosure, press coverage, and analyst following.

Regulators and Tax Agencies

Regulators and tax agencies demand accounting information for tax policies, antitrust assessments, public protection, price setting, import-export analyses, and various other uses. Timely and reliable information is crucial to effective regulatory policy. Moreover, accounting information is often central to social and economic policy. For example, governments often grant monopoly rights to electric and gas companies serving specific areas in exchange for regulation over prices charged to consumers. These prices are mainly determined from accounting measures of return.

Voters and Their Representatives

Voters and their representatives to national, state, and local governments demand accounting information for policy decisions. The decisions can involve economic, social, taxation, and other initiatives. Voters and their representatives also use accounting information to monitor government spending. We have all heard of the $1,000 hammer type stories that are uncovered while sifting through accounting data. Contributors to nonprofit organizations also demand accounting information to assess the impact of their donations.

> **NOTE**
> *Others that have an interest in financial reports include financial analysts, potential stockholders, accounting standard setters, and auditing firms.*

Financial Analysts

Financial analysts use financial statement information to both analyze and forecast the future performance of companies. The results of their efforts are used to recommend stock purchases and sales to clients, determine asking prices for new stock and bond issues, and establish the basis for merger and acquisition activities, among other uses.

B U S I N E S S   I N S I G H T

Recent court cases involving Enron, Tyco, and WorldCom (now MCI) have identified executives, including CEOs, guilty of inappropriate disclosures. These executives have received substantial fines and, in come cases, extended jail sentences. The effects have been felt by all members of corporate boards, who have witnessed lost credibility and reputation damage. Firms have also been wiped out as was the case with one of the world's largest audit firms, Arthur Andersen.

Labor Unions

Labor unions examine the financial reports of their companies prior to negotiating new or extending old contracts to determine what bargaining strategies to use based on the financial health of the firm. Their analysis often includes considering firms in the same industry to determine a multi-firm strategy. This activity is common in the U.S. automobile industry and in professional sports leagues.

B U S I N E S S   I N S I G H T

Warren Buffett on Management Talk   "Bad terminology is the enemy of good thinking. When companies or investment professionals use terms such as 'EBITDA' and 'pro forma,' they want you to unthinkingly accept concepts that are dangerously flawed. (In golf, my score is frequently below par on a pro forma basis: I have firm plans to 'restructure' my putting stroke and therefore only count the swings I take before reaching the green.)"

—Berkshire Hathaway annual report.

Supply of Information

The supply of accounting information is determined by management's estimates of the benefits and costs of disclosure. That is, management would release information provided the benefits of disclosure outweigh the costs of disclosure.

NOTE
The Sarbanes-Oxley Act requires the issuer of securities to disclose whether it has adopted a code of ethics for its senior officers.

Regulation and *bargaining power* also play roles in determining the supply of accounting information. Many areas of the world regulate the minimum levels of accounting disclosures. For example, regulators in the U.S. require financial statements, various note disclosures, and other reports on a regular basis. Moreover, some stakeholders possess ample bargaining power to obtain accounting information for themselves. These typically include private lenders and major suppliers and customers.

Recognize that the minimum, regulated supply of information is not the standard. We need only look at several annual reports to see considerable variance in the supply of accounting information. For example, differences abound on disclosures for segment operations, product performance reports, financing activities, and so forth. Both the quantity and quality of information differ across companies and over time.

Benefits of Disclosure

The benefits of supplying accounting information extend to a company's capital, labor, input, and output markets. Companies must compete in these markets. For example, capital markets provide the sources of financing; the better a company's prospects, the lower are its costs of capital (as reflected in lower interest rates or higher stock prices). The same holds for a company's recruiting efforts in labor markets and its ability to establish superior supplier-customer relations in the input and output markets.

A company's performance in these markets depends on success with its business activities *and* the market's awareness of that success. Companies reap the benefits of disclosure with good news information about their products, processes, management, and so forth. That is, there are real economic incentives for companies to disclose reliable (audited) accounting information enabling them to better compete in capital, labor, input, and output markets. Further, the markets play an important role in allocating resources in the economy.

What inhibits companies from providing false or misleading good news? There are several constraints. An important constraint imposed by stakeholders is that of audit requirements and legal repercussions associated with inaccurate accounting information. Another relates to reputation effects from disclosures over time as events either support or refute earlier news.

The reputations of senior managers and their auditing firms can be seriously affected by improper reporting. We need only consider the events surrounding **Enron, WorldCom** (currently **Verizon**), **Global Crossing, Adelphia, Tyco, Heath South, Lucent, Rite Aid**, and **Arthur Andersen**, among others.

Costs of Disclosure

The costs of supplying accounting information include its preparation and dissemination, competitive disadvantages, litigation potential, and political costs. Preparation and dissemination costs can be substantial, but much of this cost is already borne by inside managers for their own business decisions. The potential for information to yield competitive disadvantages is high. Companies are concerned that disclosures of their activities such as product or segment successes, strategic alliances or pursuits, technological or system innovations, and product or process quality improvements will harm their competitive advantages. Also, litigation costs can arise when disclosures yield expectations that are not met. Political costs also are usually linked to highly visible companies that, therefore, must be careful to not generate excess profits; for example, government defense contractors and oil companies are often targets of public scrutiny.

THE FOUR BASIC FINANCIAL STATEMENTS

Four financial statements are used to periodically report on a company's business activities. These statements are the balance sheet, income statement, statement of stockholders' equity, and statement of cash flows.

Exhibit 1.5 shows how these statements are linked across time. A balance sheet reports on a company's position at a *point in time.* The income statement, statement of stockholders' equity, and the statement of cash flows report on performance over a *period of time.* The three statements in the middle of Exhibit 1.5 (period-of-time statements) link the balance sheet from the beginning to the end of a period.

LO3 Introduce the four basic financial statements including the balance sheet, the income statement, the statement of stockholders' equity, and the statement of cash flows.

A one-year, or annual, reporting period is common, which is called the *accounting,* or *fiscal, year.* Semiannual, quarterly, and monthly reporting periods are also common. *Calendar-year* companies are those companies with a reporting period that begins on January 1 and ends on December 31. Berkshire Hathaway is a calendar-year company. Some companies choose a fiscal year ending on a date other than December 31, such as when sales and inventory are low. For example, **J. Crew Group**'s fiscal year-end is always near February 1, after the busy holiday season.

EXHIBIT 1.5 Financial Statement Links across Time

Generally Accepted Accounting Principles

External users who rely on audited financial statements expect that all companies follow the same standards and procedures in preparing their statements. Accountants have developed an overall set of standards and procedures that apply to the preparation of financial statements. These standards and procedures are called **generally accepted accounting principles (GAAP).** Generally accepted accounting principles are not immutable laws like those in the physical sciences. Instead, they are *guides to action* and can change over time. Sometimes specific principles must be altered or new principles must be formulated to fit changed economic circumstances or changes

NOTE
Financial statements are typically required when a firm requests a loan from a bank.

in business practices. As the diagram below indicates, generally accepted accounting principles are relevant for financial statements.

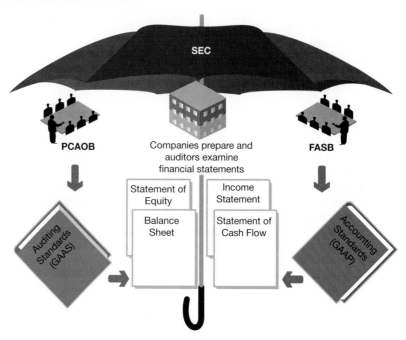

The most prominent organization concerned with the formulation of generally accepted accounting principles is the Financial Accounting Standards Board (FASB). The FASB is a nongovernmental body whose pronouncements establish U.S. GAAP. Consisting of a seven-member board, the FASB follows a process that allows for input from interested parties as it considers a new or changed accounting principle. The Securities and Exchange Commission (SEC) oversees accounting standard setting, but has granted primary responsibility to the FASB. The SEC requires that each company with publicly traded securities has its financial statements audited. The Public Company Accounting Oversight Board (PCAOB), also overseen by the SEC, approves auditing standards that govern audits of financial statements. Appendix 1A to this chapter details this regulatory environment.

Balance Sheet

NOTE
The balance sheet is also known as the statement of financial position and the statement of financial condition.

A **balance sheet** reports on investing and financing activities. It lists amounts for assets, liabilities, and equity at a point in time. The accounting equation (also called the *balance sheet equation*) is the basis of the balance sheet: Assets = Liabilities + Equity.

The balance sheet for Berkshire Hathaway for 2004 is reproduced as Exhibit 1.6. Refer to this balance sheet to verify the following amounts: assets = $188,874 million, liabilities = $102,216 million, and equity = $86,658 million. Assets equal liabilities plus equity, which reflects the equality of investing and financing totals.

Income Statement

NOTE
The income statement is also known as statement of income, statement of earnings, statement of operation, and statement of profit and loss.

An **income statement** reports on operating activities. It lists amounts for revenues less expenses over a period of time. Revenues less expenses yield the bottom-line net income amount.

Berkshire Hathaway's income statement for 2004 is shown as Exhibit 1.7. Refer to its income statement to verify the following: revenues = $74,382 million, expenses = $67,074 million, and net income = $7,308 million. Net income reflects the profit to owners for that specific period, while the line items of the statement detail how income is determined.

For manufacturing and merchandising companies, the cost of goods sold is an important measure and is also disclosed in the income statement. This measure is typically reported immediately following revenues. It is also common to report the gross profit subtotal, which is revenues less

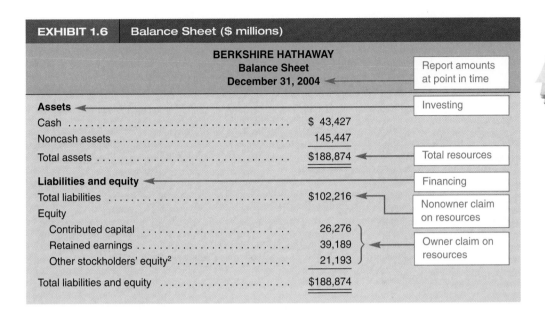

NOTE
The heading of each
financial statement
includes Who, What,
and When.

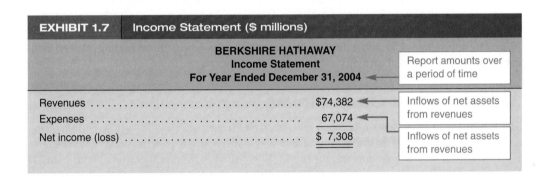

the cost of goods sold. The company's remaining expenses are then reported below gross profit. This income statement layout is:

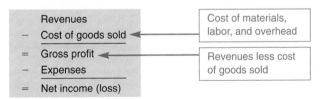

Statement of Stockholders' Equity

The **statement of stockholders' equity**, or simply *statement of equity,* reports on changes in key equity accounts over a period of time. Berkshire Hathaway's statement of stockholders' equity for 2004 is shown as Exhibit 1.8. During the recent period, its equity changed due to share issuance and income reinvestment. Berkshire Hathaway details and classifies these changes into three categories:

- Contributed capital (includes preferred stock, common stock, and additional paid-in capital)
- Retained earnings (includes cumulative net income or loss, minus dividends)
- Other stockholders' equity

Contributed capital represents the net amount contributed by shareholders (owners). Retained earnings (also called *earned capital*) represent the amount of income retained in the business and

NOTE
Dividends are reported
in the statement
of equity, and not in
the income statement.

[2] For Berkshire Hathaway, other stockholders' equity includes accumulated other comprehensive income and minority interests. These and other components of stockholders' equity are discussed in Chapters 11 and 12.

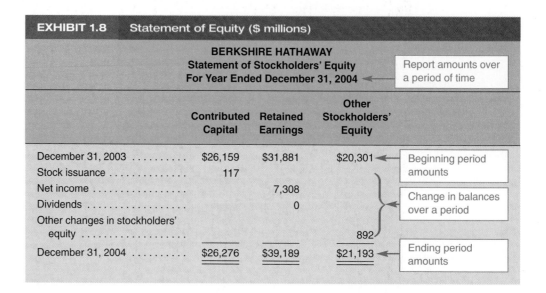

EXHIBIT 1.8   Statement of Equity ($ millions)

BERKSHIRE HATHAWAY
Statement of Stockholders' Equity
For Year Ended December 31, 2004   ← Report amounts over a period of time

	Contributed Capital	Retained Earnings	Other Stockholders' Equity	
December 31, 2003	$26,159	$31,881	$20,301 ←	Beginning period amounts
Stock issuance	117			
Net income		7,308		Change in balances over a period
Dividends		0		
Other changes in stockholders' equity			892	
December 31, 2004	$26,276	$39,189	$21,193 ←	Ending period amounts

not distributed to shareholders in the form of dividends. The change in retained earnings links consecutive balance sheets via the income statement. For Berkshire Hathaway, its recent year's retained earnings increased from $31,881 million to $39,189 million. This increase of $7,308 million is explained by net income of $7,308 million and no payment of dividends. (Note: Ending retained earnings = Beginning retained earnings + Net income − Dividends.)

Statement of Cash Flows

The **statement of cash flows** reports on net cash flows from operating, investing, and financing activities over a period of time. Berkshire Hathaway's statement of cash flows for 2004 is shown in Exhibit 1.9. The cash balance increased by $7,470 million in the recent period. Of this increase in cash, operating activities generated a $7,405 million cash inflow, investing activities generated a $221 million cash inflow, and financing activities yielded a cash outflow of $(156) million.

> **NOTE**
> Cash is critical to a firm's operations because it is necessary (eventually) for purchasing resources and paying bills.

EXHIBIT 1.9   Statement of Cash Flows ($ millions)

BERKSHIRE HATHAWAY
Statement of Cash Flows
For Year Ended December 31, 2004   ← Report amounts over a period of time

Operating cash flows	$ 7,405 ←	Net cash flow from operating
Investing cash flows	221 ←	Net cash flow from investing
Financing cash flows	(156) ←	
Net increase (decrease) in cash	7,470	Net cash flow from financing
Cash, December 31, 2003	35,957 ←	Cash amounts per balance sheet
Cash, December 31, 2004	$43,427 ←	

Berkshire Hathaway's $7,470 million net cash inflow does not equal its $7,308 million net income. Generally, a company's net cash flow for a period does *not* equal its net income. This is due to timing differences between when revenue and expense items are recognized and when cash is received and paid.

Both cash flow and net income numbers are important for business decisions. Each is used in security valuation models, and both help users of accounting reports understand and assess a company's past, present, and future business activities.

Financial Statement Linkages

Financial statements are not independent reports. They are linked. These links are shown in Exhibit 1.10 using Berkshire Hathaway's financial statements from Exhibits 1.6 through 1.9.

The left side of this exhibit shows Berkshire Hathaway's beginning-year balance sheet. Beginning-year assets equal $180,559 million, consisting of $35,957 million in cash and $144,602

EXHIBIT 1.10 Articulation of Berkshire Hathaway Financial Statements

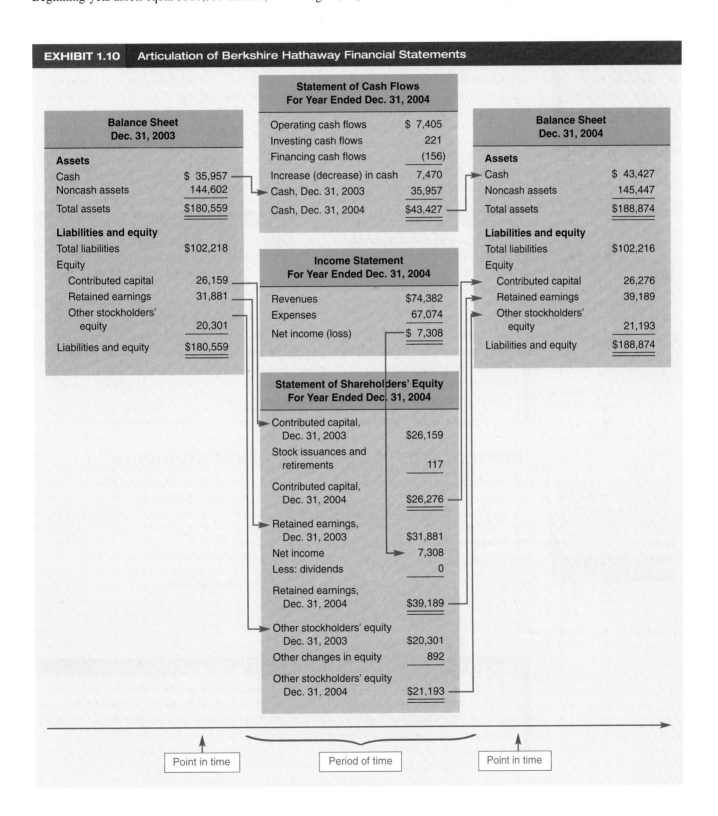

NOTE
Common formatting
pervades financial
statements:
• Dollar sign next to first
  and last amount listed
  in column
• Single rule before a
  subtraction or addition;
  double rule after a
  major total figure
• Assets listed in order
  of liquidity, which is
  nearness to cash
• Liabilities listed in order
  of due dates

million in noncash assets. These investments are financed with $102,218 million from nonowners and $78,341 million from owners. The owner portion consists of $26,159 million in contributed capital, $31,881 million in retained earnings, and $20,301 in other stockholders' equity.

Berkshire Hathaway's recent-period operating activities are reflected in the middle column of Exhibit 1.10. Its statement of cash flows explains how operating, financing, and investing activities increase the $35,957 million beginning-year cash balance to the $43,427 million year-end balance. This year-end cash balance is reported in the year-end balance sheet on the right side of the exhibit.

Berkshire Hathaway's income statement reports $7,308 million net income, which explains the change in retained earnings reported in its statement of equity (Berkshire Hathaway did not pay any dividends to its shareholders during the year).

In summary, the balance sheet is a listing of investing and financing activities at a point in time. The three statements that report on (1) cash flows, (2) income, and (3) equity explain changes over a period of time for investing and financing activities. All transactions and events reflected in these three statements impact the balance sheet. That is, the income, cash flows, and equity statements explain changes in balance sheets. This linkage is known as the *articulation* of financial statements.

YOU MAKE THE CALL

You are a Financial Analyst   Accountants, business leaders, and politicians have long debated the importance of considering the economic consequences of accounting standards (GAAP). For example, in a March 14, 1988, issue of *The Wall Street Journal,* Stanford Pensler argues that, "rules requiring amortization of 'good will' have been a major cause of the dramatic increase in acquisitions of American companies by foreign investors." Pensler's comment, however, raises a broader issue concerning the objectives of accounting standards. Should accounting standards be designed to influence behavior and effect social or economic change considered by, say, a government body or other interested group? Alternatively should such standards be designed simply to provide relevant and reliable information on which economic decisions can be made by others with a reasonable degree of confidence? What do you believe the objectives of financial reporting should be? [Answers on page 31]

Information Beyond Financial Statements

REMEMBER...
A complete analysis of a
firm's activities requires
extensive investigation of
its footnotes and the
MD&A.

Important information about a company is communicated to various decision makers through reports other than financial statements. These reports include the following:

- Management Discussion and Analysis (MD&A)
- Independent Auditor Report
- Financial statement footnotes
- Regulatory filings, including proxy statements and other SEC filings

We describe and explain the usefulness of these additional information sources throughout the book—some discussion is included in Appendix 1A to this chapter.

YOU MAKE THE CALL

You are a Shareholder   The annual report of Berkshire Hathaway describes thirteen owner-related principles the firm has followed since 1983 to "help new shareholders understand our managerial approach." Why would the company choose to include two pages in its annual report to inform readers of these principles? [Answers on page 31]

MID-CHAPTER REVIEW

The following financial information is from **Procter & Gamble**'s financial statements, for the year ended June 30, 2004 ($ millions):

Cash, ending year	$ 5,469
Cash flows from operations	9,362
Sales	51,407
Stockholders' equity	17,278
Cost of goods sold	25,076
Cash flows from financing	(414)
Total liabilities	39,770
Expenses	19,850
Noncash assets	51,579
Cash flows from investing	(9,391)
Net income	6,481
Cash, beginning year	5,912

Required
Prepare an income statement, balance sheet, and statement of cash flows for Procter & Gamble at June 30, 2004.

Solution

PROCTER & GAMBLE Income Statement For Year Ended June 30, 2004	
Sales	$51,407
Cost of goods sold	25,076
Gross profit	26,331
Expenses	19,850
Net income	$ 6,481

PROCTER & GAMBLE Balance Sheet June 30, 2004			
Cash	$ 5,469	Total liabilities	$39,770
Noncash assets	51,579	Stockholders' equity	17,278
Total assets	$57,048	Total liabilities and equity	$57,048

PROCTER & GAMBLE Statement of Cash Flows For Year Ended June 30, 2004	
Cash flows from operations	$9,362
Cash flows from investing	(9,391)
Cash flows from financing	(414)
Net increase (decrease) in cash	(443)
Cash, beginning year	5,912
Cash, ending year	$5,469

PROFITABILITY ANALYSIS

LO4 Explain the importance and basics of analyzing profitability.

There are many ways to measure company success. One crucial measure is profitability. Profitability reflects on whether or not a company is able to bring its product or service to the market in an efficient manner, and whether the market values that product or service. Companies that fail to perform on profitability are unlikely to succeed in the long run.

A key profitability metric for stakeholders and decision makers is company return on invested capital. This metric compares the level of net income with the amount of invested capital used to generate that income. Invested capital refers to total financing, which is the sum of both owner and nonowner financing. Because total financing equals total investing (assets), this return metric refers to the income generated by total assets. This section introduces the return-on-total-assets metric and the disaggregation of this metric as a motivating and learning framework for much of our subsequent analyses in this book.

Measuring Return on Assets

Return on assets (ROA), also called return on invested capital, in its simplified form is computed as:

Return on Assets (ROA) = Net Income/Average Total Assets

For example, if we invest $100 in a savings account yielding $3 at year-end, the return on assets is 3%.

A company can be assessed from the perspective of its total financing base, which by definition equals total assets (also the total of liabilities and equity). The return on assets metric reflects the return from *all* assets (financing) entrusted to it, and does not distinguish return by its sources. Alternatively, the analysis can concentrate on evaluating *operating* performance relative to operating assets. This is an important focus of Chapter 5.[4]

The income number in the numerator of the return measure reflects performance for a specific period. This implies that the asset measure used in the denominator should reflect the *average* asset level for that same period. Accordingly, we use the average asset level for ratio analysis in our examples and end-of-chapter assignments since it normally provides a better measure of capital utilization for a period and is the predominant method for analyst services, such as **S&P Compustat**. However, if circumstances dictate use of period-end amounts, then we will explicitly note the exception.

Disaggregating Return on Assets

Return on assets in its most simplified form is computed as net income divided by average total assets. This return can be disaggregated (separated) into meaningful components for profitability analysis as follows:

$$\frac{\text{Net Income}}{\text{Average Total Assets}} = \frac{\text{Net Income}}{\text{Sales}} \times \frac{\text{Sales}}{\text{Average Total Assets}}$$

The income to sales ratio is called **net profit margin**, or simply profit margin, which reflects the profitability of sales. The sales to average assets ratio is called **asset turnover**, or *total asset turnover*, which reflects effectiveness in generating sales from assets. The disaggregation of return on assets into profit margin and asset turnover is illustrated in Exhibit 1.11. (This disaggregation is sometimes called *DuPont analysis*; this is because DuPont's managers first developed and publicized this disaggregation analysis for business decisions by its managers.)

ROA can be further disaggregated to yield additional insights. For example, we can investigate profit margin (net income/sales) by analyzing its component ratios involving gross profit and individual expense items. Also, asset turnover (sales/average assets) can be broken down into turnover rates for each asset category such as receivables, inventories, and plant assets. These deeper

---

[4] This chapter uses the generic, simplified form of return on assets (Net Income/Average Assets) for a simple introduction to ratio analysis. We discuss a more useful version called return on net operating assets (RNOA) in Chapter 5.

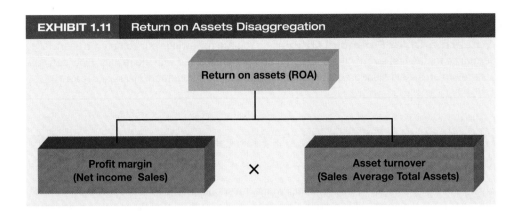

EXHIBIT 1.11   Return on Assets Disaggregation

levels of analyses yield insights into factors driving the higher-level results and can suggest areas that warrant management attention. Such analysis can lead to further efforts to enhance competitive advantages and to correct or discontinue those that are not.

There are an infinite number of combinations of profit margin and asset turnover that yield a target return on assets. To illustrate, Exhibit 1.12 graphs the 7% return on assets line for various combinations of these two profitability drivers. This exhibit also shows recent combinations of these drivers for several industries. Specifically, these points represent industry medians from over 55,000 observations over the decade and a half prior to 2005. Certain industries carry much higher profit margins with much lower asset turnovers, and vice-versa. This is basic economics at work.

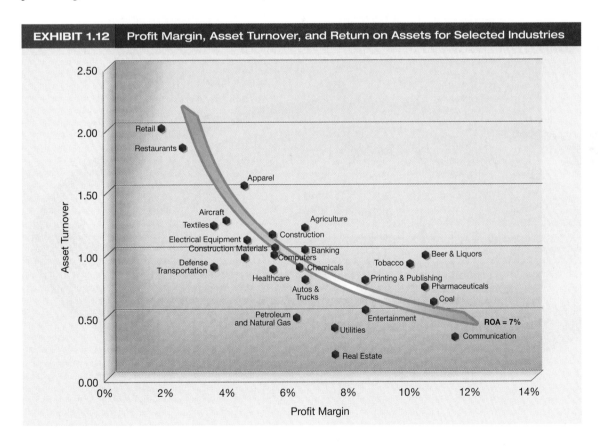

EXHIBIT 1.12   Profit Margin, Asset Turnover, and Return on Assets for Selected Industries

The key drivers of profitability are also key outputs of the financial accounting information system. Accordingly, good analysis demands that we understand accounting measurements, their limitations and strengths, and the potential for adjustments to further enrich our use of these numbers.

Berkshire Hathaway reported 2004 net income of $7.3 billion on average total assets of $184.72 billion, yielding a 3.96% return on assets, which is about average for all publicly traded companies. In his Chairman's report, Warren Buffett discusses the fact that he is finding it increasingly difficult to find undervalued investments of sufficient size to positively affect the performance of his company.

FINANCIAL ACCOUNTING AND BUSINESS ANALYSIS

LO5 Discuss the need to interpret accounting information within the broader business environment.

Analysis and interpretation of financial statements must consider the broader business context in which a company operates. This section describes how to systematically consider those broader business forces to enhance our analytical and interpretive skills. We can then better extract the insights from financial statements and better estimate future performance and firm value.

Analyzing the Competitive Environment

Financial statements are influenced by five important forces that confront the company and determine its competitive intensity: (A) industry competition, (B) buyer power, (C) supplier power, (D) product substitutes, and (E) threat of entry (for further discussion, see Porter, *Competitive Strategy: Techniques for Analyzing Industries and Competitors,* The Free Press, 1980 and 1998).

These five forces are depicted graphically in Exhibit 1.13.

EXHIBIT 1.13 Competitive Forces within the Broader Business Environment

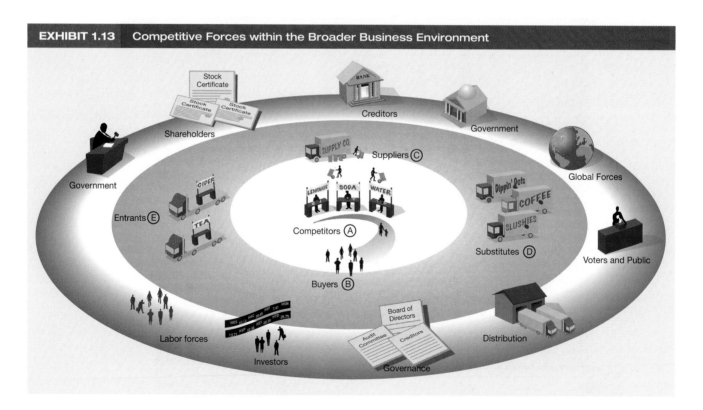

Applying Competitive Analysis for Financial Interpretations

To illustrate, we apply competitive analysis to help us interpret the financial results of **McLane Company**. McLane is a subsidiary of Berkshire Hathaway that was acquired in 2003 for cash of $1.5 billion as explained in the following note to the Berkshire annual report:

> On May 23, 2003, Berkshire acquired McLane Company, Inc., a distributor of grocery and food products to retailers, convenience stores, and restaurants. See Note 2 to the Consolidated

Financial Statements for additional information regarding the McLane acquisition. Results of McLane's business operations are included in Berkshire's consolidated results beginning on that date. McLane's revenues in 2004 totaled $23.4 billion and for the full year 2003 totaled about $22 billion. Pre-tax earnings totaled $228 million in 2004 and $225 million for the full year 2003. The comparative year-to-date increases in sales reflect the addition of new customers since Berkshire's acquisition and growth in the food service business. In 2004, approximately 33% of McLane's annual revenues were derived from sales to Wal-Mart Stores, Inc. McLane's business is marked by high sales volume and very thin profit margins.

McLane is a wholesaler of food products in that it purchases food products in finished and semi-finished form from agricultural and food-related businesses and resells them to grocery and convenience food stores. The extensive distribution network required in this business entails considerable investment.

A competitive analysis of McLane's financial results includes the following observations:

- **Industry competitors.** McLane has many competitors with food products that are difficult to differentiate.
- **Bargaining power of buyers.** A third of McLane's sales are to Wal-Mart. Wal-Mart has considerable buying power that limits seller profits. Further, the food industry is characterized by high turnover and low profit margins, which implies that cost control is key to success.
- **Bargaining power of suppliers.** McLane is large ($22 billion in annual sales), which implies its suppliers are unlikely to exert forces to increase its cost of sales.
- **Threat of substitution.** Grocery items are usually not well differentiated. This means the threat of substitution is high, which inhibits its ability to raise selling prices.
- **Threat of entry.** High investment costs (such as warehousing and logistics) are a barrier to entry in McLane's business. This means the threat of entry is relatively low.

Our analysis shows that McLane is a high-volume, low-margin company. Its ability to control costs is crucial to its financial performance, including its ability to fully utilize its assets. Evaluation of McLane's financial statements, therefore, should focus on these dimensions, and its financial statements must be evaluated within this broader environment.

Assessing the Broader Business Environment

A quality accounting analysis depends on an effective business analysis. Before we analyze accounting numbers, we must ask further questions about the company's broader business environment including:

- *Life cycle* At what stage in its life is this company? Is it a startup, experiencing growing pains? Is it strong and mature, reaping the benefits of competitive advantages? Is it nearing the end of its life, trying to milk what it can from stagnant product lines?
- *Outputs* What products does it sell? Are its products new, established, or dated? Do its products have substitutes? How complicated are its products to produce?
- *Inputs* Who are its suppliers? Are there many supply sources? Does the company depend on a few supply sources with potential for high input costs?
- *Capital* Must or should it seek capital from public markets? Is it going public? Is it seeking to use its stock to acquire another company? Is it in danger of defaulting on debt covenants? Are there incentives to tell an overly optimistic story to attract lower cost capital or to avoid default on debt?
- *Labor* Who are its managers? What are their backgrounds? Do they buy into the firm's strategy and the means of achieving it? Are they competent? What is the state of employee relations? Is labor unionized?
- *Governance* How effective is its corporate governance? Does it have a strong and independent board of directors? Does a strong audit committee of the board exist, and is it populated with outsiders? Does management have a large portion of its wealth tied to the company's stock?

■ *Risk* Is it now or expected to be subject to lawsuits from competitors or shareholders? Is it under investigation by regulators? Has it changed auditors? If so, why? Are its auditors independent? Does it face environmental or political risks?

We must consider the broader business context in which a company operates as we read and interpret its financial statements. The outer part of Exhibit 1.13 emphasizes that a review of financial statements, which reflect business activities, cannot be undertaken in a vacuum. It is contextual and can only be effectively undertaken within the framework of a thorough understanding of the broader forces that impact company performance.

CHAPTER-END REVIEW

Following are selected ratios of **Procter & Gamble**:

	Profit Margin	Asset Turnover
2003	12.0%	1.027
2004	12.6%	1.024

Required
a. Was the company profitable in 2004? What evidence supports your inference?
b. Do you interpret the change in the company's asset turnover rate as a positive development? Explain.
c. Compute the return on assets (ROA) for 2004 (show computations).

Solution
a. Procter & Gamble was profitable in 2004 as evidenced by its positive profit margin of 12.6%.
b. Asset turnover slightly decreased from 1.027 in 2003 to 1.024 in 2004. This is not a positive development as it indicates that assets are not generating the level of sales that they did in the prior year—however, this change is probably not material. Moreover, ROA increased in 2004; thus, the slight decline in turnover might be related to managerial initiatives to increase profit margin (and relatedly ROA).
c. Return on Assets (ROA) = Profit Margin × Asset Turnover = 12.6% × 1.024 = 12.9% (versus 12.3% in 2003)

SUMMARY

LO1 **Describe how companies report their business activities and how this fits with the accounting equation. (p. 5)**

■ To effectively manage a company or infer whether it is well managed, we must understand its activities as well as the competitive and regulatory environment in which it operates.

■ All corporations *plan* business activities, *finance* and *invest* is them, and then engage in *operations*.

■ Financing is obtained partly from stockholders and partly from creditors, including suppliers (operating creditors) and lenders (investing creditors).

■ Investing activities involve the acquisition and disposition of the company's productive resources called assets.

■ Operating activities include the production of goods or services that create operating revenues (sales) and expenses (costs). Operating profit (income) arises when operating revenues exceed operating expenses. Selecting the proper mix of operating activities is known as strategic management.

LO2 **Identify the users (and suppliers) of financial information. (p. 10)**

■ There are many diverse users of financial information and their benefits, as well as the firm's benefits. The benefits of disclosure of credible financial information exceed the costs of providing the information.

LO3 **Introduce the four basic financial statements including the balance sheet, the income statement, the statement of stockholders' equity, and the statement of cash flows. (p. 13)**

■ The four basic financial statements used to periodically report the company's progress are the balance sheet, the income statement, the statement of stockholders' equity, and the statement of cash flows. These statements articulate with one another.

- The balance sheet reports the company's financial position *at a point* in time. It lists the company's asset, liability, and equity items, and it typically aggregates similar items.

- The income statement reports the firm's operating activities in determining the profit earned, and thereby the firm's performance *over a period* of time.

- The stockholder's equity account reports the changes in the key equity accounts *over a period* of time.

- The statement of cash flows reports the cash flows into and out of the firm separately from operating, investing, and financing sources *over a period* of time.

Explain the importance and basics of analyzing profitability. (p. 20)   **LO4**

- One of the more important metrics used to measure a company's performance is *return on assets,* measured as income divided by average total assets. This measure can be further broken down into the company's profit margin times its asset turnover

Discuss the need to interpret accounting information within the broader business environment. (p. 22)   **LO5**

- The analysis and interpretation of financial statements must consider the broader context in which the firm operates.

- Porter's five forces, which are; industry competitors, buyer bargaining power, supplier bargaining power, substitution threats, and entry threats, provide a useful template for analyzing the competitive environment.

APPENDIX 1A: Accounting Principles and Governance Structures

Financial Accounting Environment

Information in financial statements is crucial to company valuation and, by extension, the valuation of its debt and equity securities. Financial statements affect the prices paid for its equity securities and interest rates attached to its debt securities.

The importance of financial statements means that their reliability is of paramount importance. This includes the crucial role of *ethics.* To the extent that financial performance and condition are accurately communicated to business decision makers, debt and equity securities are more accurately priced. By extension, it is also important to recognize the crucial role of financial accounting in efficient resource allocation within and across economies. We must also recognize its importance to the effectiveness of securities markets—and other markets such as labor, input, and output markets.

To illustrate its importance, imagine the consequences of a breakdown in the integrity of financial accounting. **Enron** provides a case in point. Once it became clear to the markets that Enron had not faithfully and accurately reported its financial condition and performance, people became unwilling to purchase its securities. The value of its debt and equity securities dropped precipitously and the company was unable to obtain the cash needed for operating activities. Within months of the disclosure of its financial accounting irregularities, Enron, with revenues of over $100 billion and total company value of over $60 billion, the fifth largest U.S. company, was bankrupt!

Further historical evidence of the importance of financial accounting is provided by the Great Depression of the 20th century. This depression was caused, in large part, by the failure of companies to faithfully report their financial condition and performance.

Oversight of Financial Accounting

The Great Depression led Congress to pass the 1933 Securities Act. This act had two main objectives: (1) to require disclosure of financial and other information about securities being offered for public sale; and (2) to prohibit deceit, misrepresentations, and other fraud in the sale of securities. This act also required that companies register all securities proposed for public sale and disclose information about the securities being offered, including information about company financial condition and performance. This act became and remains a foundation for contemporary financial accounting.

Congress also passed the 1934 Securities Act, which created the **Securities and Exchange Commission (SEC)** and gave it broad powers to regulate the issuance and trading of securities. The act also provided that companies with more than $10 million in assets and whose securities are held by more than 500 owners must file annual and other periodic reports, including financial statements that are available for download from the SEC's **EDGAR** database (www.sec.gov).

The SEC has ultimate authority over U.S. financial reporting, including setting accounting standards for preparing financial statements. The SEC has, however, ceded the authority to set accounting standards to businesses themselves in the form of a nongovernmental body, the American Institute of Certified Public Accountants (AICPA). Over the years, the AICPA has sponsored three (nonoverlapping in time) standard-setting organizations, each of which was governed by representatives from private industry, including accountants, investment managers, securities analysts, academics, and corporate managers.

The current standard-setting organization is the **Financial Accounting Standards Board (FASB)**, which has published over 150 accounting standards governing the preparation of financial reports. This is in addition to over 40 standards that were written by predecessor organizations to the FASB and numerous bulletins and interpretations, all of which form the body of accounting standards governing financial statements, called **Generally Accepted Accounting Principles (GAAP)**.

The standard-setting process is arduous, often lasting a decade and involving extensive comment by the public, public officials, accountants, academics, investors, analysts, and corporate preparers of financial reports. The reason for this involved process is that amendments to existing standards or the creation of new standards affect the reported financial performance and condition of companies—that is, their reported profits and other measures of financial condition. Consequently, given the widespread impact of financial accounting, there are considerable **economic consequences** as a result of accounting changes.

Choices in Financial Accounting

Some people mistakenly assume that financial accounting is an exact discipline—that is, companies select the proper standard to account for a transaction and then follow the rules. The reality is that GAAP allows companies choices in preparing financial statements. The choice of methods often yields financial statements that are markedly different from one another in terms of reported income, assets, liabilities, and equity amounts.

People often are surprised that financial statements depend on numerous estimates. For example, companies must estimate the amounts owed from customers that will eventually be collected, the length of time that buildings and equipment will be productive, the value impairments of assets, the prediction of future costs such as warranties, the prediction of future pension costs, and so on.

Accounting standard setters walk a fine line regarding choice in accounting. On one hand, they are concerned that choice in preparing financial statements will lead to abuse by those seeking to gain by influencing decisions of those who rely on those statements. On the other hand, they are concerned that companies are too diverse for a 'one size fits all' financial accounting system. Standard setters are also sensitive to the costs of reporting when crafting a new standard.

Enron exemplifies rigidity problems with accounting standards. A set of accounting standards relating to special purpose entities (SPEs) also called variable interest entities provided preparers with guidelines under which these entities are and are not aggregated with the companies that established them. Unfortunately, once guidelines are set, some people work diligently to structure these entities so as to just miss the requirements to aggregate them with the financial statements of the establishing company. This is one example of *off-balance-sheet financing*.

For most of its existence, the FASB has promulgated standards that were quite complicated and replete with guidelines. This invited abuse of the type embodied by the Enron scandal. Consequently, the pendulum has begun to swing away from such rigidity. Now, once financial statements are prepared, company management is required to step back from the details and make a judgment on whether the statements taken as a whole 'fairly present' the financial condition of the company.

Moreover, as a result of the 2002 **Sarbanes-Oxley Act**, the SEC requires the chief executive officer (CEO) of the company and its chief financial officer (CFO) to personally sign a statement attesting to the accuracy and completeness of financial statements. This requirement is an important step in restoring confidence in the integrity of financial accounting. The statements signed by both the CEO and CFO contain the following commitments:

- Both the CEO and CFO have personally reviewed the annual report
- There are no untrue statements of a material fact or the failure to state a material fact necessary to make the statements not misleading
- Financial statements fairly present in all material respects the financial condition of the company
- All material facts are disclosed to the company's auditors and board of directors
- No changes to its system of internal controls are made unless properly communicated

The prospect of personal losses is designed to make these managers more vigilant in monitoring the financial accounting system.

Regulatory and Legal Environment

Even though managers must personally attest to the completeness and accuracy of company financial statements, markets demand further assurances from outside parties to achieve the level of confidence necessary to warrant investment, credit, and other business decisions. The regulatory and legal environment provides further assurance that financial statements are complete and accurate.

Board of Directors and the Audit Committee

Law requires each publicly traded company to have a board of directors, where stockholders elect each director. This board represents the company owners and oversees management. The board also hires executive management and regularly reviews company operations.

The board of directors usually establishes several subcommittees to focus on particular governance tasks such as compensation, strategic plans, and financial management. Exhibit 1A.1 illustrates a typical organization of a company's governance structure. Corporate governance refers to the checks and balances that monitor company and manager activities. Governance committees are commonplace. One of these, the audit committee, oversees the financial accounting system.

The audit committee preferably consists solely of outside directors, excluding the CEO. As part of its oversight of the financial accounting system, the audit committee focuses on **internal controls**, which refers to the policies and

EXHIBIT 1A.1

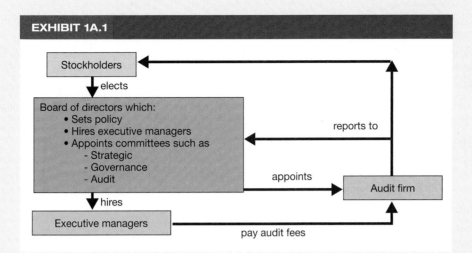

procedures used to protect assets, ensure reliable accounting, promote efficient operations, and urge adherence to company policies.

YOU MAKE THE CALL

You are a CEO   All publicly traded companies are required to have at least one member of its audit committee designated and qualified as a financial expert. What are the pros and cons of such a requirement? [Answers on page 31]

Statement of Management Responsibility

Financial statements for each publicly traded company must contain a **statement of responsibility** such as that for **DuPont** in Exhibit 1A.2.

EXHIBIT 1A.2   Responsibility for Financial Reporting

Responsibility for Financial Reporting Report of Independent Accountants

Management is responsible for the consolidated financial statements and the other financial information contained in this Annual Report on Form 10-K. The financial statements have been prepared in conformity with accounting principles generally accepted in the United States of America and are considered by management to present fairly the company's financial position, results of operations and cash flows. The financial statements include some amounts that are based on management's best estimates and judgments.

The company's system of internal controls is designed to provide reasonable assurance as to the protection of assets against loss from unauthorized use or disposition, and the reliability of financial records for preparing financial statements and maintaining accountability for assets. The company's business ethics policy is the cornerstone of our internal control system. This policy sets forth management's commitment to conduct business worldwide with the highest ethical standards and in conformity with applicable laws. The business ethics policy also requires that the documents supporting all transactions clearly describe their true nature and that all transactions be properly reported and classified in the financial records. The system is monitored by an extensive program of internal audit, and management believes that the system of internal controls at December 31, 2002, meets the objectives noted above.

The financial statements have been audited by the company's independent accountants, PricewaterhouseCoopers LLP. The purpose of their audit is to independently affirm the fairness of management's reporting of financial position, results of operations and cash flows. To express the opinion set forth in their report, they study and evaluate the internal controls to the extent they deem necessary. The adequacy of the company's internal controls and the accounting principles employed in financial reporting are under the general oversight of the Audit Committee of the Board of Directors. This committee also has responsibility for employing the independent accountants, subject to stockholder ratification. No member of this committee may be an officer or employee of the company or any subsidiary or affiliated company. The independent accountants and the internal auditors have direct access to the Audit Committee, and they meet with the committee from time to time, with and without management present, to discuss accounting, auditing and financial reporting matters.

The statement of responsibility contains several assertions by management:

1.   Financial statements are prepared by management, which assumes responsibility for them
2.   Financial statements are prepared in accordance with GAAP

3. Its system of internal controls provides *reasonable assurance* that assets are safeguarded and the information system is protected

4. Financial statements are audited by an outside auditing firm

5. Board of directors has an audit committee to oversee the financial accounting system and the system of internal controls

Management prepares financial statements—not the auditors that are hired to express an opinion on those statements. Moreover, management's interests may or may not be aligned with those of other stakeholders.

Audit Report

Financial statements for each publicly traded company must be audited by an independent audit firm. There are currently four large, international auditing firms (and other smaller firms) that are authorized by the SEC to provide auditing services for companies that issue securities to the public:

1. **Deloitte & Touche LLP**
2. **Ernst & Young LLP**
3. **KPMG LLP**
4. **PricewaterhouseCoopers LLP**

These four firms provide opinions for the majority of financial statements filed by publicly traded U.S. companies. There also are a number of regional accounting firms that provide audit services for both publicly traded and nontraded private companies.

Auditors are hired by the Audit Committee of the Board of Directors to review and express an opinion on its financial statements. The audit opinion expressed by Deloitte & Touche, LLP on the financial statements of Berkshire Hathaway is reproduced in Exhibit 1A.3.

EXHIBIT 1A.3   Audit Report for Berkshire Hathaway

INDEPENDENT AUDITORS' REPORT

To the Board of Directors and Shareholders of Berkshire Hathaway Inc.

We have audited the accompanying consolidated balance sheets of Berkshire Hathaway Inc. and subsidiaries (the "Company") as of December 31, 2004 and 2003, and the related consolidated statements of earnings, cash flows, and changes in shareholders' equity and comprehensive income for each of the three years in the period ended December 31, 2004. These financial statements are the responsibility of the Company's management. Our responsibility is to express an opinion on these financial statements based on our audits.

We conducted our audits in accordance with the standards of the Public Company Accounting Oversight Board (United States). Those standards require that we plan and perform the audit to obtain reasonable assurance about whether the financial statements are free of material misstatement. An audit includes examining, on a test basis, evidence supporting the amounts and disclosures in the financial statements. An audit also includes assessing the accounting principles used and significant estimates made by management, as well as evaluating the overall financial statement presentation. We believe that our audits provide a reasonable basis for our opinion.

In our opinion, such consolidated financial statements present fairly, in all material respects, the financial position of Berkshire Hathaway Inc. and subsidiaries as of December 31, 2004 and 2003, and the results of their operations and their cash flows for each of the three years in the period ended December 31, 2004, in conformity with accounting principles generally accepted in the United States of America.

We have also audited, in accordance with the standards of the Public Company Accounting Oversight Board (United States), the effectiveness of the Company's internal control over financial reporting as of December 31, 2004, based on the criteria established in *Internal Control–Integrated Framework* issued by the Committee of Sponsoring Organizations of the Treadway Commission and our report dated March 3, 2005, expressed an unqualified opinion on management's assessment of the effectiveness of the Company's internal control over financial reporting and an unqualified opinion on the effectiveness of the Company's internal control over financial reporting.

DELOITTE & TOUCHE LLP
Omaha, Nebraska
March 3, 2005

The basic structure of a 'clean' audit report is consistent across companies and includes these assertions:

- Financial statements *present fairly* and *in all material respects* a company's financial condition.
- Financial statements are prepared in conformity with GAAP.

- Financial statements are management's responsibility. Auditor responsibility is to express an opinion on those statements.
- Auditing involves a sampling of transactions, not investigation of each transaction.
- Audit opinion provides *reasonable assurance* that the statements are free of *material* misstatements, not a guarantee.
- Auditors review accounting policies used by management and the estimates used in preparing the statements.

The audit opinion is not based on a test of each transaction. Auditors usually develop statistical samples and infer test results to other transactions. The audit report is not a guarantee that no misstatements exist. Auditors only provide reasonable assurance that the statements are free of material misstatements. Their use of the word *reasonable* is deliberate, as they do not want to be held to an absolute standard should problems be subsequently uncovered. The word *material* is used in the sense that an item must be of sufficient magnitude to make a difference, that is, to change the perceptions or decisions of the user (such as a decision to purchase stock or extend credit).

The requirement of auditor independence is the cornerstone of effective auditing. But the company pays the audit fee. Auditing firms also often perform services for the company it audits, such as tax planning, information system design and implementation, and benchmarking analyses.

Regulators have questioned the perceived lack of independence of auditing firms and the degree to which a lack of independence compromises the ability of auditing firms to challenge a client's dubious accounting. Auditing firms reject any assertion that their independence is compromised. The Sarbanes-Oxley Act of 2002 was passed in part to address the independence issue.

YOU MAKE THE CALL

You are a member of the Board of Directors   Until recently accounting firms were permitted to earn money for consulting activities performed for clients they audited. Do you see any reason why this might not be an acceptable practice? Do you see any advantage to your firm from allowing such activity? [Answers on page 31]

BUSINESS INSIGHT

Warren Buffett on Audit Committees   "Audit committees can't audit. Only a company's outside auditor can determine whether the earnings that a management purports to have made are suspect. Reforms that ignore this reality and that instead focus on the structure and charter of the audit committee will accomplish little.

As we've discussed, far too many managers have fudged their company's numbers in recent years, using both accounting and operational techniques that are typically legal but that nevertheless materially mislead investors. Frequently, auditors knew about these deceptions. Too often, however, they remained silent. The key job of the audit committee is simply to get the auditors to divulge what they know.

To do this job, the committee must make sure that the auditors worry more about misleading its members than about offending management. In recent years auditors have not felt that way. They have instead generally viewed the CEO, rather than the shareholders or directors, as their client. That has been a natural result of day-to-day working relationships and also of the auditors' understanding that, no matter what the book says, the CEO and CFO pay their fees and determine whether they are retained for both auditing and other work. The rules that have been recently instituted won't materially change this reality. What will break this cozy relationship is audit committees unequivocally putting auditors on the spot, making them understand they will become liable for major monetary penalties if they don't come forth with what they know or suspect." —Warren Buffett, Berkshire Hathaway annual report

SEC Enforcement Actions

Companies whose securities are issued to the public must file reports with the SEC (see **www.sec.gov**). One of these reports is the 10-K, which includes the annual financial statements (quarterly statements are filed under report 10-Q). The 10-K report provides more information than the company's glossy annual report, which is partly a marketing document (although the basic financial statements are identical). In analyzing a firm, we should use the 10-K because of its additional information.

The SEC has ultimate authority to accept or reject financial statements that companies submit. Should the SEC reject the financial statements a company files, the company is then required to either resolve any disagreement or restate and refile them. Any restatement takes time and such companies usually incur a marked decline in their market value. For example, the following SEC press release is an example of SEC action against Xerox arising from its financial statements:

Washington, D.C., April 11, 2002—The Securities and Exchange Commission today filed suit against **Xerox Corporation** in connection with a wide-ranging, four-year scheme to defraud investors. The SEC's complaint alleges that from at least 1997 through 2000, Xerox used a variety of what it called 'accounting actions' and 'accounting opportunities' to meet or exceed Wall Street expectations and disguise its true operating performance from investors.

These actions, most of which violated generally accepted accounting principles (GAAP), accelerated the company's recognition of equipment revenue by over $3 billion and increased its pre-tax earnings by approximately $1.5 billion. Xerox agreed to settle the SEC's complaint by consenting to the entry of an injunction for violations of the antifraud and other provisions of the federal securities laws; restating its financials for the years 1997 to 2000; agreeing to a special review of its accounting controls; and paying an unprecedented $10 million penalty. (SEC Website, April 2002)

The SEC's power to require restatement, with its consequent potential damage to the company's reputation and stock price, is a major deterrent to those desiring to bias their financial accounts to achieve a particular goal.

Courts

Courts provide remedies to individuals or companies that can show damages as a result of material misstatements in financial numbers. Typical court actions involve shareholders that sue the company and its auditors, alleging that the company disclosed, and auditors attested to, false and misleading financial statements. The number of such shareholder suits has increased dramatically according to Stanford Law School's Securities Class Action Clearinghouse, which commented that "an increasing percentage of the complaints filed allege financial misstatements and violations of GAAP, or generally accepted accounting principles."

Both the SEC and attorneys representing shareholders in a class action suit brought one such suit against **Rite Aid Corporation**, the large drug store chain. The SEC described Rite Aid's financial accounting as follows:

Rite Aid's former senior management team engaged in a financial fraud that materially overstated the Company's net income for the fiscal years (FY) 1998, 1999, the intervening quarters and the first quarter of FY 2000. In addition, the former senior management failed to disclose material information, including related party transactions, in Proxy and Registration Statements, as well as a Form 8-K filed in February 1999. Initially in July 2000 and later in October 2000, Rite Aid restated reported cumulative pre-tax income by a total of $2.3 billion and cumulative net income by $1.6 billion. Rite Aid's massive restatement was, and to this day is, the largest financial restatement of income by a public company. As a result of the improper acts and accounting practices described below, Rite Aid violated the reporting, books and records, and internal controls provisions of the Exchange Act.

Sections 13(a) and 13(b)(2)(A) of the Exchange Act and Rules 12b-20, 13a-1, and 13a-13 require issuers to make and keep accurate books, records, and accounts, to file annual and quarterly reports with the Commission, and to keep reported information current and not misleading. Section 13(b)(2)(B) of the Exchange Act requires issuers to devise and maintain a system of internal accounting controls sufficient to provide reasonable assurances that transactions are recorded as necessary to permit preparation of financial statements in conformity with generally accepted accounting principles and to maintain the accountability of assets.

Rite Aid's internal books, records, and accounts reflected numerous transactions that were invalid or without substantiation, had no legitimate business purpose, and were recorded in violation of GAAP. Moreover, from at least 1997 to July 11, 2000, all of the annual and quarterly reports that Rite Aid filed with the Commission contained misleading financial statements. As a result, Rite Aid violated Sections 13(a) and 13(b)(2)(A) of the Exchange Act and Rules 12b-20, 13a-1, and 13a-13 thereunder.

Rite Aid's system of internal accounting controls was not designed to provide reasonable assurances that transactions were recorded as necessary to permit preparation of financial statements in conformity with GAAP or to maintain the accountability of assets. Rite Aid's system of internal accounting controls failed to prevent, and indeed facilitated, the improper accounting practices described in detail above. As a result, Rite Aid violated Section 13(b) of the Exchange Act and Rule 13(b)(2)(B) thereunder. (Source: SEC Website, April 2003)

Rite Aid's settlement agreement with shareholders provided for the following payments:

1. Rite Aid agreed to pay $193 million in damages.
2. Rite Aid's auditors agreed to pay $125 million in damages.
3. Martin Grass, Rite Aid's former chair, agreed to pay $1.45 million in damages.
4. Timothy Noonan, Rite Aid's former COO, agreed to pay $130,000 in damages.

GUIDANCE ANSWERS

YOU MAKE THE CALL

You are a Product Manager There are at least two considerations that must be balanced—namely, the disclosure requirements and your company's need to protect its competitive advantages. You must comply with all minimum required disclosures. The extent to which you offer additional disclosures depends on the sensitivity of the information; that is, how beneficial it is to your existing and potential competitors. Another consideration is how the information disclosed will impact your existing and potential investors. Disclosures such as this can be beneficial in that they convey the positive investments that are available to your company. Still, there are many stakeholders impacted by your decision and each must be given due consideration.

YOU MAKE THE CALL

You are a Financial Analyst   This question has received a lot of discussion on both sides of the question under the title "Economic Consequences." On one side are those who maintain that accounting rules should, indeed most of these folks would say must, not only reflect a rule's economic consequences but should often be designed to facilitate the attainment of a specific economic goal. A recent example is the case where the oil industry lobbied for an accounting rule that they and others believed would increase the incentive to explore and develop new oil deposits.

Those on the other side of the argument believe that accounting should try to provide data that is objective, reliable, and free from bias without considering the economic consequences of the decision that might be made. They believe that accounting rule makers have neither the insight nor the public mandate to attempt forecasts of the economic effects of financial reporting. Decisions that will affect the allocation of resources or that affect society's social structure should be made only by our elected representative.

While there are substantive points to be made on both sides, your authors would stand by those who believe that it is the job of accounting rule makers to work toward the objective of financial reporting that reflects economic reality, subject to practical measurement limitations.

YOU MAKE THE CALL

You are a Shareholder   As a shareholder, I would assume that the corporation wants me to know the philosophy of the company. The CEO, Warren Buffett, is well-known. If I am an individual investor, I have many options for investment including mutual funds, which through diversification will lower the risk of my investment. Why should I invest in his firm given the very high price of each share? A substantial part of the growth of Berkshire Hathaway has been accomplished through acquisitions. How does he decide which firms to acquire and what is his management philosophy? Basically, do I feel comfortable that his firm will act as a good steward of the funds I entrust to it.

If I am an institutional investor with a mutual fund or a pension fund, again I am interested in how the firm is managed and whether I can rely on the financial statements to give me a honest picture of the firm's financial health and profitability.

YOU MAKE THE CALL

You are a Chief Financial Officer   Financial performance is typically measured by return on assets, which can be disaggregated into the net profit margin (income/sales) and the asset turnover rate (sales/average assets). This disaggregation might lead you to a review of both the factors affecting profitability (gross margins and expense control) and how effectively your company is utilizing its assets (the turnover rates). Finding ways to increase profitability and reduce the amount of invested capital contributes to improved financial performance.

YOU MAKE THE CALL

You are a CEO   The Board of Directors is responsible to the stockholders of the corporation. In that role, one of the Board's duties, which is the responsibility of the Audit Committee, is to oversee the financial reporting of the firm to ensure that the reporting is reliable and in accordance with the rules promulgated by the Financial Accounting Standards Board. A second major responsibility of the Audit Committee is to ensure that the corporation's internal controls, which are designed to protect the corporation's assets and enforce compliance with company policy, are followed. Such responsibilities are best left to a member of the Board with substantive financial experience. Hence, a financial expert is not only required but is also an indispensable board member.

The availability of individuals with the necessary background is, however, limited. Many qualified individuals are reluctant to take on this role because of their vulnerability if the company is sued for misrepresenting its financial situation or for fraud. Further, the potential legal liability attached to the chair of the Audit Committee, typically the financial expert, means that the corporation must compensate this individual above a normal director's remuneration and provide increased director insurance.

YOU MAKE THE CALL

You are a Member of the Board of Directors   In order to perform a thorough audit, a company's auditors must gain an intimate knowledge of its operations, its internal controls, and its accounting system. Because of this familiarity, the accounting firm is in a position to provide insights and recommendations that another consulting firm might not be able to provide. However, the independence of the auditor is critical to the credibility of the audit. Audit firms lose some of their independence when they are hired as consultants. The concern is that the desire to retain a profitable consulting engagement might lead the auditors to tailor their audit opinions so as to "satisfy the customer." In order to maintain the independence of the auditor, accounting firms are now prohibited from performing consulting services for their audit clients.

KEY TERMS

Accounting equation (p. 8)

Asset turnover (p. 20)

Balance sheet (p. 14)

Capital markets (p. 9)

Covenants (p. 10)

Economic consequences (p. 26)

EDGAR database (p. 25)

Financial Accounting Standards
   Board (FASB) (p. 25)

Financing activities (p. 6)

Fundamental analysis (p. 11)

Generally accepted accounting
   principles (GAAP) (p. 13)

Income statement (p. 14)

Internal controls (p. 26)

Investing activities (p. 7)

Management discussion and
   analysis (MD&A) (p. 18)

Net profit margin (p. 20)

Operating activities (p. 9)

Return (p. 9)

Return on assets (ROA) (p. 20)

Risk (p. 9)

Sarbanes-Oxley Act (p. 26)

Securities and Exchange Commission
   (SEC) (p. 25)

Statement of cash flows (p. 16)

Statement of responsibility (p. 27)

Statement of stockholders' equity
   (p. 15)

MULTIPLE CHOICE

Multiple Choice Answers

1. c   2. a   3. a   4. d   5. b

1. Which one of the following items would be relied upon by Mr. Buffett in deciding whether to acquire a new business?
    a. Earnings before interest, taxes, depreciation, and amortization (EBITDA) of the new business
    b. The earnings projections from corporate management
    c. The footnotes to the financial statements of the new business
    d. The pro forma financial statements predicting steady growth

2. Resources used in making a product or delivering a service are known as
    a. operating assets.
    b. current assets.
    c. stockholders' equity.
    d. nonoperating assets.

3. Banks that lend money to corporations are considered
    a. investing creditors.
    b. operating creditors.
    c. both a and b above.
    d. neither a nor b above.

4. Which of the following is not one of the four basic financial reports?
    a. The balance sheet
    b. The income statement
    c. The statement of stockholders' equity
    d. The notes to the financial statements

5. Which of the following expressions is a correct statement of the accounting equation?
    a. Equity + Assets = Liability
    b. Assets − (Liabilities + Equity) = 0
    c. Liabilities − Equity = Assets
    d. Liabilities + Assets = Equity

Superscript ^{A} denotes assignments based on Appendix 1A.

DISCUSSION QUESTIONS

Q1-1. What are the three major business activities of a company that are motivated and shaped by planning activities? Explain each activity.

Q1-2. The accounting equation (Assets = Liabilities + Equity) is a fundamental business concept. Explain what this equation reveals about a company's sources and uses of funds and the claims on company resources.

Q1-3. Companies prepare four primary financial statements. What are those financial statements and what information is typically conveyed in each?

Q1-4. Does a balance sheet report on a period of time or at a point in time? Also, explain the information conveyed in that report.

Q1-5. Does an income statement report on a period of time or at a point in time? Also, explain the information conveyed in that report.

Q1-6. Does a statement of cash flows report on a period of time or at a point in time? Also, explain the information and activities conveyed in that report.

Q1-7. Explain what is meant by the articulation of financial statements.

Q1-8. The trade-off between risk and return is a fundamental business concept. Briefly describe both risk and return and their trade-off. Provide some examples that demonstrate investments of varying risk and the approximate returns that you might expect to earn on those investments.

Q1-9. Identify the five forces that influence competitive intensity and discuss the impact of each.

Q1-10. Financial statements are used by several interested stakeholders. Develop a listing of three or more potential external users of financial statements and their applications.

Q1-11. What ethical issues might managers face in dealing with confidential information?

Q1-12. Return on assets (ROA) is an important summary measure of financial performance. How is it computed? Describe what this metric reveals about company performance.

Q1-13. Refer to Exhibit 1.12 to answer (a) through (c).
    a. Discuss possible reasons for the difference in profit margin and asset turnover between the Retail and the Communication industries.
    b. Which industry is more profitable, Pharmaceuticals or Healthcare? Why do you believe this is the case?
    c. Which industry has the higher asset turnover, Restaurants or Agriculture? Why do you believe this is the case?

Q1-14.[A] Access the 2004 10-K for **Procter & Gamble** at the SEC's EDGAR database of financial reports (www.sec.gov). Who is P&G's auditor? What specific language does its auditor use in expressing its opinion and what responsibilities does it assume?

Procter & Gamble (PG)

Q1-15.[A] Business decision makers external to the company increasingly demand more financial information on business activities of companies. Discuss the reasons why companies have traditionally opposed the efforts of regulatory agencies like the SEC to require more disclosure.

Q1-16.[A] What are generally accepted accounting principles and what organization presently establishes them?

Q1-17.[A] Corporate governance has received considerable attention since the collapse of **Enron** and other accounting-related scandals. What is meant by corporate governance? What are the primary means by which sound corporate governance is achieved?

Enron (ENRNQ)

Q1-18.[A] What is the primary function of the auditor? To what does the auditor attest in its opinion?

MINI EXERCISES

M1-19. **Financing and Investing Relations, and Financing Sources** **(LO1)**
Total assets of **Dell Computer Corporation** equal $15,470 million and its equity is $4,873 million. What is the amount of its liabilities? Does Dell receive more financing from its owners or nonowners, and what percentage of financing is provided by its owners?

Dell Computer Corporation (DELL)

M1-20. **Financing and Investing Relations, and Financing Sources** **(LO1)**
Total assets of **Ford Motor Company** equal $315,920 million and its liabilities equal $304,269 million. What is the amount of its equity? Does Ford receive more financing from its owners or nonowners, and what percentage of financing is provided by its owners?

Ford Motor Company (F)

M1-21. **Applying the Accounting Equation and Computing Financing Proportions** **(LO1)**
Use the accounting equation to compute the missing financial amounts (a), (b), and (c). Which of these companies is more owner-financed? Which of these companies is more nonowner-financed?

($ millions)	Assets	=	Liabilities	+	Equity
Hewlett-Packard	$74,708		$ 36,962		$ (a)
General Mills	$18,227		$ (b)		$4,175
General Motors	$ (c)		$365,057		$6,814

Hewlett-Packard (HPQ)

General Mills (GIS)

General Motors (GM)

M1-22. **Identifying Key Numbers from Financial Statements** **(LO1, 3)**
Access the 2004 10-K for **Winn-Dixie Stores, Inc.**, at the SEC's EDGAR database for financial reports (www.sec.gov). What are Winn Dixie's dollar amounts for assets, liabilities, and equity at June 30, 2004? Confirm that the accounting equation holds in this case. What percent of Winn Dixie's assets is financed from nonowner financing sources?

Winn-Dixie Stores, Inc. (WIN)

M1-23. **Verifying Articulation of Financial Statements** (LO3)

Access the 2002 10-K for **DuPont** at the SEC's EDGAR database of financial reports (www.sec.gov). Using its December 31, 2002, consolidated statement of stockholders' equity, prepare a table showing the articulation of its retained (reinvested) earnings for calendar-year 2002.

M1-24. **Identifying Financial Statement Line Items and Accounts** (LO3)

Several line items and account titles are listed below. For each, indicate in which of the following financial statement(s) you would likely find the item or account: income statement (IS), balance sheet (BS), statement of stockholders' equity (SE), or statement of cash flows (SCF).

a.	Cash asset	*d.* Contributed capital	*g.* Cash inflow for stock issued
b.	Expenses	*e.* Cash outflow for land	*h.* Cash outflow for dividends
c.	Noncash assets	*f.* Retained earnings	*i.* Net income

M1-25.[A] **Ethical Issues and Accounting Choices** (LO2, 5)

Assume that you are a technology services provider and you must decide on whether to record revenue from the installation of computer software for one of your clients. Your contract calls for acceptance of the software by the client within six months of installation before payment is due. Although you have not yet received formal acceptance, you are confident that it is forthcoming. Failure to record these revenues will cause your company to miss Wall Street's earnings estimates. What stakeholders will be affected by your decision and how might they be affected?

M1-26.[A] **Internal Controls and Their Importance** (LO5)

The **Sarbanes-Oxley** legislation requires companies to report on the effectiveness of their internal controls. What are internal controls and their purpose? Why do you think Congress felt it to be such an important area to monitor and report on?

EXERCISES

E1-27. **Applying the Accounting Equation and Assessing Financing Contributions** (LO1)

Determine the missing amount from each of the separate situations (a), (b), and (c) below. Which of these companies is more owner-financed? Which of these companies is more nonowner-financed?

Motorola, Inc. (MOT)
Kraft Foods (KFT)
Merck & Co. (MRK)

($ millions)	Assets	=	Liabilities	+	Equity
a. Motorola, Inc.	$31,152	=	$?		$11,239
b. Kraft Foods	$?	=	$31,268		$25,832
c. Merck & Co.	$47,561	=	$29,361		$?

E1-28. **Applying the Accounting Equation and Financial Statement Articulation** (LO1, 3)

Answer the following questions. (*Hint*: Apply the accounting equation.)

Intel (INTC)

a. **Intel** had assets equal to $44,224 million and liabilities equal to $8,756 million for a recent year-end. What was the total equity for Intel's business at year-end?

JetBlue (JBLU)

b. At the beginning of a recent year, **JetBlue**'s assets were $1,378 million and its equity was $415 million. During the year, assets increased $70 million and liabilities increased $30 million. What was its equity at the end of the year?

The Walt Disney Company (DIS)

c. At the beginning of a recent year, **The Walt Disney Company**'s liabilities equaled $26,197 million. During the year, assets increased by $400 million, and year-end assets equaled $50,388 million. Liabilities decreased $100 million during the year. What were its beginning and ending amounts for equity?

E1-29. **Specifying Financial Information Users and Uses** (LO2)

Financial statements have a wide audience of interested stakeholders. Identify two or more financial statement users that are external to the company. Specify two questions for each user identified that could be addressed or aided by use of financial statements.

E1-30. **Applying Financial Statement Relations to Compute Dividends** (LO3, 4)

Colgate-Palmolive (CL)

Colgate-Palmolive reports the following dollar balances in its stockholders' equity.

($ millions)	2003	2002
Contributed capital, net . . .	$ 45.8	$ 568.7
Retained earnings	7,433.0	6,518.5
Total equity	$7,478.8	$7,087.2

During 2003, Colgate-Palmolive reported net income of $1,421.3 million. What amount of dividends, if any, did Colgate-Palmolive pay to its shareholders in 2003? Assuming it paid dividends, this dividend amount constituted what percent of its net income?

E1-31. **Computing and Interpreting Financial Statement Ratios** (LO4)

Following are selected ratios of Briggs & Stratton (manufacturer of engines).

Briggs & Stratton (BGG)

	Net Profit Margin (Net Income/Sales)	Total Asset Turnover (Sales/Average Assets)
2000	8.58%	1.76
2001	3.66%	1.18

  a.   Was the company profitable in 2001? What evidence do you have of this?
  b.   Do you interpret the change in its total asset turnover rate as a positive development? Explain.
  c.   Compute the company's return on assets (ROA) for 2001 (show computations).

E1-32. **Computing Return on Assets and Applying the Accounting Equation** (LO1, 4)

Nordstrom, Inc., reports net income of $242.8 million for its fiscal year ended January 2004. At the beginning of that year, Nordstrom had $4,096.4 million in total assets. By fiscal year-end 2004, total assets had grown to $4,465.7. What is Nordstrom's return on assets (ROA)? Does its ROA seem adequate? Explain.

Nordstrom, Inc. (JWN)

E1-33.[A] **Accounting in Society** (LO2, 5)

Financial accounting plays an important role in modern society and business.
  a.   Identify two or more external stakeholders that are interested in a company's financial statements and what their particular interests are.
  b.   What are *generally accepted accounting principles,* and what organization has primary responsibility for their formulation?
  c.   What role does financial accounting play in the allocation of society's financial resources?
  d.   What are three aspects of the accounting environment that can create ethical pressure on management?

PROBLEMS

P1-34. **Applying the Accounting Equation and Financial Statement Articulation** (LO1, 3, 5)

The following table contains financial statement information for Procter & Gamble ($ millions):

Procter & Gamble (PG)

Year	Assets	Liabilities	Equity	Net Income	Cash Dividends
2001 . . .	$?	$22,377	$12,010	$2,922	$1,943
2002 . . .	40,776	?	13,706	4,352	2,095
2003 . . .	43,706	27,520	?	5,186	2,246

Required
  a.   Compute the missing amounts for assets, liabilities, and equity for each year.
  b.   Compute return on assets for 2002 and 2003. The average ROA for all publicly traded companies is about 5.5%. How does P&G compare with this average?
  c.   What factors do you think might allow a company like P&G to reap above-average returns? (*Hint*: Consider the five forces of competitive intensity.)

P1-35. **Formulating Financial Statements from Raw Data** (LO1, 3)

Following is selected financial information from General Mills, Inc., for its fiscal year ended May 30, 2004 ($ millions):

General Mills, Inc. (GIS)

Cash asset	$ 751
Net cash from operations	1,461
Sales	11,070
Stockholders' equity	5,547
Cost of goods sold	6,584
Net cash from financing	(943)
Total liabilities	12,901
Total expenses	3,431
Noncash assets	17,697

Net cash from investing	(470)
Net income	1,055
Cash, beginning year	703

Required

a. Prepare an income statement, balance sheet, and statement of cash flows for General Mills, Inc.

b. What portion of the financing is contributed by owners?

P1-36. Formulating Financial Statements from Raw Data (LO1, 3)

Abercrombie
& Fitch (ANF)

Following is selected financial information from Abercrombie & Fitch for its fiscal year ended January 31, 2004 ($ millions):

Cash asset	$ 511
Cash flows from operations	282
Sales	1,708
Stockholders' equity	871
Cost of goods sold	991
Cash flows from financing	(92)
Total liabilities	328
Expenses	512
Noncash assets	688
Cash flows from investing	(99)
Net income	205
Cash, beginning year	420

Required

a. Prepare an income statement, balance sheet, and statement of cash flows for Abercrombie & Fitch.

b. Determine the owner and nonowner financing levels.

P1-37. Formulating Financial Statements from Raw Data (LO1, 3)

Cisco Systems,
Inc. (CSCO)

Following is selected financial information from Cisco Systems, Inc., for the year ended July 31, 2004 ($ millions):

Cash asset	$ 3,722
Cash flows from operations	7,121
Sales	22,045
Stockholders' equity	25,916
Cost of goods sold	6,919
Cash flows from financing	(7,790)
Total liabilities	9,678
Expenses	10,725
Noncash assets	31,872
Cash flows from investing	466
Net income	4,401
Cash, beginning year	3,925

Required

Prepare an income statement, balance sheet, and statement of cash flows for Cisco Systems, Inc.

P1-38. Formulating a Statement of Stockholders' Equity from Raw Data (LO1, 3)

Crocker Corporation began calendar-year 2005 with stockholders' equity of $100,000, consisting of contributed capital of $70,000 and retained earnings of $30,000. During 2005, it issued additional stock for total cash proceeds of $30,000. It also reported $50,000 of net income, of which $25,000 was paid as a cash dividend to shareholders.

Required

Prepare the 2005 statement of stockholders' equity for Crocker Corporation.

P1-39. Formulating a Statement of Stockholders' Equity from Raw Data (LO3)

EA Systems, Inc., reports the following selected information at December 31, 2005 ($ millions):

Contributed capital, December 31, 2004 and 2005	$ 550
Retained earnings, December 31, 2004	2,437
Cash dividends, 2005	281
Net income, 2005	859

Required

Use this information to prepare its statement of stockholders' equity for 2005.

P1-40. **Computing, Analyzing, and Interpreting Return on Assets** **(LO3, 4)**

Nokia manufactures, markets, and sells phones and other electronics. Total assets for Nokia are €23,920 in 2003 and €23,327 in 2002. In 2003, Nokia reported net income of €3,592 on sales of €29,455.

Nokia (NOK)

Required

a. What is Nokia's return on assets for 2003?

b. Does return on assets seem satisfactory for Nokia given that its competitors average a 12% return on assets? Explain.

c. What are total expenses for Nokia in 2003?

d. What is Nokia's average total amount of liabilities plus equity for 2003?

P1-41. **Computing, Analyzing, and Interpreting Return on Assets and its Components** **(LO4, 5)**

Abercrombie & Fitch (ANF) reported net income of $205 million on sales of $1,700 million for fiscal year ended January 31, 2004. The January 31, 2004, balance sheet of ANF reports the following ($ millions):

Abercrombie & Fitch (ANF)

	2004	2003
Total assets	$1,199	$1,023

Required

a. What is ANF's return on assets? Given that the average ROA for all publicly traded firms is about 5.5%, how does ANF compare on ROA? Explain.

b. Decompose ANF's ROA into its net profit margin and total asset turnover. Given that the average net profit margin and asset turnover rate for all publicly traded firms is about 4.3% and 1.2 times, respectively, how does ANF compare on these measures? Explain.

c. Given the competitive nature of the retail clothing industry, can you identify any reasons why ANF should report an above-average level of financial performance? (*Hint*: Recall the five forces of competitive intensity.) Explain.

P1-42. **Computing, Analyzing, and Interpreting Return on Assets and Its Components** **(LO4, 5)**

McDonald's Corporation (MCD) reported 2003 net income of $1,470 million on sales of $17,140 million. The December 31, 2003, balance sheet of MCD reports the following ($ millions):

McDonald's Corporation (MCD)

	2003	2002
Total assets	$25,525	$23,971

Required

a. What is MCD's return on assets? Given that the average ROA for all publicly traded firms is about 5.5%, how does MCD compare on ROA? Explain.

b. Decompose MCD's ROA into its net profit margin and total asset turnover. Given that the average net profit margin and asset turnover rate for all publicly traded firms is about 4.3% and 1.2 times, respectively, how does MCD compare on these measures? Explain.

c. Given the competitive nature of the food service industry, can you identify any reasons why MCD should report this level of financial performance and any potential areas of concern? (*Hint*: Recall the five forces of competitive intensity.) Explain.

CASES AND PROJECTS

C1-43. **Computing, Analyzing, and Interpreting Return on Assets** **(LO4, 5)**

Following are summary financial statement data for both Kimberly-Clark and Procter & Gamble (industry competitors) for the years 2002 and 2003:

Kimberly-Clark (KMB)

Procter & Gamble (PG)

Kimberly-Clark Corporation (KMB)			
($ millions)	**Total Assets**	**Net Sales**	**Net Income**
2002	$15,586	$13,566	$1,675
2003	16,780	14,348	1,694

Procter & Gamble Company (PG)			
($ millions)	**Total Assets**	**Net Sales**	**Net Income**
2002	$40,776	$40,169	$4,352
2003	43,706	43,373	5,186

Required

a. Compute the return on assets (net income/average assets), the net profit margin (net income/sales), and the total asset turnover (sales/average assets) for both companies for 2003.

b. Verify that return on assets is equal to the product of net profit margin and total asset turnover for both companies. Show computations.

c. Which company reports a higher return on assets for 2003? Identify one or more reasons for this difference? (*Hint*: Consider the five forces of competitive intensity.)

C1-44.   **Computing, Analyzing, and Interpreting Return on Assets and Its Components**   (LO1, 2, 4)

Wal-Mart (WMT)

Wal-Mart (WMT) reported net income of $9,100 million on sales of $258,700 million for fiscal year ended January 31, 2004. The January 31, 2004, balance sheet of WMT reports the following ($ millions):

	2004	**2003**
Total assets	$104,912	$94,808

Required

a. What is WMT's return on assets? Given that the average ROA for all publicly traded firms is about 5.5%, how does WMT compare on ROA? Explain.

b. Decompose WMT's ROA into its net profit margin and total asset turnover. Given that the average net profit margin and asset turnover rate for all publicly traded firms is about 4.3% and 1.2 times, respectively, how does WMT compare on these measures? Explain.

c. Given the competitive nature of the retailing industry, can you identify any reasons why WMT should report an above-average level of financial performance? (*Hint*: Recall the five forces of competitive intensity.) Explain.

C1-45.   **Analysis and Explanation of Risk and Return**   (LO1, 2, 4)

The trade-off between risk and return is a fundamental business concept. It underlies all business activities and management decisions.

Required

a. Identify three different types of investments and their approximate return to the investor.

b. Drawing on your solutions to (a), do you see that the concept of higher expected risk yields higher expected return? Explain.

Berkshire Hathaway
(BRKA)

c. Apply the risk and return trade-off to discuss an investment in Berkshire Hathaway stock vis-à-vis an investment in U.S. government bonds.

C1-46.   **Interpreting Financial Statement Information**   (LO3, 4, 5)

Paula Seale is negotiating the purchase of an extermination firm called Total Pest Control. Seale has been employed by a national pest control service and knows the technical side of the business. However, she knows little about accounting data and financial statements. The sole owner of the firm, Meg Krey, has provided Seale with income statements for the past three years, which show an average net income of $72,000 per year. The latest balance sheet shows total assets of $285,000 and liabilities of $45,000. Seale brings the following matters to your attention and requests advice.

1. Krey is asking $300,000 for the firm. She has told Seale that because the firm has been earning 30% on its investment, the price should be higher than the net assets on the balance sheet.

2. Seale has noticed no salary for Krey on the income statements, even though she worked half-time in the business. Krey explained that because she had other income, the firm only paid $18,000 in cash

dividends to Krey (the sole shareholder). If she purchases the firm, Seale will hire a full-time manager for the firm at an annual salary of $36,000.

3. Krey's tax returns for the past 3 years report a lower net income for the firm than the amounts shown in the financial statements. Seale is skeptical about the accounting principles used in preparing the financial statements.

Required

a. How did Krey arrive at the 30% return figure in point 1? If Seale accepts Krey's average annual income figure of $72,000, what would Seale's percentage return be, assuming that the net income remained at the same level and that the firm was purchased for $300,000?

b. Should the dividend to Krey affect the net income reported in the financial statements? What will Seale's percentage return be if she takes into consideration the $36,000 salary she plans to pay a full-time manager?

c. Could there be legitimate reasons for the difference between net income shown in the financial statements and net income reported on the tax returns, as mentioned in point 3? How might Seale obtain additional assurance about the propriety of the financial statements?

C1-47. **Management, Auditing, and Ethical Behavior** **(LO1, 5)**

Jackie Hardy, CPA, has a brother, Ted, in the retail clothing business. Ted ran the business as its sole owner for 10 years. During this 10-year period, Jackie helped Ted with various accounting matters. For example, Jackie designed the accounting system for the company, prepared Ted's personal income tax returns (which included financial data about the clothing business), and recommended various cost control procedures. Ted paid Jackie for all these services. A year ago, Ted markedly expanded the business; Ted is president of the corporation and also chairs the corporation's board of directors. The board of directors has overall responsibility for corporate affairs. When the corporation was formed, Ted asked Jackie to serve on its board of directors. Jackie accepted. In addition, Jackie now prepares the corporation's income tax returns and continues to advise her brother on accounting matters.

Recently, the corporation applied for a large bank loan. The bank wants audited financial statements for the corporation before it will decide on the loan request. Ted asked Jackie to perform the audit. Jackie replied that she cannot do the audit because the code of ethics for CPAs requires that she be independent when providing audit services.

Required

a. Why is it important that a CPA be independent when providing audit services?

b. Which of Jackie's activities or relationships impair her independence?

2

Constructing Financial Statements

LEARNING OBJECTIVES

After completing the chapter, you should be able to:

LO1 Describe and construct the balance sheet. (p. 43)

LO2 Describe and construct the income statement. (p. 53)

LO3 Describe revenue recognition and the matching principle. (p. 54)

LO4 Describe the statement of equity and its interpretation. (p. 59)

LO5 Describe the statement of cash flow and its interpretation. (p. 61)

LO6 Explain the methods applied to analyze and record transactions. (p. 62)

WALT DISNEY

R obert Iger (pictured above with Mickey Mouse) succeeded Michael Eisner as CEO of the Walt Disney Company on October 1, 2005. Since taking over at Disney, Iger has taken several steps to remake the once bureaucratic company. He has revamped Disney's management style, dismantled the corporate strategic planning group and improved operations. In what is perhaps his boldest move, on January 24, 2006, Disney agreed to acquire Pixar Animation Studios for $7.4 billion in common stock. The acquisition of Pixar is the latest of several Disney investments, not all of which have been successful. The Pixar investment and others are reported in Disney's balance sheet.

This chapter expands our knowledge and analyses of all financial statements, including the balance sheet. The balance sheet reports the resources (assets) under control of management as well as the claims against those resources (liabilities and stockholders' equity). The balance sheet contains a wealth of information, including equity investments, receivables, long-term debt and common stock. Disney's balance sheet includes investments in other companies, similar to the investment in Pixar. Its total assets equal $49,988 million, including and $10,705 million invested in attractions, buildings and equipment in its theme parks. The Disney balance sheet also reports $10,643 million in long-term borrowing and $23,791 million in equity.

This chapter also explains the preparation and analysis of the income statement. Income statements must be scrutinized for the information that they reveal about the viability of a company's products and services. We use those insights in projections of future performance. Our discussion confronts these challenges and sets the stage for more in-depth discussions and analyses.

Disney's income statement reports revenues of $27,061 million and operating expenses of $24,330 million. After subtracting income taxes, it reported net income of $1,267 million. In the final analysis, the largest asset of Disney is probably Mickey Mouse. This asset, however, is not reported on Disney's balance sheet because it cannot be reliably measured. Yet all of the income and cash flows it generates are measurable and are reported in Disney's financial statements.

Sources: *St. Petersburg Times,* March 2004; *Washington Post,* 2004; *Barrons* 2002; *Walt Disney* 2004 and 2001 10-K Report. *Business Week,* February, 2006.

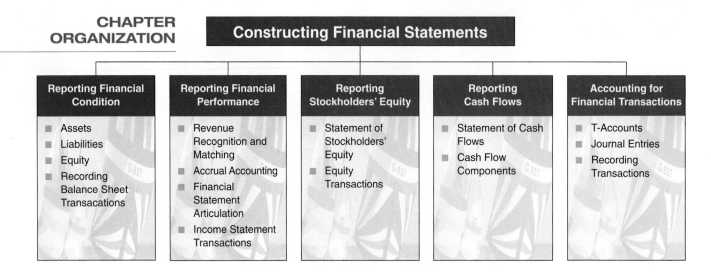

CHAPTER ORGANIZATION

Constructing Financial Statements

Reporting Financial Condition	Reporting Financial Performance	Reporting Stockholders' Equity	Reporting Cash Flows	Accounting for Financial Transactions
■ Assets ■ Liabilities ■ Equity ■ Recording Balance Sheet Transacations	■ Revenue Recognition and Matching ■ Accrual Accounting ■ Financial Statement Articulation ■ Income Statement Transactions	■ Statement of Stockholders' Equity ■ Equity Transactions	■ Statement of Cash Flows ■ Cash Flow Components	■ T-Accounts ■ Journal Entries ■ Recording Transactions

In Chapter 1, we introduced the four financial statements—the balance sheet, the income statement, the cash flow statement and the statement of stockholders' equity. In this chapter and in Chapter 3, we turn our attention to how the balance sheet and income statement are prepared. In Chapter 4, we will discuss preparation of the cash flow statement. The statement of stockholders' equity is discussed in Chapter 11.

To better understand the balance sheet and income statement, we first examine how costs flow through the financial accounting system. When a company incurs a cost, the cost is either expensed or capitalized. We say that a cost is **expensed** when it is recorded in the income statement and labeled as an expense. When a cost is **capitalized,** it is initially recorded on the balance sheet as an asset. The cost remains on the balance sheet until it expires. When the cost expires, it is transferred from the balance sheet to the income statement and labeled as an expense. Exhibit 2.1 illustrates these cost flows.

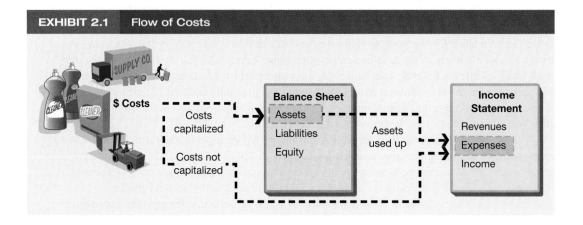

EXHIBIT 2.1   Flow of Costs

When a company incurs a cost, it usually expects to receive some benefit in return. In some cases, the benefit is realized immediately. When this happens, the cost is *expensed* immediately. For example, assume a company pays wages to its employees at the end of every week. The wages are payment for services performed by the employee during that week. The cost (wages paid to the employee) and the benefit (services provided to the company by the employee) occur at approximately the same time. In this case, the cost would be recorded in the income statement as *wage expense.*

In many cases, however, a company incurs costs that provide benefits in future periods. For example, when a company purchases equipment that it expects will last five years, the cost is incurred immediately when the equipment is purchased. However, the benefit is received gradually over a five-year period as the equipment is used. In this case, it would be inappropriate to record the entire cost as an expense at the time that the equipment is purchased. Instead, the cost of the equipment is *capitalized.* It is recorded on the balance sheet as an asset called equipment. As the equipment is used, the cost is transferred from the balance sheet to the income statement and recorded as an expense. (The process of transferring equipment costs from the balance sheet to the income statement is called **depreciation** and the resulting expense is called depreciation expense. Depreciation expense is discussed further in chapter 3.)

As another example, assume that a company signs a lease agreement to rent a building for two years at a cost of $24,000, or $1,000 per month. Also assume that the company pays the entire $24,000 in rent when it signs the lease. Because the lease gives the company the right to use the building for the next two years, it should not expense the rent payment right away. Instead, the payment is capitalized as an asset called *prepaid rent.* As the lease contract expires, the cost is transferred from the balance sheet to the income statement and labeled *rent expense.*

Tracking costs as they flow through the financial statements is a key step in understanding how the financial statements are prepared. It is important to remember that a cost is not the same as an expense. A cost does not become an expense until it is recorded in the income statement.

REPORTING FINANCIAL CONDITION

The balance sheet reports on a company's financial condition and is divided into three components: assets, liabilities, and stockholders' equity. It provides us with information about the resources available to management and the claims against those resources by creditors and shareholders. Disney reports total assets of $49,988 million, total liabilities of $26,197 million, and equity of $23,791 million. Drawing on the **accounting equation**, Disney's balance sheet is summarized as follows ($ million).

LO1 Describe and construct the balance sheet.

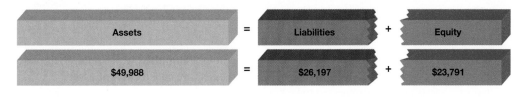

NOTE
Equity is a term used to describe the owners' claim in the company. In corporations, the terms **shareholders' equity** and **stockholders' equity** are also used to describe the owners' claim. We use all three terms interchangeably in this and subsequent chapters.

The balance sheet is prepared at a *point in time.* It is a snapshot of the financial condition of the company at that instant. For Disney, the above balance sheet amounts were reported at the close of business on September 30, 2003. Balance sheet accounts carry over from one period to the next; that is, the ending balance from one period becomes the beginning balance for the next period.

Assets

An **asset** is a resource that is expected to provide a company with future economic benefits. When a company incurs a cost to acquire future benefits, that cost is capitalized and an asset is recorded. An asset must possess two characteristics to be reported on the balance sheet:

1. It must be owned or controlled by the company.
2. It must possess expected future benefits that can be measured.

The first requirement, that the asset must be owned or controlled by the company, implies that the company has legal title to the asset or has the unrestricted right to use the asset. This requirement presumes that the cost to acquire the asset has been incurred, either by paying cash, by trading other assets, or by assuming an obligation to make future payments.

The second requirement indicates that the company expects to receive some future benefit from ownership of the asset. Benefits can be the expected cash receipts from selling the asset or from selling products produced by the asset. Benefits can also refer to the receipt of other noncash assets, such as accounts receivable or the reduction of a liability, such as when assets are given up to settle debts. It also requires that a monetary value can be assigned to the asset.

Companies acquire assets to yield a return for their shareholders. Assets are expected to produce revenues, either directly such as with inventory that is sold or indirectly such as with a manufacturing plant that produces inventories for sale. To create shareholder value, assets must yield income that is in excess of the cost of the funds utilized to acquire the assets.

The asset section of the **Walt Disney** 2003 balance sheet is shown in Exhibit 2.2. Disney reports $49,988 million of total assets as of September 30, its year-end.

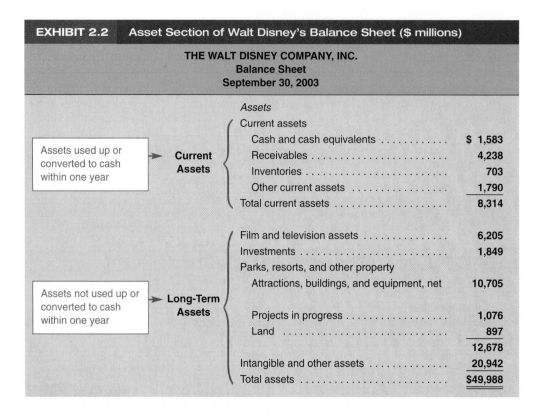

EXHIBIT 2.2 Asset Section of Walt Disney's Balance Sheet ($ millions)

THE WALT DISNEY COMPANY, INC.
Balance Sheet
September 30, 2003

Assets	
Current assets	
Cash and cash equivalents	$ 1,583
Receivables	4,238
Inventories	703
Other current assets	1,790
Total current assets	8,314
Film and television assets	6,205
Investments	1,849
Parks, resorts, and other property	
Attractions, buildings, and equipment, net	10,705
Projects in progress	1,076
Land	897
	12,678
Intangible and other assets	20,942
Total assets	$49,988

Assets used up or converted to cash within one year → **Current Assets**

Assets not used up or converted to cash within one year → **Long-Term Assets**

The assets section of a balance sheet is presented in order of **liquidity**, which refers to the ease of converting noncash assets into cash. The most liquid assets are called **current assets.**

Current assets are assets expected to be converted into cash or used in operations within the next year.[1] Some typical examples of current assets include the following asset accounts listed in order of their liquidity:

- **Cash**—currency, bank deposits, certificates of deposit and other *cash equivalents;*
- **Marketable securities**—short-term investments that can be quickly sold to raise cash;
- **Accounts receivable**—amounts due to the company from customers arising from the sale of products on credit;
- **Inventory**—goods purchased or produced for sale to customers;
- **Prepaid expenses**—costs paid in advance for rent, insurance, or other services.

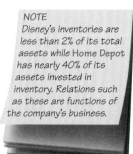

NOTE
Disney's inventories are less than 2% of its total assets while Home Depot has nearly 40% of its assets invested in inventory. Relations such as these are functions of the company's business.

The amount of current assets is an important measure of liquidity. Companies require a degree of liquidity to effectively operate on a daily basis. However, current assets are expensive to hold—they must be insured, monitored, financed, and so forth—and they typically generate returns that are less than those from non-current assets. As a result, companies seek to maintain only just enough current assets to cover liquidity needs, but not so much so as to unnecessarily reduce income.

The second section of the balance sheet reports non-current (long-term) assets. Non-current assets include the following asset accounts:

- **Property, plant and equipment (PPE)**—includes land, factory buildings, warehouses, office buildings, machinery, office equipment and other items used in the operations of the company;
- **Long-term investments**—investments that the company does not intend to sell in the near future;

---

[1]Technically, current assets include those assets expected to be converted into cash within the upcoming year or the company's operating cycle (the cash-to-cash cycle), whichever is longer. **Fortune Brands** (manufacturer of Jim Beam whiskey among other products) provides an example of the classification of inventories as a current asset with a cash conversion cycle of longer than one year. The company's inventory footnote from a recent 10-K states: "In accordance with generally recognized trade practices, bulk whiskey inventories are classified as current assets, although the majority of such inventories, due to the duration of aging processes, ordinarily will not be sold within one year."

- **Intangible and other assets**—includes patents, trademarks, franchise rights, goodwill and other items that provide future benefits, but do not possess physical substance.

Non-current assets are listed after current assets because they are not expected to expire or be converted into cash within one year.

Most assets, such as inventory and property, plant and equipment, are reported on the balance sheet at their **historical cost.** Historical cost refers to the original acquisition cost, less the portion of that cost that has expired and been transferred to the income statement. The use of historical cost to report asset values has the advantage of **reliability.** Historical costs are reliable because the acquisition cost (typically the amount of cash paid to purchase the asset) can be objectively determined and accurately measured. The disadvantage of historical costs is that some assets can be significantly undervalued on the balance sheet. For example, the land in Anaheim, California on which *Disneyland* was built more than 50 years ago, was purchased for a mere fraction of its current market value.

Some assets, such as marketable securities, are reported at current market value or **fair market value.** The market value of these assets can be easily obtained from online price quotes or from reliable sources such as the *Wall Street Journal.* Reporting certain assets at fair market value increases the **relevance** of the information presented in the balance sheet. Relevance refers to how useful the information is to those who use the financial statements for decision making. For example, marketable securities are intended to be sold for cash when cash is needed by the company to pay its obligations. Therefore, the most relevant value for marketable securities is the amount of cash that the company expects to receive when the securities are sold.

Only those asset values that can be accurately measured are reported on the balance sheet. For this reason, some of a company's most important assets are often not reflected among the reported assets of the company. For example, the well-recognized image of Mickey Mouse is absent from Disney's balance sheet. This image is referred to as an unrecognized intangible asset. Like the Coke bottle silhouette, the Kleenex name, an excellent management team, or a well-designed supply-chain, intangible assets are only measured and reported on the balance sheet when they are purchased. As a result, *internally created* intangible assets, like the Mickey Mouse image, are not reported on a balance sheet. Many of these internally created intangible assets are of enormous value.

> **NOTE**
> Excluded assets often relate to knowledge-based assets, like people and technology. This is one reason that knowledge-based industries are so difficult to analyze. Yet, excluded assets are presumably reflected in company market values. This can yield a marked difference between company market values and their book values of equity.

Liabilities and Equity—Reporting Sources of Financing

Liabilities and equity represent the sources of capital to the company that are used to finance the acquisition of assets. Liabilities are borrowed funds such as accounts payable, accrued liabilities, and obligations to lenders or bond investors. These obligations can be interest-bearing or non-interest-bearing. Equity represents capital that has been invested by the shareholders, either directly via the purchase of stock or indirectly in the form of retained earnings that reflect earnings that are reinvested in the business and not paid out as dividends. We discuss liabilities and equity in this section.

The liabilities and equity sections of the Walt Disney balance sheet are reproduced in Exhibit 2.3. Disney reports $26,197 million of total liabilities ($8,669 million + $10,643 million + $6,885 million) and $23,791 million of equity as of its 2003 year-end.

A **liability** is a probable future economic sacrifice resulting from a current or past event. The economic sacrifice can be a future cash payment to a creditor, or it can be an obligation to deliver goods or services to a customer at a future date. A liability must be reported in the balance sheet when each of the following three conditions is met:

1. The future sacrifice is probable.
2. The amount of the obligation is known or can be reasonably estimated.
3. The transaction that caused the obligation has occurred.

When conditions 1 and 2 are satisfied, but the transaction that caused the obligation has not occurred, the obligation is called an **executory contract** and no liability is reported. An example of such an obligation is a purchase order. When a company signs an agreement to purchase materials from a supplier, it commits to making a future cash payment of a known amount. However, the obligation to pay for the materials is not considered a liability until the materials are delivered. Therefore, even though the company is contractually obligated to make the cash payment to the supplier, a liability is not recorded on the balance sheet. However, information about purchase

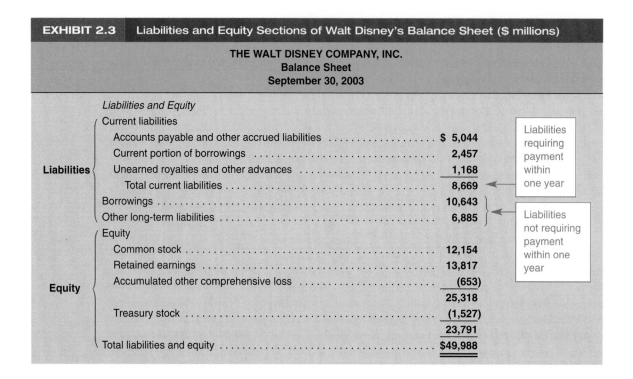

EXHIBIT 2.3 Liabilities and Equity Sections of Walt Disney's Balance Sheet ($ millions)

THE WALT DISNEY COMPANY, INC.
Balance Sheet
September 30, 2003

Liabilities and Equity

Liabilities

Current liabilities
Accounts payable and other accrued liabilities .... $ 5,044
Current portion of borrowings 2,457
Unearned royalties and other advances 1,168
    Total current liabilities .... 8,669 ← Liabilities requiring payment within one year
Borrowings 10,643
Other long-term liabilities .... 6,885 ← Liabilities not requiring payment within one year

Equity

Common stock 12,154
Retained earnings 13,817
Accumulated other comprehensive loss .... (653)
    25,318
Treasury stock .... (1,527)
    23,791
Total liabilities and equity $49,988

commitments and other executory contracts is useful to investors and creditors, and the obligations should be disclosed in the footnotes to the financial statements.

Liabilities on the balance sheet are listed in order of maturity. Debts coming due first are listed first. Obligations that are due within one year are called **current liabilities.** Some examples of common current liabilities include:

- **Accounts payable**—amounts owed to suppliers for goods and services purchased on credit terms.

- **Accrued liabilities**—obligations for expenses that have been recorded but not yet paid. Examples include accrued wages payable (wages earned by employees but not yet paid), accrued interest payable (interest on debt that has not been paid), and accrued income taxes (taxes due).

- **Unearned revenues**—an obligation created when the company accepts payment in advance for goods or services it will deliver in the future. Sometimes also called advances from customers or customer deposits.

- **Short-term notes payable**—short-term debt payable to banks or other creditors.

- **Current maturities of long-term debt**—the portion of long-term debt that is due to be paid within one year.

Analysts often compare the level of current liabilities with that of current assets. We usually prefer more current assets than current liabilities to ensure that companies have sufficient liquidity to pay their short-term debts when they mature.

Net working capital, or simply working capital, reflects the difference between current assets and current liabilities and is defined as follows:

Net Working Capital = Current Assets − Current Liabilities

The net working capital required to conduct business operations depends on the company's **operating cycle**, which is the time between paying cash for goods or employee services and receiving cash from customers—see Exhibit 2.4. The longer the operating cycle the more working capital is required.

Manufacturing companies, for example, begin with cash that is used to purchase or manufacture inventories held for resale. Inventories are often purchased on credit (accounts payable) from other companies. This financing is called **trade credit**. When inventories are sold, they are often

EXHIBIT 2.4   Operating Cycle

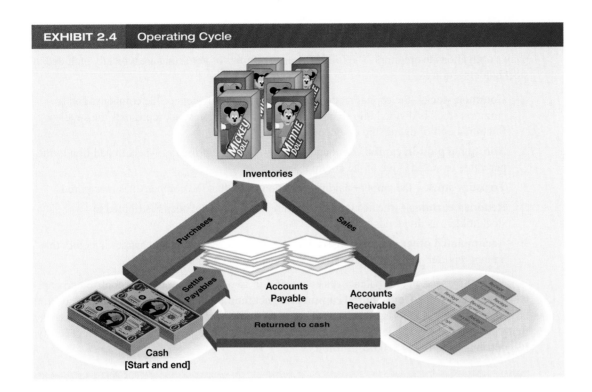

sold either on credit (accounts receivable) or for cash. When receivables are ultimately collected, a portion of the cash received is used to repay accounts payable and the remainder goes to the cash account for the next operating cycle.

Noncurrent liabilities are obligations to be paid after one year. Examples of noncurrent liabilities include:

- **Long-term debt**—amounts borrowed from creditors that are scheduled to be repaid more than one year in the future. Any portion of long-term debt that is due within one year is reclassified as a current liability called *current maturities of long-term debt*.

- **Other long-term liabilities**—various obligations, such as pension liabilities and long-term tax liabilities, that will be satisfied at least a year in the future. These items are discussed in later chapters.

Detailed information about a company's noncurrent liabilities, such as payment schedules, interest rates, and restrictive covenants, are provided in the footnotes to the financial statements.

> NOTE
> Borrowings are often titled **Notes Payable.** When a company borrows money it normally signs a promissory note agreeing to pay the money back—hence, the title notes payable.

BUSINESS INSIGHT

How Much Disney Debt Is Reasonable?   Disney reports total assets of $49,988 million, liabilities of $26,197 million, and equity of $23,791 million. Therefore, Disney finances 52% of its assets with borrowed funds and 48% with shareholder investment. This debt percentage is higher than that utilized by Viacom, but similar to other entertainment and media companies as shown below. Companies must monitor their financing sources and amounts. Too much reliance on equity capital is expensive. And, too much borrowing is risky. The level of debt that a company can effectively manage also depends on the stability and reliability of their operating cash flows that are used to pay interest and repay principal.

Company ($ millions)	Assets	Liabilities	Liabilities as % of Total Assets	Equity	Equity as % of Total Assets
Walt Disney Company ..	$49,988	$26,197	52%	$23,791	48%
News Corp, Ltd	45,478	23,779	52%	21,699	48%
Six Flags, Inc	4,245	2,605	61%	1,640	39%
Viacom, Inc	89,754	27,266	30%	62,488	70%

Equity reflects capital provided by the owners of the company. It is often referred to as a *residual interest.* That is, stockholders have a claim on any assets that are not needed to meet the company's obligations to creditors. The following are examples of items that are typically included in stockholders' equity:

- **Common stock**—the capital received from the primary owners of the company. Total common stock is divided into shares. One share of common stock represents the smallest fractional unit of ownership of a company.

- **Additional paid-in capital**—amounts received from the primary owners in addition to the par value or stated value of the common stock.

- **Treasury stock**—the amount paid for common stock that the company has reacquired.

- **Retained earnings**—the accumulated earnings that have not been distributed to stockholders as dividends.

- **Accumulated other comprehensive income or loss**—accumulated changes in equity that are not reported in the income statement; discussed in Chapter 11.

The equity section of a balance sheet consists of two basic components: contributed capital and earned capital. **Contributed capital** is the net funding that a company has received from issuing and reacquiring its equity shares. That is, the funds received from issuing shares less any funds paid to repurchase such shares. Disney's equity section reports $23,791 million in equity. Its contributed capital is $10,627 million.

BUSINESS INSIGHT

Disney's Unrecognized Liabilities   Euro Disney has been unsuccessful since the day it opened. It also suffered a major blow to its cash flows when attendance dwindled from increased global terrorism. Under 2003 accounting standards, Disney reports its investment in Euro Disney on its balance sheet at its percent ownership interest. That is, at 39% of Euro Disney's equity of $69 million, or $27 million, plus accounts and notes receivable from that venture. However, a 2004 *New York Times* article reports that:

> Under new industry accounting rules Disney will be required for the first time in the second quarter to include on the balance sheet [the assets and liabilities of] its 39 percent stake in the debt-laden Euro Disney. . . . While the addition of Euro Disney's assets and liabilities is not expected to hurt earnings per share, analysts say . . . Euro Disney is saddled with $2.5 billion in debt.

Thus, behind the reported investment amount of $27 million are assets amounting to $3,373 million and liabilities of $3,304 million, much of which is currently in default. The new accounting rules referred to in the article were enacted following the Enron scandal and are designed to provide more disclosure on the balance sheet for off-balance-sheet investments. Disney's balance sheet now recognizes those previously unrecognized liabilities.

Earned capital is the cumulative net income (and losses) that has been retained by the company (not paid out to shareholders as dividends). Earned capital typically includes retained earnings and accumulated other comprehensive income or loss. Disney's earned capital is $13,164 million ($13,817 − $653).

There is an important relation for retained earnings that reconciles its beginning and ending balances as follows:

> Beginning retained earnings
> ± Net income (loss)
> − Dividends
> = Ending retained earnings

This is a useful relation to remember, even though there are other items that sometimes impact retained earnings. We revisit this relation after our discussion of the income statement and show how it links the balance sheet and income statement.

Reported stockholders' equity is company value as determined by GAAP, and is called company **book value**. This value is different from company **market value**, which is computed by multiplying the number of outstanding common shares by the market price per share. Book value and market value can differ for several reasons, and most relate to the timing and uncertainty for recognition of transactions and events in financial statements such as the following:

- GAAP generally reports assets and liabilities at historical costs; whereas the market attempts to estimate fair market values.

- GAAP excludes resources that cannot be reliably measured such as talented management, employee morale, recent innovations and successful marketing; whereas the market attempts to value these.

- GAAP does not usually report expected future performance; whereas the market does attempt to predict and value future performance.

BUSINESS INSIGHT

Disney's Book and Market Values   Disney's market value has historically exceeded its book value of equity (see below). This is because much of Disney's market value results from intangible assets such as brand equity that are not fully reflected on its balance sheet. However, the difference between these two values has declined in recent years following abandonment of GO.com and poor performance in its television and film units as shown below. Conservative accounting depresses book value as R&D, advertising, wages, etc., are expensed rather than capitalized as assets. Intangible assets are capitalized only when purchased, and not when internally developed. Consequently, balance sheets of knowledge-based companies are, arguably, less informative.

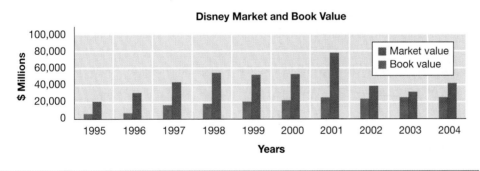

Disney Market and Book Value

Presently for U.S. companies, book value is, on average, about two-thirds of market value. This means that the market has drawn on some different information or measurement processes in valuing equity shares. A major part of this information can be found in the financial statement notes, but not all.

Eventually, all factors determining a company's market value are reflected in financial statements and book value. Assets are eventually sold and liabilities are settled. Moreover, talented management, employee morale, technological innovations, and successful marketing are all eventually recognized in profitability. The difference between book value and market value is timing. To the extent that market value is accurate, the change in stockholders' equity represents the change in company market value with a time lag.

RESEARCH INSIGHT

Market-to-Book   The *market-to-book ratio*, also called *price-to-book*, refers to a company's market value divided by its book (equity) value—it is also computed as stock price per share divided by book value per share. Research shows that the market-to-book ratio exhibits considerable variability over time. Specifically, over the past few decades, the median (50th percentile) market-to-book ratio was less than 1.0 during the mid-1970s, over 2.0 during the mid-1990s, and often between 1.0 and 2.0 during the 1960s and 1980s. Research also explores the drivers of this variability in market-to-book. One purpose of fundamental analysis is to exploit such research to arrive at *intrinsic value,* which is the worth of a stock justified by all available information.

Recording Balance Sheet Transactions

The balance sheet is the foundation of the accounting system. Every event, or transaction, that is recorded in the accounting system must be recorded so that we maintain the accounting equation:

$$\textbf{Assets = Liabilities + Equity}$$

Before a transaction is recorded, we first analyze the effect of the transaction on the accounting equation by asking the following:

- What accounts are affected by the transaction?
- What is the direction of each effect?

To maintain the equality of the accounting equation, each transaction must affect (at least) two accounts. For example, a transaction might increase assets and increase stockholders' equity by equal amounts. Another transaction might increase one asset and decrease another asset. These *dual effects* are what accountants call the **double entry accounting system.**

To illustrate the effect of transactions on the accounting equation, we consider a company called Mickey's Camera Shop. Disney employs independent contractors for some of the retail operations within its theme parks. Mickey's Camera Shop was established to sell cameras, film, batteries, picture frames and other supplies to visitors at Disney World in Orlando, Florida. The company was established on March 1, 2006. The following transactions occurred during the first few days of that month:

(1) On March 1, the company sold 12,000 shares of common stock to investors for $1 per share.

(2) On March 1, it signed a lease with Disney for retail space near the entrance of Disney World. The rent was $900 per month. Mickey's Camera Shop paid three months' rent in advance.

(3) On March 2, the company borrowed $10,000 from a local bank, giving the bank a two-year, 8% note payable.

(4) On March 2, it purchased computers and other equipment for $9,500 cash.

(5) On March 3, it took delivery of merchandise inventory costing $17,200. The inventory was purchased on credit.

We illustrate the effect of each transaction on the financial statements using the following **financial statement effects template**.

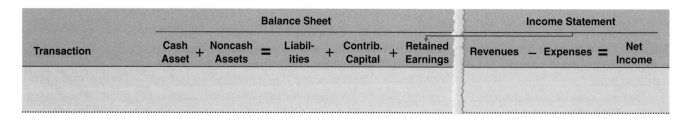

The template captures the transaction and its financial statement effects on the balance sheet and income statement. For the balance sheet, we differentiate between cash and non-cash assets so as to identify the cash effects of transactions. Likewise, equity is separated into the contributed and earned capital (retained earnings) components. Finally, income statement effects are separated into revenue and expense components, and their income effect. (By definition, any revenue or expense components impact retained earnings.) Use of this template is a convenient means to represent relatively complex financial accounting transactions and events in a simple, concise manner for both analysis and interpretation. We also separate the income statement effects from the balance sheet effects to preserve the equality of the accounting equation.

To illustrate the use of this template, let's examine the financial statement effects of the first transaction. Shareholders invested $12,000 cash in Mickey's Camera shop and the company issued 12,000 shares of common stock. Mickey's cash would increase and it would issue stock to the shareholders, which increases equity (contributed capital). This transaction is reflected as follows:

	Balance Sheet					Income Statement		
Transaction	Cash Asset +	Noncash Assets =	Liabil- ities +	Contrib. Capital +	Retained Earnings	Revenues −	Expenses =	Net Income
(1) Issue Stock for $12,000 cash	+12,000 Cash	=		+12,000 Common Stock				=

Both assets (cash) and equity (common stock) increase, and the accounting equation still applies (as it always must).

In the second transaction, Mickey's paid $2,700 ($900 × 3) in advance to Disney for three months rent. Because the cost provides benefits in future periods, the rent payment is capitalized as an asset called prepaid rent. This transaction is reflected as follows:

	Balance Sheet					Income Statement		
Transaction	Cash Asset +	Noncash Assets =	Liabil- ities +	Contrib. Capital +	Retained Earnings	Revenues −	Expenses =	Net Income
(2) Paid $2,700 for rent in advance	−2,700 Cash	+2,700 = Prepaid Rent						=

In the third transaction, Mickey's borrowed $10,000 from a local bank. This transaction increases cash and also increases liabilities:

	Balance Sheet					Income Statement		
Transaction	Cash Asset +	Noncash Assets =	Liabil- ities +	Contrib. Capital +	Retained Earnings	Revenues −	Expenses =	Net Income
(3) Borrowed $10,000 from bank	+10,000 Cash	=	+10,000 Note Payable					=

In the fourth transaction, the company purchased equipment for $9,500 in cash. Cash is decreased by $9,500 and a noncash asset called equipment is increased by $9,500.

	Balance Sheet					Income Statement		
Transaction	Cash Asset +	Noncash Assets =	Liabil- ities +	Contrib. Capital +	Retained Earnings	Revenues −	Expenses =	Net Income
(4) Purchased equipment for $9,500	−9,500 Cash	+9,500 = Equip- ment						=

Finally, on March 3, Mickey's took delivery of merchandise inventory costing $17,200. Because the merchandise was purchased on credit, this transaction increased inventory by $17,200 and increased liabilities (accounts payable) by the same amount.

	Balance Sheet					Income Statement		
Transaction	Cash Asset +	Noncash Assets =	Liabil- ities +	Contrib. Capital +	Retained Earnings	Revenues −	Expenses =	Net Income
(5) Received $17,200 of merchandise purchased on account		+17,200 = Inventory	+17,200 Accounts Payable					=

To summarize, each transaction is described in the first column of the template. Then the financial statement effects are recorded with a + or a − in the appropriate columns of the balance sheet and income statement. (None of the transactions that have been recorded so far have affected the income statement.) After each transaction, the equality of the accounting equation is maintained. If we so choose, we can prepare a balance sheet at any time, reflecting the transactions up to that point in time. After these five transactions, Mickey's balance sheet would appear as follows:

MICKEY'S CAMERA SHOP
Balance Sheet
As of March 3, 2006

Assets		Liabilities and Equity	
Cash	$ 9,800	Accounts payable	$17,200
Inventory	17,200	Total current liabilities	17,200
Prepaid rent	2,700	Notes payable	10,000
Total current assets	29,700	Total liabilities	27,200
Equipment	9,500	Equity	
Total assets	$39,200	Contributed capital	12,000
		Total liabilities and equity	$39,200

MID-CHAPTER REVIEW 1

Part 1. Enter the letter of the balance sheet category in the space next to the balance sheet items numbered 1 through 20. Enter an **X** in the space if the item is not reported on the balance sheet.

A. Current assets
B. Long-term assets
C. Current liabilities
D. Long-term liabilities
E. Equity

___ 1. Accounts receivable		___ 11. Rent expense	
___ 2. Short-term notes payable		___ 12. Cash	
___ 3. Land		___ 13. Buildings	
___ 4. Retained earnings		___ 14. Accounts payable	
___ 5. Intangible assets		___ 15. Prepaid rent	
___ 6. Common stock		___ 16. Borrowings (due in 25 years)	
___ 7. Repairs expense		___ 17. Marketable securities	
___ 8. Equipment		___ 18. Inventories	
___ 9. Treasury stock		___ 19. Additional paid-in capital	
___ 10. Investments (noncurrent)		___ 20. Unearned revenue	

Solution to Part 1.

1. A	2. A	3. B	4. E	5. B	6. E	7. X	8. B	9. E	10. B
11. X	12. A	13. B	14. C	15. A	16. D	17. A	18. A	19. E	20. C

Part 2. Record each of the following transactions in the financial statement effects template.

a. Issued common stock for $20,000 cash.
b. Purchased inventory costing $8,000 on credit.
c. Purchased equipment costing $10,000 for cash.
d. Paid suppliers $3,000 for part of the inventory purchased in *b*.

Solution to Part 2.

Transaction	Cash Asset	+	Noncash Assets	=	Liabil-ities	+	Contrib. Capital	+	Retained Earnings	Revenues	−	Expenses	=	Net Income
(a) Issued common stock for $20,000 in cash	+20,000 Cash			=			+20,000 Common Stock						=	
(b) Purchased inventory on credit			+8,000 Inventory	=	+8,000 Accounts Payable								=	
(c) Purchased equipment	−10,000 Cash		+10,000 Equip-ment	=									=	
(d) Paid suppliers	−3,000 Cash			=	−3,000 Accounts Payable								=	

REPORTING FINANCIAL PERFORMANCE

The income statement reports revenues earned during a period, the expenses incurred to generate those revenues, and the resulting net income or loss. The structure of the income statement is:

LO2 Describe and construct the income statement.

General Income Statement Format

	Revenues
−	Cost of goods sold
	Gross profit
−	Operating expenses
−	Nonoperating expenses
−	Tax expenses
	Income from continuing operations
±	Nonrecurring items
	Net income

Disney's income statement is shown in Exhibit 2.5. Disney reported net income of $1,267 million on revenues of $27,061 million. As is typical of many large companies, less than $0.05 of each dollar of revenue is brought to the bottom line—for Disney, it is $0.047 of each dollar, computed as $1,267 million divided by $27,061 million. The remainder of that revenue dollar, $0.953 (computed as $1 minus $0.047) relates to costs incurred to generate its revenues, such as wages, advertising, interest, promotion, equipment costs, and film and television production expenses.

NOTE The terms revenues and sales are used interchangeably.

EXHIBIT 2.5   Walt Disney's Income Statement ($ millions)

THE WALT DISNEY COMPANY, INC.
Income Statement
For Year Ended September 30, 2003

Revenues	$ 27,061
Costs and expenses	(24,330)
Other income (expense)	(675)
Income before income taxes	2,056
Income taxes	(789)
Net income (loss)	$ 1,267

To analyze an income statement we need to understand some terminology. **Revenues** are increases in net assets (assets less liabilities) as a result of business activities. **Expenses** are the outflow or use of assets to generate revenues, including costs of products and services sold, operating costs like wages and advertising, and nonoperating costs like interest on debt. The difference between revenues and expenses is **net income** when revenues exceed expenses, or **net loss** when expenses exceed revenues. The terms income, profit, and earnings are used interchangeably (as are revenues and sales, and expenses and costs).

Operating expenses are the usual and customary costs that a company incurs to support its main business activities. These include cost of goods sold, selling expenses, depreciation expense, amortization expense, and research and development expense. (Not all of these expenses require a cash outlay; for example, depreciation expense is a non-cash expense, as are accruals of liabilities such as wages payable, that recognize the expense in advance of cash payment.) **Non-operating revenues and expenses** relate to the company's financing and investing activities, and include interest revenue and interest expense. Business decision makers and analysts usually segregate operating and nonoperating activities as they offer different insights into company performance and condition.

It is also helpful to distinguish income from continuing operations from nonrecurring items. Many readers of financial statements are interested in forecasting future company performance and focus their analysis on sources of operating income that are expected to *persist* into the future. Nonrecurring revenues and expenses are unlikely to arise in the future and are largely irrelevant to predictions of future performance. Consequently, many decision makers identify transactions and events that are unlikely to recur and separate them from operating income in the income statement. These nonrecurring items are described in Chapter 7.

Revenue Recognition

LO3 Describe revenue recognition and the matching principle.

The **revenue recognition principle** in accounting requires that revenue be recognized (recorded) only when earned. Its application is crucial in income statement reporting. To illustrate, assume that Disney purchases inventories for $100,000 on credit (also called *on account*), which it sells later in that same period for $150,000 cash. Disney would record $150,000 in revenue because when the inventory is delivered to the customer, we say that it has been earned. Also assume Disney pays $20,000 cash for sales employee wages during the period. The income statement would appear as follows.

Revenues	$ 150,000
Cost of goods sold	(100,000)
Gross profit	50,000
Wages expense	(20,000)
Net income	$ 30,000

NOTE
Purchase of inventories on credit or on account means that the buyer does not pay the seller at the time of purchase. The buyer reports a liability (accounts payable) on its balance sheet that is later removed when payment is made. The seller reports an asset (accounts receivable) on its balance sheet until it is removed when the buyer pays.

Cost of goods sold is an expense item in the income statements of manufacturing and merchandising companies. It represents the cost of products that are sold during the period. The difference between revenues (at selling prices) and cost of goods sold (at purchase price or manufacturing cost) is called **gross profit.** Gross profit for manufacturers and merchandisers is an important number as it represents the remaining income available to cover all of the company's overhead and other expenses (selling, general, and administrative expenses).

Continuing with the above illustration, assume instead that the company sells its product on **credit** rather than cash. Does the seller still report sales revenue? The answer is yes. Under GAAP, revenues are reported when a company has *earned* those sales. Earned means that the company has done everything required under the sales agreement—no major contingencies remain—and cash is realizable or realized. Thus revenue can be recognized without cash collection. Also, the seller reports accounts receivable on its balance sheet.

NOTE
Sales on credit will not always be collected. The potential for uncollectable accounts introduces additional risk to the firm.

Credit sales mean that companies can report substantial sales revenue and assets without receiving cash. When such receivables are ultimately collected, no further revenue is recorded because it was recorded earlier when the revenue recognition criteria were met. The collection of a receivable merely involves the decrease of one asset (accounts receivable) and the increase in another asset (cash).

Next consider a different situation. Assume that Disney sells tickets for admission to Disneyland to a travel agent for $9,500. The travel agent sells these tickets to tourists as part of an excursion package for a trip scheduled to take place next year. Should Disney recognize the $9,500 in ticket sales as revenue? No. Even though the tickets were sold and cash was collected, the revenue has not been earned. Disney earns revenues from ticket sales when the service is provided. In this case, the revenue is not earned until the tourists visit Disneyland. Hence, the $9,500 would be recorded as an increase in cash and an increase in *unearned revenues,* a liability.

Matching Principle

The **matching principle** prescribes that all expenses incurred in generating revenues be recognized in the same period as the related revenues. For example, cost of goods sold, an expense, should be recognized in the same period that the corresponding sales revenue is recorded. This is true no matter when the goods are purchased or paid for. The word *incurred* does not necessarily imply paid in cash, as the company can agree to pay these costs in the future and recognize a liability on the balance sheet.

Extending our above illustration, assume that the $20,000 of employee wages for the period is for work directed toward selling the $150,000 of goods, but that these wages are not paid until the first day of the *following* period. Should wages expense be recorded in the current period? Yes. Following the matching principle, the seller must record wages expense in the current period to match the wages against the revenues it records, even though the wages are not yet paid in cash.

Unlike sales, no *external transaction or event* triggers the recording of wages expense. After $150,000 of sales and $100,000 in costs of goods sold are recorded, the financial statements are incomplete in failing to reflect employee wages necessary for their sale. The statements must be adjusted to reflect wages expense and the wages liability. More generally, managers must review financial statements before issuance to determine that all *internal transactions and events* such as this one are recorded.

These adjustments for *accrued expenses* yield the following effects: (1) an *expense* reported in the income statement, (2) a *liability* reported on the balance sheet.

When wages are ultimately paid in the following period, both cash and the wages payable liability are reduced. No expense is recorded when cash is paid because it was recorded the prior period when wages were incurred. Adjustments like this one are a focus of chapter 3.

YOU MAKE THE CALL

You are an Operations Manager   You are the operations manager on a new consumer product that was launched this period with very successful sales. The Chief Financial Officer (CFO) asks you to prepare an estimate of warranty costs to charge against those sales. You question the CFO and the need for such an estimate and reply with confidence that you hope such charges are minimal. Why does the CFO desire a warranty cost estimate? What hurdles must you address in arriving at such an estimate? [Answers on page 69]

Accrual Accounting

Accrual accounting refers to the recognition of revenue when earned (even if not received in cash) and the matching of expenses when incurred (even if not paid in cash). Accrual accounting is required under U.S. GAAP and in most other countries as it is considered most useful for business decisions. (Information about cash flows is also important and is conveyed in the statement of cash flows discussed in Chapter 4.)

Consider the case where employees earn wages for work in one period, but are paid in the next period. Because wages expense must be recognized when *incurred,* regardless of when it is paid, the company must report wages expense and recognize a liability for payment (wages payable) in the first period. The increase in expense reduces income and retained earnings.

When wages are paid in the next period, both cash and the wages payable liability are decreased. No expense is reported when the cash is paid. The expense was recognized when it was incurred in the prior period.

Accrual accounting results in matching, which is crucial for reporting the proper expense in the appropriate period's income statement. In the case of wages, the amount of the accrual is known with certainty. However, in some cases, accruals are estimated. Examples are estimating contingent liabilities such as warranty, litigation, environmental, and severance costs. These estimated accruals yield both liabilities and expenses.

> *NOTE*
> **Cash accounting** recognizes revenues only when received in cash and expenses only when paid in cash. This approach is not acceptable accounting under GAAP.

Financial Statement Articulation

Financial statements are linked within and across accounting periods, which is called **articulation.** In Chapter 1, we illustrated the articulation of the four major financial statements. The balance sheet and income statement are mainly linked via retained earnings. Recall that retained earnings is updated each period as follows.

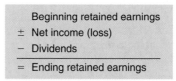

Generally, retained earnings reflect cumulative income and loss not distributed to shareholders. Exhibit 2.6 shows Walt Disney's change in retained earnings for 2003.

EXHIBIT 2.6	Walt Disney's Retained Earnings Reconciliation

THE WALT DISNEY COMPANY, INC.
Retained Earnings Reconciliation ($ millions)
For Year Ended September 30, 2003

Retained earnings, September 30, 2002	$12,979
Add: Net income (loss)	1,267
	14,246
Less: Dividends	429
Retained earnings, September 30, 2003	$13,817

This reconciliation of retained earnings provides the link between the balance sheet and income statement. Namely, the change in retained earnings is the amount by which shareholder value in the company changes for the period, as measured by GAAP. Stockholders' equity reflects that change, and the income statement details that change in value.

In the absence of owner equity transactions—such as stock issuances and purchases, and dividend payments—the change in stockholders' equity equals income or loss for the period. The income statement, thus, measures the change in company value under GAAP. This is not the same as the change in market value. However, in the long run, all value-relevant data is eventually reflected in the income statement. So, it is not surprising that stock prices react to reported income and earnings forecasts.

RESEARCH INSIGHT

Research suggests that many managers select investments that help the company meet analysts' expectations as to earnings on a per-share basis even though available alternative investments are expected to yield superior market performance.

Recording Income Statement Transactions

Earlier, we introduced the financial statement effects template as a tool to illustrate the effects of transactions on the balance sheet. In this section, we show how this template can be used to analyze income statement transactions. To do so, we extend our illustration of Mickey's Camera Shop to reflect the following events:

(6) Mickey's had cash sales of $25,000 for the week ending March 12, 2006.

(7) The cost of merchandise sold in (6) totaled $13,600.

(8) The company made payments of $14,000 to suppliers for previously purchased merchandise.

(9) Mickey's paid $1,200 cash in wages to employees for the week.

In transaction 6, Mickey's had cash sales of $25,000. This is recorded as an increase in cash and an increase in retained earnings. It is also recorded in the income statement as an increase in revenues and net income. Any change in net income must correspond to a change in retained earnings.

Transaction	Balance Sheet					Income Statement		
	Cash Asset +	Noncash Assets =	Liabil-ities +	Contrib. Capital +	Retained Earnings	Revenues −	Expenses =	Net Income
(6) Sold merchandise for $25,000 cash	+25,000 Cash	=			+25,000 Retained Earnings	+25,000 Sales Revenue		= +25,000

It is tempting to record a decrease in inventory in the above transaction. After all, the merchandise was delivered to the customers at the time of the sale. However, the cost of the merchandise that was sold is recorded in a separate entry. The matching principle requires that the cost of goods sold be recorded in the same period that the sale is recorded. Therefore, entry 7 results in a decrease in inventory and a decrease in retained earnings. A decrease in net income is also recorded due to the corresponding expense.

Transaction	Balance Sheet					Income Statement		
	Cash Asset +	Noncash Assets =	Liabil-ities +	Contrib. Capital +	Retained Earnings	Revenues −	Expenses =	Net Income
(7) Record $13,600 for the cost of merchandise sold in entry 6		−13,600 = Inventory			−13,600 Retained Earnings		−13,600 = Cost Of Goods Sold	−13,600

Once again, the change in net income equals the change in retained earnings. Next, the payment to suppliers is recorded as a decrease to cash and a corresponding decrease to accounts payable. The income statement is not affected by the payment. The cost of merchandise is reflected in the income statement when the merchandise is sold (delivered to the customer), not when it is purchased or paid for.

Transaction	Balance Sheet					Income Statement		
	Cash Asset +	Noncash Assets =	Liabil-ities +	Contrib. Capital +	Retained Earnings	Revenues −	Expenses =	Net Income
(8) Paid $14,000 to suppliers of merchandise purchased on account	−14,000 Cash	=	−14,000 Accounts Payable					=

The ninth entry is needed to record wage expense. In this case, the wages were paid in cash. Both cash and retained earnings are decreased by $1,200. A decrease of $1,200 is also recorded in the income statement for wage expense.

Transaction	Balance Sheet					Income Statement		
	Cash Asset +	Noncash Assets =	Liabil-ities +	Contrib. Capital +	Retained Earnings	Revenues −	Expenses =	Net Income
(9) Paid $1,200 in wages to employees	−1,200 Cash	=			−1,200 Retained Earnings		−1,200 = Wage Expense	−1,200

Putting these transactions together, we can prepare an income statement for Mickey's Camera Shop for the week ending March 12, 2006.

MICKEY'S CAMERA SHOP
Income Statement
For the week ended March 12, 2006

Sales revenue....................	$25,000
Cost of goods sold	13,600
Gross profit	11,400
Wage expense	1,200
Net income	$10,200

MID-CHAPTER REVIEW 2

Part 1. At December 31, 2005, the Waymire Corporation records show the following amounts. Use this information, as necessary, to prepare its 2005 income statement (ignore income taxes).

Cash	$ 3,000	Cash dividends	$ 1,000
Accounts receivable	12,000	Revenues	25,000
Office equipment	32,250	Rent expense	5,000
Land	36,000	Wages expense	8,000
Accounts payable	7,500	Utilities expense	2,000
Common stock	45,750	Other expenses	4,000

Solution to Part 1.

WAYMIRE CORPORATION
Income Statement
For Year Ended December 31, 2005

Revenues		$25,000
Expenses		
Wages expense	$8,000	
Rent expense	5,000	
Utilities expense	2,000	
Other expenses	4,000	
Total expenses		19,000
Net income		$ 6,000

Part 2. The following is selected financial information for Waymire Corporation for the year ended December 31, 2005:

Retained earnings, Dec. 31, 2005 ...	$30,000	Dividends	$1,000
Net income	$6,000	Retained earnings, Dec. 31, 2004	$25,000

Prepare the 2005 calendar-year retained earnings reconciliation for this company.

Solution to Part 2.

WAYMIRE CORPORATION
Retained Earnings Reconciliation
For Year Ended December 31, 2005

Retained earnings, Dec. 31, 2004	$25,000
Add: Net income	6,000
Less: Dividends	(1,000)
Retained earnings, Dec. 31, 2005	$30,000

Part 3. Use the listing of accounts and figures reported in part 1 along with the ending retained earnings from part 2 to prepare the December 31, 2005, balance sheet for Waymire Corporation .

Solution to Part 3.

WAYMIRE CORPORATION
Balance Sheet
December 31, 2005

Cash	$ 3,000	Accounts payable	$ 7,500
Accounts receivable	12,000		
Office equipment	32,250	Common stock	45,750
Land	36,000	Retained earnings	30,000
Total assets	$83,250	Total liabilities and equity . . .	$83,250

REPORTING STOCKHOLDERS' EQUITY

The statement of stockholders' equity is a reconciliation of the beginning and ending balances of stockholders' equity accounts.

The statement of stockholders' equity for Walt Disney is shown in Exhibit 2.7.

LO4 Describe the statement of equity and its interpretation.

EXHIBIT 2.7   Walt Disney's Statement of Stockholders' Equity

THE WALT DISNEY COMPANY, INC.
Statement of Stockholders' Equity
For Year Ended September 30, 2003

(in millions)	Common Stock	Retained Earnings	Other Equity	Total Shareholders' Equity
Balance at September 30, 2002	$12,107	$12,979	$(1,641)	$23,445
Exercise of stock options and other stock	47	—	29	76
Dividends ($0.21 per Disney share)	—	(429)	—	(429)
Other comprehensive loss, net	—	—	(568)	(568)
Net income	—	1,267	—	1,267
Balance at September 30, 2003	$12,154	$13,817	$(2,180)	$23,791

Focusing on contributed capital and retained earnings, there were three changes to Disney's stockholders' equity in 2003. (Changes in accumulated other comprehensive income are discussed in later chapters.)

1. Disney issued $76 million of common shares ($47 million common stock + $29 million in treasury stock) for the exercise of stock options and restricted stock. This transaction is similar to the first transaction we recorded for Mickey's Camera Shop. (Stock options are discussed in Chapter 11.)

2. Disney paid dividends of $429 million to shareholders.

3. Disney reported net income of $1,267 million.

In sum, total stockholders' equity begins the year at $23,445 million and ends 2003 with a balance of $23,791 million for a net increase of $346 million.

YOU MAKE THE CALL

You are an Analyst Callaway Golf Company reports a balance in retained earnings of $437.3 million at December 31, 2004. This compares to $466.4 million one year earlier in 2003. In 2004, Callaway reported a net loss of $10.1 million. What can explain the additional decrease in retained earnings? [Answers on page 69]

Equity Transactions

Earlier we illustrated the effect of issuing common stock on the balance sheet of Mickey's Camera Shop. To complete our illustration, we illustrate one final transaction—a dividend payment.

(10) On March 12, Mickey's Camera Shop paid a $500 cash dividend to shareholders.

To record the dividend payment, we decrease cash and decrease retained earnings, as follows:

	Balance Sheet							Income Statement		
Transaction	**Cash Asset**	**+ Noncash Assets**	**= Liabil- ities**	**+ Contrib. Capital**	**+ Retained Earnings**			**Revenues**	**− Expenses =**	**Net Income**
(10) Paid a $500 cash dividend to shareholders	−500 Cash		**=**		−500 Retained Earnings					**=**

No revenue or income is recorded from a stock issuance. Similarly, no expense is recorded from a dividend. This is always the case. Companies cannot report revenues and expenses from capital transactions (transactions with its stockholders' relating to their investment in the company).

Because the equality of the accounting equation is always maintained, we can update Mickey's balance sheet at this time. The balance in retained earnings is $9,700 (net income of $10,200 − cash dividends of $500).

MICKEY'S CAMERA SHOP
Balance Sheet
As of March 12, 2006

Assets		Liabilities and Equity	
Cash	$ 19,100	Accounts payable	$ 3,200
Inventory	3,600	Total current liabilities	3,200
Prepaid rent	2,700	Notes payable	10,000
Total current assets	25,400	Total liabilities	13,200
Equipment	9,500	Equity	
Total assets	$34,900	Contributed capital	12,000
		Retained earnings	9,700
		Total equity	21,700
		Total liabilities and equity	$34,900

REPORTING CASH FLOWS

The balance sheet and income statement are prepared using accrual accounting, in which revenues are recognized when earned and expenses when incurred (matched). This matching means that companies can sometimes report income even though no cash is received. There have been companies that reported positive income up to the time they declared bankruptcy. This situation can occur from cash shortages—such as when cash expectations do not materialize or when customers either refuse to pay or cannot pay.

To assess cash flows, we must assess a company's cash management. Obligations to employees, creditors, and others are usually settled with cash. Also, stock prices are linked to the expected future cash generating ability of the company. Illiquid companies (those lacking cash) are at risk of failure and typically reflect poor investing activities. Given the importance of cash management, the SEC and FASB require disclosure of the statement of cash flows in addition to the balance sheet, income statement, and statement of equity.

The income statement provides information about the economic viability of the company's products and services. It tells us whether the market sufficiently values the company's products and services at prices that cover its costs and that also provide a reasonable return to the providers of capital (lenders and stockholders). On the other hand, the statement of cash flows provides information about the company's ability to generate cash from those same transactions. The statement of cash flows tells us from what sources the company has generated its cash, and what it has done with the cash generated.

> **LO5** Describe the statement of cash flow and its interpretation.

Cash Flow Components

The statement of cash flows is formatted to report cash inflows and outflows by the three primary business activities:

- *Cash flows from operating activities*   Cash flows from the company's transactions and events that relate to its primary operations.
- *Cash flows from investing activities*   Cash flows from acquisitions and divestitures of investments and long-term assets.
- *Cash flows from financing activities*   Cash flows from issuances of and payments toward equity, borrowings, and long-term liabilities.

The net cash flows from these three sections yield the change in cash for the period.

In analyzing the statement of cash flows, we should not necessarily conclude that the company is better off if cash increases and worse off if cash decreases. It is not the cash change that is most important, but the reasons for the change. For example, what are the sources of the cash inflows? Are these sources transitory? Are these sources mainly from operating activities? To what uses have cash inflows been put? Such questions and answers are key to properly using the statement of cash flows.

Exhibit 2.8 summarizes Walt Disney's statement of cash flows. Disney reported $2,901 million in net cash inflows from operating activities in 2003. This amount is substantially in excess of its net income of $1,267 million.

EXHIBIT 2.8	Walt Disney's Statement of Cash Flows ($ millions)

THE WALT DISNEY COMPANY, INC.
Statement of Cash Flows
For Year Ended September 30, 2003

Cash provided by operations	2,901
Cash used by investing activities	(1,034)
Cash used by financing activities	(1,523)
Increase (decrease) in cash and cash equivalents	344
Cash and cash equivalents, beginning of year	1,239
Cash and cash equivalents, end of year	$ 1,583

Disney reported a net cash outflow of $1,034 million for investing activities, mainly for investments in its parks, resorts, and property. Disney also used $1,523 million in financing activities, mainly to pay cash dividends and to settle (repay) borrowings.

Overall, Disney's cash flow picture is adequate. It is generating positive operating cash flows, it is reinvesting cash in its infrastructure (parks and resorts) that benefits future performance, and it is retiring some debt.

ACCOUNTING FOR FINANCIAL TRANSACTIONS

LO6 Explain the methods applied to analyze and record transactions.

The financial statement effects template is a useful tool for illustrating the effects of a transaction on the balance sheet and income statement. However, when representing individual transactions or analyzing individual accounts, the financial statement effects template can be cumbersome and impractical.

T-Accounts

Accountants use a graphic representation of an account called a **T-account,** so named because it looks like a large T. The typical form of a T-account is

Account Title	
Debits	Credits
(Dr.)	(Cr.)

One side of the T-account is used to record increases to the account and the other side is used to record decreases.

Accountants represent individual transactions using the journal entry. A **journal entry** is an accounting entry in the financial records (journals) of a company. This is the *bookkeeping* aspect of accounting. Even if many of us never make a journal entry for a company, we will interact with accounting and finance professionals who do, and who will use this language. Further, journal entries and T-accounts can help in reconstructing transactions and interpreting their financial effects.

Accountants describe increases and decreases in accounts using the terms *debit* and *credit.* The left side of each account is the debit side (abbreviated Dr.) and the right side of each account is the credit side (abbreviated Cr.). In some accounts, increases are recorded on the debit (left) side of the account and decreases are recorded on the credit (right) side of the account. In other accounts, just the opposite is true—increases are credits and decreases are debits. An easy way to remember what the words debit and credit reflect is to visualize a balance sheet in "T" account form with assets on the left and liabilities and equity on the right as follows.

NOTE
Debit and credit are accounting terms meaning left and right, respectively.

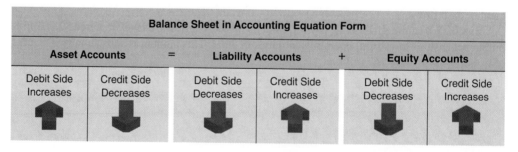

Balance Sheet in Accounting Equation Form

Asset Accounts		=	**Liability Accounts**		+	**Equity Accounts**	
Debit Side Increases	Credit Side Decreases		Debit Side Decreases	Credit Side Increases		Debit Side Decreases	Credit Side Increases

REMEMBER . . .
The rule that total debits equal total credits for each entry is known as double-entry accounting, or the duality of accounting.

Thus, assets are assigned a *normal debit balance* because they are on the left side. Liabilities and equity are assigned a *normal credit balance* because they are on the right side. So, to reflect an increase in an asset, we debit the asset account. To reflect an increase in a liability or equity account we credit the account. Conversely, to reflect a decrease in an asset account, we credit it. To reflect a decrease in a liability or equity account we debit it.

The balance sheet must always balance (assets = liabilities + equity). So too must total debits equal total credits in each journal entry. There can, however, as we shall see, be more than one debit and one credit in an entry. These so-called *compound entries* still adhere to the rule: **total debits equal total credits for each entry.** This important relation is extended below to show the *expanded accounting equation* in T-account form with the inclusion of debit (Dr.) and credit (Cr.) rules. Equity is expanded to reflect increases from capital stock and revenues and to reflect decreases from dividends and expenses.

Assets	=	Liabilities	+	Equity						
Assets	=	**Liabilities**	+	**Common Stock**	−	**Dividends**	+	**Revenues**	−	**Expenses**
Dr. for increases / Cr. for decreases		Dr. for decreases / Cr. for increases		Dr. for decrease / Cr. for increases		Dr. for increased / Cr. for decreases		Dr. for decreases / Cr. for increases		Dr. for increases / Cr. for decreases
Normal (Dr.)		Normal (Cr.)		Normal (Cr.)		Normal (Dr.)		Normal (Cr.)		Normal (Dr.)

Recall that income (revenues less expenses) feeds directly into retained earnings. Also, anything that increases equity is a credit and anything that decreases equity is a debit. So, to reflect an increase in revenues (which increase equity), we credit the revenue account, and to reflect an increase in an expense account (which reduces equity), we debit it.

To summarize, the following table reflects the use of the terms debit and credit to reflect increases and decreases to the general balance sheet and the income statement relations.

Accounting Relation		Debit	Credit
Balance sheet	Assets (A)	Increase	Decrease
	Liabilities (L)	Decrease	Increase
	Equity (SE)	Decrease	Increase
Income statement	Revenue (R)	Decrease	Increase
	Expense (E)	Increase	Decrease

The basic component of an accounting system is the **account,** which is an individual record of increases and decreases. An account is created for each important asset, liability, and equity item. This includes individual accounts for each important revenue and expense (recall that revenues and expenses yield income, which is part of retained earnings). Balance sheet accounts are called **permanent accounts**. The distinguishing feature of permanent accounts is that any balance in the account at the end of the period is carried forward as the beginning balance for the next period. Revenue and expense accounts are called **temporary accounts** because they are considered temporary subdivisions of retained earnings.

A two-column Cash T-account follows. There is a beginning balance of $2,500. Increases in cash have been placed on the left side of the Cash T-account and the decreases have been placed on the right side. The ending balance of cash is $3,700. An account balance is determined by totaling the left side and the right side money columns and entering the difference on the side with the largest total. The T-account is an extremely simple record that can be summarized in terms of four money elements: (1) beginning balance, (2) additions, (3) deductions, and (4) ending balance.

+	Cash (A)	−	
Beg. bal.	2,500		
(a)	4,000	1,500	(b)
(d)	200	500	(c)
		1,000	(e)
End. bal.	3,700		

Dates and other related data are usually omitted in T-accounts, but it is customary to *key* entries with a number or a letter to identify the similarly coded transaction. The type and number of accounts used by a business depend on the complexity of its operations and the degree of detail demanded by decision makers.

The Journal Entry

The journal entry records each transaction by summarizing the debits and credits. To illustrate the use of journal entries and T-accounts, assume that Disney: (1) Paid employees $10,000 cash wages, and (2) Paid $20,000 cash to acquire ride equipment. The journal entries and T-accounts reflecting these two transactions follow. The T-accounts can be viewed as reflecting the company *ledger,* which is a listing of all accounts and their dollar balances.

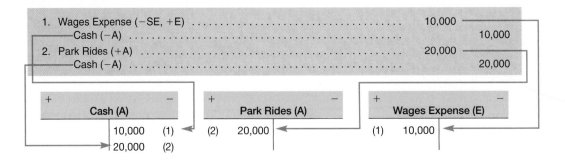

For journal entries, debits are recorded first followed by the credits. Credits are commonly indented. An alternative presentation is to utilize the abbreviation *dr* to denote debits and *cr* to denote credits that precede the account title.

Recording Transactions

To illustrate the use of journal entries and T-accounts to record transactions, we return to the example of Mickey's Camera Shop. We will use the same transactions we recorded earlier in the financial statement effects template. The entire template showing all ten transactions is reproduced below.

Transaction	Cash Asset	+	Noncash Assets	=	Liabil- ities	+	Contrib. Capital	+	Retained Earnings		Revenues	−	Expenses	=	Net Income
					Balance Sheet								**Income Statement**		
(1) Issue Stock for $12,000 cash	+12,000 Cash			=			+12,000 Common Stock							=	
(2) Paid $2,700 for rent in advance	−2,700 Cash		+2,700 Prepaid Rent	=										=	
(3) Borrowed $10,000 from bank	+10,000 Cash			=	+10,000 Note Payable									=	
(4) Purchased equipment for $9,500	−9,500 Cash		+9,500 Equip- ment	=										=	
(5) Received $17,200 of merchandise purchased on account			+17,200 Inventory	=	+17,200 Accounts Payable									=	
(6) Sold merchandise for $25,000 cash	+25,000 Cash			=					+25,000 Retained Earnings		+25,000 Sales Revenue			=	+25,000
(7) Record $13,600 for the cost of merchandise sold in entry 6			−13,600 Inventory	=					−13,600 Retained Earnings				−13,600 Cost Of Goods Sold	=	−13,600

(table continues on the next page)

Transaction	Cash Asset	+	Noncash Assets	=	Liabil- ities	+	Contrib. Capital	+	Retained Earnings	Revenues	–	Expenses	=	Net Income
(8) Paid $14,000 to suppliers of merchandise purchased on account	−14,000 Cash			=	−14,000 Accounts Payable								=	
(9) Paid $1,200 in wages to employees	−1,200 Cash			=					−1,200 Retained Earnings			−1,200 Wage Expense	=	−1,200
(10) Paid a $500 cash dividend to shareholders	−500 Cash			=					−500 Retained Earnings				=	

Journal entries representing each of the ten transactions are recorded chronologically as follows:

```
(1)  Cash (+A) .........................................  12,000
         Common stock (+SE) .............................          12,000
         Issued 12,000 shares of common stock.
(2)  Prepaid rent (+A) ..................................   2,700
         Cash (−A) ......................................           2,700
         Paid three months' rent in advance.
(3)  Cash (+A) .........................................  10,000
         Bank note payable (+L) .........................          10,000
         Borrowed $10,000 on a 2-year, 8% note.
(4)  Equipment (+A) .....................................   9,500
         Cash (−A) ......................................           9,500
         Purchased equipment for cash.
(5)  Inventory (+A) .....................................  17,200
         Accounts payable (+L) ..........................          17,200
         Received shipment of merchandise for inventory.
(6)  Cash (+A) .........................................  25,000
         Sales revenue (+R, +SE) ........................          25,000
         To record sales for the week of March 12.
(7)  Cost of goods sold (+E, −SE) .......................  13,600
         Inventory (−A) .................................          13,600
         To record the cost of merchandise sold during the week of March 12.
(8)  Accounts payable (−L) ..............................  14,000
         Cash (−A) ......................................          14,000
         Paid $14,000 to suppliers for merchandise received.
(9)  Wage expense (+E, −SE) .............................   1,200
         Cash (−A) ......................................           1,200
         Paid wages to employees.
(10) Retained earnings (−SE) ............................     500
         Cash (−A) ......................................             500
         Paid a cash dividend.
```

Each of these journal entries is then posted to the appropriate T-accounts, which represent the general ledger and are as follows. See that: Assets = Liabilities + Equity. Specifically, $34,900 assets ($19,100 + $2,700 + $2,700 + $3,600 + $9,500) = $13,200 liabilities ($3,200 + $10,000) + $21,700 equity ($12,000 − $500 + $25,000 − $13,600 − $1,200).

+ Cash (A) −			
(1)	12,000	2,700	(2)
(3)	10,000	9,500	(4)
(6)	25,000	14,000	(8)
		1,200	(9)
		500	(10)
End.	19,100		

+ Prepaid rent (A) −	
(2)	2,700
End.	2,700

+ Inventory (A) −			
(5)	17,200		
		13,600	(7)
End.	3,600		

+ Equipment (A) −	
(4)	9,500
End.	9,500

− Accounts payable (L) +			
		17,200	(5)
(8)	14,000		
		3,200	End.

− Note payable (L) +			
		10,000	(3)
		10,000	End.

− Common stock (SE) +			
		12,000	(1)
		12,000	End.

− Retained earnings (SE) +	
(10)	500

− Sales revenue (R) +			
		25,000	(6)

+ Cost of goods sold (E) −	
(7)	13,600

+ Wage expense (E) −	
(9)	1,200

To review, the balance sheet accounts are *permanent accounts*. Ending balances in asset, liability and equity accounts carry over to the next accounting period and become the beginning balances for that period. Revenue and expense accounts, on the other hand, are *temporary accounts*. Each period, these accounts begin with a balance of $0. In Chapter 3 we will learn how to complete the accounting process using journal entries and T-accounts, and prepare the balance sheet and income statement from these account balances.

CHAPTER-END REVIEW

The following accounts appear in the ledger of G. Pownall, an attorney: Cash; Accounts Receivable; Office Equipment; Prepaid Subscriptions; Accounts Payable; Common Stock; Retained Earnings; Legal Fees Earned; Salaries Expense; Rent Expense; and Utilities Expense. (a) Analyze and enter the following transactions of the firm into the financial statement effects template. (b) Prepare journal entries for each of the transactions 1 through 10. (c) Set up T-accounts for each of the ledger accounts and post the journal entries to those T-accounts—key all entries with the number identifying the transaction. Determine the ending balance for each account.

(1) Pownall started the law firm by contributing $19,500 cash to the business in exchange for common stock.
(2) Purchased $10,400 in office equipment on account.
(3) Paid $700 cash for this period's office rent.
(4) Paid $9,600 cash for subscriptions to online legal databases covering the next three periods.
(5) Billed clients $11,300 for services rendered.
(6) Made $6,000 cash payment on account for the equipment purchased in transaction 2.
(7) Paid $2,800 cash for legal assistant's salary for this period.
(8) Collected $9,400 cash from clients previously billed in transaction 5.
(9) Received $180 invoice for this period's utilities; it is paid early in the next period.
(10) Paid $1,500 cash for dividends to shareholders.

Solutions
a.   Financial statement effects template

Transaction	Balance Sheet						Income Statement		
	Cash Asset	+ Noncash Assets	= Liabil- ities	+ Contrib. Capital	+ Retained Earnings		Revenues	− Expenses	= Net Income
(1) Issued common stock	+19,500 Cash		=	+19,500 Common Stock				=	
(2) Purchased office equipment on account		+10,400 Office Equipment	= +10,400 Accounts Payable					=	
(3) Paid rent expense	−700 Cash		=		−700 Retained Earnings			−700 Rent Expense	= −700
(4) Paid for subscriptions in advance	−9,600 Cash	+9,600 Prepaid Subscriptions	=					=	
(5) Billed clients for services rendered		+11,300 Accounts Receivable	=		+11,300 Retained Earnings		+11,300 Legal Fees Earned	=	+11,300
(6) Payment of accounts payable	−6,000 Cash		= −6,000 Accounts Payable					=	
(7) Paid salary for legal assistant	−2,800 Cash		=		−2,800 Retained Earnings			−2,800 Salaries Expense	= −2,800
(8) Collected cash from client	+9,400 Cash	−9,400 Accounts Receivable	=					=	
(9) Utility expense			= −180 Accounts Payable		−180 Retained Earnings			−180 Utilities Expense	= −180
(10) Paid cash dividends	−1,500 Cash		=		−1,500 Retained Earnings			=	

b. Journal entries for transactions.

```
 1. Cash (+A) ..............................................    19,500
       Common Stock (+SE) ...............................              19,500
 2. Office Equipment (+A) ..............................    10,400
       Accounts Payable (+L) ............................              10,400
 3. Rent Expense (+E, −SE) ............................       700
       Cash (−A) .........................................                 700
 4. Prepaid Subscriptions (+A) ........................     9,600
       Cash (−A) .........................................               9,600
 5. Accounts Receivable (+A) ..........................    11,300
       Legal Fees Earned (+R, +SE) ....................              11,300
 6. Accounts Payable (−L) .............................     6,000
       Cash (−A) .........................................               6,000
 7. Salaries Expense (+E, −SE) .......................     2,800
       Cash (−A) .........................................               2,800
 8. Cash (+A) ..............................................     9,400
       Accounts Receivable (−A) .........................               9,400
 9. Utilities Expense (+E, −SE) .......................       180
       Accounts Payable (+L) ............................                 180
10. Retained Earnings (−SE) ..........................     1,500
       Cash (−A) .........................................               1,500
```

c.   T-accounts with transactions and ending balances entered and keyed.

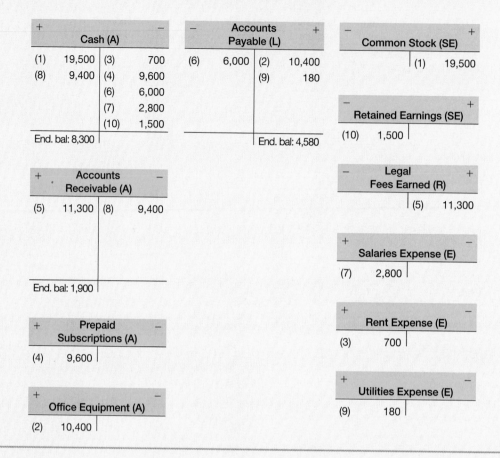

SUMMARY

LO1   **Describe and construct the balance sheet. (p. 43)**

- Assets, which reflect investment activities, are reported (in order of their liquidity) as current assets (expected to be used typically within a year) and long-term (or plant) assets.
- Assets are reported at their historical cost and not at market values (with few exceptions) and are restricted to those that can be reliably measured.
- Not all assets are reported on the balance sheet; a company's intellectual capital, often one of its more valuable assets, is one example.
- For an asset to be recorded, it must be owned or controlled by the company and carry future economic benefits.
- Liabilities and equity are the sources of company financing; ordered by maturity dates.

LO2   **Describe and construct the income statement. (p. 53)**

- The income statement presents the revenues, expenses, and net income recognized by the company during the accounting period.
- Net income (or loss) is the increase (decrease) in net assets that results from business activities.
- Net income is determined based on the use of accrual accounting.

LO3   **Describe revenue recognition and the matching principle. (p. 54)**

- Revenues must be recognized only when they have been earned and realized (or realizable).
- Expenses incurred to generate revenues should be recognized in the same period as the revenues.

LO4   **Describe the statement of equity and its interpretation. (p. 59)**

- The statement of stockholders' reports transactions resulting in changes in equity accounts during the accounting period.

■ Transactions between the company and its owners, such as dividend payments, are not reported in the income statement.

Describe the statement of cash flow and its interpretation. (p. 61)   **LO5**

■ The cash flow statement details the sources and uses of cash during the period.

■ Cash flows are delineated by activity: operating activities, investing activities, or financing activities.

■ Cash flow from operations differs from net income because of the use of accrual accounting.

Explain the methods applied to analyze and record transactions. (p. 62)   **LO6**

■ Transactions are recorded in the accounting system using journal entries.

■ Journal entries are posted to a general ledger, represented by "T-accounts."

■ Accountants use "debits" and "credits" to record transactions in the accounts

GUIDANCE ANSWERS

YOU MAKE THE CALL

You are an Operations Manager   The CFO desires a warranty cost estimate to match against the sales generated from the new product. To arrive at such an estimate, you must estimate the number and types of deficiencies in your product and the costs associated with each per the warranty provisions. This is often a difficult task for product engineers because it forces them to focus on the product failures and costs associated with them.

YOU MAKE THE CALL

You are an Analyst   In 2004, Callaway paid cash dividends of $19.0 million (net) despite reporting the loss. The loss and dividend payments account for the change in retained earnings ($466.4 − $10.1 − $19.0 = $437.3). The following year (2005), Callaway reported net income of $13.3 million, but paid dividends of $19.6 million, further reducing retained earnings to $431.0 million.

KEY TERMS

Account (p. 63)

Accounting equation (p. 43)

Accounts payable (p. 46)

Accounts receivable (p. 44)

Accrual accounting (p. 55)

Accrued liabilities (p. 46)

Accumulated other comprehensive income or loss (p. 48)

Additional paid-in capital (p. 48)

Articulation (p. 56)

Asset (p. 43)

Book value (p. 49)

Capitalized (p. 42)

Cash (p. 44)

Cash accounting (p. 55)

Common stock (p. 48)

Contributed capital (p. 48)

Credit (p. 54)

Current assets (p. 44)

Current maturities of long-term debt (p. 46)

Current liabilities (p. 46)

Depreciation (p. 43)

Double entry accounting system (p. 50)

Earned capital (p. 48)

Equity (p. 43, 48)

Executory contract (p. 45)

Expensed (p. 42)

Expenses (p. 54)

Fair market value (p. 45)

Financial statement effects template (p. 50)

Gross profit (p. 54)

Historical costs (p. 45)

Intangible and other assets (p. 45)

Inventory (p. 44)

Journal entry (p. 62)

Liability (p. 45)

Liquidity (p. 44)

Long-term debt (p. 47)

Long-term investments (p. 44)

Market value (p. 49)

Marketable securities (p. 44)

Matching principle (p. 55)

Net income (p. 54)

Net loss (p. 54)

Net working capital (p. 46)

Non-current liabilities (p. 47)

Non-operating expenses (p. 54)

Non-operating revenues (p. 54)

Notes payable (p. 47)

Operating cycle (p. 46)

Operating expenses (p. 54)

Other long-term liabilities (p. 47)

Permanent account (p. 63)

Prepaid expenses (p. 44)

Property, Plant and Equipment (PPE) (p. 44)

Relevance (p. 45)

Reliability (p. 45)

Retained earnings (p. 48)

Revenue recognition principle (p. 54)

Revenues (p. 54)

Shareholders' Equity (p. 43)

Short-term notes payable (p. 46)

Stockholders' Equity (p. 43)

T-account (p. 62)

Temporary account (p. 63)

Trade credit (p. 46)

Treasury stock (p. 48)

Unearned revenues (p. 46)

MULTIPLE CHOICE

1. Which of the following conditions must exist for an item to be recorded as an asset?
   a. Item is not owned or controlled by the company
   b. Future benefits from the item cannot be reliably measured
   c. Item must be a tangible asset
   d. Item must be expected to yield future benefits

2. Company assets that are excluded from the company financial statements
   a. are presumably reflected in the company's stock price.
   b. include all of the company's intangible assets.
   c. are known as intangible assets.
   d. include investments in other companies.

3. If an asset declines in value, which of the following must be true?
   a. A liability also declines
   b. Equity also declines
   c. Either a liability or equity also declines or another asset increases in value
   d. Neither a nor b can occur

4. Which of the following is true about accrual accounting?
   a. Accrual accounting does not require matching.
   b. Accrual accounting is required under GAAP.
   c. Accrual accounting recognizes revenue only when cash is received.
   d. Recognition of a prepaid asset is not an example of accrual accounting.

5. Which of the following is one of the three major sections of the statement of cash flows?
   a. Cash flows from operating activities
   b. Net income from cash flows
   c. Operating expenses from cash activities
   d. Net income from operating cash flows

DISCUSSION QUESTIONS

Q2-1. The balance sheet consists of assets, liabilities, and equity. Define each category and provide two examples of accounts reported within each category.

Q2-2. Two important concepts that guide income statement reporting are the revenue recognition principle and the matching principle. Define and explain each of these two guiding principles.

Q2-3. GAAP is based on the concept of accrual accounting. Define and describe accrual accounting.

Q2-4. What is the statement of stockholders' equity? What useful information is contained in that statement?

Q2-5. What is the statement of cash flows? What useful information is contained in that statement?

Q2-6. Describe the flow of costs for the purchase of a machine. At what point do such costs become expenses? Why is it necessary to match the expenses related to the machine in the same period with the revenues it produces?

Q2-7. What are the two essential characteristics of an asset?

Q2-8. What does the concept of liquidity refer to? Explain.

Q2-9. What does the term *current* denote when referring to assets?

Q2-10. Assets are recorded at historical costs even though current market values might, arguably, be more relevant to financial statement readers. Describe the reasoning behind historical cost usage.

Q2-11. Identify three intangible assets that are likely to be *excluded* from the balance sheet because they cannot be reliably measured.

Q2-12. What are accrued liabilities? Provide an example.

Q2-13. What three conditions must be satisfied to require reporting of liability on the balance sheet?

Q2-14. Define net working capital. Explain how increasing the amount of trade credit can reduce the net working capital for a company.

Q2-15. What is the difference between company *book value* and *market value*? Explain why these two amounts can be different.

Q2-16. On December 31, 2006, Miller Company had $700,000 in total assets and owed $220,000 to creditors. If this corporation's common stock totaled $300,000, what amount of retained earnings is reported on its December 31, 2006, balance sheet?

MINI EXERCISES

M2-17. Determining Retained Earnings and Net Income (LO1)

The following information is reported for Kinney Corporation at the end of 2006.

Accounts Receivable	$ 23,000	Retained Earnings	$?
Accounts Payable	11,000	Supplies	9,000
Cash	8,000	Equipment	138,000
Common Stock	110,000		

a. Compute the amount of retained earnings at the end of 2006.

b. If the amount of retained earnings at the beginning of 2006 was $30,000, and $12,000 in cash dividends were declared and paid during 2006, what was its net income for 2006?

M2-18. Applying the Accounting Equation (LO1)

Determine the missing amount in each of the following separate company cases.

	Assets	Liabilities	Equity
a.	$200,000	$85,000	?
b.	?	$32,000	$28,000
c.	$ 93,000	?	$52,000

M2-19. Applying the Accounting Equation (LO1)

Determine the missing amount in each of the following separate company cases.

	Assets	Liabilities	Equity
a.	$375,000	$105,000	?
b.	?	$ 43,000	$ 11,000
c.	$878,000	?	$422,000

M2-20. Applying the Accounting Equation (LO1)

Determine the following for each separate company case:

a. The stockholders' equity of Blaccionere Corporation, which has assets of $450,000 and liabilities of $326,000.

b. The liabilities of Sloan & Dechow, Inc., which has assets of $618,000 and stockholders' equity of $165,000.

c. The assets of Clem Corporation, which has liabilities of $400,000, common stock of $200,000, and retained earnings of $185,000.

M2-21. Analyzing Transaction Effects on Equity (LO6)

Would each of the following transactions increase, decrease, or have no effect on equity?

a. Paid cash to acquire supplies.

b. Paid cash for dividends to shareholders.

c. Paid cash for salaries.

d. Purchased equipment for cash.

e. Shareholders invested cash in business in exchange for common stock.

f. Rendered service to customers on account.

g. Rendered service to customers for cash.

M2-22. Identifying and Classifying Financial Statement Items (LO1, 2)

For each of the following items, identify whether they would most likely be reported in the balance sheet (B) or income statement (I).

a.	Machinery ____	e.	Common stock ____	i.	Taxes expense ____
b.	Supplies expense ____	f.	Factory buildings ____	j.	Cost of goods sold ____
c.	Prepaid advertising ____	g.	Receivables ____	k.	Long-term debt ____
d.	Advertising expense ____	h.	Taxes payable ____	l.	Treasury stock ____

M2-23. Computation and Comparison of Income and Cash Flow Measures (LO1, 4)

Healy Corporation recorded service revenues of $100,000 in 2005, of which $70,000 were for credit and $30,000 were for cash. Moreover, of the $70,000 credit sales for 2005, it collected $20,000 cash on those receivables before year-end 2005. The company also paid $25,000 cash for 2005 wages. Its employees also earned another $15,000 in wages for 2005, which were not yet paid at year-end 2005. (a) Compute the company's net income for 2005. (b) How much net cash inflow or outflow did the company generate in 2005? Explain.

M2-24. Classifying Items in Financial Statements (LO1, 2, 3, 4)

Next to each item, indicate whether it would most likely be reported: on the balance sheet (B), the income statement (I), the statement of cash flow (CF), or the statement of stockholders' equity (SE).

a.	Liabilities ___	d.	Revenues ___	g.	Assets ___
b.	Net Income ___	e.	Financing cash flows ___	h.	Expenses ___
c.	Cash ___	f.	Dividends ___	i.	Equity ___

M2-25. Classifying Items in Financial Statements (LO1, 2, 3, 4)

For each of the following items, indicate whether it is most likely reported on the balance sheet (B), the income statement (I), the statement of cash flow (CF), or the statement of stockholders' equity (SE).

a.	Accounts receivable ___	e.	Notes payable ___
b.	Cash received from land sale ___	f.	Supplies expense ___
c.	Net income ___	g.	Land ___
d.	Stockholder's equity ___	h.	Supplies ___

M2-26. Classifying Items in Financial Statements (LO1, 2, 3, 4)

For each of the following items, indicate whether it is most likely reported on the balance sheet (B), the income statement (I), the statement of cash flow (CF), or the statement of stockholders' equity (SE).

a.	Cash (year-end balance) ___	e.	Dividends ___
b.	Advertising expense ___	f.	Accounts payable ___
c.	Common stock ___	g.	Cash paid to purchase equipment ___
d.	Printing fees earned ___	h.	Equipment ___

M2-27. Computing Company Performance Using the Accounting Equation (LO3)

World Wrestling Entertainment (WWE)

Use your knowledge of accounting relations to complete the following table for World Wrestling Entertainment, Inc.

	2003	2004
Beginning retained earnings	$89,089	$?
Net income (loss)	?	48,192
Dividends	0	15,060
Ending retained earnings	69,634	?

M2-28. Analyzing Transactions using the Accounting Equation (LO1, 6)

Following the example in *a* below, indicate the effects of transactions *b* through *i* on assets, liabilities, and equity, including identifying the individual accounts affected.

- a. Rendered legal services to clients for cash
  - ANSWER: Increase assets (Cash)
    - Increase equity (Revenues)
- b. Purchased office supplies on account
- c. Issued additional common stock in exchange for cash
- d. Paid amount due on account for office supplies purchased in *b*
- e. Borrowed cash (and signed a six-month note) from bank
- f. Rendered legal services and billed clients
- g. Paid cash to acquire a desk lamp for the office
- h. Paid cash to cover interest on note payable to bank
- i. Received invoice for this period's utilities

M2-29. Analyzing Transactions using the Accounting Equation (LO1, 6)

Following the example in *a* below, indicate the effects of transactions *b* through *i* on assets, liabilities, and equity, including identifying the individual accounts affected.

- a. Paid cash to acquire a computer for use in office
  - ANSWER: Increase assets (Office Equipment)
    - Decrease assets (Cash)
- b. Rendered services and billed client
- c. Paid cash to cover rent for this period
- d. Rendered services to client for cash
- e. Received amount due from client in *b*
- f. Purchased an office desk on account
- g. Paid cash to cover this period's employee salaries
- h. Paid cash to cover desk purchased in *f*
- i. Declared and paid a cash dividend

M2-30. Constructing a Retained Earnings Reconciliation from Financial Data (LO3)

Following is financial information from Johnson & Johnson for the year ended December 28, 2003. Prepare the 2003 calendar-year retained earnings reconciliation for Johnson & Johnson ($ millions).

Retained earnings, Dec. 29, 2002	$26,571	Dividends	$2,746
Net earnings	7,197	Retained earnings, Dec. 28, 2003	?
Other retained earnings changes	(519)		

M2-31. Analyzing Transactions to Compute Net Income (LO2)

Guay Corp., a start-up company, provided services that were acceptable to its customers and billed those customers for $350,000 in 2004. However, Guay collected only $280,000 cash in 2004, and the remaining $70,000 of 2004 revenues were collected in 2005. Guay employees earned $200,000 in 2004 wages that were not paid until the first week of 2005. How much net income does Guay report for 2004? For 2005 (assuming no new transactions)?

M2-32. Analyzing Transactions using the Financial Statement Effects Template (LO1, 2, 3, 4, 6)

Report the effects for each of the following independent transactions using the financial statement effects template provided.

	Balance Sheet					Income Statement		
Transaction	Cash Asset +	Noncash Assets =	Liabil- ities +	Contrib. Capital +	Retained Earnings	Revenues –	Expenses =	Net Income
a. Issue stock for $1,000 cash		=						=
b. Purchase inventory for $500 cash		=						=
c. Sold inventory for $2,000 on credit		=						=
d. Record $500 for cost of inventory sold in c		=						=
e. Receive $2,000 cash on receivable from c		=						=

M2-33. Refer to the transactions in M2-32. (LO6)

(1) Prepare journal entries for each of the transactions a through d. (2) Set up T-accounts for each of the accounts used in part (1) and post the journal entries to those T-accounts.

M2-34. Refer to the transactions in M2-32. (LO5)

For each transaction indicate (1) its effect on the cash flow statement—source of cash, use of cash, or no effect on cash, and (2) its placement into one of the three sections of the statement of cash flows—operating, investing, financing—or its 'no effect' on the statement of cash flows.

EXERCISES

E2-35. Constructing Balance Sheets (LO1, 6)

The following balance sheet data are reported for Parker, Inc., at May 31, 2006.

Accounts Receivable	$18,300	Accounts Payable	$ 5,200
Notes Payable	20,000	Cash	12,200
Equipment	55,000	Common Stock	42,500
Supplies	16,400	Retained Earnings	?

Assume that on June 1, 2006, only the following two transactions occurred.

June 1 Purchased additional equipment costing $15,000, giving $2,000 cash and a $13,000 note payable.
    2 Declared and paid a $7,000 cash dividend.

a. Prepare its balance sheet at May 31, 2006.

b. Prepare its balance sheet at June 1, 2006.

E2-36. **Applying the Accounting Equation to Compute Missing Data** (LO1, 2)

For each of the four separate situations *1* through *4* below, compute the unknown amounts referenced by the letters *a* through *d* shown.

	1	2	3	4
Beginning				
Assets	$28,000	$12,000	$28,000	$ (d)
Liabilities	18,600	5,000	19,000	9,000
Ending				
Assets	30,000	26,000	34,000	40,000
Liabilities	17,300	(b)	15,000	19,000
During Year				
Common Stock Issued	2,000	4,500	(c)	3,500
Revenues	(a)	28,000	18,000	24,000
Cash Dividends Paid	5,000	1,500	1,000	6,500
Expenses	8,500	21,000	11,000	17,000

E2-37. **Preparing Balance Sheets and Computing Income** (LO1, 2, 6)

Balance sheet information for Lang Services at the end of 2006 and 2007 follows.

	December 31, 2007	December 31, 2006
Accounts Receivable	$22,800	$17,500
Accounts Payable	1,800	1,600
Cash	10,000	8,000
Equipment	32,000	27,000
Supplies	4,700	4,200
Accounts Payable	25,000	25,000
Stockholders' Equity	?	?

a. Prepare its balance sheet for December 31 of each year.

b. Lang Services raised $5,000 cash through issuing additional common stock early in 2007, and it declared and paid a $17,000 cash dividend in December 2007. Compute its net income or loss for 2007.

E2-38. **Constructing Balance Sheets and Determining Income** (LO1, 2, 6)

Following is balance sheet information for Lynch Services at the end of 2005 and 2006.

	December 31, 2006	December 31, 2005
Accounts Payable	$ 6,000	$ 9,000
Cash	23,000	20,000
Accounts Receivable	42,000	33,000
Land	40,000	40,000
Building	250,000	260,000
Equipment	43,000	45,000
Mortgage Payable	90,000	100,000
Supplies	20,000	18,000
Common Stock	220,000	220,000
Retained Earnings	?	?

a. Prepare balance sheets at December 31 of each year.

b. The firm declared and paid a cash dividend of $10,000 in December 2006. Compute its net income for 2006 (*Hint:* The net increase in retained earnings equals net income less the dividend.).

E2-39. Constructing Balance Sheets (LO1, 6)

The following balance sheet data are reported for Normand Catering at May 31, 2006.

Accounts Receivable	$18,300	Accounts Payable	$ 5,200
Notes Payable	20,000	Cash	12,200
Equipment	55,000	Capital Stock	42,500
Supplies	16,400	Retained Earnings	?

Assume that on June 1, 2006, only the following two transactions occurred:

June 1   Purchased additional equipment costing $15,000, giving $2,000 cash and a $13,000 note payable.
    1   Declared and paid a cash dividend of $7,000.

a.   Prepare its balance sheet at May 31, 2006.
b.   Prepare its balance sheet at June 1, 2006.

E2-40. Constructing Financial Statements from Transaction Data (LO1, 2, 6)

Baiman Corporation commences operations at the beginning of January. It provides its services on credit and bills its customers $30,000 for January sales. Its employees also earn January wages of $12,000 that are not paid until the first of February. Complete the following statements for the month-end of January.

Income Statement	
Sales	$
Wages expense	
Net income (loss)	$

Balance Sheet	
Cash	$
Accounts receivable	
Total assets	$
Wages payable	$
Retained earnings	
Total liabilities and equity	$

E2-41. Identifying and Classifying Balance Sheet and Income Statement Accounts (LO1, 2)

Following are selected accounts for Procter & Gamble.

Procter & Gamble (PG)

($ millions)	Amount	Classification
Sales	$43,373	
Accumulated depreciation	10,438	
Depreciation expense	1,703	
Retained earnings	11,686	
Net income	5,186	
Property, plant & equipment	13,104	
Selling, general & administrative expense	13,009	
Accounts receivable	3,038	
Total liabilities	27,520	
Stockholders' equity	16,186	

(*a*)   Indicate the appropriate classification of each account as appearing in either its balance sheet (B) or its income statement (I).
(*b*)   Using the data, compute its amounts for total assets and for total expenses.
(*c*)   Compute its net profit margin (net income/sales) and its debt-to-equity ratio (total liabilities/stockholders' equity).

E2-42. Identifying and Classifying Balance Sheet and Income Statement Accounts (LO1, 2, 4)

Following are selected accounts for Target Corporation.

Target Corporation (TGT)

($ millions)	Amount	Classification
Sales	$48,163	
Accumulated depreciation	6,178	
Depreciation expense	1,320	
Retained earnings	9,648	
Net income	1,841	
Property, plant & equipment	16,969	
Selling, general & administrative expense	11,534	
Accounts receivable	5,776	
Total liabilities	20,327	
Stockholders' equity	11,065	

(*a*) Indicate the appropriate classification of each account as appearing in either its balance sheet (B) or its income statement (I).

(*b*) Using the data, compute its amounts for total assets and for total expenses.

(*c*) Compute its net profit margin (net income/sales) and its debt-to-equity ratio (total liabilities/stockholders' equity).

E2-43. Identifying and Classifying Balance Sheet and Income Statement Accounts (LO1, 3, 5)

Briggs & Stratton (BGG)

Following are selected accounts for Briggs & Stratton.

($ millions)	Amount	Classification
Sales	$1,658	
Accumulated depreciation	506	
Depreciation expense	64	
Retained earnings	821	
Net income	81	
Property, plant & equipment	371	
Selling, general & administrative expense	178	
Accounts receivable	202	
Total liabilities	960	
Stockholders' equity	515	

(*a*) Indicate the appropriate classification of each account as appearing in either its balance sheet (B) or its income statement (I).

(*b*) Using the data, compute its amounts for total assets and for total expenses.

(*c*) Compute its net profit margin (net income/sales) and its debt-to-equity ratio (total liabilities/stockholders' equity).

E2-44. Preparing Balance Sheets and Computing Income (LO1, 2, 3)

Balance sheet information for Kennedy Services at the end of 2005 and 2006 follows.

	December 31, 2006	December 31, 2005
Accounts Payable	$ 12,000	$ 18,000
Cash	46,000	40,000
Accounts Receivable	84,000	66,000
Land	80,000	80,000
Building	500,000	520,000
Equipment	86,000	90,000
Mortgage Payable	180,000	200,000
Supplies	40,000	36,000
Common Stock	440,000	440,000
Retained Earnings	?	?

a. Prepare its balance sheet for December 31 of each year.

b. The company declared and paid a $20,000 cash dividend in December 2006. Compute its net income for 2006.

E2-45.   Identifying and Classifying Balance Sheet and Income Statement Accounts   (LO1, 3, 5)

Following are selected accounts for **Kimberly-Clark**.

Kimberly-Clark
(KMB)

($ millions)	Amount	Classification
Sales	$14,348	
Accumulated depreciation	6,916	
Depreciation expense	759	
Retained earnings	9,494	
Net income	1,694	
Property, plant & equipment	8,263	
Selling, general & administrative expense	2,376	
Accounts receivable	1,955	
Total liabilities	10,014	
Stockholders' equity	6,766	

a.   Indicate the appropriate classification of each account as appearing in either its balance sheet (B) or its income statement (I).

b.   Using the data, compute its amounts for total assets and for total expenses.

c.   Compute its net profit margin (net income/sales) and its debt-to-equity ratio (total liabilities/stockholders' equity).

d.   Which of the accounts would be included in a statement of cash flows?

E2-46.   Identifying and Classifying Balance Sheet and Income Statement Accounts   (LO1, 3, 5)

Following are selected accounts for **YUM! Brands**.

YUM! Brands (YUM)

($ millions)	Amount	Classification
Sales	$8,380	
Accumulated depreciation	2,326	
Depreciation expense	401	
Retained earnings	204	
Net income	617	
Property, plant & equipment	3,280	
Selling, general & administrative expense	973	
Accounts receivable	169	
Total liabilities	4,500	
Stockholders' equity	1,120	

a.   Indicate the appropriate classification of each account as appearing in either its balance sheet (B) or its income statement (I).

b.   Using the data, compute its amounts for total assets and for total expenses.

c.   Compute its net profit margin (net income/sales) and its debt-to-equity ratio (total liabilities/stockholders' equity).

d.   Which of the accounts would be included in a statement of cash flows?

E2-47.   Constructing Balance Sheets   (LO1, 2, 3)

The following balance sheet data are reported for Bettis Contractors at June 30, 2006.

Accounts Payable	$ 8,900	Common Stock	$100,000
Cash	14,700	Retained Earnings	?
Supplies	30,500	Notes Payable	30,000
Equipment	98,000	Accounts Receivable	9,200
Land	25,000		

Assume that during the next two days only the following three transactions occurred:

July 1   Paid $5,000 cash toward the notes payable owed

2   Purchased equipment for $10,000, paying $2,000 cash and an $8,000 note payable for the remaining balance

2   Declared and paid a $5,500 cash dividend

a. Prepare a balance sheet at June 30, 2006.
b. Prepare a balance sheet at July 2, 2006.

E2-48. **Analyzing Transactions using the Financial Statement Effects Template** (LO1, 2, 3)
Record the effect of each of the following independent transactions using the financial statement effects template provided.

	Balance Sheet							Income Statement		
Transaction	Cash Asset	+ Noncash Assets	=	Liabil- ities	+	Contrib. Capital	+ Retained Earnings	Revenues	− Expenses	= Net Income
a. $500 of wages are earned by employees but not yet paid			=							=
b. $2,000 of inventory is purchased on credit			=							=
c. Sold inventory for $3,000 on credit			=							=
d. Record $2,000 for cost of inventory sold in c			=							=
e. Collected $3,000 cash from the transaction c			=							=
f. $5,000 of equipment is acquired for cash			=							=
g. Record of depreciation of $1,000 on equipment from transaction e			=							=
h. Paid $10,000 on a note payable that came due			=							=
i. Paid $2,000 cash interest on borrowings			=							=

E2-49. **Recording Transactions in Journal Entries and T-Accounts** (LO2)
Use the information in Exercise 2-48 to complete the following.
1. Prepare journal entries for each of the transactions a through g.
2. Set up T-accounts for each of the accounts used in part (1) and post the journal entries to those T-accounts.

E2-50. **Analyzing Cash Effects of Transactions** (LO6)
Use the information in Exercise 2-48 to complete the following.
1. For each transaction indicate its effect on the cash flow statement—source of cash, use of cash, or no effect on cash.
2. For each transaction indicate its placement into one of the three sections of the statement of cash flows—operating, investing, financing—or its 'no effect' on the statement of cash flows.

PROBLEMS

P2-51. **Preparing a Balance Sheet and Computing Net Income** (LO1, 2)
At the beginning of 2006, Barth Company reported the following balance sheet.

Assets		Liabilities	
Cash	$ 4,800	Accounts Payable	$12,000
Accounts Receivable	14,700	**Equity**	
Equipment	10,000	Common Stock	47,500
Land	50,000	Retained Earnings	20,000
Total Assets	$79,500	Total liabilities and Equity	$79,500

Required

a. At the end of 2006, Barth Corporation reported the following assets and liabilities: Cash, $8,800; Accounts Receivable, $18,400; Equipment, $9,000; Land, $50,000; and Accounts Payable, $7,500. Prepare a year-end balance sheet for Barth. (*Hint:* Report equity as a single total.)

b. Assuming that Barth did not issue any common stock during the year but paid $12,000 cash in dividends, what was its net income or net loss for 2006?

c. Assuming that Barth issued an additional $13,500 common stock early in the year but paid $21,000 cash in dividends before the end of the year, what was its net income or net loss for 2006?

P2-52. **Analyzing and Interpreting the Financial Performance of Competitors** (LO1, 2, 3)

Abercrombie & Fitch and Nordstrom are major retailers that concentrate in the higher-end clothing lines. Following are selected data from their fiscal-year 2003 financial statements:

Abercrombie & Fitch (ANF)

Nordstrom (JWN)

($ millions)	ANF	JWN
Total liabilities and equity	$1,199	$4,466
Net income	195	205
Sales	1,596	1,708

Required

a. What is the total amount of assets invested in (1) ANF and (2) JWN? What are the total expenses for each company (1) in dollars and (2) as a percentage of sales?

b. What is the return on average assets for (1) ANF and (2) JWN? Note: ANF's total assets at the beginning of 2003 are $995 million and JWN's beginning 2003 assets are $4,096 million.

P2-53. **Constructing and Analyzing Balance Sheet Numbers from Incomplete Data** (LO1, 2, 3, 4)

Selected balance sheet amounts for 3M Company, a manufacturer of consumer and business products, for five recent years follow:

3M Company (MMM)

($ millions)	Current Assets	Long-Term Assets	Total Assets	Current Liabilities	Long-Term Liabilities	Total Liabilities	Stockholders' Equity
1999	$6,066	$?	$13,896	$3,819	$?	$7,607	$6,289
2000	?	8,143	14,522	4,754	3,237	7,991	?
2001	6,296	8,310	?	?	4,011	8,520	6,086
2002	6,059	9,270	?	4,457	4,879	?	5,993
2003	?	9,880	17,600	5,082	4,633	9,715	?

Required

a. Compute the missing balance sheet amounts for each of the five years shown.

b. What types of accounts would you expect to be included in current assets? In long-term assets?

P2-54. **Analyzing, Reconstructing and Interpreting Balance Sheet Data** (LO1, 2, 3, 4)

Selected balance sheet amounts for Abercrombie & Fitch, a retailer of name-brand apparel at premium prices, for five recent fiscal-years follow ($ millions):

Abercrombie & Fitch (ANF)

	Current Assets	Long-Term Assets	Total Assets	Current Liabilities	Long-Term Liabilities	Total Liabilities	Stockholders' Equity
2000	$?	$158	$ 458	$138	$?	$147	$311
2001	304	284	?	155	10	165	?
2002	405	?	771	?	12	175	595
2003	601	394	?	211	?	245	750
2004	753	?	1,199	?	48	328	871

Required

a. Compute the missing balance sheet amounts for each of the five years shown.

b. What asset category would you expect to constitute the majority of its current assets?

    c. Has the proportion of current and long-term assets changed markedly over the past five years? Explain.

    d. Does the company appear to be conservatively financed; that is, financed by a greater proportion of equity than of debt? Explain

P2-55. **Analyzing Transactions using the Financial Statement Effects Template and Preparing an Income Statement** (LO2, 3)

On December 1, 2006, I. Emig formed Emig Services, which provides career and vocational counseling services to graduating college students. The following transactions took place during December, and company accounts include the following: Cash, Accounts Receivable, Land, Accounts Payable, Note Payable, Common Stock, Retained Earnings, Dividends, Counseling Services Revenue, Rent Expense, Advertising Expense, Interest Expense, Salary Expense, and Utilities Expense.

  1. Raised $7,000 cash through common stock issuance
  2. Paid $750 cash for December rent on its furnished office space
  3. Received $500 invoice for December advertising expenses
  4. Borrowed $15,000 cash from bank and signed note payable for that amount
  5. Received $1,200 cash for counseling services rendered
  6. Billed clients $6,800 for counseling services rendered
  7. Paid $2,200 cash for secretary salary
  8. Paid $370 cash for December utilities
  9. Declared and paid a $900 cash dividend
 10. Purchased land for $13,000 cash to use for its own facilities
 11. Paid $100 cash to bank as December interest expense on note payable

Required

a. Report the effects for each of the separate transactions 1 through 11 using the financial statement effects template. Total all columns and prove that (1) assets equal liabilities plus equity at December 31, and (2) revenues less expenses equal net income for December.

b. Prepare an income statement for the month of December.

P2-56. **Recording Transactions in Journal Entries and T-Accounts** (LO2)
Use the information in Problem 2-55 to complete the following requirements.

Required

1. Prepare journal entries for each of the transactions *1* through *11*.
2. Set up T-accounts for each of the accounts used in part 1 and post the journal entries to those T-accounts.

P2-57. **Analyzing, Reconstructing and Interpreting Balance Sheet Data** (LO1, 2, 3, 4)

Albertsons Inc. (ABS)

Selected balance sheet amounts for Albertsons Inc., a grocery company, for five recent fiscal-years follow ($ millions):

	Current Assets	Long-Term Assets	Total Assets	Current Liabilities	Long-Term Liabilities	Total Liabilities	Stockholders' Equity
2000	$4,582	$?	$15,701	$4,055	$?	$ 9,999	$5,702
2001	4,300	11,778	?	3,395	6,989	?	5,694
2002	?	11,358	15,967	3,582	6,470	10,052	?
2003	4,268	10,943	?	3,448	?	10,014	5,197
2004	4,419	?	15,394	?	6,328	10,013	5,381

Required

a. Compute the missing balance sheet amounts for each of the five years shown.

b. What asset category would you expect to constitute the majority of its current assets? Of its long-term assets?

c. Is the company conservatively financed; that is, is it financed by a greater proportion of equity than of debt? Explain.

P2-58. **Constructing and Analyzing Balance Sheet Numbers from Incomplete Data** (LO1, 2, 3, 4)

Harley-Davidson, Inc. (HDI)

Selected balance sheet amounts for Harley-Davidson, Inc., a motorcycle manufacturer, for five recent years follow ($ millions):

	Current Assets	Long-Term Assets	Total Assets	Current Liabilities	Long-Term Liabilities	Total Liabilities	Stockholders' Equity
1999	$?	$1,163	$2,112	$518	$?	$ 951	$1,161
2000	1,297	1,139	?	498	533	1,031	?
2001	1,665	?	3,118	?	646	1,362	1,756
2002	2,067	?	3,861	990	?	1,628	2,233
2003	2,729	2,194	?	956	1,010	?	2,958

Required

a. Compute the missing amounts for each of the five years shown.
b. What asset categories would you expect to be included in its current assets? In its long-term assets?
c. Is the company conservatively financed; that is, is it financed by a greater proportion of equity than of debt? Explain.

P2-59. Analyzing, Reconstructing, and Interpreting Income Statement Data (LO1, 2, 3)

Selected income statement information for Nike, Inc., a manufacturer of athletic footwear, for five recent fiscal-years follows ($ millions):

Nike, Inc. (NKE)

	Sales	Cost of Goods Sold	Gross Profit	Operating Expenses	Operating Income	Non-operating Income	Net Income
1999	$?	$5,295	$3,482	$?	$ 837	$386	$451
2000	8,995	5,216	?	2,813	966	387	?
2001	9,489	?	3,901	2,903	999	?	590
2002	?	5,781	4,112	3,060	1,052	389	?
2003	10,697	6,074	?	?	1,246	772	474

Required

a. Compute the missing amounts for each of the five years shown.
b. Compute the gross profit margin (gross profit/sales) for each of the five years and comment on its level and any trends that are evident.
c. What would you expect to be the major cost categories constituting its operating expenses?

P2-60. Analyzing Transactions using the Financial Statement Effects Template and Preparing an Income Statement (LO2, 3)

On June 1, 2006, a group of pilots in Melbourne, Australia, formed Outback Flights by issuing common stock for $50,000 cash. The group then leased several amphibious aircraft and docking facilities, equipping them to transport campers and hunters to outpost camps owned by various resorts in remote parts of Australia. The following transactions occurred during June 2006, and company accounts include the following: Cash, Accounts Receivable, Prepaid Insurance, Accounts Payable, Common Stock, Retained Earnings, Dividends, Flight Services Revenue, Rent Expense, Entertainment Expense, Advertising Expense, Insurance Expense, Wages Expense, and Fuel Expense.

1. Issued common stock for $50,000 cash
2. Paid $4,800 cash for June rent of aircraft, dockage, and dockside office
3. Received $1,600 invoice for the cost of a reception to entertain resort owners in June
4. Paid $900 cash for June advertising in various sport magazines
5. Paid $1,800 cash for insurance premium for July
6. Rendered flight services for various groups for $22,700 cash
7. Billed client $2,900 for transporting personnel, and billed various firms for $13,000 in flight services
8. Paid $1,500 cash to cover accounts payable
9. Received $13,200 on account from clients in transaction 6
10. Paid $16,000 cash to cover June wages
11. Received $3,500 invoice for the cost of fuel used during June
12. Declared and paid a $3,000 cash dividend

Required

a. Report the effects for each of the separate transactions 1 through 12 using the financial statement effects template. Total all columns and prove that (1) assets equal liabilities plus equity at June 30, and (2) revenues less expenses equal net income for June.
b. Prepare an income statement for the month of June.

P2-61. **Recording Transactions in Journal Entries and T-Accounts** (LO2)

Use the information in Problem 2-60 to complete the following requirements.

Required

1. Prepare journal entries for each of the transactions 1 through 12.
2. Set up T-accounts for each of the accounts used in part 1 and post the journal entries to those T-accounts.

P2-62. **Constructing and Analyzing Income Statement Numbers from Incomplete Data** (LO1, 2, 3)

Starbucks
Corporation (SBUX)

Selected income statement information for Starbucks Corporation, a coffee-related restaurant chain, for five recent fiscal-years follows ($ millions):

	Sales	Cost of Goods Sold	Gross Profit	Operating Expenses	Operating Income	Non-operating Income	Net Income
1999	$?	$1,336	$344	$187	$157	$ 55	$?
2000	2,169	1,737	?	240	192	?	95
2001	2,649	?	567	?	252	71	181
2002	?	2,598	691	390	301	86	?
2003	4,076	?	869	482	?	118	268

Required

a. Compute the missing amounts for each of the five years shown.
b. Compute the gross profit margin (gross profit/sales) for each of the five years and comment on its level and any trends that are evident.
c. What would you expect to be the major cost categories constituting its operating expenses?

P2-63. **Analyzing, Reconstructing, and Interpreting Income Statement Data** (LO1, 2, 3)

Target Corporation
(TGT)

Selected income statement information for Target Corporation, a department store chain, for five recent fiscal-years follows:

($ millions)	Sales	Cost of Goods Sold	Gross Profit	Operating Expenses	Operating Income	Non-operating Income	Net Income
2000	$?	$23,029	$10,673	$ 8,344	$2,329	$1,185	$?
2001	36,903	25,295	?	9,130	2,478	?	1,264
2002	39,888	?	12,642	?	2,747	1,379	1,368
2003	?	29,260	14,657	11,393	3,264	1,610	?
2004	48,163	31,790	?	12,854	3,519	?	1,841

Required

a. Compute the missing amounts for each of the five years shown.
b. Compute the gross profit margin (gross profit/sales) for each of the five years and comment on its level and any trends that are evident.
c. What would you expect to be the major cost categories constituting its operating expenses?

P2-64. **Constructing a Complete Set of Financial Statements** (LO1, 2, 3, 4, 5)

The records of Geyer, Inc., show the following information after all transactions are recorded for 2006.

Notes Payable	$ 4,000	Supplies	$ 6,100
Service Fees Earned	67,600	Cash	4,200
Supplies Expense	9,700	Accounts Receivable	10,600
Insurance Expense	1,500	Advertising Expense	1,700
Miscellaneous Expense	200	Salaries Expense	30,000
Common Stock (beg. month)	4,000	Rent Expense	7,500
Accounts Payable	1,800	Retained Earnings (beg. month) ...	6,200

Geyer, Inc., raised $1,400 cash through the issuance of additional common stock during this year and it declared and paid a $13,500 cash dividend near year-end.

Required

a. Prepare its income statement for 2006.

b. Prepare its statement of stockholders' equity for 2006.

c. Prepare its balance sheet at December 31, 2006.

d. Prepare its statement of cash flows for 2006.

P2-65. Analyzing Transactions using the Financial Statement Effects Template and Preparing Financial Statements (LO1, 2, 3, 4, 5)

Schrand Aerobics, Inc., rents studio space (including a sound system) and specializes in offering aerobics classes. On January 1, 2006, its beginning account balances are as follows: Cash, $5,000; Accounts Receivable, $5,200; Equipment, $0; Notes Payable, $2,500; Accounts Payable, $1,000; Common Stock, $5,500; Retained Earnings, $1,200; Dividend, $0; Services Revenue, $0; Rent Expense, $0; Advertising Expense, $0; Wages Expense, $0; Utilities Expense, $0; Interest Expense, $0. The following transactions occurred during January.

1. Paid $600 cash toward accounts payable
2. Paid $3,600 cash for January rent
3. Billed clients $11,500 for January classes
4. Received $500 invoice from supplier for T-shirts given to January class members as an advertising promotion
5. Collected $10,000 cash from clients previously billed for services rendered
6. Paid $2,400 cash for employee wages
7. Received $680 invoice for January utilities expense
8. Paid $20 cash to bank as January interest on notes payable
9. Declared and paid $900 cash dividend to stockholders
10. Paid $4,000 cash on January 31 to purchase sound equipment to replace the rental system

Required

a. Using the financial statement effects template, enter January 1 beginning amounts in the appropriate columns of the first row. (*Hint:* Beginning balances for columns can include amounts from more than one account.)

b. Report the effects for each of the separate transactions *1* through *10* in the financial statement effects template set up in part *a*. Total all columns and prove that (1) assets equal liabilities plus equity at January 31, and (2) revenues less expenses equal net income for January.

c. Prepare its income statement for January 2006.

d. Prepare its statement of stockholders' equity for January 2006.

e. Prepare its balance sheet at January 31, 2006.

P2-66. Recording Transactions in Journal Entries and T-Accounts (LO2)

Use the information in Problem 2-65 to complete the following requirements.

Required

1. Prepare journal entries for each of the transactions 1 through 10.
2. Set up T-accounts, including beginning balances, for each of the accounts used in part 1. Post the journal entries to those T-accounts.

P2-67. Analyzing Cash Effects of Transactions (LO6)

Use the information in Problem 2-65 to complete the following requirements.

Required

1. For each transaction 1 through 10, indicate its effect on the cash flow statement as a source of cash, use of cash, or no cash effect.
2. For each transaction 1 through 10, indicate its placement into one of the three sections of the statement of cash flows—operating, investing, financing—or 'no effect' for the statement of cash flows.

P2-68. Analyzing Transactions using the Financial Statement Effects Template and Preparing Financial Statements (LO1, 2, 3, 4, 5)

Kross, Inc., provides appraisals and feasibility studies. On January 1, 2006, its beginning account balances are as follows: Cash, $6,700; Accounts Receivable, $14,800; Notes Payable, $2,500; Accounts Payable, $600; Retained Earnings, $12,400; and Common Stock, $6,000. The following transactions occurred during January, and company accounts include the following: Cash, Accounts Receivable, Vehicles, Accounts Payable, Note Payable, Services Revenue, Rent Expense, Interest Expense, Salary Expense, Utilities Expense, Dividends, Common Stock, and Retained Earnings.

1. Paid $950 cash for January rent
2. Received $8,800 cash on customers' accounts

3. Paid $500 cash toward accounts payable
4. Received $1,600 cash for services performed for customers
5. Borrowed $5,000 cash from bank and signed note payable for that amount
6. Billed the city $6,200 for services performed, and billed other credit customers for $1,900 in services
7. Paid $4,000 cash for salary of assistant
8. Received $410 invoice for January utilities expense
9. Declared and paid a $6,000 cash dividend
10. Paid $9,800 cash to acquire a vehicle (on January 31) for business use
11. Paid $50 cash to bank for January interest on notes payable

Required

a. Using the financial statement effects template, enter January 1 beginning amounts in the appropriate columns of the first row. (*Hint:* Beginning balances for columns can include amounts from more than one account.)

b. Report the effects for each of the separate transactions 1 through 11 in the financial statement effects template set up in part *a*. Total all columns and prove that (1) assets equal liabilities plus equity at January 31, and (2) revenues less expenses equal net income for January.

c. Prepare its income statement for January 2006.

d. Prepare its statement of stockholders' equity for January 2006.

e. Prepare its balance sheet at January 31, 2006.

f. Prepare its statement of cash flows for January 2006

P2-69. **Recording Transactions in Journal Entries and T-Accounts** (LO2)
Use the information in Problem 2-68 to complete the following requirements.

Required

1. Prepare journal entries for each of the transactions 1 through 11.
2. Set up T-accounts, including beginning balances, for each of the accounts used in part 1. Post the journal entries to those T-accounts.

P2-70. **Analyzing Cash Effects of Transactions** (LO6)
Use the information in Problem 2-68 to complete the following requirements.

Required

1. For each transaction 1 through 11, indicate its effect on the cash flow statement as a source of cash, use of cash, or no cash effect.
2. For each transaction 1 through 11, indicate its placement into one of the three sections of the statement of cash flows—operating, investing, financing—or 'no effect' for the statement of cash flows.

CASES AND PROJECTS

C2-71. **Constructing Financial Statements from Cash Flow Data** (LO1, 2, 3, 4, 5)
Sarah Penney operates the Wildlife Picture Gallery, selling original art and signed prints received on consignment (rather than purchased) from recognized wildlife artists throughout the country. The firm receives a 30% commission on all art sold and remits 70% of the sales price to the artists. All art is sold on a strictly cash basis.

Sarah began the business on March 1, 2006. The business received a $10,000 loan from a relative of Sarah to help her get started; it took on a note payable agreeing to pay the loan back in one year. No interest is being charged on the loan, but the relative does want to receive a set of financial statements each month. On April 1, 2006, Sarah asks for your help in preparing the statements for the first month.

Sarah has carefully kept the firm's checking account up to date and provides you with the following complete listing of the cash receipts and cash disbursements for March 2006.

Cash Receipts	
Original investment by Sarah Penney	$ 6,500
Loan from relative	10,000
Sales of art	95,000
Total cash receipts	111,500
Cash Disbursements	
Payments to artists for sales made	54,000
Payment of March rent for gallery space	900
Payment of March wages to staff	4,900
Payment of airfare for personal vacation of Sarah (vacation will be in April)	500
Total cash disbursements	60,300
Cash balance, March 31, 2006	$51,200

Sarah also gives you the following documents she has received:
1. A $350 invoice for March utilities; payment is due by April 15, 2006.
2. A $1,700 invoice from Careful Express for the shipping of artwork sold in March; payment is due by April 10, 2006.
3. Sarah signed a one-year lease for the gallery space; as an incentive to sign the lease, the landlord reduced the first month's rent by 25%; the monthly rent starting in April is $1,200.

In your discussions with Sarah, she tells you that she has been so busy that she is behind in sending artists their share of the sales proceeds. She plans to catch up within the next week.

Required

From the above information, prepare the following financial statements for Wildlife Picture Gallery: (*a*) income statement for the month of March 2006; (*b*) statement of stockholders' equity for the month of March 2006; and (*c*) balance sheet as of March 31, 2006. To organize and record all data needed, you might wish to use T-accounts to construct the company's accounts.

C2-72. **Financial Records and Ethical Behavior** **(LO6)**

Andrea Frame and her supervisor are sent on an out-of-town assignment by their employer. At the supervisor's suggestion, they stay at the Spartan Inn (across the street from the Luxury Inn). After three days of work, they settle their lodging bills and leave. On the return trip, the supervisor gives Andrea what appears to be a copy of a receipt from the Luxury Inn for three nights of lodging. Actually, the supervisor indicates that he prepared the Luxury Inn receipt on his office computer and plans to complete his expense reimbursement request using the higher lodging costs from the Luxury Inn.

Required

What are the ethical considerations that Andrea faces when she prepares her expense reimbursement request?

CHAPTER

3

Adjusting Accounts for Financial Statements

LEARNING OBJECTIVES

After completing the chapter, you should be able to:

FEDEX
CORPORATION

Getty Images

Several years ago Frederick Smith, an undergraduate student at Yale University, wrote a term paper detailing the inadequacies of the passenger route systems used by most airfreight shippers. In his paper, Smith suggested that there was a need for a freight system designed specifically for shipments requiring expedited service, such as medicines, computer parts, and electronics. A few years later, Federal Express was born (later renamed FedEx Corporation).

FedEx revenues now approach $30 billion per year and it provides services to over 220 countries and territories around the world. On an average day, FedEx ships more than 6 million packages through its express, ground, freight, and expedited delivery services. In 2005, FedEx was rated the "6th Most Admired American Company" and the "World's 8th Most Admired Company" according to *Fortune Magazine*. Fortune ranked it 20th of the Best Large Companies to work for in 2006.

Through the years, FedEx has become synonymous with overnight delivery. More recently, FedEx has expanded its business to include non-expedited delivery service, which has traditionally been dominated by United Parcel Service (UPS). With its acquisition of Roadway Package System (a subsidiary of Caliber Systems), FedEx entered the small package, ground delivery market. FedEx Ground has grown from $1 billion in annual revenues to over $4.7 billion in 2005. FedEx's share of the ground delivery segment is estimated at 18%, with most of its growth coming from rival UPS.

FedEx Ground's tremendous growth is due, in part, to its 14,000 independent drivers (contractors). By hiring independent contractors, FedEx Ground avoids large expenses such as health insurance, overtime pay, vacation pay, and expense reimbursement that would be incurred if employees were used. As a result of these cost savings, FedEx is able to offer ground service comparable to that of UPS but at greater savings. On average, FedEx Ground delivery is less expensive than UPS Ground delivery, and a growing number of informed customers have taken advantage of the savings.

FedEx Ground also benefits from its independent contractors' entrepreneurial spirit. Since independent contractors essentially run their own business, they approach their work as business owners trying to maximize their profits and minimize their costs. FedEx Ground drivers are constantly trying to make their routes more profitable, and nearly 20% of the drivers manage multiple routes. According to *BusinessWeek*, 300 FedEx Ground drivers each grossed over $250,000 in 2004 by expanding the number of routes they manage.

In this chapter, we consider the typical business activities that an independent contractor engages in while working as a FedEx Ground driver. We look at several transactions that occur during the course of conducting business and then learn about the accounting adjustments necessary

(Continued on next page)

(Continued from previous page)

to produce accurate financial statements that reflect these activities. In the process, we discover the importance of accounting adjustments for creating high quality accounting information that is used to make effective business decisions.

Sources: *FedEx.com* Website, January 2006; *FedEx 10-K Report*, 2005; *FedEx Annual Report*, 2005; *BusinessWeek*, November 28, 2005, pp. 42–43.

CHAPTER ORGANIZATION

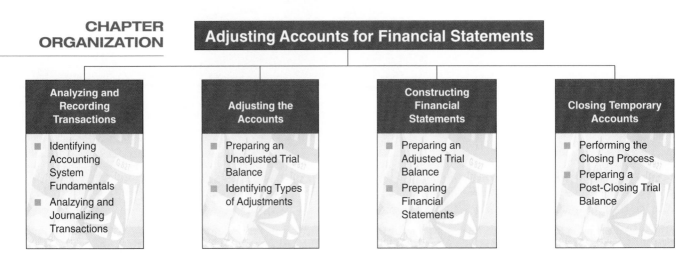

Adjusting Accounts for Financial Statements

Analyzing and Recording Transactions
- Identifying Accounting System Fundamentals
- Analzying and Journalizing Transactions

Adjusting the Accounts
- Preparing an Unadjusted Trial Balance
- Identifying Types of Adjustments

Constructing Financial Statements
- Preparing an Adjusted Trial Balance
- Preparing Financial Statements

Closing Temporary Accounts
- Performing the Closing Process
- Preparing a Post-Closing Trial Balance

The double-entry accounting system introduced in Chapter 2 provides us with a framework for the analysis of business activities. This chapter describes the procedures companies use to account for the operations of a business during a specific time period. All companies, regardless of size or complexity, perform accounting steps, known as the *accounting cycle*, to accumulate and report their financial information. An important step in the accounting cycle is the *adjusting* process. This chapter focuses on the accounting cycle with emphasis on the adjusting process.

ACCOUNTING CYCLE

LO1 Identify the major steps in the accounting cycle.

Companies engage in business activities. These activities are analyzed for their financial impact, and the results from that analysis are entered into the accounting information system. When management needs financial statements, the financial data often requires adjustment prior to financial statements being prepared. At the end of the accounting period, the company *closes the books*. This closing process prepares accounts for the next accounting period.

The process described constitutes the major steps in the **accounting cycle**—a sequence of activities to accumulate and report financial statements. The steps are analyze, record, adjust, report, and close. Exhibit 3.1 shows the sequence of major steps in the accounting cycle.

EXHIBIT 3.1 Accounting Cycle—Abbreviated

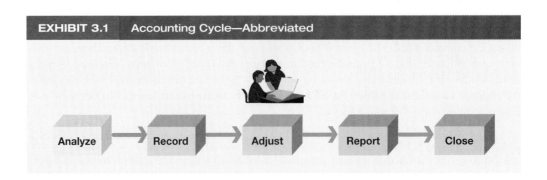

Analyze → Record → Adjust → Report → Close

The steps in the accounting cycle do not occur with equal frequency. That is, companies analyze and record daily transactions throughout the accounting period, but they only adjust and report when management requires financial statements, often monthly or quarterly, but at least annually. Closing occurs once during the accounting cycle, at the period-end.

The annual (one-year) accounting period adopted by a company is known as its **fiscal year**. Companies with fiscal year ends on December 31 are said to be on a **calendar-year**. About 60% of companies are on a calendar-year basis. Many companies prefer to have their accounting year coincide with their "natural" year; that is, the fiscal year ends when business is slow. For example, Limited, a specialty retailer, ends its fiscal year on the Friday nearest January 31. The Boston Celtics, a professional basketball team, ends its fiscal year on June 30, during its off-season.

ANALYZING AND RECORDING TRANSACTIONS

The purpose of this section is to (1) review the analysis and recording of transactions as described in Chapter 2, and (2) to establish a case example that we will use to illustrate the adjusting and closing of accounts in the next section. For this purpose, we use a typical independent contractor of FedEx Corporation. FedEx employs independent contractors for ground and home deliveries, among other services. These contractors acquire their own trucks, and experience related truck and delivery expenses, which often include rent expenses for truck storage. In return, FedEx contractors earn service fees for delivering packages and commissions based on the number of packages handled. Our illustration uses the December 2006 transactions of FedEx–DeFond, an independent FedEx contractor operating out of Los Angeles, California. This business was organized by M. DeFond on December 1, 2006. FedEx–DeFond's fiscal year-end is December 31, so its first accounting period is only one month long.

LO2 Explain the process of journalizing and posting transactions.

FedEx Corporation ($ mil)

Assets $20,404 = Liabilities $10,816 + Equity $9,588

Accounting System Fundamentals

This section reviews several accounting fundamentals for FedEx–DeFond.

Chart of Accounts

A chart of accounts facilitates transaction analysis and the preparation of entries. FedEx–DeFond's **chart of accounts** is in Exhibit 3.2, and lists the titles and numbers of all accounts found in its general ledger. The account titles are grouped into the five major sections of the general ledger (assets, liabilities, equity, revenues, and expenses).

General Journal

A **journal**, or *book of original entry*, is a tabular record in which business activities are analyzed in terms of debits and credits and recorded in chronological order before they are entered in the general ledger. A journal, therefore, organizes information by date rather than by account. The complete analysis for one transaction is shown in a journal before the next transaction analysis is recorded. The word *journalize* means to record a transaction in a journal.

The **general journal** is a journal with enough flexibility so that any type of business transaction can be recorded in it. The procedure for recording entries in the general journal is as follows:

1. Indicate the year, month, and day of the entry.
2. Enter titles of the accounts affected. Recall, accounts to receive debits are entered close to the left margin and are recorded first; accounts to receive credits are then recorded and commonly indented.
3. Place the appropriate money amounts in the left (Debit) and right (Credit) money columns.

Each transaction entered in the journal must be stated in terms of equal dollar amounts of debits and credits—the double-entry system at work. The account titles cited must correspond to those in the general ledger.

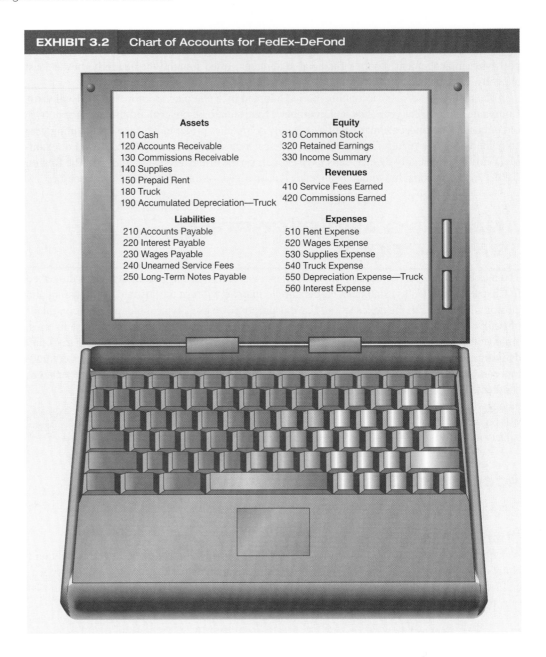

EXHIBIT 3.2   Chart of Accounts for FedEx–DeFond

Assets
110 Cash
120 Accounts Receivable
130 Commissions Receivable
140 Supplies
150 Prepaid Rent
180 Truck
190 Accumulated Depreciation—Truck

Liabilities
210 Accounts Payable
220 Interest Payable
230 Wages Payable
240 Unearned Service Fees
250 Long-Term Notes Payable

Equity
310 Common Stock
320 Retained Earnings
330 Income Summary

Revenues
410 Service Fees Earned
420 Commissions Earned

Expenses
510 Rent Expense
520 Wages Expense
530 Supplies Expense
540 Truck Expense
550 Depreciation Expense—Truck
560 Interest Expense

Posting Entries to General Ledger

After transactions are journalized, the debits and credits in each journal entry are transferred to their related general ledger accounts. This transcribing process is called posting to the general ledger, or simply **posting**. Journalizing and posting occur simultaneously when recordkeeping is automated. When records are kept manually, posting from the general journal can be done daily, every few days, or at the end of a month. Today, computers are used extensively to perform mechanical accounting tasks such as posting.

Analyzing and Journalizing Transactions

Exhibit 3.3 lists the December transactions of FedEx–DeFond. Most of its revenue transactions are payments in cash or on account with FedEx Corporation. Its expense transactions involve costs of supplies, wages, and truck expenses.

Many transactions affect several accounting periods, and the accounting for these transactions after their initial occurrence often requires further analysis. Examples from Exhibit 3.3 include:

EXHIBIT 3.3	Transactions for FedEx–DeFond for 2006	
Event	**Date**	**Description**
(1)	Dec. 1	M. DeFond deposited $20,000 in the company's bank account to start the business in exchange for common stock of the company.
(2)	1	Purchased $950 in supplies by paying $250 cash and the remainder to be paid in 60 days.
(3)	1	Paid facilities rent for six months, December–May, $3,600.
(4)	1	Purchased truck for $54,000 and signed two-year note payable for $54,000 with annual interest at 10% due each November 30.
(5)	2	Signed contract with FedEx Corporation to perform services for four months, December–March, at $2,500 per month; received $10,000 cash in advance.
(6)	2	Signed one-year contract with FedEx Corporation to provide potential customers with promotional literature. For distributing the literature, FedEx–DeFond will receive a $500 monthly commission, payable at the end of every 3 months; the first $1,500 commission will be paid February 28, 2007.
(7)	10	Performed services for FedEx Corporation and received $650 cash.
(8)	12	Billed FedEx Corporation for $1,580 in services rendered on account.
(9)	13	Paid assistant's wages for first two weeks of December, $540.
(10)	19	Received $800 cash from FedEx Corporation toward its account.
(11)	21	Performed service for FedEx Corporation and received $520 cash.
(12)	27	Paid assistant's wages for second two weeks of December, $540.
(13)	29	FedEx–DeFond paid $800 cash for dividends.
(14)	30	Paid December truck expenses (gas and oil) of $1,600.
(15)	31	Billed FedEx Corporation for $2,700 in services rendered on account.

transaction (3), where the rent payment covers six months; transaction (4), where the truck is used for several years and the note payable extends two years; transaction (5), where the contract runs for four months; and transaction (6), where the contract runs for one year. We illustrate the subsequent accounting for these transactions as part of the adjusting process in the next section.

Panel A of Exhibit 3.4 presents the completed financial statement effects template. Panel B of Exhibit 3.4 presents the journal entries for FedEx–DeFond's December transactions. Review each of the 14 transaction to make sure it is understood. (The completed T-accounts for each of these transactions appear in Exhibit 3.5.)

A journal entry that involves more than two accounts is called a **compound journal entry**. The journal entry for transaction 2 in Exhibit 3.4 is a compound journal entry and involves three accounts. The debit of $950 to Supplies is offset by credits of $250 to Cash and $700 to Accounts Payable. Any number of accounts can appear in a compound entry; but, regardless of how many accounts are used, the total of the debit amounts must always equal the total of the credit amounts.

Transaction 3 is the payment of rent for six months; the journal entry debits Prepaid Rent for $3,600 and credits Cash for $3,600. Prepaid Rent is an asset account; therefore, it is debited because the time period covered by the rental payment extends beyond the current accounting period (which is the month of December). Asset accounts are debited when payments are made in advance for services to be received over more than just the current accounting period. Other examples include the advance payment of insurance premiums for coverage that extends beyond the current accounting period (debit Prepaid Insurance) and the payment in advance for advertising services that extend beyond the current period (debit Prepaid Advertising).

Transaction 5 relates to a contract entered into by the local FedEx–DeFond with the national FedEx Corporation. The mere signing of a contract does not normally require a journal entry because a contract is just an agreement by each party to do something, and neither party has performed yet. This is also the case with event 6; no entry is made in the general journal because FedEx Corporation has not yet paid anything, and FedEx–DeFond has not yet distributed any promotional literature. In transaction 5, however, FedEx–DeFond receives payment in advance for four months

EXHIBIT 3.4   Recording FedEx–DeFond's Transactions

Panel A: Transactions Analyzed Using Financial Statement Effects Template

Event	Cash Asset	+	Noncash Assets	=	Liabil-ities	+	Contrib. Capital	+	Retained Earnings	Revenues	−	Expenses	=	Net Income
(1) Contributed $20,000 cash in exchange for common stock	+20,000 Cash			=			+20,000 Common Stock						=	
(2) Purchased $950 in supplies with $250 cash and $700 on account	−250 Cash		+950 Supplies	=	+700 Accounts Payable								=	
(3) Paid 6 months rent in advance with $3,600 cash	−3,600 Cash		+3,600 Prepaid Rent	=									=	
(4) Purchased $54,000 truck with a note payable			+54,000 Truck	=	+54,000 Notes Payable								=	
(5) Received $10,000 cash for future services	+10,000 Cash			=	+10,000 Unearned Service Fees								=	
(6) No entry recorded														
(7) Received $650 cash for services performed	+650 Cash			=					+650 Retained Earnings	+650 Service Fees Earned			=	+650
(8) Billed FedEx Corp. $1,580 for services rendered			+1,580 Accounts Receivable	=					+1,580 Retained Earnings	+1,580 Service Fees Earned			=	+1,580
(9) Paid $540 cash for wages	−540 Cash			=					−540 Retained Earnings			−540 Wage Expense	=	−540
(10) Received $800 cash from FedEx Corp. towards its account	+800 Cash		−800 Accounts Receivable	=									=	
(11) Received $520 cash for services performed	+520 Cash			=					+520 Retained Earnings	+520 Service Fees Earned			=	+520
(12) Paid $540 cash for wages	−540 Cash			=					−540 Retained Earnings			−540 Wages Expense	=	−540
(13) Paid $800 cash dividend	−800 Cash			=					−800 Retained Earnings				=	
(14) Paid $1,600 cash for truck expenses	−1,600 Cash			=					−1,600 Retained Earnings			−1,600 Truck Expense	=	−1,600
(15) Billed FedEx Corp. $2,700 for services performed			+2,700 Accounts Receivable	=					+2,700 Retained Earnings	+2,700 Service Fees Earnings			=	+2,700

EXHIBIT 3.4	Recording FedEx–DeFond's Transactions (continued)

Panel B: Transactions Analyzed in Journal Entry Form

Dec. 1 (1)	Cash (+A) .... Common Stock (+SE) .... *Owner invested cash to start business.*	20,000			20,000
1 (2)	Supplies (+A) .... Cash (−A) .... Accounts Payable (+L) .... *Purchased supplies for $950.* *Terms: $250 down, remainder due in 60 days.*	950			250 700
1 (3)	Prepaid Rent (+A) .... Cash (−A) .... *Paid rent for December–May.*	3,600			3,600
1 (4)	Truck (+A) .... Long-Term Notes Payable (+L) .... *Purchased truck with two-year note payable.*	54,000			54,000
2 (5)	Cash (+A) .... Unearned Service Fees (+L) .... *Received advance on 4-month contract at $2,500 per month.*	10,000			10,000
10 (7)	Cash (+A) .... Service Fees Earned (+R, +SE) .... *Services rendered for cash.*	650			650
12 (8)	Accounts Receivable (+A) .... Service Fees Earned (+R, +SE) .... *Services rendered on account.*	1,580			1,580
13 (9)	Wages Expense (+E, −SE) .... Cash (−A) .... *Paid wages for first two weeks of December.*	540			540
19 (10)	Cash (+A) .... Accounts Receivable (−A) .... *Received $800 on account from FedEx.*	800			800
21 (11)	Cash (+A) .... Service Fees Earned (+R, +SE) .... *Services rendered for cash.*	520			520
27 (12)	Wages Expense (+E, −SE) .... Cash (−A) .... *Paid wages for second two weeks of December.*	540			540
29 (13)	Retained Earnings (−SE) .... Cash (−A) .... *Paid $800 cash for dividends.*	800			800
30 (14)	Truck Expense (+E, −SE) .... Cash (−A) .... *Paid cash for December gas and oil.*	1,600			1,600
31 (15)	Accounts Receivable (+A) .... Service Fees Earned (+R, +SE) .... *Services rendered on account.*	2,700			2,700

of services. The receipt of this payment requires a journal entry debiting Cash for $10,000 and crediting Unearned Service Fees for $10,000. Unearned Service Fees is a liability account and represents the obligation of FedEx–DeFond to provide 4 months of service for which payment has already been received.

Exhibit 3.5 presents the general ledger accounts of FedEx–DeFond in T-account form. These ledger accounts received the postings from the journal entries in Exhibit 3.4. Trace several of the postings from the general journal to these ledger accounts. Each of the accounts in Exhibit 3.5 reports an unadjusted balance, and only those accounts with multiple entries have a separately totaled unadjusted balance.

EXHIBIT 3.5   FedEx–DeFond's Transactions Using T-accounts

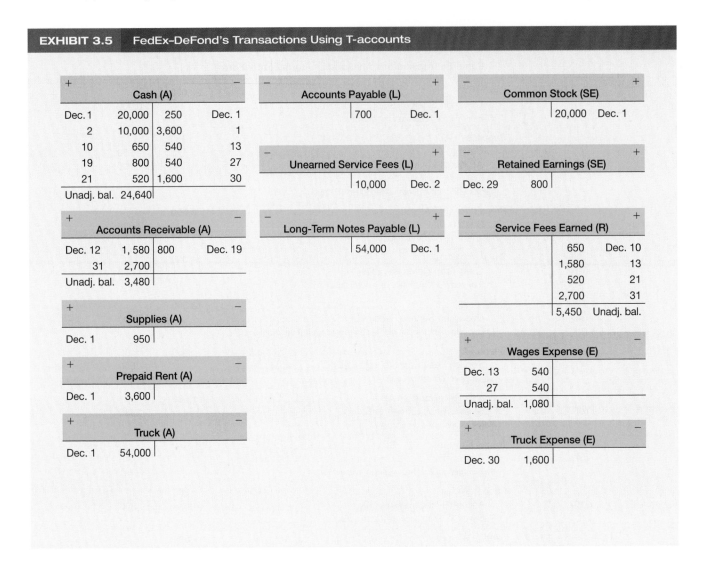

ADJUSTING THE ACCOUNTS

LO3 Describe the adjusting process and illustrate adjusting entries.

It is important that accounts in financial statements be properly reported. For many accounts, the balances shown in the general ledger after all transactions are posted are not the proper balances for financial statements. Thus, when it is time to prepare financial statements, management must review account balances and make proper adjustments to these balances. The adjustments required are based on accrual accounting and generally accepted accounting principles. This section focuses on these issues.

Preparing an Unadjusted Trial Balance

The adjustment process begins with a trial balance of all general ledger accounts—it is only necessary to list those that currently carry a dollar balance. It is called an **unadjusted trial balance** because it shows account balances before any adjustments are made. The purpose of an unadjusted trial balance is to be sure the general ledger is in balance before management adjusts the accounts. Showing all general ledger account balances in one place also makes it easier to review accounts and determine which account balances require adjusting. The unadjusted trial balance of FedEx–DeFond at December 31 is in Exhibit 3.6.

EXHIBIT 3.6	Unadjusted Trial Balance

FedEx–DeFond
Unadjusted Trial Balance
December 31, 2006

	Debit	Credit
Cash	$24,640	
Accounts Receivable	3,480	
Supplies	950	
Prepaid Rent	3,600	
Truck	54,000	
Accounts Payable		$ 700
Unearned Service Fees		10,000
Long-Term Notes Payable		54,000
Common Stock		20,000
Retained Earnings	800	
Service Fees Earned		5,450
Wages Expense	1,080	
Truck Expense	1,600	
Totals	$90,150	$90,150

Types of Adjustments

Following are the four general types of adjustments made at the end of an accounting period.

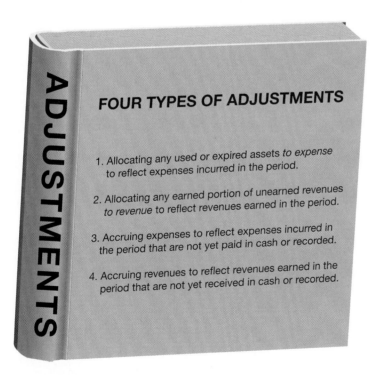

ADJUSTMENTS

FOUR TYPES OF ADJUSTMENTS

1. Allocating any used or expired assets *to expense* to reflect expenses incurred in the period.

2. Allocating any earned portion of unearned revenues *to revenue* to reflect revenues earned in the period.

3. Accruing expenses to reflect expenses incurred in the period that are not yet paid in cash or recorded.

4. Accruing revenues to reflect revenues earned in the period that are not yet received in cash or recorded.

Journal entries made to reflect these adjustments are known as **adjusting entries**. Each adjusting entry usually affects a balance sheet account (an asset or liability account) and an income statement account (an expense or revenue account), but never affects the cash account. The first two types of adjustments—allocating assets to expense and allocating unearned revenues to revenue— are often referred to as **deferrals**. The distinguishing characteristic of a deferral is that the adjustment deals with an amount previously recorded in a balance sheet account; the adjusting entry

REMEMBER . . .
Chapter 2 explained that revenue recognition and matching are two key accounting principles that determine net income under accrual accounting. In general, accrual accounting recognizes revenues when services are performed or when goods are sold and it recognizes expenses in the period that they help to generate the recorded revenues.

decreases the balance sheet account and increases an income statement account. The last two types of adjustments—accruing expenses and accruing revenues—are often referred to as **accruals**. The unique characteristic of an accrual is that the adjustment deals with an amount not previously recorded in any account; the adjusting entry increases both a balance sheet account and an income statement account.

Type 1: Allocating Assets to Expenses—Prepaids

Many cash outlays benefit several accounting periods. Examples are purchases of buildings, equipment, and supplies; prepayments of rent and advertising; and payments of insurance premiums covering several periods. These outlays are debited to an asset account when the expenditure occurs. Then at the end of each accounting period, the estimated portion of the outlay that has expired in that period, or has benefited that period, is transferred to an expense account.

We can usually see when adjustments of this type are needed by inspecting the unadjusted trial balance for costs that benefit several periods. Looking at the December 31 trial balance of FedEx–DeFond (Exhibit 3.6), for example, adjustments are required to record the costs of supplies, prepaid rent, and the truck for the month of December.

Supplies In December, FedEx–DeFond purchased $950 of supplies and recorded the outlay in an asset account, Supplies. During December, supplies were used up as services were provided. The cost of supplies used is an expense for December that reduces the amount of supplies. It is not necessary, however, to record the expense as each individual supply item is used. Instead, at the end of December the company assesses the supplies still available. A total of $510 of supplies remain at month-end, indicating that $440 ($950 − $510) of supplies have been used in the month. Thus, at period-end, an adjusting entry transfers this amount to an expense account, Supplies Expense. This is identified as adjustment (a) in the template, journal entry, and T-accounts as follows. (The entire set of T-accounts reflecting the transactions and adjustments for FedEx–DeFond appear in Exhibit 3.8.)

	Balance Sheet						Income Statement		
Transaction	**Cash Asset**	**+ Noncash Assets**	**= Liabil-ities**	**+ Contrib. Capital**	**+ Retained Earnings**		**Revenues**	**− Expenses =**	**Net Income**
(a) Adjusting entry to record supplies used		−440 = Supplies			−440 Retained Earnings			−440 Supplies Expense	= −440

NOTE
Many transactions reflected in ledger accounts affect net income of more than one period. Likewise, other events that are not yet recorded in accounts affect the current period's income. The adjusting process identifies these situations and results in proper revenues and expenses recorded in the current period.

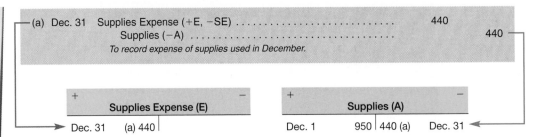

(a) Dec. 31   Supplies Expense (+E, −SE)   440
                 Supplies (−A)   440
                 To record expense of supplies used in December.

+ Supplies Expense (E) −			− Supplies (A) +
Dec. 31 (a) 440		Dec. 1 950	440 (a) Dec. 31

When this adjusting entry is posted, it properly reflects the $440 December expense for supplies and reduces the asset account, Supplies, to $510, the actual amount of the asset remaining at December 31.

Prepaid Rent On December 1, FedEx–DeFond paid six months' rent in advance and debited the $3,600 payment to Prepaid Rent, an asset account. As each day passes and the rented space is occupied, rent expense is being incurred, and the prepaid rent is decreasing. It is not necessary to record rent expense on a daily basis because financial statements are not prepared daily. At the end of an accounting period, however, an adjustment must be made to recognize the proper amount of rent expense for the period and to decrease prepaid rent by that amount. On December 31, one month's rent has been used up, so FedEx–DeFond transfers $600 ($3,600/6 months) from Prepaid Rent to Rent Expense. This is identified as adjustment (b) in the template, journal entry, and T-accounts as follows.

Transaction	Balance Sheet									Income Statement			
	Cash Asset	+	Noncash Assets	=	Liabil-ities	+	Contrib. Capital	+	Retained Earnings	Revenues	−	Expenses	= Net Income
(b) Adjusting entry to record expiration of prepaid rent			−600 Prepaid Rent	=					−600 Retained Earnings			−600 Rent Expense	= −600

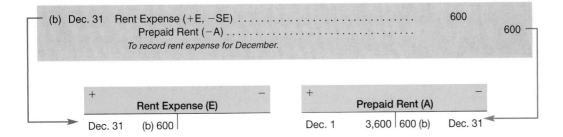

(b) Dec. 31   Rent Expense (+E, −SE)   600
                  Prepaid Rent (−A)   600
                  To record rent expense for December.

+ Rent Expense (E) −	+ Prepaid Rent (A) −
Dec. 31 (b) 600	Dec. 1 3,600 | 600 (b) Dec. 31

The posting of this adjusting entry creates the proper rent expense of $600 for December in the Rent Expense ledger account and reduces the Prepaid Rent balance to the amount that is prepaid as of December 31, which is $3,000.

Examples of other prepaid expenses for which similar adjustments are made include prepaid insurance and prepaid advertising. When insurance premiums are paid, the amount is debited to Prepaid Insurance. At the end of an accounting period, the adjusting entry to record the portion of insurance coverage that expired during the period must debit Insurance Expense and credit Prepaid Insurance. Similarly, when advertising services are purchased in advance, the payment is debited to Prepaid Advertising. At the end of an accounting period, an adjustment is needed to recognize the cost of any of the prepaid advertising used during the period. The adjusting entry debits Advertising Expense and credits Prepaid Advertising.

Depreciation The process of allocating the costs of equipment, vehicles, and buildings to the periods benefiting from their use is called **depreciation**. Each accounting period in which such assets are used must reflect a portion of their cost as expense because these assets helped generate revenue for those periods. This periodic expense is known as *depreciation expense*. Periodic depreciation expense is an estimate. The procedure we use here estimates the annual amount of depreciation expense by dividing the asset cost by its estimated useful life. This method is called **straight-line depreciation** (used by over 80% of companies).

When recording depreciation expense, the asset amount is not reduced directly. Instead, the reduction is recorded in a contra account (labeled XA in the journal entries and T-accounts) called *Accumulated Depreciation*. **Contra accounts** are so named because they are used to record reductions in or offsets against a related account. The Accumulated Depreciation account normally has a credit balance and appears in the balance sheet as a deduction from the related asset amount. Use of the contra asset Accumulated Depreciation allows the original cost of the asset to be reported in the balance sheet, followed by the accumulated depreciation.

The truck purchased by FedEx–DeFond for $54,000 is expected to last six years. Straight-line depreciation recorded on the truck is $9,000 ($54,000/6 years) per year, or $750 ($9,000/12 months) per month. At the end of December, FedEx–DeFond makes the adjustment (c), as shown in the following template, journal entry, and T-accounts.

NOTE
Contra accounts are used to provide more information to users of financial statements. For example, Accumulated Depreciation is a contra asset reported in the balance sheet, which enables users to estimate asset age. For FedEx–DeFond, the balance sheet reveals that its Truck asset is nearly new as its accumulated depreciation is only $750, which is 1.4% of its $54,000 original cost.

Transaction	Balance Sheet									Income Statement			
	Cash Asset	+	Noncash Assets	=	Liabil-ities	+	Contrib. Capital	+	Retained Earnings	Revenues	−	Expenses	= Net Income
(c) Adjusting entry to depreciation on truck			−750 Accumulated Depreciation— Truck	=					−750 Retained Earnings			−750 Depreciation Expense	= −750

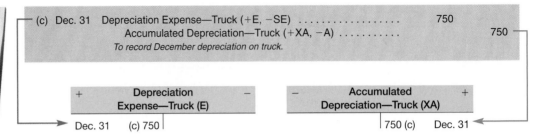

REMEMBER . . .
An increase in the contra asset account Accumulated Depreciation reduces the book value of the asset.

(c) Dec. 31   Depreciation Expense—Truck (+E, −SE) 750
                Accumulated Depreciation—Truck (+XA, −A)   750
                To record December depreciation on truck.

+	Depreciation Expense—Truck (E)	−		−	Accumulated Depreciation—Truck (XA)	+
Dec. 31	(c) 750				750 (c)	Dec. 31

When this entry is posted, it properly reflects the cost of using this asset during December, and the correct expense ($750) appears in the December income statement. On the balance sheet, the accumulated depreciation is subtracted from the asset amount. The resulting balance (cost less accumulated depreciation), which is the asset's **book value**, represents the unexpired asset cost to be applied as an expense against future periods. For example, the December 31, 2006, balance sheet reports the truck with a book value of $53,250, as follows.

Truck $54,000
Less: Accumulated Depreciation 750 $53,250

Type 2: Allocating Unearned Revenues to Revenue—Deferred Revenues

Companies often receive fees for services before services are rendered. Such transactions are recorded by debiting Cash and crediting a liability account for the **unearned revenue**—also referred to as **deferred revenue**. This account reflects the obligation for performing future services. As services are performed, revenue is earned. At period-end, an adjusting entry records the revenue that was earned in the current accounting period and the liability amount that was reduced.

Deferred Service Revenue During December, FedEx–DeFond entered into a transaction that generated an advance receipt of revenues. On December 2, the firm signed a four-month contract to perform services for the national FedEx Corporation at $2,500 per month, with the entire contract price of $10,000 received in advance. The entry made on December 2 increased Cash and Unearned Service Fees, both by $10,000. On December 31, FedEx–DeFond makes the adjustment (d) in the following template, journal entry, and T-accounts (it transfers $2,500, the revenue earned in December, to Service Fees Earned and it reduces the liability, Unearned Service Fees, by the same amount).

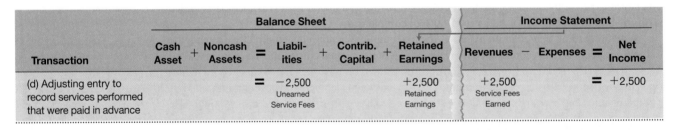

		Balance Sheet					Income Statement		
Transaction	Cash Asset	+ Noncash Assets	= Liabil- ities	+ Contrib. Capital	+ Retained Earnings		Revenues	− Expenses	= Net Income
(d) Adjusting entry to record services performed that were paid in advance			= −2,500 Unearned Service Fees		+2,500 Retained Earnings		+2,500 Service Fees Earned		= +2,500

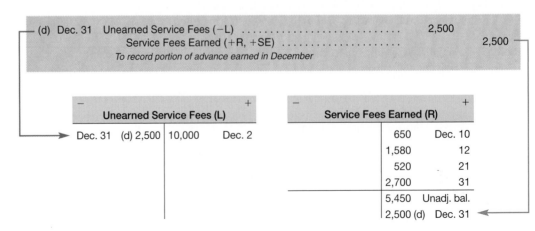

(d) Dec. 31   Unearned Service Fees (−L) 2,500
                Service Fees Earned (+R, +SE)   2,500
                To record portion of advance earned in December

−	Unearned Service Fees (L)	+		−	Service Fees Earned (R)	+
Dec. 31 (d) 2,500		10,000 Dec. 2			650	Dec. 10
					1,580	12
					520	21
					2,700	31
					5,450	Unadj. bal.
					2,500 (d)	Dec. 31

After this entry is posted, the liability account shows a balance of $7,500, the amount of future services still owing, and the Service Fees Earned account reflects the $2,500 earned in December.

Other examples of revenues received in advance include rental payments received in advance by real estate management companies, insurance premiums received in advance by insurance companies, subscription revenues received in advance by magazine and newspaper publishers, and membership fees received in advance by health clubs. In each case, a liability account is set up when the advance payment is received. Later, an adjusting entry is made to reflect the revenues earned from the services provided or products delivered during the period.

YOU MAKE THE CALL

You are the Chief Accountant   REI requires customers of its travel-vacation business to make an initial deposit equal to 10% of the trip cost when the trip is reserved. REI's refunding policy is to return the entire deposit if the customer informs REI of the trip's cancellation two or more months in advance of the trip. REI will refund 50% of the deposit if a customer cancels between 30 and 60 days prior to the trip, and there is no refund if notification occurs within 30 days of the trip. REI's cancellation rate is very low. How should you account for deposits, and when should revenue be recorded? [Answers on page 117]

Type 3: Accruing Expenses

Companies often incur expenses before paying for them. Wages, interest, utilities, and taxes are examples of expenses that are incurred before cash payment is made. Usually the payments are made at regular intervals of time, such as weekly, monthly, quarterly, or annually. If the accounting period ends on a date that does not coincide with a scheduled cash payment date, an adjusting entry is required to reflect the expense incurred since the last cash payment. Such an expense is referred to as an **accrued expense**. FedEx–DeFond has two such required adjustments at December 31—wages and interest.

Accrued Wages   A FedEx–DeFond employee is paid every two weeks at the rate of $270 for each 6-day work week (this employee is required to work 4 hours per work day). The employee was paid $540 on December 13 and on December 27. Both these dates fell on Saturday, and Sunday is a nonwork day. At the close of business on Wednesday, December 31, the employee has worked three days (Monday, Tuesday, and Wednesday) during December for which wages are not paid until January. An additional wages expense of $135 must be recorded in the income statement for December because the employee earned 3 more days' wages (3 days × [$270/6 days]). At the end of December, FedEx–DeFond makes the adjustment (e) in the template, journal entry, and T-accounts that follow.

	Balance Sheet							Income Statement		
Transaction	**Cash Asset** +	**Noncash Assets** =	**Liabil-ities** +	**Contrib. Capital** +	**Retained Earnings**		**Revenues** −	**Expenses** =	**Net Income**
(e) Adjusting entry to record wages earned but not yet paid		=	+135 Wages Payable		−135 Retained Earnings				−135 Wages Expense =	−135

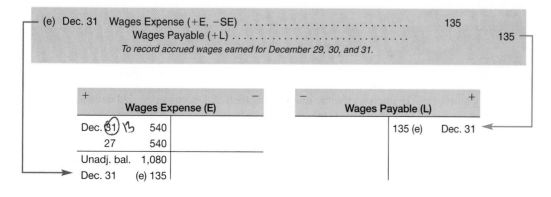

(e) Dec. 31   Wages Expense (+E, −SE)   135
                    Wages Payable (+L)   135
              To record accrued wages earned for December 29, 30, and 31.

+ Wages Expense (E) −		− Wages Payable (L) +	
Dec. 31 540			135 (e) Dec. 31
27 540			
Unadj. bal. 1,080			
Dec. 31 (e) 135			

This adjustment enables the firm to reflect as December expense the cost of all wages *incurred* during the month rather than just the wages *paid*. In addition, the balance sheet shows the liability for unpaid wages at the end of the period.

When this employee is paid on the next regular payday in January, the company must make sure that the three days' pay accrued at the end of December is not again charged to expense. For example, when the employee is paid $540 on Saturday, January 10, the following entry is made.

Jan. 10	Wages Payable (−L)	135	
	Wages Expense (+E, −SE)	405	
	Cash (−A)		540

This entry eliminates the liability recorded in Wages Payable at the end of December and debits Wages Expense for only those wages earned by the employee in January. (Another method of avoiding dual charges is that of *reversing entries*, which is explained in intermediate courses.)

Accrued Interest   On December 1, 2006, FedEx–DeFond signed a two-year note payable for $54,000 to finance the purchase of its truck. The annual interest rate on the note is 10%, with interest payable each November 30. The first year's interest of $5,400 ($54,000 × 10%) is due on November 30, 2007. An adjusting entry is needed at December 31, 2006, to reflect the interest expense for December. December's interest is $450 ($5,400/12 months), and at the end of December FedEx–DeFond makes the adjustment (f) in the template, journal entry, and T-accounts that follow.

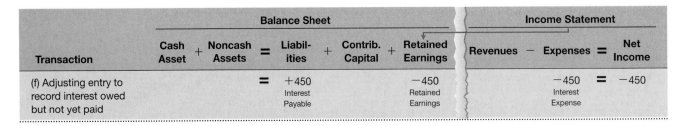

		Balance Sheet					Income Statement		
Transaction	**Cash Asset** +	**Noncash Assets** =	**Liabil-ities** +	**Contrib. Capital** +	**Retained Earnings**	**Revenues** −	**Expenses** =	**Net Income**
(f) Adjusting entry to record interest owed but not yet paid			= +450 Interest Payable		−450 Retained Earnings		−450 Interest Expense	= −450

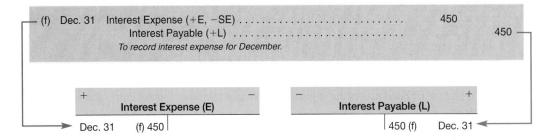

(f) Dec. 31	Interest Expense (+E, −SE)	450	
	Interest Payable (+L)		450
	To record interest expense for December.		

+	Interest Expense (E)	−		−	Interest Payable (L)	+
Dec. 31 (f) 450					450 (f) Dec. 31	

When this entry is posted to the general ledger, the accounts show the correct interest expense for December and the liability for one month's interest that has accrued by December 31.

When the first year's interest of $5,400 is paid on November 30, 2007, management must not forget that $450 of that amount relates to 2006. For example, assume that FedEx–DeFond prepares only year-end financial statements in 2007 and makes no 2007 adjustments for interest through the end of November. On November 30, 2007, the following entry to record the interest payment on that date is made.

Nov. 30	Interest Payable (−L)	450	
	Interest Expense (+E, −SE)	4,950	
	Cash (−A)		5,400

This entry eliminates the interest payable that was accrued on December 31, 2006, and debits Interest Expense for $4,950, the correct interest expense for the first 11 months of 2007.

Type 4: Accruing Revenues

Revenues from services should be recognized in the period the services are performed. Yet a company may provide services during a period that are neither paid for by clients or customers nor billed at the end of the period. The value of these services represents revenue that should be included in the firm's current period accrual income statement. To accomplish this, end-of-period adjusting entries are made to reflect any revenues for the period that have been earned and realized, but are not received for or billed. Such accumulated revenue is often called **accrued revenue**.

Accrued Commissions FedEx–DeFond entered into a contract with FedEx Corporation on December 2 that requires a December 31 adjusting entry to accrue revenue. Under the one-year contract, FedEx–DeFond agreed to distribute promotional literature to FedEx customers in exchange for a monthly commission of $500, payable at the end of every 3 months. (A commission represents a payment to an employee or agent for specific services rendered and is usually a percentage of the amounts involved in the related transaction, such as a commission to a real estate broker for selling a home. A commission can be a fixed amount, as is the case for FedEx–DeFond's contract with FedEx Corporation.) By December 31, FedEx–DeFond has earned one month's commission, and it makes the adjustment (g) in the following template, journal entry, and T-accounts.

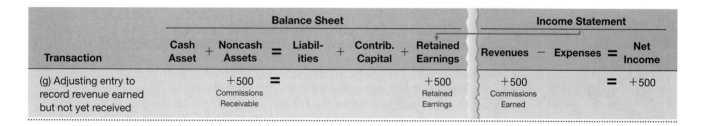

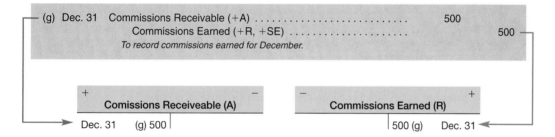

When this entry is posted, a $500 normal balance is created in a new asset account, Commissions Receivable, reflecting FedEx–DeFond's claim to receive revenues already earned. A new revenue account, Commissions Earned, also has a $500 normal balance created. A different revenue account is used because a different activity generates the revenue—distributing promotional literature as contrasted with delivery services.

When FedEx–DeFond receives the first $1,500 commission payment on February 28, 2007, management must recall that $500 was earned and recorded in 2006. On February 28, 2007, the following entry is made to record the commission received.

Feb. 28	Cash (+A)	1,500	
	Commissions Receivable (−A)		500
	Commissions Earned (+R, +SE)		1,000
	To record receipt of quarterly commission.		

This entry eliminates the Commissions Receivable set up on December 31, 2006, and records $1,000 of commissions earned, the proper amount of revenue from commissions for the first two months of 2007.

Another example of an adjusting entry to accrue revenue involves a company that loans money on which interest is earned but not yet collected by period-end. The interest must be reflected in the net income of the period in which it is earned. Thus, an adjusting entry is made debiting Interest Receivable and crediting Interest Income for the amount of interest earned.

Exhibit 3.7 summarizes accounting adjustments and the financial impacts of the related adjusting entries.

| EXHIBIT 3.7 | Summary of Accounting Adjustments |

Accounting Adjustment	Examples	Adjusting Entry	Financial Effects If Not Adjusted	
			Balance Sheet	Income Statement
Prepaid expenses	Expiration of prepaid rent, insurance, and advertising	Dr. Expense Cr. Asset	Asset overstated Equity overstated	Expense understated
Unearned revenues	Delivery on advances from clients, gift cards, and subscribers	Dr. Liability Cr Revenue	Liability overstated Equity understated	Revenue understated
Accrued expenses	Incurred but unpaid wages, interest, and tax expenses	Dr. Expense Cr. Liability	Liabilty understated Equity overstated	Expense understated
Accrued revenues	Earned but not received service, sales, and interest revenues	Dr. Asset Cr. Revenue	Asset understated Equity understated	Revenue understated

MID-CHAPTER REVIEW

The following transactions relate to **The Sony Corporation** with selected and assumed numbers. Prepare the accounting adjustment for each transaction using both the financial statement effects template and the journal entry.

a. The Supplies and Parts balance on December 31, the company's accounting year-end, reveals $100,000 available. This amount reflects its beginning-year balance and all purchases for the year. A physical inventory indicates that much of this balance has been used in service operations, leaving supplies and parts valued at $9,000 remaining at year-end December 31.

b. A $5,000 bill for December and January rent on the warehouse was received on December 30 but has not yet been paid or recorded.

c. A building holding its offices was purchased for $400,000 five years ago. The building's life was estimated at 8 years.

d. An executive was hired on December 15 with an annual $120,000 salary. Payment and work are to start on January 15. No entry has yet been made to record this event.

e. A services contract is signed with the local university on December 1. Sony received $1,200 cash on December 1 as a retainer for the months of December and January, but it has not yet been recorded. Sony retains the money whether the university requires its assistance or not.

f. Employees are paid on the first day of the month following the month in which work is performed. Wages earned in December, but not yet paid or recorded as of December 31, amount to $25,000.

Required

1. For each of the 6 transactions described: (1) enter their effects in the financial statement effects template, and (2) prepare the related journal entries and T-accounts. Sony's ledger includes the following ledger accounts and unadjusted normal balances at December 31: Cash $80,000; Accounts Receivable $95,000; Supplies and Parts $100,000; Building $400,000; Accumulated Depreciation— Building $200,000; Land $257,500; Accounts Payable $20,000; Wages Payable $25,000; Unearned Revenue $0; Common Stock $80,000; Retained Earnings $380,000; Services Revenue $720,000; Rent Expense $27,500; Depreciation Expense $0; Wages Expense $440,000; Supplies and Parts Expense $0.

2. Set up T-accounts for all ledger accounts in part 1 and enter the beginning unadjusted balance, the adjustments from part 1, and the adjusted ending balance.

Part 1 Solution

a.

	Balance Sheet						Income Statement		
Transaction	Cash Asset	+ Noncash Assets	= Liabil- ities	+ Contrib. Capital	+ Retained Earnings		Revenues	− Expenses	= Net Income
(a) Adjusting entry to record supplies and parts used		−91,000 Supplies and Parts	=		−91,000 Retained Earnings			−91,000 Supplies and Parts Expense	= −91,000

| (a) | Dec. 31 | Supplies and Parts Expense (+E, −SE) . . . . | 91,000 | |
| | | Supplies and Parts (−A) . . . . | | 91,000 |

b.

	Balance Sheet					Income Statement		
Transaction	Cash Asset	+ Noncash Assets	= Liabil- ities	+ Contrib. Capital	+ Retained Earnings	Revenues	− Expenses	= Net Income
(b) Adjusting entry to record rent expense accrued but not yet paid			= +2,500 Accounts Payable		−2,500 Retained Earnings		−2,500 Rent Expense	= −2,500

| (b) | Dec. 31 | Rent Expense (+E, −SE) . . . . | 2,500 | |
| | | Accounts Payable (+L) . . . . | | 2,500 |

NOTE
The $2,500 rent for January is not recorded because it is not yet incurred as of December 31.

c.

	Balance Sheet					Income Statement		
Transaction	Cash Asset	+ Noncash Assets	= Liabil- ities	+ Contrib. Capital	+ Retained Earnings	Revenues	− Expenses	= Net Income
(c) Adjusting entry to record depreciation on building		−50,000 = Accumulated Depreciation— Building			−50,000 Retained Earnings		−50,000 Depreciation Expense	= −50,000

| (c) | Dec. 31 | Depreciation Expense (+E, −SE) . . . . | 50,000 | |
| | | Accumulated Depreciation—Building (+XA, −A) . . . | | 50,000 |

d. No entry required; the executive has not yet begun work and thus no expense is incurred.

e.

	Balance Sheet					Income Statement		
Transaction	Cash Asset	+ Noncash Assets	= Liabil- ities	+ Contrib. Capital	+ Retained Earnings	Revenues	− Expenses	= Net Income
(e) Adjusting entry to record cash advance, of which a part is earned	+1,200 Cash		= +600 Unearned Revenue		+600 Retained Earnings	+600 Service Revenue		= +600

(e)	Dec. 31	Cash (+A)	1,200	
		Unearned Revenue (+L)		600
		Service Revenue (+R, +SE)		600

f.

	Balance Sheet					Income Statement		
Transaction	Cash Asset	+ Noncash Assets	= Liabil- ities	+ Contrib. Capital	+ Retained Earnings	Revenues	− Expenses	= Net Income
(f) Adjusting entry to record wages earned but not yet paid			= +25,000 Wages Payable		−25,000 Retained Earnings		−25,000 Wages Expense	= −25,000

| (f) | Dec. 31 | Wages Expense (+E, −SE) . . . . | 25,000 | |
| | | Wages Payable (+L) . . . . | | 25,000 |

Part 2 Solution

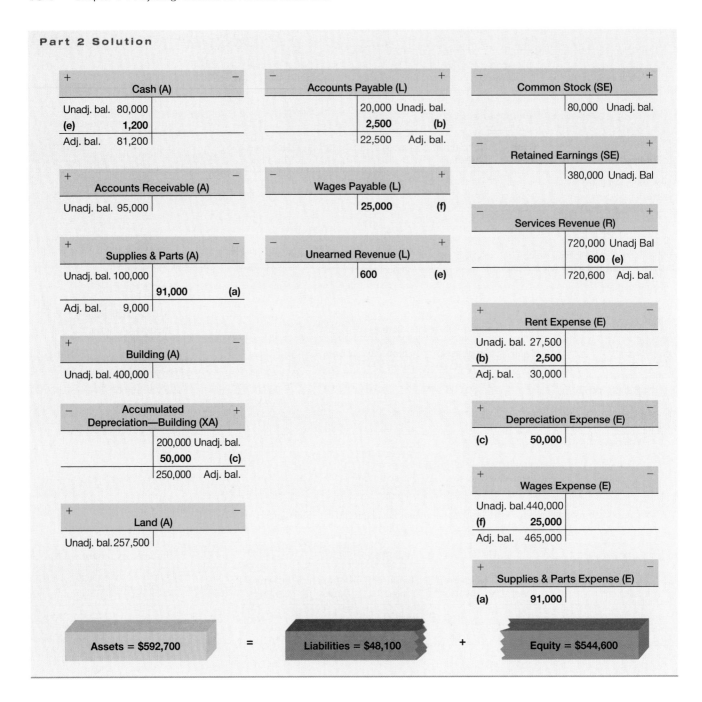

CONSTRUCTING FINANCIAL STATEMENTS FROM ADJUSTED DATA

This section explains the preparation of financial statements from the adjusted financial accounts.

LO4 Prepare financial statements from adjusted accounts.

Preparing an Adjusted Trial Balance

After adjustments are recorded and posted, the company prepares an adjusted trial balance. The **adjusted trial balance** lists all the general ledger account balances after adjustments. Much of the content for company financial statements is taken from an adjusted trial balance. Exhibit 3.8 shows the general ledger accounts for FedEx–DeFond after adjustments, in T-account form.

The adjusted trial balance at December 31 for FedEx–DeFond is prepared from its general ledger accounts and is in the right-hand two columns of Exhibit 3.9. We show the unadjusted balances along with the adjustments to highlight the adjustment process.

EXHIBIT 3.8   General Ledger Accounts after Adjustments

Cash (A)

+		–	
Dec. 1	20,000	250	Dec. 1
2	10,000	3,600	1
10	650	540	13
19	800	540	27
21	520	1,600	30
Unadj. bal.	24,640		

Accounts Receivable (A)

+		–	
Dec. 12	1, 580	800	Dec. 19
31	2,700		
Adj. bal.	3,480		

Supplies (A)

+		–	
Dec. 1	950	440 (a)	Dec. 31
Adj. bal.	510		

Prepaid Rent (A)

+		–	
Dec. 1	3,600	600 (b)	Dec. 31
Adj. bal.	3,000		

Truck (A)

+		–
Dec. 1	54,000	

Commissions Receivable (A)

+		–
Dec. 31	(g) 500	

Accumulated Depreciation—Truck (XA)

–		+	
		750 (c)	Dec. 31

Accounts Payable (L)

–	+	
	700	Dec. 1

Unearned Service Fees (L)

–		+	
Dec. 31	(d) 2,500	10,000	Dec. 2
		7,500	Adj. bal.

Long-Term Notes Payable (L)

–	+	
	54,000	Dec. 1

Interest Payable (L)

–	+	
	450 (f)	Dec. 31

Wages Payable (L)

–	+	
	135 (e)	Dec. 31

Common Stock (SE)

–	+	
	20,000	Dec. 1

Retained Earnings (SE)

–		+
Dec. 29	800	

Service Fees Earned (R)

–	+	
	650	Dec. 10
	1,580	12
	520	21
	2,700	31
	5,450	Unadj. bal.
	2,500 (d)	Dec. 31
	7,950	Adj. Bal

Commissions Earned (R)

–	+	
	500 (g)	Dec. 31

Wages Expense (E)

+		–
Dec. 13	540	
27	540	
Unadj. bal.	1,080	
Dec. 31	(e) 135	
Adj. bal.	1,215	

Truck Expense (E)

+		–
Dec. 30	1,600	

Supplies Expense (E)

+		–
Dec. 31	(a) 440	

Rent Expense (E)

+		–
Dec. 31	(b) 600	

Depreciation Expense—Truck (E)

+		–
Dec. 31	(c) 750	

Interest Expense (E)

+		–
Dec. 31	(f) 450	

Assets = $85,380   =   Liabilities = $62,785   +   Equity = $22,595

EXHIBIT 3.9   Unadjusted and Adjusted Trial Balances

FedEx–DeFond
Trial Balance
December 31, 2006

	Unadjusted Trial Balance		Adjustments		Adjusted Trial Balance	
	Debit	Credit	Debit	Credit	Debit	Credit
Cash	$24,640				$24,640	
Accounts Receivable	3,480				3,480	
Commissions Receivable			(g) 500		500	
Supplies	950			(a) 440	510	
Prepaid Rent	3,600			(b) 600	3,000	
Truck	54,000				54,000	
Accumulated Depreciation—Truck .				(c) 750		$ 750
Accounts Payable		$ 700				700
Interest Payable				(f) 450		450
Wages Payable				(e) 135		135
Unearned Service Fees		10,000	(d) 2,500			7,500
Long-Term Notes Payable		54,000				54,000
Common Stock		20,000				20,000
Retained Earnings	800				800	
Service Fees Earned		5,450		(d) 2,500		7,950
Commissions Earned				(g) 500		500
Rent Expense			(b) 600		600	
Wages Expense	1,080		(e) 135		1,215	
Supplies Expense			(a) 440		440	
Truck Expense	1,600				1,600	
Depreciation Expense—Truck			(c) 750		750	
Interest Expense			(f) 450		450	
Totals	$ 90,150	$ 90,150	$ 5,375	$ 5,375	$ 91,985	$91,985

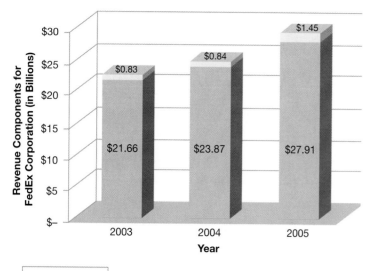

Preparing Financial Statements

A company prepares its financial statements from the adjusted trial balance (and sometimes other supporting information). The set of financial statements consists of the income statement, statement of stockholders' equity, balance sheet, and statement of cash flows. We illustrate these financial statements for FedEx–DeFond.

Income Statement

The income statement reports a company's revenues and expenses. FedEx–DeFond's adjusted trial balance contains two revenue accounts and six expense accounts. These revenues and expenses are reported in FedEx–DeFond's income statement for December as shown in Exhibit 3.10. Its net income for December is $3,395.

EXHIBIT 3.10 | Income Statement

FedEx–DeFond
Income Statement
For Month Ended December 31, 2006

Revenues

Service Fees Earned	$7,950	
Commissions Earned	500	
Total Revenues		$8,450

Expenses

Rent Expense	600	
Wages Expense	1,215	
Supplies Expense	440	
Truck Expense	1,600	
Depreciation Expense—Truck	750	
Interest Expense	450	
Total Expenses		5,055
Net Income		$3,395

Statement of Stockholders' Equity

The statement of stockholders' equity reports the events causing the major equity components to change during the accounting period. Exhibit 3.11 shows FedEx–DeFond's statement of stockholders' equity for December. A review of its common stock account in the general ledger provides some of the information for this statement; namely, its balance at the beginning of the period and stock issuances during the period. (Because December is the first month of FedEx–DeFond's existence, the beginning common stock is zero; later periods begin with the ending balance of the prior period.) The net income (or net loss) amount comes from the income statement. Dividends during the period are reflected in the retained earnings balance from the adjusted trial balance.

EXHIBIT 3.11 | Statement of Stockholders' Equity

FedEx–DeFond
Statement of Stockholders' Equity
For Month Ended December 31, 2006

	Common Stock	Retained Earnings	Total
Balances, December 1, 2006	$ 0	$ 0	$ 0
Issuance of Common Stock	20,000	—	20,000
Net Income	—	3,395	3,395
Cash Dividends	—	(800)	(800)
Balances, December 31, 2006	$20,000	$ 2,595	$22,595

Balance Sheet

The balance sheet reports a company's assets, liabilities, and equity. The assets and liabilities for FedEx–DeFond's balance sheet at December 31, 2006, shown in Exhibit 3.12, come from the adjusted trial balance in Exhibit 3.9. The amounts reported for Common Stock and Retained Earnings in the balance sheet are taken from the statement of stockholder's equity for December (Exhibit 3.11).

EXHIBIT 3.12   Balance Sheet

FedEx–DeFond
Balance Sheet
December 31, 2006

Assets			Liabilities		
Cash		$24,640	Accounts Payable	$	700
Accounts Receivable		3,480	Interest Payable		450
Commissions Receivable		500	Wages Payable		135
Supplies		510	Unearned Service Fees		7,500
Prepaid Rent		3,000	Long-Term Notes Payable		54,000
Truck	$ 54,000		Total Liabilities		62,785
Less: Accumulated Depreciation	750	53,250	**Equity**		
			Common Stock		20,000
			Retained Earnings		2,595
Total Assets		$85,380	Total Liabilities and Equity		$85,380

Statement of Cash Flows

The statement of cash flows reports information about cash inflows and cash outflows for a period of time. The cash flows are classified into operating, investing, and financing categories. The procedures for preparing a statement of cash flows are discussed in a later chapter. For completeness, we present FedEx–DeFond's statement of cash flows for December in Exhibit 3.13 (there were no investing cash flows in December).

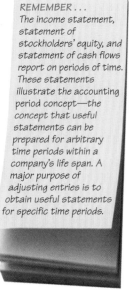
EXHIBIT 3.13   Statement of Cash Flows

FedEx–DeFond
Statement of Cash Flows
For Month Ended December 31, 2006

Cash Flows from Operating Activities	
Cash Received for Services	$11,970
Cash Paid for Supplies	(250)
Cash Paid for Rent	(3,600)
Cash Paid for Employee Wages	(1,080)
Cash Paid for Gas and Oil	(1,600)
Net Cash Provided by Operating Activities	5,440
Cash Flows from Investing Activities	0
Cash Flows from Financing Activities	
Issuance of common stock	20,000
Payment of dividends	(800)
Net Cash Provided by Financing Activities	19,200
Net Increase in Cash	$24,640
Cash balance, December 1, 2006	0
Cash balance, December 31, 2006	$24,640

CLOSING TEMPORARY ACCOUNTS

LO5 Describe the process of closing temporary accounts.

Temporary accounts consist of revenues, expenses, and dividends (if a separate Dividends account is used). These accounts accumulate data that relate to a specific accounting period. As such, their balances are reported in period financial statements—the income statement and statement of stockholders' equity. At the end of each accounting period, the balances of these temporary accounts are transferred to a permanent account—the Retained Earnings account. This part of the accounting cycle is referred to as **closing procedures.**

A temporary account is *closed* when an entry is made that changes its balance to zero. The entry is equal in amount to the account's balance but is opposite to the balance as a debit or credit. An account that is closed is said to be closed *to* the account that receives the offsetting debit or credit. Thus, a closing entry simply transfers the balance of one account to another account. When closing entries bring temporary account balances to zero, the temporary accounts are then ready to accumulate data for the next accounting period.

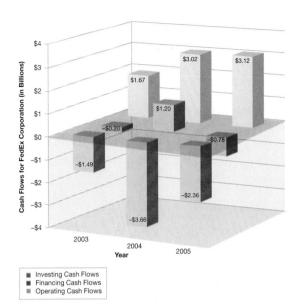

 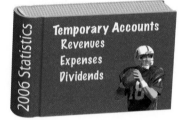

Closing Process

A summary account, titled Income Summary, is traditionally used to close the temporary revenue and expense accounts. The entries for opening and closing Income Summary occur only during the closing process. The entries to close temporary accounts are as follows.

1. **Close revenue accounts.** Debit each revenue account for an amount equal to its balance, and credit Income Summary for the total of revenues.

2. **Close expense accounts.** Credit each expense account for an amount equal to its balance, and debit Income Summary for the total of expenses.

After these temporary accounts are closed, the balance of Income Summary equals the period's net income (if a credit balance) or net loss (if a debit balance). The final closing step is as follows.

3. **Close Income Summary.** In the case of net income, debit Income Summary and credit Retained Earnings for net income. In the case of net loss, debit Retained Earnings and credit Income Summary for net loss.

The closing process is graphically portrayed as follows.

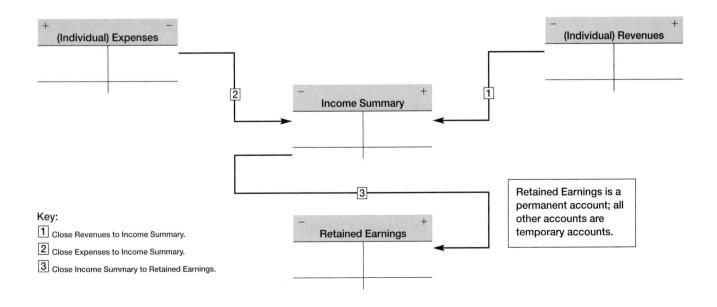

Key:
1 Close Revenues to Income Summary.
2 Close Expenses to Income Summary.
3 Close Income Summary to Retained Earnings.

Closing Steps Illustrated

Exhibit 3.14 illustrates the entries for closing revenues and expenses to Income Summary for FedEx–DeFond. The effects of these entries in T-accounts are shown below the entries.

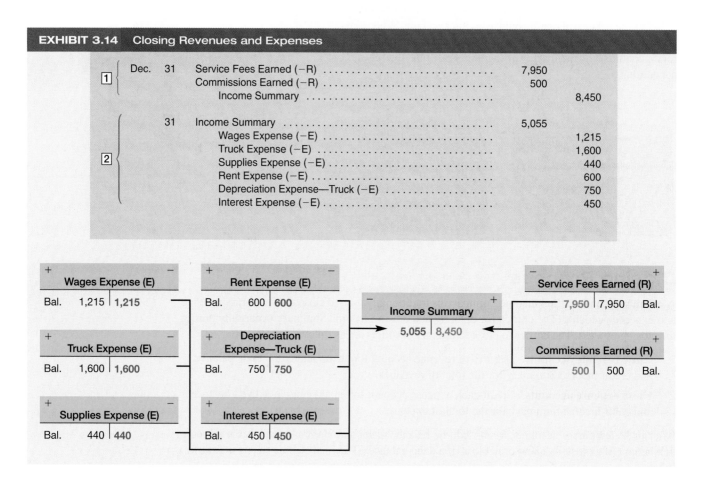

EXHIBIT 3.14 Closing Revenues and Expenses

	Dec.	31	Service Fees Earned (−R)	7,950	
1			Commissions Earned (−R)	500	
			Income Summary		8,450
		31	Income Summary	5,055	
2			Wages Expense (−E)		1,215
			Truck Expense (−E)		1,600
			Supplies Expense (−E)		440
			Rent Expense (−E)		600
			Depreciation Expense—Truck (−E)		750
			Interest Expense (−E)		450

After these two steps, the balance of Income Summary is a credit equal to net income of $3,395. The closing procedure is completed by closing the Income Summary account to the Retained Earnings account. This entry is shown in Exhibit 3.15. The effect of this entry on the general ledger, in T-account form, is also diagrammed.

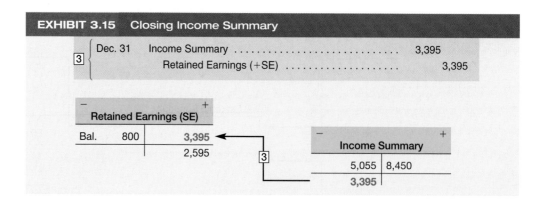

EXHIBIT 3.15 Closing Income Summary

| | Dec. 31 | Income Summary | 3,395 | |
| 3 | | Retained Earnings (+SE) | | 3,395 |

Preparing a Post-Closing Trial Balance

After closing entries are recorded and posted to the general ledger, all temporary accounts have zero balances. At this point a **post-closing trial balance** is prepared. A balancing of this trial balance is evidence that an equality of debits and credits has been maintained in the general ledger throughout the adjusting and closing process and that the general ledger is in balance to start the next accounting period. Only balance sheet accounts appear in a post-closing trial balance. The post-closing trial balance for FedEx–DeFond is in Exhibit 3.16.

EXHIBIT 3.16	**Post-Closing Trial Balance**		
FedEx–DeFond **Post-Closing Trial Balance** **DECEMBER 31, 2006**			
		Debit	**Credit**
Cash		$ 24,640	
Accounts Receivable		3,480	
Commissions Receivable		500	
Supplies		510	
Prepaid Rent		3,000	
Truck		54,000	
Accumulated Depreciation—Truck			$ 750
Accounts Payable			700
Interest Payable			450
Wages Payable			135
Unearned Service Fees			7,500
Long-Term Notes Payable			54,000
Common Stock			20,000
Retained Earnings			2,595
		$ 86,130	$ 86,130

SUMMARIZING THE ACCOUNTING CYCLE

The sequence of accounting procedures known as the *accounting cycle* occurs each fiscal year (period) and represents a systematic process for accumulating and reporting financial data of a company. Exhibit 3.17 expands on Exhibit 3.1 to include descriptions of the five major steps in the accounting cycle.

LO6 Summarize the accounting cycle.

EXHIBIT 3.17	**Accounting Cycle**

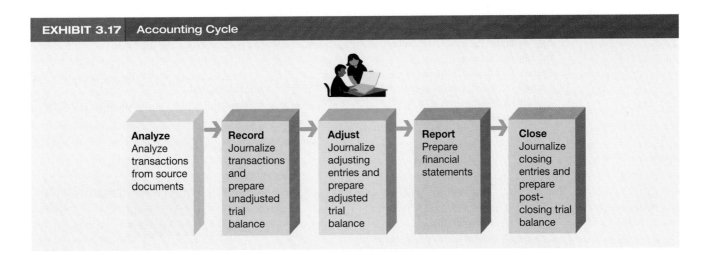

Analyze Analyze transactions from source documents → **Record** Journalize transactions and prepare unadjusted trial balance → **Adjust** Journalize adjusting entries and prepare adjusted trial balance → **Report** Prepare financial statements → **Close** Journalize closing entries and prepare post-closing trial balance

CHAPTER-END REVIEW

Assume that Abbott Laboratories, Inc., operates with an accounting fiscal-year ending June 30. The company's accounts are adjusted annually and closed on that date. Its unadjusted trial balance ($ millions) as of June 30, 2006, is as follows.

Abbott Laboratories, Inc. Unadjusted Trial Balance June 30, 2006		
	Debit	**Credit**
Cash	$ 1,000	
Accounts Receivable	9,200	
Prepaid Insurance	6,000	
Supplies	31,300	
Equipment	270,000	
Accumulated Depreciation—Equipment		$ 60,000
Accounts Payable		3,100
Unearned Fees		4,000
Fees Revenue		150,000
Wages Expense	58,000	
Rent Expense	22,000	
Common Stock		120,400
Retained Earnings		60,000
Totals	$397,500	$397,500

Additional Information
1. Abbott acquired a two-year insurance policy on January 1, 2006. The policy covers fire and casualty; Abbott had no coverage prior to January 1, 2006.
2. An inventory of supplies was taken on June 30 and the amount available was $6,300.
3. All equipment was purchased on July 1, 2003 for $270,000. The equipment's life is estimated at 9.
4. Abbott received a $4,000 cash payment on April 1, 2006, from Beave Clinic for diagnostic work to be provided uniformly over the next 4 months, beginning April 1, 2006. The amount was credited to Unearned Fees. The service was provided per the agreement.
5. Unpaid and unrecorded wages at June 30, 2006, were $600.
6. Abbott rents facilities for $2,000 per month. Abbott has not yet made or recorded the payment for June 2006.

Required
1. Prepare the necessary adjusting entries and enter them in T-accounts. Number the entries per above. Abbott's ledger includes the following ledger accounts and unadjusted normal balances at June 30: Cash $1,000; Accounts Receivable $9,200; Supplies $31,300; Prepaid Insurance $6,000; Equipment $270,000; Accumulated Depreciation—Equipment $60,000; Accounts Payable $3,100; Wages Payable $0; Rent Payable $0; Unearned Fees $4,000; Common Stock $120,400; Retained Earnings $60,000; Fees Revenue $150,000; Rent Expense $22,000; Insurance Expense $0; Depreciation Expense $0; Wages Expense $58,000; Supplies Expense $0. Use "Unadj. bal." to denote the unadjusted balance in each account when such a balance exists, and use "Adj. bal." to denote the adjusted balance.
2. Prepare its adjusted trial balance.
3. Prepare its closing journal entries and post them to the T-accounts (key the entries).
4. Prepare its balance sheet as of June 30, 2006, and its income statement and statement of stockholders' equity for the year ended June 30, 2006.

Solutions
Part 1

1. June 30	Insurance Expense (+E, −SE)*		1,500	
	Prepaid Insurance (−A)			1,500
	* $6,000 ÷ 4			
2. June 30	Supplies Expense (+E, −SE)*		25,000	
	Supplies (−A)			25,000
	* $31,300 − $6,300			
3. June 30	Depreciation Expense (+E, −SE)*		30,000	
	Accumulated Depreciation—Equipment (+XA, −A)			30,000
	* ($270,000 − $0) ÷ 9			
4. June 30	Unearned Fees (−L)		3,000	
	Fees Revenue (+R, +SE)			3,000

5. June 30	Wages Expense (+E, −SE)	....	600	
	Wages Payable (+L)	....		600
6. June 30	Rent Expense (+E, −SE)	....	2,000	
	Rent Payable (+L)	....		2,000

Cash (A) (+ −)
Unadj. bal.	1,000	
Adj. bal.	1,000	

Accounts Payable (L) (− +)
	3,100	Unadj. bal.
	3,100	Adj. bal.

Common Stock (SE) (− +)
	120,400	Unadj. bal.
	120,400	Adj. bal.

Accounts Receivable (A) (+ −)
Unadj. bal.	9,200	
Adj. bal.	9,200	

Unearned Fees (L) (− +)
(4)	3,000	4,000	Unadj. bal.
		1,000	Adj. bal.

Retained Earnings (SE) (− +)
	60,000	Unadj. bal.
	60,000	Adj. bal.

Prepaid Insurance (A) (+ −)
Unadj. bal.	6,000	1,500	(1)
Adj. bal.	4,500		

Wages Payable (L) (− +)
	600	(5)
	600	Adj. bal.

Fees Revenue (R) (− +)
	150,000	Unadj. bal.
	3,000	(4)
	153,000	Adj. bal.

Supplies (A) (+ −)
Unadj. bal.	31,300	25,000	(2)
Adj. bal.	6,300		

Rent Payable (L) (− +)
	2,000	(6)
	2,000	Adj. bal.

Insurance Expense (E) (+ −)
(1)	1,500	
Adj. bal.	1,500	

Equipment (A) (+ −)
Unadj. bal.	270,000	
Adj. bal.	270,000	

Supplies Expense (E) (+ −)
(2)	25,000	
Adj. bal.	25,000	

Accumulated Depreciation—Equipment (XA) (− +)
	60,000	Unadj. bal.
	30,000	(3)
	90,000	Adj. bal.

Depreciation Expense (E) (+ −)
(3)	30,000	
Adj. bal.	30,000	

Rent Expense (E) (+ −)
Unadj. bal.	22,000	
(6)	2,000	
Adj. bal.	24,000	

Wage Expense (E) (+ −)
Unadj. bal.	58,000	
(5)	600	
Adj. bal.	58,600	

Assets = $201,000 = Liabilities = $6,700 + Equity = $194,300

Part 2

Abbott Laboratories, Inc. Adjusted Trial Balance June 30, 2006	Debits	Credits
Cash	$ 1,000	
Accounts Receivable	9,200	
Prepaid Insurance	4,500	
Supplies	6,300	
Equipment	270,000	
Accumulated Depreciation—Equipment		$ 90,000
Accounts Payable		3,100
Rent Payable		2,000
Wages Payable		600
Unearned Fees		1,000
Fees Revenue		153,000
Wages Expense	58,600	
Rent Expense	24,000	
Insurance Expense	1,500	
Supplies Expense	25,000	
Depreciation Expense	30,000	
Common Stock		120,400
Retained Earnings		60,000
Totals	$430,100	$430,100

Part 3

a.	Income Summary	139,100	
	Insurance Expense (−E)		1,500
	Supplies Expense (−E)		25,000
	Depreciation Expense (−E)		30,000
	Rent Expense (−E)		24,000
	Wages Expense (−E)		58,600
b.	Fees Revenue (−R)	153,000	
	Income Summary		153,000
c.	Income Summary	13,900	
	Retained Earnings (+SE)		13,900

+ Cash (A) −	
Unadj. bal. 1,000	
Adj. bal. 1,000	

− Accounts Payable (L) +	
	3,100 Unadj. bal.
	3,100 Adj. bal.

− Common Stock (SE) +	
	120,400 Unadj. bal.
	120,400 Adj. bal.

+ Accounts Receivable (A) −	
Unadj. bal. 9,200	
Adj. bal. 9,200	

− Unearned Fees (L) +	
(4) 3,000	4,000 Unadj. bal.
	1,000 Adj. bal.

− Retained Earnings (SE) +	
	60,000 Unadj. bal.
	13,900 (c)
	73,900 Adj. bal.

+ Prepaid Insurance (A) −	
Unadj. Bal 6,000	1,500 (1)
Adj. bal. 4,500	

− Wages Payable (L) +	
	600 (5)
	600 Adj. bal.

− Fees Revenue (R) +	
	150,000 Unadj. bal.
(b) 153,000	3,000 (4)
	0 Adj. bal.

+ Supplies (A) −		
Unadj. bal. 31,300	25,000	(2)
Adj. bal. 6,300		

− Rent Payable (L) +		
	2,000	(6)
	2,000	Adj. bal.

+ Insurance Expense (E) −		
(1)	1,500	1,500	(a)
Adj. bal.	0	

+ Equipment (A) −	
Unadj. bal. 270,000	
Adj. bal. 270,000	

+ Supplies Expense (E) −		
(2)	25,000	25,000	(a)
Adj. bal.	0	

− Accumulated Depreciation—Equipment (XA) +		
	60,000	Unadj. bal.
	30,000	(3)
	90,000	Adj. bal.

+ Depreciation Expense (E) −		
(3)	30,000	30,000	(a)
Adj. bal.	0	

+ Rent Expense (E) −		
Unadj. bal. 22,000		
(6) 2,000		
24,000	24,000	(a)
Adj. bal. 0		

+ Wage Expense (E) −		
Unadj. bal. 58,000		
(5) 600		
58,600	58,600	(a)
Adj. bal. 0		

− Income Summary +		
(a)	139,100	153,000	(b)
(c)	13,900		
		0	Adj. bal.

Assets = $201,000 = **Liabilities = $6,700** + **Equity = $194,300**

Part 4

Abbott Laboratories, Inc.
Balance Sheet
June 30, 2006

Assets			Liabilities		
Cash		$ 1,000	Accounts Payable		$ 3,100
Accounts Receivable		9,200	Unearned Fees		1,000
Prepaid Insurance		4,500	Wages Payable		600
Supplies		6,300	Rent Payable		2,000
Total Current Assets		21,000	Total Current Liabilities		6,700
Equipment, original cost	270,000		Equity		
Less Accumulated Depreciation	90,000	180,000	Retained Earnings		73,900
Total Assets		$201,000	Common Stock		120,400
			Totals Liabilities and Equity . . .		$201,000

Abbott Laboratories, Inc.
Income Statement
For Year Ended June 30, 2006

Sales Revenues		$153,000
Expenses		
Insurance Expense	$ 1,500	
Supplies Expense	25,000	
Depreciation Expense	30,000	
Rent Expense	24,000	
Wages Expense	58,600	
Total Expense		139,100
Net Income		$ 13,900

Abbott Laboratories, Inc.
Statement of Stockholders' Equity
For Year Ended June 30, 2006

	Common Stock	Retained Earnings	Total
Balance at June 30, 2005	$120,400	$60,000	$180,400
Net Income		13,900	13,900
Balance at June 30, 2006	$120,400	$73,900	$194,300

Abbott's statement of stockholders' equity is much simpler than the usual statement because we have focused on the adjustment and closing process. In doing so, we did not consider additional activities in which corporations commonly engage, such as paying dividends, issuing stock, and repurchasing stock. (Requirements did not ask for a statement of cash flows. Neither the adjusting nor closing entries, which were our focus, involve cash transactions. The next chapter is devoted to the statement of cash flows.)

SUMMARY

LO1 **Identify the major steps in the accounting cycle (in order). (p. 88)**

▪ The major steps in the accounting cycle are

    a. Analyze   b. Record   c. Adjust   d. Report   e. Close

LO2 **Explain the process of journalizing and posting transactions. (p. 89)**

▪ Transactions are initially recorded in a journal; the entries are in chronological order, and the journal shows the total effect of each transaction or adjustment.

▪ Posting is the transfer of information from a journal to the general ledger accounts.

LO3 **Describe the adjusting process and illustrate adjusting entries. (p. 94)**

▪ Adjusting entries achieve the proper recognition of revenues and the proper matching of expenses with those revenues; adjustments are summarized as follows.

Adjustment	Adjusting Entry
Adjusting prepaid expenses	Increase expense
	Decrease asset
Adjusting unearned revenues	Decrease liability
	Increase revenue
Accruing expenses	Increase expense
	Increase liability
Accruing revenues	Increase asset
	Increase revenue

Prepare financial statements from adjusted accounts. (p. 104)   **LO4**

■   An income statement, statement of stockholders' equity, balance sheet, and statement of cash flows are
    prepared from an adjusted trial balance and other information.

Describe the process of closing temporary accounts. (p. 108)   **LO5**

■   *Closing the books* means closing (yielding zero balances) revenues and expenses—that is, all temporary
    accounts. Revenue and expense account balances are transferred to the Income Summary account. The balance
    of the Income Summary account is closed to the Retained Earnings account.

Summarize the accounting cycle. (p. 111)   **LO6**

■   Major steps in the accounting cycle are: analyze, record, adjust, report, and close.

Identify and explain the principles underlying financial accounting. (p. 118)   **LO7**

■   Each of the following is an important accounting principle: accounting entity, consistency, accounting period,
    revenue recognition, measuring unit, matching, objectivity, conservatism, historical cost, materiality, going
    concern, and full disclosure. (These concepts are discussed in the appendix to this chapter.)

GUIDANCE ANSWERS

YOU MAKE THE CALL

You are the Chief Accountant   Deposits represent a liability and should be included in REI's current liabilities at the time the cash or check is received. The account that would be used may have several names, including advances, trip deposits, and unearned revenues. Revenue should not be recognized until the trip has been
completed. It is not unusual for events to occur that result in a refund of some portion or even all of the traveler's total
payment. In the present case involving a low cancellation rate, waiting until the trip is over is not only conservative reporting, but is likely more efficient bookkeeping as well.

YOU MAKE THE CALL

You are the Bank Loan Officer   The value shown on Hertz's books will be the purchase price, though
perhaps reduced for the time the fleet has been in use. However, the bank would want to know the current market
value of the fleet, not its book value, and the bank would then adjust this market value. The current market value of
a single car can be found in used-car market quotes. If the bank ultimately becomes the owner of the fleet, it will
need to sell the cars, probably a few at a time through wholesalers. Therefore, the adjusted market value and the
book value are likely to differ for several reasons, including:

1. Hertz would have been able to buy the fleet at a reduced value due to buying regularly in large volume
   (market value higher than used-car quotes).
2. Hertz is likely to have kept the cars in better condition than would the average buyer (market value higher
   than used-car quotes).
3. The bank would reduce the value by some percentage due to the costs associated with disposing of the
   fleet (including the wholesaler's discount) and the length of the bank loan (reduction to the value as otherwise determined).

YOU MAKE THE CALL

You are an Auditor   All maintenance expenditures are made to ensure future revenues. Logically, under the
matching principle, these expenditures should be capitalized and written off over the future use of the asset to generate returns. Capitalizing maintenance expenditures today decreases expenses and increases reported income. In
the future the maintenance expenditures would be gradually written off as expenses, reducing reported income.
The issue is entirely one of timing. An auditor, however, would need to consider the rules that accountants have established for maintenance expenditures. The term, as used in accounting, considers maintenance to be expenditures designed to achieve the initial economic life and/or productivity expected for the asset. Examples include
machine lubrication, sharpening, and replacing small components. Accounting requires that such items be expensed in the period made. Matching is sacrificed for conservatism. WorldCom capitalized these expenditures. An
auditor should neither recommend this practice nor approve it. Expenditures that increase the life or the productivity of an asset from its original expectation would be appropriately capitalized. The replacement of an aircraft engine or reconfiguration to carry more passengers, or a major overhaul would qualify for capitalization.

APPENDIX 3A: Fundamental Principles (Assumptions) of Accounting

LO7 Identify and explain the principles underlying financial accounting.

This appendix considers several fundamental principles that underlie financial accounting. Terms such as *principle, concept, standard, assumption,* and *convention* are used to refer to one or more of them. Regardless of the term used, each of these principles influences the application of accounting. These key principles are shown here.

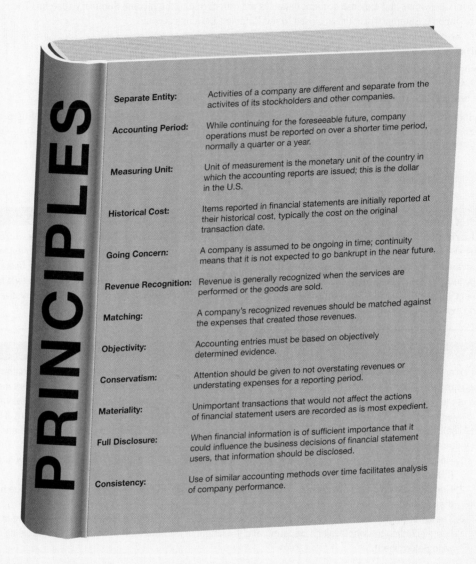

PRINCIPLES

Separate Entity:	Activities of a company are different and separate from the activites of its stockholders and other companies.
Accounting Period:	While continuing for the foreseeable future, company operations must be reported on over a shorter time period, normally a quarter or a year.
Measuring Unit:	Unit of measurement is the monetary unit of the country in which the accounting reports are issued; this is the dollar in the U.S.
Historical Cost:	Items reported in financial statements are initially reported at their historical cost, typically the cost on the original transaction date.
Going Concern:	A company is assumed to be ongoing in time; continuity means that it is not expected to go bankrupt in the near future.
Revenue Recognition:	Revenue is generally recognized when the services are performed or the goods are sold.
Matching:	A company's recognized revenues should be matched against the expenses that created those revenues.
Objectivity:	Accounting entries must be based on objectively determined evidence.
Conservatism:	Attention should be given to not overstating revenues or understating expenses for a reporting period.
Materiality:	Unimportant transactions that would not affect the actions of financial statement users are recorded as is most expedient.
Full Disclosure:	When financial information is of sufficient importance that it could influence the business decisions of financial statement users, that information should be disclosed.
Consistency:	Use of similar accounting methods over time facilitates analysis of company performance.

The last five items listed—objectivity, conservatism, materiality, full disclosure, and consistency—can be thought of as constraints.

Separate Entity Principle

Perhaps the most fundamental concept in accounting is the separate entity principle. An accounting entity is an economic unit with identifiable boundaries, for which companies accumulate and report financial information. Before companies can analyze and report activities, they must identify the particular entity (and its boundaries) for which they are accounting. Every financial report specifies the entity in its heading. In accumulating financial information, we must separate the activities of an accounting entity from the other economic and personal activities of its owners. Also, data for two or more corporations can be combined to provide financial reports for a larger economic entity. For example, a parent corporation and its wholly-owned subsidiaries (corporations in their own right) can consolidate their individual financial reports into a set of consolidated statements covering the parent corporate group.

Accounting Period Principle

The economic life of an accounting entity can be divided into specific periods—typically, one year for financial reporting purposes. The operations of most businesses are virtually continuous except for some changes associated with cyclical time periods, seasons, or dates. Thus, any division of the total life of a business into

NOTE
When a company's operating cycle exceeds one year, such as wineries, shipbuilders, and bridge developers, their interim reporting periods cover multiple years.

segments based on annual periods is artificial. Accounting reports can cover any period. For instance, investors and creditors usually receive quarterly *interim* financial reports and management often receives monthly financial reports. Proper accounting requires that both the entity and the period be identified in financial reports.

Measuring Unit Principle

The unit of measure in accounting is the basic unit of money. Economic activity must be expressed in a common unit of measure so that data can be easily classified, summarized, and reported. The measuring unit principle specifies that a monetary unit (dollar in the U.S.) is used to measure and record an entity's economic activity. When all assets, liabilities, and equity are stated in monetary terms, they can be added or subtracted, as necessary, to prepare financial statements. Also, various relationships among financial statement components can be computed to help interpret the statements. Recording and reporting in monetary terms imposes two limitations on the financial accounting process. First, only items that may be expressed in monetary terms are brought into the information system. Some economic resources and obligations are sometimes excluded from the accounting information system because there is no agreement as to how to express them monetarily. For example, human resources (workforce) is not recorded and reported as an asset in financial statements. The second limitation is that the U.S. dollar (or any other currency) is not a stable unit of measure. Inflation causes a currency's purchasing power to decline through time. Failure to adjust for this can cause distortions in financial statements because amounts are expressed in dollars of different values.

Historical Cost Principle

Asset measures are based on the prices (costs) paid to acquire the assets. The historical cost principle states that assets are initially recorded at the amounts paid to acquire the assets. Land, for example, that is purchased for $75,000 cash, is recorded at its $75,000 cost. Cost is considered the proper initial measure because, at the time an asset is acquired, cost represents the fair value of the asset as agreed to by both the buyer and seller. Cost also is the general basis used to report an asset at subsequent times while it is still held by a company. A year later, for example, the land purchased could be appraised at $90,000, but the company continues to report it at $75,000 because that amount was verified by engaging in an exchange transaction with another entity. The $90,000 appraisal has not been verified by an exchange transaction. In this context, the cost measure is often referred to as *historical cost* (a cost measure that continues to be utilized through time). Historical cost is probably the most objective and verifiable basis for reporting assets. Historical costs are often reduced over time to reflect asset expirations. There are a few cases in which current market values (rather than historical costs) are used to measure assets at dates after their acquisition date.

> *NOTE*
> *When a company is acquired at a price in excess of the market value of its identifiable net assets, the additional price paid is recorded as goodwill. This goodwill could be due in part to the acquired company's intellectual capital.*

YOU MAKE THE CALL

You are the Bank Loan Officer   Hertz, the rental car firm, has a fleet of relatively new automobiles that it rents to customers for usually short periods. Suppose that Hertz applied to your bank for a loan and offered their fleet of cars as collateral. Would you, as the loan officer, be satisfied with the value shown on Hertz's balance sheet as a measure of the fleet's value? If not, what value would you prefer and how might you estimate that value? [Answers on page 117]

Going Concern Principle

In the absence of evidence to the contrary, a company is assumed to have an indefinite life. The going concern concept assumes that an entity will continue to operate indefinitely and will not be sold or liquidated. This principle supports the use of historical cost to measure assets, such as supplies and equipment that will be used in operating the business. The going concern principle implies that the firm will operate long enough to use up the supplies and equipment. As they are used up, their costs will be reflected as costs of operations. Information about the current market values or liquidation values of assets that are going to be used in operations rather than sold is not considered to be particularly relevant information. Sometimes there is strong evidence that the entity is not going to operate indefinitely into the future. In this rare case, the going concern principle is not used, and amounts other than historical cost can prove useful. Throughout this book, however, we will use the going concern principle.

Revenue Recognition Principle

Revenue is generally recognized when services are performed or goods are sold. Business entities exist to provide services and/or sell goods to their customers. The revenue recognition principle states that revenue should be recorded when the services are performed or the goods are sold. The revenue recognition principle requires two conditions to exist before revenue is recorded: The revenue must be *earned* and *realized*. Normally, both conditions are not met until services are performed or goods are sold. An entity *earns* revenue by putting forth the economic effort to provide services or to sell goods. A department store, for example, earns revenue by doing such things as buying merchandise, displaying it in convenient locations, and providing sales clerks to answer questions. An entity *realizes* revenue either by receiving payment for the services and goods or by establishing a claim to receive payment. The involvement of a customer creates realization; that is, services are provided *for* a customer and goods are sold *to* a customer. The customer is a party outside the entity whose involvement confirms the revenue.

> *NOTE*
> *Companies in processed foods, such as General Mills, typically report annual financial statements in late spring. Retailers such as Wal-Mart commonly report annual statements at calendar year-end when the Christmas season concludes.*

NOTE
Cash-basis accounting contrasts with accrual accounting. Under cash-basis accounting, revenues are recorded when cash is received from operating activities and expenses are recorded when cash payments related to operating activities are made. Cash-basis accounting does not attempt to match expenses with revenues. Thus, cash-basis accounting is not consistent with generally accepted accounting principles.

Matching Principle

To the extent feasible, all expenses related to given revenue are matched with and deducted from that revenue in the determination of net income. The matching concept states that net income is determined by linking, or matching, expenses incurred with the related revenues recognized. Expenses are recorded in the period they help to generate the recorded revenues. There is a linkage, therefore, between expenses and revenues: Expenses are incurred to generate revenues. Together, the revenue recognition principle and the matching concept define accrual accounting. In accrual accounting, revenues are recognized when they are both earned and realized (revenue recognition principle) and expenses are recorded in the period they help to generate the recorded revenues (matching concept). The recording of accrual revenues and expenses does not rely on the receipt or payment of cash.

YOU MAKE THE CALL

You are an Auditor   WorldCom, whose fraudulent accounting is estimated to have cost stockholders $11 billion, followed a practice of capitalizing (recognizing amounts as assets on the balance sheet) its maintenance expenditures to the tune of $3.9 billion. Is this approach consistent with the matching principle? As an auditor, would you recommend this practice? What is the impact of this practice on reported income? [Answers on page 117]

Objectivity Principle

Whenever possible, accounting entries must be based on objectively determined evidence. The usefulness of accounting reports is enhanced when the underlying data are objective and verifiable. The objectivity principle dictates that the recording of transactions should be based on reliable and verifiable evidence. Amounts recorded should be supported by actual invoices, physical counts, and other relatively bias-free evidence whenever possible. Undocumented opinions of management or others do not provide a good basis for accounting determinations. As we shall see, however, it is often necessary to incorporate estimates. Even when a certain amount of subjectivity cannot be avoided, it is important that such estimates be supported by some type of objective analysis if possible.

Conservatism Principle

Accounting measurements take place in a context of uncertainties, and possible errors in measurement of net assets and income should tend toward understatement rather than overstatement. Accounting determinations are often based on estimates of future events and are therefore subject to a range of optimistic or pessimistic interpretations. Many past abuses were perpetrated on financial statement users who were given overly optimistic measurements of assets and estimates of income. Conservatism is a reaction to situations in which uncertainties exist about the outcomes of transactions in progress. In contrast to intentional understatements of net assets and income, conservative accounting is applied when one is unsure of the proper measure to use. For example, if two estimates of future amounts to be received are about equally likely, conservatism requires the less optimistic estimate be used. Thus, possible errors in measuring net assets and income should tend toward understatement rather than overstatement.

RESEARCH INSIGHT

Research has documented a decline in the value relevance of accounting information, particularly earnings, over the past few decades. The decline has been attributed by some to conservatism in reporting. However, recent research has not been able to establish an association between this decrease in value relevance and conservatism despite using several alternative measures of conservative accounting. One explanation offered for the research finding is that conservatism favors more objective measures while avoiding additional estimation, thereby increasing reliability. If true, conservative accounting measurement could lead to greater relevance. The issue remains unresolved at this time and conservatism in reporting continues.

Materiality Principle

Accounting transactions so insignificant that they would not affect the actions of financial statement users are recorded as is most expedient. Applying sound accounting procedures requires effort and costs money. When the amounts involved are too small to markedly affect the overall picture, the application of theoretically correct accounting procedures is hardly worth its cost. For example, assets represent items with future economic benefit to an entity. Yet the costs of some assets are so small that it makes little sense to track them in the accounts for their entire future economic lives. Thus, the concept of materiality permits a firm to expense the costs of such items as small tools, pencil sharpeners, and wastebaskets when acquired because they are "immaterial" in amount. Many firms set dollar limits—such as $100—below which the costs of all items are expensed. The concept of materiality is relative—an immaterial amount for FedEx Corporation can be material for smaller companies. Beware that although a given series of transactions may *each* be considered immaterial in amount, their aggregate effect could be material in certain circumstances.

Full Disclosure Principle

All information necessary for users' understanding of financial statements must be disclosed. Accounting reports must provide useful information to various parties interested in a company's financial performance and condition. Often facts or conditions exist that, although not specifically part of the data in the accounts, have considerable influence on the understanding and interpretation of financial statements. For example, assume that FedEx Corporation is a defendant in a $100-billion liability lawsuit. Or suppose FedEx Corporation has signed noncancelable lease contracts that will cost $75 billion per year for five years. To inform users properly, the full disclosure principle requires that companies disclose all important financial facts and circumstances, including lawsuits and lease commitments.

Consistency Principle

Accounting reports are prepared on a basis consistent with the preceding period, unless otherwise disclosed. In many instances, more than one method of applying a generally accepted accounting principle is possible. In other words, two firms that have identical operating situations might each choose a different—but equally acceptable—accounting method and report different amounts for the same types of transactions. Changes in accounting methods that lead to different reported values can affect reported income. Such a situation justifies the consistency principle. Consistency means that the same accounting methods are used from one accounting period to the next. Consistency enhances the utility of financial statements when comparative data for a firm are analyzed. Still, it is sometimes appropriate for a firm to change an accounting method. Indeed, progress in improving accounting data almost dictates that some changes will occur. In these cases, financial statement users should know when and to what extent reported income changes due to a change in accounting method.

KEY TERMS

Accounting cycle (p. 88)	Chart of accounts (p. 89)	General journal (p. 89)
Accruals (p. 96)	Closing procedures (p. 108)	Journal (p. 89)
Accrued expense (p. 99)	Compound journal entry (p. 91)	Post-closing trial balance (p. 110)
Accrued revenue (p. 101)	Contra account (p. 97)	Posting (p. 90)
Adjusted trial balance (p. 104)	Deferrals (p. 95)	Straight-line depreciation (p. 97)
Adjusting entries (p. 95)	Deferred revenue (p. 98)	Unadjusted trial balance (p. 94)
Book value (p. 98)	Depreciation (p. 97)	Unearned revenue (p. 98)
Calendar-year (p. 89)	Fiscal year (p. 89)	

MULTIPLE CHOICE

1. A journal entry that contains more than two accounts is called
    a.   a posted journal entry.
    b.   an adjusting journal entry.
    c.   an erroneous journal entry.
    d.   a compound journal entry.

2. Posting refers to the process whereby journal entry information is transferred from
    a.   journal to general ledger accounts.
    b.   general ledger accounts to a journal.
    c.   source documents to a journal.
    d.   a journal to source documents.

3. Which of the following is an example of an adjusting entry?
    a.   Recording the purchase of supplies on account
    b.   Recording depreciation expense on a truck
    c.   Recording cash received from customers for services rendered
    d.   Recording the cash payment of wages to employees

4. An adjusting entry to record utilities expense used during a month for which no cash has yet been paid is an example of
   a. adjusting prepaid assets to reflect expenses incurred during the accounting period.
   b. adjusting unearned revenues to reflect revenues earned during the accounting period.
   c. accruing expenses to reflect expenses incurred during the period that are not yet paid or recorded.
   d. accruing revenues to reflect revenues earned during the period that are not yet received or recorded.

5. Which of the following procedures is part of the closing process?
   a. Close each unearned revenue account to the Income Summary account.
   b. Close each prepaid expense account to the Income Summary account.
   c. Close the Income Summary account to the Retained Earnings account.
   d. Close the Retained Earnings account to the Income Summary account.

Superscript [A] denotes assignments based on Appendix 3A.

DISCUSSION QUESTIONS

Q3-1 What are the five major steps in the accounting cycle? List them in their proper order.

Q3-2 What does the term *fiscal year* mean?

Q3-3 What are three examples of source documents that underlie business transactions?

Q3-4 What is the nature and purpose of a general journal?

Q3-5 Explain the process of posting.

Q3-6 What is a compound journal entry?

Q3-7 What is a chart of accounts? Give an example of a coding system for identifying different types of accounts.

Q3-8 Why is the adjusting step of the accounting cycle necessary?

Q3-9 What four different types of adjustments are frequently necessary at the close of an accounting period? Give examples of each type.

Q3-10 On January 1, Prepaid Insurance was debited with the cost of a two-year premium, $1,872. What adjusting entry should be made on January 31 before financial statements are prepared for the month?

Q3-11 What is a contra account? What contra account is used in reporting the book value of a depreciable asset?

Q3-12 At the beginning of January, the first month of the accounting year, the Supplies account had a debit balance of $825. During January, purchases of $260 worth of supplies were debited to the account. Although only $630 of supplies were still available at the end of January, the necessary adjusting entry was omitted. How will the omission affect (a) the income statement for January, and (b) the balance sheet prepared at January 31?

Q3-13 The publisher of *International View*, a monthly magazine, received two-year subscriptions totaling $9,720 on January 1. (a) What entry should be made to record the receipt of the $9,720? (b) What entry should be made at the end of January before financial statements are prepared for the month?

Q3-14 Globe Travel Agency pays an employee $475 in wages each Friday for the five-day work week ending on that day. The last Friday of January falls on January 27. What adjusting entry should be made on January 31, the fiscal year-end?

Q3-15 The Bayou Company earns interest amounting to $360 per month on its investments. The company receives the interest every six months, on December 31 and June 30. Monthly financial statements are prepared. What adjusting entry should be made on January 31?

Q3-16 Which groups of accounts are closed at the end of the accounting year?

Q3-17 What are the three major steps in the closing process?

Q3-18 What is the purpose of a post-closing trial balance? Which of the following accounts should *not* appear in the post-closing trial balance: Cash; Unearned Revenue; Prepaid Rent; Depreciation Expense; Utilities Payable; Supplies Expense; and Retained Earnings?

Q3-19[A] Dehning Corporation is an international manufacturer of films and industrial identification products. Included among its prepaid expenses is an account titled Prepaid Catalog Costs; in recent years, this account's size has ranged between $2,500,000 and $4,000,000. The company states that catalog costs are initially capitalized and then written off over the estimated useful lives of the publications (generally eight months). Identify and briefly discuss the accounting principles that support Dehning Corporation's handling of its catalog costs.

Q3-20[A]   How would you describe, in one sentence, each of the following accounting principles?

accounting entity	consistency	going concern	measuring unit
accounting period	cost	matching	objectivity
conservatism	full disclosure	materiality	revenue recognition

MINI EXERCISES

M3-21. Journalizing Transactions in Template, Journal Entry Form, and T-Account Forms   (LO2)

Creative Designs, a firm providing art services for advertisers, began business on June 1, 2006. The following accounts in its general ledger are needed to record the transactions for June: Cash; Accounts Receivable; Supplies; Office Equipment; Accounts Payable; Common Stock; Retained Earnings; Service Fees Earned; Rent Expense; Utilities Expense; and Salaries Expense. Record the following transactions for June (a) using the financial statement effects template, and (b) in journal entry form. (c) Set up T-accounts for each of the ledger accounts and post the entries to them (key those numbers in T-accounts by date).

June	1	Anne Clem invested $12,000 cash to begin the business in exchange for common stock.
	2	Paid $950 cash for June rent.
		Purchased $6,400 of office equipment on account.
	6	Purchased $3,800 of art materials and other supplies; paid $1,800 cash with the remainder due within 30 days.
	11	Billed clients $4,700 for services rendered.
	17	Collected $3,250 cash from clients on their accounts.
	19	Paid $3,000 cash toward the account for office equipment firm (see June 3).
	25	Paid $900 cash for dividends.
	30	Paid $350 cash for June utilities.
	30	Paid $2,500 cash for June salaries.

M3-22. Journalizing and Posting Transactions   (LO2)

Minute Maid, a firm providing house cleaning services, began business on April 1, 2006. The following accounts in its general ledger are needed to record the transactions for April: Cash; Accounts Receivable; Supplies; Prepaid Van Lease; Equipment; Notes Payable; Accounts Payable; Common Stock; Retained Earnings; Cleaning Fees Earned; Wages Expense; Advertising Expense; and Van Fuel Expense. Record the following transactions for April (a) using the financial statement effects template, and (b) in journal entry form. (c) Set up T-accounts for each of the ledger accounts and post the entries to them (key those numbers in T-accounts by date).

April	1	A. Falcon invested $9,000 cash to begin the business in exchange for common stock.
	2	Paid $2,850 cash for six months' lease on van for the business.
	3	Borrowed $10,000 cash from bank and signed note payable agreeing to repay it in 1 year plus 10% interest.
	3	Purchased $5,500 of cleaning equipment; paid $2,500 cash with the remainder due within 30 days.
	4	Paid $4,300 cash for cleaning supplies.
	7	Paid $350 cash for advertisements to run in newspaper during April.
	21	Billed customers $3,500 for services performed.
	23	Paid $3,000 cash on account to cleaning equipment firm (see April 3).
	28	Collected $2,300 cash from customers on their accounts.
	29	Paid $1,000 cash for dividends.
	30	Paid $1,750 cash for April wages.
	30	Paid $995 cash to service station for gasoline used during April.

M3-23. Journalizing Transactions and Adjusting Accounts   (LO2, 3)

Deluxe Building Services offers janitorial services on both a contract basis and an hourly basis. On January 1, 2006, Deluxe collected $20,100 in advance on a six-month contract for work to be performed evenly during the next six months.

a.   Prepare the entry on January 1 to record the receipt of $20,100 cash for contract work (1) using the financial statements effect template and (2) in journal entry form.

b.   Prepare the adjusting entry to be made on January 31, 2006 for the contract work done during January (1) using the financial statements effect template and (2) in journal entry form.

c.   At January 31, a total of 30 hours of hourly rate janitor work was unbilled. The billing rate is $19 per hour. Prepare the adjusting entry needed on January 31, 2006 (1) using the financial statements effect template and (2) in journal entry form. (Note: The firm uses the account Fees Receivable to reflect amounts due but not yet billed.)

M3-24.   **Adjusting Accounts**   (LO3)

Selected accounts of Ideal Properties, a real estate management firm, are shown below as of January 31, 2006, before any adjusting entries have been made.

	Debits	Credits
Prepaid Insurance	$6,660	
Supplies	1,930	
Office Equipment	5,952	
Unearned Rent Revenue		$ 5,250
Salaries Expense	3,100	
Rent Revenue		15,000

Monthly financial statements are prepared. Using the following information, record the adjusting entries necessary on January 31 (1) using the financial statements effect template and (2) in journal entry form.

a.   Prepaid Insurance represents a three-year premium paid on January 1, 2006.

b.   Supplies of $850 were still available on January 31.

c.   Office equipment is expected to last eight years.

d.   On January 1, 2006, Ideal Properties collected six months' rent in advance from a tenant renting space for $875 per month.

e.   Accrued salaries of $490 are not recorded as of January 31.

M3-25.   **Inferring transactions from financial statements**   (LO2, 3, 4)

Dick's Sporting
Goods, Inc. (DKS)

Dick's Sporting Goods, Inc., a retailer of sporting goods equipment, apparel, and footwear, operates 234 stores in 33 states. For the year ended January 29, 2005, Dick's purchased merchandise inventory costing $1,363,427 ($ thousands). Assume that all purchases were made on account. The following T-accounts reflect information contained in the company's 2005 and 2004 balance sheets.

+	Inventories (A)	−		−	Accounts Payable (L)	+
2004 Bal. 254,360					118,383	2004 Bal.
	⋮				⋮	
2004 Bal. 457,618					211,685	2005 Bal.

a.   Prepare the entry, using the financial statement effects template and in journal entry form, to record its purchases.

b.   What amount did Dick's pay in cash to its suppliers for fiscal-year 2005? Explain.

c.   Prepare the entry, using the financial statement effects template and in journal entry form, to record cost of goods sold for the year ended January 29, 2005.

M3-26.   **Preparing a Statement of Stockholders' Equity**   (LO4)

On December 31, 2005, the credit balance of the Common Stock and Retained Earnings accounts were $30,000 and $18,000, respectively, for Architect Services Company. Its stock issuances for 2006 totaled $6,000, and it paid $9,700 cash toward dividends in 2006. After revenue and expense accounts were closed at December 31, 2006, the Income Summary account had a credit balance of $29,900. Prepare a 2006 statement of stockholders' equity for Architect Services.

M3-27.   **Applying Closing Procedures**   (LO5)

Assume you are in the process of closing procedures for Echo Corporation. You have already closed all revenue and expense accounts to zero balances, and the Income Summary account shows a single debit entry for $308,800 and a single credit entry for $347,400. The Retained Earnings account has a credit balance of $99,000. Prepare entry(ies) to complete the closing process at December 31, 2006 (1) using the financial statements effect template and (2) in journal entry form.

M3-28.   **Preparing Closing Entries**   (LO5)

The adjusted trial balance at December 31, 2006, for Fontaine Company includes the following selected accounts.

	Debit	Credit
Commissions Earned		$ 84,900
Wages Expense	$ 36,000	
Insurance Expense	1,900	
Utilities Expense	8,200	
Depreciation Expense	9,800	
Retained Earnings		72,100

Prepare entries to close these accounts (a) using the financial statement effects template, and (b) in journal entry form. (c) Set up T-accounts for each of the ledger accounts and post the entries to them. After these entries are posted, what is the balance of the Retained Earnings account?

M3-29. **Inferring Transactions from Financial Statements** (LO2, 3, 4)

Barnes & Noble, Inc., sells books through its Barnes & Noble bookstores and superstores, and through B. Dalton Booksellers, which are located primarily in shopping malls. For the year ended January 29, 2005, Barnes & Noble purchased merchandise inventory at a cost of $2,680,478 ($ thousands). Assume that all purchases were made on account. The following T-accounts reflect information contained in the company's 2005 and 2004 balance sheets.

Barnes & Noble Inc. (BKS)

+			−
Merchandise Inventories (A)			
2004 Bal. 1,289,807			
⋮			
2005 Bal. 1,274,578			

−			+
Accounts Payable (L)			
		639,939	2004 Bal.
		⋮	
		745,073	2005 Bal.

a. Prepare the entry, using the financial statement effects template and in journal entry form, to record its purchases.

b. What amount did Barnes & Noble pay in cash to its suppliers for fiscal-year 2005? Explain.

c. Prepare the entry, using the financial statement effects template and in journal entry form, to record cost of goods sold for the year ended January 29, 2005.

M3-30. **Preparing Entries Across Two Periods** (LO2, 3, 5)

Hatcher Company closes its accounts on December 31 each year. On December 31, 2006, Hatcher accrued $600 of interest income that was earned on an investment but not yet received or recorded (the investment will pay interest of $900 cash on January 31, 2007). On January 31, 2007, the company received the $900 cash as interest on the investment. Prepare entries using both the financial statement effects template and in journal entry form to (a) accrue the interest earned on December 31; (b) close the Interest Income account on December 31 (the account has a year-end balance of $2,400 after adjustments); and (c) record the cash receipt of interest on January 31.

EXERCISES

E3-31. **Closing Entries** (LO5)

The adjusted trial balance as of December 31, 2006, for Doherty Consulting Company contains the following selected accounts.

	Debit	Credit
Service Fees Earned		$ 80,300
Rent Expense	$ 20,800	
Salaries Expense	45,700	
Supplies Expense	5,600	
Depreciation Expense	10,200	
Retained Earnings		67,000

Prepare entries to close these accounts (a) using the financial statement effects template, and (b) in journal entry form. (c) Set up T-accounts for each of the ledger accounts and post the entries to them. After these entries are posted, what is the balance of the Retained Earnings account?

E3-32. **Adjusting Entries** (LO6)

For each of the following separate situations, prepare the necessary adjusting entry accounts (a) using the financial statement effects template, and (b) in journal entry form.

a. Unrecorded depreciation on equipment is $610.

b. The Supplies account has an unadjusted balance of $2,990. Supplies still available at the end of the period total $1,100.

c. On the date for preparing financial statements, an estimated utilities expense of $390 has been incurred, but no utility bill has yet been received or paid.

d. On the first day of the current period, rent for four periods was paid and recorded as a $2,800 debit to Prepaid Rent and a $2,800 credit to Cash.

e. Nine months ago, Hartford Insurance Company sold a one-year policy to a customer and recorded the receipt of the premium by debiting Cash for $624 and crediting Unearned Premium Revenue for

Hartford Insurance Company (HIG)

$624. No adjusting entries have been prepared during the nine-month period. Annual financial statements are now being prepared.

f. At the end of the period, employee wages of $965 have been incurred but not paid or recorded.

g. At the end of the period, $300 of interest has been earned but not yet received or recorded.

E3-33. Preparing Entries Across Two Periods (LO2, 3, 5)

Micron Company closes its accounts on December 31 each year. The company works a five-day work week and pays its employees every two weeks. On December 31, 2006, Micron accrued $4,700 of salaries payable. On January 9, 2007, the company paid salaries of $12,000 cash to employees. Prepare entries using the financial statement effects template and in journal entry form to (a) accrue the salaries payable on December 31; (b) close the Salaries Expense account on December 31 (the account has a year-end balance of $250,000 after adjustments); and (c) record the salary payment on January 9.

E3-34. Financial Analysis using Adjusted Data (LO3)

Selected T-account balances for Clikeman Company are shown below as of January 31, 2007; adjusting entries have already been posted. The firm uses a calendar-year accounting period but prepares *monthly* adjustments.

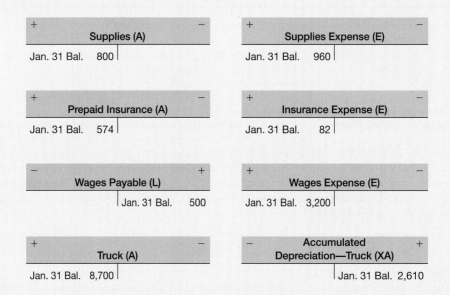

a. If the amount in Supplies Expense represents the January 31 adjustment for the supplies used in January, and $620 worth of supplies were purchased during January, what was the January 1 beginning balance of Supplies?

b. The amount in the Insurance Expense account represents the adjustment made at January 31 for January insurance expense. If the original insurance premium was for one year, what was the amount of the premium and on what date did the insurance policy start?

c. If we assume that no beginning balance existed in Wages Payable or Wages Expense on January 1, how much cash was paid as wages during January?

d. If the truck has a useful life of five years, what is the monthly amount of depreciation expense and how many months has Clikeman owned the truck?

E3-35. Preparing Adjusting Entries (LO3)

Wayne Thomas began Thomas Refinishing Service on July 1, 2006. Selected accounts are shown below as of July 31, before any adjusting entries have been made.

	Debit	Credit
Prepaid Rent	$5,700	
Prepaid Advertising	630	
Supplies	3,000	
Unearned Refinishing Fees		$ 600
Refinishing Fees Revenue		2,500

Using the following information, prepare the adjusting entries necessary on July 31 (1) using the financial statement effects template, and (2) in journal entry form. (3) Set up T-accounts for each of the ledger accounts and post the entries to them.

a. On July 1, the firm paid one year's rent of $5,700 in cash.
b. On July 1, $630 cash was paid to the local newspaper for an advertisement to run daily for the months of July, August, and September.
c. Supplies still available at July 31 total $1,100.
d. At July 31, refinishing services of $800 have been performed but not yet recorded or billed to customers. The firm uses the account Fees Receivable to reflect amounts due but not yet billed.
e. A customer paid $600 in advance for a refinishing project. At July 31, the project is one-half complete.

E3-36. Inferring Transactions from Financial Statements (LO2, 3, 4)

Winnebago Industries manufactures and sells motor homes as well as retail parts and accessories, throughout the United States and Canada. The following information is taken from Winnebago's fiscal 2005 10-K report.

Winnebago
Industries (WGO)

Selected Balance Sheet Data	2005	2004
Inventories	$120,655	$130,733
Accrued Compensation Liability	16,380	21,217

a. Winnebago spent $844,919 to purchase and manufacture inventories for its fiscal year ended 2005. Prepare the entry, using the financial statement effects template and in journal entry form, to record cost of goods sold for its fiscal year ended 2005.
b. Assume that Winnebago reported compensation expense of $175,657 for its fiscal year ended 2005. What amount of compensation was paid to its employees for 2005?

E3-37. Preparing Closing Procedures (LO5)

The adjusted trial balance of Parker Corporation, prepared December 31, 2006, contains the following selected accounts.

	Debit	Credit
Service Fees Earned		$ 92,500
Interest Income		2,200
Salaries Expense	$ 41,800	
Advertising Expense	4,300	
Depreciation Expense	8,700	
Income Tax Expense	9,900	
Retained Earnings		42,700

Prepare entries to close these accounts (a) using the financial statement effects template, and (b) in journal entry form. (c) Set up T-accounts for each of the ledger accounts and post the entries to them. After these entries are posted, what is the balance of the Retained Earnings account?

E3-38. Inferring Transactions from Financial Statements (LO2, 3, 4)

Ethan Allen Interiors, Inc., a leading manufacturer and retailer of home furnishings and accessories, sells products through an exclusive network of 313 retail stores. All of Ethan Allen's products are sold by special order. Customers generally place a deposit equal to 25% to 50% of the purchase price when ordering. Orders take 4 to 12 weeks to be delivered. Selected fiscal-year information from the company's balance sheets is as follows ($ thousands).

Ethan Allen
Interiors (ETH)

Selected Balance Sheet Data	2005	2004
Inventories	$186,479	$186,895
Customer Deposits Liability	53,654	56,026

a. In fiscal 2005, Ethan Allen collected customer deposits equal to $307,684 and reported total sales revenue of $949,012. Prepare entries, using the financial statement effects template and in journal entry form, to record customer deposits and its sales revenue for fiscal year 2005.

b. During fiscal 2005, Ethan Allen purchased or manufactured inventory at a cost of $487,542. Prepare the adjusting entry, using the financial statement effects template and in journal entry form, that it made to record cost of sales.

E3-39. **Preparing Financial Statements and Closing Procedures** (LO4, 5)
The adjusted trial balance for Emig Corporation is as follows.

	Debit	Credit
Emig Corporation		
Adjusted Trial Balance		
December 31, 2006		
Cash	$ 4,000	
Accounts Receivable	6,500	
Equipment	78,000	
Accumulated Depreciation		$ 14,000
Notes Payable		10,000
Common Stock		43,000
Retained Earnings		12,600
Service Fees Earned		71,000
Rent Expense	18,000	
Salaries Expense	37,100	
Depreciation Expense	7,000	
Totals	$158,600	$158,600

(a) Prepare its income statement and statement of stockholders' equity (cash dividends were $8,000 and there were no stock issuances or repurchases) for the current year, and its balance sheet for the current year-end. (b) Prepare entries to close its temporary accounts (1) using the financial statement effects template, and (2) in journal entry form. (c) Set up T-accounts for each of the ledger accounts and post the closing entries to them. After these entries are posted, what is the balance of the Retained Earnings account?

PROBLEMS

P3-40. **Journalizing and Posting Transactions, and Preparing a Trial Balance and Adjustments** (LO2, 3)
Mark Lang opened Lang Roofing Service on April 1, 2006. Transactions for April are as follow:

Apr. 1 Lang contributed $11,500 cash to the business in exchange for common stock.
2 Paid $6,100 cash for the purchase of a used truck.
2 Purchased $3,100 of ladders and other equipment; paid $1,000 cash, with the balance due in 30 days.
3 Paid $2,880 cash for two-year premium toward liability insurance.
5 Purchased $1,200 of supplies on account.
5 Received an advance of $1,800 cash from a customer for roof repairs to be done during April and May.
12 Billed customers $5,500 for roofing services performed.
18 Collected $4,900 cash from customers on their accounts.
29 Paid $675 cash for truck fuel used in April.
30 Paid $100 cash for April newspaper advertising.
30 Paid $2,500 cash for assistants' wages.
30 Billed customers $4,000 for roofing services performed.

Required
a. Set up a general ledger in T-account form for the following accounts: Cash; Accounts Receivable; Supplies; Prepaid Insurance; Trucks; Accumulated Depreciation—Trucks; Equipment; Accumulated Depreciation—Equipment; Accounts Payable; Unearned Roofing Fees; Common Stock; Retained Earnings; Fuel Expense; Advertising Expense; Wages Expense; Insurance Expense; Supplies Expense; Depreciation Expense—Trucks; and Depreciation Expense—Equipment.
b. Record these transactions for April (1) using the financial statement effects template, and (2) in journal entry form. (3) Post these entries to their T-accounts (key numbers in T-accounts by date).
c. Prepare an unadjusted trial balance at April 30, 2006.

d.   Prepare entries to adjust the books for Insurance Expense, Supplies Expense, Depreciation Expense—Trucks, Depreciation Expense—Equipment, and Roofing Fees Earned: (1) using the financial statement effects template, and (2) in journal entry form. Supplies still available on April 30 amount to $400. Depreciation for April was $125 on the truck and $35 on equipment. One-fourth of the roofing fee received in advance was earned by April 30. (3) Post adjusting entries to their T-accounts.

P3-41.   **Preparing an Unadjusted Trial Balance and Adjustments**   (LO3)
Photomake Company, a commercial photography studio, has just completed its first full year of operations on December 31, 2006. General ledger account balances before year-end adjustments follow; no adjusting entries have been made to the accounts at any time during the year. Assume that all balances are normal.

Cash	$ 2,150	Accounts Payable	$ 1,910
Accounts Receivable	3,800	Unearned Photography Fees	2,600
Prepaid Rent	12,600	Common Stock	24,000
Prepaid Insurance	2,970	Photography Fees Earned	34,480
Supplies	4,250	Wages Expense	11,000
Equipment	22,800	Utilities Expense	3,420

An analysis of the firm's records discloses the following.
1.   Photography services of $925 have been rendered, but customers have not yet paid or been billed. The firm uses the account Fees Receivable to reflect amounts due but not yet billed.
2.   Equipment, purchased January 1, 2006, has an estimated life of 10 years.
3.   Utilities expense for December is estimated to be $400, but the bill will not arrive or be paid until January of next year.
4.   The balance in Prepaid Rent represents the amount paid on January 1, 2006, for a 2-year lease on the studio.
5.   In November, customers paid $2,600 cash in advance for photos to be taken for the holiday season. When received, these fees were credited to Unearned Photography Fees. By December 31, all of these fees are earned.
6.   A 3-year insurance premium paid on January 1, 2006, was debited to Prepaid Insurance.
7.   Supplies available at December 31 are $1,520.
8.   At December 31, wages expense of $375 has been incurred but not paid or recorded.

Required
a.   Prove that debits equal credits for Photomake's unadjusted account balances by preparing its unadjusted trial balance at December 31, 2006.
b.   Prepare its adjusting entries: (1) using the financial statement effects template, and (2) in journal entry form.
c.   Set up T-accounts and post adjusting entries to them.

P3-42.   **Preparing Adjusting Entries, Financial Statements, and Closing Entries**   (LO3, 4, 5)
Kattelus Carpet Cleaners ended its first month of operations on June 30, 2006. Monthly financial statements will be prepared. The unadjusted account balances are as follows.

Kattelus Carpet Cleaners
Unadjusted Trial Balance
June 30, 2006

	Debit	Credit
Cash	$ 1,180	
Accounts Receivable	450	
Prepaid Rent	3,100	
Supplies	2,520	
Equipment	4,440	
Accounts Payable		$ 760
Common Stock		2,000
Retained Earnings		5,300
Service Fees Earned		4,650
Wages Expense	1,020	
	$ 12,910	$ 12,910

The following information is also available.
1. The balance in Prepaid Rent was the amount paid on June 1 for the first 4 months' rent.
2. Supplies available at June 30 were $820.
3. Equipment, purchased June 1, has an estimated life of five years.
4. Unpaid and unrecorded wages at June 30 were $210.
5. Utility services used during June were estimated at $300. A bill is expected early in July.
6. Fees earned for services performed but not yet billed on June 30 were $380. It uses the account Fees Receivable to reflect amounts due but not yet billed.

Required
a. Prepare its adjusting entries at June 30, 2006: (1) using the financial statement effects template, and (2) in journal entry form.
b. Set up T-accounts and post the adjusting entries to them.
c. Prepare its income statement for June and its balance sheet at June 30, 2006.
d. Prepare entries to close its temporary accounts (1) using the financial statement effects template, and (2) in journal entry form. Post the closing entries to the T-accounts.

P3-43. **Preparing Adjusting Entries** (LO3)
The following information relates to December 31 adjustments for Kwik Print Company. The firm's fiscal year ends on December 31.
1. Weekly salaries for a five-day week total $1,800, payable on Fridays. December 31 of the current year is a Tuesday.
2. Kwik Print has $20,000 of notes payable outstanding at December 31. Interest of $200 has accrued on these notes by December 31, but will not be paid until the notes mature next year.
3. During December, Kwik Print provided $900 of printing services to clients who will be billed on January 2. The firm uses the account Fees Receivable to reflect amounts due but not yet billed.
4. Starting December 1, all maintenance work on Kwik Print's equipment is handled by Richardson Repair Company under an agreement whereby Kwik Print pays a fixed monthly charge of $400. Kwik Print paid six months' service charge in advance on December 1, debiting Prepaid Maintenance for $2,400.
5. The firm paid $900 on December 15 for a series of radio commercials to run during December and January. One-third of the commercials have aired by December 31. The $900 payment was debited to Prepaid Advertising.
6. Starting December 16, Kwik Print rented 400 square feet of storage space from a neighboring business. The monthly rent of $0.80 per square foot is due in advance on the first of each month. Nothing was paid in December, however, because the neighbor agreed to add the rent for one-half of December to the January 1 payment.
7. Kwik Print invested $5,000 in securities on December 1 and earned interest of $38 on these securities by December 31. No interest will be received until January.
8. Annual depreciation on the firm's equipment is $2,175. No depreciation has been recorded during the year.

Required
Prepare its adjusting entries required at December 31: (1) using the financial statement effects template, and (2) in journal entry form.

P3-44. **Preparing Financial Statements and Closing Entries** (LO4, 5)
The following adjusted trial balance is for Trueman Consulting at December 31, 2006. The company had stock issuances or repurchases during 2006.

	Debit	Credit
Cash	$ 2,700	
Accounts Receivable	3,270	
Supplies	3,060	
Prepaid Insurance	1,500	
Equipment	6,400	
Accumulated Depreciation—Equipment		$ 1,080
Accounts Payable		845
Long-Term Notes Payable		7,000
Common Stock		1,000
Retained Earnings		3,305
Service Fees Earned		58,400

continued

	Debit	Credit
Rent Expense	12,000	
Salaries Expense	33,400	
Supplies Expense	4,700	
Insurance Expense	3,250	
Depreciation Expense—Equipment	720	
Interest Expense	630	
	$ 74,530	$ 74,530

Required

a. Prepare its income statement and statement of stockholders' equity for 2006 and its balance sheet at December 31, 2006.

b. Prepare entries to close its accounts (1) using the financial statement effects template, and (2) in journal entry form.

P3-45. **Preparing Closing Entries** (LO5)

The following adjusted trial balance is for Bayou Company at December 31, 2006.

	Debit	Credit
Cash	$ 3,500	
Accounts Receivable	8,000	
Prepaid Insurance	3,600	
Equipment	72,000	
Accumulated Depreciation		$ 12,000
Accounts Payable		600
Common Stock		30,000
Retained Earnings		19,100
Service Fees Earned		97,200
Miscellaneous Income		4,200
Salaries Expense	42,800	
Rent Expense	13,400	
Insurance Expense	1,800	
Depreciation Expense	8,000	
Income Tax Expense	8,800	
Income Tax Payable		$ 8,800
	$166,900	$166,900

Required

a. Prepare closing entries (1) using the financial statement effects template, and (2) in journal entry form.

b. After its closing entries are posted, what is the balance for the Retained Earnings account?

c. Prepare its post-closing trial balance.

P3-46. **Preparing Entries Across Two Periods** (LO2, 3, 5)

The following selected accounts appear in Shaw Company's unadjusted trial balance at December 31, 2006, the end of its fiscal year (all accounts have normal balances).

Prepaid Advertising	$ 1,200	Unearned Service Fees	$ 5,400
Wages Expense	43,800	Service Fees Earned	87,000
Prepaid Insurance	3,420	Rental Income	4,900

Required

a. Prepare its adjusting entries at December 31, 2006, (1) using the financial statement effects template, and (2) in journal entry form. Additional information is as follows.

  1. Prepaid advertising at December 31 is $800.
  2. Unpaid wages earned by employees in December are $1,300.
  3. Prepaid insurance at December 31 is $2,280.
  4. Unearned service fees at December 31 are $3,000.

5.   Rent revenue of $1,000 owed by a tenant is not recorded at December 31.
b.   Prepare entries on January 4, 2007, using the financial statement effects template and in journal entry form, to record (1) payment of $2,400 cash in wages and (2) cash receipt from the tenant of the $1,000 rent revenue.

P3-47.   Journalizing and Posting Transactions, and Preparing a Trial Balance and Adjustments   (LO2, 3)
Market-Probe, a market research firm, had the following transactions in June 2007, its first month of operations.

June 1   B. May invested $24,000 cash in the firm in exchange for common stock.
1   The firm purchased the following: office equipment, $11,040; office supplies, $2,840. Terms are $4,400 cash with the remainder due in 60 days. (Make a compound entry.)
2   Paid $875 cash for June rent.
2   Contracted for 3 months' advertising in a local newspaper at $310 per month and paid for the advertising in advance.
2   Signed a 6-month contract with a customer to provide research consulting services at a rate of $3,200 per month. Received two months' fees in advance. Work on the contract started immediately.
10   Billed various customers $5,800 for services rendered.
12   Paid $3,600 cash for two weeks' salaries (5-day week) to employees.
15   Paid $1,240 cash to employee for travel expenses to conference.
18   Paid $520 cash to post office for bulk mailing of research questionnaire (postage expense).
26   Paid $3,600 cash for two weeks' salaries to employees.
28   Billed various customers $5,200 for services rendered.
30   Collected $7,800 cash from customers on their accounts.
30   Paid $1,500 cash for dividends.

Required
a.   Set up a general ledger in T-account form for the following accounts: Cash; Accounts Receivable; Office Supplies; Prepaid Advertising; Office Equipment; Accumulated Depreciation—Office Equipment; Accounts Payable; Salaries Payable; Unearned Service Fees; Common Stock; Retained Earnings; Service Fees Earned; Salaries Expense; Advertising Expense; Supplies Expense; Rent Expense; Travel Expense; Depreciation Expense—Office Equipment; and Postage Expense.
b.   Record these transactions (1) using the financial statement effects template, and (2) in journal entry form. (3) Post these entries to their T-accounts (key numbers in T-accounts by date).
c.   Prepare an unadjusted trial balance at June 30, 2007.
d.   Prepare adjusting entries (1) using the financial statement effects template and (2) in journal entry form, that reflect the following information at June 30, 2007:
Office supplies available, $1,530
Accrued salaries, $725
Estimated life of office equipment is 8 years
Adjusting entries must also be prepared for advertising and service fees per the June transactions. (3) Post adjusting entries to their T-accounts.

P3-48.   Preparing an Unadjusted Trial Balance and Adjustments   (LO3)
DeliverAll, a mailing service, has just completed its first full year of operations on December 31, 2006. Its general ledger account balances before year-end adjustments follow; no adjusting entries have been made to the accounts at any time during the year. Assume that all balances are normal.

Cash	$ 2,300	Accounts Payable	$ 2,700
Accounts Receivable	5,120	Common Stock	9,530
Prepaid Advertising	1,680	Mailing Fees Earned	86,000
Supplies	6,270	Wages Expense	38,800
Equipment	42,240	Rent Expense	6,300
Notes Payable	7,500	Utilities Expense	3,020

An analysis of the firm's records reveals the following.
1.   The balance in Prepaid Advertising represents the amount paid for newspaper advertising for 1 year. The agreement, which calls for the same amount of space each month, covers the period from February 1, 2006, to January 31, 2007. DeliverAll did not advertise during its first month of operations.
2.   Equipment, purchased January 1, has an estimated life of eight years.

3. Utilities expense does not include expense for December, estimated at $325. The bill will not arrive until January 2007.
4. At year-end, employees have earned $1,200 in wages that will not be paid or recorded until January.
5. Supplies available at year-end amounted to $1,520.
6. At year-end, unpaid interest of $450 has accrued on the notes payable.
7. The firm's lease calls for rent of $525 per month payable on the first of each month, plus an amount equal to 1/2% of annual mailing fees earned. The rental percentage is payable within 15 days after the end of the year.

Required

a. Prove that debits equal credits for its unadjusted account balances by preparing its unadjusted trial balance at December 31, 2006.
b. Prepare its adjusting entries: (1) using the financial statement effects template, and (2) in journal entry form.
c. Set up T-accounts and post adjusting entries to them.

P3-49. Preparing Adjusting Entries (LO3)

Wheel Place Company began operations on March 1, 2006, to provide automotive wheel alignment and balancing services. On March 31, 2006, the unadjusted balances of the firm's accounts are as follows.

Wheel Place Company Unadjusted Trial Balance March 31, 2006		
	Debit	**Credit**
Cash	$ 1,900	
Accounts Receivable	3,820	
Prepaid Rent	4,770	
Supplies	3,700	
Equipment	36,180	
Accounts Payable		$ 2,510
Unearned Service Revenue		1,000
Common Stock		38,400
Service Revenue		12,360
Wages Expense	3,900	
	$ 54,270	$ 54,270

The following information is also available.

1. The balance in Prepaid Rent was the amount paid on March 1 to cover the first 6 months' rent.
2. Supplies available on March 31 amounted to $1,720.
3. Equipment has an estimated life of nine years.
4. Unpaid wages at March 31 were $560.
5. Utility services used during March were estimated at $390; a bill is expected early in April.
6. The balance in Unearned Service Revenue was the amount received on March 1 from a car dealer to cover alignment and balancing services on cars sold by the dealer in March and April. The Wheel Place agreed to provide the services at a fixed fee of $500 each month.

Required

a. Prepare its adjusting entries at March 31, 2006 (1) using the financial statement effects template, and (2) in journal entry form.
b. Set up T-accounts and post the adjusting entries to them.
c. Prepare its income statement for March and its balance sheet at March 31, 2006.
d. Prepare entries to close its temporary accounts (1) using the financial statement effects template, and (2) in journal entry form. Post the closing entries to the T-accounts.

P3-50. Preparing Financial Statements and Closing Entries (LO4, 5)

Trails, Inc., publishes magazines for skiers and hikers. The firm has the following adjusted trial balance at December 31, 2006.

	Debit	Credit
Cash	$ 3,400	
Accounts Receivable	8,600	
Supplies	4,200	
Prepaid Insurance	930	
Office Equipment	66,000	
Accumulated Depreciation		$ 11,000
Accounts Payable		2,100
Unearned Subscription Revenue	10,000	
Salaries Payable	3,500	
Common Stock		25,000
Retained Earnings		23,220
Subscription Revenue		168,300
Advertising Revenue		49,700
Salaries Expense	100,230	
Printing and Mailing Expense	85,600	
Rent Expense	8,800	
Supplies Expense	6,100	
Insurance Expense	1,860	
Depreciation Expense	5,500	
Income Tax Expense	1,600	
	$292,820	$292,820

Required

a. Prepare its income statement and statement of stockholders' equity for 2006, and its balance sheet at December 31, 2006.

b. Prepare entries to close its accounts (1) using the financial statement effects template, and (2) in journal entry form.

P3-51. Preparing Closing Entries (LO3)

The following adjusted trial balance is for Okay Moving Service at December 31, 2006.

	Debit	Credit
Cash	$ 3,800	
Accounts Receivable	5,250	
Supplies	2,300	
Prepaid Advertising	3,000	
Trucks	28,300	
Accumulated Depreciation—Trucks		$ 10,000
Equipment	7,600	
Accumulated Depreciation—Equipment		2,100
Accounts Payable		1,200
Unearned Service Fees		2,700
Common Stock		5,000
Retained Earnings		15,550
Service Fees Earned		72,500
Wages Expense	29,800	
Rent Expense	10,200	
Insurance Expense	2,900	
Supplies Expense	5,100	
Advertising Expense	6,000	
Depreciation Expense—Trucks	4,000	
Depreciation Expense—Equipment	800	
	$109,050	$109,050

Required

a.   Prepare closing entries (1) using the financial statement effects template, and (2) in journal entry form.

b.   After its closing entries are posted, what is the balance for the Retained Earnings account?

c.   Prepare its post-closing trial balance.

P3-52.   Preparing Entries Across Two Periods   (LO2, 3, 5)

The following selected accounts appear in Marcinko Company's unadjusted trial balance at December 31, 2006, the end of its fiscal year (all accounts have normal balances).

Prepaid Maintenance	$2,700	Commission Fees Earned ...	$84,000
Supplies	8,400	Rent Expense	10,800
Unearned Commission Fees ..	8,500		

Required

a.   Prepare its adjusting entries at December 31, 2006 (1) using the financial statement effects template, and (2) in journal entry form. Additional information is as follows.

   1.   On September 1, 2006, the company entered into a prepaid equipment maintenance contract. Marcinko Company paid $2,700 to cover maintenance service for 6 months, beginning September 1, 2006. The $2,700 payment was debited to Prepaid Maintenance.

   2.   Supplies available on December 31 are $3,200.

   3.   Unearned commission fees at December 31 are $4,000.

   4.   Commission fees earned but not yet billed at December 31 are $2,800. (*Note:* Debit Fees Receivable.)

   5.   Marcinko Company's lease calls for rent of $900 per month payable on the first of each month, plus an annual amount equal to 1% of annual commissions earned. This additional rent is payable on January 10 of the following year. (*Note:* Use the adjusted amount of commissions earned in computing the additional rent.)

b.   Prepare entries on January 10, 2007, using both the financial statement effects template and in journal entry form, to record (1) the billing of $4,600 in commissions earned (includes the $2,800 of commissions earned but not billed at December 31) and (2) the cash payment of the additional rent owed for 2006.

P3-53.   Preparing Adjusting Entries, Financial Statements, and Closing Entries   (LO3, 4, 5)

Wilkinson Card Shop is a small retail shop. Wilkinson's balance sheet at year-end 2006 is as follows. The following information details transactions and adjustments that occurred during 2007.

   1.   Sales total $145,850 in 2007; all sales were cash sales.

   2.   Inventory purchases total $76,200 in 2007; at December 31, 2007, inventory totals $14,500.

   3.   Accounts payable totals $4,100 at December 31, 2007.

   4.   Annual store rent for 2007 totals $24,000 and was paid on March 1, 2007, covering the next 12 months. The balance in prepaid rent at December 31, 2006, was the balance remaining from the advance rent payment in 2006.

   5.   Wages are paid every other week on Friday; during 2007, Wilkinson paid $12,500 cash for wages. At December 31, 2007 (a Wednesday), Wilkinson owed employees unpaid and unrecorded wages of $350.

   6.   Depreciation on equipment totals $1,700 in 2007.

Wilkinson Card Shop **Balance Sheet** **December 31, 2006**	
Cash	$ 8,500
Inventories	12,000
Prepaid rent	3,800
Total current assets	24,300
Equipment	7,500
Less accumulated depreciation	(3,000)
Equipment, net	4,500
Total Assets	$ 28,800
Accounts payable	$ 5,200
Wages payable	100
Total liabilities	5,300
Total equity	23,500
Total liabilities and equity	$ 28,800

Required

a. Prepare any necessary adjusting entries at December 31, 2007 (1) using the financial statement effects template, and (2) in journal entry form.

b. Set up T-accounts and post the adjusting entries to them.

c. Prepare its income statement for 2007, and its balance sheet at December 31, 2007.

d. Prepare entries to close its temporary accounts (1) using the financial statement effects template, and (2) in journal entry form. Post the closing entries to the T-accounts.

PC3-54. Applying the Entire Accounting Cycle (LO2, 3, 4, 5, 6)

Howe Tax Services began business on December 1, 2006. Its December transactions are as follows.

Dec. 1 Howe invested $20,000 in the business in exchange for common stock.

2 Paid $1,200 cash for December rent to Star Realty.

2 Purchased $1,080 of supplies on account.

3 Purchased $9,500 of office equipment; paying $4,700 cash with the balance due in 30 days.

8 Paid $1,080 cash on account for supplies purchased December 2.

14 Paid $900 cash for assistant's wages for 2 weeks' work.

20 Performed consulting services for $3,000 cash.

28 Paid $900 cash for assistant's wages for 2 weeks' work.

30 Billed clients $7,200 for December consulting services.

31 Paid $1,800 cash for dividends.

Required

a. Set up a general ledger in T-account form for the following accounts: Cash; Accounts Receivable; Fees Receivable; Supplies; Office Equipment; Accumulated Depreciation—Office Equipment; Accounts Payable; Wages Payable; Common Stock; Retained Earnings; Income Summary; Consulting Revenue; Supplies Expense; Wages Expense; Rent Expense; and Depreciation Expense.

b. Record these transactions (1) using the financial statement effects template, and (2) in journal entry form. (3) Post these entries to their T-accounts (key numbers in T-accounts by date).

c. Prepare an unadjusted trial balance at December 31, 2006.

d. Journalize the adjusting entries at December 31 (using both the financial statement effects template and journal entry form), drawing on the following information.

1. Supplies available at December 31 are $710.

2. Accrued wages payable at December 31 are $270.

3. Depreciation for December is $120.

4. Howe has spent 30 hours on an involved tax fraud case during December. When completed in January, his work will be billed at $75 per hour. (*Note*: It uses the account Fees Receivable to reflect amounts earned but not yet billed.)

Then post adjusting entries to their T-accounts.

e. Prepare an adjusted trial balance at December 31, 2006.

f. Prepare a December 2006 income statement and statement of stockholders' equity, and a December 31, 2006, balance sheet.

g. Record its closing entries (1) using the financial statement effects template and (2) in journal entry form. Post these entries to their T-accounts.

h. Prepare a post-closing trial balance at December 31, 2006.

CASES AND PROJECTS

C3-55. Preparing Adjusting Entries, Financial Statements, and Closing Entries (LO3, 4, 5)

Seaside Surf Shop began operations on July 1, 2006, with an initial investment of $50,000. During the initial 3 months of operations, the following cash transactions were recorded in the firm's checking account.

Deposits	
Initial investment by owner . . .	$ 50,000
Collected from customers	81,000
Borrowed from bank	10,000
	$141,000

continued

Checks drawn	
Rent	$ 24,000
Fixtures and equipment	25,000
Merchandise inventory	62,000
Salaries	6,000
Other expenses	13,000
	$130,000

Additional information

a.   Most sales were for cash, however, the store accepted a limited amount of credit sales; at September 30, 2006, customers owed the store $9,000.

b.   Rent was paid on July 1 for six months.

c.   Salaries of $3,000 per month are paid on the 1st of each month for salaries earned in the month prior.

d.   Inventories are purchased for cash; at September 30, 2006, inventory worth $21,000 was available.

e.   Fixtures and equipment were expected to last five years with zero salvage value.

f.   The bank charges 12% annual interest (1% per month) on its bank loan.

Required

a.   Prepare any necessary adjusting entries at September 30, 2006 (1) using the financial statement effects template, and (2) in journal entry form.

b.   Set up T-accounts and post the adjusting entries to them.

c.   Prepare its income statement for 2007 and its balance sheet at December 31, 2007.

d.   Analyze the statements from part *c* and assess the company's performance over its initial 3 months.

C3-56.   Analyzing Transactions, Impacts on Financial Ratios, and Loan Covenants   (LO2, 3)
Wyland Consulting, a firm started three years ago by Reyna Wyland, offers consulting services for material handling and plant layout. Its balance sheet at the close of 2006 is as follows.

Wyland Consulting Balance Sheet December 31, 2006				
Assets			**Liabilities**	
Cash		$ 3,400	Notes Payable	$30,000
Accounts Receivable . .		22,875	Accounts Payable	4,200
Supplies		13,200	Unearned Consulting Fees . . .	11,300
Prepaid Insurance		4,500	Wages Payable	400
Equipment	$68,500		Total Liabilities	45,900
Less: Accumulated			**Equity**	
Depreciation	23,975	44,525	Common Stock	8,000
Total Assets		$88,500	Retained Earnings	34,600
			Total liabilities and Equity	$88,500

Earlier in the year Wyland obtained a bank loan of $30,000 cash for the firm. One of the provisions of the loan is that the year-end debt-to-equity ratio (ratio of total liabilities to total equity) cannot exceed 1.0. Based on the above balance sheet, the ratio at the end of 2006 is 1.08. Wyland is concerned about being in violation of the loan agreement and requests assistance in reviewing the situation. Wyland believes that she might have overlooked some items at year-end. Discussions with Wyland reveal the following.

1.   On January 1, 2006, the firm paid a $4,500 insurance premium for 2 years of coverage; the amount in Prepaid Insurance has not yet been adjusted.

2.   Depreciation on the equipment should be 10% of cost per year; the company inadvertently recorded 15% for 2006.

3.   Interest on the bank loan has been paid through the end of 2006.

4. The firm concluded a major consulting engagement in December, doing a plant layout analysis for a new factory. The $6,000 fee has not been billed or recorded in the accounts.

5. On December 1, 2006, the firm received an $11,300 advance payment from Croy Corporation for consulting services to be rendered over a 2-month period. This payment was credited to the Unearned Consulting Fees account. One-half of this fee was earned by December 31, 2006.

6. Supplies costing $4,800 were available on December 31; the company has made no entry in the accounts.

Required

a. What is the correct debt-to-equity ratio at December 31, 2006?

b. Is the firm in violation of its loan agreement? Prepare computations to support the correct total liabilities and total equity figures at December 31, 2006.

C3-57.   **Ethics, Accounting Adjustments, and Auditors   (LO2, 3)**

It is the end of the accounting year for Juliet Javetz, controller of a medium-sized, publicly held corporation specializing in toxic waste cleanup. Within the corporation, only Javetz and the president know that the firm has been negotiating for several months to land a large contract for waste cleanup in Western Europe. The president has hired another firm with excellent contacts in Western Europe to help with negotiations. The outside firm will charge an hourly fee plus expenses, but has agreed not to submit a bill until the negotiations are in their final stages (expected to occur in another 3 to 4 months). Even if the contract falls through, the outside firm is entitled to receive payment for its services. Based upon her discussion with a member of the outside firm, Javetz knows that its charge for services provided to date will be $150,000. This is a material amount for the company.

Javetz knows that the president wants negotiations to remain as secret as possible so that competitors will not learn of the contract the company is pursuing in Europe. In fact, the president recently stated to her, "This is not the time to reveal our actions in Western Europe to other staff members, our auditors, or the readers of our financial statements; securing this contract is crucial to our future growth." No entry has been made in the accounting records for the cost of contract negotiations. Javetz now faces an uncomfortable situation. The company's outside auditor has just asked her if she knows of any year-end adjustments that have not yet been recorded.

Required

a. What are the ethical considerations that Javetz faces in answering the auditor's question?

b. How should Javetz respond to the auditor's question?

C3-58.   **Inferring Adjusting Entries from Financial Statements   (LO2, 3, 4)**

J. Jill Group (JILL)

J. Jill Group, Inc., a specialty retailer of women's apparel, markets its products through retail stores and catalogs. Selected information from its 2004 and 2003 balance sheets is as follows ($ thousands).

Selected Balance Sheet Data	2004	2003
Prepaid catalog costs asset	$ 3,894	$ 4,106
Advertising credits receivable	21	123
Unearned gift certificate revenue	6,108	4,698

The following excerpts are from J. Jill's 2004 10-K report.

Catalog costs in our direct segment are considered direct response advertising and as such are capitalized as incurred and amortized over the expected sales life of each catalog, which is generally a period not exceeding six months.

The Company periodically enters into arrangements with certain national magazine publishers whereby the Company includes magazine subscription cards in its catalog mailings in exchange for advertising credits or discounts on advertising.

Required

a. Assume that J. Jill spent $62,550 to design, print, and mail catalogs in 2004. Also assume that it received advertising credits of $849. Prepare the entry, using the financial statement effects template and in journal entry form, that J. Jill would have recorded when these costs were incurred.

b. Prepare the adjusting entry, using the financial statement effects template and in journal entry form, that would be necessary to record its amortization of prepaid catalog costs.

c. How do advertising credits expire? Prepare the adjusting entry, using both the financial statement effects template and in journal entry form, that J. Jill would record to reflect expired advertising credits.

d.   Assume that J. Jill sold gift certificates valued at $19,175 in 2004. Prepare the entry, using the financial statement effects template and in journal entry form, that J. Jill would make to record these sales. Next, prepare the entry, using the financial statement effects template and in journal entry form, that it make to record merchandise sales to customers who pay with gift certificates.

C3-59.   **Reviewing the Accounting Cycle and Preparing Financial Statements**   (LO2, 3, 4, 5)

Pacific
Sunwear (PSUN)

Pacific Sunwear of California is a specialty retailer of casual apparel, accessories, and footwear for teens and young adults. The company operates a total of 1,005 retail stores in 50 states and Puerto Rico under the names "Pacific Sunwear," "PacSun," and "d.e.m.o." Pacific Sunwear's balance sheet is as follows.

Pacific Sunwear of California, Inc.
Consolidated Balance Sheet
January 31, 2004

($ thousands)

ASSETS

Cash and cash equivalents	$109,640
Short-term investments	66,235
Accounts receivable	5,194
Merchandise inventories	147,751
Prepaid rent	10,711
Other prepaid expenses	5,781
Total current assets	345,312
Net property and equipment	272,869
Goodwill	6,492
Other assets	11,589
Total assets	$636,262

LIABILITIES AND SHAREHOLDERS' EQUITY

Accounts payable	$ 38,668
Accrued compensation and benefits	27,660
Unearned gift card revenue	4,618
Income taxes payable	15,019
Short-term debt and other current liabilities	22,688
Current portion of long-term debt	1,886
Total current liabilities	110,539
Long-term debt, net of current portion	1,455
Deferred rent and lease incentives	81,321
Deferred compensation and other	10,925
Deferred income taxes, net	3,290
Total liabilities	207,530
Common stock	139,661
Retained earnings	289,071
Total shareholders' equity	428,732
Total liabilities and shareholders' equity	$636,262

The following list of transactions for the period starting February 1, 2004, and ending January 29, 2005, are consistent with information provided in Pacific Sunwear's 10-K report ($ thousands).

1.   Cash sales totaled $1,111,600; credit sales totaled $74,350.
2.   Collections on accounts receivable totaled $71,415.
3.   Sales of gift cards amounted to $49,580; gift card sales are not recognized as revenue until the cards are redeemed for merchandise.
4.   Purchased merchandise inventory for $642,305; all merchandise was purchased on account.
5.   Payments on accounts receivable amounted to $642,220.
6.   Opened 118 new stores; all store space is rented. Received cash incentives for store design and improvements of $13,188 from landlords; these incentives are recorded as deferred lease incentives.
7.   Paid rent of $143,165; record as prepaid rent.

8. Paid insurance premiums and license fees of $11,737; recorded as other prepaid expenses.
9. Paid maintenance and utilities costs totaling $15,402.
10. Purchased property and equipment for $86,730; of this amount, $4,084 was financed with short-term debt and $654 was financed with long-term debt, and the remainder was paid in cash.
11. Disposed of property and equipment, recognizing a loss of $3,692.
12. Payments on short-term debt and other current liabilities totaled $10,557.
13. Payments on long-term debt, including the current portion of long-term debt, totaled $2,056.
14. Paid interest expense of $142.
15. Cash invested in other assets totaled $2,657.
16. Purchased short-term investments for $12,988.
17. Received interest on investments of $2,031.
18. Paid advertising costs of $11,400.
19. Paid compensation and benefits of $213,912; this payment included the amount owed under accrued compensation and benefits on January 31, 2004.
20. Paid income taxes of $15,019 for 2002 and, in addition, made estimated tax payments of $52,297 for 2003.
21. During 2003, the company repurchased some of its outstanding common stock; some of the shares were reissued, while the remaining shares were retired. These transactions resulted in a decrease to common stock of $77,602.

Required

a. Set up a general ledger in T-account form for the accounts listed in Pacific Sunwear's balance sheet and record each account's opening balance as of January 31, 2004.
b. Record each of these transactions (1) using the financial statement effects template, and (2) in journal entry form. (3) Post these entries to their T-accounts (key numbers in T-accounts by transaction number). Open new accounts as needed.
c. Prepare an unadjusted trial balance as of January 29, 2005.
d. Journalize its adjusting entries at January 29 (using both the financial statement effects template and journal entry form), drawing on the following information.

1. Gift cards worth $43,812 were redeemed for merchandise during the year.
2. Merchandise inventory on hand at January 29, 2005 was valued at $175,081.
3. The balance in prepaid rent was $12,476 on January 29, 2005.
4. The balance in other prepaid expenses was $7,467.
5. Depreciation expense was $51,685.
6. Deferred compensation increased by $2,465. The balance in accrued compensation and benefits was $22,427 on January 29, 2005.
7. Total income tax expense for 2004 was determined to be $64,998, of which $6,708 was recorded as deferred income taxes.
8. Long-term debt of $1,536 was reclassified as the current portion of long-term debt.
Then post adjusting entries to their T-accounts.

e. Prepare an adjusted trial balance at January 29, 2005.
f. Prepare its income statement for the year ended January 29, 2005, and its balance sheet as of January 29, 2005.
g. Record its closing entries (1) using the financial statement effects template, and (2) in journal entry form. Post these entries to their T-accounts.
h. Prepare its post-closing trial balance at January 29, 2005.

CHAPTER 4

Reporting Cash Flows

LEARNING OBJECTIVES

After completing the chapter, you should be able to:

LO1 Explain the framework and usefulness of the statement of cash flows. (p. 145)

LO2 Construct the net operating cash flows section of the statement of cash flows. (p. 149)

LO3 Prepare the investing and financing sections of the statement of cash flows. (p. 156)

LO4 Compute and interpret ratios that reflect on a company's ability to satisfy its current liabilities and remain solvent. (p. 162)

LO5 Compute and interpret free cash flow. (p. 163)

STARBUCKS

Premiums in Coffee

Starbucks Corporation is the leading retailer, roaster, and brander of specialty coffee in the world. It has nearly 10,000 retail locations in North America, Latin America, Europe, the Middle East, and the Pacific Rim. Starbucks sells high quality coffee and the "Starbucks Experience." It also produces and sells bottled Frappuccino® coffee drinks, Starbucks DoubleShot™ coffee drink, and a line of superpremium ice creams through its joint venture partnerships. Its Tazo Tea's line of premium teas and Hear Music's compact discs further add to its product offerings. Seattle's Best Coffee® and Torrefazione Italia® Coffee brands also help Starbucks appeal to a broader consumer base.

Starbucks' fiscal year 2005 resulted in $6.369 billion in total net revenues, a 20% year-over-year growth, and $494.467 million in net income, a 24% year-over-year growth. It also reported an 8% comparable store sales growth, which represents the 14th consecutive year of 5% or greater growth. Recently, Starbucks was recognized by *Fortune* magazine as number 8 on its list of America's Most Admired Companies and number 34 in its ranking of 100 Best Companies to Work For. Starbucks was also listed among *Business Ethics* magazine's 100 Best Corporate Citizens.

Product lines of the major U.S. brewed coffee sellers are well defined. On the high end there is Starbucks, with 7,302 U.S. locations. It has made its expensive cappuccinos, frappuccinos, espressos, and lattes part of the common lexicon. On the other end, there is **Dunkin' Donuts**, with approximately 4,400 stores in the U.S. Dunkin' Donuts is the largest seller of regular, nonflavored brewed coffee in the U.S. fast-food outlets. It has an estimated 17% market share, compared with an estimated 15% for **McDonald's Corporation** and 6% for Starbucks.

The Wall Street Journal recently reported that "there's a new brew-haha in Latte-land . . . Starbucks increasingly is looking for growth by opening stores in blue-collar communities where Dunkin' Donuts would typically dominate . . . At the same time, Dunkin' Donuts, a unit of United Kingdom spirits group **Allied Domecq PLC**, wants to lure Starbucks' well-heeled customers with a line of Italian brews that it claims it can deliver faster, cheaper, and simpler."

Although competition exists, Starbucks' recent 2005 performance is difficult to top. In the last 12 years, Starbucks' sales have increased from $285 million to over $6 billion and its income has increased from $29 million to nearly $500 million. It currently ranks among the 500 largest companies in assets and profits, and in the top 200 in revenues and market value. Starbucks ranks sixth

(Continued on next page)   **143**

(Continued from previous page)

in earnings-per-share growth over the last ten years. Since its IPO in 1992, its shares have risen by an eye-popping 3,500% (as of late 2005).

During this same period of time, Starbucks' net income and operating cash flows have increased by over twenty-fold each. This information is graphically portrayed as follows:

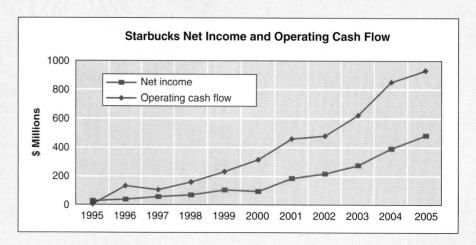

Both net income and operating cash flows are important in assessing the financial health of a company and its value. Starbucks is generating much more cash than it is reporting in income. Why is this? What does it mean? In this chapter, we describe the process of constructing the statement of cash flows. We also describe how we can use and interpret the statement of cash flows to aid both internal and external decisions makers.

Sources: Ball and Leung, "Latte Versus Latte—Starbucks, Dunkin' Donuts Seek Growth by Capturing Each Other's Customers," *The Wall Street Journal* 9 September 2005, *Fortune* 18 April 2005; Starbucks 2005, 2004 and 2003 *Annual Reports* and *10-K Reports*; Starbucks Website, *The Wall Street Journal* February 2004.

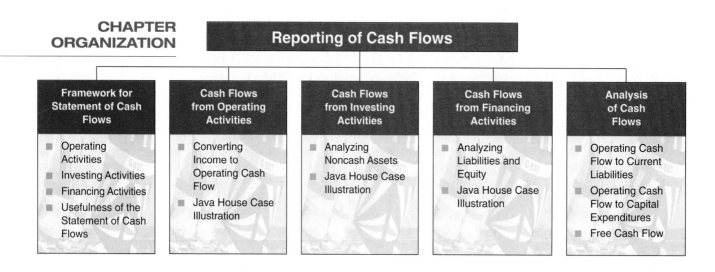

INTRODUCTION

The **statement of cash flows** is a financial statement that summarizes information about the flow of cash into and out of a company. In this chapter, we discuss the preparation, analysis, and interpretation of the statement of cash flows.

The statement of cash flows complements the balance sheet and the income statement. The balance sheet reports the company's financial position at a point in time (the end of each period) whereas the statement of cash flows explains the change in one of its components—cash—from one balance sheet date to the next. The income statement reveals the results of the company's operating activities for the period, and these operating activities are a major contributor to the change in cash as reported in the statement of cash flows.

The statement of cash flows explains the change in a firm's cash *and* cash equivalents. **Cash equivalents** are short-term, highly liquid investments that are (1) easily convertible into a known cash amount and (2) close enough to maturity that their market value is not sensitive to interest rate changes (generally, investments with initial maturities of three months or less). Treasury bills, commercial paper (short-term notes issued by corporations), and money market funds are typical examples of cash equivalents.

> REMEMBER . . .
> A CASH EQUIVALENT is a short-term, highly liquid investment with an original maturity of less than three months.

When preparing a statement of cash flows, the cash and cash equivalents are added together and treated as a single sum. The addition is done because the purchase and sale of investments in cash equivalents are considered to be part of a firm's overall management of cash rather than a source or use of cash. As statement users evaluate and project cash flows, for example, it should not matter whether the cash is readily available, deposited in a bank account, or invested in cash equivalents. Transfers back and forth between a firm's cash account and its investments in cash equivalents, therefore, are not treated as cash inflows and cash outflows in its statement of cash flows.

When discussing the statement of cash flows, managers generally use the word *cash* rather than the phrase *cash and cash equivalents.* We will follow the same practice.

FRAMEWORK FOR THE STATEMENT OF CASH FLOWS

In analyzing the statement of cash flows, we must not necessarily conclude that the company is better off if cash increases and worse off if cash decreases. It is not the cash change that is most important, but the reasons for that change. For example, what are the sources of cash inflows? Are these sources transitory? Are these sources mainly from operating activities?

> **LO1** Explain the framework and usefulness of the statement of cash flows.

We must also review the uses of cash. Has the company invested its cash in operating areas to strengthen its competitive position? Is it able to comfortably meet its debt obligations? Has it diverted cash to creditors or investors at the expense of investing the cash in the company operating activities. Such questions and answers are key to properly applying the statement of cash flows for business decisions.

The statement of cash flows classifies cash receipts and payments into one of three categories: operating activities, investing activities, or financing activities. Classifying cash flows into these categories identifies the effects on cash of each of the major activities of a firm. The combined effects on cash of all three categories explain the net change in cash for the period. The period's net change in cash is then reconciled with the beginning and ending amounts of cash.

Exhibit 4.1 reproduces Starbucks' statement of cash flows ($ thousands). During 2005 Starbucks reported net income of $494.467 million and generated $923.608 million of cash from operating activities. The company used $221.308 million of cash for investing activities and used $673.827 million of cash from financing activities. In sum, Starbucks increased its cash reserves by $28.756 million, from $145.053 million at the beginning of fiscal 2005 to $173.809 million at the end of fiscal 2005.

Operating Activities

A company's income statement mainly reflects the transactions and events that constitute its operating activities. Generally, the cash effects of these operating transactions and events determine the net cash flow from operating activities. The usual focus of a firm's **operating activities** is on selling goods or rendering services, but the activities are defined broadly enough to include any cash receipts or payments that are not classified as investing or financing activities. For example, cash received from collection of receivables and cash payments to purchase inventories are treated as cash flows from operating activities. The following are examples of cash inflows and outflows relating to operating activities.

> REMEMBER . . .
> CASH FLOW FROM OPERATING ACTIVITIES (cash flow from operations) refers to cash inflows and outflows directly related to income from normal operations.

EXHIBIT 4.1	Statement of Cash Flows for Starbucks Corporation	
Fiscal Year Ended ($ thousands)	**Oct 2, 2005**	**Oct 3, 2004**
Operating Activities		
Net earnings	$494,467	$388,973
Adjustments to reconcile net earnings to net cash provided by operating activities		
Depreciation and amortization	367,207	314,047
Provision for impairments and asset disposals	20,157	13,568
Deferred income taxes, net	(31,253)	(3,770)
Equity in income of investees	(49,633)	(31,801)
Distributions of income from equity investees	30,919	38,328
Tax benefit from exercise of nonqualified stock options	109,978	63,405
Net accretion of discount and amortization of premium on marketable securities	10,097	11,603
Cash provided (used) by changes in operating assets and liabilities		
Accounts receivable	(49,311)	(24,977)
Inventories	(121,618)	(77,662)
Accounts payable	9,717	27,948
Accrued compensation and related costs	22,711	54,929
Deferred revenue	53,276	47,590
Other operating assets and liabilities	56,894	36,356
Net cash provided by operating activities	923,608	858,537
Investing Activities		
Purchase of available-for-sale securities	(643,488)	(887,969)
Maturity of available-for-sale securities	469,554	170,789
Sale of available-for-sale securities	626,113	452,467
Acquisitions, net of cash acquired	(21,583)	(7,515)
Net additions to equity investments, other investments, and other assets	(7,915)	(64,747)
Net additions to property, plant, and equipment	(643,989)	(412,537)
Net cash used by investing activities	(221,308)	(749,512)
Financing Activities		
Proceeds from issuance of common stock	163,555	137,590
Borrowings under revolving credit facility	277,000	
Principal payments on long-term debt	(735)	(722)
Repurchase of common stock	(1,113,647)	(203,413)
Net cash provided (used) by financing activities	(673,827)	(66,545)
Effect of exchange rate changes on cash and cash equivalents	283	3,111
Net increase in cash and cash equivalents	28,756	45,591
Cash and cash equivalents, beginning of period	145,053	99,462
Cash and cash equivalents, end of period	$173,809	$145,053

Operating Activities

Cash Inflows

1. Cash receipts from customers for sales made or services rendered.
2. Cash receipts of interest and dividends.
3. Other cash receipts that are not related to investing or financing activities, such as insurance proceeds, lawsuit settlements, and refunds received from suppliers.

Cash Outflows

1. Cash payments to employees or suppliers.
2. Cash payments to purchase inventories.
3. Cash payments of interest to creditors.
4. Cash payments of taxes to government.
5. Other cash payments that are not related to investing or financing activities, such as contributions to charity and lawsuit settlements.

Investing Activities

A firm's transactions involving (1) the acquisition and disposal of property, plant, and equipment (PPE) assets and intangible assets, (2) the purchase and sale of stocks, bonds, and other securities (that are not cash equivalents), and (3) the lending and subsequent collection of money constitute the basic components of its **investing activities**. The related cash receipts and payments appear in the investing activities section of the statement of cash flows. Examples of these cash flows follow:

REMEMBER . . .
CASH FLOWS FROM INVESTING ACTIVITIES are cash inflows and outflows related to acquiring or selling productive assets and the investments in securities of other companies.

Cash Inflows

1. Cash receipts from sales of property, plant, and equipment (PPE) assets and intangible assets.
2. Cash receipts from sales of investments in stocks, bonds, and other securities (other than cash equivalents).
3. Cash receipts from repayments of loans by borrowers.

Cash Outflows

1. Cash payments to purchase property, plant, and equipment (PPE) assets and intangible assets.
2. Cash payments to purchase stocks, bonds, and other securities (other than cash equivalents).
3. Cash payments made to lend money to borrowers.

Financing Activities

A firm engages in **financing activities** when it obtains resources from owners, returns resources to owners, borrows resources from creditors, and repays amounts borrowed. Cash flows related to these transactions are reported in the financing activities section of the statement of cash flows. Examples of these cash flows follow:

REMEMBER . . .
CASH FLOWS FROM FINANCING ACTIVITIES are cash inflows and outflows related to external sources of financing (owners and nonowners).

Cash Inflows

1. Cash receipts from issuances of common stock and preferred stock and from sales of treasury stock.
2. Cash receipts from issuances of bonds payable, mortgage notes payable, and other notes payable.

Cash Outflows

1. Cash payments to acquire treasury stock.
2. Cash payments of dividends.
3. Cash payments to settle outstanding bonds payable, mortgage notes payable, and other notes payable.

Paying cash to settle such obligations as accounts payable, wages payable, interest payable, and income tax payable are operating activities, not financing activities. Also, cash received as interest and dividends and cash paid as interest (not dividends) are classified as cash flows from operating activities.

Usefulness of Classifications

The classification of cash flows into three categories of activities helps financial statement users interpret cash flow data. To illustrate, assume that Starbucks, Peets, and Espresso Royale each reports a $100,000 cash increase during the current year. Information from their current year statements of cash flows is summarized in Exhibit 4.2.

EXHIBIT 4.2	Summary Information for Three Competitors		
	Starbucks	**Peets**	**Espresso Royale**
Net cash provided by operating activities	$100,000	$ 0	$ 0
Cash flows from investing activities			
Sale of property, plant, and equipment (PPE)	0	100,000	0
Cash flows from financing activities			
Issuance of notes payable	0	0	100,000
Net increase in cash	$100,000	$100,000	$100,000

Although each company's net cash increase was the same, the source of the increase varied by company. This variation affects the analysis of the cash flow data, particularly for potential short-term creditors who must evaluate the likelihood of obtaining repayment in the future for any funds loaned to the company. Based only on these cash flow data, a potential creditor would feel more comfortable lending money to Starbucks than to either Peets or Espresso Royale. This choice is because Starbucks' cash increase came from its operating activities, whereas both Peets and Espresso Royale could only break even on their cash flows from operations. Also, Peets' cash increase came from the sale of property, plant, and equipment (PPE) assets, a source that is not likely to recur regularly. Espresso Royale's cash increase came entirely from borrowed funds. This means Espresso Royale faces additional cash burdens in the future when the interest and principal payments on the note payable become due.

Noncash Investing and Financing Activities

Another objective of cash flow reporting is to present summary information about a firm's investing and financing activities. Many of these activities affect cash and are therefore already included in the investing and financing sections of the statement of cash flows. Some significant investing and financing events, however, do not affect current cash flows. Examples of **noncash investing and financing activities** are the issuance of stocks, bonds, or leases in exchange for property, plant, and equipment (PPE) assets or intangible assets; the exchange of long-term assets for other long-term assets; and the conversion of long-term debt into common stock. Information about these events must be reported as a supplement to the statement of cash flows.

Noncash investing and financing transactions generally do affect *future* cash flows. Issuing bonds payable to acquire equipment, for example, requires future cash payments for interest and principal on the bonds. Alternatively, converting bonds payable into common stock eliminates future cash payments related to the bonds. Knowledge of these types of events, therefore, is helpful to users of cash flow data who wish to assess a firm's future cash flows.

Information on noncash investing and financing transactions is disclosed in a schedule that is separate from the statement of cash flows. The separate schedule is reported either immediately below the statement of cash flows or among the notes to the financial statements.

BUSINESS INSIGHT

Objectivity of Cash   Usefulness of financial statements is enhanced when the underlying data are objective and verifiable. Measuring cash and the changes in cash are among the most objective measurements that accountants make. Thus, the statement of cash flows is arguably the most objective financial statement. This characteristic of the statement of cash flows is welcomed by those investors and creditors interested in evaluating the quality of a firm's income.

Usefulness of the Statement of Cash Flows

A statement of cash flows shows the periodic cash effects of a firm's operating, investing, and financing activities. Distinguishing among these different categories of cash flows helps users compare, evaluate, and predict cash flows. With cash flow information, creditors and investors are better able to assess a firm's ability to settle its liabilities and pay its dividends. A firm's need for outside financing is also better evaluated when using cash flow data. Over time, the statement of cash flows permits users to observe and access management's investing and financing policies.

A statement of cash flows also provides information useful in evaluating a firm's financial flexibility. *Financial flexibility* refers to a firm's ability to generate sufficient amounts of cash to respond to unanticipated needs and opportunities. Information about past cash flows, particularly cash flows from operations, helps in assessing financial flexibility. An evaluation of a firm's ability to survive an unexpected drop in demand, for example, should include a review of its past cash flows from operations. The larger these cash flows, the greater is the firm's ability to withstand adverse changes in economic conditions. Other financial statements, particularly the balance sheet and the related notes, also contain information useful for judging financial flexibility.

Some investors and creditors find the statement of cash flows useful in evaluating the *quality* of a firm's income. As we know, determining income under accrual accounting procedures requires many accruals, deferrals, allocations, and valuations. These adjustment and measurement procedures introduce more subjectivity into income determination than some financial statement users prefer. These users prefer a more objective performance measure—**cash flow from operations divided by net income.** To these users, the higher this ratio is, the higher is the quality of income. The ratios of cash flow from operations to net income for Starbucks were 2.21 ($858,537/$388,973) in 2004, and 1.87 ($923,608/$494,467) for 2005. Although the ratio declined, it is still a strong value and indicates that Starbucks' income is of high quality.

CASH FLOWS FROM OPERATING ACTIVITIES

The first section of a statement of cash flows presents a firm's net cash flow from operating activities. Two alternative formats are used to report the net cash flow from operating activities: the *indirect method* and the *direct method. Both methods report the same amount of net cash flow from operating activities.* (Net cash flows from investing and financing activities are prepared in the same manner under both the indirect and direct methods; only the format for cash flows from operating activities differ.)

In Chapter 3, the statement of cash flows for the FedEx–DeFond Company was prepared using the direct method. The direct method is logical and relatively easy to follow. In practice, however, nearly all statements of cash flows are presented using what is called the **indirect method.** Under this method, the cash flow from operations section begins with net income and applies a series of adjustments to net income to convert it to a cash-basis income number, which is the net cash flow from operating activities. The adjustments to net income do not represent specific cash flows, however, so the indirect method does not report any detail concerning individual operating cash inflows and outflows.

Accountants estimate that *more than 98% of companies preparing the statement of cash flows use the indirect method.* The indirect method is popular because (1) it is easier and less expensive to prepare than the direct method and (2) the direct method requires a supplemental disclosure showing the indirect method (thus, essentially requiring the company to report both methods).

The remainder of this chapter discusses the preparation of the statement of cash flows. Only the indirect method is presented in this section, using an example and illustration. We first make each of the required adjustments to net income in the operating section and then discuss each adjustment. The direct method is presented in Appendix 4A.

LO2 Construct the net operating cash flows section of the statement of cash flows.

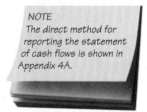

NOTE
The direct method for reporting the statement of cash flows is shown in Appendix 4A.

Use of Direct and Indirect Method

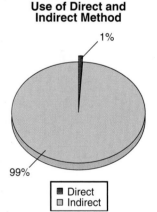

1%

99%

■ Direct
□ Indirect

BUSINESS INSIGHT

Comparison of Accrual and Cash-Basis Amounts   Accountants compute net income, shown on the income statement, using accrual accounting procedures. The net cash flow from operating activities may be larger, smaller, or about the same amount. Financial data from recent annual reports of three companies bear this out.

	Net Income or (Loss)	Net Cash Provided (Used) by Operating Activities
JC Penney	$ (928) million	$ 748 million
General Motors	4,063 million	(4,648) million
GlaxoSmithKline	8,022 million	8,694 million

To prepare a statement of cash flows, we need a firm's income statement, comparative balance sheets, and some additional data taken from the accounting records. Exhibit 4.3 presents this information for Java House. We use these data to prepare Java's 2005 statement of cash flows using the indirect method.

EXHIBIT 4.3 Financial Data of Java House

Java House Income Statement For Year Ended December 31, 2005		
Sales		$250,000
Cost of goods sold . . .	$148,000	
Wages expense	52,000	
Insurance expense . . .	5,000	
Depreciation expense .	10,000	
Income tax expense . .	11,000	226,000
Income from operations		24,000
Gain on sale of land . .		8,000
Net income		$ 32,000

Additional Data for 2005

1. Purchased all long-term stock investments for cash at year-end.
2. Sold land costing $20,000 for $28,000 cash.
3. Acquired $60,000 patent at year-end by issuing common stock.
4. All accounts payable relate to merchandise purchases.
5. Issued common stock for $10,000 cash.
6. Declared and paid cash dividends of $13,000.

Java House Balance Sheet		
	Dec. 31, 2005	Dec. 31, 2004
Assets		
Cash	$ 35,000	$ 10,000
Accounts receivable	39,000	34,000
Inventory	54,000	60,000
Prepaid insurance	17,000	4,000
Long-term investments	15,000	—
PPE assets	180,000	200,000
Accumulated depreciation	(50,000)	(40,000)
Patent	60,000	—
Total assets	$350,000	$ 268,000
Liabilities and Equity		
Accounts payable	$ 10,000	$ 19,000
Income tax payable	5,000	3,000
Common stock	260,000	190,000
Retained earnings	75,000	56,000
Total liabilities and equity	$350,000	$ 268,000

Java's statement of cash flows explains the $25,000 increase in cash that occurred during 2005 (from $10,000 to $35,000) by classifying the firm's cash flows into operating, investing, and financing categories. To get the information to construct the statement we do the following:

1. **Use the indirect method to determine the net cash flow from operating activities.** We apply a series of adjustments to the firm's net income. The adjustments include changes in various current asset and current liability accounts.
2. **Determine cash flows from investing activities.** We do this by analyzing changes in noncurrent asset accounts.
3. **Determine cash flows from financing activities.** We do this by analyzing changes in liability and equity accounts.

The *indirect method* presents the net cash flow from operating activities by applying a series of adjustments to net income to convert it to a cash-basis amount. The adjustment amounts represent differences between revenues, expenses, gains, and losses recorded under accrual accounting and the related operating cash inflows and outflows. The adjustments are added to or subtracted from net income, depending on whether the related cash flow is more or less than the accrual amount. Exhibit 4.4 portrays this process.

EXHIBIT 4.4 Indirect Method Operating Adjustments

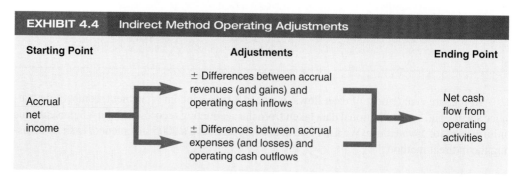

Starting Point	Adjustments	Ending Point
Accrual net income	± Differences between accrual revenues (and gains) and operating cash inflows ± Differences between accrual expenses (and losses) and operating cash outflows	Net cash flow from operating activities

Converting Income to Operating Cash Flow

Exhibit 4.5 summarizes the adjustments to net income in determining operating cash flows. These are the adjustments applied under the indirect method of computing cash flow from operations.

EXHIBIT 4.5	Converting Net Income to Operating Cash Flows	
Business Account or Activity	**Adjustment to Net Income**	
Allocations of noncurrent prepaid expenses*	Added	
Allocations of noncurrent unearned revenues†	Subtracted	
Divestiture of noncurrent assets	Losses added	Gains subtracted
Divestiture of noncurrent liabilities	Losses added	Gains subtracted
Current assets (noncash)	Increases subtracted	Decreases added
Current liabilities‡	Increases added	Decreases subtracted

*Examples are allocations of long-term asset costs such as depreciation, amortization, and depletion.

†Examples are allocations of long-term unearned revenues such as subscriptions, gift certificates, and service contracts.

‡Excludes short-term debt, current portion of long-term debt, and dividends payable.

Exhibit 4.6 identifies several specific adjustments to convert net income to net cash flow from operating activities. The first several adjustments cover depreciation expense, amortization expense, and gains and losses from investing and financing activities. The remaining adjustments relate to the effects on cash flow of changes in current assets and current liabilities. If there is a net loss for the period, the indirect method begins with the net loss. It is possible for the net amount of add-backs to exceed the loss so that there is a positive net cash flow from operating activities even when there is an accrual net loss.

> REMEMBER . . .
> The INDIRECT METHOD of presenting the operating activites section of the cash flow statment adjusts net income to get cash flow from operating activities.

EXHIBIT 4.6	Adjustments to Convert Net Income to Net Cash Flow from Operating Activities
Add to Net Income	**Deduct from Net Income**
Depreciation expense	
Amortization expense	
Depletion expense	
Losses (investing and financing)	Gains (investing and financing)
Decrease in accounts receivable	Increase in accounts receivable
Decrease in inventory	Increase in inventory
Decrease in prepaid expenses	Increase in prepaid expenses
Increase in accounts payable	Decrease in accounts payable
Increase in accrued liabilities	Decrease in accrued liabilities

Java House Case Illustration

We next explain these adjustments and illustrate them with Java House's data from Exhibit 4.3

Depreciation and Amortization Expenses

Depreciation and amortization expenses represent write-offs of previously recorded assets; so-called noncash expenses. Because depreciation, amortization, and depletion expenses are subtracted in computing net income, we add these expenses to net income as we convert it to a related net operating cash flow. Adding these expenses to net income eliminates them from the income statement and is a necessary adjustment to obtain cash income. Java House had $10,000 of 2005 depreciation expense, so this amount is added to Java's net income of $32,000.

Net income	$32,000
Add: Depreciation	**10,000**

To better understand, consider the following journal entry for depreciation.

Depreciation Expense (+E, −SE)	10,000	
Asset—Accumulated Depreciation (+XA, −A)		10,000

The expense reduces net income but *no* cash is involved. The cash was spent when the asset was acquired. Cash was credited at that time. Because net income is considered the initial sources of cash in the operating section of the statement of cash flows, we must add back the noncash depreciation expense deducted from revenues in computing net income.

Gains and Losses Related to Investing or Financing Activities

If the income statement contains gains and losses that relate to investing or financing activities, these gains (losses) must be subtracted (added) back to net income in computing cash flows from operations. Gains and losses from the sale of investments, PPE assets, or intangible assets illustrate gains and losses from investing (not operating) activities. A gain or loss from the retirement of bonds payable is an example of a financing gain or loss. The full cash flow effect from these types of events is reported in the investing or financing sections of the statement of cash flows. Therefore, the related gains or losses must be eliminated as we convert net income to net cash flow from operating activities. To eliminate their impact on net income, gains are subtracted and losses are added to net income. Java House had an $8,000 gain from the sale of land in 2005. This gain relates to an investing activity, so it is subtracted from Java's net income.

Net income	$32,000
Add: Depreciation	10,000
Deduct: Gain on sale of land	**(8,000)**

Again, the following journal entry for the gain is helpful for our understanding.

Cash (+A)	28,000	
Gain on Sale of Land (+R, +SE)		8,000
Land (−A)		20,000

Cash is increased as we can see from the entry. Further, the gain is included in the company's net income. However, the entire $28,000, which included the gain of $8,000, is reported in the cash flows from investing section of the statement of cash flows. Thus, the gain is included twice in the statement. We correct this double counting by deducting the gain from net income.

Accounts Receivable Change

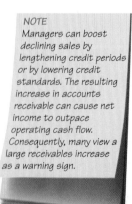

NOTE
Managers can boost declining sales by lengthening credit periods or by lowering credit standards. The resulting increase in accounts receivable can cause net income to outpace operating cash flow. Consequently, many view a large receivables increase as a warning sign.

Credit sales increase accounts receivable; cash collections on account decrease accounts receivable. If, overall, accounts receivable decrease during a year, then cash collections from customers exceed credit sales revenue by the amount of the decrease. Because sales are added in computing net income, the decrease in accounts receivable is added to net income. In essence, this adjustment replaces the sales amount with the larger amount of cash collections from customers. If accounts receivable increase during a year, then sales revenue exceeds the cash collections from customers by the amount of the increase. Because sales are added in computing net income, the increase in accounts receivable is subtracted from net income as we convert it to a net cash flow from operating activities. In essence, this adjustment replaces the sales amount with the smaller amount of cash collections from customers. Java's accounts receivable increased $5,000 during 2005, so this increase is subtracted from net income under the indirect method.

Net income	$32,000
Add: Depreciation	10,000
Deduct: Gain on sale of land	(8,000)
Deduct: Accounts receivable increase	**(5,000)**

Credit sales increase revenues and thereby net income. But, they do not immediately bring in cash. To see this, consider the original journal entry.

Accounts Receivable (+A)	5,000	
Sales (+R, +SE)		5,000

Income increases but there is no additional cash. We must adjust net income by subtracting the credit sales of the period still represented by accounts receivable from net income.

Inventory Change

The adjustment for an inventory change is one of two adjustments to net income that together cause the cost of goods sold expense to be replaced by an amount representing the cash paid during the period for merchandise purchased. The second adjustment, which we examine shortly, is for the change in accounts payable. The effect of the inventory adjustment alone is to adjust net income for the difference between the cost of goods sold and the cost of merchandise purchased during the period. The cost of merchandise purchased increases inventory; the cost of goods sold decreases inventory. An overall decrease in inventory during a period must mean, therefore, that the cost of merchandise purchased was less than the cost of goods sold by the amount of the decrease. Because cost of goods sold was subtracted in computing net income, the inventory decrease is added to net income. After this adjustment, the effect of the cost of goods sold on net income has been replaced by the smaller cost of merchandise purchased. Similarly, if inventory increased during a period, the cost of merchandise purchased is larger than the cost of goods sold by the amount of the increase. To replace the cost of goods sold with the cost of merchandise purchased, the inventory increase is subtracted from net income. Java's inventory decreased $6,000 during 2005, so this decrease is added to net income.

> **NOTE**
> An unexpected inventory increase can cause income to outpace operating cash flow. Inventory growth can signal lack of planned sales growth. An inventory decline can signal expected lower sales. However, an increase in inventory could indicate a buildup for expected future sales.

Net income	$32,000
Add: Depreciation	10,000
Deduct: Gain on sale of land	(8,000)
Deduct: Accounts receivable increase	(5,000)
Add: Inventory decrease	**6,000**

As further explanation, consider the following journal entry, assuming Java purchased $148,000 of inventory.

Inventory (+A)	142,000	
Cash (−A)		142,000

At purchase, there is no impact on income, but cash of $142,000 is used. When the inventory is later applied in producing products that are sold or in providing services, an expense is recognized. Java's income statement in Exhibit 4.3 indicates that Java used $148,000. Its original (summary) entry follows.

Cost of Sales (+E, −SE)	148,000	
Inventory (−A)		148,000

The $148,000 expense is deducted in determining net income but it exceeds the cash of $142,000 used to purchase inventory. The difference of $6,000, also the decrease in the inventory account ($54,000 −$60,000, see Exhibit 4.3), did not require a cash outflow this period and must be added back to net income as an adjustment in the operating section to adjust for the noncash portion of expense.

Why is this use of cash not considered a cash flow from investing? The reason is that inventories are assumed to be quickly used by the company in its operating activities. Thus, adjustment for changes in inventories and other current operating assets (and liabilities) are part of the cash flows from operations section.

Prepaid Expenses Change

Cash prepayments of various expenses increase a firm's prepaid expenses. When the related expenses for the period are subsequently recorded, the prepaid expenses decrease. An overall decrease in prepaid expenses for a period means that the cash prepayments were less than the related expenses. Because the expenses were subtracted in determining net income, the indirect method adds the decrease in prepaid expenses to net income as it is converted to a cash flow amount. The effect of the addition is to replace the expense amount with the smaller cash payment amount. Similarly, an increase in prepaid expenses is subtracted from net income because an increase means that the cash prepayments during the year were more than the related expenses. Java's prepaid insurance increased $13,000 during 2005, so this increase is deducted from net income.

Net income	$32,000
Add: Depreciation	10,000
Deduct: Gain on sale of land	(8,000)
Deduct: Accounts receivable increase	(5,000)
Add: Inventory decrease	6,000
Deduct: Prepaid insurance increase	**(13,000)**

Prepayments are similar to inventories in their cash flow effects. Cash outflow occurs when the prepayment is made. For Java House, prepaid insurance increased by $13,000. One way this could have occurred was if Java House purchased additional prepaid insurance for $13,000. The following journal entry would be recorded to reflect such payment.

Prepaid Insurance (+A)	13,000	
Cash (−A)		13,000

Since the insurance premium provides coverage for a future period, an asset is debited and the cash expenditure is not reflected in the income statement at this time. Nevertheless, the cash payment is an operating cash flow and should be subtracted to obtain cash flow from operations.

Accounts Payable Change

When merchandise is purchased on account, accounts payable increase by the amount of the goods' cost. Accounts payable decrease when cash payments are made to settle the accounts. An overall decrease in accounts payable during a year means that cash payments for purchases were more than the cost of the purchases. An accounts payable decrease, therefore, is subtracted from net income under the indirect method. The deduction, in effect, replaces the cost of merchandise purchased with the larger cash payments for merchandise purchased. (Recall that the earlier inventory adjustment replaced the cost of goods sold with the cost of merchandise purchased.) In contrast, an increase in accounts payable means that cash payments for purchases were less than the cost of purchases for the period. Thus, an accounts payable increase is added to net income as it is converted to a cash flow amount. Java House shows a $9,000 decrease in accounts payable during 2005. This decrease is subtracted from net income.

Net income	$32,000
Add: Depreciation	10,000
Deduct: Gain on sale of land	(8,000)
Deduct: Accounts receivable increase	(5,000)
Add: Inventory decrease	6,000
Deduct: Prepaid insurance increase	(13,000)
Deduct: Accounts payable decrease	**(9,000)**

One way to think about accounts payable is to recall that any reduction of accounts payable uses cash. If accounts payable increase, no cash is involved. The original (summary) entry is as follows.

Merchandise (+A)	9,000	
Accounts Payable (+L)		9,000

An adjustment is needed to subtract the increase in accounts payable to reflect the additional cash used in operating activities. (A decrease in accounts payable would be added.)

Accrued Liabilities Change

Changes in accrued liabilities are interpreted the same way as changes in accounts payable. A decrease means that cash payments exceeded the related expense amounts; an increase means that cash payments were less than the related expenses. Decreases are subtracted from net income; increases are added to net income. Java has one accrued liability, income tax payable, and it increased by $2,000 during 2005. The $2,000 increase is added to net income.

Net income	$32,000
Add: Depreciation	10,000
Deduct: Gain on sale of land	(8,000)
Deduct: Accounts receivable increase	(5,000)
Add: Inventory decrease	6,000
Deduct: Prepaid insurance increase	(13,000)
Deduct: Accounts payable decrease	(9,000)
Add: Income tax payable increase	**2,000**

As with accounts payable, cash is used in the payment of these accounts. For example, a decrease in accrued income taxes payable would indicate the use of cash. However, accrued taxes increased for Java House. Taxes are an expense of operations and are a deduction to obtain net income. But if a portion of the tax is accrued as a liability, only the difference is paid in cash. For Java, the entry based on the tax expense of $11,000 from the income statement of Exhibit 4.3 is as follows.

Income Tax Expense (+E, −SE)	11,000	
Cash (−A)		9,000
Income Taxes Payable (+L)		2,000

No cash is used and an adjustment (an addition in this case) is required for the increase in the accrued income taxes from $3,000 to $5,000 to obtain cash flow from operations (see the balance sheet in Exhibit 4.3).

We have now identified the adjustments to convert Java's net income to its net cash flow from operating activities. The operating activities section of the statement of cash flows is shown in Exhibit 4.7 under the indirect method:

EXHIBIT 4.7	**Java's Net Cash Flows from Operations**
Net income	$32,000
Add (deduct) items to convert net income to cash basis:	
Depreciation	10,000
Gain on sale of land	(8,000)
Accounts receivable increase	(5,000)
Inventory decrease	6,000
Prepaid insurance increase	(13,000)
Accounts payable decrease	(9,000)
Income tax payable increase	2,000
Net cash provided by operating activities	$15,000

To summarize, net cash flows from operating activities begin with net income (loss) and eliminates noncash expenses (such as depreciation) and any gains and losses that are properly reported in the investing and financing sections. Next, cash inflows (outflows) relating to changes in the level of current operating assets and liabilities are added (subtracted) to yield net cash flows from operating activities. During the period, Java earned cash operating profits of $34,000 ($32,000 + $10,000 − $8,000), but used $19,000 of cash (−$5,000 + $6,000 − $13,000 − $9,000 + $2,000) to increase net working capital. Cash outflows relating to the increase in net working capital are a common occurrence for growing companies, and this net asset increase must be financed by the company, just like the increase in PPE assets.

BUSINESS INSIGHT

Starbucks' Add-Backs for Operating Cash Flow   Starbucks reports $494.467 million of net income for 2005 and $923.608 million of operating cash inflows. The difference between these numbers is mainly due to $367.207 million of depreciation expense that is included in net income. Depreciation is a noncash charge; an expense not requiring cash payment. It is added back to income in computing operating cash flows. Starbucks also reports a $20.157 million asset impairment (write-down). This, too, is a noncash charge and is added back in computing operating cash flows. Starbucks subtracts $31.253 million for deferred taxes, indicating that cash payments of taxes are greater than tax expense reported in income (deferred income taxes are discussed in Chapter 7). Starbucks subtracts $49.633 million for equity in income of investees, meaning that it reported equity income that it did not receive in cash in the form of dividends (see Chapter 12). Its tax benefit relating to stock options arises from the tax credits it receives when employees exercise options. It reports no expense relating to these options in its income statement. The $10.097 million relating to accretion of discounts (premiums) on marketable securities indicates it reported that amount as an expense that does not require cash payment (see Chapter 10).

YOU MAKE THE CALL

You are the Securities Analyst   You are analyzing a company's statement of cash flows. The company has two items relating to its accounts receivable. First, the company finances the sale of its products to some customers with notes receivable; the increase to notes receivable is classified as an investing activity. Second, the company sells its accounts receivable to another company. As a result, the sale of receivables is reported as an asset sale, which reduces receivables and yields a gain or loss on sale. This action increases its operating cash flows. How should you interpret these items in the cash flow statement?
[Answer on p. 166]

CASH FLOWS FROM INVESTING ACTIVITIES

Analyzing Remaining Noncash Assets

Investing activities cause changes in asset accounts. Usually the accounts affected (other than cash) are noncurrent asset accounts such as property, plant and equipment assets and long-term investments, although short-term investment accounts can also be affected. To determine the cash flows from investing activities, *we analyze changes in all noncash asset accounts not used in computing net cash flow from operating activities.* Our objective is to identify any investing cash flows related to these changes.

Java House Case Illustration

Analyze Change in Long-Term Investments

Java's comparative balance sheets show that long-term investments increased $15,000 during 2005. The increase means that investments must have been purchased, and the additional data reported indicates that cash was spent to purchase long-term stock investments. Purchasing stock is an investing activity. Thus, a $15,000 purchase of stock investments is reported as a cash outflow from investing activities in the statement of cash flows. The entire $28,000, which includes the gain, is reported in the investing section.

Analyze Change in Property, Plant, and Equipment Assets

Java's PPE assets decreased $20,000 during 2005. PPE assets decrease as the result of disposals, and the additional data for Java House indicate that land was sold for cash in 2005. Selling land is an investing activity. Thus, the sale of land for $28,000 is reported as a cash inflow from investing activities in the statement of cash flows.

Analyze Change in Accumulated Depreciation

Java's accumulated depreciation increased $10,000 during 2005. Accumulated depreciation increases when depreciation expense is recorded. Java's 2005 depreciation expense was $10,000, so the total change in accumulated depreciation is the result of the recording of depreciation expense. As previously discussed, there is no cash flow related to the recording of depreciation expense, and we have previously adjusted for this expense in our computation of net cash flows from operating activities.

Analyze Change in Patent

We see from the comparative balance sheets that Java had an increase of $60,000 in a patent. The increase means that a patent was acquired, and the additional data indicate that common stock was issued to obtain the patent. This event is a noncash investing (acquiring a patent) and financing (issuing common stock) transaction that must be disclosed as supplementary information to the statement of cash flows.

We can now finalize the cash flows provided by the investing activities section of Java House's statement of cash flows (see Exhibit 4.8).

> REMEMBER...
> Investing activities on the cash flow statement include (1) cash outflows to acquire plant assets and short- and long-term investments, and (2) cash inflows from sales of plant assets and short- and long-term investments.

EXHIBIT 4.8	Java's Cash Flows Provided by Investing Activites
Purchase of stock investments	$(15,000)
Sale of land	28,000
Net cash inflows from investing activites	$13,000

BUSINESS INSIGHT

Starbucks' Investing Activities   Starbucks spent $643.989 million on property, plant and equipment in 2005. However, not all investing activities contribute to operations, as do PPE investments. Starbucks also generated $452.179 million ($469.554 + $626.113 − $643.488) from transactions in securities. It also spent $29.498 million ($21.583 + $7,915) for acquisitions and other investments, for a total of $221.308 used for investing activities.

CASH FLOWS FROM FINANCING ACTIVITIES

Analyzing Remaining Liabilities and Equity

Financing activities cause changes in liability and stockholders' equity accounts. Usually the accounts affected are noncurrent accounts such as bonds payable and common stock, although a current liability such as short-term notes payable, or the short-term portion of long-term debt due in the next year, can also be affected. To determine the cash flows from financing activities, *we analyze changes in all liability and stockholders' equity accounts that were not used in computing net cash flow from operating activities.* Our objective is to identify any financing cash flows related to these changes.

Java House Case Illustration

Analyze Change in Common Stock

REMEMBER . . .
Cash inflows from financing activites include cash from the issuance for short- and long-term debt and common stock. Cash outflows include cash principal payments on short- and long-term debt, cash paid for stock buybacks, and cash dividend payments.

Java's common stock increased $70,000 during 2005. Common stock increases when shares of stock are issued. As noted in discussing the patent increase, common stock with a $60,000 par value was issued in exchange for a patent. This event is disclosed as a noncash investing and financing transaction. The other $10,000 increase in common stock, as noted in the additional data, resulted from an issuance of stock for cash. Issuing common stock is a financing activity, so a $10,000 cash inflow from a stock issuance appears as a financing activity in the statement of cash flows.

Analyze Change in Retained Earnings

Retained earnings grew from $56,000 to $75,000 during 2005—a $19,000 increase. This increase is the net result of Java's $32,000 of net income (which increased retained earnings) and a $13,000 cash dividend (which decreased retained earnings). Because every item in Java's income statement was considered in computing the net cash provided by operating activities, only the cash dividend remains to be considered. Paying a cash dividend is a financing activity. Thus, a $13,000 cash dividend appears as a cash outflow from financing activities in the statement of cash flows. We have now completed the analysis of all of Java's noncash balance sheet accounts and can prepare the 2005 statement of cash flows. Exhibit 4.10 shows this statement.

If there are cash inflows and outflows from similar types of investing and financing activities, the inflows and outflows are reported separately (rather than reporting only the net difference). For example, proceeds from the sale of plant assets are reported separately from outlays made to acquire plant assets. Similarly, funds borrowed are reported separately from debt repayments, and proceeds from issuing stock are reported separately from outlays to acquire treasury stock.

We can now reproduce the financing section of Java House's statement of cash flows, (see Exhibit 4.9).

EXHIBIT 4.9	Java's Cash Flows from Financing Activities.
Issuance of common stock	$10,000
Payments of dividends	(13,000)
Net cash outflows from financing activities	($ 3,000)

BUSINESS INSIGHT

Starbucks' Financing Activities   Starbucks experienced cash outflows of $950.092 million ($163.555 million − $1,113.647 million) from repurchases of common stock, net of issuances. Only stock issued for cash is reflected in the statement of cash flows. Stock issued in connection with acquisitions is not reflected because it does not involve cash. Issuance of stock is often related to the exercise of employee stock options, and companies frequently repurchase stock to offset the dilution caused by the issuance of additional shares. Starbucks also reports a cash outflow of approximately $0.735 million relating to the repayment of long-term debt. The net effect is a decrease in cash of $673.827 million from financing activities.

SUPPLEMENTAL DISCLOSURES FOR INDIRECT METHOD

When the indirect method is used in the statement of cash flows, three separate disclosures are required: (1) two specific operating cash outflows—cash paid for interest and cash paid for income taxes, (2) a schedule or description of all noncash investing and financing transactions, and (3) the firm's policy for determining which highly liquid, short-term investments are treated as cash equivalents. A firm's policy regarding cash equivalents is placed in the financial statement notes. The other two separate disclosures are reported either in the notes or at the bottom of the statement of cash flows.

Java House Case Illustration

Java House incurred no interest cost during 2005. It did pay income taxes. Our discussion of the $2,000 change in income tax payable during 2005 revealed that the increase meant that cash tax payments were less than income tax expense by the amount of the increase. Income tax expense was $11,000, so the cash paid for income taxes was $2,000 less than $11,000, or $9,000.

Java House did have one noncash investing and financing event during 2005: the issuance of common stock to acquire a patent. This event, as well as the cash paid for income taxes, is disclosed as supplemental information to the statement of cash flows in Exhibit 4.10.

REMEMBER . . .
Noncash investing and financing activities are investing and financing activities that do not involve cash.

EXHIBIT 4.10	Statement of Cash Flows Using the Indirect Method with Supplemental Disclosures

Java House
Statement of Cash Flows
For Year Ended December 31, 2005

Net cash flow from operating activities		
Net income	$32,000	
Add (deduct) items to convert net income to cash basis		
Depreciation	10,000	
Gain on sale of land	(8,000)	
Accounts receivable increase	(5,000)	
Inventory decrease	6,000	
Prepaid insurance increase	(13,000)	
Accounts payable decrease	(9,000)	
Income tax payable increase	2,000	
Net cash provided by operating activities		$15,000
Cash flows from investing activities		
Purchase of stock investments	(15,000)	
Sale of land	28,000	
Net cash provided by investing activities		13,000
Cash flows from financing activities		
Issuance of common stock	10,000	
Payment of dividends	(13,000)	
Net cash used by financing activities		(3,000)
Net increase in cash		25,000
Cash at beginning of year		10,000
Cash at end of year		$35,000

Supplemental Information

Supplemental cash flow disclosure	
Cash paid for income taxes	$ 9,000
Schedule of noncash investing and financing activities	
Issuance of common stock to acquire patent	$60,000

MID-CHAPTER REVIEW

The comparative balance sheets and income statement for Dye's PC Shop are as follows.

DYE'S PC SHOP Comparative Balance Sheets			
	Year-End 1	Year-End 2	Change from Prior Period
Assets			
Cash	$ 10,000	$ 15,000	$ 5,000
Accounts receivable	30,000	50,000	20,000
Inventories	100,000	125,000	25,000
Total current assets	140,000	190,000	50,000
Long-term assets, gross	200,000	250,000	50,000
Accumulated depreciation	(20,000)	(30,000)	10,000
Long-term assets, net	180,000	220,000	40,000
Total assets	$320,000	$410,000	90,000
Liabilities			
Accounts payable	$ 40,000	$ 60,000	$20,000
Bonds payable, long-term	200,000	180,000	(20,000)
Equity			
Common stock	50,000	100,000	50,000
Retained earnings	30,000	70,000	40,000
Total liabilities and equity	$320,000	$410,000	90,000

DYE'S PC SHOP Income Statement For Year Ended Year 2		
Sales		$ 300,000
Cost of goods sold	$190,000	
Expenses		
Salaries expense	50,000	
Depreciation expense	10,000	250,000
Net income*		$ 50,000

*Cash dividends declared and paid during Year 2 were $10,000.

Required

a. Compute the operating cash flow section of the statement of cash flows.
b. Compute the investing and financing sections of the statement of cash flows and present them as part of the complete statement of cash flows.

Solution

a. The operating cash flows section begins with net income of $50,000 and then adjusts it for any non-cash operating or nonoperating items not impacting cash, and then for changes in current assets and current liabilities. First, we identify one noncash operating item—depreciation expense of $10,000—which needs to be added back to income. No other operating or nonoperating items not impacting cash are identified in net income. Second, the identified changes in current assets and current liabilities, as they reflect cash inflows and outflows, are as follows.

	Amount	As Reflected in Cash Flows
Increase in accounts receivable	$20,000	$(20,000)
Increase in inventories	25,000	(25,000)
Increase in accounts payable	20,000	20,000
Net change in working capital (excluding cash) ..	25,000	(25,000)

Consequently, the net cash flows from operations of Dye's PC Shop for Year 2—as computed from adjustments to net income—are as follows.

Net income	$50,000
Depreciation	10,000
Increase in accounts receivable	(20,000)
Increase in inventories	(25,000)
Increase in accounts payable	20,000
Net cash flow from operating activities	$35,000

b. We next compute the cash flows from investing and financing activities. First, to compute net cash flows from investing activities, we recognize that these flows mainly arise from long-term asset purchases and sales. PC Shop's asset purchases were $50,000 for Year 2 (there were no asset sales); this is revealed by the balance sheet increase in long-term assets, which is reflected as a cash outflow from investing activities.

Second, to compute the net cash flows from financing activities, we recognize that these flows mainly arise from changes in long-term liability and the equity accounts. For Dye's PC Shop, the bond repayment ($20,000 outflow), stock issuance ($50,000 inflow), and dividend payment ($10,000 outflow) are relevant. The net cash flows from financing activities, therefore, yield a $20,000 net cash inflow.

The complete statement of cash flows is as follows.[1]

DYE'S PC SHOP
Statement of Cash Flows
For Year Ended Year 2

Cash flows from operating activities	
Net income	$50,000
Adjustments to net income to get operating cash flows	
Depreciation expense	10,000
Accounts receivable increase	(20,000)
Inventories increase	(25,000)
Accounts payable increase	20,000
Net cash from operating activities	35,000
Cash flows from investing activities	
Purchase of long-term assets	(50,000)
Net cash flow from investing activities	(50,000)
Cash flows from financing activities	
Cash paid to retire bonds	(20,000)
Cash received from stock issuance	50,000
Cash paid for dividends	(10,000)
Net cash flow from financing activities	20,000
Net increase in cash	$ 5,000
Cash, beginning Year 2	10,000
Cash, ending Year	$15,000

[1] When looking at published 10-Ks, the amounts reported in the statement of cash flows do not always agree with what we would compute them to be using the reported income statement and changes in the reported balance sheet accounts. Reasons for this include: (1) The statement of cash flows includes only transactions involving cash receipt or payment. If an asset is acquired for noncash assets or seller financing, there is no cash involved and, therefore, it does not impact the statement of cash flows. Instead, such a purchase is described in a note as a *noncash investing and financing activity*. An example of this would be assets acquired under lease from the manufacturer. (2) When a company acquires another company in a stock transaction, the consolidated balance sheet reflects the increase in assets and liabilities, but no cash is paid. This acquisition is not reflected in the statement of cash flows but, instead, is described in a note to the statement of cash flows as a *noncash investing and financing activity*. For example, in 2001 (the year of the ABC acquisition), Disney reports a cash outflow relating to acquisitions of $(8,432) million, which is the $10.1 billion cash portion of the purchase price less the cash acquired on ABC's balance sheet. The remainder of the purchase price ($8.8 billion) paid in stock is not reflected on its statement of cash flows. (3) Several items affect the balance sheet but do not affect the income statement. That is, they are charged to stockholders' equity accounts directly and do not run through the incom statement. Examples are unrealized gains (losses) on available-for-sale securities, the recognition of minimum pension liability, foreign currency translation gains and losses, and gains and losses on some derivative (hedging) transactions. These topics are covered in later chapters.

YOU MAKE THE CALL

You are the Chief Accountant   The July 27, 2005, Wall Street Journal reported that Cendant has "agreed to sell its marketing services division for $1.83 million, ending ownership of a business that staggered the company with a $500 million accounting fraud." How would the sale be reflected in Cendant's cash flow statement? [Answer on page 167]

ANALYSIS OF CASH FLOWS

LO4 Compute and interpret ratios that reflect on a company's ability to satisfy its current liabilities and remain solvent.

Data from the statement of cash flows enter into various financial ratios. Two such ratios are:

1. Operating Cash Flow to Current Liabilities
2. Operating Cash Flow to Capital Expenditures.

Operating Cash Flow to Current Liabilities

The **operating cash flow to current liabilities ratio** is a measure of the ability to liquidate current liabilities and is calculated as:

> **Operating Cash Flow to Current Liabilities = Net Cash Flow from Operating Activities/Average Current Liabilities**

Net cash flow from operating activities is obtained from the statement of cash flows; it represents the excess amount of cash derived from operations during the year after deducting working capital needs and payments required on current liabilities. The denominator is the average of the beginning and ending current liabilities for the year. Starbucks' current liabilities averaged $986.628 million in 2005 ([$1,226.996 + $746.259]/2), yielding an operating cash flow to current liabilities ratio of 0.936, computed as $923.608/$986.628.

To illustrate, the following amounts are taken from the 2004 financial statements for **Gannett Co., Inc.**, a diversified news and information company that publishes *USA Today*.

Net cash flow from operating activities	$1,586 million
Current liabilities at beginning of the year . . .	962 million
Current liabilities at end of the year	1,005 million

Gannett's operating cash flow to current liabilities ratio is 1.61, $1,586/[($962 + 1,005)/2]. Gannett's operating cash flow to current liabilities ratio for the preceding year was 1.54. The higher this ratio, the stronger is a firm's ability to settle current liabilities as they come due. The increase in Gannett's ratio from 1.54 to 1.61 is favorable.

Operating Cash Flow to Capital Expenditures

To remain competitive, an entity must be able to replace, and expand when appropriate, its property, plant, and equipment. A ratio that helps assess a firm's ability to do so from internally generated cash flow is the **operating cash flow to capital expenditures ratio**, which is computed as follows.

> **Operating Cash Flow to Capital Expenditures = Net Cash Flow from Operating Activities/Annual Capital Expenditures**

The numerator in this ratio comes from the first section of the statement of cash flows—the section reporting the net cash flow from operating activities. Information for the denominator can be found in one or more places in the financial statements or in the Management Discussion and Analysis section of the 10-K report. Data on capital expenditures are part of the required industry segment disclosures in notes to the financial statements. Capital expenditures are often also shown in the investing activities section of the statement of cash flows. Also, capital expenditures often appear in the comparative selected financial data presented as supplementary information to the financial statements. Finally, management's discussion and analysis of the statements commonly identifies the annual capital expenditures.

A ratio in excess of 1.0 means that the firm's current operating activities are providing cash in excess of the amount needed to provide the desired level of plant capacity and would normally be considered a sign of financial strength. This ratio is also viewed as an indicator of long-term solvency—a ratio exceeding 1.0 means that there is operating cash flow in excess of capital needs that can then be used to repay outstanding long-term debt. Starbucks spent $643.989 million on capital expenditures in 2005, which yields an operating cash flow to capital expenditures ratio of 1.434, computed as $923.608/$643.989. (Some would also include net acquisitions of $21.583 million and net additions to equity investments of $7.915 million in capital expenditures; in this case the ratio would equal 1.371.)

The interpretation of this ratio for a firm is influenced by its trend in recent years, the ratio size being achieved by other firms in the same industry, and the stage of the firm's life cycle. A firm in the early stages of its life cycle when periods of rapid expansion occur, is expected to experience a lower ratio than a firm in the mature stage of its life cycle when maintenance of plant capacity is more likely than expansion of capacity. Starbucks' ratio decreased from 2.08 in 2004 to 1.434 in 2005. This indicates a slight reduction in its ability to fund capital expenditures at current levels.

To illustrate the ratio's computation, **Abbott Laboratories** (a manufacturer of pharmaceutical and other health care products) reported capital expenditures in a recent year of $1,247 million. In the same year, Abbott's net cash flow from operating activities was $3,746 million. Abbott's operating cash flow to capital expenditures ratio for that year is $3,746 million/$1,247 million = 3.0. Following are recent operating cash flow to capital expenditures ratios for several companies:

Colgate-Palmolive (consumer grocery products)	5.85
Lockheed Martin (aerospace)	2.63
Verizon Communications (telecommunications)	1.89
Harley-Davidson (motorcycle manufacturer)	4.12
Home Depot (home products)	1.87

NOTE Another measure is the quality of income ratio (Operating Cash Flow/Net Income), which reflects the portion of income generated in cash. A higher ratio implies greater ability to fund activities from operating cash flow. A higher ratio also implies a lower likelihood of aggressive revenue recognition to increase income.

Free Cash Flow

Free cash flow is a measure of a company's ability to apply its resources to new endeavors. Free cash flows to the firm are often defined as *net cash flows from operations +/- net cash flows from investing activities*. As we progress through the book and learn more, we better develop the notion of free cash flows. We eventually determine that free cash flows equal net operating profit that is not used to grow operating assets - this strict definition of free cash flows is on page 687. For this chapter, however, we assume that free cash flows are approximated by the inexact measure in italics above.

Free cash flow reflects on the funds available for buying back stock, paying down debt, or returning funds to stockholders in the form of dividends. The concept is also used in mergers and acquisitions to indicate cash that would be available to the acquirer for investment. We revisit this concept in later chapters.

LO5 Compute and interpret free cash flow.

NOTE Free cash flow has another common, though slightly different, definition: Free Cash Flow = Operating Cash Flow – Dividends – Capital Expenditures.

RESEARCH INSIGHT

Is the Cash Flow Statement Useful? Some analysts rely on cash flow forecasts to value common stock. Research shows that both net income and operating cash flows are correlated with stock prices, but that stock prices are more highly correlated with net income than with cash flows. So, do we need both statements? Evidence suggests that by using *both* net income and cash flow information, we can improve our forecasts of *future* cash flows. Also, net income and cash flow together are more highly correlated with stock prices than either net income or cash flow alone. This suggest that, for purposes of stock valuation, information from the cash flow statement complements information from the income statement.

CHAPTER-END REVIEW

Espresso Royale's income statement and comparative balance sheets are as follows.

Espresso Royale Income Statement For Year Ended December 31, 2005		
Sales		$ 385,000
Dividend income		5,000
Net Sales		390,000
Cost of goods sold	$233,000	
Wages expense	82,000	
Advertising expense	10,000	
Depreciation expense	11,000	
Income tax expense	17,000	
Loss on sale of investments	2,000	355,000
Net income		$ 35,000

Espresso Royale Comparative Balance Sheets		
	Dec 31, 2005	**Dec 31, 2004**
Assets		
Cash	$ 8,000	$ 12,000
Accounts receivable	22,000	28,000
Inventory	94,000	66,000
Prepaid advertising	12,000	9,000
Long-term investments—Available-for-sale	30,000	41,000
Fair value adjustment to investments	—	(1,000)
Plant assets	178,000	130,000
Accumulated depreciation	(72,000)	(61,000)
Total assets	$272,000	$224,000
Liabilities and Equity		
Accounts payable	$ 27,000	$ 14,000
Wages payable	6,000	2,500
Income tax payable	3,000	4,500
Common stock	139,000	125,000
Retained earnings	97,000	79,000
Unrealized loss on investments	—	(1,000)
Total liabilities and equity	$272,000	$224,000

Cash dividends of $17,000 were declared and paid during 2005. Plant assets were purchased for cash in 2005, and, later in the year, additional common stock was issued for cash. Investments costing $11,000 were sold for cash at a $2,000 loss in 2005; an unrealized loss of $1,000 on these investments had been recorded in 2004 (at December 31, 2005, the cost and fair value of unsold investments are equal).

Required
a. Compute the change in cash that occurred during 2005.
b. Prepare a 2005 statement of cash flows using the indirect method.
c. Compute the company's (1) operating cash flow to current liabilities ratio, (2) operating cash flow to capital expenditure ratio, and (3) free cash flow.

Solution
a. $8,000 ending balance − $12,000 beginning balance = $4,000 decrease in cash
b. (1) Use the indirect method to determine the net cash flow from operating activities.
   ▪ Adjustments to convert Espresso Royale's net income of $35,000 to a net cash provided by operating activities of $38,000 are shown in the following statement of cash flows.

(2) Analyze changes in remaining noncash asset (and contra asset) accounts to determine cash flows from investing activities.
- Long-Term Investments: $11,000 decrease resulted from sale of investments for cash at a $2,000 loss. Cash received from sale of investments = $9,000 ($11,000 cost − $2,000 loss).
- Fair Value Adjustment to Investments: $1,000 decrease resulted from the elimination of this account balance (and the Unrealized Loss of Investments) at the end of 2005. No cash flow effect.
- Plant Assets: $48,000 increase resulted from purchase of plant assets for cash. Cash paid to purchase plant assets = $48,000.
- Accumulated Depreciation: $11,000 increase resulted from the recording of 2005 depreciation. No cash flow effect.

(3) Analyze changes in remaining liability and stockholders' equity accounts to determine cash flows from financing activities.
- Common Stock: $14,000 increase resulted from the issuance of stock for cash. Cash received from issuance of common stock = $14,000.
- Retained Earnings: $18,000 increase resulted from net income of $35,000 and dividend declaration of $17,000. Cash dividends paid = $17,000.
- Unrealized Loss on Investments: $1,000 decrease resulted from the elimination of this account balance (and the Fair Value Adjustment to Investments) at the end of 2005. No cash flow effect.

The statement of cash flows is as follows.

Espresso Royale Statement of Cash Flows For Year Ended December 31, 2005		
Net cash flow from operating activities		
Net income	$35,000	
Add (deduct) items to convert net income to cash basis		
Depreciation	11,000	
Loss on sale of investments	2,000	
Accounts receivable decrease	6,000	
Inventory increase	(28,000)	
Prepaid advertising increase	(3,000)	
Accounts payable increase	13,000	
Wages payable increase	3,500	
Income tax payable decrease	(1,500)	
Net cash provided by operating activities		$38,000
Cash flows from investing activities		
Sale of investments	9,000	
Purchase of plant assets	(48,000)	
Net cash used by investing activities		(39,000)
Cash flows from financing activities		
Issuance of common stock	14,000	
Payment of dividends	(17,000)	
Net cash used by financing activities		(3,000)
Net decrease in cash		(4,000)
Cash at beginning of year		12,000
Cash at end of year		$ 8,000

c. Operating cash flow to current liabilities ratio = 1.33. This is computed as $38,000 [($36,000 + $21,000)/2].
Operating cash flow to capital expenditure ratio = 0.79. This is computed as $38,000/$48,000.
Free cash flow = $(1,000). This is computed as $38,000 − $39,000.

SUMMARY

Explain the framework and usefulness of the statement of cash flows. (p. 145)

LO1

- The statement of cash flows summarizes information about the flow of cash into and out of the business.
- The statement of cash flows classifies the cash flows into three categories: cash flows from operations, cash flows from investing, and cash flows from financing activities.

LO2   **Construct the net operating cash flows section of the statement of cash flows. (p. 149)**

- The cash flows from the operation section of the statement begins with net income, which is the primary source of cash for most firms. Net income is determined on an accrual basis and must be adjusted before it represents cash flows. This approach is called the indirect method of preparation and is used by over 98% of reporting businesses.

- The adjustments made to net income include adding back noncash expenses, such as depreciation, and subtracting the increase in working capital (current assets less current liabilities), which represents a use of funds.

LO3   **Prepare the investing and financing sections of the statement of cash flows. (p. 156)**

- Cash investment outlays are captured in the investing section along with any cash receipts from asset disposals. Because cash receipts include any gain on sale (or reflect any loss), the gain (loss) must be subtracted from (added to) net income in the operating section to avoid double counting.

- Cash obtained from the issuance of securities or borrowings, and any repayments of debt, are disclosed in the financing section. Cash dividends are also included in this section. Interest payments are included in the operating section of the statement.

- Some events, for example assets donated to the firm, provide resources to the business that are important but which do not involve cash outlays. These events are disclosed separately, along with the statement of cash flows as supplementary disclosures or in the notes.

- Notes to financial statements also disclose cash payments for interest and for taxes.

LO4   **Compute and interpret ratios that reflect on a company's ability to satisfy its current liabilities and remain solvent. (p. 162)**

- Two ratios of importance that are based on cash flows include:

  - Operating cash flow to current liabilities—a measure of the adequacy of current operations to cover current liability payments.

  - Operating cash flow to capital expenditures—a reflection of a company's ability to replace or expand its activities based on the level of current operations.

LO5   **Compute and interpret free cash flow. (p. 163)**

- Free cash flow is defined as: Cash Flow from Operations ± Net Cash Flow from Investing.

- Free cash flow is a measure of a company's ability to apply its resources to new endeavors.

GUIDANCE ANSWERS

YOU MAKE THE CALL

You are a Business Consultant   The inventory purchased on credit has no impact on the cash flow statement as the below journal entry indicated.

Inventory (+A)   XXX
    Accounts payable (+L).   XXX

There is no cash involved. Another way to look at the situation is to observe that the increase in the inventory (a use of cash) is offset by the increase in the liability (a source of cash) in the adjustments to net income that are made in the operating section of the cash flow statement.

YOU MAKE THE CALL

You are the Securities Analyst   Many companies, but not all, treat customers' notes receivable as an investing activity. In 2005, the SEC became concerned with this practice and issued letters to a number of companies objecting to this accounting classification. "Presenting cash receipts from receivables generated by the sale of inventory as investing activities in the company's consolidated statements of cash flows is not in accordance with GAAP," wrote the chief accountant for the SEC's division of corporation finance, in her letter to the companies ("Little Campus Lab Shakes Big Firms—Georgia Tech Crew's Report Spurs Change in Accounting for Operating Cash Flow," March 1, 2005, *The Wall Street Journal*). The SEC's position is that these notes receivable are an operating activity and analysts are certainly justified in treating them likewise. Concerning the sale of receivables, the transaction can be treated as a sale with a consequent reduction in receivables and a gain or loss on the sale recorded in the income statement. Many analysts treat this as a financing activity and argue that the cash inflow should not be regarded as an increase in operating cash flows. Bottom line: many argue that operating cash flows do not increase as a result of these two transactions and analysts should adjust the statement of cash flows to properly classify the financing of notes receivable as an operating activity and the sale of receivables as a financing activity.

APPENDIX 4A: Direct Method Reporting for Statement of Cash Flows

To prepare a statement of cash flows, we need a firm's income statement, comparative balance sheets, and some additional data taken from the accounting records. Exhibit 4.3 presents this information for Java House. We use these data to prepare Java's 2005 statement of cash flows using the direct method. Java's statement of cash flows explains the $25,000 increase in cash that occurred during 2005 (from $10,000 to $35,000) by classifying the firm's cash flows into operating, investing, and financing categories. To get the information to construct the statement, we do the following:

1. **Use the direct method to determine individual cash flows from operating activities.** We use changes that occurred during 2005 in various current asset and current liability accounts.
2. **Determine cash flows from investing activities.** We do this by analyzing changes in noncurrent asset accounts.
3. **Determine cash flows from financing activities.** We do this by analyzing changes in liability and stockholders' equity accounts.

The net cash flows from investing and financing are identical to those prepared using the indirect method. Only the format of the net cash flows from operating activities differs between the two methods, not the total amount of cash generated from operating activities.

CASH FLOWS FROM OPERATING ACTIVITIES

The **direct method** presents net cash flow from operating activities by showing the major categories of operating cash receipts and payments. The operating cash receipts and payments are usually determined by converting the accrual revenues and expenses to corresponding cash amounts. It is efficient to do it this way because the accrual revenues and expenses are readily available in the income statement.

Convert Revenues and Expenses to Cash Flows

Exhibit 4A.1 summarizes the procedures for converting individual income statement items to corresponding cash flows from operating activities.

EXHIBIT 4A.1 Adjustments to Convert Income Statement Items to Operating Activity Cash Flows

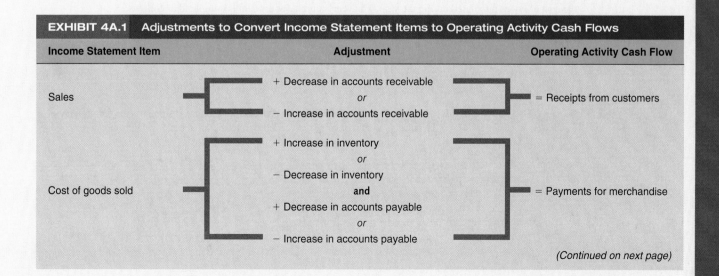

(Continued on next page)

EXHIBIT 4A.1	Adjustments to Convert Income Statement Items to Operating Activity Cash Flows *(Continued)*	
Income Statement Item	**Adjustment**	**Operating Activity Cash Flow**

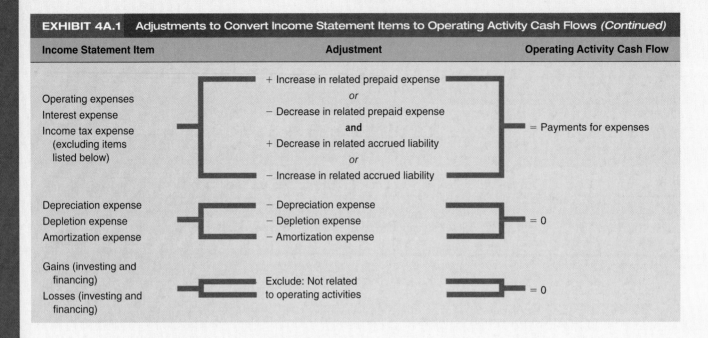

Operating expenses
Interest expense
Income tax expense
(excluding items
listed below)

+ Increase in related prepaid expense
or
– Decrease in related prepaid expense
and
+ Decrease in related accrued liability
or
– Increase in related accrued liability

= Payments for expenses

Depreciation expense
Depletion expense
Amortization expense

– Depreciation expense
– Depletion expense
– Amortization expense

= 0

Gains (investing and
financing)
Losses (investing and
financing)

Exclude: Not related
to operating activities

= 0

Java House Case Illustration

We next explain and illustrate the process of converting Java House's 2005 revenues and expenses to corresponding cash flows from operating activities under the direct method.

Convert Sales to Cash Received from Customers

> **REMEMBER . . .**
> The direct method for reporting operating cash flows is prepared by adjusting each item on the income statement from an accrual basis to a cash basis.

During 2005, accounts receivable increased $5,000. This increase means that during 2005, cash collections on account (which decrease accounts receivable) were less than credit sales (which increase accounts receivable). We compute cash received from customers as follows (this computation assumes that no accounts were written off as uncollectible during the period).

Sales	$250,000
– Increase in accounts receivable	(5,000)
= Cash received from customers	$245,000

Convert Cost of Goods Sold to Cash Paid for Merchandise Purchased

The conversion of cost of goods sold to cash paid for merchandise purchased is a two-step process. First, cost of goods sold is adjusted for the change in inventory to determine the amount of purchases during the year. Then the purchases amount is adjusted for the change in accounts payable to derive the cash paid for merchandise purchased. Inventory decreased from $60,000 to $54,000 during 2005. This $6,000 decrease indicates that the cost of goods sold exceeded the cost of goods purchased during the year. The year's purchases amount is computed as follows.

Cost of goods sold	$148,000
– Decrease in inventory	(6,000)
= Purchases	$142,000

During 2005, accounts payable decreased $9,000. This decrease reflects the fact that cash payments for merchandise purchased on account (which decrease accounts payable) exceeded purchases on account (which increase accounts payable). The cash paid for merchandise purchased, therefore, is computed as follows.

Purchases	$142,000
+ Decrease in accounts payable	9,000
= Cash paid for merchandise purchased	$151,000

Convert Wages Expense to Cash Paid to Employees

No adjustment to wages expense is needed. The absence of any beginning or ending accrued liability for wages payable means that wages expense and cash paid to employees as wages are the same amount: $52,000.

Convert Insurance Expense to Cash Paid for Insurance

Prepaid insurance increased $13,000 during 2005. The $13,000 increase reflects the excess of cash paid for insurance during 2005 (which increases prepaid insurance) over the year's insurance expense (which decreases prepaid insurance). Starting with insurance expense the cash paid for insurance is computed as follows.

Insurance expense	$ 5,000
+ Increase in prepaid insurance	13,000
= Cash paid for insurance	$18,000

Eliminate Depreciation Expense and Other Noncash Operating Expenses

Depreciation expense is a noncash expense. Because it does not represent a cash payment, depreciation expense is eliminated as we convert accrual expense amounts to the corresponding amounts of cash payments. If Java House had any amortization expense or depletion expense, it would eliminate them for the same reason. The amortization of an intangible asset and the depletion of a natural resource are noncash expenses.

Convert Income Tax Expense to Cash Paid for Income Taxes

The increase in income tax payable from $3,000 at December 31, 2004, to $5,000 at December 31, 2005, means that 2005's income tax expense (which increases income tax payable) was $2,000 more than 2005's tax payments (which decrease income tax payable). If we start with income tax expense, then we calculate cash paid for income taxes as follows.

Income tax expense	$11,000
− Increase in income tax payable	(2,000)
= Cash paid for income taxes	$ 9,000

Omit Gains and Losses Related to Investing and Financing Activities

The income statement may contain gains and losses related to investing or financing activities. Examples include gains and losses from the sale of plant assets and gains and losses from the retirement of bonds payable. Because these gains and losses are not related to operating activities, we omit them as we convert income statement items to various cash flows from operating activities. The cash flows relating to these gains and losses are reported in the investing activities or financing activities sections of the statement of cash flows. Java House had an $8,000 gain from the sale of land in 2005. This gain resulted from an investing activity; no related cash flow appears within the operating activities category.

We have now applied the adjustments to convert each accrual revenue and expense to the corresponding operating cash flow. We use these individual cash flows to prepare the operating activities section of the statement of cash flows, see Exhibit 4A.2

EXHIBIT 4A.2	Direct Method Operating Section of Statement of Cash Flows		
Cash received from customers			$ 245,000
Cash paid for merchandise purchased		$151,000	
Cash paid to employees		52,000	
Cash paid for insurance		18,000	
Cash paid for income taxes		9,000	230,000
Net cash provided by operating activities			$ 15,000

CASH FLOWS FROM INVESTING AND FINANCING

The reporting of investing and financing activities in the statement of cash flows is identical under the indirect and direct methods. Thus, we simply refer to the previous sections in this chapter for explanations.

Supplemental Disclosures

When the direct method is used for the statement of cash flows, three separate disclosures are required: (1) a reconciliation of net income to the net cash flow from operating activities, (2) a schedule or description of all noncash investing and financing transactions, and (3) the firm's policy for determining which highly liquid, short-term investments are treated as cash equivalents. The firm's policy regarding cash equivalents is placed in the financial statement notes. The other two separate disclosures are reported either in the notes or at the bottom of the statement of cash flows.

The required reconciliation is essentially the indirect method of computing cash flow from operating activities. *Thus, when the direct method is used in the statement of cash flows, the indirect method is a required separate disclosure.* We discussed the indirect method earlier in this appendix.

Java House did have one noncash investing and financing event during 2005: the issuance of common stock to acquire a patent. This event is disclosed as supplemental information to the statement of cash flows in Exhibit 4.10.

APPENDIX-END REVIEW

Espresso Royale's income statement and comparative balance sheets are as follows.

Espresso Royale Income Statement For Year Ended December 31, 2005		
Sales		$ 385,000
Dividend income		5,000
Net Sales		390,000
Cost of goods sold	$233,000	
Wages expense	82,000	
Advertising expense	10,000	
Depreciation expense	11,000	
Income tax expense	17,000	
Loss on sale of investments	2,000	355,000
Net income		$ 35,000

ESPRESSO ROYALE Comparative Balance Sheets	Dec 31, 2005	Dec 31, 2004
Assets		
Cash	$ 8,000	$ 12,000
Accounts receivable	22,000	28,000
Inventory	94,000	66,000
Prepaid advertising	12,000	9,000
Long-term investments—Available-for-sale	30,000	41,000
Fair value adjustment to investments	—	(1,000)
Plant assets	178,000	130,000
Accumulated depreciation	(72,000)	(61,000)
Total assets	$272,000	$224,000
Liabilities and Equity		
Accounts payable	$ 27,000	$ 14,000
Wages payable	6,000	2,500
Income tax payable	3,000	4,500
Common stock	139,000	125,000
Retained earnings	97,000	79,000
Unrealized loss on investments	—	(1,000)
Total liabilities and equity	$272,000	$224,000

Cash dividends of $17,000 were declared and paid during 2005. Plant assets were purchased for cash in 2005, and later in the year, additional common stock was issued for cash. Investments costing $11,000 were sold for cash at a $2,000 loss in 2005; an unrealized loss of $1,000 on these investments had been recorded in 2004 (at December 31, 2005, the cost and fair value of unsold investments are equal).

Required

a. Compute the change in cash that occurred during 2005.

b. Prepare a 2005 statement of cash flows using the direct method.

Solution

a. $8,000 ending balance − $12,000 beginning balance = $4,000 decrease in cash

b. (1) Use the direct method to determine the individual cash flows from operating activities.
- $385,000 sales + $6,000 accounts receivable decrease = $391,000 cash received from customers
- $5,000 dividend income = $5,000 cash received as dividends
- $233,000 cost of goods sold + $28,000 inventory increase − $13,000 accounts payable increase = $248,000 cash paid for merchandise purchased
- $82,000 wages expense − $3,500 wages payable increase = $78,500 cash paid to employees
- $10,000 advertising expense + $3,000 prepaid advertising increase = $13,000 cash paid for advertising
- $17,000 income tax expense + $1,500 income tax payable decrease = $18,500 cash paid for income taxes

(2) Analyze changes in remaining noncash asset (and contra asset) accounts to determine cash flows from investing activities.
- Long-term investments: $11,000 decrease resulted from sale of investments for cash at a $2,000 loss. Cash received from sale of investments = $9,000 ($11,000 cost − $2,000 loss).
- Fair value adjustment to investments: $1,000 decrease resulted from the elimination of this account balance (and the unrealized loss on investments) at the end of 2005. No cash flow effect.
- Plant assets: $48,000 increase resulted from purchase of plant assets for cash. Cash paid to purchase plant assets = $48,000.
- Accumulated depreciation: $11,000 increase resulted from the recording of 2005 depreciation. No cash flow effect.

(3) Analyze changes in remaining liability and stockholders' equity accounts to determine cash flows from financing activities.
- Common stock: $14,000 increase resulted from the issuance of stock for cash. Cash received from issuance of common stock = $14,000.
- Retained earnings: $18,000 increase resulted from net income of $35,000 and dividend declaration of $17,000. Cash dividends paid = $17,000.
- Unrealized loss on investments: $1,000 decrease resulted from the elimination of this account balance (and the fair value adjustment to investments) at the end of 2005. No cash flow effect.

The statement of cash flows under the direct method is as follows.

Espresso Royale Statement of Cash Flows For Year Ended December 31, 2005		
Cash flows from operating activities		
Cash received from customers	$391,000	
Cash received as dividends	5,000	
Cash paid for merchandise purchased	(248,000)	
Cash paid to employees	(78,500)	
Cash paid for advertising	(13,000)	
Cash paid for income taxes	(18,500)	
Net cash provided by operating activities		$38,000
Cash flows from investing activities		
Sale of investments	9,000	
Purchase of plant assets	(48,000)	
Net cash used by investing activities		(39,000)
Cash flows from financing activities		
Issuance of common stock	14,000	
Payment of dividends	(17,000)	
Net cash used by financing activities		(3,000)
Net decrease in cash		(4,000)
Cash at beginning of year		12,000
Cash at end of year		$ 8,000

KEY TERMS

Cash equivalents (p. 145)

Depreciation and amortization
    expenses (p. 151)

Direct method (p. 167)

Financing activities (p. 147)

Free cash flow (p. 163)

Indirect method (p. 149)

Investing activities (p. 147)

Noncash investing and financing
    activities (p. 148)

Operating activities (p. 145)

Operating cash flow to current
    liabilities ratio (p. 162)

Operating cash flow to capital
    expenditures ratio (p. 162)

Statement of cash flows (p. 144)

MULTIPLE CHOICE

1. Which of the following is not disclosed in a statement of cash flows?
    a. a transfer of cash to a cash equivalent investment
    b. the amount of cash at year-end
    c. cash outflows from investing activities during the period
    d. cash inflows from financing activities during the period

2. Which of the following events appear in the cash flows from investing activities section of the statement of cash flows?
    a. cash received as interest
    b. cash received from issuance of common stock
    c. cash purchase of equipment
    d. cash payment of dividends

3. Which of the following events appear in the cash flows from financing activities section of the statement of cash flows?
    a. cash purchase of equipment
    b. cash purchase of bonds issued by another company
    c. cash received as repayment for funds loaned
    d. cash purchase of treasury stock

4. Tyler Company has a net income of $49,000 and the following related items:

Depreciation expense	$ 5,000
Accounts receivable increase	2,000
Inventory decrease	10,000
Accounts payable decrease	4,000

Using the indirect method, what is Tyler's net cash flow from operations?

    a. $42,000
    b. $46,000
    c. $58,000
    d. $38,000

Refer to information in Exhibits 4.3 and 4.10 for questions 5–6.

5. Free Cash flow for Java House in 2005 is
    a. $43,000.
    b. $28,000.
    c. $15,000.
    d. $0.

6. The operating cash flow to current liabilities ratio for Java House in 2005 is
    a. 3.00.
    b. 2.00.
    c. 1.00.
    d. 0.81.

Superscript ᴬ denotes assignments based on Appendix 4A.

DISCUSSION QUESTIONS

Q4-1. What is the definition of *cash equivalents*? Give three examples of cash equivalents.

Q4-2. Why are cash equivalents included with cash in a statement of cash flows?

Q4-3. What are the three major types of activities classified on a statement of cash flows? Give an example of a cash inflow and a cash outflow in each classification.

Q4-4. In which of the three activity categories of a statement of cash flows would each of the following items appear? Indicate for each item whether it represents a cash inflow or a cash outflow:
 a. Cash purchase of equipment.
 b. Cash collection on loans.
 c. Cash dividends paid.
 d. Cash dividends received.
 e. Cash proceeds from issuing stock.
 f. Cash receipts from customers.
 g. Cash interest paid.
 h. Cash interest received.

Q4-5. Traverse Company acquired a $3,000,000 building by issuing $3,000,000 worth of bonds payable. In terms of cash flow reporting, what type of transaction is this? What special disclosure requirements apply to a transaction of this type?

Q4-6. Why are noncash investing and financing transactions disclosed as supplemental information to a statement of cash flows?

Q4-7. Why is a statement of cash flows a useful financial statement?

Q4-8. What is the difference between the direct method and the indirect method of presenting net cash flow from operating activities?

Q4-9. In determining net cash flow from operating activities using the indirect method, why must we add depreciation back to net income? Give an example of another item that is added back to net income under the indirect method.

Q4-10. Vista Company sold for $98,000 cash land originally costing $70,000. The company recorded a gain on the sale of $28,000. How is this event reported in a statement of cash flows using the indirect method?

Q4-11. A firm uses the indirect method. Using the following information, what is its net cash flow from operating activities?

Net income	$88,000
Accounts receivable decrease	13,000
Inventory increase	9,000
Accounts payable decrease	3,500
Income tax payable increase	1,500
Depreciation expense	6,000

Q4-12. What separate disclosures are required for a company that reports a statement of cash flows using the indirect method?

Q4-13. If a business had a net loss for the year, under what circumstances would the statement of cash flows show a positive net cash flow from operating activities?

Q4-14.ᴬ A firm is converting its accrual revenues to corresponding cash amounts using the direct method. Sales on the income statement are $925,000. Beginning and ending accounts receivable on the balance sheet are $58,000 and $44,000, respectively. What is the amount of cash received from customers?

Q4-15.ᴬ A firm reports $86,000 wages expense in its income statement. If beginning and ending wages payable are $3,900 and $2,800, respectively, what is the amount of cash paid to employees?

Q4-16.ᴬ A firm reports $43,000 advertising expense in its income statement. If beginning and ending prepaid advertising are $6,000 and $7,600, respectively, what is the amount of cash paid for advertising?

Q4-17.ᴬ Rusk Company sold equipment for $5,100 cash that had cost $35,000 and had $29,000 of accumulated depreciation. How is this event reported in a statement of cash flows using the direct method?

Q4-18.ᴬ What separate disclosures are required for a company that reports a statement of cash flows using the direct method?

Q4-19. How is the operating cash flow to current liabilities ratio calculated? Explain its use.

Q4-20. How is the operating cash flow to capital expenditures ratio calculated? Explain its use.

Q4-21. The statement of cash flows provides information that may be useful in predicting future cash flows, evaluating financial flexibility, assessing liquidity, and identifying financing needs. It is not, however, the best financial statement for learning about a firm's financial performance during a period; information about periodic financial performance is provided by the income statement. Two basic principles—the revenue recognition principle and the matching concept—work to distinguish the income statement from the statement of cash flows. (a) Define the revenue recognition principle and the matching concept. (b) Briefly explain how these two principles work to make the income statement a better report on periodic financial performance than the statement of cash flows.

MINI EXERCISES

M4-22. Classification of Cash Flows (LO1)
For each of the items below, indicate whether the cash flow relates to an operating activity, an investing activity, or a financing activity.
a. Cash receipts from customers for services rendered.
b. Sale of long-term investments for cash.
c. Acquisition of plant assets for cash.
d. Payment of income taxes.
e. Bonds payable issued for cash.
f. Payment of cash dividends declared in previous year.
g. Purchase of short-term investments (not cash equivalents) for cash.

M4-23. Classifying Cash Flow Statement Components (LO1)

Dole Food Company, Inc.

The following table presents selected items from the 2004 cash flow statement of **Dole Food Company, Inc.** For each item, determine whether the amount would be disclosed in the cash flow statement under operating activities, investing activities, or financing activities. (Dole uses the indirect method of reporting.)

Dole Food Company, Inc.
Selected Items from Its Cash Flow Statement

1 Cash dividends paid
2 Change in inventories
3 Depreciation and amortization
4 Long-term debt repayments
5 Change in accounts payable and accrued liabilities
6 Net income
7 Proceeds from sales of assets
8 Provision for deferred income taxes
9 Change in prepaid expenses and other assets
10 Short-term debt borrowings
11 Capital additions

M4-24. Classification of Cash Flows (LO1)
For each of the items below, indicate whether it is (1) a cash flow from an operating activity, (2) a cash flow from an investing activity, (3) a cash flow from a financing activity, (4) a noncash investing and financing activity, or (5) none of the above.
a. Paid cash to retire bonds payable at a loss.
b. Received cash as settlement of a lawsuit.
c. Acquired a patent in exchange for common stock.
d. Received advance payments from customers on orders for custom-made goods.
e. Gave large cash contribution to local university.
f. Invested cash in 60-day commercial paper (a cash equivalent).

M4-25. Classifying Cash Flow Statement Components (LO1)

Pacific Sunwear (PSUN)

The following table presents selected items from the 2004 cash flow statement of **Pacific Sunwear.** For each item determine whether the amount would be disclosed in the cash flow statement under operating activities, investing activities, or financing activities. (Pacific Sunwear uses the indirect method of reporting.)

Pacific Sunwear of California, Inc. Selected Items from its Cash Flow Statement
1 Depreciation and amortization
2 Proceeds from exercise of stock options
3 Loss on disposal of equipment
4 Change in accrued liabilities
5 Repayments of long-term debt obligations
6 Changes in income taxes payable and deferred income taxes
7 Change in accounts receivable
8 Purchases of property and equipment
9 Repurchase and retirement of common stock
10 Purchases of available-for-sale short-term investments

M4-26. Net Cash Flow from Operating Activities (Indirect Method) (LO2)

The following information was obtained from Galena Company's comparative balance sheets. Assume that Galena Company's 2005 income statement showed depreciation expense of $8,000, a gain on sale of investments of $9,000, and a net income of $45,000. Calculate the net cash flow from operating activities using the indirect method.

	Dec 31, 2005	Dec 31, 2004
Cash	$ 19,000	$ 9,000
Accounts receivable	44,000	35,000
Inventory	55,000	49,000
Prepaid rent	6,000	8,000
Long-term investments	21,000	34,000
Plant assets	150,000	106,000
Accumulated depreciation	40,000	32,000
Accounts payable	24,000	20,000
Income tax payable	4,000	6,000
Common stock	121,000	92,000
Retained earnings	106,000	91,000

M4-27. Classifying Cash Flow Statement Components and Determining Their Effects (LO1, 2, 3)

The following table presents selected items from the 2004 cash flow statement of Ethan Allen Interiors.

Ethan Allen Interiors (ETH)

a. For each item determine whether the amount would be disclosed in the cash flow statement under operating activities, investing activities, or financing activities. (Assume it uses the indirect method of reporting.)

b. For each item, determine whether the effect on cash flow is positive, negative, or indeterminate.

Ethan Allen Interiors Inc. and Subsidiaries Consolidated Statements of Cash Flows—Selected Items
1 Purchases of short-term investments
2 Payment of cash dividends
3 Depreciation and amortization
4 Provision for deferred income taxes
5 Decrease in customer deposits
6 Capital expenditures
7 Increase in income taxes and accounts payable
8 Payments on long-term debt and capital leases
9 Gain on disposal of property, plant, and equipment
10 Increase in prepaid and other current assets
11 Net proceeds from issuance of common stock
12 Proceeds from the disposal of property, plant, and equipment
13 Net income
14 Decrease in inventories
15 Borrowings on revolving credit facility

M4-28. **Net Cash Flow from Operating Activities (Indirect Method)** (LO2)

Cairo Company had a $21,000 net loss from operations for 2005. Depreciation expense for 2005 was $8,600 and a 2005 cash dividend of $6,000 was declared and paid. Balances of the current asset and current liability accounts at the beginning and end of 2005 follow. Did Cairo Company's 2005 operating activities provide or use cash? Use the indirect method to determine your answer.

	Ending	Beginning
Cash	$ 3,500	$ 7,000
Accounts receivable	16,000	25,000
Inventory	50,000	53,000
Prepaid expenses	6,000	9,000
Accounts payable	12,000	8,000
Accrued liabilities	5,000	7,600

M4-29. **Classifying Cash Flow Statement Components and Determining Their Effects** (LO1, 2, 3)

Nordstrom,
Inc. (JWN)

The following table presents selected items from the 2004 cash flow statement of Nordstrom, Inc.

a. For each item, determine whether the amount would be disclosed in the cash flow statement under operating activities, investing activities, or financing activities. (Nordstrom uses the indirect method of reporting.)

b. For each item, determine whether the effect on cash flow is positive, negative, or indeterminate.

Nordstrom, Inc. Consolidated Statement of Cash Flows—Selected Items
1   Increase in accounts receivable
2   Capital expenditures
3   Purchases of short-term investments
4   Deferred income taxes
5   Principal payments on long-term debt
6   Increase in merchandise inventories
7   Decrease in income taxes payable
8   Proceeds from employee stock purchase plan
9   Increase in accounts payable
10 Net earnings
11 Repurchase of common stock
12 Increase in accrued salaries, wages, and related benefits
13 Proceeds from sale of assets
14 Cash dividends paid
15 Depreciation and amortization of buildings and equipment

M4-30.[A] **Operating Cash Flows (Direct Method)** (LO2)

Calculate the cash flow for each of the following cases.

a. Cash paid for rent:

Rent expense	$60,000
Prepaid rent, beginning year	10,000
Prepaid rent, end of year	8,000

b. Cash received as interest:

Interest income	$16,000
Interest receivable, beginning year	3,000
Interest receivable, end of year	3,700

c. Cash paid for merchandise purchased:

Cost of goods sold	$98,000
Inventory, beginning year	19,000
Inventory, end of year	22,000
Accounts payable, beginning year	11,000
Accounts payable, end of year	7,000

M4-31.[A] **Operating Cash Flows (Direct Method)** **(LO2)**

Howell Company's current year income statement reports the following:

Sales	$825,000
Cost of goods sold	550,000
Gross profit	$275,000

Howell's comparative balance sheets show the following (accounts payable relate to merchandise purchases):

	End of Year	Beginning of Year
Accounts receivable	$ 71,000	$ 60,000
Inventory	109,000	96,000
Prepaid expenses	3,000	8,000
Accounts payable	31,000	37,000

Compute Howell's current-year cash received from customers and cash paid for merchandise purchased.

EXERCISES

E4-32. **Classifying Cash Flow Statement Components and Preparing the Statement of Cash Flow** **(LO1, 2, 3)**

The table below contains data from the 2004 cash flow statement of Target Corporation.

Target (TGT)

Target Corporation Consolidated Statement of Cash Flows ($ millions)	
Proceeds from sale of discontinued operations	$4,255
Net earnings	3,198
Depreciation and amortization	1,259
Increase in accounts paybale	823
Cash balance at the beginning of 2004	708
Increase in accrued liabilities	319
Deferred income tax provision	233
Stock issued as a result of stock option exercises	146
Loss on disposal of fixed assets, net	59
Proceeds from disposals of fixed assets	56
Additions to long-term debt	10
Other operating cash flow adjustments	(12)
Decrease in income taxes payable	(78)
Dividends paid	(272)
Increase in accounts receivable	(448)
Increase in inventory	(853)
Repurchase of stock	(1,290)
Gain on disposal of discontinued operations, net of tax	(1,313)
Reductions of long-term debt	(1,487)
Expenditures for property and equipment	(3,068)

a. For each item, indicate whether the item is operating, investing, or financing.
b. Prepare the cash flow statement (indirect method) using the data from the table.
c. Compute Target's cash balance as of the end of 2004.

E4-33. Net Cash Flow from Operating Activities (Indirect Method) (LO2)

Lincoln Company owns no plant assets and reported the following income statement for the current year:

Sales		$750,000
Cost of goods sold	$470,000	
Wages expense	110,000	
Rent expense	42,000	
Insurance expense	15,000	637,000
Net income		$113,000

Additional balance sheet information about the company follows:

	End of Year	Beginning of Year
Accounts receivable	$54,000	$49,000
Inventory	60,000	66,000
Prepaid insurance	8,000	7,000
Accounts payable	22,000	18,000
Wages payable	9,000	11,000

Use the information to calculate the net cash flow from operating activities under the indirect method. Also, compute its (1) operating cash flow to current liabilities ratio and (2) operating cash flow to capital expenditure ratio. (Assume current liabilities consist of accounts payable and wages payable.)

E4-34. Classifying Cash Flow Statement Components and Preparing the Statement of Cash Flow (LO1, 2, 3)

Oakley, Inc. (OO)

The table below contains data from the 2004 cash flow statement of Oakley, Inc.

Oakley, Inc. and Subsidiaries Consolidated Statements of Cash Flows ($ thousands)	
Net income	$41,550
Increase in receivables, net	(23,717)
Acquisitions of property and equipment	(29,615)
Cash and cash equivalents at December 31, 2003	49,211
Decrease in income taxes payable	(7,580)
Net proceeds from issuance of common shares	3,458
Increase in accrued expenses and other current liabilities	5,763
Dividends	(10,208)
Increase in accounts payable	5,751
Deferred income taxes, net	2,331
Increase in accrued warranty	186
Repayments of bank borrowings	(2,853)
Increase in deposits	362
Acquisitions of businesses	(450)
Increase in other assets (investments)	(491)
Increase in prepaid expenses and other	(974)
Depreciation and amortization	31,879
Loss on disposition of equipment	639
Other noncash expenses	1,403
Proceeds from bank borrowings	3,416
Proceeds from sale of property and equipment	311
Increase in inventories	(12,711)
Repurchase of common shares	(5,923)

a. For each item, indicate whether the item is operating, investing, or financing.

b. Prepare the cash flow statement (indirect method) using the data from the table.

c. Compute Oakley's cash balance as of the end of 2004.

d. Oakley's cash flow statement reports "Proceeds from bank borrowings" and "Repayments of bank borrowings." Why might both have occurred in the same period? Compute its net change in bank borrowings. Why does Oakley present both amounts in the cash flow statement rather than simply showing the net change?

E4-35. Statement of Cash Flows (Indirect Method) (LO2, 3)

Use the following information about Lund Corporation for 2005 to prepare a statement of cash flows under the indirect method.

Accounts payable increase	$ 9,000
Accounts receivable increase	4,000
Accrued liabilities decrease	3,000
Amortization expense	6,000
Cash balance, beginning of 2005	22,000
Cash balance, end of 2005	15,000
Cash paid as dividends	29,000
Cash paid to purchase land	90,000
Cash paid to retire bonds payable at par	60,000
Cash received from issuance of common stock	35,000
Cash received from sale of equipment	17,000
Depreciation expense	29,000
Gain on sale of equipment	4,000
Inventory decrease	13,000
Net income	76,000
Prepaid expenses increase	2,000

E4-36. Reconciling Changes in Balance Sheet Accounts (LO1, 2, 3)

The following table presents selected items from the 2004 and 2003 balance sheets and 2004 income statement of Lowe's Companies, Inc.

Lowe's Companies, Inc. (LOW)

Lowe's Companies, Inc. ($ millions)				
Selected Balance Sheet Data			**Selected Income Statement Data**	
	2004	**2003**		**2004**
Merchandise inventories	$5,982	$ 4,584	Cost of merchandise sold ..	$24,165
Property, net of depreciation ..	13,911	11,819	Depreciation expense	902
Accounts payable	2,687	2,212	Net income	2,176
Retained earnings	9,634	7,574		

a. Compute the cash paid for merchandise inventories in 2004. Assume all merchandise was purchased on account.

b. Compute the net cost of property acquired in 2004

c. Compute the cash dividends paid in 2004

E4-37. Investing and Financing Cash Flows (LO3)

During 2005, Paxon Corporation's long-term investments account (at cost) increased $15,000, which was the net result of purchasing stocks costing $80,000 and selling stocks costing $65,000 at a $6,000 loss. Also, its bonds payable account decreased $40,000, the net result of issuing $100,000 of bonds at $103,000 and retiring bonds with a face value (and book value) of $140,000 at a $9,000 gain. What items and amounts appear in the (a) cash flows from investing activities and (b) cash flows from financing activities sections of its 2005 statement of cash flows?

E4-38. Reconciling Changes in Balance Sheet Accounts (LO1, 2, 3)

The following table presents selected items from the 2004 and 2003 balance sheets and 2004 income statement of Borders Group, Inc.

Borders Group, Inc. (BGP)

Borders Group, Inc. ($ millions)				
Selected Balance Sheet Data			**Selected Income Statement Data**	
	2004	**2003**		**2004**
Merchandise inventories	$1,306.9	$1,235.6	Cost of merchandise sold	$2,803.6
Property and equipment	635.6	671.8	Depreciation expense	112.9
Trade accounts payable	615.1	595.9	Loss on sale of property and equipment	2.4
Retained earnings	539.0	432.2	Net Income	131.9

  a. Compute the cash paid for merchandise inventories in 2004. Assume all merchandise was purchased on account.
  b. Borders reported expenditures for property and equipment of $115.5 million in 2004. Compute the cash proceeds from the sale of property and equipment in 2004.
  c. Determine the cash dividends paid in 2004.
  d. For each part a, b, and c, prepare journal entries to record the cash transactions.

E4-39.[A] **Operating Cash Flows (Direct Method)**   (LO2)
Calculate the cash flow for each of the following cases.
  a. Cash paid for advertising:

Advertising expense	$62,000
Prepaid advertising, beginning of year	11,000
Prepaid advertising, end of year	15,000

  b. Cash paid for income taxes:

Income tax expense	$29,000
Income tax payable, beginning of year	7,100
Income tax payable, end of year	4,900

  c. Cash paid for merchandise purchased:

Cost of goods sold	$180,000
Inventory, beginning of year	30,000
Inventory, end of year	25,000
Accounts payable, beginning of year	10,000
Accounts payable, end of year	12,000

E4-40.[A] **Statement of Cash Flows (Direct Method)**   (LO2, 3)
Use the following information about the 2005 cash flows of Mason Corporation to prepare a statement of cash flows under the direct method.

Cash balance, end of 2005	$ 12,000
Cash paid to employees and suppliers	148,000
Cash received from sale of land	40,000
Cash paid to acquire treasury stock	10,000
Cash balance, beginning of 2005	16,000
Cash received as interest	6,000
Cash paid as income taxes	11,000
Cash paid to purchase equipment	89,000
Cash received from customers	194,000
Cash received from issuing bonds payable ..	30,000
Cash paid as dividends	16,000

E4-41.[A] **Operating Cash Flows (Direct Method)**   (LO2)
Refer to the information in Exercise 4-33. Calculate the net cash flow from operating activities using the direct method. Show a related cash flow for each revenue and expense. Also, compute its (1) operating cash flow to current liabilities ratio and (2) operating cash flow to capital expenditure ratio. (Assume current liability consist of accounts payable and wages payable.)

PROBLEMS

P4-42. Estimating and Interpreting Operating Cash Flows (LO1, 2, 3, 4)

The 2004 and 2003 balance sheets (condensed) of Robert Mondavi are as follows.

Robert Mondavi

Robert Mondavi Corporation Condensed Balance Sheets		
($ thousands)	2004	2003
Cash	$ 48,960	$ 1,339
Receivables and other current assets	101,574	108,656
Inventories	387,940	392,635
Total current assets	538,474	502,630
Property, plant and equipment, and other noncurrent assets	439,696	458,547
Total assets	$978,170	$961,177
Accounts payable and accrued expenses	$ 63,602	$ 57,146
Short-term debt and current portion of long-term debt	18,910	14,837
Total current liabilities	82,512	71,983
Long-term debt	363,289	397,889
Other long-term liabilities	52,569	40,311
Total liabilities	498,370	510,183
Stockholders' equity	479,800	450,994
Total liabilities and stockholders' equity	$978,170	$961,177

In addition, the 2004 income statement reported net income of $25,584 and depreciation and amortization expense of $25,348 ($ thousands). Assume that other long-term liabilities includes deferred income taxes and other operating liabilities.

Required

a. Use information in the comparative balance sheets to verify the following:

Change in cash = Change in liabilities + Change in stockholders' equity − Change in noncash assets

b. Calculate its cash flow from operations based on the data provided.
c. Calculate Mondavi's operating cash flow to current liabilities ratio.
d. Explain (as best you can) any difference between operating cash flow and net income.
e. Which items in Mondavi's cash flow statement do you suspect analysts watch most closely? Why?

P4-43. Reconciling and Computing Operating Cash Flows from Net Income (LO2)

Petroni Company reports the following selected results for its calendar year 2005.

Net income	$135,000
Depreciation expense	25,000
Gain on sale of assets	5,000
Accounts receivable increase	10,000
Accounts payable increase	6,000
Prepaid expenses decrease	3,000
Wages payable decrease	4,000

Required

Prepare the operating section only of Petroni Company's statement of cash flows for 2005 under the indirect method of reporting.

P4-44. Statement of Cash Flows (Indirect Method) (LO2, 3)

Wolff Company's income statement and comparative balance sheets follow.

Wolff Company
Income Statement
For Year Ended December 31, 2005

Sales		$ 635,000
Cost of goods sold	$430,000	
Wages expense	86,000	
Insurance expense	8,000	
Depreciation expense	17,000	
Interest expense	9,000	
Income tax expense	29,000	579,000
Net income		$ 56,000

Wolff Company
Balance Sheets

	Dec. 31, 2005	Dec. 31, 2004
Assets		
Cash	$ 11,000	$ 5,000
Accounts receivable	41,000	32,000
Inventory	90,000	60,000
Prepaid insurance	5,000	7,000
Plant assets	250,000	195,000
Accumulated depreciation	(68,000)	(51,000)
Total assets	$329,000	$248,000
Liabilities and Stockholders' Equity		
Accounts payable	$ 7,000	$ 10,000
Wages payable	9,000	6,000
Income tax payable	7,000	8,000
Bonds payable	130,000	75,000
Common stock	90,000	90,000
Retained earnings	86,000	59,000
Total liabilities and equity	$329,000	$248,000

Cash dividends of $29,000 were declared and paid during 2005. Also in 2005, plant assets were purchased for cash, and bonds payable were issued for cash. Bond interest is paid semiannually on June 30 and December 31. Accounts payable relate to merchandise purchases.

Required

a. Compute the change in cash that occurred during 2005.
b. Prepare a 2005 statement of cash flows using the indirect method.

P4-45.   **Preparing the Statement of Cash Flows (Indirect Method)**   (LO1, 2, 3)

Columbia Sportswear
Company (COLM)

The 2004 and 2003 balance sheets for **Columbia Sportswear Company** follow. In addition, the following information is reported ($ thousands):

- 2004 net income was $138,624. Tax expense was $76,297. Columbia did not pay cash dividends in 2004.
- During 2004, Columbia sold property, plant and equipment for $40 cash, and recognized a loss of $541 in the sale.
- Depreciation of property, plant and equipment totaled $18,544 in 2004. Amortization of intangible assets totaled $84.
- Assume all expenditures for property, plant and equipment, and other assets were paid in cash.
- Other liabilities consist of various long-term operating liabilities.

Required

a. Prepare the cash flow statement for 2004 using the indirect method.
b. Compute the income taxes that Columbia paid in cash in 2004.
c. Evaluate Columbia's policy of not paying cash dividends. Does it have sufficient cash flow and cash resources to pay a dividend? Explain.

At December 31 ($ thousands)	2004	2003
Columbia Sportswear Company		
Consolidated Balace Sheets		
Assets		
Cash and cash equivalents	$130,023	$104,135
Short-term investments	160,205	160,450
Accounts receivable	267,653	206,024
Inventories	165,426	126,808
Deferred income taxes	22,190	17,442
Prepaid expenses and other current assets	10,536	5,371
Total current assets	756,033	620,230
Property, plant, and equipment	155,013	126,247
Goodwill, intangibles and other assets	38,398	37,289
Total assets	$949,444	$783,766
Liabilities and Shareholders' Equity		
Accounts payable	$ 78,309	$ 62,432
Accrued liabilities	49,789	42,303
Income taxes payable	11,819	8,069
Long-term debt (including current maturities)	16,434	20,931
Other liabilities	1,481	0
Deferred income taxes	11,425	9,202
Total liabilites	169,194	142,937
Shareholders' equity	780,250	640,829
Total liabilities and shareholder's equity	$949,444	$783,766

P4-46. **Statement of Cash Flows (Indirect Method)** (LO2, 3)

Arctic Company's income statement and comparative balance sheets follow.

Arctic Company
Income Statement
For Year Ended December 31, 2005

Sales		$728,000
Cost of goods sold	$534,000	
Wages expense	190,000	
Advertising expense	31,000	
Depreciation expense	22,000	
Interest expense	18,000	
Gain on sale of land	(25,000)	770,000
Net loss		$(42,000)

Arctic Company
Balance Sheets

	Dec. 31, 2005	Dec. 31, 2004
Assets		
Cash	$ 49,000	$ 28,000
Accounts receivable	42,000	50,000
Inventory	107,000	113,000
Prepaid advertising	10,000	13,000
Plant assets	360,000	222,000
Accumulated depreciation	(78,000)	(56,000)
Total assets	$490,000	$370,000

(table continues on the next page)

Arctic Company Balance Sheets		
	Dec. 31, 2005	Dec. 31, 2004
Liabilities and Stockholders' Equity		
Accounts payable	$ 17,000	$ 31,000
Interest payable	6,000	—
Bonds payable	200,000	—
Common stock	245,000	245,000
Retained earnings	52,000	94,000
Treasury stock	(30,000)	—
Total liabilities and equity	$490,000	$370,000

During 2005, Arctic sold land for $70,000 cash that had originally cost $45,000. Arctic also purchased equipment for cash, acquired treasury stock for cash, and issued bonds payable for cash in 2005. Accounts payable relate to merchandise purchases.

Required

a. Compute the change in cash that occurred during 2005.

b. Prepare a 2005 statement of cash flows using the indirect method.

P4-47. **Preparing the Statement of Cash Flows (Indirect Method)** (LO1, 2, 3, 4, 5)

Campbell Soup Company (CPB)

The 2005 and 2004 balance sheets for Campbell Soup Company follow. In addition, the following information is available.

▪ Fiscal 2005 net earnings were $707 million. Taxes on earnings (tax expense) were $323 million. (Fiscal 2005 refers to the 52 weeks ended July 31, 2005.)

▪ During fiscal 2005, Campbell acquired $369 million in plant assets and intangibles, paying $332 million in cash and issuing long-term debt of $37 million for the remainder.

▪ Depreciation and amortization of plant assets and intangibles total $279 million in fiscal 2005.

▪ During fiscal 2005, Campbell repurchased some of its common stock and reissued the shares as part of its stock based compensation plans. These transactions resulted in net decreases in shareowners' equity and cash of $31 million.

Required

a. Prepare the cash flow statement for fiscal 2005 using the indirect method.

b. Compute the income taxes that Campbell paid in cash in fiscal 2005.

c. Compute its operating cash flow to current liabilities ratio and its free cash flow.

Campbell Soup Company Consolidated Balance Sheets		
($ millions)	July 31, 2005	August 1, 2004
Assets		
Cash and cash equivalents	$ 40	$ 32
Accounts receivable	509	490
Inventories	782	782
Prepaid expenses	181	164
Total current assets	1,512	1,468
Plant assets and intangibles, net of depreciation	5,114	5,044
Investments	150	150
Total assets	$ 6,776	$ 6,662
Liabilities and Shareholders' Equity		
Notes payable	$ 451	$ 810
Payable to suppliers and others	624	607
Accrued liabilities	606	594
Accrued income taxes	251	250
Dividend payable	70	65
Total current liabilities	2,002	2,326

(table continues on the next page)

Campbell Soup Company
Consolidated Balance Sheets

($ millions)	July 31, 2005	August 1, 2004
Long-term debt and other liabilities	2,746	2,709
Deferred income taxes	342	332
Deferred compensation and benefits	416	421
Total liabilites	5,506	5,788
Shareowners' equity	1,270	874
Total liabilities and shareowners' equity	$ 6,776	$ 6,662

P4-48. **Statement of Cash Flows (Indirect Method)** **(LO2, 3, 4, 5)**
Dair Company's income statement and comparative balance sheets follow.

Dair Company
Income Statement
For Year Ended December 31, 2005

Sales		$ 700,000
Cost of goods sold	$440,000	
Wages and other operating expenses	95,000	
Depreciation expense	22,000	
Amortization expense	7,000	
Interest expense	10,000	
Income tax expense	36,000	
Loss on bond retirement	5,000	615,000
Net income		$ 85,000

Dair Company
Balance Sheets

	Dec. 31, 2005	Dec. 31, 2004
Assets		
Cash	$ 27,000	$ 18,000
Accounts receivable	53,000	48,000
Inventory	103,000	109,000
Prepaid expenses	12,000	10,000
Plant assets	360,000	336,000
Accumulated depreciation	(87,000)	(84,000)
Intangible assets	43,000	50,000
Total assets	$ 511,000	$ 487,000
Liabilities and Stockholders' Equity		
Accounts payable	$ 32,000	$ 26,000
Interest payable	4,000	7,000
Income tax payable	6,000	8,000
Bonds payable	60,000	120,000
Common stock	252,000	228,000
Retained earnings	157,000	98,000
Total liabilities and equity	$ 511,000	$ 487,000

During 2005, the company sold for $17,000 cash old equipment that had cost $36,000 and had $19,000 accumulated depreciation. Also in 2005, new equipment worth $60,000 was acquired in exchange for $60,000 of bonds payable, and bonds payable of $120,000 were retired for cash at a loss. A $26,000 cash dividend was declared and paid in 2005. Any stock issuances were for cash.

Required

a. Compute the change in cash that occurred in 2005.
b. Prepare a 2005 statement of cash flows using the indirect method.
c. Prepare separate schedules showing (1) cash paid for interest and for income taxes and (2) noncash investing and financing transactions.
d. Compute its (1) operating cash flow to current liabilities ratio, (2) operating cash flow to capital expenditure ratio, and (3) free cash flow.

P4-49. **Interpreting the Statement of Cash Flows** **(LO1, 4, 5)**

Staples, Inc. (SPLS)

Following is the statement of cash flows of Staples, Inc.

In thousands	Year Ended January 31, 2004
Operating activities	
Net income	$ 490,211
Adjustments to reconcile net income to net cash provided by operating activities:	
Depreciation and amortization	282,811
Asset impairment and other charges	—
Store closure charge	—
Deferred income taxes (benefit) expense	(13,725)
Other	36,434
Change in assets and liabilities, net of companies acquired	
(Increase) decrease in receivables	(4,218)
Decrease (increase) in merchandise inventories	147,130
Increase in prepaid expenses and other assets	(34)
(Decrease) increase in accounts payable	(27,266)
Increase in accrued expenses and other current liabilities	95,549
Increase in other long-term obligations	12,840
Net cash provided by operating activities	1,019,732
Investing activities	
Acquisition of property and equipment	(277,793)
Acquisition of businesses, net of cash acquired	(2,910)
Proceeds from sales and maturities of short-term investments	—
Purchase of short-term investments	(834,100)
Proceeds from sales and maturities of long-term investments	—
Purchase of long-term investments	—
Acquisition of lease rights	—
Net cash used in investing activities	(1,114,803)
Financing activities	
Proceeds from sale of capital stock	389,793
Proceeds from borrowings	—
Payments on borrowings	(325,235)
Repayments under receivables securitization agreement	(25,000)
Termination of interest rate swap agreement	—
Purchase of treasury stock	(4,287)
Net cash provided by (used in) financing activities	35,271
Effect of exchange rate changes on cash	21,376
Net (decrease) increase in cash and cash equivalents	(38,424)
Cash and cash equivalents at beginning of period	495,889
Cash and cash equivalents at end of period	$ 457,465

Required

a. Staples reports net income of $490.211 million and net cash inflows from operating activities of $1,019.732 million. Part of the difference relates to depreciation of $282.811 million. Why does Staples add this amount in the computation of operating cash flows?

b. Staples reports a positive amount of $147.130 million relating to merchandise inventories. What does this signify about the change in the dollar amount of inventories during the year? Might this positive cash inflow be of some concern? Explain.

c. Staples reports a cash outflow of $1,114.803 million relating to investing activities. Is this cash outflow a cause for concern? Explain.

d. Staples net cash flows from financing activities is $35.271 million. Does this relatively small amount imply that there is no informational value in this category for the year? Explain.

e. Staples cash balance decreased by $38.424 million during the year. Is this a cause for concern? Explain. Does Staples present a "healthy" cash flow picture for the year? Explain.

P4-50. Statement of Cash Flows (Indirect Method) (LO2, 3, 4, 5)

Rainbow Company's income statement and comparative balance sheets follow.

Rainbow Company Income Statement For Year Ended December 31, 2005		
Sales		$ 750,000
Dividend income		15,000
Net sales		765,000
Cost of goods sold	$ 440,000	
Wages and other operating expenses	130,000	
Depreciation expense	39,000	
Patent amortization expense	7,000	
Interest expense	13,000	
Income tax expense	44,000	
Loss on sale of equipment	5,000	
Gain on sale of investments	(10,000)	668,000
Net income		$ 97,000

Rainbow Company Balance Sheets		
	Dec. 31, 2005	**Dec. 31, 2004**
Assets		
Cash and cash equivalents	$ 19,000	$ 25,000
Accounts receivable	40,000	30,000
Inventory	103,000	77,000
Prepaid expenses	10,000	6,000
Long-term investments—Available-for-sale	—	50,000
Fair value adjustment to investments	—	7,000
Land	190,000	100,000
Buildings	445,000	350,000
Accumulated depreciation—Buildings	(91,000)	(75,000)
Equipment	179,000	225,000
Accumulated depreciation—Equipment	(42,000)	(46,000)
Patents	50,000	32,000
Total assets	$903,000	$781,000

(table continues on the next page)

Rainbow Company Balance Sheets		
	Dec. 31, 2005	**Dec. 31, 2004**
Liabilities and Stockholders' Equity		
Accounts payable	$ 20,000	$ 16,000
Interest payable	6,000	5,000
Income tax payable	8,000	10,000
Bonds payable	155,000	125,000
Preferred stock ($100 par value)	100,000	75,000
Common stock ($5 par value)	379,000	364,000
Paid-in capital in excess of par value—Common	133,000	124,000
Retained earnings	102,000	55,000
Unrealized gain on investments	—	7,000
Total liabilities and equity	$903,000	$781,000

During 2005, the following transactions and events occurred:
1. Sold long-term investments costing $50,000 for $60,000 cash. Unrealized gains totaling $7,000 related to these investments had been recorded in earlier years. At year-end, the fair value adjustment and unrealized gain account balances were eliminated.
2. Purchased land for cash.
3. Capitalized an expenditure made to improve the building.
4. Sold equipment for $14,000 cash that originally cost $46,000 and had $27,000 accumulated depreciation.
5. Issued bonds payable at face value for cash.
6. Acquired a patent with a fair value of $25,000 by issuing 250 shares of preferred stock at par value.
7. Declared and paid a $50,000 cash dividend.
8. Issued 3,000 shares of common stock for cash at $8 per share.
9. Recorded depreciation of $16,000 on buildings and $23,000 on equipment.

Required
a. Compute the change in cash and cash equivalents that occurred during 2005.
b. Prepare a 2005 statement of cash flows using the indirect method.
c. Prepare separate schedules showing (1) cash paid for interest and for income taxes and (2) noncash investing and financing transactions.
d. Compute its (1) operating cash flow to current liabilities ratio, (2) operating cash flow to capital expenditure ratio, and (3) free cash flow.

P4-51.[A] **Statement of Cash Flows (Direct Method)** (LO2, 3)
Refer to the data for Wolff Company in Problem 4-44.

Required
a. Compute the change in cash that occurred during 2005.
b. Prepare a 2005 statement of cash flows using the direct method.

P4-52.[A] **Statement of Cash Flows (Direct Method)** (LO2, 3)
Refer to the data for Arctic Company in Problem 4-46.

Required
a. Compute the change in cash that occurred during 2005.
b. Prepare a 2005 statement of cash flows using the direct method.

P4-53.[A] **Statement of Cash Flows (Direct Method)** (LO2, 3)
Refer to the data for Dair Company in Problem 4-48.

Required
a. Compute the change in cash that occurred in 2005.
b. Prepare a 2005 statement of cash flows using the direct method. Use one cash outflow for "cash paid for wages and other operating expenses." Accounts payable relate to inventory purchases only.

c. Prepare separate schedules showing (1) a reconciliation of net income to net cash flow from operating activities (see Exhibit 4A.1) and (2) noncash investing and financing transactions.

P4-54.[A] **Statement of Cash Flows (Direct Method)** (LO2, 3)
Refer to the data for Rainbow Company in Problem 4-50.

Required

a. Compute the change in cash that occurred in 2005.

b. Prepare a 2005 statement of cash flows using the direct method. Use one cash outflow for "cash paid for wages and other operating expenses." Accounts payable relate to inventory purchases only.

c. Prepare separate schedules showing (1) a reconciliation of net income to net cash flow from operating activities (see Exhibit 4A.1) and (2) noncash investing and financing transactions.

CASES AND PROJECTS

C4-55. **Using the Cash Flow Statement to Construct the Balance Sheet** (LO2, 3)

Based in San Diego, Aldila, Inc. produces high-quality graphite golf shafts and sells its products to most domestic and many foreign golf club manufacturers including Callaway, TaylorMade, Ping and Acushnet. Aldila's 2004 cash flow statement follows, along with its December 31, 2003, balance sheet.

Aldila, Inc.
Callaway
TaylorMade
Ping
Acushnet

Aldila, Inc. Consolidated Statements of Cash Flows	
For Year Ended December 31 ($ thousands)	**2004**
Cash flows from Operating Activities	
Net income	$ 9,320
Adjustments to reconcile net income to net cash provided by operating activities	
Depreciation	1,422
Loss on disposal of property, plant and equipment	32
Income of joint venture, noncash	(285)
Changes in assets and liabilities	
Accounts receivable	(601)
Inventories	(514)
Deferred tax assets	(2,204)
Prepaid expenses and other assets	52
Accounts payable	1,146
Accrued expenses	1,320
Income taxes receivable/payable	(1,013)
Deferred rent and other long-term liabilities	(19)
Net cash provided by operating activities	8,656
Cash Flows from Investing Activities	
Purchases of property, plant and equipment	(1,871)
Proceeds from sales of property, plant and equipment	3
Investment in marketable securities	(4,971)
Distributions from joint venture	1,500
Net Cash (used for) provided by investing activities	(5,339)
Cash Flows from Financing Activities	
Proceeds from issuance of common stock	2,064
Dividend payments	(769)
Net cash provided by (used for) financing activities	1,295
Net Increase in Cash and Cash Equivalents	$ 4,612
Supplemental Disclosure of Noncash Transactions	
Reclassification of assets from other assets to property, plant and equipment	$55

Aldila, Inc. Consolidated Balance Sheets		
At December 31 ($ thousands)	**2003**	**2004**
Assets		
Cash and cash equivalents	$ 6,919	$
Marketable securities	—	
Accounts receivable	4,613	
Income taxes receivable	—	
Inventories	7,778	
Prepaid expenses and other current assets	399	
Total current assets	9,709	
Property, plant and equipment	4,776	
Investment in joint venture	4,287	3,072
Deferred tax assets	—	
Other assets	241	
Total assets	$ 29,013	$ 42,075
Liabilities and Shareholders' Equity		
Accounts payable	$ 3,067	$
Accrued expensese	1,461	
Deferred rent	39	
Total liabilities	4,567	
Common stock and additional paid-in capital	41,851	
Accumulated deficit	(17,405)	
Total stockholders' equity	24,446	
Total liabilities and stockholders' equity	$ 29,013	$

Required

a. Complete the missing amounts from the December 31, 2004, balance sheet.

b. Compute the operating cash flow to current liabilities ratio (assume all liabilities are current).

c. Compute its free cash flow.

C4-56. **Interpreting the Statement of Cash Flows** (LO2, 3)

Amgen, Inc. (AMGN)

Following is the statement of cash flows of Amgen, Inc.

Year Ended December 31 (In millions)	2003	2002
Cash flows from operating activities		
Net income (loss)	$ 2,259.5	$ (1,391.9)
Write-off of acquired in-process R&D	—	2,991.8
Depreciation and amortization	686.5	447.3
Tax benefits related to employee stock options	268.6	251.6
Deferred income taxes	(189.6)	174.7
Other noncash expenses	99.0	24.9
Cash provided by (used in) changes in operating assets and liabilities, net of acquisitions		
Trade receivables, net	(255.5)	(121.9)
Inventories	(167.7)	(101.7)
Other current assets	(32.8)	(5.2)
Accounts payable	74.0	11.0
Accrued liabilities	824.6	(31.8)
Net cash provided by operating activities	3,566.6	2,248.8

(table continues on the next page)

Year Ended December 31 (In millions)	2003	2002
Cash flows from investing activities		
Purchases of property, plant, and equipment	(1,356.8)	(658.5)
Purchases of marketable securities	(5,320.3)	(2,952.8)
Proceeds from sales of marketable securities	3,338.6	1,621.5
Proceeds from maturities of marketable securities	370.8	778.2
Cash paid for Immunex, net of cash acquired	—	(1,899.0)
Proceeds from sale of Leukine® business	—	389.9
Purchase of certain rights from Roche	—	(137.5)
Other	(242.5)	(5.6)
Net cash used in investing activities	(3,210.2)	(2,863.8)
Cash flows from financing activities		
Issuance of zero-coupon convertible notes, net of issuance costs . . .	—	2,764.7
Repayment of debt	(123.0)	—
Net proceeds from issuance of common stock upon exercise of employee stock options and in connection with employee stock purchase plan	529.0	427.8
Repurchases of common stock	(1,801.0)	(1,420.4)
Other	23.5	5.5
Net cash (used in) provided by financing activities	(1,371.5)	1,777.6
(Decrease) increase in cash and cash equivalents	(1,015.1)	1,162.6
Cash and cash equivalents at beginning of period	1,851.7	689.1
Cash and cash equivalents at end of period	$ 836.6	$ 1,851.7

Required

a. Amgen reports that it generated $3,566.6 million in net cash from operating activities in 2003. Yet, its net income for the year amounted to only $2,259.5 million. Much of this difference is the result of depreciation. Why is Amgen adding depreciation to net income in the computation of operating cash flows?

b. Amgen reports net cash inflows of $268.6 million in tax benefits arising from employee stock options. These relate to tax benefits the company realizes when employees exercise stock options. Since employees will only exercise stock options when the market price of the stock is above the exercise price, do you feel that this is a reliable source of cash for the company? Explain.

c. Amgen is reporting $(255.5) million relating to trade receivables. What does the sign on this amount signify about the change in receivables during the year?

d. Amgen reports $824.6 million relating to accrued liabilities. Describe what this relates to and its implications for Amgen's future cash flows.

e. Does the composition of Amgen's cash flow present a "healthy" picture for 2003? Explain.

f. Compute its (1) operating cash flow to current liabilities ratio, (2) operating cash flow to capital expenditure ratio, and (3) free cash flow. (Assume current liabilities consist of accounts payable and accrued liabilities.) Comment on the measures computed.

CHAPTER 5

Financial Statements and Profitability Analysis

LEARNING OBJECTIVES

After completing the chapter, you should be able to:

LO1 Define return on equity (ROE) and explain its application to the analysis of company operating performance. (p. 197)

LO2 Describe Level 1 disaggregation of ROE into return on net operating assets (RNOA) and return on nonoperating activities (FLEV × Spread), and apply and interpret these components. (p. 199)

LO3 Distinguish between operating and nonoperating assets and liabilities. (p. 201)

LO4 Describe Level 2 disaggregation of return on net operating assets (RNOA) into net operating profit margin (NOPM) and net operating asset turnover (NOAT). (p. 207)

LO5 Describe Level 3 disaggregation of net operating profit margin and of net operating asset turnover into metrics of operating performance and financial condition. (p. 211)

Courtesy of 3M

3M
COMPANY

3M is an industrial conglomerate that seeks to balance slowdowns in one industry with up-turns in others. It has a strong tradition of discipline and quality and it has a focus on measuring and rewarding performance. 3M has produced several world-famous brands such as Scotch® tape and Post-it® notes. Still, 3M is primarily a nuts-and-bolts type producer. It provides duct tape, turbines, and electronic gear that keep the industrial world humming.

The key to 3M's success is its research. Over the decades, 3M scientists and engineers have developed sandpaper, magnetic audiotape, molds and glues for orthodontia, lime-yellow traffic signs, respirators, floppy disks, and Scotchgard™. To this day, 3M draws its identity from its research success. 3M devotes more than $1 billion to research each year and has 1,000 scientists and engineers around the world searching for the next breakthrough.

Income has increased 35% since 2001. 3M's income for 2003 topped off at $2.4 billion on net sales of $18.23 billion, yielding a 13.2% net profit margin. Importantly, its return on equity (ROE), as shown below and defined as net income/average equity, has improved since 2001, when restructuring costs cut into 3M's income as its new CEO refocused activities.

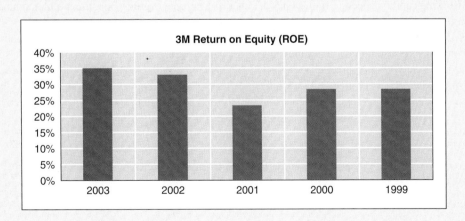

3M's increase in ROE has been accompanied by an increase in its stock price. By early 2006, 3M shares were valued at $73 per share, which is 25% higher than in 2001. The Dow Jones Industrial Average, by contrast, shows no net (percent) increase for the same time period.

(Continued on next page)

(Continued from previous page)

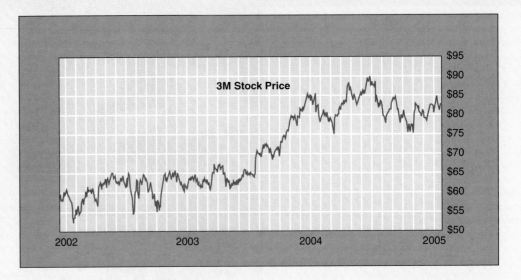

What was 3M's secret? There is no doubt that one of the most urgent problems at 3M was its ballooning costs. Costs had grown at twice the rate of sales in the years prior to 2001. Cost-control efforts generated an immediate savings of $500 million in 2001. That same year, 3M also streamlined purchasing, which generated another $100 million in savings.

One key to cost savings at 3M is its *Six Sigma* cost-cutting program, which was successfully applied at **GE** and a number of other companies now led by former GE executives. 3M is using Six Sigma for everything from focusing sales efforts to developing new kinds of duct tape.

Efforts are paying off. In 2003, sales rose in each of 3M's businesses except telecom, and income was up in all but the industrial division. Further, cash flows swelled by 27%, to $3.77 billion, and 3M's operating income margin widened by over a percentage point to 20.4%. 3M also increased its inventory turnover, which contributed to its increases in cash flows and profitability.

3M also increased its acquisitions. The hope is that these acquisitions will help sales grow 10% annually, nearly double the rate of the past decade. Fortunately, 3M has the cash flows and the flexibility necessary to go shopping.

3M has funded its cash outflows for acquisitions in part with cash inflows from improved working capital management. For example, 3M's average collection period for its receivables has been reduced from 63 days in 1999 to 54 days in 2003. Increased production efficiencies and lower cost raw materials have boosted inventory turnover from 3.8 times per year to 4.5 times. As a result, the working capital needed to run 3M has declined as a percent of sales, boosting both income and cash flows.

3M's management has brought operating discipline to the business, including a renewed focus on measures used to evaluate financial performance. This chapter and the next focus on such measures. A key to company success is ROE. This chapter explains ROE and focuses on *disaggregation of ROE,* also called DuPont analysis (after DuPont's management that first successfully applied it). ROE disaggregation focuses on the drivers of ROE. This chapter also introduces liquidity and solvency analysis—another important aspect of company success. Specifically, we describe the factors relevant to credit analysis and its use in setting debt ratings and terms.

Sources: *BusinessWeek*, April 2004 and August 2002; *Financial Times*, July 2002; *Fortune Magazine*, August 2002; 3M 10-K report, 2005, 2004, and 2003.

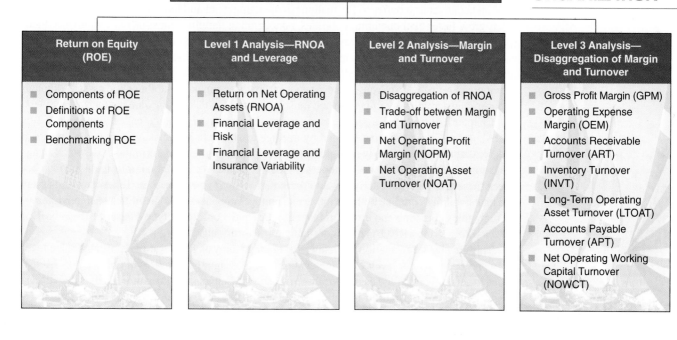

CHAPTER
ORGANIZATION

Financial Statements and Profitability Analysis

Return on Equity (ROE)
- Components of ROE
- Definitions of ROE Components
- Benchmarking ROE

Level 1 Analysis—RNOA and Leverage
- Return on Net Operating Assets (RNOA)
- Financial Leverage and Risk
- Financial Leverage and Insurance Variability

Level 2 Analysis—Margin and Turnover
- Disaggregation of RNOA
- Trade-off between Margin and Turnover
- Net Operating Profit Margin (NOPM)
- Net Operating Asset Turnover (NOAT)

Level 3 Analysis—Disaggregation of Margin and Turnover
- Gross Profit Margin (GPM)
- Operating Expense Margin (OEM)
- Accounts Receivable Turnover (ART)
- Inventory Turnover (INVT)
- Long-Term Operating Asset Turnover (LTOAT)
- Accounts Payable Turnover (APT)
- Net Operating Working Capital Turnover (NOWCT)

INTRODUCTION

Effective financial statement analysis and interpretation begin with an understanding of the kinds of questions that are both important and can be aided by financial analysis. Then, determining which questions to ask is a function of the type of analysis we plan to conduct. Different stakeholders of a company have different analysis requirements. Consider the following:

Stakeholder	Types of Questions Guiding Analysis of Financial Statements
Creditor	Can the company pay the interest and principal on its debt? Does the company rely too much on nonowner financing?
Investor	Does the company earn an acceptable return on invested capital? Is the gross profit margin growing or shrinking? Does the company effectively use nonowner financing?
Manager	Are costs under control? Are company markets growing or shrinking? Do observed changes reflect opportunities or threats? Is the allocation of investment across different assets too high or too low?

A crucial aspect of analysis is identifying the business activities that drive company success. Namely, does company return on invested capital result from operating activities or nonoperating (often called *financial*) activities? The distinction between operating and nonoperating activities is important as it plays a key role in effective analysis.

Operating activities are the core activities of a company. They are the activities required to deliver a company's products or services to its customers. Operating activities include research and development of products, the establishment of supply chains, the assemblage of administrative and productive product support, the promotion and marketing of products, and after-sale customer services.

Operating activities are reflected on the balance sheet, for example, by receivables and inventories net of payables and accruals, and by long-term operating assets net of long-term operating liabilities. On the income statement, operating activities are reflected in revenues, costs of goods sold, and operating expenses such as selling, general, and administrative expenses. Operating activities have the most long-lasting (persistent) effects on the future profitability and cash flows of the company and, thus, are the primary value drivers for company stakeholders. It is for this reason that operating activities play such a prominent role in effective profitability analysis.

Nonoperating activities primarily relate to the investing and financing activities of a company. They are reflected on the balance sheet as nonoperating (financial) assets and liabilities, which expand and contract as a buffer to fluctuations in operating asset and liability levels. When operating assets grow faster than operating liabilities, nonoperating liabilities must increase to finance them (per the accounting equation). These liabilities contract when assets decline and can even turn negative, resulting in financial assets invested temporarily in marketable securities to provide some return until those funds are needed again for operations. On the income statement, nonoperating activities are reflected in expenses and revenues from those financial liabilities and assets. Although nonoperating activities are important and must be carefully managed, they are not the value drivers.

Chapter 1 introduced a simple measure of financial performance called *return on assets* (ROA), defined as net income divided by average total assets. ROA is a widely quoted measure and, for that reason, it is one we should know. Net income in the ROA formula, however, is an aggregation of both operating and nonoperating components. Accordingly, it fails to distinguish between these two important activities and drivers of company performance. Likewise, total assets and total liabilities combine both operating and nonoperating assets and liabilities.[1] Effective analysis segregates operating and nonoperating activities and, consequently, we describe the *return on net operating assets* (RNOA) that is arguably more informative.

This chapter's explanation of financial statement analysis begins at the most aggregate level and works down to three levels of disaggregation. The most aggregate level is *return on equity* (ROE), which is generally regarded as the summary measure of financial performance. ROE is then disaggregated into key drivers of profitability and asset utilization. The framework of ROE disaggregation is depicted in Exhibit 5.1.

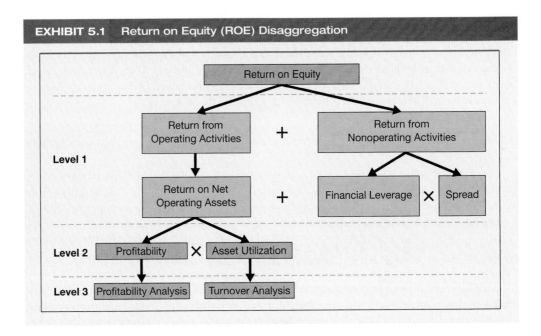

EXHIBIT 5.1   Return on Equity (ROE) Disaggregation

ROE disaggregation serves to answer several important questions in analyzing financial performance. Examples are:

- What is driving the company's financial performance?
    - Is it related solely to profitability?
    - What aspects of company profitability are important?
- Is the company effectively managing its balance sheet (investing and financing activities)?
- Is the company relying more on operating or nonoperating activities?
- Do its assets generate sufficient revenues?

---

[1] An alternate definition for return on assets is: ROA = (Net income + *After-tax interest expense*) / Average total assets. While the numerator in this formulation seeks to focus on operating income, the denominator (total assets) still includes nonoperating (financial) components.

These are but a sampling of questions that an analysis of ROE through its disaggregation can help answer.

The first level of disaggregation separates ROE into two basic drivers: return from operating activities and return from nonoperating activities. This approach identifies drivers by business activities. The second level of analysis examines the drivers of return on operating activities: profitability and asset utilization. A third level of disaggregation explores both of those components of return on operating activities for further insights into the drivers of company performance.

RETURN ON EQUITY (ROE)

Return on equity (ROE) is the ultimate measure of performance from the shareholders' perspective. It is computed as follows:

LO1 Define return on equity (ROE) and explain its application to the analysis of company operating performance.

$$\text{ROE} = \text{Net Income/Average Equity}$$

Net income is the bottom line from the income statement. Net income includes revenues from all sources, both operating and nonoperating. It also includes expenses from all sources, including cost of goods sold, selling, general, and administrative expenses, and nonoperating (financial) expenses like interest. Net income does not include dividend payments as they are not a deductible expense in the computation of GAAP income; instead, dividends are considered a distribution of income.

Components of ROE

ROE is disaggregated into operating and nonoperating components as follows.

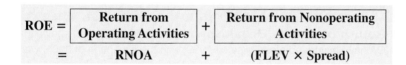

$$\text{ROE} = \boxed{\begin{array}{c}\textbf{Return from} \\ \textbf{Operating Activities}\end{array}} + \boxed{\begin{array}{c}\textbf{Return from Nonoperating} \\ \textbf{Activities}\end{array}}$$

$$= \quad \text{RNOA} \quad + \quad (\text{FLEV} \times \text{Spread})$$

NOTE
3M's ROE for 2003 is 34.6%; computed as $2,403 ÷ [($5,993 + $7,885) ÷ 2].

Definitions of ROE Components

This is an important disaggregation, and the definitions for these variables along with their typical components are in Exhibit 5.2—this table includes additional variables that are subsequently

EXHIBIT 5.2	Key Ratio Definitions
Ratio	**Definition**
ROE: return on equity	Net Income/Average Equity
RNOA: return on net operating assets	NOPAT/Average NOA
NOPAT: net operating profit after tax	Sales and other operating revenues less operating expenses such as cost of sales, taxes, selling, general, and administrative; it excludes nonoperating revenues and expenses such as those from financial assets and liabilities
NOA: net operating assets	Current and long-term operating assets less current and long-term operating liabilities; it excludes investments in securities, short- and long-term interest-bearing debt, and capitalized lease obligations
FLEV: financial leverage	Average NFO/Average Equity
NFO: net financial obligations	Financial (nonoperating) obligations less financial (nonoperating) assets
Spread	RNOA − NFR
NFR: net financial rate	NFE/Average NFO
NFE: net financial expense	NOPAT − Net income; it includes interest expense less revenues from nonoperating assets, net of tax

NOTE
These ratio definitions are important and are referred to throughout the book.

defined. The previous formula emphasizes the two key drivers of ROE: operating (RNOA) and nonoperating (FLEV × Spread) activities. Stakeholders prefer ROE to be driven by operating activities.

Benchmarking ROE

For a recent 34-year period, the median ROE achieved by all publicly traded U.S. companies was 12.2% (from Nissim and Penman, 2001, *Review of Accounting Studies* 6 (1), pp. 109–154). Most of this ROE is driven by RNOA as illustrated in the following table of median values for those companies and years.

ROE Disaggregation*	ROE	=	RNOA	+	(FLEV	×	Spread)
1st quartile (25th percentile)	6.3%		6.0%	+	0.05	×	−0.5%
Median (50th percentile)	12.2%	≈	10.3%	+	0.40	×	3.3%
3rd quartile (75th percentile)	17.6%		15.6%	+	0.93	×	10.3%

*Numbers in the table are medians (50th percentile) and quartiles (25th or 75th percentile); thus, the equation does not exactly equal ROE.

This table shows that companies are, on average, conservatively financed with a greater proportion of equity than net financial obligations (evident from FLEV < 1.0). Also, companies earn, on average, a positive spread on borrowed monies (3.3%). This is not always the case, however, as evidenced by the lowest 25% of companies. Most important, RNOA is, on average, approximately 84% of ROE (10.3%/12.2%).

BUSINESS INSIGHT

3M's Return on Equity Breakdown   The following graph shows that 3M's ROE and RNOA have increased steadily since 1999, with the exception of 2001, which was impacted by costs of its restructuring program.

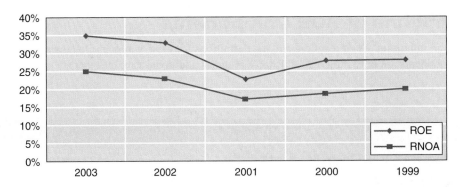

ROE exceeds RNOA in all years. The difference between ROE and RNOA lines is the return from nonoperating activities (FLEV × Spread). Because ROE exceeds RNOA for 3M, it shows that 3M is, on average, able to invest borrowed funds with a return exceeding its borrowing rate. The following data underlying this graph shows that 3M's financial leverage is only slightly higher than the 0.40 median for U.S. companies. Specifically, for 2003, and per the ROE disaggregation, 3M's ROE of 34.6% equals its RNOA of 24.7% plus its FLEV × Spread of 9.9%.

(in percents)	2003	2002	2001	2000	1999
ROE	34.6%	32.7%	22.7%	27.8%	28.0%
RNOA	24.7	22.5	16.8	18.4	19.6
FLEV	45.5	51.9	45.4	42.5	41.5
Spread	21.8	19.5	14.8	15.8	16.9

LEVEL 1 ANALYSIS—RNOA AND LEVERAGE

This section drills down one level in ROE disaggregation analysis to investigate the two main drivers of ROE: the return on net operating assets (RNOA) and the return from nonoperating activities (FLEV × Spread) as illustrated in Exhibit 5.3. We first discuss the return on net operating assets, followed by a discussion of the effects of financial leverage, including its advantages and disadvantages.

LO2 Describe Level 1 disaggregation of ROE into return on net operating assets (RNOA) and return on nonoperating activities (FLEV x Spread), and apply and interpret these components.

EXHIBIT 5.3	Level 1 of ROE Disaggregation

To illustrate computation of the measures described in this chapter, we use the financial information from 3M Company as provided in Exhibits 5.4 and 5.5.

EXHIBIT 5.4	3M Balance Sheet Information

3M COMPANY
Balance Sheet Information

At December 31	2003	2002	2001
Cash	$ 1,836	$ 618	$ 616
Receivables	2,714	2,527	2,482
Inventories	1,816	1,931	2,091
Other current assets	1,354	983	1,107
Total current assets	7,720	6,059	6,296
Property, plant and equipment, net	5,609	5,621	5,615
Investments	218	238	275
Intangibles	2,693	2,167	1,250
Deposits and other assets	1,360	1,244	1,170
Total assets	17,600	15,329	14,606
Notes payable	1,202	1,237	1,373
Accounts payable	1,087	945	753
Accrued liabilities	436	411	539
Income taxes	880	518	596
Other current liabilities	1,477	1,346	1,248
Total current liabilities	5,082	4,457	4,509
Long-term debt	1,735	2,140	1,520
Other long-term liabilities	2,898	2,739	2,491
Total liabilities	9,715	9,336	8,520
Common stock, net	9	5	5
Capital in excess of par	287	291	291
Retained earnings	14,010	12,748	11,914
Treasury stock	4,641	4,767	4,633
Other equities	(1,780)	(2,284)	(1,491)
Shareholder equity	7,885	5,993	6,086
Total liabilities and equity	$17,600	$15,329	$14,606

EXHIBIT 5.5   3M Income Statement Information

3M COMPANY
Income Statement Information

For Year Ended December 31	2003	2002	2001
Net sales	$18,232	$16,332	$16,054
Cost of good sold	9,285	8,496	8,749
Gross profit	8,947	7,836	7,305
R & D expenditures	1,102	1,070	1,084
Selling, general & admin expense	4,132	3,720	3,948
Operating income	3,713	3,046	2,273
Interest expense	56	41	87
Income before taxes	3,657	3,005	2,186
Income taxes	1,202	966	702
Minority interest income	52	65	54
Net income	$ 2,403	$ 1,974	$ 1,430

Return on Net Operating Assets (RNOA)

The **return on net operating assets** (RNOA) is normally the most important driver of ROE. It is computed as follows:

$$RNOA = NOPAT/Average\ NOA$$

where
NOPAT is net operating profit after tax
NOA is net operating assets

Both NOPAT and NOA are explained in detail below. RNOA reflects the operating side of the business (the other is the nonoperating, or financial, side). To appreciate the importance of RNOA, we must first understand the difference between the operating and nonoperating assets and liabilities (equity is always nonoperating).

EXHIBIT 5.6   Distinguishing Operating and Nonoperating Assets and Liabilities

Typical GAAP Balance Sheet
[Nonoperating (Financial) Items Highlighted]

Current assets
Cash and cash equivalents
Short-term investments
Accounts receivable
Inventories
Prepaid expenses
Deferred income tax assets

Long-term assets
Long-term investments in securities
Property, plant & equipment, net
Natural resources
Equity method investments
Intangible assets
Deferred income tax assets
Capitalized lease assets
Other long-term assets

Current liabilities
Short-term notes and interest payable
Accounts payable
Accrued liabilities
Deferred income tax liabilities
Current maturities of long-term debt   *Nonop*

Long-term liabilities
Bonds and notes payable
Capitalized lease obligations
Pension and other postretirement liabilities
Deferred income tax liabilities

Minority interest

Total stockholders' equity

Operating and Nonoperating Assets and Liabilities

Exhibit 5.6 presents a typical balance sheet with the nonoperating (financial) assets and liabilities highlighted. All other assets and liabilities are considered operating.

Operating assets and liabilities are those necessary to conduct the company's business. These include current operating assets such as cash, accounts receivable, inventories, prepaid expenses, and short-term deferred tax assets. It also includes current operating liabilities such as accounts payable, accrued liabilities, and short-term deferred tax liabilities. **Net operating working capital (NOWC)** equals operating current assets less operating current liabilities.

The current nonoperating assets include short-term investments in marketable securities. The current nonoperating liabilities include short-term interest-bearing notes payable, interest payable, and current maturities of long-term interest-bearing liabilities (and capitalized lease obligations).

Long-term operating assets include property, plant, and equipment (PPE), long-term investments related to strategic acquisitions (equity method investments, goodwill, and acquired intangible assets), deferred tax assets, and capitalized lease assets. Long-term operating liabilities include pensions and other postretirement liabilities and deferred income tax liabilities.

Long-term nonoperating assets include long-term investments in marketable securities and nonstrategic investments, and investments in nonoperating assets (such as discontinued operations prior to sale). Long-term nonoperating liabilities include bonds and other long-term interest-bearing liabilities, and any noncurrent portion of capitalized leases. Stockholders' equity includes all of the components of contributed and earned capital, net of treasury stock and other comprehensive income, plus minority interest recognized from business combinations.

LO3 Distinguish between operating and nonoperating assets and liabilities.

NOTE Discontinued operations are, by definition, not part of the continuing operating activities of the company. Although not financial in nature, we classify them as nonoperating as they represent an investment in the process of disposition.

Distinction Between Operating and Nonoperating Activities

The distinction between operating and nonoperating activities is summarized in Exhibit 5.7. **Net operating assets (NOA)** of the company consist of current and long-term operating assets less current and long-term operating liabilities. Stated differently, net operating assets consist of net operating working capital plus long-term net operating assets.

EXHIBIT 5.7	Simplified Operating and Nonoperating Balance Sheet	
	Assets	**Liabilities**
Net Operating Assets (NOA) .... (Assets – Liabilities)	Current Operating Assets / Long-Term Operating Assets	Current Operating Liabilities / Long-Term Operating Liabilities
Net Financial Obligations (NFO) . (Liabilities – Assets)	Financial Assets (Nonoperating)	Financial Obligations (Nonoperating)
		Equity
Equity (NOA–NFO)		Stockholders' Equity
	Total Assets	Total Liabilities and Equity

Nonoperating assets and liabilities are primarily financial in nature, and typically represent investments in marketable securities and discontinued operations, and borrowings in interest-bearing debt. **Net financial obligations (NFO)** are the net of financial (nonoperating) obligations less financial (nonoperating) assets. Net financial obligations are positive if financial obligations exceed financial assets and negative otherwise.

Because the accounting equation stipulates that Assets = Liabilities + Equity, we can also net this adjusted (reformulated) balance sheet to yield the following identity:

Net Operating Assets (NOA) = Net Financial Obligations (NFO) + Stockholders' Equity

The RNOA computation and analysis also require that we distinguish between operating and nonoperating profit. **Net operating profit after tax (NOPAT)**, the numerator of RNOA, is the after-tax profit earned from net operating assets. It includes sales less: cost of goods sold (COGS), operating expenses (OE) such as selling, general, and administrative (SG&A) expenses, and taxes on pretax operating profit.[2] Items excluded from NOPAT include interest revenue and expense, dividend revenue, and income or loss from discontinued operations.[3] More generally, NOPAT is computed as follows:

$$\text{NOPAT} = (\text{Sales} - \text{Operating Expenses}) \times [1 - (\text{Tax Expense}/\text{Pretax Income})]$$

Sales less operating expense yields pretax operating profits. The expression (Tax Expense/Pretax Income) yields the effective tax rate for the period. Multiplying pretax operating profit by one minus the effective tax rate yields net operating profit after tax, or NOPAT.[4]

The operating versus nonoperating distinction is different from the core (also called permanent and persistent) versus transitory distinction for earnings components that was discussed in Chapter 2. Exhibit 5.8 lists typical income statement items categorized by operating versus nonoperating and by core versus transitory. (Items listed are meant to give a general idea of the composition of these categories and are not a complete listing.)

EXHIBIT 5.8	Distinguishing Operating, Nonoperating, Core, and Transitory Income	
	Core	**Transitory**
Operating	Sales; cost of goods sold; selling, general, and administrative expenses; research and development; income taxes	Operating asset write-downs; nonrecurring restructuring accruals; gains and losses on sales of operating assets
Nonoperating	Dividends; interest revenues and expenses; hedging gains and losses	Debt retirement gains and losses; gains and losses on discontinued operations

RESEARCH INSIGHT

Ratio Behavior over Time How do ROE, RNOA, and NFR ratios behave over time? Following is a graph of these ratios over a recent 34-year period (from graph B, p.134, of Nissim and Penman, 2001, *Review of Accounting Studies* 6 (1), pp. 109–154, with permission of Springer Science and Business Media). There is considerable variability in these ratios over time. Also, the proportion of RNOA to ROE is greater for some periods of time than for others. Yet, in all periods, RNOA exceeds the net financial rate, NFR. This is evidence of a positive effect, on average, for ROE from financial leverage.

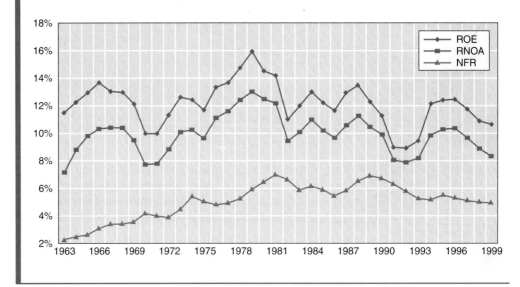

---

[2]Earnings on equity method investments (covered in Chapter 12) are operating so long as the equity method investment is classified as a strategic acquisition.

[3]Net income or loss on discontinued operations, and the gain or loss on sale of its net assets, are treated as nonoperating items.

[4]In Chapter 2, we distinguished between nonrecurring items and income from continuing operations when we presented the income statement. For purposes of analysis, some of these nonrecurring items may relate to operations and should, therefore, be included in the calculation of NOPAT. We discuss nonrecurring items in detail in Chapter 7.

Financial Leverage and Risk

Management strives to increase ROE, and both RNOA and **financial leverage (FLEV)** are the drivers of ROE. Financial leverage (FLEV) is defined as average net financial obligations divided by average equity. Thus, one way to increase ROE is to increase RNOA through improved operating performance. The other way to increase ROE is with the successful use of financial leverage. Increased leverage, however, is associated with increased risk.

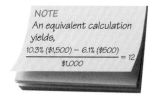

To illustrate the effect on ROE of increased financial leverage, assume that a company is financed solely with equity. This means that a $1,000 shareholder investment yields $1,000 in assets that earn a RNOA of, say, 10.3%. Alternatively, assume that this company is financed with $1,000 in shareholder equity and $500 in nonowner financing costing 6.1% after tax. In this case the ROE is 12.4%, computed as 10.3% + [($500/$1,000) × (10.3% − 6.1%)]. ROE is 10.3% without leverage, but 12.4% with leverage, a difference of 2.1%. The source of this difference is the $500 of debt-financed assets with a spread of 4.2% (10.3% − 6.1%); yielding a dollar increase of $21 or 2.1% of our $1,000 equity investment. This shows the beneficial effect on ROE from financial leverage *when a positive spread is achieved.*

If increases in financial leverage increase ROE, why are all companies not 100% debt financed? The answer is because debt is risky. Debt is a contractual obligation that must be met regardless of the company's current financial status. If not met, creditors can ultimately force payment, which can lead to company bankruptcy and liquidation, much to the detriment of shareholders who are *residual claimants* and can potentially lose their entire investment.

Higher financial leverage also results in a higher cost of debt for the company (this is explained later in the chapter). Several credit-rating companies such as **Standard & Poor's** and **Moody's Investors Service** rate publicly traded debt. Those ratings partly determine the debt's interest rate—with lower quality ratings yielding higher interest rates and vice versa. So, all else equal, higher financial leverage lowers a company's debt rating and increases the interest rate it must pay.

Debtholders (creditors) also typically require a company to execute a loan agreement that places varying restrictions on its operating activities. These restrictions, called *covenants*, help safeguard debtholders in the face of increased risk (recall, debtholders do not have a voice on the board of directors). These debt covenants also impose a cost on the company via restrictions on its activities, and these restrictions become more stringent with increased reliance on nonowner financing.

Financial Leverage and Income Variability

Financial leverage can also affect income variability. To illustrate, we must first define variable and fixed costs. **Variable costs** are those that change in proportion to changes in sales volume. **Fixed costs** are those that do not change with changes in sales volume (over a reasonable range).

Debt with a fixed rate of interest introduces fixed costs into the cost structure. The effect of fixed interest costs on income variability is evidenced in Exhibit 5.9.

EXHIBIT 5.9	Cases showing Financial Leverage and Income Variability		
	Case 1	**Case 2**	**Case 3**
Sales	$10,000	$8,000	$12,000
Variable costs (40%)	4,000	3,200	4,800
Fixed costs	2,000	2,000	2,000
Net income	$ 4,000	$2,800	$ 5,200
Percentage change in sales	—	(20)%	20%
Percentage change in income	—	(30)%	30%

A given percentage change in revenues generates a greater percentage change in income. Exhibit 5.9 shows that a 20% change in revenues (cases 2 and 3) generates a 30% income change. Leverage is a *magnifier*—positive when revenues increase, and negative when revenues decrease.

The effect of financial leverage (fixed costs) on ROE is shown in Exhibit 5.10. For a given increase or decrease in revenues, the change in ROE is greater for a higher leverage (fixed cost) company.

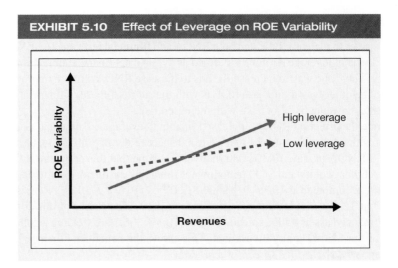

EXHIBIT 5.10   Effect of Leverage on ROE Variability

Thus, although a higher level of ROE is desirable, there is a difference between high ROE generated by operating activities (RNOA) and high ROE generated from high levels of financial leverage (FLEV). As illustrated above, use of financial leverage can benefit shareholders. Financial leverage, however, is a double-edged sword. Its downside is an increased level of risk in the form of a higher probability of financial distress and bankruptcy if debt payments cannot be made and with greater variability in net income and ROE.

MID-CHAPTER REVIEW 1

Caterpillar, Inc., is a manufacturer of construction equipment. It consists of two segments: one manufactures equipment and the other provides financing (loans and leases) to customers. The finance company is like other financial institutions with high financial leverage and a small spread on loan rates over the cost of debt it incurs to finance those loans. The comparative balance sheets and income statements for Caterpillar are as follows.

Caterpillar, Inc. Balance Sheets		
December 31 ($ millions)	2003	2002
Assets		
Current assets		
Cash and short-term investments	$ 342	$ 309
Receivables—trade and other	3,666	2,838
Receivables—finance	7,605	6,748
Deferred and refundable income taxes	707	781
Prepaid expenses	1,424	1,224
Inventories	3,047	2,763
Total current assets	16,791	14,663
Property, plant and equipment—net	7,290	7,046
Long-term receivables—trade and other	82	66
Long-term receivables—finance	7,822	6,714
Investments in unconsolidated affiliated companies	800	747
Deferred income taxes	616	711
Intangible assets	239	281
Goodwill	1,398	1,402
Other assets	1,427	1,117
Total assets	**$36,465**	**$32,747**

(continued)

Caterpillar, Inc.
Balance Sheets *(Continued)*

December 31 ($ millions)	2003	2002
Liabilities		
Current liabilities		
Short-term borrowings		
Machinery and engines	$ 72	$ 64
Financial products	2,685	2,111
Accounts payable	3,100	2,269
Accrued expenses	1,638	1,620
Accrued wages, salaries, and employee benefits	1,802	1,779
Dividends payable	127	120
Deferred and current income taxes payable	216	70
Long-term debt due within one year		
Machinery and engines	32	258
Financial products	2,949	3,654
Total current liabilities	12,621	11,945
Long-term debt due after one year		
Machinery and engines	3,367	3,403
Financial products	10,711	8,193
Liability for postemployment benefits	3,172	3,333
Deferred income taxes and other liabilities	516	401
Total liabilities	30,387	27,275
Stockholders' equity		
Common stock of $1.00 par value; Authorized shares: 900,000,000		
Issued shares (2003 and 2002—407,447,312) at paid-in amount	1,059	1,034
Treasury stock (2003—63,685,272 shares; 2002—63,192,245 shares) at cost	(2,914)	(2,669)
Profit employed in the business	8,450	7,849
Accumulated other comprehensive income	(517)	(742)
Total stockholders' equity	6,078	5,472
Total liabilities and stockholders' equity	$36,465	$32,747

Caterpillar, Inc.
Income Statements

For Year Ended December 31 ($ millions)	2003	2002
Sales and revenues		
Sales of machinery and engines	$21,048	$18,648
Revenues of financial products	1,715	1,504
Total sales and revenues	22,763	20,152
Operating costs		
Costs of goods sold	16,945	15,146
Selling, general, and administrative expenses	2,470	2,094
Research and development expenses	669	656
Interest expense of financial products	470	521
Other operating expenses	521	411
Total operating costs	21,075	18,828

(Continued)

Caterpillar, Inc. Income Statements *(Continued)*		
For Year Ended December 31 ($ millions)	2003	2002
Operating profit	**1,688**	1,324
Interest expense excluding financial products	246	279
Other income (expense)	35	69
Consolidated profit before taxes	**1,477**	1,114
Provision for income taxes	398	312
Profit of consolidated companies	1,079	802
Equity in profit (loss) of unconsolidated affiliated companies	20	(4)
Profit	**$ 1,099**	$ 798

Required

Using Caterpillar's (CAT) financial information, compute the following for 2003 (refer to Exhibits 5.2, 5.3, 5.6, and 5.7 for guidance).

1. Balance sheet amounts
   a. Net operating working capital (NOWC)
   b. Net operating long-term assets (NOLTA)
   c. Net operating assets (NOA) (Note: a + b = c)
   d. Net financial obligations (NFO)
   e. Shareholders' equity
   f. Confirm that c = d + e

2. Income statement amounts
   a. Net operating profit after tax (NOPAT)
   b. Net income
   c. Net financial expense
   d. Confirm that c = a − b

3. Financial ratios and measures
   a. Return on equity (ROE)
   b. Return on net operating assets (RNOA)
   c. Financial leverage (FLEV)
   d. Net financial rate (NFR)
   e. Spread
   f. Confirm: ROE = RNOA + (FLEV × Spread)

4. What insights do you draw about Caterpillar's financial performance from its Level 1 analysis of ROE?

Solution

1. a. Net operating working capital (NOWC) .... $ 9,908
      NOWC = Current Operating Assets − Current Operating Liabilities
         = ($16,791 − $0) − [$12,621 − ($2,685 + $72) − ($32 + $2,949)]
   b. Net operating long-term assets (NOLTA) 15,986
      NOLTA = Long-Term Operating Assets − Long-Term Operating Liabilities
         = [($36,465 − $16,791) − $0] − ($516 + $3,172)
   c. Net operating assets (NOA) 25,894
      NOA = Operating Assets − Operating Liabilities
         = ($36,465 − $0) − ($30,387 − $2,757 − $2,981 − $14,078)
   d. Net financial obligations (NFO) $19,816
      NFO = Nonoperating Liabilities − Nonoperating Assets
         = ($2,757 + $2,981 + $14,078) − $0
   e. Stockholders' equity (given) 6,078
   f.   c = d + e
      25,894 = 19,816 + 6,078 (confirmed)

2. a. Net operating profit after tax (NOPAT) 1,253
      NOPAT = [Net Operating Profit × (1 − Effective Tax Rate)]
            + Other Income, net of tax
      NOPAT = {$1,688 × [1 − ($398/$1,477)]} + 20
      Note: CAT's income statement references "equity in profit (loss) of unconsolidated affiliated companies." We cover the concept of equity income of unconsolidated

affiliates in Chapter 12. For now, just know that this amount is presented after tax (so no tax adjustment is necessary). Absent knowledge that these affiliates are conducting nonoperating activities, it is customary to include them as operating activities.

b. Net income (given) 1,099
c. Net financial expense (NFE) = ($246 − $35) × [1 − ($398/$1,477)]   154
d.   c = a − b
$154 = $1,253 − $1,099 (confirmed)

3. a. Return on equity (ROE) 19.0%
ROE = Net Income/Average Stockholders' Equity
= $1,099/[($6,078 + $5,472)/2]
b. Return on net operating assets (RNOA) 5.1%
RNOA = NOPAT/Average NOA
= $1,253/[($25,894 + $23,155)/ 2]
c. Financial leverage (FLEV) 324.7%
FLEV = Average NFO/Average Stockholders' Equity
= [($19,816 + $17,683)/2]/[($6,078 + $5,472)/2]
d. Net financial rate (NFR) 0.8%
NFR = NFE/Average NFO
= $154/[($19,816 + $17,683)/2]
e. Spread 4.3%
Spread = RNOA − NFR
= 5.1% − 0.8%
f. 19.0% = 5.1% + (3.247 × 4.3%)

4. Much of CAT's ROE of 19% is driven by financial leverage, as RNOA is only 5.1%. CAT's financial statements include its manufacturing and financial subsidiaries. The financial subsidiary, like many captive finance subsidiaries, is quite large and highly financially leveraged. As a result, the consolidated (combined) balance sheet reflects this leverage. Leverage in a financial subsidiary is usually not as problematic as if it were solely in the manufacturing company; this is because the financial subsidiary's cash flows are unlikely cyclical. As long as its cash flows are relatively stable, it can handle a higher debt load. The business model for this financial subsidiary, then, is low margins and high financial leverage to yield the target ROE. This is the business model for a typical financial institution.

YOU MAKE THE CALL

You are a Business Reporter   You are a reporter for *The Wall Street Journal* and Caterpillar reports an ROE for 2003 of 19%, while 3M reports an ROE of 35% for the same period. What factors might explain the difference in the reported ROE values? [Answers on page 217]

LEVEL 2 ANALYSIS—MARGIN AND TURNOVER

This section focuses on Level 2 analysis, which disaggregates RNOA into net operating profit margin (NOPM) and net operating asset turnover (NOAT). The purpose here is to identify the key drivers of RNOA. Nearly all goals of financial analysis are future oriented. Examples are predicting future operating income, pricing companies' securities, forming opinions about companies' debt-paying abilities, evaluating alternate strategies, and making managerial decisions. Understanding the drivers of financial performance (RNOA) is key to effectively predicting future performance. To highlight the development of our analytical framework, Exhibit 5.11 presents the Level 1 disaggregation of ROE into operating (RNOA) and nonoperating components (FLEV × Spread) and the Level 2 disaggregation of RNOA into its components: net operating profit margin (NOPM) and net operating asset turnover (NOAT). The latter is the focus of this section.

LO4 Describe Level 2 disaggregation of return on net operating assets (RNOA) into net operating profit margin (NOPM) and net operating asset turnover (NOAT).

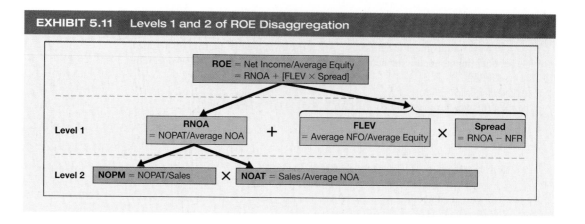

EXHIBIT 5.11   Levels 1 and 2 of ROE Disaggregation

Disaggregation of RNOA

Level 2 analysis focuses on the disaggregation of RNOA into its two basic components, profit margin and asset turnover, as follows:

$$\textbf{RNOA} = \textbf{NOPAT/Average Net Operating Assets} = \underbrace{\textbf{NOPAT/Sales}}_{\textbf{Margin}} \times \underbrace{\textbf{Sales/Average Net Operating Assets}}_{\textbf{Turnover}}$$

The ratio of NOPAT (net operating profit after tax) to sales is the *net operating profit margin* (NOPM). It reflects the percentage of each sales dollar that the company is realizing in after-tax operating profit. The ratio of sales to net operating assets is the *net operating asset turnover* (NOAT). Turnover reflects the productivity of assets. Namely, how much revenue does the firm realize from a dollar of operating asset investment.

Management and its stakeholders prefer that both margin and turnover be higher rather than lower as both increase RNOA and, thus, ROE. The next section describes the trade-off between margin and turnover, and how that translates into company performance.

Trade-Off Between Margin and Turnover

An infinite number of combinations of net operating profit margin and net operating asset turnover yield a given RNOA. As depicted in Exhibit 5.12, industries tend to reach RNOA equilibria, which are determined by fundamental business characteristics (data points represent industry medians from over 55,000 observations for the 15 years prior to 2005). That is, some industries, like communication and pharmaceuticals, are capital intensive with relatively low turnover. Accordingly, for such industries to achieve a required RNOA, they must obtain a higher profit margin. Service companies, such as retailers and restaurants, in contrast, carry fewer assets and can operate on lower operating profit margins to achieve a similar RNOA because their asset turnover is far greater.

One implication of Exhibit 5.12 is that we must be careful in evaluating performances of companies in different industries. A higher profit margin in the communication industry than that in the apparel industry is not necessarily the result of better management. Instead, the communication industry requires a higher profit margin to offset its lower asset turnover (resulting from the capital intensity of its industry) to achieve an equivalent return on net operating assets.

The margin and turnover trade-off is obvious when comparing the communication and apparel industries. However, the analysis of conglomerates that are mixtures of several industries is more challenging. Their margins and turnover rates are a weighted average of the margins and turnover rates for the various industries that constitute the company. For example, like Caterpillar, **General Motors Corporation (GM)** is a blend of a manufacturing company and a financial subsidiary **(GMAC)**. Each of these industries has its own margin and turnover equilibrium, and the margin and turnover for GM on a consolidated basis is a weighted average of the two.

EXHIBIT 5.12	Margin and Turnover Combinations for a given RNOA Operating Cycle

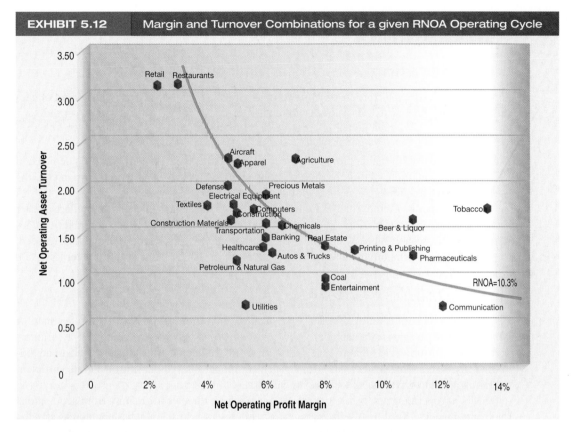

Net Operating Profit Margin (NOPM)

The analysis of profit margin relates to the income statement. Profit margin can be used to compare one income statement number with another, where sales is the usual denominator. It is commonly used to compare the performance of one company over time and/or its performance vis-à-vis its competitors.

The **net operating profit margin (NOPM)** is a useful summary measure of operating performance as it encompasses both the gross profit on sales and operating expenses.[5] It is computed as follows:

$$\text{Net Operating Profit Margin (NOPM)} = \text{NOPAT/Sales}$$

BUSINESS INSIGHT

The 3M Margin   The following chart shows that 3M's net operating profit margin has increased from 11.6% of sales in 1999 to 13.7% in 2003. The 2001 decline was due to 3M's $568 million pretax restructuring costs, consisting mainly of expected severance costs as it downsized its employee base.

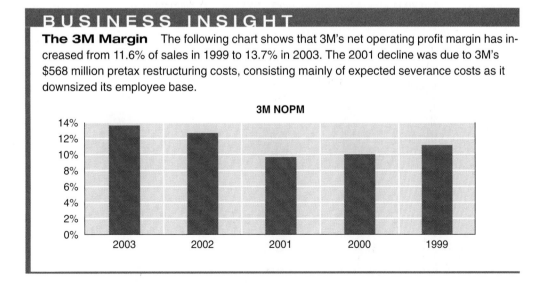

3M NOPM

---

[5]Another common measure of performance is **net profit margin** (net income/sales), sometimes called **return on sales**. This measure uses net income, which encompasses both operating and financial components. Our focus on net operating profit margin is to distinguish between operating and nonoperating (financial) components of net profit margin.

The NOPM is one of the two drivers of RNOA. It is a summary measure of company profitability.

Net Operating Asset Turnover (NOAT)

Asset turnover reflects the productivity of company assets. That is, it reflects the amount of capital required to generate a dollar of sales volume. The general form of an asset turnover ratio is:

$$\text{Asset Turnover} = \text{Sales/Average Assets}$$

A turnover ratio uses measures from both the income statement and balance sheet. As depicted in Exhibit 5.12, capital-intensive companies have lower turnover rates than service companies as the amount of assets required to generate a dollar of sales is less for services.

Our interest in asset turnover arises from the following observation: higher turnover reflects greater sales inflow for a given level of assets. Although turnover does not directly impact profitability, it does so indirectly as asset holding costs (such as interest, insurance, warehousing, and logistics) are reduced.

One of the most important measures of turnover is the **net operating asset turnover (NOAT)**, which is defined as:

$$\text{Net Operating Asset Turnover (NOAT)} = \text{Sales/Average Net Operating Assets}$$

For 3M, its 2003 net operating asset turnover is 1.81. Its turnover ratio of 1.81 implies that 3M generates $1.81 in sales from each dollar invested in net operating assets. Another way of interpreting the 1.81 turnover is that for each additional sales dollar, 3M must invest $0.55 in net operating assets (computed as $1/1.81). Thus, each additional sales dollar must generate sufficient operating profit to offset the added investment cost.

3M's net operating assets have increased over the past three years, mainly from acquisitions of other companies. Specifically, its average net operating working capital has not increased to the extent that sales have increased, and its net property, plant, and equipment (PPE) assets have not increased during this period, as capital expenditures have equaled depreciation. Instead, goodwill and other intangible assets account for most of the growth in its net operating assets.

It is crucial that companies monitor their asset utilization. They must also take action if asset growth is excessive. For example, they can sell excess capacity of underutilized assets or outsource production of some products. Later in this chapter we explore means to monitor, analyze, and interpret the effective use of net operating assets.

BUSINESS INSIGHT

Turnover at 3M The following chart shows 3M's net operating asset turnover, which is reasonably steady during the past five years. Its largest value is 1.83 times in 2000 and its lowest is 1.75 in 2001 (the restructuring year). 3M's net operating asset turnover is below the 1.97 median for all publicly traded firms.

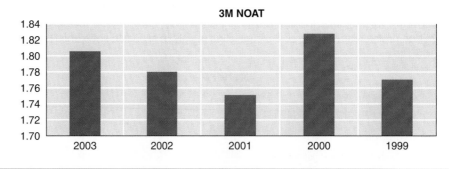

MID-CHAPTER REVIEW 2

Refer to the Mid-Chapter Review 1 for the financial statements of Caterpillar, Inc.

Required

Using Caterpillar's financial information, compute the following for 2003 (refer to Exhibit 5.11 for guidance).

1. Net operating profit margin and net operating asset turnover
   a. Net operating profit margin (NOPM)
   b. Net operating asset turnover (NOAT)
   c. Confirm: RNOA = $a \times b$
2. What insights do you draw about Caterpillar's financial performance from its Level 2 analysis of ROE?

Solution

1. a. Net operating profit margin (NOPAT/Sales = $1,253 / $22,763) 5.5%
   b. Net operating asset turnover (NOAT) . . . .   0.93 times
      NOAT = $22,763 /([$25,894 + $23,155]/ 2)
   c. RNOA: 5.1% = 5.5% × 0.93 (confirms *Mid-Chapter Review 1*, part 3b) 5.1%

2. CAT's RNOA is relatively low as it is within the bottom quartile of median RNOAs for publicly traded companies (RNOA of under 6%)—see table in the earlier part of this chapter. Also, CAT is in a capital intensive industry. The median turnover of net operating assets for all companies is 1.94, and CAT is well below that level (0.93). Although its NOPM approximates the median for all companies, its low NOAT hinders its ability to achieve acceptable returns on net operating assets.

YOU MAKE THE CALL

You are the Entrepreneur   You are analyzing the performance of your startup company. Your analysis of RNOA reveals the following (industry benchmarks in parentheses): RNOA is 16% (10%), NOPM is 18% (17%), and NOAT is 0.89 (0.59). What interpretations do you draw that are useful for managing your company? [Answers on page 217]

LEVEL 3 ANALYSIS—DISAGGREGATION OF MARGIN AND TURNOVER

This section focuses on Level 3 analysis, which highlights the disaggregation of profit margin and asset turnover to better understand the drivers of RNOA. Again, understanding the drivers of financial performance (RNOA) is key to predicting future company performance. To help frame our presentation, Exhibit 5.13 shows the full analytical framework for disaggregation of ROE into Level 1 components, the return from operating activities (RNOA) and the return from nonoperating activities (FLEV × Spread), the Level 2 disaggregation of RNOA into profit margin (NOPM) and asset turnover (NOAT), and the Level 3 analysis of the drivers of operating profit margin and asset turnover.

LO5   Describe Level 3 disaggregation of net operating profit margin and of net operating asset turnover into metrics of operating performance and financial condition.

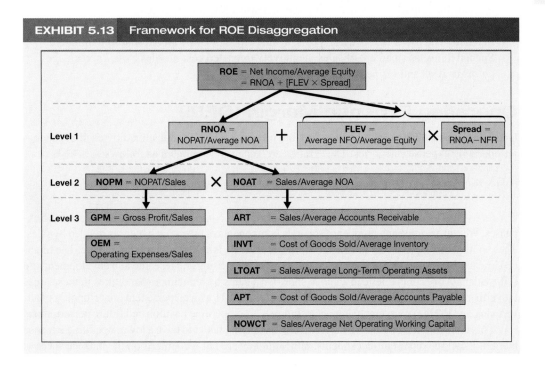

EXHIBIT 5.13   Framework for ROE Disaggregation

Gross Profit Margin (GPM)

Gross profit is net sales less cost of goods sold. It represents the **markup** of selling price over costs that the company has incurred in manufacturing or purchasing the goods sold. Analysis of gross profit *dollars* is not usually meaningful as it results from both the unit markup and the number of units sold—either or both can change over time or differ across companies. Instead, we focus on gross profit margin, which is defined as follows:

$$\text{Gross Profit Margin (GPM)} = \text{Gross Profit/Net Sales}$$

Conducting gross profit analysis in ratio form serves two objectives. First, it mitigates any problem arising when comparing different sized companies. Second, it allows us to focus on average markup per unit sold, which abstracts from the volume of units sold in our analysis.

Analysis of gross profit margin provides insight into a company's average markup on its product cost through selling prices. A higher gross profit margin is preferred to a lower one. A higher gross profit margin also means that a company has more flexibility in product pricing. Such companies are historically more profitable.

Two main factors determine gross profit margin:

1. Competition. When competition intensifies, more substitutes become available, which limits a company's ability to raise prices and pass on cost increases to customers.

2. Product mix. When lower-priced, higher-volume products increase in proportion to higher-priced, lower-volume products, gross profit margin declines.

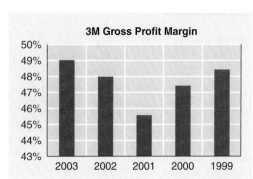

Absent product mix changes, a decline in gross profit margin is generally viewed negatively as it suggests that a company's products have lost some competitive advantage. Reasons can include failures in product quality, style, or technology.

3M's gross profit margin has improved in recent years. However, in 2001, its GPM declined by 1.9 percentage points, which is substantial. In its 10-K for that year, 3M reports that special items, principally related to its restructuring program, accounted for 1.7 of the 1.9 points of that decline.

3M credits the reductions in its cost of goods sold to its manufacturing efficiencies and purchasing initiatives. Following is an excerpt from its 2003 10-K that provides part of 3M's explanation:

Cost of sales in 2003 benefited from . . . projects aimed at improving manufacturing throughput, yield and productivity. 3M's global sourcing initiative has helped mitigate the impact of raw material price increases. Raw material costs were essentially flat versus 2002. In 2002, gross margins were positively impacted by improved plant efficiencies and lower raw material costs, again helped by 3M's global sourcing initiative. Special items, as a percent of sales, negatively impacted cost of sales by 0.7 percentage points in 2002 and 1.7 percentage points in 2001.

Operating Expense Margin (OEM)

Operating expense ratios (percents) reflect the proportion of sales consumed by each of the major operating expense categories. These ratios are generally computed as follows:

$$\text{Operating Expense Margin (OEM)} = \text{Operating Expenses/Net Sales}$$

The focus is on any changes over time in the proportion of company sales invested in operating expenses. We can examine any number of separate components of operating expenses divided by sales. These outlays must produce a satisfactory return and create long-term shareholder value. The financial impacts from some expenditures, such as those in advertising and research and development, are self-evident. Also, companies can achieve short-term gains by reducing expenditures in these areas (advertising and R&D outlays are expensed under GAAP). However, persistent underfunding of advertising and R&D can adversely impact a company's competitive position and future performance.

This is an important point. Namely, it is not necessarily better to have a lower operating expense margin. Expenses represent investments, although they are not recognized on the balance sheet as assets. As with any investment, we must expect an acceptable return. The objective, then, is not necessarily to reduce operating expenses. Instead, it is to *optimize* them—make sure that they are producing an acceptable return, the aim being to increase RNOA.

3M has two large operating expenses: R&D costs and selling, general, and administrative (SG&A) expenses. 3M's percent of sales invested in R&D has remained constant for the past five years. Its business depends on R&D to maintain its competitive advantage. Cutbacks in R&D for short-run profits are probably at the cost of long-run profits.

3M's SG&A expense as a percentage of sales has decreased from 23.6% to 22.2% in the past five years. This 1.4 percentage point decrease is substantial for a mature company of this size and reflects 3M's commitment to cost control.

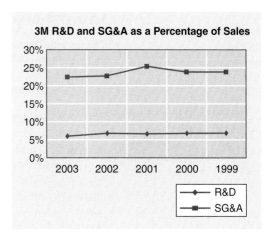

Accounts Receivable Turnover (ART)

Disaggregation of total asset turnover gives further insights into the drivers of RNOA. The **accounts receivable turnover (ART)** is one of those disaggregates. It provides insights into the sales impact of accounts receivable. That is, receivables are an asset, just like inventories and equipment, and the accounts receivable turnover reflects the investment in receivables required to generate a dollar of sales. This turnover ratio is:

Accounts Receivable Turnover (ART) = Net Sales/Average Accounts Receivable

The higher this turnover ratio, the lower the required investment. Generally, companies want a higher receivables turnover, as this reflects greater sales for a given level of accounts receivable.

3M's accounts receivable turnover ratio increased from 5.79 times in 1999 to 6.96 times in 2003. This is a marked increase that should enhance its profitability and cash flow.

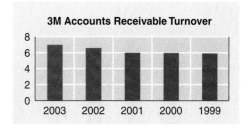

Although companies desire to minimize their investment in accounts receivable, the extension of credit is one of the marketing tools available to a company. Each tool has its cost. While the cost of advertising is easy to see, the cost of credit extension is less evident.

Receivables are an asset that must be financed like any other asset. In addition, receivables entail collection risk and require additional overhead in the form of credit and collection departments. On the other hand, reducing collection overhead costs with an overly restrictive credit policy hurts sales. Receivables must, therefore, be effectively managed.

An intuitive formulation of a measure related to accounts receivable turnover is the **average collection period**, which is:

Average Collection Period = Accounts Receivable/Average Daily Sales

This metric reflects how long accounts receivable are outstanding, on average.

For 3M, the average collection period has been reduced from 64.4 days in 1999 to 54.3 days in 2003. More timely collection of receivables reduces the probability of noncollection. Also, the reduction in receivables increases cash flow. For these reasons, 3M's more timely collection of receivables over the past five years is a positive development.

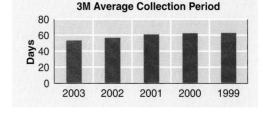

To assess whether an average collection period of 54.3 days is good or bad, we can compare it to the company's credit policies. For example, if invoice terms are net 60 days, experience tells us to expect the average collection period to be about 30 days. Credit terms vary by industry, but are usually 90 days or less. Accordingly, average collection periods longer than 60 days are unusual and, thus, warrant investigation.[6]

---

[6]Companies with captive finance subsidiaries, and those that offer leasing of their manufactured products, report longer average collection periods that arise from the length of the financing, not necessarily as a result of uncollectible accounts.

Inventory Turnover (INVT)

The **inventory turnover (INVT)** ratio provides insight into the inventory investment required to support the current sales volume. It is computed as follows:

Inventory Turnover (INVT) = Cost of Goods Sold/Average Inventory

This ratio uses cost of goods sold (COGS) as a measure of sales volume because the denominator, inventory, is reported at cost, not retail. Accordingly, both the numerator and denominator are measured at cost.

The inventory turnover for 3M increased from 3.82 times per year in 1999 to 4.95 times per year in 2003. This is a substantial improvement in inventory turns. In its 2003 10-K, 3M attributes much of this success to "projects aimed at improving manufacturing throughput, yield, and productivity." In addition, 3M cites its "global sourcing initiative," which has helped to control raw materials costs, a main component of its inventory.

When inventory turnover declines, concerns arise about uncompetitive products. (Inventory turnover is also determined by changes in product mix.) Further, such declines add costs. Namely, inventory requires warehouse space and logistics, personnel to monitor and manage them, financing costs, and insurance coverage. Also, the longer inventory sits, the greater is the likelihood of its being damaged or stolen, going out of style, or becoming technologically obsolete. Companies want enough inventory to meet customer demand without stock-outs, and no more.

Analysis of inventory is aided by the following complementary measure that reflects the number of days of sales in inventory:

Average Inventory Days Outstanding = Inventory/Average Daily Cost of Goods Sold

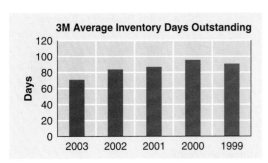

This result gives us some indication of the length of time that inventories sit prior to sale.

For 3M, and commensurate with its increased inventory turnover shown above, we see a reduction in its average inventory days outstanding from 91.2 days in 1999 to 71.4 days in 2003. Although 71.4 days can seem like a long time for inventories to remain unsold, this time includes the time from the purchase of the raw materials, through the manufacturing process, to the time the finished goods are sold.

We want the company inventory cycle to be as short as possible. One way in which companies can reduce inventory cycle is to minimize their raw materials through good inventory management methods such as just-in-time deliveries—which means that inventory sits with suppliers. Similarly, companies can achieve reductions in work-in-progress inventory by efficient production processes that eliminate bottlenecks. Finally, companies can minimize finished goods inventory by producing to orders, not estimated demand, if possible. These management tools increase inventory turnover and reduce the inventory days outstanding.

Long-Term Operating Asset Turnover (LTOAT)

Long-term operating asset turnover (LTOAT) reflects capital intensity relative to sales and is defined as:

Long-Term Operating Asset Turnover (LTOAT) = Net Sales/Average Long-Term Operating Assets

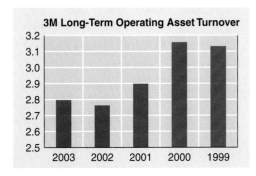

where net long-term operating assets equals long-term operating assets less long-term operating liabilities. An alternate way of computing net long-term operating assets is to compute Net Operating Assets (NOA) minus Net Operating Working Capital (NOWC).

Capital intensive industries, like manufacturing companies, require large investments in long-term operating assets. Accordingly, such companies have lower long-term operating asset turnovers than do less capital intensive companies, like service businesses.

Higher is better for long-term operating asset turnover. Companies desire to minimize the investment in long-term operating assets required to generate a dollar of sales.

Long-term operating asset turnover for 3M in 2003 is 2.8 times, compared with 3.1 times in 1999. During the intervening five years, 3M grew in asset size, but not in terms of long-term operating asset purchases, which have remained fairly constant (capital expenditures approximating depreciation). Instead, 3M's increase in long-term operating assets are in the form of goodwill and other intangible assets acquired from acquisitions of other companies. The LTOAT ratio does not distinguish between long-term operating assets purchased individually or as part of a larger corporate acquisition.

Accounts Payable Turnover (APT)

Net operating working capital, defined as current operating assets less current operating liabilities, is financed in large part by accounts payable (also called *trade credit* or *trade payables*). Accounts payable represent amounts that one company owes another arising from the purchase of goods. Such payables usually represent interest-free financing and are, therefore, less expensive than using available funds or borrowed money to finance purchases or production. Accordingly, companies use trade credit whenever possible. This is called *leaning on the trade.*

The **accounts payable turnover** reflects on management's success in using trade credit to finance purchases of goods. It is computed as:

Accounts Payable Turnover (APT) = Cost of Goods Sold/Average Accounts Payable

Payables are reported at cost, not retail prices. Thus, for consistency with the denominator, cost of goods sold (not sales) is used in the numerator. Management desires to use trade credit to the greatest extent possible for financing. This means that management desires a lower accounts payable turnover.

For 3M, its accounts payable turnover rate has declined from 10.4 times per year in 2001 to 9.1 times per year in 2003. This decline in accounts payable turnover indicates that these obligations are remaining unpaid for a longer period of time. Again, this is generally interpreted as positive, which reflects management's effective use of low-cost financing.

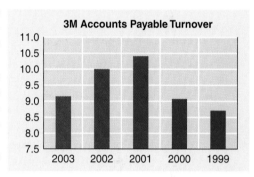

A metric analogous to accounts payable turnover is that of **average payable days outstanding**, which is computed as:

Average Payable Days Outstanding = Accounts Payable/ Average Daily Cost of Goods Sold

Management hopes to extend the payable days outstanding number to as long as possible provided they do not harm their supply channel relationships.

For 3M, its accounts payable remain unpaid for 40 days in 2003, up from 35 days two years ago. 3M is, therefore, leaning on the trade to a greater extent than it has in the recent past. The increase in payable days outstanding increases cash flow because it reflects greater use of a noninterest-bearing source of funding. So, all else equal, cash flow and profits increase.

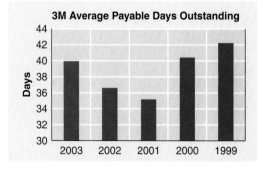

Payment policies must be managed with care as increasing payables correspond with increasing receivables on suppliers' balance sheets, thus increasing suppliers' costs. As a result, if suppliers' bargaining power is greater than the buyers, then suppliers attempt to recoup those costs with higher selling prices. In the extreme, suppliers can refuse to sell to such buyers. Even when buyers possess bargaining leverage, they do not want to exact too high of a cost from suppliers. This is because buyers need a healthy supplier network for a consistent supply source at an acceptable quality level.

Net Operating Working Capital Turnover (NOWCT)

Net operating working capital is the investment in short-term net operating assets. It is one of the two general categories of net operating assets (the other being net long-term operating assets). Management's effectiveness in using operating working capital turnover is reflected in the following metric:

Net Operating Working Capital Turnover (NOWCT) = Net Sales/Average Net Operating Working Capital

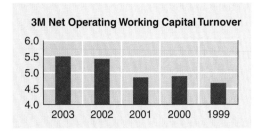

3M Net Operating Working Capital Turnover

A lower operating working capital turnover reflects a greater investment in working capital for each dollar of sales. Working capital turns more quickly when receivables and inventories turn more quickly, and it also turns more quickly when companies lean on the trade (when payables turn more slowly).

3M has been successful in increasing its net operating working capital turnover from 4.7 times a year in 1999 to 5.5 times a year in 2003. This performance is mainly due to increasing turnover for receivables and inventories, and a decreasing turnover for payables.

RNOA (and ROE) disaggregation gives us insight into the drivers of company success. Knowing the drivers of operating performance is crucial in forecasting future performance, which is the ultimate object of most analyses. Still, we must remember that to fully understand the drivers of operating performance, we must analyze the company's business, not just its financial reports. That analysis entails an understanding of the company's markets, its products, its execution, and a number of other strategic factors.

CHAPTER-END REVIEW

Refer to the Mid-Chapter Review 1 for the financial statements of **Caterpillar, Inc.**

Required

Using Caterpillar's financial information, compute the following for 2003.

1. Profit margins
   a. Gross profit margin on machinery and engines (GPM)
   b. Selling, general, and administrative costs as a percentage of total sales and revenues (SGAM for short)

2. Asset turnovers
   a. Accounts receivable turnover (ART) for machinery and engines
   b. Average collection period (Accounts Receivable/Average Daily Sales)
   c. Inventory turnover (INVT) on machinery and engines
   d. Average machinery and engine inventory days outstanding (Inventories/Average Daily COGS for Machinery and Engines)
   e. Long-term operating asset turnover (LTOAT); use total sales and revenues in the numerator
   f. Accounts payable turnover (APT); use machinery and engines COGS
   g. Average payable days outstanding (Accounts Payable/Average Daily COGS)

Solution

1.	a.	Gross profit margin (GPM)	19.5%	($21,048 − $16,945)/$21,048
	b.	SG&A Expenses / Total Sales and Revenues	10.9%	$2,470/$22,763
2.	a.	ART (Sales/Average Accounts Receivable)	6.47 times	$21,048/[($3,666 + $2,838)/2]
	b.	Average collection period	63.57 days	$3,666/($21,048/365)
	c.	INVT (COGS/Average Inventory)	5.83 times	$16,945/[($3,047 + $2,763)/2]
	d.	Average inventory days outstanding	65.63 days	$3,047/($16,945/365)
	e.	LTOAT (Sales/Average Long-Term Operating Assets)	1.21 times	$22,763/[($19,674 + $18,084)/2]
	f.	APT (COGS/Average Accounts Payable)	6.31 times	$16,945/[($3,100 + 2,269)/2]
	g.	Average payable days outstanding	66.77 days	$3,100/($16,945/365)

SUMMARY

LO1 **Define return on equity (ROE) and explain its application to analysis of company operating performance. (p. 197)**

■ Return on equity is net income divided by average equity. It provides insights into the drivers of company profitability, including the source as either operating or nonoperating activities and whether sufficient revenues are generated from assets.

Describe Level 1 disaggregation of ROE into return on net operating assets (RNOA) and return on nonoperating activities (FLEV × Spread), and apply and interpret these components. (p. 199)   LO2

■ ROE is disaggregated into return on net operating activities (RNOA) and the return on nonoperating activities (Financial Leverage × Spread). This disaggregation is referred to as *Level 1 analysis*.

■ RNOA is net operating profit after tax (NOPAT) divided by average net operating assets (NOA).

Distinguish between operating and nonoperating assets and liabilities. (p. 201)   LO3

■ Operating assets and liabilities are those necessary to conduct company business.

■ Nonoperating assets and liabilities are mainly *financial* in nature, and commonly consist of investments in marketable securities and discontinued operations, and borrowings with interest-bearing debt.

Describe Level 2 disaggregation of return on net operating assets (RNOA) into net operating profit margin (NOPM) and net operating asset turnover (NOAT). (p. 207)   LO4

■ RNOA is disaggregated into net operating profit margin (NOPM) multiplied by net operating asset turnover (NOAT). These two components are analyzed separately in evaluating company performance and strategy. They are the two drivers of RNOA and are crucial in comparative analysis of competitors. This is referred to as *Level 2 analysis*.

■ NOPM measures the percent of each dollar realized in after tax profits.

■ NOAT impacts profits in that higher turnover reduces asset holding costs such as insurance and logistics.

■ ROE is increased if a company borrows at a rate below what it can earn on its operating assets (RNOA). The difference, measured by the spread multiplied by leverage, can increase the total return to stockholders.

■ Reliance on leverage carries the risk that contractual payment obligations accompanying increased debt must be met. Failure to do so can lead to outside intervention in company operations and potential bankruptcy.

Describe Level 3 disaggregation of net operating profit margin and of net operating asset turnover into metrics of operating performance and financial condition. (p. 211)   LO5

■ *Level 3 analysis* refers to the disaggregation of both profit margin and asset turnover to better assess the drivers of RNOA.

■ Disaggregates of net operating profit margin (NOPM): gross profit margin (GPM) and operating expense margin (OEM).

■ Disaggregates of net operating asset turnover (NOAT): accounts receivable turnover (ART), inventory turnover (INVT), long-term operating asset turnover (LTOAT), accounts payable turnover (APT), and net operating working capital turnover (NOWCT).

GUIDANCE ANSWERS

YOU MAKE THE CALL

You are a Business Reporter   Several factors that could influence the difference in result include: (1) the firms are in different industries, (2) the extensive use of financial leverage by 3M compared to Caterpillar, (3) the possibility that 3M could be simply better managed, and (4) macro economic and international factors could be having very different impacts on the two companies' fortunes.

YOU MAKE THE CALL

You are the Entrepreneur   Your firm is doing well over all for a start-up. However, most of the success is due to asset turnover while margins are doing at best average compared to the competition. If your products are new and easily copied by the competition, your margins (and also turnover) could easily drop to a point where you would no longer be competitive. A market study should be made and compared to the initial company business plan to see how valid the assumptions contained in the initial strategic plan could be altered to reflect what has been learned during operations to date.

KEY TERMS

Accounts payable turnover (APT) (p. 215)

Accounts receivable turnover (ART) (p. 213)

Average collection period (p. 213)

Average inventory days outstanding (p. 214)

Average payable days outstanding (p. 215)

Financial leverage (FLEV) (p. 203)

Fixed costs (p. 203)

Gross profit margin (GPM) (p. 212)

Inventory turnover (INVT) (p. 214)

Long-term operating asset turnover (LTOAT) (p. 214)

Markup (p. 212)

Net financial obligations (NFO) (p. 201)

Net financial expense (NFE) (p. 197)

Net financial rate (NFR) (p. 197)

Net operating assets (NOA) (p. 201)

Net operating assets turnover (NOAT) (p. 210)

Net operating profit after tax (NOPAT) (p. 201)

Net operating profit margin (p. 209)

Net operating working capital (NOWC) (p. 201)

Net operating working capital turnover (NOWCT) (p. 215)

Net profit margin (p. 209)

Operating expense margin (OEM) (p. 212)

Return on assets (ROA) (p. 196)

Return on equiy (ROE) (p. 197)

Return on net operating assets (RNOA) (p. 200)

Return on sales (p. 209)

Spread (p. 197)

Variable costs (p. 203)

MULTIPLE CHOICE

1. ROA is limited as a measure of operating performance because
   a. it excludes nonoperating components.
   b. it fails to consider company equity.
   c. its denominator includes nonoperating assets.
   d. its numerator fails to include important operating revenues.

2. If ROE exceeds the return on net operating assets (RNOA), the difference must be due to
   a. a positive return from nonoperating activities.
   b. increasing financial leverage (FLEV).
   c. a negative spread.
   d. Both a and b.

3. Which of the following items is a nonoperating asset?
   a. intangible assets
   b. deferred tax liabilities
   c. investments in government securities
   d. leased equipment (an asset)

4. If additional assets are purchased using borrowed funds, which of the following must be true?
   a. The asset addition will decrease NOPAT.
   b. The asset addition will decrease FLEV.
   c. The asset addition will increase NOWC.
   d. The asset addition will increase NFO.

5. A company has the following values: NOPM = 0.07; NOPAT = $1,900; Average NOA = $37,320, and NFO = $13,254. NOAT equals
   a. 0.05.
   b. 0.73.
   c. 0.36.
   d. NOAT is not determinable because its sales cannot be computed from the information provided.

DISCUSSION QUESTIONS

Q5-1. Explain in general terms the concept of return on investment. Why is this concept important in the analysis of financial performance?

Q5-2. (a) Explain how an increase in financial leverage can increase a company's ROE. (b) Given the potentially positive relation between financial leverage and ROE, why don't we see companies with 100% financial leverage (entirely nonowner financed)?

Q5-3. Identify two factors that can yield a decline in the gross profit margin. Should a reduction in the gross profit margin always be interpreted negatively? Explain.

Q5-4. When might a reduction in operating expenses as a percentage of sales denote a short-term gain at the cost of long-term performance?

Q5-5. Describe the concept of asset turnover. What does the concept mean and why it is so important to understanding and interpreting financial performance?

Q5-6. How might a company increase its accounts receivable turnover?

Q5-7. How can a company increase its inventory turnover?

Q5-8. By what means might a company increase its long-term operating asset turnover?

Q5-9. Why might a reduction in the accounts payable turnover rate not be considered favorable?

Q5-10. What insights do we take away from the graphical relation between profit margin and asset turnover?

MINI EXERCISES

M5-11. Identify and Compute Net Operating Assets and its Components (LO3)

Target
Corporation (TGT)

Following is the actual balance sheet for **Target Corporation**. Identify and compute its net operating assets and its components: net operating working capital and net operating long-term assets.

(millions)	January 31, 2004
Assets	
Cash and cash equivalents	$ 716
Accounts receivable, net	5,776
Inventory	5,343
Other	1,093
Total current assets	12,928
Property and equipment	
Land	3,629
Buildings and improvements	13,091
Fixtures and equipment	5,432
Construction-in-progress	995
Accumulated depreciation	(6,178)
Property and equipment, net	16,969
Other	1,495
Total assets	$31,392
Liabilities and shareholders' investment	
Accounts payable	$ 5,448
Accrued liabilities	1,618
Income taxes payable	382
Current portion of long-term debt and notes payable	866
Total current liabilities	8,314
Long-term debt	10,217
Deferred income taxes and other	1,796
Shareholders' investment	
Common stock	76
Additional paid-in-capital	1,341
Retained earnings	9,645
Accumulated other comprehensive income	3
Total shareholders' investment	11,065
Total liabilities and shareholders' investment	$31,392

M5-12. Identify and Compute NOPAT and NFE (LO3)

Following is the actual income statement for Target Corporation. Identify and compute its net operating profit after tax (NOPAT) and its net financial expense (NFE).

Target Corporation (TGT)

(millions)	Year-Ended January 31, 2004
Sales	$46,781
Net credit card revenues	1,382
Total revenues	48,163
Cost of sales	31,790
Selling, general, and administrative expense	10,696
Credit card expense	838
Depreciation and amortization	1,320
Interest expense	559
Earnings before income taxes	2,960
Provision for income taxes	1,119
Net earnings	$ 1,841

M5-13. Compute RNOA, NOPAT Margin, and NOA Turnover (LO2, 4)

Selected balance sheet and income statement information for Target Corporation, a department store retailer, follows ($ millions)

Target Corporation (TGT)

a. Compute its 2004 return on net operating assets (RNOA).

b. Disaggregate its RNOA from *a* into net operating profit margin (NOPM) and net operating asset turnover (NOAT). Show that RNOA = NOPM × NOAT.

c. Compute its net operating working capital turnover (NOWCT) and its long-term operating asset turnover (LTOAT).

Company	Ticker	2004 Sales	2004 NOPAT	2004 Net Operating Working Capital	2003 Net Operating Working Capital	2004 Net Operating Assets	2003 Net Operating Assets	2003 Long-Term Operating Assets	2004 Long-Term Operating Assets
Target Corp	TGT	$48,163	$2,189	$5,480	$5,387	$22,148	$20,604	$18,464	$16,668

The Walt Disney Company (DIS)

M5-14. Identify and Compute Net Operating Assets and its Components (LO3)

Following is the actual fiscal year-end 2003 balance sheet for The Walt Disney Company. Identify and compute net operating assets (NOA) and its components: net operating working capital (NOWC) and net operating long-term assets (NOLTA).

(in millions)	September 30, 2003
Assets	
Current assets	
Cash and cash equivalents	$ 1,583
Receivables	4,238
Inventories	703
Television costs	568
Deferred income taxes	674
Other current assets	548
Total current assets	8,314
Film and television costs	6,205
Investments	1,849
Parks, resorts and other property, at cost	
Attractions, buildings and equipment	19,499
Accumulated depreciation	(8,794)
	10,705
Projects in progress	1,076
Land	897
	12,678
Intangible assets, net	2,786
Goodwill	16,966
Other assets	1,190
Total assets	$49,988
Liabilities and Shareholders' Equity	
Current liabilities	
Accounts payable and other accrued liabilities	$ 5,044
Current portion of borrowings	2,457
Unearned royalties and other advances	1,168
Total current liabilities	8,669
Borrowings	10,643
Deferred income taxes	2,712
Other long-term liabilities	3,745
Minority interests	428
Shareholders' equity	
Common stock—Disney, $.01 par value	
Authorized—3.6 billion shares, Issued—2.1 billion shares	12,154
Retained earnings	13,817
Accumulated other comprehensive loss	(653)
Treasury stock, at cost, 86.7 million and 81.4 million Disney shares	(1,527)
	23,791
Total liabilities and equity	$49,988

M5-15. **Identify and Compute NOPAT and NFE** **(LO3)**

Following is the actual fiscal year-end 2003 income statement for **The Walt Disney Company**. Identify and compute its net operating profit after tax (NOPAT) and its net financial expense (NFE).

The Walt Disney Company (DIS)

(in millions)	Year Ended September 30, 2003
Revenues	$ 27,061
Costs and expenses	(24,330)
Amortization of intangible assets	(18)
Gain on sale of businesses	16
Net interest expense	(793)
Equity in the income of investees	334
Restructuring and impairment charges	(16)
Income before income taxes, minority interests and the cumulative effect of accounting change	2,254
Income taxes	(789)
Minority interests share of income	(127)
Income before the cumulative effect of accounting changes	1,338
Cumulative effect of accounting change	
Multiple element revenue accounting	(71)
Net income (loss)	$ 1,267

M5-16. **Compute RNOA, NOPAT Margin, and NOA Turnover** **(LO2, 4)**

Selected balance sheet and income statement information for **The Walt Disney Company**, an operator of theme parks and media companies, follows ($ millions).

The Walt Disney Company (DIS)

Company	Ticker	2004 Sales	2004 NOPAT	2003 Net Operating Working Capital	2002 Net Operating Working Capital	2003 Net Operating Assets	2002 Net Operating Assets	2003 Long-Term Operating Assets	2002 Long-Term Operating Assets
Walt Disney	DIS	$27,061	$1,899	$2,102	$1,693	$37,319	$38,009	$41,674	$42,196

a. Compute its 2003 return on net operating assets (RNOA).

b. Disaggregate its RNOA from *a* into net operating profit margin (NOPM) and net operating asset turnover (NOAT). Show that RNOA = NOPM × NOAT.

c. Compute its net operating working capital turnover (NOWCT) and its long-term operating asset turnover (LTOAT).

M5-17. **Compute and Interpret Asset Turnover Ratios** **(LO4, 5)**

Selected balance sheet and income statement information from **Toys "R" Us, Inc.**, for 2003 follows ($ millions).

Toys "R" Us, Inc. (TOY)

Company	Sales	Cost of Goods Sold	Average Accounts Receivable	Average inventory	Average Long-Term Operating Assets
Toys "R" US	$11,566	$7,849	$174	$2,157	$4,821

a. Compute the following asset turnover ratios:
1. Accounts receivable turnover (ART)
2. Inventory turnover (INVT)
3. Long-term operating asset turnover (LTOAT)

b. What are some characteristics of the Toys "R" Us business that would likely lead to the levels of turnover identified in *a*?

EXERCISES

E5-18. Compute and Interpret RNOA, Profit Margin, and Asset Turnover of Competitors (LO2, 4)

Selected balance sheet and income statement information for the department store retailers Target Corporation and Wal-Mart Stores follows ($ millions).

Company	Ticker	2004 Sales	2004 NOPAT	2004 Net Operating Working Capital	2003 Net Operating Working Capital	2004 Net Operating Assets	2003 Net Operating Assets	2004 Long-Term Operating Assets	2003 Long-Term Operating Assets
Target Corp	TGT	$48,163	$2,189	$5,480	$5,387	$22,148	$20,604	$18,464	$16,668
Wal-Mart Stores	WMT	258,681	9,601	3,370	3,994	71,573	66,211	70,491	64,086

a. Compute the 2004 return on net operating assets (RNOA) for each company.
b. Disaggregate RNOA from a into net operating profit margin (NOPM) and net operating asset turnover (NOAT) for each company.
c. Compute the 2004 net operating working capital turnover (NOWCT) and long-term operating asset turnover (LTOAT) for each company.
d. Discuss any differences in these ratios for each company. Your interpretation should reflect the distinct business strategies of each company.

E5-19. Compute, Disaggregate, and Interpret RNOA of Competitors (LO2, 4)

Selected balance sheet and income statement information for the clothing retailers Abercrombie & Fitch and The GAP, Inc., follows ($ millions).

Company	Ticker	2003 Sales	2003 NOPAT	2003 Net Operating Working Capital	2002 Net Operating Working Capital	2003 Net Operating Assets	2002 Net Operating Assets	2003 Long-Term Operating Assets	2002 Long-Term Operating Assets
Abercrombie & Fitch	ANF	$ 1,708	$ 203	$ 463	$ 374	$ 861	$ 740	$ 447	$ 394
Gap, Inc	GPS	15,854	1,150	2,056	3,152	5,710	7,314	3,654	4,162

a. Compute the 2004 return on net operating assets (RNOA) for each company.
b. Disaggregate RNOA from a into net operating profit margin (NOPM) and net operating asset turnover (NOAT) for each company.
c. Compute the 2004 net operating working capital turnover (NOWCT) and long-term operating asset turnover (LTOAT) for each company.
d. Discuss any differences in these ratios for each company. Your interpretation should reflect the distinct business strategies of each company.

E5-20. Compute, Disaggregate, and Interpret RNOA of Competitors (LO2, 4)

Selected balance sheet and income statement information for the grocery retailers Albertsons, Inc., and Kroger Company follows ($ millions).

Company	Ticker	2004 Sales	2004 NOPAT	2004 Net Operating Working Capital	2003 Net Operating Working Capital	2004 Net Operating Assets	2003 Net Operating Assets	2004 Long-Term Operating Assets	2003 Long-Term Operating Assets
Albertsons, Inc	ABS	$35,436	$809	$1,254	$939	$10,705	$10,573	$10,975	$10,943
Kroger Co	KR	53,791	562	281	310	12,375	12,424	14,565	14,536

a. Compute the 2004 return on net operating assets (RNOA) for each company.
b. Disaggregate RNOA from a into net operating profit margin (NOPM) and net operating asset turnover (NOAT) for each company.
c. Compute the 2004 net operating working capital turnover (NOWCT) and long-term operating asset turnover (LTOAT) for each company.
d. Discuss any differences in these ratios for each company. Your interpretation should reflect the distinct business strategies of each company.

E5-21. **Compute, Disaggregate, and Interpret RNOA of Competitors** (LO3)

Selected balance sheet and income statement information for the soft drink manufacturers Coca-Cola and PepsiCo follows ($ millions).

Coca-Cola (KO)
PepsiCo (PEP)

Company	Ticker	2003 Sales	2003 NOPAT	2003 Net Operating Working Capital	2002 Net Operating Working Capital	2003 Net Operating Assets	2002 Net Operating Assets	2003 Long-Term Operating Assets	2002 Long-Term Operating Assets
Coca-Cola Co	KO	$21,044	$4,342	$3,296	$2,581	$19,393	$17,071	$18,946	$17,054
PepsiCo Inc	PEP	26,971	3,649	(75)	716	12,986	12,065	18,397	17,061

a. Compute the 2003 return on net operating assets (RNOA) for each company.
b. Disaggregate RNOA from *a* into net operating profit margin (NOPM) and net operating asset turnover (NOAT) for each company.
c. Compute the 2003 net operating working capital turnover (NOWCT) and long-term operating asset turnover (LTOAT) for each company.
d. Discuss any differences in these ratios for each company. Your interpretation should reflect the distinct business strategies of each company.

E5-22. **Compute, Disaggregate, and Interpret RNOA of Competitors** (LO2, 4)

Selected balance sheet and income statement information for the drug retailers CVS Corporation and Walgreen Company follows ($ millions).

a. Compute the 2003 return on net operating assets (RNOA) for each company.

CVS
Corporation (CVS)
Walgreen
Company (WAG)

Company	Ticker	2003 Sales	2003 NOPAT	2003 Net Operating Working Capital	2002 Net Operating Working Capital	2003 Net Operating Assets	2002 Net Operating Assets	2003 Long-Term Operating Assets	2002 Long-Term Operating Assets
CVS Corp	CVS	$26,588	$ 877	$3,331	$2,913	$7,098	$6,310	$4,047	$3,663
Walgreen Co	WAG	32,505	1,150	2,938	2,211	7,196	6,230	5,048	4,712

b. Disaggregate RNOA from *a* into net operating profit margin (NOPM) and net operating asset turnover (NOAT) for each company.
c. Compute the 2003 net operating working capital turnover (NOWCT) and long-term operating asset turnover (LTOAT) for each company.
d. Discuss any differences in these ratios for each company. Your interpretation should reflect the distinct business strategies of each company.

E5-23. **Compute, Disaggregate, and Interpret RNOA of Competitors** (LO2, 4)

Selected fiscal year balance sheet and income statement information for the athletic shoe and apparel manufacturers Nike, Inc., and Reebok International follows ($ millions).

Nike, Inc. (NKE)
Reebok
International (RBK)

Company	Ticker	2004 Sales	2004 NOPAT	2004 Net Operating Working Capital	2003 Net Operating Working Capital	2004 Net Operating Assets	2003 Net Operating Assets	2004 Long-Term Operating Assets	2003 Long-Term Operating Assets
Nike Inc	NKE	$12,253	$962	$3,255	$3,048	$5,216	$4,824	$2,380	$2,034
Reebok Ltd	RBK	3,485	174	1,169	1,053	1,432	1,300	263	247

a. Compute the 2004 return on net operating assets (RNOA) for each company.
b. Disaggregate RNOA from *a* into net operating profit margin (NOPM) and net operating asset turnover (NOAT) for each company.
c. Compute the 2004 net operating working capital turnover (NOWCT) and long-term operating asset turnover (LTOAT) for each company.
d. Discuss any differences in these ratios for each company. Your interpretation should reflect the distinct business strategies of each company.

Abercrombie &
Fitch (ANF)

Wal-Mart
Stores (WMT)

E5-24. **Compute and Interpret Asset Turnover Ratios of Competitors** (LO4, 5)

Selected balance sheet and income statement information from Abercrombie & Fitch and Wal-Mart Stores for fiscal 2004 follows ($ millions)

Company	Sales	Cost of Goods Sold	Average Accounts Receivable	Average inventory	Average Long-Term Operating Assets
Abercrombie & Fitch	$ 1,708	$ 990	$ 8	$ 184	$ 420
Wal-Mart Stores	258,681	198,747	1,411	25,506	67,288

a. Compute the following asset turnover ratios for each company:
1. Accounts receivable turnover
2. Inventory turnover
3. Long-term operating asset turnover
b. What are some characteristics of their respective business activities that would likely lead to the levels of turnover identified in a?

Harley-Davidson,
Inc. (HDI)

Target
Corporation (TGT)

E5-25. **Compute and Interpret Asset Turnover Ratios of Competitors** (LO4, 5)

Selected balance sheet and income statement information from the motorcycle manufacturing company, Harley-Davidson, Inc., and from the retailing company, Target Corporation, follows ($ millions).

Company	Sales	Cost of Goods Sold	Average Accounts Receivable	Average inventory	Average Long-Term Operating Assets
Harley-Davidson	$ 4,624	$ 2,959	$ 110	$ 213	$ 1,994
Target Corp	48,163	31,790	5,670	5,052	17,566

a. Compute the following asset turnover ratios for each company:
1. Accounts receivable turnover
2. Inventory turnover
3. Long-term operating asset turnover
b. What are some characteristics of their respective business activities that would likely lead to the levels of turnover identified in a?

PROBLEMS

Procter &
Gamble (PG)

P5-26. **Analysis and Interpretation of Company Profitability** (LO1, 2, 3, 4)

Balance sheets and income statements for Procter & Gamble follow. Refer to these financial statements to answer the requirements below.

Procter & Gamble Company Comparative Balance Sheets				
For June 30 ($ millions)	2003	2002	2001	2000
Cash and cash equivalents	$ 5,912	$ 3,427	$ 2,306	$ 1,415
Investment securities	300	196	212	185
Accounts receivable	3,038	3,090	2,931	2,910
Inventories	3,640	3,456	3,384	3,490
Other current (operating) assets	2,330	1,997	2,056	2,146
Total current assets	15,220	12,166	10,889	10,146
Property, plant and equipment, gross	23,542	23,070	22,821	23,221
Accumulated depreciation	10,438	9,721	9,726	9,529
Property, plant and equipment, net	13,104	13,349	13,095	13,692
Goodwill and intangible assets	13,507	13,430	8,300	8,786
Other noncurrent (operating) assets	1,875	1,831	2,103	1,742
Total assets	$43,706	$40,776	$34,387	$34,366

(Continued)

Procter & Gamble Company
Comparative Balance Sheets (Continued)

For June 30 ($ millions)	2003	2002	2001	2000
Accounts payable	$ 2,795	$ 2,205	$ 2,075	$ 2,209
Debt due within one year	2,172	3,731	2,233	3,241
Accrued and other liabilities	7,391	6,768	5,538	4,691
Total current liabilities	12,358	12,704	9,846	10,141
Deferred income taxes	1,396	1,077	894	625
Long-term debt	11,475	11,201	9,792	9,012
Other noncurrent liabilities	2,291	2,088	1,845	2,301
Total liabilities	27,520	27,070	22,377	22,079
Preferred stock	1,580	1,634	1,701	1,737
Common stock	1,297	1,301	1,296	1,306
Additional paid-in capital	2,931	2,490	2,057	1,794
Retained earnings	13,692	11,980	10,451	10,710
Other equities	(3,314)	(3,699)	(3,495)	(3,260)
Shareholders' equity	16,186	13,706	12,010	12,287
Total liabilities and equity	$43,706	$40,776	$34,387	$34,366

Procter & Gamble Company
Comparative Income Statements

Year Ended June 30 ($ millions)	2003	2002	2001	2000
Net sales	$43,377	$40,238	$39,244	$39,951
Cost of goods sold	22,141	20,989	22,102	21,514
Gross profit	21,236	19,249	17,142	18,437
Selling, general & administrative expense	13,383	12,571	12,406	12,483
Operating income	7,853	6,678	4,736	5,954
Other nonoperating income, net	238	308	674	304
Interest expense	561	603	794	722
Income before income taxes	7,530	6,383	4,616	5,536
Income taxes	2,344	2,031	1,694	1,994
Net earnings	$ 5,186	$ 4,352	$ 2,922	$ 3,542

Required

a. Compute the following profitability ratios for each year shown:
1. Gross profit margin (GPM).
2. Operating expense margin (OEM)—also called SG&A margin.
3. Net operating profit margin (NOPM).

b. Your results in part *a* should have revealed an increase in net operating profit margin (NOPM).
1. Is this increase due to an increase in the gross profit margin or a decrease in operating expenses, or both? Provide evidence and explain your answer.
2. Consider how much control that companies have or do not have over gross profit margin. What factors must exist to allow companies to increase selling prices of their products? In what ways can they improve gross profit margin by lowering product manufacturing costs? Explain.

c. What are the usual components of operating expense for a company like Procter and Gamble? For which of these components are companies likely able to achieve expense reductions? To what extent are these expense reductions a short-term gain at the cost of long-term performance? Explain.

P5-27. Analysis and Interpretation of Asset Turnover Ratios (LO3, 4, 5)

Refer to the financial information for **Procter & Gamble** in Problem 5-26 to answer the following.

Procter & Gamble (PG)

Required

a. Compute the following turnover ratios and analysis measures for 2001 through 2003:
1. Accounts receivable turnover and the average collection period.
2. Inventory turnover and the average inventory days outstanding.
3. Long-term operating asset turnover.

b. Results from part *a* should reveal a slight improvement in receivables turnover from 2001 to 2003. How can a company like P&G realize an improvement in this ratio? Explain.

c. Results from part *a* should reveal no discernible improvement in inventory turnover from 2001 to 2003. How can a manufacturer like P&G realize an improvement in its inventory turnover? Explain.

d. Results from part *a* should reveal a slight decline in long-term operating asset turnover from 2001 to 2003. Why is it so difficult for companies to impact this ratio? Can you think of ways in which a company can achieve an improvement in this ratio? Explain.

P5-28. **Disaggregation and Interpretation of Company ROE** (LO1, 2, 3)

Procter &
Gamble (PG)

Refer to the financial information for Procter & Gamble in Problem 5-26 to answer the following.

Required

a. Compute the following for 2001 through 2003:
1. Net operating profit margin (NOPM).
2. Return on net operating assets (RNOA).
3. Financial leverage (FLEV).
4. Net financial rate (NFR).
5. Spread.
6. Return on equity (ROE).
7. Confirm that ROE from the formula, ROE = RNOA + (FLEV × Spread), equals that computed in part (6).

b. Drawing on results from part *a*, does P&G depend more on operations (RNOA) or financial leverage to drive its ROE? Explain.

P5-29. **Analysis and Interpretation of Company Profitability** (LO3, 4, 5)

Merck & Co. (MRK)

Actual balance sheets and income statements for Merck & Co. follow ($ millions). Refer to these financial statements to answer the requirements below.

Merck & Co. Comparative Balance Sheets			
December 31 ($ millions)	2003	2002	2001
Assets			
Current Assets			
Cash and cash equivalents	$ 1,201.0	$ 2,243.0	$ 2,144.0
Short-term investments	2,972.0	2,728.2	1,142.6
Accounts receivable	4,023.6	5,423.4	5,215.4
Inventories	2,554.7	2,964.3	3,579.3
Prepaid expenses and taxes	775.9	1,027.5	880.3
Total current assets	11,527.2	14,386.4	12,961.6
Investments	7,941.2	7,255.1	6,983.5
Property, Plant, and Equipment (at cost)			
Land	356.7	336.9	315.2
Buildings	8,016.9	7,336.5	6,653.9
Machinery, equipment and office furnishings	11,018.2	10,883.6	9,807.0
Construction in progress	1,901.9	2,426.6	2,180.4
	21,293.7	20,983.6	18,956.5
Less allowance for depreciation	7,124.7	6,788.0	5,853.1
	14,169.0	14,195.6	13,103.4
Goodwill	1,085.4	4,127.0	4,127.0
Other Intangibles, Net	864.0	3,114.0	3,364.0
Other Assets	5,000.7	4,483.1	3,481.7
Total Assets	$40,587.5	$47,561.2	$44,021.2

(Continued)

Merck & Co.
Comparative Balance Sheets (*Continued*)

December 31 ($ millions)	2003	2002	2001
Liabilities and Stockholders' Equity			
Current Liabilities			
Loans payable and current portion of long-term debt	$ 1,700.0	$ 3,669.8	$ 4,066.7
Trade accounts payable	735.2	2,413.3	1,895.2
Accrued and other current liabilities	3,772.8	3,365.6	3,213.2
Income taxes payable	2,538.9	2,118.1	1,573.3
Dividends paya'ble	822.7	808.4	795.8
Total current liabilities	9,569.6	12,375.2	11,544.2
Long-Term Debt	5,096.0	4,879.0	4,798.6
Deferred Income Taxes and Noncurrent Liabilities	6,430.3	7,178.2	6,790.8
Minority Interests	3,915.2	4,928.3	4,837.5
Stockholders' Equity			
Common stock, one cent par value			
Authorized—5,400,000,000 shares			
Issued—2,976,230,393 shares—2003			
Issued—2,976,198,757 shares—2002	29.8	29.8	29.8
Other paid-in capital	6,956.6	6,943.7	6,907.2
Retained earnings	34,142.0	35,434.9	31,489.6
Accumulated other comprehensive income (loss)	65.5	(98.8)	10.6
	41,193.9	42,309.6	38,437.2
Less treasury stock, at cost			
754,466,884 shares—2003			
731,215,507 shares—2002	25,617.5	24,109.1	22,387.1
Total stockholders' equity	15,576.4	18,200.5	16,050.1
Total Liabilities and Equity	$40,587.5	$47,561.2	$44,021.2

Merck & Co.
Comparative Income Statements

Year Ended December 31 ($ millions)	2003	2002	2001
Sales	$22,485.9	$21,445.8	$21,199.0
Costs, Expenses and Other			
Materials and production	4,315.3	3,907.1	3,624.8
Marketing and administrative	6,394.9	5,652.2	5,700.6
Research and development	3,178.1	2,677.2	2,456.4
Acquired research	101.8	—	—
Equity income from affiliates	(474.2)	(644.7)	(685.9)
Other (income) expense, net	(81.6)	202.3	155.0
	13,434.3	11,794.1	11,250.9
Income from Continuing Operations Before Taxes	9,051.6	9,651.7	9,948.1
Taxes on Income	2,462.0	2,856.9	2,894.9
Income from Continuing Operations	6,589.6	6,794.8	7,053.2
Income from Discontinued Operations, Net of Taxes . .	241.3	354.7	228.6
Net Income	$ 6,830.9	$ 7,149.5	$ 7,281.8

Required

a. Compute the following profitability ratios for each year shown:
1. Gross profit margin (GPM). (*Hint*: Materials and production are MRK's cost of goods sold.)
2. Operating expense margin (OEM). (*Hint*: Include acquired research for 2003 in R&D expense.)
3. Taxes on income as a percentage of income before taxes.
4. Net operating profit margin (NOPM).

b. Your results in part *a* should have revealed a decrease in net operating profit margin (NOPM) from 2002 to 2003.
   1. Which component(s) of operating profit (from part *a*) contribute to this decrease? Provide evidence and explain your answer.
   2. Consider how much control that companies have or do not have over gross profit margin. What market factors adversely affect GPM? Explain.
c. MRK's R&D costs as a percent of sales have increased over the past 3 years. How do you interpret changes in the level of R&D costs? Explain.

P5-30. Analysis and Interpretation of Asset Turnover Ratios (LO3, 4, 5)

Merck & Co. (MRK)

Refer to the financial information for Merck & Co. in Problem 5-29 to answer the following requirements.

Required

a. Compute the following turnover ratios and analysis measures for 2002 and 2003:
   1. Accounts receivable turnover and the average collection period.
   2. Inventory turnover and the average inventory days outstanding.
   3. Long-term operating asset turnover.
b. Results from part *a* should reveal an improvement in receivables turnover from 2002 to 2003. Considering the customer base for product sales, how can a company like MRK realize an improvement in this ratio? Explain.
c. Results from part *a* should reveal an improvement in inventory turnover from 2002 to 2003. How can a manufacturer like MRK realize an improvement in its inventory turnover? Explain.
d. Results from part *a* should reveal an improvement in long-term operating asset turnover from 2002 to 2003. Why is it so difficult for companies to impact this ratio? Can you think of ways in which a company can achieve an improvement in this ratio? Explain.

P5-31. Disaggregation and Interpretation of Company ROE (LO1, 2, 3)

Merck & Co. (MRK)

Refer to the financial information for Merck & Co. in Problem 5-29 to answer the following.

Required

a. Compute the following for 2002 and 2003:
   1. Net operating profit margin (NOPM).
   2. Net operating asset turnover ((NOAT).
   3. Return on net operating assets (RNOA).
   4. Confirm that RNOA from the formula, RNOA = NOPM $\times$ NOAT, and using results from (1) and (2), equals that computed in part (3).
   5. Financial leverage (FLEV). (*Hint*: FLEV is negative when financial assets exceed financial liabilities.)
   6. Net financial rate (NFR).
   7. Spread.
   8. Return on equity (ROE).
   9. Confirm that ROE from the formula, ROE = RNOA + (FLEV $\times$ Spread), and using results from (3), (5) and (7), equals that computed in part (8).
b. Results from part *a* indicate that MRK's RNOA is greater than its ROE for 2003. This means that FLEV has a negative impact. How do you interpret this result? Explain.

P5-32. Disaggregation and comparison of ROE.

McDonald's Corporation (MCD)
Wendy's International, Inc. (WEN)
Applebee's International, Inc. (APPB)
Outback Steakhouse, Inc. (OSI)

The following table contains selected data from the 2004 10-K reports of McDonald's Corporation, Wendy's International, Inc., Applebee's International, Inc., and Outback Steakhouse, Inc. All four companies are listed in the same industry classification as retail eating places.

($ thousands)	McDonald's Corporation	Wendy's International	Applebee's International	Outback Steakhouse
Revenues	$19,064,700	$3,635,438	$1,111,634	$3,201,750
NOPAT	2,519,066	64,061	108,707	165,096
Net Income	2,278,500	52,035	110,865	156,057
Average Net Operating Assets	45,133,900	2,458,451	497,836	1,236,987
Average Stockholders' Equity	13,091,700	1,737,148	474,935	1,046,813

a. Calculate the return on equity (ROE) for each company.
b. Calculate the return on net operating assets (RNOA) for each company.
c. For each company, calculate financial leverage (FLEV) and the net financial rate (NFR).

d. Confirm that ROE = RNOA + FLEV × Spread.

e. Disaggregate the RNOA into net operating profit margin (NOPM) and net operating asset turnover (NOAT). Confirm that RNOA = NOPM × NOAT.

f. Compare the ratios of these four companies. What can you infer from this comparison about the relative profitability of each firm?

P5-33. Disaggregation and comparison of ROE.

The following table contains selected data from the 2004 10-K reports of **Dell, Inc.**, **Apple Computer**, and **Sun Microsystems, Inc.**

Dell, Inc. (DELL)
Apple Computer
(AAPL)
Sun Microsystems,
Inc. (SUNW)

($ millions)	Dell	Apple	Sun Microsystems
Revenues	$49,205	$8,279	$11,070
NOPAT	2,912	235	(219)
Net Income	3,043	276	(107)
Average Net Operating Assets	3,203	2,969	6,101
Average Stockholders' Equity	6,383	4,650	6,579

a. Calculate the return on equity (ROE) for each company.

b. Calculate the return on net operating assets (RNOA) for each company.

c. For each company, calculate financial leverage (FLEV) and the net financial rate (NFR).

d. Confirm that ROE = RNOA + FLEV × Spread.

e. Disaggregate the RNOA into net operating profit margin (NOPM) and net operating asset turnover (NOAT). Confirm that RNOA = NOPM × NOAT.

f. Compare the ratios of these three companies. What can you infer from this comparison about the relative profitability of each firm?

CASES AND PROJECTS

C5-34. Analysis and Interpretation of Company Profitability

Refer to the actual comparative balance sheets and income statements for **Colgate-Palmolive Company** that follow to answer the requirements below.

Colgate-Palmolive
Company (CL)

Required

a. Compute the following analysis measures for 2003:
1. Net operating profit margin (NOPM).
2. Return on net operating assets (RNOA).
3. Financial leverage (FLEV).
4. Net financial rate (NFR).
5. Spread.
6. Return on equity (ROE).
7. Confirm that ROE from the formula, ROE = RNOA + (FLEV × Spread), and using results from (2), (3) and (5), equals that computed in part (6).

b. Drawing on results from part *a*, does Colgate depend more on operations (RNOA) or financial leverage to drive its ROE? Explain.

c. Compute the following profitability ratios for 2003:
1. Gross profit margin (GPM).
2. Operating expense margin (OEM)—also called SG&A margin.
3. Net operating profit margin (NOPM)—*see part a.*

d. Consider how much control that companies have or do not have over gross profit margin. What factors must exist to allow them to increase selling prices of their products? In what ways can they improve gross profit margin by lowering product manufacturing costs? Explain.

e. What components of selling, general and administrative expense are companies likely able to use to achieve expense reductions? To what extent are these expense reductions a short-term gain at the cost of long-term performance? Explain.

f. Compute the following turnover ratios and analysis measures for 2003:
1. Accounts receivable turnover.
2. Average collection period.
3. Inventory turnover.
4. Average inventory days outstanding.

g. How can a company like Colgate realize an improvement in its accounts receivable turnover? Explain.

h. How can a manufacturer like Colgate realize an improvement in its inventory turnover? Explain.

Colgate-Palmolive Company
Comparative Income Statements

Year Ended December 31 ($ millions)	2003	2002	2001
Net sales	$9,903.4	$9,294.3	$9,084.3
Cost of sales	4,456.1	4,224.2	4,234.9
Gross profit	5,447.3	5,070.1	4,849.4
Selling, general & administrative expenses	3,296.3	3,034.0	2,920.1
Other (income) expense, net	(15.0)	23.0	94.5
Operating profit	2,166.0	2,013.1	1,834.8
Interest expense, net	124.1	142.8	166.1
Income before income taxes	2,041.9	1,870.3	1,668.7
Provision for income taxes	620.6	582.0	522.1
Net income	$1,421.3	$1,288.3	$1,146.6

Colgate-Palmolive Company
Comparative Balance Sheets

December 31 ($ millions)	2003	2002
Assets		
Current Assets		
Cash and cash equivalents	$ 265.3	$ 167.9
Receivables (less allowances of $43.6 and $45.9, respectively)	1,222.4	1,145.4
Inventories	718.3	671.7
Other current assets	290.5	243.1
Total current assets	2,496.5	2,228.1
Property, plant and equipment, net	2,542.2	2,491.3
Goodwill	1,299.4	1,182.8
Other intangible assets, net	597.6	608.5
Other assets	543.1	576.5
Total assets	$7,478.8	$7,087.2
Liabilities and Shareholders' Equity		
Current Liabilities		
Notes and loans payable	$ 103.6	$94.6
Current portion of long-term debt	314.4	298.5
Accounts payable	753.6	728.3
Accrued income taxes	183.8	121.7
Other accruals	1,090.0	905.6
Total current liabilities	2,445.4	2,148.7
Long-term debt	2,684.9	3,210.8
Deferred income taxes	456.0	488.8
Other liabilities	1,005.4	888.6
Total liabilities	6,591.7	6,736.9
Shareholders' Equity		
Preferred stock	292.9	323.0
Common stock, $1 par value (1,000,000,000 shares authorized, 732,853,180 shares issued)	$ 732.9	$ 732.9
Additional paid-in capital	1,126.2	1,133.9
Retained earnings	7,433.0	6,518.5
Accumulated other comprehensive income	(1,866.8)	(1,865.6)
	7,718.2	6,842.7

(Continued)

Colgate-Palmolive Company Comparative Balance Sheets (*Continued*)		
December 31 ($ millions)	2003	2002
Unearned compensation	(331.2)	(340.1)
Treasury stock, at cost	(6,499.9)	(6,152.3)
Total shareholders' equity	887.1	350.3
Total liabilities and shareholders' equity	$ 7,478.8	$ 7,087.2

C5-35. **Analysis and Interpretation of Profit Margin, Asset Turnover, and RNOA for Several Companies** (LO1, 2, 3, 4, 5)

Net operating profit margin (NOPM) and net operating asset turnover (NOAT) for several selected companies for 2003 follow:

Company	NOPM	NOAT
Albertsons, Inc	2.20%	3.59
Alcoa, Inc	5.93%	1.51
Caterpillar, Inc	6.96%	1.99
Home Depot, Inc	6.64%	2.72
McDonalds Corporation	12.61%	0.89
SBC Communications, Inc	10.62%	0.79
Southwest Airlines	5.08%	0.74
Target Corporation	4.54%	2.23

Albertsons, Inc (ABS)

Alcoa, Inc (AA)

Caterpillar, Inc (CAT)

Home Depot, Inc (HD)

McDonalds Corporation (MCD)

SBC Communications, Inc (SBC)

Southwest Airlines (LUV)

Target Corporation (TGT)

Required

a. Graph NOPM and NOAT for each of these companies. Do you see a pattern revealed that is similar to that shown in this chapter? Explain. (Note that the graph in the chapter is based on medians for selected industries. The graph for this problem uses fewer companies than in the chapter and, thus, will not be as smooth.)

b. Consider the trade-off between profit margin and asset turnover. How can we evaluate companies on the profit margin and asset turnover trade-off? Explain.

C5-36. **Analysis and interpretation of profitability.**

The balance sheets and income statement from the 2004 10-K report of Advanced Medical Optics, Inc. is presented below ($ thousands).

Advanced Medical Optics, Inc. (AMO)

Advanced Medical Optics, Inc. Balance Sheets		
	2004	2003
Assets		
Current Assets		
Cash and equivalents	$ 49,455	$ 46,104
Trade receivables, net	189,465	130,423
Inventories	85,028	41,596
Deferred income taxes	40,250	24,124
Other current assets	12,627	10,245
Total current assets	376,825	252,492
Property, plant and equipment, net	118,639	68,136
Deferred income taxes		7,556
Other assets	41,825	27,079
Intangible assets, net	147,895	369
Goodwill	391,350	105,713
Total assets	$1,076,534	$461,345

(Continued)

Advanced Medical Optics, Inc.
Balance Sheets (Continued)

	2004	2003
Liabilities and Stockholders' Equity		
Current liabilities		
Current portion of long-term debt	$1,950	$2,328
Accounts payable	77,824	35,605
Accrued compensation	31,451	24,507
Other accrued expenses	67,042	46,866
Income taxes	15,656	5,995
Total current liabilities	193,923	115,301
Long-term debt, net of current portion	550,643	233,611
Deferred income taxes	29,570	
Other liabilities	26,128	19,241
Stockholders' equity		
Common stock, $.01 par value	371	294
Additional paid-in capital	310,437	54,064
Retained earnings (accumulated deficit)	(104,389)	24,981
Accumulated other comprehensive income	69,874	13,868
Less treasury stock, at cost (1,379 and 997 shares)	(23)	(15)
Total stockholders' equity	276,270	93,192
Total liabilities and stockholders' equity	$1,076,534	$461,345

Advanced Medical Optics, Inc.
Income Statement

	2004
Net sales	$742,099
Cost of sales	306,164
Gross profit	435,935
Selling, general and administrative	329,197
Research and development	45,616
In-process research and development	28,100
Operating income	33,022
Non-operating expense:	
Interest expense	26,933
Unrealized loss on derivative instruments	403
Loss due to exchange of 3½% Convertible Senior Subordinated Notes due 2023	116,282
Other, net	10,620
	154,238
Earnings (loss) before income taxes	(121,216)
Provision for income taxes	8,154
Net earnings (loss)	($129,370)

Required

a. Compute net operating profit after taxes (NOPAT), net financial expense (NFE), net operating assets (NOA), and net financial obligations (NFO) for 2004 and 2003.

b. Compute AMO's return on equity (ROE).

c. Show how ROE is disaggregated into return on net operating assets (RNOA), financial leverage (FLEV) and spread.

d. Disaggregate RNOA by computing the net operating profit margin (NOPM) and net operating asset turnover (NOAT).

e. Calculate components of AMO's net operating profit margin (NOPM), including gross profit margin (GPM) and other relevant operating expense margin (OEM) ratios.

f. Calculate AMO's accounts receivable turnover (ART), inventory turnover (INVT), and accounts payable turnover (APT) ratios.

g. Notice that AMO reported a loss of $116,282 due to the exchange of convertible notes. What impact does this nonrecurring (or transitory) loss have on the ratios computed in questions a through d above? How does the loss affect your interpretation of these ratios?

C5-37. Analysis and interpretation of profitability.

The balance sheets and income statements from the January 2005 (fiscal 2004) 10-K of Nordstrom, Inc. are presented below.

Nordstrom, Inc. (JWN)

Nordstrom, Inc. Balance Sheets		
($ thousands)	January 29, 2004	January 31, 2003
Assets		
Current Assets		
Cash and cash equivalents	$ 360,623	$ 340,281
Short-term investments	41,825	176,000
Accounts receivable, net	645,663	666,811
Investment in asset backed securities	422,416	272,294
Merchandise inventories	917,182	901,623
Current deferred tax assets	131,547	121,681
Prepaid expenses and other	53,188	46,153
Total current assets	2,572,444	2,524,843
Land, buildings and equipment, net	1,780,366	1,807,778
Goodwill, net	51,714	51,714
Tradename, net	84,000	84,000
Other assets	116,866	100,898
Total assets	$4,605,390	$4,569,233
Liabilities and Shareholders' Equity		
Current liabilities:		
Accounts payable	$ 482,394	$ 458,809
Accrued salaries, wages and related benefits	287,904	276,007
Other current liabilities	354,201	314,753
Income taxes payable	115,556	66,157
Current portion of long-term debt	101,097	6,833
Total current liabilities	1,341,152	1,122,559
Long-term debt, net	929,010	1,227,410
Deferred property incentives, net	367,087	407,856
Other liabilities	179,147	177,399
Shareholders' equity:		
Common stock, no par value: 500,000 shares authorized; 135,665 and 138,377 shares issued and outstanding	552,655	424,645
Unearned stock compensation	(299)	(597)
Retained earnings	1,227,303	1,201,093
Accumulated other comprehensive earnings	9,335	8,868
Total shareholders' equity	1,788,994	1,634,009
Total liabilities and shareholders' equity	$4,605,390	$4,569,233

	Nordstrom, Inc. Income Statements	
($ thousands) Fiscal year	**2004**	**2003**
Net sales.	$7,131,388	$6,448,678
Cost of sales and related buying and occupancy costs	(4,559,388)	(4,215,546)
Gross profit	2,572,000	2,233,132
Selling, general and administrative expenses	(2,020,233)	(1,899,129)
Operating income	551,767	334,003
Interest expense, net	(77,428)	(90,952)
Other income including finance charges, net	172,942	155,090
Earnings before income taxes	647,281	398,141
Income tax expense	(253,831)	(155,300)
Net earnings	$ 393,450	$ 242,841

Required

a. Compute net operating profit after taxes (NOPAT), net financial expense (NFE), net operating assets (NOA), and net financial obligations (NFO) for fiscal 2004 and 2003.

b. Compute Nordstrom's 2004 return on equity (ROE).

c. Show how ROE is disaggregated into return on net operating assets (RNOA), financial leverage (FLEV) and SPREAD.

d. Disaggregate RNOA by computing the net operating profit margin (NOPM) and net operating asset turnover (NOAT).

CHAPTER 6

Financial Statements, Liquidity and Solvency Analysis

LEARNING OBJECTIVES

After completing the chapter, you should be able to:

LO1 Define and discuss financial ratios for analyzing short-term liquidity. (p. 238)

LO2 Define and discuss financial ratios for analyzing long-term solvency. (p. 242)

LO3 Describe financial distress and techniques used to predict the likelihood of bankruptcy. (p. 244)

LO4 Explain the limitations of ratio analysis. (p. 246)

LO5 Describe vertical and horizontal analyses of financial statements. (p. 247)

3M
COMPANY

Courtesy of 3M

Many stakeholders, including managers, owners, prospective investors, creditors, labor unions, government agencies, and the public, are interested in the data appearing in a company's financial statements. These stakeholders are often interested in the profitability and financial strength of the company in question, although such factors as size, growth, and efforts made to meet its social responsibilities are also of interest.

Chapter 5 applied ROE disaggregation to 3M's financial statements to identify and understand the key drivers of 3M's profitability. This chapter extends the financial analysis of 3M to include credit analysis. Credit analysis uses measures of liquidity and solvency to answer questions that stakeholders, particularly creditors, ask, such as: Will debt be paid when due? Will interest payments be met? Does the company generate sufficient cash to meet its short-term financial obligations? What is the likelihood that the company will go bankrupt and, therefore, default on its financial obligations?

Various techniques are used to perform credit analysis. In the following pages, we illustrate some widely used methods of credit evaluation.

CHAPTER ORGANIZATION

Financial Statements, Liquidity and Solvency Analysis

Liquidity Analysis	Solvency Analysis	Limitation of Ratio Analysis	Vertical and Horizontal Analysis
■ Average Cash Cycle ■ Current Ratio ■ Quick Ratio ■ Operating Cash Flow to Current Liabilities	■ Debt-to-Equity ■ Long-term Debt-to-Equity ■ Times Interest Earned ■ Operating Cash Flow to Liabilities ■ Gross Profit Margin and Return on Sales ■ Bankruptcy Prediction	■ GAAP Limitations ■ Company Changes ■ Impact of Conglomerates ■ A Means to an End	■ Common-size Financial Statements ■ Comparative Financial Statements

INTRODUCTION

ROE disaggregation in Chapter 5 focused mainly on profitability analysis. Yet, liquidity and solvency are also important in analyzing a company. This later analysis is often put under the umbrella of *credit analysis* because of the importance of liquidity and solvency for creditors. However, credit analysis is also important for lenders, underwriters, managers of start-ups and growth companies, and even investors (given that creditors enjoy senior standing in liquidation).

Liquidity refers to cash: how much cash the company has, how much cash the company is generating, and how much can be raised on short notice. Moreover, liquidity is a matter of survival since most obligations are settled with cash. **Solvency** refers to the ability to meet obligations; mainly obligations to creditors, including lessors. Solvency is equally crucial since an insolvent company is a failed company. The following sections introduce measures of liquidity and solvency, and discuss tools and measures of credit analysis, including measure of vertical and horizontal analysis.

LIQUIDITY ANALYSIS

LO1 Define and discuss financial ratios for analyzing short-term liquidity.

This section describes several useful measures in our analysis of liquidity. Liquidity is the ability of a company to cover its short-term obligations. The measures in this chapter are illustrated using the 3M accounting information from Exhibit 6.2.

Average Cash (Operating) Cycle

The **cash (operating) cycle** is the period of time from when cash is invested in inventories, until the inventories are sold and receivables are collected (see Exhibit 6.1). It is the cycle from "cash to cash." Companies generally want to minimize the cash cycle provided that they achieve acceptable inventory levels and customer credit terms, and that relationships with suppliers are not damaged as a result of excessive "leaning on the trade." The **average cash cycle** is measured as follows:

EXHIBIT 6.1	Cash Operating Cycle

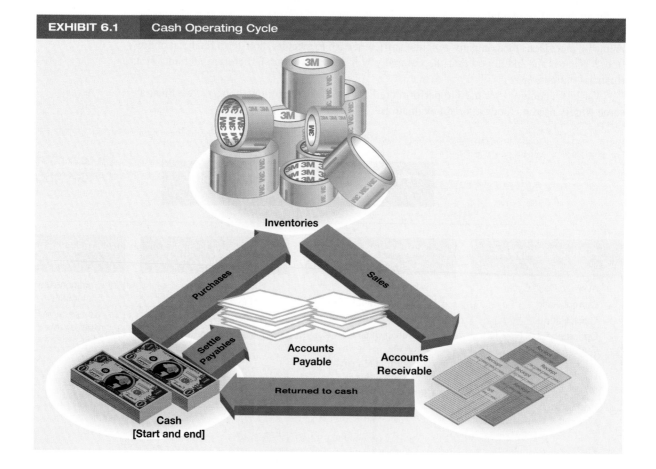

$$\text{Average Cash Cycle} = \begin{array}{c}\textbf{Average}\\ \textbf{Collection}\\ \textbf{Period}\end{array} + \begin{array}{c}\textbf{Modified Average}\\ \textbf{Inventory Days}\\ \textbf{Outstanding}\end{array} - \begin{array}{c}\textbf{Modified Average}\\ \textbf{Payable Days}\\ \textbf{Outstanding}\end{array}$$

The modified measures refer to their computation *using sales in the denominator* instead of cost of goods sold. This allows for the summation of days outstanding.

For 3M, the average collection period is 54.3 days, the modified average inventory days outstanding is 36.4 days, and the modified average payable days outstanding is 21.8 days. 3M's average cash cycle (modified to compute all ratios based on sales) is as follows:

Average collection period	54.3	days
+ Modified average inventory days outstanding	36.4	days
− Modified average payable days outstanding	(21.8)	days
Average cash cycle	68.9	days

This means 3M takes about 69 days to convert its cash to inventories, then to receivables, and finally back into cash. Over the past five years, 3M has been able to reduce its cash cycle from 91 days in 1999 to 69 days in 2003. This is a marked improvement. The quicker a company is able to cycle from cash to cash, the greater is its cash flow. Its aim, therefore, is to *optimize,* not necessarily minimize, investment in receivables, inventories, and payables. Not extending credit and not having goods available for sale would minimize receivables and inventories, but this would be counter-productive. So, the aim is not to minimize but to optimize receivables, inventories and payables so as to maximize shareholder value. This is known as *working capital management.*

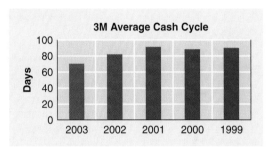

Current Ratio

Current assets are those assets that a company expects to convert into cash within the next year (or operating cycle if longer than one year). Current liabilities are those liabilities that a company expects to mature within the next year (or operating cycle if longer than one year). Companies typically desire more current assets than current liabilities as that implies more expected cash inflows than cash outflows in the short run.

One measure of liquidity is the relative magnitude of current assets and current liabilities. The difference between them is *net working capital.* However, since the dollar amount of net working capital is difficult to compare across companies of different sizes, the **current ratio (CR)** is often used. It is computed as follows:

Current Ratio = Current Assets/Current Liabilities

A current ratio greater than 1.0 implies positive net working capital. In general, companies prefer more liquid assets to less and a higher current ratio to a smaller one. (A too high current ratio is possible, and is indicative of inefficient asset use.) A current ratio less than 1.0 is not always bad for at least two reasons:

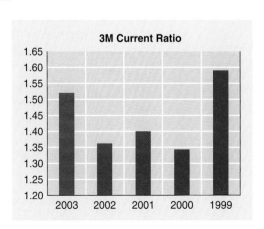

1. A cash-and-carry company (like a grocery store where payment is typically made in cash) can have consistently large operating cash inflows and potentially few current assets (and a low current ratio), but still be liquid due to those large cash inflows.

2. A company can efficiently manage its working capital by minimizing receivables and inventories and maximizing payables, and still be liquid. **Dell Computer** and **Wal-Mart**, for example, use their buying power to exact extended credit terms from suppliers. Further, because both companies are mainly cash-and-carry businesses, their current ratios are less than 1.0 and both are highly liquid.

The aim of current ratio analysis is to discern if a company is having, or is likely to have, difficulty meeting short-term obligations. Using the data in Exhibit 6.2, 3M's current ratio stands at a healthy 1.52 ($7,720/$5,082) in 2003. Over the past five years, it has fluctuated within a range of 1.34 to 1.59.

EXHIBIT 6.2	3M Financial Statement Information		
3M COMPANY **Financial Statement Information**			
(in millions)	**2003**	**2002**	**2001**
Balance Sheet Information (at December 31)			
Cash	$ 1,836	$ 618	$ 616
Receivables	2,714	2,527	2,482
Inventories	1,816	1,931	2,091
Other current assets	1,354	983	1,107
Total current assets	7,720	6,059	6,296
Property, plant and equipment, net	5,609	5,621	5,615
Investments	218	238	275
Intangibles	2,693	2,167	1,250
Deposits and other assets	1,360	1,244	1,170
Total assets	$17,600	$15,329	$14,606
Notes payable	$ 1,202	$ 1,237	$ 1,373
Accounts payable	1,087	945	753
Accrued liabilities	436	411	539
Income taxes	880	518	596
Other current liabilities	1,477	1,346	1,2488
Total current liabilities	5,082	4,457	4,509
Long-term debt	1,735	2,140	1,520
Other long-term liabilities	2,898	2,739	2,491
Total liabilities	9,715	9,336	8,520
Common stock, net	9	5	5
Capital in excess of par	287	291	291
Retained earnings	14,010	12,748	11,914
Treasury stock	4,641	4,767	4,633
Other equities	(1,780)	(2,284)	(1,491)
Shareholder equity	7,885	5,993	6,086
Total liabilities and equity	$17,600	$15,329	$14,606
Income Statements Information (for year end Dec. 31)			
Net sales	$18,232	$16,332	$16,054
Cost of good sold	9,285	8,496	8,749
Gross profit	8,947	7,836	7,305
R & D expenditures	1,102	1,070	1,084
Selling, general & admin expense	4,132	3,720	3,948
Operating Income	3,713	3,046	2,273
Interest expense	56	41	87
Income before taxes	3,657	3,005	2,186
Income taxes	1,202	966	702
Minority interest income	52	65	54
Net income	$ 2,403	$ 1,974	$ 1,430
Cash Flow Information (for year ended Dec. 31)			
Net cash provided by operating activities	$ 3,773	$ 2,992	$ 3,078
Net cash used in investing activities	(969)	(1,927)	(1,050)
Net cash used in financing activities	(1,627)	(1,021)	(1,716)

Quick Ratio

The **quick ratio (QR)** is a variant of the current ratio. It focuses on current assets that are considered *quick assets,* which are those assets likely to be converted to cash within a short period of time. Quick assets generally include cash, marketable securities, and accounts receivable; it excludes inventories and prepaid assets. The quick ratio follows:

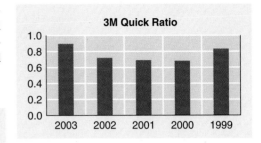

Quick Ratio = (Cash + Marketable Securities + Accounts Receivables)/ Current Liabilities

The quick ratio reflects a company's ability to meet its current liabilities without liquidating inventories that could require markdowns. It is a more stringent test of liquidity compared to the current ratio.

3M's quick ratio is 0.90 [($1,836 + $2,714)/$5,082] as of 2003. Over the past five years, 3M's quick ratio has ranged from 0.67 to its current level of 0.90.

Operating Cash Flow to Current Liabilities Ratio

Cash is ultimately required to settle current liabilities. The **operating cash flow to current liabilities ratio** focuses on the ability of a company to pay current liabilities, as they become due, from its cash flow from operations. It is calculated as follows.

Operating Cash Flow to Current Liabilities = Net Cash Flow from Operating Activities/ Average Current Liabilities

Working capital components are constantly changing as a company engages in its operating activities—inventory is bought and sold, services are rendered, receivables are collected, employees work, suppliers provide various goods and services, and payments are made to employees and suppliers. This ratio relates the net cash available as a result of these activities for the period to the average current liabilities outstanding during the period. The higher the ratio, the stronger the company's ability to settle current liabilities as they are due.

3M's operating cash flow to current liabilities ratio for 2003 and 2002 are as follows.

2003: $3,773 / [($5,082 + $4,457) /2] = 0.79
2002: $2,992 / [($4,457 + $4,509) /2] = 0.67

Even though 3M's current liabilities increased from 2002 to 2003, its operating cash flow to current liabilities ratio improved from 0.67 to 0.79. This is due to a 26% increase in its operating cash flow, from $2,992 to $3,773.

MID-CHAPTER REVIEW 1

Refer to Chapter Review 1 in chapter 5 on page 204 for the financial statements of Caterpillar, Inc.

Required
Using Caterpillar's financial information, compute the following for 2003.

1. Liquidity measures
   a. Average cash operating cycle for machinery and engines
   b. Current ratio
   c. Quick ratio
2. What insights do you draw about Caterpillar's liquidity from the analytical measures in part 1?

Solution

1. a. Cash cycle

Average collection period	63.57 days	$3,666/($21,048/365)
Modified average inventory days outstanding .	52.84 days	$3,047/($21,048/365)
Modified average payable days outstanding . . .	(53.76) days	$3,100/($21,048/365)
Average cash cycle	62.65 days	63.57 + 52.84 − 53.76
b. Current ratio	1.33	$16,791/$12,621
c. Quick ratio	0.92	($342 + $3,666 + $7,605)/$12,621

2. The average cash cycle is 62.7 days. This is a reasonably quick conversion from cash-to-cash. John Deere (a competitor), for example, reports a cash-to-cash cycle of 70 days for the same period. Both of these computations are on trade receivables and inventories only and do not include the receivables and inventories arising from long-term financing of equipment sales through their respective financial subsidiaries. CAT's current ratio of 1.33 is also reasonably strong as is its quick ratio of 0.92. Neither ratio indicates liquidity problems.

SOLVENCY ANALYSIS

LO2 Define and discuss financial ratios for analyzing long-term solvency.

Solvency analysis is aided by financial leverage ratios. Financial leverage refers to the extent of borrowed funds in a company's capital structure. We examine financial leverage ratios for insight into company solvency, that is, the risk of bankruptcy. We consider several ratios in addition to FLEV, which we discussed in connection with ROE disaggregation.

Debt-to-Equity

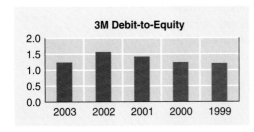

3M Debit-to-Equity

One common measure of financial leverage is the ratio of **debt-to-equity (DE)**, which is defined as:

> **Debt-to-Equity = Total Liabilities/Stockholders' Equity**

A higher debt-to-equity ratio reflects a greater proportion of debt in a company's capital structure. 3M's debt-to-equity ratio has fluctuated from 1.21 to 1.56 in the past five years. It currently sits at the lower end of this range at 1.23.

BUSINESS INSIGHT

Microsoft's Debt-to-Equity Some corporations enjoy having little or no long-term debt in their financial structure. In its fiscal 2004 balance sheet, Microsoft reported $2.846 billion long-term liabilities (of which $1.790 billion reflect long-term unearned revenue). Microsoft had total assets of $81.732 billion, current liabilities of $13.974 billion, and equity of $64.912 billion at its 2004 fiscal year-end. Microsoft's debt-to-equity ratio at that point was 0.26, computed as $16.82 billion/$64.912 billion. Also, its cash and short-term investments were 60% of its total assets.

Long-Term Debt-to-Equity

Another common measure of leverage is **long-term debt-to-equity (LTDE)**. It focuses on long-term financing and is defined as follows:

> **Long-Term Debt-to-Equity = Long-Term Debt/Stockholders' Equity**

This ratio implicitly assumes that current liabilities are covered by current assets and, thus, only long-term debt must be funded from operating cash flows. Accordingly, it is important to examine long-term debt relative to the stockholders' investment.

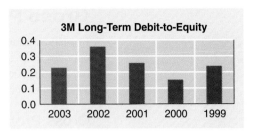

3M's long-term debt-to-equity ratio has fluctuated between 0.15 and 0.36 during the past five years, and the company has a conservative level of 0.22 as of 2003 ($1,735/$7,885). The marked difference between 3M's debt-to-equity ratio of 1.23 and its long-term debt-to-equity ratio of 0.22 relates to the concentration of its liabilities in short-term noninterest-bearing debt. This is a consequence of 3M's aggressive working capital management program.

Times Interest Earned

Another useful perspective on solvency analysis is to compare operating flows to liabilities. One approach considers how much income is available to service debt given the debt level and its repayment terms. A common measure is **times interest earned (TIE)**, defined as follows:

> **Times Interest Earned = Earnings before Interest and Taxes/Interest Expense**

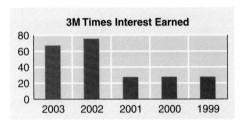

The numerator is similar to net operating profits after-tax (NOPAT), but it is *pre-tax* instead of after-tax. Times interest earned reflects the income available to pay interest expense in relation to interest requirements.

Management wants this ratio to be reasonably high so that there is little risk of default. 3M's times interest earned is robust and currently stands at 66.3 times ($3,713/$56). This reflects a comfortable margin of coverage and is at the second highest level in the past five years.

Operating Cash Flow to Liabilities

Another variation in comparing operating flows to liabilities is to examine the **operating cash flow to liabilities (OCFL)** ratio, defined as:

> **Operating Cash Flow to Liabilities = Net Cash Flow from Operations/Total Liabilities**

This ratio links operating cash flows with the debt level. Companies prefer this ratio to be higher rather than lower.

3M's operating cash flow to total liabilities ratio is 0.39 as of 2003 ($3,773/$9,715). Further, it has fluctuated from a low of 0.29 to a high of 0.41 over the past five years.

Overall, there are several variations in leverage ratios. The basic idea is to construct measures that best reflect a company's credit risk exposure. There is no best financial leverage ratio. As with all ratios, there are several variations in formulas and approaches. Still to be sure we are measuring the risk we wish to measure, we must compute ratios ourselves from raw data and not rely on financial reporting services whose definitions are uncertain, inappropriate, and sometimes wrong.

$$QR = \frac{68.58}{16.355} = 4.19$$

YOU MAKE THE CALL

You are the Bank Loan Officer   Peet's Coffee and Tea began as a coffee house in Berkeley, California. In recent years, Peet's has been expanding to other metropolitan locations around the country. The Chief Financial Officer for Peet's has asked your bank for a one year, $1.5 million bank loan to accelerate their expansion to an additional five cities. The CFO provided the following financial statement information ($ millions): Current assets $95.478; Cash $13.9; Marketable securities $49.75; Accounts receivable $4.928; Current liabilities $16.355; Total liabilities $19.635; Stockholders' equity $126.324; Net cash flow from operations $6.737. Should you approve the loan? [Answer on page 257]

$$\frac{CA}{CL} = \frac{95.478}{16.355} = 5.84$$

Gross Profit Margin and Return on Sales

In analyzing long-term solvency, we need to consider how efficiently and effectively a company operates in its quest for profits. Profitability is the focus of Chapter 5, but there are a few additional ratios that are occasionally used by creditors to determine a company's long-term solvency. These ratios include gross profit margin and return on sales.

Gross Profit Margin

3M's Sales Breakdown

51% Cost of Sales

49% Gross Profit

The **gross profit margin (GPM)** is a closely watched ratio for both merchandisers and manufacturers. The ratio is computed as follows.

> **Gross Profit Margin = Gross Profit/Net Sales**

This ratio reflects the net impact on profitability if there are changes in a company's pricing structure, sales mix, and merchandise costs. Both managers and analysts monitor movements in the gross profit margin. 3M's gross profit margin for 2003 was 49%, computed as $8,947/$18,232. Its 49% is a whole percentage point increase over its 48% in 2002.

Return on Sales

NOTE
Return on sales is also called **net profit margin.**

Another measure of operating performance is **return on sales**. As an overall test of operating efficiency, this ratio reveals the percentage of each dollar of net sales that remains as net profit. Return on sales is computed as follows.

> **Return on Sales = Net Income/Net Sales**

3M's Return in Sales

51% Cost of Sales

36% Additional Expenses

13% Return on Sales

When common-size income statements are prepared, the return on sales equals the net income percentage. 3M's return on sales for 2003 was 13.2%, computed as $2,403/$18,232. This percentage is 1.1% greater than its 12.1% in 2002.

Return on sales and gross profit margins are most effectively used when analyzing similar companies in the same industry or when comparing different periods for the same company. These ratios vary widely by industry. Retail jewelers, for example, have much larger gross profit margins (industry average around 40%) and returns on sales (industry average around 5%) than retail grocers (industry averages are about 20% for gross profit margin and about 2% for return on sales).

Bankruptcy Prediction

LO3 Describe financial distress and techniques used to predict the likelihood of bankruptcy.

Lenders, bankers, and debt raters are concerned with default risk, which is the risk a company is unable to honor its debt obligations. One way to assess this risk is to review a company's financial characteristics in relation to prior experience with bankrupt companies. Statistical models often aid in this process and are used to draw inferences on the degree of financial distress.

A well-known model of financial distress is **Altman's Z-score**. Altman's Z-score uses multiple ratios to get a predictor of financial distress. This predictor classifies or predicts the likelihood of bankruptcy or nonbankruptcy. Five financial ratios makeup the Z-score:

$X1$ = Working Capital/Total Assets

$X2$ = Retained Earnings/Total Assets

$X3$ = Earnings before Interest and Taxes/Total Assets

$X4$ = Shareholders' Equity/Total Liabilities

$X5$ = Sales/Total Assets.

In brief, $X1$ reflects liquidity, $X2$ reflects cumulative retained profitability, $X3$ reflects profitability, $X4$ reflects leverage, and $X5$ reflects total asset turnover.

The Altman Z-score is computed as:

$$\text{Z-score} = (0.717 \times X1) + (0.847 \times X2) + (3.107 \times X3) + (0.420 \times X4) + (0.998 \times X5)$$

The Z-score is then interpreted as follows. (The model is from Altman, *Corporate Financial Distress*, New York: John Wiley, 1983, pp. 120–124; this model is more generalizable than his earlier 1968 model that can only be applied to publicly traded companies.)

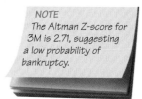

NOTE
The Altman Z-score for 3M is 2.71, suggesting a low probability of bankruptcy.

$$\textbf{Z-score} < 1.20 \rightarrow \text{high probability of bankruptcy}$$
$$\textbf{Z-score} > 2.90 \rightarrow \text{low probability of bankruptcy}$$
$$1.20 \le \textbf{Z-score} \le 2.90 \rightarrow \text{gray or ambiguous area.}$$

Another source of data on default risk is information services. For example, **Standard & Poor's**, which sells debt ratings, uses several accounting ratios to assess default risk (*S&P Compustat* also provides the Z-score for companies). A discussion of debt ratings and accounting ratios is in Chapter 10.

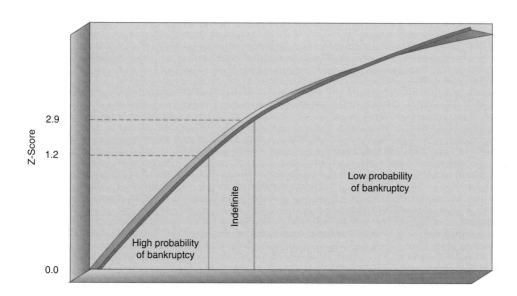

MID-CHAPTER REVIEW 2

Refer to Mid-Chapter Review 1 in chapter 5 on page 204 for the financial statements of Caterpillar, Inc.

Required
Using Caterpillar's financial information, compute the following for 2003.

1. Solvency measures
   a. Debt-to-equity
   b. Long-term debt-to-equity
   c. Times interest earned
   d. Operating cash flow to liabilities (note: CAT's 2003 net cash flows from operations is $2,066 million)
   e. Gross Profit Margin
   f. Return on Sales

2. What insights do you draw about Caterpillar's solvency from the analytical measures in part 1?

Solution

1. *a.*	Debt-to-equity	5.00	$30,387/$6,078
b.	Long-term debt-to-equity	2.92	($30,387 − $12,621)/$6,078
c.	Times interest earned	3.06 times*	($1,477 + $246 + $470)/($246 + $470)
d.	Operating cash flow to liabilities	0.07	$2,066/$30,387
e.	Gross Profit Margin	19.5%	100X ($21,048 − $16,945)/$21,048
f.	Return on Sales	5.2%	$1,099/$21,048

*Many analysts would properly add the $30.77 million profit from affiliated companies to the numerator, computed as $20/ (1–0.35) assuming a 35% tax rate. This gives a times interest earned of 3.11.

2. CAT's debt-to-equity and long-term debt-to-equity ratios are fairly high and reflect the long-term financing related to its leasing operations. Remember, CAT finances a substantial portion of its equipment sales via its captive finance subsidiary. The balance sheet of that subsidiary, which is consolidated with the manufacturing company parent, is similar to a bank balance sheet (meaning that it is highly leveraged and reliant on a relatively small spread of lease returns over the cost of the financing to support the leasing activities). Given CAT's adequate times interest earned ratio, our concern with CAT's financial leverage is moderated.

LIMITATIONS OF RATIO ANALYSIS

LO4 Explain the limitations of ratio analysis.

The quality of financial statement analysis depends on the quality of financial information. Analysis cannot be blindly conducted because of various accounting conventions and the flexibility afforded companies in preparing financial statements. Instead, any analysis must be aware of GAAP limitations, the current company environment, competitive pressures, and structural and strategic company changes. This section discusses some of the factors that can limit the usefulness of financial accounting information for ratio analysis.

GAAP Limitations

Several limitations in GAAP can distort financial ratios. They include the following:

1. **Measurability.** Financial statements reflect what can be reliably measured. This results in nonrecognition of some assets, generally items that confer a competitive advantage, and are internally developed. Examples are brand value, a superior management team, employee skills, and a superior supply chain.

2. **Noncapitalized costs.** Related to measurability is the expensing of assets that cannot be identified with enough precision to warrant capitalization. Examples are brand equity costs from promotional activities, and research and development costs on future products.

3. **Historical costs.** Assets and liabilities are typically recorded at original acquisition or issuance costs. Subsequent increases in value are not recorded until realized, and declines in value are only recognized if deemed permanent.

There are other limitations that we subsequently discuss throughout later chapters.

Company Changes

Many companies acquire and divest subsidiaries with regularity. Such changes impair the comparability of company ratios across time. Companies also change strategies, such as product pricing, R&D, and financing. We must understand the effects of such changes on ratio analysis and accordingly adjust our inferences.

Companies also behave differently at different points in their life cycles. Specifically, growth companies possess a different profile than do mature companies. Also, seasonal effects can markedly impact analysis of financial statements at different times of the year.

Impact of Conglomerates

Most companies are blends of several businesses. Many consist of a parent company and multiple subsidiaries, often pursuing different lines of business. Several manufacturers, for example, have a finance subsidiary, like the GMAC subsidiary for General Motors. Financial statements of such companies are a combination (consolidation) of the financial statements of the parent and its subsidiaries. Consequently, such consolidated statements impair comparability with other competitors.

   Analysis of these conglomerates is difficult and often requires breaking them apart into their component businesses and separately analyzing each line of business. Fortunately, some financial information for major lines of business are provided in the 10-K report, but these disclosures are limited.

A Means to an End

Too many individuals compute and examine ratios in their analysis as if such ratios are reality. Ratios are not reality, but they reflect reality. Reality is the innumerable transactions and events that occur each day between a company and various parties. Reality also is a company's marketing and management philosophies, its human resource activities, its financing activities, its strategic initiatives, and its product management. In our analysis we must learn to look through the numbers and ratios to better understand the operational factors that drive financial results. Our overriding purpose in analysis is to understand the past and present to better predict the future.

> **NOTE**
> Ratios are often assigned a degree of importance that is not always deserved; one reason is that they give an appearance of being exact.

RESEARCH INSIGHT

Fundamental Analysis and Stock Prices   Financial statement analysis highlights relations across and within financial statements that are relevant to investment and credit decisions. Research shows that financial statements capture much of the same economic information that is reflected in stock prices. But, can financial statement analysis help us predict future stock prices? Investors who practice *fundamental analysis* attempt to identify under-priced and over-priced stocks by analyzing financial statements and other information. Research has examined investment strategies based on an aggregation of common financial ratios, such as return on net operating assets and asset turnover. The strategies yield investment returns, suggesting evidence of information in financial statements that is not immediately reflected in stock prices. However, because financial markets are competitive, it is difficult to *consistently* make more than a normal return.

VERTICAL AND HORIZONTAL ANALYSIS

Companies organize and operate in all sizes, which presents difficulties in comparing the numbers in financial statements across such companies. There are several methods that attempt to overcome this hurdle. When evaluating a company's financial statements for two or more years, analysts often use *horizontal analysis*. This type of analysis is useful in detecting improvement or deterioration in a company's performance and is also useful for spotting trends. The term *vertical analysis* describes the study of a single year's financial statements. This section begins by examining vertical analysis and concludes with horizontal analysis. These analyses are illustrated using the financial statements of 3M.

LO5 Describe vertical and horizontal analyses of financial statements.

Vertical Analysis

Vertical analysis is one way to overcome size differences. Its approach is to express the financial statements in ratio form. Specifically, it is common to express income statement items as a percentage of net sales and all balance sheet items as a percentage of total assets. Such a ratio-formed financial statement is prepared by dividing each individual financial statement amount under analysis by its base amount as follows:

$$\text{Common-Size Percent } (\%) = (\text{Analysis Amount/Base Amount}) \times 100$$

The resulting *common-size comparative financial statements* facilitate comparative analysis *across companies* of different sizes, and help highlight any changes in strategies or operations *across time*. The common-size balance sheet and income statement for **3M Company** are presented in Exhibits 6.3 and 6.4.

Exhibit 6.3 reveals that 3M's total assets in dollars have increased by 26% since 1999. However, it is the *composition* of the balance sheet, the proportion invested in each asset category, that we are interested in. Liquidity has generally improved as cash now represents 10.43% of total assets, up from 4.22% in 2001. Yet, not all of that cash is sitting in 3M's checking account. GAAP categorizes cash and cash equivalents in the same account, the latter being temporary investments. Why would 3M build such liquidity? Perhaps, it desires the capacity to quickly react to strategic moves by competitors and to be able to quickly take advantage of investment opportunities, like the acquisition of a company.

The increased accounts receivable and inventory turnover are evidenced in their reduced proportion of total assets. Receivables now constitute 15.4% of total asserts, down from nearly 20% in 2000 (not shown). Also, inventories make up 10.3% of total assets compared with 14.3% in 2001.

It is interesting that plant assets (net) have decreased as a percentage of total assets, from 38.4% in 2001 to 31.9% in 2003. Yet, this category of assets has not decreased (in dollars), as purchases of plant assets have equaled depreciation expense. All of the growth in long-term operating assets

NOTE
The base amount used to prepare common-size balance sheets is total assets.

EXHIBIT 6.3   3M's Common-Size Comparative Balance Sheet

3M COMPANY
Common-Size Comparative Balance Sheets

At December 31 (in millions)	2003	2002	2001	2003	2002	2001
Cash	$ 1,836	$ 618	$ 616	10.43%	4.03%	4.22%
Receivables	2,714	2,527	2,482	15.42	16.49	16.99
Inventories	1,816	1,931	2,091	10.32	12.60	14.32
Other current assets	1,354	983	1,107	7.69	6.41	7.58
Total current assets	7,720	6,059	6,296	43.86	39.53	43.11
Property, plant and equipment, net	5,609	5,621	5,615	31.87	36.67	38.44
Investments	218	238	275	1.24	1.55	1.88
Intangibles	2,693	2,167	1,250	15.30	14.14	8.56
Deposits and other assets	1,360	1,244	1,170	7.73	8.12	8.01
Total assets	$17,600	$15,329	$14,606	100.00%	100.00%	100.00%
Notes payable	$ 1,202	$ 1,237	$ 1,373	6.83%	8.07%	9.40%
Accounts payable	1,087	945	753	6.18	6.16	5.16
Accrued liabilities	436	411	539	2.48	2.68	3.69
Income taxes	880	518	596	5.00	3.38	4.08
Other current liabilities	1,477	1,346	1,2488	8.39	8.78	8.54
Total current liabilities	5,082	4,457	4,509	28.88	29.08	30.87
Long-term debt	1,735	2,140	1,520	9.86	13.96	10.41
Other long-term liabilities	2,898	2,739	2,491	16.47	17.87	17.05
Total liabilities	9,715	9,336	8,520	55.20%	60.90%	58.33%
Common stock, net	9	5	5	0.05	0.03	0.03
Capital in excess of par	287	291	291	1.63	1.90	1.99
Retained earnings	14,010	12,748	11,914	79.60	83.16	81.57
Treasury stock	4,641	4,767	4,633	26.37	31.10	31.72
Other equities	(1,780)	(2,284)	(1,491)	(10.11)	(14.90)	(10.21)
Shareholders' equity	7,885	5,993	6,086	44.80	39.10	41.67
Total liabilities and equity	$17,600	$15,329	$14,606	100.00%	100.00%	100.00%

EXHIBIT 6.4	3M's Common-Size Comparative Income Statements					

3M COMPANY
Common-Size Comparative Income Statements

For Year Ended December 31 (in millions)	2003	2002	2001	2003	2002	2001
Net sales	$18,232	$16,332	$16,054	100.00%	100.00%	100.00%
Cost of good sold	9,285	8,496	8,749	50.93	52.02	54.50
Gross profit	8,947	7,836	7,305	49.07	47.98	45.50
R & D expenditures	1,102	1,070	1,084	6.04	6.55	6.75
Selling, general & admin expense	4,132	3,720	3,948	22.66	22.78	24.59
Operating Income	3,713	3,046	2,273	20.37	18.65	14.16
Interest expense	56	41	87	0.31	0.25	0.54
Income before taxes	3,657	3,005	2,186	20.06	18.40	13.62
Income taxes	1,202	966	702	6.59	5.91	4.37
Minority interest income	52	65	54	0.29	0.40	0.34
Net income	$ 2,403	$ 1,974	$ 1,430	13.18%	12.09%	8.91%

> **NOTE**
> The base amount used to prepare common-size income statements is net sales.

has resulted from acquisitions, in the form of intangible assets, which were nonexistent five years ago, now constitute 15.3% of total assets.

Total liabilities have not changed appreciably as a percentage of total capitalization—55.2% in 2003 versus 58.3% in 2001. Current liabilities are at a slightly higher level. Stockholders' equity stands at 44.8% of total capitalization in 2003 versus 41.7% in 2001.

Exhibit 6.4 shows the common-size income statement. 3M has done a remarkable job of controlling its cost of goods sold. Gross profit is 49.07% of sales in 2003, up from 45.5% in 2001. Also, overhead cost control has reduced SG&A expenses to 22.66% of sales in 2003, versus 24.59% in 2001. R&D expenses are slightly reduced as a proportion of sales and this is somewhat less than positive given the importance of this cost center to 3M's competitive position and future performance. Finally, 3M is carrying $13.18 cents out of each sales dollar to the bottom line in 2003. This compares favorably with 8.91% in 2001.

Overall, 3M is financially healthy, with high liquidity and relatively low financial leverage, and it is profitable. The operating discipline in recent years is evident in 3M's control over working capital and operating costs.

Horizontal Analysis

Horizontal analysis is the scrutiny of financial data *across time*. Comparing data across two or more consecutive periods assists in analyzing company performance and in predicting future performance. Horizontal analysis includes examination of absolute dollar changes and percent changes. The *dollar change* for a financial statement account is computed as follows:

$$\textbf{Dollar Change} = \textbf{Analysis Period Amount} - \textbf{Base Period Amount}$$

The *percent change* (%) for an account is computed as follows:

$$\textbf{Percent Change} = \textbf{[(Analysis Period Amount} - \textbf{Base Period Amount)/}$$
$$\textbf{Base Period Amount]} \times \textbf{100}$$

The percent change is not interpretable when the base period amount is negative or zero, or when the analysis period amount is negative.

Comparative Balance Sheets

The form of horizontal analysis encountered most often is **comparative financial statements** for two or more years, showing dollar and percentage changes for important items and classification totals. Dollar increases and decreases are divided by the earliest year's data to obtain percentage changes. The 2003 and 2002 balance sheets for 3M are in Exhibit 6.5.

When examining comparative financial statements, we focus our immediate attention on substantive changes. Although percentage changes are helpful in identifying items to focus on, sometimes they can be misleading. An unusually large percentage change can occur because the dollar amount of the base year is small. This is illustrated by the percentage increase of nearly 70% for income taxes in Exhibit 6.5. Large percentage changes also frequently occur in items whose dollar amounts are not large compared with other items on the statements. Instead, attention is directed first to changes in totals: current assets, total assets, current liabilities, and so on. Next, changes in important individual items, such as receivables, inventories, payables, and debt would be examined.

These changes can also be linked to changes in income statement items or cash flows to determine whether they are favorable. For example, 3M Company's total assets increased 14.82%, and net sales increased 11.63% (look ahead to Exhibit 6.6). That is, a fairly large percentage increase in sales was accompanied by an increase in assets. Further, inventories actually decreased by 5.96% as both sales and assets increased. This result reflects favorably on 3M's efficiency in

EXHIBIT 6.5	3M's Comparative Balance Sheets			
	3M COMPANY **Comparative Balance Sheets**			
At December 31 (in millions)	**2003**	**2002**	**Dollar Change**	**Percent Change**
Cash	$ 1,836	$ 618	$1,218	197.09%
Receivables	2,714	2,527	187	7.40
Inventories	1,816	1,931	(115)	−5.96
Other current assets	1,354	983	371	37.74
Total current assets	7,720	6,059	1,66,	27.41
Property, plant, and equipment, net	5,609	5,621	(12)	−0.21
Investments	218	238	(20)	−8.40
Intangibles	2,693	2,167	526	24.27
Deposits and other assets	1,360	1,244	116	9.32
Total assets	$17,600	$15,329	$ 2,271	14.82%
Notes payable	$ 1,202	$1,237	$ (35)	−2.83%
Accounts payable	1,087	945	142	15.03
Accrued liabilities	436	411	25	6.08
Income taxes	880	518	362	69.88
Other current liabilities	1,477	1,346	131	9.73
Total current liabilities	5,082	4,457	625	14.02
Long-term debt	1,735	2,140	(405)	−18.93
Other long-term liabilities	2,898	2,739	159	5.81
Total liabilities	9,715	9,336	379	4.06%
Common stock, net	9	5	4	80.00%
Capital in excess of par	287	291	(4)	−1.37
Retained earnings	14,010	12,748	1,262	9.90
Treasury stock	4,641	4,767	(126)	−2.64
Other equities	(1,780)	(2,284)	504	−22.07
Shareholders' equity	7,885	5,993	1,892	31.57
Total liabilities and equity	$17,600	$15,329	$2,271	14.82%

EXHIBIT 6.6	3M's Comparative Income Statements			

3M COMPANY
Comparative Income Statements

For Year Ended Dec. 31 (in millions)	2003	2002	Dollar Change	Percent Change
Net Sales	$18,232	$16,332	$1,900	11.63%
Cost of goods sold	9,285	8,496	789	9.29
Gross profit	8,947	7,836	1,111	14.18
R & D expenditures	1,102	1,070	32	2.99
Selling, general & admin. expense	4,132	3,720	412	11.08
Operating income	3,713	3,046	667	21.90
Interest expense	56	41	15	36.59
Income before taxes	3,657	3,005	652	21.70
Income taxes	1,202	966	236	24.43
Minority interest income	52	65	(13)	−20.00
Net income	$ 2,403	$ 1,974	$ 429	21.73%

operations. Also, 3M's 11.63% increase in sales was accompanied by an increase in accounts receivable of only 7.40%; on the surface, 3M's sales growth was not associated with a relaxation in credit policy.

Comparative Income Statements

Exhibit 6.6 shows 3M's **comparative income statements**. We see from these income statements that 3M's 14.18% gross profit increase outstripped the 11.63% increase in sales, indicating a higher mark-up rate in 2003. Moreover, net income increased 21.73%; therefore, expenses have not grown proportionately, which is a favorable finding. The concern, if any, is that R&D spending increased only 2.9%. Our concern is that 3M management is not sufficiently investing in 3M future product development.

From this limited analysis of 3M's comparative financial statements, we might conclude that operating performance for 2003 was generally favorable when compared with that for 2002. Further analysis using techniques described in later sections of this chapter, however, will cause us to modify that opinion.

Trend analysis

Trend analysis is a type of horizontal analysis. In this case a base period is chosen, and then all subsequent period amounts are defined relative to the base. Specifically, the **trend percent** (%) is defined as follows:

Trend Percent = (Analysis Period Amount/Base Period Amount) × 100

Trend percents are often graphed to give a visual representation of the data. To illustrate trend analysis, we use the 3M data from Exhibit 6.7 and prior reports.

EXHIBIT 6.7	3M's Revenues and Expenses				

3M COMPANY
Revenues and Expenses

(in millions)	2003	2002	2001	2000	1999
Revenues	$18,232	$16,332	$16,054	$16,699	$15,723
Cost of goods sold	9,285	8,494	8,749	8,787	8,126
Selling, general, & administrative expenses	4,132	3,720	3,948	3,938	3,600

The base period here is 1999 and the trend percent is computed in each subsequent year by dividing that year's amount by its 1999 amount. For instance, the revenue trend percent for 2003 is 116.0%, computed as $18,232/$15,723. The trend percents—using the data from Exhibit 6.7— are shown in Exhibit 6.8.

EXHIBIT 6.8	3M's Trend Percents for Revenues and Expenses				
3M COMPANY Trend Percents for Revenues and Expenses					
	2003	**2002**	**2001**	**2000**	**1999**
Revenues	116.0%	103.9%	102.1%	106.2%	100%
Cost of goods sold	114.3	104.5	107.7	108.1	100%
Selling, general, & administrative expenses	114.8	103.3	109.7	109.4	100%

Graphical depictions often aid analysis of trend percents. Exhibit 6.8 shows the trend percents from Exhibit 6.9 in a *line graph*, which can help us identify trends and detect changes in direction or magnitude. It reveals that the trend lines were not favorable for 3M prior to 2001. Since that time the trends are more favorable. This result bodes well for 3M because its most recent year shows substantial sales growth. That is, 3M shows an ability to control key expenses as it expands.

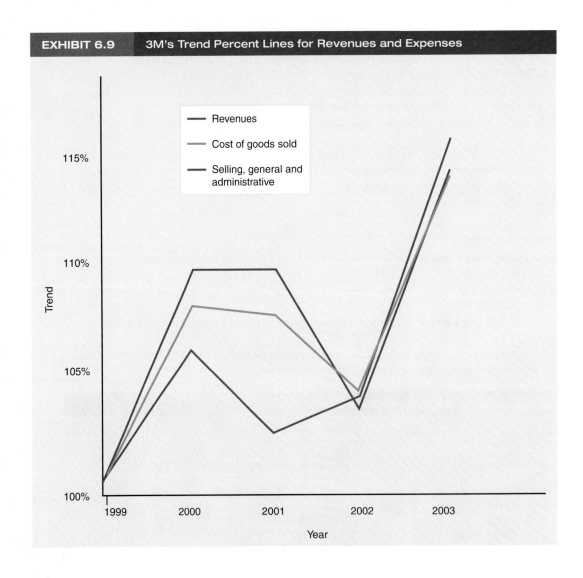

EXHIBIT 6.9   3M's Trend Percent Lines for Revenues and Expenses

CHAPTER-END REVIEW

Part 1

Income statement data from eGames, Inc., from 2006 and 2007 is as follows.

eGAMES, INC. Comparative Income Statements		
For Year Ended December 31 ($ millions)	2007	2006
Net sales	$415,000	$320,000
Cost of goods sold	290,000	230,000
Gross profit	125,000	90,000
Operating expenses		
Selling expenses	39,500	27,300
Administrative expenses	49,640	32,600
Total operating expenses	89,140	59,900
Income before interest expense and taxes	35,860	30,100
Interest expense	3,000	2,400
Income before income taxes	32,860	27,700
Income tax expense	14,100	12,300
Net income	$ 18,760	$ 15,400

a. Prepare common-size comparative income statements for each year.
b. Compare and comment on the common-size income statements from requirement a.
c. Prepare comparative income statements, showing increases or decreases in both dollars and percentages for each line item.
d. Comment on the changes between the two years from requirement c.

Part 1 Solution

a.

eGAMES, INC. Common-Size Comparative Income Statements		
For Year Ended December 31 ($ millions)	2007	2006
Net sales	100.0%	100.0%
Cost of goods sold	69.9	71.9
Gross profit	30.1	28.1
Operating expenses		
Selling expenses	9.5	8.5
Administrative expenses	12.0	10.2
Total operating expenses	21.5	18.7
Income before interest and taxes	8.6	9.4
Interest expense	0.7	0.8
Income before income taxes	7.9	8.6
Income tax expense	3.4	3.8
Net income	4.5%	4.8%

b. Net income as a percent of sales decreased slightly in 2007 relative to 2006 (4.5% vs. 4.8%), despite an increase in gross margin (30.1% vs. 28.1%). The decrease was largely due to an increase in selling and administrative expenses as a percent of sales.

c.

eGAMES, INC. Comparative Income Statements				
For Year End December 31 ($ millions)	**2007**	**2006**	**Increase (Decrease)**	**Percent Change**
Net sales	$415,000	$320,000	$95,000	29.7%
Cost of goods sold	290,000	230,000	60,000	26.1
Gross profit	125,000	90,000	35,000	38.9
Operating expenses				
Selling expenses	39,500	27,300	12,200	44.7
Administrative expenses	49,640	32,600	17,040	52.3
Total operating expenses	89,140	59,900	29,240	48.8
Income before interest expense and taxes	35,860	30,100	5,760	19.1
Interest expense	3,000	2,400	600	25.0
Income before income taxes	32,860	27,700	5,160	18.6
Income tax expense	14,100	12,300	1,800	14.6
Net income	$ 18,760	$ 15,400	$ 3,360	21.8%

d. The 21.8% growth in net income is substantial, but smaller than the 29.7% growth in sales and the 38.9% growth in gross profit. The discrepancy is due to the 48.8% increase in selling and administrative expenses. It appears as if eGames is spending large amounts on selling and administrative expenses in order to grow sales and gain market share.

Part 2
Balance sheet data from eGames, Inc., from 2006 and 2007 is as follows.

eGAMES, INC. Comparative Balance Sheets		
At December 31 ($ millions)	**2007**	**2006**
Assets		
Cash and cash equivalents	$ 5,500	$ 4,200
Short-term investments	2,500	—
Accounts receivable, net	59,600	52,000
Inventory	75,000	63,000
Prepaid expenses	900	600
Total current assets	143,500	119,800
Long-term investments	800	—
Property, plant, and equipment, net	48,000	44,000
Total assets	$192,300	$163,800
Liabilities		
Notes payable	$ 3,500	$ 3,000
Accounts payable	25,100	24,100
Accrued liabilities	30,000	27,300
Total current liabilities	58,600	54,400
Long-term bonds payable	25,000	20,000
Total liabilities	83,600	74,400
Stockholders' equity		
Common stock	34,600	27,500
Retained earnings	74,100	61,900
Total stockholders' equity	108,700	89,400
Total liabilities and stockholders' equity	$192,300	$163,800

a. Prepare common-size comparative balance sheets for each year (use total assets as the base amount for computing percentages).
b. Compare and comment on the common-size balance sheets from requirement a.
c. Prepare comparative balance sheets, showing increases or decreases in both dollars and percentages for each line item.
d. Comment on the changes between the two years from requirement c.

Part 2 Solution

a.

eGAMES, INC. Common-Size Comparative Balance Sheets		
At December 31 ($ millions)	2007	2006
Assets		
Cash and cash equivalents	2.86%	2.56%
Short-term investments	1.30	—
Accounts receivable, net	30.99	31.75
Inventory	39.00	38.46
Prepaid expenses	0.47	0.37
Total current assets	74.62	73.14
Long-term investments	0.42	—
Property, plant, and equipment, net	24.96	26.86
Total assets	100.00%	100.00%
Liabilities		
Notes payable	1.82%	1.83%
Accounts payable	13.05	14.71
Accrued liabilities	15.60	16.67
Total current liabilities	30.47	33.21
Long-term bonds payable	13.00	12.21
Total liabilities	43.47	45.42
Stockholders' equity		
Common stock	17.99	16.79
Retained earnings	38.53	37.79
Total stockholders' equity	56.53	54.58
Total liabilities and stockholders' equity	100.00%	100.00%

*Percents are rounded to hundredths and thus may not exactly sum to totals.

b. Current assets make up 74.6% of total assets and current liabilities make up more than 2/3 of total liabilities. Comparing current assets and current liabilities as a percent of total assets reveals that eGames' short-term liquidity improved slightly from 2006 to 2007. Also, total liabilities declined slightly as a percent of total assets, improving long-term solvency.

c.

eGAMES, INC. Comparative Balance Sheets				
At December 31 ($ millions)	2007	2006	Increase (Decrease)	Percent Change
Assets				
Cash and cash equivalents	$ 5,500	$ 4,200	$ 1,300	31.0%
Short-term investments	2,500	—	2,500	—
Accounts receivable, net	59,600	52,000	7,600	14.6

(continued)

eGAMES, INC.
Comparative Balance Sheets (continued)

At December 31 ($ millions)	2007	2006	Increase (Decrease)	Percent Change
Inventory	$ 75,000	$ 63,000	$12,000	19.0%
Prepaid expenses	900	600	300	50.0
Total current assets	143,500	119,800	23,700	19.8
Long-term investments	800	—	800	—
Property, plant, and equipment, net	48,000	44,000	4,000	9.1
Total assets	$192,300	$163,800	$28,500	17.4
Liabilities				
Notes payable	$ 3,500	$ 3,000	$ 500	16.7
Accounts payable	25,100	24,100	1,000	4.1
Accrued liabilities	30,000	27,300	2,700	9.9
Total current liabilities	58,600	54,400	4,200	7.7
Long-term bonds payable	25,000	20,000	5,000	25.0
Total liabilities	83,600	74,400	9,200	12.4
Stockholders' equity				
Common stock	34,600	27,500	7,100	25.8
Retained earnings	74,100	61,900	12,200	19.7
Total stockholders's equity	108,700	89,400	19,300	21.6
Total liabilities and stockholders' equity	$192,300	$163,800	$28,500	17.4

d. With the exception of prepaid expenses and cash, working capital accounts increased at a slower rate than did sales. This indicates that eGames is doing a good job of managing working capital during a growth period. The 25% increase in long-term debt is not alarming given a similar percent increase in common stock.

SUMMARY

LO1 Define and discuss financial ratios for analyzing short-term liquidity. (p. 238)

■ Several liquidity and solvency ratios that underlie a credit worthiness analysis of any company are discussed in this chapter including:

■ Liquidity Ratios:
   • Average cash (operating) cycle (ACC)
   • Current ratio (CR)
   • Quick ratio (QR)

■ The average cash operating cycle (ACC) is the time from investing cash in inventories until the receivable is paid in cash. Company's generally try to keep this time as short as possible subject to supplier and customer concerns.
   • ACC = Ave. Collection Period + Inv. Days Out. Payable Days Out.
   [Accounts Receivable ÷ (Sales ÷ 365)] + [Inv. ÷ (Ave. Sales ÷ 365)] − [Accounts Payable ÷ (Sales ÷ 365)]

■ The importance of the current ratio (CR) depends on the type of business. Ratios greater than one are often considered sufficient, but ratios of less than one can be sufficient if the company appears to be able to meet its short-term obligations including interest and current debt repayments.
   • Current Ratio = Current Assets ÷ Current Liabilities

■ The quick ratio (QR) includes only cash, marketable securities, and receivables. It indicates the company's ability to meet its current obligations without liquidating other assets.
   • Quick Ratio = (Cash + Marketable Securities + Accounts Receivable) ÷ Current Liabilities

■ Operating cash flow to current liabilities ratio focuses on the ability of the firm to pay its current liabilities.
   • Operating cash flow to current liabilities = Net Cash Flow from Operations/Average Current Liabilities

Define and discuss financial ratios for analyzing long-term solvency. (p. 242)   **LO2**

■ Solvency Ratios:
  • Debt-to-equity (DE)
  • Long-term debt-to-equity (LTDE)
  • Times interest earned (TIE)
  • Operating cash flow to liabilities (OCFL)

■ The debt-to-equity (DE) ratio reflects the proportion of the company funded by non-equity sources. The larger the ratio, the more financial risk that is assumed by the company. However, if the spread is positive, the return to stockholders will be greater.

  • Debt-to-Equity = Total Liabilities ÷ Stockholders' Equity

■ The long-term debt-to-equity (LTDE) ratio assumes that current liabilities are covered by current assets. If true, the long-term debt can be covered by operating cash flows.

  • Long-term Debt-to-Equity = Long-tern Debt ÷ Stockholder's Equity

■ The times interest earned (TIE) measures how much of the company's income is available to service its interest bearing debt. Companies prefer a large value so the risk of default is minimal.

  • Times Interest Earned = Income before interest and taxes ÷ Interest Expense

■ The operating cash flow to liabilities (OCFL) ratio is another good measure of the company's ability to pay its current debts. While other measures exist, the above are indicative of credit-risk exposure.

■ Gross profit margin reflects the net impact on profitability of changes in company pricing structure and sales mix.

  • Gross Profit Margin = Gross Profit/Net Sales

■ Gross profit margin reflects the net impact on profitability of changes in company pricing structure and sales mix.

■ Return on sales reflects on overall operating efficiency; it reveals the percentage of each dollar of net sales that remains as net income.

  • Return on Sales = Net Income/Net Sales

Describe financial distress and techniques used to predict the likelihood of bankruptcy. (p. 244)   **LO3**

■ Altman's Z-score is used as a measure of the risk that a company will be unable to honor its debt obligations.

Explain the limitations of ratio analysis. (p. 246)   **LO4**

■ Ratios are limited for several reasons, including:
  • Omitted assets and liabilities from financial statements
  • Use of historical values of long-term assets and liabilities
  • Company changes over time due to acquisitions and divestitures
  • Companies are a blend of different business
  • Company strategy changes over its life cycle and changes in competition

Explain describe vertical and horizontal analysis of financial statements. (p. 247)   **LO5**

■ Vertical analysis deals with the study of financial statement data for a single year.

■ Common-size comparative financial statements express items on a financial statement as a percentage of a key item, such as expressing income statement items as a percentage of net sales.

■ USE OF Horizontal analysis typically relies on dollar and percentage changes in comparative financial statements for two or more years.

■ Analyzing trend percentages of key figures, such as net sales, net income, and total assets for a number of years, as related to a base year, is part of horizontal analysis.

GUIDANCE ANSWERS

YOU MAKE THE CALL

You are the Bank Loan Officer   Yes, based on the information supplied. The firm's ability to cover the interest payments is indicated by strong current and quick ratios of 1.75 and 1.45 respectively. Operating income is positive. Long-term debt will be just under $5 million including the new borrowing, but even with an interest rate of 10%, interest payments will be less than 8% of operating cash flow.

KEY TERMS

Altman's Z-Score (p. 244)

Average cash (operating) cycle (p. 238)

Common-size comparative financial statements (p. 248)

Comparative balance sheets (p. 250)

Comparative financial statements (p. 250)

Comparative income statement (p. 251)

Current ratio (p. 239)

Debt-to-equity (p. 242)

Dollar change (p. 249)

Fundamental analysis (p. 247)

Gross profit margin (p. 244)

Horizontal analysis (p. 249)

Impact of conglomerates (p. 246)

Liquidity (p. 238)

Liquidity analysis (p. 238)

Long-term debt-to-equity (p. 242)

Net working capital (p. 239)

Operating cash flow to current liabilities ratio (p. 241)

Operating cash flow to liabilities (p. 243)

Percent change (p. 249)

Quick ratio (p. 241)

Return on sales (p. 244)

Solvency (p. 238)

Solvency analysis (p. 242)

Times interest earned (TIE) (p. 243)

Trend analysis (p. 251)

Trend percent (p. 251)

Vertical analysis (p. 247)

MULTIPLE CHOICE

Use the following information to answer questions 1 through 3.

THERMO COMPANY
Balance Sheet
December 31 2006

Cash	$ 40,000	Current liabilities	$ 80,000
Accounts receivable (net)	80,000	Bonds payable	120,000
Inventory	130,000	Common stock	200,000
Plant and equipment (net)	250,000	Retained earnings	100,000
Total assets	$500,000	Total liabilities and equity	$500,000

Net sales for 2006 were $800,000, gross profit was $320,000, and net income was $36,000. The income tax rate was 40%. At December 31, 2005, accounts receivable (net) were $76,000, inventory was $110,000, and stockholders' equity was $260,000. The bonds payable were outstanding all year and 2006 interest expense was $12,000.

1. The current ratio of Thermo Company at December 31, 2006, calculated from this data, was 3.13, and the working capital was $170,000. Which of the following would happen if the company paid $20,000 of its current liabilities on January 1, 2007?
   a. Both the current ratio and the working capital would decrease.
   b. Both the current ratio and the working capital would increase.
   c. The current ratio would increase, but the working capital would remain the same.
   d. The current ratio would increase, but the working capital would decrease.

2. What is the company's debt-to-equity ratio at year-end 2006?
   a. .67   b. 4   c. 6   d. 3.69

3. What is the company's times interest earned ratio for 2006?
   a. 4   b. 3   c. 5   d. 6

4. Suppose that a company's average inventory days outstanding is 200, average payable days outstanding is 40, and the cost of goods sold is $10 million. If the average collection period is 60 days and sales were $20 million, what is the company's average cash cycle? (*Hint:* To compute the modified values from the nonmodified values, multiply the nonmodified values by the ratio of cost of goods sold divided by sales.)
   a. 72 days
   b. 140 days
   c. 180 days
   d. 300 days

5. A company's current ratio is 2 and its quick ratio is 1. What can be said about the sum of the company's cash + marketable securities + accounts receivable?
   a. The sum exceeds the current liabilities.
   b. The sum is equal to the sum of the current liabilities.
   c. The sum is equal to ½ of the total current liabilities.
   d. None of the above is correct.

Multiple Choice Answers
1. c   2. a   3. d   4. b   5. b

DISCUSSION QUESTIONS

Q6-1. What is the cash cycle? What objective does management have regarding the cash cycle?

Q6-2. Explain the concept of liquidity and why it is crucial to company survival.

Q6-3. How does the quick ratio differ from the current ratio?

Q6-4. For each of the following ratios, is a high ratio or low ratio considered, in general, a positive sign?
  a. Current ratio.
  b. Quick ratio.
  c. Operating cash flow to current liabilities ratio.
  d. Times Interest Earned
  e. Debt-to-Equity

Q6-5. What is the importance of the debt-to-equity ratio and how is it computed?

Q6-6. Why do we compute the times interest earned ratio and how is it calculated?

Q6-7. Under what circumstances can return on sales be used to appraise the profitability of a company? Can this ratio be used to compare the profitability of companies from different industries? Explain.

Q6-8. What are two inherent limitations of financial statement data?

Q6-9. How do horizontal analysis and vertical analysis of financial statements differ?

Q6-10. "Analysts should focus attention on each item showing a large percentage change from one year to the next." Is this statement correct? Comment.

Q6-11. What are trend percentages and how are they calculated? What pitfalls must an analyst avoid when preparing trend percentages?

Q6-12. What are common-size financial statements and how are they used?

Q6-13. What item is the base figure (that is, 100%) in a common-size income statement? a common-size balance sheet?

MINI EXERCISES

M6-14. Working Capital and Short-Term Liquidity Ratios (LO1)

Bell Company has a current ratio of 2.85 (2.85:1) on December 31, 2008. On that date its current assets are as follows.

Cash	$ 26,400
Short-term investments	49,000
Accounts receivable (net)	169,000
Inventory	200,000
Prepaid expenses	11,600
	$456,000

Bell Company's current liabilities at December 31, 2007, were $135,000 and during 2008 its operating activities provided a net cash flow of $50,000.
  a. What are the company's current liabilities on December 31, 2008?
  b. What is the company's working capital on December 31, 2008?
  c. What is the quick ratio on December 31, 2008?
  d. What is the 2008 operating cash flow to current liabilities ratio?

M6-15. Working Capital and Short-Term Liquidity Ratios (LO1)

Favor Company has a current ratio of 2.08 (2.08:1) on December 31, 2007. On that date its current assets are as follows.

Cash and cash equivalents	$ 28,000
Short-term investments	87,000
Accounts receivable (net)	125,000
Inventory	178,500
Prepaid expenses	9,980
	$428,480

Favor Company's current liabilities at December 31, 2006, were $192,000 and during 2007 its operating activities provided a net cash flow of $33,830.

a. What are the company's current liabilities on December 31, 2007?
b. What is the company's working capital on December 31, 2007?
c. What is the quick ratio on December 31, 2007?
d. What is the 2007 operating cash flow to current liabilities ratio?

M6-16. Compute and Interpret Liquidity and Solvency Ratios (LO1, 2)

Toys "R" Us, Inc.
(TOY)

Selected balance sheet and income statement information from Toys "R" Us, Inc., for 2002 through 2004 follows ($ millions):

	2004	2003	2002
Current assets	$4,684	$3,586	$2,631
Current liabilities	2,772	2,378	1,974
Earnings before interest and taxes	265	471	200
Interest expense	127	110	109
Total liabilities	5,987	5,354	4,635
Stockholders' equity	4,231	4,043	3,441

a. Compute the current ratio for each year and discuss any trend in liquidity. What additional information about the accounting numbers comprising this ratio might be useful in helping you assess liquidity? Explain.
b. Compute times interest earned and the debt-to-equity ratio for each year and discuss any trends for each. Do you have any concerns about Toys "R" Us's extent of financial leverage and its ability to meet interest obligations? Explain.
c. What is your overall assessment of Toys "R" Us's liquidity and solvency from the analyses in a and b? Explain.

M6-17. Ratios Analyzing Profitability (LO2)

The following information is available for Buhler Company.

Annual Data	2008	2007
Net sales	$8,600,000	$8,000,000
Gross profit	3,053,000	2,736,000
Net income	567,600	488,000

Year-End Data	Dec. 31, 2008	Dec. 31, 2007
Total assets	$6,500,000	$6,100,000
Stockholders' equity	3,800,000	3,200,000

Calculate the following ratios for 2008:
a. Gross profit margin
b. Return on sales

M6-18. Ratios Analyzing Profitability (LO2)

The following information is available for Crest Company.

Annual Data	2008	2007
Net sales	$6,400,000	$6,000,000
Cost of goods sold	4,006,400	3,720,000
Net income	307,200	264,000

Year-End Data	Dec. 31, 2008	Dec. 31, 2007
Total assets	$ 2,850,000	$ 2,360,000
Stockholders' equity	1,900,000	1,800,000

Calculate the following ratios for 2008:
a. Gross profit margin
b. Return on sales

M6-19. Ratios Analyzing Long-Term Solvency (LO2)

The following information is available for Antler Company.

Annual Data	2007	2006
Interest expense	$ 88,000	$ 82,000
Income tax expense	203,500	185,000
Net income	496,500	395,000
Capital expenditures	320,000	400,000
Net cash provided by operating activities	425,000	390,000

Year-End Data	Dec. 31, 2008	Dec. 31, 2007
Total liabilities	$ 2,200,000	$1,900,000
Total equity	4,000,000	3,600,000

Calculate the following:

a.   2007 year-end debt-to-equity ratio

b.   2007 times interest earned ratio

M6-20. Ratios Analyzing Long-Term Solvency (LO2)

The following information is available for Percy Company.

Annual Data	2007	2006
Interest expense	$175,000	$166,000
Income tax expense	216,000	117,000
Net income	294,000	273,000
Capital expenditures	440,000	350,000
Net cash provided by operating activities	247,000	223,000

Year-End Data	Dec. 31, 2008	Dec. 31, 2007
Total liabilities	$3,300,000	$2,900,000
Total equity	2,200.000	1,900,000

Calculate the following:

a.   2007 year-end debt-to-equity ratio

b.   2007 times interest earned ratio

M6-21. Comparative Income Statements (LO5)

Consider the following income statement data from Ross Company for 2007 and 2008.

	2008	2007
Sales	$525,000	$450,000
Cost of goods sold	336,000	279,000
Selling expenses	105,000	99,000
Administrative expenses	60,000	54,000
Income tax expense	7,800	5,400

a.   Prepare comparative income statements, showing increases or decreases in both dollars and percentages for each line item.

b.   Comment on the results from the analysis in part *a.*

M6-22. Common-Size Income Statements (LO5)

Refer to the income statement data in Mini Exercise 6-21.

a.   Prepare common-size comparative income statements for each year.

b.   Compare the common-size comparative income statements in part *a* and comment on the results.

EXERCISES

E6-23. **Analysis of Year-to-Year Changes in Ratios** (LO1, 2)

Selected information follows for Brimmer Company, taken from its 2007 and 2008 financial statements.

	2008	2007
Net sales	$910,000	$840,000
Cost of goods sold	575,000	542,000
Interest expense	20,000	20,000
Income tax expense	27,000	24,000
Net income	61,000	52,000
Net cash flow from operating activities	65,000	55,000
Capital expenditures	42,000	45,000
Accounts receivable (net), December 31	126,000	120,000
Inventory, December 31	196,000	160,000
Stockholders' equity, December 31	450,000	400,000
Total assets, December 31	730,000	660,000

Required

a. Compute the following ratios for 2008. The 2007 results are given for comparative purposes.

		2007 Ratios
1.	Gross profit margin	35.5%
2.	Return on sales	6.2%
3.	Times interest earned ratio	4.80

b. Comment on the changes between the two years.

E6-24. **Compute and Interpret Liquidity and Solvency Ratios** (LO1, 2)

The Walt Disney Company (DIS)

Selected balance sheet and income statement information from The Walt Disney Company for 2001 through 2003 follows ($ millions):

	Current Assets	Current Liabilities	Pretax Income	Interest Expense	Total Assets	Stockholders' Equity
2001	$ 7,029	$ 6,219	$ 1,283	$ 606	$ 43,699	$ 22,672
2002	7,849	7,819	2,190	759	50,045	23,445
2003	8,314	8,669	2,254	699	49,988	23,791

a. Compute the current ratio for each year and discuss any trend in liquidity. Do you believe the company is sufficiently liquid? Explain. What additional information about the accounting numbers comprising this ratio might be useful in helping you assess liquidity? Explain.

b. Compute times interest earned and the debt-to-equity ratio for each year and discuss any trends for each. Do you have any concerns about the company's extent of financial leverage and its ability to meet interest obligations? Explain.

c. What is your overall assessment of the company's liquidity and solvency from the analyses in a and b? Explain.

E6-25. **Analysis of Year-to-Year Changes in Ratios** (LO1, 2)

Selected information follows for Cycle Company, taken from its 2007 and 2008 financial statements.

	2008	2007
Net sales	$675,000	$520,000
Cost of goods sold	407,700	310,000
Interest expense	18,000	14,000
Income tax expense	6,200	5,100
Net income	24,600	20,300
Net cash flow from operating activities	29,500	26,500
Capital expenditures	40,000	25,000
Accounts receivable (net), December 31	182,000	128,000
Inventory, December 31	225,000	180,000
Stockholders' equity, December 31	205,000	165,000
Total assets, December 31	460,000	350,000

Required

a. Compute the following ratios for 2008. The 2007 results are given for comparative purposes.

		2007 Ratios
1.	Gross profit margin	40.4%
2.	Return on sales	3.9%
3.	Times interest earned ratio	2.81

b. Comment on the changes between the two years.

E6-26. Compute and Interpret Liquidity and Solvency Ratios (LO1, 2)

Selected balance sheet and income statement information from Verizon Communications, Inc., for 2001 through 2003 follows ($ millions):

Verizon Communications, Inc. (VZ)

	Current Assets	Current Liabilities	Pretax Income	Interest Expense	Total Assets	Stockholders' Equity
2001	$23,187	$38,020	$3,496	$3,737	$170,795	$32,539
2002	20,921	27,047	7,472	3,422	167,468	32,616
2003	18,293	26,570	6,344	2,941	165,968	33,466

a. Compute the current ratio for each year and discuss any trend in liquidity. Do you believe the company is sufficiently liquid? Explain. What additional information about the accounting numbers comprising this ratio might be useful in helping you assess liquidity? Explain.

b. Compute times interest earned and the debt-to-equity ratio for each year and discuss any trends for each. Do you have any concerns about the company's extent of financial leverage and its ability to meet interest obligations? Explain.

c. What is your overall assessment of the company's liquidity and solvency from the analyses in *a* and *b*? Explain.

E6-27. Trend Percentages (LO5)

Net sales, net income, and total assets for Vibrant Controls, Inc., for five consecutive years follow (Vibrant manufactures pollution controls).

($ thousands)	2008	2007	2006	2005	2004
Net sales	$94,700	$88,400	$84,250	$79,800	$71,500
Net income	4,790	4,160	3,900	3,650	3,200
Total assets	54,900	51,000	48,700	45,400	42,500

Required

a. Compute trend percentages for each line item, using 2004 as the base year.

b. Compute return on sales for each year. (Rates above 2.8% are considered good for manufacturers of pollution controls; rates above 6.4% are considered very good.)

c. Comment on the results of your analysis from parts a and b.

E6-28. Compute and Interpret Liquidity and Solvency Ratios (LO1, 2)

Selected balance sheet and income statement information from Wal-Mart Stores, Inc., for fiscal 2002 through 2004 follows ($ millions):

Wal-Mart Stores, Inc. (WMT)

	Current Assets	Current Liabilities	Pretax Income	Interest Expense	Total Assets	Stockholders' Equity
2002	$28,246	$27,282	$10,751	$1,456	$ 83,451	$35,102
2003	30,483	32,617	12,719	1,187	94,685	39,337
2004	34,421	37,418	14,193	1,140	104,912	43,623

a. Compute the current ratio for each year and discuss any trend in liquidity. Do you believe the company is sufficiently liquid? Explain. What additional information about the accounting numbers comprising this ratio might be useful in helping you assess liquidity? Explain.

b. Compute times interest earned and the debt-to-equity ratio for each year and discuss any trends for each. Do you have any concerns about the company's extent of financial leverage and its ability to meet interest obligations? Explain.

c. What is your overall assessment of the company's liquidity and solvency from the analyses in *a* and *b*? Explain.

E6-29. Comparative Balance Sheet (LO5)

The following balance sheet data are for Best Buyer, an electronics and appliance retailer, at February 26, 2005, and February 27, 2004 ($ thousands).

	Feb. 26, 2005	Feb. 27, 2004
Cash and cash equivalents	$ 59,872	$ 7,138
Receivables	52,944	37,968
Merchandise inventories	637,950	249,991
Other current assets	13,844	9,829
Total current assets	764,610	304,926
Property and equipment, net	172,724	126,442
Other assets	15,160	7,774
Total assets	$952,494	$439,142
Current liabilities	$402,028	$186,005
Long-term liabilities	239,022	70,854
Total liabilities	641,050	256,859
Common stock	2,087	1,149
Additional paid-in capital	224,089	137,151
Retained earnings	85,268	43,983
Total stockholders' equity	311,444	182,283
Total liabilities and equity	$952,494	$439,142

a. Prepare comparative balance sheets, showing increases or decreases in both dollars and percentages for each line item.

b. Comment on the results from the analysis in part *a*.

E6-30. Common-Size Balance Sheets (LO5)

Refer to the balance sheet data in Exercise 6-29.

a. Prepare common-size comparative balance sheets for each year (use total assets as the base amount for computing percentages).

b. Compare the common-size comparative balance sheets in part *a* and comment on the results.

E6-31. Compute and Interpret Liquidity and Solvency Ratios (LO1, 2)

Viacom, Inc.
(VIA)

Selected balance sheet and income statement information from Viacom, Inc., for 2001 through 2003 follows ($ millions):

	Current Assets	Current Liabilities	Pretax Income	Interest Expense	Total Assets	Stockholders' Equity
2001	$7,206	$7,562	$ 656	$963	$90,810	$62,717
2002	7,167	7,341	3,695	848	89,754	62,488
2003	7,736	7,585	2,861	776	89,849	63,205

a. Compute the current ratio for each year and discuss any trend in liquidity. Do you believe the company is sufficiently liquid? Explain. What additional information about the accounting numbers comprising this ratio might be useful in helping you assess liquidity? Explain.

b. Compute times interest earned and the debt-to-equity ratio for each year and discuss any trends for each. Do you have any concerns about the company's extent of financial leverage and its ability to meet interest obligations? Explain.

c. What is your overall assessment of the company's liquidity and solvency from the analyses in *a* and *b*? Explain.

PROBLEMS

P6-32. Analysis using Liquidity Ratios and Common-Size Income Statements (LO1, 2, 3)

The following financial statements are for Waverly Company for 2007 and 2008. During 2008, management obtained additional bond financing to enlarge its production facilities. The company faced higher production costs during the year for such things as fuel, materials, and freight. Because of temporary government price controls, a planned price increase on products was delayed several months. As a holder of both its common and preferred stock, you decide to analyze its financial statements for 2007 and 2008.

WAVERLY COMPANY
Balance Sheets

At December 31 ($ thousands)	2008	2007
Assets		
Cash and cash equivalents	$ 18,000	$ 12,000
Accounts receivable, net	55,000	43,000
Inventory	120,000	105,000
Prepaid expenses	20,000	14,000
Plant and other assets, net	471,000	411,000
Total assets	$684,000	$585,000
Liabilities and Stockholders' Equity		
Current liabilities	$ 90,000	$ 82,000
10% bonds payable	225,000	160,000
9% preferred stock	75,000	75,000
Common stock	200,000	200,000
Retained earnings	94,000	68,000
Total liabilities and equity	$684,000	$585,000

WAVERLY COMPANY
Income Statements

For Year Ended December 31 ($ thousands)	2008	2007
Sales	$820,000	$678,000
Cost of goods sold	541,200	433,920
Gross profit	278,800	244,080
Selling and administrative expenses	171,400	149,200
Income before interest expense and taxes	107,400	94,880
Interest expense	22,500	16,000
Income before income taxes	84,900	78,880
Income tax expense	22,900	21,300
Net income	$ 62,000	$ 57,580
Other financial data		
Net cash provided by operating activities	$ 65,200	$ 60,500
Preferred (cash) dividends	6,750	6,750

Required

a. Compute the following for each year: current ratio, quick ratio, operating cash flow to current liabilities ratio (current liabilities were $78,000,000 at December 31, 2006), debt-to-equity ratio, and times interest earned ratio.

b. Compute common-size comparative income statements for each year.

c. Comment on the results of your analysis in parts a and b.

P6-33. Analysis and Interpretation of Liquidity and Solvency (LO1, 2, 3)

Balance sheets and income statements for **Procter & Gamble** follow. Refer to these financial statements to answer the requirements below.

Procter & Gamble (PG)

PROCTER & GAMBLE COMPANY
Comparative Balance Sheets

For June 30 ($ millions)	2003	2002	2001	2000
Cash and cash equivalents	$ 5,912	$ 3,427	$ 2,306	$ 1,415
Investment securities	300	196	212	185

(continued)

PROCTER & GAMBLE COMPANY
Comparative Balance Sheets (continued)

For June 30 ($ millions)	2003	2002	2001	2000
Accounts receivable	3,038	3,090	2,931	2,910
Inventories	3,640	3,456	3,384	3,490
Other current (operating) assets	2,330	1,997	2,056	2,146
Total current assets	15,220	12,166	10,889	10,146
Property, plant and equipment, gross	23,542	23,070	22,821	23,221
Accumulated depreciation	10,438	9,721	9,726	9,529
Property, plant and equipment, net	13,104	13,349	13,095	13,692
Goodwill and intangible assets	13,507	13,430	8,300	8,786
Other noncurrent (operating) assets	1,875	1,831	2,103	1,742
Total assets	$43,706	$40,776	$34,387	$34,366
Accounts payable	$ 2,795	$ 2,205	$ 2,075	$ 2,209
Debt due within one year	2,172	3,731	2,233	3,241
Accrued and other liabilities	7,391	6,768	5,538	4,691
Total current liabilities	12,358	12,704	9,846	10,141
Deferred income taxes	1,396	1,077	894	625
Long-term debt	11,475	11,201	9,792	9,012
Other noncurrent liabilities	2,291	2,088	1,845	2,301
Total liabilities	27,520	27,070	22,377	22,079
Preferred stock	1,580	1,634	1,701	1,737
Common stock	1,297	1,301	1,296	1,306
Additional paid-in capital	2,931	2,490	2,057	1,794
Retained earnings	13,692	11,980	10,451	10,710
Other equities	(3,314)	(3,699)	(3,495)	(3,260)
Shareholders' equity	16,186	13,706	12,010	12,287
Total liabilities and equity	$43,706	$40,776	$34,387	$34,366

PROCTER & GAMBLE COMPANY
Comparative Income Statements

Year Ended June 30 ($ millions)	2003	2002	2001	2000
Net sales	$43,377	$40,238	$39,244	$39,951
Cost of goods sold	22,141	20,989	22,102	21,514
Gross profit	21,236	19,249	17,142	18,437
Selling, general & administrative expense	13,383	12,571	12,406	12,483
Operating income	7,853	6,678	4,736	5,954
Other nonoperating income, net	238	308	674	304
Interest expense	561	603	794	722
Income before income taxes	7,530	6,383	4,616	5,536
Income taxes	2,344	2,031	1,694	1,994
Net earnings	$ 5,186	$ 4,352	$ 2,922	$ 3,542

Required

a. Compute its current ratio and quick ratio for 2001 through 2003. Do the trends, if any, in these ratios indicate that P&G is becoming more or less liquid? Use computations to support your analysis and inferences.

b. Compute P&G's debt-to-equity ratio and times interest earned for 2001 through 2003. Do these ratios indicate that P&G is becoming more or less solvent? Explain.

c. Compute the Altman Z-Score of P&G for 2003. Does this score indicate any concerns about P&G's financial condition? Explain.

P6-34. **Ratios Compared with Industry Averages** (LO 1, 2)

Assume you own common stock of Phantom Corporation, a paper manufacturer, and you are analyzing the company's performance for the most recent year. The following data are taken from its most recent annual report.

At December 31	Current Year	Prior Year
Quick assets	$ 600,000	$ 552,000
Inventory and prepaid expenses	372,000	312,000
Other assets	4,788,000	4,176,000
Total assets	$5,760,000	$5,040,000
Current liabilities	$ 624,000	$ 540,000
10% bonds payable	1,440,000	1,440,000
8% preferred stock	480,000	480,000
Common stock	2,700,000	2,160,000
Retained earnings	516,000	420,000
Total liabilities and equity	$5,760,000	$5,040,000

For the current year, net sales amount to $11,280,000, net income is $573,600, and preferred (cash) dividends declared and paid are $38,400.

Required

a. Compute the following measures for the current year:
1. Return on sales
2. Quick ratio
3. Current ratio
4. Debt-to-equity ratio

b. Trade association statistics and information provided by credit agencies reveal the following data on industry norms.

	Median	Upper Quartile
Return on sales	4.9%	8.6%
Quick ratio	1.0	1.8
Current ratio	1.8	3.0
Debt-to-equity ratio	1.08	0.66

Analyze and interpret Phantom Corporation's performance in light of industry performance.

P6-35. **Analysis using Liquidity Ratios and Common-Size Income Statements** (LO 0)

Consider the following financial statements for Vega Company for 2007 and 2008. During 2008, management obtained additional bond financing to enlarge its production facilities. The plant addition produced a new high-margin product, which is supposed to improve its average rate of gross profit and its return on sales. As a potential investor, you analyze the financial statements for 2007 and 2008.

VEGA COMPANY Balance Sheets		
At December 31 ($ thousands)	**2008**	**2007**
Assets		
Cash	$ 21,000	$ 16,100
Accounts receivable, net	39,000	21,400
Inventory	105,000	72,000
Prepaid expenses	1,500	3,000
Plant and other assets, net	463,500	427,500
Total assets	$630,000	$540,000
Liabilities and stockholders' equity		
Current liabilities	$ 76,000	$ 45,000
9% bonds payable	187,500	150,000
8% preferred stock	60,000	60,000
Common stock	225,000	225,000
Retained earnings	81,500	60,000
Total liabilities and equity	$630,000	$540,000

VEGA COMPANY
Income Statements

For Year Ended December 31 ($ thousands)	2008	2007
Sales	$840,000	$697,500
Cost of goods sold	552,000	474,000
Gross profit	288,000	223,500
Selling and administrative expenses	231,000	174,000
Income before interest expense and taxes	57,000	49,500
Interest expense	16,800	13,500
Income before income taxes	40,200	36,000
Income tax expense	14,100	12,600
Net income	$ 26,100	$ 23,400
Other financial data		
Net cash provided by operating activities	$ 30,000	$ 25,000
Preferred (cash) dividends	4,800	4,800

Required

a. Compute the following for each year: current ratio, quick ratio, operating cash flow to current liabilities ratio (current liabilities were $42,000,000 at December 31, 2006), debt-to-equity ratio, and times interest earned ratio.

b. Compute common-size comparative income statements for each year.

c. Comment on the results of your analysis in parts *a* and *b*.

P6-36. Ratios Compared with Industry Averages (LO1, 2)

Packard Plastics, Inc., manufactures various plastic and synthetic products. Financial statement data for the company are as follows.

($ thousands, except per share data)	2008
Net sales	$815,000
Cost of goods sold	540,000
Net income	50,500
Dividends	14,000
Earnings per share	4.04

PACKAGED PLASTICS, INC.
Balance Sheets

At December 31 ($ thousands)	2008	2007
Assets		
Cash	$ 4,100	$ 2,700
Accounts receivable, net	66,900	60,900
Inventory	148,000	140,000
Total current assets	219,000	203,600
Plant assets, net	215,000	194,000
Other assets	5,300	3,900
Total assets	$439,300	$401,500
Liabilities and stockholders' equity		
Notes payable—banks	$ 31,000	$ 25,000
Accounts payable	27,600	23,000
Accrued liabilities	25,100	24,800
Total current liabilities	83,700	72,800
10% bonds payable	150,000	150,000
Total liabilities	233,700	222,800
Common stock	125,000	125,000

(continued)

PACKAGED PLASTICS, INC.
Balance Sheets

At December 31 ($ thousands)	2008	2007
Retained earnings	80,600	53,700
Total stockholders' equity	205,600	178,700
Total liabilities and equity	$439,300	$401,500

Required

a. Using the company data provided, compute measures 1 through 5 below for 2008.
b. Compare the performance of this company relative to the industry averages reported below.
c. Based on your findings, comment on the company's overall operations.

Median Ratios for Competitors

1.	Quick ratio	1.2
2.	Current ratio	1.9
3.	Debt-to-equity ratio	0.95
4.	Gross profit margin	32.7%
5.	Return on sales	3.5%

P6-37. **Analysis and Interpretation of Liquidity and Solvency** (LO1, 2, 3)

Actual balance sheets and income statements for Merck & Co. (MRK) follow. Refer to these financial statements to answer the requirements below.

Merck & Co. (MRK)

MERCK & CO.
Comparative Balance Sheets

December 31 ($ millions)	2003	2002	2001
Assets			
Current Assets			
Cash and cash equivalents	$ 1,201.0	$ 2,243.0	$ 2,144.0
Short-term investments	2,972.0	2,728.2	1,142.6
Accounts receivable	4,023.6	5,423.4	5,215.4
Inventories	2,554.7	2,964.3	3,579.3
Prepaid expenses and taxes	775.9	1,027.5	880.3
Total current assets	11,527.2	14,386.4	12,961.6
Investments	7,941.2	7,255.1	6,983.5
Property, Plant, and Equipment (at cost)			
Land	356.7	336.9	315.2
Buildings	8,016.9	7,336.5	6,653.9
Machinery, equipment and office furnishings	11,018.2	10,883.6	9,807.0
Construction in progress	1,901.9	2,426.6	2,180.4
	21,293.7	20,983.6	18,956.5
Less allowance for depreciation	7,124.7	6,788.0	5,853.1
	14,169.0	14,195.6	13,103.4
Goodwill	1,085.4	4,127.0	4,127.0
Other Intangibles, Net	864.0	3,114.0	3,364.0
Other Assets	5,000.7	4,483.1	3,481.7
	$40,587.5	$47,561.2	$44,021.2
Liabilities and Stockholders' Equity			
Current Liabilities			
Loans payable and current portion of long-term debt	$ 1,700.0	$ 3,669.8	$ 4,066.7
Trade accounts payable	735.2	2,413.3	1,895.2
Accrued and other current liabilities	3,772.8	3,365.6	3,213.2

(continued)

MERCK & CO.
Comparative Balance Sheets

December 31 ($ millions)	2003	2002	2001
Income taxes payable	2,538.9	2,118.1	1,573.3
Dividends payable	822.7	808.4	795.8
Total current liabilities	9,569.6	12,375.2	11,544.2
Long-term debt	5,096.0	4,879.0	4,798.6
Deferred Income Taxes and Noncurrent Liabilities	6,430.3	7,178.2	6,790.8
Minority Interests	3,915.2	4,928.3	4,837.5
Stockholders' Equity			
Common stock, one cent par value			
Authorized—5,400,000,000 shares			
Issued—2,976,230,393 shares—2003			
Issued—2,976,198,757 shares—2002	29.8	29.8	29.8
Other paid-in capital	6,956.6	6,943.7	6,907.2
Retained earnings	34,142.0	35,434.9	31,489.6
Accumulated other comprehensive income (loss)	65.5	(98.8)	10.6
	41,193.9	42,309.6	38,437.2
Less treasury stock, at cost			
754,466,884 shares—2003			
731,215,507 shares—2002	25,617.5	24,109.1	22,387.1
Total stockholders' equity	15,576.4	18,200.5	16,050.1
	$40,587.5	$47,561.2	$44,021.2

MERCK & CO.
Comparative Income Statements

December 31 ($ millions)	2003	2002	2001
Sales	$22,485.9	$21,445.8	$21,199.0
Costs, expenses and other			
Materials and production	4,315.3	3,907.1	3,624.8
Marketing and administrative	6,394.9	5,652.2	5,700.6
Research and development	3,178.1	2,677.2	2,456.4
Acquired research	101.8	—	—
Equity income from affiliates	(474.2)	(644.7)	(685.9)
Other (income) expense, net	(81.6)	202.3	155.0
	13,434.3	11,794.1	11,250.9
Income from Continuing Operations Before Taxes	9,051.6	9,651.7	9,948.1
Taxes on Income	2,462.0	2,856.9	2,894.9
Income from Continuing Operations	6,589.6	6,794.8	7,053.2
Income from Discontinued Operations, Net of Taxes	241.3	354.7	228.6
Net Income	$ 6,830.9	$ 7,149.5	$ 7,281.8

Required

a. Compute its current ratio and quick ratio for 2001 through 2003. Do the trends, if any, in these ratios indicate that MRK is becoming more or less liquid? Use computations to support your analysis and inferences.

b. Compute MRK's debt-to-equity ratio and times interest earned for 2001 through 2003. Do these ratios indicate that MRK is becoming more or less solvent? Explain.

P6-38. **Analysis and Interpretation of Trend Percentages** (LO5)

Sales of automotive products for Ford Motor Company and General Motors Corporation for the five years 1989–2004 are as follows.

Ford Motor Company (F)

General Motors Corporation (GM)

Sales of Automotive Products ($ millions)	2002	2003	2004	2005	2006
Ford Motor Company	$82,879	$81,844	$72,051	$ 84,407	$ 91,568
General Motors Corporation	99,106	97,312	94,828	103,005	108,027

Net sales for Pfizer, Inc., and Abbott Laboratories for the five years 1989–2004 are as follows.

Pfizer, Inc. (PFE)

Abbott Laboratories (ABT)

Net Sales ($ millions)	2002	2003	2004	2005	2006
Pfizer, Inc.	$5,672	$6,406	$6,950	$7,230	$7,478
Abbott Laboratories	5,380	6,159	6,877	7,852	8,408

Required

a. Compute trend percentages for all four companies, using 2002 as the base year.

b. Comment on the trend percentage of Ford Motor Company and General Motors Corporation.

c. Comment on the trend percentages of Pfizer, Inc., and Abbott Laboratories.

P6-39. **Ratios Compared with Industry Averages** (LO1, 2)

You are analyzing the performance of Lumite Corporation, a manufacturer of personal care products, for the current year. The following data are taken from its most recent annual report.

At December 31	Current Year	Prior Year
Quick assets	$ 290,000	$ 250,000
Inventory and prepaid expenses	945,000	820,000
Other assets	4,165,000	3,700,000
Total assets	$5,400,000	$4,770,000
Current liabilities	$ 500,000	$ 400,000
10% bonds payable	1,300,000	1,300,000
7% preferred stock	900,000	900,000
Common stock	1,900,000	1,800,000
Retained earnings	800,000	370,000
Total liabilities and equity	$5,400,000	$4,770,000

For the current year, net sales are $8,600,000, net income is $675,000, and preferred (cash) dividends declared and paid are $63,000.

Required

a. Compute the following for the current year:
1. Return on sales
2. Quick ratio
3. Current ratio
4. Debt-to-equity ratio

b. Trade association statistics and information provided by credit agencies reveal the following data on industry norms.

	Median	**Upper Quartile**
Return on sales	3.7%	10.6%
Quick ratio	1.0	1.8
Current ratio	2.2	3.7
Debt-to-equity ratio	1.07	0.37

Analyze and interpret Lumite Corporation's performance in light of industry performance.

Colgate-Palmolive
Company
(CL)

P6-40. **Analysis and Interpretation of Liquidity, Solvency, and Bankruptcy Prediction** (LO1, 2, 3)
Refer to the actual comparative balance sheets and income statements for **Colgate-Palmolive Company** that follow to answer the requirements below.

Required

a. Compute its current ratio and quick ratio for 2001 through 2003. Do the trends, if any, in these ratios indicate that Colgate is becoming more or less liquid? Use computations to support your analysis and inferences.

b. Compute Colgate 's debt-to-equity ratio and times interest earned for 2001 through 2003. Do these ratios indicate that Colgate is becoming more or less solvent? Explain.

c. Compute the Altman Z-Score of Colgate for 2003. Does this score indicate any concerns about its financial condition? Explain.

COLGATE-PALMOLIVE COMPANY
Comparative Income Statements

For Year Ended December 31 ($ millions)	2003	2002	2001
Net Sales	$9,903.4	$9,294.3	$9,084.3
Cost of sales	4,456.1	4,224.2	4,234.9
Gross profit	5,447.3	5,070.1	4,849.4
Selling, general & administrative expenses	3,296.3	3,034.0	2,920.1
Other (income) expense, net	(15.0)	23.0	94.5
Operating profit	2,166.0	2,013.1	1,834.8
Interest expense, net	124.1	142.8	166.1
Income before income taxes	2,041.9	1,870.3	1,668.7
Provision for income taxes	620.6	582.0	522.1
Net income	$1,421.3	$1,288.3	$1,146.6

COLGATE-PALMOLIVE COMPANY
Comparative Balance Sheets

December 31 ($ millions)	2003	2002
Assets		
Cash and cash equivalents	$ 265.3	$ 167.9
Receivables (less allowances of $43.6 and $45.9, respectively)	1,222.4	1,145.4
Inventories	718.3	671.7
Other current assets	290.5	243.1
Total current assets	2,496.5	2,228.1
Property, plant and equipment, net	2,542.2	2,491.3
Goodwill	1,299.4	1,182.8
Other intangible assets, net	597.6	608.5
Other assets	543.1	576.5
Total assets	$7,478.8	$7,087.2
Liabilities and Shareholders' Equity		
Notes and loans payable	$ 103.6	$ 94.6
Current portion of long-term debt	314.4	298.5
Accounts payable	753.6	728.3
Accrued income taxes	183.8	121.7
Other accruals	1,090.0	905.6
Total current liabilities	2,445.4	2,148.7
Long-term debt	2,684.9	3,210.8
Deferred income taxes	456.0	488.8
Other liabilities	1,005.4	888.6
Total liabilities	6,591.7	6,736.9

(continued)

COLGATE-PALMOLIVE COMPANY Comparative Balance Sheets		
December 31 ($ millions)	2003	2002
Shareholders' Equity		
Preferred stock	$ 292.9	$ 323.0
Common stock, $1 par value (1,000,000,000 shares authorized, 732,853,180 shares issued)	732.9	732.9
Additional paid-in capital	1,126.2	1,133.9
Retained earnings	7,433.0	6,518.5
Accumulated other comprehensive income	(1,866.8)	(1,865.6)
	7,718.2	6,842.7
Unearned compensation	(331.2)	(340.1)
Treasury stock, at cost	(6,499.9)	(6,152.3)
Total shareholders' equity	887.1	350.3
Total liabilities and shareholders' equity	$7,478.8	$7,087.2

P6-41.   Ratios Compared with Industry Averages   (LO1, 2)

Avery Instrument, Inc., is a manufacturer of measuring instruments. Financial statement data for the company follows.

($ thousands, except per share data)	2008
Net sales	$210,000
Cost of goods sold	125,000
Net income	8,300
Cash dividends	2,600
Earnings per Share	4.15

AVERY INSTRUMENT, INC. Balance Sheets		
($ thousands)	2008	2007
Assets		
Cash	$ 18,300	$ 18,000
Accounts receivable, net	46,000	41,000
Inventory	39,500	43,700
Total current assets	103,800	102,700
Plant assets, net	52,600	50,500
Other assets	15,600	13,800
Total assets	$172,000	$167,000
Liabilities and stockholders' equity		
Notes payable—banks	$ 6,000	$ 6,000
Accounts payable	22,500	18,700
Accrued liabilities	16,500	21,000
Total current liabilities	45,000	45,700
9% bonds payable	40,000	40,000
Total liabilities	85,000	85,700
Common stock	50,000	50,000
Retained earnings	37,000	31,300
Total stockholders' equity	87,000	81,300
Total liabilities and equity	$172,000	$167,000

Required

a. Using the company data provided, compute measures 1 through 6 below for 2008.
b. Compare the performance of this company relative to the industry averages reported below.
c. Based on your findings, comment on the company's overall operations.

Median Ratios for Competitors

1.	Quick ratio	1.3
2.	Current ratio	2.4
3.	Debt-to-equity ratio	0.73
4.	Gross profit margin	42.8%
5.	Return on sales	4.5%
6.	Return on assets	7.6%

Toys "R" Us (TOY)
Gillette Company (G)

P6-42. **Analysis and Interpretation of Financial Statement Quarterly Data** (LO2, 4)

Quarterly data follow for Companies "C" and "D." One of these companies is Toys "R" Us, a children's specialty retail chain; its fiscal year ends on the Saturday nearest January 31. The other company is Gillette Company, a manufacturer of blades, razors, and toiletries; its reports are on a calendar-year basis.

($ thousands)	First Quarter	Second Quarter	Third Quarter	Fourth Quarter	Year
Company C					
Net sales	$1,216.6	$1,237.3	$1,339.7	$1,617.2	$5,410.8
Gross profit	753.1	773.6	839.0	1,000.8	3,366.5
Company D					
Net sales	$1,172.5	$1,249.1	$1,345.8	$3,401.8	$7,169.2
Gross profit	362.5	384.6	423.2	1,030.3	2,200.6

Required

a. Compute the percent of annual net sales generated each quarter by Company C. Round to the nearest percent.
b. Compute the percent of annual net sales generated each quarter by Company D. Round to the nearest percent.
c. Which company is most subject to seasonal fluctuation in sales? Explain.
d. Which company is Toys "R" Us? Gillette Company? Explain.

CASES AND PROJECTS

Gibson
Greetings, Inc.
Hon Industries, Inc.

C6-43. **Analysis and Interpretation of Financial Statement Quarterly Data** (LO2, 4)

Quarterly data follow for Companies "A" and "B." One of these companies is Gibson Greetings, Inc., which manufactures and sells greeting cards. The other company is Hon Industries, Inc., which manufactures and sells office furniture. Both companies report on a calendar-year basis.

($ thousands)	First Quarter	Second Quarter	Third Quarter	Fourth Quarter	Year
Company A					
Net sales	$186,111	$177,537	$203,070	$213,608	$780,326
Gross profit	55,457	53,643	64,024	69,374	242,498
Company B					
Net sales	$ 84,896	$ 83,796	$ 42,137	$235,336	$546,165
Gross profit	53,900	52,983	66,018	104,961	277,862

Required

a. Compute the percent of annual net sales generated each quarter by Company A. Round to the nearest percent.
b. Compute the percent of annual net sales generated each quarter by Company B. Round to the nearest percent.
c. Which company is most subject to seasonal fluctuation in sales? Explain.
d. Which company is Gibson Greetings, Inc.? Hon Industries, Inc.? Explain.
e. Which company's quarterly data are probably most useful for predicting annual results? Explain.

C6-44. **Ratio Analysis and Bank Loan Decisions** (LO1, 2)

Crescent Paints, a paint manufacturer, has been in business for five years. The company has had modest profits and has not experienced operating difficulties until this year (2008). Assume that you are a loan officer at

Granite Bank, and Crescent Paints' president, Alice Becknell, meets with you to discuss her company's working capital problems. Becknell explains that expanding her company has created difficulties in meeting obligations when they come due and in taking advantage of cash discounts offered by manufacturers for timely payment. Accordingly, she would like to borrow $50,000 from Granite Bank. At your request, Becknell submits the following financial data for the past two years.

For Year Ended December 31	2007	2006
Net sales	$2,000,000	$1,750,000
Cost of goods sold	1,320,000	1,170,000
Net income	42,000	33,600
Cash dividends	22,000	18,000

At December 31	2005
Total assets	$1,100,000
Accounts receivable, net	205,000
Inventory	350,000

CRESCENT PAINTS
Balance Sheets

At December 31	2007	2006
Assets		
Cash	$ 31,000	$ 50,000
Accounts receivable, net	345,000	250,000
Inventory	525,000	425,000
Prepaid expenses	11,000	6,000
Total current assets	912,000	731,000
Plant assets, net	483,000	444,000
Total assets	$1,395,000	$1,175,000
Liabilities and stockholders' equity		
Notes payable—banks	$ 100,000	$ 35,000
Accounts payable	244,500	190,000
Accrued liabilities	96,000	85,000
Total current liabilities	440,000	310,000
10% mortgage payable	190,000	250,000
Total liabilities	630,000	560,000
Common stock	665,000	535,000
Retained earnings	100,000	80,000
Total stockholders' equity	765,000	615,000
Total liabilities and equity	$1,395,000	$1,175,000

You compute the following measures 1 through 4 for both years from the data provided and then compare those ratios with the following median ratios for paint manufacturers provided by a commercial credit firm.

Median Ratios for Competitors

1.	Current ratio	2.5
2.	Quick ratio	1.3
3.	Debt-to-equity ratio	0.78
4.	Return on sales	2.4%

Required

Based on your analysis, decide whether and under what circumstances you would grant Becknell's request for the new loan. Explain the reasons for your decision.

C6-45.   **Management Advances, Ratio Implications, and Ethics**   (LO1, 2, 4)

Chris Nelson, new assistant controller for Grand Company, is preparing for the company's year-end closing procedures. On December 30, 2007, a memorandum from the controller directed Nelson to make a journal entry debiting Cash and crediting Long-Term Advances to Officers for $1,000,000. Not finding the $1,000,000 in the cash deposit prepared for the bank that day, Nelson went to the controller for further explanation. In response, the controller took from her desk drawer a check for $1,000,000 payable to Grand Company from Jason Grand, chief executive officer of the company. Attached to the check was a note from Jason Grand saying that if this check was not needed, to return it to him next week.

"This check is paying off a $1,000,000 advance the company made to Jason Grand six years ago," reported the controller. "Mr. Grand has done this every year since the advance; each time we have returned the check to him in January of the following year. We plan to do so again this time. In fact, when Mr. Grand retires in four years, I expect the board of directors will forgive this advance. However, if the company really needed the cash, we would deposit the check."

"Then why go through this process each year?" inquired Nelson.

"It dresses up our year-end balance sheet," replied the controller. "Certain financial statement ratios are improved markedly. Also, notes to the financial statements don't have to reveal a related-party loan. Besides, lots of companies engage in year-end transactions designed to dress up their financial statements."

Required

a.   What financial statement ratios are improved by making the journal entry suggested in the controller's memorandum?

b.   Is the year-end handling of Jason Grand's advance an ethical practice? Explain.

Reporting Operating Income

Courtesy of Cisco Systems

TRANSITORY ITEMS
SURFACE AT CISCO

After a decade of 80% annual growth, Cisco Systems, Inc., ran smack into the tech decline in 2001. When its Chief Executive John Chambers failed to implement new strategic initiatives, his reputation as one of the world's top CEOs plummeted like the networking giant's stock. This was especially so after the company took a massive $2.2 billion inventory write-down, which seemed to undermine Cisco's claims of cutting-edge e-efficiency (BusinessWeek 2003).

Cisco is the worldwide leader in networking for the Internet. Its engineers have been prominent in the development of Internet Protocol (IP)-based networking technologies in the core areas of routing and switching, along with advancing technologies in areas such as IP telephony, wireless LAN, storage networking, and home networking. Its products are seemingly everywhere:

- Cisco routers and switches are a crucial component of all networks, including the Internet.

- Cisco wireless network and IP telephony products allow people to communicate freely and reduce the cost of long distance communications.

- Cisco wireless technology allows employees to connect to corporate networks over a virtual private network (VPN), and it has medical applications such as telerobotics that aid in surgery. Commercial applications include wireless displays on shopping carts, targeted advertisements, and quick checkout.

- Virtual classrooms, powered by Cisco's switching technology and web collaboration software, are part of the distance learning evolution.

John Chambers recently commented to BusinessWeek, "success in the 1990s was often based on how fast could you get to market and how fast could you blow a product through your distribution [channels]." In the wake of the 2001 market decline, Chambers remarked, "Our market changed dramatically in terms of what customers expected, we needed to have engineering and manufacturing and professional services and [sales] and customer support working together in a way that wasn't required before."

Cisco, in short, had to restructure its business from the ground up. Such a restructuring would be expensive. In a footnote to its annual report, Cisco described its restructuring program as follows:

Due to macroeconomic and capital spending issues affecting the networking industry, the Company announced a restructuring program to prioritize its initiatives around high-growth areas of its business, focus on profit contribution, reduce expenses, and improve efficiency. This restructuring program includes a worldwide workforce reduction, consolidation of excess facilities, and restructuring of certain business functions.

(Continued on next page)   **279**

(Continued from previous page)

Cisco's restructuring program translated into the following cost implications (10-K report):

■ *Workforce reduction.* Elimination of about 6,000 jobs, yielding severance payments and fringe benefits.

■ *Facilities consolidation.* Closure of corporate and sales offices and operational centers, yielding lease termination (buyout) costs, losses on disposal of properties and equipment, and vendor payments to terminate supply agreements.

■ *Impairment of goodwill and other purchased intangible assets.* These costs reflect the amounts by which asset book values exceed their market values.

■ *Inventory write-down.* These costs reflect the amounts by which inventory book values exceed their market values as well as the costs of honoring existing purchase commitments.

Many of the costs comprising Cisco's restructuring program involve considerable estimation. For example, Cisco had to identify the employees to terminate, all 6,000 of them. It had to then separate those that would be retiring and not be replaced, from those that might be induced to accept early retirement packages, from those that would be terminated outright. Further, it had to estimate the severance costs for each. Cisco also had to estimate asset market values and the cost of lease buyouts. Write-down of goodwill and other intangible assets required that it estimate the cash flows to be realized from each investment. Finally, the inventory write-down required that it estimate market values for a substantial amount of unusable inventory.

As this chapter explains, companies must report the expected restructuring costs when they are estimated, *not* when they are subsequently paid. Accordingly, Cisco reported a special charge of $1,170 million as described in the following table from its 2001 restructuring footnote:

	Total Charge	Noncash Charges	Cash Payments	Restructuring Liabilities at July 28, 2001
Workforce reduction	$ 397	$ (71)	$(265)	$ 61
Consolidation of excess facilities and other charges	484	(141)	(18)	325
Impairment of goodwill and purchased intangible assets	289	(289)	—	—
Totals	$1,170	$(501)	$(283)	$386

Beyond this $1,170 million charge, Cisco took another charge of $2,250 million. Cisco's total special charges of $3.4 billion contributed to its 2001 net loss of $1 billion.

Cisco's stock had reached a per share high of just over $80 prior to the announcement of its restructuring program. Within three months of that announcement, its stock had declined to $50 per share. By the first anniversary of the announcement, Cisco's stock had plummeted to under $20, one-fourth of its peak value. As the following chart indicates, despite generating nearly $5.5 billion of net income in the two years since its restructuring plan went into effect, the market has yet to embrace Cisco's stock

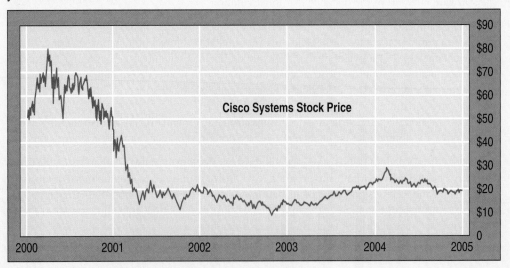

Cisco Systems Stock Price

Cisco's restructuring costs fall into a general class of income statement items called *transitory items*. Transitory items result from events that are unlikely to recur. This chapter describes transitory items, together with other items related to company operating activities. Many of these items reflect important events with enormous dollar amounts.

What does this mean for Cisco? Well, as Chambers noted to *BusinessWeek,* "Jack Welch [former General Electric CEO] said it best. He said, 'John, you'll never have a great company until you go through the really tough times. What builds a company is not just how you handle the successes, but it's the way you handle the real challenges.'" The materials in this chapter provide give you insights into how we might better assess the likelihood of such success.

Sources: *Cisco Systems, Inc.,* 2005, 2004, 2003 and 2001 10-K Reports; *The Wall Street Journal,* February 7, 2005; *BusinessWeek,* November/December 2003.

INTRODUCTION

The income statement is the primary source of information about recent company performance. This information is used to predict future performance for investment purposes and to assess the credit worthiness of a company. The income statement is also used to evaluate the quality of management.

This chapter describes the information reported in the income statement and its analysis implications. The central questions that the income statement attempts to answer are

- How profitable is the company? and
- Will the current profitability level persist?

To answer these questions, it is helpful to partition income producing activities along two dimensions. As in chapter 5, we separate income generated by operating activities from income (or expenses) caused by other, nonoperating activities. We also distinguish recurring (or persistent) sources of income from those sources that are nonrecurring (or transitory).

Operating activities refer to the primary transactions and events of a company. These include the purchase of goods from suppliers, the conversion of goods into finished products, the promotion and distribution of goods, the sale of goods to customers, and post-sale customer support. Operating activities are reported in the income statement under items such as sales, cost of goods sold, and selling, general, and administrative expenses. They represent a company's primary activities, and they must be executed successfully for a company to remain consistently profitable.

Nonoperating activities relate to the financial (borrowing) and securities investment activities of a company. These activities are typically reported in the income statement under items such as interest revenues and expenses, dividend revenues, and gains and losses on sales of securities. Distinguishing income components by operating versus nonoperating is an important part of effective financial statement analysis because operating activities drive company performance. It is of interest, for example, to know whether company profitability results from operating activities, or whether poor performing operating activities are being masked by income from nonoperating activities.

It is also useful to separate income statement components into core versus transitory activities. **Core (or persistent) components** of income are those that are most likely to persist and are, therefore, the most relevant for projecting future financial performance. **Transitory components** of income are those that are not recurring. Presumably, projections of future financial performance are improved if we can identify and exclude transitory components from those projections.

Proper identification of core and transitory components is motivated by valuation objectives. Core components, because they are relatively long-lasting, carry a greater weight in the valuation of securities. For instance, changes in the level of core income per share commonly impact stock price by a factor of 10 or more, while transitory income components normally affect stock price dollar-for-dollar. Because valuation of a company's stock is based on expectations of future company performance, core operating components carry more weight than transitory nonoperating sources of income.

Exhibit 7.1 shows the income statements of Adler Corporation for 2006, 2005, and 2004. To the left of each item we insert its identification as either "core-operating," "core-nonoperating," or "transitory." Note that the items labeled "transitory" do not appear in the income statement in every year. (It is also useful to separate transitory items into operating and nonoperating, which requires a close examination of the footnotes.)

Specifically, sales, cost of goods sold, and most selling, general, and administrative expenses are categorized as both operating and core activities. On the other hand, operating activities such as sales and write-downs of operating assets, and company restructurings are unlikely to recur and, therefore, are transitory. Similarly, investment related income from dividends and interest is non-operating but recurring, hence its designation as a core activities. Gains and losses on debt retirements and sales of investments are also nonoperating, but are transitory.

This chapter is divided into three main sections. The first section focuses on reporting core operating components of income, including discussion of revenue and expense recognition, and a discussion of income tax expense reporting. The second section focuses on the transitory components of income, including items reported in the income statement after income from continuing operations. The third section examines the practice of earnings management.

EXHIBIT 7.1	Distinguishing Core-operating, Core-nonoperating, and Transitory Components of the Income Statement

ADLER CORPORATION
Income Statements ($ millions)

Year ended December 31	2006	2005	2004
Sales revenue	$22,900	$19,700	$15,200
Cost of goods sold	10,200	9,600	6,900
Gross profit	12,700	10,100	8,300
Operating expenses			
Sales and marketing	3,100	2,220	1,840
General and administrative	960	680	430
Research and development	1,210	970	650
Total operating expenses	5,270	3,870	2,920
Operating income	7,430	6,230	5,380
Other income and expenses			
Gain on sale of land	—	290	—
Dividend income	210	190	140
Interest expense	(1,100)	(840)	(730)
Total other income and expenses	(890)	(360)	(590)
Income before income taxes	6,540	5,870	4,790
Provision for income taxes	2,610	2,390	1,880
Income from continuing operations	3,930	3,480	1,090
Loss from discontinued operations	—	—	(1,200)
Extraordinary gain	300	—	—
Net income (loss)	$ 4,230	$ 3,480	$ (110)

Labels at left of table: Core-operating (Sales and marketing through Operating income), Transitory (Gain on sale of land), Core-nonoperating (Dividend income, Interest expense), Core-operating (Provision for income taxes), Transitory (Loss from discontinued operations, Extraordinary gain).

BUSINESS INSIGHT

Ratio Equilibrium Each industry tends to evolve and reach an equilibrium level for its operating activities, which depend on its core operations. For example, some industries require a high level of selling, general and administrative (SG&A) expenses, perhaps due to high advertising demands, high level of employee skills required, or necessary research and development (R&D) to remain competitive. Review the following table of selected operating margins for companies in various industries. (Gross profit divided by sales is GPM; selling, general and administrative expenses divided by sales is SGAM; research and development divided by sales is R&DM; and net income divided by sales is NPM.)

	GPM	SGAM	R&DM	NPM
Cisco Systems	76.5%	41.9%	16.6%	19.0%
Intel Corporation	68.7	31.9	15.1	11.6
Pfizer, Inc.	90.5	49.5	16.0	28.4
Procter & Gamble	53.7	30.0	3.8	12.0
Wal-Mart Stores	23.1	16.7	0.0	3.3

Cisco, Intel, Pfizer, and Proctor & Gamble report high gross profit margins (GPM). This does not necessarily suggest they are better managed than Wal-Mart. Instead, their industries are structured to require higher levels of gross profit to cover other expenses (such as SG&A, R&D, and advertising) necessary for the industry to survive. Wal-Mart, on the other hand, is in a "penny business." Since it sells undifferentiated consumer products, its competitive advantage must lie in cost control. Wal-Mart reports the lowest ratios of any of the companies listed.

OPERATING INCOME COMPONENTS

This section examines the core operating components of income. We review revenue recognition criteria and illustrate revenue recognition methods that are used to account for bundled sales transactions, long-term contracts, and installment sales. We then discuss a number of revenue recognition scenarios that warrant special scrutiny. Finally, we turn to expense recognition and highlight accounting for income tax expense.

Revenue Recognition

Revenue recognition refers to the timing and amount of revenue reported by the company. The decision of when to recognize revenue depends on relatively simple criteria. Despite their simplicity, most SEC enforcement actions against companies for inaccurate, and sometimes fraudulent, financial reporting are for improper (usually premature) revenue recognition. Determining whether the criteria for revenue recognition are met is often subjective and subject to abuse. This is especially so for companies facing market pressures to meet income targets.

> **LO1** Describe the criteria for determining when revenue is recognized.

GAAP dictates two **revenue recognition criteria** that must be met for revenue to be recognized (and reported) on the income statement. Revenue must be (1) **realized or realizable**, and (2) **earned**. *Realized or realizable* means that the company's net assets increase. That is, it receives an asset or satisfies a liability as a result of a transaction or event. *Earned* means that the seller has executed its duties under the terms of the sales agreement and that the title has passed to the buyer, as long as no right of return or other contingencies exist.

> NOTE
> International financial reporting standards (IRRS) for revenue recognition are similar to U.S. GAAP.

The SEC is so concerned about aggressive (premature) revenue recognition that it recently issued *Staff Accounting Bulletin (SAB) 101* to address this issue. *SAB 101* states that revenue is earned and realized, or realizable, when all of the following criteria have been met: (1) there is persuasive evidence that a sales agreement exists; (2) delivery has occurred or services have been rendered; (3) the seller's price is fixed or determinable; and (4) collectibility is reasonably assured.

Many companies recognize revenues when the product or service is delivered to the customer. For these companies, delivery occurs at the same time, or shortly after, the sale takes place. Complications arise if there is uncertainty about collectibility or when the sale is contingent on product performance, product approval, or similar contingencies. In some industries, it is standard practice to allow customers to return the product within a specified period of time. When the customer retains a **right of return,** it is sometimes inappropriate to recognize revenue at the time of delivery. If the return period is long or the amount of returns is difficult to estimate, revenues should not be recognized until the return period expires. Similarly, products sold on consignment cannot be recorded as sales revenue until sold by the consignee.

Bundled Sales

Another revenue recognition complication arises when two or more products or services are sold under the same sales agreement for one lump-sum price. **Bundled sales** such as this are commonplace in the software industry, where developers sell software, training, maintenance, and customer support in one transaction. In these circumstances, GAAP requires that the sales price be allocated among the various elements of the sale in proportion to their fair value. Revenue allocated to the elements that have not been delivered (such as maintenance and customer support) must be deferred and recognized as the service is rendered in future periods.

To illustrate a bundled sales transaction, assume that Cisco Systems sells its virtual classroom product to a university for a price of $800,000. The product includes three elements: hardware, software licenses, and customer support for the duration of the five-year license agreement. The $800,000 in revenue would be allocated as shown in Exhibit 7.2.

EXHIBIT 7.2	Allocation of Sales Revenue in a Bundled Sale		
Product element	**Price if sold separately**	**Percentage of total price**	**Revenue allocated to element**
Hardware	$ 300,000	$300,000 / $1,000,000 = 30%	$800,000 × 30% = $240,000
Software	500,000	$500,000 / $1,000,000 = 50%	$800,000 × 50% = 400,000
Customer support	200,000	$200,000 / $1,000,000 = 20%	$800,000 × 20% = 160,000
Totals	$1,000,000	100%	$800,000

Cisco would record $240,000 in revenue when the hardware is delivered and $400,000 in revenue when the software is delivered. The $160,000 in customer support revenue would be recognized ratably over five years ($32,000 each year).

BUSINESS INSIGHT

Cisco's Revenue Recognition   Following is an excerpt from Cisco Systems' policies on revenue recognition as reported in footnotes to its recent annual report.

We recognize product revenue when persuasive evidence of an arrangement exists, delivery has occurred, the fee is fixed or determinable, and collectibility is reasonably assured. In instances where final acceptance of the product, system, or solution is specified by the customer, revenue is deferred until all acceptance criteria have been met . . . Service revenue is generally deferred and, in most cases, recognized ratably over the period during which the services are to be performed . . . Contracts and customer purchase orders are generally used to determine the existence of an arrangement. Shipping documents and customer acceptance, when applicable, are used to verify delivery . . . When a sale involves multiple elements, such as sales of products that include services, the entire fee from the arrangement is allocated to each respective element based on its relative fair value and recognized when revenue recognition criteria for each element are met.

Cisco's criteria for revenue recognition mirror SEC guidance. The key components are that revenue is *earned* and that proceeds are *realized or realizable*. For Cisco, earned means that delivery to and acceptance by the customer occurs, or that Cisco is available to perform service commitments, even if not called upon.

Revenue Recognition for Long-term Contracts

LO2 Illustrate revenue and expense recognition for long-term contracts.

Challenges arise in determining revenue recognition for companies with long-term sales contracts (spanning more than one year) such as construction companies and defense contractors. For these companies, revenue is often recognized using the **percentage-of-completion method**, which recognizes revenue by determining the costs incurred under the contract relative to its total expected costs.

Percentage-of-Completion Method

To illustrate this method, assume that Built-Rite Construction signs a $10 million contract to construct a building. The company estimates $7.5 million in construction costs, yielding an expected gross profit of $2.5 million. Further assume that Built-Rite incurs $4.5 million in construction costs during the first year of construction, and the remaining $3 million in costs during the second year. The amount of revenue and gross profit that Built-Rite would report each year is illustrated in Exhibit 7.3.

EXHIBIT 7.3	Revenue Recognition Using the Percentage-of-Completion Method			
Year	Percentage completed	Revenue recognized	Expense recognized	Gross profit
1	$4,500,000 / $7,500,000 = 60%	$10,000,000 × 60% = $ 6,000,000	$4,500,000	$1,500,000
2	$3,000,000 / $7,500,000 = 40%	$10,000,000 × 40% = $ 4,000,000	$3,000,000	$1,000,000
Totals	100%	$10,000,000	$7,500,000	$2,500,000

Using the percentage-of-completion method, Built-Rite would report $1.5 million in gross profit from this project in the first year and $1.0 million in the second year.

Revenue recognition policies for these types of contracts are disclosed in a manner typical to the following from the 2004 10-K report footnotes of **Raytheon Company**:

> Sales under long-term government contracts are recorded under the percentage of completion method. Incurred costs and estimated gross margins are recorded as sales as work is performed based on the percentage that incurred costs bear to estimated total costs utilizing the Company's estimates of costs and contract value . . . Since many contracts extend over a long period of time, revisions in cost and contract value estimates during the progress of work have the effect of adjusting earnings applicable to performance in prior periods in the current period.

The percentage-of-completion method of revenue recognition requires an estimate of total costs. This estimate is made at the beginning of the contract and is typically the one used to initially bid the contract. However, estimates are inherently inaccurate. If the estimate changes during the construction period, the percentage-of-completion is computed as the total costs incurred to date divided by the *current* estimate of total anticipated costs (costs incurred to date plus total estimated costs to complete).

If total construction costs are underestimated to date, the percentage-of-completion is overestimated (the denominator is too low) and too much revenue and gross profit are recognized to date. The estimation process inherent in this method has the potential for inaccurate or, even, improper revenue recognition. Estimates of remaining costs to complete projects are also difficult to verify for auditors. This uncertainty adds additional risk to financial statement analysis.

To justify use of the percentage-of-completion method, a company must have a signed contract with the customer that specifies a fixed or determinable price. In addition, collection must be reasonably assured. When a long-term project fails to meet these criteria, all revenue should be deferred until the contract is complete. This is known as the **completed contract method**. Exhibit 7.4 provides a comparison the gross profit calculations using each of these two accounting methods for the Built-Rite Construction contract described earlier.

EXHIBIT 7.4	Comparison of the Percentage-of-Completion and Completed Contract Methods				
Percentage-of-Completion Method			Completed Contract Method		
	Year 1	Year 2		Year 1	Year 2
Revenues	$6,000,000	$4,000,000	Revenues	$0	$10,000,000
Expenses	4,500,000	3,000,000	Expenses	0	7,500,000
Gross profit	$1,500,000	$1,000,000	Gross profit	$0	$ 2,500,000

The total revenue and gross profit are the same under either revenue recognition method. Likewise, there is no difference in the costs incurred to construct the building. The only difference between the percentage-of-completion method and the completed contract method is *when* the revenue and gross profit are reported in the income statement.

REMEMBER . . .
GAAP requires use of the percentage-of-completion method whenever management can reasonably estimate revenues and expenses.

NOTE
Application of percentage-of-completion enhances earnings quality relative to the complete contract method. However, poor or biased estimates for applying percentage-of-completion can reduce or reverse the improvement in earnings quality.

Installment Method

Although rare, there are circumstances where collectibility cannot be reasonably assured, even though all other revenue recognition criteria are met. In these situations, GAAP requires that revenue recognition must be delayed until cash is collected. The **installment method** recognizes revenue when cash is collected, and records costs and gross profit in proportion to the amount of cash collected.

To illustrate, assume that inventory costing $65,000 is sold on credit for $100,000, yielding an expected gross profit of $35,000. Further, assume that the customer makes a $20,000 cash payment in the first year, a $50,000 cash payment in the second year, and the remaining $30,000 cash is paid in year three. The gross profit percentage is 35% ($35,000 / $100,000). The revenue, expense, and gross profit recognized each year are shown in Exhibit 7.5.

EXHIBIT 7.5	Revenue Recognition Using the Installment Method		
Year	Revenue recognized (cash collected)	Expense recognized	Gross profit (cash collected × 35%)
1	$ 20,000	$13,000	20,000 × 35% = $ 7,000
2	50,000	32,500	50,000 × 35% = 17,500
3	30,000	19,500	30,000 × 35% = 10,500
Totals	$100,000	$65,000	$35,000

In the installment method, revenue is not recorded until it has been collected in cash. Expenses and gross profit are then matched in proportion to the revenues. In the event that the customer defaults on the sales contract, the product would be repossessed and returned to inventory. A loss would be recorded if the value of the repossessed inventory is less than the outstanding (unpaid) receivable.

BUSINESS INSIGHT

Disney's Revenue Recognition The Walt Disney Company uses a method similar to the installment method to determine the amount of production cost to match against film and television revenues. Following is an excerpt from its 10-K.

Film and television production and participation costs are expensed based on the ratio of the current period's gross revenues to estimated remaining total gross revenues from all sources on an individual production basis. Television network series costs and multi-year sports rights are charged to expense based on the ratio of the current period's gross revenues to estimated remaining total gross revenues from such programs or straight-line, as appropriate.

Production costs are recorded on the balance sheet as inventory when paid. As film and television revenues are recognized, the company recognizes a portion of production costs to match against revenues in computing income. The costs recognized are equal to the proportion of total revenues recognized in the period to the total expected revenues to be recognized over the life of the film or television show. Thus, estimates of both costs and income depend on the quality of its revenue estimates, an imprecise estimate.

Potential Abuses of Revenue Recognition

This section presents five situations that illustrate questionable or improper revenue recognition practices. Each of these cases involves inherent risks for certain industries and companies that are subject to similar transactions and events. The potential abuses range in severity from misleading to fraudulent. Financial statement users must be cognizant of these risks when analyzing and interpreting financial performance. Be forewarned, however, that these examples do not represent an exhaustive list of creative revenue recognition tactics.

- *Case 1: Pending execution of sales agreements.* Companies seeking to boost current period revenues have resorted to sales recognition upon delivery of product to customers when the requisite sales approval has yet to be received by period-end, although it is expected shortly thereafter. The SEC's position is that if the company's practice is to obtain sales authorization, revenue is not recognized until such approval is obtained, even though product delivery is made and approval by the customer is anticipated.

■ *Case 2: Gross versus net revenues.* Some companies use their distribution network to act as agents for others, selling other companies' goods at a slight markup for a sales "commission." There are increasing reports of companies that inflate revenues by reporting such transactions on a gross basis (reporting both sales and cost of goods sold) instead of reporting only the commission (sales less cost of goods sold) earned. The incentives for such reporting are high for some dot.com companies and start-ups that believe the market prices of their stocks are based on revenue growth and not profitability. Reporting revenues at gross rather than net would have enormous impact on valuations of those companies. The SEC prescribes that such sales be reported on a net basis.

■ *Case 3: Barter transactions.* Some barter transactions are concocted to create the illusion of revenue. Examples include the advertising swaps engaged in by some dot.com companies, and the excess capacity swaps of fiber optic communications businesses. An example of the latter is a company selling excess capacity in one region to a competitor and, simultaneously, purchasing excess capacity from that competitor in another region. Typically, these situations are equal exchanges of similar products not providing income to either party. Further, these examples do not represent a culmination of the normal earning process (for example, fiber optic networks are created to sell communications services to end users, not to swap capacity with others).

■ *Case 4: Nonrefundable fees.* Sellers sometimes receive fees that are nonrefundable to the customer. An example is a health club fee or a cellular phone activation fee. Some sellers wish to record these cash receipts as revenue to boost current sales and income. Although cash is received and nonrefundable, revenue is not recognized until the product is delivered or service performed. Until that time, the cash received is reported as an asset on the balance sheet and a liability (deferred revenue) is reported as an obligation to deliver product or perform service. Once the obligation is settled, the liability is removed and revenue is reported.

■ *Case 5: Channel stuffing.* Some sellers use their market power over customers to induce (or even require) them to purchase more goods than necessary to satisfy customer demand, thus increasing period-end sales and incomes of sellers. This practice is called channel stuffing. If no side agreements exist for product returns, the practice is acceptable per GAAP, but is discouraged. However, when return rights exist, such revenue should not be recognized.

In sum, revenue can only be recognized when it is earned and when it is realized or realizable. These criteria demand that the seller has performed its obligations (no contingencies exist) and the buyer is an independent party with the financial capacity to cover amounts owed.

YOU MAKE THE CALL

You are the Controller   While evaluating the performance of your sales staff, you notice that one of the sales people consistently meets his quarterly sales quotas but never surpasses his goals by very much. You also discover that his customers often return an unusually large amount of product at the beginning of each quarter. What might be happening here? How would you investigate for potential abuse? [Answer, p. 306]

Expense Recognition

In addition to determining when to recognize revenues, to properly measure and report a company's performance we must also decide when to recognize expenses. The **matching principle** was introduced in Chapter 2 and discussed in Appendix 3A. The matching principle requires that expenses should be recognized in the same period that the associated revenue is recognized. Expense recognition can be generally divided into the following three approaches.

■ **Direct association**. Any cost that can be *directly* associated with a specific source of revenue should be recognized at the same time that the related revenue is recognized. An example of direct association is matching cost of goods sold with sales revenue. The cost of acquiring or producing inventory is recorded in the inventory asset account until the item is sold; at that point, the cost is transferred to expenses. Any costs that will be incurred in the future, but can be directly associated with current revenues, should also be estimated and matched against those revenues. An example of such an expense is expected warranty costs.

■ **Immediate recognition**. Many expenses are necessary for generating revenues and income but cannot be directly linked with specific revenues. These costs can be associated with all of the revenues of an accounting period, but not with any specific sales transaction that occurred during that period. Examples include most administrative and marketing costs, as well as financing costs such as interest expense. Because these costs are more closely associated with a period of time than with specific revenues, these costs are recognized as expenses in the period when the costs are incurred. Other expense items, such as research and development (R&D) expense, are recognized immediately because of GAAP requirements.

■ **Systematic allocation**. Costs that benefit more than one accounting period and cannot be associated with specific revenues or assigned to a specific period must be allocated across all of the periods benefited. The most common example is depreciation expense. When an asset is purchased, it is capitalized (recorded in an asset account) and then converted into an expense over the duration of its useful life according to a depreciation formula or schedule established by management.

BUSINESS INSIGHT

Cisco R&D Cisco spends about $3.1 billion annually for R&D compared with its revenues of $18.8 billion, or about 16.5%. This reflects a high percent of revenues devoted to R&D in comparison with nontechnology companies, but typifies companies that compete in the high-tech arena. Following is the R&D-expense-to-sales ratio for Cisco and some of its competitors.

	2003	2002	2001
Cisco Systems	16.5%	18.5%	20.1%
Nortel Networks	20.2	18.7	17.0
Juniper Networks	25.3	44.5	24.8
3Com	12.1	19.2	21.1

Income Tax Expense

LO3 Explain how income taxes are reported in financial statements..

Companies maintain two sets of books, one for reporting to their shareholders and another for reporting to tax authorities. This practice is neither illegal nor unethical. In fact, it is necessary. Financial accounting is concerned with presenting information in the financial statements that is useful to investors and creditors. These statements are prepared in accordance with GAAP. Tax returns, on the other hand, are prepared to report to tax authorities such as the Internal Revenue Service (IRS) and must comply with whatever tax regulations are established by these agencies. Because tax authorities have different objectives from shareholders, it is not surprising that income tax regulations differ from GAAP.

The difference between GAAP and tax regulations means that income before income taxes, as presented in the income statement, will differ from taxable income in the tax return. Taxable income is used to calculate the company's tax obligation for that period. Usually this involves multiplying taxable income by the tax rate. However, in the income statement prepared for shareholders, the calculation of income tax expense is less straightforward.

NOTE
Book income refers to income before income taxes, as reported in financial statements. Taxable income refers to income reported in the income tax return.

To illustrate the challenge of measuring tax expense, refer to the Built-Rite Construction example presented earlier. Assume for this example that Built-Rite uses the percentage-of-completion method to recognize revenue and gross profit in the income statement, but uses the completed contract method for tax reporting. Also assume a 35% tax rate. The company's tax returns for years 1 and 2 would show the following:

Built-Rite Construction IRS Tax Returns		
	Year 1	**Year 2**
Revenues	$0	$10,000,000
Expenses	0	7,500,000
Gross profit (taxable income)	$0	$ 2,500,000
Income tax obligation (35%)	$0	$ 875,000

Based on these tax returns, Built-Rite would pay no taxes in year 1 and $875,000 in year 2. Now let's look at the following Built-Rite income statement as reported to shareholders.

Built-Rite Construction Income statements		
	Year 1	**Year 2**
Revenues	$6,000,000	$4,000,000
Expenses	4,500,000	3,000,000
Gross profit (income before income taxes)	$1,500,000	$1,000,000
Provision for income taxes	???	???
Net income	???	???

In year 1, income before income taxes ($1,500,000) is higher than taxable income ($0). In year 2, the difference *reverses*. Income before income taxes ($1,000,000) is lower than taxable income ($2,500,000). Because this difference between the two statements reverses, the difference is called a **temporary difference**. Most differences between financial and tax reporting are temporary differences. Differences which do not reverse are called **permanent differences**.

How much should Built-Rite report as a provision for income taxes (income tax expense) in year 1? In year 2? One possible answer is to expense the same amount that is calculated on the tax return. It is easy to see how this approach can distort net income. In the Built-Rite example, all of the tax expense would be reported in year 2, even though most of the pretax income is reported in year 1.

A more reasonable approach (and the one that is acceptable for GAAP) is to recognize tax expense based on the *temporary difference* between the tax return and the income statement. Following this approach, the income statements appear as follows.

Built-Rite Construction Income statements		
	Year 1	**Year 2**
Revenues	$6,000,000	$4,000,000
Expenses	4,500,000	3,000,000
Gross profit (income before income taxes)	$1,500,000	$1,000,000
Provision for income taxes	525,000	350,000
Net income	$ 975,000	$ 650,000

The tax expense of $525,000 ($1,500,000 x 35%) that is recognized in year 1 will be paid in cash in year 2 when the temporary difference reverses. As a consequence, the entry to record income tax expense in year 1 appears as follows using the financial statement effect template and in journal entry form.

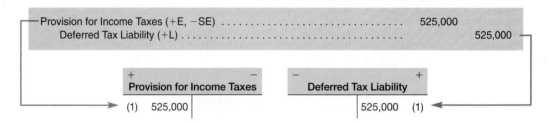

Transaction	Balance Sheet					Income Statement		
	Cash Asset +	Noncash Assets =	Liabil- ities +	Contrib. Capital +	Retained Earnings	Revenues −	Expenses =	Net Income
(1) Recording income tax expense		=	+525,000 Deferred Tax Liability		−525,000 Retained Earnings		−525,000 Provision for Income Taxes	= −525,000

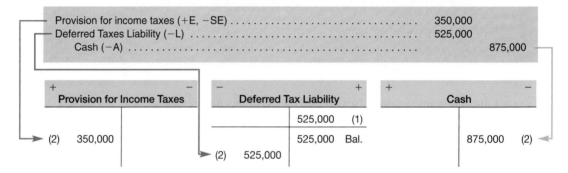

Provision for Income Taxes (+E, −SE) 525,000
   Deferred Tax Liability (+L)   525,000

+ Provision for Income Taxes −	− Deferred Tax Liability +
(1) 525,000	525,000 (1)

The account called **Deferred Tax Liability** (also called *Deferred Taxes*) is reported on the balance sheet as a liability. When reported as a liability, deferred taxes represent taxes to be paid in the future when taxable income is higher than financial reporting income. In year 2, when the temporary difference reverses, the entry to record tax expense and tax payments would be:

Provision for income taxes (+E, −SE) 350,000
Deferred Taxes Liability (−L) 525,000
   Cash (−A)   875,000

+ Provision for Income Taxes −	− Deferred Tax Liability +	+ Cash −
(2) 350,000	525,000 (1)	875,000 (2)
	525,000 Bal.	
	(2) 525,000	

A *Deferred Tax Liability* arises when tax reporting income is less than financial reporting income. When this occurs, the tax expense reported on the income statement is greater than the current tax due from the tax return. This implies that the taxes will be paid when the temporary differences reverse. In addition to differences in revenue recognition for long-term contracts, deferred tax liabilities are also caused by the use of different depreciation methods for financial reporting and tax reporting.

A **Deferred Tax Asset** arises when tax reporting income is higher than financial reporting income. In this situation, the deferred tax asset expires when the temporary difference reverses. Examples of temporary differences that lead to deferred tax assets include costs of uncollectible accounts receivable, warranty costs, and some pension expenses. For example, estimated warranty costs reduce reported pretax income and thereby tax expense on the income statement. These costs, however, cannot be deducted on the company's tax return until they are paid in cash. Thus, the recognized tax expense is less then the tax liability due currently (the debit is less than the credit) creating a deferred tax asset.[1]

To see how income tax expense is disclosed, Cisco Systems's tax footnote to its income statement is shown in Exhibit 7.6. Cisco's $1,435 million tax expense reported in its income statement consists of the following two components (organized by federal, state, and foreign taxing authorities):

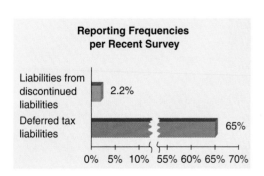

Reporting Frequencies per Recent Survey

Liabilities from discontinued liabilities   2.2%

Deferred tax liabilities   65%

0% 5% 10% 55% 60% 65% 70%

---

[1] When a company has both deferred tax assets and deferred tax liabilities, the assets and liabilities are first separated into current and long-term amounts. The current deferred tax assets and current deferred tax liabilities are then reported *net* in the balance sheet under current assets or current liabilities, whichever is greater. Long-term amounts are treated similarly. It is not uncommon, therefore to see a company report deferred tax assets under current assets in the balance sheet, while reporting deferred tax liabilities under long-term liabilities.

1. *Current tax expense.* Amount currently payable (in cash) to tax authorities.
2. *Deferred tax expense.* Effect on tax expense from changes in deferred tax liabilities and deferred tax assets.

EXHIBIT 7.6	Income Tax Expense Footnote for Cisco
Year Ended ($ millions)	**July 26, 2002**
Federal	
Current	$1,041
Deferred	6
	1,047
State	
Current	138
Deferred	2
	140
Foreign	
Current	270
Deferred	(22)
	248
Total	$1,435

Companies must disclose the components of deferred tax liabilities and assets. Cisco's deferred tax footnote to its balance sheet (shown in Exhibit 7.7) reports deferred tax assets of $3,826 million. Many of these deferred tax assets relate to expenses that are included in financial reporting income, but are not yet deductible for tax reporting until paid (such as allowance for doubtful accounts, severance accruals in restructuring expenses, inventory allowances, investment provisions, and in-process R&D expenses). These deferred tax assets represent future reductions of the company's tax liability and are, therefore, classified as assets. Deferred tax liabilities arise when expenses are greater for tax purposes than for financial reporting purposes, such as when companies use accelerated depreciation for tax purposes and straight-line for financial reporting.

EXHIBIT 7.7	Deferred Taxes Footnote for Cisco
($ millions)	**July 26, 2003**
Assets	
Allowance for doubtful accounts and returns	$ 228
Sales-type and direct-financing leases	297
Loan reserves	123
Inventory allowances and capitalization	247
Investment provisions	654
In-process R&D, goodwill, and purchased intangible assets	608
Deferred revenue	899
Credits and net operating loss carryforwards	261
Other	509
Total deferred tax assets	3,826
Liabilities	
Purchased intangible assets	(233)
Unrealized gains on investments	(142)
Total deferred tax liabilities	(375)
Total	$3,451

The procedure for computing income tax expense is to first calculate the tax obligation (from the company's tax return), then compute any changes in deferred tax liabilities or assets. From these two amounts, we can then calculate tax expense as follows.

Tax Expense = Tax Obligation − Changes in Deferred Tax Assets and Liabilities

Analysis of deferred taxes can yield useful insights. An increase in deferred tax liabilities indicates that a company is reporting higher profits in its income statement than in its tax return. The difference between reported corporate profits and taxable income increased substantially in the late 1990s, just prior to the stock market decline. The following quote from CFO Magazine (November 2002) implies that such differences should be carefully monitored.

> Fueling the sense that something [was] amiss [was] the growing gap between the two sets of numbers. In 1992, there was no significant difference between pretax book income and taxable net income . . . By 1996, according to IRS data, a $92.5 billion gap had appeared. By 1998 [prior to the market decline], the gap was $159 billion—a fourth of the total taxable income reported . . . If people had seen numbers showing very significant differences between book numbers for trading and tax numbers, they would have wondered if those [income] numbers were completely real.

Although an increase in deferred tax liabilities can legitimately result, we must be aware of the possibility that such differences can be the result of improper revenue recognition or other questionable accounting practices.

Other Expenses in Income

Core operating income includes sales, cost of goods sold, and the usual selling, general, and administrative expenses. It also includes income taxes. In addition to these items, there are several other expense items that would be classified as part of core operating income. These expenses include:

- Employee stock option expenses (whether reported in the income statement or in the notes)
- Service cost portion of pension expense
- Research and development expenses
- Gains and losses deriving from foreign currency translation and commodity hedges

In contrast, *core nonoperating* components include:

- Interest revenue and expense
- Dividend income
- Pension expenses, excluding service costs
- Unrealized gains and losses on financial investments classified as trading securities

Stock options, pensions, research and development, and financial investments are covered in later chapters. The appendix to this chapter discusses foreign currency translation effects on income.

MID-CHAPTER REVIEW

Following are two footnotes from the 2005 annual report of Adler Corporation.

Note 2: Revenue Recognition
Revenue from long-term government contracts is recognized using the percentage of completion method of accounting. Production costs are capitalized by project and are expensed based on the ratio of current period costs to estimated total contract costs. Revenue from contracts with private organizations is recognized using the completed contract method.

Note 9: Income Taxes
The provision for income taxes includes the following

($ thousands)	2005
Current provision	
Domestic	$1,342
Foreign	146
Deferred provision (credit)	
Domestic	960
Foreign	(58)
Total	$2,390

Required
1. Speculate as to possible reasons why Adler Corporation uses different revenue recognition policies for long-term government contracts and for contracts with private organizations.
2. (a) What is the amount of income tax expense reported on its income statement? (b) How much of its income tax expense is payable in cash? (c) Assuming that its deferred tax liability increased; identify an example that could account for such a change.
3. Prepare the entry, using both the financial statement effects template and in journal entry form, to record its income tax expense for 2005.

Solution
1. The terms of the contract are likely different for government contracts and contracts with private organizations. To justify the use of the percentage-of-completion method, there must be a contract that specifies a fixed or determinable price. The contracts for private organizations might have more ambiguity as far as the pricing is concerned. Alternatively, Adler most likely has experience that would indicate that government contracts are less likely to be cancelled.
2. (a) $2,390,000; (b) $1,488,000, computed as $1,342,000 in domestic taxes plus $146,000 in foreign taxes; (c) Deferred tax liabilities increase when taxable income is less than GAAP income. This situation arises when plant assets are being depreciated faster for tax purposes than in the financial statements, or when revenue is recognized later in the tax return. In this instance, we could conclude that Adler is reporting revenue on its tax return for government contracts using the completed contract method.
3.

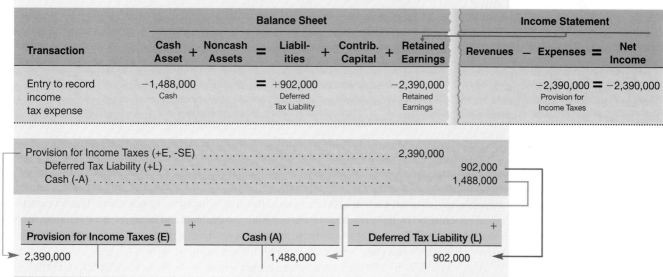

TRANSITORY INCOME COMPONENTS

The prior section focused on core-operating components of income. This section focuses on another aspect of income reporting—that of transitory (nonrecurring) sources of income. Isolating transitory earnings is useful for two reasons. First, to evaluate company performance or management quality, it is helpful to make comparisons of current performance with prior years and with other companies facing similar economic circumstances. It is easier to make these comparisons if we focus on recurring (core) income components. Transitory income components are likely to be specific to one company and one accounting period, making them irrelevant for comparative purposes. Second, estimation of company value involves forecasts of income and cash flows. Such forecasts are better when we can identify any transitory effects in income and cash flows and then eliminate them from projections. Core earnings and cash flows are more *persistent* and, therefore, are more useful in estimating company value.

> **LO4** Identify transitory components of income, and distinguish between transitory and core elements.

Accounting standards attempt to distinguish some transitory income components. Two of the transitory components GAAP identifies are discontinued operations and extraordinary items. These items are reported in the income statement immediately below income from continuing operations (so-called *below the line* items). This section describes these components and considers their analysis implications. We also consider additional transitory components, including gains and losses on asset sales and restructuring costs.

Discontinued Operations

Discontinued operations refer to any separately identifiable business unit that the company sells or intends to sell. The income or loss of the discontinued operations (net of tax), and the after-tax gain or loss on sale of the unit, are reported in the income statement below income from continuing operations. The segregation of discontinued operations means that its revenues and expenses are *not* reported with revenues and expenses from continuing operations.

To illustrate, assume that Cisco's reported results appeared as follows.

	Continuing Operations	Discontinued Operations	Total
Revenues	$10,000	$3,000	$13,000
Expenses	7,000	2,000	9,000
Pretax income	3,000	1,000	4,000
Tax expense (40%)	1,200	400	1,600
Net income	$ 1,800	$ 600	$ 2,400

The reported income statement would then appear with the separate disclosure for discontinued operations (shown in bold, separately net of any related taxes) as follows.

Revenues	$10,000
Expenses	7,000
Pretax income	3,000
Tax expense (40%)	1,200
Income from continuing operations	1,800
Income from discontinued operations, net	**600**
Net income	$ 2,400

> **REMEMBER . . .**
> Income, gains, and losses from discontinued operations are reported separately from other items to alert readers to their transitory nature.

Revenues and expenses reflect those of the continuing operations only, and the (persistent) income from continuing operations is reported net of its related tax expense. Results from the (transitory) discontinued operations are collapsed into one line item and reported separately net of any related taxes. This includes any gain or loss from sale of the discontinued unit's net assets. The net income figure is unchanged by this presentation, but our ability to evaluate and interpret income information is vastly improved. The segregation of discontinued operations is made in the current year and for the two prior year's comparative results reported in the income statement.

Best Buy's 2004 fiscal-year income statement presentation of discontinued operations is in Exhibit 7.8—see boldface numbers. Its income statement reflects the 2004 net loss from its discontinued operations in Musicland up to the point of its sale plus the loss from sale of Musicland's net assets.

EXHIBIT 7.8	Income Statement with Discontinued Operations for Best Buy
($ millions)	**2004**
Revenue	$24,547
Cost of goods sold	18,350
Gross profit	6,197
Selling, general and administrative expenses	4,893
Operating income	1,304
Net interest (expense) income	(8)
Earnings from continuing operations before income tax expense	1,296
Income tax expense	496
Earnings from continuing operations	800
Loss from discontinued operations, net of $17 tax	**(29)**
Loss on disposal of discontinued operations, net of $0 tax	**(66)**
Net earnings	$ 705

Best Buy also separately identifies the assets and liabilities of its discontinued operations on its 2004 fiscal year-end balance sheet in Exhibit 7.9—see the boldface numbers. Because Best Buy's discontinued operations in Musicland were sold during fiscal year 2004, its net assets in Musicland are no longer a component of its fiscal year-end 2004 balance sheet.

EXHIBIT 7.9	Balance Sheet with Discontinued Operations for Best Buy	
($ millions)	February 28, 2004	March 1, 2003
Assets		
Current assets		
Cash and cash equivalents	$2,600	$1,914
Receivables	343	312
Merchandise inventories	2,607	2,077
Other current assets	174	198
Current assets of discontinued operations	—	**397**
Total current assets	5,724	4,898
Property and equipment		
Land and buildings	484	208
Leasehold improvements	861	719
Fixtures and equipment	2,151	2,108
Property under master and capital lease	78	54
	3,574	3,089
Less accumulated depreciation and amortization	1,330	1,027
Net property and equipment	2,244	2,062
Goodwill, net	477	429
Intangible assets	37	33
Other assets	170	115
Noncurrent assets of discontinued operations	—	**157**
Total assets	$8,652	$7,694
Liabilities and Shareholders' Equity		
Current liabilities		
Accounts payable	$2,535	$2,195
Unredeemed gift card liabilities	300	222
Accrued compensation and related expenses	269	174
Accrued liabilities	649	538
Accrued income taxes	380	374
Current portion of long-term debt	368	1
Current liabilities of discontinued operations	—	**320**
Total current liabilities	4,501	3,824
Long-term liabilities	247	287
Long-term debt	482	828
Noncurrent liabilities of discontinued operations	—	**25**
Shareholders' equity		
Common stock, $.10 par value: Authorized—1 billion shares; Issued and outstanding—324,648,000 and 321,966,000 shares, respectively	32	32
Additional paid-in capital	836	778
Retained earnings	2,468	1,893
Accumulated other comprehensive income	86	27
Total shareholders' equity	3,422	2,730
Total liabilities and shareholders' equity	$8,652	$7,694

Extraordinary Items

Extraordinary items refer to transitory events that are both unusual *and* infrequent. Their effects are segregated and reported separately in income statements following income from continuing operations. Management makes the determination of whether an event is unusual and infrequent for reporting purposes. Further, management often has incentives to classify unfavorable items as extraordinary, which means they are reported separately from continuing operation (*below-the-line*). These incentives derive from investors who tend to focus more on items included in income from continuing operations and less on those items not included in continuing operations.

GAAP provides the following guidance in determining whether or not an item is extraordinary:

- *Unusual nature.* The underlying event or transaction must possess a high degree of abnormality and be clearly unrelated to, or only incidentally related to, the ordinary activities of the entity, taking into account the entity's operating environment.

- *Infrequency of occurrence.* The underlying event or transaction must be of a type that would not reasonably be expected to recur in the foreseeable future, taking into account the entity's operating environment.

The following items are generally *excluded* from extraordinary items:

- Write-down or write-off of assets
- Foreign currency gains and losses
- Gains and losses from disposal of specific assets or business segment
- Effects of a strike
- Accrual adjustments related to long-term contracts
- Costs of defense against a takeover
- Costs incurred as a result of the September 11, 2001, events

Extraordinary items are reported separately (net of tax) and below income from continuing operations on the income statement.

Gains and Losses on Asset Sales

Assets are recorded at cost when purchased. Subsequently, most assets are reported at adjusted historical cost (acquisition cost less any depreciation, amortization, or depletion), even if they appreciate in value. An asset is written down from this book (carrying) value only if a permanent decline (impairment) in value occurs. However, when an asset is sold, the company recognizes a gain or loss equal to the difference between the selling price and its book value. This gain or loss is computed as follows:

Gain or Loss on Asset Sale = Asset Sale Proceeds − Asset Book Value

To illustrate, assume that Cisco sells a machine for $10,000 when its book value is $8,000. The book value is computed from its acquisition cost of $12,000 less accumulated depreciation of $4,000. Cisco would report a gain of $2,000 ($10,000 − $8,000). The gain is reported in income from continuing operations (usually included among SG&A expense as an offset to other expense accounts), and it serves to increase reported income. The entry to record this sale, using both the financial statement effects template and in journal form, is as follows. (Accumulated depreciation is a contra asset account, designated XA. Contra assets are introduced in Chapter 3 and accumulated depreciation is covered in detail in Chapter 9.)

	Balance Sheet					Income Statement		
Transaction	Cash Asset	+ Noncash Assets	= Liabil- ities	+ Contrib. Capital	+ Retained Earnings	Revenues	− Expenses	= Net Income
Entry to record asset sale	+10,000 Cash	−12,000 Machine	=		+2,000 Retained Earnings	+2,000 Gain on Asset Sale		= +2,000
		+4,000 Accumulated Depreciation						

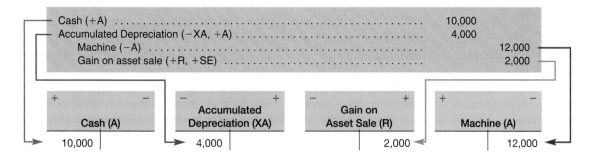

To generalize, all gains and losses from asset sales are reported in income. Further, gains and losses are reported from sales of both short-term and long-term assets. Companies can even sell assets such as accounts receivable to raise cash, which yield reported gains and losses. Companies sometimes sell investments or entire subsidiaries, which also yield reported gains and losses. Each of these gains and losses is computed in the same manner: Asset Sale Proceeds − Asset Book Value.

Even though companies usually report gains and losses from asset sales as part of income from continuing operations, such gains and losses are transitory. Sales of depreciated operating assets are routine and are expected to occur in almost any accounting period. However, nonroutine sales, such as the sale of a large operating facility or an entire subsidiary are not a recurring part of operations. Moreover, the gains and losses from these asset sales, whether routine or nonroutine, are nonrecurring and cannot be easily predicted. Consequently, our analysis should exclude them from computation of core (persistent) income.

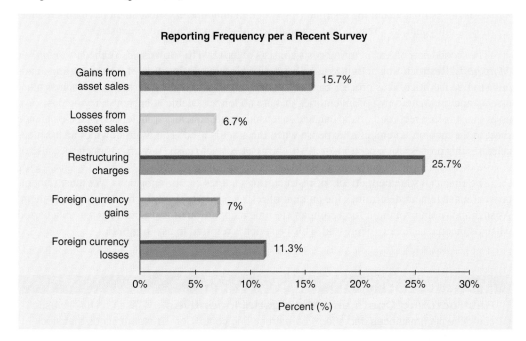

The general challenge for our analysis is to identify those transitory gains and losses. Accounting standards require that companies need only disclose *material* gains and losses. Material items are normally separately disclosed, either as a line item in the income statement or in the notes. However, even when material, some companies include gains on asset sales in SG&A expenses as an offset to expenses, thereby reducing SG&A expenses and making the company look more efficient than it is.

BUSINESS INSIGHT

IBM's Spinoff   IBM sold its Global Network to AT&T, the gain for which was included in (and as an offset to) its 1999 SG&A expenses. By including this gain as part of SG&A expense, its quarterly expenses were reduced by 13.7% from the previous year's quarter and made IBM appear more efficient that it was. Analysis reveals that without this gain, IBM's quarterly SG&A expenses actually *increased* by 0.7% over the prior year's quarter.

Restructuring Costs

Restructuring costs are similar to discontinued operations, except that they do not involve the sale of a separately identifiable business unit. These costs typically involve activities such as consolidating production facilities, reorganizing sales operations, outsourcing some activities, or discontinuing product lines within a business unit. Restructuring costs are a substantial expense item in many companies' income statements. They tend to be large in magnitude and, as a result, GAAP requires enhanced disclosure, either as a separate line item in the income statement or in a footnote. These costs are typically transitory because companies do not engage in restructuring activities every year. As such, these costs should be reclassified to a transitory category for analysis purposes when companies include them in income from continuing operations. The reporting of restructuring costs in the income statement typically consists of two parts:

REMEMBER...
Management's ability to reduce income from restructuring charges and later reverse some of that charge (creating subsequent period income) reduces earnings quality.

1. Employee severance costs
2. Asset write-downs

The first of these, **employee severance costs**, represent accrued (estimated) costs for termination of employees as part of a restructuring program. Accruing these costs proceeds in two steps:

1. Estimating total costs of terminating or relocating selected employees. Costs might include severance pay (typically a number of weeks of pay based on how long the employee has worked for the company), outplacement costs, and relocation or retraining costs for those employees remaining.
2. Reporting total estimated costs as an expense (and a liability) in the period when those costs are estimated and the restructuring program announced. Subsequent payments reduce this liability and, as a result, do not usually yield any major future expenses.

NOTE
An asset write-down might also be made in a period when net income is otherwise unusually high (income smoothing) to relieve future periods of the charge.

The second part of restructuring costs consists of **asset write-downs**, also called *write-offs* or *charge-offs*. Restructuring activities usually involve closure or relocation of manufacturing or administrative facilities. This process can require the write-down of long-term assets (such as plant assets), and the write-down of inventories that are no longer salable at current carrying costs. An asset's cost is first recorded on the balance sheet and is subsequently transferred from the balance sheet to the income statement as expense when the asset is used. The write-down of an asset accelerates this process for a portion, or all, of the asset cost. No cash flow effects occur because of a write-down other than some potential tax benefits.

The financial statement effects of restructuring charges can be enormous. We must remember that management determines the amount of restructuring costs and when to recognize them. As such, it is not uncommon for a company to time recognition of restructuring costs in a period when its income is already depressed. This behavior is referred to as a **big bath**.

RESEARCH INSIGHT

Restructuring Costs and Managerial Incentives   Research has investigated the circumstances and effects of restructuring costs. Some research finds that stock prices increase upon announcement of a restructuring as if the market appreciates the company's candor. Research also finds that many companies that reduce income through restructuring costs later reverse those costs, resulting in a substantial income boost for the period of reversal. These reversals often occur when their absence would have yielded an earnings decline. Whether or not the market responds favorably to trimming the fat or simply disregards such transitory items as uninformative, managers have incentives to exclude such income-decreasing items from operating income. These incentives are contractually-based, extending from debt covenants and restrictions to managerial bonuses.

NOTE
Liabilities from restructurings are known as constructive liabilities—arising not from an obligation, but from management intent.

The FASB has tightened rules relating to restructuring costs in an effort to mitigate abuses. For example, a company is required to have a formal restructuring plan that is approved by its board of directors before any restructuring charges are reported. Also, a company must identify the relevant employees and notify them of its plan. In each subsequent year, the company must disclose in its footnotes the original amount of the liability (accrual), how much of that liability is settled in the current period (such as employee payments), how much of the original liability has been reversed because of cost overestimation, any new accruals for unforeseen costs, and the current balance of the liability.

BUSINESS INSIGHT

Cisco's Restructuring   Cisco's restructuring activity in 2001 included a $397 million charge for workforce reduction (mainly severance and benefit payments) and a $484 million charge for consolidation of facilities, including the write-down of plant assets and lease termination payments to landlords. The status of these charges and the ensuing two years' results are shown in the following footnote to Cisco's 2003 annual report:

($ millions)	Workforce Reduction	Consolidation of Excess Facilities and Other Charges
Initial charge in the third quarter of fiscal 2001	$ 397	$ 484
Noncash charges	(71)	(141)
Cash payments	(265)	(18)
Balance at July 28, 2001	61	325
Adjustments	(35)	128
Cash payments	(26)	(131)
Balance at July 27, 2002	—	322
Adjustments	—	45
Cash payments	—	(72)
Balance at July 26, 2003	**$ —**	**$ 295**

For its $397 million initial workforce reduction charge, $265 million cash was paid to employees and $71 million was noncash charges, leaving a $61 million first-year balance. In the second year, $26 million cash was paid to employees and the remaining $35 million was eliminated as an adjustment. Cisco reports that this $35 million was transferred from the workforce reduction account to the consolidation of facilities account. For the $484 million initial accrual on facilities consolidation, $18 million was paid in cash and $141 million was noncash charges, leaving a $325 million first-year balance. In the second year, the accrual was increased by $128 million, including the $35 million reclassification discussed above and a further $93 million "due to changes in real estate market conditions." This additional $93 million impacted its 2002 income. The second-year's accrual balance was $322 million after a reduction of $131 million for cash payments. In fiscal 2003, continued deterioration of the real estate market yielded a further accrual of $45 million, which also affected 2003 income. Cisco ended 2003 with a balance of $295 million after cash payments of $72 million.

In sum, of the total restructuring charges relating to workforce reduction and consolidation of facilities, $881 million ($397 million + $484 million) affected 2001 income, $93 million ($128 million − $35 million) affected 2002 income, and $45 million affected 2003 income.

YOU MAKE THE CALL

You are the Financial Analyst   You are analyzing the financial statements of a company that has reported a large restructuring cost, involving both employee severance and asset write-downs, in its income statement. How do you interpret and treat this cost in your analysis of its current and future period profitability? [Answer, p. 306]

BUSINESS INSIGHT

Pro Forma Income and Managerial Motives Income from continuing operations per GAAP, once a key measure of company performance, is often supplemented or even supplanted by pro forma income in company financial statements and press releases. **Pro forma income** begins with the GAAP income from continuing operations (that excludes discontinued operations and extraordinary items), and then excludes other transitory items (most notably, restructuring charges), and some additional items such as expenses arising from acquisitions, compensation expense in the form of stock options, and research and development expenditures.

The purported motive of pro forma income is to eliminate transitory items so as to enhance year-to-year comparability. Although this might be justified on the basis that the resulting income has greater predictive ability, important information is lost in the process. Accounting is beneficial in reporting how effective management has been in its stewardship of invested capital. Asset write-downs, liability accruals, and other charges that are eliminated in the process often reflect outcomes of poor management decisions. Our analysis must not blindly eliminate information contained in nonrecurring items by focusing solely on pro forma income.

Critics of pro forma income argue that the items excluded by managers from GAAP income are inconsistent across companies and time. They contend that a major motive for pro forma income is to mislead stakeholders. Legendary investor Warren Buffet puts pro forma in context (Berkshire Hathaway, Annual Report): "When companies or investment professionals use terms such as 'EBITDA' and 'pro forma,' they want you to unthinkingly accept concepts that are dangerously flawed."

In summary, *transitory operating* income components include restructuring costs, asset impairment write-downs, and gains and losses on sales of operating assets. *Transitory nonoperating* components include gains and losses on the sale of most financial investments, and any income, gains, and losses from discontinued operatings and their disposal. Extraordinary gains and losses are always considered transitory, but are classified as either operating or nonoperating, depending on their source. Distinguishing between core and transitory components of income requires judgment. We conclude this section by examining Cisco's 2003 income statement in Exhibit 7.10.

Cisco's income statement components are generally viewed as operating with the exception of its $660 million interest income and $(529) million in other income (loss). The footnotes to Cisco's 10-K reveal that other income (loss) relates primarily to its investments that are deemed impaired. Cisco's sole transitory item is its $4 million in-process R&D expense, which is normally nonrecurring for Cisco. Amortization expense is the regular recurring cost allocation of intangible assets (similar to depreciation for tangible assets) and is not transitory.[2]

EXHIBIT 7.10	Cisco System's Income Statement
Year Ended ($ millions)	**July 26, 2003**
Net sales	
Product	$15,565
Service	3,313
Total net sales	18,878
Cost of sales	
Product	4,594
Service	1,051
Total cost of sales	5,645
Gross margin	**13,233**
Operating expenses	
Research and development	3,135
Sales and marketing	4,116
General and administrative	702
Amortization of purchased intangible assets	394
In-process research and development	4
Total operating expenses	8,351
Operating income (loss)	**4,882**
Interest income	660
Other income (loss), net	(529)
Interest and other income (loss), net	131
Income (loss) before provision for income taxes	**5,013**
Provision for income taxes	1,435
Net income (loss)	**$ 3,578**

[2] **Standard & Poor's (S&P)** is a major player in the analyst community, providing investment information to equity investors and bond ratings to fixed-income investors. S&P has its own definition of "core income," which is similar to the one here: including items such as employee stock options expense and gains and losses from hedging of foreign currencies and commodities, and excluding items such as goodwill write-downs, gains and losses from asset sales, merger and acquisition costs, and litigation expenses and insurance proceeds.

In the next section, we discuss managerial discretion in the reporting of core-operating and transitory income components. This practice is known as *earnings management.*

EARNINGS MANAGEMENT

Management choices about accounting principles, estimates, disclosure, and presentation of income components are an inevitable part of financial reporting. **Earnings management** occurs when management uses this discretion to mask the underlying economic performance of a company. There are many motives for earnings management, but these motives generally fall into one of two categories:

1. desire to mislead some financial statement users about the financial performance of the company to gain economic advantage, or
2. desire to influence legal contracts that use reported accounting numbers to specify contractual obligations and outcomes.[3]

LO5 Discuss earnings management and explain how it affects analysis and interpretation of financial statements.

REMEMBER... Earnings management is claimed as part of management's tools used to meet earnings targets.

Earnings Management Tactics

Earlier in this chapter, we identified five situations that represent questionable application of revenue recognition criteria. However, not all earnings management tactics involve revenue recognition. In some cases, financial statement presentation is the concern. Below, we identify several additional examples of potentially misleading income reporting.

REMEMBER... Earnings management involves earnings quality and management ethics. For the latter, management must consider both legal and personal ethical standards of conduct.

- *Case 6: Mischaracterizing extraordinary and unusual items.* This tactic often involves reporting transitory or nonoperating gains as operating revenues or as a reduction of operating expenses. For example, gains on sales of assets might be netted against SG&A expenses or extraordinary gains might be reported in income from continuing operations. These misclassifications do not impact net income, but can distort key financial ratios and make it difficult to identify core (recurring) income from operations. Misclassifications are often justified on the grounds that they are "immaterial." However, in a market environment where even a 1% change in core-operating profit can have an impact on stock prices, these items should be properly disclosed.

- *Case 7: Strategic timing of transitory gains and losses.* Management has some discretion about when to report certain transitory gains and losses. As such, it is not uncommon for a company to report the recognition of a transitory item in a particular period in order to achieve predetermined income targets. One strategy is to take a *big bath* by recording a transitory loss in a period of already depressed income. Another strategy is to time such gains and losses so that the company maintains a steady improvement in income each year. This practice is known as **income smoothing**. Given adequate disclosure, the astute reader of the financial statements will separate transitory income items from core operating income, making these *income management* tactics transparent.

- *Case 8: Mischaracterizing transactions as arm's-length.* Transfers of inventories or other assets to related entities typically are not recorded until later arm's-length sales occur. Sometimes sales are disguised as being sold to unrelated entities to inflate income when (1) the buyer is a related party to the seller, or (2) financing is provided or guaranteed by the seller, or (3) the buyer is a special-purpose entity that fails to meet independence requirements. This financial reporting practice is not consistent with GAAP and may be fraudulent.

- *Case 9: Selling undervalued assets.* This earnings management tactic involves selling specific assets that are carried at a book value that is well below fair market value. An example is the sale of low-cost inventory layers (see Chapter 8), which boosts gross margin and income for the current period, albeit at the cost of having to later replenish inventories with higher-cost goods. Another example is the sale of securities for which unrealized gains exist while holding others with unrealized losses. Such activities are acceptable under GAAP, although required disclosures can be a deterrent.

[3] See Healy, Paul M., and James M. Wahlen, "A Review of Earnings Management Literature and Its Implications for Standard Setting." *Accounting Horizons,* December 1999.

NOTE
The percentage-of-completion method gives management an opportunity to manage reported earnings. Management can adjust estimates of the degree of completion and/or expenses to accelerate or delay income recognition. Auditors and other information users must be alert to this risk.

Case 10: Misleading or biased estimates. The use of estimates in accrual accounting is extensive. For example, we discussed the use of estimated construction costs in applying the percentage-of-completion method of revenue recognition. Estimates are also used to determine uncollectible accounts, warranty costs, pension costs, and the useful life of depreciable assets. Although changes in estimates are sometimes warranted by changing conditions, these changes can have a significant impact on reported net income and, thus, be misleading if not properly disclosed. Furthermore, estimates that are intentionally biased represent an unethical or fraudulent misrepresentation of a company's financial performance.

The consequence of earnings management is that the usefulness of the information presented in the income statement is compromised. **Quality of earnings** is a term that analysts often use to describe the extent to which reported income reflects the underlying economic performance of a company. Financial statement users must be especially careful to examine the quality of a company's earnings before using that information to evaluate performance or value its securities.

Accounting Changes

Within GAAP, management has considerable discretion to choose and apply accounting methods to report income. Occasionally, it is desirable or even necessary, to change these accounting practices. A **change in accounting principle** results from adoption of a generally accepted accounting principle different from the one previously used for reporting purposes. An example of such a change would be the adoption of a different method of depreciating plant and equipment assets from the method previously used (there are several depreciation methods acceptable under GAAP).

Any change in principle must be justified as preferable from a financial reporting perspective. The usual claim is that its adoption would yield higher quality financial statements. It is unacceptable to change an accounting principle simply because it would have a desirable affect on reported income or tax liabilities.

Companies are required to report a change in accounting principle through *retrospective* application of the new method to all prior periods. In other words, the income statements from all prior periods presented must be restated to report income as if the newly adopted accounting principle had been in use all along. Similarly, balance sheet amounts must be restated to be consistent with income reporting.

A **change in an accounting estimate** is unlike a change in accounting principle. For example, a change from one depreciation method to another is a change in accounting principle. However, if a company continues to use the same depreciation method, but changes the period of time (useful life) over which it depreciates its assets, this is a change in accounting estimate. A change in accounting estimate is applied prospectively (current and future periods only) from the date of change. No adjustment or restatement of prior periods' income statements is required.

Changes in accounting principles or estimates can sometimes hide other issues. Disclosures about the change should be studied closely to ascertain how the change affects current earnings and projections of future income.

R E S E A R C H   I N S I G H T

Pro Forma Income   Transitory items in income such as discontinued operations, restructuring charges and extraordinary items make it difficult for investors to determine what portion of income is sustainable into the future. The past decade has seen more companies reporting pro forma income, which purportedly excludes the effects of nonrecurring or non-cash items that companies feel are unimportant for valuation purposes. Research, however, provides no evidence that more exclusions via pro forma income leads to more predictable future cash flows. More important, investors appear to be misled by the exclusions at the time of the pro forma income release. Research also finds that companies issuing pro forma income are more likely to be young companies concentrated in technology and business services. Too often, these companies are characterized by below-average sales and income when they choose to report pro forma income. Evidence also shows that the pro forma income can exceed GAAP income by as much as 20 percent.

CHAPTER-END REVIEW

Following is the 2005 income statement reported by Aboody Corporation.

(in millions, except per share amounts)	2005
Revenues	$973
Cost of sales	425
Selling, general and administrative expenses	82
Purchased in-process research and development charges	15
Loss on sale of subsidiary	33
Merger-related costs	11
Restructuring costs	91
Equity in earnings of unconsolidated affiliates	9
Other costs (revenues)—net	(27)
Income from continuing operations before taxes and other items	334
Provision for income taxes	120
Minority interests' share of income	4
Income from continuing operations	210
Discontinued operations	
Income from operations of discontinued business—net of tax	22
Gain on sale of discontinued business—net of tax	8
Discontinued operations—net of tax	30
Net income	$240

Required

a. Identify the components in its income statement that are likely transitory.

b. Compute a net income figure absent the transitory components identified in part a.

Solution

a. The following five income components of Aboody are usually identified as transitory by analysts:

- *Purchased in-process research and development charges.* GAAP requires that research and development projects purchased in an acquisition of a company be written off immediately if they have not reached technological feasibility when acquired. This is a one-time write-off and is properly characterized as transitory.

- *Loss on sale of subsidiary.* This item rests in the category of gains and losses on asset sales. This is considered a one-time loss and is characterized as transitory.

- *Merger-related costs.* These are one-time (transitory) costs incurred in connection with the acquisition of another company.

- *Restructuring costs.* These are one-time (transitory) costs as part of a restructuring plan.

- *Discontinued operations.* This item reflects income earned in connection with a business unit that was sold. The gain on sale is transitory as it is a one-time occurrence. The income from operations was not a past transitory item as it regularly occurred, but it is properly identified as transitory this period because it will not persist into the future.

b. Net income absent the transitory items identified in part (a) is computed as follows ($ millions):

$$\$240 + [(\$15 + \$33 + \$11 + \$91) \times (1 - \{120/334\})] - \$30 = \underline{\$306}$$

The *adjusted* income number of $306 million is markedly higher ($66 million) from the reported net income of $240 million. This case emphasizes the importance of adjusting income for any transitory items when analyzing current performance and forecasting future performance. (The ratio $120/$334 is the effective tax rate. Items reported "net of tax" do not require adjustment for tax.)

SUMMARY

Describe the criteria for determining when revenue is recognized. (p. 283)   LO1

- Revenue is recognized when it is earned and realized (or realizable).

Illustrate revenue and expense recognition for long-term contracts. (p. 284)   LO2

- Long-term contracts are recorded using the percentage-of-completion (**POC**) method when a signed contract exists with a fixed or determinable price, collection is reasonably assured, and the cost of completing the contract can be estimated.

- The completed contract method is used when the conditions for using **POC** are not met.
- The installment method is used for long-term sales contracts when collection of cash is not assured.

LO3 **Explain how income taxes are reported in financial statements. (p. 288)**

- Deferred tax assets and liabilities are reported in the balance sheet to reflect temporary differences between the measurement of income in the financial statements and the calculation of taxable income in the tax return.
- Tax expense is calculated as the sum of the tax due on the tax return plus the change in deferred tax assets and liabilities.

LO4 **Identify transitory components of income, and distinguish between transitory and core elements. (p. 293)**

- Transitory components of income are nonrecurring revenues and expenses, such as extraordinary items, discontinued operations, and restructuring charges.
- Because these items are nonrecurring, they do not provide information about future performance of the company.
- While some transitory items are detailed on the income statement, others can only be identified by studying the footnotes.

LO5 **Discuss earnings management and explain how it affects analysis and interpretation of financial statements. (p. 301)**

- Earnings management occurs when management uses its discretion to mask the underlying economic performance of a company.
- The consequence of earnings management is that the usefulness of the information presented in the income statement is compromised.

APPENDIX 7A: Foreign Currency Translation Effects

Many companies conduct operations outside of their domestic countries and in other currencies. Some companies purchase assets in foreign currencies, borrow money in foreign currencies, and transact business with their customers in foreign currencies. Some companies even have subsidiaries whose entire balance sheet and income statement are stated in foreign currencies.

Financial statements prepared according to U.S. GAAP must be reported in $US. This means that financial statements of any foreign subsidiaries must be translated into $US before they are consolidated with those of the U.S. parent company. This translation process can markedly alter both the balance sheet and income statement.

Balance Sheet Effects

Consider a foreign subsidiary that conducts its business in Euros and prepares its financial statements in Euros. Assume that the Euro strengthens vis-à-vis the $US during the current period—that is, each Euro can now purchase more $US as the $US has weakened. When the balance sheet is translated into $US, the assets and liabilities are reported at higher $US than before the Euro strengthened. This result is shown in accounting equation format in Exhibit 7A.1.[4]

EXHIBIT 7A.1	**Balance Sheet Effects of Euro Strengthening versus the Dollar**				
Currency	**Assets**	**=**	**Liabilities**	**+**	**Equity**
$US weakens	Increase	=	Increase	+	Increase
$US strengthens	Decrease	=	Decrease	+	Decrease

The amount necessary to balance the accounting equation is reported in the equity section and is called a **foreign currency translation** adjustment. It is included in *other comprehensive income* and does not impact reported net income. Since assets are greater than liabilities for solvent companies, the cumulative translation adjustment is usually positive for local currencies that strengthen vis-à-vis the $US, with the opposite effect when the dollar strengthens. (In the unusual case when liabilities exceed assets, equity exhibits the opposite effects.) The cumulative translation adjustment remains in equity unless the subsidiary is sold, at which time it is recognized in income.

Exhibit 7A.2 shows an excerpt from the statement of stockholders' equity of Ford Motor Company. Ford's cumulative foreign currency translation is $(1,291) million at the beginning of 2003, which increases to $1,593 million

---

[4] We assume that the company is translating the statements of its foreign subsidiary using the **current rate method**, which is required for subsidiaries operating independently from the parent and is the method most commonly used. Under the current rate method, most items in the balance sheet are translated using exchange rates in effect at the period-end consolidation date and the income statement is translated using the average exchange rate for the period. An alternative procedure is the temporal method, which is covered in advanced courses.

by year-end. The $2,884 million positive swing primarily reflects a weakening of the $US vis-à-vis the foreign currencies in which Ford conducted its business in 2003. That is, as the $US weakened, assets and liabilities of foreign subsidiaries are translated into more $US, resulting in an increase in equity to maintain the accounting equation. These unrealized gains (and losses) remain in other comprehensive income as long as the subsidiary is owned, fluctuating between positive and negative amounts as the value of the $US fluctuates. However, when the subsidiary is sold, any existing foreign currency translation adjustment relating to that subsidiary is immediately recognized in current income with the gain or loss from sale of the subsidiary.

EXHIBIT 7A.2 Foreign Currency Translation for Ford Motor Company ($ millions)

| Year Ended December 31, 2003 | Capital Stock | Capital in Excess of Par Value of Stock | Retained Earnings | Other Comprehensive Income/(Loss) | | | Other | Total |
				Foreign Currency Translation	Minimum Pension Liability	Derivative Instruments and Other		
Balance at beginning of year ...	$19	$5,420	$8,659	$(1,291)	$(5,776)	$ 536	$(1,977)	$ 5,590
Comprehensive income (loss)								
Net income			495					495
Foreign currency translation ..				3,075				3,075
Net gain on derivative instruments (net of tax of $430) .				(191)		989		798
Minimum pension liability (net of tax of $1,208)					2,243			2,243
Net holding gain (net of tax of $1)						1		1
Comprehensive income								6,612
Common Stock issued for employee benefit plans and other		(46)						(46)
Treasury stock							228	228
Cash dividends			(733)					(733)
Balance at end of year	$19	$5,374	$8,421	$1,593	$(3,533)	$1,526	$(1,749)	$11,651

Income Statement Effects

A change in the strength of the $US vis-à-vis foreign currencies does affect reported income in the following manner: changes in foreign currency yield changes in revenues, expenses, and income for the foreign subsidiary (where revenues and expenses are translated at the average exchange rate for the period). Thus, even when translation of the balance sheet does not affect reported income, translation of the income statement does. Specifically, assuming a company is profitable, when the foreign currency strengthens ($US weakens), the subsidiary's revenues, expenses, and income increases. On the other hand, when the $US strengthens, the subsidiary's revenues, expenses, and income decrease.

To illustrate the income statement effects of foreign exchange fluctuations, consider the following footnote from **McDonald's Corporation** 2003 10-K.

> In 2003, foreign currency translation had a positive impact on consolidated revenues, operating income and earnings per share due to the strengthening of several major currencies, primarily the Euro.

As the Euro and other currencies strengthen vis-à-vis the $US, McDonald's reported revenues are translated into more $US, resulting in a reported revenues increase. Specifically, McDonald's revenues increased from $15,406 million in 2002 to $17,140 million in 2003. However, 5% of this 11% increase is due to the foreign currency translation effect as evident in the following footnote from McDonald's 2003 10-K ($ millions):

Total Revenues	2003	2002	Increase (Decrease)	Increase (Decrease) Excluding Currency Translation
U.S.	$ 6,039	$ 5,423	11%	11%
Europe	5,875	5,136	14	—
APMEA	2,447	2,368	3	(3)
Latin America	859	814	6	14
Canada	778	633	23	9
Other	1,142	1,032	11	11
Total revenues	$17,140	$15,406	11%	6%

Although McDonald's reports that 2003 total revenues increase by 11%, the weakening $US accounts for 5% of this increase. That is, excluding currency effects, McDonald's revenues increased only 6%. McDonald's also reports (not shown here) that 9% of its 34% increase in 2003 operating profit was due to the weakening $US.

We must remember that for companies deriving a major portion of their revenues and profits in international currencies, we must be cognizant of the effects of currency fluctuations on reported revenues, expenses, and profits.

GUIDANCE ANSWERS

YOU MAKE THE CALL

You are the Controller The sales person may be channel stuffing (case 5) or delivering product and recording sales without a confirmed sales order (case 1). The unusual amount of returns suggests that sales revenues are most likely being recognized prematurely. To investigate, you could examine specific sales orders from customers who returned goods early in the following quarter, or contact customers directly. Most companies delay bonuses until after an appropriate return period expires and only credits the sales staff with *net* sales.

YOU MAKE THE CALL

You are the Financial Analyst There are two usual components to a restructuring charge: asset write-downs (such as inventories, property, plant, and goodwill) and severance costs. Write-downs occur when the cash flow generating ability of an asset declines, thus reducing its current market value below its book value reported on the balance sheet. Arguably, this decline in cash flow generating ability did not occur solely in the current year and, most likely, has developed over several periods. Delays in loss recognition, such as write-downs of assets, are not uncommon. Thus, prior period income is arguably not as high as reported, and the current period loss is not as great as is reported. Turning to severance costs, their recognition can be viewed as an investment decision by the company that is expected to increase future cash flows (through decreased wages). If this cost accrual is capitalized on the balance sheet, current period income is increased and future period income would bear the amortization of this "asset" to match against future cash flow benefits from severance. This implies that current period income is not as low as reported; however, this adjustment is not GAAP as such severance costs cannot be capitalized. Yet, we can make such an adjustment in our analysis.

KEY TERMS

Asset write-down (p. 298)

Big bath (p. 298)

Bundled sales (p. 284)

Change in accounting estimate (p. 302)

Change in accounting principles (p. 302)

Completed contract method (p. 285)

Core components (p. 281)

Current rate method (p. 304)

Deferred tax asset (p. 290)

Deferred tax liability (p. 290)

Direct association (p. 287)

Discontinued operations (p. 294)

Earned (p. 283)

Earnings management (p. 301)

Employee severance costs (p. 298)

Extraordinary items (p. 295)

Foreign currency translation (p. 304)

Immediate recognition (p. 288)

Income smoothing (p. 301)

Installment method (p. 286)

Matching principle (p. 287)

Percentage-of-completion method (p. 284)

Permanent differences (p. 289)

Pro forma income (p. 300)

Quality of earnings (p. 302)

Realized (or realizable) (p. 283)

Restructuring costs (p. 298)

Revenue recognition (p. 283)

Revenue recognition criteria (p. 283)

Right of return (p. 284)

Systematic allocation (p. 288)

Temporary differences (p. 289)

Transitory components (p. 282)

MULTIPLE CHOICE

1. Which of the following best describes the condition(s) that must be present for the recognition of revenue?
   a. Revenue must be earned and collected.
   b. There are no uncertainties in measurement of income.
   c. Revenue must be earned and realizable.
   d. Expenses must be measurable and directly associated with the revenues.

2. A company's projects extend over several years and collection of receivables is reasonably certain. Each of its projects has a contract that specifies a price, and reliable estimates can be made of the extent of progress and cost to complete each project. The method that the company should use to account for construction revenue is the
   a. installment method.
   b. percentage-of-completion method.
   c. completed-contract method.
   d. sales method.

3. The installment method of recognizing revenue
   a. is used only in cases in which no reasonable basis exists for estimating the collectibility of receivables.
   b. is not a generally accepted accounting method under any circumstances.
   c. is used for book purposes only if it is also used for tax purposes.
   d. is used by most firms that make installment sales.

4. Which of the following is *not* an acceptable basis for the recognition of expenses?
   a. Systematic and rational allocation
   b. Direct association
   c. Immediate recognition
   d. Cash disbursement only

5. The amount of income reported for tax purposes
   a. is normally greater than the net income reported to stockholders.
   b. must be computed according to GAAP.
   c. is called deferred income taxes.
   d. can differ from income determined for financial reporting purposes.

6. An ice storm destroyed a building of a company located in Tucson, Arizona. This loss should be reported as a(n)
   a. extraordinary loss.
   b. prior period adjustment.
   c. loss from continuing operations.
   d. loss from discontinued operations.

7. A company reported a large restructuring charge on its income statement in 2002; it has since experienced consistently rising earnings while sales remained flat. This would most likely be an example of
   a. misclassification of unusual or extraordinary items.
   b. creative acquisition accounting.
   c. big bath accounting.
   d. income smoothing.

8. When management selectively excludes some revenues, expenses, gains, and losses from earnings calculated using generally accepted accounting principles, it is an example of
   a. income smoothing.
   b. big bath accounting.
   c. cookie jar accounting.
   d. pro forma earnings.

Multiple Choice Answers
1.c   2.b   3.a   4.d   5.d   6.a   7.c   8.d

Superscript ^{A} denotes assignments based on Appendix 7A

DISCUSSION QUESTIONS

Q7-1. What are the criteria that guide firms in recognition of revenue? What does each of the criteria mean? How are the criteria met for a company like **Abercrombie & Fitch**, a clothing retailer? How are the criteria met for a construction company that builds offices under long-term contracts with developers?

Abercrombie & Fitch (ANF)

Q7-2. Why are discontinued operations reported separately from continuing operations in the income statement?

Q7-3. What are the criteria for categorizing an event as an extraordinary item? Provide an example of an event that would properly be categorized as an extraordinary item and one that would not.

Q7-4. How does the proper accounting treatment for a change in accounting *principle* differ from that for a change in accounting *estimate?*

Q7-5. What is the concept of *materiality* and why is it so important to an understanding of financial statements?

Q7-6. Identify the two typical categories of restructuring costs and their effects on the balance sheet and the income statement. Explain the concept of a *big bath* and why restructuring costs are often identified with this event.

Q7-7. Why might companies want to manage earnings? Describe some of the tactics that some companies use to manage earnings.

Q7-8.   Under what circumstances would a tax payment be recorded as deferred income taxes?

Q7-9.   What is the concept of *pro forma income* and why has this income measure been criticized?

Q7-10. Why does GAAP allow management to make estimates of amounts that are included in financial statements? Does this improve the usefulness of financial statements? Explain.

Q7-11. How can management's decisions about how to report immaterial transactions result in earnings management?

Q7-12. How might earnings forecasts that are published by financial analysts encourage companies to manage earnings?

MINI EXERCISES

M7-13. Computing Percentage-of-Completion Revenues   (LO1, 2)

Bartov Corporation agreed to build a warehouse for $2,500,000. Expected (and actual) costs for the warehouse follows: 2003, $400,000; 2004, $1,000,000; and 2005, $500,000. The company completed the warehouse in 2005. Compute revenues, expenses, and income for each year 2003 through 2005 using the percentage-of-completion method.

M7-14. Assessing Revenue Recognition of Companies   (LO1, 2)

Identify and explain when each of the following companies should recognize revenue.

The GAP (GPS)

Merck & Company (MRK)

John Deere (DE)

Bank of America (BAC)

Johnson Controls (JCI)

a.   **The GAP:** The GAP is a retailer of clothing items for all ages.

b.   **Merck & Company:** Merck engages in the development, manufacturing, and marketing of pharmaceutical products. It sells its drugs to retailers like CVS and Walgreen.

c.   **John Deere:** Deere manufactures heavy equipment. It sells equipment to a network of independent distributors, who in turn sell the equipment to customers. Deere provides financing and insurance services both to distributors and customers.

d.   **Bank of America:** Bank of America is a banking institution. It lends money to individuals and corporations and invests excess funds in marketable securities.

e.   **Johnson Controls:** Johnson Controls manufactures products for the US Government under long-term contracts.

M7-15. Assessing Risk Potential for Revenue Recognition   (LO1, 2)

BannerAD Corporation (BANR)

BannerAD Corporation manages a Website in which it sells products on consignment from sellers. It pays these sellers a portion of the sales price, absent its commission. Identify at least two potential revenue recognition problems relating to such sales.

M7-16. Estimating Revenue Recognition with Right of Return   (LO1, 2)

The GAP (GPS)

The GAP offers an unconditional return policy. It normally expects 2% of sales at retail selling prices to be returned at some point prior to the expiration of the return period. Assuming that it records total sales of $5 million for the current period, how much revenue can it record for this period?

M7-17. Percentage-of-Completion and Completed Contract Methods (LO1, 2)

Halsey Building Company signed a contract to build an office building for $40,000,000. The scheduled construction costs follow.

Year	Cost
2004	$ 9,000,000
2005	15,000,000
2006	6,000,000
Total	$30,000,000

The building is completed in 2006.

For each year, compute the revenue, expense, and gross profit reported for this construction project using each of the following methods.

a.   Percentage-of-completion method

b.   Completed contract method

M7-18. Revenue Recognition and Bundled Sales. (LO1, 2)

A.J. Smith Electronics is a retail consumer electronics company that also sells extended warranty contracts for many of the products that it carries. The extended warranty provides coverage for three years beyond expiration of the manufacturer's warranty. In 2006, A.J. Smith sold extended warranties amounting to $1,700,000. The warranty coverage for all of these begin in 2007 and run through 2009. The expected cost of providing warranty services on these contracts is $500,000.

a. How should A.J. Smith recognize revenue on the extended warranty contracts?

b. Estimate the revenue, expense, and gross profit reported from these contracts in the year(s) that the revenue is recognized.

c. In 2007, as a special promotion, A.J. Smith sold a digital camera (retail price $300), a digital photograph printer (retail price $125), and an extended warranty contract for each (total retail price $75) as a package for a special price of $399. The extended warranty covers the period from 2008 through 2010. The company sold 200 of these camera-printer packages. Compute the revenue that A.J. Smith should recognize in each year from 2007 through 2010.

M7-19.[A] **Interpreting Foreign Currency Translation Disclosure** **(Appendix)**

Bristol-Myers Squibb (BMY)

Bristol-Myers Squibb (BMY) reports accumulated other comprehensive income (loss) as part of its statement of stockholders' equity as reported in the following footnote from its 10-K report:

Dollars in Millions	Foreign Currency Translation	Available for Sale Securities	Deferred Loss on Effective Hedges	Minimum Pension Liability Adjustment	Accumulated Other Comprehensive Income/(Loss)
Balance at December 31, 2002 (Restated)	$(724)	$ 1	$ (87)	$ (94)	$(904)
Other comprehensive income (loss)	233	23	(171)	(36)	49
Balance at December 31, 2003	$(491)	$24	$(258)	$(130)	$(855)

a. What effect(s) does the $233 million foreign currency translation amount have on BMY's stockholders' equity?

b. Describe the exchange rate environment ($US vis-à-vis other world currencies) that gives rise to the effect identified in part *a.*

M7-20. **Recording Gains and Losses on Asset Sales** **(LO4)**

Virchick Company disclosed the following assets in its annual report.

At December 31 ($ millions)	2006
Machine, at cost	$60,000
Less accumulated depreciation	45,000
Machine, net	$15,000

a. Assume that Virchick sold the machine for $12,100 cash. Record this asset sale (1) using the financial statement effects template, and (2) in journal entry form. (3) Post the entry to T-accounts.

b. Assume that Virchick sold the machine for $17,500 cash. Record this asset sale (1) using the financial statement effects template, and (2) in journal entry form. (3) Post the entry to T-accounts.

M7-21. **Recording Gains and Losses on Asset Sales** **(LO4)**

Whittington Company's reports the following information on the value of a company automobile. An independent appraiser assessed the fair market value of the automobile at $7,200.

At December 31 ($ millions)	2006
Automobile, at cost	$40,000
Less accumulated depreciation	35,000
Automobile, net	$ 5,000

a. Assume that Whittington Company sold the automobile for $6,500 cash. Record this asset sale (1) using the financial statement effects template, and (2) in journal entry form. (3) Post the entry to T-accounts.

b. Assume that Whittington Company sold the automobile for $9,500 cash. Record this asset sale (1) using the financial statement effects template, and (2) in journal entry form. (3) Post the entry to T-accounts.

EXERCISES

E7-22. **Assessing Revenue Recognition Timing** (LO1)

Discuss and justify when each of the following businesses should recognize revenues:

a. A clothing retailer like **The Limited**.

b. A contractor like **Boeing Corporation** that performs work under long-term government contracts.

c. A grocery store like **Albertsons**.

d. A producer of television shows like **MTV** that syndicates its content to television stations.

e. A residential real estate developer who constructs only speculative houses and later sells these houses to buyers.

f. A banking institution like **Bank of America** that lends money for home mortgages.

g. A manufacturer like **Harley-Davidson**.

h. A publisher of magazines such as **Time-Warner**.

E7-23. **Assessing Revenue Recognition Timing and Income Measurement** (LO1)

Discuss and justify when each of the following businesses should recognize revenue and identify any income measurement issues that are likely to arise.

a. **RealMoney.Com**, a division of **TheStreet.Com** provides investment advice to customers for an up-front fee. It provides these customers with password-protected access to its Website where customers can download certain investment reports. Real Money has an obligation to provide updates on its Website.

b. **Oracle** develops general ledger and other business application software that it sells to its customers. The customer pays an up-front fee to gain the right to use the software and a monthly fee for support services.

c. **Intuit** develops tax preparation software that it sells to its customers for a flat fee. No further payment is required and the software cannot be returned, only exchanged if defective.

d. A developer of computer games sells its software with a 10-day right of return period during which the software can be returned for a full refund. After the 10-day period has expired, the software cannot be returned.

E7-24. **Constructing and Assessing Income Statements Using Percentage-of-Completion** (LO1, 2)

Assume that **General Electric Company** agreed in May 2004 to construct a nuclear generator for NSTAR, a utility serving the Boston area. The contract price of $500 million is to be paid as follows: $200 million at the time of signing; $100 million on December 31, 2004; and $200 million at completion in May 2005. General Electric incurred the following costs in constructing the generator: $100 million in 2004, and $300 million in 2005.

a. Compute the amount of General Electric's revenue, expense, and income for both 2004 and 2005 under the percentage-of-completion revenue recognition method.

b. Compute the amount of GE's revenue, expense, and income for both 2004 and 2005 using the installment method.

c. Discuss whether you believe that the percentage of completion method or the installment method provides a good measure of GE's performance under the contract.

E7-25. **Constructing and Assessing Income Statements Using Percentage-of-Completion** (LO1, 2)

On March 15, 2003, Frankel Construction contracted to build a shopping center at a contract price of $120 million. The schedule of expected (equals actual) cash collections and contract costs follows:

Year	Cash Collections	Cost Incurred
2003	$ 30 million	$15 million
2004	50 million	40 million
2005	40 million	30 million
Total	$120 million	$85 million

a. Calculate the amount of revenue, expense, and income for each of the three years 2003 through 2005 using (1) the percentage-of-completion method, (2) the completed contract method, and (3) the installment method.

b. Discuss which method you believe provides the best measure of the construction company's performance under this contract.

E7-26. **Interpreting the Income Tax Expense Footnote Disclosure** (LO3)

The income tax footnote to the financial statements of **FedEx** follows.

The components of the provision for income taxes for the years ended May 31 were as follows:

In millions	2002	2001
Current provision		
Domestic		
Federal	$333	$310
State and local	39	43
Foreign	41	36
	413	389
Deferred provision (credit)		
Domestic		
Federal	21	(43)
State and local	3	(3)
Foreign	(2)	—
	22	(46)
	$435	$343

- *a.* What is the amount of income tax expense reported in FedEx's 2002 income statement?
- *b.* How much of its 2002 income tax expense is payable in cash? Explain.
- *c.* One possible reason for the $22 million deferred tax expense in 2002 is that deferred tax liabilities increased during that year. Provide an example that gives rise to an increase in the deferred tax liability.
- *d.* Record 2002 income tax expense for FedEx (1) using the financial statement effects template, and (2) in journal entry form. (3) Post the entry to T-accounts.

E7-27. Identifying Operating and Transitory Income Components (LO4)

Following is the Dow Chemical income statement.

Dow Chemical (DOW)

- *a.* Identify the components in its statement that you would consider operating.
- *b.* Identify those components that you would consider transitory.

(In millions) For Year Ended December 31	2002
Net sales	$27,609
Cost of sales	23,780
Research and development expenses	1,066
Selling, general, and administrative expenses	1,598
Amortization of intangibles	65
Merger-related expenses and restructuring	280
Asbestos-related charge	828
Equity in earnings of nonconsolidated affiliates	40
Sundry income—net	54
Interest income	66
Interest expense and amortization of debt discount	774
Income (loss) before income taxes and minority interests	(622)
Provision (credit) for income taxes	(280)
Minority interests' share of income	63
Income (loss) before cumulative effect of changes in accounting principles	(405)
Cumulative effect of changes in accounting principles	67
Net income (loss) available for common stockholders	$ (338)

E7-28. Revenue Recognition and the Installment Method. (LO1, 2)

Bryant Company sold a software package to Cheng, Inc., for $2,500,000. The sales price is to be paid in installments, with $1,000,000 due in 2005, $750,000 due in 2006, $500,000 due in 2007, and $250,000 due in 2008. The cost of the software is $450,000. Cheng, Inc., is a start-up company that has been struggling to make a profit. As a result, there is some concern that Cheng, Inc., may be unable to meet its payment demands.

a. Compute the revenue, expense, and gross profit that would be reported each year using the installment method.

b. Assume that Cheng, Inc., defaults on this contract in 2007 before that year's payment is collected. What effect would this event have on Bryant's financial statements?

E7-29. Percentage-of-Completion and Completed Contract Methods. (LO1, 2)
Philbrick Company signed a three-year contract to provide sales training to the employees of Elliot Company. The contract price is $1,200 per employee and the estimated number of employees to be trained is 400. The expected number to be trained in each year and the expected training costs follow.

Year	Number of employees	Training costs incurred
2005	125	$ 60,000
2006	200	75,000
2007	75	40,000
Total	400	$175,000

a. For each year, compute the revenue, expense, and gross profit reported assuming revenue is recognized using the following method.
1. Percentage-of-completion method, where percentage-of-completion is determined by the number of employees trained.
2. Percentage-of-completion method, where percentage-of-completion is determined by the costs incurred.
3. Completed contract method.

b. Which method do you believe is most appropriate in this situation? Explain.

E7-30. Recording Income Tax Expense (LO3)

Nike, Inc. (NKE)

For the year ended May 31, 2005, Nike, Inc., reported a provision for income taxes of $648.2 million. Of this amount, $585.3 million was paid in cash during that year. The following additional information was taken from Nike's income tax footnote.

Provision for income taxes consists of the following ($ millions)	2005
Current	$622.8
Deferred	25.4
Total	$648.2

a. Record Nike's provision for income taxes for 2005 (1) using the financial statement effects template, and (2) in journal entry form. (3) Post the entry to T-accounts.

b. Explain how the provision for income taxes affects Nike's financial statements. (*Hint*: Use the financial statements effects template.)

E7-31. Recording Income Tax Expense (LO3)

Boeing Company (BA)

Boeing Company disclosed the following information in a footnote to its annual report. That footnote also disclosed that during 2004, Boeing received a cash refund of $896 million from the IRS.

Expense for taxes on income consisted of the following ($ millions)	2004
Taxes paid or currently payable	$(493)
Deferred income taxes	633
Income tax expense	$ 140

a. Record Boeing's provision for income taxes for 2004 (1) using the financial statement effects template, and (2) in journal entry form. (3) Post the entry to T-accounts.

b. What factors might explain the refund that Boeing received in 2004?

c. Explain how the provision for income taxes affects Boeing's financial statements. (*Hint*: Use the financial statements effects template.)

E7-32. Recording Gains on the Sale of Long-term Assets (LO4)
Capettini Company reported the following assets in its 2006 balance sheet.

Property and buildings, at cost	2006
Land	$1,200,000
Building	2,500,000
Less accumulated depreciation	1,950,000
Net book value	$1,750,000

a. Early in 2007, Capettini sold the land and building for $2,600,000 cash. Record this asset sale (1) using the financial statement effects template, and (2) in journal entry form. (3) Post the entry to T-accounts.

b. How would any gain or loss on the transaction in part a be reported in the company's 2007 income statement?

c. Assume that an independent appraisal determined that the fair market value of the land was $2,200,000 and the building was worth $400,000. Would this information alter your answers to parts a or b? Explain.

E7-33. Reporting Restructuring Charges (LO4)

Pepsico reported restructuring charges of $150 million in its 2004 income statement. The following additional details were disclosed in its footnotes.

Pepsico (PEP)

Restructuring charges included the following	2004
Asset impairment–planned closure of 4 plants	$ 93
Employee severance and related costs	29
Contract termination and other exit costs	28
Total	$150

Pepsico's contract termination costs include, for example, the cost to buy out the remaining years on lease agreements, or penalties paid for canceling purchase contracts.

a. Assume that none of these costs had yet been paid in cash in 2004. Record these restructuring charges (1) using the financial statement effects template, and (2) in journal entry form. (3) Post the entry to T-accounts.

b. Should restructuring charges be classified as discontinued operations? Why or why not?

E7-34. Changing Accounting Estimates and Earnings Management (LO5)

Ten years ago, Sloan Corporation began operating out of a new building that had cost Sloan $15 million to construct. At that time, Sloan's management assumed that the building had a useful life of 25 years. Today, ten years later, management revised its estimate of the useful life of the building to 30 years.

a. How would the change in the estimated useful life of the building impact Sloan's balance sheet?

b. How would the change in the estimated useful life of the building impact Sloan's income statement?

c. What possible incentives might management have to overestimate or underestimate the useful life of a long-term asset?

E7-35. Incentives for Earnings Management (LO5)

Harris Corporation pays senior management an annual bonus from a bonus pool. The size of the bonus pool is determined as follows.

Reported net income	Bonus pool
Less than or equal to $10 million	$0
Greater than $10 million, but less than or equal to $20 million	10% of income in excess of $10 million
Greater than $20 million	$1 million

a. Assume that senior management expects current earnings to be $21 million and next year's earnings to be $18 million. What incentive does management of Harris Corporation have for managing earnings?

b. Assume that senior management expects current earnings to be $17 million and next year's earnings to be $24 million. What incentive does management of Harris Corporation have for managing earnings?

c. Assume that senior management expects current earnings to be $9.5 million and next year's earnings to be $12 million. What incentive does management of Harris Corporation have for managing earnings?

d. How might the bonus plan be structured to minimize the incentives for earnings management?

E7-36.[A] **Analyzing and Interpreting Foreign Currency Translation Adjustments** (Appendix)

Honeywell
International, Inc.
(HON)

Honeywell International, Inc., reports $10,729 million of stockholders' equity in its 2003 10-K, which is reported as follows:

(In millions, except per share amounts)	Shares	Amount	Additional Paid-in Capital	Shares	Amount	Accumulated Other Nonowner Changes	Retained Earnings	Total Shareowners' Equity
Balance at December 31, 2002	957.6	$958	$3,409	(103.1)	$(3,783)	$(1,109)	$ 9,450	$ 8,925
Net income							1,324	1,324
Foreign exchange translation adjustments						551		551
Minimum pension liability adjustment						369		369
Nonowner changes in shareowners' equity								2,244
Common stock issued for employee savings and option plans (including related tax benefits of $19)			75	9.3	182			257
Repurchases of common stock				(1.9)	(62)			(62)
Cash dividends on common stock ($.75 per share)							(645)	(645)
Other owner changes			2	.4	8			10
Balance at December 31, 2003	957.6	$958	$3,486	(95.3)	$(3,655)	$ (189)	$10,129	$10,729

a. How did foreign currency translation adjustments affect stockholders' equity for Honeywell in 2003? Explain.

b. Describe the accounting for foreign currency translation. What scenario of exchange rates for the $US vis-à-vis foreign currency is consistent with the translation adjustments reported for Honeywell?

c. How did the foreign currency translation adjustments reported in its stockholders' equity affect Honeywell's 2003 reported income? What other related effects might be reflected in its 2003 income statement?

d. Under what circumstances will the cumulative foreign currency translation adjustments in stockholders' equity impact reported income in the income statement?

PROBLEMS

P7-37. **Analyzing and Interpreting Revenue Recognition Policies and Risks** (LO1)

Amazon.com (AMZN)

Amazon.com, Inc., provides the following explanation of its revenue recognition policies from its 10-K report.

The Company generally recognizes revenue from product sales or services rendered when the following four revenue recognition criteria are met: persuasive evidence of an arrangement exists, delivery has occurred or services have been rendered, the selling price is fixed or determinable, and collectibility is reasonably assured.

The Company evaluates the criteria outlined in EITF Issue No. 99-19, "Reporting Revenue Gross as a Principal versus Net as an Agent," in determining whether it is appropriate to record the gross amount of product sales and related costs or the net amount earned as commissions. Generally, when the Company is the primary obligor in a transaction, is subject to inventory risk, has latitude in establishing prices and selecting suppliers, or has several but not all of these indicators, revenue is recorded gross as a principal. If the Company is not the primary obligor and amounts earned are determined using a fixed percentage, a fixed-payment schedule, or a combination of the two, the Company generally records the net amounts as commissions earned.

Product sales (including sales of products through the Company's Syndicates Stores program), net of promotional gift certificates and return allowances, are recorded when the products are shipped and title passes to customers. Return allowances are estimated using historical experience.

Commissions received on sales of products from Amazon Marketplace, Auctions and zShops are recorded as a net amount since the Company is acting as an agent in such transactions. Amounts earned are recognized as net sales when the item is sold by the third-party seller and our collectibility is reasonably assured. The Company records an allowance for refunds on such commissions using historical experience.

The Company earns revenues from services, primarily by entering into business-to-business strategic alliances, including providing the Company's technology services such as search, browse and personalization; permitting third parties to offer products or services through the Company's Websites; and powering third-party Websites, providing fulfillment services, or both. These strategic alliances also include miscellaneous marketing and promotional agreements. As compensation for the services the Company provides under these agreements, it receives one or a combination of cash and equity securities. If the Company receives non-refundable, up-front payments, such amounts are deferred until service commences, and are then recognized on a straight-line basis over the estimated corresponding service period. Generally, the fair value of consideration received, whether in cash, equity securities, or a combination thereof, is measured when agreement is reached, and any subsequent appreciation or decline in the fair value of the securities received does not affect the amount of revenue recognized over the term of the agreement. To the extent that equity securities received or modified after March 16, 2000 are subject to forfeiture or vesting provisions and no significant performance commitment exists upon signing of the agreements, the fair value of the securities and corresponding revenue is determined as of the date of the respective forfeiture or as vesting provisions lapse. The Company generally recognizes revenue from these services on a straight-line basis over the period during which the Company performs services under these agreements, commencing at the launch date of the service.

Outbound shipping charges to customers are included in net sales.

Required

a. Identify and discuss the main revenue recognition policies for its two primary sources of business revenues.

b. Identify and describe potential areas for revenue recognition shams in a business such as Amazon.

P7-38. Analyzing, Interpreting, and Forecasting with Discontinued Operations (LO4)

AOL Time-Warner reports the following footnote relating to its discontinued operations in its 2002 10-K report.

AOL Time-Warner (AOL)

In the third quarter of 2002, the Company's results of operations have been adjusted to reflect the results of certain cable television systems held in the TWE-Advance/Newhouse Partnership ("TWE-A/N") as discontinued operations for all periods presented herein. For 2002, for the six months ended June 30, 2002 (e.g., the most recent reported period prior to the deconsolidation), the net impact of the deconsolidation of these systems was a reduction of the Cable segment's previously reported revenues, EBITDA and operating income of $715 million, $333 million and $206 million, respectively. For the year ended December 31, 2001, the net impact of the deconsolidation of these systems was a reduction of the Cable segment's previously reported revenues, EBITDA and operating income of $1,247 billion, $571 million and $313 million, respectively. The discontinued operations did not impact the Company's results in 2000 because the Company's ownership interest in these cable television systems was acquired in the Merger. As of December 31, 2001, the discontinued operations had current assets and total assets of approximately $64 million and $2.7 billion, respectively, and current liabilities and total liabilities of approximately $210 million and $963 million, respectively, including debt assumed in the restructuring of TWE-A/N.

Required

a. Describe the accounting treatment according to GAAP for discontinued operations

b. How did AOL Time-Warner's treatment of its discontinued operations impact its 2001 (1) income statement and (2) balance sheet?

c. How do you believe the operating results of the discontinued segment should be interpreted when evaluating the 2002 financial performance for AOL Time-Warner?

P7-39. **Analyzing and Interpreting Income Components and Disclosures** **(LO4, 5)**

Xerox Corporation
(XRX)

The income statement for Xerox Corporation follows.

Year Ended December 31 (in millions)	2002	2001	2000
Revenues			
Sales	$ 6,752	$ 7,443	$ 8,839
Service, outsourcing and rentals	8,097	8,436	8,750
Finance income	1,000	1,129	1,162
Total revenues	15,849	17,008	18,751
Costs and Expenses			
Costs of sales	4,197	5,170	6,080
Cost of service, outsourcing and rentals	4,530	4,880	5,153
Equipment financing interest	401	457	498
Research and development expenses	917	997	1,064
Selling, administrative and general expenses	4,437	4,728	5,518
Restructuring and asset impairment charges	670	715	475
Gain on sale of half of interest in Fuji Xerox	—	(773)	—
Gain on affiliate's sale of stock	—	(4)	(21)
Gain on sale of China operations	—	—	(200)
Other expenses, net	445	444	551
Total costs and expenses	15,597	16,614	19,118
Income (Loss) before Income Taxes (Benefits), Equity Income, Minorities' Interests and Cumulative Effect of Change in Accounting Principle	252	394	(367)
Income taxes (benefits)	60	497	(70)
Income (Loss) before Equity Income, Minorities' Interests and Cumulative Effect of Change in Accounting Principle	192	(103)	(297)
Equity in net income of unconsolidated affiliates	54	53	66
Minorities' interests in earnings of subsidiaries	(92)	(42)	(42)
Income (Loss) before Cumulative Effect of Change in Accounting Principle	154	(92)	(273)
Cumulative effect of change in accounting principle	(63)	(2)	—
Net Income (Loss)	$ 91	$ (94)	$ (273)

Required

a. Xerox reports three main sources of income: sales, services, and finance income. Describe the usual and proper revenue recognition policy for each of these sources.

b. Xerox reports restructuring costs of $670 million in 2002. It also reports restructuring costs in each of 2001 and 2000. (1) Describe the two typical categories of restructuring costs and the accounting for each. (2) How do you recommend treating these costs for analysis purposes? (3) Should regular recurring restructuring costs be treated differently than isolated occurrences of such costs for analysis purposes?

c. Xerox reports various gains on the sales of its subsidiaries as negative expenses in 2000 and 2001. (1) Describe in general terms how Xerox computes these gains. (2) How should such gains be treated for analysis purposes? (3) Do you believe Xerox is trying to influence the reader of its income statement by inclusion of these gains in its expense section?

d. Xerox reports $445 million in expenses labeled as 'Other expenses, net.' How can a company use the concept of materiality to minimize the disclosure relating to such items and, therefore, to potentially obscure its actual financial performance?

P7-40. Identifying Operating and Transitory Income Components   (LO4)

Following is the Pfizer, Inc., income statement.

a.   Identify the components in its statement that you would consider operating.

b.   Identify those components that you would consider transitory.

Pfizer, Inc. (PFE)

Year Ended December 31 (millions)	2002
Revenues	$32,373
Costs and expenses	
Cost of sales	4,045
Selling, informational and administrative expenses	10,846
Research and development expenses	5,176
Merger-related costs	630
Other (income) deductions—net	(120)
Income from continuing operations before provision for taxes on income, minority interests and cumulative effect of a change in accounting principle	11,796
Provision for taxes on income	2,609
Minority interests	6
Income from continuing operations before cumulative effect of a change in accounting principle	9,181
Discontinued operations	
Income from operations of discontinued businesses—net of tax	278
Gain on sale of discontinued business—net of tax	77
Discontinued operations—net of tax	355
Income before cumulative effect of a change in accounting principle	9,536
Cumulative effect of a change in accounting principle—net of tax	(410)
Net income	$ 9,126

P7-41. Analyzing and Interpreting Restructuring Costs and Effects   (LO4)

Dell Computer Corporation reported $587 million of charges in connection with a prior year restructuring of its operations as described in the following footnote from its 2003 10-K report.

Dell Computer Corporation (DELL)

($ millions)	Total Charge	Cumulative Payments	Noncash Charges	Liability at January 31, 2003
Employee separations	$184	$(184)	$ —	$—
Facility consolidations	224	(130)	(79)	15
Other asset impairments and exit costs	179	(27)	(152)	—
Total	$587	$(341)	$(231)	$15

Required

a.   Identify the three components of Dell's restructuring charge and the related expense amounts for each. For each component, what portion of its charge was paid in cash?

b.   What was the effect on the balance sheet and the income statement of Dell's noncash charges?

CASES AND PROJECTS

C7-42. **Analyzing and Interpreting Gains and Losses on Asset (Subsidiary) Sales** (LO4)

Altria Group, Inc., formerly Phillip Morris Companies, Inc., sold its **Miller Brewing** subsidiary. Following is a footnote to its 10-K report, which describes that transaction.

On May 30, 2002, ALG announced an agreement with SAB to merge Miller into SAB. The transaction closed on July 9, 2002, and SAB changed its name to SABMiller plc ("SABMiller"). At closing, ALG received 430 million shares of SABMiller valued at approximately $3.4 billion, based upon a share price of 5.12 British pounds per share, in exchange for Miller, which had $2.0 billion of existing debt. The shares in SABMiller owned by ALG resulted in a 36% economic interest in SABMiller and a 24.9% voting interest. The transaction resulted in a pre-tax gain of approximately $2.6 billion or approximately $1.7 billion after-tax. The gain was recorded in the third quarter of 2002. Beginning with the third quarter of 2002, ALG's ownership interest in SABMiller is being accounted for under the equity method. Accordingly, ALG's investment in SABMiller of approximately $1.9 billion is included in other assets on the consolidated balance sheet at December 31, 2002. In addition, ALG records its share of SABMiller's net earnings, based on its economic ownership percentage, in minority interest in earnings and other, net, on the consolidated statement of earnings.

Required

a. Identify (1) the total value received by Altria in exchange for Miller, (2) the book value of Altria's investment in the Miller Brewing subsidiary, and (3) the pretax and after-tax gains recognized by Altria from the Miller transaction.

b. How much of the purchase price was received in cash by Altria? Explain.

c. How should the gain from this transaction be interpreted in an analysis of Altria, especially with respect to projections of Altria's future cash flows?

C7-43. **Interpreting the Income Tax Expense Footnote** (LO3)

The income tax footnote to the 2005 financial statements of **Ethan Allen Interiors, Inc.**, follows.

Income tax expense attributable to income from operations consists of the following for the fiscal years ended June 30 (in thousands).

	2005	2004	2003
Current			
Federal	$39,423	$42,997	$35,909
State	6,724	6,500	5,152
Total current	46,147	49,497	41,061
Deferred			
Federal	3,445	132	3,934
State	490	(12)	355
Total deferred	3,935	120	4,289
Income tax expense	$50,082	$49,617	$45,350

a. What amount of income tax expense is reported in Ethan Allen's 2005 income statement?

b. How much of its 2005 income tax expense is payable in cash? Explain.

c. Assume that Ethan Allen's deferred tax expense is due to an increase in deferred tax liabilities. Provide an example that would be consistent with this explanation.

d. Assume that Ethan Allen's deferred tax expense is due to a decrease in a deferred tax asset. The deferred tax asset was recorded in 2004 as a result of restructuring charges recorded that year. Explain how restructuring charges would create a deferred tax asset. What would cause that asset to decrease in value?

Reporting Short-Term Operating Assets

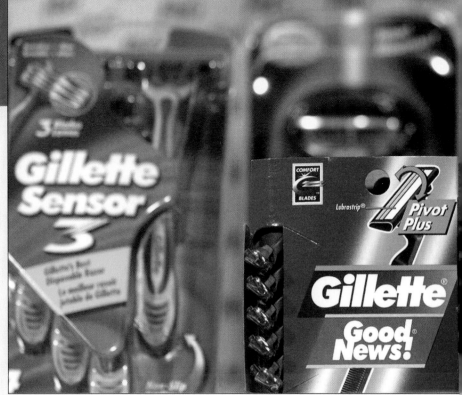

GILLETTE COMPANY

A **Hair-Raising Turnaround** "Three years ago, we made a commitment. We said that we're going to transform this Company from a chronic underperformer to a producer of consistent, sustainable earnings growth—the kind of growth that would take us to the top tier of industry performers over time . . . I'm pleased to report that we are delivering on those commitments. Three years of solid progress allows us to say something . . . that this Company hasn't been able to say in several years . . . Gillette had record earnings per share." (The Gillette Company 2003 Annual Report, Chair's letter)

Gillette reported record sales and earnings in 2003, three years after James Kilts assumed the top job. Sales rose 9%, to $9.25 billion, up from $8.45 billion in 2002. Net income rose 14%, to $1.39 billion, up from $1.22 billion in 2002; similar increases occurred in 2004.

Gillette's turnaround and its recent results "trounced Wall Street's estimates . . . 'If anybody had doubted the company's ability to produce solid numbers, that has got to be put to bed,' said William H. Steele, an analyst at Banc of America Securities. Mr. Steele credits Mr. Kilts for much of the improvement. Shares rose $2.41, or 6.2%, to $41.20 a share . . . [and] marks the first time in more than four years that Gillette shares have surpassed $40" (*The Wall Street Journal,* April 2004).

Gillette is a global manufacturer of a variety of consumer products. It has five major segments:

- **Blades and Razors.** Gillette is the world leader in blades and razors with such brands as M3Power, Mach3Turbo, Mach3, SensorExcel, Sensor, Atra, and Trac II.

- **Duracell.** Gillette is the world leader in alkaline batteries with such products as Duracell CopperTop, Duracell Ultra alkaline batteries, and Duracell rechargeable batteries.

- **Oral Care.** Gillette is the world leader in manual and power toothbrushes, sold under the Oral-B brand.

- **Braun.** Gillette sells electric shavers under the Braun brand and hair epilators under the Silk-Epil brand. It also sells Braun household and personal diagnostic appliances.

- **Personal Care.** Gillette sells shaving preparations, skin care products, and antiperspirants/deodorants under brands such as, Satin Care, Right Guard, Soft & Dri, and Dry Idea.

As the following chart shows, Gillette's stock price has consistently trotted upward, after reaching a low point shortly after Kilts, formerly CEO of Nabisco, joined the company in early 2001.

(Continued on next page)

(Continued from previous page)

The company hailed its earnings and stock price turnaround as evidence that its multiyear restructuring aimed at both slimming a bloated manufacturing process and renegotiating supplier agreements was bearing fruit. A heavy investment in advertising and marketing also paid off with higher sales, and two new Gillette disposable razors were well received.

Management of its net operating assets, including working capital, was crucial to creation of shareholder value. Gillette focused intently on its management of net operating assets and has realized substantial accomplishments, including the following:

- It reorganized its supply chain and gained a better handle on receivables. Its receivables are turning over at a rate of 6.6 times a year, up from 3.5 times a year five years ago.

- It pursued a cost-reduction program, aiming to build more efficient production lines, offer some workers early retirement, and consolidate operations. Inventories are turning over at a rate of three times a year, up from two times a year just four years ago.

- It shifted factory and warehouse operations from London to Eastern Europe to trim costs; it moved manufacturing of its Sensor razor from its high-tech Berlin plant to Eastern European; and it realigned some razor production from the Czech Republic to St. Petersburg.

This chapter focuses on the reporting and analysis of receivables and inventories. These assets comprise a substantial part of operating assets for most companies and must be managed effectively to achieve high performance. Moreover, management decisions in accounting for operating assets can markedly affect both the balance sheet and the income statement. We explain the effects of accounting choices for the reporting of these assets on financial statements, and how this knowledge is used to enhance analysis and interpretation of working capital. [A final note: In late 2005, Gillette merged with Procter & Gamble.]

Sources: *The Wall Street Journal* 2004 and 2003; *Gillette* 2004 and 2003 Annual Report; *Gillette* 2004 10-K Report and 2005 press release.

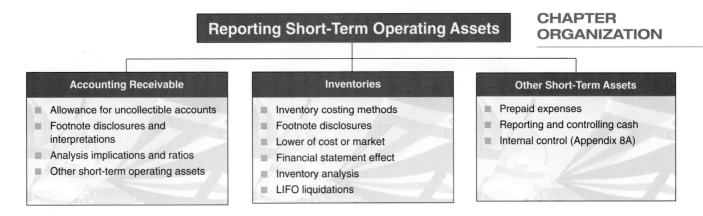

INTRODUCTION

Management of net operating assets is crucial to achieving high company performance and creating shareholder value. To manage and assess net operating assets, we need to understand how they are measured and reported. This chapter describes the reporting and measuring of operating working capital, mainly receivables and inventories. Chapter 9 focuses on long-term operating assets such as property, plant and equipment.

The current asset section of Gillette's 2003 balance sheet ($ millions) is presented below. We highlight two important components of current assets, trade receivables and inventories.

> **NOTE**
> The phrase *trade receivables* refers to accounts receivable from customers.

Cash and cash equivalents	$ 681
Trade receivables, less allowances of $53	920
Other receivables	351
Inventories	1,094
Deferred income taxes	322
Other current assets	282
Total current assets	$3,650

Receivables are usually a major part of operating working capital. They must be carefully managed as they represent a substantial asset for most companies and are an important marketing tool. GAAP requires companies to report receivables at the amount they expect to collect, necessitating an estimation of uncollectible accounts. These estimates determine the receivables reported on the balance sheet and expenses reported on the income statement. Accordingly, it is important that companies accurately assess uncollectible accounts and report them. It is also necessary that readers of financial reports understand management's accounting choices and their effects on reported balance sheets and income statements.

Inventory is another major component of operating working capital. Inventories usually constitute one of the three largest asset amounts (with receivables and long-term operating assets). Also, cost of goods sold, which flows from inventory, is often the largest expense category for retailing and manufacturing companies. GAAP allows several acceptable methods for inventory accounting, and these choices can markedly impact the balance sheets and income statements, especially for companies experiencing relatively high inflation, coupled with slowly turning inventories.

ACCOUNTS RECEIVABLE

Our discussion of operating assets begins with accounts receivable. To help frame our discussion, we refer to the following graphic as we proceed through the chapter.

Income Statement
Sales
Cost of goods sold
Selling, general & administrative
Income taxes
Net income

Balance Sheet	
Cash	Current liabilities
Accounts receivable	Long-term liabilities
Inventory	
Property, plant, and equipment, net	Shareholders' equity
Investments	

We use this graphic to highlight the financial statement item (accounts receivable) that is the focus of this section. We also highlight the income statement items that are affected by uncollectible accounts receivable and by credit sales. This section explains the accounting, reporting, and analysis of these and related items.

When companies sell to other companies, they usually do not expect cash upon delivery as is common with retail customers. Instead, they offer credit terms, and the resulting sales are called **credit sales** or *sales on account.*[1] An account receivable on the seller's balance sheet is always matched by a corresponding account payable on the buyer's balance sheet. Accounts receivable are reported on the balance sheet of the seller at **net realizable value,** which is the net amount the seller expects to collect.

Companies establish credit policies (to determine which customers receive credit) by weighing the expected losses from uncollectible accounts against the expected profits generated by offering credit. Sellers know that some buyers will be unable to pay their accounts when they become due. Buyers, for example, can suffer business downturns that are beyond their control, which limit their cash available to meet liabilities. They must, then, make choices concerning which of their liabilities to pay. Liabilities to the IRS, to banks, and to bondholders are usually paid, as those creditors have enforcement powers and can quickly seize assets and disrupt operations, leading to bankruptcy and eventual liquidation. Buyers also try to cover their payroll, as they cannot exist without employees. Then, if there is cash remaining, these customers will pay suppliers to ensure a continued flow of goods.

When a customer faces financial difficulties, suppliers are often the last creditors to receive payment and are often not paid in full. Consequently, there is risk in the collectibility of accounts receivable. This *collectibility risk* is crucial to analysis of accounts receivable.

Gillette reports $920 million of trade accounts receivable in the current asset section of its 2003 balance sheet.

Its receivables are reported net of allowances for uncollectible accounts of $53 million. This reporting means the total amount owed to Gillette is $973 million ($920 million + $53 million), but Gillette *estimates* that $53 million are uncollectible and reports on its balance sheet only the amount expected to be collected.

We might ask why Gillette would sell to companies from whom they do not expect to collect the amounts owed. The answer is they would not *if* they knew beforehand who those companies were. That is, Gillette probably cannot identify those companies that constitute the $53 million in uncollectible accounts as of its statement date. Yet, Gillette knows from past experience that a certain portion of its receivables will prove uncollectible. GAAP requires it to estimate the dollar amount of uncollectible accounts each time it issues its financial statements (even if it cannot identify specific accounts that are uncollectible), and to report its accounts receivable at the resulting *net realizable value* (total receivables less an **allowance for uncollectible accounts**).

---

[1] An example of common credit terms are 2/10, net 30. These terms indicate that the seller offers the buyer an early-pay incentive, which in this case is a 2% discount off the cost if the buyer pays within 10 days of billing. If the buyer does not take advantage of the discount, it must pay 100% of the invoice cost within 30 days of billing. From the seller's standpoint, offering the discount is often warranted because it receives cash more quickly, and it hopes to invest the monies to yield a return greater than the discount it is offering. The buyer often wishes to avail itself of attractive discounts even if it has to borrow money to do so. If the discount is not taken, however, the buyer should withhold payment as long as it can (at least for the full net period) so as to maximize its available cash while the seller will exert whatever pressure it can to collect the amount due as quickly as possible. There is normal tension between sellers and buyers in this regard.

Allowance for Uncollectible Accounts

The amount of expected uncollectible accounts is usually estimated based on an **aging analysis**. When aging the accounts, an analysis of receivables is performed as of the balance sheet date. Specifically, each customer's account balance is categorized by the number of days or months that the related invoices are outstanding. Based on prior experience, or on other available statistics, uncollectible (bad debt) percentages are applied to each of these categorized amounts, with larger percentages applied to older accounts. The result of this analysis is a dollar amount for the allowance for uncollectible accounts (also called allowance for doubtful accounts) at the balance sheet date.

LO1 Estimate uncollectible accounts receivable.

To illustrate, Exhibit 8.1 shows an aging analysis for a seller that began operations this year and is owed $100,000 of accounts receivable at year-end. Those accounts listed as current consist of those outstanding that are still within their original credit period. As an example, an invoice with terms 2/10, net 30, which has been outstanding for 30 days or less as of the financial statement date is current. Accounts listed as 1–60 days past due are those 1 to 60 days past their due date. This classification would include an account that is 45 days outstanding for a net 30-day invoice. This same logic applies to all aged categories.

> REMEMBER . . .
> Short-term receivables are valued and reported at net realizable value—the net amount expected to be received in cash. Determining net realizable value requires an estimation of uncollectible receivables.

EXHIBIT 8.1	Aging of Accounts Receivable		
Age of Accounts Receivable	Receivable Balance	Estimated Percent Uncollectible	Estimated Uncollectible Accounts
Current	$ 50,000	2%	$1,000
1–60 days past due	30,000	3	900
61–90 days past due	15,000	4	600
Over 90 days past due	5,000	8	400
Total	$100,000		$2,900

The calculation illustrated in exhibit 8.1 also reflects the seller's experience with uncollectible accounts, which manifests itself in the uncollectible percentages for each aged category. For example, on average, 3% of buyers' accounts that are 1–60 days past due prove uncollectible for this seller. Hence, it estimates a potential loss of $900 for those $30,000 in receivables for that aged category.[2]

How does the accounting system record this estimate? Recall that the amount that appears in the balance sheet as accounts receivable represents a collection of individual accounts—one or more receivables for each customer. Because we need to keep track of exactly how much each customer owes us, we cannot simply subtract estimated uncollectables from accounts receivable.

Thus, we introduce a new type of account—the **contra-asset account**. A *contra-asset* account is directly associated with an asset account, but serves to offset the asset account. Whenever we need to reduce the reported balance of an asset, we do not wish to subtract the amount directly from the asset itself, we record the reduction in a contra-asset account—in this case, allowance for uncollectible accounts. To illustrate, we use the data from Exhibit 8.1. First the summary journal entry to reflect credit sales follows (the template effects are shown later in this section).

(1) Accounts Receivable (+A)	100,000	
Sales (+R, +SE)		100,000

> NOTE
> The term provision is sometimes used as a substitute for expense; often used when the reported expense is an estimate.

At year-end, uncollectible accounts are estimated and recorded as follows as **bad debt expense** (also called *provision for uncollectible accounts*):

(2) Bad debt expense (+E, −SE)	2,900	
Allowance for uncollectible accounts (+XA, −A)		2,900

---

[2] Another means to estimate uncollectible accounts is to use the **percentage of sales.** To illustrate, if a company reports sales of $100,000 and estimates the provision at 3% of sales, it would report a bad debts expense of $3,000 instead of $2,900. This results in an allowance balance of $3,000 instead of $2,900 using the aging analysis. The percentage of sales method computes bad debts expense (the addition to the allowance balance), whereas the aging method computes the allowance balance (with bad debts expense being the amount needed to yield that balance). Thus, these methods nearly always report different values for the allowance, net accounts receivable, and bad debts expense.

The allowance for uncollectible accounts is a contra-asset account. It offsets (reduces) accounts receivable. These entries are posted in their corresponding T-accounts as follows.

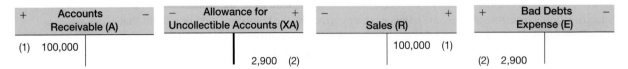

This accounting treatment serves three purposes. First, the balance in accounts receivable is reported in the balance sheet net of estimated uncollectible accounts as follows.

Accounts receivable, net of $2,900 in allowances $97,100

The $97,100 is the net realizable value of the accounts receivable. Second, the original value of accounts receivable is preserved. The individual accounts that add up to the $100,000 in accounts receivable have not been altered. Third, bad debts expense of $2,900, which is part of the cost of offering credit to customers, is matched against the $100,000 sales generated on credit and reported in the income statement. Bad debt expense is usually included in SG&A expenses.

The allowance for uncollectible accounts is increased by bad debts expense (estimated provision for uncollectibles) and decreased when an account is written off. Because the allowance for uncollectible accounts is a contra-asset account, credit entries increase its balance. The greater the balance in the contra-asset account, the more the corresponding asset account is offset.

An individual account is written off when the seller decides that it is uncollectible. To illustrate a write-off, assume that in the next period (year 2), the company described above receives notice that one of its customers, owing $500 at the time, has declared bankruptcy. The seller's attorneys believe that the legal costs necessary to collect the amount would exceed the $500 owed. The seller could then decide to write off the account with the following entry.

(3) Allowance for uncollectible accounts (−XA, +A)   500
      Accounts receivable (−A)   500

Posting this entry to the respective T-accounts yields the following.

Exhibit 8.2 summarizes the effects of this write-off on the individual accounts.

EXHIBIT 8.2	Effects of an Accounts Receivable Write-Off		
Account	**Before Write-Off**	**Effects of Write-Off**	**After Write-Off**
Accounts receivable	$100,000	$ (500)	$ 99,500
Less: Allowance for uncollectible accounts	2,900	500	2,400
Accounts receivable, net of allowance	$ 97,100		$ 97,100

The net amount of accounts receivable that is reported in the balance sheet after the write-off is the same amount that was reported before the write-off. This is always the case. The individual account receivable was reduced and the contra-asset was reduced by the same amount. Also no entry was made to the income statement. The expense was estimated and recorded in the period when the credit sales were recorded.

To complete the illustration, assume that management estimate that another $600 should be added to the allowance account at the end of year 2. The entry to record the year 2 provision follows.

(4) Bad debt expense (+E, −SE)	600	
Allowance for uncollectible accounts (+XA, −A)		600

This entry is the same (albeit with a different dollar amount) as was entered to record the estimate in year 1. A reconciliation of allowance for uncollectible accounts for the two years follows.

	Year 1	Year 2
Allowance for uncollectible accounts, beginning balance	$ 0	$2,900
Add: provision for uncollectible accounts (bad debt expense estimate)	2,900	600
Subtract: write-offs of uncollectible accounts receivable	0	500
Allowance for uncollectible accounts, ending balance	$2,900	$3,000

To summarize, the *main balance sheet and income statement effects occur when the provision is made to the allowance for uncollectible accounts.* Accounts receivable (net) is reduced, and that reduction is reflected in the income statement as bad debts expense (usually part of selling, general, and administrative expenses). The net income reduction yields a corresponding equity reduction (via reduced retained earnings). Importantly, the main financial statement effects are at the point of *estimation*, not upon the event of *write-off.* In this way, sales are matched with bad debts expense, and accounts receivable are matched with its expected uncollectible accounts. Exhibit 8.3 illustrates each of the transactions discussed in this section using the financial statement effects template:

LO2 Analyze effects of uncollectible accounts on financial statements and footnotes.

EXHIBIT 8.3	Financial Statement Effects of Key Accounts Receivable Transactions

	Balance Sheet						Income Statement		
Transaction	Cash Asset	+ Noncash Assets	= Liabil- ities	+ Contrib. Capital	+ Retained Earnings		Revenues	− Expenses	= Net Income
a. Sales of $100,000 on credit		+100,000 = Accounts Receivable			+100,000 Retained Earnings		+100,000 Sales		= +100,000
b. Estimate $2,900 in bad debts		−2,900 = Allowance for Uncollectibles			−2,900 Retained Earnings			−2,900 Bad Debts Expense	= −2,900
c. Write-off $500 in accounts receivable		−500 = Accounts Receivable +500 Allowance for Uncollectibles							=
d. Estimated $600 in more bad debts		−600 = Allowance for Uncollectibles			−600 Retained Earnings			−600 Bad Debts Expense	= −600

Footnote Disclosures, and Interpretations

To illustrate the typical footnote disclosure related to accounts receivable, consider Gillette and its disclosure relating to its allowance for uncollectible accounts:

> With respect to trade receivables, concentration of credit risk is limited, due to the diverse geographic areas covered by Gillette operations. The Company's largest customer, Wal-Mart Stores, Inc. and its affiliates, accounted for 13% of consolidated net sales in 2003, and 12% of consolidated net sales in both 2002 and 2001. These sales occurred primarily in North America and were across all product segments. At December 31, 2003 and 2002, 44% and 40% of the Company's accounts receivable were from customers in North America, respectively. Wal-Mart Stores, Inc. represented 23% and 17% of the North American accounts receivable at December 31, 2003 and 2002, respectively. Using the best information available, the Company has provided an allowance for doubtful accounts based on estimated bad-debt loss.

Given the large concentration of its receivables with **Wal-Mart**, Gillette does not have much risk related to their collection. (Note Wal-Mart's power over suppliers—it represents 23% of Gillette's receivables but only 13% of its sales.)

Gillette provides a footnote reconciliation of its allowance for uncollectible (doubtful) accounts for the past three years as shown in Exhibit 8.4.

EXHIBIT 8.4	Reconciliation of Gillette's Allowance for Uncollectible Accounts			
Allowance for Doubtful Accounts **Years ended December 31 (millions)**		**2003**	**2002**	**2001**
Balance at beginning of year		$73	$69	$81
Additions		19	37	30
Deductions		(39)	(33)	(42)
Balance at end of year		$53	$73	$69

The reconciliation of Gillette's allowance account provides insight into the level of its provision (bad debts expense) per year relative to its actual write-offs. For example, the 2003 provision of $19 million was much less than the 2003 write-offs of $39 million. Its allowance account declined as a result; that is, Gillette utilized amounts accrued in one or more prior years to absorb losses in the current year. For this entire three-year period, Gillette has increased the allowance account by a cumulative total of $86 million ($19 million + $37 million + $30 million) and has written off accounts equal to an aggregate amount of $114 million ($39 million + $33 million + $42 million). As a result, the allowance account has been reduced by a cumulative amount of $28 million during the past three years.

On a percentage basis, the 2003 allowance account represents 5.4% of gross accounts receivable [$53 million/($920 million + $53 million)]. The 2002 allowance account represents 5.7% of gross accounts receivable [$73 million/($1,202 million + $73 million)]. Gillette, therefore, has reduced the 2003 allowance account as a percentage of gross accounts receivable compared to 2002.

The reduction in Gillette's allowance account results from greater write-offs and a lower provision. Since 2003 additions to the allowance account are reduced relative to 2002, Gillette appears to be living off the allowance account established in prior years. A question we must ask at the end of 2003 is whether the allowance account is adequate to absorb expected losses. If not, then Gillette's receivables are overstated on its balance sheet and its income is also overstated (because too little bad debt expense is recognized).

Analysis Implications and Ratios

This section considers analysis of accounts receivable and its provision for uncollectible accounts.

Adequacy of Allowance Account

A company makes two representations when reporting accounts receivable (net) in the current asset section of its balance sheet:

1. It expects to collect the asset amount reported on the balance sheet (remember, accounts receivable are reported net of allowance for uncollectible accounts).

2. It expects to collect the asset amount within the next year (implied from its classification as a current asset).

From an analysis viewpoint, we scrutinize the adequacy of a company's provision for its uncollectible accounts. If the provision is inadequate, the cash ultimately collected will be less than what the company is reporting as net receivables.

How can an outsider assess the adequacy of the allowance account? One answer is to examine the percentage of the allowance account to gross accounts receivable. For Gillette, the 2003 percentage is 5.4% (see above), a slight decline from the prior year. What does such a decline signify? Perhaps the overall economic environment has improved, rendering write-offs less likely. Perhaps the company has improved its credit underwriting or receivables collection efforts. Such new initiatives are likely to be discussed in the MD&A section of its financial report. Or perhaps the company's customer mix has changed and it is now selling to more creditworthy customers (or, it eliminated a risky customer class).

The important point is that we must be comfortable with the percentage of uncollectible accounts reported by the company. We must remember that management has control over the adequacy and reporting of the allowance account—albeit with audit assurances.

Earnings Management

The main financial statement effects of uncollectible accounts are normally at the point of estimation, not on the event of write-off. Further, the amount and timing of the uncollectible provision is largely controlled by management. Although external auditors assess the reasonableness of the allowance for uncollectible accounts, auditors do not possess the inside knowledge and experience of management and are, therefore, at an information disadvantage, particularly if a dispute arises.

Experience tells us that many companies have previously used the allowance for uncollectible accounts to shift income from one year into another. For example, by underestimating the provision, bad debt expense is reduced in the current period, thus increasing current period income. In one or more future periods, when write-offs occur, it must then increase the provision to make up for the underestimated provision of the current period. This adjustment reduces income in future periods. Income has, thus, been shifted from a future period into the current period.

Why would a company want to engage in shifting income from a later period into the current period? Perhaps it is a lean year and the company is in danger of missing income targets. For example, internal targets affect manager bonuses and external targets set by the market influence stock prices. Perhaps the company is in danger of defaulting on loan agreements tied to income levels. The reality is that pressures to meet income targets are great and these pressures can cause companies to bend the rules.

We should also consider whether a company engages in shifting income from the current period to one or more future periods. For example, when a company overestimates the current period uncollectible provision it reduces current period income. Then, in future lean periods, the company can reduce its allowance account as a percentage of gross accounts receivable, thereby increasing income in these future periods.

Why would a company want to shift income from the current period to one or more future periods? Perhaps current times are good and the company wants to "bank" some of that income for future periods—sometimes called a **cookie jar reserve.** It can then draw on that reserve, if necessary, to boost income in one or more future lean years. Perhaps another reason for a company to shift income from the current period is that it does not wish to unduly inflate current market expectations and pressures for future period income. Or, perhaps the company is experiencing a very bad year and it feels that overestimating the provision will not drive income materially lower than it already is. Thus, the company decides to take a big bath and create a reserve that can be used in future periods. **Sears** (now **Macy's**) provides an interesting example as described in the Business Insight below.

Use of the allowance for uncollectible accounts to shift income is a source of concern. This concern is especially critical for banks because the allowance for loan losses is usually a large component of their balance sheet and loan loss expense is a major component of reported income. Our analysis must scrutinize the allowance for uncollectible accounts to identify any changes from past practices or industry norms and, then, to justify those changes before accepting them as valid.

Accounts Receivable Turnover and Average Collection Period

Total asset turnover is computed as sales divided by average total assets. An important compliment to this measure is the accounts receivables turnover (ART), which is defined as:

> **Accounts Receivable Turnover = Sales/Average Accounts Receivable**

Accounts receivable turnover reveals how many times receivables have turned (been collected) during the period. More turns indicate that receivables are being collected more quickly.

A companion measure to accounts receivable turnover is the average collection period (ACP) for accounts receivable, also called *days sales outstanding (DSO)*, which is defined as:

> **Average Collection Period = Accounts Receivable/Average Daily Sales**

where average daily sales equals sales divided by 365 days. The average collection period indicates how long, on average, the receivables are outstanding before being collected.

To illustrate, assume that sales are $1,000, ending accounts receivable are $230, and the average accounts receivable is $200. The accounts receivable turnover is 5, computed as

NOTE
Technically, net credit sales should be used in the numerator as receivables arise from credit sales and the inclusion of cash sales inflates the ratio. Typically, however, outsiders do not know the level of cash sales and total sales must be used, most of which are likely to be credit sales.

BUSINESS INSIGHT

Sears' Cookie Jar   The Heard on the Street column in *The Wall Street Journal* (1996) reported the following: "Analyst David Poneman argues that Sears' earnings growth this year of 24%, or $134 million, has been aided by a 1993 balance-sheet maneuver that softens the impact of soaring levels of bad credit-card debt among its 50 million cardholders. Wall Street got a wake-up call in the second quarter, when Sears increased its provision for bad credit-card debt by $254 million, up 73% from the year earlier. Then in the third quarter, it made another $286 million provision, a 53% increase. Yet the retailer posted a 22% gain in third-quarter net. How so? 'Sears is using its superabundant balance sheet to smooth out its earnings,' says Mr. Poneman. He says Sears has a 'quality-of-earnings' issue."

Poneman is referring to a $2 billion reserve for credit losses that Sears set up in 1993. As it turned out, the reserve was higher than needed. Three years later, Sears still had a nearly $1 billion reserve on its balance sheet. That's nearly twice the size of reserves at most credit-card companies as a percentage of receivables. The credit-card reserve was part of a big bath that also included restructuring charges that Sears took in 1993. Such charges and reserves can be a big help for a new CEO (which Sears had) who wishes to show a pattern of improving results in future years. Poneman says the big addition to reserves "moved income out of 1992 and 1993 and into 1995 and 1996." Why is that bad? The overly large reserve allowed Sears to prop up its earnings at a time when losses in its credit-card unit were soaring. Sears' credit-card delinquencies had risen by $420 million in 1996. Poneman asserts that "Considering that increased delinquencies exceed year-to-date increased earnings, it could be argued that the increase in Sears' year-to-date earnings has depended entirely on its over-reserved condition."

$1,000/200, and the average collection period (days sales outstanding) is 84 days, computed as $230/($1,000/365).

The accounts receivable turnover and the average collection period yield valuable insights on at least two dimensions:

1. *Receivables quality*   A change in receivable turnover (and collection period) provides insight into accounts receivable quality. If turnover slows (collection period lengthens), the reason could be deterioration in collectibility of receivables. However, before reaching this conclusion, consider at least three alternative explanations:
   a. A seller can extend its credit terms. If the seller is attempting to enter new markets or take market share from competitors, it may extend credit terms to attract buyers.
   b. A seller can take on longer-paying customers. For example, facing increased competition, many computer and automobile companies began leasing their products, thus reducing the cash outlay for customers and stimulating sales. The change in mix away from cash sales and toward leasing had the effect of reducing receivables turnover and increasing the collection period.
   c. The seller can increase the allowance provision. Receivables turnover is often computed using net receivables (after the allowance for uncollectible accounts). Overestimating the provision reduces net receivables and increases turnover.
2. *Asset utilization*   Asset turnover is an important measure of financial performance, both by managers for internal performance goals, as well as by the market in evaluating companies. High-performing companies must be both efficient (controlling margins and operating expenses) and productive (getting the most out of their asset base). An increase in receivables ties up cash as the receivables must be financed, and slower-turning receivables carry increased risk of loss. One of the first "low hanging fruits" that companies pursue in efforts to improve asset utilization is efficiency in receivables collection.

Exhibit 8.5 shows the accounts receivable turnover for Gillette and three of its peer competitors as identified by Gillette in its 10-K.

The improvement in Gillette's receivable turnover over the 2001–2003 period from 4.2 times to 6.6 times is evident, and it now exceeds the turnover for Energizer. Nevertheless, Gillette's turnover is still less than Colgate-Palmolive and markedly lower than Procter & Gamble. The two latter companies also have large sales to Wal-Mart.

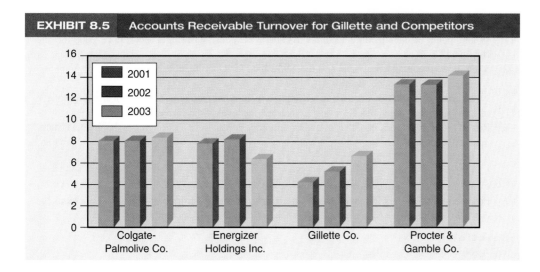

EXHIBIT 8.5   Accounts Receivable Turnover for Gillette and Competitors

A possible cause for these differences in turnover is the relative sizes of these companies. Gillette is a $9.3 billion (sales) company, Colgate-Palmolive is a $9.9 billion company, and Proctor & Gamble, is a $43.4 billion company. P&G's greater size likely confers some negotiating advantage even against a behemoth like Wal-Mart (with 2003 sales of $256 billion).

To appreciate differences in accounts receivable turnover rates across industries, examine the comparison of Gillette with companies in other industries illustrated in Exhibit 8.6:

Gillette and **Fortune Brands** have similar accounts receivable turnover. These companies are comparable in that both manufacture and sell consumer products. Fortune Brands' products include Titleist golf balls and equipment, Moen faucets, and Jim Beam whiskey. **Caterpillar**, on the other hand, is a heavy equipment producer that finances much of its equipment sales with intermediate-term loans and leases. Thus, its accounts receivable turnover is much lower. At the other end is **Dell Computer**. Much of Dell's sales occur on a cash basis via the Internet and, hence, its accounts receivable turnover is very high.

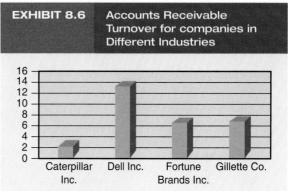

EXHIBIT 8.6   Accounts Receivable Turnover for companies in Different Industries

YOU MAKE THE CALL

You Are the Receivables Manager   You are analyzing your receivables turnover report for the period, and you are concerned that the average collection period is lengthening. What specific actions can you take to reduce the average collection period? [Answers on page 350]

MID-CHAPTER REVIEW

At December 31, 2005, Engel Company had a balance of $770,000 in its Accounts Receivable account and an unused balance of $7,000 in its Allowance for Uncollectible Accounts. The company then analyzed and aged its accounts receivable as follows:

Current	$468,000
1–60 days past due	244,000
61–180 days past due	38,000
Over 180 days past due	20,000
Total accounts receivable	$770,000

In the past, the company experienced losses as follows: 1% of current balances, 5% of balances 0–60 days past due, 15% of balances 61–180 days past due, and 40% of balances over 180 days past due. The company bases its provision for credit losses on the aging analysis.

Required

1. What amount of uncollectible accounts (bad debts) expense will Engel report in its 2005 income statement?
2. Show how Accounts Receivable and the Allowance for Uncollectible Accounts appear in its December 31, 2005, balance sheet.
3. Assume that Engel's allowance for uncollectible accounts has maintained an historical average of 2% of gross accounts receivable. How do you interpret the level of the current allowance percentage?
4. Report the effects for each of the following summary transactions a through c in the financial statement effects template.
    a. Credit sales of $770,000.
    b. Bad debts expense estimated at $23,580.
    c. Write-off $5,000 in customer accounts.
5. Prepare journal entries for each of the transactions a through c from part 4. Set up T-accounts for each of the accounts used and post the journal entries to those T-accounts.

Solution

1. As of December 31, 2005,

Current	$468,000	×	1% =	$ 4,680
1–60 days past due	244,000	×	5% =	12,200
61–180 days past due	38,000	×	15% =	5,700
Over 180 days past due	20,000	×	40% =	8,000
Amount required				$30,580
Unused allowance balance				7,000
Provision				$23,580 2005 bad debts expense

2. Current assets section of balance sheet.

Accounts receivable, net of $30,580 in allowances $739,420

3. Engel Company has markedly increased the percentage of the allowance for uncollectible accounts to gross accounts receivable—from the historical 2% to the current 4% ($30,580/$770,000). There are at least two possible interpretations:
    a. The quality of Engel Company's receivables has declined. Possible causes include the following: (1) Sales can stagnate and the company can feel compelled to sell to lower quality accounts to maintain sales volume; (2) It may have introduced new products for which average credit losses are higher; and (3) Its administration of accounts receivable can become lax.
    b. The company has intentionally increased its allowance account above the level needed for expected future losses so as to reduce current period income and "bank" that income for future periods (income shifting).
4. Transaction effects shown in the financial statement effects template.

	Balance Sheet					Income Statement		
Transaction	Cash Asset	+ Noncash Assets	= Liabil- ities	+ Contrib. Capital	+ Retained Earnings	Revenues	− Expenses	= Net Income
a. Credit sales of $770,000		+770,000 = Accounts Receivable			+770,000 Retained Earnings	+770,000 Sales		= +770,000
b. Estimate $23,580 in bad debts		−23,580 = Allowance for Uncollectibles			−23,580 Retained Earnings		−23,580 Bad Debts Expense	= −23,580
c. Write-off $5000 in accounts receivable		−5,000 = Accounts Receivable +5,000 Allowance for Uncollectibles						=

5. Journal entries and postings to T-accounts.

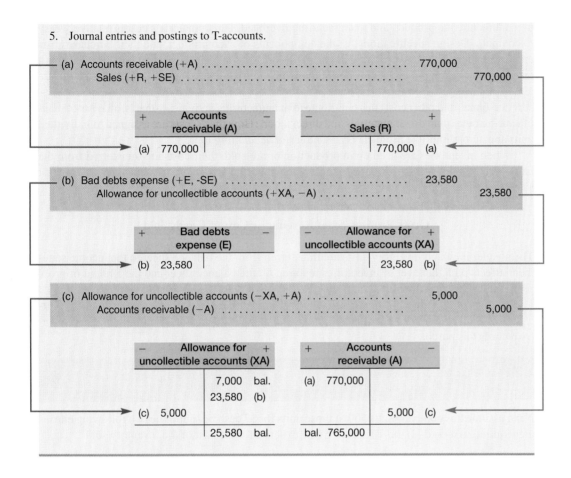

INVENTORIES

The second of the two major components of operating working capital is inventory. To help frame this discussion, we again refer to the following graphic. We highlight inventory, which is a major asset for most manufacturers and merchandisers. We also highlight cost of goods sold on the income statement, which reflects the flow of inventory costs to match against related sales. This section explains the accounting, reporting, and analysis of inventory and related items.

Income Statement	Balance Sheet	
Sales	Cash	Current liabilities
Cost of goods sold	Accounts receivable	Long-term liabilities
Selling, general & administrative	Inventory	
Income taxes	Property, plant, and equipment, net	Shareholders' equity
Net income	Investments	

Inventory is reported on the balance sheet at its purchase price or the cost to manufacture those goods if internally produced. Such prices and costs typically vary over time with changes in market conditions. Consequently, the cost per unit of the goods available for sale likely varies from period to period—even if the quantity of goods available remains the same.

When inventory is purchased or produced, it is capitalized and carried on the balance sheet as an asset until it is sold, at which time its cost is transferred from the balance sheet to the income statement as an expense (cost of goods sold). The process by which costs are removed from the balance sheet is important. For example, if higher cost units are transferred from the balance sheet when a sale is recorded, then gross profit (sales less cost of goods sold) is lower. Conversely, if lower cost units are transferred to cost of goods sold, gross profit is higher.

For purchased inventories (such as those with merchandisers), the amount of cost capitalized is the purchase price. For manufacturers, cost capitalization is more difficult, as **manufacturing costs** consist of three components: cost of direct materials used in the product, cost of direct labor

> **NOTE**
> *Only one inventory account appears in the financial statements of a merchandiser. A manufacturer normally has three inventory accounts: Raw Materials, Work in Process, and Finished Goods.*

to manufacture the product, and manufacturing overhead. Direct materials cost is relatively easy to compute. Design specifications list the components of each product, and their purchase costs are readily determined. The direct labor cost per unit of inventory is based on how long each unit takes to construct and the rates for each individual working on that product. Overhead costs are also capitalized into inventory, and include the costs of plant asset depreciation, utilities, supervisory personnel, and other costs that contribute to manufacturing activities—that is, all costs of manufacturing other than direct materials and direct labor. (How these costs are assigned to individual units and across multiple products is a *managerial accounting* topic.)

When inventories are used up in production or are sold, their costs are transferred from the balance sheet to the income statement as cost of goods sold (COGS). COGS is then matched against sales revenue to yield **gross profit**:

$$\text{Gross Profit} = \text{Sales Revenue} - \text{Cost of Goods Sold}$$

The manner in which inventory costs are transferred from the balance sheet to the income statement affects both the level of inventories reported on the balance sheet and the amount of gross profit (and net income) reported on the income statement.

To illustrate the inventory purchasing and selling cycle, assume that a startup company purchases 800 units of merchandise inventory at a cost of $4 cash per unit. The following journal entry records this purchase.

(1) Inventory (+A)	3,200	
Cash (−A)		3,200

Next, assume this company sells 500 of those units for $7 cash per unit. The two following entries are required to record (a) the sales and (b) the expense for the cost of the inventory sold.

(2a) Cash (+A)	3,500	
Sales (+R, +SE)		3,500
(2b) Cost of Goods Sold (+E, −SE)	2,000	
Inventory (−A)		2,000

These entries would be posted to the following T-accounts as shown.

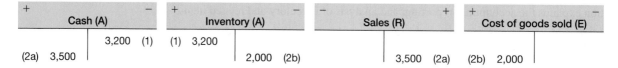

The gross profit from this sale is $1,500 ($3,500 - $2,000). Also, $1,200 worth of merchandise remains in inventory (300 units × $4 per unit). This set of transactions is summarized in the following financial statement effects template.

	Balance Sheet						Income Statement		
Transaction	**Cash Asset**	**+ Noncash Assets**	**= Liabilities**	**+ Contrib. Capital**	**+ Retained Earnings**		**Revenues**	**− Expenses =**	**Net Income**
(1) Purchased 800 units of inventory at $4 cash per unit	−3,200 Cash	+3,200 Inventory	=						=
(2a) Sold 500 units of inventory for $3,500 cash	+3,500 Cash		=		+3,500 Retained Earnings		+3,500 Sales		= +3,500
(2b) Record cost of goods sold with 2a		−2,000 Inventory	=		−2,000 Retained Earnings			−2,000 Cost of Goods Sold	= −2,000

Inventory Costing Methods

Computation of cost of goods sold is important and is shown in Exhibit 8.7.

EXHIBIT 8.7	Cost of Goods Sold Computation

	Beginning inventory (prior period balance sheet)
+	Inventory purchases and/or production
	Cost of goods available for sale
−	Ending inventory (current period balance sheet)
	Cost of goods sold (current income statement)

The cost of inventory available at the beginning of a period is a carryover from the ending inventory balance of the prior period. Current period purchases of inventory (or costs of newly manufactured inventories) are added to the costs of beginning inventory on the balance sheet, yielding the total cost of goods (inventory) available for sale. Then, the total cost of goods available either end up in cost of goods sold for the period (reported on the income statement) or is carried forward as inventory to start the next period (reported on the balance sheet). This cost flow is graphically shown in Exhibit 8.8.

LO3 Account for inventory and cost of goods sold using different costing methods.

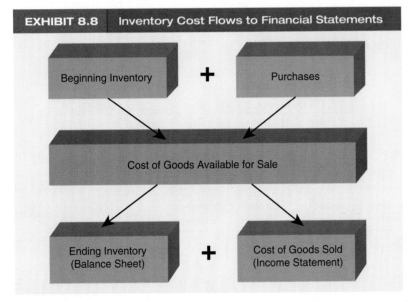

EXHIBIT 8.8	Inventory Cost Flows to Financial Statements

Beginning Inventory + Purchases

Cost of Goods Available for Sale

Ending Inventory (Balance Sheet) + Cost of Goods Sold (Income Statement)

Understanding the flow of inventory costs is important. If the beginning inventory plus all inventory purchased or manufactured during the period is sold, then COGS is equal to the cost of the goods available for sale. However, when inventory remains at the end of a period, companies must identify the cost of those inventories that have been sold and the cost of those inventories that remain. The issue involves determining the sequence in which inventories have been sold and GAAP allows for several options.

To illustrate the possible cost flow assumptions that companies can adopt, assume that Exhibit 8.9 reflects the inventory records of Butler company.

EXHIBIT 8.9	Summary Inventory Records for Butler Company

Inventory on January 1, 2005	500 units	@ $ 100 each	$50,000
Inventory purchased in 2005	200 units	@ $ 170 each	34,000
Total cost of goods available for sale in 2005	700 units		$84,000

Butler company began the period with inventories consisting of 500 units that it purchased at a total cost of $50,000 ($100 each). During the period the company purchased additional 200 units costing $34,000. The total cost of goods that are available for sale for this period equals $84,000.

Butler company sold 450 units during 2005 at a selling price of $250 per unit for total sales revenue of $112,500. Accordingly, the company must remove the cost of the 450 units sold from its reported inventories on the balance sheet and match this cost against the revenues generated from the goods sold (reported as cost of goods sold). Which costs should management remove from the balance sheet and report as cost of goods sold in the income statement: the units costing $100 each, the units costing $170 each, or some combination of both? Three inventory costing methods are commonly used, and all are acceptable under GAAP.

First-In, First-Out (FIFO)

The **first-in, first-out (FIFO)** inventory costing method transfers costs from inventory in the order that they were initially recorded. That is, FIFO assumes that the first costs recorded in inventory (first-in) are the first costs transferred from inventory (first-out). Conversely, the last units purchased are the units that remain in inventory at year-end. Applying FIFO to the data in Exhibit 8.9 means that the costs relating to the 450 units sold are all taken from its *beginning* inventory, which consists of 500 units. The company's cost of goods sold and gross profit, using FIFO, is computed as follows:

Sales	$112,500
COGS (450 @ $100 each)	45,000
Gross profit	$ 67,500

The journal entry to record cost of goods sold computed using FIFO, along with its posting to T-accounts, follows.

Cost of goods sold (+E, −SE)	45,000	
Inventory (−A)		45,000

+ Inventory (A) −	+ Cost of Goods Sold (E) −
45,000	45,000

The effects of these inventory purchases and cost of goods sold on its financial statements follow.

Transaction	Balance Sheet					Income Statement		
	Cash Asset	+ Noncash Assets	= Liabil-ities	+ Contrib. Capital	+ Retained Earnings	Revenues	− Expenses	= Net Income
(1) Purchased 200 units @ $170 each	−34,000 Cash	+34,000 Inventory	=					=
(2) Sold 450 units of inventory		−45,000 Inventory			−45,000 Retained Earnings		−45,000 Cost of Goods Sold	= −45,000

The cost remaining in inventory and reported on its 2005 year-end balance sheet is $39,000 ($84,000 − $45,000; also computed 50 × $100 + 200 × $170).

Last-In, First-Out (LIFO)

The **last-in, first-out (LIFO)** inventory costing method transfers the most recent costs that were recorded in inventory. That is, we assume that the most recent costs recorded in inventory (last-in) are the first costs transferred from inventory (first-out). Conversely, the first units purchased are the units that remain in inventory at year-end. The company's cost of goods sold and gross profit, using LIFO, is computed as follows:

Sales		$112,500
COGS: (200 @ $170 each = $34,000)		
(250 @ $100 each = $25,000)		59,000
Gross profit		$ 53,500

The cost remaining in inventory and reported on its 2005 balance sheet is $25,000 (84,000 − $59,000; also computed 250 × $100).

Average Cost (AC)

The **average cost (AC)** method computes the cost of goods sold as an average of the cost to purchase all of the inventories that were available for sale during the period as follows:

Sales	$112,500
COGS (450 @ $120 [$84,000/700 units] each)	54,000
Gross profit	$58,500

The average cost of $120 per unit is determined from the total cost of goods available for sale divided by the number of units available for sale ($84,000/700 units). The cost remaining in inventory and reported on its 2005 balance sheet is $30,000 ($84,000 − $54,000; also computed 250 × $120).

Footnote Disclosures

Notes to the financial statements describe, at least in general terms, the inventory accounting method used by a company. To illustrate, **Gillette** reports $1,094 million in inventory on its 2003 balance sheet as a current asset. Gillette includes a general footnote on inventory along with more specific disclosures in other footnotes. Following is an excerpt from Gillette's general footnote related to inventories:

> Inventories are stated at the lower of cost or market. Cost is determined on a first-in, first-out (FIFO) basis.

This footnote includes at least two items of interest for our analysis of inventory:

1. Gillette uses the FIFO method of inventory costing.
2. Inventories are reported at the lower of cost or market—lower of cost or market (LCM) means that inventory is written down if its replacement cost declines below its FIFO cost reported on the balance sheet.

Gillette includes another footnote that provides further details on its manufacturing inventories.

> *NOTE*
> *Standards require the consistent application of costing methods from one period to another.*

Inventories At December 31 (millions)	2003	2002
Raw materials and supplies	$ 114	$115
Work in process	196	191
Finished goods	784	622
Total inventories	$1,094	$928

This disclosure separately reports its inventory costs by the three stages in its production cycle:

- **Raw materials and supplies** These are costs of direct materials and inputs into the production process, including for example base chemicals in raw state, plastic and steel for manufacturing, and incidental direct materials such as screws and lubricants.
- **Work in process** These are costs of partly finished products (also called work-in-progress) in the manufacturing process.
- **Finished goods** These are the costs of products that are completed and awaiting sale.

Gillette's raw materials and work-in-process inventories have roughly remained at 2002 levels despite a 9.5% increase in sales. This result likely reflects its cost reduction and production efficiency programs initiated in 2002–2003. On the other hand, its finished goods inventory has increased.

Caterpillar, Inc. reports the following disclosure to its 2003 10-K regarding its inventories.

> *REMEMBER…*
> *Standards require financial statement disclosure of (1) the composition of the inventory (in the balance sheet or a separate schedule in the notes), (2) significant or unusual inventory financing arrangements, and (3) inventory costing methods employed (which can differ for different types of inventory).*

> Inventories are stated at the lower of cost or market. Cost is principally determined using the last-in, first-out (LIFO) method. The value of inventories on the LIFO basis represented about 80% of total inventories at December 31, 2003, 2002 and 2001.
>
> If the FIFO (first-in, first-out) method had been in use, inventories would have been $1,863 million, $1,977 million and $1,923 million higher than reported at December 31, 2003, 2002 and 2001, respectively.

Most of CAT's inventories are reported using LIFO.[5] The use of LIFO has reduced the carrying amount of its 2003 inventories by $1,863 million. Had it used FIFO, its inventories would have been reported at $4,910 million rather than the $3,047 million that is reported on its balance sheet as of 2003. This

---

[5]Neither the IRS nor GAAP requires use of a single inventory costing method. That is, companies are allowed to, and frequently do, use different inventory costing methods for different pools of their inventories (such as spare parts versus finished goods).

difference, referred to as the **LIFO reserve**, is the amount LIFO inventories must be adjusted to equal FIFO inventories.

Why do companies disclose such details on inventory, and why is so much attention paid to inventory in financial statement analysis? First, the magnitude of a company's investment in inventory is often large—impacting both balance sheets and income statements. Second, risks of inventory losses are often high, as they are tied to technical obsolescence and consumer tastes. Third, it can provide insight into future performance—both good and bad. Fourth, high inventory levels result in substantial costs for the company, such as:

- Financing costs to purchase inventories (when not purchased on credit)
- Storage costs of inventories (such as warehousing and related facilities)
- Handling costs of inventories (including wages)
- Insurance costs of inventories

Consequently, companies seek to minimize the amount of inventories, provided this does not exceed the cost of insufficient inventory (stock-out and resulting lost sales and delays in production, as machines and employees sit idle awaiting inventories to process).

LO4 Apply the lower of cost or market rule to value inventory

Lower of Cost or Market

Gillette's inventory disclosures make reference to the cost of its inventories not exceeding market value. This is important, as companies are required to write down the carrying amount of inventories on the balance sheet, *if* the reported cost (using FIFO, for example) exceeds market value (determined by current replacement cost). This process is called reporting inventories at the **lower of cost or market (LCM)**. Should the replacement cost (market value) be less than reported cost, the inventories must be written down from cost to market, resulting in the following financial statement effects.

- Inventory book value is written down to current market value (replacement cost), reducing total assets.
- Inventory write-down is reflected as an expense (part of cost of goods sold) on the income statement, reducing current period gross profit, income, and equity.

REMEMBER...
If inventory declines in value below its original cost, for whatever reason, the inventory is written down to reflect this loss.

The most common occurrence of inventory write-downs is in connection with restructuring activities. These write-downs are included in cost of goods sold.

The write-down of inventories can potentially shift income from one period to another. If, for example, inventories were written down below current replacement cost (too conservative), future gross profit would be increased as lower future costs would be reflected in cost of goods sold. GAAP anticipates this possibility by requiring that inventories not be written down below a floor that is equal to net realizable value less a normal markup. Although this does allow some discretion (and the ability to manage income), the net realizable value and markup values must be substantiated by auditors.

The chapter-end review provides an illustration of the mechanics for the lower of cost or market rule.

Financial Statement Effects of Inventory Costing

LO5 Evaluate how inventory costing impacts management decisions and outsiders' interpretations of financial statements

This section describes the financial statement effects of different inventory costing methods.

Income Statement Effects

The three inventory costing methods described yield differing levels of gross profit for our illustrative example as shown in Exhibit 8.10

The underlying cost behavior of this case is important; the illustrative company's unit costs are subject to inflation and, as a result, inventory costs have risen during this period (from $100 per unit to $170 per unit). The higher gross profit reported under FIFO (vis-à-vis LIFO) is because it matches older, lower cost inventory against current selling prices. To generalize: in an inflationary environment, FIFO yields higher gross profit than does LIFO or average cost.

EXHIBIT 8.10	Income Effects from Inventory Costing Methods		
	Sales	Cost of Goods Sold	Gross Profit
FIFO	$ 112,500	$ 45,000	$ 67,500
LIFO	112,500	59,000	53,500
Average cost	112,500	54,000	58,500

> **NOTE**
> *If ending inventory is misstated, then (1) the inventory, retained earnings, working capital, and current ratio in the balance sheet is misstated, and (2) the cost of goods sold and net income in the income statement is misstated.*

The gross profit impact from FIFO is determined by two effects. First, goods previously purchased at a lower cost can now be sold at a higher selling price (due to inflation). Second, the longer those goods sit in inventory as inflation occurs, the greater the holding gain from inflation. In recent years, such gains have been minimal due to minimal inflation and increased management focus on reducing inventory quantities through improved manufacturing processes and better inventory controls. The FIFO gross profit effect can still arise, however, in industries subject to high inflation and slow inventory turnover.

Balance Sheet Effects

The ending inventory using LIFO for our illustration is less than that reported using FIFO. In periods of rising costs, using LIFO generally yields ending inventories that are markedly lower than FIFO. As a result, balance sheets using LIFO do not accurately represent the cost that a company would incur to replace its current investment in inventories.

Caterpillar (CAT), for example, reports 2003 inventories under LIFO costing $3,047 million. As disclosed in the footnotes to its 10-K, if CAT valued these inventories using FIFO, the reported amount would be $1,863 million greater, a 61% increase. This result suggests that over $1,863 million currently invested in inventories is omitted from CAT's balance sheet.

Cash Flow Effects

The increased gross profit using FIFO results in higher pretax income and, consequently, higher taxes payable (assuming FIFO is also used for tax reporting). Conversely, the use of LIFO in an inflationary environment results in a reduced tax liability.

Use of LIFO has reduced the dollar amount of CAT's inventories by $1,863 million, resulting in a cumulative increase in cost of goods sold and a cumulative decrease in gross profit and pretax profit of that same amount.[7] The decrease in cumulative pretax profits reduces CAT's tax bill by $652 million ($1,863 million × 35% assumed corporate tax rate), which increases CAT's cumulative operating cash flow by that same amount. The increased cash flow from tax savings is often cited as a compelling reason for management to adopt LIFO.

For analysis purposes, we can use the LIFO reserve to adjust the balance sheet and income statement to achieve comparability between companies that utilize different inventory costing methods. For example, if we wanted to compare CAT with another company using FIFO, we can add the LIFO reserve to its LIFO inventory. As explained above, this $1,863 million increase in 2003 inventories would have increased its cumulative pretax profits by $1,863 million and taxes by $652 million. Thus, the balance sheet adjustments involve increasing inventories by $1,863 million, tax liabilities by $652 million, and retained earnings by the remaining after-tax amount of $1,211 million (computed as $1,863 − $652).

> **NOTE**
> *When a company adopts LIFO in its tax filings, the IRS requires it to use LIFO for reporting to its shareholders (in its 10-K). This requirement is known as the LIFO conformity rule.*

To adjust the income statement from LIFO to FIFO, we use the *change* in LIFO reserve (for CAT, it changes from $1,977 million in 2002 to $1,863 million in 2003). CAT's 2003 pretax income *increases* by $114 million from the *decrease* in LIFO reserve. This means that had it been using FIFO, its COGS would have been $114 million higher, and gross profit and pretax income would have been $114 million lower. This result shows that use of LIFO does not always yield lower pretax profit as costs do not always rise. Companies can also sustain reductions in the LIFO reserve if inventories are liquidated as described below.

Tools of Inventory Analysis

This section describes several useful tools for analysis of inventory and related accounts.

---

[7] Recall: Cost of Goods Sold = Beginning Inventories + Purchases − Ending Inventories. Thus, as ending inventories decrease, cost of goods sold increases.

RESEARCH INSIGHT

LIFO and Stock Prices The value-relevance of inventory disclosures depends at least partly on whether investors rely more on the income statement or the balance sheet to assess future cash flows. Under LIFO, cost of goods sold reflects current costs, whereas FIFO ending inventory reflects current costs. This implies that LIFO enhances the usefulness of the income statement to the detriment of the balance sheet. This trade-off partly motivates the required LIFO reserve disclosure (the adjustment necessary to restate LIFO ending inventory and cost of good sold to FIFO).

Research suggests that LIFO-based income statements better reflect stock prices than do FIFO income statements that are restated using the LIFO reserve. Research also shows a negative relation between stock prices and LIFO reserve—meaning that higher magnitudes of LIFO reserve are associated with lower stock prices. This is consistent with the LIFO reserve being viewed as an inflation indicator (for either current or future inventory costs) detrimental to company value.

Gross profit analysis

The gross profit margin (GPM) is gross profit divided by sales. This ratio is important and is monitored by management and outsiders. The gross profit margin of **Gillette** for each of the past three years is shown in Exhibit 8.11.

The gross profit margin is commonly used instead of the dollar amount of gross profit as it allows for comparisons across companies and over time. A decline in GPM is usually cause for concern because it indicates that the company has less ability to pass on to customers increased costs

EXHIBIT 8.11 Gross Profit Margin for Gillette			
	2003	**2002**	**2001**
Revenues	$ 9,252	$ 8,453	$ 8,084
Cost of goods sold	3,708	3,511	3,407
Gross profit	$ 5,544	$ 4,942	$ 4,677
Gross profit margin	59.9%	58.5%	57.9%

in its products. Since companies try to charge the highest price the market will bear, we can safely assume that a decline in GPM is the result of market forces beyond the company's control. Some possible reasons for a GPM decline are:

- Product line is stale. Perhaps it is out of fashion and the company must resort to markdowns to reduce overstocked inventories. Or, perhaps the product lines have lost their technological edge, yielding reduced demand.

- New competitors enter the market. Perhaps substitute products are now available from competitors, yielding increased pressure to reduce selling prices.

- General decline in economic activity. Perhaps an economic downturn reduces product demand. The recession of the early 2000s led to reduced gross profits for many companies.

- Inventory is overstocked. Perhaps the company overproduced goods and finds itself in an overstock position. This can require reduced selling prices to move inventory.

Gillette increased its 2003 gross profit margin 2 percentage points above that for 2001, a substantial increase for a two-year period. Following is Gillette's discussion of its gross profit improvement from its 2003 10-K:

> Gross profit was $5.54 billion in 2003, $4.94 billion in 2002, and $4.68 billion in 2001. As a percent of net sales, gross profit was 59.9% in 2003, 58.5% in 2002, and 57.9% in 2001. The improvement in gross profit was due to favorable product mix, cost-savings initiatives, and manufacturing efficiencies, which more than offset higher European-based costs due to exchange and $50 million in incremental provisions to realign European blade and razor manufacturing and distribution.

Competitive pressures mean that companies rarely have the opportunity to affect gross profit with price increases. Most improvements in gross profit that we witness are likely the result of better management of supply chains, production processes, or distribution networks. Companies that win typically do so because of better performance on basic business processes. This is one of Gillette's primary objectives.

Inventory Turnover

Inventory turnover (INVT) is a useful measure of inventory management and is computed as follows:

LO6 Define and apply the receivables turnover and inventory turnover ratios.

$$\textbf{Inventory Turnover = Cost of Goods Sold/Average Inventory}$$

Cost of goods sold is in the numerator because inventory is reported at cost. Inventory turnover indicates how many times inventory turns (is sold) during a period. More turns indicate that inventory is being sold more quickly.

Average inventory days outstanding (AIDO), also called *days inventory outstanding,* is a companion measure to inventory turnover and is computed as follows:

$$\textbf{Average Inventory Days Outstanding = Inventory/Average Daily Cost of Goods Sold}$$

where average daily cost of goods sold equals cost of goods sold divided by 365 days.

Average inventory days outstanding indicates how long, on average, inventories are *on the shelves* before being sold. For example, if cost of goods sold is $1,200 and average (and ending) inventories are $300, inventories are turning four times and are on the shelves 91.25 days ($300/[$1,200/365]) on average. This performance might be an acceptable turnover for the retail fashion industry where it needs to sell out its inventories each retail selling season, but it would not be acceptable for the grocery industry.

Analysis of inventory turnover is important for at least two reasons:

1. *Inventory quality.* Inventory turnover can be compared with those of prior periods and competitors. Higher turnover is viewed favorably, implying that products are salable, preferably without undue discounting of selling prices. Conversely, lower turnover implies that inventory is on the shelves for a longer period of time, perhaps from excessive purchases or production, missed fashion trends or technological advances, increased competition, and so forth. Our conclusions about higher or lower turnover must consider alternative explanations including:
   a. Company product mix can change to higher margin, slower turning inventories or vice-versa. This can occur from business acquisitions and the resulting consolidated inventories.
   b. A company can change its promotion policies. Increased, effective advertising is likely to increase inventory turnover. Advertising expense is in SG&A, not COGS. This means the cost is in operating expenses, but the benefit is in gross profit and turnover. If the promotion campaign is successful, the positive effects in margin and turnover should offset the promotion cost in SG&A.
   c. A company can realize improvements in manufacturing efficiency and lower investments in direct materials and work-in-process inventories. Such improvements reduce inventory and, consequently, increase inventory turnover. Although positive, it does not yield any information about the desirability of a company's product line.
2. *Asset utilization.* Companies strive to optimize their inventory investment. Carrying too much inventory is expensive, and too little inventory risks stock-outs and lost sales (current and future). There are operational changes that companies can make to reduce inventory:
   a. Improved manufacturing processes can eliminate bottlenecks and the consequent build-up of work-in-process inventories.
   b. Just-in-time (JIT) deliveries from suppliers that provide raw materials to the production line when needed can reduce the level of raw materials required.
   c. Demand-pull production, in which raw materials are released into the production process when final goods are demanded by customers instead of producing for estimated demand, can reduce inventory levels. **Dell Computer** produces for actual, rather than estimated, demand; as its computers are manufactured after the customer order is received.

Reducing inventories reduces inventory carrying costs, thus improving profitability and increasing cash flow (asset reduction is reflected as a cash inflow adjustment in the statement of cash flows). However, if inventories get too low, production can be interrupted and sales lost.

There is normal tension between the sales side of a company that argues for depth and breadth of inventory and the finance side that monitors inventory carrying costs and seeks to maximize cash flow. Companies, therefore, seek to *optimize* inventory investment, not *minimize* it.

Exhibit 8.12 compares Gillette's inventory turnover with the peer companies it identifies in its 2003 10-K. Although Gillette's inventory turnover has improved over the past two years, it is about the same as Energizer, which is the lower performer. Further, inventory turnover for both Procter and Gamble and Colgate-Palmolive are markedly better than that for Gillette.

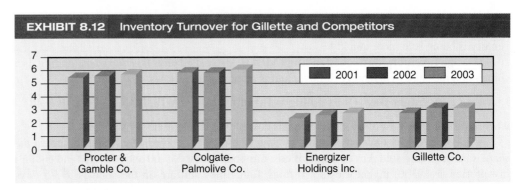

EXHIBIT 8.12 Inventory Turnover for Gillette and Competitors

It is also instructive to compare the consumer products manufacturing industry represented by Gillette against some other companies and industries as illustrated in Exhibit 8.13.

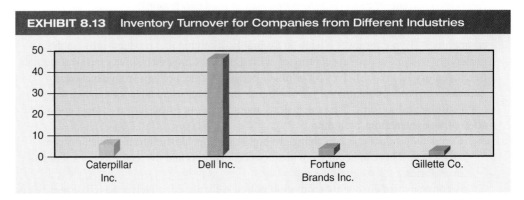

EXHIBIT 8.13 Inventory Turnover for Companies from Different Industries

Dell's production management expertise is well known. It effectively utilizes its buying power over suppliers and its just-in-time delivery processes to minimize the investment in and cost of raw materials. Its production process is so efficient that work-in-process inventories are virtually zero. (Dell reports less work-in-process inventories than Gillette and has nearly four times the sales!) Dell also produces to order instead of for finished goods inventory. As a result, it reports finished goods inventories that are less than one-tenth of those for Gillette. Consequently, Dell's inventory turnover is nearly off the chart. However, Gillette reasonably compares with the others. For example, Gillette's inventory turnover is slightly less than that for Fortune Brands (3.0 times versus 3.6 times per year) but is less than the 5.4 times per year of Caterpillar.

YOU MAKE THE CALL

You Are the Plant Manager   You are analyzing your inventory turnover report for the month and are concerned that the average inventory days outstanding is lengthening. What actions can you take to reduce average inventory days outstanding? [Answer on page 350]

LIFO Liquidation

When companies use LIFO inventory costing, the most recent costs of purchasing inventory are transferred to cost of goods sold, while older costs remain in ending inventory. Each time inventory is purchased at a different price a new *layer* (also called a **LIFO layer**) is added to the inventory balance. As long as purchases equal or exceed the quantity sold, older cost layers remain in inventory— sometimes for several years. On the other hand, when the quantity sold exceeds the quantity purchased, inventory costs from these older cost layers are transferred to cost of goods sold. This situation is called **LIFO liquidation**. Because these older costs are usually much lower than current replacement costs, LIFO liquidation normally yields a boost to current gross profit as these older costs are matched against current revenues.

To illustrate LIFO liquidation, we return to the example of Butler Company presented in exhibit 8.7 Recall that at the beginning of 2005, Butler company's inventory consisted of 500 units costing $50,000. During the year, Butler purchased 200 units costing $170 each and sold 450 units. The calculation of cost of goods sold and ending inventory is shown in Exhibit 8.14.

EXHIBIT 8.14	Calculation of LIFO Inventory and Cost of Goods Sold	
Inventory, January 1, 2005	500 units @ $100 each	$50,000
Inventory purchased during 2005	200 units @ $170 each	34,000
Cost of goods available for sale in 2005	700 units (200 units @ $170 each + 500 units @ $100 each)	84,000
Cost of goods sold in 2005	450 units (200 units @ $170 each + 250 units @ $100 each)	59,000
Inventory, December 31, 2005	250 units @ $100	$25,000

We can see from this illustration that cost of goods available for sale consists of two LIFO layers: 500 units at $100 each (the older layer) and 200 units at $170 each (the newer layer). We can also see what happens when Butler liquidates LIFO inventory layers. by selling 450 units (250 more than the 200 units purchased in 2005) the company had to partially liquidate the older LIFO layer. The inventory at the end of the year now consists of one layer made up of 250 units @ $100 each. This is portrayed graphically as follows.

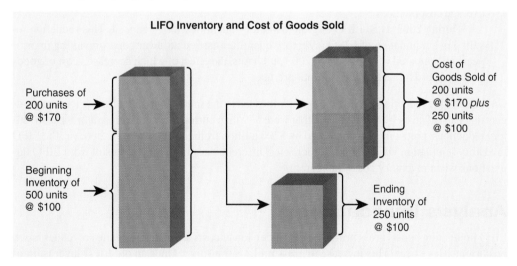

What would have happened if Butler had purchased 450 units at the cost of $170 each instead of just 200 units? The result is shown in Exhibit 8.15.

EXHIBIT 8.15	Calculation of LIFO Cost of Goods Sold with Additional Purchase	
Inventory, January 1, 2005	500 units @ $100 each	$ 50,000
Inventory purchased during 2005	450 units @ $170 each	76,500
Cost of goods available for sale in 2005	950 units (450 units @ $170 each + 500 units @ $100 each)	126,500
Cost of goods sold in 2005	450 units @ $170 each	76,500
Inventory, December 31, 2005	500 units @ $100	$ 50,000

Thus, if Butler had purchased an additional 250 units before December 31, the older layer of inventory would not have been liquidated. As a result, the company would have increased its cost of goods sold to $76,500 as compared to $59,000 without the additional purchase. That is, the LIFO liquidation results in $17,500 *lower* cost of goods sold and $17,500 *higher* gross profit. This case is portrayed graphically as follows.

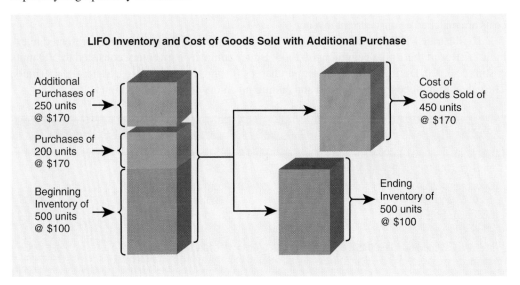

LIFO Inventory and Cost of Goods Sold with Additional Purchase

Additional Purchases of 250 units @ $170

Purchases of 200 units @ $170

Beginning Inventory of 500 units @ $100

Cost of Goods Sold of 450 units @ $170

Ending Inventory of 500 units @ $100

The effect of LIFO liquidation is evident in the following footnote from **General Motors Corporation**'s 2003 10-K.

> Inventories are stated generally at cost, which is not in excess of market. The cost of approximately 92% of U.S. inventories is determined by the last-in, first-out (LIFO) method. Generally, the cost of all other inventories is determined by either the first-in, first-out (FIFO) or average cost methods.
>
> During 2003, U.S. LIFO eligible inventory quantities were reduced. This reduction resulted in a liquidation of LIFO inventory quantities carried at lower costs prevailing in prior years as compared with the cost of 2003 purchases, the effect of which decreased cost of goods sold by approximately $200 million, pre-tax.

REMEMBER
The effect of LIFO liquidations is that costs from prior periods are matched against sales reported in current dollars. This can distort net income.

GM reports that reductions in inventory quantities led to the sale (at current selling prices) of products that carried costs from prior years that were less than current costs. As a result of these inventory reductions, pretax income increased by $200 million from lower COGS. In this case, the LIFO inventory liquidation yielded a profit increase. Different income effects can result from LIFO liquidations when inventory costs fluctuate.

Analysis Implications

LIFO liquidation boosts gross profit because older, lower costs are matched against revenues based on current sales prices. This increase in gross profit is transitory. Once an old LIFO layer is liquidated, it can only be replaced at current prices. The transitory boost in gross profit temporarily distorts the gross profit margin (GPM) ratio.

It is important that we ask why the LIFO liquidation happened. Involuntary LIFO liquidations result from circumstances beyond the company's control, such as disruptions in supply due to a natural disaster. Voluntary LIFO liquidations are the result of a management decision to reduce inventory levels. While this is sometimes the result of efforts to lower costs and improve efficiency, it can also be the consequence of earnings management.

While a voluntary LIFO liquidation may be the result of earnings management, we should remember that the extra gross profit that is reported is taxable. These tax consequences provide an incentive for companies to *avoid* LIFO liquidations by maintaining inventories at levels equal to or greater than beginning inventory quantities. Maintaining these inventory levels can be inefficient; leading to higher inventory holding costs. However, in the short run, the tax savings can be greater than the costs.

On one hand, management could liquidate LIFO inventories to report higher earnings. On the other hand, management may hold too much inventory to avoid paying extra taxes. Neither of these inventory management tactics is in the best interest of stockholders in the long run.

OTHER SHORT-TERM OPERATING ASSETS

Accounts receivable and inventories make up a majority of the noncash, short-term operating assets for most companies. Although typically less substantial, another important short-term operating asset is prepaid expenses. Prepaid expenses are separately identified in the balance sheet or included under an account title similar to Other Current Assets, and are reported in the current asset section of the balance sheet after any inventories.[4]

LO7 Understand accounting for prepaid expenses and the reporting of cash.

Prepaid expenses result from transactions that require the purchaser to pay cash in advance for future services and rights. Examples are prepaid insurance premiums and prepaid rent. When the insurance premium and rent are paid, future benefits exist and assets are recorded. The payment is not expensed immediately. Instead, it is matched with the revenue of that (future) period benefited from that payment.

To illustrate, assume that Sinha Company pays a $3,000 annual fire insurance premium on April 1, 2006. The premium provides insurance coverage for twelve months beginning April 1, 2006 and ending March 31, 2007. The initial premium payment is recorded as prepaid insurance as follows:

(1) Prepaid insurance (+A)	3,000	
Cash (−A)		3,000

At Sinha's 2006 calendar year-end, it records an adjusting entry to reflect that portion of the insurance premium expired. Nine months have passed since the policy was prepaid and, thus, Sinha records $2,250 ($3,000 × 9/12) of insurance expense as follows.

(2) Insurance expense (+E, −SE)	2,250	
Prepaid insurance (−A)		2,250

Posting these two entries to its 2006 T-accounts shows that $750 of unexpired insurance coverage remains in the prepaid insurance account at year-end.

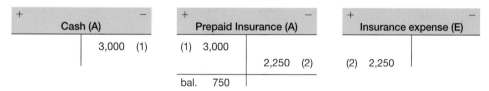

The financial statements effects of these transaction are summarized here.

	Balance Sheet					Income Statement		
Transaction	Cash Asset	+ Noncash Assets	= Liabil-ities	+ Contrib. Capital	+ Retained Earnings	Revenues −	Expenses =	Net Income
(1) Paid fire insurance premium	−3,000 Cash	+3,000 Prepaid Insurance	=					=
(2) Record insurance expense adjusting entry		−2,250 Prepaid Insurance	=		−2,250 Retained Earnings		−2,250 Insurance Expense	= −2,250

[4]Many companies also report a deferred income tax asset among current assets in the balance sheet. Recall from chapter 7 that deferred tax assets arise when income reported to tax authorities is higher that the income reported in the income statement. When these temporary differences are expected to reverse within one year, the deferred tax asset is classified as a current asset. A more detailed discussion is presented in the appendix to chapter 9.

Reporting and Controlling Cash

A company may have only one cash account in the general ledger or it may have multiple cash accounts, such as Cash in Bank, Cash on Hand, and Petty Cash. Cash in Bank includes checking accounts and savings accounts. Cash on Hand includes cash items not yet deposited in the bank. Petty Cash is used for small disbursements.

When a company has several bank accounts, it may maintain a separate general ledger account for each account rather than one overall Cash in Bank account. Although a company may prepare for internal use a balance sheet that shows each individual bank account separately, the balance sheet that the company prepares for external users typically shows the combined balances of all bank accounts and other cash accounts under the single heading Cash. Management wants the detail so it can monitor and control the various accounts and on-hand amounts. Most external users are interested only in the total amount of cash and its relationship to other items on the financial statements.

Cash is a current asset and is shown first in the balance sheet listing of assets. Sometimes a company's total cash includes one or more compensating balances. A **compensating balance** is a minimum amount that a bank requires a firm to maintain in a bank account as part of a borrowing arrangement. Compensating balances related to short-term borrowings are current assets, which if significant, are reported separately from the cash amount among the current assets. Compensating balances related to long-term borrowings are reported as long-term assets.

A company may combine certain short-term, highly liquid investments with cash and present a single amount called **cash and cash equivalents** in the balance sheet. Treasury bills and money market funds are examples of investments that may be considered as cash equivalents. A company presents this combined amount on the balance sheet so it ties to the statement of cash flows.

> REMEMBER...
> Cash is reported as a current asset in the balance sheet. Cash equivalents are often reported together with cash as "Cash and cash equivalents."

Internal Control of Cash

Most companies develop elaborate internal controls to protect cash because it is their most liquid asset. Cash is highly desirable, easily taken and concealed, and quickly converted into other assets. In addition, a high percentage of a company's transactions involve cash. Cash is received from customers and cash is paid to suppliers and employees. A company receives cash from customers, for example, as payments on account and as payments for cash sales. The appendix to this chapter discusses internal control of cash and procedures for preparing bank reconciliations.

CHAPTER-END REVIEW

Part 1

At the beginning of the current period, Hutton Company holds 1,000 units of its only product with a per unit cost of $18. A summary of purchases during the current period follows:

		Units	Unit Cost	Cost
Beginning Inventory		1,000	$18.00	$18,000
Purchases:	#1	1,800	18.25	32,850
	#2	800	18.50	14,800
	#3	1,200	19.00	22,800
Goods available for sale		4,800		$88,450

During the current period, Hutton sells 2,800 units.

Required

1. Assume that Hutton uses the first-in, first-out (FIFO) method. Compute the cost of goods sold for the current period and the ending inventory balance.
2. Assume that Hutton uses the last-in, first-out (LIFO) method. Compute the cost of goods sold for the current period and the ending inventory balance.
3. Assume that Hutton uses the average cost (AC) method. Compute the cost of goods sold for the current period and the ending inventory balance.

4. As manager, which one of these three inventory costing methods would you choose:
   a. To reflect what is probably the physical flow of goods? Explain.
   b. To minimize income taxes for the period? Explain.
5. Assume that Hutton utilizes the LIFO method and instead of purchasing lot #3, the company allows its inventory level to decline and delays purchasing lot #3 until the next period. Compute cost of goods sold under this scenario and discuss the effect of LIFO liquidation on profit.
6. Record the effects of each of the following summary transactions *a* and *b* in the financial statement effects template.
   a. Purchased inventory for $70,450 cash.
   b. Sold $50,850 of inventory for $85,000 cash.
7. Prepare journal entries for each transaction *a* and *b* from part 6. Set up T-accounts for each of the accounts used and post the journal entries to those T-accounts.

Solution

Preliminary computation: Units in ending inventory = 4,800 available − 2,800 sold = 2,000

1. First-in, first-out (FIFO)

Cost of goods sold computation:	Units		Cost		Total
	1,000	@	$18.00	=	$18,000
	1,800	@	$18.25	=	32,850
	2,800				**$50,850**
Cost of goods available for sale			$88,450		
Less: Cost of goods sold			50,850		
Ending inventory ($22,800 + $14,800)			**$37,600**		

2. Last-in, first-out (LIFO)

Cost of goods sold computation:	Units		Cost		Total
	1,200	@	$19.00	=	$22,800
	800	@	$18.50	=	14,800
	800	@	$18.25	=	14,600
	2,800				**$52,200**
Cost of goods available for sale			$88,450		
Less: Cost of goods sold			52,200		
Ending inventory ($18,000 + [1,000 × $18.25])			**$36,250**		

3. Average cost (AC)

Average unit cost = $88,450/4,800 = $18.427
Cost of goods sold = 2,800 × $18.427 = **$51,596**
Ending inventory = 2,000 × $18.427 = **$36,854**

4. *a.* FIFO in most circumstances reflects physical flow. For example, FIFO would apply to the physical flow of perishables and to situations where the earlier items acquired are moved out first because of risk of deterioration or obsolescence.
   b. LIFO results in the lowest ending inventory amount during periods of rising costs, which in turn yields the lowest net income and the lowest income taxes.
5. Last-in, first-out with LIFO liquidation

Cost of goods sold computation:	Units		Cost		Total
	800	@	$18.50	=	$14,800
	1,800	@	$18.25	=	32,850
	200	@	$18.00	=	3,600
	2,800				**$51,250**
Cost of goods available for sale			$65,650		
Less: Cost of goods sold			51,250		
Ending inventory (800 × $18)			**$14,400**		

The company's LIFO gross profit has increased by $950 ($52,200 − $51,250). This increase is from LIFO liquidation, which is the reduction of inventory quantities that results in matching older (lower) cost layers against current selling prices. The company has, in effect, dipped into lower cost layers to boost current period profit—all from a simple delay of inventory purchases.

6. Transaction effects shown in the financial statement effects template.

	Balance Sheet						Income Statement		
Transaction	Cash Asset	+ Noncash Assets	= Liabilities	+ Contrib. Capital	+ Retained Earnings		Revenues	− Expenses	= Net Income
(a) Purchased $70,450 of inventory	−70,450 Cash	+70,450 Inventory	=						=
(b1) Sold $50,850 of inventory		−50,850 Inventory	=		−50,850 Retained Earnings			−50,850 Cost of Goods Sold	= −50,850
(b2) Sold Inventory for $85,000 cash	+85,000 Cash		=		+85,000 Retained Earnings		+85,000 Sales		= +85,000

7. Journal entries and postings to t-accounts.

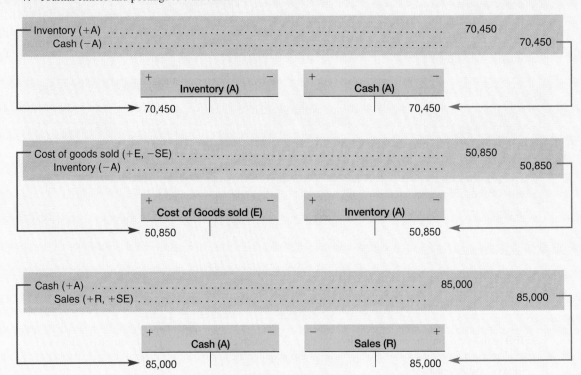

Part 2

Venner Company had the following inventory at December 31, 2006

			Unit Price	
		Quantity	Cost	Market
Fans				
Model X1	....	300	$18	$19
Model X2	....	250	22	24
Model X3	....	400	29	26
Heaters				
Model B7	....	500	24	28
Model B8	....	290	35	32
Model B9	....	100	41	38

Required

1. Determine ending inventory by applying the lower of cost or market rule to
   a. Each item of inventory
   b. Each major category of inventory.
   c. Total inventory.
2. Which of the LCM procedures from requirement *a* results in the lowest net income for 2006? Explain.

Solution

1.

| Item | Quantity | Per Unit | | Inventory Amounts | | |
		Cost	Market	Cost	Market	LCM (by Item)
Fans						
Model X1	300	$18	$19	$ 5,400	$ 5,700	$ 5,400
Model X2	250	22	24	5,500	6,000	5,500
Model X3	400	29	26	11,600	10,400	10,400
Totals				$22,500	$22,100	$21,300
Heaters						
Model B7	500	24	28	$12,000	$14,000	$12,000
Model B8	290	35	32	10,150	9,280	9,280
Model B9	100	41	38	4,100	3,800	3,800
Totals				26,250	27,080	25,080
Totals				$48,750	$49,180	$46,380

a. As shown in this schedule, applying the lower of cost or market rule to each item of the inventory results in an ending inventory amount of $46,380.

b. Applying the lower of cost or market rule to each major category of the inventory result sin an ending inventory amount of $48,350, calculated as follows:

Fans	$22,100
Heaters	26,250
	$48,350

c. As shown in this schedule, applying the lower of cost or market rule to the total inventory results in an ending inventory amount of $48,750.

2. The LCM procedure that results in the lowest ending inventory amount also results in the lowest net income for the year (the lower the ending inventory amount, the higher the cost of goods sold). Applying the lower of cost or market rule to each item of the inventory results in the lowest net income for the year.

SUMMARY

Estimate uncollectible accounts receivable (p. 325).   **LO1**

▪ Uncollectible accounts are usually estimated by aging the accounts receivable.

Analyze effects of uncollectible accounts on financial statements and footnotes (p. 327).   **LO2**

▪ Estimate uncollectible accounts are recorded as bad debt expense in the income statement in the same year that credit sales are recorded.

▪ The contra-asset account, allowance for uncollectible accounts is credited to offset accounts receivable.

▪ Write-offs of uncollectible accounts are deducted from accounts receivable and from the allowance accounts.

Accounts for inventory and cost of goods sold using different costing methods (p. 335).   **LO3**

▪ FIFO places the cost of the most recent purchases in ending inventory and older costs in the cost of goods sold.

▪ LIFO places the cost of the most recent purchases in cost of goods sold and older costs in inventory.

▪ The average cost method computes an averages unit cost which is used to value inventories *and* cost of goods sold.

LO4 **Apply the lower of cost or marker rule to value inventory (p. 338).**

- If the market value of inventory falls below its cost, the inventory is written down to market value, thereby reducing total assets.
- The loss is added to cost of goods sold and reported in the income statement.

LO5 **Evaluate how inventory costing impacts management decisions and outsider's interpretations of financial statements (p. 338).**

- If LIFO is used for the reporting, it must be used for financial reporting.
- Companies that use LIFO have an incentive to hold inventories to avoid LIFO *liquidation* and the resulting higher income taxes.
- LIFO distorts the inventory turnover ratio because inventories are often severely undervalued (relative to current cost of goods sold). Management can boost earnings by liquidating these undervalued inventories.

LO6 **Define and apply the receivables turnover and inventory turnover ratios (p. 341).**

- Accounts receivable turnover is defined as Sales / Average Accounts Receivable
- Inventory turnover is defined as Cost of Goods Sold / Average Inventory
- These ratios provide insight into how efficiently the company is managing these key working capital assets.

LO7 **Understand accounting for prepaid expenses and the reporting of cash (p. 345).**

- Prepaid expenses result from transactions that require a company to pay cash in advance for future benefits.
- Companies usually report various cash accounts, along with highly liquid investments, under the heading cash and cash equivalents.
- Companies develop elaborate internal controls to protect cash because it is their most liquid asset.

LO8 **(Appendix 8A) Define internal control and explain internal controls involving cash, including bank reconciliations (p. 351).**

- Internal controls are measures undertaken by a company to ensure the reliability of its accounting data, protect its assets, and make sure that its policies are followed.
- A prevention control is designed to deter problems before they arise. A detection control is designed to discover problems after they arise.
- The procedure used to prepare a bank reconciliation involves four steps.
  - Trace outstanding items on the bank reconciliations for the pervious month to the current bank statement.
  - Compare the deposits made during the month to the deposits on the bank statement.
  - Compare the checks issued during the month to the checks on the bank statement.
  - Scan the bank statement for charges and credits not yet reflected in the general ledger.

GUIDANCE ANSWERS

YOU MAKE THE CALL

You Are the Receivables Manager First, you must realize that the extension of credit is an important tool in the marketing of your products, often as important as advertising and promotion. Given that receivables are necessary, there are some methods we can use to speed their collection. (1) We can better screen the customers to whom we extend credit. (2) We can negotiate advance or progress payments from customers. (3) We can use bank letters of credit or other automatic drafting procedures so that billings must not be sent. (4) We can make sure products are sent as ordered to reduce disputes. (5) We can improve administration of past due accounts to provide for more timely notices of delinquencies and better collection procedures.

YOU MAKE THE CALL

You Are the Plant Manager Companies need inventories to avoid lost sales opportunities; however, there are several ways to minimize inventory needs. (1) We can reduce product costs by improving product design to eliminate costly features not valued by customers. (2) We can use more cost-efficient suppliers; possibly including production in lower wage-rate parts of the world. (3) We can reduce raw material inventories with just-in-time delivery from suppliers. (4) We can eliminate bottlenecks in the production process that increase work-in-process inventories. (5) We can manufacture for orders rather than for estimates of demand to reduce finished goods inventories. (6) We can improve warehousing and distribution to reduce duplicate inventories. (7) We can monitor product sales and adjust product mix as demand changes to reduce finished goods inventories.

APPENDIX 8A: Internal Controls

Internal controls are steps undertaken by a company to ensure the reliability of its accounting data, protect its assets from theft or unauthorized use, make sure that employees are following the company's policies and procedures, and evaluate the performance of employees to function according to the plans developed by management.

LO8 Define internal control and explain internal controls involving cash, including bank reconciliations.

Management is responsible for designing, installing, and monitoring internal controls throughout the company. In designing the controls, management tries to attain "reasonable assurance" rather than "absolute assurance" that the controls will meet their objectives. Management does this by balancing the benefit derived from installing a control against the cost of installing and maintaining the control. The benefit should exceed the cost.

Internal controls exist in many forms, including policies, procedures, records, equipment, supervision, and insurance. An internal control can be either a prevention control or a detection control. A company establishes a **prevention control** to deter problems before they arise. A company establishes a **detection control** to discover problems soon after they arise. Prevention controls are generally more desirable than detection controls.

A company should incorporate the following concepts when it designs its internal controls:

1. Establish clear lines of authority and responsibility.
2. Separate incompatible work functions.
3. Use control numbers on all business documents
4. Maintain adequate accounting records.
5. Conduct internal audits.

Establish Lines of Authority and Responsibility

The organization structure of a company defines the lines of authority and responsibility within the company. When a company assigns authority to an employee to perform certain functions, it also makes that employee responsible for accomplishing certain objectives. This structure provides the overall framework for planning, directing, and controlling the company's operations. It informs the employees about who is in charge of what functions and to whom each person reports.

Separate Incompatible Work Functions

When allocating various duties within the transaction processing system, management should make sure that too much responsibility is not assigned to any one employee. No individual employee should be able to perpetrate and conceal irregularities in the transaction processing system. to accomplish this, management must separate three functions: the authorization function, the recording function, and the custody function. Ideally, for any particular transaction, an individual employee should have authority to perform only one of these three functions.

For example, if an employee "authorizes" a sales transaction by approving the customer's credit, that employee should not "record" the transaction in the accounting records or have physical "custody" of the merchandise sold or the cash received from the customer. This separation is an important preventive control.

Use Control Numbers on All Business Documents

All business documents such as purchase orders, invoices, credit memos, and checks should have control numbers preprinted on them. Each control number should be unique for that type of document. The bank checks that you use to pay your personal bills have control numbers on them, usually in the upper right-hand corner. You refer to them as *check numbers.*

To provide proper controls to the accounting process, a company should use the documents in strict numerical sequence. Then, for each type of business document, periodically account for all the numbers in the sequence to make sure that all of them were processed. Use of control numbers with this type of reconciliation helps to ensure that a company records all transactions and it does not record a transaction multiple times. This important preventive control contributes to the accuracy of the data in the accounting system.

Maintain Adequate Records

We have already discussed many control that help ensure that a company has adequate accounting records. These controls include using the double-entry approach to recording transactions (debits = credits), preparing trial balances (total debits = total credits), and taking physical inventory counts.

Many internal controls related to maintaining adequate records involve comparisons. A company periodically makes a physical inspection to compare the data in the plant assets subsidiary ledger to plant assets actually in use. This inspection identifies missing assets and assets not recorded in the ledger. Both require adjustment of the general ledger accounts. Similarly, a company periodically confirms the amounts owed to supplier (accounts payable) and amounts due from customers (accounts receivable) by contacting the suppliers and customers.

Conduct Internal Audits

In a small company, internal auditing is a function that a company assigns to an employee who has other duties as well. In a large company, internal auditing is assigned to an independent department that reports to top management or the board of directors of a corporation. **Internal auditing** is a company function that provides independent appraisals of the company's financial statements, its internal controls, and its operations.

The appraisal of its internal controls involves two phases. First the internal auditor determines whether sufficient internal controls are in place. Second, the internal auditor determines whether the internal controls in place are actually functioning as planned. After completing the appraisal, the internal auditor makes recommendations to management on additional controls that are needed and improvements that are required in existing controls.

REMEMBER . . .
Common techniques to control cash are (1) Using bank accounts, (2) the imprest petty cash system, (3) physical protection of cash balances, and (4) reconciliation of bank balances.

Banking Controls

When a company opens a checking account at a bank, the bank requires each company employee who will sign checks to sign a signature card. The bank files the signature cards. Occasionally, a bank employee compares the signatures on checks to the authorized signatures on the signature cards.

A **check** is a written order signed by a checking account owner (also known as the *maker*) directing the bank (also known as the *payer*) to pay a specified amount of money to the person or company named on the check (also knows as the *payee*). A check is a negotiable instrument; it can be transferred to another person or company by writing "pay to the order of" and the name of the other person or company on the back of the check and then signing the back of the check.

Bank Statement

At the end of each month, the bank prepares a bank statement for each checking account and sends it to the person or company that owns the checking account. Exhibit 8A.1 is the bank statement from Anchor National Bank for Wilson Corporation's checking account as of November 30, 2006.

EXHIBIT 8A.1 Bank Statement of Wilson

NATIONAL BANK
123 Center Street
Chicago, IL 60505

Wilson Corporation
1847 Elmwood Avenue
Westmont, IL 60559

Account Number   27-31020558
Statement Date   November 30, 2006

Deposits and Credits		Checks and Debits			Daily Balance	
Date	**Amount**	**Number**	**Date**	**Amount**	**Date**	**Amount**
Nov 01	420.00	149	Nov 02	125.00	Nov 01	6,060.30
Nov 02	630.00	154	Nov 03	56.25	Nov 02	6,565.30
Nov 07	560.80	155	Nov 10	135.00	Nov 03	6,509.05
Nov 10	480.25	156	Nov 08	315.10	Nov 07	6,801.19
Nov 14	525.00	157	Nov 07	233.26	Nov 08	6,486.09
Nov 17	270.25	158	Nov 11	27.14	Nov 10	6,831.34
Nov 21	640.20	159	Nov 18	275.00	Nov II	6804.20
Nov 26	300.00CM	160	Nov 15	315.37	Nov 14	7,329.20
Nov 26	475.00	16!	Nov 17	76.40	Nov 15	7,013.83
Nov 30	471.40	162	Nov 21	325.60	Nov 17	7,207.68
		163	Nov 21	450.00	Nov 18	6,932.68
		164	Nov 23	239.00	Nov 21	6,731.58
		165	Nov 21	65.70	Nov 23	6,492.58
		166	Nov 28	482.43	Nov 26	7,262.58
		169	Nov 28	260.00	Nov 28	6,520.15
		170	Nov 30	122.50	Nov 30	6,488.95
		171	Nov 30	370.10		
			Nov 07	35.4ORT		
			Nov 26	5.00DM		
			Nov 30	10.00SC		

Beginning Balance	+	Deposits and Credits	−	Checks and Debits	=	Ending Balance
$5,640.30	+	$4,772.90	−	$3,924.25	=	$6,488.95

Item Codes:	EC: Error Correction	DM: Debit Memo	CM: Credit Memo
	SC: Service Charge	OD: Overdraft	RT: Returned Item
	IN: Interest Earned		

In the body of the statement, the bank lists Wilson's deposits and other credits on the left, Wilson's checks (in numerical order) and other debits in the center, and Wilson's daily account balance on the right. Daily balance is the balance in the account as of the end of each day listed. The bank presents a summary calculation of Wilson's ending account balance near the bottom of the statement.

BUSINESS INSIGHT

Debits or Credit? Debit and credit terminology may seem backward on a bank statement. Debits decrease the account balance and credits increase the account balances. When a company deposits cash in its checking account, the bank debits Cash and credits a liability account. The subsidiary ledger for this liability contains the customers' account balances. The statement sent to each company is a statement of its account in the bank's liability subsidiary ledger. As with any liability, debits decrease its balance and credits increase its balance.

Bank Reconciliation

The internal auditor or other designated employee prepares a bank reconciliation as of the end of each month. A **bank reconciliation** is a schedule that (1) accounts for all differences between the ending balance on the bank statement and the ending balance of the Cash account in the general ledger and (2) determines the reconciled cash balance as of the end of the month. The person preparing the bank reconciliation needs access to the bank statement, the general ledger, cash receipts records, and cash disbursements records to prepare the reconciliation.

Exhibit 8A.2 outlines the structure of a company's bank reconciliation. The bank reconciliation is really two schedules prepared side-by-side. The schedule on the left includes bank items, and the schedule on the right includes items related to the company's general ledger.

The schedule on the left begins with the ending balance of the bank statement (the month-end balance according to the bank's records). The person preparing the reconciliation adds (1) deposits not yet recorded by the bank, called **deposits in transit,** and (2) any corrections not yet made by the bank that will increase the bank balance. The preparer subtracts (1) checks not yet recorded by the bank, called **outstanding checks,** and (2) any corrections not yet made by the bank that will decrease the bank balance. The resulting total is the *reconciled cash balance at the end of the month.*

The schedule on the right begins with the ending balance in the Cash account in the company's general ledger. The preparer adds (1) items recorded as cash receipts by the bank but not yet recorded in the company's journals and

EXHIBIT 8A.2	Structure of a Company's Bank Reconciliation

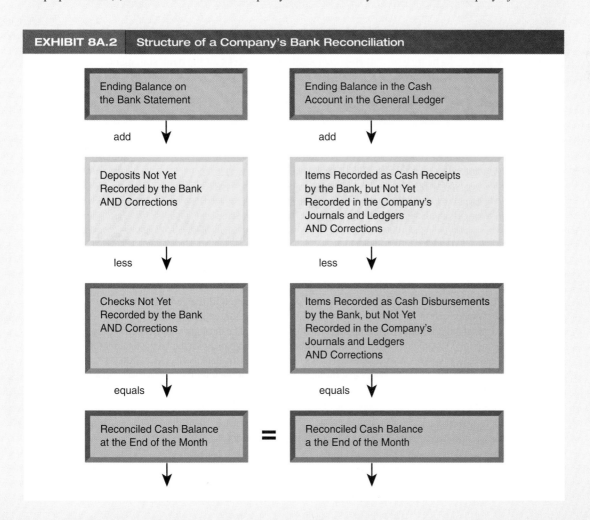

ledgers and (2) any corrections not yet made by the company that will increase the general ledger cash balance. The preparer subtracts (1) items recorded as cash disbursements by the bank but not yet recorded in the company's journals and ledgers and (2) any corrections not yet made by the company that will decrease the general ledger cash balance. The resulting total is the reconciled cash balance at the end of the month. The totals of the two schedules should be the same.

Bank Reconciliation Procedure   Assume that the internal auditor of Wilson corporation is preparing the November 30, 2006, bank reconciliation. He or she uses the following procedures to reconcile the November 30, 2006, bank statement balance of $6,488.95 to the November 30, 2006, general ledger blanch of $5,322.69:

1. **Trace outstanding items on the bank reconciliation for the previous month to the current bank statement.** Any item on the previous reconciliation that still has not been processed by the bank must appear on the current reconciliation. The October 31, 2006, reconciliation included the following:

Deposit in transit		$420.00
Outstanding checks	Number 149	$125.00
	Number 154	56.25
	Number 155	135.00

The November 30, 2006, bank statement includes the $420 deposit and all three checks listed above. Therefore, none of these items will appear on the November 30 reconciliation.

2. **Compare the deposits made during the month to the deposits on the bank statement.** Wilson Corporation made the following deposits during November:

November 2	$630.00	November 21	$640.20
November 7	560.80	November 26	475.00
November 10	480.25	November 29	471.40
November 14	525.00	November 30	225.00
November 17	270.25		

All of these deposits appear on the bank statement except for the November 30 deposit of $225. The $225 deposit will appear on the left side of the November 30 reconciliation as a deposit in transit.

3. **Compare the checks being issued during the month to the checks on the bank statement.**   Wilson Corporation issued the following checks during November:

Number 156	$315.10	Number 161	$ 76.40
Number 157	233.25	Number 162	325.60
Number 158	27.14	Number 163	450.00
Number 159	275.00	Number 164	239.00
Number 160	315.37	Number 165	65.70
Number 166	482.43	Number 170	122.50
Number 167	301.66	Number 171	370.10
Number 168	149.50	Number 172	450.00
Number 169	260.00	Number 173	240.50

Four of the check—number 167, 168, 172, and 173—do not appear on the bank statement. These four checks will appear on the left side of the November 30 reconciliation as outstanding checks.

4. **Scan the bank statement for charges and credits not yet reflected in the general ledger.** Wilson Corporation's bank statement contains a charge of $35.40 for a returned item, a debit memo of $5.00, and a service charge of $10.00 in the checks and other debits column. The deposits and other credits column contains a credit memo for $300.00. Supplemental information sent by the bank with the bank statement reveals that the bank charged a $35.40 NSF check against Wilson's account, that the bank collected a $300.00 note for Wilson, and charged a $5.00 collection fee, and that the service charge for the month of November was $10.00. These four items have not yet been recorded by Wilson Corporation. Therefore, they must be listed on the right side of the reconciliation.

After the four preceding procedures have been complete, the November 30, 2006 bank reconciliation for Wilson Corporation appears as shown in Exhibit 8A.3. Note that both the left side and the right side of the reconciliation end with a reconciled cash balance and what the two amounts are the same. This reconciled cash balance is the amount that will appear in the November 30, 2006 balance sheet.

EXHIBIT 8A.3 Bank Reconciliation for Wilson Corporation

WILSON CORPORATION
BANK RECONCILIATION
NOVEMBER 30, 2006

Balance from bank statement		$6,488.95	Balance from general ledger			$5,322.69
Add: Deposits in transit		225.00	Add: Collection of note	$300.00		
			Less: Collection fee	5.00	295.00	
		6,713.95			5,617.69	
Less: Outstanding checks			Less: NSF check	35.40		
No. 167	$301.66		Service charge	10.00	45.40	
No. 168	149.50					
No. 172	450.00					
No. 173	240.50	1,141.66				
Reconciled cash balance		$5,572.29	Reconciled cash balance			$5,572.29

Before Wilson Corporation prepares its financial statements for November, Wilson must make journal entries to bring the balance in the cash account into agreement with the reconciled cash balance on the bank reconciliation. These entries incorporate the items on the company's side of the reconciliation. Wilson makes the following entries:

Nov. 30	Cash	295.00	
	Miscellaneous Expense	5.00	
	Notes receivable		300.00
Nov. 30	Accounts Receivable	35.40	
	Cash		35.40
30	Miscellaneous Expense	10.00	
	Cash		10.00

APPENDIX END REVIEW

At December 31, 2003, the Cash account in Tyler Company's general ledger had a debit balance of $18,434.27. The December 31, 2006, bank statement showed a balance of $19,726.40. In reconciling the two amounts, you discover the following:

1. Bank deposits made by Tyler on December 31, 2006, amounting to $2,145.40 do not appear on the bank statement.
2. A noninterest-bearing note receivable from Smith Company for $2,000, left with the bank for collection, was collected by the bank near the end of December. The bank credited the proceeds, less a $5 collection charge, on the bank statement. Tyler Company has not recorded the collection.
3. Accompanying the bank statement is a debit memorandum indicating that John Miller's check for $450 was charged against Tyler's bank account on December 30 because of insufficient funds.
4. Check No. 586, written for an advertising expense of $869.10, was recorded as $896.10 by Tyler Company.
5. A comparison of the paid checks returned by the bank with the recorded disbursements revealed the following checks still outstanding at December 31, 2006:

No. 561	$306.63	No. 591	$190.00
No. 585	440.00	No. 592	282.50
No. 588	476.40	No. 593	243.00

6. The bank mistakenly charges Tyler Company's account for check-printing costs of $30.50, which should have been charged to Tylor Company.
7. The bank charged Tyler Company's account $42.50 for rental of a safe deposit box. No entry has been made in Tyler's records for this expense.

Required

a. Prepare a bank reconciliation at December 31, 2006.

b. Prepare any necessary journal entries at December 31, 2006.

Solution

a.

TYLER COMPANY
Bank Reconciliation
December 31, 2006

Balance from bank statement		$19,726.40	Balance from general ledger			$18,434.27
Add: Deposits not credited by bank		2,145.40	Add: Collection of note	$2,000.00		
Error by bank (Check printing charge of Taylor Co.)		30.50	Less: Collection charge	5.00	1,995.00	
		21,902.30	Error in recording check No. 586		27.00	
					20,456.27	
Less: Outstanding checks			Less:			
No. 561	$306.63		NSF check	450.00		
No. 585	440.00		Charge for safe deposit box	42.50	492.50	
No. 588	476.40					
No. 591	190.00					
No. 592	282.50					
No. 593	243.00	1,938.53				
Reconciled cash balance		$19,963.77	Reconciled cash balance			$19,963.77

b.

Dec. 31	Cash	1,995.00	
	Miscellaneous Expense	5.00	
	Notes receivable—Smith Company		2,000.00
	To record collection of Smith's note by bank, less collection charge.		
31	Cash	27.00	
	Advertising Expense		27.00
	To correct error in recording advertising expense.		
31	Accounts Receivable—John Miller	450.00	
	Cash		450.00
	To reclassify NSF check as an account receivable.		
31	Miscellaneous Expense	42.50	
	Cash		42.50
	To record rental expense of safe deposit box.		

KEY TERMS

Manufacturing costs (p. 333)	Payer (p. 352)	Receivables quality (p. 330)
Net realizable value (p. 324)	Percentage of sales (p. 325)	Reconciled cash balance (p. 353)
Outstanding checks (p. 353)	Raw materials and	Work in process (p. 337)
Payee (p. 352)	supplies (p. 337)	

MULTIPLE CHOICE

1. If bad debt expense is determined by estimating uncollectible accounts receivable, the entry to record the write-off of a specific uncollectible account would decrease
    a. allowance for uncollectible accounts.
    b. net income.
    c. net book value of accounts receivable.
    d. bad debt expense.

2. If management intentionally underestimates bad debt expense, then net income is
    a. overstated and assets are understated.
    b. understated and assets are overstated.
    c. understated and asset are understated.
    d. overstated and assets are overstated.

3. When the current year's ending inventory amount is overstated, then the
    a. current year's cost of goods sold is overstated.
    b. current year's total assets are understated.
    c. current year's net income is overstated.
    d. next year's income is overstated.

4. In a period of rising prices, the inventory cost allocation method that tends to result in the lowest reported net income is
    a. LIFO.
    b. FIFO.
    c. Average cost.
    d. Specific identification.

5. Which of the following inventory costing methods most closely reports the current cost of inventory on the balance sheet?
    a. LIFO
    b. FIFO
    c. Average cost
    d. Specific identification

6. In a period of increasing prices, the LIFO method tends to
    a. understate inventory turnover and overvalue inventory balances.
    b. overstate inventory turnover and undervalue inventory balances.
    c. understate inventory turnover and undervalue inventory balances.
    d. overstate inventory turnover and understate cost of goods sold.

Multiple Choice Answers
1. a   2. d   3. c   4. a   5. b   6. b

Superscript ^{A} denotes assignments based on Appendix 8A

DISCUSSION QUESTIONS

Q8-1. Explain how management can shift income from one period into another by its estimation of uncollectible accounts.

Q8-2. Why do relatively stable inventory costs reduce the importance of management's choice of an inventory costing method?

Q8-3. What is one explanation for increased gross profit during periods of rising inventory costs when FIFO is used?

Q8-4. If inventory costs are rising, which inventory costing method—first-in, first-out; last-in, first-out; or average cost—yields the (a) lowest ending inventory? (b) lowest net income? (c) largest ending inventory? (d) largest net income? (e) greatest cash flow assuming that method is used for tax purposes?

Q8-5. Even though it may not reflect their physical flow of goods, why might companies adopt last-in, first-out inventory costing in periods when costs are consistently rising?

Q8-6. In a recent annual report, Kaiser Aluminum Corporation made the following statement in reference to its inventories: "The Company recorded pretax charges of approximately $19.4 million because of a reduction in the carrying values of its inventories caused principally by prevailing lower prices for alumina, primary aluminum, and fabricated products." What basic accounting principle caused Kaiser Aluminum to record this $19.4 million pretax charge? Briefly describe the rationale for this principle.

Q8-8. During an examination of Wallace Company's financial statements, you notice that the allowance for uncollectible accounts has decreased as a percentage of accounts receivable. What are the possible explanations for this change?

Q8-9. Under what circumstances would it be correct to say that a company would be better off with more uncollectible accounts?

Q8-10. Estimating the bad debt expense by aging accounts receivable generally results in smaller errors than the percentage of credit sales approach. Can you explain why?

Q8-11. Analysts claim that it is more difficult to forecast net income for a company that uses LIFO. Why might this be true?

Q8-12.^A Define and contrast *prevention controls* and *detection controls*. Which are more desirable?

Q8-13.^A Yates Company is reviewing its internal procedures to try to improve internal control. It specifically wants to separate incompatible work functions. What three types of work functions must be separated to improve internal control?

Q8-14.^A What is the purpose of a bank reconciliation?

Q8-15.^A In preparing a bank reconciliation, how should you determine (a) deposits not recorded in the bank statement and (b) outstanding checks?

MINI EXERCISES

M8-16. Estimating Uncollectible Accounts and Reporting Accounts Receivables (LO1, 2)
Mohan Company estimates its uncollectible accounts by aging its accounts receivable and applying percentages to various aged categories of accounts. Mohan computes a total of $2,100 in estimated losses as of December 31, 2005. Its Accounts Receivable has a balance of $98,000, and its Allowance for Uncollectible Accounts has an unused balance of $500 before adjustment at December 31, 2005.
    a. What is the amount of bad debt expense that Mohan will report in 2005?
    b. Determine the net amount of accounts receivable reported in current assets at December 31, 2005.
    c. Set up T-accounts for both Bad Debt Expense and for Allowance for Uncollectible Accounts. Enter any beginning balances and effects from the information above (including your results from parts *a* and *b*). Explain the numbers for each of your T-accounts.

M8-17. Explaining the Allowance Method for Accounts Receivable (LO1, 2)
At a recent board of directors meeting of Ascot, Inc., one of the directors expressed concern over the allowance for uncollectible accounts appearing in the company's balance sheet. "I don't understand this account," he said. "Why don't we just show accounts receivable at the amount owed to us and get rid of that allowance?" Respond to that director's question, include in your response (a) an explanation of why the company has an allowance account, (b) what the balance sheet presentation of accounts receivable is intended to show, and (c) how the matching principle relates to the analysis and presentation of accounts receivable.

M8-18. Analyzing the Allowance for Uncollectible Accounts (LO2)

Kraft Foods, Inc.
(KFT)

Following is the current asset section from Kraft Foods, Inc., balance sheet:

At December 31 ($ millions)	2003	2002
Cash and cash equivalents	$ 514	$ 215
Receivables (less allowances of $114 and $119)	3,369	3,116
Inventories		
Raw materials	1,375	1,372
Finished product	1,968	2,010
	3,343	3,382
Deferred income taxes	681	511
Other current assets	217	232
Total current assets	$8,124	$7,456

    a. Compute the gross amount of accounts receivable for both 2003 and 2002. Compute the percentage of the allowance for uncollectible accounts relative to the gross amount of accounts receivable for each of these years.
    b. How do you interpret the change in the percentage of the allowance for uncollectible accounts relative to total accounts receivable computed in (a)?

M8-19. Analyzing accounts receivable changes. (LO2)

The comparative balance sheets of Sloan Company reveal that accounts receivable (before deducting allowances) increased by $15,000 in 2006. During the same time period, the allowance for uncollectible accounts increased by $2,100. If sales revenue was $120,000 in 2006 and bad debt expense was 2% of sales, how much cash was collected from customers during the year?

M8-20. Evaluating Accounts Receivable Turnover for Competitors (LO6)

Procter & Gamble (PG) and Colgate-Palmolive (CL) report the following sales and accounts receivable balances ($ millions):

Procter & Gamble (PG)

Colgate-Palmolive (CL)

	Procter & Gamble		Colgate-Palmolive	
	Sales	Accounts Receivable	Sales	Accounts Receivable
2003	$43,373	$3,038	$9,903	$1,222
2002	40,169	3,090	9,294	1,145

a. Compute the 2003 accounts receivable turnover for both companies.
b. Identify and discuss a potential explanation for the difference between these competitors' accounts receivable turnover.

M8-21. Analyzing accounts receivable changes. (LO2)

In 2006, Grant Corporation recorded credit sales of $3,200,000 and bad debt expense of $42,000. Write-offs of uncollectible accounts totaled $39,000 and one account, worth $12,000, that had been written of in an earlier year was collected in 2006.
a. Prepare journal entries to record each of these transactions.
b. If net accounts receivable increased by $220,000, how much cash was collected from customers during the year? Prepare a journal entry to record cash collections.
c. Set up T-accounts and post each of the transactions in parts a and b to them.
d. Record each of the above transactions in a financial statement effects template to show the effect of these entries on the balance sheet and income statement.

M8-22. Accounting for prepaid expenses. (LO7)

On May 31, 2006, Virchick Company paid $2,700 cash for a one-year insurance policy. The premium provides insurance from June 1, 2006, through May 31, 2007. Virchick's fiscal year ends on December 31, 2006.
a. Prepare (1) the journal entry, and (2) the financial statement effects template, to record payment of the insurance premium.
b. Open T-accounts and post the transaction recorded in part a.
c. Prepare the necessary year-end adjusting entry to record the expired insurance premium; also, show its impact using the financial statement effects template. Post the entry to the prepaid insurance T-account and determine the year-end balance that would be reported in Virchick's balance sheet.

M8-23. Computing Cost of Goods Sold and Ending Inventory under FIFO, LIFO, and Average Cost (LO3)

Assume that Gode Company reports the following initial balance and subsequent purchase of inventory:

Beginning inventory, 2005	1,000 units @ $100 each	$100,000
Inventory purchased in 2005	2,000 units @ $150 each	300,000
Cost of goods available for sale in 2005	3,000 units	$400,000

Assume that 1,700 units are sold during 2005. Compute the cost of goods sold for 2005 and the balance reported as ending inventory on its 2005 balance sheet under the following inventory costing methods:
a. FIFO
b. LIFO
c. Average Cost

M8-24. Inferring purchases using cost of goods sold and inventory balances. (LO3)

Geiger Corporation, a retail company, reported inventories of $1,320,000 in 2005 and $1,460,000 in 2006. The 2006 income statement reported cost of goods sold of $6,980,000.
a. Compute the amount of inventory purchased during 2006.
b. Prepare journal entries to record (1) purchases, and (2) cost of goods sold.
c. Post the journal entries in part b to their respective T-accounts.
d. Record each of the transactions in part b in the financial statement effects template to show the effect of these entries on the balance sheet and income statement.

M8-25. Computing Cost of Goods Sold and Ending Inventory (LO3, 5)

Bartov Corporation reports the following beginning inventory and purchases for 2005:

Beginning inventory, 2005	400 units @ $10 each	$ 4,000
Inventory purchased in 2005	700 units @ $12 each	8,400
Cost of goods available for sale in 2005 . . .	1,100 units	$12,400

Bartov sells 600 of these units in 2005. Compute its cost of goods sold for 2005 and the ending inventory reported on its 2005 balance sheet under each of the following inventory costing methods:

a. FIFO
b. LIFO
c. Average Cost

M8-26. Computing and Evaluating Inventory Turnover (LO6)

Sears (S)

Kmart (KMRT)

Sears and Kmart reported the following information in their respective 10-K reports, prior to their merger:

	Sears			K-Mart		
($ millions)	Sales	COGS	Inventories	Sales	COGS	Inventories
2003	$41,124	$26,202	$5,335	$23,253	$17,638	$3,238
2002	41,366	25,646	5,115	30,762	24,228	4,825

a. Compute the 2003 inventory turnover for each of these two retailers.
b. Discuss any changes that are evident in inventory turnover across years and companies from (a).
c. Describe ways that a retailer can improve its inventory turnover.

M8-27. Inferring purchases using cost of goods sold and inventory balances. (LO3)

Penno Company reported inventories of $23,560,000 in 2006 and $25,790,000 in 2005. Cost of goods sold totaled $142,790,000 in 2006.

a. Prepare the journal entry to record cost of goods sold.
b. Set up a T-account for inventory and post the cost of goods sold entry from part a to this account.
c. Using the T-account from b, determine the amount of inventory that was purchased in 2006. Prepare a journal entry to record those purchases.
d. Using the financial statement effects template, show the effects of the entries in parts a and c on the balance sheet and income statement.

M8-28. Determining Lower of Cost or Market (LO4)

The following data refer to Froning company's ending inventory.

Item code	Quantity	Unit Cost	Unit Market
LXC	60	$45	$48
KWT	210	38	34
MOR	300	22	20
NES	100	27	32

Determine the ending inventory amount by applying the lower of cost or market rule to (a) each item or inventory and (b) the total inventory.

M8-29.[A] Analyzing Internal Controls (LO8)

Each of the following unrelated procedures has been designed to strengthen internal control. Explain how each of these procedures strengthens internal control.

a. Western Corporations's photocopy machines are activated by keying a code number. Each employee is assigned a different, confidential code number. Each copy machine keeps tract of the number of copies run under each employee number.
b. Picket Company's bank requires a signature card on file for each Picket company employee who is authorized to sign checks.
c. Fast Stop Convenience Stores have programmed their cash registers to imprint a blue star on every 300th receipt printed. A sign by each cash register states that the customer will receive $2 if his or her receipt has a blue star on it.

M8-30.[A] **Preparing a Bank Reconciliation** (LO8)

Use the following information to prepare a bank reconciliation for Young Company at June 30, 2006.
1. Balance per Cash account, June 30, $7,055.80.
2. Balance per bank statement, June 30, $7,300.25.
3. Deposits not reflected on bank statement, $725
4. Outstanding checks, June 30, $1,260.45
5. Service charge on bank statement not recorded in books, $11.
6. Error by bank—Yertel company check charged on Young Company's bank statement, $550.
7. Check for advertising expense, $250, incorrectly recorded in books at $520.

M8-31.[A] **Preparing a Bank Reconciliation** (LO8)

Use the following information to prepare a bank reconciliation for Dillon Company at April 30, 2006.
1. Balance per Cash account, April 30, $6,042.10.
2. Balance per bank statement, April 30, $6,300.28
3. Deposits not reflected on bank statement, $650.
4. Outstanding checks, April 30, $1,140.18
5. Service charge on bank statement not recorded in books. $12
6. Error by bank—Dillard Company check charged on Dillard Company check charges on Dillon Company's bank statement, $400.
7. Check for advertising expense, $130, incorrectly recorded in books at $310.

EXERCISES

E8-32. **Estimating Uncollectible Accounts and Reporting Accounts Receivable** (LO1, 2)

LaFond Company analyzes its accounts receivable at December 31, 2005, and arrives at the aged categories below along with the percentages that are estimated as uncollectible.

Age Group	Accounts Receivable	Estimated Loss %
1–30 days past due	$ 90,000	1%
31–60 days past due	20,000	2
61–120 days past due	11,000	5
121–180 days past due	6,000	10
Over 180 days past due	4,000	25
Total accounts receivable	$131,000	

The unused balance of the allowance for uncollectible accounts is $520 on December 31, 2005, before any adjustments.
a. What amount of bad debts expense will LaFond report for 2005?
b. What is the balance of accounts receivable that it reports on its December 31, 2005, balance sheet?
c. Set up T-accounts for both Bad Debts Expense and for the Allowance for Uncollectible Accounts. Enter any unadjusted balances along with the dollar effects of the information described (including your results from parts a and b). Explain the numbers in each of the T-accounts.

E8-33. **Analysis of accounts receivable and allowance for doubtful accounts.** (LO2, 6)

Ethan Allen Interiors, Inc. reported the following amounts in its 2005 10-K report ($ thousands).

	2005	2004
Accounts receivable, less allowance for doubtful accounts of $2,102 at June 30, 2005 and $2,194 at June 30, 2004	28,019	26,967

Sales revenue totaled $949,012,000 and the footnotes revealed that the company recorded bad debt expense of $563,000 in fiscal 2005.
a. Prepare the journal entry to record accounts receivable written off as uncollectible in 2005 along with its dollar impacts in the financial statement effects template. Enter the results in T-accounts (including any balances available).
b. What amount of cash was collected from customers in 2005?
c. Compute the accounts receivable turnover for 2005.

E8-34. **Analyzing and Reporting Receivable Transactions and Uncollectible Accounts (using percentage of sales method)** (LO1, 2)

At the beginning of 2005, Penman Company had the following account balances in its financial records:

Accounts Receivable	$122,000
Allowance for Uncollectible Accounts	7,900

During 2005, its credit sales were $1,173,000 and collections on credit sales were $1,150,000. The following additional transactions occurred during the year:

Feb. 17   Wrote off Nissim's account, $3,600.
May 28   Wrote off Weiss's account, $2,400.
Dec. 15   Wrote off Ohlson's account, $900.
Dec. 31   Recorded the provision for uncollectible accounts at 0.8% of credit sales for the year. (*Hint*: The allowance account is increased by 0.8% of credit sales regardless of any prior write-offs.)

Compute and show how accounts receivable and the allowance for uncollectible accounts are reported in its December 31, 2005, balance sheet.

E8-35. **Interpreting the Accounts Receivable Footnote** (LO2)

Hewlett-Packard
Company (HP)

Hewlett-Packard Company (HP) reports the following trade accounts receivable in its 10-K report:

October 31 (In millions)	2003	2002
Accounts receivable, net of allowance for doubtful accounts of $347 and $410 as of October 31, 2003 and 2002, respectively	$8,921	$8,456

HP's footnotes to its 10-K provide the following additional information relating to its allowance for doubtful accounts:

For Year Ended October 31 (In millions)	2003	2002	2001
Allowance for doubtful accounts			
Balance, beginning of period.	$410	$275	$171
Amount acquired through acquisition	—	141	—
Additions to allowance	29	90	206
Deductions, net of recoveries	(92)	(96)	(102)
Balance, end of period	$347	$410	$275

a. What is the gross amount of accounts receivables for HP in each of its fiscal years 2002 and 2003?
b. What is the percentage of the allowance for doubtful accounts to gross accounts receivable for each of its fiscal years 2002 and 2003?
c. What amount of bad debt expense has HP reported in each of its fiscal years 2001 through 2003? How does its reported expense compare with the amounts of its accounts receivable actually written off? (Identify the amounts and explain.)
d. Explain the changes in the allowance for doubtful accounts from 2001 through 2003. Does it appear that HP increased or decreased its allowance for doubtful accounts in any particular year beyond what seemed reasonable? (*Hint*: T-accounts can help with this analysis.)

E8-36. **Estimating Bad Debts Expense and Reporting of Receivables** (LO1, 2)

At December 31, 2005, Sunil Company had a balance of $375,000 in its accounts receivable and an unused balance of $4,200 in its allowance for uncollectible accounts. The company then aged its accounts as follows:

Current	$304,000
0–60 days past due	44,000
61–180 days past due	18,000
Over 180 days past due	9,000
Total accounts receivable	$375,000

The company has experienced losses as follows: 1% of current balances, 5% of balances 0–60 days past due, 15% of balances 61–180 days past due, and 40% of balances over 180 days past due. The company continues to base its provision for credit losses on this aging analysis and percentages.

a. What amount of bad debt expense does Sunil report on its 2005 income statement?
b. Show how accounts receivable and the allowance for uncollectible accounts are reported in its December 31, 2005, balance sheet.
c. Set up T-accounts for both Bad Debts Expense and for the Allowance for Uncollectible Accounts. Enter any unadjusted balances along with the dollar effects of the information described (including your results from parts a and b). Explain the numbers in each of the T-accounts.

E8-37. Estimating Uncollectible Accounts and Reporting Receivables over Multiple Periods (LO1, 2)
Barth Company, which has been in business for three years, makes all of its sales on credit and does not offer cash discounts. Its credit sales, customer collections, and write-offs of uncollectible accounts for its first three years follow:

Year	Sales	Collections	Accounts Written Off
2003	$751,000	$733,000	$5,300
2004	876,000	864,000	5,800
2005	972,000	938,000	6,500

a. Barth uses the allowance method of recognizing credit losses that provides for such losses at the rate of 1% of sales. (Hint: This means the allowance account is increased by 1% of credit sales regardless of any write-offs and unused balances.) What amounts for accounts receivable and the allowance for uncollectible accounts are reported on its balance sheet at the end of 2005? What total amount of bad debts expense appears on its income statement for each of the three years?
b. Comment on the appropriateness of the 1% rate used to provide for bad debts based on your results in part (a). (Hint: T-accounts can help with this analysis.)

E8-38. Accounting for prepaid expenses. (LO7)
At December 31, 2006, the balance sheet of Collins Company reports the following.

At December 31	2006
Prepaid rent	$16,000

On May 1, 2007, Collins made an annual rent prepayment of $54,000 cash. The existing prepaid rent was fully expired on April 30, 2007. The rent payment covered the period from May 1, 2007, through April 30, 2008.
a. Prepare the journal entry to record the rent payment on May 1, 2007.
b. Open T-accounts and post the journal entry from part a to the appropriate accounts.
c. Prepare the journal entry (or entries) to adjust the prepaid rent account at year-end. Post this entry to the prepaid rent T-account.
d. Using the financial statement effects template, show how the entries in parts a and c affect the balance sheet and income statement.

E8-39. Applying and Analyzing Inventory Costing Methods (LO3, 5)
At the beginning of the current period, Chen carried 1,000 units of its product with a unit cost of $20. A summary of purchases during the current period follows:

	Units	Unit Cost	Cost
Beginning Inventory	1,000	$20	$20,000
Purchases: #1	1,800	22	39,600
#2	800	26	20,800
#3	1,200	29	34,800

During the current period, Chen sold 2,800 units.
a. Assume that Chen uses the first-in, first-out method. Compute its cost of goods sold for the current period and the ending inventory balance.
b. Assume that Chen uses the last-in, first-out method. Compute its cost of goods sold for the current period and the ending inventory balance.
c. Assume that Chen uses the average cost method. Compute its cost of goods sold for the current period and the ending inventory balance.
d. Which of these three inventory costing methods would you choose to:
1. Reflect what is probably the physical flow of goods? Explain.
2. Minimize income taxes for the period? Explain.
3. Report the largest amount of income for the period? Explain.

E8-40. **Analysis of Inventory Footnote Disclosure** (LO5)

General Electric Company reports the following footnote in its 10-K report:

INVENTORIES December 31 (In millions)	2003	2002
Raw materials and work in process	$4,530	$4,894
Finished goods	4,376	4,379
Unbilled shipments	281	372
	9,187	9,645
Less revaluation to LIFO	(632)	(606)
	$8,555	$9,039

The company reports its inventories using the LIFO inventory costing method.

a. At what dollar amount are inventories reported on its 2003 balance sheet?

b. At what dollar amount would inventories have been reported on GE's 2003 balance sheet had it used FIFO inventory costing?

c. What *cumulative* effect has the use of LIFO inventory costing had, as of year-end 2003, on its pretax income compared with the pretax income it would have reported had it used FIFO inventory costing? Explain.

d. Assuming a 35% income tax rate, by what *cumulative* dollar amount has GE's tax liability been affected by use of LIFO inventory costing as of year-end 2003? Has the use of LIFO inventory costing increased or decreased its cumulative tax liability?

e. What effect has the use of LIFO inventory costing had on GE's pretax income and tax liability for 2003 (assume a 35% income tax rate)?

E8-41. **Computing Cost of Sales and Ending Inventory** (LO3)

Stocken Company has the following financial records for the current period:

	Units	Unit Cost
Beginning inventory	100	$46
Purchases: #1	650	42
#2	550	38
#3	200	36

Ending inventory at the end of this period is 350 units. Compute the ending inventory and the cost of goods sold for the current period using (a) first-in, first out, (b) average cost, and (c) last-in, first-out.

E8-42. **Determining Lower of Cost or Market** (LO4)

Crane Company had the following inventory at December 31, 2006.

		Unit Price	
	Quantity	Cost	Market
Desks			
Model 9001	70	$190	$210
Model 9002	45	280	268
Model 9003	20	350	360
Cabinets			
Model 7001	120	60	64
Model 7002	80	95	88
Model 7003	50	130	126

Required

a. Determine the ending inventory amount by apply the lower of cost or market rule to
   1. Each item of inventory.
   2. Each major category of inventory.
   3. Total inventory.

b. Which of the LCM procedures from requirement *a* results in the lowest net income for 2006? Explain.

E8-43. **Analysis of Inventory and Footnote Disclosure** (LO3, 5)

The current asset section of the Kraft Foods, Inc., balance sheet follows ($ millions):

Kraft Foods, Inc.

At December 31	2003	2002
Cash and cash equivalents	$ 514	$ 215
Receivables (less allowances of $114 and $119)	3,369	3,116
Inventories		
Raw materials	1,375	1,372
Finished product	1,968	2,010
	3,343	3,382
Deferred income taxes	681	511
Other current assets	217	232
Total current assets	$8,124	$7,456

Kraft also reports the following footnote to its 2003 10-K report:

Note 6. Inventories

The cost of approximately 39% and 43% of inventories in 2003 and 2002, respectively, was determined using the LIFO method. The stated LIFO amounts of inventories were approximately $155 million and $215 million higher than the current cost of inventories at December 31, 2003 and 2002, respectively.

Notice that not all of Kraft's inventories are reported using the same inventory costing method (companies can use different inventory costing methods for different inventory pools).

a. At what dollar amount are Kraft's inventories reported on its 2003 balance sheet?

b. At what dollar amount would inventories have been reported on Kraft's 2003 balance sheet had it used FIFO inventory costing?

c. What *cumulative* effect has the use of LIFO inventory costing had, as of year-end 2003, on its pretax income compared with the pretax income it would have reported had it used FIFO inventory costing? Explain.

d. Assuming a 35% income tax rate, by what *cumulative* dollar amount has Kraft's tax liability been affected by use of LIFO inventory costing as of year-end 2003? Has the use of LIFO inventory costing increased or decreased its cumulative tax liability?

e. What effect has the use of LIFO inventory costing had on Kraft's pretax income and tax liability for 2003 (assume a 35% income tax rate)?

E8-44. **Analysis of Inventories using LIFO inventory Footnote** (LO5)

The footnote below is from the 2004 10-K report of Whole Foods Market, Inc. a Texas based retail grocery chain.

Whole Foods Market, Inc. (WFMI)

Inventories

We value our inventories at the lower of cost of market. Cost was determined using the last-in, first-out ("LIFO") method for approximately 94.2% and 96.4% of inventories in fiscal years 2004 and 2003, respectively. Under the LIFO method, the cost assigned to items sold is based on the cost of the most recent items purchased. As a result, the cost of the first items purchased remain in inventory and are used to value ending inventory. The excess of estimated current costs over LIFO carrying value, or LIFO reserve, was approximately $11.2 million and $9.1 million at September 26, 2004 and September 28, 2003, respectively. Costs for the balance of inventories are determined by the first-in, first-out ("FIFO") method.

Whole Foods operates the world's largest chain of natural and organic food stores. In 2004, Whole Foods reported sales revenue of $3,865 million and cost of goods sold of $2,523 million. The following information was extracted from the company's 2004 balance sheet ($ thousands):

	2003	2002
Merchandise inventories	152,912	123,904

1. Calculate the amount of inventories purchased by Whole Foods in 2004.
2. What amount of gross profit would Whole Foods have reported if the FIFO method had been used to value all inventories?
3. Calculate the gross profit margin (GPM) as reported and assuming that the FIFO method had been used to value all inventories.

E8-45. **Internal Control** (LO7)

Each of the following unrelated procedures has been designed to strengthen internal control. Explain how each of these procedures strengthens internal control.

a. After preparing a check for a cash disbursement, the accountant for Travis Lumber Company cancels the supporting business documents (purchase order, receiving report, and invoice) by stamping them PAID.

b. The salespeople for Davis Department Store give each customer a cash register receipt along with the proper change. A sign on each cash register states that no refunds or exchanges are allowed without the related cash register receipt.

c. The ticket-taker at the Exquire Theater tears each admission ticket in half and gives one half back to the ticket purchaser.

d. John Renald's restaurant provides servers with prenumbered customer's checks. The servers are to void checks with mistakes on them and issue new ones rather than make corrections on them. Voided checks must be given to the manager every day.

E8-46.[A] **Internal Control** (LO8)

The Mountain Twister amusement ride had the following system of internal control over cash receipts. All persons pay the same price for a ride. A person taking the ride pays cash to the cashier and receives a prenumbered ticket. The tickets are issued in strict number sequence. The individual then walks to the ride site, hands the ticket to the ticket-taker (who controls the number of people getting on each ride), and passes through a turnstile. At the end of each day, the beginning ticket number is subtracted from the ending ticket number to determine the number of tickets sold. The cash is counted and compared with the number of tickets sold. The turnstile records how many people pass through it. At the end of each day, the beginning turnstile count is subtracted from the ending count to determine the number of riders that day. The number of riders is compared with the number of tickets sold.

Required

Which internal control feature would reveal each of the following irregularities?

a. The ticket-taker lets her friends on the ride without tickets.

b. The cashier gives his friends tickets without receiving cash from them.

c. The cashier give too much change.

d. The ticket-taker returns the tickets she has collected to the cashier. The cashier then resells these tickets and splits the proceeds with the ticket-taker.

e. A person sneaks into the ride line without paying the cashier.

E8-47.[A] **Bank Reconciliation Components** (LO8)

Identify the amount asked for in each of the following situations.

a. Munsing Company's May 31 bank reconciliation shows deposits in transit of $1,400. The general ledger Cash in Bank account shows total cash receipts during June of $57,300. The June bank statement shows total cash deposits of $55,900 (and no credit memos). What amount of deposits in transit should appear in the June 30 bank reconciliation?

b. Sandusky Company's August 31 bank reconciliation shows outstanding checks of $2,100. The general ledger Cash in Bank account shows total cash disbursements (all by check) during September of $50,300. The September bank statement shows $49,200 of checks clearing the bank. What amount of outstanding checks should appear in the September 30 bank reconciliation?

c. Fremont Corporation's March 31 bank reconciliation shows deposits in transit of $800. The general ledger Cash in Bank account shows total cash receipts during April of $38,000. The April bank statement shows total cash deposits of $37,000 (including $1,300 from the collection of a note; the note collection has not yet been recorded by Fremont.) What amount of deposits in transit should appear in the April 30 bank reconciliation?

E8-48.[A] **Bank Reconciliation Components** (LO8)

Identify the amount asked for in each of the following situations:

a. Howell Company's August 31 bank reconciliation shows deposits in transit of 42,400. The general ledger Cash in Bank account shows total cash receipts during September of $91,200. The September bank statement shows total cash deposits of $88,000 (and no credit memos). What amount of deposits in transit should appear in the September 30 bank reconciliation?

b. Wright Corporation's March 31 bank reconciliation shows deposits in transit of $1,600. The general ledger Cash in Bank account shows total cash receipts during april of $63,100. The April bank statement shows total cash deposits of $66,200 (including $2,000 from the collection of a note; the note collection has not yet been recorded by Wright). What amount of deposits in transit should appear in the April 30 bank reconciliation?

c. Braddock Company's October 31 bank reconciliations shows outstanding checks of $2,600. The general ledger Cash in Bank account shows total cash disbursements (all by check) during November of $68,700. The November bank statement shows $67,200 of checks clearing the bank. What amount of outstanding checks should appear in the November 30 bank reconciliation?

PROBLEMS

P8-49.   **Interpreting Accounts Receivable and Footnote Disclosure**   **(LO1, 2)**

Following is the current asset section from the **W.W. Grainger, Inc.**, balance sheet:

W.W. Grainger, Inc.
(GWW)

($ 000s)	2003	2002	2001
Cash and cash equivalents	$ 402,824	$ 208,528	$ 168,846
Accounts receivable (less allowances for doubtful accounts of $24,736, $26,868 and $30,552, respectively)	431,896	423,240	454,180
Inventories	661,247	721,178	634,654
Prepaid expenses and other assets	37,947	36,665	37,477
Deferred income taxes	99,499	95,336	97,454
Total current assets	$1,633,413	$1,484,947	$1,392,611

Grainger reports the following footnote relating to its receivables:

ALLOWANCE FOR DOUBTFUL ACCOUNTS

The following table shows the activity in the allowance for doubtful accounts:

	For Years Ended December 31		
($ 000s)	2003	2002	2001
Balance at beginning of period	$26,868	$30,552	$23,436
Provision for uncollectible accounts	9,263	13,328	21,483
Write-off of uncollectible accounts, less recoveries	(11,713)	(17,054)	(14,290)
Miscellaneous adjustments	318	42	(77)
Balance at end of period	$ 24,736	$ 26,868	$ 30,552

Required

a. What amount do customers owe Grainger at each of the year-ends 2001 through 2003?

b. What percentage of those accounts receivable in *a* does Grainger feel are uncollectible? (*Hint*: Percentage of uncollectible accounts = Allowance for uncollectible accounts/Gross accounts receivable.)

c. What amount of bad debts expense did Grainger report in its income statement for each of the years 2001 through 2003?

d. Explain the change in the balance of the allowance for uncollectible accounts from 2002 to 2003. Specifically, did the allowance increase or decrease as a percentage of gross accounts receivable, and why?

e. If Grainger had kept its 2003 allowance for uncollectible accounts at the same percentage of gross accounts receivable as it was in 2002, by what amount would its profit have changed (ignore taxes)? Explain.

P8-50.   **Analyzing and Interpreting Receivables and its Related Ratios**   **(LO2, 6)**

Following is the current asset section from **AOL Time Warner**'s balance sheet ($ millions):

AOL Time Warner

December 31	2002	2001
Current assets		
Cash and equivalents	$ 1,730	$ 719
Receivables, less allowances of $2,379 and $1,889 million	5,667	6,054
Inventories	1,896	1,791
Prepaid expenses and other current assets	1,862	1,687
Total current assets	$11,155	$10,251

During 2002, AOL reported a $98,700 million net loss, all of which was attributed to the write off of goodwill that it recognized in the merger of AOL and Time Warner. Sales were $40,961 million in 2002 and $37,166 million in 2001.

Required

a. What is AOL's gross amount of receivables at the end of (1) 2002 and (2) 2001?

b. For both 2002 and 2001, compute the ratio of (1) the allowance for uncollectible accounts to gross receivables and (2) gross receivables to sales. Identify and interpret the changes in these ratios over these two years.

c. Compute both the receivables turnover and the average collection period for 2002. Does the collection period (days sales in receivables) appear reasonable given AOL's lines of business? Explain.

d. Given the large loss reported in 2002, it is reasonable to consider whether AOL took a big bath by writing off other assets or padding reserves such as the allowance for uncollectible accounts. Do your results from (b) suggest that this might be the case? Explain. What might be another explanation for the relative increase in the allowance for uncollectible accounts?

P8-51.   **Analysis of Inventory and its Footnote Disclosure**   (LO4, 5)

Caterpillar, Inc. (CAT)

The current asset section of the **Caterpillar, Inc.**, balance sheet follows ($ millions):

December 31	2003	2002
Current assets		
Cash and short-term investments	$ 342	$ 309
Receivables—trade and other	**3,666**	2,838
Receivables—finance	**7,605**	6,748
Deferred and refundable income taxes	**707**	781
Prepaid expenses	**1,424**	1,224
Inventories	**3,047**	2,763
Total current assets	**$16,791**	$14,663

CAT also provides the following footnote to its 2003 10-K report:

Inventories are stated at the lower of cost or market. Cost is principally determined using the last-in, first-out (LIFO) method. The value of inventories on the LIFO basis represented about 80% of total inventories at December 31, 2003, 2002 and 2001.

If the FIFO (first-in, first-out) method had been in use, inventories would have been $1,863 million, $1,977 million and $1,923 million higher than reported at December 31, 2003, 2002 and 2001, respectively.

Notice that not all of CAT's inventories are reported using the same inventory costing method (companies can use different inventory costing methods for different inventory pools).

a. At what dollar amount is CAT's inventories reported on its 2003 balance sheet?

b. At what dollar amount would inventories have been reported on CAT's 2003 balance sheet had it used FIFO inventory costing?

c. What *cumulative* effect has the use of LIFO inventory costing had, as of year-end 2003, on its pretax income compared with the pretax income it would have reported had it used FIFO inventory costing? Explain.

d. Assuming a 35% income tax rate, by what *cumulative* dollar amount has CAT's tax liability been affected by use of LIFO inventory costing as of year-end 2003? Has the use of LIFO inventory costing increased or decreased its cumulative tax liability?

e. What effect has the use of LIFO inventory costing had on CAT's pretax income and tax liability for 2003 (assume a 35% income tax rate)?s

P8-52.   **Analysis of Inventories using LIFO Inventory Footnote**   (LO3, 5, 6)

Hormel Foods
Corporation (HRL)

Note C from the 2005 10-K report of **Hormel Foods Corporation** follows.

Inventories

Principal components of inventories are:

(In Thousands)	October 30, 2004	October 30, 2003
Finished products	$258,941	$229,530
Raw materials and work-in-process	126,139	130,841
Materials and supplies	77,329	76,563
LIFO reserve	(36,754)	(33,721)
Total	$425,655	$403,213

Inventoriable expenses, packages, supplies, and turkey products amounting to approximately $85.5 million at October 30, 2004, and $91.1 million at October 25, 2003, are stated at cost determined by the last-in, first-out method are are $36.8 million and $33.7 million lower in the respective years than such inventories determined under the first-in, first-out method.

Hormel reported cost of goods sold of $3,658,870,000 and pretax income of $364,565,000 in 2004.

Required

a. What amount of cost of goods sold and pretax income would Hormel report if the FIFO method were used to value all inventories?

b. The company's effective tax rate was 36.5% in 2004. What amount of income taxes did the company save by using LIFO in 2004.

c. Calculate the inventory turnover ratio for 2004, using inventories and cost of goods sold as reported.

d. Calculate the inventory turnover ratio assuming that Hormel used FIFO to value all of its inventories. Compare your answer to the turnover ratio calculated in *c*.

P8-53. **Analyzing and Interpreting Inventories and its Related Ratios and Disclosures** (LO5, 6)

The current asset section from **The Stride Rite Corporation**'s annual report follows ($ thousands):

The Stride Rite
Corporation (SRR)

	November 28, 2003	November 29, 2002
Current Assets		
Cash and cash equivalents	$103,272	$ 73,105
Accounts and notes receivable, less allowances of $9,406 in 2003 and $12,250 in 2002	51,058	48,075
Inventories	81,925	98,213
Deferred income taxes	14,393	20,588
Prepaid expenses and other current assets	19,452	14,131
Total current assets	$270,100	$254,112

Stride Rite reports the following related to its gross profit ($ thousands):

	Years Ended	
	2003	**2002**
Net sales	$550,124	$532,400
Cost of sales	340,614	337,951
Gross profit	$209,510	$194,449

Stride Rite further reports the following footnote related to its inventories:

> **INVENTORIES** The cost of inventories, which consist primarily of finished product, at November 28, 2003 and November 29, 2002 was determined on a last-in, first-out (LIFO) basis. During 2003, the LIFO reserve decreased by $1,610,000 to $10,875,000 at November 28, 2003. If all inventories had been valued on a first-in, first-out (FIFO) basis, net income would have been lower by $1,019,000 ($.03 per share) in 2003. The LIFO reserve decreased in 2002 and increased in 2001, by $758,000 and $314,000, respectively. If all inventories had been valued on a FIFO basis, net income would have been lower by $516,000 ($.01 per share) in 2002 and would have been higher by $223,000 (less than $.01 per share) in 2001.
>
> During 2003 and 2002, reductions in certain inventory quantities resulted in the sale of products carried at costs prevailing in prior years which were different from current costs. As a result of these inventory reductions, net income was increased by $141,000 (less than $.01 per share) and decreased by $120,000 (less than $.01 per share) in 2003 and 2002, respectively.

Required

a. Compute the ratio of inventories to total current assets for both 2003 and 2002. Is the change you observe for the ratio a positive development for a company such as Stride Rite? Explain.

b. Compute inventory turnover for both 2003 and 2002 (2001 ending inventories were $112,481). Interpret and explain the change in inventory turnover as positive or negative for the company.

c. What inventory costing method does Stride Rite use? What effect has the use of this method (relative to FIFO or LIFO) had on its reported income over the three years, 2001–2003? Explain.

d. Stride Rite reports that it decreased certain inventory quantities. Why do you believe Stride Rite reduced its inventory quantities? Is this development positive or negative for a company such as Stride Rite? Explain.

e. What effect did reductions in inventory quantities have on Stride Rite's reported income for 2003 and for 2002? Explain.

P8-54. **Internal Control** **(LO8)**

Each of the following lettered paragraphs briefly describes an independent situation involving some aspect of internal control.

Required

Answer the questions at the end of each paragraph or numbered section.

a. A doughnut shop uses a cash register that produces a printed receipt for each sale. The register also prints each transaction on a paper tape that is locked inside the cash register. Only the supervisor has access to the locked-in tape. A prominently displayed sign promises a free doughnut to any customer who is not given the cash register receipt with his or her purchase. How is this procedure an internal control device for the doughnut shop?

b. Jason Miller, a swindler, sent several businesses invoices requesting payment for office supplies that had never been ordered or delivered to the businesses. A 5% discount was offered for prompt payment. What internal control procedures should prevent this swindle from being successful?

c. The cashier for Uptown Cafeteria is located at the end of the food line. After customers have selected their food items, the cashier rings up the prices of the food and the customer pays the bill. The customer line frequently stalls while a person paying searches for the correct amount of cash. To speed things up, the cashier often collects money from the next customer or two who have the correct change without ringing up their food on the register. After the first customer finally pays, the cashier rings up the amount for the customers who have already paid. (1) What is the internal control weakness in this procedure? (2) How might the internal control over the collection of cash from the cafeteria customers be strengthened?

P8-55.[A] **Bank Reconciliation** **(LO8)**

On July 31, 2006, Sullivan Company's Cash in Bank account had a balance of 47,216.60. On that date, the bank statement indicated a balance of $9,098.55. Comparison of returned checks and bank advices revealed the following:

1. Deposits in transit July 31 amounted to $3,576.95.
2. Outstanding checks July 31 totaled $1,467.90.
3. The bank erroneously charged a $325 check of Solomon Company against the Sullivan bank account.
4. A $25 bank service charge has not yet been recorded by Sullivan Company.
5. Sullivan neglected to record $44,000 borrowed from the bank on a 10% six-month note. The bank statement shows the $4,000 as a deposit.
6. Included with the returned checks is a memo indicating that J. Martin's check for $640 had been returned NSF. Martin, a customer, had sent the check to pay an account of $660 less a $20 discount.
7. Sullivan Company recorded a $109 payment for repairs as $1,090.

Required

a. Prepare a bank reconciliation for Sullivan Company at July 31, 2006

b. Prepare the general journal entry or entries necessary to bring the Cash in Bank account into agreement with the reconciled cash balance on the bank reconciliation.

P8-56.[A] **Bank Reconciliation** **(LO8)**

The bank reconciliation made by Winton, Inc., on August 31, 2006, showed a deposit in transit of $1,280 and two outstanding checks, No. 597 for $830 and No. 603 for $640. The reconciled cash balance on August 31 was $14,110.

The following bank statement is available for September:

Bank Statement

TO   Winton, Inc.
     St. Louis, Mo

September 30, 2006
STATE BANK

Date	Deposits	No.	Date	Charges	Date	Balance
					Aug. 31	$14,300
Sept. 1	$1,280	597	Sept. 1	$ 830	Sept. 1	14,750
2	1,120	607	5	1,850	2	15,870
5	850	608	5	1,100	5	13,770
9	744	609	9	552	8	13,130
15	1,360	610	8	640	9	13,322
17	1,540	611	17	488	15	14,008
25	1,028	612	15	674	17	5,060
30	680	614	25	920	25	15,168
		NSF	29	1,028	29	4,140
		SC	30	96	30	14,784

A list of deposits made and checks written during September is shown below:

Deposits Made		Checks Written	
Sept. 1	$1,120	No. 607	$1,850
4	850	608	1,100
8	744	609	552
12	1,360	610	640
16	1,540	611	488
24	1,028	612	746
29	680	613	310
30	1,266	614	920
	$8,588	615	386
		616	420
			$7,412

The Cash in Bank account balance on September 30 was $15,286. In reviewing checks returned by the bank, the accountant discovered that check No. 612, written for $674 for advertising expense, was recorded in the cash disbursements journal as $746. The NSF check for $1,028, which Winton deposited on September 24, was a payment on account from customer D. Walker.

Required
a.   Prepare a bank reconciliation for Winton, Inc., at September 30, 2006.
b.   Prepare the necessary journal entries to bring the Cash in Bank account into agreement with the reconciled cash balance on the bank reconciliation.

CASES AND PROJECTS

C8-57.   Analysis of accounts receivable allowances and turnover ratios.   (LO1, 2, 6)
Oakley, Inc. manufactures and markets fashion eyewear, apparel, footwear and watches. The current asset section of the company's consolidated balance sheet and portions of the income statements for 2002 and 2003 are presented below. The following footnote provides details on Oakley's accounting for uncollectible accounts, and sales returns.

Oakley, Inc. (OO)

Accounts Receivable Valuation Allowances					
(in thousands)	Balance at beginning of period	Additions charged to cost and expense	Deductions	Adjustments	Balance at end of period
For the year ended December 31, 2003:					
Allowance for doubtful accounts	$2,606	$1,738	$(?,???)	$ —	$2,623
Sales return reserve	$5,825	$4,707	$(?,???)	$ —	$7,049

OAKLEY, INC. AND SUBSIDIARIES Consolidated Balance Sheets		
(in thousands, except share and per share data)	December 31, 2003	December 31, 2002
ASSETS		
Cash and cash equivalents	$ 49,211	$ 22,248
Accounts receivable, less allowances of $9,672 (2003) and $8,431 (2002)	77,989	68,116
Inventories, net (Note 3)	98,691	87,007
Other receivables	3,386	5,008
Deferred and prepaid income taxes	9,965	10,686
Prepaid expenses and other assets	8,062	6,271
Total current assets	$247,286	$199,336

OAKLEY, INC. AND SUBSIDIARIES Consolidated Statements of Income			
Year Ended December 31 ($ thousands)	2003	2002	2001
Net sales	$521,549	$489,552	$429,267
Cost of goods sold	226,846	211,962	174,332
Gross profit	$294,703	$277,590	$254,935

Required

1. Prepare journal entries (and related T-accounts) along with their impacts on the financial statement effects template to record bad debt expense and accounts receivable write-offs for 2003.
2. Oakley has also established an allowance for returns. How do returns differ from doubtful accounts? Under what circumstances might this difference affect the accounting for returns?
3. Calculate the accounts receivable turnover ratio for 2003.
4. Calculate the inventory turnover ratio and gross profit margin for 2003.

C8-58. **Evaluating Turnover Rates for Different Companies** (LO6)

Following are asset turnover rates for accounts receivable; inventory; and property, plant, and equipment (PPE) for **Best Buy** (retailer of consumer products), **Carnival** (vacation cruise line), **Caterpillar** (manufacturer of heavy equipment), **Harley-Davidson** (manufacturer of motorcycles), **Microsoft** (software company), **Oracle** (software company), and **Sharper Image** (retailer of specialty consumer products):

Best Buy (BBY)

Carnival (CCL)

Caterpillar (CAT)

Harley-Davidson (HDI)

Microsoft (MSFT)

Oracle (ORCL)

Sharper Image (SHRP)

	Receivables Turnover	Inventory Turnover	PPE Turnover
Best Buy Co., Inc.	74.94	7.16	10.58
Carnival Corporation	43.88	25.23	0.47
Caterpillar Inc.	2.18	5.37	3.18
Harley-Davidson, Inc.	4.96	12.97	4.47
Microsoft Corporation	6.24	7.00	14.33
Oracle Corporation	4.17	n.a.	9.25
Sharper Image Corporation	50.57	4.21	10.79

Required

a. Interpret and explain differences in receivables turnover for the retailers (Best Buy and Sharper Image) vis-à-vis that for the manufacturers (Caterpillar and Harley-Davidson).

b. Interpret and explain the difference in inventory turnover for Harley-Davidson versus Sharper Image. Why do you believe Oracle's inventory turnover is reported as n.a.?

c. What are some general observations you might draw regarding the relative levels of these turnover rates across the different industries?

Reporting Long-Term Operating Assets

LEARNING OBJECTIVES

After completing the chapter, you should be able to:

LO1 Describe and distinguish between tangible and intangible assets. (p. 377)

LO2 Determine which costs to capitalize and report as assets and which costs to expense. (p. 378)

LO3 Apply different depreciation methods to allocate the cost of assets over time. (p. 381)

LO4 Determine the effects of asset sales and impairments on financial statements. (p. 384)

LO5 Describe the accounting and reporting for intangible assets. (p. 390)

LO6 Analyze the effects of tangible and intangible assets on key performance measures. (p. 395)

LO7 Explain the accounting for acquisition and depletion of natural resources. (p. 395)

LO8 *Appendix 9A*—Explain and illustrate the reporting for deferred income taxes. (p. 399)

Getty Images

PROCTER & GAMBLE

Head and Shoulders Above Competitors

Procter & Gamble (P&G) has successfully reinvented itself . . . again. It has shed its image as the "lumbering giant" of its industry with new products and directed marketing. Its annual sales now exceed $50 billion, which far exceeds competitors such as Colgate-Palmolive and Kimberly-Clark. P&G has also focused on its higher margin products such as those in beauty care. This strategy has improved its profit margin and provided much needed dollars for marketing activities. Its advertising budget is up to nearly 11% of sales, which is nearly double the budget of some of its key competitors.

P&G's financial performance has been equally impressive. Its return on average equity (ROE) in 2004 was 38.7%, with RNOA comprising 52% of it. Although more financially leveraged than the average publicly traded company, there is little need for concern because P&G generates over $9 billion in operating cash flow, which is more than sufficient to cover its $2 billion in interest and principal payments on long-term debt. P&G also generates sufficient cash to allow it to pay dividends in excess of $2.5 billion annually to shareholders.

P&G's product stable is impressive. It consists of numerous well-recognized household brands—a partial listing follows by business segment:

- **Fabric and Home Care**—Tide, Downy, Joy, Cascade, Mr. Clean, Bounce, Swiffer, and Febreze

- **Beauty Care**—Head & Shoulders, Pantene, Olay, Clairol, Max Factor, Old Spice, and Ivory

- **Baby and Family Care**—Pampers, Charmin, Bounty, and Puffs

- **Health Care**—Crest, Vicks, Fixodent, PUR, and Pepto-Bismol

- **Snacks and Beverages**—Pringles and Folgers

Sales of its products are distributed across each of these business segments as illustrated in the following chart:

(Continued on next page)

(Continued from previous page)

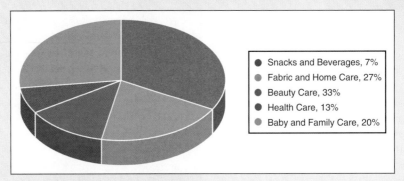

- Snacks and Beverages, 7%
- Fabric and Home Care, 27%
- Beauty Care, 33%
- Health Care, 13%
- Baby and Family Care, 20%

P&G's recent successes have coincided with new leadership. A.G. Lafley took the helm in 2000. Since assuming the top job, he has guided P&G to successive increases in sales, income, and cash flows. In turn, increases have driven impressive gains in stock prices.

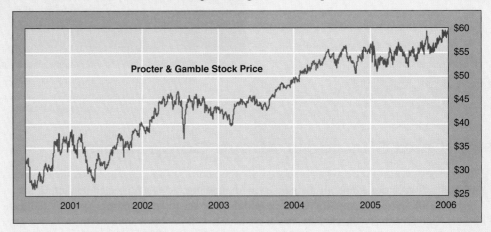

Lafley's innovation and market savvy have consistently propelled P&G. *Business Week* (2004) reports: "From its Swiffer mop to battery-powered Crest SpinBrush toothbrushes and Whitestrip tooth whiteners, P&G has simply done a better job than rivals." Clayton C. Daley Jr., P&G's chief financial officer, adds "We are growing market share in 70% of our businesses. That doesn't happen unless you have strong innovation."

In this chapter we explore the reporting and analysis of long-term operating assets. In order to maintain growth in sales, income, and cash flows, capital intensive companies like P&G must be diligent in managing long-term operating assets. As is the case with P&G, many companies have made large investments in innovation. These investments are not always reflected adequately in the balance sheet. Management's choices and GAAP rules concerning the reporting of long-term operating assets can have a marked impact on the analysis and interpretation of financial statements.

Sources: Procter & Gamble 2004 & 2005 10-K Reports; *Procter & Gamble* 2004 Annual Report; *BusinessWeek,* 4 October 2004; *The Wall Street Journal,* January 2005.

CHAPTER ORGANIZATION

Reporting Long-Term Operating Assets

Property, Plant, and Equipment
- Determination of which costs to capitalize
- Depreciation methods
- Asset sales and impairments
- Footnote disclosures
- Analysis implications

Intangible Assets
- Research and development costs
- Patents, trademarks, and franchises
- Amortization and impairment
- Goodwill
- Footnote disclosures
- Analysis implications

Natural Resources
- Cost capitalization and depletion
- Depletion recognition

INTRODUCTION

Investments in long-term operating assets usually represent the largest component of a company's balance sheet. Effectively managing long-term operating assets is crucial, because these investments affect company performance for several years and are frequently irreversible. To evaluate how well a company is managing operating assets, we need to understand how they are measured and reported.

This chapter describes the accounting, reporting, and analysis of long-term operating assets including tangible and intangible assets. **Tangible assets** are assets that have physical substance. They are frequently included in the balance sheet as *property, plant and equipment*, and include land, buildings, machinery, fixtures and equipment. **Intangible assets**, such as trademarks and patents, do not have physical substance, but provide the owner with specific rights and privileges.

Long-term operating assets have two common characteristics. First, unlike inventory, these assets are not acquired for resale. Instead, they are necessary to produce and deliver the products and services that generate revenues for the company. Second, these assets help produce revenues for multiple accounting periods. Consequently, accountants focus considerable attention on how they are reported in the balance sheet and how these costs are transferred over time to the income statement as expenses.

To illustrate the size and importance of long-term operating assets, the asset section (only) of P&G's balance sheet is reproduced in Exhibit 9.1. We can see that in 2004, P&G's net investment in property, plant and equipment totaled approximately $14.1 billion and its intangible assets represent a $23.9 billion investment. Together, these two categories of assets make up two-thirds of P&G's total assets.

LO1 Describe and distinguish between tangible and intangible assets.

EXHIBIT 9.1	Procter & Gamble Balance Sheet (assets only)	
	June 30	
Amounts in millions	2004	2003
Assets		
Current Assets		
Cash and cash equivalents	$ 5,469	$ 5,912
Investment securities	423	300
Accounts receivable	4,062	3,038
Inventories		
Materials and supplies	1,191	1,095
Work in process	340	291
Finished goods	2,869	2,254
Total inventories	4,400	3,640
Deferred income taxes	958	843
Prepaid expenses and other receivables	1,803	1,487
Total current assets	17,115	15,220
Property, Plant, and Equipment		
Buildings	5,206	4,729
Machinery and equipment	19,456	18,222
Land	642	591
	25,304	23,542
Accumulated depreciation	(11,196)	(10,438)
Net property, plant, and equipment	14,108	13,104
Goodwill and Other Intangible Assets		
Goodwill	19,610	11,132
Trademarks and other intangible assets, net	4,290	2,375
Net Goodwill and Other Intangible Assets	23,900	13,507
Other Noncurrent Assets	1,925	1,875
Total Assets	$ 57,048	$ 43,706

This chapter is divided into two main sections. The first section focuses on accounting for tangible property, plant, and equipment and the related depreciation expense that is reported each period in the income statement. The second section examines measurement and reporting of intangible assets and natural resources.

PROPERTY, PLANT, AND EQUIPMENT (PPE)

For many companies, the largest category of operating assets is its long-term property, plant, and equipment (PPE) assets. To frame this discussion, we again refer to the following graphic where we highlight PPE assets on the balance sheet, and selling, general and administrative expenses on the income statement. Selling, general and administrative expense usually includes the allocation of asset costs, such as depreciation and asset write-downs, that are matched against sales. This section explains the accounting, reporting, and analysis of PPE assets and related items.

Income Statement	Balance Sheet	
Sales	Cash	Current liabilities
Cost of goods sold	Accounts receivable	Long-term liabilities
Selling, general & administrative	Inventory	
Income taxes	Property, plant, and equipment, net	Shareholders' equity
Net income	Investments	

Determining Costs to Capitalize

LO2 Determine which costs to capitalize and report as assets and which costs to expense.

When a company acquires an asset, it must first decide which portion of the cost should be included among the expenses of the current period and which costs should be **capitalized** as part of the asset and reported in the balance sheet. Outlays to acquire **PPE** are called **capital expenditures**. Expenditures that are recorded as an asset must possess each of the following two characteristics:

1. The asset is owned or controlled by the company.
2. The asset is expected to provide future benefits.

All costs incurred to acquire an asset and prepare it for its intended use should be capitalized and reported in the balance sheet. These costs would include the purchase price of the asset plus any of the following: installation costs, taxes, shipping costs, legal fees, and set-up or calibration costs.

Determining the specific costs that should be capitalized requires judgment. There are two important considerations to address when deciding which costs to capitalize. First, companies can only capitalize costs that are *directly linked* to future benefits. Incidental costs or costs that would be incurred regardless of whether the asset is purchased should not be capitalized. Second, the costs capitalized as an asset can be no greater than the expected future benefits to be derived from use of the asset. This requirement means that if a company reports a $200 asset, we can reasonably expect that it will derive at least $200 in expected future cash inflows from the use and ultimate disposition of the asset.

Sometimes, companies construct assets for their own use rather than purchasing a similar asset from another company. In this case, all of the costs incurred to construct the asset—including materials, labor, and a reasonable amount of overhead—should be included in the cost that is capitalized. In addition, in many cases, a portion of the interest expense incurred during the construction period should also be capitalized as part of the asset's cost. This interest is called capitalized interest. Capitalizing some of a company's interest cost as part of the cost of a self-constructed asset reduces interest expense in the current period and increases depreciation expense in future periods when the asset is placed in service.

Once an asset is placed in service, additional costs are often incurred to maintain and improve the asset. Routine repairs and maintenance costs are necessary to realize the full potential benefits of ownership of the asset and should be treated as expenses of the period in which the maintenance is performed. However, if the cost can be considered an *improvement or betterment* of the asset, the cost should be capitalized. An improvement or betterment is an outlay that either enhances the usefulness of the asset or extends the asset's useful life beyond the original expectation.

BUSINESS INSIGHT

Federal authorities arrested **WorldCom**'s chief financial officer, Scott Sullivan and its controller (chief accounting officer), David Myers, in August 2002 for allegedly conspiring to alter the telecommunications giant's financial statements to meet analyst expectations. They were accused of *cooking the books* so the company would not show a loss for 2001 and subsequent quarters (U.S. v. Sullivan et al., No. 02–1511, complaint unsealed, S.D.N.Y., 8/1/2002). According to the criminal complaint, WorldCom failed to generate enough revenue to offset its costs. These costs were fees charged by third-party telecommunications companies for access to their networks that allowed WorldCom to enlarged its service area. Many of these access-leases required WorldCom to pay a fixed sum to the outside network regardless of whether WorldCom actually made use of all or part of the capacity agreed upon.

WorldCom obtained these leases in anticipation of an increase internet-related business that did not materialize. Instead of reporting the loss, its executives shifted operating costs to its capitalized assets. By capitalizing these costs (moving them from the income statement to the balance sheet), World Com was able disguise these costs as an asset to be allocated as future costs. When questioned by internal auditors, Sullivan allegedly said the costs were pre-paid capacity associated with underutilized lines.

Contrary to WorldCom's usual practices and prevailing accounting principles, no support existed for its capitalization, alleges FBI agents. Further, other officials within WorldCom expressed concerns about the propriety of its capitalization to no avail. Myers did admit that the amounts were capitalized based on historical margins (ratio of line costs to revenues), and he acknowledged no support for that. Myers also said he was uncomfortable with capitalization, but that once it started it was difficult to stop.

Although the WorldCom case also involved alleged fraud, an astute analyst would have suspected something was amiss from analysis of WorldCom's long-term asset turnover (Sales/Average long-term assets) as shown below. The obvious decline in turnover reveals that its assets constituted an ever-increasing percent of total sales during 1995 to 2002, by quarter. This finding does not, in itself, imply fraud. It does, however, raise serious questions that should have been answered by World Com executives in meetings with analysts.

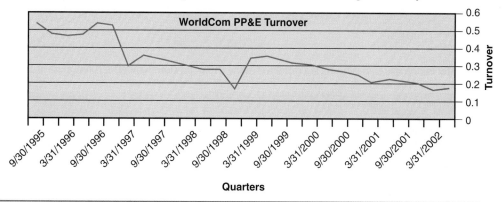

YOU MAKE THE CALL

You are the Company Accountant   Your company has just purchased a plot of land as a building site for an office building. After the purchase, you discover that the building site was once the site of an oil well. Before construction can commence, your company must spend $40,000 to properly cap the oil well and prepare the site to meet current environmental standards. How should you account for the $40,000 clean-up cost? [Answers on page 398]

Depreciation

Once an asset has been recorded in the balance sheet, the cost must be transferred over time from the balance sheet to the income statement and reported as an expense. The *matching principle* requires that we match the cost of the asset with the revenues that it helped to generate. The nature of long-term operating assets is that they benefit more than one period. As a consequence, it is impossible to match a specific portion of the cost *directly* to the revenues of a particular period. Instead, we rely on a *systematic allocation* to assign a portion of the asset's cost to each period benefited. This systematic allocation of cost is called **depreciation**.

The concept of systematic allocation of an asset's cost is important. When depreciation expense is recorded, the reported value of the asset (also called the *book value* or *carrying value*) is reduced. Naturally, it is tempting to infer that the market value of the asset is lower as a result. However, this reported value does not reflect the market value of the asset. The market value of the asset may decline by more or less than the amount of depreciation expense, and can even increase in some periods. Depreciation expense should only be interpreted as an assignment of costs to an accounting period and not a measure of the decline in market value of the asset.

The amount of cost that is allocated to a given period is recorded as depreciation expense in the income statement and **accumulated depreciation** in the balance sheet. Accumulated depreciation is a contra-asset account (denoted "XA" in the journal entry). Like all contra-asset accounts, it offsets the balance in the corresponding asset account. To illustrate, assume that Dehning Company purchases a heavy-duty delivery truck for $100,000 and decides to record $18,000 of depreciation expense in the first year of operation. The following entries would be recorded.

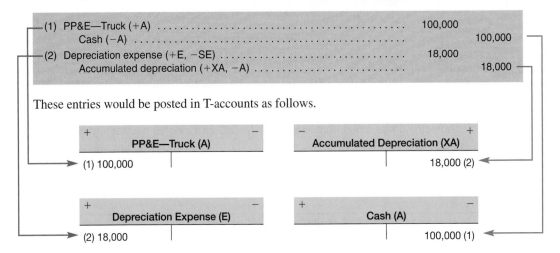

The effects of these transactions are reflected in the financial statement effects template as follows.

	Balance Sheet						Income Statement		
Transaction	Cash Asset	+ Noncash Assets	= Liabil- ities	+ Contrib. Capital	+ Retained Earnings		Revenues	− Expenses	= Net Income
(1) Purchased delivery truck	−100,000 Cash	+100,000 PP&E— Truck	=						
(2) Depreciation of delivery truck		−18,000 Accumulated Depreciation— Truck	=		−18,000 Retained Earnings			−18,000 Depreciation Expense	= −18,000

The asset would be presented in the balance sheet at period-end at its net book value.

Delivery truck, at cost	$100,000
Less accumulated depreciation.	18,000
Delivery truck, net	$ 82,000

By presenting the information using a contra-asset account, the original acquisition cost of the asset is preserved in the asset account. The net book value of the asset reflects the acquisition cost less the balance in the accumulated depreciation account. The balance in the accumulated depreciation account is the sum of the depreciation expense that has been recorded to date. To extend the illustration one more year, assume that Dehning Company records another $18,000 of depreciation in year 2. Now the balance sheet would report the following:

Delivery truck, at cost	$100,000
Less accumulated depreciation	36,000
Delivery truck, net	$ 64,000

Accumulated depreciation now includes the sum of the first and second years' depreciation ($36,000), and the net book value of the asset has been reduced to $64,000.

Depreciation Methods

Two estimates are required to compute the amount of depreciation expense to record each period.

1. **Useful life**. The useful life is the period of time over which the asset is expected to provide economic benefits to the company. The useful life is not the same as the physical life of the asset. An asset may or may not provide economic benefits to the company for its entire physical life. This useful life should not exceed the period of time that the company intends to use the assets. For example, if a company has a policy of replacing automobiles every two years, the useful life should be set at no longer than two years, even if the automobiles physically last three years or more.

2. **Residual(or salvage)value**. The residual value is the expected realizable value of the asset at the end of its useful life. This value may be the disposal or scrap value, or it may be an estimated resale value for a used asset.

LO3 Apply different depreciation methods to allocate the cost of assets over time.

These factors must be estimated when the asset is acquired. The **depreciation base**, also called the *nonrecoverable cost*, is the portion of the cost that is depreciated. The depreciation base is the capitalized cost of the asset less the estimated residual value. This amount is allocated over the useful life of the asset according to the *depreciation method* that the company has selected.

To illustrate alternative depreciation methods, we return to the example presented earlier. Assume that Dehning Company purchases a delivery truck for $100,000. The company expects the truck to last five years and estimates a residual value of $10,000. The depreciation base is $90,000 ($100,000 – 10,000). We illustrate the three most common depreciation methods:

1. Straight-line method
2. Double-declining-balance method
3. Units-of-production method

Straight-Line Method

Under the **straight-line method**, depreciation expense is recorded evenly over the useful life of the asset. That is, the same amount of depreciation expense is recorded each year. The **depreciation rate** is equal to one divided by the useful life. In our example, $1/5 = 0.2$ or 20% per year. The depreciation base and depreciation rate follow.

Depreciation Base	**Depreciation Rate**
Cost − Salvage value	1/Estimated useful life
= $100,000 − $10,000	= 1/5 years = 20%
= $90,000	

Depreciation expense per year for this asset is $18,000, computed as $90,000 × 20%. For the asset's first full year of usage, $18,000 of depreciation expense is reported in the income statement. At the end of that first year the asset is reported on the balance sheet as follows:

Truck, at cost	$100,000
Less accumulated depreciation	18,000
Truck, net	$ 82,000

Accumulated depreciation is the sum of all depreciation expense that has been recorded to date. The asset **book value (BV)**, or *net book value* or *carrying value,* is cost less accumulated depreciation. Although the word "value" is used here, it does not refer to market value. Depreciation is a cost allocation concept (transfer of costs from the balance sheet to the income statement), not a valuation concept.

In the second year of usage, another $18,000 of depreciation expense is recorded in the income statement and the net book value of the asset on the balance sheet follows:

Truck, at cost	$100,000
Less accumulated depreciation	36,000
Truck, net	$ 64,000

Accumulated depreciation now includes the sum of the first and second years' depreciation ($36,000), and the net book value of the asset is now reduced to $64,000. After the fifth year, a total of $90,000 of accumulated depreciation will be recorded, yielding a net book value for the truck of $10,000, its estimated salvage value.

Double-Declining-Balance Method

GAAP allows companies to use **accelerated depreciation** methods. Accelerated depreciation methods record more depreciation expense in the early years of an asset's useful life and less expense in the later years. The total depreciation expense recorded *over the entire useful life* of the asset is the same as with straight-line depreciation. The only difference is in the amount of depreciation recorded for *any given year*.

The **double-declining-balance (DDB) method** is an accelerated depreciation method that computes the depreciation rate as twice the straight-line rate. This double rate is then multiplied by the net book value of the asset, which declines each period as accumulated depreciation increases. For Dehning Company, the depreciation base and the depreciation rate are computed as follows:

Depreciation Base	Depreciation Rate
Net Book Value = Cost − Accumulated Depreciation	2 × SL rate = 2 × 20% = 40%

REMEMBER . . .
When calculating DDB depreciation, the depreciation rate is multiplied by the book value; residual value is not subtracted from book value.

The depreciation expense for the first year of usage for this asset is $40,000, computed as $100,000 × 40%. At the end of the first full year, $40,000 of depreciation expense is reported on the income statement (compared with $18,000 under the SL method), and the asset is reported on the balance sheet as follows:

Truck, at cost	$100,000
Less accumulated depreciation	40,000
Truck, net	$ 60,000

In the second year, $24,000 ($60,000 × 40%) of depreciation expense is reported in the income statement and the net book value of the asset on the balance sheet follows:

Truck, at cost	$100,000
Less accumulated depreciation	64,000
Truck, net	$ 36,000

The double-declining-balance method continues to record depreciation expense in this manner until the salvage amount is reached, at which point the depreciation process is discontinued. This leaves a net book value equal to the salvage value as with the straight-line method. The DDB depreciation schedule for the life of this asset is in Exhibit 9.2.

The depreciation expense in the fifth year is not calculated as 40% × $12,960 because the resulting depreciation would reduce the net book value below the $10,000 residual value. Instead, the residual value ($10,000) is subtracted from the remaining book value ($12,960), resulting in depreciation expense of $2,960.

EXHIBIT 9.2	Double-Declining-Balance Depreciation Schedule		
Year	Book Value at Beginning of Year	Depreciation Expense	Book Value at End of Year
1.	$100,000	100,000 × 40% = $40,000	$60,000
2.	60,000	60,000 × 40% = 24,000	36,000
3.	36,000	36,000 × 40% = 14,400	21,600
4.	21,600	21,600 × 40% = 8,640	12,960
5.	12,960	12,960 − 10,000 = 2,960*	10,000

*The formula value of $5,184 ($12,960 × 40%) is not reported because it would depreciate the asset below salvage value. Only the $2,960 needed to reach salvage value is reported as depreciation.

Exhibit 9.3 compares the depreciation expense and net book value for both the SL and DDB methods. During the first two years, the DDB method yields higher depreciation expense in comparison with the SL method. Beginning in the third year, this pattern reverses and the SL method produces higher depreciation expense. Over the asset's life, the same $90,000 in total depreciation expense is recorded, leaving a residual value of $10,000 on the balance sheet under both methods.

EXHIBIT 9.3	Comparison of Straight-Line and Double-Declining-Balance Depreciation			
	Straight-Line		Double-Declining-Balance	
Year	Depreciation Expense	Book Value at End of Year	Depreciation Expense	Book Value at End of Year
1.	$18,000	$82,000	$40,000	$60,000
2.	18,000	64,000	24,000	36,000
3.	18,000	46,000	14,400	21,600
4.	18,000	28,000	8,640	12,960
5.	18,000	10,000	2,960	10,000
	$90,000		$90,000	

All depreciation methods yield the same salvage value

Total depreciation over asset life is identical for all methods

Units-of-Production Method

Under the **units-of-production method**, the useful life of the asset is defined in terms of the number of units of service provided by the asset. For instance, this could be the number of units produced, the number of hours that a machine is operated, or, as with Dehning Company's delivery truck, the number of miles driven. To illustrate, assume that Dehning Company estimates that the delivery truck will provide 150,000 miles of service before it is sold for its residual value of $10,000. The depreciation rate is expressed in terms of a cost per mile driven, computed as follows:

$$\frac{\$100,000 - 10,000}{150,000 \text{ miles}} = \$0.60 \text{ per mile}$$

If the delivery truck is driven 35,000 miles in year 1, the depreciation expense for that year would be $21,000 (35,000 × $0.60). This method produces an amount of depreciation that varies from year to year as the use of the asset varies.

Most companies use the straight-line method for financial reporting purposes and an accelerated depreciation method for tax returns.[1] The reason is that in the early years of the asset's useful life, straight-line depreciation yields higher income on shareholder reports, whereas accelerated depreciation yields lower taxable income. As we discovered in chapter 7, this difference between financial reporting and tax reporting results in a deferred tax liability. Even though this difference

[1] The IRS mandates the use of MACRS (Modified Accelerated Cost Recovery System) for tax purposes. This method fixes the useful life for various classes of assets, assumes no salvage value, and generally produces depreciation amounts consistent with the double-declining-balance method.

reverses in later years, companies prefer to defer the tax payments so that the cash savings can be invested to produce earnings. Further, even with the reversal in the later years of an asset's life, if total depreciable assets are growing at a fast enough rate, the additional first-year depreciation on newly acquired assets more than offsets the lower depreciation expense on older assets, yielding an indefinite deferral of taxable income and taxes paid. Deferred income taxes are discussed further in the appendix at the end of this chapter.

Changes in Accounting Estimates

The estimates required in the depreciation process are made when the asset is acquired. When necessary, companies can, and do, change these estimates during the useful lives of assets.

To illustrate, Delta and several other airlines changed their depreciation lives on aircraft in the late 1990s and early 2000s. Following is the disclosure describing this action in Delta Air Lines' 1999 10-K:

> **Depreciation and Amortization** Effective July 1, 1998, the Company increased the depreciable life of certain new generation aircraft types from 20 to 25 years. Owned flight equipment is depreciated on a straight-line basis to a residual value equal to 5% of cost.

Analysts are usually critical of changes in estimates, especially when they result in an increase in current income. For example, the Center for Financial Research and Analysis (CFRA) assessed the Delta announcement as follows:

> Delta Air Lines, Inc. ("DAL") extended the life of certain new generation aircraft types on July 1, 1998 to 25 years from 20 years. Furthermore, the Company's residual values for aircraft changed from a policy of 5% of the cost of the aircraft to *between* 5% to 10% of the cost. This change reduced depreciation expense by $92 million for the fiscal year ended June 1999, resulting in a boost to reported earnings of $0.37 [per share]. Absent the change CFRA estimates DAL's fiscal 1999 earnings would have been $6.83 rather than the reported $7.20. Furthermore, we find this change particularly unusual since DAL recorded a charge of $107 million to write-down to estimated fair value aircraft parts and obsolete flight equipment and parts during the September 1999 quarter.

Delta's change in the depreciable life and residual value of its aircraft is a *change in estimate*. When either the useful life or residual value estimates change, the change is applied prospectively. That is, companies use the new estimates from the date of the change going forward and do not restate the financial statements of prior periods.

Asset Sales and Impairments

This section discusses gains and losses from asset sales and computation and disclosure of asset impairments.

Gains and Losses on Asset Sales

LO4 Determine the effects of asset sales and impairments on financial statements.

The gain or loss on the sale (disposition) of a long-term asset is computed as follows.

> **Gain or Loss on Asset Sale = Proceeds from Sale − Book Value of Asset Sold**

The book (carrying) value of an asset is its acquisition cost less accumulated depreciation. When an asset is sold, its acquisition cost and related accumulated depreciation are removed from the balance sheet and any gain or loss is reported in income from continuing operations. To illustrate such a transaction, assume that Dehning Company decided to sell the delivery truck after four years of straight-line depreciation. From Exhibit 9.3, we know that the book value of the truck is $28,000 ($100,000 − $72,000). If the truck is sold for $30,000, the journal entry to record the sale follows.

Cash(+A)	30,000	
Accumulated depreciation (−XA, +A)	72,000	
PP&E—Truck (−A)		100,000
Gain on the sale of truck (+R, +SE)		2,000

This entry would be reflected in the financial statements as follows.

	Balance Sheet						Income Statement		
Transaction	Cash Asset	+ Noncash Assets	= Liabil-ities	+ Contrib. Capital	+ Retained Earnings		Revenues	− Expenses =	Net Income
(1) Sold delivery truck	+30,000 Cash	−100,000 = PP&E—Truck +72,000 Accumulated Depreciation— Truck			+2,000 Retained Earnings		+2,000 Gain on sale of truck		= +2,000

Gains and losses on asset sales can be large, and analysts must be aware of these transitory operating income components. Further, if the gains are deemed immaterial, companies often include such gains and losses in general line items of the income statement—often as an offset to selling, general and administrative expenses.

To illustrate, DuPont provides the following footnote disclosure to its 10-K relating to the sale of DuPont Pharmaceuticals' net assets to Bristol-Myers Squibb Company ($ millions):

GAIN ON SALE OF DUPONT PHARMACEUTICALS

On October 1, 2001, the company sold substantially all of the net assets of DuPont Pharmaceuticals to Bristol-Myers Squibb Company and recorded net proceeds of $7,798. The net assets sold to Bristol-Myers Squibb as of the date of sale and included within the accompanying Consolidated Balance Sheet at December 31, 2000, consisted of the following:

	October 1, 2001	December 31, 2000
Current assets	$ 584	$ 484
Property, plant and equipment, net	356	374
Other assets, net	1,041	1,139
Current liabilities	(282)	(392)
Noncurrent liabilities	(288)	(244)
Net assets sold	$1,411	$1,361

As a result of this transaction, the company recorded a pretax gain of $6,136, which included charges that are a direct result of the decision to divest DuPont Pharmaceuticals. The after-tax gain on this transaction was $3,866.

DuPont sold a subsidiary company, carried on its balance sheet at a net book value of $1,411 million, for $7,798 million. The pretax gain of $6,387 million, less transaction costs of $251 million and taxes of $2,270 million, resulted in an after-tax gain of $3,866 million ($6,387 − $251 − $2,270). DuPont reported net income of $4,339 million in that year, 89% of which is attributable to the gain on the sale of this subsidiary.

Asset Impairments

Property, plant, and equipment (PPE) assets are reported at their net book values (original cost less accumulated depreciation). This is the case even if market values of these assets increase subsequent to acquisition. As a result, there can be unrecognized gains hidden in the balance sheet.

However, if market values of PPE assets subsequently decrease—and it can be determined that the asset value is permanently impaired—then companies must recognize losses on those assets. **Impairment** of PPE assets is determined by comparing the sum of *expected* future (undiscounted) cash flows from the asset with its net book value. If these expected cash flows are greater than net book value, no impairment is deemed to exist. However, if the sum of expected cash flows is less than net book value, the asset is deemed impaired and it is written down to its current market value (generally, the discounted present value of those expected cash flows). Exhibit 9.4 depicts this impairment analysis.

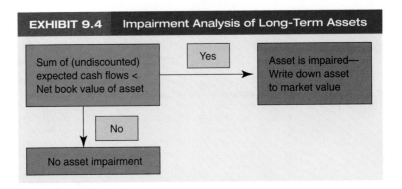

EXHIBIT 9.4 Impairment Analysis of Long-Term Assets

When a company records an impairment charge, assets are reduced by the amount of the write-down and the loss is recognized in the income statement, which reduces current period income. These effects are illustrated in Exhibit 9.5.

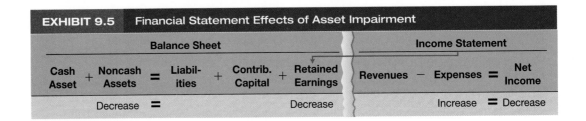

EXHIBIT 9.5 Financial Statement Effects of Asset Impairment

Balance Sheet						Income Statement		
Cash Asset	+ Noncash Assets	= Liabilities	+ Contrib. Capital	+ Retained Earnings		Revenues	− Expenses	= Net Income
	Decrease =			Decrease			Increase	= Decrease

Once a depreciable asset is written off, future depreciation charges are reduced by the amount written off. This is because that portion of the asset's cost that is written off is permanently removed from the balance sheet and cannot be subsequently depreciated. It is important to note that management determines if and when to recognize asset impairments. Write-downs of long-term assets are often recognized in connection with a restructuring program.

Analysis of asset write-downs present two potential challenges:

1. *Insufficient write-down.* Assets sometimes are impaired to a larger degree than is recognized. This can arise if management is overly optimistic about future prospects or is reluctant to recognize the full loss in income. Underestimation of an impairment causes current income to be overstated and income in future years to be lower.

2. *Aggressive write-down.* This *big bath* scenario can arise if income is currently and severely depressed. Management's view is that the market will not penalize the firm for an extra write-off, and that doing so purges the balance sheet of costs that would otherwise reduce future years' income. This leads to income being overstated for several years after the write-down.

Neither of these cases is condoned under GAAP. Yet, since management is estimating future cash flows for the impairment test and such estimates are difficult to verify, it has some degree of latitude over the timing and amount of the write-off and can use that discretion to manage reported income.

Footnote Disclosure

Procter & Gamble provides the following footnote to describe its accounting for PPE assets.

Property, Plant and Equipment
Property, plant and equipment are recorded at cost reduced by accumulated depreciation. Depreciation expense is recognized over the assets' estimated useful lives using the straight-line method. Machinery and equipment includes office furniture and equipment (15-year life), computer equipment and capitalized software (3- to 5-year lives) and manufacturing equipment (3- to 20-year lives). Buildings are depreciated over an estimated useful life of 40 years.

Estimated useful lives are periodically reviewed and, where appropriate, changes are made prospectively. Where certain events or changes in operating conditions occur, asset lives may be adjusted and an impairment assessment may be performed on the recoverability of the carrying amounts.

The note details P&G's depreciation method (straight-line) and the estimated useful lives of various classes of PPE assets. From this note, we can also infer that there was no material asset impairment recorded during the period covered by the report. If asset values were impaired, it would have been disclosed in this note or in a separate note.

Analysis Implications

This section considers two measures useful for analysis of long-term asset utilization and age.

PPE Turnover

A crucial issue in analysis of PPE assets is their productivity (or efficient utilization). For example, what level of plant assets is necessary to generate a dollar of revenues? How capital intensive is the company and its competitors? PPE turnover is often used for insights into asset utilization and to address these and similar questions. It is defined as follows:

$$\text{PPE Turnover (PPET)} = \text{Sales/Average PPE Assets}$$

P&G's 2004 PPE asset turnover is 3.8 times, up from 3.3 in 2003. Although its turnover has improved, it remains in the middle range among companies that P&G competes with, as shown in the following chart.[2]

PPE Turnover for P&G and Its Competitors

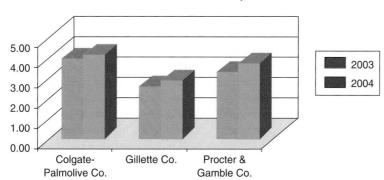

Companies prefer that PPE turnover be higher rather than lower. A higher PPE turnover implies a lower capital investment for a given level of sales. The result is an increase in profitability (as asset carrying costs are less) and an increase in cash flow.

PPE turnover is lower for *capital intensive* manufacturing companies like P&G than it is companies in service or knowledge based industries. To this point, consider the following chart of plant asset turnover for companies from different industries.

PPE Turnover for Companies from Different Industries

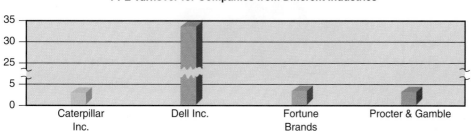

---

[2]Early in 2005 P&G announced a proposed acquisition of Gillette. The acquisition was approved on October 1, 2005. P&G financial statements will reflect this acquisition in 2006.

Dell's PPE turnover far surpasses the PPET of these other companies. P&G's PPE turnover of 3.8 times compares more favorably with the remaining companies (**Caterpillar** is 3.2 times and **Fortune Brands** is 4.6 times). Nevertheless, P&G must constantly strive to improve its PPE asset utilization to remain competitive.

YOU MAKE THE CALL

You are the Division Manager   You are the division manager for a main operating division of your company. You are concerned that a declining PPE turnover adversely affecting your division's RNOA. What specific actions can you take to increase PPE turnover?

[Answers on page 398]

Percent Depreciated

P&G reports that the useful lives of its depreciable assets range from 3 to 5 years for computer equipment and software to 40 years for buildings. It might be of interest to know whether a company's assets are relatively old or new.

We can estimate the percent of a company's depreciable assets that have been depreciated, reflecting the portion of depreciable assets that are no longer productive, as follows:

Percent Depreciated = Accumulated Depreciation/Depreciable Asset Cost

Using this ratio, we can see that P&G's assets are 45.4% depreciated, computed as follows:

$$45.4\% = \$11,196 \text{ million} / (\$25,304 \text{ million} - \$642 \text{ million})$$

In this computation, $642 million in land cost is subtracted in the denominator because it is not a depreciable asset.

If assets were replaced evenly each year, the average asset would be 50% depreciated. P&G's depreciable assets are slightly younger than this benchmark. If, for example, depreciable assets are 80% depreciated, we might need to project a higher level of capital expenditures to replace assets in the near future. On the other hand, a low percent depreciated implies that a company is utilizing newer assets. If the cost of purchasing assets is generally increasing, we would expect that owning newer assets would result in higher depreciation charges than would owning older assets. We also expect that older assets are less efficient and require higher maintenance costs.

Examining the ratios of Colgate-Palmolive and Gillette shows that both companies have a percent depreciated ratio that is near the 50% mark, but that P&G has a slightly lower ratio than these competitors.

Percent Depreciated for P&G and Competitors

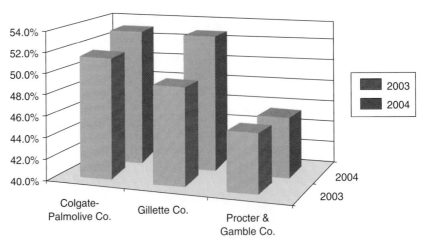

MID-CHAPTER REVIEW

On January 2, Lev Company purchases equipment for use in fabrication of a part for one of its key products. The equipment costs $95,000, and its estimated useful life is five years, after which it is expected to be sold for $10,000.

Required

1. Compute depreciation expense for each year of the equipment's useful life for each of the following depreciation methods:
   a. Straight-line
   b. Double-declining-balance
2. Assume that Lev Company uses the straight-line depreciation method.
   a. Prepare journal entries to record the initial purchase of the equipment on January 2, and the year-end depreciation adjustment on December 31.
   b. Post the journal entries from part a to T-accounts.
   c. Show the effects of these entries on the balance sheet and the income statement using the financial statement effects template.
3. Show how the equipment is reported on Lev's balance sheet at the end of the third year assuming straight-line depreciation.
4. Assume that this is the only depreciable asset the company owns and that it uses straight-line depreciation. Using the depreciation expense computed in *1a* and the balance sheet presentation from 3, estimate the percent depreciated for this asset at the end of the third year.

Solution

1a. Straight-line

Depreciation expense = ($95,000 − $10,000)/5 years = $17,000 per year

1b. Double-declining-balance (twice straight-line rate = 2 × (100%/5) = 40%

Year	Book Value × Rate	Depreciation Expense
1	$95,000 × 0.40 =	$38,000
2	($95,000 − $38,000) × 0.40 =	22,800
3	($95,000 − $60,800) × 0.40 =	13,680
4	($95,000 − $74,480) × 0.40 =	8,208
5	($95,000 − $82,688) × 0.40	2,312*

*The formula value of $4,925 is not reported because it would depreciate the asset below residual value. Only the $2,312 needed to reach residual value is depreciated.

2a.

PPE—Equipment (+A)	95,000	
Cash (−A)		95,000
Depreciation expense (+E, −SE)	17,000	
Accumulated depreciation (+XA, −A)		17,000

2b.

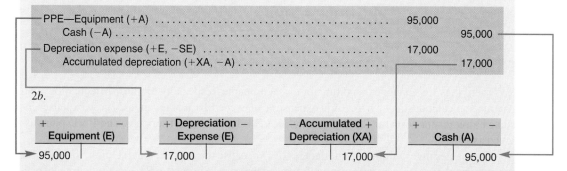

	Balance Sheet						Income Statement		
Transaction	Cash Asset	+ Noncash Assets	= Liabil- ities	+ Contrib. Capital	+ Retained Earnings		Revenues	− Expenses	= Net Income
(a) Purchased equipment	−95,000 Cash	+95,000 Equipment	=						=
(b) Recorded annual depreciation		−17,000 Accumulated depreciation	=		−17,000 Retained Earnings			−17,000 Depreciation Expense	= −17,000

3.

Equipment, cost....................	$95,000
Less accumulated depreciation........	51,000
Equipment, net	$44,000

Equipment is reported on Lev's balance sheet at its net book value of $44,000.

4. The percent depreciated is computed as: Accumulated Depreciation/Depreciable Asset Cost = $51,000/$95,000 = 53.7%. The equipment is more than one-half depreciated at the end of the third year. Again, the lack of knowledge of salvage value has resulted in an underestimate of the percent depreciated. Still, this estimate is useful in that in that we know that the company's asset is over one-half depreciated and is likely to require replacement in about 2 years (less than one-half of its useful life of 5 years). This replacement will become a cash outflow or financing need when it arises and should be considered in our projections of future cash flows.

INTANGIBLE ASSETS

LO5 Describe the accounting and reporting for intangible assets.

Intangible assets are assets that lack physical substance but provide future benefits to the owner in the form of specific property rights or legal rights. For many companies, these assets have become an important source of competitive advantage and company value.

For financial accounting purposes, intangible assets are classified as either *identifiable intangible assets* or *goodwill*. Identifiable intangible assets generally fall into one of two categories. The first category is assets that are the product of contractual or other legal rights. These include patents, trademarks, copyrights, franchises, license agreements, broadcast rights, mineral rights, and non-competition agreements. The second category of intangible assets includes benefits that are not contractually or legally defined, but can be separated from the company and sold, transferred or exchanged. Examples include customer lists, unpatented technology, formulas, processes, and databases.

The issues involved in reporting intangible assets are conceptually similar to those of accounting for property, plant and equipment. We must first decide which costs to capitalize and then we need to determine how and when those costs will be transferred to the income statement. However, intangible assets often pose a particularly difficult problem for accountants. This problem arises because the benefits provided by these assets are uncertain and difficult to quantify. In addition, the useful life of an intangible asset is often impossible to estimate with confidence.

As was the case with property, plant and equipment, intangible assets are either purchased from another individual or company or internally developed. Like PPE assets, the cost of purchased intangible assets is capitalized. Unlike PPE assets, though, we generally do not capitalize the cost of internally developed intangible assets. Research and development (R&D) costs, and the patents and technologies that are created as a result of R&D, serve as a useful example.

Research and Development Costs

R&D activities are a major expenditure for most companies, especially for those in technology and pharmaceutical industries where R&D expenses can exceed 10% of revenues. These expenses include employment costs for R&D personnel, R&D related contract services, and R&D plant asset costs.

Companies invest millions of dollars in R&D because they expect that the future benefits resulting from these activities will eventually exceed the costs. Successful R&D activities create new products that can be sold and new technologies that can be utilized to create and sustain a competitive advantage. Unfortunately, only a fraction of R&D projects reach commercial production and it is difficult to predict which projects will be successful. Moreover, it is often difficult to predict when the benefits will be realized, even if the project is successful.

Because of the uncertainty surrounding the benefits of R&D, accounting for R&D activities follows a uniform method—*expense costs as incurred*. This approach applies to all R&D costs incurred prior to the start of commercial production, including the salaries and wages of personnel engaged in R&D activities, the cost of materials and supplies, and the equipment and facilities used in the project. Should any of the R&D activities prove successful, the benefits should result in higher net income in future periods.

If equipment and facilities are purchased for a specific R&D project, their cost is expensed immediately even though their useful life would typically extend beyond the current period. The expensing of R&D equipment and facilities is in stark contrast to the capitalization-and-depreciation of non-R&D plant assets. The expensing of R&D plant assets is mandated unless those assets have alternative future uses (in other R&D projects or otherwise). For example, a general research facility housing multi-use lab equipment should be capitalized and depreciated like any other depreciable asset. However, project-directed research buildings and equipment with no alternate uses must be expensed.

BUSINESS INSIGHT

R&D Costs at Cisco Systems   Cisco spends about $3.1 billion annually for R&D compared with its revenues of $18.8 billion, or about 16.5%. This reflects a high percent of revenues devoted to R&D in comparison with nontechnology companies, but typifies companies that compete in the high-tech arena. Following is the R&D-expense-to-sales ratio (also called R&D intensity) for Cisco and some of its competitors.

	2003	2002	2001
Cisco Systems	16.5%	18.5%	20.1%
Nortel Networks	20.2	18.7	17.0
Juniper Networks	25.3	44.5	24.8
3Com	12.1	19.2	21.1

Patents

Successful research and development activity often leads a company to obtain a **patent** for its discoveries. A patent is an exclusive right to produce a product or use a technology. Patents are granted to protect the inventor of the new product or technology by preventing other companies from copying the innovation. The market value of a patent depends on the commercial success of the product or technology. For example, a patent on the formula for a new drug to treat diabetes could be worth billions of dollars.

If a patent is purchased from the inventor, the purchase price is capitalized and reported in the balance sheet as an intangible asset. On the other hand, if the patent is developed internally, only the legal costs and registration fees are capitalized. The R&D cost to develop the new product or technology is expensed as incurred. This accounting illustrates the marked difference between purchased and internally created intangible assets.

Trademarks

A **trademark** is a registered name, logo, package design, image, jingle, or slogan that is associated with a product. Many trademarks are easily recognizable, such as the Nike "swoosh," the shape of a CocaCola bottle, McDonald's golden arches, and the musical tones played in computer advertisements featuring Intel computer chips. Companies spend millions of dollars developing and protecting trademarks and their value is enhanced by advertising programs that increase their recognition. If a trademark is purchased from another company, the purchase price is capitalized. However, the cost of internally developed trademarks is expensed as incurred. Likewise, all advertising costs are expensed immediately, even if the value of a trademark is enhanced by the advertisement. For this reason, most trademarks are not presented in the balance sheet.

Franchise Rights

A **franchise** is a contractual agreement that gives a company the right to operate a particular business in an area for a particular period of time. For example, a franchise may give the owner the right to operate a number of fast-food restaurants in a particular geographic region for twenty years. *Operating rights* and *licenses* are similar to franchise rights, except that they are typically granted by government agencies. Most franchise rights are purchased and, as a result, the purchase price should be capitalized and presented as an intangible asset in the balance sheet.

Amortization and Impairment of Identifiable Intangible Assets

When intangible assets are acquired and capitalized, a determination must be made as to whether the asset has a **definite life**. Examples of intangible assets with a definite lives include patents and franchise rights. An intangible asset with a definite life must be *amortized* over the expected useful life of the asset. **Amortization** is the systematic allocation of the cost of an intangible asset to the periods benefited. Like the depreciation of tangible assets, amortization is motivated by the matching principle.

Amortization expense is generally recorded using the straight-line method. The expense is included in the income statement as a component of operating income, and is often included among selling, general and administrative expenses. The cost of the intangible asset is presented in the balance sheet net of accumulated amortization.

To illustrate, assume that Landsman Company spent $100,000 in early 2006 to purchase a patent. The journal entry to record the capitalization of this cost follows.

(1) Patent (+A)	100,000	
Cash (−A)		100,000

Although the patent had a remaining legal life of 12 years, Landsman estimated that the useful life of the patent was 5 years. Thus the intangible asset has a definite life. The entry to record the annual amortization expense at the end of 2006 follows.

(2) Amortization expense (+E, −SE)	20,000	
Accumulated amortization (+XA, −A)		20,000

These entries are posted to the T-accounts as follows.

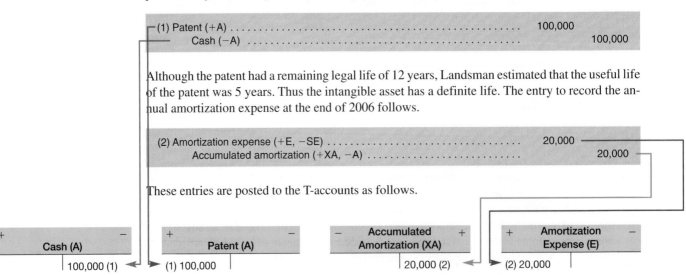

The financial statement effects template reflects these transactions as follows.

	Balance Sheet						Income Statement		
Transaction	**Cash Asset** +	**Noncash Assets** =	**Liabil- ities** +	**Contrib. Capital** +	**Retained Earnings**		**Revenues** −	**Expenses** =	**Net Income**
(1) Purchased patent	−100,000 Cash	+100,000 = Patent						=	
(2) Annual amortization expense		−20,000 = Accumulated Amortization— Patent			−20,000 Retained Earnings			−20,000 = Amortization Expense	−20,000

Some identifiable intangible assets, such as some trademarks, have **indefinite lives**. For these assets, the expected useful life extends far enough into the future that it is impossible for management to estimate a useful life. An intangible asset with an indefinite life should not be amortized until the useful life of the asset can be specified. That is, no expense is recorded until management can reasonably estimate the useful life of the asset.

Although intangible assets with indefinite lives are not subject to amortization, they must be tested annually to determine if their value has been impaired. The impairment test is slightly different than the impairment test used to evaluate PPE assets. The intangible asset is impaired if the book value of the asset exceeds its fair market value and the write-down is equal to the difference between the book value and the market value.

To illustrate, assume that Norell Company purchased a trademark for $240,000 and determined that the intangible asset had an indefinite life. The entry to record the purchase of the trademark follows.

(1) Trademark (+A)	240,000	
Cash (− A)		240,000

In 2006, changes in regulations caused Norell to conclude that the value of the trademark had been impaired. They estimated the current fair market value was $100,000, resulting in a loss of $140,000 ($240,000 – $100,000). The journal entry to record the impairment of the trademark would be as follows.

(2) Loss due to impairment of trademark (+E, −SE)	140,000	
Trademark (−A)		140,000

If the value of the trademark subsequently decreases further, additional impairment losses would be recorded. However, increases in the fair market value of the asset would not be recorded. Furthermore, if, at any time, Norell determined that the trademark had a definite life, the company would begin amortizing the remaining value over the remaining estimated life.

Goodwill

Goodwill is an intangible asset that is recorded only when one company acquires another company. **Goodwill** is defined as the excess of the purchase price paid for a company over the fair market value of its *identifiable* net assets (assets minus the liabilities assumed). The identifiable net assets include any *identifiable intangible assets* acquired in the purchase. Therefore, goodwill can neither be linked to any identifiable source, nor can it be sold or separated from the company. It represents the value of the acquired company above and beyond the specific identifiable assets listed on the balance sheet.

By definition, goodwill has an indefinite life. Once it is recorded in the balance sheet, it is not amortized. Instead, it is subject to an annual impairment test. Goodwill is impaired when the market value of the acquired business is less than the recorded book value. If this occurs, goodwill is written down to an imputed value. The goodwill write-down (also called a goodwill write-off) results in the immediate transfer of some or all of a company's goodwill book value from the balance sheet to the income statement as an expense. The book value of the intangible assets is immediately reduced and a corresponding expense is reported in the income statement. Like the impairment write-down of tangible assets, the write-down of goodwill is a discretionary expense whose amount and timing are largely determined by management (with auditor acceptance).

It is commonplace to see goodwill write-downs for unsuccessful acquisitions, particularly those from the acquisition boom of the late 1990s. Goodwill write-downs usually represent material amounts. For example, **AOL Time-Warner** wrote off $54 billion of goodwill in the second quarter of 2002, which arose from the $106 billion merger of AOL and Time-Warner. This write-off exceeded the *total revenues* of 483 of the Fortune 500 companies (*Fortune*, 2002). Goodwill write-downs are usually transitory, but are typically reported by companies in income from continuing operations. For analysis purpose we normally classify them as operating and transitory unless they are recurring.

Footnote Disclosures

The book value of intangible assets exceeded the value of PPE assets in P&G's balance sheet (refer to Exhibit 9.1). In addition to the amount reported in the balance sheet, P&G provides the following two footnotes that more fully describe its intangible assets.

NOTE 1: Summary of Significant Accounting Policies—Goodwill and Other Intangible Assets

The cost of intangible assets with determinable useful lives is amortized to reflect the pattern of economic benefits consumed, principally on a straight-line basis over the estimated periods benefited. Goodwill and indefinite-lived intangibles are not amortized, but are evaluated annually for impairment. The Company evaluates a number of factors to determine whether an indefinite life is appropriate, including the competitive environment, market share, brand history, operating plan and the macroeconomic environment of the country in which the brand is sold. Due to the nature of the Company's business, there are a number of brand intangibles that have been determined to have indefinite lives. If it is determined that a brand intangible does not have an indefinite life, the Company's policy is to amortize such assets over the expected useful life, which generally ranges from 5 to 20 years. Patents, technology and other intangibles with contractual terms are amortized over their respective contractual lives. Other non-contractual intangible assets with determinable lives are amortized over periods ranging from 5 to 20 years.

NOTE 4: Goodwill and Intangible Assets

The change in net carrying amount of goodwill for the years ended June 30, 2004 and 2003 was allocated by reportable business segment as follows ($ millions):

	2004	2003
Goodwill, net, beginning of year	$11,132	$10,966
Acquisitions	7,830	–
Translation adjustments and other	648	166
End of year	$19,610	$11,132

Identifiable intangible assets as of June 30, 2004 and 2003 were comprised of:

Intangible assets with determinable lives	June 30, 2004 Gross carrying amount	June 30, 2004 Accumulated amortization	June 30, 2003 Gross carrying amount	June 30, 2003 Accumulated amortization
Trademarks	1,012	155	499	85
Patents and technology	518	250	492	204
Other	554	165	316	140
	2,084	570	1,307	429
Trademarks with indefinite lives, net	2,776		1,497	
	$4,860	$570	$2,804	$429

There are two observations that we can make from these disclosures. First, P&G has purchased a significant amount of intangible assets by acquiring other companies. We can infer this from the large amount of goodwill assets reported in the balance sheet. Second, most of P&G's identifiable intangible assets are trademarks and most have indefinite lives. Hence, we might expect that the amount of amortization expense in any given year would be small.

YOU MAKE THE CALL

You are a Financial Analyst   Early in 2005, P&G announced their plans to purchase the Gillette Company. How will this acquisition alter the intangible assets reported in P&G's balance sheet? [Answers on page 398]

Analysis Implications

Because internally generated intangible assets are not capitalized, an important component of a company's assets is potentially hidden from users of the financial statements. Moreover, differential treatment of purchased and internally created assets makes it difficult to compare companies. If one company generates its patents and trademarks internally, while another company purchases these intangibles, their balance sheets can differ dramatically, even if the two companies are otherwise very similar.

LO6 Analyze the effects of tangible and intangible assets on key performance measures.

These hidden intangible assets can distort our analysis of the financial statements. For example, when a company expenses R&D costs, especially R&D equipment and facilities that can potentially benefit more than one period, both the income statement and balance sheet are distorted. Net income, assets and stockholders' equity are all understated.

The income statement effects may be small if a company regularly purchases R&D assets and the amount of purchases is relatively constant from year-to-year. Specifically, after the average useful life is reached, say in 5 to 10 years, the expensing of current year purchases will be approximately the same as the depreciation that would have been reported had the assets been capitalized. Thus, the income statement effect is mitigated. However, the recorded assets and equity are still understated. This accounting produces an upward bias in asset turnover ratios, RNOA and ROE.

NATURAL RESOURCES

An important asset for some companies consists of natural resources such as oil reserves, mineral deposits or timberlands. These assets are often referred to as **wasting assets**, because the asset is consumed as it is used.

LO7 Explain the accounting for acquisition and depletion of natural resources.

Cost Capitalization and Depletion

The acquisition cost of a natural resource, plus any costs incurred to prepare the asset for its intended use, should be capitalized and reported among PPE assets in the balance sheet.

When the natural resource is used or extracted, inventory is created. The cost of the resource is transferred from the long-term asset account into inventory and, once the inventory is sold, to the income statement as cost of goods sold. The process of transferring costs from the resource account into inventory is called **depletion**.

Depletion is very much like depreciation of tangible operating assets, except that the amount of depletion recorded each period should reflect the amount of the resource that was actually extracted or used up during that period. As a result, depletion is usually calculated using the units-of-production method. The depletion rate is calculated as follows:

$$\text{Depletion rate per unit consumed} = \frac{\text{Acquisition cost} - \text{Residual value}}{\text{Estimated quantity of resource available}}$$

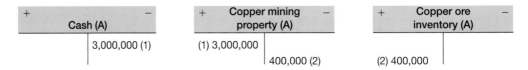

The calculation requires an estimate of the quantity of the resource available, which usually requires the assistance of experts, such as geologists or engineers, who are trained to make these determinations.

Depletion Recognition

Once the depletion rate is determined, the annual depletion is calculated by multiplying the depletion rate times the quantity of resource depleted during the period. This amount is subtracted from the natural resource asset account and added to inventory. Ultimately, the depletion becomes part of the cost of goods sold when the inventory is sold.

Illustration

To illustrate accounting for natural resources, assume that Nichols Company acquired property for $3,000,000 for the development of a copper mine. Nichols estimated that the mine would produce 1,500,000 tons of ore, and once mining is completed, the property could be sold for $600,000. The journal entry to record the purchase of the property follows.

(1) Copper mining property (+A)	3,000,000	
Cash (−A)		3,000,000

The depletion expense per ton of ore would be calculated as follows:

$$\frac{\$3,000,000 - \$600,000}{1,500,000 \text{ tons}} = 1.60 \text{ per ton}$$

If Nichols were to recover 250,000 tons of ore in 2006, the journal entry to record depletion of the copper mine would be as follows.

(2) Copper ore inventory (+A)	400,000	
Copper mining property (−A)		400,000

Posting these entries to T-accounts results in the following.

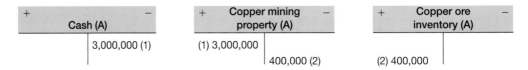

The depletion would remain in the inventory account until the copper ore is sold.

CHAPTER-END REVIEW

In 2002, Bowen Company's R&D department developed a new production process that significantly reduced the time and cost required to manufacture its product. R&D costs were $120,000. The process was patented on July 1, 2002. Legal costs and fees to acquire the patent totalled $12,500. Bowen estimated the useful life of the patent at 10 years.

On July 1, 2004, Bowen sold the non-exclusive right to use the new process to Kennedy Company for $90,000. Because Bowen retained the patent, the agreement allows Kennedy to use, but not sell, the new technology for a period of 5 years. Both Bowen Company and Kennedy Company have December 31 fiscal years.

On July 1, 2006, another competitor obtained a patent on a new process that made Bowen's patent obsolete.

Required

1. How should Bowen Company account for the R&D costs and legal costs incurred to obtain the patent? Prepare the appropriate journal entries necessary to account for the costs incurred in 2002.
2. What amount of amortization expense would Bowen record each year? Prepare a journal entry to record amortization expense on December 31, 2002.

3. Open T-accounts and post the entries from questions 1 and 2 to them.
4. How would Kennedy Company record the acquisition of the rights to use the new technology? Prepare a journal entry to record the purchase of the technology rights.
5. What effect would the new patent registered by the other competitor have on Bowen Company? On Kennedy Company? Prepare a journal entry to record the impairment loss for Kennedy Company.

Solution

1. Bowen Company would expense the $120,000 in R&D costs in 2002. The $12,500 in legal fees to obtain the patent would be capitalized. As a result, the book value of the patent would be $12,500 on July 1, 2002. The journal entries to record these costs would be as follows:

(i) R&D expense (+E, −SE)	120,000	
Cash (−A)		120,000
(ii) Patent (+A)	12,500	
Cash (−A)		12,500

2. Each year, beginning on July 1, 2002, Bowen would record amortization expense of $1,250 (12,500/10). For 2002, six months of amortization expense, or $625, would be recorded ($1,250/2). The journal entry would be as follows:

(iii) Amortization expense (+E, −SE)	625	
Accumulated amortization (+XA, −A)		625

3.

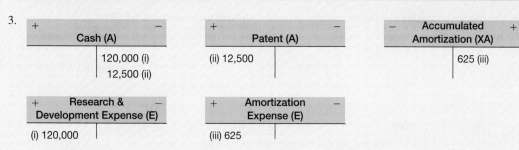

4. Because Kennedy purchased the right to use the technology, the purchase price can be capitalized as an intangible asset and amortized over the 5-year length of the agreement. Kennedy would record amortization expense of $18,000 (90,000/5) each year, beginning July 1, 2004. (Bowen would recognize the $90,000 as revenue.) The journal entry that Kennedy Company would need to record the acquisition of the technology rights would be as follows:

(i) Technology rights (+A)	90,000	
Cash (−A)		90,000

5. Given that the patent is obsolete, both Bowen Company and Kennedy Company would record impairment losses. Bowen would write off the unamortized balance in the patent account, resulting in a loss of $7,500 (12,500 − 1,250 × 4). Kennedy Company would write off the remaining value of the technology agreement, recording an impairment loss of $54,000 (90,000 − 18,000 × 2). Kennedy's journal entry would be as follows:

(i) Loss due to impairment of technology rights (+E, −SE)	54,000	
Technology rights (−A)		54,000

SUMMARY

Describe and distinguish between tangible and intangible assets. (p. 377)   **LO1**

▪ Tangible assets, including land, buildings, machinery and equipment are assets with physical substance and are usually classified as property, plant and equipment.

▪ Intangible assets are long-term assets lacking in physical substance, such as patents, trademarks, franchise rights and goodwill.

Determine which costs to capitalize and report as assets and which costs to expense. (p. 378)   **LO2**

▪ All costs incurred to acquire an asset and prepare it for its intended use should be capitalized and reported in the balance sheet.

■ The cost of self-constructed assets should include all costs incurred during construction, including the interest cost of financing the construction.

LO3 **Apply different depreciation methods to allocate the cost of assets over time. (p. 381)**

■ Depreciation methods generally fall into three categories:

(1) Straight-line depreciation

(2) Accelerated depreciation, such as the double-declining-balance method

(3) Units of production method

LO4 **Determine the effects of asset sales and impairments on financial statements. (p. 384)**

■ The sale of a long-term asset will result in a gain or loss if the proceeds from the sale are greater than or less than the book value of the asset.

■ If the expected benefits (undiscounted cash flows) derived from an asset fall below its book value, the asset is impaired and should be written down to fair market value.

LO5 **Describe the accounting and reporting for intangible assets. (p. 390)**

■ For the most part, internally generated intangible asserts are not recognized in the balance sheet.

■ Intangible assets purchased from other companies are capitalized and presented separately in the balance sheet.

■ Intangible assets with definite lives are amortized using the straight-line method.

■ Intangible assets with indefinite lives are not amortized.

LO6 **Analyze the effects of tangible and intangible assets on key performance measures. (p. 395)**

■ PPE turnover and long-term asset turnover ratios provide insights into the capital intensity of a company and how efficiently the company is utilizing these investments.

■ The ratio of accumulated depreciation divided by the cost of depreciable assets measures the percent depreciated.

LO7 **Explain the accounting for acquisition and depletion of natural resources. (p. 395)**

■ Natural resources are valued at acquisition cost plus the cost to develop the resource.

■ Natural resources are depleted using a method similar to the units-of-production method.

LO8 *Appendix 9A—Explain and illustrate the reporting for deferred income taxes. (p. 399)*

GUIDANCE ANSWERS

YOU MAKE THE CALL

You are the Company Accountant   Any cost that is necessary in order to bring an asset into service should be capitalized as a part of the cost of the asset. In this case, your company cannot build an office building on this property until the oil well is properly capped. Therefore, the $40,000 cost of capping the oil well should be capitalized as part of the cost of the land.

YOU MAKE THE CALL

You are the Division Manager   To increase PPE turnover one must either increase sales or reduce PPE assets. The first step is to identify unproductive or inefficiently utilized assets. Unnecessary assets can be sold, and some processes can be outsourced. Also, by reducing down time, effective maintenance practices will increase asset productivity.

YOU MAKE THE CALL

You are the Financial Analyst   Gillette is an established company with several well recognized trademarks. These trademarks will most likely appear on P&G's balance sheet as intangible assets with indefinite lives. In addition, P&G's goodwill asset will likely increase significantly.

APPENDIX 9A: Deferred Income Taxes

The concept of deferred income taxes was introduced in Chapter 7. As we learned in that chapter, businesses measure income to report to shareholders as well as to tax authorities, and the objectives of these measurements differ. Income is reported to shareholders (and potential shareholders) to inform investors about the operating performance of the company and to help them estimate future potential earnings and cash flows. These reported income numbers are measured in accordance with GAAP. On the other hand, income reported to tax authorities must comply with the relevant tax regulations, which can be significantly different from GAAP.

LO8 Explain and illustrate the reporting for deferred income taxes.

Differences between taxable income and pretax income on the income statement are either permanent or temporary. **Permanent differences** between GAAP income and tax income arise because some revenues and expenses recorded in the income statement are never recognized in the tax return. Alternatively, some tax deductions are never recorded as expenses in the financial statements.

Temporary differences, on the other hand, are differences between tax and financial reporting that are expected to *reverse* in a future year. That is, the difference between the two statements is temporary. For example, an expense might be deductible for income taxes in the current year, but not recognized in the financial statements until a future year. When the expense is deducted on the tax return, but not the income statement, a temporary difference is created. When that expense is recognized in the income statement in a later period, the temporary difference is said to reverse.

Temporary differences between tax and financial reporting complicate the measurement of income tax expense in the income statement. The effect of these temporary differences is recorded in **deferred income taxes**. Total income tax expense for any given year is equal to the current tax obligation plus (or minus) any changes in deferred income taxes. To illustrate the effects of temporary differences on the calculation of income tax expense, consider the 2006 tax return for Murray Company.

Murray Company 2006 Tax Return	
Income before depreciation	$800
Depreciation	200
Taxable income	600
Income tax (at 40%)	$240

The tax amount of $240 is actually payable for 2006, as determined by the tax regulations. However, this amount is *not* the amount of income tax expense that the company would report in its income statement. Like many companies, Murray Company uses straight-line depreciation for financial reporting and accelerated depreciation for tax reporting. Over the life of an asset, the total depreciation expense is the same under straight-line and accelerated methods. However, accelerated depreciation reports higher depreciation amounts and lower asset values than the straight-line method.

To see how the difference in depreciation methods affects income tax expense, refer to the information provided in Exhibit 9A.1.

EXHIBIT 9A.1	Comparison of Book Value and Tax basis of PPE	
Murray Company Book Value and Tax Basis of Plant & Equipment		
	2006	2005
Plant & equipment—book value		
Plant and equipment, at cost	$1,500	$1,500
Accumulated depreciation	600	450
Plant and equipment, net book value	$ 900	$1,050
Plant & equipment—tax basis		
Plant and equipment, at cost	$1,500	$1,500
Accumulated depreciation	1,100	900
Plant and equipment, net book value	$ 400	$ 600

The difference between the book value of plant and equipment and the tax basis of the same assets is solely due to the different depreciation methods used for financial and tax reporting purposes. When the assets were purchased, the cost was $1,500. This amount was the same for financial and tax reporting purposes. The different depreciation methods have caused the net book value to differ from the tax basis, as summarized in the following table:

Calculation of temporary differences in PPE values for Murray Company		
	2006	**2005**
Net book value	$900	$1,050
Tax basis	400	600
Temporary difference	$500	$ 450

These differences are temporary, because they are expected to reverse in future years. Once the assets are fully depreciated, the net book value *and* the tax basis will be $0.

The amount of deferred income taxes is computed by multiplying the temporary difference by the tax rate. In this example, the tax rate is 40%. Murray's deferred tax liability is calculated as follows:

Calculation of Deferred Tax Liability for Murray Company		
	2006	**2005**
Temporary difference between book value and tax basis of PPE assets	$500	$450
Tax rate	× 40%	× 40%
Deferred tax liability	$200	$180

The deferred tax liability increased by $20 in 2006 ($200 − $180). We can now calculate and record income tax expense for the year. The procedure for calculating income tax expense is to first compute the tax obligation from the company's tax return, then to compute any changes in deferred tax liabilities or assets by multiplying the tax rate by the temporary differences. From these two amounts, we can then calculate tax expense as follows.

$$\text{Tax Expense} = \text{Tax Obligation} \pm \text{Changes in Deferred Tax Assets and Liabilities}$$

In this example, the necessary journal entry to record tax expense is as follows:

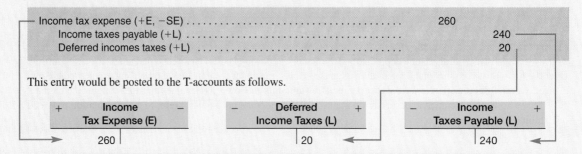

```
Income tax expense (+E, −SE) .....................................  260
    Income taxes payable (+L) .....................................         240
    Deferred incomes taxes (+L) ...................................          20
```

This entry would be posted to the T-accounts as follows.

+ Income Tax Expense (E) −	− Deferred Income Taxes (L) +	− Income Taxes Payable (L) +
260	20	240

Deferred tax liabilities arise when tax reporting income is less than financial reporting income. When this occurs, a temporary difference is created because the book value of net assets on the financial statements will be greater than the tax basis of net assets. This implies that the taxes will be paid when the temporary differences reverse.

Deferred tax assets arise when tax reporting income is higher than financial reporting income. In this situation, a temporary difference is created because the book value of net assets on the financial statements is less than the tax basis of net assets. The deferred tax asset expires when the temporary difference reverses. Examples of temporary differences that lead to deferred tax assets include costs of uncollectible accounts receivable, warranty costs, and some pension expenses. For example, estimated bad debt expenses reduce reported pretax income on the income statement, but the losses from uncollectible accounts cannot be deducted on the company's tax return until the write-off occurs. Thus, the recognized tax expense is less than the tax liability due currently (the debit is less than the credit) creating a deferred tax asset.

When a company has both deferred tax assets and deferred tax liabilities, the assets and liabilities are first separated into current and long-term amounts. The current deferred tax assets and current deferred tax liabilities are then reported *net* in the balance sheet under current assets or current liabilities, whichever is greater. Long-term amounts are treated similarly. It is not uncommon, therefore, to see a company report deferred tax assets under current assets in the balance sheet, while reporting deferred tax liabilities under long-term liabilities.

KEY TERMS

Accelerated depreciation (p. 382)

Amortization (p. 392)

Book value (or carrying value) (p. 380, 382)

Capital expenditures (p. 378)

Capitalized (p. 378)

MULTIPLE CHOICE

1. Burgstahler Corporation bought a lot to construct a new corporate office building. An older building on the lot was razed immediately so that the office building could be constructed. The cost of razing the older building should be
   a. recorded as part of the cost of the land.
   b. written off as a loss in the year of purchase.
   c. written off as an extraordinary item in the year of purchase.
   d. recorded as part of the cost of the new building.

2. The purpose of recording periodic depreciation of long-term PPE assets is to
   a. report declining asset values on the balance sheet.
   b. allocate asset costs over the periods benefited by use of the assets.
   c. account for costs to reflect the change in general price levels.
   d. set aside funds to replace assets when their economic usefulness expires.

3. When the estimate of an asset's useful life is changed,
   a. depreciation expense for all past periods must be recalculated.
   b. there is no change in the amount of depreciation expense recorded for future years.
   c. only depreciation expense for current and future years is changed.
   d. only depreciation expense in the current year is affected.

4. If the sale of a depreciable asset results in a loss, the proceeds from the sale were
   a. less than current market value.
   b. greater than cost.
   c. greater than book value.
   d. less than book value.

5. Which of the following principles best describes the current method of accounting for research and development costs?
   a. Revenue recognition method
   b. Systematic and rational allocation
   c. Immediate recognition as an expense
   d. Income tax minimization

6. Goodwill should be recorded in the balance sheet as an intangible asset only when
   a. it is sold to another company.
   b. it is acquired through the purchase of another business.
   c. a company reports above normal earnings for five or more consecutive years.
   d. it can be established that a definite benefit or advantage has resulted from some item such as a good reputation.

Multiple Choice Answers
1. a 2. b 3. c 4. d 5. c 6. b

Superscript ^Adenotes assignments based on Appendix 9A.

DISCUSSION QUESTIONS

Q9-1. How should companies account for costs, such as maintenance or improvements, which are incurred after an asset is acquired?

Q9-2. What is the effect of capitalized interest on the income statement in the period that an asset is constructed? What is the effect in future periods?

Q9-3. Why is the recognition of depreciation expense necessary to properly match revenues and expenses?

Q9-4. Why do companies use accelerated depreciation for income tax purposes, when the total depreciation taken over the asset's useful life is identical to straight-line depreciation?

Q9-5. How should a company treat a change in an asset's estimated useful life or residual value? Which period(s)—past, present, or future—is affected by this change?

Q9-6. What factors determine the gain or loss from the sale of a long-term operating asset?

Q9-7. When is a PPE asset considered to be impaired? How is the impairment loss determined?

Q9-8. What is the proper accounting treatment for research and development costs? Why are R&D costs not capitalized under GAAP?

Q9-9. Why are some intangible assets amortized while others are not? What is meant by an intangible asset with an "indefinite life"?

Q9-10. Under what circumstances should a company report goodwill in its balance sheet? What is the affect of goodwill on the income statement?

Q9-11.^A What are two examples of temporary differences that will result in the recognition of deferred tax liabilities?

Q9-12.^A During 2007, its first year of operations, Penno, Inc., recorded $20,000 of sales revenue in its financial statements that will not be reported as revenue on its income tax return until 2008. The tax rate is 40% for 2007 and 2008. what amount of deferred tax liability related to this temporary difference should appear in Penno's December 31, 2007, balance sheet?

Q9-13.^A A firm records an outlay as an asset in 2006 but deducts the outlay as an expense on its 2006 income tax return. In 2007 the entire amount will be expensed for financial reporting. In 2006, tax rates enacted into law were 35% for 2006 and 40% for 2007. Which rate is used in determining the deferred tax liability at December 31, 2006? Explain.

Q9-14.^A When are deferred tax liabilities classified as current liabilities? As long-term liabilities?

MINI EXERCISES

M9-15. **Determining whether to capitalize or expense** **(LO2)**
For each of the following items, indicate whether the cost should be capitalized or expensed immediately:
a. Paid $1,200 for routine maintenance of machinery
b. Paid $5,400 to rent equipment for two years
c. Paid $2,000 to equip the production line with new instruments that measure quality
d. Paid $20,000 to repair the roof on the building
e. Paid $1,600 to refurbish a machine, thereby extending its useful life
f. Purchased a patent for $5,000

M9-16. **Computing Depreciation under Straight-Line and Double-Declining-Balance** **(LO3)**
A delivery van costing $18,000 is expected to have a $1,500 salvage value at the end of its useful life of 5 years. Assume that the truck was purchased on January 1, 2005. Compute the depreciation expense for 2006 (its second year) under each of the following depreciation methods:
a. Straight-line.
b. Double-declining balance.

M9-17. **Computing depreciation under alternative methods** **(LO3)**
Equipment costing $130,000 is expected to have a residual value of $10,000 at the end of its 6-year useful life. The equipment is metered so that the number of units processed is counted. The equipment is designed to process 1,000,000 units in its lifetime. In 2006 and 2007, the equipment processed 180,000 units and 140,000 units respectively. Calculate the depreciation expense for 2006 and 2007 using each of the following methods:
a. Straight-line.
b. Double-declining balance
c. Units of production.

M9-18. Recording the sale of PPE assets (LO4)

As part of a renovation of its showroom, O'Keefe Auto Dealership sold furniture and fixtures that were eight years old for $3,500 in cash. The assets had been purchased for $40,000 and had been depreciated using the straight-line method with no residual value and a useful life of ten years.

a. Prepare a journal entry to record this transaction.

b. Show how the sale of the furniture and fixtures affects the balance sheet and income statement using the financial statement effects template.

M9-19. Recording the sale of PPE assets (LO4)

Gaver Company sold machinery that had originally cost $75,000 for $25,000 in cash. The machinery was three years old and had been depreciated using the double declining balance method assuming a five year useful life and a residual value of $5,000.

a. Prepare a journal entry to record this sale.

b. Using the financial statement effects template, show how the sale of the machinery affects the balance sheet and income statement.

M9-20. Computing Depreciation under Straight-Line and Double-Declining-Balance for Partial Years (LO3)

A machine costing $145,800 is purchased on May 1, 2005. The machine is expected to be obsolete after three years (36 months) and, thereafter, no longer useful to the company. The estimated salvage value is $5,400. Compute depreciation expense for both 2005 and 2006 under each of the following depreciation methods:

a. Straight-line.

b. Double-declining balance.

M9-21. Computing double-declining-balance depreciation (LO3)

Swieringa Company purchased a machine for $24,000. For each of the following sets of assumptions, prepare a depreciation schedule (all years) for this machine assuming that Swieringa uses the double-declining balance depreciation method.

Useful life	Residual value
a. Five years	$4,000
b. Eight years	$2,000
c. Ten years	$ 0

M9-22. Computing double declining-balance depreciation (LO3)

DeFond Company purchased equipment for $50,000. For each of the following sets of assumptions, prepare a depreciation schedule (all years) for this equipment assuming that DeFond uses the double-declining balance depreciation method.

Useful life	Residual value
a. Four years	$8,000
b. Five years	$3,000
c. Ten years	$1,000

M9-23. Computing and recording depletion expense (LO7)

The Nelson Oil Company estimated that the oil reserve that it acquired would produce 4 million barrels of oil. The company extracted 300,000 barrels the first year, 500,000 barrels in 2007, and 600,000 barrels in 2008. Nelson paid $32,000,000 for the oil reserve.

a. Compute the depletion expense for each year—2006, 2007 and 2008.

b. Prepare the journal entries to record (i) the acquisition of the oil reserve, and (ii) the depletion for 2006.

c. Open T-accounts and post the entries from part *b* in the accounts.

M9-24. Computing and Comparing PPE Turnover for Two Companies (LO6)

Texas Instruments and Intel Corporation report the following information:

Texas Instruments (TXN)

Intel Corporation (INTC)

($ millions)	Texas Instruments		Intel Corp	
	Sales	PPE, net	Sales	PPE, net
2003	$9,834	$4,132	$30,141	$16,661
2002	8,383	4,794	26,764	17,847

a. Compute the 2003 PPE turnover for both companies. Comment on any difference you observe.

b. Discuss ways in which high-tech manufacturing companies like these can increase their PPE turnover.

M9-25. **Assessing Research and Development Expenses** (LO5, 6)

Abbott Laboratories reports the following income statement (in partial form):

Year Ended December 31 ($ 000s)	2003
Net sales	$19,680,561
Cost of products sold	9,473,416
Research and development	1,733,472
Acquired in-process research and development	100,240
Selling, general and administrative	5,050,901
Total operating cost and expenses	16,358,029
Operating earnings	$ 3,322,532

a. Compute the percent of net sales that Abbott Laboratories spends on research and development (R&D). How would you assess the appropriateness of its R&D expense level?

b. Using the financial statement effects template, describe how the accounting for R&D expenditures affects Abbot Laboratories' balance sheet and income statement.

M9-26.[A] **Computing and reporting deferred income taxes** (LO8)

Fisk, Inc., purchased $600,000 of construction equipment on January 1, 2006. The equipment is being depreciated on a straight-line basis over six years with no expected salvage value. MACRS depreciation is being used on the firm's tax returns. At December 31, 2008, the equipment's book value is $300,000 and its tax basis is $173,000 (this is Fisk's only temporary difference). Over the next three years, straight-line depreciation will exceed MACRS depreciation by $31,000 in 2009, $31,000 in 2010, and $65,000 in 2011. Assume that the income tax rate in effect for all years is 40%.

a. What amount of deferred tax liability should appear in Fisk's December 31, 2008, balance sheet?

b. What amount of deferred tax liability should appear in Fisk's December 31, 2009, balance sheet?

c. What amount of deferred tax liability should appear in Fisk's December 31, 2010, balance sheet?

d. Where should the deferred tax liability accounts be classified in Fisk's 2008, 2009, and 2010 year-end balance sheets?

EXERCISES

E9-27. **Recording asset acquisition, depreciation, and disposal** (LO2, 3, 4)

On January 2, 2006, Hutton Company acquired a machine for $85,000. In addition to the purchase price, Hutton spent $2,000 for shipping and installation, and $2,500 to calibrate the machine prior to use. The company estimates that the machine has a useful life of five years and residual value of $7,000.

a. Prepare journal entries to record the acquisition costs.

b. Calculate the annual depreciation expense using straight-line depreciation and prepare a journal entry to record depreciation expense for 2006.

c. On December 31, 2009, Hutton sold the machine to another company for $12,000. Prepare the necessary journal entry to record the sale.

E9-28. **Computing Straight-Line and Double-Declining-Balance Depreciation** (LO3)

On January 2, Haskins Company purchases a laser cutting machine for use in fabrication of a part for one of its key products. The machine cost $80,000, and its estimated useful life is five years, after which the expected salvage value is $5,000. Compute depreciation expense for each year of the machine's useful life under each of the following depreciation methods:

a. Straight-line

b. Double-declining balance

E9-29. **Computing Depreciation, Asset Book Value, and Gain or Loss on Asset Sale** (LO3, 4)

Sloan Company uses its own executive charter plane that originally cost $800,000. It has recorded straight-line depreciation on the plane for six full years, with an $80,000 expected salvage value at the end of its estimated 10-year useful life. Sloan disposes of the plane at the end of the sixth year.

a. At the disposal date, what is the (1) cumulative depreciation expense and (2) net book value of the plane?

  b. Prepare a journal entry to record the disposal of the plane assuming that the sales price is
    1. Cash equal to the book value of the plane.
    2. $195,000 cash.
    3. $600,000 cash.

E9-30. **Computing Straight-Line and Double-Declining-Balance Depreciation** (LO3)

On January 2, 2005, Dechow Company purchases a machine to help manufacture a part for one of its key products. The machine cost $218,700 and is estimated to have a useful life of six years, with an expected salvage value of $23,400.

  Compute each year's depreciation expense for 2005 and 2006 for each of the following depreciation methods.

  a. Straight-line.
  b. Double-declining-balance.

E9-31. **Computing Depreciation, Asset Book Value, and Gain or Loss on Asset Sale** (LO3, 4)

Palepu Company owns and operates a delivery van that originally cost $27,200. Straight-line depreciation on the van has been recorded for three years, with a $2,000 expected salvage value at the end of its estimated six-year useful life. Depreciation was last recorded at the end of the third year, at which time Palepu disposes of this van.

  a. Compute the net book value of the van on the sale date.
  b. Compute the gain or loss on sale of the van if its sales price is for:
    1. Cash equal to book value (of van).
    2. $15,000 cash.
    3. $12,000 cash.

E9-32. **Computing depreciation and accounting for a change of estimate** (LO3)

Lambert Company acquired machinery costing $110,000 on January 2, 2006. At that time, Lambert estimated that the useful life of the equipment was 6 years and that the residual value would be $15,000 at the end of its useful life. Compute depreciation expense for this asset for 2006, 2007, and 2008 using the

  a. straight-line method.
  b. double-declining balance method.
  c. Assume that on January 2, 2008, Lambert revised its estimate of the useful life to 7 years and changed its estimate of the residual value to $10,000. What effect would this have on depreciation expense in 2008 for each of the above depreciation methods?

E9-33. **Computing depreciation and accounting for a change of estimate** (LO3)

In January 2006, Rankine Company paid $8,500,000 for land and a building. An appraisal estimated that the land had a fair market value of $2,500,000 and the building was worth $6,000,000. Rankine estimated that the useful life of the building was 30 years, with no residual value.

  a. Calculate annual depreciation expense using the straight-line method.
  b. Calculated depreciation for 2006 and 2007 using the double-declining balance method.
  c. Assume that in 2008, Rankine changed its estimate of the useful life of the building to 25 years. If the company is using the double-declining balance method of depreciation, what amount of depreciation expense would Rankine record in 2008?

E9-34. **Estimating and Percent Depreciated** (LO6)

The property and equipment footnote from the Deere & Company balance sheet follows ($ millions):

Deere & Company (DE)

PROPERTY AND DEPRECIATION

A summary of property and equipment at October 31 in millions of dollars follows:

	Useful Lives (Years)	2003
Land		$ 68
Buildings and building equipment	10–33	1,366
Machinery and equipment.	12	2,705
Dies, patterns, tools, etc	8	932
All other.	3–8	671
Construction in progress		92
Total at cost.		5,834
Less accumulated depreciation		3,758
Property and equipment—net.		$2,076

During 2003, the company reported $631.4 million of depreciation expense.

a. Estimate the percent depreciated of Deere's depreciable assets. How do you interpret this figure?

E9-35. **Computing and Evaluating Receivables, Inventory and PPE Turnovers** (LO6)

3M Company
(MMM)

3M Company reports the following financial statement amounts in its 10-K report:

($ millions)	Sales	Cost of Sales	Receivables	Inventories	PPE
2003	$18,232	$8,321	$3,162	$1,816	$5,609
2002	16,332	7,482	2,840	1,931	5,621
2001	16,079	7,462	2,786	2,091	5,615

Required

a. Compute the receivables, inventory, and PPE turnover ratios for both 2003 and 2002.

b. What changes are evident in the turnover rates of 3M for these years? Discuss ways in which a company such as 3M can improve its turnover within each of these three areas.

E9-36. **Identifying and accounting for intangible assets** (LO5)

In 2006, Holthausen Company acquired the assets of Leftwich Company including several intangible assets. These include a patent on Leftwich's primary product, a device called a plentiscope. Leftwich carried the patent on its books for $1,500, but Holthausen believes that the fair market value is $200,000. The patent expires in seven years, but competitors can be expected to develop competing patents within three years. Holthausen believes that, with expected technological improvements, the product is marketable for at least 20 years.

The registration of the trademark for the Leftwich name is scheduled to expire in 15 years. However, the Leftwich brand name, which Holthausen believes is worth $500,000, could be applied to related products for many years beyond that.

As part of the acquisition, Leftwich's principle researcher left the company. As part of the acquisition, he signed a five-year non-competition agreement that prevents him from developing competing products. Holthausen paid the scientist $300,000 to sign the agreement.

a. What amount should be capitalized for each of the identifiable intangible assets?

b. What amount of amortization expense should Holthausen record in 2006 for each asset?

E9-37. **Computing and recording depletion expense** (LO7)

In 2006, Eldenburg Mining Company purchased land for $7,200,000 that had a natural resource reserve estimated to be 500,000 tons. Development and road construction costs on the land were $420,000, and a building was constructed at a cost of $50,000. When the natural resources are completely extracted, the land has an estimated residual value of $1,200,000. In addition, the cost to restore the property to comply with environmental regulations is estimated to be $800,000. Production in 2006 and 2007 was 60,000 tons and 85,000 tons, respectively.

a. Compute the depletion charge for 2006 and 2007. (You should include depreciation on the building, if any, as part of the depletion charge.)

b. Prepare a journal entry to record each year's depletion expense as determined in (a).

E9-38. **Computing and interpreting percent depreciated and PPE turnover** (LO6)

Adams Golf
Company

The following footnote is from the 2004 10-K of Adams Golf Company, a Texas based manufacturer of golf equipment:

Property and Equipment, net		
Property and equipment consist of the following at December 31, 2004 and 2003:		
Equipment	$ 1,789	$ 1,711
Computers and software	8,866	8,635
Furniture and fixtures	662	629
Leaseholds improvements	186	181
Accumulated depreciation and amortization	(10,783)	(10,241)
	$ 720	$ 915

a. Calculate the percent depreciated ratio for each year.

b. Sales revenue totaled $56,762 in 2004 and the average net operating assets was $24,878 (all values are in $ thousands). Calculated the PPE turnover ratio (PPET) and the net operating asset turnover ratio (NOAT).

c. Comment on these ratios. Do you notice anything unusual?

E9-39. **Evaluating R&D expenditures of companies** (LO5, 6)

R&D intensity is measured by the ratio of research and development expense to sales revenue. The following table compares the R&D intensity for various companies.

Company	R&D Intensity
Adams Golf	3.25%
Callaway Golf	3.27%
Apple Computer	5.91%
Dell Computer	0.94%
Intel, Corp.	13.97%
Motorola, Inc.	9.77%
Baxter International	5.44%
Advanced Medical Optics	6.15%
Pfizer, Inc.	14.62%
Merck & Co.	17.48%

Adams Golf
Callaway Golf
Apple Computer
Dell Computer
Intel, Corp.
Motorola, Inc.
Baxter International
Advanced Medical Optics
Pfizer, Inc.
Merck & Co.

a. Comment on the differences among these companies. To what extent are the differences related to industry affiliation?

b. What other factors (besides industry affiliation) might determine a company's R&D intensity?

E9-40. **Computing and Assessing Plant Asset Impairment** (LO4)

Zeibart Company purchases equipment for $225,000 on July 1, 2000, with an estimated useful life or 10 years and expected salvage value of $25,000. Straight-line depreciation is used. On July 1, 2004, economic factors cause the market value of the equipment to decline to $90,000. On this date, Zeibart examines the equipment for impairment and estimates $125,000 in future cash inflows related to use of this equipment.

a. Is the equipment impaired at July 1, 2004? Explain.

b. If the equipment is impaired on July 1, 2004, compute the impairment loss and prepare a journal entry to record the loss.

c. What amount of depreciation expense would Zeibart record for the 12 months from July 1, 2004 through June 30, 2005? Prepare a journal entry to record this depreciation expense.

d. Using the financial statement effects template, show how the entries in parts b and c affect Zeibart Company's balance sheet and income statement.

E9-41.[A] **Computing and reporting deferred income taxes** (LO8)

Early in January 2007, Wade, Inc., purchased equipment costing $16,000 and debited the amount to the Equipment account. The equipment had a two-year useful life and was depreciated $8,000 in each of the years 2007 and 2008. Wade deducted the entire $16,000 as an expense on its 2007 income tax return. Wade had no other plant assets and the accounting for this equipment represented the only difference between Wade's financial statements and income tax returns. Wade's income before depreciation expense and income taxes was $236,000 in 2007 and $245,000 in 2008. Tax rates enacted into law at December 31, 2007, were 40% for both 2007 and 2008.

a. What amount of deferred tax liability should be reported in Wade's year-end balance sheets for 2007 and 2008?

b. Prepare journal entries to record income taxes at December 31, 2007, and December 31, 2008.

c. Assume that the tax rates enacted into law at December 31, 2007, are 35% for 2007 and 40% for 2008. Prepare journal entries to record income taxes at December 31, 2007, and December 31, 2008.

E9-42.[A] **Calculating and recording income tax expense** (LO8)

Lougee Company began operations in 2006. The company reported $24,000 in depreciation expense on its income statement in 2006 and $26,000 in 2007. On its tax returns, Lougee deducted $32,000 for depreciation in 2006 and $37,000 in 2007. The 2007 tax return shows a tax obligation of $19,200 based on a tax rate of 40%.

a. Determine the temporary difference between the book value of depreciable assets and the tax basis of these assets at the end of 2006 and 2007.

b. Calculate the deferred tax liability for each year.

c. Calculate the income tax expense for 2007.

d. Prepare a journal entry to record income tax expense and post this entry to T-accounts.

E9-43.[A] **Calculating and recording income tax expense** (LO8)

Yetman Company began operations in 2006. The company reported $130,000 in depreciation expense on its income statement in 2006 and $128,000 in 2007. On its tax returns, Yetman deducted $140,000 for depreciation in 2006 and $122,000 in 2007. The 2007 tax return shows a tax obligation of $45,150 based on a tax rate of 35%.

a. Determine the temporary difference between the book value of depreciable assets and the tax basis of these assets at the end of 2006 and 2007.

b. Calculate the deferred tax liability for each year.

c. Calculate the income tax expense for 2007.

d. Prepare a journal entry to record income tax expense and post this entry to T-accounts.

PROBLEMS

P9-44. **Computing and recording gain or loss on asset sale** (LO4)

Nordstrom
Corporation (JWN)

The following information was provided in a footnote to the 2005 10-K report of Nordstrom Corporation.

Note 10: Land, Buildings and Equipment		
($ thousands)	January 29, 2005	January 31, 2004
Total land, buildings and equipment, at cost	4,090,973	3,928,936
Less accumulated depreciation and amortization	(2,310,607)	(2,121,158)
Land, buildings and equipment, net	$1,780,366	$1,807,778

Also, its cash flow statement revealed the following information ($ thousands):

■ Depreciation expense was $264,769.

■ Capital expenditures totaled $246,851.

■ Proceeds from the sale of land, buildings and equipment totaled $5,473.

Required

Using this information, prepare a journal entry to record the sale of land, buildings and equipment.

P9-45. **Analyzing and Assessing Research and Development Expenses** (LO5, 6)

Agilent
Technologies, Inc.
(A)
Hewlett-Packard
(HPQ)

Agilent Technologies, Inc., the high-tech spin-off from Hewlett-Packard, reports the following operating loss for 2003 in its 10-K ($ millions):

Net revenue	
Products	$5,240
Services and other	816
Total net revenue	6,056
Costs and expenses	
Cost of products	3,195
Cost of services and other	567
Total costs	3,762
Research and development	1,051
Selling, general and administrative	1,968
Total costs and expenses	6,781
Loss from operations	$ (725)

a. What percentage of its total net revenue is Agilent spending on research and development?

b. How are its balance sheet and income statement affected by the accounting for R&D costs?

c. Agilent reports a loss from operations for 2003. Identity and explain the implications if Agilent had reduced its 2003 R&D spending by $800 million and reported an operating profit. Consider its reduction of R&D costs relative to the no reduction scenario.

P9-46. **Analyzing PPE accounts and recording PPE transactions, including discontinued operations** (LO3, 4)

Target Corporation
(TGT)

The 2004 and 2003 income statements and balance sheets (asset section only) for Target Corporation follow, along with its footnote describing Target's accounting for property, plant and equipment. Target's cash flow statement for fiscal 2004 reported capital expenditures of $3,068 million and a loss on disposal of property, plant and equipment of $69 million. In addition, assets from discontinued operations were sold for a gain of $1,999. Prepare journal entries to record the following:

    a.   Depreciation expense
    b.   Amortization expense
    c.   Capital expenditures
    d.   Disposal of property, plant and equipment
    e.   Sale of assets from discontinued operations

Property and Equipment

Property and equipment are recorded at cost, less accumulated depreciation. Depreciation is computed using the straight-line method over estimated useful lives.

Depreciation expense for the years 2004, 2003, and 2002 was $1,232 million, $1,068 million and $942 million, respectively. Accelerated depreciation methods are generally used for income tax purposes. Repair and maintenance costs were $453 million, $393 million and $355 million in 2004, 2003 and 2002, respectively.

Target Corporation Consolidated Income Statement

(in millions)	2004	2003
Sales...	$45,682	$40,928
Net credit card revenues.................................	1,157	1,097
Total revenues..	46,839	42,025
Cost of sales..	31,445	28,389
Selling, general and administrative expense	9,797	8,657
Credit card expense	737	722
Depreciation and amortization	1,259	1,098
Earnings from continuing operations before interest and taxes	3,601	3,159
Net interest expense......................................	570	556
Earnings from continuing operations before taxes	3,031	2,603
Provision for income taxes	1,146	984
Earnings from continuing operations	1,885	1,619
Earnings from discontinued operations, net of $46 and $116 tax.............	75	190
Gain on disposal of discontinued operations, net of $761 tax	1,238	—
Net earnings	$ 3,198	$ 1,809

Target Corporation Consolidated Balance Sheets
(Asset Section Only)

(in millions)	January 29, 2005	January 31, 2004
Assets		
Cash and cash equivalents..................................	$ 2,245	$ 708
Accounts receivable, net....................................	5,069	4,621
Inventory...	5,384	4,531
Other current assets	1,224	1,000
Current assets of discontinued operations	—	2,092
Total current assets.......................................	13,922	12,952
Property and equipment		
Land	3,804	3,312
Buildings and improvements................................	12,518	11,022
Fixtures and equipment	4,988	4,577
Construction-in-progress...................................	962	969
Accumulated depreciation..................................	(5,412)	(4,727)
Property and equipment, net...............................	16,860	15,153
Other non-current assets	1,511	1,377
Non-current assets of discontinued operations..............	—	1,934
Total assets...	$32,293	$31,416

P 9-47.[A] **Computing and reporting deferred income taxes** (LO8)

Miner Corporation paid $12,000 on December 31, 2006, for equipment with a three-year useful life (2007–2009) and debited the payment to Equipment. The equipment will be depreciated $4,000 per year in 2007, 2008, and 2009. Miner took the $12,000 payment as an expense on its 2006 income tax return. This amount is Miner's only temporary difference between its books and its tax return. Miner's income tax rate is 40%.

Required

a. What amount of deferred tax liability should appear in Miner's December 31, 2006, balance sheet?
b. Where should the deferred tax liability be classified in the balance sheet at December 31, 2006?
c. What amount of deferred tax liability should appear in Miner's December 31, 2007, balance sheet?

P9-48.[A] **Computing and reporting deferred income taxes** (LO8)

Buckeye Corporation paid $12,000 on December 31, 2006, for special equipment with a two-year useful life and debited the payment to Equipment. The equipment was depreciated $6,000 per year in 2007 and 2008. Buckeye owned no other plant assets. Buckeye deducted the entire $12,000 as an expense on its 2006 income tax return. This represented the only difference between Buckeye's financial statements and income tax returns. Buckeye's income before depreciation expense and income taxes was $320,000 in 2006, $400,000 in 2007, and $420,000 in 2008. Tax rates enacted into law at December 31, 2006, were 35% for 2006, 35% for 2007, and 40% for 2008.

Required

a. What is the book value of equipment at December 31, 2006; December 31, 2007; and December 31, 2008?
b. What is the tax basis of equipment at December 31, 2006; December 31, 2007; and December 31, 2008?
c. What amount of deferred tax liability should be reported in the year-end balance sheets for 2006, 2007, and 2008?
d. Prepare journal entries to record income taxes at December 31, 2006; December 31, 2007; and December 31, 2008.

P9-49.[A] **Interpreting income tax footnotes** (LO8)

Williams-Sonoma, Inc. (WSM)

The following information was presented in the footnotes of the 2005 10-K for **Williams-Sonoma, Inc.** (all dollar amounts in thousands):

Significant components of our deferred tax accounts are as follows:		
Deferred tax asset (liability)	**Jan. 30, 2005**	**Feb. 1, 2004**
Current		
Compensation	$14,667	$12,587
Inventory	11,357	10,357
Accrued liabilities	13,725	11,971
Customer deposits	19,342	470
Prepaid catalog costs	(20,540)	(14,871)
Other	464	18
Total current	**39,015**	**20,532**
Noncurrent		
Depreciation	(18,634)	(3,511)
Deferred rent	8,275	1,151
Deferred lease incentives	(11,595)	(7,271)
Other	897	744
Total noncurrent	**(21,057)**	**(8,887)**
Total	$17,958	$11,645

a. For the year ended January 30, 2005, Williams-Sonoma reported a current tax obligation (based on its tax return) of $125,225. What amount of income tax expense did the company report in its income statement?
b. Prepare a journal entry to record income tax expense for the year ended January 30, 2005.
c. Williams-Sonoma reported that the net book value of property, plant and equipment was $852,412 at January 30, 2005. Given a tax rate of 38.5%, what was the tax basis of these assets?
d. Williams-Sonoma reported prepaid catalog expenses of $53,520 as a current asset in its January 30, 2005 balance sheet. They provided the following note to explain this prepaid expense:

Prepaid Catalog Expenses Prepaid catalog expenses consist of direct costs, including creative design, paper, printing, postage and mailing costs for all of our direct response catalogs. Such costs are capitalized as prepaid catalog expenses and are amortized over their expected period of future benefit. . . . Each catalog is generally fully amortized over a six to nine month period, with the majority of the amortization occurring within the first four to five months.

Required

Explain how this prepaid expense results in a temporary difference between tax and financial reporting.

CASES AND PROJECTS

C9-50. **Reporting PPE transactions and asset impairments** (LO3, 4)

Robert Mondavi, Inc. is a leading producer and marketer of premium table wines. Its brands include Robert Mondavi Winery, Robert Mondavi Private Selection and Woodbridge. Woodbridge accounted for 75% by volume and 57% by net revenue of the Company's sales in fiscal 2003. The Company's smaller wineries include Byron in Santa Maria and Arrowood in Sonoma, as well as four international joint ventures. Presented below are the 2002 and 2003 balance sheets (asset sections only) as well as income statements for 2001 through 2003. Selected notes are also provided.

Robert Mondavi, Inc.

Required

1. Mondavi recorded depreciation expense of $23,565,000 in 2003. In addition, a loss for asset impairment of $5,347,000 was charged to income and credited to accumulated depreciation (see note 5). How are these two events recorded in journal entries and presented in the financial statements?
2. Mondavi purchased PPE assets for $25,524,000 in 2003. Note 5 explains that some properties that were designated for sale were sold at a gain during the year. In addition, Mondavi sold additional PPE assets. The total cash proceeds from these asset sales amounted to $24,967,000. Prepare journal entries to record these transactions.
3. Calculate the PPE turnover ratio, the inventory turnover ratio and the percent depreciated for Mondavi in 2003.

ROBERT MONDAVI, INC.
BALANCE SHEETS (Asset section only)

June 30 ($ 000s)	2003	2002
Assets		
Current assets		
Cash.	$ 1,339	$ —
Accounts receivable, net	96,111	92,555
Inventories	394,389	388,574
Prepaid expenses and other current assets	12,545	12,179
Total current assets	504,384	493,308
Property, plant and equipment, net	302,015	323,582
Investments in joint ventures	30,763	27,220
Other assets.	11,674	11,455
Total assets	$848,836	$855,565

ROBERT MONDAVI, INC.
CONSOLIDATED STATEMENTS OF INCOME

YEAR ENDED JUNE 30 ($ 000s)	2003	2002	2001
Net revenues	$452,673	$441,358	$480,969
Cost of goods sold	278,208	249,020	264,739
Gross profit.	174,465	192,338	216,230
Selling, general and administrative expense . . .	129,993	125,760	132,496
Special charges, net.	2,111	12,240	—
Operating income.	42,361	54,338	83,734

(table continues on the next page)

ROBERT MONDAVI, INC. CONSOLIDATED STATEMENTS OF INCOME			
YEAR ENDED JUNE 30 ($ 000s)	2003	2002	2001
Other income (expense)			
Interest..............................	(21,442)	(22,062)	(21,411)
Other	6,585	8,550	8,069
Income before income taxes	27,504	40,826	70,392
Provision for income taxes................	10,177	15,310	27,098
Net income............................	$ 17,327	$ 25,516	$ 43,294

NOTE 1: SUMMARY OF SIGNIFICANT ACCOUNTING POLICIES
Property, plant and equipment
Property, plant and equipment is stated at cost. Maintenance and repairs are expensed as incurred. Costs incurred in developing vineyards, including related interest costs, are capitalized until the vineyards become commercially productive. The cost of property, plant and equipment sold or otherwise disposed of and the related accumulated depreciation are removed from the accounts at the time of disposal with resulting gains and losses included in Other Income (Expense) in the Consolidated Statements of Income.

Depreciation and amortization is computed using the straight-line method, with the exception of barrels. which are depreciated using an accelerated method, over the estimated useful lives of the assets amounting to 20 to 30 years for vineyards, 45 years for buildings, 3 to 20 years for production machinery and equipment and 3 to 10 years for other equipment. Leasehold improvements are amortized over the estimated useful lives of the improvements or the terms of the related lease, whichever is shorter.

NOTE 4: PROPERTY, PLANT AND EQUIPMENT
The cost and accumulated depreciation of property, plant and equipment consist of the following:

	2003	2002
Land..	$ 58,664	$ 58,592
Vineyards...................................	80,211	80,211
Buildings	72,934	70,776
Production machinery and equipment	168,817	177,172
Other equipment	59,077	41,397
Vineyards under development.................	2,767	21,255
Construction in progress	6,925	16,528
	449,395	461,866
Less, accumulated depreciation	147,380	138,284
	$302,015	$323,582

NOTE 5: ASSETS HELD FOR SALE
During fiscal 2003, the Company determined that certain of its vineyard and other assets were no longer expected to fit its long-term grape sourcing needs or meet its long-term financial objectives. At that time, assets with a combined book value of $47,042 were identified for potential future sale. These assets are expected to be held and used while the Company develops a plan to sell the assets. During fiscal 2003, the Company recorded asset impairment charges of $5,347 to write-down the value of certain vineyard properties to fair value. One of these properties was disposed of during fiscal 2003 for amounts in excess of book value, less selling costs, which resulted in a gain of $7,312. These amounts are included in Special Charges, Net in the Consolidated Statements of Income. The Company believes that the carrying value of the remaining assets available for sale, amounting to $36,681 as of June 30,2003, is recoverable and it does not exceed fair value.

C9-51. **Interpreting and Applying Disclosures on Property and Equipment** (LO6)
Following are selected income statement; balance sheet; and land, buildings, and equipment (PPE) disclosures from **Rohm and Haas Company** (a specialty chemical company).

Rohm and Haas
Company (ROH)

For Years Ended December 31 ($ millions)	2002	2001	2000
Net sales	$5,727	$5,666	$6,349
Cost of goods sold	3,910	4,008	4,342
Gross profit	1,817	1,658	2,007
Selling and administrative expense	879	861	933
Research and development expense	260	230	224
Interest expense	132	182	241
Amortization of goodwill and other intangibles	69	156	159
Purchased in-process research and development	—	—	13
Provision for restructuring and asset impairments	177	320	13
Share of affiliate earnings, net	15	12	18
Other income, net	5	15	46
Earnings (loss) from continuing operations before income taxes, extraordinary item and cumulative effect of accounting change	320	(64)	488

December 31 ($ millions)	2002	2001
Assets		
Cash and cash equivalents	$ 295	$ 92
Receivables, net	1,184	1,220
Inventories	765	712
Prepaid expenses and other current assets	299	397
Total current assets	2,543	2,421
Land, building and equipment, net of accumulated depreciation	2,954	2,905
Investments in and advances to affiliates	170	152
Goodwill, net of accumulated amortization	1,617	2,159
Other intangible assets, net of accumulated amortization	1,861	2,257
Other assets	561	484
Total Assets	$9,706	$10,378

NOTE 15: LAND, BUILDING AND EQUIPMENT, NET

(in millions)	2002	2001
Land	$ 142	$ 114
Buildings and improvements	1,541	1,421
Machinery and equipment	4,926	4,482
Capitalized interest	292	272
Construction in progress	345	318
Less: accumulated depreciation	4,292	3,702
Total	$2,954	$2,905

The principal lives (in years) used in determining depreciation rates of various assets are: buildings and improvements (10–50); machinery and equipment (5–20); automobiles, trucks and tank cars (3–10); furniture and fixtures, laboratory equipment and other assets (5–10); capitalized interest (11).

NOTE 5: PROVISION FOR RESTRUCTURING AND ASSET IMPAIRMENTS

2002   In 2002, we recognized $177 million for restructuring and asset impairments. This charge is comprised of $191 million for the impairment of certain long-lived assets and costs associated with workforce reductions initiated in 2002. Of the total 2002 charges, $158 million was non-cash in nature and comprised of asset impairments recorded to reduce the carrying value of certain identified assets to their fair values, which were calculated using cash flow analyses . . . The largest, single asset write-down was $121 million, recorded to write-down certain long-lived intangible and fixed assets of the Printed Wiring Board business in the

Electronic Materials segment in accordance with SFAS No.144, "Accounting for the Impairment or Disposal of Long-Lived Assets." The remaining $37 million of non-cash charges, recorded during 2002, related largely to the closure of two European plants and other building and equipment impairments.

2001   In 2001, we launched a repositioning initiative to enable several of our businesses to respond to structural changes in the global marketplace. In connection with these repositioning initiatives, we recognized a $330 million restructuring and asset impairment charge in the second quarter of 2001 . . . The largest component of the 2001 repositioning charge related to the full and partial closure of certain manufacturing and research facilities across all business groups and included exit costs related to the liquid polysulfide sealants business in Adhesives and Sealants and part of the dyes business in Performance Chemicals. Approximately 75% of the asset write-downs were in the North American region.

Required

a.   Compute the PPE (land, buildings and equipment) asset turnover for 2002 and 2001 (net PPE assets for 2000 is $2,916 million). Interpret and explain any change in turnover. Does the level of its PPE turnover suggest that Rohm and Haas is capital intensive? Explain. Do you believe that Rohm and Haas' balance sheet reflects all of the assets it uses to conduct operations? Explain.

b.   Rohm and Haas reported depreciation expense of $388 million in 2002. Assuming that Rohm and Haas uses straight-line depreciation, estimate the useful life, on average, for its depreciable PPE assets?

c.   By what percentage are Rohm and Haas' assets depreciated at year-end 2002? What implication does the assets used up computation have for forecasting cash flows?

d.   Rohm and Haas reported large expenses in 2002 and 2001 related to asset impairment charges with its restructuring program. Describe the accounting process by which the impairment charge is determined. How do these charges affect its cash flows for 2002 and 2001? How should you treat these charges for analysis purposes?

CHAPTER 10

Reporting Nonowner Financing

LEARNING OBJECTIVES

After completing the chapter, you should be able to:

LO1 Analyze and distinguish between operating liabilities and nonoperating liabilities. (p. 420)

LO2 Identify and account for current operating liabilities. (p. 420)

LO3 Describe and account for current nonoperating (financial) liabilities. (p. 426)

LO4 Explain and illustrate the pricing of long-term nonoperating liabilities. (p. 430)

LO5 Analyze and account for financial statement effects of long-term nonoperating liabilities. (p. 433)

LO6 Explain how debt ratings are determined and how they impact the cost of debt. (p. 438)

Verizon Communications

Getty Images

Verizon Communications Inc. began doing business in 2000, when Bell Atlantic Corporation merged with GTE Corporation. Verizon is one of the world's leading providers of communications services. It is the largest provider of wire line and wireless communications in the U.S., and is the largest of the Baby Bells as of 2004 with $68 billion in revenues and $166 billion in assets. Verizon is the third largest long distance carrier for U.S. consumers, and it is the largest directory publisher in the world (Verizon 2004 10-K).

When Ivan Seidenberg became sole CEO of Verizon in mid-2002 (and its chairman in late 2003), the Internet frenzy had cooled and Verizon's stock price had plunged, falling from an all-time high of $70 in late 1999 to $27 in mid-2002. Since then, the stock has rebounded somewhat, but continued to trade below $35 per share in early 2006 and continues to decline.

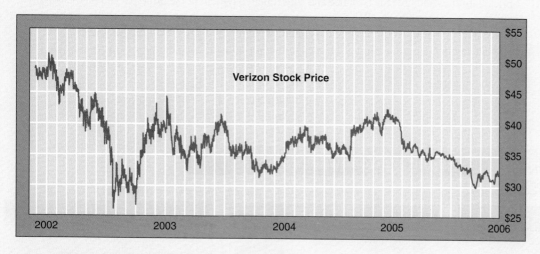

Verizon survived the internet and telecom downturn, but it faces a formidable new challenger: cable. Cable companies spent an estimated $75 billion in recent years upgrading their infrastructure to offer customers discounted bundled packages of local voice, high-speed Internet connections, and video. They could grab a quarter of the local voice market over the next decade as they deploy new voice over Internet protocol (VOIP) technology, estimates John Hodulik, a UBS telecom analyst." (*BusinessWeek* 2004)

(Continued on next page)

(Continued from previous page)

Phone companies have historically drawn their power and profits from both networks of switches and the lines that lead to nearly every home. "Having watched this industry for 35 years," says Bruce Gordon, president of Verizon's retail division, "I don't believe it's a network that will take us into the next decade." (*Business Week* 2003) Further, Verizon's revenue mix has changed in the past few years. Its change in revenue mix is as much due to the declining land-line segment as it is to the rise in newer technologies, as traditional phone service revenues continue to decline.(Verizon 10-K). Despite the enormous investment in physical plant to support this segment of its business, Verizon must now shift its strategic focus to wireless and high-speed connectivity.

Faced with growing competition from cable-TV companies and others, Verizon plans to spend $20 billion to $40 billion over the next decade to build fiber-optic connections to every home and business it serves. *BusinessWeek* says "this means speeds of 5 to 10 megabits per second, up to 20 times faster than today's typical broadband connections . . . that's fast enough to provide voice, video, and digital-TV signals on a single connection to the customer." Verizon is also deploying wireless technology faster than rivals and setting up Wi-Fi hotspots, committing itself to a massive network upgrade.

The demand for new capital spending is coming at an inopportune time for Verizon. Saddled with a debt load of over $45 billion as of 2003, half of which matures over the next five years, Verizon must also provide for the payment of over $4 billion in stock dividends annually plus nearly $17 billion in accumulated employee pensions and health-care costs. Verizon is concerned. Faced with a question from a stockholder why Verizon isn't repurchasing its stock given its decline in value, Seidenberg said "our number-one priority for using free cash flow over the last two years has been reducing debt." (Verizon 2003 10-K)

"'Verizon, like the rest of the industry, is in a tough spot,' says Moody's analyst Dennis Saputo, who has the company's A1 credit rating on review for a possible downgrade. 'They have an increasing business risk with substitution and competition, and they are trying to offset that risk by lowering debt and improving the balance sheet. They're damned if the do and damned if they don't . . . Right now, as competition is increasing, this isn't a good time to be cutting capital investments." (TheStreet.Com 2003)

This chapter focuses on liabilities—that is, short-term and long-term obligations. Liabilities (also called debt) are one of two financing sources for a company. The other is shareholder financing. Bonds and notes are a major part of most companies' liabilities. In this chapter, we show how to price liabilities and how the issuance and subsequent payment of the principal and interest on them affect financial statements. We also discuss the required disclosures that enable us to effectively analyze a company's ability to make its liability payments as they mature.

The actor, James Earl Jones, intones in the Verizon ad, "make progress every day." Verizon is seeking to do just that as it allocates its available cash flow between strategic investment and debt payments.

Sources: *BusinessWeek* 2003; *TheStreet.Com* 2003; *Verizon* 2005, 2004 and 2003 Annual Reports; *Verizon* 2005, 2004 and 2003 10-Ks.

CHAPTER ORGANIZATION

Reporting Nonowner Financing

Short-Term Current Liabilities	Long-Term Liabilities	Interest Concepts and Computations
■ Accounts Payable ■ Accrued Liabilities ■ Short-Term Debt ■ Current Maturities of Long-Term Debt	■ Pricing and Cost of Debt ■ Reporting Debt Financing ■ Debt Ratios and Debt Cost ■ Bond Repurchases	■ Present and Future Values ■ Single Amounts and Annuities

INTRODUCTION

The accounting equation (Assets = Liabilities + Equity) is a useful tool in helping us think about how the balance sheet and income statement are constructed, the linkages between the financial statements, and the effects of transactions on financial statements. The accounting equation is also useful in helping us think about the statements from another perspective, namely, how the business is financed. Consider the following representation of the accounting equation:

$$\text{Assets} = \text{Liabilities} + \text{Equity}$$
$$\text{Uses} = \text{Sources}$$

Assets represent investments (uses of funds) that management has made. They include current operating assets such as cash, accounts receivable, and inventories. They also include long-term operating assets such as manufacturing and administrative facilities. Most companies also invest a portion of funds in nonoperating assets such as treasury bills and money market funds, that provide the liquidity a company needs to conduct transactions and to react to market opportunities and changes.

Just as asset disclosures provide us with information on where a company invests its funds, the disclosures on liabilities and equity inform us as to how those assets are financed. These are the sources of funds. To be successful, a company must not only invest funds wisely, but must also be astute in the manner in which it raises funds.

Companies hope to finance their assets at the lowest possible cost. Current liabilities (such as accounts payable and accrued liabilities) are generally non-interest-bearing. As a result, firms try to maximize the financing of their assets using these sources of funds.

Current liabilities, as the name implies, are short-term in nature, generally requiring payment within the coming year. As a result, they are not a suitable source of funding for long-term assets that generate cash flows over several years. Instead, companies often finance long-term assets with long-term liabilities that require payments over several years. Generally, companies try to link the cash outflows of the financing source with the cash inflows of the asset class to which they relate. As such, long-term financing is usually in the form of bonds, notes, and stock issuances.

When a company acquires assets, and finances them with liabilities, its financial leverage increases. Also, the magnitude of required liability payments increases proportionally with the level of liability financing, and those larger payments imply a higher probability of default should a downturn in business occur. Increasing levels of liabilities, then, make the company riskier to investors who, consequently, demand a higher return on the financing they provide to the company. This assessment of risk is part of liquidity and solvency analysis.

This chapter describes and assesses *on-balance-sheet financing,* namely current and noncurrent liabilities, where the financing effects are reported on financial statements. If companies can find a way to purchase assets and have neither the asset, nor its related financing, appear on the balance sheet, they can report higher levels of income (and asset turnover) and thereby appear less risky. It is this basic idea that has spawned off-balance-sheet financing, which is the focus of Chapter 13.

CURRENT LIABILITIES

Liabilities are separated into current and long-term. Current liabilities are due within 1 year. Long-term liabilities are due beyond 1 year. The focus of this section is on current liabilities. Most current liabilities such as those related to utilities, wages, insurance, rent, and taxes, generate a corresponding impact on selling, general and administrative expenses. **Verizon**'s current liabilities as taken from its balance sheet follows.

At December 31 ($ millions)	2003	2002
Current liabilities		
Debt maturing within one year	$ 5,967	$ 9,267
Accounts payable and accrued liabilities	14,699	12,642
Liabilities of discontinued operations	—	1,007
Other	5,904	5,013
Total current liabilities	$26,570	$27,929

Verizon reports four categories of current liabilities: (1) long-term liability (debt) obligations that are scheduled for payment in the upcoming year, (2) accounts payable and accrued liabilities, (3) current liabilities from discontinued operations (these operations were sold in 2003, hence they are no longer part of Verizon's operations in 2004), and (4) other current liabilities, which consist mainly of customer deposits, dividends declared but not yet paid, and miscellaneous short-term obligation too small to list separately.

Analysis and interpretation of return on net operating assets (RNOA) requires that we separate current liabilities into operating and nonoperating components. These two components primarily consist of:

LO1 Analyze and distinguish between operating liabilities and nonoperating liabilities.

1. Current operating liabilities
    ■ **Accounts payable** Obligations to others for amounts owed on purchases of goods and services. These are usually non-interest-bearing.
    ■ **Accrued liabilities** Obligations for which there is no related external transaction in the current period. These include, for example, accruals for employee wages earned but yet unpaid, accruals for taxes (usually quarterly) on payroll and current period profits, and accruals for other liabilities such as rent, utilities, and insurance. Accruals are made to properly reflect the liabilities owed as of the statement date and the expenses incurred in the period. Each one is journalized by a debit to an expense account and a credit to a related liability.

2. Current nonoperating liabilities
    ■ **Short-term interest-bearing debt** Short-term bank borrowings and notes expected to mature in whole or in part during the upcoming year; including any accrued interest payable on these obligations.
    ■ **Current maturities of long-term debt** Long-term borrowings that are scheduled to mature in whole or in part during the upcoming year including any accrued interest for the period on these obligations.

The remainder of this section describes current *operating* liabilities except for the last section, which discusses current *nonoperating* liabilities.

Accounts Payable

LO2 Identify and account for current operating liabilities.

Accounts payable, which are part of current operating liabilities, arise from the purchase of goods and services from others. Accounts payable are normally non-interest-bearing and, thus, are an inexpensive financing source. Verizon reports $14,699 million in accounts payable and accrued liabilities. Its accounts payable represent $4,130 million, or 28%, of this total amount.

Accounting for a typical purchase of goods on account, which results in accounts payable, and the ultimate sale of those goods follows:

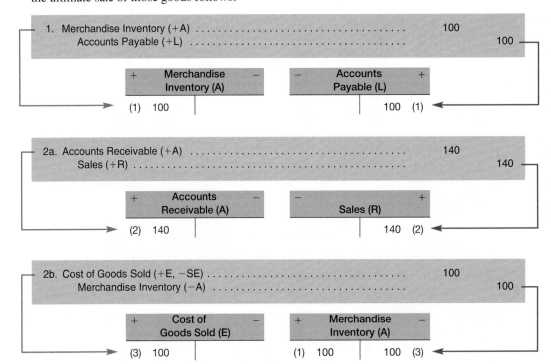

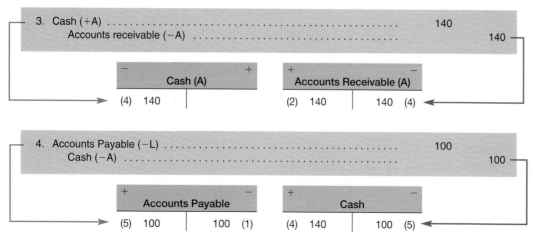

3. Cash (+A) 140
    Accounts receivable (−A) 140

	− Cash (A) +		+ Accounts Receivable (A) −
(4) 140		(2) 140	140 (4)

4. Accounts Payable (−L) 100
    Cash (−A) 100

	+ Accounts Payable −		+ Cash −
(5) 100	100 (1)	(4) 140	100 (5)

Transaction	Balance Sheet					Income Statement		
	Cash Asset	+ Noncash Assets	= Liabil- ities	+ Contrib. Capital	+ Retained Earnings	Revenues	− Expenses	= Net Income
1. Purchase $100 of inventory on credit		+100 Inventory	= +100 Accounts Payable					=
2a. Sale of $100 inventory on credit for $140		+140 Accounts Receivable	=		+140 Retained Earnings	+140 Sales		= +140
2b. Record $100 cost of sales with transaction 2a		−100 Inventory	=		−100 Retained Earnings		−100 Cost of Goods Sold	= −100
3. Cash received from accounts receivable	+140 Cash	−140 Accounts Receivable	=					=
3. Cash paid to settle accounts payable	−100 Cash		= −100 Accounts Payable					=

The journal entries, T-accounts, and financial statement effects template reveal several impacts related to the usual purchase of goods on account and their ultimate sale:

- Purchase of inventory is reflected on the balance sheet as an increase in inventory and an increase in accounts payable.

- Sale of inventory involves two components—revenue and cost. The revenue part reflects the increase in sales revenue and the increase in accounts receivable (revenue is recognized when earned, even though cash is not yet received).

- The cost part of the sales transaction reflects the decrease in inventory and the increase in cost of goods sold (COGS). COGS is reported in the income statement and matched against revenues reported (this expense is recognized because the inventory asset is sold, even though inventory-related payables may not yet be paid).

- Cash payment of accounts payable is solely a balance sheet transaction and does not impact income statement accounts (expense relating to purchase of inventories is recognized when the asset is sold or used up, not when the liability is paid).

- Collection of the receivable reduces accounts receivable and increases cash. It is solely a balance sheet transaction and does not impact income statement accounts.

Accounts payable reflect a source of interest-free financing. Increased payables reduce the amount of net operating working capital, current assets, and current liabilities because these payables are deducted from current operating assets in the computation of net operating working capital. Also, increased payables mean increased cash flow (because increased liabilities increase net cash from operating activities). An increase in accounts payable also increases profitability because it causes a reduction in the level of interest-bearing debt that is required to finance operating assets. RNOA increases when companies make use of this low cost financing source. Our analysis, however, must be aware of excessive 'leaning on the trade' because short-term income gains can yield long-term costs such as damaged supply channels.[1, 2]

MID-CHAPTER REVIEW 1

3M's accounts payable turnover (cost of goods sold/average accounts payable—see Chapter 5 for a discussion) decreased from 10.4 in 2001 to 9.1 in 2003.

a. Does this change indicate that accounts payable have increased or decreased relative to cost of goods sold? Explain.
b. What effect does this change have on 3M's net cash flows from operating activities?
c. What management concerns, if any, might this change in accounts payable turnover pose?

Solution

a. We know that accounts payable turnover is computed as cost of goods sold divided by accounts payable. Thus, a decline in accounts payable turnover indicates that accounts payable have increased relative to cost of goods sold (all else equal).
b. An increase in accounts payable results in an increase in net cash flows from operating activities. This is a case of the company *leaning on the trade*.
c. Increased accounts payable (and accrued liabilities) reduce net operating working capital, with consequent improvement in profitability and cash flow. As a result, the increase in payables is desirable, provided that the company does not damage relations with its suppliers. Analysts must be aware of the potentially damaging consequences of leaning on the trade to a much greater extent than is customary.

Accrued Liabilities

Accrued liabilities are identified at the end of an accounting period to reflect liabilities and expenses that have been incurred during the period but are not yet recognized in financial statements.[3] **Verizon** reports details of its $10,569 million accrued liabilities and its $4,130 million accounts payable in the following footnote to its 10-K report:

December 31 ($ millions)	2003	2002
Accounts payable	$ 4,130	$ 4,851
Accrued expenses	2,995	2,796
Accrued vacation pay	824	960
Accrued salaries and wages	3,376	2,171
Interest payable	633	669
Accrued taxes	2,741	1,195
Total	$14,699	$12,642

Verizon accrues liabilities for the following expenses: miscellaneous accrued expenses, accrued vacation pay, accrued salaries and wages, interest payable, and accrued taxes. These accruals are

---

[1]We must be careful, however, that excessive delays the in payment of payables can result in suppliers charging a higher price for their goods or, ultimately, refusing to sell to certain buyers. This situation is a hidden "financing" cost that, even though it is not interest, is a real cost.

[2]Accounts payable often carry credit terms such as 2/10, net 30. These terms give the buyer, for example, 2% off the invoice price of goods purchased if paid within 10 days. Otherwise the entire invoice is payable within 30 days. By its failure to take a discount, the buyer is effectively paying a 2% interest charge to use its funds for an additional 20 days. Because there are approximately 18 such 20-day periods in a year (365/20), this equates to an annual rate of interest of about 36%. Thus, borrowing funds at less than 36% to pay this liability within the discount period would be cost effective and good management.

[3]Accruals can also be made for recognition of revenue and a corresponding receivable. An example of this might be revenue recognition on a long-term contract that has reached a particular milestone, or for interest earned on an investment in bonds that is still outstanding at period-end.

typical of most companies. The accruals are recognized with a liability on the balance sheet and a corresponding expense on the income statement. This reporting means that liabilities increase, current income decreases, and equity reporting decreases. When an accrued liability is ultimately paid, both cash and the liability are decreased (but no expense is recorded because it was recognized previously).

Accounting for Accruals

Accounting for a typical accrued liability, that of accrued wages, follows:

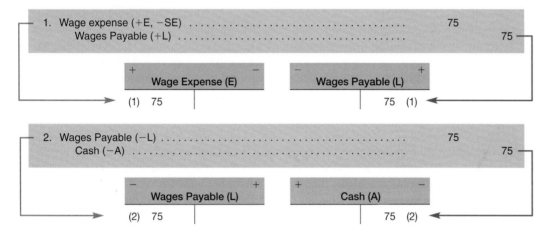

The following financial statement effects result from this accrual of employee wages:

- Employees have worked during a period and have not yet been paid. The effect of this accrual is to increase wages payable on the balance sheet and to recognize wages expense on the income statement. Failure to recognize this liability and associated expense would understate liabilities on the balance sheet and overstate income.

- Employees are paid in the following period, resulting in a cash decrease and a reduction in wages payable. This payment does not result in expense because the expense was recognized in the prior period when incurred.

The accrued wages illustration relates to events that are fairly certain. We know, for example, when wages are incurred but not paid. Other examples of such accruals are rental costs, insurance premiums due but not yet paid, and taxes owed.

Some accrued liabilities, however, are less certain than others. Consider a company facing a lawsuit. Should it record the possible liability and related expense? The answer depends on the likelihood of occurrence and the ability to estimate the obligation. Specifically, if the obligation is *probable* **and** the amount *estimable,* then a company will recognize this obligation, called a **contingent liability**. If an obligation is only *reasonably possible,* regardless of the company's ability to estimate the amount, the contingent liability is not reported on the balance sheet and is merely disclosed in the footnotes. All other contingent liabilities that are less than reasonably possible are not accrued although disclosure in a note is permitted but not required.

All accrued liabilities result in a liability on the balance sheet and an expense on the income statement. Management has some latitude in determining the amount and timing for accruals. This latitude can lead to misreporting of income and liabilities (unintentional or otherwise). For example, if accruals are underestimated, then liabilities are underestimated, income is overestimated, and

You are the Analyst   The FCM Corporation recognized accrued environmental liabilities in excess of $170 million in 2003. What conditions needed to be met before these liabilities could be reported? The company also indicated in a footnote that, if only the range could be estimated but with no single value in the range being more likely, only the lower bound on the range would be reported. Why would the firm report this way? Would you consider FCM's reporting to be conservative? Explain.

  Merck currently faces potential law suits related to its arthritis drug Vioxx that analysts estimate could potentially amount to $50 billion. The firm has already lost one case at trial, currently on appeal. Consistent with the reporting practice of other firms, Merck is unlikely to accrue a liability for these claims while they are still being litigated. Why is this reporting used? How would you as an analyst compensate for this reporting? [Answers on page 444]

retained earnings are overestimated. In subsequent periods when an understated accrued liability is reversed (it is recognized in the account), reported income is lower than it should be; this is because prior period income was higher than it should have been. (The reverse holds for overestimated accruals.) The over and under reporting of accruals, therefore, results in the shifting of income from one period into another. We must be keenly aware of this potential for income shifting as we analyze the financial condition of a company.

  Experience tells us that accrued liabilities that are linked with restructuring programs[4] (including severance accruals and accruals for asset write-downs), with the estimation of legal and environmental liabilities, and with business acquisitions are too often problematic. Namely, these accruals too often represent early (aggressive) recognition of expenses, leading to an understatement of income, in a desire to relieve future periods of these expenses. The reduction in income due to the overestimation of expenses allows for income to increase in future years when the management decides that the accrual can be reversed because it was too large initially. This behavior can occur, for example, under a new management that wants to show earnings growth in the future, or under current management when an unexpected increase in earnings can be pushed into a future year when it is needed by overestimating the current accruals. The terms "clearing the decks" and "taking a big bath" have both been applied to such accounting shenanigans. An example of the journal entry in an acquisition that would create such an accrued liability is;

Reorganization expense (+E, −SE)	***	
Accrued liabilities (+L)		***

This liability could be aggregated with other accrued liabilities requiring us to diligently peruse the footnotes to discern its individual amount. In future years, some or all of the accrued liability could be reversed, increasing income for the new period. Accrued liabilities set up to smooth income over future periods are called "**cookie jar reserves**." The name is rightly deserved. Accordingly, we must monitor any change or unusual activity with accrued liabilities.

Estimating Accruals

Several accrued liabilities require estimates of their amounts. Warranty liabilities are an important example. Warranties are commitments made by manufacturers to their customers to repair or replace defective products within a specified period of time. The expected cost of this commitment usually is reasonably estimated at the time of sale based on past experience. As a result, GAAP requires manufacturers to record the expected cost of warranties as a liability, and to record the related expected warranty expense in the income statement to match against the sales revenue reported for that period.

---

[4]Restructuring charges often occur when one company acquires another. Such acquisitions often involve estimating expenses for laying off workers, and realigning sales organizations and territories, and moving equipment among other future cash outlays. These expenses need to be accrued to accurately reflect the company's current financial situation.

To illustrate, the effects of an accrual of a $1,000 warranty liability are as follows:

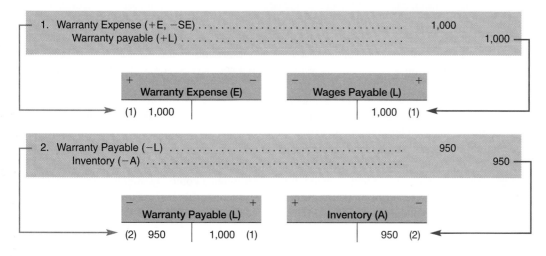

	Balance Sheet					Income Statement		
Transaction	Cash Asset	+ Noncash Assets	= Liabil- ities	+ Contrib. Capital	+ Retained Earnings	Revenues	− Expenses	= Net Income
1. Accrue $1,000 of expected warranty costs on goods sold this period			= +1,000 Warranty Payable		−1,000 Retained Earnings		−1,000 Warranty Expense	= −1,000
2. Next period's costs (sent $950 in replacement products) to cover failures under warranty		−950 Inventory	= −950 Warranty Payable					=

Reporting of warranty liabilities has the same effect on financial statements as does the accrual of wages expense in the previous section. That is, a liability is recorded on the balance sheet and an expense is reported in the income statement, reducing income by the warranty accrual. When the defective product is later replaced (or repaired), the liability is reduced together with the cost of the inventory (or other assets) spent to satisfy the claim. (Only a portion of the products estimated to fail does so in the current period; we expect other product failures in future periods. Management monitors this estimate and adjusts it if failure is higher or lower than expected.) As in the accrual of wages, the expense is reported when it is incurred and the liability is estimated at that time, not when payments are made.

Ford Motor Company reports $5,443 million of warranty liability on its 2003 balance sheet. Its footnotes reveal the following additional information:

> **Product Performance, Warranty**—Estimated warranty costs and additional service actions are accrued for at the time the vehicle is sold to a dealer. Included in the warranty cost accruals are costs for basic warranty coverage's on vehicles sold. Estimates for warranty costs are made based primarily on historical warranty claim experience. The following is a tabular reconciliation of the product warranty accrual (in millions):

Product Warranty Liability	2003	2002
Beginning balance	$ 5,401	$ 4,739
Payments made during the year	(3,524)	(3,508)
Changes in accrual related to warranties issued during the year	3,562	3,489
Changes in accrual related to pre-existing warranties	(266)	595
Foreign currency translation and other	270	86
Ending balance	$ 5,443	$ 5,401

Of the $5,401 million balance at the beginning of 2003, $3,524 million in cost was incurred to replace or repair defective products during the year, reducing the liability by this amount. This cost can be in the form of cash paid to customers or to employees as wages, and in the form of parts used for repairs. Ford accrued an additional $3,562 million in new warranty liabilities in 2003 and recorded additional minor adjustments amounting to a net increase in the liability of $4 million ($270 million − $266 million). It is important to realize that only the increase in the liability resulting from additional accruals impacts the income statement (like the provision for uncollectible accounts receivable), reducing income through the additional warranty expense. Payments per the warranty obligation reduce the preexisting liability.

GAAP requires that the warranty liability reflect the estimated amount of cost that the company expects to incur as a result of warranty claims. This amount is often a difficult estimate to make and is prone to error. There is also the possibility that a company might underestimate its warranty liability to report higher current income, or overestimate it so as to depress current income and create an additional liability on the balance sheet (*cookie jar reserve*) that can be used to absorb future warranty costs without the need to record additional expense. Doing so would shift income from the current period to one or more future periods. Warranty liabilities must, therefore, be examined closely and compared with sales levels. Any deviations from the historical relation of the warranty liability to sales, or that reported by competitors, should be investigated.

MID-CHAPTER REVIEW 2

Hayn Company's employees worked during the current month and earned $10,000 in wages, which are not paid until the first of next month. Must Hayn recognize any wages liability and expense for the current month? Explain with reference to journal entries, t-accounts, and the financial statement effects template.

Solution

Yes. Liabilities and expenses must be recognized when incurred, regardless of when payment is made, and matched with the revenues they helped generate. Failure to recognize the wages owed and wages expense to employees for the period would understate liabilities and overstate income. Hayn must reflect the wages earned and the related expense in its financial statements as follows:

The appropriate journal entry would be:

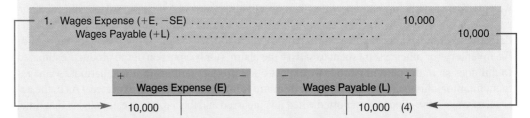

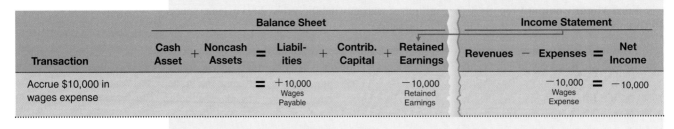

	Balance Sheet						Income Statement		
Transaction	Cash Asset	+ Noncash Assets	= Liabil- ities	+ Contrib. Capital	+ Retained Earnings		Revenues −	Expenses =	Net Income
Accrue $10,000 in wages expense			= +10,000 Wages Payable		−10,000 Retained Earnings			−10,000 Wages Expense =	−10,000

Current Nonoperating (Financial) Liabilities

LO3 Describe and account for current nonoperating (financial) liabilities.

Current nonoperating (financial) liabilities include short-term bank loans, the accrual of interest on those loans, and the current maturities of long-term debt. Companies generally try to structure their financing so that debt service requirements (payments) of those financing obligations coincide with the cash inflows from the assets financed. This strategy means that current assets are usually financed with current liabilities, and that long-term assets are financed with long-term liabilities (and equity) sources.

To illustrate, a seasonal company's investment in current assets tends to fluctuate during the year as depicted in the graphic below:

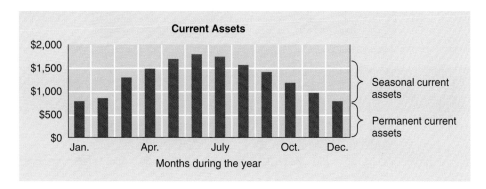

This particular company does most of its selling in the summer months. More inventory is purchased and manufactured in the early spring than at any other time of the year. Sales of the company's manufactured goods are also greater during the summer months, giving rise to accounts receivable that are higher than normal during the fall. The peak working capital level is reached at the height of the selling season and is lowest when the business slows in the off-season. There is a permanent level of working capital required for this business (about $750), and a seasonal component (maximum of about $1,000). Different businesses exhibit different patterns in their working capital requirements, but many have permanent and seasonal components.

The existence of permanent and seasonal current operating assets often requires financing sources for liabilities that consist of permanent and seasonal components. Again, let's assume the company exhibits current asset levels according to the graphic above. Because a portion of these assets is invested in inventories that are financed, in part, with accounts payable and accruals, we expect there is a relatively permanent level of current operating liabilities that also exhibit a seasonal component that fluctuates with the level of operations. These payables are generally non-interest-bearing and, thus, provide low-cost financing that should be used to the greatest extent possible. Additional financing needs are covered by short-term interest- bearing debt.

This section focuses on current nonoperating liabilities, which include short-term debt (and its interest) and any current maturities of long-term liabilities. These liabilities create interest expenses.

Short-Term Interest-Bearing Debt

Seasonal swings in working capital are often financed with a bank line of credit (short-term debt). In this case the bank provides a commitment to lend up to a given level with the understanding that the amounts borrowed are repaid in full sometime during the year. An interest-bearing note is evidence of such borrowing.

When these short-term funds are borrowed, the cash received is reported on the balance sheet together with an increase in liabilities (notes payable). The note is reported as a current liability because the expectation is that it will be paid within a year. This borrowing has no effect on income or equity. The borrower incurs (and the lender earns) interest on the note as time passes. GAAP requires the borrower to accrue the interest liability and the related interest expense each time financial statements are issued.

To illustrate, assume that Verizon borrows $1,000 cash from 1st Bank on January 1. The note bears interest at a 12% annual (3% quarterly) rate, and the interest is payable on the first of each subsequent quarter (April 1, July 1, October 1, January 1). Assuming that Verizon issues calendar-quarter financial statements, this borrowing results in the following financial statement effects for the period January 1 through April 1:

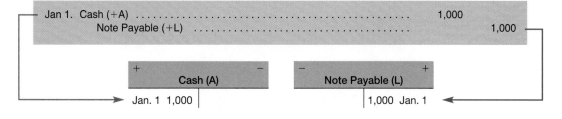

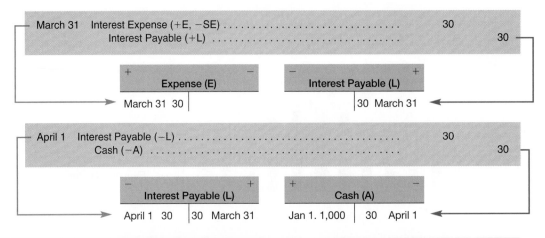

Transaction	Balance Sheet						Income Statement		
	Cash Asset	+ Noncash Assets	= Liabil- ities	+ Contrib. Capital	+ Retained Earnings		Revenues	− Expenses	= Net Income
(1) Jan 1, Borrowed $1,000 cash by issuing note payable	+1,000 Cash		= +1,000 Note Payable						=
(2) Mar 31, Interest accrues on 12% note payable			= +30 Interest Payable		−30 Retained Earnings			−30 Interest Expense	= −30
(3) Apr 1, Cash paid to cover interest due	−30 Cash		= −30 Interest Payable						=

The January 1 borrowing is reflected by an increase in cash and notes payable. On March 31, this company issues its quarterly financial statements. Although interest is not paid until April 1, the company has incurred three months' interest obligation as of March 31. Failure to recognize this liability and the expense incurred would not fairly present the financial condition of the company. Accordingly, the quarterly accrued interest is computed as follows:

$$\text{Interest Expense} = \text{Principal} \times \text{Annual Rate} \times \text{Portion of Year Outstanding}$$
$$\$30 = \$1,000 \times 12\% \times 3/12$$

The subsequent interest payment on April 1 is reflected in the financial statements as a reduction of cash and a reduction of the interest payable liability accrued on March 31. There is no expense reported on April 1, because it was recorded the previous day (March 31) when the financial statements were prepared. (For fixed-maturity borrowings specified in days, such as a 90-day note, we use a 365-day year for interest accrual computations, see Mid-Chapter Review 3 below.)

Current Maturities of Long-Term Debt

Payments that must be made during the upcoming 12 months on long-term debt (such as for a mortgage) or the maturity of a bond or note are reported as current liabilities called *current maturities of long-term debt*. All companies are required to provide a schedule of the maturities of its long-term debt in the footnotes to financial statements. To illustrate, the current liability section from the balance sheet of **Verizon** follows. Verizon reports $5,967 million in long-term debt due within one year.

December 31 ($ millions)	2003
Current liabilities	
Debt maturing within one year	$ 5,967
Accounts payable and accrued liabilities	14,699
Liabilities of discontinued operations	—
Other	5,904
Total current liabilities	$26,570

MID-CHAPTER REVIEW 3

Gigler Company borrowed $10,000 on a 90-day, 6% note payable dated January 15. The bank accrues interest daily based on a 365-day year. Use journal entries, t-accounts, and the financial statement effects template to show the implications (amounts and accounts) of the January 31 month-end interest accrual.

Solution
The related journal entry to recognize the accrual of interest is:

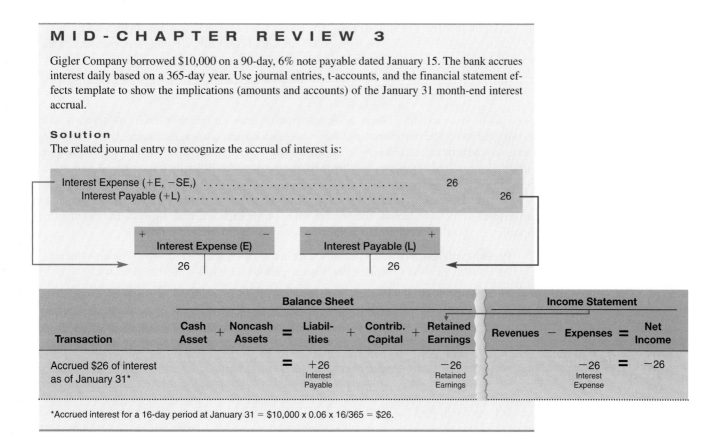

	Balance Sheet					Income Statement		
Transaction	Cash Asset	+ Noncash Assets	= Liabil-ities	+ Contrib. Capital	+ Retained Earnings	Revenues	− Expenses	= Net Income
Accrued $26 of interest as of January 31*			= +26 Interest Payable		−26 Retained Earnings		−26 Interest Expense	= −26

*Accrued interest for a 16-day period at January 31 = $10,000 x 0.06 x 16/365 = $26.

LONG-TERM LIABILITIES

Companies usually require some long-term liabilities in their capital structure to fund their long-term assets. Long-term liabilities of smaller amounts can be readily obtained from banks, private placements with insurance companies, and other credit sources. However, when a large amount of financing is required, the issuance of bonds (and notes) in capital markets is a cost-efficient way to raise capital. The following discussion uses bonds for illustration, but much of it is readily applied to notes. Long-term financing can also be obtained by issuing stock. We discuss this possibility in the next chapter. We will find that stock is less risky to the company, but more risky to those who hold the stock.

Bonds and notes are structured like any other borrowing. The borrower receives cash and agrees to pay it back with interest. Generally, the entire **face amount** (principal) of the bond or note is repaid at maturity and interest payments are made (usually semiannually) in the interim.

Companies wishing to raise funds in the bond market normally work with an underwriter (e.g., **Merrill Lynch**) to set the terms of the bond issue. The underwriter sells individual bonds (usually in $1,000 denominations) from this general bond issue to its retail clients and professional portfolio managers (e.g., **The Vanguard Group**), and it receives a fee for underwriting the bond issue. These bonds often become investments for retirement plans and insurance companies.

Once sold, the bonds can be traded in the secondary market between investors just like stocks. Market prices of bonds fluctuate daily despite the fact that the company's obligation for payment of principal and interest normally remains fixed throughout the life of the bond. This occurs because bonds compete with other possible investments, and become more or less desirable depending on the general level of interest rates offered by competing securities and the financial condition of the borrowing company.

The following section analyzes and interprets the reporting for bonds. We first examine the mechanics of bond pricing. In a subsequent section, we address the accounting for and reporting of bonds.

Pricing of Debt

Two different interest rates are crucial for understanding how the debt is priced.

LO4 Explain and illustrate the pricing of long-term nonoperating liabilities.

■ **Coupon (contract** or **stated) rate** The coupon rate of interest is stated in the bond contract. It is used to compute the dollar amount of (semiannual) interest payments that are paid to bondholders during the life of the bond issue.

■ **Market (yield) rate** The market rate is the interest rate that investors expect to earn on the investment for this debt security. This rate is used to price the bond issue.

The coupon (contract) rate is used to compute interest payments and the market (yield) rate is used to price the bond. The coupon rate and the market rate are nearly always different. This result is because the coupon rate is fixed prior to issuance of the bond and normally remains so throughout its life. Market rates of interest, on the other hand, fluctuate continually with the supply and demand for bonds in the market place, general macroeconomic conditions, and the financial condition of borrowers.

The bond price, both its initial sales price and the price it trades at in the secondary market subsequent to issuance, equals the present value of the expected cash flows to the bondholder. Specifically, bondholders normally expect to receive two different cash flows:

1. **Periodic interest payments** (usually semiannual) during the bond's life. These payments are often in the form of equal cash flows at periodic intervals, called an **annuity**.

2. **Single payment** of the face (principal) amount of the bond at maturity.

The bond price equals the present value of the periodic interest payments plus the present value of the principal payment at maturity. We next illustrate the purchase of bonds at three different prices: at par, at a discount, and at a premium.

Bonds Issued at Par

When a bond is issued at par, its coupon rate is identical to the market rate. Under this condition, a $1,000 bond sells for $1,000 in the market. To illustrate bond pricing, assume that investors wish to value a bond with a face amount of $10 million, a 6% annual coupon rate with interest payable semiannually (3% semiannual rate), and a maturity of 10 years.[5] Investors purchasing this issue receive the following cash flows:

	Number of Payments	Dollars per Payment	Total Cash Flows
Semiannual interest payments	10 years × 2 = 20	$10,000,000 × 3% = $ 300,000	$ 6,000,000
Principal payment at maturity	1	$10,000,000	10,000,000
			$16,000,000

Specifically, the bond agreement dictates that the borrower makes 20 semiannual payments of $300,000 each, computed as $10,000,000 × (6%/2), plus the $10,000,000 face amount at maturity, for a total of $16 million in cash flows. (When pricing bonds, identify the *number* of interest payments and use that number when computing the present value of both the interest payments and the principal (face) payment at maturity.)

The bond price is the present value of the interest annuity plus the present value of the principal payment. Assuming that investors desire a 6% annual market rate (yield), the bond sells for $10,000,000 million, which is computed as follows:

	Payment	Present Value Factor[a]	Present Value
Interest	$ 300,000	14.87747[b]	$ 4,463,200[d]
Principal	$10,000,000	0.55368[c]	5,536,800
			$10,000,000

[a]Mechanics of using tables to compute present values are explained in Appendix 10A at the end of this chapter. Present value factors are taken from Appendix A near the end of the book.
[b]Present value of ordinary annuity for 20 periods discounted at 3% per period.
[c]Present value of single payment in 20 periods hence discounted at 3% per period.
[d]Rounded.

---

[5]Semiannual interest payments are typical for bonds. With semiannual interest payments, the issuer pays bondholders two interest payments per year. In this case, the semiannual interest rate is the annual rate divided by two.

Because the bond contract pays investors a 6% annual rate when investors demand a 6% market rate given the bond's (company's) credit rating and term, investors purchase these bonds at the **par (face) value** of $1,000 per bond, ($10 million in total).

Discount Bonds

As a second illustration, assume that the company's risk characteristics are such that investors demand an 8% annual yield (4% semiannual) for the 6% coupon bond, while all other details remain the same. The bond now sells for $8,640,999, computed as follows:

	Payment	Present Value Factor	Present Value
Interest	$ 300,000	13.59033[a]	$ 4,077,099
Principal	$10,000,000	0.45639[b]	4,563,900
			$ 8,640,999

[a]Present value of ordinary annuity for 20 periods discounted at 4% per period.
[b]Present value of single payment in 20 periods hence discounted at 4% per period.

Since the bond carries a coupon rate *lower* than that which investors demand, the bond is less desirable and sells at a **discount**. More generally, bonds sell at a discount whenever the coupon rate is less than the market rate.[6]

Premium Bonds

As a third illustration, assume that investors demand a 4% annual yield (2% semiannual) for the 6% coupon bonds, while all other details remain the same. The bond now sells for $11,635,129, computed as follows:

	Payment	Present Value Factor	Present Value
Interest	$ 300,000	16.35143[a]	$ 4,905,429
Principal	$10,000,000	0.67297[b]	6,729,700
			$11,635,129

[a]Present value of ordinary annuity for 20 periods discounted at 2% per period.
[b]Present value of single payment in 20 periods hence discounted at 2% per period.

Since the bond carries a coupon rate higher than that which investors demand, the bond is more desirable and sells at a **premium.** More generally, bonds sell at a premium whenever the coupon rate is greater than the market rate. Exhibit 10.1 summarizes this relation for bond pricing.

EXHIBIT 10.1	Coupon Rate, Market Rate, and Bond Pricing
Coupon rate > market rate →	Bond sells at a **premium** (above face amount)
Coupon rate = market rate →	Bond sells at **par** (at face amount)
Coupon rate < market rate →	Bond sells at a **discount** (below face amount)

Exhibit 10.2 shows an announcement (called a *tombstone*) of the recent General Electric $5 billion debt issuance. It is 5% debt, paying 2.5% semiannual interest, maturing in 2013, with an issue price of 99.626 (valued at a discount). GE's underwriters took 0.425 in fees (more than $21 million) for underwriting and selling this debt issue.[7]

Effective Cost of Debt

When a bond sells for par, the cost to the issuing company is the cash interest paid. In our first illustration where the bond was issued at par, the *effective cost* of the bond is the 6% interest paid by the issuer.

---

[6]Bond prices are often stated in percent form. For example, a bond sold at par is said to be sold at 100 (that is, 100% of par). The bond sold at $8,640,999 is said to be sold at 86.41 (86.41% of par, computed as $8,640,999/$10,000,000).

[7]The tombstone makes clear that if we purchase any of these notes (in denominations of $1,000) after the semiannual interest date, we must pay accrued interest in addition to the purchase price. This interest is returned to us in the regular interest payment. (This procedure makes the bookkeeping easier for the issuer/underwriter.)

EXHIBIT 10.2 Announcement (Tombstone) of Debt Offering to Public

General Electric Company

$5,000,000,000
5% Notes due 2013

Issue price: 99.626%

We will pay interest on the notes semiannually on February 1 and August 1 of each year, beginning August 1, 2003. The notes will mature on February 1, 2013. We may not redeem the notes prior to maturity.

The notes will be unsecured obligations and rank equally with our other unsecured debt securities that are not subordinated obligations. The notes will be issued in registered form in denominations of $1,000.

Neither the Securities and Exchange Commission nor any state securities commission has approved or disapproved of the notes or determined if this prospectus supplement or the accompanying prospectus is truthful or complete. Any representation to the contrary is a criminal offense.

	Per Note	Total
Public Offering Price(1)	99.626%	$4,981,300,000
Underwriting Discounts	.425%	$ 21,250,000
Proceeds to General Electric Company (before expenses)	99.201%	$4,960,050,000

(1) Plus accrued interest from January 28, 2003, if settlement occurs after that date.

The underwriters expect to deliver the notes in book-entry form only through the facilities of The Depository Trust Company, Clearstream, Luxembourg or the Euroclear System, as the case may be, on or about January 28, 2003.

Joint Bookrunners

Lehman Brothers	**Morgan Stanley**	**Salomon Smith Barney**

Senior Co-Managers

Banc of America Securities LLC	Credit Suisse First Boston	Deutsche Bank Securities
Goldman. Sachs & Co.	JPMorgan	Merrill Lynch & Co.
	UBS Warburg	

Co-Managers

Banc One Capital Markets, Inc.	Barclays Capital	Blaylock & Partners, L.P.
BNP PARIBAN	Dresdner Kleinwort Wasserstein	Guzman & Company
HSBC	Loop Capital Markets	Ormes Capital Markets, Inc.
Utendahl Capital Partners, L.P.	The Williams Capital Group, L.P.	

When a bond sells at a discount, the issuer's effective cost consists of two parts: (1) the cash interest paid and (2) the discount incurred. The discount, which is the difference between par and the lower issue price, is a cost that must eventually be reflected in the issuer's income statement as an expense. This fact means that the effective cost of a discount bond is greater than if the bond had sold at par. A discount is a cost and, like any other cost, must eventually be transferred from the balance sheet to the income statement as an expense.

When a bond sells at a premium, the issuer's effective cost consists of (1) the cash interest paid and (2) a cost reduction due to the premium received. The premium is a benefit that must eventually find its way from the balance sheet to the income statement as a *reduction* of interest expense. As a result of the premium, the effective cost of a premium bond is less than if the bond had sold at par.

Bonds are priced to yield the return (market rate) demanded by investors, which results in the effective rate of a bond *always* equaling the yield (market) rate demanded by investors, regardless of the coupon (stated) rate of the bond. Bond prices are set by the market so as to always yield the rate demanded by investors based on the terms and qualities of the bond. Companies cannot influence the effective cost of debt by raising or lowering the coupon rate. We discuss the factors affecting the yield demanded by investors later in the chapter.

The effective cost of debt is ultimately reflected in the amount reported in the issuer's income statement as interest expense. This amount can be, and usually is, different from the cash interest paid. The two are the same only for a bond issued at par. The next section discusses how management reports bonds on the balance sheet and interest expense on the income statement.

REPORTING OF DEBT FINANCING

This section identifies and describes the financial statements effects of bond transactions.

LO5 Analyze and account for financial statement effects of long-term nonoperating liabilities.

Financial Statement Effects of Debt Issuance

Bonds Issued at Par

When a bond sells at par, the issuing company receives the cash proceeds and accepts an obligation to make payments per the bond contract. Specifically, cash is increased and a liability (bonds payable) is increased by the same amount. Using the facts from our earlier illustration, the issuance of bonds at par has the following financial statement effects (there is no revenue or expense at bond issuance):

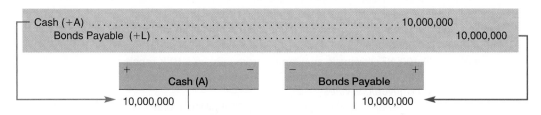

Transaction	Balance Sheet							Income Statement		
	Cash Asset	+	Noncash Assets	=	Liabil- ities	+	Contrib. Capital	+	Retained Earnings	Revenues − Expenses = Net Income
Issue bonds at par for cash	+10,000,000 Cash			=	+10,000,000 Bond Payable, Net					=

Discount Bonds

When a bond is sold at a discount, the cash proceeds and net bond liability are recorded at the amount of the proceeds received (not the face amount of the bond). Again, using the facts above from our bond discount illustration, the financial statement effects follow:

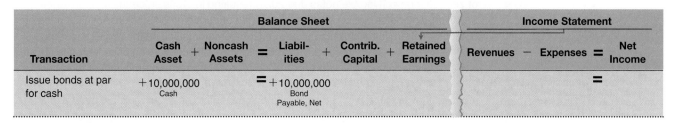

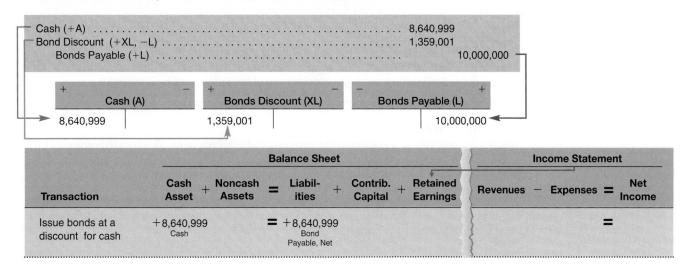

Transaction	Balance Sheet							Income Statement		
	Cash Asset	+	Noncash Assets	=	Liabil- ities	+	Contrib. Capital	+	Retained Earnings	Revenues − Expenses = Net Income
Issue bonds at a discount for cash	+8,640,999 Cash			=	+8,640,999 Bond Payable, Net					=

For the discount bond case, cash is increased by the proceeds from the sale of the bonds, and the liability increases by the same amount. However, the net liability consisting of the two components shown below is reported on the balance sheet.

Bonds payable, face	$10,000,000
Less bond discount	(1,359,001)
Bonds payable, net	$ 8,640,999

Bonds are reported on the balance sheet net of any discount (or plus any premium). When the bond matures, however, the company is obligated to repay $10 million. Accordingly, at maturity, the bond liability must read $10 million, the amount that is owed. Therefore, between the bond issuance and its maturity, the discount must decline to zero. This reduction of the discount over the life of the bond is called **amortization.** The next section shows how discount amortization results in additional interest expense in the income statement. This amortization causes the effective interest expense to be greater than the periodic cash interest payments based on the coupon rate.

BUSINESS INSIGHT

Verizon's Zero Coupon Debt   Zero coupon bonds and notes, called *zeros,* do not carry a coupon rate. However, the pricing of these bonds and notes is done in the same manner as those with coupon rates—the exception is the absence of an interest annuity. This means that the price is the present value of just the principal payment at maturity; hence the bond is sold at a *deep discount.* (For example, in the case of the 6% bond, suppose there is no coupon rate, and hence no interest payments. The only payment would be the return of principal 10 years away. We already know that the present value of this single payment is $4,563,900. The bond would be a "zero" and sell for $4,563,900 resulting in a substantial discount of $5,436,100.) Following is an example from Verizon's 10-K report:

Zero-Coupon Convertible Notes
In May 2001, Verizon . . . issued approximately $5.4 billion in principal amount at maturity of zero-coupon convertible notes due 2021, resulting in gross proceeds of approximately $3 billion. The notes are convertible into shares of our common stock at an initial price of $69.50 per share if the closing price of Verizon common stock on the NYSE exceeds specified levels or in other specified circumstances. The conversion price increases by at least 3% a year. The initial conversion price represents a 25% premium over the May 8, 2001 closing price of $55.60 per share. There are no scheduled cash interest payments associated with the notes. The zero-coupon convertible notes are callable by Verizon . . . on or after May 15, 2006. In addition, the notes are redeemable at the option of the holders on May 15th in each of the years 2004, 2006, 2011 and 2016. As of December 31, 2003, the zero-coupon notes were classified as long-term debt maturing within one year since they are redeemable on May 15, 2004.

Verizon's zero-coupon convertible notes have a maturity value of $5.4 billion and mature in 2021. No interest is paid in the interim. The notes were sold for $3 billion. The difference between the $3 billion sales proceeds and the $5.4 billion maturity value represents Verizon's interest costs, which is the return to the investor. The effective cost of the debt is the interest rate that equates the issue price and maturity value, or approximately 3%. These notes are also convertible—an increasingly popular form of debt discussed in Chapter 11.

Premium Bonds

When a bond is sold at a premium, the cash proceeds and net bond liability are recorded at the amount of the proceeds received (not the face amount of the bond). Again, using the facts above from our premium bond illustration, the financial statement effects follow:

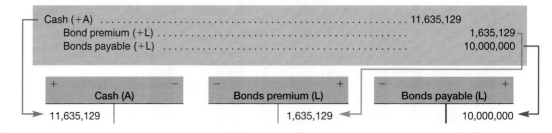

	Balance Sheet						Income Statement		
Transaction	Cash Asset	+ Noncash Assets	= Liabil- ities	+ Contrib. Capital	+ Retained Earnings		Revenues	− Expenses =	Net Income
Issue bonds at a premium for cash	+11,635,129 Cash		= +11,635,129 Bond Payable, net						=

The net bond liability amount reported on the balance sheet, again, consists of two parts:

Bonds payable, face	$10,000,000
Add bond premium	1,635,129
Bonds payable, net	$11,635,129

The $10 million must be repaid at maturity, and the premium is amortized to zero over the life of the bond. The premium represents a *benefit,* which yields a *reduction* in interest expense on the income statement.

Effects of Discount and Premium Amortization

For bonds issued at par, interest expense reported on the income statement equals the cash interest payment. However, for bonds issued at a discount or premium, interest expense reported on the income statement consists of one of the following two components:

Cash interest paid		Cash interest paid
+ Amortization of discount	or	− Amortization of premium
Interest expense		Interest expense

Specifically, periodic amortization of a discount is added to the cash interest paid to get interest expense for a discount bond. Amortization of the discount reflects the additional cost the issuer incurs from issuance of the bonds at a discount and its recognition, via amortization, as an increase to interest expense. For a premium bond, the premium is a benefit the issuer receives at issuance. Amortization of the premium reduces interest expense over the debt term. In both cases, interest expense on the income statement represents the *effective cost* of debt (the *nominal cost* of debt is the cash interest paid).

Companies amortize discounts and premiums using the effective interest method. To illustrate, recall the assumptions of the discount bond above-face amount of $10 million, a 6% annual coupon rate payable semiannually (3% semiannual rate), a maturity of 10 years, and a market (yield) rate of 8% annual (4% semiannual). These facts resulted in a bond issue price of $8,640,999. Exhibit 10.3 shows the first two and final two periods of a bond discount amortization table for this bond.

EXHIBIT 10.3	Bond Discount Amortization Table				
	[A] ([E] × market%) Interest Expense	[B] (Face × coupon%) Cash Interest Paid	[C] ([A] − [B]) Discount Amortization	[D] (Prior bal − [C]) Discount Balance	[E] (Face − [D]) Bond Payable Net
Period					
0				$1,359,001	$ 8,640,999
1	$345,640	$300,000	$45,640	1,313,361	8,686,639
2	347,466	300,000	47,466	1,265,895	8,734,105
⋮	⋮	⋮	⋮	⋮	⋮
19	392,458	300,000	92,458	96,087	9,902,188
20	396,088	300,000	96,088	0	10,000,000

The interest period is denoted in the left-most column. Period 0 is the point at which the bond is issued, and period 1 and following are successive six-month periods (recall, interest is paid semi-annually). Column [A] is interest expense, which is reported in the income statement. This col-umn is computed as the carrying amount of the bond at the beginning of the period (column [E]) multiplied by the 8% yield rate (4% semiannual) used to compute the bond issue price. Column [B] is cash interest paid, which is a constant $300,000 per the bond contract (face amount × coupon rate). Column [C] is discount amortization, which is the difference between interest expense and cash interest paid. Column [D] is the discount balance, which is the previous balance of the discount less the discount amortization in column [C]. Column [E] is the net bond payable, which is the $10 million face amount less the unamortized discount from column [D].

Amounts for interest periods 0, 1, 2, 19, and 20 are shown in the table. The amortization process continues until period 20, at which time the discount balance is 0 and the net bond payable is $10 million (the maturity value). An amortization table reveals the financial statement effects of the bond for its duration.[8] Specifically, we see the income statement effects in column [A], the cash effects in column [B], and the balance sheet effects in columns [C], [D] and [E].

To illustrate amortization of a premium bond, we use the assumptions of the premium bond above-$10 million face value, a 6% annual coupon rate payable semiannually (3% semiannual rate), a maturity of 10 years, and a 4% annual market (yield) rate (2% semiannual). These parameters resulted in a bond issue price of $11,635,129. Exhibit 10.4 shows the first and last two periods of a bond premium amortization table for this bond.

EXHIBIT 10.4	Bond Premium Amortization Table				
	[A] *([E] × market%)* **Interest** **Expense**	**[B]** *(Face × coupon%)* **Cash** **Interest Paid**	**[C]** *([A] − [B])* **Premium** **Amortization**	**[D]** *(Prior bal − [C])* **Premium** **Balance**	**[E]** *(Face − [D])* **Bond** **Payable Net**
Period					
0				$1,635,129	$11,635,129
1	$232,703	$300,000	$67,297	1,567,832	11,567,832
2	231,357	300,000	68,643	1,499,188	11,499,188
⋮	⋮	⋮	⋮	⋮	⋮
19	203,883	300,000	96,117	98,018	10,099,068
20	201,981	300,000	98,018	0	10,000,000

Interest expense is computed using the same process that we used for discount bonds. The difference is that the yield rate is 4% (2% semiannual) in the premium case. Also, cash interest paid follows from the bond contract (face amount 3 coupon rate), and the other columns' computations reflect the premium amortization. After period 20, the premium is fully amortized (equals zero) and the net bond payable balance is $10 million, the amount owed at maturity. Again, an amortization table reveals the financial statement effects of the bond—the income statement effects in column [A], the cash effects in column [B], and the balance sheet effects in columns [C], [D] and [E].

> ## BUSINESS INSIGHT
>
> **A Simpler Approach**   General Accepted Accounting Principles allow a simpler approach when the difference in the resulting interest cost is not material. The approach allows the discount or premium to be amortized using the straight-line method over the life of the bond. In the case of the 6% percent bond that we have been discussing, the discount amortized each six-month period would be $67,950 ($1,359,001/20 periods). Interest would increase by $67,950 each six-month period from $300,000 to $367,950. In the premium case, the amortization each interest period, would be $81,756 ($1,635,129/20), causing interest expense to be reduced by $81,756 each six-month period, from $300,000 to $218,244. The straight line method should not be used in the case of deep discount bonds, the zero coupon bond being one example.

Financial Statement Effects of Bond Repurchase

Companies report bonds payable at *historical (adjusted) cost.* Specifically, net bonds payable amounts follow from the amortization table, as do the related cash flows and income statement

---

[8]A fully completed amortization table is shown in Appendix 10B for illustrative purposes.

numbers. All financial statement relations are established at the time the bonds are issued and do not subsequently change.

Once issued, however, bonds are free to trade in secondary markets between bondholders. The yield rate, used in these transactions to compute bond prices, changes based on the level of interest rates in the economy and the perceived creditworthiness of the bond issuer.

Companies can and sometimes do repurchase (also called *redeem*) their bonds prior to maturity. The bond indenture (contract agreement), often includes a **call provision** giving the company the right to repurchase its bond. Alternatively, the company can repurchase bonds in the open market. When a bond repurchase occurs, a gain or loss usually results, and is computed as follows:

Gain or Loss on Bond Repurchase = Bonds Payable, Net—Repurchase Payment

The net bonds payable, also referred to as the *book (carrying) value of the bond,* is the net amount reported on the balance sheet. If the issuer pays more to retire the bonds than the amount carried on its balance sheet, a loss is reported on its income statement, usually called *loss on bond retirement.* The issuer reports a *gain on bond retirement* if the repurchase price is less than the net bonds payable.

GAAP dictates that any gains or losses on bond repurchases are reported as part of ordinary income unless they meet the criteria for treatment as an extraordinary item (unusual and infrequent, see Chapter 7). Relatively few debt retirements meet these criteria and, hence, most gains and losses on bond repurchases are reported as part of income from continuing operations.

The question arises as to how gains and losses on the redemption of bonds should affect our analysis of a company's profitability. We have argued before that bonds and notes payable represent nonoperating items. Therefore, activities including the refunding of bonds and any gain or loss resulting from such activity should be omitted from our computation of net operating profit after tax (NOPAT). The gain or loss on repurchase is exactly offset by the present value of the future cash flow implications of the repurchase (Appendix 10B demonstrates this).

Another analysis issue involves assessing the market values of bonds and other long-term liabilities. This information is relevant for some investors and creditors in revealing unrealized gains and losses (similar to that reported for marketable securities). GAAP requires companies to provide information about current market values of their long-term liabilities in footnotes (see Verizon's fair value of debt disclosure in the next section). However, these market values are *not* reported on the balance sheet and changes in these market values are not reflected in net income. We must make our own adjustments to the balance sheet and income statement if we want them to reflect changes in market values of liabilities.

Financial Statement Footnotes

Companies are required to disclose details about their long-term liabilities, including the amounts borrowed under each debt issuance, the interest rates, maturity dates, and other key provisions. Following is **Verizon**'s disclosure for its long-term debt ($ millions):

Long-Term Debt
Outstanding long-term obligations are as follows:

At December 31	Interest Rates %	Maturities	2003
Notes payable	1.24–10.05	2004–2032	$17,364
Telephone subsidiaries—debentures and			
first/refunding mortgage bonds	2.00– 7.00	2004–2042	13,417
	7.15– 7.65	2006–2032	3,625
	7.85– 9.67	2010–2031	2,184
Other subsidiaries—debentures and other	6.36– 8.75	2004–2028	3,926
Zero-coupon convertible notes,			
net of unamortized discount of $2,198	3.00% yield	2021	3,244
Employee stock ownership plan loans:			
GTE guaranteed obligations	9.73	2005	119
NYNEX debentures	9.55	2010	175
			Continued

At December 31	Interest Rates %	Maturities	2003
Capital lease obligations (average rate 7.9%) other lease-related debt (average rate 6.0%)			521
Property sale holdbacks held in escrow, vendor and other	4.00– 6.00	2004–2005	99
Unamortized discount, net of premium			(81)
Total long-term debt, including current maturities			44,593
Less: debt maturing within one year			(5,180)
Total long-term debt			$39,413

Verizon reports a book value for long-term debt of $44,593 million at year-end 2003. Of this amount, $5,180 million matures in the next year, hence its classification as a current liability (current maturities of long-term debt) and the remainder matures after 2004. Verizon also reports $81 million in unamortized discount (net of unamortized premium) on this debt.

In addition to amounts, rates, and due dates on its long-term debt, Verizon also reports aggregate maturities for the five years subsequent to its balance sheet date as follows:

Maturities of Long-Term Debt
Maturities of long-term debt outstanding at December 31, 2003 are $5.2 billion in 2004, $5.5 billion in 2005, $3.9 billion in 2006, $2.5 billion in 2007, $2.5 billion in 2008 and $25.1 billion thereafter.

This reporting reveals that Verizon is required to make principal payments of $19.6 billion in the next five years, with $10.7 billion of that coming due in the next two years. Such maturities are important as a company must meet its required payments, negotiate a rescheduling of the indebtedness, or refinance the debt to avoid default. The latter (default) usually has severe consequences as debt holders have legal remedies available to them, that can result in bankruptcy of the company.

Verizon's disclosure on the market value of its total debt follows:

At December 31, 2003 ($ millions)	Carrying Amount	Fair Value
Short- and long-term debt	$45,140	$48,685

As of 2003, indebtedness with a book value of $45,140 million had a market value of $48,685 million, resulting in an unrecognized liability (and loss if the debt is redeemed) of $3,545 million (due mainly to a decline in interest rates subsequent to bond issuance). The justification for not recognizing unrealized gains and losses on the balance sheet and income statement is that such amounts can reverse with future fluctuations in interest rates. Further, because only the face amount of debt is repaid at maturity, unrealized gains and losses that arise during intervening years are not necessarily relevant. This approach is based on is the same logic used to justify the nonrecognition of gains and losses on held-to-maturity investments in debt securities, a topic covered in Chapter 12.

DEBT RATINGS AND THE COST OF DEBT

LO6 Explain how debt ratings are determined and how they impact the cost of debt.

Earlier in the chapter we learned that the effective cost of debt to the issuing company is the market (yield) rate of interest used to price the bond, regardless of the bond coupon rate. The market rate of interest is usually defined as the yield on U.S. Government borrowings such as treasury bills, notes, and bonds, called the *risk-free rate,* plus a *spread* (also called risk premium).

Yield Rate = Risk-Free Rate + Spread

Treasury yields (risk-free rates) vary with the maturity of the security, generally increasing as the term increases as shown in the following graph as of 2005:

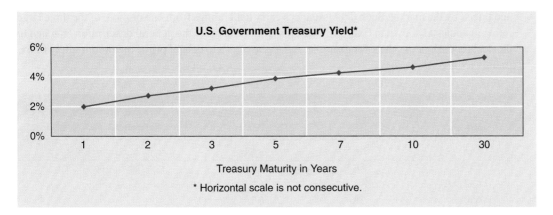

The rate of interest that a company must pay on its debt is a function of the maturity of that debt and the creditworthiness of the issuing company. The rate it pays in excess of the treasury (risk-free) rate for a given debt maturity and risk level of issuer is illustrated in the following graph as of 2005:

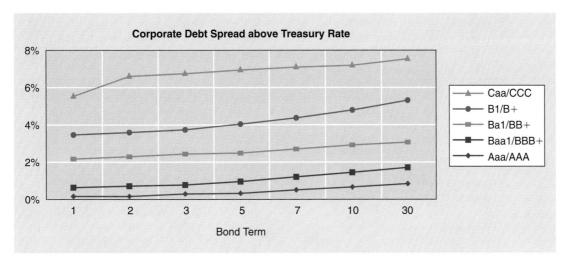

For all maturities, the required market rate increases (shifts upward) as debt quality moves from Aaa/AAA debt, which is the highest quality debt reflected in the line nearest to zero, to the Caa/CCC debt, which is the lowest quality debt reflected in the line nearest to 8%. That is, higher credit-rated issuers warrant a lower rate than lower credit-rated issuers. This difference is substantial. For example, for the 10-year bond, the treasury bond yield is 4.71%, while the Aaa/AAA corporate bond yield is 5.31% (a 0.60% or 60 basis-point spread). However, the low quality, high risk Caa/CCC bond yield is 11.86% (4.71% + 7.15%), which is a 7.15% or 715 basis point spread.

RESEARCH INSIGHT

Accounting Conservatism and Cost of Debt   Research indicates that companies applying more conservative accounting incur a lower cost of debt. Research also suggests that while accounting conservatism can lead to lower quality accounting income (because such income does not fully reflect economic reality), creditors are more confident in the numbers and view them as more credible. Evidence also implies that companies can lower the required return demanded by creditors (the spread) by issuing high quality financial reports that include enhanced footnote disclosures and detailed supplemental reports.

A company's debt rating, also referred to as credit quality and creditworthiness, is related to default risk. **Default** refers to the nonpayment of interest and principal or the failure to adhere to the various terms and conditions (covenants) of the bond indenture. Companies seeking to obtain bond financing from the capital markets, normally first seek a rating on their proposed debt issuance from one of several rating agencies such as **Standard & Poor's, Moody's Investors Service**, or **Fitch**. The aim of rating agencies is to rate debt so that its default risk is more accurately determined and priced by the market. Such debt issuances carry debt ratings from one or more of the three large rating agencies as shown in Exhibit 10.5. This exhibit includes the general description attached to the debt for each rating class-for example, AAA is assigned to debt of prime maximum safety (maximum creditworthiness).

EXHIBIT 10.5	Corporate Debt Ratings and Descriptions		
Moody's	**S&P**	**Fitch**	**Description**
Aaa	AAA	AAA	Prime Maximum Safety
Aa1	AA+	AA+	High Grade, High Quality
Aa2	AA	AA	
Aa3	AA−	AA−	
A1	A+	A+	Upper-Medium Grade
A2	A	A	
A3	A−	A−	
Baa1	BBB+	BBB+	Lower-Medium Grade
Baa2	BBB	BBB	
Baa3	BBB−	BBB−	
Ba1	BB+	BB+	Non-Investment Grade
Ba2	BB	BB	Speculative
Ba3	BB−	BB−	
B1	B+	B+	Highly Speculative
B2	B	B	
B3	B−	B−	
Caa1	CCC+	CCC	Substantial Risk
Caa2	CCC		In Poor Standing
Caa3	CCC−		
Ca			Extremely Speculative
C			May be in Default
		DDD	Default
		DD	
	D	D	

YOU MAKE THE CALL

You Are the Vice President of Finance   Your company is currently rated B1/B+ by credit rating agencies. You are considering possible financial and other restructurings of the company to increase your credit rating. What types of restructurings might you consider? What benefits will your company receive from those restructurings? What costs will your company incur to implement such restructurings? [Answers on page 444]

Verizon bonds are rated A1/A+ as of 2004. It is this rating that, in conjunction with the maturity of its bonds, establishes the market interest rate and consequent selling price. There are a number of considerations that affect the rating of a bond. Standard & Poor's list the following factors among its credit rating criteria:

> **Business Risk**
>   Industry characteristics
>   Competitive position (e.g., marketing, technology, efficiency, regulation)
>   Management
> **Financial Risk**
>   Financial characteristics
>   Financial policy
>   Profitability
>   Capital structure
>   Cash flow protection
>   Financial flexibility

Debt ratings are set from the point of view of the debt investor. Debt investors are mainly interested in assessing the probability that the interest and principal payments are made on time by the borrower. If a company defaults on its debt, debt holders possess several legal remedies, including the potential to require asset liquidation to settle obligations. However, in this eventuality, debt holders rarely realize the entire amounts owed to them.

Standard and Poor's uses several financial ratios to assess default risk. A listing of these ratios, together with median averages for various risk classes as of 2005, is shown in Exhibit 10.6. In examining the ratios, recall that debt is regarded as increasingly more risky as we move from the first column, AAA, to the last, CCC.[9]

EXHIBIT 10.6	Ratio Values for Different Risk Classes of Corporate Debt*						
Three-Year Medians	**AAA**	**AA**	**A**	**BBB**	**BB**	**B**	**CCC**
EBIT interest coverage (×)	21.4	10.1	6.1	3.7	2.1	0.8	0.1
EBITDA interest coverage (×)	26.5	12.9	9.1	5.8	3.4	1.8	1.3
FFO/total debt (%)	128.8	55.4	43.2	30.8	18.8	7.8	1.6
Free oper. cash flow/total debt (%)	84.2	25.2	15.0	8.5	2.6	(3.2)	(12.9)
Return on capital (%)	34.9	21.7	19.4	13.6	11.6	6.6	1.0
Operating income/sales (%)	27.0	22.1	18.6	15.4	15.9	11.9	11.9
Long-term debt/capital (%)	13.3	28.2	33.9	42.5	57.2	69.7	68.8
Total debt/capital (incl. STD) (%)	22.9	37.7	42.5	48.2	62.6	74.8	87.7

*Corporate Ratings Criteria-Adjusted Key Financial Ratios, Standard & Poor's Ratings, Released 2002, Standard & Poor's, a division of The McGraw-Hill Companies (reproduced with permission).

A review of these ratios indicates that the following factors are considered relevant by S&P in evaluating the ability of a company to meet its debt service requirements:

1. Liquidity (ratios 1 through 4)
2. Profitability (ratios 5 and 6)
3. Solvency (ratios 7 and 8)

These ratios are variants of the ratios we describe in Chapters 5 and 6, especially those used to assess solvency.

There are other relevant factors in setting debt ratings including the following:

---

[9] Definitions for the key ratios in this Exhibit are:

$$\text{EBIT interest coverage} = \frac{\text{Earnings from continuing operations before interest and taxes}}{\text{Gross interest incurred before subtracting (1) capitalized interest and (2) interest income}}$$

$$\text{EBITDA interest coverage} = \frac{\text{Earnings from continuing operations before interest and taxes, depreciation, and amortization}}{\text{Gross interest incurred before subtracting (1) capitalized interest and (2) interest income}}$$

$$\text{Funds from operations/total debt} = \frac{\text{Net income from continuing operations plus depreciation, amortization, deferred income taxes, and other noncash items}}{\text{Long-term debt plus current maturities, commercial paper, and other short-term borrowings}}$$

$$\text{Free operating cash flow/total debt} = \frac{\text{Funds from operations minus capital expenditures, minus (plus) the increase (decrease) in working capital (excluding changes in cash, marketable securities, and short-term debt)}}{\text{Long-term debt plus current maturities, commercial paper, and other short-term borrowings}}$$

$$\text{Return on capital} = \frac{\text{Earnings from continuing operations before interest and taxes}}{\text{Average of beginning of year and end of year capital, including short-term debt, current maturities, long-term debt, noncurrent deferred taxes, and equity}}$$

$$\text{Operating income/sales} = \frac{\text{Sales minus cost of goods manufactured (before depreciation and amortization), selling, general and administrative, and research and development costs}}{\text{Sales}}$$

$$\text{Long-term debt/capital} = \frac{\text{Long-term debt}}{\text{Long-term debt} + \text{shareholders' equity (including preferred stock) plus minority interest}}$$

$$\text{Total debt/capital} = \frac{\text{Long-term debt plus current maturities, commercial paper, and other short-term borrowings}}{\text{Long-term debt plus current maturities, commercial paper, and other short-term borrowings} + \text{shareholders' equity (including preferred stock) plus minority interest}}$$

- **Collateral** Companies can provide security for debt in the form of mortgages on assets. To the extent debt is secured, the debt holder is in a preferred position vis-à-vis other creditors.

- **Covenants** Debt agreements (indentures) can contain restrictions on the issuing company to protect debt holders. Examples are restrictions on excessive dividend payment, on other company acquisitions, on further borrowing, and on maintaining minimum levels for key liquidity and solvency ratios. These covenants provide debt holders some means of control over the issuer's operations because, unlike equity investors, they do not have voting rights.

- **Options** Debt obligations involve contracts between the borrowing company and debt holders. Options are sometimes written into debt contracts. Examples are options to convert debt into stock (so that debt holders have a stake in value creation) and options allowing the issuing company to repurchase its debt before maturity (usually at a premium).

RESEARCH INSIGHT

Valuation of Debt Options Debt instruments can include features such as conversion options, under which the debt can be converted to common stock. Such conversion features are not accounted for separately under GAAP. Instead, convertible debt is accounted for just like debt with no conversion features (unless the conversion option can be separately traded). However, option-pricing models can be used to estimate the value of such debt features even when no market for those features exist. Empirical results suggest that those debt features represent a substantial part of debt value. These findings contribute to the current debate regarding the separation of compound financial instruments into debt and equity portions for financial statement presentation and analysis.

CHAPTER-END REVIEW

On January 1, 2005, Hogan Company issues $300,000 of 15-year, 10% bonds payable for $351,876, yielding an effective interest rate of 8%. Interest is payable semiannually on June 30 and December 31. (1) Show computations to confirm the issue price of $351,876, and (2) provide Hogan's journal entries, t-accounts, and complete financial statement effects template for (a) bond issuance, (b) semiannual interest payment and premium amortization on June 30, 2005, and (c) semiannual interest payment and premium amortization on December 31, 2005.

Solution

1. Issue price for $300,000, 15-year, 10% semiannual bonds discounted at 8%:

Present value of principal payment ($300,000 × 0.30832)	$ 92,496
Present value of semiannual interest payments ($15,000 × 17.29203)	259,380
Issue price of bonds	$351,876

2.

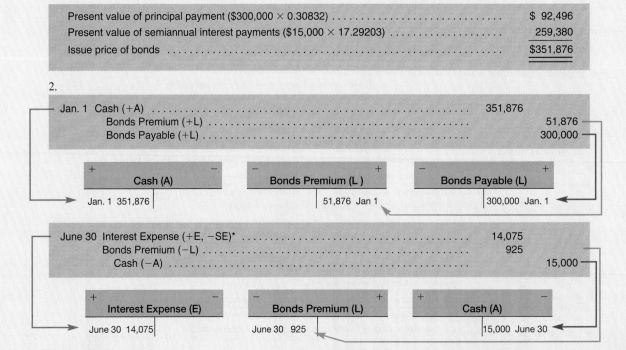

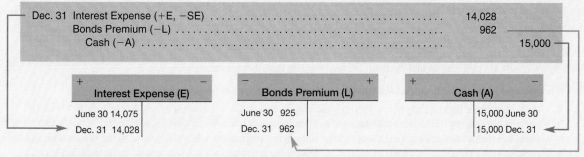

```
Dec. 31  Interest Expense (+E, −SE) ....................................  14,028
              Bonds Premium (−L) ..........................................       962
                   Cash (−A) ...................................................             15,000
```

*If the straight-line method of amortizing the discount had been used, each six-month period's entry would have been;

```
Interest expense (+E,−SE) amount plugged ...................................  12,406.20
Bonds Premium (−L) [$51,876÷20] ..........................................         2,593.80
     Cash (−A) ...................................................................              15,000
```

Transaction	Cash Asset	+	Noncash Assets	=	Liabil-ities	+	Contrib. Capital	+	Retained Earnings		Revenues	−	Expenses	=	Net Income
a. Issuance	+351,876 Cash			=	+351,876 Bond Payable, Net										=
b. Interest and amortization[1]	−15,000 Cash			=	−925 Bond Payable, Net				−14,075 Retained Earnings				−14,075 Interest Expense	=	−14,075
c. Interest and amortization[2]	−15,000 Cash			=	−962 Bond Payable, Net				−14,038 Retained Earnings				−14,038 Interest Expense	=	−14,038

Balance Sheet | Income Statement

[1]$300,000 × 0.10 × 6/12 5 $15,000 cash payment; 0.04 × $351,876 = $14,075 interest expense; the difference is the bond premium amortization, a reduction of the net bond carrying amount.

[2]0.04 × ($351,876 − $925) = $14,038 interest expense. The difference between this amount and the $15,000 cash payment is the premium amortization, a reduction of the net bond carrying amount.

SUMMARY

Analyze and distinguish between operating liabilities and nonoperating liabilities. (p. 420) LO1

- Operating liabilities are obligations related to the primary activities of the business; nonoperating liabilities are "financial" in nature and are part of business financing activities.

Identify and account for current operating liabilities. (p. 420) LO2

- Current liabilities are short-term and generally noninterest bearing; accordingly, firms try to maximize the financing of their assets using these sources of funds.
- RNOA increases when firms make use of accounts payable increases to finance operating assets; a firm must avoid excessive "leaning on the trade" for short-term gains that can damage long-term supplier relationships.
- Accrued liabilities reflect liabilities and expenses that have been incurred during the period, but which have not yet been recognized in financial statements.
- While all accruals result in a liability on the balance sheet and an expense on the income statement, management has latitude in determining (in some cases, estimating) their amount and timing; this discretion offers the opportunity for managing earnings.

Describe and account for current nonoperating (financial) liabilities. (p. 426) LO3

- Management will generally try to assure that the debt service on financial (nonoperating) liabilities coincides with the cash flows from the assets financed.
- When large amounts of financing are required for, say, plant and equipment, firms find that bonds, notes, and other forms of long-term financing provide a cost-efficient means of raising capital.

Explain and illustrate the pricing of long-term nonoperating liabilities. (p. 430) LO4

- The coupon rate indicated on a bond contract determines the periodic interest payment. The required return on any bond called the market (yield or effective) rate is determined by market conditions and rarely equals the coupon (contract) rate. The market rate is used to price the bond and determines the effective cost of the debt to the issuer.

- If the market rate is below the coupon rate, the bond will sell at a premium to its face value, assuring that the owner of the bond earns only the market rate of interest. If the market rate exceeds the coupon rate, the bond will sell at a discount so that the bond is bought at less than its face value.

LO5 **Analyze and account for financial statement effects of long-term nonoperating liabilities. (p. 433)**

- A discount for a bond selling below its face value represents additional interest expense over time to the issuer because the issuer received less than face value upon issuance, but must pay the holder the face value at the bond's maturity; this discount represents additional interest beyond the coupon payment to the holder. The premium on a bond selling above its face value lowers the interest cost to the issuer and the interest revenue received by the holder.

- Gains and losses on bonds repurchased, equal to the difference between the book value and the cash paid, are required to be reported in operating income, unless extraordinary; they do not represent operating activities and should be removed from operating cash flows in our analysis.

LO6 **Explain how debt ratings are determined and how they affect the cost of debt. (p. 438)**

- The market rate of interest to a firm reflects a premium for risk added to the current risk-free rate (the rate on U.S. Treasury securities with a similar life). The additional risk premium will reflect the credit worthiness of the particular issuer. Credit agencies play an important role in this process by issuing debt ratings.

- Borrowing is typically secured by covenants that place the issuer in a superior position to other creditors and covenants that put restrictions on the borrower's activities; bonds can also contain options including for conversion or repurchase.

GUIDANCE ANSWERS

YOU MAKE THE CALL

You Are the Analyst   Accrued liabilities must be probable and estimable before they can be reported in the balance sheet. FCM's reporting is not conservative, because in using the lower bound of a range of values, it may be understating its liabilities (and overstating equity).

As the defendant in the Vioxx lawsuits, Merck's management would argue that these claims are not probable, because they expect to win in court. As an analyst, you might believe otherwise and add an estimated liability to Merck's balance sheet.

YOU MAKE THE CALL

You Are the Vice President of Finance   The types of restructurings you might consider are those yielding a strengthening of the financial ratios typically used to assess liquidity and solvency by the rating agencies. Such restructurings typically include inventory reduction to generate cash, the reallocation of cash outflows from investing activities (PPE) to debt reduction, and issuing stock for cash used to reduce debt (an equity for debt recapitalization). These actions increase liquidity or reduce financial leverage and, thus, should yield an improved debt rating. An improved dept rating gives your company access to more debt holders as your current debt rating is below investment grade and is not a suitable investment for many professionally managed portfolios. It also yields a lower interest rate on your debt. Offsetting these benefits are costs such as the following: (1) potential loss of sales from inventory stock outs; (2) potential future cash flow reductions and loss of market power from reduced investing in PPE; and (3) costs of equity issuances (which is more than debt since investors demand a higher return to compensate for added risk and the lack of tax deductibility of dividends vis-à-vis interest payments), which can yield a net increase in the total cost of capital. All cost and benefits must be assessed before you pursue any restructurings.

APPENDIX 10A: Compound Interest

This appendix explains the concepts of present and future value.

Present Value Concepts

Would we rather receive a dollar now or a dollar one year from now? Most of us would answer, "a dollar now." Intuition tells us that a dollar received now is more valuable than the same amount received sometime in the future. Sound reasons exist for choosing the earlier dollar, the most obvious of which concerns risk. Because the future is uncertain, an event can prevent us from receiving the dollar at the later date. To avoid this risk, we choose the earlier date. Another reason for choosing the earlier date is that the dollar received now could be invested. That is, one year from now, we have the dollar and the interest earned on that dollar.

Present Value of a Single Amount

Risk and interest factors yield the following generalizations: (1) the right to receive an amount of money now-its **present value**—is worth more than the right to receive the same amount later-its future value; (2) the longer we must wait to receive an amount, the less attractive the receipt is (the difference between the present value of an amount and its future value is a function of interest, that is, Principal $\times$ Interest Rate $\times$ Time); and (3) the more risk associated with any situation, the higher the interest rate.

To illustrate, let's compute the present value equivalent to receiving $100 one year from now if money can be invested at 10%. We recognize intuitively that, with a 10% interest rate, we should accept less than $100. We base this estimate on the realization that the $100 received in the future must equal the present value (100%) plus interest (10%) on the present value. Thus, the $100 future receipt must be 1.10 times the present value. Dividing $100/1.10, we obtain a present value of $90.91 (rounded). This means that we would do as well to accept $90.91 now as to wait one year and receive $100. To confirm the equality of the $90.91 receipt now to a $100 receipt one year later, we calculate the future value of $90.91 at 10% for one year as follows:

$$\$90.91 \times 1.10 \times 1 \text{ year} = \$100 \text{ (rounded)}$$

To generalize, we compute the present value of a future receipt by *discounting* the future receipt back to the present at an appropriate interest rate. We present this schematically below:

$$\begin{array}{ccc} \textbf{Present Value} & \leftarrow \quad \textbf{Discounted for} \quad \leftarrow & \textbf{Future Value} \\ \$90.91 & \textbf{1 year at 10\%} & \$100 \end{array}$$

If either the time period or the interest rate were increased, the resulting present value would decrease. If more than one time period is involved, our future receipts include interest on interest. This is called *compounding*.

Present Value Tables

Table 1 in Appendix A near the end of the book can be used to compute the present value amounts in this section. A present value table provides multiplies for many combinations of time periods and interest rates that, when applied to the dollar amount of a future cash flow, determines its present value.

Present value tables are used as follows. First, determine the number of interest compounding periods involved (three years compounded annually are 3 periods, and three years compounded semiannually are 6 periods). The extreme left-hand column indicates the number of periods.

Next, determine the interest rate per compounding period. Interest rates are usually quoted on a *per year* (annual) basis. The rate per compounding period is the annual rate divided by the number of compounding periods per year. For example, an interest rate of 10% per year would be 10% per period if compounded annually, and 5% per period if compounded semiannually.

Finally, locate the present value factor, which is that value to the right of the appropriate number of compounding periods and beneath the appropriate interest rate per compounding period. Multiply this factor by the number of dollars involved.

All values in Table 1 are less than 1.0 because the present value is always smaller than the $1 future amount. As the interest rate increases (moving from left to right in the table) or the number of periods increases (moving from top to bottom), the present value multiplies decline. This illustrates two important facts: (1) present values decline as interest rates increase, and (2) present values decline as the time to receipt lengthens. Consider the following two cases:

Case 1. Compute the present value of $100 to be received one year from today, discounted at 10% interest compounded annually:

> Number of periods (one year, annually) = 1
> Rate per period (10%/1) = 10%
> Multiplier = 0.90909
> Present value = $100.00 X 0.90909 = $90.91 (rounded)

Case 2. Compute the present value of $116.99 to be received two years from today, discounted at 8% compounded *semiannually:*

> Number of periods (two years, semiannually) = 4
> Rate per period (8%/2) = 4%
> Multiplier = 0.85480
> Present value = $116.99 x 0.85480 = $100.00 (rounded)

Present Value of an Annuity

We can compute the present value of any single future amount (or series of future amounts) using present value tables like Table 1. One frequent pattern of amounts, however, is subject to a more convenient treatment. This pattern, known as an **annuity**, can be described as *equal amounts equally spaced over a period.*

To illustrate, assume $100 is to be received at the end of each of the next three years as an annuity. When annuity amounts occur at the *end of each period,* the annuity is called an *ordinary annuity.* As shown below, the present value of this ordinary annuity can be computed from Table 1 by computing the present value of each of the three individual receipts and summing them (assume a 10% annual rate compounded semiannually).

Case 3.

Future Receipts (ordinary annuity)			PV Multiplier (Table 1)		Present Value
Year 1	Year 2	Year 3			
$100			× 0.95238	=	$ 95.24
	$100		× 0.90703	=	90.70
		$100	× 0.86384	=	86.38
			2.72325		$272.32

Table 2 in Appendix A provides a single multiplier for computing the present value of a series of future amounts in the ordinary annuity form. Referring to Table 2 in the three periods hence row and the 5% column, we see that the multiplier is 2.72325. When applied to the $100 annuity amount, the multiplier gives a present value of $272.33. As shown above, the same present value (with 1 cent rounding error) is derived—as was calculated—using several multiplies from Table 1. For annuities of 5, 10, or 20 years, considerable computations are avoided by using annuity tables.

Bond Valuation

We already learned that (1) a bond agreement specifies a pattern of future cash flows-usually a series of interest payments and a single payment of the face amount at maturity, and (2) bonds are sold at premiums or discounts to adjust their coupon rates to the prevailing market rate at issuance. The selling price (or valuation) of a bond that yields a specific rate is determined as follows:

1. Use Table 1 to compute the present value of the future principal payment at the desired (effective) rate.
2. Use Table 2 to compute the present value of the future series of interest payments at the desired (effective) rate.
3. Add the present values from steps 1 and 2.

We illustrate in Exhibit 10A.1 the pricing of a $100,000 issuance of 8%, 4-year bonds paying interest semiannually and sold on the date of issue to yield (1) 8%, (2) 10% or (3) 6%. The price of 8% bonds sold to yield 8% is the face (or par) value of the bonds. A bond issue price of $93,537 (discount bond) yields 10%. A bond issue price of $107,019 (premium bond) yields 6%.

Future Value Concepts
Future Value of a Single Amount
The **future value** of a single sum is the amount that a specific investment is worth at a future date if invested at a given rate of compound interest. To illustrate, suppose that we decide to invest $6,000 in a savings account that pays 6% annual interest and we intend to leave the principal and interest in the account for five years. We assume that interest is credited to the account at the end of each year. The balance in the account at the end of five years is determined using Table 3 in Appendix A, which gives the future value of a dollar after a given number of time periods, as follows:

Principal	×	Factor	=	Future Value
$6,000	×	1.33823	=	$8,029

The factor 1.33823 is in the row for five periods and the column for 6%.

Next, suppose that the interest is credited to the account semiannually rather than annually. In this situation, there are now 10 compounding periods, and we use a 3% semiannual rate (one-half the annual rate because there are two compounding periods per year). The future value calculation follows:

Principal	×	Factor	=	Future Value
$6,000	×	1.34392	=	$8,064

Future Value of an Annuity
If, instead of investing a single amount at the beginning of a series of periods, we invest a specified amount *each period,* then we are investing in an annuity. To illustrate, assume we decide to invest $2,000 at the end of each year for five years at an 8% annual rate of return. To determine the accumulated amount of principal and interest, we refer to Table 4 in Appendix A, which furnishes the future value of a dollar invested at the end of each period. The factor 5.867 is in the row for five periods and the column for 8%, and the calculation is as follows:

| EXHIBIT 10A.1 | Calculation of Bond Price Using Present Value Tables |

(1) $100,000 of 8%, 4-year bonds with interest payable semiannually priced to yield 8%.

Future Cash Flows	Multiplier (Table 1)	Multiplier (Table 2)	Present Values at 4% Semiannually
Principal payment, $100,000 (a single amount received 8 semiannual periods hence)	0.73069		$ 73,069
Interest payments, $4,000 at end of each of 8 semiannual periods		6.73274	26,931
Present value (issue price) of bonds			$100,000

(2) $100,000 of 8%, 4-year bonds with interest payable semiannually priced to yield 10%.

Future Cash Flows	Multiplier (Table 1)	Multiplier (Table 2)	Present Values at 5% Semiannually
Principal payment, $100,000 (a single amount received 8 semiannual periods hence)	0.67684		$67,684
Interest payments, $4,000 at end of each of 8 semiannual periods		6.46321	25,853
Present value (issue price) of bonds			$93,537

(3) $100,000 of 8%, 4-year bonds with interest payable semiannually priced to yield 6%.

Future Cash Flows	Multiplier (Table 1)	Multiplier (Table 2)	Present Values at 3% Semiannually
Principal repayment, $100,000 (a single amount received 8 semiannual periods hence)	0.78941		$ 78,941
Interest payments, $4,000 at end of each of 8 semiannual periods		7.01969	28,078
Present value (issue price) of bonds			$107,019

Periodic Payment	×	Factor	=	Future Value
$2,000	×	5.86660	=	$11,733

If, instead, we decide to invest $1,000 at the end of each six months for five years at an 8% annual rate of return, we would use the factor for 10 periods at 4%, as follows:

Periodic Payment	×	Factor	=	Future Value
$1,000	×	12.00611	=	$12,006

APPENDIX 10B: Economics of Gains and Losses on Bond Repurchases

Is a reported gain or loss on bond repurchases before maturity of economic substance? The short answer is no. To illustrate, assume that on January 1, a company issues $50 million face value bonds with an 8% annual coupon rate. The interest is to be paid semiannually (4% each semiannual period) for a term of five years (10 semiannual periods), at which time the principal is due and payable. The bond issue price, if investors demand a 10% annual return (5% semiannually) on their investment, is computed as follows:

Present value of semiannual interest ($2,000,000 × 7.72173)	=	$15,443,460
Present value of principal ($50,000,000 × 0.61391)	=	30,695,500
Present value of bond	=	$46,138,960

This bond's amortization table follows:

Period	[A] ([E] × market%) Interest Expense	[B] (Face × coupon%) Cash Interest Paid	[C] ([A] − [B]) Discount Amortization	[D] (Prior bal − [C]) Discount Balance	[E] (Face − [D]) Bond Payable, Net
0				$3,861,040	$46,138,960
1	$2,306,948	$2,000,000	$306,948	3,554,092	46,445,908
2	2,322,295	2,000,000	322,295	3,231,797	46,768,203
3	2,338,410	2,000,000	338,410	2,893,386	47,106,614
4	2,355,331	2,000,000	355,331	2,538,056	47,461,944
5	2,373,097	2,000,000	373,097	2,164,959	47,835,041
6	2,391,752	2,000,000	391,752	1,773,206	48,226,794
7	2,411,340	2,000,000	411,340	1,361,867	48,638,133
8	2,431,907	2,000,000	431,907	929,960	49,070,040
9	2,453,502	2,000,000	453,502	476,458	49,523,542
10	2,476,458	2,000,000	476,458	0	50,000,000

Next, assume we are at period 6 (three years after issuance) and the market rate of interest for this bond has risen from 10% at the time of issuance to 12% currently. The firm then decides to retire (redeem) the outstanding bond issue and finances it through issuance of a new bond issue. That is, it issues bonds with a face amount equal to the market value of the existing issue and uses the proceeds to retire the existing issue. The new issue will have a term of two years (four semiannual periods), the remaining life of the existing bond issue.

At the end of the third year, there are four semiannual payments of interest remaining in the amount of $2,000,000 each plus the repayment of the face amount of the bond at the end of the fourth period. The present value of this cash flow stream, discounted at the current 12% annual rate (6% semiannual rate) is:

Present value of semiannual interest ($2,000,000 x 3.46511)	=	$ 6,930,220
Present value of principal ($50,000,000 3 0.79209)	=	39,604,500
Present value of bond	=	$46,534,720

This means the company pays $46,534,720 to redeem a bond that is on its books at a carrying amount of $48,226,794. The difference of $1,692,074 is reported as a gain on repurchase (also called *redemption*). GAAP requires this gain be reported in income from continuing operations unless it meets the tests for treatment as an extraordinary item (both un-usual and infrequent).

Although the company reports a gain in its income statement, has it actually realized an economic gain? Consider that this company issues new bonds when the previous ones are redeemed that carry a coupon rate of 12% (6% semi-annually) for $46,534,720. Since we assume that those bonds are sold with a coupon rate equal to the market rate, they will sell at par (no discount or premium). The interest expense per six-month period, therefore, equals the interest paid in the amount of $2,792,083 ($46,534,720 × 6%). Total expense for the four-period life of the bond is $11,168,333 ($2,792,083 × 4). That amount, plus the $46,534,720 face amount of bonds due at maturity, results in total bond pay-ments of $57,703,053. Had this company not redeemed the bonds, it would have paid four additional interest payments of $2,000,000 each plus the face amount of $50,000,000 at maturity, for total bond payments of $58,000,000. On the surface, it appears that the firm is able to save $296,947 by redeeming the bonds and, therefore, reports a gain.[10]

However, this gain is misleading. Specifically, this gain has two components. First, interest payments increase by $792,083 per year ($2,792,083 − $2,000,000). Second, the face amount of the bond that must be repaid in four years decreases by $3,465,280 ($50,000,000 − $46,534,720). To evaluate whether a real gain has been realized, we must con-sider the present value of these cash outflows and savings. The present value of the increased interest outflow, a four-period annuity of $792,083 discounted at 6% per period, is **$2,744,655** ($792,083 × 3.46511). The present value of the reduced maturity amount, $3,465,280 in four periods hence, is **$2,744,814** ($3,465,280 × 0.79209)—note: the two amounts differ by $159, and would be equal if we used more significant digits.

This analysis shows there is no real economic gain. The present value of the increased interest payments exactly offsets the present value of the decreased amount due at maturity. Why, then, does GAAP yield a gain? The answer lies in use of historical costing. Bonds are reported at amortized cost, that is, the face amount less any applicable discount or plus any premium. These amounts are a function of the bond issue price and its yield rate at issuance, which are both

---

[10]Also, total interest expense on the new bond issue is $3,168,333 ($11,168,333 − $8,000,000) more than it would have recorded under the old issue. So, although it is recording a present gain, it also incurs future higher interest costs which are not recognized under GAAP.

fixed for the bond duration. Market prices for bonds, however, vary continually with changes in market interest rates. Companies do not adjust bond liabilities for these changes in market value. As a result, when bonds are redeemed, their carrying amount differs from market value and GAAP reports a gain or loss equal to this difference.

KEY TERMS

Annuity (p. 430)

Book (carrying) value (p. 437)

Call provision (p. 437)

Collateral (p. 442)

Contingent liability (p. 423)

Cookie jar reserve (p. 424)

Coupon (contract or stated) rate (p. 430)

Covenants (p. 439)

Current maturities of long-term debt (p. 428)

Default (p. 439)

Discount (p. 431)

Effective cost (p. 431)

Face amount (or principal) (p. 429)

Future value (p. 445)

Gain on bond retirement (p. 437)

Leaning on the trade (p. 422)

Loss on bond retirement (p. 437)

Market (yield) rate (p. 430)

Nominal cost (p. 435)

On-balance-sheet financing (p. 419)

Options (p. 442)

Ordinary annuity (p. 446)

Par (face) value (p. 431)

Periodic interest payments (p. 430)

Premium (p. 431)

Present value (p. 445)

Redeem (p. 437)

Risk-free rate (p. 438)

Short-term interest-bearing debt (p. 420)

Spread (or risk premium) (p. 438)

Tombstone (p. 431)

MULTIPLE CHOICE

1. Which of the following statements is correct? A decrease in accrued wages liability:
   a. decreases cash flows from operations.
   b. decreases working capital.
   c. increases NOPAT.
   d. increases net non-operating (financial) assets.

2. On April 1, 2005, a firm borrows $12,000 at an annual interest rate of 10% with payments required semiannually on September 30 and March 31. How much interest payable and how much interest expense should appear on the firm's books at the end of the firm's fiscal year, December 31, 2005?
   a. $900 payable and $300 expense.
   b. $300 payable and $900 expense.
   c. $600 payable and $600 expense.
   d. $900 payable and $600 expense.

3. A firm issues $30,000,000 of 10-year bonds and receives $29.5 million in cash. Which of the following statements is correct?
   a. The bonds do not have a coupon rate because they are zeros.
   b. The market rate exceeds the coupon rate.
   c. The contract rate exceeds the market rate.
   d. The bonds were issued at par.

4. A firm issues $5 million of ten-year 6 percent notes with interest paid semiannually. At issuance the firm received $5,817,565 cash reflecting a 4% yield. What is the amount of premium written off against interest expense in the first year the notes are outstanding?
   a. $48,318
   b. $24,527
   c. $67,297
   d. $33,649

Multiple Choice Answers 1. a 2. b 3. b 4. c

Superscript ^{A}(^{B}) denotes assignments based on Appendix 10A (10B).

DISCUSSION QUESTIONS

Q10-1. What do the term current liabilities mean? What assets are usually used to settle current liabilities?

Q10-2. What is an accrual? How do accruals impact the balance sheet and the income statement?

Q10-3. What is the difference between a bond coupon rate and its market interest rate (yield)?

Q10-4. How does issuing a bond at a premium or discount affect the bond's *effective* interest rate vis-à-vis the coupon (stated) rate?

Q10-5. Why do companies report a gain or loss on the repurchase of their bonds (assuming the repurchase price is different from bond book value)? Is this gain or loss a real economic gain or loss?

Q10-6. How do debt ratings affect the cost of borrowing for a company?

Q10-7.[B] How would you interpret a company's reported gain or loss on the repurchase of its bonds?

Q10-8. What do the following terms mean? (a) term loan, (b) bonds payable, (c) trustee, (d) secured bonds, (e) serial bonds, (f) call provision, (g) convertible bonds, (h) face value, (i) nominal rate, (j) bond discount, (k) bond premium, and (l) amortization of bond premium or discount.

Q10-9. What are the advantages and disadvantages of issuing bonds rather than common stock?

Q10-10. A $3,000,000 issue of a 10-year, 9% bonds was sold at 98 plus accrued interest three months after the bonds were dated. What net amount of cash is received?

Q10-11. How does issuing bonds at a premium or discount "adjust the contract rate to the applicable market rate of interest"?

Q10-12. Regardless of whether premium or discount is involved, what generalization can be made about the change in the book value of bonds payable during the period in which they are outstanding?

Q10-13. If the effective interest amortization method is used for bonds payable, how does the periodic interest expense change over the life of the bonds when they are issued (a) at a discount and (b) at a premium?

Q10-14. How should premium and discount on bonds payable be presented in the balance sheet?

Q10-15. On April 30, 2006, one year before maturity, Weber Company retired $200,000 of 9% bonds payable at 101. The book value of the bonds on April 30 was $197,600. Bond interest was last paid on April 30, 2006. What is the gain or loss on the retirement of the bonds?

Q10-16. Brownlee Company borrowed money by issuing a 20-year mortgage note payable. The note will be repaid in equal monthly installments. The interest expense component of each payment decreases with each payment. Why?

MINI EXERCISES

M10-17. Analyzing and Computing Financial Statement Effects of Bond Interest (LO5)

DeFond Company gave a creditor a 90-day, 8% note payable for $7,200 on December 16.

a. Prepare the journal entry to record the year-end December 31st accounting adjustment DeFond must make.

b. Post the journal entries from part *a* to their respective T-accounts.

c. Record the transaction from part *a* in the financial statement effects template.

Transaction	Balance Sheet						Income Statement		
	Cash Asset	+ Noncash Assets	= Liabil-ities	+ Contrib. Capital	+ Retained Earnings		Revenues	− Expenses	= Net Income

M10-18. Analyzing and Determining the Amount of a Liability

For each of the following situations, indicate the liability amount, if any, which is reported on the balance sheet of Basu, Inc., at December 31, 2005.

a. Basu owes $110,000 at year-end 2005 for its inventory purchases.

b. Basu agreed to purchase a $28,000 drill press in January 2006.

c. During November and December of 2005, Basu sold products to a firm and warranted them against product failure for 90 days. Estimated 2006 costs of honoring this warranty are $2,200.

d. Basu provides a profit-sharing bonus for its executives equal to 5% of its reported pretax annual income. The estimated pretax income for 2005 is $600,000. Bonuses are not paid until January of the following year.

M10-19. Interpreting Relations between Bond Price, Coupon, Yield, and Rating (LO4)

Boston Scientific (BSX)

The following notice appeared in *The Wall Street Journal* regarding a bond issuance by **Boston Scientific (BSX)**:

> **Boston Scientific Corp.**—$500 million of notes was priced with the following terms in two parts via joint lead managers Merrill Lynch & Co., UBS Securities and Wachovia:
>
> Amount: $250 million; Maturity: Jan. 12, 2011; Coupon: 4.25%; Price: 99.476;
> Yield: 4.349%; Ratings: Baa1 (Moody's), A− (S&P).
>
> Amount: $250 million; Maturity: Jan. 12, 2017; Coupon: 5.125%; Price: 99.926;
> Yield: 5.134%; Ratings: Baa1 (Moody's), A− (S&P).

a. Discuss the relation between the coupon rate, issuance price, and yield for the 2011 issue.
b. Compare the yields on the two bond issues. Why are the yields different when the bond ratings are the same?

M10-20. Determining Gain or Loss on Bond Redemption (LO5)
On April 30, 2005, one year before maturity, Easton Company retired $200,000 of its 9% bonds payable at the current market price of 101 (101% of the bond face amount, or $200,000 × 1.01 = $202,000). The bond book value on April 30, 2005, is $197,600 reflecting an unamortized discount of $2,400. Bond interest is presently fully paid and recorded up to the date of retirement. What is the gain or loss on retirement of these bonds? Is this gain or loss a real economic gain or loss? Explain.

M10-21. Interpreting Bond Footnote (LO5)
Bristol-Myers Squibb (BMY) reports the following maturities schedule for its long-term debt in its 2003 10-K report:

Bristol-Myers Squibb (BMY)

Dollars in Millions	Total	2004	2005–2006	2007–2008	Later Years
Long-Term Debt	$8,522	$13	$2,616	$545	$5,348

Payments Due by Period

a. What does the $2,616 million indicate for the 2005-2006 time period?
b. What implications does this payment schedule have for your evaluation of BMY's liquidity and solvency?

M10-22. Classifying Debt Accounts into the Balance Sheet or Income Statement (LO2,3)
Indicate the proper financial statement classification (balance sheet or income statement) for each of the following accounts:
a. Gain on Bond Retirement
b. Discount on Bonds Payable
c. Mortgage Notes Payable
d. Bonds Payable
e. Bond Interest Expense
f. Bond Interest Payable (due next period)
g. Premium on Bonds Payable
h. Loss on Bond Retirement

M10-23. Interpreting Bond Footnote Disclosures (LO5)
Comcast Corporation reports the following footnote to the long-term debt section of its 2003 10-K report:

Comcast Corporation (CMC)

Debt Covenants
Certain of our subsidiaries' loan agreements require that we maintain financial ratios based on debt, interest and operating income before depreciation and amortization, as defined in the agreements. In addition, certain of our subsidiary loan agreements contain restrictions on dividend payments and advances of funds to us. We were in compliance with all financial covenants for all periods presented. As of December 31, 2003, $50 million of our cash, cash equivalents and short-term investments is restricted under contractual or other arrangements. Restricted net assets of our subsidiaries were approximately $368 million as of December 31, 2003.

a. The financial ratios to which Comcast refers are similar to those discussed in the section on debt ratings and the cost of debt. What effects might these ratios have on the degree of freedom that management has in running Comcast?
b. Violation of debt covenants is a serious event that typically triggers an 'immediately due and payable' provision in the debt contract. What pressures might you envision for management if the company's ratios are near their covenant limits?
c. Comcast reports that certain of its assets are restricted by its bond covenants. What implications do these restrictions have on your analysis of the company and its liquidity and solvency position?

M10-24. Analyzing Financial Statement Effects of Bond Redemption (LO5)
Holthausen Corporation issued $400,000 of 11%, 20-year bonds at 108 on January 1, 2000. Interest is payable semiannually on June 30 and December 31. Through January 1, 2005, Holthausen amortized $5,000 of the bond premium. On January 1, 2005, Holthausen retires the bonds at 103.
a. Prepare journal entries to record the transactions.
b. Post the journal entries from part a to their respective T-accounts.
c. Record each of the transactions from part a in the financial statement effects template.

M10-25. Analyzing Financial Statement Effects of Bond Redemption (LO5)
Dechow, Inc., issued $250,000 of 8%, 15-year bonds at 96 on July 1, 2000. Interest is payable semiannually on December 31 and June 30. Through June 30, 2006, Dechow amortized $3,000 of the bond discount. On July 1, 2006, Dechow retired the bonds at 101.
a. Prepare journal entries to record the transactions.
b. Post the journal entries from part a to their respective T-accounts.
c. Record each of the transactions from part a in the financial statement effects template

M10-26. Analyzing and Computing Accrued Interest on Notes (LO5)

Compute any interest accrued for each of the following notes payable owed by Penman, Inc., as of December 31, 2005 (use a 365-day year):

Lender	Issuance Date	Principal	Coupon Rate (%)	Term
Nissim	11/21/05	$18,000	10%	120 days
Klein	12/13/05	14,000	9	90 days
Bildersee	12/19/05	16,000	12	60 days

M10-27. Debt Ratings and Capital Structure (LO6)

General Mills reports the following information in the Management Discussion & Analysis section of its 2003 10-K report:

> Free cash flow allowed us to reduce debt to $9.0 billion at the end of 2003. As we complete the integration of Pillsbury, we expect our free cash flow to increase, and have set a target to pay down a cumulative $2 billion of our total adjusted debt over the next three years, including at least $450 million in fiscal 2004. The goal of our debt reduction plan is to return to a mid-A rating for our corporate debt. Currently, Standard and Poor's Corporation has ratings of "BBB+" on our publicly held long-term debt.

a. Why will debt reduction result in a higher debt rating for General Mills' bonds?

b. What effect will a higher debt rating have on General Mills' financing costs? Explain.

M10-28. Computing Bond Issue Price (LO4)

Bushman, Inc., issues $500,000 of 9% bonds that pay interest semiannually and mature in 10 years. Compute the bond issue price assuming that the bonds' market rate is:

a. 8% per year compounded semiannually.

b. 10% per year compounded semiannually.

M10-29. Computing Issue Price for Zero Coupon Bonds (LO4)

Bushman, Inc., issues $500,000 of zero coupon bonds that mature in 10 years. Compute the bond issue price assuming that the bonds' market rate is:

a. 8% per year compounded semiannually.

b. 10% per year compounded semiannually.

M10-30. Financial Statement Effects of Accounts Payable Transactions (LO3, 5)

Petroni Company had the following transactions relating to its accounts payable:

1. Purchases $300 of inventory on credit.
2. Sells $300 of inventory for $420 on credit (cost side recorded in part *c*).
3. Records $300 cost of sales with transaction *b*.
4. $300 cash paid to settle accounts payable from *a*.
5. $420 cash received from accounts receivable in *b*.

Required

a. Prepare journal entries to record the transactions.

b. Post the journal entries from part *a* to their respective T-accounts.

c. Record each of the transactions from part *a* in the financial statement effects template.

M10-31. Computing Bond Issue Price and Preparing an Amortization Table in Excel (LO4, 5)

On January 1, 2005, Bushman, Inc., issues $500,000 of 9% bonds that pay interest semiannually and mature in 10 years (December 31, 2014).

a. Using the Excel PRICE worksheet function, compute the issue price assuming that the bonds' market rate is 8% per year compounded semiannually. (Use 100 for the redemption value to get a price as a percentage of the face amount, and use 1 for the basis.)

b. Prepare an amortization table in Excel to demonstrate the amortization of the book (carrying) value to the $500,000 maturity value at the end of the 20th semiannual period.

M10-32. Recording and Assessing the Effects of Bond Financing (LO5)

On December 31, 2006, Lynch Company issued $800,000 of 10-year, 9% bonds payable for $750,232, yielding an effective interest rate of 10%. Interest is payable semiannually on June 30 and December 31.

a. Prepare journal entries to record (1) the issuance of the bonds, (2) the semiannual interest payment and discount amortization on December 31, 2007. Round amounts to the nearest dollar.

b. Post the journal entries from part *a* to their respective T-accounts.

c. Record each of the transactions from part *a* in the financial statement effects template.

M10-33. Recording and Assessing the Effects of Bond Financing (LO5)

On December 31, 2006, Emig Company issued $300,000 of 15-year, 10% bonds payable for $351,780, yielding an effective interest rate of 8%. Interest is payable semiannually on June 30 and December 31.

a. Prepare journal entries to record (1) the issuance of the bonds, (2) the semiannual interest payment and premium amortization (effective interest method) on June 30, 2007, and (3) the semiannual interest payment and premium amortization (effective interest method) on June 30, 2007, and (3) the semiannual interest payment and discount amortization on December 31, 2007. Round amounts to the nearest dollar.

b. Post the journal entries from part *a* to their respective T-accounts.

c. Record each of the transactions from part *a* in the financial statement effects template.

M10-34. Reporting the Effects of Bond Financing (LO1, 2, 3)
Indicate the proper financial statement classification for each of the following accounts:

> Gain on Bond Retirement (material amount)
> Discount on Bonds Payable
> Mortgage Notes Payable
> Bonds Payable
> Bond Interest Expense
> Bond Interest Payable
> Premium on Bonds Payable

M10-35. Recording and Assessing the Effects of Retiring Bonds (LO5)
Hanouille Company issued $400,000 of 11%, 20-year bonds at 108 on January 1, 2006. Interest is payable semiannually on July 1 and January 1. Through January 1, 2011, Hanouille amortized $5,000 of the bond premium. On January 1, 2011, Hanouille retired the bonds at 103 (after making the interest payment on that date).

a. Prepare the journal entry to record the bond retirement on January 1, 2011.

b. Post the journal entry from part *a* to their respective T-accounts.

c. Record the transaction from part *a* in the financial statement effects template.

M10-36. Recording and Assessing the Effects of Installment Loans (LO4, 5)
On December 31, 2006, Thomas, Inc., borrowed $700,000 on a 12%, 15-year mortgage note payable. The note is to be repaid in equal semiannual installments of $50,854 (payable on June 30 and December 31).

a. Prepare journal entries to record (1) the issuance of the mortgage note payable, (2) the payment of the first installment on June 30, 2007, and (3) the payment of the second installment on December 31, 2007. Round amounts to the nearest dollar.

b. Post the journal entries from part *a* to their respective T-accounts.

c. Record each of the transactions from part *a* in the financial statement effects template.

M10-37. Determining Bond Prices (LO4)
Lunar, Inc., plans to issue $900,000 of 10% bonds that will pay interest semiannually and mature in five years. Assume that the effective interest rate is 12% per year compounded semi-annually.

Compute the selling price of the bonds. Use Tables I and II in Appendix A near the end of the book.

EXERCISES

E10-38. Analyzing and Computing Accrued Warranty Liability and Expense (LO2)
Waymire Company sells a motor that carries a 60-day unconditional warranty against product failure. Waymire estimates that between the sale and lapse of the product warranty, 2% of the 69,000 units sold this period will require repair at an average cost of $50 per unit. Warranty costs for 1,000 known failures are already reflected in its financial statements, resulting in a current warranty liability of $10,000 on the balance sheet.

a. How much *additional* warranty expense must Waymire report in its income statement and what amount of *additional* warranty liability must it report on its balance sheet for this year?

b. What analysis issues do we need to consider with respect to the amount of reported warranty liability?

E10-39. Analyzing Contingencies and Assessing Liabilities (LO2)
The following independent situations represent various types of liabilities. Analyze each situation and indicate which of the following is the proper accounting treatment for the company in boldface type: (a) record in accounts, (b) disclose in a financial statement footnote, or (c) neither record nor disclose.

1. A stockholder has filed a lawsuit against Clinch Corporation. Clinch's attorneys have reviewed the facts of the case. Their review revealed that similar lawsuits have never resulted in a cash award and it is highly unlikely that this lawsuit will either.

2. Foster Company signed a 60-day, 10% note when it purchased items from another company.

3. The Department of Environment Protection notifies Shevlin Company that a state where it has a plant is filing a lawsuit for groundwater pollution against Shevlin and another company that has a

plant adjacent to Shevlin's plant. Test results have not identified the exact source of the pollution. Shevlin's manufacturing process often produces by-products that can pollute ground water.

4. Sloan Company manufactured and sold products to a retailer that sold the products to consumers. The Sloan Company warranty offers replacement of the product if it is found to be defective within 90 days of the sale to the consumer. Historically, 1.2% of the products are returned for replacement.

E10-40. Analyzing and Computing Accrued Wages Liability and Expense (LO2)
Demski Company pays its employees on the 1st and 15th of each month. It is March 31 and Demski is preparing financial statements for this quarter. Its employees have earned $25,000 since the 15th of this month and have not yet been paid. How will Demski's balance sheet and income statement change to reflect the accrual of wages that must be made at March 31? What balance sheet and income statement accounts would be incorrectly reported if Demski failed to make this accrual (for each account indicates whether it would be overstated or understated)?

E10-41. Analyzing and Reporting Financial Statement Effects of Bond Transactions (LO5)
On January 1, 2005, Hutton Corp. issued $300,000 of 15-year, 10% bonds payable for $351,876, yielding an effective interest rate of 8%. Interest is payable semiannually on June 30 and December 31.
a. Show computations to confirm the issue price of $351,876.
b. Prepare journal entries to record the bond issuance, semiannual interest payment, and premium amortization on June 30, 2005, and semiannual interest payment and premium amortization on December 31, 2005.
c. Post the journal entries from part *b* to their respective T-accounts.
d. Record each of the transactions from part *b* in the financial statement effects template.

E10-42. Analyzing and Reporting Financial Statement Effects of Bond Transactions (LO5)
On January 1, 2005, Piotroski, Inc., borrowed $700,000 on a 12%, 15-year mortgage note payable. The note is to be repaid in equal semiannual installments of $50,854 (payable on June 30 and December 31).
a. Prepare journal entries to record the issuance of the mortgage not payable, payment of the first installment on June 30, 2005, and payment of the second installment on December 31, 2005.
b. Post the journal entries from part *a* to their respective T-accounts.
c. Record each of the transactions from part *a* in the financial statement effects template.

E10-43. Computing the Bond Issue Price (LO4)
D'Souza, Inc., issues $900,000 of 10% bonds that pay interest semiannually and mature in five years. Assume that the market interest (yield) rate is 12% per year compounded semiannually. Compute the bond issue price.

E10-44. Effects of Bond Credit Ratings Changes (LO6)

AT&T (T)

AT&T reports the following footnote to its 2003 10-K:

Credit Ratings and Related Debt Implications
During 2003, AT&T's long-term credit ratings were lowered by both Standard & Poor's (S&P) and Fitch. As of December 31, 2003, our credit ratings were as follows:

Credit Rating Agency	Short-Term Rating	Long-Term Rating	Outlook
Standard & Poor's	A-2	BBB	Stable
Fitch	F-2	BBB	Negative
Moody's	P-2	Baa2	Negative

Our access to capital markets as well as the cost of our borrowings is affected by our debt ratings. The rating action by S&P in July 2003, triggered a 25 basis point interest rate step-up on approximately $10 billion in notional amount of debt ($1.3 billion of which matured in November 2003). This step-up was effective for interest payment periods that began after November 2003, resulting in an expected increase in interest expense of approximately $15 million in 2004. Further debt rating downgrades could require AT&T to pay higher rates on certain existing debt and post cash collateral for certain interest-rate and equity swaps if we are in a net payable position.

If AT&T's debt ratings are further downgraded, AT&T's access to the capital markets may be restricted and/or such replacement financing may be more costly or have additional covenants than we had in connection with our debt at December 31, 2003. In addition, the market environment for financing in general, and within the telecommunications sector in particular, has been adversely affected by economic conditions and bankruptcies of other telecommunications providers. If the financial markets become more cautious regarding the industry/ratings category we operate in, our ability to obtain financing would be further reduced and the cost of any new financings may be higher.

a. What are some typical financial ratios that credit rating companies use to evaluate the relative riskiness of borrowers?

    b.   Why might a reduction its credit ratings result in higher interest costs and restrict AT&T's access to credit markets?

    c.   What type of actions can AT&T take to improve its credit ratings?

E10-45. **Analyzing and Reporting Financial Statement Effects of Bond Transactions** (LO5)

Lundholm, Inc., which reports financial statements each December 31, is authorized to issue $500,000 of 9%, 15-year bonds dated May 1, 2005, with interest payments on October 31 and April 30. Assuming the bonds are sold at par on May 1, 2005.

    a.   Prepare journal entries to record the bond issuance, payment of the first semiannual period's interest, and retirement of $300,000 of the bonds at 101 on November 1, 2006.

    b.   Post the journal entries from part *a* to their respective T-accounts.

    c.   Record each of the transactions from part *a* in the financial statement effects template

E10-46. **Analyzing and Reporting Financial Statement Effects of Bond Transactions** (LO?)

On January 1, 2005, McKeown, Inc., issued $250,000 of 8%, 9-year bonds for $220,775, yielding a market (yield) rate of 10%. Semiannual interest is payable on June 30 and December 31 of each year.

    a.   Show computations to confirm the bond issue price.

    b.   Prepare journal entries to record the bond issuance, semiannual interest payment, and discount amortization on June 30, 2005, and semiannual interest payment and discount amortization on December 31, 2005.

    c.   Post the journal entries from part *b* to their respective T-accounts.

    d.   Record each of the transactions from part *b* in the financial statement effects template.

E10-47. **Analyzing and Reporting Financial Statement Effects of Bond Transactions** (LO5) $PV = 879,172$

On January 1, 2005, Shields, Inc., issued $800,000 of 9%, 20-year bonds for $878,948, yielding a market (yield) rate of 8%. Semiannual interest is payable on June 30 and December 31 of each year.

    a.   Show computations to confirm the bond issue price.

    b.   Prepare journal entries to record the bond issuance, semiannual interest payment, and premium amortization on June 30, 2005, and semiannual interest payment and premium amortization on December 31, 2005.

    c.   Post the journal entries from part *b* to their respective T-accounts.

    d.   Record each of the transactions from part *b* in the financial statement effects template.

E10-48. **Bond Pricing, Interest Rates, and Financial Statements** (LO4)

Following is a price quote for $1.6 billion of 5.625% coupon bonds issued by **Abbott Laboratories (ABT)** that mature in July 2006 (from www.bondpage.com):

Abbott
Laboratories
(ABT)

Ratings Industry	Issue Call Information	Coupon Maturity Pmt Months	Price YTM
A1/AA	Abbott Labs	5.625	104.069
Industrial	Non Callable, Make Whole Calls	07-01-2006 Jan, Jul	2.982

This quote indicates that Abbott's bonds have a market price of 104.069 (104.069% of face value), resulting in a yield of 2.982%.

    a.   Assuming that these bonds were originally issued at or close to par value, what does the above market price reveal about the direction that interest rates have changed since Abbott issued its bonds? (Assume that Abbott's debt rating has remained the same.)

    b.   Does the change in interest rates since the issuance of these bonds affect the amount of interest expense that Abbott is reporting in its income statement? Explain.

    c.   If Abbott Labs was to repurchase its bonds at the above market price of 104.069, how would the repurchase affect its current income?

    d.   Assuming that the bonds remain outstanding until their maturity, at what market price will the bonds sell on their due date of July 1, 2006?

E10-49.[A] **Computing Present Values of Single Amounts and Annuities** (LO4)

Refer to Tables 1 and 2 in Appendix A near the end of the book to compute the present value for each of the following amounts:

    a. $90,000 received 10 years hence if the annual interest rate is

        1.   8% compounded annually.

        2.   8% compounded semiannually.

    b. $1,000 received at the end of each year for the next eight years if money is worth 10% per year compounded annually.

c. $600 received at the end of each six months for the next 15 years if the interest rate is 8% per year compounded semiannually.

d. $500,000 inheritance 10 years hence if money is worth 10% per year compounded annually.

E10-50. Analyzing and Reporting Financial Statement Effects of Bond Transactions (LO5)

On January 1, 2005, Trueman Corp. issued $600,000 of 20-year, 11% bonds for $554,860, yielding a market (yield) rate of 12%. Interest is payable semiannually on June 30 and December 31.

a. Confirm the bond issue price.

b. Prepare journal entries to record the bond issuance, semiannual interest payment, and discount amortization on June 30, 2005, and semiannual interest payment and discount amortization on December 31, 2005.

c. Post the journal entries from part *b* to their respective T-accounts.

d. Record each of the transactions from part *b* in the financial statement effects template.

E10-51. Analyzing and Reporting Financial Statement Effects of Bond Transactions (LO5)

On January 1, 2005, Verrecchia Company issued $400,000 of 5-year, 13% bonds for $446,208, yielding a market (yield) rate of 10%. Interest is payable semiannually on June 30 and December 31.

a. Show computations to confirm the bond issue price.

b. Prepare journal entries to record the bond issuance, semiannual interest payment, and premium amortization on June 30, 2005, and semiannual interest payment and premium amortization on December 31, 2005.

c. Post the journal entries from part *b* to their respective T-accounts.

d. Record each of the transactions from part *b* in the financial statement effects template.

E10-52. Recording and Assessing the Effects of Bond Financing (LO5)

On December 31, 2006, Anderson Company issued $600,000 of 20-year, 11% bonds payable for $554,718, yielding an effective interest rate of 12%. Interest is payable semiannually on June 30 and December 31.

a. Prepare journal entries to reflect (1) the issuance of the bonds, (2) the semiannual interest payment and discount amortization (effective interest method) on June 30, 2007, and (3) the semiannual interest payment and discount amortization on December 31, 2007. Round amounts to the nearest dollar.

b. Post the journal entries from part *a* to their respective T-accounts.

c. Record each of the transactions from part *a* in the financial statement effects template.

E10-53. Recording and Assessing the Effects of Bond Financing (LO5)

On December 31, 2006, Parker Company issued $400,000 of five-year, 13% bonds payable for $446,372, yielding an effective interest rate of 10%. Interest is payable semiannually on June 30 and December 31.

a. Prepare journal entries to reflect (1) the issuance of the bonds, (2) the semiannual interest payment and premium amortization (effective interest method) on June 30, 2007, and (3) the semiannual interest payment and premium amortization on December 31, 2007. Round amounts to the nearest dollar.

b. Post the journal entries from part *a* to their respective T-accounts.

c. Record each of the transactions from part *a* in the financial statement effects template.

E10-54. Recording and Assessing the Effects of Retiring Bonds (LO5)

Norwalk, Inc., issued $250,000 of 8%, 15-year bonds at 96 on June 30, 2006. Interest is payable semiannually on December 31 and June 30. Through June 30, 2012, Norwalk amortized $3,000 of the bond discount. On June 30, 2012, Norwalk retired the bonds at 101 (after making the interest payment on that date).

a. Prepare the journal entry to record the bond retirement on June 30, 2012.

b. Post the journal entries from part *a* to their respective T-accounts.

c. Record each of the transactions from part *a* in the financial statement effects template.

E10-55 Reporting and Interpreting Bond Disclosures (LO2, 3, 5)

The adjusted trial balance for the Haas Corporation at the end of 2006 contains the following accounts:

$ 25,000	Bond Interest Payable
600,000	9% Bonds Payable due 2009
500,000	10% Bonds Payable due 2005
19,000	Discount on 9% Bonds Payable
15,000	Premium on 10% Bonds Payable
170,500	Zero Coupon Bonds Payable due 2011
100,000	8% Bonds Payable due 2007

Prepare the long-term liabilities section of the balance sheet. Indicate the proper balance sheet classification for accounts listed above that do not belong in the long-term liabilities section.

E10-56. Recording and Assessing the Effects of Installment Loans (LO4, 5)

On December 31, 2006, Dehning, Inc., borrowed $500,000 on an 8%, 10-year mortgage note payable. The note is to be repaid in equal quarterly installments of $18,278 (beginning March 31, 2007).

a. Prepare journal entries to reflect (1) the issuance of the mortgage note payable, (2) the payment of the first installment on March 31, 2007, and (3) the payment of the second installment on June 30, 2007. Round amounts to the nearest dollar.

b. Post the journal entries from part *a* to their respective T-accounts.

c. Record each of the transactions from part *a* in the financial statement effects template.

E10-57. Determining Bond Prices (LO4)

Tide, Inc., plans to issue $500,000 of 9% bonds that will pay interest semiannually and mature in 10 years. Assume that the effective interest is 8% per year compounded semiannually.

Compute the selling price of the bonds. Use Tables I and II (in Appendix A near the end of the book).

PROBLEMS

P10-58. Interpreting Term Structures of Coupon and Yield Rates (LO4, 5, 6)

Lockheed Martin reports $6,072 million of long-term debt outstanding as of December 2003 in the following schedule to its 10-K report:

Lockheed Martin (LMT)

Type (Maturity Dates) (In millions, except interest rate data)	Range of Interest Rates	2003	2002
Floating rate convertible debentures (2033)	0.93%	$1,000	$ —
Other debentures (2013–2036)	7.0–9.1%	3,388	4,198
Notes (2004–2022)	6.5–9.0%	1,778	3,099
Other obligations (2004–2017)	1.0–10.5%	42	260
		6,208	7,557
Less current maturities		(136)	(1,365)
		$6,072	$6,192

Bond pricing information relating to its Other Debentures follows (from www.bondpage.com):

Ratings Industry	Issue Call Information	Coupon Maturity Pmt Months	Price YTM LY
Baa2/BBB	Lockheed Martin Corp	8.200	119.002
Industrial	Non Callable	12-01-2009	3.976
		Jun,Dec	Mat
Baa2/BBB	Lockheed Martin Corp	7.650	122.278
Industrial	Non Callable	05-01-2016	5.058
		May,Nov	Mat
Baa2/BBB	Lockheed Martin Corp	8.500	137.654
Industrial	Non Callable, Make Whole Calls	12-01-2029	5.666
		Jun,Dec	Mat

Required

a. Although the coupon rates on these debentures range from 7.65% to 8.5%, the market (yield) rate ranges from 3.976% to 5.666%. Discuss how and why these two rates differ.

b. Rank the yields in order of maturity. Do you see a pattern? Discuss the relation between the yield rate and the term to maturity.

P10-59. Preparing an Amortization Schedule and Recording the Effects of Bonds (LO4, 5)

On December 31, 2006, Sullivan, Inc., issued $250,000 of 8%, 9-year bonds for $220,900, yielding an effective interest rate of 10%. Semiannual interest is payable on June 30 and December 31 each year. The firm uses the effective interest method to amortize the discount.

Required

a. Prepare an amortization schedule showing the necessary information for the first two interest periods. Round amounts to the nearest dollar.

    b.   Prepare the journal entries (1) for the bond issuance on December 31, 2006, (2) to record the bond interest payment and discount amortization at June 30, 2007, and (3) to record the bond interest payment and discount amortization at December 31, 2007.

    c.   Post the journal entries from part *b* to their respective T-accounts.

    d.   Record each of the transactions from part *b* in the financial statement effects template.

P10-60. **Recording and Assessing the Effects of Bond Financing (with Accrued Interest)** **(LO4, 5)**

Eskew, Inc., which closes its books on December 31, is authorized to issue $500,000 of 9%, 15-year bonds dated May 1, 2006, with interest payments on November 1 and May 1.

Required

Assuming that the bonds were sold at 100 plus accrued interest on October 1, 2006, prepare the necessary journal entries, post the journal entries to their respective t-accounts, and record each transaction in the financial statement effects template.

    a.   The bond issuance.

    b.   Payment of the first semiannual period's interest on November 1, 2006.

    c.   Accrual of bond interest expense at December 31, 2006.

    d.   Payment of the semiannual interest on May 1, 2007. (The firm does not make reversing entries.)

    e.   Retirement of $300,000 of the bonds at 101 on May 1, 2011 (immediately after the interest payment on that date).

P10-61. **Preparing an Amortization Schedule and Recording the Effects of Bonds** **(LO4, 5)**

On March 31, 2006, Strong, Inc., issued $800,000 of 9%, 20-year bonds for $878,948, yielding an effective interest rate of 8%. Semiannual interest is payable on September 30 and March 31 each year. The firm uses the effective interest method to amortize the premium.

Required

    a.   Prepare an amortization schedule showing the necessary information for the first two interest periods. Round amounts to the nearest dollar.

    b.   Prepare the journal entries (1) for the bond issuance on March 31, 2006, (2) to record the bond interest payment and premium amortization at September 30, 2006, (3) the adjusting entry to record interest expense and premium amortization at December 31, 2006, the close of the firm's accounting year, and (4) the entry to record the bond interest payment and premium amortization at March 31, 2007.

    c.   Post the journal entries from part *b* to their respective T-accounts.

    d.   Record each of the transactions from part *b* in the financial statement effects template.

P10-62. **Interpreting Debt Footnotes on Interest Rates and Expense** **(LO4, 5)**

CVS Corporation
(CVS)

CVS Corporation discloses the following footnote in its 10-K relating to its debt:

BORROWING AND CREDIT AGREEMENTS

Following is a summary of the Company's borrowings as of the respective balance sheet dates:

In millions	Jan. 3, 2004	Dec. 28, 2002
Commercial paper	$ —	$ 4.8
5.5% senior notes due 2004	300.0	300.0
5.625% senior notes due 2006	300.0	300.0
3.875% senior notes due 2007	300.0	300.0
8.52% ESOP notes due 2008	163.2	194.4
Mortgage notes payable	12.2	13.0
Capital lease obligations	0.9	0.9
	1,076.3	1,113.1
Less:		
Short-term debt	—	(4.8)
Current portion of long-term debt	(323.2)	(32.0)
	$ 753.1	$1,076.3

CVS also discloses the following:

    Interest expense, net—Interest expense was $53.9 million, $54.5 million and $65.2 million and interest income was $5.8 million, $4.1 million and $4.2 million in 2003, 2002 and 2001, respectively. Interest paid totaled $64.9 million in 2003, $60.7 million in 2002 and $75.2 million in 2001.

Required

a.   What is the average interest rate that CVS paid on its long-term debt (all of the reported interest rates relate to long-term debt)?

b.   Does your computation in (a) seem reasonable given the disclosure relating to specific bond issues? Explain.

c.   Why can the amount of interest paid be different from the amount of interest expense recorded in the income statement?

P10-63.   Recording and Assessing the Effects of Bond Financing (with Accrued Interest)   (LO4, 5)

Chaney, Inc., which closes its books on December 31, is authorized to issue $800,000 of 9%, 20-year bonds dated March 1, 2006, with interest payments on September 1 and March 1.

Required

Assuming that the bonds were sold at 100 plus accrued interest on July 1, 2006, prepare the necessary journal entries, post the journal entries to their respective t-accounts, and record each transaction in the financial statement effects template.

a.   The bond issuance.

b.   Payment of the semiannual interest on September 1, 2006.

c.   Accrual of bond interest expense at December 31, 2006.

d.   Payment of the semiannual interest on March 1, 2007. (The firm does not make reversing entries.)

e.   Retirement of $200,000 of the bonds at 101 on March 1, 2006 (immediately after the interest payment on that date).

P10-64.   Preparing an Amortization Schedule and Recording the Effects of Bonds   (LO4, 5)

On December 31, 2006, Kasznik, Inc., issued $720,000 of 11%, 10-year bonds for $678,852, yielding an effective interest rate of 12%. Semiannual interest is payable on June 30 and December 31 each year. The firm uses the effective interest method to amortize the discount.

Required

a.   Prepare an amortization schedule showing the necessary information for the first two interest periods. Round amounts to the nearest dollar.

b.   Prepare the journal entries for (1) the bond issuance on December 31, 2006, (2) to record bond interest expense and discount amortization at June 30, 2007, and (3) to record bond interest expense and discount amortization at December 31, 2007.

c.   Post the journal entries from part *b* to their respective T-accounts.

d.   Record each of the transactions from part *b* in the financial statement effects template.

P10-65.   Preparing an Amortization Schedule and Recording the Effects of Bonds   (LO4, 5)

On April 30, 2006, Cheng, Inc., issued $250,000 of 6%, 15-year bonds for $206,690, yielding an effective interest rate of 8%. Semiannual interest is payable on October 31 and April 30 each year. The firm uses the effective interest method to amortize the discount.

Required

a.   Prepare an amortization schedule showing the necessary information for the first two interest periods. Round amounts to the nearest dollar.

b.   Prepare the journal entries (1) for the bond issuance on April 30, 2006, (2) to record the bond interest payment and discount amortization at October 31, 2006, (3) the adjusting entry to record bond interest expense and discount amortization at December 31, 2006, the close of the firm's accounting year, and (4) to record the bond interest payment and discount amortization at April 30, 2007.

c.   Post the journal entries from part *b* to their respective T-accounts.

d.   Record each of the transactions from part *b* in the financial statement effects template.

P10-66.   Recording and Assessing the Effects of Installment Loans   (LO4, 5)

On December 31, 2007, Wasley Corporation borrowed $500,000 on a 10%, 10-year mortgage note payable. The note is to be repaid with equal semiannual installments, beginning June 30, 2008.

Required

a.   Compute the amount of the semiannual installment payment. Use the appropriate table (in Appendix A near the end of the book) and round amount to the nearest dollar.

b.   Prepare the journal entry (1) to record Wasley 's borrowing of funds on December 31, 2007, (2) to record Wasley 's installment payment on June 30, 2008, and (3) to record Wasley's installment payment on December 31, 2008. (Round amounts to the nearest dollar.)

c.   Post the journal entries from part *b* to their respective T-accounts.

d.   Record each of the transactions from part *b* in the financial statement effects template.

P10-67.   Recording and Assessing the Effects of Installment Loans   (LO4, 5)

On December 31, 2007, Watts Corporation borrowed $950,000 on an 8%, five-year mortgage note payable. The note is to be repaid with equal quarterly installments, beginning March 31, 2008.

Required

a. Compute the amount of the quarterly installment payment. Use the appropriate table (in Appendix A near the end of the book) and round amount to the nearest dollar.

b. Prepare the journal entries (1) to record the borrowing of funds by Watts Corporation on December 31, 2007, (2) to record the installment payment by Watts Corporation on March 31, 2008, and (3) to record the installment payment by Watts Corporation on June 30, 2008.

c. Post the journal entries from part *b* to their respective T-accounts.

d. Record each of the transactions from part *b* in the financial statement effects template.

P10-68. Computing Present Values (LO4)

Use the interest tables in Appendix A near the end of the book (or a calculator) to answer the following. Compute the present value of each of the following items.

Required

a. $90,000 10 years hence if the annual interest rate is
   1. 8% compounded annually.
   2. 8% compounded semiannually.
   3. 8% compounded quarterly.

b. $1,000 received at the end of each year for the next eight years if money is worth 10% per year compounded annually.

c. $600 received at the end of each period of six months for the next 15 years if the interest rate is 8% per year compounded semiannually.

d. $500,000 inheritance 10 years hence if money is worth 10% per year compounded annually.

e. $2,500 received each half-year for the next 10 years, plus a single sum of $85,000 at the end of 10 years if the interest rate is 12% per year compounded semiannually.

P10-69. Determining Bond Sinking-Fund Contribution and Future Values (LO4)

Use the interest tables in Appendix A near the end of the book (or a calculator) to compute the following amounts requested.

Required

a. A firm issued $800,000 of 10-year bonds payable. The bond agreement requires annual year-end contributions to a sinking fund in order to accumulate $800,000 to retire the bonds at maturity. Calculate the amount of the annual contribution if an 8% rate of return is expected.

b. Calculate the future value of a single amount of $7,000 invested for 15 years at 10% compounded annually.

c. Calculate the future value of a single amount of $7,000 invested for 15 years at 10% compounded semiannually.

d. Calculate the future value of an annuity of $20,000 invested at the end of each year for eight years at an annual rate of 8%.

e. Calculate the future value of an annuity of $10,000 invested at the end of each six months for eight years at an annual rate of 8%.

CASES AND PROJECTS

C10-70. Analyzing and Interpreting Liability Accruals in Financial Statements and Notes (Lo2, 3, 5)

International Paper (IP)

Refer to the financial statements and disclosures for **International Paper (IP)**—selected pages are shown below—to answer the following requirements.

In millions, for Year Ended December 31	2000
Net Sales	$28,180
Costs and Expenses	
Cost of products sold	20,082
Selling and administrative expenses	2,283
Depreciation and amortization	1,916
Distribution expenses	1,104
Taxes other than payroll and income taxes	287
Merger integration costs	54
Restructuring and other charges	949
Total Costs and Expenses	26,675
Reversals of reserves no longer required	34

(Continued on next page)

(Continued from previous page)

In millions, for Year Ended December 31	2000
Earnings before Interest, Income Taxes, Minority Interest and Extraordinary Items	1,539
Interest expense, net	816
Earnings before Income Taxes, Minority Interest and Extraordinary Items	723
Income tax provision	117
Minority interest expense, net of taxes	238
Earnings before Extraordinary Items	368
Impairment losses on businesses to be sold, net of taxes	(541)
Net gain on sales of investments and businesses, net of taxes and minority interest	315
Net Earnings	$ 142

In millions at December 31	2000
Assets	
Current Assets	
Cash and temporary investments	$ 1,198
Accounts and notes receivable, less allowances of $128	3,433
Inventories	3,182
Assets of businesses held for sale	1,890
Other current assets	752
Total Current Assets	10,455
Plants, Properties and Equipment, net	16,011
Forestlands	5,966
Investments	269
Goodwill	6,310
Deferred Charges and Other Assets	3,098
Total Assets	$42,109
Liabilities and Common Shareholders' Equity	
Current Liabilities	
Notes payable and current maturities of long-term debt	$ 2,115
Accounts payable	2,113
Accrued payroll and benefits	511
Liabilities of businesses held for sale	541
Other accrued liabilities	2,133
Total Current Liabilities	7,413
Long-Term Debt	12,648
Deferred Income Taxes	4,699
Other Liabilities	2,155
Minority Interest	1,355
International Paper-Obligated Mandatorily Redeemable Preferred Securities of Subsidiaries Holding International Paper Debentures	1,805
Common Shareholders' Equity	
Common stock, $1 par value, 484.2 shares	484
Paid-in capital	6,501
Retained earnings	6,308
Accumulated other comprehensive income (loss)	(1,142)
	12,151
Less: Common stock held in treasury, at cost, 2.7 shares	117
Total Common Shareholders' Equity	12,034
Total Liabilities and Common Shareholders' Equity	$42,109

6. Special Items Including Restructuring and Business Improvement Actions

2000: Special items reduced 2000 net earnings by $601 million, 1999 net earnings by $352 million and 1998 net earnings by $98 million. The following table and discussion presents the impact of special items for 2000:

In millions, Year-Ended December 31, 2000	Earnings (Loss) Before Income Taxes and Minority Interest	Earnings (Loss) After Income Taxes and Minority Interest
Before special and extraordinary items	$1,692	$ 969
Merger-related expenses	(54)	(33)
Restructuring and other charges	(824)	(509)
Provision for legal reserves	(125)	(80)
Reversals of reserves no longer required	34	21
After special items	$ 723	$ 368

During 2000, special charges before taxes and minority interest of $969 million ($601 million after taxes and minority interest) were recorded. These special items included a $54 million pre-tax charge ($33 million after taxes) for merger-related expenses, an $824 million charge before taxes and minority interest ($509 million after taxes and minority interest) for asset shutdowns of excess internal capacity and cost reduction actions, a $125 million pre-tax charge ($80 million after taxes) for additional Masonite legal reserves and a $34 million pre-tax credit ($21 million after taxes) for the reversals of reserves no longer required.

The merger-related expenses of $54 million consisted primarily of travel, systems integration, employee retention, and other one-time cash costs related to the Champion acquisition and Union Camp merger.

The $824 million charge for the asset shutdowns of excess internal capacity and cost reduction actions consisted of a $71 million charge in the second quarter of 2000 and a $753 million charge in the fourth quarter of 2000. The second quarter charge of $71 million consisted of $40 million of asset write-downs and $31 million of severance and other charges. The fourth quarter charge of $753 million consisted of $536 million of asset write-downs and $217 million of severance and other charges.

7. Businesses Held for Sale

During 2000, International Paper announced plans to sell by the end of 2001, approximately $5 billion of assets that are not strategic to its core businesses.

In the third quarter of 2000, the assets of Masonite and Zanders were written down to their fair market values based on estimated sales proceeds. This resulted in an extraordinary pre-tax charge of $460 million ($310 million after taxes). In the fourth quarter of 2000, Fine Papers, the Chemical Cellulose pulp business and International Paper's Flexible Packaging businesses in Argentina (included in Other) were written down to their fair market values based on estimated sales proceeds, resulting in an extraordinary pre-tax charge of $373 million ($231 million after taxes). These charges are presented as extraordinary items, net of taxes, in the consolidated statement of earnings in accordance with the pooling-of-interests rules.

The assets of the businesses held for sale, totaling $1.9 billion, are included in "assets of businesses held for sale" in current assets in the accompanying consolidated balance sheet. The liabilities of these businesses, totaling $541 million, are included in "liabilities of businesses held for sale" in current liabilities in the accompanying consolidated balance sheet.

Required

a. What amount of net income did IP report for 2000? List the descriptions and amounts of all transitory items in IP's income statement.

b. In Note 6, IP reports a $969 million charge for 2000. What are the four major components of this charge?

c. IP reports a total charge of $824 million relating to "asset shutdowns of excess internal capacity and cost reduction actions" in its Note 6. What amount of this charge related to asset write-downs and what amount related to severance and other charges?

d. What did the $125 million (PR_TX) special charge item relate to (per Note 6)?

e. IP reports $541 million (net of tax) in "Impairment losses on businesses to be sold, net of tax" on its income statement. To what does this item relate?

f. IP reports $34 million in "Reversals of reserves no longer required" on its income statement. Briefly interpret what this item means.

g. Do you believe that IP's accruals provide investors with relevant information? Explain. How might a company use accruals to misrepresent its financial condition? What might you examine to analyze the appropriateness of accruals?

C10-71. Analyzing Bond Rates, Yields, Prices, and Credit Ratings (LO4, 5, 6)

Reproduced below is the long-term debt footnote from the 10-K report of **Southwest Airlines**:

Long-Term Debt

(In thousands)	2002
8¾% Notes due 2003	$ 100,000
Aircraft Secured Notes due 2004	175,000
8% Notes due 2005	100,000
Pass Through Certificates	585,661
7⅞% Notes due 2007	100,000
French Credit Agreements	50,024
6½% Notes due 2012	385,000
7⅞% Debentures due 2027	100,000
Capital leases	100,563
	1,696,248
Less current maturities	130,454
Less debt discount and issue costs	13,013
	$1,552,781

On March 1, 2002, the Company issued $385 million senior unsecured Notes (Notes) due March 1, 2012. The Notes bear interest at 6.5 percent, payable semi-annually beginning on September 1, 2002. Southwest used the net proceeds from the issuance of the Notes, approximately $380.2 million, for general corporate purposes, including the repayment of the Company's credit facility in March 2002.

As of December 31, 2002, aggregate annual principal maturities (not including interest on capital leases) for the five-year period ending December 31, 2007, were $130 million in 2003, $207 million in 2004, $142 million in 2005, $542 million in 2006, $114 million in 2007, and $561 million thereafter.

Reproduced below is the rating of Southwest Airlines's $385 million, 6.5% note issuance, due in 2012. The rating is from **Fitch Ratings, Ltd.**:

				Ratings			
				Long	Short		
Maturity Date	Currency	Total Amount	Coupon Rate	Term	Term	CUSIP	ISIN
01-MAR-2012	USD	$385,000,000	6.5%	A	—	844741AV0	US844741AV08

Following is a price quote on those same Southwest Airline's $385 million notes:

Ratings	Ticker	Description	Coupon	Maturity	YTC/YTM	Price
Baa1/A	LUV	Southwest Airls Co	6.500	03-01-2012	4.721	111.631

This quote indicates that the Southwest Airlines notes with a 6.5% coupon rate trades at 111.631 (111.631% of par) resulting in a yield to the investor of 4.721%.

Required

a. What is the amount of long-term debt reported on Southwest's 2002 balance sheet? What are the scheduled maturities for this indebtedness? Why is information relating to a company's scheduled maturities of debt useful in an analysis of its financial condition?

b. Southwest reported $106 million in interest expense in its 2002 income statement. In the note to its statement of cash flows, Southwest indicates that the cash portion of this expense is $80 million. What could account for the difference between interest expense and interest paid? Explain.

c. Southwest's long-term debt is rated "A" by Fitch and similarly by other credit rating agencies. What factors would be important to consider in attempting to quantify the relative riskiness of Southwest compared with other borrowers? Explain.

d. Southwest's $385 million 6.5% notes traded at 111.631, or 111.631% of par. What is the current dollar value of these notes per this trading price? How is the difference between this value and the $385 million face amount of the issue reflected in Southwest's financial statements? What effect would the repurchase of this entire note issue have on Southwest's financial statements? What does the 111.631 price tell you about the general trend in interest rates since Southwest sold this bond issue? Explain.

C10-72. **Evaluating Debt Financing versus Equity Financing** (LO4, 5, 6)

Stober Corporation has total assets of $5,200,000 and has been earning an average of $800,000 before income taxes for the past several years. The firm is planning to expand plant facilities to manufacture a new product and needs an additional $2,000,000 in funds, on which it expects to earn 18% before income tax. The income tax rate is expected to be 40% for the next several years. The firm has no long-term debt outstanding and presently has 75,000 shares of common stock outstanding. The firm is considering three alternatives:

1. Obtain the $2,000,000 by issuing 25,000 shares of common stock at $80 per share.
2. Obtain the $2,000,000 by issuing $1,000,000 of 10%, 20-year bonds at face value and 12,500 shares of common stock at $80 per share.
3. Obtain the $2,000,000 by issuing $2,000,000 of 10%, 20-year bonds at face value.

Required

As a stockholder of Stober Corporation, which alternative would you prefer if your main concern is enhancing the firm's earnings per share? (*Hint:* Divide net income by the number of outstanding common shares to determine earnings per share.)

C10-73. **Assessing Debt Financing, Company Interests, and Managerial Ethics** (LO4, 5, 6)

Knox Corporation is in the third quarter of the current year, and projections are that net income will be down about $600,000 from the previous year. Knox's return on assets is also projected to decline from its usual 15% to approximately 13%. If earnings do decline, this year will be the second consecutive year of decline. Knox's president is quite concerned about these projections (and his job) and has called a meeting of the firm's officers for next week to consider ways to "turn things around—and fast."

Margot O'Brien, treasurer of Knox Corporation, has received a memorandum from his assistant, Lorie Marsh. O'Brien had asked Marsh if she had any suggestions as to how Knox might improve its earnings performance for the current year. Marsh's memo reads as follows:

As you know, we have $3,000,000 of 8%, 20-year bonds payable outstanding. We issued these bonds 10 years ago at face value. When they mature, we would probably replace them with other bonds. The economy right now is in a phase of high inflation, and interest rates for bonds have soared to about 16%. My proposal is to replace these bonds right now. More specifically, I propose:

1. Immediately issue $3,000,000 of 20-year, 16% bonds payable. These bonds will be issued at face value.
2. Use the proceeds from the new bonds to buy back and retire our outstanding 8% bonds. Because of the current high rates of interest, these bonds are trading in the market at $1,900,000.
3. The benefits to Knox are that (a) the retirement of the old bonds will generate a $1,100,000 gain for the income statement and (b) there will be an extra $1,100,000 of cash available for other uses.

O'Brien is intrigued by the possibility of generating a $1,100,000 gain for the income statement. However, he is not sure this proposal is in the best long-run interests of the firm and its stockholders.

Required

a. How is the $1,100,000 gain calculated from the retirement of the old bonds? Where would this gain be reported in Knox's income statement?
b. Why might this proposal not be in the best long-run interests of the firm and its stockholders?
c. What possible ethical conflict is present in this proposal?

Reporting Owner Financing

LEARNING OBJECTIVES

After completing the chapter, you should be able to:

LO1 Describe business financing through stock issuances. (p. 469)

LO2 Explain and account for the issuance and repurchase of stock. (p. 472)

LO3 Describe how operations increase the equity of a business. (p. 477)

LO4 Explain and account for dividends and stock splits. (p. 477)

LO5 Define and illustrate comprehensive income. (p. 483)

LO6 Describe and illustrate the earnings per share computation. (p. 485)

LO7 Explain and interpret the reporting of convertible securities. (p. 489)

LO8 Discuss stock rights and the accounting for stock options. (p. 490)

LO9 *Appendix 11A—Analyze the reporting for equity carve outs, including sell-offs, spin-offs, and split-offs. (p. 495)*

Getty Images

PFIZER

Surviving Drug Wars

Pfizer is a research-based, global pharmaceutical company that discovers, develops, manufactures, and markets leading prescription medicines for humans and animals. The following six drugs account for $23.5 billion (52%) of its $45.2 billion in sales (Pfizer 2004 and 2003 10-K reports): Lipitor $9,231; Norvasc $4,336; Zoloft $3,118; Neurontin $2,702; Zithromax $2,010; and Celebrex $2,132. While Pfizer's products enjoy success, they highlight the challenge of managing a large, modern pharmaceutical company. For example, Lipitor, the bestselling drug in the world, loses its patent protection in four years. Pfizer's current answer to this challenge is to combine Lipitor with a powerful new drug in the hope of even greater market share and a new patent. The new compound, Torcetrapib, is aimed at reducing heart attacks at a greater level than the one-third or so seen with Lipitor alone.

The question is whether the new duo (Torcetrapib) will arrive in time to stop the usual 80% plunge in sales that occurs when a drug goes off-patent. Pfizer is spending a staggering $800 million putting the combo pill through final-stage trials in an all-out effort to show it prevents both plaque buildup and heart disease deaths. Another $90 million has already been committed to build a factory in Ireland to produce the combo.

If the pill falls short, Pfizer's income could plummet in the next decade. However, if it works, the drugmaker could easily dominate the industry for many years to come. Best of all, the new combo would get Pfizer patent protection, which Lipitor loses, until 2020 (Forbes 2004). The company has also recently received the good news that the FDA recommended approval of Exubera, the first inhaled version of insulin, a potential sales blockbuster (WSJ September 2005).

The pulling of Bextra from the market in November 2005 and the loss of patent protection on key drug products such as the antibiotic Zithromax, are not the only problems facing Pfizer's Hank McKinnell, its CEO since 2001. A bitter fight continues over U.S. trade policy and the lives of millions of Americans involving whether the U.S. should permit imports of prescription drugs from Canada. Presently, it is generally illegal for U.S. residents to buy pharmaceuticals north of the border or from anywhere abroad without a federal waiver. Yet, for many Americans, the lure of such purchases is intense because many of the same products are available in the U.S. are also in Canada at prices 30% to 50% lower.

While the U.S. pharmaceutical industry has produced an overwhelming share of medical breakthroughs, **Merck & Co.** CEO Raymond Gilmartin cautions that U.S. competitiveness hinges on industries such as pharmaceuticals that are at the forefront of innovation. Still, despite its high-

(Continued on next page)   **467**

(Continued from previous page)

tech image, the pharmaceutical industry is less adept at manufacturing than we might expect. Factory processes are often so antiquated that companies typically can't even pinpoint the causes of snafus. "Manufacturing has been the poor stepchild of the pharmaceutical industry," asserts Jeffrey T. Macher of Georgetown University. (*BusinessWeek* 2004)

Drugmakers are now tackling manufacturing concerns with new approaches. A host of technologies, such as Raman spectroscopy and chemical imaging, are being investigated in the desire to help determine the distribution of active ingredients in a pill or the size of the granules. Companies such as Pfizer and **Abbott Laboratories** are spending tens of millions per year to install such new technology and processes in plants. (*BusinessWeek* 2004)

Shareholders, however, are less than confident. By early 2006, Pfizer's stock price had declined to just over $20 per share, reflecting weaker sales of key medicines including Lipitor and Celebrex.

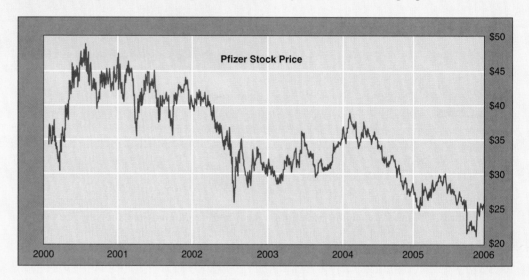

Pfizer commanded a below-average market multiple of 16.5 based on projected 2004 earnings per share of $2.11. That's a rare position for Pfizer, which typically has traded at a large premium to the S&P 500. Pfizer's admirers believe its growth potential is underappreciated and that the stock could rise to the mid $40s over the next year. But the market remains cautious because of the challenges facing the pharmaceutical industry. (*Barrons* 2004) By early 2006, the multiple exceeded $20 on projected earnings per share of slightly below $1.00.

One of the keys to Pfizer's present strategy has been to increase its size to spread its high overhead over a broader sales base. As part of this growth strategy, in 2000, Pfizer merged with **Warner-Lambert Company**, and in 2003, it acquired **Pharmacia** for $56 billion, making it the largest pharmaceutical company in the world. Under the terms of the merger agreement, each outstanding share of Pharmacia common stock was exchanged for 1.4 shares of Pfizer common stock. Also, each share of Pharmacia Series C convertible perpetual preferred stock was exchanged for a newly created class of Pfizer Series A convertible perpetual preferred stock with substantially similar rights. In December of 2005, Pfizer increased its quarterly dividend by 26% to 0.24 per share to appease investors restless over its sliding stock price. (WSJ 2005)

Companies like Pfizer issue stock for several reasons, including acquisitions and share purchases by employees under stock purchase and stock option plans. They also frequently engage in share repurchase programs and seek to unlock hidden value through sales, spin-offs, and split-offs of subsidiaries.

This chapter describes the accounting for equity transactions, including sales and repurchases of stock, dividends and stock splits, equity carve-outs, comprehensive income, and convertible securities. During 2003, Pfizer's stockholders' equity was impacted by earnings and other comprehensive income, issuance of stock in the Pharmacia acquisition, repurchases of common stock in the open market, the payment of dividends, the issuance of stock for employee stock option exercise, and the conversion to common of preferred shares. We discuss each of these transactions in this chapter.

Sources: *The Wall Street Journal* (2005 and 2004), *Barrons* (2004), Forbes (2004), *BusinessWeek* (2004), *Pfizer* 2005, 2004 and 2003 10-K Reports

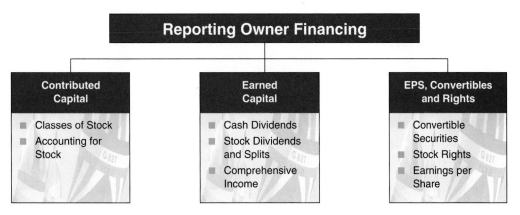

INTRODUCTION

A company finances its assets (other than through operating cash flows) from one of two sources: either it borrows funds from debtholders or it obtains funds from shareholders. On average, companies obtain about half of their external financing from borrowed sources and the other half from shareholder investment. This chapter describes the issues relating to stockholders' equity, including the accounting for stock transactions (sales and repurchases of stock, and dividends), the accounting for stock options, and the computation of earnings per share. We also discuss the issue of equity carve outs, a process by which companies seek to unlock substantial shareholder value via spin-offs and split-offs of business units into separate companies. Finally, we discuss the accounting for convertible securities, an increasingly prevalent financing vehicle.

LO1 Describe business financing through stock issuances.

When a company issues stock to the investing public, it records the receipt of cash (or other assets) and an increase in stockholders' equity, representing investment in the company by shareholders. The increase in cash and equity is equal to the market price of the stock on the issue date multiplied by the number of shares sold.

Like bonds, stockholders' equity is accounted for at *historical cost*. Consequently, fluctuations in the market price of the issuer's stock subsequent to the initial public offering do not directly affect the financial statements of the issuing company. This occurs because these transactions are between outside parties not involving the issuer. When and if stock is repurchased and subsequently resold, the issuer's stockholders' equity decreases (increases) by the purchase (sales) price of the shares.

There is an important difference between accounting for stockholders' equity and accounting for transactions involving assets and liabilities: *there is never any gain or loss reported on the purchase and sale of stock or the payment of dividends.* Instead, these "gains and losses" are reflected as increases and decreases in the contributed capital component of the issuing company's stockholders' equity.

This chapter focuses on the two broad categories of shareholder investment: contributed capital and earned capital. Exhibit 11.1 provides an illustration of this breakdown using **Pfizer**'s stockholders' equity as of 2003. Its equity consists of the following four groupings: two classes of stock (preferred and common, including additional paid-in capital and the employee benefit trust), treasury (repurchased) stock, retained earnings, and accumulated other comprehensive income.

EXHIBIT 11.1	Stockholders' Equity from Pfizer's Balance Sheet	
	Shareholders' Equity (millions, except preferred shares issued)	**Dec. 31, 2003**
Contributed capital	Preferred stock, without par value, at stated value; 27 shares authorized; 5,445 issued in 2003	$ 219
	Common stock, $.05 par value; 12,000 shares authorized; issued: 2003—8,702	435
	Additional paid-in capital	66,396
	Employee benefit trust	(1,898)
	Treasury stock, shares at cost; issued: 2003—1,073	(29,352)
Earned capital	Retained earnings	29,382
	Accumulated other comprehensive income	195
	Total shareholders' equity	$ 65,377

Pfizer, like other companies, has two broad categories of stockholders' equity:

1. **Contributed capital** This section reports the proceeds received by the issuing company from original stock issuances. Contributed capital often includes common stock, preferred stock, and additional paid-in capital. Netted against these capital accounts is treasury stock, the amounts paid to repurchase shares of the issuer's stock from its investors less the proceeds from the resale of such shares. Collectively, these accounts are generically referred to as contributed capital (or *paid-in capital*).

2. **Earned capital** This section consists of (a) retained earnings, which represent the cumulative income and losses of the company less any dividends to shareholders, and (b) accumulated other comprehensive income (AOCI), which includes changes to equity that are not included in income and are, therefore, not reflected in retained earnings. For Pfizer, AOCI includes foreign currency translation adjustments, changes in market values of derivatives, unrecognized gains and losses on available-for-sale securities, and minimum pension liability adjustments.

We discuss each of these two categories in turn. For each section, we provide a graphic that displays the part of stockholders' equity in the balance sheet impacted by the discussion of that section.

CONTRIBUTED CAPITAL

We begin our discussion with contributed capital. Contributed capital represents the cumulative cash inflow that the company has received from the sale of various classes of stock, less the net cash that it has paid out to repurchase its stock from the market. The contributed capital of Pfizer is highlighted in the following graphic:

Shareholders' Equity (millions, except preferred shares issued)	Dec. 31, 2003
Preferred stock, without par value, at stated value; 27 shares authorized; 5,445 issued in 2003	$ 219
Common stock, $.05 par value; 12,000 shares authorized; issued: 2003—8,702	435
Additional paid-in capital	66,396
Employee benefit trust	(1,898)
Treasury stock, shares at cost; issued: 2003—1,073	(29,352)
Retained earnings	29,382
Accumulated other comprehensive income	195
Total shareholders' equity	$ 65,377

Pfizer's contributed capital consists of paid-in and additional paid-in capital for both its preferred and common stock, less costs of treasury stock (repurchased shares) and the reduction of stockholders' equity arising from its employee benefit trust.[1]

Classes of Stock

There are two general classes of stock: preferred and common. The difference between the two lies in the respective legal rights conferred upon each class.

Preferred Stock
Preferred stock generally has some preference, or priority, with respect to common stock. Two typical preferences are:

---

[1]Its employee benefit trust (also called *employee stock ownership plan,* or *ESOP*) purchases company stock for the benefit of its employees with borrowed funds. Common stock increases from those purchases of shares; but until the debt is paid, the company reports an offset (reduction) in stockholders' equity equal to the unpaid debt. This explains the negative amount reported in its employee benefit trust account. As of 2003, Pfizer reports an unpaid balance of $1,898 million.

1. **Dividend preference**   Preferred shareholders receive dividends on their shares before common shareholders do. If dividends are not paid in a given year, those dividends are normally forgone. However, some preferred stock contracts include a *cumulative provision* stipulating that any forgone dividends must first be paid to preferred shareholders, together with the current year's dividends, before any dividends are paid to common shareholders.

2. **Liquidation preference**   If a company fails, its assets are sold (liquidated) and the proceeds are paid to the debtholders and shareholders, in that order. Shareholders, therefore, have a greater risk of loss than do debtholders. Among shareholders, the preferred shareholders receive payment in full before any proceeds are paid to common shareholders. This liquidation preference makes preferred shares less risky than common shares. Any liquidation payment to preferred shares is normally at its par value, although it is sometimes specified in excess of par; called a *liquidating value*.

The preferred stock of Pfizer is described in its financial statement notes:

> In connection with our acquisition of Pharmacia in 2003, we issued a newly created class of Series A convertible perpetual preferred stock (7,500 shares designated) in exchange for and with rights substantially similar to Pharmacia's Series C convertible perpetual preferred stock. The Series A convertible perpetual preferred stock is held by an Employee Stock Ownership Plan ("Preferred ESOP") Trust and provides dividends at the rate of 6.25%, which are accumulated and paid quarterly. The per-share stated value is $40,300 and the preferred stock ranks senior to our common stock as to dividends and liquidation rights. Each share is convertible, at the holder's option, into 2,547.87 shares of our common stock with equal voting rights. The Company may redeem the preferred stock, at any time or upon termination of the Preferred ESOP, at its option, in cash, in shares of common stock or a combination of both at a price of $40,300 per share.

Following are several important features of the Pfizer preferred stock:

- Shareholders control the number of shares issued—called *authorized shares*. The number of authorized shares can only be increased by an affirmative shareholder vote. There are 27 million preferred shares authorized, of which 5,445 shares are issued as of 2003. The articles of incorporation set the number of shares authorized for issuance. Once that limit is reached, shareholders must approve any increase in authorized shares.

- Pfizer preferred stock is convertible into common stock at the option of the holder and at a predetermined exchange rate. A preferred share is convertible, at the holder's option, into 2,547.87 common shares.

- Pfizer preferred stock pays a dividend of 6.25% of its par (stated) value of $40,300. This feature means that each preferred share is entitled to annual dividends of $2,518.75 ($40,300 × 6.25%), payable quarterly.

- Pfizer preferred stock is *cumulative*. This feature provides preferred shareholders with protection that unpaid dividends (called *dividends in arrears*) must be paid to them before any dividends are paid to common shareholders.

- Pfizer preferred stock has a preference with respect to dividends and liquidation; meaning that preferred shareholders are paid before common shareholders.

- Pfizer can redeem (repurchase) its preferred stock at any time in cash, common stock, or both.

Pfizer's cumulative preferred shares carry a dividend yield of 6.25%. This dividend yield compares favorably with the $0.60 per share (1.7% yield on a $35 share price) paid to its common shareholders at the time Pharmacia was acquired in 2003. Generally, preferred stock can be an attractive investment for shareholders seeking higher dividend yields, especially when tax laws wholly or partially exempt such dividends from taxation. Such exemption is not available for interest payments received by debtholders.

There are two additional features sometimes seen in preferred stock agreements:

1. **Conversion feature**   The yield on preferred stock, especially when coupled with a cumulative feature, is similar to the interest rate on a bond or note. Further, preferred shareholders receive the par value at liquidation like debtholders receive face value. The

fixed yield and liquidation value for the preferred stock limit the upside potential return of preferred shareholders. This constraint can be overcome by inclusion of a *conversion feature* that allows preferred stockholders to convert their shares into common shares at their option at a predetermined conversion ratio. Some preferred contracts give the company an option to force conversion.

2. **Participation feature**   Preferred shares sometimes carry a *participation feature* that allows preferred shareholders to share ratably with common stockholders in dividends. The dividend preference over common shares can be a benefit when dividend payments are meager, but a fixed dividend yield limits upside potential if the company performs exceptionally well. This limitation can be overcome with a participation feature.

Common Stock

Pfizer has also issued common stock, which it describes as follows (shares in millions):

Common stock, $.05 par value; 12,000 shares authorized; issued: 2003—8,702

The Pfizer common stock has the following important characteristics:

■ Pfizer common stock has a par value of $0.05 per share. The **par value** is an arbitrary amount set by company organizers at the time of formation. Generally, par value has no substance from a financial reporting or statement analysis perspective (there are some legal implications, which are usually minor). Its main impact is in specifying the allocation of proceeds from stock issuances between the two contributed capital accounts on the balance sheet: common stock and additional paid-in capital.

■ Pfizer has authorized the issuance of 12,000 million shares. As of 2003, 8,702 million shares are issued yielding a value of $435 = $.05(8,702). When shares are first issued the number of shares outstanding equals those issued. Any shares subsequently repurchased as treasury stock are deducted from issued shares to derive *outstanding shares.*[2]

Accounting for Stock Transactions

LO2 Explain and account for the issuance and repurchase of stock.

We cover the accounting for stock transactions in this section, including the accounting for stock issuances and for stock repurchases.

Stock Issuance

Stock issuances, whether common or preferred, yield an increase in both assets and stockholders' equity. Companies use stock issuances to obtain cash and other assets for use in their business. (The chart to the side shows the largest stock issuances for 2004.)

Stock issuances increase assets (cash) by the number of shares sold multiplied by the issuance price of the stock on the issue date. Equity increases by the same amount, which is reflected in contributed capital accounts. Specifically, assuming the issuance of common stock (initial public offering, or IPO for short), the common stock account increases by the number of shares sold multiplied by its par value and the additional paid-in capital account increases for the remainder.

2004's Top 10 Global Stock Issuances	
ISSUER	**AMOUNT (billions)**
ENEL	$9.5
France Telecom	6.2
Royal Bank of Scotland	4.8
Belgacom	4.4
GE	3.8
Bayerische Hypo-Vereinsbk	3.7
Deutsche Telekom	3.7
Electric Power Day	3.4
Total	3.2
Genworth Financial	2.9

---

[2]Generally, issued shares equal outstanding shares plus treasury shares.

To illustrate, assume that Pfizer issues 10,000 shares at a market price of $43 cash per share. This stock issuance has the following financial statement effects.

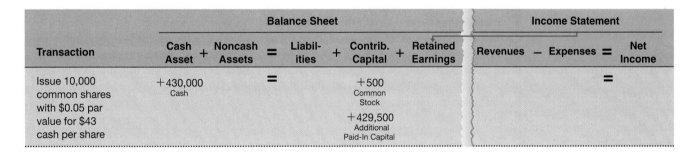

Transaction	Balance Sheet						Income Statement		
	Cash Asset	+ Noncash Assets	= Liabil- ities	+ Contrib. Capital	+ Retained Earnings		Revenues	– Expenses =	Net Income
Issue 10,000 common shares with $0.05 par value for $43 cash per share	+430,000 Cash		=	+500 Common Stock +429,500 Additional Paid-In Capital					=

The associated journal entry and T-accounts follow.

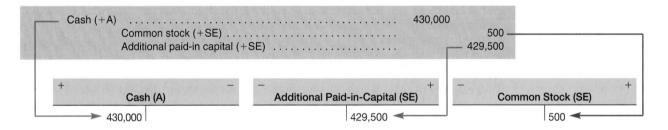

Cash (+A) 430,000
    Common stock (+SE) 500
    Additional paid-in capital (+SE) 429,500

+ Cash (A) –		– Additional Paid-in-Capital (SE) +		– Common Stock (SE) +	
430,000			429,500		500

Specifically, the following financial statement effects of the stock issuance are:

1. Cash increases by $430,000 (10,000 shares × $43 per share)
2. Common stock increases by the $500 par value of shares sold (10,000 shares × $0.05 par value)[3]
3. Additional paid-in capital increases by the $429,500 difference between the issue price and par value ($430,000 − $500)[4]

Once shares are issued, they are freely traded among investors. The proceeds of those sales and their associated gains and losses on sales do not affect the issuing company and are not recorded

---

[3]Stock can also be issued as "no par" or as "no par with a stated value." For no par stock, the common stock account is increased by the entire proceeds of the sale and no amount is assigned to additional paid-in capital. For no par stock with a stated value, the stated value is treated just like par value, that is, common stock is increased by the number of shares multiplied by the stated value, and the remainder is assigned to the additional paid-in capital account.

[4]Stock issuance affects only the balance sheet. There is never any revenue or gain from stock issuance reported in the income statement.

in its accounting records. Further, fluctuations in the issuing company's stock price subsequent to issuance do not directly affect its financial statements. Hence, the equity section of the balance sheet cannot be used to obtain the current market value of the company. The market value is given by the product of the number of common shares outstanding times the per share price of the stock.

Refer again to the following report of common stock on Pfizer's balance sheet (in millions):

Common stock, $.05 par value; 12,000 shares authorized; issued: 2003—8,702	$ 435
Additional paid-in capital	66,396

Pfizer's common stock, in the amount of $435 million, equals the number of shares issued multiplied by the common stock's par value: 8,702 million × $0.05 = $435 million. Total proceeds from stock issuances are $66,831 million, or $7.68 per share ($66,831 million/8,702 million shares). The balance of the proceeds from stock issuances ($66,396 million) is included in the additional paid-in capital account.

RESEARCH INSIGHT

Stock Issuance and Stock Returns   Research shows that, historically, companies issuing equity securities experience unusually low stock returns for several years following those offerings. Evidence suggests that this poor performance is partly due to overly optimistic estimates of long-term growth for these companies by equity analysts that impact the offering price. This over-optimism is most pronounced when the analyst is employed by the brokerage firm that underwrites the issue. There is also evidence that companies manage earnings upward prior to an equity offering. This evidence means the observed decrease in returns following an issuance likely reflects the market's negative reaction, on average, to earnings management. The result is a classic "chicken or egg" dilemma: do stock returns decline following issuance because analysts or managers are skewing performance measures upward, or do managers skew performance measures upward because they anticipate that investors rationally adjust those measures downward?

Stock Repurchase

Pfizer provides the following description of its stock repurchase program in notes to its 10-K report.

We continue to purchase our common stock via open market purchases or in privately negotiated transactions as circumstances and prices warrant. Purchased shares under each of the share-purchase programs are available for general corporate purposes.

In December 2003, we announced a $5 billion share-purchase program, which we expect to be completed by the end of 2004. In July 2002, we announced a $16 billion share-purchase program (increased from the initial $10 billion) authorized by our board of directors, which we completed in November 2003. In total, under the June 2002 program we purchased approximately 508 million shares. In May 2002, we completed the share-purchase program authorized in June 2001. In total, under the June 2001 program we purchased 120 million shares at a total cost of approximately $4.8 billion.

Pfizer initiated several stock buyback programs in the past three years. One reason a company will repurchase shares is if it feels that the market undervalues them. The logic is that the repurchase sends a positive signal to the market about the company's financial condition that positively impacts its share price and, thus, allows the company to resell those shares for a "gain." Any such gain on resale is *never* reflected in the income statement. Instead, the excess of the resale price over the repurchase price is added to additional paid-in capital. GAAP prohibits companies from reporting gains via stock transactions with their own shareholders.

Another reason shares are repurchased is to offset the dilutive effects of an employee stock option program. When an employee exercises stock options, the number of shares outstanding increases. These additional shares reduce earnings per share and are, therefore, viewed as *dilutive*. In response, many companies repurchase an equivalent number of shares in a desire to keep outstanding shares constant.

A stock repurchase represents a downsizing of the company. The repurchase has the opposite financial statement effects from a stock issuance. That is, cash is reduced by the price of the shares repurchased (number of shares repurchased multiplied by the purchase price per share) and stockholders' equity is reduced by the same amount. The reduction in equity is achieved by increasing a contra equity account called **treasury stock**. *A contra equity account is a negative equity account,* which reduces stockholders' equity. Thus, when a contra equity account increases, total equity decreases.

Any subsequent reissuance of treasury stock does not yield a gain or loss. Instead, the difference between the proceeds received and the repurchase price of the treasury stock is reflected as an increase or decease to additional paid-in capital.

To illustrate, assume that 3,000 common shares of Pfizer previously issued for $43 are later repurchased for $40. This repurchase has the following financial statement effects.

	Balance Sheet						Income Statement		
Transaction	Cash Asset	+ Noncash Assets	= Liabil-ities	+ Contrib. Capital	+ Retained Earnings		Revenues	− Expenses =	Net Income
Repurchase 3,000 common shares for $40 cash per share	−120,000 Cash		=	−120,000 Treasury Stock Increase					=

The related journal entry and T-accounts follow.

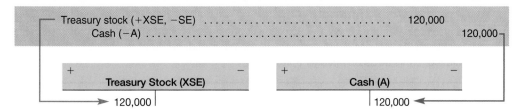

Treasury stock (+XSE, −SE) 120,000
    Cash (−A) 120,000

+ Treasury Stock (XSE) −		+ Cash (A) −
120,000		120,000

Assets (cash) and equity both decrease. Treasury stock (a contra equity account) increases by $120,000, which reduces stockholders' equity by that same amount.

Assume that these 3,000 shares are then subsequently resold for $42 cash per share. This resale of treasury stock has the following financial statement effects.

	Balance Sheet						Income Statement		
Transaction	Cash Asset	+ Noncash Assets	= Liabil-ities	+ Contrib. Capital	+ Retained Earnings		Revenues	− Expenses =	Net Income
Reissue 3,000 treasury (common) shares for $42 cash per share	+126,000 Cash		=	+120,000 Treasury Stock Decrease +6,000 Additional Paid-In Capital					=

If the reissue price is below the repurchase price, then additional paid-in capital is reduced until it reaches a zero balance, after which retained earnings is reduced.

The related journal entry and T-accounts follow.

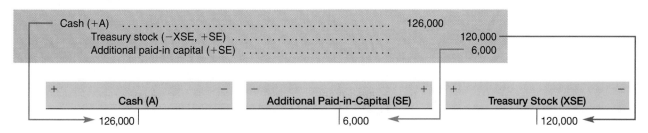

Cash (+A) 126,000
    Treasury stock (−XSE, +SE) 120,000
    Additional paid-in capital (+SE) 6,000

+ Cash (A) −	− Additional Paid-in-Capital (SE) +	+ Treasury Stock (XSE) −
126,000	6,000	120,000

Cash assets increase by $126,000 (3,000 shares × $42 per share), the treasury stock account is reduced by the $120,000 cost of the treasury shares issued, and the $6,000 excess (3,000 shares × $2 per share) is reported as an increase in additional paid-in capital. Again, there is no effect on the income statement—companies are prohibited from reporting gains and losses from repurchases and reissuances of their own stock.

The treasury stock section of **Pfizer**'s balance sheet is reproduced below.

At December 31 (millions)	2003
Treasury stock, shares at cost; issued: 2003—1,073	$(29,352)

Pfizer has repurchased a cumulative total of 1,073 million shares of its common stock for $29,352 million, an average repurchase price of $27.35 per share. This compares with total contributed capital of $65,152 million ($219 million + $435 million + $66,396 million − $1,898 million; see page 8-5). Thus, about 45% of its original contributed capital has been repurchased. Although some of Pfizer's treasury purchases were to offset increases in shares outstanding due to the exercise of stock options, it appears that most of these purchases are motivated by a perceived low stock price by Pfizer management. When there have been several repurchases and sales of treasury stock, a question arises as to which shares were sold. Typically the solution is to assume a flow such as the first shares repurchased are the first ones to be treated as sold.

YOU MAKE THE CALL

You Are the Chief Financial Officer   You believe that your company's stock price is lower than its real value. You are considering various alternatives to increase that price, including the repurchase of company stock in the market. What are some considerations relating to this decision? [Answer, p. 495]

MID-CHAPTER REVIEW 1

Plesko Corporation reported the following transactions relating to its stock accounts in 2005.

Jan 15   Issued 10,000 shares of $5 par value common stock at $17 cash per share
Mar 31   Purchased 2,000 shares of its own common stock at $15 cash per share.
June 25   Reissued 1,000 shares of its treasury stock at $20 cash per share.

Provide the appropriate journal entry for each transaction, post the journal entries to the related e-account, and show the financial impact of each transaction using the financial statement effects template.

Solution

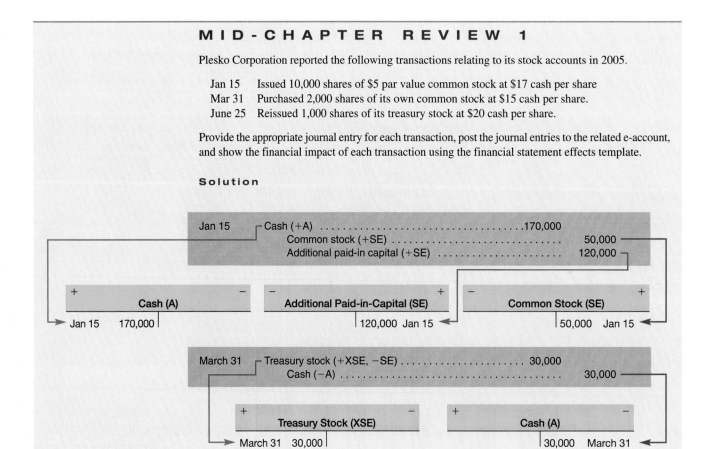

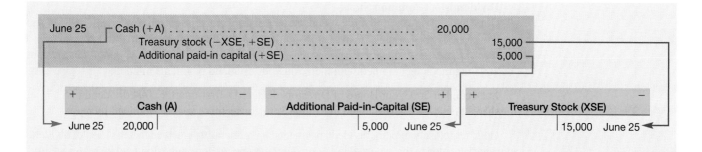

Transaction	Balance Sheet					Income Statement		
	Cash Asset +	Noncash Assets =	Liabil- ities +	Contrib. Capital +	Retained Earnings	Revenues −	Expenses =	Net Income
Jan. 15	+170,000 Cash	=		+170,000ᵃ				=
Mar. 31	−30,000 Cash	=		−30,000ᵇ				=
June 25	+20,000 Cash	=		+20,000ᶜ				=

ᵃCommon stock increases by $50,000 and additional paid-in capital by $120,000.

ᵇTreasury stock increases by $30,000, which reduces contributed capital by that same amount.

ᶜTreasury stock declines by its $15,000 cost (1,000 shares × $15 per share) and additional paid-in capital increases by $5,000. Total contributed capital, thus, increases by $20,000.

EARNED CAPITAL

We now turn our attention to the earned capital portion of stockholders' equity. Earned capital represents the cumulative profit that has been retained by the company. Recall that earned capital is increased by income earned and decreased by any losses incurred. Earned capital is also decreased by dividends paid to shareholders. Not all dividends are paid in the form of cash, however. In fact, companies can pay dividends in many forms, including property (like land, for example) or additional shares of stock. We cover both cash and stock dividends in this section. Earned capital also includes the positive or negative effects of accumulated other comprehensive income (AOCI). The earned capital of Pfizer is highlighted in the following graphic:

LO3 Describe how operations increase the equity of a business.

Shareholders' Equity (millions, except preferred shares issued)	Dec. 31, 2003
Preferred stock, without par value, at stated value; 27 shares authorized; 5,445 issued in 2003	$ 219
Common stock, $.05 par value; 12,000 shares authorized; issued: 2003—8,702	435
Additional paid-in capital	66,396
Employee benefit trust	(1,898)
Treasury stock, shares at cost; issued: 2003—1,073	(29,352)
Retained earnings	29,382
Accumulated other comprehensive income	195
Total shareholders' equity	$ 65,377

Cash Dividends

Many companies, but not all, pay dividends. Their reasons for dividend payments are varied. Most dividends are paid in cash on a quarterly basis. The following is a description of **Pfizer**'s dividend policy from its 2003 10-K.

LO4 Explain and account for dividends and stock splits.

Dividends on Common Stock

Our dividend payout ratios [dividends/net income] were approximately 111.1% in 2003 and 35.6% in 2002. The significant change in the ratio in 2003 compared to 2002 is primarily a result of the impact that certain non-cash charges relating to purchase accounting had on our 2003 net income combined with increasing our dividend payments in 2003.

In December 2003, our Board of Directors declared a first-quarter 2004 dividend of $.17 per share. The 2004 cash dividend marks the 37th consecutive year of dividend increases.

Outsiders closely monitor dividend payments. It is generally perceived that the level of dividend payments is related to the expected long-term core income. Accordingly, dividend increases are usually accompanied by stock price increases, and companies rarely reduce their dividends unless absolutely necessary. Dividend reductions are, therefore, met with substantial stock-price declines.

Pfizer's short-run dividend payment history, as reported in its 10-K, follows.

		Quarter		
	First	Second	Third	Fourth
2003				
Cash dividends paid per common share	$.15	$.15	$.15	$.15
2002				
Cash dividends paid per common share	$.13	$.13	$.13	$.13

This dividend information shows that Pfizer increased its quarterly dividend from $0.13 cents per share in 2002 to $0.15 cents per share in 2003.

Financial Effects of Cash Dividends

Cash dividends reduce both cash and retained earnings by the amount of the cash dividends paid. To illustrate, Pfizer paid $4,771 million in 2003 cash dividends on its common and preferred shares. The financial statement effects of this cash dividend payment are reflected as a reduction in assets (cash) and a reduction in retained earnings as follows.

	Balance Sheet					Income Statement		
Transaction	Cash Asset	+ Noncash Assets	= Liabil- ities	+ Contrib. Capital	+ Retained Earnings	Revenues	– Expenses =	Net Income
Paid $4,771 million cash dividends on common and preferred shares	−4,771 mil. Cash		=		−4,771 mil. Retained Earnings			=

The related journal entry and T-accounts follow.

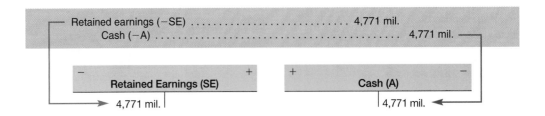

Dividend payments have no effect on profitability. They are a direct reduction to retained earnings and bypass the income statement.

Preferred stock dividends have priority over those for common shares, including unpaid prior years' preferred dividends (dividends in arrears) when preferred stock is cumulative. To illustrate, assume that Hanna Company has 15,000 shares of $50 par value, 8% preferred stock outstanding and 50,000 shares of $5 par value common stock outstanding. During its first three years in business, assume that Hanna declares $20,000 dividends in the first year, $260,000 of dividends in the second year, and $60,000 of dividends in the third year. If the preferred stock is cumulative, the total amount of dividends paid to each class of stock in each of the three years would be:

	Preferred Stock	Common Stock
Year 1		
Current year dividend ($750,000 × 8%; but only $20,000 is paid, leaving $40,000 in arrears)	$20,000	
Balance to common		$ 0
Year 2		
Arrearage from Year 1 ([$750,000 × 8%] − $20,000)	40,000	
Current year dividend ($750,000 × 8%)	60,000	
Balance to common [$260,000 − ($40,000 + $60,000)]		160,000
Year 3		
Current year dividend ($750,000 × 8%)	60,000	
Balance to common		0

MID-CHAPTER REVIEW 2

Finn Corporation has outstanding 10,000 shares of $100 par value, 5% preferred stock and 50,000 shares of $5 par value common stock. During its first three years in business, Finn declared no dividends in the first year, $300,000 of cash dividends in the second year, and $80,000 of cash dividends in the third year.

a. If the preferred stock is cumulative, determine the total amount of dividends paid to each class of stock for each of the three years.
b. If the preferred stock is not cumulative, determine the total amount of dividends paid to each class of stock for each of the three years.

Solution

a.

	Preferred Stock	Common Stock
Year 1	$ 0	$ 0
Year 2		
Arrearage from Year 1 ($1,000,000 × 5%)	50,000	
Current year dividend ($1,000,000 × 5%)	50,000	
Balance to common		200,000
Year 3		
Current year dividend ($1,000,000 × 5%)	50,000	
Balance to common		30,000

b.

	Preferred Stock	Common Stock
Year 1	$ 0	$ 0
Year 2		
Current year dividend ($1,000,000 × 5%)	50,000	
Balance to common		250,000
Year 3		
Current year dividend ($1,000,000 × 5%)	50,000	
Balance to common		30,000

Stock Dividends and Splits

Dividends need not be paid in cash. Many companies pay dividends in the form of additional shares of stock. Companies can also distribute additional shares to their stockholders with a stock split. We cover both of these distributions in this section.

Stock Dividends

When dividends are paid in the form of the company's stock, retained earnings are reduced and contributed capital is increased. However, the amount by which retained earnings are reduced depends on the proportion of the outstanding shares distributed to the total outstanding shares on the issue date. Exhibit 11.2 illustrates two possibilities depending on whether stock dividends are classified as either small stock dividends or large stock dividends. The break point is 20–25% of the outstanding shares. (When the number of additional shares issued as a stock dividend is so great that it has, or is reasonably expected to have, the effect of materially reducing the share market value, the transaction is of the nature of a stock split; the 20–25% guideline is used for that purpose.) What the proper accounting is if the dividend falls within the 20 to 25 percent interval is unspecified (presumably it is the management's choice).

EXHIBIT 11.2	Analysis of Stock Dividend Effects	
Percentage of Outstanding Shares Distributed	**Retained Earnings**	**Contributed Capital**
Less than 20–25% (*small stock dividend*)	Reduce by **market value** of shares distributed	Common stock increased by (dividend shares × par value per share); additional paid-in capital increased for the balance
More than 20–25% (*large stock dividend*)	Reduce by **par value** of shares distributed	Common stock increased by (dividend shares × par value per share)

For *small stock dividends,* retained earnings are reduced by the *market* value of the shares distributed (dividend shares × market price per share) and contributed capital is increased by the same amount. For the contributed capital increase, the common stock is increased by the par value of the shares distributed and the remainder (dividend shares × [market value per share − par value per share] increases additional paid-in capital. For *large stock dividends,* retained earnings are reduced by the *par* value of the shares distributed (dividend shares × par value per share), and common stock is increased by the same amount (no change to additional paid-in capital).

To illustrate the financial statement effects of dividends, assume that a company has 1 million shares of $5 par common stock outstanding. It then declares a small-stock dividend of 15% of the outstanding shares (1,000,000 shares × 15% = 150,000 shares) when the market price of the stock is $30 per share. This small stock dividend has the following financial statement effects:

	Balance Sheet						Income Statement		
Transaction	**Cash Asset** +	**Noncash Assets** =	**Liabil- ities** +	**Contrib. Capital** +	**Retained Earnings**	**Revenues** −	**Expenses** =	**Net Income**
Distribute 150,000 shares as a *small* stock dividend		=		+750,000 Common Stock				=
				+$3,750,000 Additional Paid-In Capital	−$4,500,000 Retained Earnings			

The related journal entry and T-accounts follow.

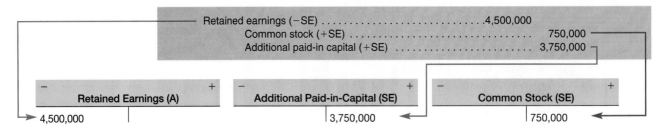

Retained earnings (−SE)	4,500,000	
Common stock (+SE)		750,000
Additional paid-in capital (+SE)		3,750,000

Retained Earnings (A)		Additional Paid-in-Capital (SE)		Common Stock (SE)	
−	+	−	+	−	+
4,500,000			3,750,000		750,000

Retained earnings are reduced by $4,500,000, which equals the market value of the small stock dividend (150,000 shares × $30 market price per share). The increase in contributed capital is treated as follows: common stock is increased by the par value of $750,000 (150,000 shares × $5 par value), and the remainder of $3,750,000 increases additional paid-in capital. Similar to cash dividend payments, the stock dividends, whether large or small, never impact income.

Next, assume instead that a company declares a large stock dividend of 70% of the 1 million outstanding common ($5 par) shares when the market price of the stock is $30 per share. This large stock dividend has the following financial statement effects:

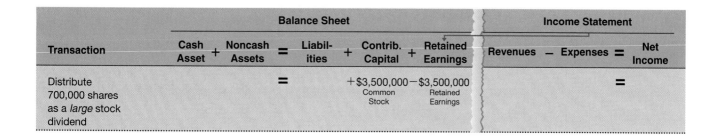

The related journal entry and T-accounts follow.

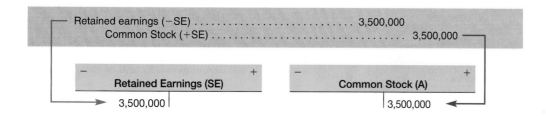

Retained earnings are reduced by $3,500,000, which equals the par value of the large stock dividend (700,000 shares × $5 par value per share). Common stock is increased by the par value of $3,500,000. There is no effect on additional paid-in capital because the dividend is reported at par value.

For both large and small stock dividends, companies are required to show comparable shares outstanding for all prior periods for which earnings per share (EPS) is reported in the statements. The reasoning is that a stock dividend has no effect on the ownership percentage of each common stockholder. As such, to show a dilution in reported EPS would erroneously suggest a decline in profitability when it is simply due to an increase in shares outstanding.

Stock Splits

A stock split is a proportionate distribution of shares and, as such, is similar in substance to a stock dividend. A typical stock split is 2-for-1, which means that the company distributes one additional share for each share owned by a shareholder. Following the distribution, and even though each investor owns twice as many shares, their percentage ownership in the company is unchanged.

A stock split is not a monetary transaction and, as such, there are no financial statement effects. However, companies must disclose the new number of shares outstanding for all periods presented in the financial statements. Further, many states require that the par value of shares be proportionately adjusted as well (for example, halved for a 2-for-1 split).

If state law requires that par value not be reduced for a stock split, this event should be described as a *stock split affected in the form of a dividend.* The following disclosure from **Pfizer**'s annual report provides such an example:

> We affected a three-for-one stock split of our common stock in the form of a 200% stock dividend in 1999 and a two-for-one split of our common stock in the form of a 100% stock dividend in 1997. All share and per share information in this report reflects both splits.

MID-CHAPTER REVIEW 3

The stockholders' equity of Zhang Corporation at December 31, 2005, follows.

5% preferred stock, $100 par value, 10,000 shares authorized; 4,000 shares issued and outstanding	$ 400,000
Common stock, $5 par value, 200,000 shares authorized; 50,000 shares issued and outstanding	250,000
Paid-in capital in excess of par value—Preferred stock	40,000
Paid-in capital in excess of par value—Common stock	300,000
Retained earnings	656,000
Total stockholders' equity	$1,646,000

Prepare journal entries for each of the following transactions that occurred during 2006, post the journal entries to the appropriate t-accounts, and show the impact of each transaction using the financial statement effects template.

Apr. 1   Declared and issued an 100% stock dividend on all outstanding shares of common stock when the market value of the stock was $11 per share.

Dec. 7   Declared and issued a 3% stock dividend on all outstanding shares of common stock when the market value of the stock was $7 per share.

Dec 31   Declared and paid a cash dividend of $1.20 per share on all outstanding common shares.

Solution

	Balance Sheet							Income Statement		
Transaction	Cash Asset	+ Noncash Assets	=	Liabil-ities	+	Contrib. Capital	+ Retained Earnings	Revenues	− Expenses =	Net Income
Apr. 1			=		+	250,000	− 250,000[1]			=
Dec. 7			=		+	21,000	− 21,000[2]			=
Dec. 31	−123,600		=				− 123,600[3]			=

[1]This large stock dividend reduces retained earnings at the par value of shares distributed (50,000 shares × 100% × $5 par value = $250,000). Contributed capital (common stock) increases by the same amount.

[2]This small stock dividend reduces retained earnings at the market value of shares distributed (3% × 100,000 shares × $7 per share = $21,000). Contributed capital increases by the same amount ($15,000 to common stock and $6,000 to paid-in capital).

[3]At the time of the cash dividend, there are 103,000 shares outstanding. The cash paid is, therefore, 103,000 shares × $1.20 per share = $123,600.

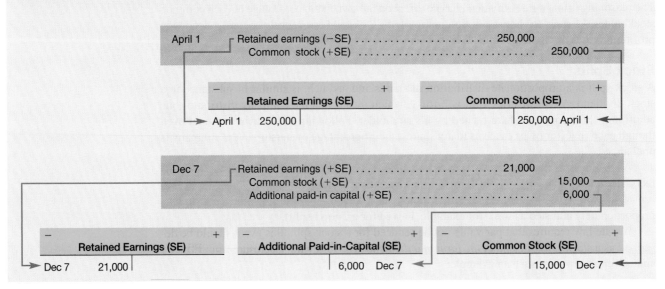

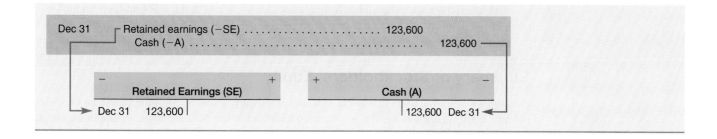

Comprehensive Income

Comprehensive income is a more inclusive notion of company performance than net income. It includes all recognized changes in equity that occur during a period except those resulting from contributions by and distributions to owners.

LO5 Define and illustrate comprehensive income.

Specifically, comprehensive income includes (and net income excludes) foreign currency adjustments, unrealized changes in market values of available-for-sale securities, minimum pension liability adjustments, and changes in market values of certain derivative investments. Comprehensive income includes the effects on a company of some economic events that are often outside of management's control. Accordingly, some observers assert that net income is a measure of management's performance, while comprehensive income is a measure of company performance.

Pfizer reports the following components of its comprehensive income from its 2004 10-K report.

(Millions)	Retained Earnings	Accumulated Other Comprehensive Income (Expense)
Balance December 31, 2002	$30,243	$(1,875)
Comprehensive income		
Net income	3,910	
Other comprehensive income—net of tax		
Currency translation adjustment		2,070
Net unrealized gain on available-for-sale securities		68
Minimum pension liability		(68)
Total other comprehensive income		2,070
Cash dividends declared—		
common stock	(4,764)	
preferred stock	(7)	
Balance December 31, 2003	**$29,382**	**$ 195**

Pfizer's total other comprehensive income includes the three following items that affect stockholders' equity and are not reflected in net income:

1. **Currency translation adjustment** ($2,070 million). This adjustment is the unrecognized gain on assets and liabilities denominated in foreign currencies. A gain implies that the $US has weakened relative to foreign currencies; such as when assets denominated in foreign currencies are translated in more $US. (Chapter 7 explains accounting for foreign currency translation.)

2. **Net unrealized gain on available-for-sale securities** ($68 million). Unrealized gains and losses on available-for-sale securities are not reflected in net income. Instead, these gains are accumulated in a separate equity account until the securities are sold. (Chapter 12 explains accounting for investments).

3. **Minimum pension liability** ($68 million). This is the additional pension liability that must be recorded under GAAP because some of Pfizer's pension plans are underfunded. The

$68 million unrealized gain on available-for-sale securities and the $68 million minimum pension liability are unrelated and the same dollar amount is coincidental. (Chapter 13 explains pension accounting.)

Summary of Stockholders' Equity

A summary of transactions that affect stockholders' equity is included in the statement of shareholders' equity. This statement reports a reconciliation of the beginning and ending balances of important stockholders' equity accounts. **Pfizer**'s statement of stockholders' equity follows:

(Millions, Except Preferred Shares)	Preferred Stock Shares	Preferred Stock Stated Value	Common Stock Shares	Common Stock Par Value	Additional Paid-In Capital	Employee Benefit Trust Shares	Employee Benefit Trust Fair Value	Treasury Stock Shares	Treasury Stock Cost	Retained Earnings	Accum. Other Compre-hensive Inc./(Exp.)	Total
Balance December 31, 2002	—	—	6,829	$341	$ 9,368	(58)	$(1,786)	(667)	$(16,341)	$30,243	$(1,875)	$ 19,950
Comprehensive income:												
Net income										3,910		3,910
Other comprehensive income—net of tax:												
Currency translation adjustment											2,070	2,070
Net unrealized gain on available-for-sale securities											68	68
Minimum pension liability											(68)	(68)
Total other comprehensive income											2,070	2,070
Total comprehensive income												5,980
Pharmacia acquisition	6,019	$242	1,817	91	55,402							55,735
Cash dividends declared—												
common stock										(4,764)		(4,764)
preferred stock										(7)		(7)
Stock option transactions . . .			52	3	1,374	5	175	(1)	(20)			1,532
Purchases of common stock								(407)	(13,037)			(13,037)
Employee benefit trust transactions—net					112	(1)	(287)	1	10			(165)
Preferred stock—conversions and redemptions	(574)	(23)			23				6			6
Other			4	—	117			1	30	—		147
Balance December 31, 2003	5,445	$219	8,702	$435	$66,396	(54)	$(1,898)	(1,073)	$(29,352)	$29,382	$ 195	$ 65,377

Pfizer's statement of shareholders' equity reveals the following key transactions for 2003:

- Net income plus other comprehensive income increased shareholders' equity by $5,980 million.

- Pfizer issued 6,019 preferred shares with a total par (stated) value of $242 million as part of Pharmacia's acquisition in 2003. It also issued 1,817 million common shares, which increased common stock by $91 million (1,817 million shares × $0.05 par value) and additional paid-in (contributed) capital by $55,402 million, representing the remaining value of the shares issued.

- Dividend payments to preferred and common shareholders decreased stockholders' equity by $4,771 million ($4,764 million + $7 million).

- Issuance of shares as a result of the exercise of employee stock options increased equity by $1,532 million.

- Stock repurchases decreased equity by $13,037 million.

- Employee benefit trust transactions reduced stockholders' equity by $165 million.

■ Conversion of preferred stock into common stock reduced the preferred stock account and increased the common stock account, for a net increase in stockholders' equity of $6 million.

■ Other transactions increased stockholders' equity by $147 million.

One final point: the financial press sometimes refers to a measure called **book value per share**. This is the net book value of the company that is available to common shareholders, defined as: stockholders' equity less preferred stock (and preferred additional paid-in capital) divided by the number of common shares outstanding (issued common shares less treasury shares). Pfizer's book value per share is computed as: ($65,377 million − $219 million)/(8,702 million shares − 1,073 million shares) = $8.54 book value per common share.

MID-CHAPTER REVIEW 4

The stockholders' equity of Sloan Corporation at December 31, 2005, follows.

Common stock, $5 par value, 400,000 shares authorized; 160,000 shares issued and outstanding	$800,000
Paid-in capital in excess of par value	920,000
Retained earnings	513,000

During 2006, the following transactions occurred:

June 28 Declared and issued a 10% common stock dividend when the market value is $11 per share.
Dec. 5 Declared and paid a cash dividend of $1.25 per share.
Dec. 31 Updated retained earnings for net income of $412,000

Compute the year-ending balance of retained earnings for 2005.

Solution

Retained Earnings Reconciliation For Year Ended December 31, 2006		
Retained earnings, December 31, 2005		$513,000
Add: Net income		412,000
		925,000
Less: Cash dividends declared [160,000 + .10(160,000)][$1.25]	$220,000	
Stock dividends declared (160,000)(.10)($11)	176,000	396,000
Retained earnings, December 31, 2006		$529,000

EPS, CONVERTIBLES, AND STOCK RIGHTS

Earnings Per Share

The income statement reports earnings per share (EPS) numbers. At least one, and potentially two, EPS figures are reported: basic and diluted. The difference between the two measures follows:

LO6 Describe and illustrate the earnings per share computation.

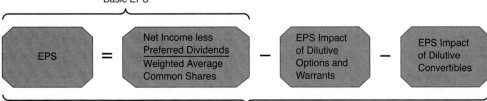

Basic EPS is computed as: (Net income − Dividends on preferred stock)/Weighted average of common shares outstanding for the year. The subtraction of preferred stock dividends yields the income per common share available for dividend payments to common shareholders. The preferred dividends are subtracted because this portion of net income does not accrue to the common stockholders.

Computation of **diluted EPS** reflects the added shares issued if all stock options and convertible securities had been exercised at the beginning of the year. To illustrate, assume a company has outstanding employee stock options for 10,000 shares. To compute diluted EPS, we assume that the options are exercised at the beginning of the year and, thus, increase the denominator by 10,000 shares. Notice that diluted EPS never exceeds basic EPS.

Companies can have a variety of convertible securities, like convertible bonds, that are potentially converted into common stock. To compute diluted EPS for convertible bonds, the company would increase the denominator by the number of shares that would be issued to the holders and eliminate the after-tax interest that would have been foregone had the bonds been converted. Similar adjustments can be made for convertible preferred stock by reflecting the additional common shares outstanding and eliminating the dividends that would have been paid on the preferred stock. The increase in the number of shares for the diluted EPS computation would be reduced by the shares that could have been repurchased with the proceeds of the option exercise, thus reducing the net increase in common shares outstanding.

The earnings per share section of Cisco's income statement is in Exhibit 11.3. Notice that diluted EPS never exceeds basic EPS. Given the near identical results for basic and diluted EPS, we know that Cisco has few dilutive securities.[5]

EXHIBIT 11.3	Earnings per Share Section of Cisco's Income Statement	
($ millions, except per share data)	**July 26, 2003**	**July 27, 2002**
Net sales	$18,878	$18,915
Net income (loss)	3,578	1,893
Net income (loss) per share—basic	0.50	0.26
Net income (loss) per share—diluted	0.50	0.25
Shares used in per-share calculation—basic	7,124	7,301
Shares used in per-share calculation—diluted	7,223	7,447

EPS figures are often used as a method of comparing operating results for companies of different sizes under the assumption that the number of shares outstanding is proportional to the income level (that is, a company twice the size of another will report double the income and will have double the common shares outstanding, leaving EPS approximately equal for the two companies). This assumption is erroneous. Management controls the number of common shares outstanding. Different companies also have different philosophies regarding share issuance and repurchase. For example, consider that most companies report annual EPS of less than $5, while Berkshire Hathaway reported EPS of $5,308 for 2003! This is because Berkshire Hathaway has so few common shares outstanding, not necessarily because it has stellar profits.

Cisco's earnings-per-share (EPS) reporting was used to illustrate the basic reporting of this closely watched ratio. We shall now consider Pfizer's reporting as shown on its income statement and refer further to footnote 17 of the company's financial report to explain the more complex reporting likely to be encountered in any serious effort to analyze a company. Pfizer's consolidated income statement is given in Exhibit 11.3. Pfizer has what is referred to as a complex capital structure because it includes equity contracts, such as options, and convertible securities (convertible preferred stock in this case).

Our attention will focus on the portion of the income statement beginning with net income. The section begins about half way down the statement. Consider first the reporting of Pfizer's basic EPS. The EPS of $1.51 reported for 2004 represents the outcome of dividing net income of $11,357

---

[5]The effects of dilutive securities are only included if they are, in fact, dilutive. If they are *antidilutive,* inclusion would actually increase EPS. As a result, they are excluded from the computation. An example of an antidilutive security is employee stock options whose exercise price is greater than the current market price. These *underwater* options are antidilutive and are therefore excluded from the EPS computation. Cisco excludes 838 million of underwater stock options from its 2003 EPS computation.

EXHIBIT 11.4	Consolidated Statement of Income		
Pfizer Inc and Subsidiary Companies			
YEAR ENDED DECEMBER 31 (Millions, Except per Common Share Data)		**2004**	**2003**
Revenues		$52,516	$44,736
Costs and Expenses			
Costs of Sales[a]		7,541	9,589
Selling, informational and administrative expenses[a]		16,903	15,108
Research and Developmnet expenses[a]		7,684	7,487
Amortization of intangible assets		3,364	2,187
Merger-related in-process research and development charges		1,071	5,052
Merger-related costs		1,193	1,058
Other (income)/deductions — net		753	1,009
Income from continuing operations before provision for taxes on income, minority interests and cumulative effect of change in accounting principles		14,007	3,246
Provision for taxes on income		2,665	1,614
Minority interests		10	3
Income from continuing operations before cumulative effect of change in accounting principles		11,332	1,629
Discontinued operations			
Income (loss) from operations of discontinued business and product lines—net of tax		(22)	26
Gains on sales of discontinued businesses and product lines—net of tax		51	2,285
Discontinues operations — net of tax		29	2,311
Income before cumulative effect of change in accounting principles		11,361	3,940
Cumulative effect of change in accounting principles—net of tax		—	(30)
Net income		$11,361	$ 3,910
Earnings per common share — basic			
Income from continuing operations		$ 1.51	$ .22
Discontinued operations		—	.32
Net income		$ 1.51	$ .54
Earnings per common share — diluted			
Income from continuing operations before cumulative effect of change in accounting principles		$ 1.49	$ .22
Discontinued operations		—	.32
Net income		$ 1.49	$ .54
Weighted-average shares — basic		7,531	7,213
Weighted-average shares — diluted		7,614	7,286

[a]Exclusive of amortization of intangible assets, except as disclosed in Note 1K, *Amortization of Intangible Assets, Depreciation and Certain Long-Lived Assets.*

million, equal to $11,361 less preferred dividends of $4 million, by the average number of outstanding shares over the year of 7,351 million shares. The number of shares used in the divisor is obtained from the EPS footnote and does not equal the number of shares reported as outstanding on the balance sheet (8,702 at the start of the year and 8,754 at the end). The reason for this difference is that the firm both issued and purchased its stock during the year causing the average number of shares to diverge from the amounts outstanding at the respective year's ends.

The basic EPS reported in the income statement shows an additional line to report separately the amount of EPS produced by discontinued operations. No operations were discontinued in 2004 so the line is blank, but the effect on the prior two years is reported. The tax impact on the firm of its discontinued operations is combined with the operating results to assure that the complete effect of the discontinued activity is reflected in the calculation. A similar treatment would report the impact of any extraordinary items, had they occurred during the period. (Pfizer's income statement also shows a line indicating the cumulative effect of a change in accounting principle, net of tax, for example, a change in the method of depreciation).[6]

[6]Under a new standard issued by the FASB (FSA 154), the cumulative effects of changes in accounting principles will be applied retrospectively to all prior reported periods for which the effect can be estimated. The Statement is effective for fiscal years beginning after December 15, 2005.]

The last section of the income statement reports diluted earnings per share. As the term implies the reported number will never exceed basic earnings per share. The calculation is designed to show earnings per share at the lowest it could be if all dilutive equity contracts and convertible securities with a dilutive effect were converted into common stock. For Pfizer there are two such securities: options and convertible preferred stock. The calculations are complex and we will not cover them here. Suffice it to say, for any converted securities, the additional common shares resulting from considering the options exercised and the preferred converted are added to the denominator while any savings (preferred dividends, in Pfizer's case) would be added back to the numerator. The dividends were initially subtracted to obtain basic EPS, but if the stock had been converted, it would not be paid. In the case of a convertible bond, the interest no longer to be paid would be added to the numerator net of the related tax savings. Options that are in the money, that is, when the strike price is less than the market price of the stock, will always be dilutive. Other securities will not always be dilutive and that is why the math must be done. Any calculation that increases EPS after the options are considered is ignored in the reporting, assuring that the most dilutive possible situation is reported.

Pfizer shows that the additional shares of common, associated with the possible dilution, increased to 7,614 million. Diluted EPS is $11,357/7,614 = $1.49. Again the additional breakdown of this amount will be shown for discontinued operations and extraordinary items. Because the numerator of the calculation changed, we know that the conversion feature of the preferred stock was a factor in the decline of EPS from $1.51 to $1.49. However, we also see that the impact of dilution was minimal.

The notes to Pfizer's financial statements indicate that the company's outstanding stock options represent the equivalent of 359 million shares of its common stock during 2004. However, these options were not considered in determining diluted earnings per share because the options were not in the money and hence would have been anti-dilutive.

Most analysts have chosen to concentrate their attention on diluted EPS versus basic EPS as the more important measure, but the value of the EPS number is influenced by a number of factors including the number of common shares outstanding. For this reason comparisons are more useful over time than across firms. In addition, management's ability to influence the net income number as well as the number of shares outstanding provides a lot of discretion in what EPS value is reported. For these reasons, EPS is of limited value in evaluating a firm's operational performance.

MID-CHAPTER REVIEW 5

In the discussion of Pfizer's stock options suppose all the options were exercised when the stock price was at $32. Authorized but unissued common stock was used.

1. Prepare the journal entries, post the journal entries to the related t-accounts, and illustrate the impact of the transaction using the financial statement effects template.
2. What would be the impact on the firm's basic and diluted earnings per share?
3. Would there be any effects on the company's equity section?

Solution

1.

Transaction	Balance Sheet							Income Statement		
	Cash Asset	+	Noncash Assets	=	Liabil- ities	+	Contrib. Capital	+	Retained Earnings	Revenues − Expenses = Net Income
Exercise 100,000 options at a price of $32 using unissued common stock, $.05 par value	+3,200,000 Cash			=			+5,000 Common Stock +$3,195,000 Additional Paid-In Capital			=

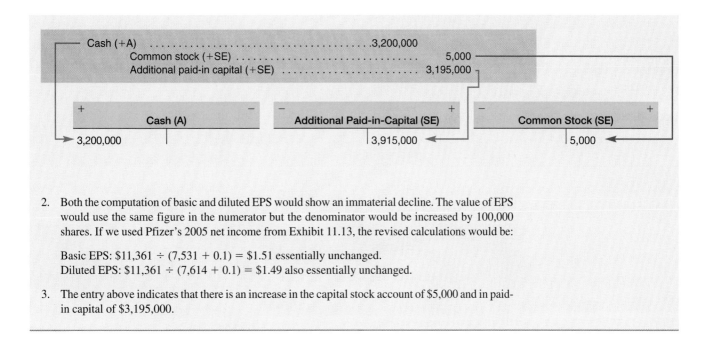

2. Both the computation of basic and diluted EPS would show an immaterial decline. The value of EPS would use the same figure in the numerator but the denominator would be increased by 100,000 shares. If we used Pfizer's 2005 net income from Exhibit 11.13, the revised calculations would be:

Basic EPS: $11,361 ÷ (7,531 + 0.1) = $1.51 essentially unchanged.
Diluted EPS: $11,361 ÷ (7,614 + 0.1) = $1.49 also essentially unchanged.

3. The entry above indicates that there is an increase in the capital stock account of $5,000 and in paid-in capital of $3,195,000.

Convertible Securities

Convertible securities are debt and equity securities that provide the holder with an option to convert those securities into other securities. Convertible debentures, for example, are debt securities that give the holder the option to convert the debt into common stock at a predetermined conversion price. Preferred stock can also contain a conversion privilege. Pfizer provides an example of the latter in its description of the Pharmacia acquisition.

> On April 16, 2003, Pfizer acquired Pharmacia for a purchase price of approximately $56 billion, which included the issuance of approximately 1.8 billion shares of Pfizer common stock, 180 million options on Pfizer common stock, six thousand shares of Pfizer Series A convertible perpetual preferred stock (convertible into 15.5 million shares of Pfizer common stock), and vested share awards, as well as transaction costs.

LO7 Explain and interpret the reporting of convertible securities.

Conversion privileges offer an additional benefit to the holder of a security. That is, debtholders and preferred stockholders carry senior positions as claimants in bankruptcy, and carry a fixed-interest or dividend yield. With a conversion privilege, they can enjoy the residual benefits of common shareholders should the company perform well.

A conversion option is valuable and yields a higher price for the securities than they would otherwise command. However, conversion privileges impose a cost on common shareholders. That is, the higher market price received for convertible securities is offset by the cost imposed on the subordinate (common) securities. In addition, conversion into common shares dilutes the ownership percentage of existing holders of the firm's common stock.

Accounting for the issuance of a convertible security is straightforward: the conversion option is *not* valued on the balance sheet unless it is detachable from the security (and, thus, separately salable). Instead, the convertible preferred stock or convertible debt is recorded just like preferred stock or debt that does not have a conversion feature.

When securities are converted, the book value of the converted security is removed from the balance sheet and a corresponding increase is made to contributed capital. To illustrate, assume that Pfizer has convertible bonds with a face value of $1,000 and an unamortized premium of $100. Its holders convert them into 20 shares of $10 par value common stock. The financial statement effects of this conversion follow:

Transaction	Balance Sheet					Income Statement		
	Cash Asset +	Noncash Assets =	Liabil- ities +	Contrib. Capital +	Retained Earnings	Revenues –	Expenses =	Net Income
$1,100 book value bonds are converted into 20 common shares of $10 par value		=	−1,100 Bonds Payable, net	+200 Common Stock +900 Additional Paid-In Capital			=	

The related journal entry and T-accounts follow.

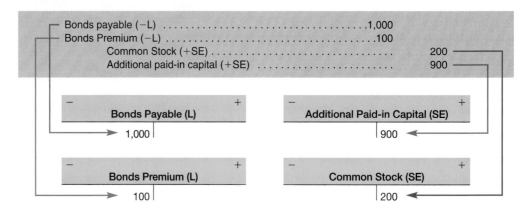

The key financial statement effects of this transaction are:

- The bond's face value ($1,000) and unamortized premium ($100) of the bonds are removed from the balance sheet
- Common stock increases by the par value of the shares issued (20 shares ×$10 par = $200) and additional paid-in capital increases for the balance ($900)
- There is no effect on income from this conversion unless an interest accrual is required.

Accounting for conversion of preferred shares is similar. That is, preferred stock is removed from the balance sheet and common stock is issued at a price equal to the book value of the converted preferred shares.

One final note, the potentially dilutive effect of convertible securities is taken into account in the computation of diluted earnings per share (EPS). Specifically, the diluted EPS computation assumes conversion at the beginning of the year (or when the security is issued if during the year). The earnings available to common shares in the numerator are increased by any forgone after-tax interest expense or preferred dividends, and the additional shares to be issued in the conversion increase the shares outstanding in the denominator.

Stock Rights

LO8 Discuss stock rights and the accounting for stock options.

Corporations often issue **stock rights** that give the holder an option to acquire a specified number of shares of capital stock under prescribed conditions and within a stated period. The evidence of stock rights is a certificate called a **stock warrant**. Stock rights are issued for several reasons that included the following.

- To compensate outside parties (such as underwriters, promoters, board members and other professionals) for services provided to the company
- As a preemptive right that gives existing stockholders the first chance to buy additional shares when the corporation decides to raise additional equity capital through share issuances.
- To compensate officers and other employees of the corporation; rights in this form are referred to as **stock options**.

- To enhance the marketability of other securities issued by the company; an example is issuing rights to purchase common stock with convertible bonds.

Stock rights or warrants specify the:

- Number of rights represented by the warrant
- Option price per share (which can be zero)
- Number of rights needed to obtain a share of the stock
- Expiration date of the rights
- Instructions for the exercise of rights

Accounting for stock rights is complex. The goals of this discussion are to understand the essence of (1) stock rights issued to current stockholders and (2) stock options issued to employees and others.

Stock rights issued to current stockholders have three important dates: (1) Announcement date of the rights offering; (2) Issuance date of the rights; and (3) Expiration date of the rights. Between the announcement date and the issuance date, the price of the stock will reflect the value of the rights. After the issuance date, the shares and the rights trade separately. Shareholders can exercise their rights, sell their stock, or allow the rights to lapse.

To illustrate, assume on December 10, 2002, Pfizer announces the issue of rights to purchase one additional share of its $0.05 par value common for every 10 shares currently held on January 1, 2003. The price per share is $20 and the rights expire September 1, 2003. Assume further that half of the rights are exercised and the other half lapse without being exercised. Using the data in Exhibit 11.1, the accounting follows:

- No recognition is required at the announcement date and at the issuance date.
- The first entry is made when the first stock right is exercised. We give only the summary entry that would be appropriate after September 1, 2003.

Jan 1: To record the issuance of 763 million shares of common stock on exercise of half of the stock rights:

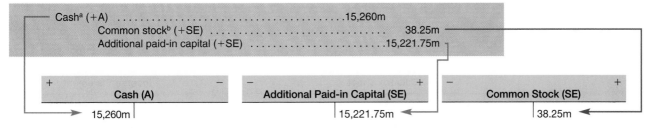

^a[(8,702mil. − 1,073mil.) ÷ 10][$20] = $15,260mil. [See Exhibit 11.1. The 1,073mil. figure represents the treasury shares that were issued but were repurchased and are no longer outstanding.]
^b[(8,702mil − 1,073mil) ÷ 10][$.05] = $38.15mil

The financial statement effects follow.

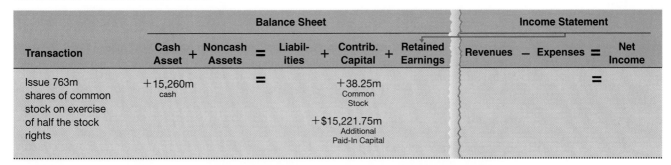

Transaction	Balance Sheet						Income Statement		
	Cash Asset	+	Noncash Assets	=	Liabil- ities	+	Contrib. Capital	+ Retained Earnings	Revenues − Expenses = Net Income
Issue 763m shares of common stock on exercise of half the stock rights	+15,260m cash			=			+38.25m Common Stock +$15,221.75m Additional Paid-In Capital		=

Stock Options

Accounting for stock options has been a contentious issue for a number of years. Accounting standard setters, on the one hand, argue that the options to purchase a corporation's stock at a discount (or even without a discount) are valuable. They point to the willingness of senior management and others to accept stock options instead of cash in payment for services rendered as evidence of their value. Thus the FASB has concluded that the fair value of each stock option award must be recognized as an expense on the firm's income statement.

On the other hand, senior managements of start-up firms typically argue that it is necessary in the face of cash shortages to compensate those providing service at least partly using stock options. If these option grants are treated as an expense, it will cause their firms to appear less profitable, thereby stifling investment and business growth. Those arguing against recognizing an expense also point to the difficulties in obtaining precise values for these options. Pfizer estimates that its stock-option expense for the second half of 2005 will amount to $201 million.

These difficulties are real, but methods of valuing options do exist that provide reasonable estimates of option values. The FASB decided that such awards are expenses and most publicly traded firms are required to report the associated expense for fiscal years beginning after December 15, 2005.

It will be interesting to see what impact the new accounting requirements have on the use of alternate means of compensating professionals for services provided. There are already indications that some firms are moving to restricted stock and performance shares as ways to address the matter. Pfizer is one of these firms and plans to reduce the number of options granted and, instead, grant restricted stock units.

To illustrate stock option accounting, suppose that on January 1, 2006, Pfizer grants options to purchase 100,000 shares to senior management as part of its 2005 performance bonus plan. The options are granted at $30, (the current price), and can be exercised anytime during the next 5 years. The firm uses an accepted valuation method (not discussed here) to obtain a value of $10 per share. The accounting and financial statement effects follow.

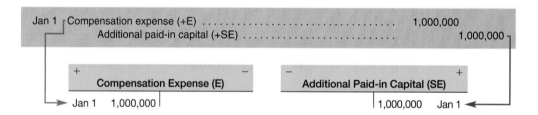

The financial statement effects follow.

	Balance Sheet						Income Statement		
Transaction	Cash Asset	+ Noncash Assets =	Liabil- ities	+ Contrib. Capital	+ Retained Earnings		Revenues	– Expenses =	Net Income
100,000 options granted at $30, the current price and value at $10 per share		=		+$1,000,000 Additional Paid-In Capital	–$1,000,000 Retained Earnings			–$1,000,000 Compensaton Expense	= –$1,000,000

Next, suppose that its stock price rises and all options are exercised on November 15 with the stock being issued from treasury shares purchased previously at $25. The accounting and financial statement effects follow.

	Balance Sheet						Income Statement		
Transaction	Cash Asset	+ Noncash Assets	= Liabil- ities	+ Contrib. Capital	+ Retained Earnings		Revenues	− Expenses =	Net Income
Exercise of 100,000 options using treasury shares purchased at $25 a share	+3,000,000 Cash		=	+2,500,000 Treasury Stock +500,000 Additional Paid-In Capital					=

YOU MAKE THE CALL...

As the CEO Your Board of Directors indicates that it intends to recommend that your company stop granting employee stock options because of the FASB's decision to require their expensing at fair value. What is likely to be the Board's reasoning and how would you respond? [Answer pg. 495]

BUSINESS INSIGHT

Agilent's Stock-Option Drag Agilent's earnings are poised to suffer in 2006 when the new rules requiring the expensing of stock option awards takes effect. For the six months ended April 30, 2005, Agilent's net income would fall from the reported $198 million to a less than stellar $98 million, a 51% decline! Instead of earning $0.76 per share, EPS would have reached only $0.31 and the firm's price/earnings multiple would be 34 rather than 84. Things were even worse in 2004 when Agilent would have found net income to be only 34% of the rejected amount. And this level of reduction is not confined to Agilent. Par for the course for 13 rivals shows a reduction to 77% of reported net income. Watch for substantial reductions in 2006 net income for those firms relying heavily on stock-based pay.

CHAPTER-END REVIEW

Kallapur, Inc. has issued convertible debentures: each $1,000 bond is convertible into 200 shares of $1 par common. Assume that the bonds were sold at a discount, and that each bond has a current unamortized discount equal to $150.

Required

1. Prepare journal entries for the transaction.
2. Post the journal entries to the related T-accounts.
3. Using the financial statement effects template, illustrate the effects of the conversion of one of its bonds.

Solution

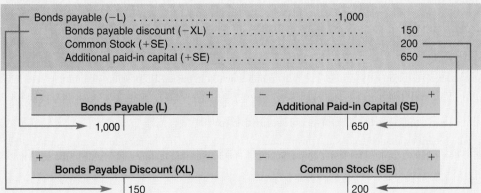

	Balance Sheet					Income Statement		
Transaction	**Cash Asset** + **Noncash Assets**	=	**Liabil- ities**	+ **Contrib. Capital**	+ **Retained Earnings**	**Revenues** − **Expenses**	=	**Net Income**
Conversion of an $850 book-value bond into 200 common shares of $1 par value		=	−850 Bonds Payable, net	+200 Common Stock +650 Additional Paid-In Capital			=	

SUMMARY

Describe business financing through stock issuances. (p. 469)

LO1
- Contributed capital represents the cumulative cash inflow that the company has received from the sale of various classes of stock, preferred and common.

- Preferred stock receives preference in terms of dividends before common and if cumulative receives all dividends not paid in the past before common dividends can be paid. Preferred stock can also be designated as convertible into common stock at the holder's option and at a predetermined conversion ratio. Voting privileges reside only with the common stock.

LO2

Explain and account for the issuance and repurchase of stock. (p. 472)

- Common stock is often repurchased by the firm for use in stock award programs or to signal management confidence in the company. Repurchased stock is either cancelled or held for reissue. The repurchase is debited to a contra equity account titled treasury stock.

LO3 ### Describe how operations increase the equity of a business. (p. 477)

- Earned capital, called retained earnings, represents the cumulative profit that has been retained by the company. Earned capital is increased by income earned and decreased by losses and dividends declared by the firm. Earned capital also includes the effects of items included in other comprehensive income.

LO4 ### Explain and account for dividends and stock splits. (p. 477)

- Dividends in the form of stock decrease retained earnings and increase contributed capital by an equivalent amount.

- A stock split is a proportionate distribution similar in substance to a stock dividend. The new number of shares outstanding must be disclosed. Otherwise, no further required accounting is required unless the state of incorporation requires that the par value be proportionally adjusted.

LO5 ### Define and illustrate comprehensive income. (p. 483)

- Comprehensive Income includes several additional items not recognized in net income including: adjustments for changes in foreign exchange rates, unrealized changes in available-for-sale securities, minimum pension liability adjustments. The concept is designed to highlight impacts on income that are beyond management's control.

LO6 ### Describe and illustrate the earnings per share computation. (p. 485)

- Earnings per share is a closely watched number reported for all publicly traded firms. Basic EPS is computed as the ratio of net income (less preferred dividends) to the average number of outstanding shares for the period. The value of this performance metric is subject to all the difficulties in measuring net income including the fact that net income can increase due to an acquisition that can have no impact on the number of outstanding shares.

- Most analysts are more interested in what is termed diluted earnings per share. This conservative calculation, which never exceeds basic EPS, reflects the maximum reduction in basic EPS possible assuming conversion of the convertible securities.

LO7 ### Explain and interpret the reporting of convertible securities. (p. 489)

- Convertible securities are debt and equity instruments, including stock rights that allow these securities to be exchanged for other securities, typically common stock. The convertible feature adds value to the security to which it is attached.

Discuss stock rights and the accounting for stock options. (p. 490)

- Stock options, one form of stock right, allow the holders to exchange them at a specified (strike) price for common stock. This right is valuable and should create as an expense when granted to an employee or other individual. Expense recognition is appropriate; using the value obtained using an options-pricing model, even though the calculation is not precise. The option will not be exercised unless the market price of the common stock exceeds the strike price. (The option is said to be "in the money.")

Appendix 11A—**Analyze the reporting for equity carve outs, including sell-offs, spin-offs, and split-offs. (p. 495)**

- Equity carve-outs are corporate divestitures of business units allowing the market to value these units individually.

- Equity carve-outs are usually non-cash transactions and always transitory. Any gain or loss resulting from the carve-out transaction should be interpreted similar to discontinued operations.

GUIDANCE ANSWERS

YOU MAKE THE CALL

You Are the Chief Financial Officer   Several points must be considered. (1) Treasury shares are likely to prop up earnings per share (EPS). While the numerator (earnings) is likely dampened by the use of cash for the stock repurchase, EPS is likely to increase because of the reduced shares in the denominator. (2) Another motivation is that, if the shares are sufficiently undervalued (in management's opinion), the stock repurchase and subsequent resale can provide a better return than some alternative investments. (3) Stock repurchases send a strong signal to the market that management feels its stock is undervalued. This is more credible than merely making that argument with analysts. On the other hand, company cash is diverted from other investments. This is bothersome if such investments are mutually exclusive either now or in the future.

YOU MAKE THE CALL

As the CEO   The Board is likely to be concerned primarily that the additional expense will lower net income from operations. In addition, the Board will indicate that the expense will be aggregated into other expenses and not subject to separate evaluation. Finally the Board will argue that the amounts are disclosed in the footnotes, require no cash outlay and hence mislead investors as to the profitability of the corporation.

While you could respond that granted options are an expense because they represent compensation to the receiving employee, you should also observe that reporting the estimated cost of stock options is proper full disclosure and gives a conservative bias to the firm's reporting that could increase the perceived quality of its reporting thereby lowering the firm's cost of capital. Finally, if all else fails, you simply note that expensing options is or shortly will be requires under GAAP. That should settle the matter.

APPENDIX 11A: Equity Carve Outs

Corporate divestitures, or **equity carve outs**, are increasingly common as companies seek to increase shareholder value through partial or total divestiture of operating units. Generally, equity carve outs are motivated by the notion that consolidated financial statements often obscure the performance of individual business units, thus complicating their evaluation by outsiders. Corporate managers are concerned that this difficulty in assessing the performance of individual business units limits their ability to reach full valuation. Maximization of shareholder value is, therefore, not attained. In response, conglomerates have divested subsidiaries so that the market can individually price them.

Sell-Offs

Equity carve outs take many forms. Several of the more common variety are discussed here. The first and simplest form of divestiture is the outright sale of a business unit, called a **sell-off**. In this case, the company sells its equity interest to an unrelated party. When a company sells the business unit, it accounts for this sale similar to the sale of any other asset. Specifically, any excess (deficit) of cash received over the book value of the business unit sold is recorded as a gain (loss) on the sale.

To illustrate, **Pfizer** reported a 2003 gain on the sale of its Adams confectionery products business unit in its income statement as follows:

> In March 2003, we sold the Adams confectionery products business, formerly part of our Consumer Healthcare segment, to Cadbury Schweppes plc for $4.2 billion in cash. We recognized a gain on the sale of this business of $3,091 million ($1,824 million net of tax) in 2003.

The financial statement effects of this transaction follow:

- Pfizer received $4,200 million cash.
- The Adams's subsidiary was carried on Pfizer's balance sheet as an equity method investment with a book value of $1,109 million.
- Pfizer's gain on sale equaled the sale proceeds less the book value: $4,200 million − $1,109 million = $3,091 million gain on sale.
- The gain on sale, though transitory, is reported in its 2003 income from continuing operations.
- Pfizer subtracts the gain from net income in its statement of cash flows to compute net cash flows from operations since it is not deemed an operating cash flow. Instead, the $4,200 million cash proceeds are reported as a cash inflow from investing activities.

Spin-Offs

A **spin-off** is another form of divestiture. In this case, the company distributes the subsidiary shares that it owns as a dividend to its shareholders who, then, own shares in the subsidiary directly rather than through the parent company. In recording this dividend, retained earnings are reduced by the book value of the equity method investment and the subsidiary's investment account is removed from the balance sheet.

The spin-off of **Limited Too** subsidiary by its parent company, **The Limited, Inc.** (now Limited Brands), is an example of this form of equity carve out. The Limited described this spin-off as follows:

> On July 15, 1999, the Company's Board of Directors approved a formal plan to spin-off Limited Too. The record date for the spin-off was August 11, 1999, with Limited shareholders receiving one share of Too, Inc. (the successor company to Limited Too) common stock for every seven shares of Limited common stock held on that date. The spin-off was completed on August 23, 1999. The Company recorded the spin-off as a $25 million dividend, which represented the carrying value of the net assets underlying the common stock distributed. As part of the transaction, the Company received total proceeds of $62 million that included a $50 million dividend from TOO and a $12 million repayment of advances to TOO. During the second quarter of 1999, the Company recognized a $13.1 million charge for transaction costs related to the spin-off.

The important financial statement facts and effects of this transaction follow:

- Limited's shareholders received 1 share of Limited Too stock for every 7 shares of The Limited that they owned.
- Limited recorded the distribution as a dividend. Retained earnings were reduced by the book value (carrying amount) of the equity method investment, and the investment was removed from its assets.
- This distribution had no effect on The Limited's profitability in the year of the distribution. Instead, the distribution reduced the retained earnings component of its shareholders' equity.

Split-Offs

The **split-off** is a third form of equity carve out. In this case, the parent exchanges stock in the subsidiary that it owns in return for shares in the parent owned by its shareholders. After completing this transaction, the subsidiary is an independent publicly traded company.

The parent treats acquisition of its own shares from its shareholders like the purchase of treasury stock. As such, the treasury stock account is increased and the equity method investment account is reduced, reflecting the distribution of that asset. The dollar amount recorded for this treasury stock depends on how the distribution is set up. There are two possibilities:

1. **Pro rata distribution.** Shares are distributed to stockholders on a pro rata basis. Namely, a shareholder owning 10% of the outstanding stock of the parent company receives 10% of the shares of the subsidiary distributed. The treasury stock account is recorded at the book value of the investment in the subsidiary. The accounting is similar to repurchase of treasury stock for cash, except that shares of the subsidiary are paid to shareholders instead of cash.

2. **Non pro rata distribution.** This case is like a tender offer where stockholders can accept or reject the distribution. The treasury stock account is recorded at the *market value* of the shares of the subsidiary

distributed. Because the investment account can only be reduced by its book value, a gain or loss on distribution is recorded in the income statement for the difference.[7]

The **Limited** split-off of **Abercrombie & Fitch** (A&F) in 1998 provides an excellent example of both variants of the split-off. To illustrate, we begin with The Limited's income statement.

($ 000s)	2000	1999	1998
Net sales	$10,104,606	$ 9,766,220	$ 9,364,750
Costs of goods sold, buying and occupancy	(6,667,389)	(6,443,063)	(6,424,725)
Gross income	3,437,217	3,323,157	2,940,025
General, administrative and store operating expenses	(2,561,201)	(2,415,849)	(2,256,332)
Special and nonrecurring items, net	(9,900)	23,501	1,740,030
Operating income	866,116	930,809	2,423,723
Interest expense	(58,244)	(78,297)	(68,528)
Other income, net	20,378	40,868	59,915
Minority interest	(69,345)	(72,623)	(63,616)
Gain on sale of subsidiary stock	—	11,002	—
Income before income taxes	758,905	831,759	2,351,494
Provision for income taxes	331,000	371,000	305,000
Net income	$ 427,905	$ 460,759	$ 2,046,494

Limited reports "special and nonrecurring items, net" of $1,740 million in 1998. This amount includes a $1,651 million in gain from the A&F split-off. Although Limited describes this gain as special and nonrecurring, Limited *included* it in income from continuing operations. This reporting highlights the potential for large transitory items in income from continuing operations.

Limited describes this split-off in the notes to its 2000 annual report as follows:

> On May 19, 1998, the Company completed a tax-free exchange offer to establish A&F as an independent company. A total of 94.2 million shares of the Company's common stock were exchanged at a ratio of 0.86 of a share of A&F common stock for each Limited share tendered. In connection with the exchange, the Company recorded a $1.651 billion tax-free gain. This gain was measured based on the $21.81 per share market value of the A&F common stock at the expiration date of the exchange offer. In addition, on June 1, 1998, a $5.6 million dividend was effected through a pro rata spin-off to shareholders of the Company's remaining 6.2. million A&F shares. Limited shareholders of record as of the close of trading on May 29, 1998 received .013673 of a share of A&F for each Limited share owned at that time.

Key financial statement facts and effects of this transaction follow:

▪ Limited exchanged shares that it owned in A&F for some of the Limited shares owned by its shareholders. This splits off the subsidiary as an independent company.

▪ Limited recorded treasury stock at the market value of A&F on the exchange date. Because the investment is removed from its balance sheet at its book value, the difference between these two amounts is recorded as a gain of $1,651 million.

▪ Limited's statement of cash flows adds back the gain to remove it from operating cash flows because the A&F split-off does not involve any cash flows.

▪ Limited was unable to exchange all of the A&F shares it owned via the tender offer. It then distributed the remaining 6.2 million shares on a pro rata basis. No gain is recorded on this part of the transaction.

Analysis of Equity Carve Outs

Sell-offs, spin-offs, and split-offs all involve the divestiture of an operating segment. They are usually stock transactions and, as a result, do not involve cash inflow. Finally, they are all one-time occurrences. Yet, because they can result in substantial gains and can markedly alter the balance sheet, we must think about how they should be interpreted.

---

[7]The SEC also allows companies to record the difference as an adjustment to additional paid-in capital. The usual practice, as might be expected, is for companies to report any gain as part of income.

Equity carve outs are usually noncash and are always transitory. The company does, of course, lose the cash flows (positive or negative) of the divested business unit. As such, the divestiture should be treated like any other discontinued operation. Any recognized gain or loss from divestiture is treated as a nonoperating (investing) activity. The sale price of the divested unit reflects the valuation of *future expected* cash flows by the purchaser and is best viewed as a nonoperating (investing) activity by the seller. Income (and cash flows) of the divested unit up to the date of sale, however, is part of operations.

APPENDIX REVIEW

Blacconiere Company announced the split-off of its Salamon subsidiary. Blacconiere reported a gain from the split-off. (1) Describe the accounting for a split-off. (2) Why was Blacconiere able to report a gain on this transaction?

Solution
1. In a split-off, shares of the parent company owned by its shareholders are exchanged for shares of the subsidiary owned by the parent. If the distribution is non pro rata, the parent can report a gain equal to the difference between the fair market value of the subsidiary and its book value on the parent's balance sheet.
2. Blacconiere met the conditions described in part 1, which enabled it to report a gain.

KEY TERMS

Basic EPS (p. 486)	Earned capital (p. 470)	Sell-off (p. 495)
Book value per share (p. 485)	Equity carve outs (p. 495)	Spin-off (p. 496)
Contributed capital (p. 470)	Liquidation preference (p. 471)	Split-off (p. 496)
Conversion feature (p. 471)	Minimum pension liability (p. 483)	Stock options (p. 490)
Convertible securities (p. 489)	Non pro rata distribution (p. 496)	Stock rights (p. 490)
Currency translation adjustment (p. 483)	Participation feature (p. 472)	Stock warrant (p. 490)
Diluted EPS (p. 486)	Par value (p. 472)	Treasury stock (p. 475)
Dividend preference (p. 471)	Preferred stock (p. 470)	
	Pro rata distribution (p. 496)	

MULTIPLE CHOICE

1. Suppose Pfizer issues 100,000 shares of its common stock, $0.05 par value, to obtain a warehouse and the accompanying land when the price of the stock is $22.00. Which one of the following statements is **not** true?
   a. The newly acquired assets will increase total assets by $2.2 billion
   b. Retained earnings are unaffected
   c. The common stock account increases by $5,000
   d. Total shareholders' equity increases by $2,195,000

2. Assume Pfizer resells 10,000 shares of its stock for $22 that were purchased when the market price of the stock is $25. Which one of the following statements holds?
   a. Additional paid-in capital decreases by $30,000
   b. The treasury stock account increases by $30,000
   c. Additional paid-in capital decreases by $30,000
   d. The treasury stock account increases by $30,000

3. Suppose Pfizer declares a 200,000 common stock dividend (par $0.05) when the market value of a share is $20.00. Which one of the following statements is true?
   a. The common stock account increases by $10,000
   b. Additional paid-in capital decreases by $3.99 billion
   c. Retained earnings increases by $4 billion
   d. Additional paid-in capital increases by $4billion

4. Consider Exhibit 11.14. Which one of the following statements is **not** true concerning Pfizer's stock option transactions for 2003?
   a. The acquisition cost of the treasury shares issued was $20 million
   b. Pfizer's additional paid in capital increased by $1,532 million
   c. Pfizer's stock option transactions increased the number of shares outstanding by 56 million shares
   d. Stock option activity decreased the value of the Employee Benefit Trust.

5. Which of the following statements is **not** true in relation to diluted EPS (DEPS)?
   a. Stock options that are in the money will always cause DEPS to be less than basic EPS.
   b. Convertible bonds, if dilutive, will cause changes in both the numerator and the denominator of DEPS.
   c. Stock analysts tend to concentrate their attention on DEPS instead of basic EPS.
   d. Pfizer's only equity contract that can lead to dilution is stock options.

DISCUSSION QUESTIONS

Q11-1. Define *par value stock*. What is the significance of a stock's par value from an accounting and analysis perspective?

Q11-2. What are the basic differences between preferred stock and common stock? What are the typical features of preferred stock?

Q11-3. What features make preferred stock similar to debt? Similar to common stock?

Q11-4. What is meant by dividend arrearage on preferred stock? If dividends are two years in arrears on $500,000 of 6% preferred stock, and dividends are declared at the end of this year, what amount of total dividends must preferred shareholders receive before any distributions are made to common shareholders?

Q11-5. Distinguish between authorized stock and issued stock. Why might the number of shares issued be more than the number of shares outstanding?

Q11-6. Describe the difference between contributed capital and earned capital. Specifically, how can earned capital be considered as an investment by the company's shareholders?

Q11-7. How does the account "additional paid-in capital" (APIC) arise? What inferences, if any, can you draw from the amount of APIC as reported on the balance sheet relative to the common stock amount in relation to the financial condition of the company?

Q11-8. Define *stock split*. What are the major reasons for a stock split?

Q11-9. Define *treasury stock*. Why might a corporation acquire treasury stock? How is treasury stock reported in the balance sheet?

Q11-10. If a corporation purchases 600 shares of its own common stock at $10 per share and resells them at $14 per share, where would the $2,400 increase in capital be reported in the financial statements? Why is no gain reported?

Q11-11. A corporation has total stockholders' equity of $4,628,000 and one class of $2 par value common stock. The corporation has 500,000 shares authorized; 300,000 shares issued; 260,000 shares outstanding; and 40,000 shares as treasury stock. What is its book value per share?

Q11-12. What is a stock dividend? How does a common stock dividend distributed to common shareholders affect their respective ownership interests?

Q11-13. What is the difference between the accounting for a small stock dividend and the accounting for a large stock dividend?

Q11-14. Employee stock options have a potentially dilutive effect on earnings per share (EPS) that is recognized in the diluted EPS computation. What can companies do to offset these dilutive effects and how might this action affect the balance sheet?

Q11-15. What information is reported in a statement of stockholders' equity?

Q11-16. What items are typically reported under the stockholders' equity category of other comprehensive income (OCI)?

Q11-17. What is the difference between a spin-off and a split-off? Under what circumstances can either result in the recognition of a gain in the income statement?

Q11-18. Describe the accounting for a convertible bond. Can the conversion ever result in the recognition of a gain in the income statement?

MINI EXERCISES

M11-19. Analyzing and Identifying Financial Statement Effects of Stock Issuances (LO2, 6)
On June 1, 2005, Beatty Corp., issues (*a*) 8,000 shares of $50 par value preferred stock at $68 cash per share and it issues (*b*) 12,000 shares of $1 par value common stock at $10 cash per share. Indicate the financial statement effects of these two issuances using the financial statement effects template. How would each issue effect basic EPS?

M11-20. Analyzing and Identifying Financial Statement Effects of Stock Issuances (LO2)
On September 1, 2005, Magliolo, Inc., (*a*) issues 18,000 shares of $10 par value preferred stock at $48 cash per share and (*b*) issues 120,000 shares of $2 par value common stock at $37 cash per share.
   a. Prepare the journal entries for the two issuances.
   b. Post the journal entries from *a* to the related T-accounts.
   c. Using the financial statement effects template, illustrate the effects of these two issuances.

Cisco Systems,
Inc. (CSCO)

M11-21. Distinguishing between Common Stock and Additional Paid-in Capital (LO1)

Following is the 2003 stockholders' equity section from the Cisco Systems, Inc., balance sheet (in millions, except par value).

Shareholders' equity	July 26, 2003
Preferred stock, no par value: 5 shares authorized; none issued and outstanding	$ —
Common stock and additional paid-in capital, $0.001 par value: 20,000 shares authorized: 6,998 shares issued and outstanding	21,116
Retained earnings	6,559
Accumulated other comprehensive income	354
Total shareholders' equity	$28,029

For the $21,116 million reported as "common stock and additional paid-in capital," what portion is common stock and what portion is additional paid-in capital? Explain.

M11-22. Identifying and Analyzing Financial Statement Effects of Stock Issuance and Repurchase (LO2)

On January 1, 2005, Bartov Company issues 5,000 shares of $100 par value preferred stock at $250 cash per share. On March 1, the company repurchases 5,000 shares of previously issued $1 par value common stock at $83 cash per share.

a. Prepare the journal entries for the two issuances.

b. Post the journal entries from *a* to the related T-accounts.

c. Using the financial statement effects template, illustrate the effects of these two issuances.

M11-23. Assessing the Financial Statement Effects of a Stock Split (LO4, 6)

Procter & Gamble
Company (PG)

Procter & Gamble Company discloses the following footnote to its 2004 10-K report.

> **Stock Split**   In March 2004, the Company's Board of Directors approved a two-for-one stock split effective for common and preferred shareholders of record as of May 21, 2004. The financial statements, notes and other references to share and per share data have been restated to reflect the stock split for all periods presented.

This note to its 2004 balance sheet further indicates that amounts have been "restated for two-for-one stock split effective May 21, 2004." What restatements has P&G made to its balance sheet as a result of this action?

M11-24 Computing Basic and Diluted Earnings per Share (LO6)

Zeller Corporation began 2006 with 120,000 shares of common stock and 16,000 shares of convertible preferred stock outstanding. On March 1 an additional 10,000 shares of common stock were issued. On August 1, another 16,000 shares of common stock were issued. On November 1, 6,000 shares of common stock were acquired for the treasury. The preferred stock has a $2 per-share dividend rate, and each share may be converted into one share of common stock. Zeller Corporation's 2006 net income is $501,000.

a. Compute basic earnings per share for 2006,

b. Compute diluted earnings per share for 2006.

c. If the required stock were not convetible, Zeller Corporation would have a simple capital structure. How would this change Zeller's earnings per share presentation?

M11-25. Proving Common Stock and Treasury Stock Balances (LO2, 6)

Abercrombie & Fitch
(ANF)

Following is the stockholders' equity section from the Abercrombie & Fitch balance sheet ($ thousands).

Shareholders' Equity	Feb. 1, 2003
Common stock—$.01 par value: 150,000,000 shares authorized, 97,268,877 shares outstanding	$ 1,033
Paid-in capital	142,577
Retained earnings	714,475
	858,085
Less: Treasury stock, at average cost	(108,558)
Total shareholders' equity	$ 749,527

a. Assuming that A&F has repurchased 6,031,123 shares that comprise its 2003 treasury stock account, show the computation to yield the $1,033,000 balance reported for its common stock.

b. If this repurchase took place March 31, what would be the effect on the denominator of the basic EPS calculation?

M11-26. Identifying and Analyzing Financial Statement Effects of Cash Dividends (LO4)

Freid Corp. has outstanding 6,000 shares of $50 par value, 6% preferred stock, and 40,000 shares of $1 par value common stock. The company has $328,000 of retained earnings. At year-end, the company declares and pays the regular $3 per share cash dividend on preferred stock and a $2.20 per share cash dividend on common stock.

a. Prepare the journal entries for the two dividend payments.
b. Post the journal entries from *a* to the related T-accounts.
c. Using the financial statement effects template, illustrate the effects of these two dividend payments.

M11-27. Analyzing and Identifying Financial Statement Effects of Stock Dividends (LO4)

Dutta Corp. has outstanding 70,000 shares of $5 par value common stock. At year-end, the company declares and issues a 4% common stock dividend when the market price of the stock is $21 per share.

a. Prepare the journal entries for the stock dividend declaration and payment.
b. Post the journal entries from a to the related T-accounts.
c. Using the financial statement effects template, illustrate the effects of this dividend declaration and payment.

M11-28. Analyzing, Identifying and Explaining the Effects of a Stock Split (LO4, 6)

On September 1, 2005, Weiss Company has 250,000 shares of $15 par value ($165 market value) common stock that are issued and outstanding. Its balance sheet on that date shows the following account balances relating to the common stock.

Common stock	$3,750,000
Paid-in capital in excess of par value	2,250,000

On September 2, Weiss splits its stock 3-for-2 and reduces the par value to $10 per share.
a. How many shares of common stock are issued and outstanding immediately after the stock split?
b. What is the dollar balance of the common stock account immediately after the stock split?
c. What is the likely reason that Weiss Company split its stock?
d. What is the effect on the denominator of the basic EPS calculation?

M11-29. Distributing Cash Dividends to Preferred and Common Shareholders (LO4)

Dechow Company has outstanding 20,000 shares of $50 par value, 6% cumulative preferred stock and 80,000 shares of $10 par value common stock. The company declares and pays cash dividends amounting to $160,000.
a. If no arrearage on the preferred stock exists, how much in total dividends, and in dividends per share, is paid to each class of stock?
b. If one year's dividend arrearage on the preferred stock exists, how much in total dividends, and in dividends per share, is paid to each class of stock?

M11-30. Analyzing and Preparing a Retained Earnings Reconciliation (LO6)

Use the following data to prepare the 2005 retained earnings reconciliation for Bamber Company.

Total retained earnings, December 31, 2004	$347,000
Stock dividends declared and paid in 2005	28,000
Cash dividends declared and paid in 2005	35,000
Net income for 2005	94,000

M11-31. Accounting for Large Stock Dividend and Stock Split (LO4)

Watts Corporation has 40,000 shares of $10 par value common stock outstanding and retained earnings of $820,000. The company declares a 100% stock dividend. The market price at the declaration is $17 per share.
a. Prepare the general journal entries for (1) the declaration of the dividend and (2) the issuance of the dividend.
b. Assume that the company splits its stock two shares for one share and reduces the par value from $10 to $5 rather than declaring a 100% stock dividend. How does the accounting for the stock split differ from the accounting for the 100% stock dividend?

M11-32. Computing Basic and Diluted Earnings per Share (LO6)

During 2006, Park Corporation had 50,000 shares of $10 par value common stock and 10,000 shares of 8%, $50 par value convertible preferred stock outstanding. Each share of preferred stock may be converted into three shares of common stock. Park Corporation's 2006 net income was $440,000.
a. Compute the basic earnings per share for 2006.
b. Compute the diluted earnings per share for 2006.

M11-33. Computing Earnings per Share (LO6)

Kingery Corporation began the year with a simple structure consisting of 38,000 shares of common stock outstanding. On May 1, 10,000 additional shares were issued, and another 1,000 shares were issued on September 1. The company had a net income for theyear of $234,000.

a. Compute the earnings per share of common stock.

b. Assume that the company also had 6,000 shares of 6%, $50 par value cumulative preferred stock outstanding throughout the year. Compute the earnings per share of common stock.

M11-34. Defining and Computing Earnings per Share (LO6)

3M Company (MMM)

3M Company reports the following basic and diluted earnings per share in its 2002 10-K report (shares in million).

a. Describe the accounting definitions for basic and diluted earnings per share.

b. Identify the 3M numbers that make up both EPS computations.

Weighted average common shares outstanding—basic	390.0
Earnings per share—basic	$5.06
Weighted average common shares outstanding—diluted	395.0
Earnings per share—diluted	$4.99

M11-35. Analyzing Stock Option Expense for Income (LO7)

Merck & Company (MRK)

Merck & Company reports the following footnote disclosure to its 10-K report.

The effect on net income and earnings per common share if the Company had applied the fair value method for recognizing employee stock-based compensation is as follows:

Years Ended December 31 ($ millions)	2003	2002	2001
Net income, as reported	$6,830.9	$7,149.5	$7,281.8
Compensation expense, net of tax			
Reported	4.9	1.2	(0.1)
Fair value method	(559.4)	(487.9)	(400.9)
Pro forma net income	$6,276.4	$6,662.8	$6,980.8

a. How much expense is currently reported in Merck's income statement relating to its stock options?

b. How much expense would have been reported had Merck valued its employee stock options using the fair value method? What woud have been the effect on net income if this alternative method had been applied?

c. Is the expense in (b) a cash expense? How would your answer change, if at all, if you knew that Merck repurchases shares of its stock in the open market to offset the dilutive effect of shares issued when these stock options are exercised?

M11-37. Interpretation of a Spin-Off Disclosure (LO7, 9)

Bristol-Myers Squibb (BMY)

Bristol-Myers Squibb discloses the following in notes to its 2003 10-K report.

The Company spun off Zimmer Holdings, Inc. (Zimmer), in a tax-free distribution, resulting in a common stock dividend of $156 million.

a. Describe the difference between a spin-off and a split-off.

b. What effects did BMY's spin-off have on its balance sheet and its income statement?

M11-38. Interpretation of a Proposed Split-Off Disclosure (LO8)

Viacom, Inc. (VIA)

Viacom, Inc. reports the following footnote in its 2003 10-K.

SUBSEQUENT EVENT

On February 10, 2004, the Company announced that its Board of Directors authorized the Company to pursue the divestiture of Viacom's approximately 81.5% interest in Blockbuster, based on the conclusion that Blockbuster would be better positioned as a company completely independent of Viacom. The Company anticipates that the divestiture would be achieved through a tax-free split-off, but will also continue to consider other alternatives. The transaction is subject to further approval of the Viacom Board and an assessment of market conditions. The split-off, which would result in a reduction of Viacom's outstanding shares, is expected to be completed by mid-2004. If the Company determines to split-off Blockbuster any difference between the fair market value of Blockbuster and its net book value at the time of the split-off will be recognized as a gain or loss for accounting purposes. The actual amount of the gain or loss will depend upon the fair market value and the net book value of Blockbuster at the time of the split-off as well as the exchange ratio used in the split-off.

a. Describe the accounting for a split-off.
b. How will the proposed split-off result in a reduction of Viacom's outstanding shares?
c. Under what circumstances will Viacom be able to report a gain for this proposed split-off?

M11-39. Interpretation of Disclosure related to the Split-Off of AT&T Wireless   (LO7, 9)

AT&T reports the following footnote to its 2003 10-K.

AT&T (T)

In 2001, we realized a tax-free noncash gain on the disposition of discontinued operations of $13.5 billion, representing the difference between the fair value of the AT&T Wireless tracking stock at the date of the split-off and our book value of AT&T Wireless.

a. Describe the accounting for a split-off.
b. Describe the circumstances that allowed AT&T to recognize a gain on this split-off.
c. How should you interpret the gain from this split-off in your analysis of AT&T for 2003?

M11-40. Analyzing Financial Statement Effects of Convertible Securities   (LO6, 7)

Jetblue Airways Corporation reports the following footnote to its 2002 10-K.

Jetblue Airways
Corporation (JBLU)

Convertible Redeemable Preferred Stock and Stockholders' Equity

Effective with our initial public offering on April 17, 2002, our authorized shares of capital stock were increased to 500 million shares of common stock and 25 million shares of preferred stock and all outstanding shares of our convertible redeemable preferred stock were converted to common stock on a one-for-one basis. The holders of our common stock are entitled to one vote per share on all matters which require a vote by the Company's stockholders as outlined in the articles of incorporation and the by-laws.

a. Describe the effects on Jetblue's balance sheet of the conversion of its preferred stock.
b. Did this conversion impact its 2002 net earnings? Explain.
c. Discuss the effect of this action on the calculation of basic and diluted EPS.

EXERCISES

E11-40. Identifying and Analyzing Financial Statement Effects of Stock Transactions   (LO2, 6)

Lipe Company reports the following 2005 transactions relating to its stock accounts.

Feb 20   Issued 10,000 shares of $1 par value common stock at $25 cash per share
Feb 21   Issued 15,000 shares of $100 par value, 8% preferred stock at $275 cash per share.
Jun 30   Purchased 2,000 shares of its own common stock at $15 cash per share.
Sep 25   Sold 1,000 shares of the treasury stock at $21 cash per share.

a. Prepare the journal entries for these transactions.
b. Post the journal entries from *a* to the related T-accounts.
c. Using the financial statement effects template, illustrate the effects of these transactions.
d. Indicate the impact of each transaction on the calculation of EPS.

E11-41. Analyzing and Identifying Financial Statement Effects of Stock Transactions   (LO2)

McNichols Corp. reports the following transactions relating to its stock accounts in 2005.

Jan 15   Issued 25,000 shares of $5 par value common stock at $17 cash per share
Jan 20   Issued 6,000 shares of $50 par value, 8% preferred stock at $78 cash per share.
Mar 31   Purchased 3,000 shares of its own common stock at $20 cash per share.
June 25   Sold 2,000 shares of the treasury stock at $26 cash per share.
July 15   Sold the remaining 1,000 shares of treasury stock at $19 cash per share.

a. Prepare the journal entries for these transactions.
b. Post the journal entries from *a* to the related T-accounts.
c. Using the financial statement effects template, illustrate the effects of these transactions.

E11-42. Analyzing and Computing Average Issue Price and Treasury Stock Cost   (LO2, 6)

Following is the stockholders' equity section from the Abercrombie & Fitch balance sheet.

Abercrombie & Fitch
(ANF)

(Thousands)	February 1, 2003
Shareholders' Equity	
Common stock—$.01 par value: 150,000,000 shares authorized, 97,268,877 shares outstanding	$ 1,033
Paid-in capital	142,577
Retained Earnings	714,475
	858,085
Less: Treasury stock, at average cost	(108,558)
Total shareholders' equity	$ 749,527

a. Assuming that A&F has repurchased 6,031,123 shares that constitute its treasury stock, compute the number of shares that it has issued?

b. At what average issue price were the A&F shares issued?

c. At what average cost were the A&F treasury stock shares purchased?

d. How should Treasury Stock be treated in calculating EPS?

E11-43. Analyzing and Distributing Cash Dividends to Preferred and Common Stocks (LO4)

Moser Company began business on March 1, 2003. At that time, it issued 20,000 shares of $60 par value, 7% cumulative preferred stock and 100,000 shares of $5 par value common stock. Through the end of 2005, there has been no change in the number of preferred and common shares outstanding.

a. Assume that Moser declared and paid cash dividends of $0 in 2003, $183,000 in 2004, and $200,000 in 2005. Compute the total cash dividends and the dividends per share paid to each class of stock in 2003, 2004, and 2005.

b. Assume that Moser declared and paid cash dividends of $0 in 2003, $84,000 in 2004, and $150,000 in 2005. Compute the total cash dividends and the dividends per share paid to each class of stock in 2003, 2004, and 2005.

E11-44. Computing Basic and Diluted Earnings per Share (LO6)

Nichols Corporation began the year 2006 with 25,000 shares of common stock and 5,000 shares of convertible preferred stock outstanding. On May 1, an additional 9,000 shares of common stock were issued. On July 1, 6,000 shares of common stock were acquired for the treasury. On September 1, the 6,000 treasury shares of common stock were reissued. The preferred stock has a $4 per-share dividend rate, and each share may be converted into two shares of common stock. Nichols Corporation's 2006 net income is $230,000.

a. Compute earnings per share for 2006.

b. Compute diluted earnings per share for 2006.

c. If the preferred stock were not convertible, Nichols Corporation would have a simple capital structure. How would this change Nichol's earnings per share presentation?

E11-45. Analyzing and Distributing Cash Dividends to Preferred and Common Stocks (LO4, 6)

Potter Company has outstanding 15,000 shares of $50 par value, 8% preferred stock and 50,000 shares of $5 par value common stock. During its first three years in business, it declared and paid no cash dividends in the first year, $280,000 in the second year, and $60,000 in the third year.

a. If the preferred stock is cumulative, determine the total amount of cash dividends paid to each class of stock in each of the three years.

b. If the preferred stock is noncumulative, determine the total amount of cash dividends paid to each class of stock in each of the three years.

c. How should each type of preferred dividends be treated in calculating EPS?

E11-46. Analyzing and Computing Issue Price, Treasury Stock Cost, and Shares Outstanding (LO2, 4)

Altria (MO)

Following is the stockholders' equity section from Altria's balance sheet ($ million).

December 31	2003
Stockholders' Equity	
Common stock, par value $0.331/3 per share (2,805,961,317 shares issued)	$ 935
Additional paid-in capital	4,813
Earnings reinvested in the business	47,008
Accumulated other comprehensive losses (including currency translation of $1,578)	(2,125)
Cost of repurchased stock (768,697,895 shares)	(25,554)
Total stockholders' equity	$ 25,077

a. Show the computation to derive the $935 million for common stock.
b. At what average price has Altria issued its common stock?
c. How many shares of Altria common stock are outstanding as of December 31, 2003?
d. At what average cost has Altria repurchased its treasury stock as of December 31, 2003?
e. Why would a company such as Altria want to repurchase more than $25 billion of its common stock?

E11-47. **Analyzing and Distributing Cash Dividends to Preferred and Common Stocks** (LO4)
Skinner Company began business on June 30, 2003. At that time, it issued 18,000 shares of $50 par value, 6% cumulative preferred stock and 90,000 shares of $10 par value common stock. Through the end of 2005, there has been no change in the number of preferred and common shares outstanding.
a. Assume that Skinner declared and paid cash dividends of $63,000 in 2003, $0 in 2004, and $378,000 in 2005. Compute the total cash dividends and the dividends per share paid to each class of stock in 2003, 2004, and 2005.
b. Assume that Skinner declared and paid cash dividends of $0 in 2003, $108,000 in 2004, and $189,000 in 2005. Compute the total cash dividends and the dividends per share paid to each class of stock in 2003, 2004, and 2005.

E11-48. **Analyzing and Identifying Financial Statement Effects of Dividends** (LO4)
Chaney Company has outstanding 25,000 shares of $10 par value common stock. It also has $405,000 of retained earnings. Near the current year-end, the company declares and pays a cash dividend of $1.90 per share and declares and issues a 4% stock dividend. The market price of the stock at the declaration date is $35 per share.
a. Prepare the journal entries for these two separate dividend transactions.
b. Post the journal entries from *a* to the related T-accounts.
c. Using the financial statement effects template, illustrate the effects of these two separate dividends.

E11-49. **Identifying and Analyzing Financial Statement Effects of Dividends** (LO4)
The stockholders' equity of Revsine Company at December 31, 2004, appears below.

Common stock, $10 par value, 200,000 shares authorized;
  80,000 shares issued and outstanding $800,000
Paid-in capital in excess of par value 480,000
Retained earnings 305,000

During 2005, the following transactions occurred:

May 12   Declared and issued a 7% stock dividend; the common stock market value was $18 per share.
Dec. 31   Declared and paid a cash dividend of 75 cents per share.

a. Prepare the journal entries for these transactions.
b. Post the journal entries from *a* to the related T-accounts.
c. Using the financial statement effects template, illustrate the effects of these transactions.
d. Prepare a retained earnings reconciliation for 2005 assuming that the company reports 2005 net income of $283,000.
e. What is the impact of the May 12th transaction on the calculation of EPS?

E11-50. **Analyzing and Identifying Financial Statement Effects of Dividends** (LO4)
The stockholders' equity of Kinney Company at December 31, 2004, is shown below:

5% preferred stock, $100 par value, 10,000 shares authorized;
  4,000 shares issued and outstanding .... $ 400,000
Common stock, $5 par value, 200,000 shares authorized;
  50,000 shares issued and outstanding 250,000
Paid-in capital in excess of par value—preferred stock 40,000
Paid-in capital in excess of par value—common stock 300,000
Retained earnings 656,000
Total stockholders' equity $1,646,000

The following transactions, among others, occurred during 2005.

Apr. 1   Declared and issued a 100% stock dividend on all outstanding shares of common stock. The market value of the stock was $11 per share.
Dec. 7   Declared and issued a 3% stock dividend on all outstanding shares of common stock. The market value of the stock was $14 per share.

Dec. 20   Declared and paid (1) the annual cash dividend on the preferred stock and (2) a cash dividend of 80 cents per common share.

a. Prepare the journal entries for these transactions.
b. Post the journal entries from a to the related T-accounts.
c. Using the financial statement effects template, illustrate the effects of these transactions.
d. Prepare a 2005 retained earnings reconciliation assuming that the company reports 2005 net income of $253,000.

E11-51. Analyzing, Identifying and Explaining the Effects of a Stock Split   (LO4)
On March 1 of the current year, Xie Company has 400,000 shares of $20 par value common stock that are issued and outstanding. Its balance sheet shows the following account balances relating to common stock.

Common stock	$8,000,000
Paid-in capital in excess of par value	3,400,000

On March 2, Xie Company splits its common stock 2-for-1 and reduces the par value to $10 per share.
a. How many shares of common stock are issued and outstanding immediately after the stock split?
b. What is the dollar balance in its common stock account immediately after the stock split?
c. What is the dollar balance in its paid-in capital in excess of par value account immediately after the stock split?
d. What is the effect of a stock split on the calculation of EPS?

E11-52. Analyzing and Computing Issue Price, Treasury Stock Cost, and Shares Outstanding   (LO4)

Caterpillar, Inc. (CAT)

Following is the stockholders' equity section of the Caterpillar, Inc., balance sheet.

December 31 ($ millions)	2003	2002
Stockholders' equity		
Common stock of $1.00 par value		
Authorized shares: 900,000,000		
Issued shares (2003 and 2002—407,447,312) at paid-in amount	**$ 1,059**	$ 1,034
Treasury stock (2003—63,685,272 shares;		
2002—63,192,245 shares) at cost	**(2,914)**	(2,669)
Profit employed in the business	**8,450**	7,849
Accumulated other comprehensive income	**(517)**	(742)
Total stockholders' equity	**$ 6,078**	$ 5,472

a. How many shares of Caterpillar common stock are outstanding at year-end 2003?
b. What does the phrase "at paid-in amount" mean?
c. At what average cost has Caterpillar repurchased its stock as of year-end 2003?
d. Why would a company such as Caterpillar want to repurchase its common stock?
e. Explain how the repurchase affects the computation of EPS.

E11-53. Effects of Equity Changes from Convertible Preferred and Employee Stock Options   (LO2, 6, 8)

Jetblue Airways Corporation (JBLU)

Following is the 2002 statement of stockholders' equity for JetBlue Airways Corporation ($ 000s).
a. Discuss the linkage between changes in convertible redeemable preferred stock, common stock, and additional paid-in capital accounts for 2002.
b. Assuming that 811,623 shares were issued to employees under the stock option plan in 2002, discuss the effects on stockholders' equity and EPS of the exercise of employee stock options in 2002. JetBlue's stock traded in the $20 per share range during that same period.

($ thousands)	Convertible Redeemable Preferred Stock	Common Stock	Additional Paid-In Capital	Accumulated Deficit/ Retained Earnings	Unearned Compensation	Accumulated Other Comprehensive Income	Total
Balance at December 31, 2001	$ 210,441	$ 65	$ 3,868	$(33,117)	$(2,983)	$ —	$ (32,167)
Net income	—	—	—	54,908	—	—	54,908
Other comprehensive income ...	—	—	—	—	—	187	187
Total comprehensive income							55,095
Accrued undeclared dividends on preferred stock	5,955	—	—	(5,955)	—	—	(5,955)
Proceeds from initial public offering, net of offering expenses	—	101	168,177	—	—	—	168,278
Conversion of redeemable preferred stock	(216,394)	461	215,933	—	—	—	216,394
Exercise of common stock options	—	8	1,058	—	—	—	1,066
Tax benefit of stock options exercised	—	—	6,568	—	—	—	6,568
Unearned compensation on common stock options, net of forfeitures	—	—	8,144	—	(8,144)	—	—
Amortization of unearned compensation	—	—	—	—	1,713	—	1,713
Stock issued under crewmember stock purchase plan	—	3	3,711	—	—	—	3,714
Other	(2)	—	12	(45)	—	—	(33)
Balance at December 31, 2002	$ —	$638	$407,471	$ 15,791	$(9,414)	$187	$414,673

(Stockholders' Equity (Deficit))

E11-54. **Analyzing and Computing Issue Price, Treasury Stock Cost, and Shares Outstanding** (LO2)

Following is the stockholders' equity and minority interest sections of the Merck & Co., Inc., balance sheet. Merck & Company (MRK)

($ millions)	Dec. 31, 2003
Minority interests	$ 3,915.2
Stockholders' equity	
Common stock, one cent par value	
Authorized—5,400,000,000 shares	
Issued—2,976,230,393 shares—2003	29.8
Other paid-in capital	6,956.6
Retained earnings	34,142.0
Accumulated other comprehensive income	65.5
	41,193.9
Less treasury stock, at cost	
754,466,884 shares—2003	25,617.5
Total stockholders' equity	$15,576.4

a. Explain the derivation of the $29.8 million in the common stock account.
b. At what average issue price were the Merck common shares issued at?
c. At what average cost was the Merck treasury stock purchased at?
d. How many common shares are outstanding as of December 31, 2003?

E11-55. Assessing Effects of Employee Stock Options for Income and EPS (LO7)

Viacom, Inc. (VIA)

Viacom, Inc., reports the following footnote disclosure in its 10-K report ($ millions, except per share).

Year Ended December 31	2003	2002
Net earnings (loss)	$1,416.9	$ 725.7
Option expense, net of tax	(252.9)	(200.3)
Net earnings (loss) after option expense	$1,164.0	$ 525.4
Basic earnings (loss) per share		
Net earnings (loss) as reported	$ .81	$ .41
Net earnings (loss) after option expense	$ .67	$ .30
Diluted earnings (loss) per share		
Net earnings (loss) as reported	$ .80	$ .41
Net earnings (loss) after option expense	$ .66	$ .30

a. Viacom is currently accounting for its employee stock options using *APB 25*. Summarize the accounting for stock options under this current standard.
b. By what amount (and percent) would Viacom's 2003 net earnings be affected had it valued employee stock options when granted and recognized using the fair value as expense? By what amount (and percent) would diluted earnings per share be affected by this alternate accounting treatment?
c. Is stock options expense a cash expense? How would your answer differ, if at all, if you knew that Viacom repurchases shares of its stock in the open market to offset the dilutive effects of the issuance of additional shares to employees under its stock option program?
d. Following declines in the stock market, the market price of the shares under option can fall below the exercise price. How would this affect diluted earnings per share?

E11-56. Interpretation of a Split-Off Disclosure (LO4, 6, 9)

IMS Health (RX)

IMS Health reports the following footnote to its 2003 10-K related to the split-off of its CTS subsidiary.

CTS Split-OFF
On February 6, 2003, the Company completed an exchange offer to distribute its majority interest in CTS. The Company exchanged 0.309 shares of CTS class B common shares for each share of the Company that was tendered. Under terms of the offer, the Company accepted 36,540 IMS common shares tendered in exchange for all 11,291 CTA common shares that the Company owned. As the offer was oversubscribed, the Company accepted tendered IMS shares on a pro-rata basis in proportion to the number of shares tendered. The proration factor was 21.115717%.

As a result of this exchange offer, during 2003, the Company recorded a net gain from discontinued operations of $496,887. This gain was based on the Company's closing market price on February 6, 2003 multiplied by the 36,540 shares of IMS common shares accepted in the offer, net of the Company's carrying value of CTS and after deducting direct and incremental expenses related to the exchange offer.

a. Describe the accounting procedures for a split-off.
b. Describe the circumstances that allowed IMS to recognize a gain on this split-off.
c. How should you interpret this gain in your analysis of the company for 2003?
d. How does a split-off affect the calculation of EPS?

PROBLEMS

P11-57. Analyzing and Identifying Financial Statement Effects of Stock Transactions (LO2, 6)
The stockholders' equity section of Gupta Company at December 31, 2004, follows.

8% preferred stock, $25 par value, 50,000 shares authorized;	
6,800 shares issued and outstanding	$170,000
Common stock, $10 par value, 200,000 shares authorized;	
50,000 shares issued and outstanding	500,000
Paid-in capital in excess of par value—preferred stock	68,000
Paid-in capital in excess of par value—common stock	200,000
Retained earnings	270,000

During 2005, the following transactions occurred:

Jan. 10   Issued 28,000 shares of common stock for $17 cash per share.
Jan. 23   Purchased 8,000 shares of common stock for the treasury at $19 cash per share.
Mar. 14   Sold one-half of the treasury shares acquired January 23 for $21 cash per share.
July 15   Issued 3,200 shares of preferred stock for $128,000 cash.
Nov. 15   Sold 1,000 of the treasury shares acquired January 23 for $24 cash per share.

Required
a.   Prepare the journal entries for these transactions.
b.   Post the journal entries from a to the related T-accounts.
c.   Using the financial statement effects template, illustrate the effects of each transaction.
d.   Indicate the impact of each transaction on the calculation of EPS.
e.   Prepare the December 31, 2005, stockholders' equity section of the balance sheet assuming the company reports 2005 net income of $59,000.

P11-58. Analyzing and Identifying Financial Statement Effects of Stock Transactions   (LO2, 6)
The stockholders' equity of Sougiannis Company at December 31, 2004, follows.

7% Preferred stock, $100 par value, 20,000 shares authorized;	
5,000 shares issued and outstanding	$ 500,000
Common stock, $15 par value, 100,000 shares authorized;	
40,000 shares issued and outstanding	600,000
Paid-in capital in excess of par value—preferred stock	24,000
Paid-in capital in excess of par value—common stock	360,000
Retained earnings	325,000
Total stockholders' equity	$1,809,000

The following transactions, among others, occurred during the year.

Jan. 12   Announced a 3-for-1 common stock split, reducing the par value of the common stock to $5 per share. The authorized shares were increased to 300,000 shares.
Sept. 1   Acquired 10,000 shares of common stock for the treasury at $10 cash per share.
Oct. 12   Sold 1,500 treasury shares acquired September 1 at $12 cash per share.
Nov. 21   Issued 5,000 shares of common stock at $11 cash per share.
Dec. 28   Sold 1,200 treasury shares acquired September 1 at $9 cash per share.

Required
a.   Prepare the journal entries for these transactions.
b.   Post the journal entries from a to the related T-accounts.
c.   Using the financial statement effects template, illustrate the effects of each transaction.
d.   Indicate the impact of each transaction on the calculation of EPS.
e.   Prepare the December 31, 2005, stockholders' equity section of the balance sheet assuming that the company reports 2005 net income of $83,000.

P11-59. Identifying and Analyzing Financial Statement Effects of Stock Transactions (LO2, 9)

The stockholders' equity of Verrecchia Company at December 31, 2004, follows.

Common stock, $5 par value, 350,000 shares authorized;	
150,000 shares issued and outstanding	$750,000
Paid-in capital in excess of par value	600,000
Retained earnings	346,000

During 2005, the following transactions occurred.

Jan. 5	Issued 10,000 shares of common stock for $12 cash per share.
Jan. 18	Purchased 4,000 shares of common stock for the treasury at $14 cash per share.
Mar 12	Sold one-fourth of the treasury shares acquired January 18 for $17 cash per share.
July 17	Sold 500 shares of the remaining treasury stock for $13 cash per share.
Oct. 1	Issued 5,000 shares of 8%, $25 par value preferred stock for $35 cash per share. This is the first issuance of preferred shares from the 50,000 authorized shares.

Required

a. Prepare the journal entries for these transactions.
b. Post the journal entries from *a* to the related T-accounts.
c. Using the financial statement effects template, illustrate the effects of each transaction.
d. Prepare the December 31, 2005, stockholders' equity section of the balance sheet assuming that the company reports net income of $72,500 for the year.
e. How will each transaction affect the calculation of EPS?

P11-60. Identifying and Analyzing Financial Statement Effects of Stock Transactions (LO2)

Following is the stockholders' equity of Dennis Corporation at December 31, 2004.

8% preferred stock, $50 par value, 10,000 shares authorized;	
7,000 shares issued and outstanding	$ 350,000
Common stock, $20 par value, 50,000 shares authorized;	
25,000 shares issued and outstanding	500,000
Paid-in capital in excess of par value—preferred stock	70,000
Paid-in capital in excess of par value—common stock	385,000
Retained earnings	238,000
Total stockholders' equity	$1,543,000

The following transactions, among others, occurred during the year.

Jan. 15	Issued 1,000 shares of preferred stock for $62 cash per share.
Jan. 20	Issued 4,000 shares of common stock at $36 cash per share.
May 18	Announced a 2-for-1 common stock split, reducing the par value of the common stock to $10 per share. The authorization was increased to 100,000 shares.
June 1	Issued 2,000 shares of common stock for $60,000 cash.
Sept. 1	Purchased 2,500 shares of common stock for the treasury at $18 cash per share.
Oct. 12	Sold 900 treasury shares at $21 cash per share.
Dec. 22	Issued 500 shares of preferred stock for $59 cash per share.

Required

a. Prepare the journal entries for these transactions.
b. Post the journal entries from *a* to the related T-accounts.
c. Using the financial statement effects template, illustrate the effects of each transaction.

P11-61. Analyzing and Interpreting Equity Accounts and Comprehensive Income (LO2 LO5, 7)

Procter & Gamble
Company (PG)

Following is the stockholders' equity section of the balance sheet for Procter & Gamble Company and its statement of stockholders' equity.

June 30 (Amounts in millions)	2003	2002
Shareholders' Equity		
Convertible Class A preferred stock, stated value $1 per share (600 shares authorized)	**$ 1,580**	$ 1,634
Non-Voting Class B preferred stock, stated value $1 per share (200 shares authorized)	**—**	—
Common stock, stated value $1 per share (5,000 shares authorized; shares outstanding: 2003—1,297.2, 2002—1,300.8)	**1,297**	1,301
Additional paid-in capital	**2,931**	2,490
Reserve for ESOP debt retirement	**(1,308)**	(1,339)
Accumulated other comprehensive income	**(2,006)**	(2,360)
Retained earnings	**13,692**	11,980
Total Shareholders' Equity	**$16,186**	$13,706

Dollars in millions/ Shares in thousands	Common Shares Outstanding	Common Stock	Preferred Stock	Additional Paid-In Capital	Reserve for ESOP Debt Retirement	Accumulated Other Comprehensive Income	Retained Income	Total	Total Comprehensive Income
Balance June 30, 2002	1,300,770	$1,301	$1,634	$2,490	$(1,339)	$(2,360)	$11,980	$13,706	
Net earnings							5,186	5,186	$5,186
Other comprehensive income									
Financial statement translation						804		804	804
Net investment hedges, net of $251 tax						(418)		(418)	(418)
Other, net of tax benefits						(32)		(32)	(32)
Total comprehensive income									$5,540
Dividends to shareholders									
Common							(2,121)	(2,121)	
Preferred, net of tax benefit							(125)	(125)	
Treasury purchases	(14,138)	(14)		6			(1,228)	(1,236)	
Employee plan issuances	7,156	7		384				391	
Preferred stock conversions	3,409	3	(54)	51				—	
ESOP debt guarantee reduction					31			31	
Balance June 30, 2003	1,297,197	$1,297	$1,580	$2,931	$(1,308)	$(2,006)	$13,692	$16,186	

Required

a. How many shares of convertible class A preferred stock are issued at fiscal year-end 2003?

b. What does the term *convertible* mean?

c. Show (confirm) the computation yielding the $1,297 million for common stock at year-end 2003.

d. Assuming that the convertible class A preferred stock was sold at par value, at what average price were the common shares issued at as of year-end 2003?

e. What is the accumulated other comprehensive income account? Explain.

f. What items are included in the $5,540 million 'total comprehensive income' at year-end 2003? How do these items affect stockholders' equity?

g. What amount of cash dividends was paid in 2003 for each of P&G's classes of stock?

P11-62. Analyzing and Interpreting Equity Accounts and Comprehensive Income (LO5, 7)

Following is the stockholders' equity section of **Fortune Brands** balance sheet and its statement of stockholders' equity.

Fortune Brands (FO)

December 31 (In millions, except per share amounts)	2003	2002
Minority interest in consolidated subsidiaries	$ 369.5	$ 398.9
Stockholders' equity		
$2.67 Convertible Preferred stock	7.5	7.9
Common stock, par value $3.125 per share, 229.6 shares issued	717.4	717.4
Paid-in capital	126.7	116.0
Accumulated other comprehensive loss	(106.2)	(177.6)
Retained earnings	4,942.2	4,529.9
Treasury stock, at cost	(2,968.1)	(2,880.4)
TOTAL STOCKHOLDERS' EQUITY	$ 2,719.5	$ 2,313.2

(In millions except per share amounts)	$2.67 Convertible Preferred Stock	Common Stock	Paid-In Capital	Accumulated Other Comprehensive Loss	Retained Earnings	Treasury Stock, At Cost	Total
Balance at December 31, 2002	$ 7.9	$717.4	$116.0	$(177.6)	$4,529.9	$(2,880.4)	$2,313.2
Comprehensive income							
Net income	—	—	—	—	579.2	—	579.2
Foreign exchange adjustments	—	—	—	76.0	—	—	76.0
Minimum pension liability adjustments	—	—	—	(4.6)	—	—	(4.6)
Total comprehensive Income	—	—	—	71.4	579.2	—	650.6
Dividends ($1.14 per share)	—	—	—	—	(166.9)	—	(166.9)
Purchases (4.1 shares)	—	—	—	—	—	(204.5)	(204.5)
Tax benefit on exercise of stock options	—	—	27.6	—	—	—	27.6
Conversion of preferred stock and delivery of stock plan shares (3.3 shares) and sale of stock in a subsidiary	(0.4)	—	(16.9)	—	—	116.8	99.5
Balance at December 31, 2003	$ 7.5	$717.4	$126.7	$(106.2)	$4,942.2	$(2,968.1)	$2,719.5

Required

a. Explain the "$2.67" as reported in the convertible preferred stock account title.

b. Show (confirm) the computation that yields the $717.4 million common stock in 2003.

c. Assuming that the convertible preferred stock was sold at par value, at what average price were the common shares issued at as of year-end 2003?

d. What accounts typically comprise the accumulated other comprehensive income (or loss) account? What accounts are included in Fortune Brands' accumulated comprehensive income and loss adjustments for 2003?

e. Assuming that there are 83,305,000 shares in treasury at year-end 2003, show how the $166.9 million in dividends is computed. What effect did the dividend payment of $1.14 per common share have on the stockholders' equity of Fortune Brands?

P11-63. Interpretation of Footnote on Convertible Debentures (LO6, 7)

Lucent Technologies (LU)

Lucent Technologies reports the following footnote to its 2003 10-K related to its convertible debentures.

2.75% series A and B debentures

During the third quarter of fiscal 2003, we sold 2.75% Series A Convertible Senior Debentures and 2.75% Series B Convertible Senior Debentures for an aggregate amount of $1.6 billion, net of the underwriters discount and related fees and expenses of $46 million. The debentures were issued at a price of $1,000 per debenture and were issued under our universal shelf. The debentures rank equal in priority with all of the existing and future unsecured and unsubordinated indebtedness and senior in right of payment to all of the existing and future subordinated indebtedness. The terms governing the debentures limit our ability to create liens, secure certain indebtedness and merge with or sell substantially all of our assets to another entity.

The debentures are convertible into shares of common stock only if (1) the average sale price of our common stock is at least equal to 120% of the applicable conversion price, (2) the average trading price of the debentures is less than 97% of the product of the sale price of the common stock and the conversion rate, (3) the debentures have been called for redemption by us or (4) certain specified corporate actions occur.

Required

a. How did Lucent initially account for the issuance of its bonds, assuming that the conversion option is not detachable and separately salable?

b. How will Lucent account for the conversion of its bonds, if and when conversion occurs? Specifically, will Lucent recognize any gain or loss related to conversion? Explain.

c. How is the convertible bond treated in the computation of basic and diluted earnings per share (EPS)?

d. How should you treat the existence of its convertible bonds in your analysis of the company?

P11-64. Analyzing and Interpreting Employee Stock Option Disclosures and Adjustments (LO7)

eBay, Inc., reports the following footnote for its employee stock options from its 10-K report.

eBay, Inc. (EBAY)

Generally accepted accounting principles provide companies with the option of either recognizing the fair value of option grants as an operating expense or disclosing the impact of fair value accounting in a note to the financial statements. Consistent with predominant industry practice, we account for stock-based employee compensation arrangements using the intrinsic value method, which calculates compensation expense based on the difference, if any, on the date of the grant, between the fair value of our stock and the exercise price and have elected to disclose the impact of fair value accounting for option grants. Had we elected to recognize the fair value of option grants as an operating expense, our reported net income would have been substantially reduced, as follows (in thousands).

Year Ended December 31	2001	2002
Net income, as reported	$ 90,448	$ 249,891
Add: Amortization of stock-based compensation expense determined under the intrinsic value method	3,091	5,953
Deduct: Total stock-based compensation expense determined under fair value based method for all awards, net of tax	(211,526)	(192,902)
Pro forma net income (loss)	$(117,987)	$ 62,942

Required

a. Describe the accounting for employee stock options under GAAP.

b. How does eBay's accounting for its stock options impact its reported 2002 income? Explain.

CASES AND PROJECTS

C11-65. Interpretation of Disclosure on Convertible Preferred Securities (LO7)

Lucent Technologies reports the following footnote to its 2003 10-K related to its convertible preferred stock.

Lucent Technologies (LU)

Mandatorily Redeemable Convertible Preferred Stock

We have 250,000,000 shares of authorized preferred stock. During fiscal 2001, we designated and sold 1,885,000 shares of non-cumulative 8% redeemable convertible preferred stock having an initial liquidation preference of $1,000 per share, subject to accretion. The net proceeds were $1.8 billion, including fees of $54 million. . . . Holders of the preferred stock have no voting rights, except as required by law, and rank junior to our debt obligations. In addition, upon our dissolution or liquidation, holders are entitled to the liquidation preference plus any accrued and unpaid dividends prior to any distribution of net assets to common shareowners . . . Each trust preferred security is convertible at the option of the holder into 206.6116 shares of our common stock.

Required

a. Describe the meaning of the terms or phrases: *non-cumulative, 8%, convertible,* and *liquidation preference.*

b. Describe the general impact on Lucent's balance sheet when it issued the preferred shares. (*Hint:* Aggregate all equity into the contributed capital account, that is, do not break out par value and additional paid-in capital.)

c. Assume that its preferred stock is converted in full. Describe the general impact on Lucent's balance sheet at the conversion of the preferred shares if:

(1) The conversion is paid in cash.

(2) The preferred stock is converted into common stock

(*Hint:* Aggregate all equity into the contributed capital account, that is, do not break out par value and additional paid-in capital).

d. How should you treat the existence of its convertible stock for your analysis of the company?

C11-66. Corporate Takeover, Stock Ownership, and Managerial Ethics (LO1, 2, 3, 8)

Ron King, chairperson of the board of directors and chief executive officer of Image, Inc., is pondering a recommendation to make to the firm's board of directors in response to actions taken by Jack Hatcher. Hatcher recently informed King and other board members that he (Hatcher) had purchased 15% of the voting stock of Image at $12 per share and is considering an attempt to take control of the company. His effort to take control would include offering $16 per share to stockholders to induce them to sell shares to him. Hatcher also indicated that he would abandon his takeover plans if the company would buy back his stock at a price 50% over its current market price of $13 per share.

King views the proposed takeover by Hatcher as a hostile maneuver. Hatcher has a reputation of identifying companies that are undervalued (that is, their underlying net assets are worth more than the price of the outstanding stock), buying enough stock to take control of such a company, replacing top management, and, on occasion, breaking up the company (that is, selling off the various divisions to the highest bidder). The process has proven profitable to Hatcher and his financial backers. Stockholders of the companies taken over also benefited because Hatcher paid them attractive prices to buy their stock.

King recognizes that Image is currently undervalued by the stock market but believes that eventually the company will significantly improve its financial performance to the long-run benefit of its stockholders.

Required

What are the ethical issues that King should consider in arriving at a recommendation to make to the board of directors regarding Hatcher's offer to be "bought out" of his takeover plans?

C11-67. Shareholders' Meeting, Managerial Communications, and Financial Interpretations (LO1, 2, 3, 8)

The stockholders' equity section of Pillar Corporation's comparative balance sheet at the end of 2006 and 2007 is presented below. It is part of the financial data just reviewed at a stockholders' meeting.

	December 31, 2007	December 31, 2006
Common Stock, $10 Par Value, 600,000 shares authorized; issued at December 31, 2007, 275,000 shares; 2006, 250,000 shares	$2,750,000	$2,500,000
Paid-in Capital in Excess of Par	4,575,000	4,125,000
Retained Earnings (see Note)	2,960,000	2,825,000
Total Stockholders' Equity	$10,285,000	$9,450,000

Note: Availability of retained earnings for cash dividends is restricted by $2,000,000 due to a planned plant expansion.

The following items were also disclosed at the stockholders' meeting: net income for 2007 was $1,220,000; a 10% stock dividend was issued December 14, 2007; when the stock dividend was declared, the market value was $28 per share; the market value per share at December 31, 2007, was $26; management plans to borrow $500,000 to help finance a new plant addition, which is expected to cost a total of $2,300,000; and the customary $1.54 per share cash dividend had been revised to $1.40 when declared and issued the last week of December 2007. As part of its investor relations program, during the stockholders' meeting management asked stockholders to write any questions they might have concerning the firm's operations or finances. As assistant controller, you are given the stockholders' questions.

Required

Prepare brief but reasonably complete answers to the following questions:

a. What did Pillar do with the cash proceeds from the stock dividend issued in December?

b. What was my book value per share at the end of 2006 and 2007?

c. I owned 7,500 shares of Pillar in 2006 and have not sold any shares. How much more or less of the corporation do I own at December 31, 2007, and what happened to the market value of my interest in the company?

d. I heard someone say that stock dividends don't give me anything I didn't already have. Why did you issue one? Are you trying to fool us?

e. Instead of a stock dividend, why didn't you declare a cash dividend and let us buy the new shares that were issued?

f. Why are you cutting back on the dividends I receive?

g. If you have $2,000,000 put aside in retained earnings for the new plant addition, which will cost $2,300,000, why are you borrowing $500,000 instead of just the $300,000 needed?

C11-68. Stock Buybacks, Corporate Accountability, and Managerial Ethics   (LO2, 3, 6, 8)

Liz Plummer, vice president and general counsel, chairs the Executive Compensation Committee for Sunlight Corporation. Four and one-half years ago, the compensation committee designed a performance bonus plan for top management that was approved by the board of directors. The plan provides an attractive bonus for top management if the firm's earnings per share grows each year over a five-year period. The plan is now in its fifth year; for the past four years, earnings per share has grown each year. Last year, earnings per share was $1.95 (net income was $7,800,000 and the weighted average common shares outstanding was 4,000,000). Sunlight Corporation has no preferred stock and has had 4,000,000 common shares outstanding for several years. Plummer has recently seen an estimate that Sunlight's net income this year will decrease about 5% from last year because of a slight recession in the economy.

Plummer is disturbed by an item on the agenda for the board of directors meeting on June 20 and an accompanying note from Rob Libby. Libby is vice president and chief financial officer for Sunlight. Libby is proposing to the board that Sunlight buy back 600,000 shares of its own common stock on July 1. Libby's explanation is that the firm's stock is undervalued now and that Sunlight has excess cash available. When the stock subsequently recovers in value, Libby notes. Sunlight will reissue the shares and generate a nice increase in contributed captial.

Libby's Note to Plummer merely states, "Look forward to your support of my proposal at the board meeting."

Required

Why is Plummer disturbed by Libby's proposal and note? What possible ethical problem does Plummer face when Libby's proposal is up for a vote at the board meeting?

Reporting Intercorporate Investments

LEARNING OBJECTIVES

After completing the chapter, you should be able to:

LO1 Explain and interpret the three levels of investor influence over an investee—passive, significant, and controlling. (p. 519)

LO2 Describe and analyze accounting for passive investments. (p. 520)

LO3 Explain and analyze accounting for investments with significant influence. (p. 529)

LO4 Describe and analyze accounting for investments with control. (p. 534)

LO5 *Appendix 12A*—Illustrate and analyze accounting mechanics for equity method investments. (p. 546)

LO6 *Appendix 12B*—Apply equity method accounting mechanics to consolidations. (p. 547)

LO7 *Appendix 12C*—Discuss the reporting of derivative securities. (p. 549)

Getty Images

HEWLETT-PACKARD

HP Gambles on COMPAQ

The *Wall Street Journal* ran an article in August 2002 on Hewlett-Packard Company under the heading, "H-P Posts Big Loss Due to Compaq Purchase." *The WSJ* reported that "HP posted a $2.03 billion fiscal third-quarter net loss . . . reflecting nearly $3 billion of restructuring costs and merger-related charges." This article further fueled the ongoing debate over the wisdom of HP's recent merger with Compaq Computer Corporation.

One year later, Forbes concluded, "The chief executive of Hewlett-Packard has pulled off the biggest merger in high-tech history. . . . One year into the [$24.2 billion] purchase of Compaq Computer, she has cut $3.5 billion in annual costs, a billion dollars more and a year earlier than promised. And despite erasing 17,000 jobs since the merger, HP has gained market share in key categories, scored 3,000 new patents and debuted 367 new products. It just won a ten-year, $3 billion outsourcing deal with Procter & Gamble." (*Forbes,* August 2003) HP was a $45 billion (in sales) company prior to its merger with Compaq. (*Associated Press Newswires,* 2003).

HP's sales now exceed $70 billion and its operations are organized into five business segments:

- **Imaging and Printing Group**—provides home and business imaging, printing and publishing devices and systems, digital imaging products, printer supplies, and consulting services.

- **Personal Systems Group**—provides commercial personal computers (PCs), consumer PCs, workstations, handheld computing devices, digital entertainment systems, calculators, and other accessories, software and services for commercial and consumer markets.

- **Enterprise Systems Group**—provides servers, storage, and software solutions.

- **HP Services**—provides a portfolio of IT services including customer support, consulting and integration, and managed services.

- **HP Financial Services**—supports and enhances HP's global product and service solutions, providing a range of financial management services.

In 2003, its first full year following the Compaq merger, HP reported net income of $2.5 billion. *Forbes* lauded its performance: "HP has slashed billions in costs by overhauling its data processing operations and its supply chain. . . . In merging its systems with Compaq's, HP erected a single communications network linking more than a quarter of a million PCs and handhelds; it handles 26 million e-mails a day. HP also cut the number of software applications it uses from 7,000

(Continued on next page)   **517**

(Continued from previous page)

to 5,000, and of components it buys from 250,000 to 25,000. A huge part of the company's success so far has come from the $3 billion in annual cost cuts. Half the savings comes from cutting jobs. However, a large portion comes from the price concessions that HP can extract from its suppliers now that it orders huge volumes of PC components and other supplies. That, in turn, allows it to pressure rivals, even the ultra-lean Dell, on price." (*Forbes,* 2003)

HP purchased Compaq for $24.2 billion. From an accounting standpoint, acquiring a company is like acquiring any other asset. That is, it is recorded on the balance sheet at its fair market value on the date of acquisition. Each tangible asset (such as receivables, inventories, and plant assets) and any liabilities assumed by the purchaser must be appraised, as must any acquired identifiable intangible assets (such as trademarks, customer lists, licenses, franchise agreements, leases, contracts, software, and patented and unpatented technology). Any purchase price in excess of the fair market value of the tangible and identifiable intangible net assets is assigned to *goodwill.*

The purchaser's financial reports reflect the operating activities of the acquired company from the date of acquisition. For HP, that meant Compaq's results are reflected in HP's income statement from the May 2001 acquisition date, which involved five months in the initial year of acquisition given HP's year-end is October. From the purchaser's view, this accounting is the same whether it acquires 25% or 100%, the difference lies in whether the acquired company is treated as an equity method investment or is consolidated. We cover both methods in this chapter.

There is subjectivity in the allocation of the purchase price in acquisitions, and some assets are depreciated and amortized over longer periods than others. Such allocation decisions can materially impact the acquirer's near-term and long-term reported profitability. Further, the cost of goodwill never impacts the income statement unless it becomes impaired and is written down. Finally, many financial statements reflect results of acquisitions made under a previous accounting standard (pooling-of-interest) that reported acquired assets at the acquired company's book value rather than fair market value at the time of sale, as is current practice. This chapter covers all of these issues related to the reporting and analysis of consolidation accounting.

There are three methods of accounting for intercorporate investments depending on the perceived level of influence or control that the acquiring company has over the company that is acquired. The choice of method is typically determined by the percent of the company that is acquired. Each of these accounting methods affects the balance sheet and the income statement differently. We will consider the reporting and analysis of intercorporate investments, and their effects on the various financial statements. We will also consider what is being reported on the balance sheet and what is not. We highlight these issues as we progress through the discussion.

Sources: Hewlett-Packard 10-K report, 2005, 2004 and 2003; *The Wall Street Journal,* August 2002 and 2003; *Forbes,* August 2003; *Associated Press Newswires,* 2003, *USA Today* 2005.

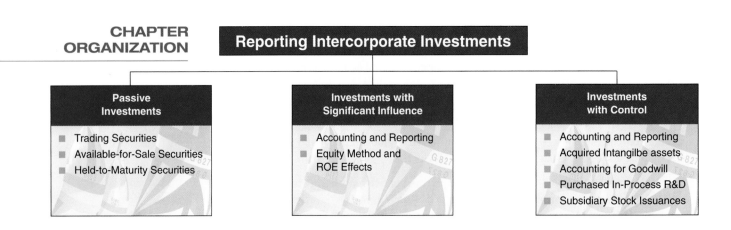

CHAPTER ORGANIZATION

Reporting Intercorporate Investments

Passive Investments
- Trading Securities
- Available-for-Sale Securities
- Held-to-Maturity Securities

Investments with Significant Influence
- Accounting and Reporting
- Equity Method and ROE Effects

Investments with Control
- Accounting and Reporting
- Acquired Intangilbe assets
- Accounting for Goodwill
- Purchased In-Process R&D
- Subsidiary Stock Issuances

INTRODUCTION

Many companies purchase the common stock of other companies. These purchases, called *inter-corporate investments,* are often aimed at strategic activities such as the following:

LO1 Explain and interpret the three levels of investor influence over an investee—passive, significant, and controlling.

- **Short-term investment of excess cash.** Companies often generate excess cash for investment either during slow times of the year (after receivables are collected and before seasonal production begins) or for liquidity needs (such as to counter strategic moves by competitors or to quickly respond to acquisition opportunities).

- **Alliances for strategic purposes.** Companies often acquire an equity interest in others for strategic purposes, such as gaining access to their research and development activities, to supply or distribution markets, or to their production and marketing expertise.

- **Market penetration or expansion.** Acquisitions of controlling interests in other companies can achieve vertical or horizontal integration in existing markets or can be avenues to penetrate new and growth markets.

Accounting for intercorporate investments follows one of three different methods, each of which affects the balance sheet and the income statement differently, often substantially. To help assimilate the materials in this chapter, Exhibit 12.1 provides a graphical depiction of accounting for investments.

The accounting for intercorporate investments depends on the degree of influence or control that the investor company (purchaser) can exert over the investee company (the company whose securities are being purchased). GAAP identifies three levels of influence/control:

1. **Passive.** In this case the purchasing company is merely an investor and cannot exert influence over the investee company. The purchaser's goal for this investment is to realize dividends and capital gains. Generally, passive investor status is presumed if the investor company owns less than 20% of the outstanding voting stock of the investee.

2. **Significant influence.** A company can sometimes exert significant influence over, but not control, the activities of the investee company. This level of influence can result from the percentage of voting stock owned. It also can result from legal agreements, such as a license to use technology, a formula, or a trade secret like production know-how. It also can occur when the investor company is the sole supplier or customer of the investee. Generally, significant influence is presumed if the investor company owns 20% to 50% of the voting stock of the investee.

3. **Control.** When a company has control over another, it has the ability to elect a majority of the board of directors and, as a result, the ability to affect its strategic direction and hiring of executive management. Control is generally presumed if the investor company owns more than 50% of the outstanding voting stock of the investee company. Control can

EXHIBIT 12.1 Intercorporate Investment Diagram

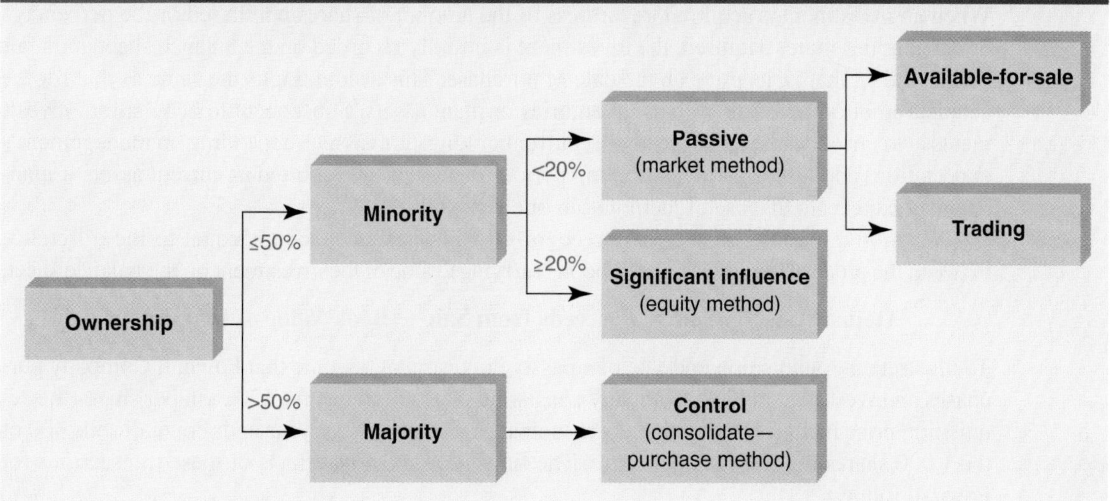

sometimes occur at less than 50% stock ownership by virtue of legal agreements, technology licensing, or other contractual means.

Once the level of influence/control is determined, the appropriate accounting method is applied as outlined in Exhibit 12.2.

EXHIBIT 12.2	Investment Type, Accounting Treatment, and Financial Statement Effects			
	Accounting	Balance Sheet Effects	Income Statement Effects	Cash Flow Effects
Passive	Market method	Investment account is reported at current market value	Dividends and capital gains affect income Interim changes in market value may or may not affect income depending on classification	Dividend and sale proceeds are cash inflows Purchases are cash outflows
Significant influence	Equity method	Investment account equals percent owned of investee company's equity*	Dividends reduce investment account Investor reports income equal to percent owned of investee income Capital gains are income	Dividend and sale proceeds are cash inflows Purchases are cash outflows
Control	Consolidation	Balance sheets of investor and investee are combined	Income statements of investor and investee are combined (and sale of investee yields capital gain or loss)	Cash flows of investor and investee are combined (and sale/purchase of investee yields cash inflow/outflow)

*Investments are often acquired at purchase prices in excess of book value (on average, market prices are 1.5 times book value for public companies). In this case the investment account exceeds the proportionate ownership of the investee's equity. We discuss this situation later in the chapter.

There are two basic reporting issues with investments: (1) how investment income should be recognized and (2) at what amount (cost or fair market value) the investment should be reported on the balance sheet. We next discuss both of these issues under each of the three investment types.

PASSIVE INVESTMENTS

LO2 Describe and analyze accounting for passive investments.

Short-term investments of excess cash typically involve passive investments. Passive means that the investor does not possess sufficient ownership to enable it to exert "significant influence" over the investee company or to control it outright. The *market method* is used to account for passive investments.

Acquisition and Sale

When an investment is acquired, regardless of the amount of shares purchased or the percentage of outstanding shares acquired, the investment is initially recorded on the balance sheet at its fair market value, that is, its price on the date of purchase. This accounting is the same as that for the acquisition of other assets such as inventories or plant assets. Subsequent to acquisition, investments are carried on the balance sheet as current or long-term assets, depending on management's expectations about their ultimate holding period (the assets are reported as current assets if management expects to dispose of them within one year).

When investments are sold, any recognized gain or loss on sale is equal to the difference between the proceeds received and the book (carrying) value of the investment on the balance sheet.

Gain or Loss on Sale = Proceeds from Sale − Book Value of Investment Sold

To illustrate the acquisition and sale of a passive investment, assume that Pownall Company purchases an investment in King Company consisting of 1,000 shares for $20 cash per share (the acquisition price includes transaction costs such as brokerage). Near year-end, Pownall sells 400 of the 1,000 shares for $30 cash per share. The financial statement effects of these transactions for Pownall follow:

	Balance Sheet						Income Statement		
Transaction	**Cash Asset** +	**Noncash Assets** =	**Liabil- ities** +	**Contrib. Capital** +	**Retained Earnings**	**Revenues** −	**Expenses** =		**Net Income**
1. Purchase 1,000 common shares for $20 cash per share	−20,000 Cash	+20,000 = Investments							=
2. Sell 400 common shares for $30 cash per share	+12,000 Cash	−8,000 = Investments			+4,000 Retained Earnings	+4,000 Gain on Sale			= +4,000

The related journal entries and T-accounts follow.

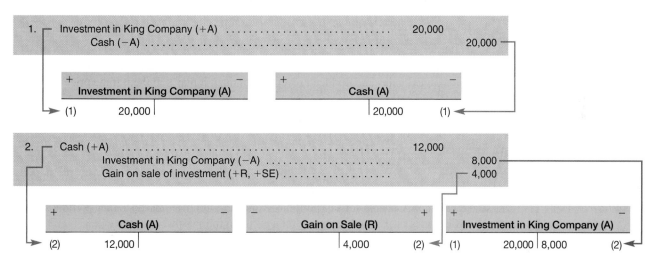

1. Investment in King Company (+A) 20,000
        Cash (−A) 20,000

+ Investment in King Company (A) −		− Cash (A) +	
(1)	20,000		20,000 (1)

2. Cash (+A) 12,000
        Investment in King Company (−A) 8,000
        Gain on sale of investment (+R, +SE) 4,000

+ Cash (A) −		− Gain on Sale (R) +		+ Investment in King Company (A) −	
(2)	12,000		4,000 (2)	(1) 20,000	8,000 (2)

The gain or loss on sale is reported as a component of *other income,* which is commonly commingled with interest and dividend revenue.

Accounting for the purchase and sale of investments is the same as with any other asset. Further, there is no difference in accounting for purchases and sales across the different types of passive investments discussed in this section. However, there are differences in accounting for the different passive investments *between* their purchase and their sale. We next address this issue.

Mark-to-Market versus Cost

If an investment in these marketable securities has an active market with published prices, that investment is reported on the balance sheet at its market value as of the balance sheet date. If such a market does not exist, that investment is reported at its historical cost. **Market value** is the published price (as listed on a stock exchange) multiplied by the number of shares owned. This is one of very few assets that are reported at market value instead of historical cost.[1]

There is a trade-off between the *objectivity* of historical cost and the *relevance* of market value. All things equal, we prefer to know current market values of assets as these are more relevant in determining the market value of the company. However, for most assets, market values cannot be reliably determined. Their use would introduce excess subjectivity into the financial reporting process.[2]

---

[1]Other assets reported at market value include (1) derivative securities (such as forward contracts, options, and futures) that are purchased to provide a hedge against price fluctuations or to eliminate other business risks (such as interest or exchange rate fluctuations), and (2) inventories and long-term assets that must be written down to market when permanent declines in value occur.

[2]Early in 2006, the FASB proposed allowing firms to use current market value to report financial assets (called the *fair value option*). The effect of this option would be to allow companies to report any financial assets and liabilities at fair market value and recognize changes in value in the income statement. This treatment is currently reserved only for trading securities. This change, if adopted, would take affect at the end of 2007 and have the greatest potential impact on the financial statements of financial institutions and insurance companies.

In the case of marketable securities, market prices result from numerous transactions between willing buyers and sellers. Market prices in this case provide an unbiased (objective) estimate of value to report on the balance sheet. This market method of accounting for marketable securities yields fluctuations in the asset side of the balance sheet with corresponding fluctuations in equity (liabilities are unaffected). This is reflected in the following accounting equation:

$$\text{Assets} \uparrow\downarrow = \text{Liabilities} + \text{Equity} \uparrow\downarrow$$

An important issue is whether such changes in equity should be reported as income (with a consequent change in retained earnings), or whether they should bypass the income statement and directly impact equity via *other comprehensive income (OCI)*. The answer differs depending on the classification of the securities, which we explain in the next section.

Investments Marked to Market

The following two classifications of marketable securities require the investment to be reported on the balance sheet at current market value (*marked-to-market*):

1. **Available-for-sale (AFS).** These are investments in securities that management intends to hold for capital gains and dividend revenue; although it may sell them if the price is right.
2. **Trading (T).** These are investments in securities that management intends to actively buy and sell for trading profits as market prices fluctuate.

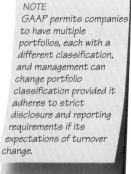

NOTE
GAAP permits companies to have multiple portfolios, each with a different classification, and management can change portfolio classification provided it adheres to strict disclosure and reporting requirements if its expectations of turnover change.

Investments in both equity and debt securities qualify for these classifications. (Equity securities refer to those with ownership interest, whereas debt securities have no ownership interest.) Management's assignment of securities between these two classifications depends on the degree of turnover (transaction volume) it expects in the investment portfolio, which reflects its intent to actively trade the securities or not. Available-for-sale portfolios exhibit less turnover than do trading portfolios. Once that classification is established, reporting for a portfolio follows that in Exhibit 12.3.

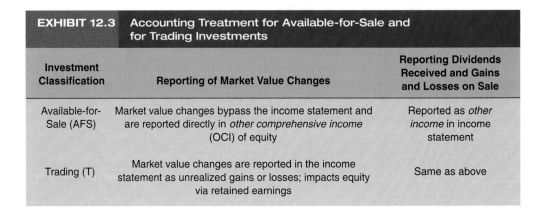

EXHIBIT 12.3	**Accounting Treatment for Available-for-Sale and for Trading Investments**	
Investment Classification	**Reporting of Market Value Changes**	**Reporting Dividends Received and Gains and Losses on Sale**
Available-for-Sale (AFS)	Market value changes bypass the income statement and are reported directly in *other comprehensive income (OCI)* of equity	Reported as *other income* in income statement
Trading (T)	Market value changes are reported in the income statement as unrealized gains or losses; impacts equity via retained earnings	Same as above

Both available-for-sale (AFS) and trading (T) investments are reported at current market values (marked-to-market) on the statement date. Whether the change in market value affects current income depends on the investment classification: available-for-sale securities have no income affect; trading securities have an income affect. The impact on equity is similar for both classifications, with the only difference being whether the change is reflected in retained earnings or in the other comprehensive income (OCI) of equity. Dividends and any gains or losses on security sales are reported in the other income section of the income statement for both classifications.

Market Adjustments

To illustrate the accounting for changes in market value subsequent to purchase (and before sale), assume that Pownall's investment in King Co. (600 remaining shares purchased for $20 per share) increases in value to $25 per share at year-end. The investment must be marked to market to reflect the $3,000 unrealized gain ($5 per share increase for 600 shares). The financial statements are affected as follows.

Transaction	Balance Sheet					Income Statement		
	Cash Asset +	Noncash Assets =	Liabil-ities +	Contrib. Capital +	Retained Earnings	Revenues −	Expenses =	Net Income
If available-for-sale portfolio:								
$5 increase in market value of King Co. investment		+3,000 Investments =			+3,000 OCI			=
If trading portfolio:								
$5 increase in market value of King Co. investment		+3,000 Investments =			+3,000 Retained Earnings	+3,000 Unrealized Gain		= +3,000

The related journal entries and T-accounts follow.

> **REMEMBER**
> When trading securities are marked-to-market, the unrealized gain is recorded as revenue and reported in the income statement. For available-for-sale investments, unrealized gains are reported as other comprehensive income.

*The gain is reported in other comprehensive income (O.C.I.) for AFS securities.

Under both classifications, the investment account is increased by $3,000 to reflect the increase in market value of the shares owned. When accounted for as available-for-sale, the unrealized gain is reflected as an increase in Other Comprehensive Income (OCI), typically viewed as a component of retained earnings. However, when accounted for as trading, the unrealized gain is recorded as income, thus increasing both reported income and retained earnings for that period. (Our illustration uses a portfolio with only one security for simplicity. Portfolios usually consist of multiple securities, and the unrealized gain or loss is computed based on the total cost and total market value of the entire portfolio.)

These market adjustments are only applied to publicly traded securities. Companies sometimes purchase securities for which current market values are unavailable. Examples are investments in start-up companies, privately held corporations, and in local bond offerings. Investments in non-publicly traded companies are accounted for at cost as we discuss later in this section.

Financial Statement Disclosures

Companies are required to disclose cost and market value information on their investment portfolios in footnotes to financial statements. **American Express Company** reports its accounting policies for its investments in the following footnote to its 10-K report:

> **Investments**   Generally, investment securities are carried at fair value on the balance sheet with unrealized gains (losses) recorded in equity, net of income tax provisions (benefits). Gains and losses are recognized in results of operations upon disposition of the securities. In addition, losses are also recognized when management determines that a decline in value is other-than-temporary, which requires judgment regarding the amount and timing of recovery.

This footnote reveals that American Express generally accounts for its investments as available-for-sale. We know this because it reports that unrealized gains and losses are "recorded in equity."

It also reports that these investments are reported on its balance sheet at market value. Following is the investments line item from the asset section of American Express' balance sheet ($ millions):

December 31	2003
Investments	$57,067

American Express' investment portfolio is carried as an asset with a current market value of $57,067 million. Unrealized gains and losses on its available-for-sale investments bypass its income statement (they do not affect current income), and are reported as a component of equity called other comprehensive income (OCI). Gains and losses on the *sale* of investments, however, are reported in current income. Also, as American Express reports in its footnote, if investments suffer a decline in value prior to sale that is deemed "other-than-temporary," they are written down to current market value and that loss is reported in current income.

Footnotes to the American Express 10-K provide further information about the composition of its investment portfolio ($ millions):

American Express: Summary of Investments at December 31:

	2003
Available-for-Sale, at fair value	$52,278
Investment loans (fair value: $4,116)	3,794
Trading	995
Total	$57,067

This note reveals that of the $57,067 million in investments, $52,278 million are classified as available-for-sale, with the remainder classified as either investment (commercial) loans or trading securities. Investment loans are reported at cost because no liquid market exists for these investments. (The reported "fair value" is computed based on projected cash flows and prevailing interest rates, and is not based on reference to a published market price.) The trading portfolio is reported at current market value with unrealized gains and losses reported in current income.

American Express provides additional (required) disclosures on both the cost and unrealized gains and losses for its available-for-sale investments as follows:

(Millions)	Cost	Gross Unrealized Gains	Gross Unrealized Losses	Fair Value
Corporate debt securities	$20,144	$ 883	$(110)	$20,917
Mortgage and other asset-backed securities	16,674	279	(84)	16,869
State and municipal obligations	7,138	479	(5)	7,612
Structured investments	2,828	24	(60)	2,792
Foreign government bonds and obligations	1,378	60	(3)	1,435
U.S. Government and agencies obligations	1,150	17	—	1,167
Other	1,474	21	(9)	1,486
Total	$50,786	$1,763	$(271)	$52,278

For each investment, American Express reports its cost, fair market value, and gross unrealized gains and losses; the latter reflect differences between cost and market. American Express reports that the cost of its investment portfolio is $50,786 million, and that there are unrealized gains (losses) of $1,763 ($271) million as of December 31, 2003. The total market value of $52,278 million at December 31, 2003 is the amount reported on its balance sheet. The reported fair value is the cost and all unrealized gains less all unrealized losses.

American Express' net unrealized gain of $1,492 million ($1,763 million − $271 million) is reported net of $561 million in estimated tax; yielding a reported balance of $931 million in the other comprehensive income section of its stockholders' equity as follows ($ millions):

December 31	2003
Shareholders' Equity	
Common shares, $.20 par value, authorized 3.6 billion shares; issued and outstanding 1,284 million shares in 2003	$ 257
Additional paid-in capital	6,081
Retained earnings	8,793
Other comprehensive income (loss), net of tax	
Net unrealized securities gains	931
Net unrealized derivatives losses	(446)
Foreign currency translation adjustments	(278)
Minimum pension liability	(15)
Accumulated other comprehensive income	192
Total shareholders' equity	$15,323

There is sometimes confusion because of the difference between the amount reported in the investment footnote and the amount reported in other comprehensive income. This difference arises because the net unrealized gain of $1,492 million ($1,763 million − $271 million) reported in the investment footnote is pretax and the $931 million reported in the other comprehensive income section of stockholders' equity is after-tax (reflecting a nearly 38% tax rate).

Investments Marked to Cost

Investments for which no current market values exist must be accounted for using the cost method. Under the **cost method**, the investment is continually reported at its historical cost, and any cash dividends and interest received are recognized in current income.

Debt securities that management intends to hold to maturity are reported using the cost method. These debt securities are classified as **held-to-maturity** (HTM). Exhibit 12.4 identifies the reporting of these securities.

EXHIBIT 12.4	Accounting Treatment for Held-to-Maturity Investments	
Investment Classification	**Reporting of Market Value Changes**	**Reporting Dividends Received and Gains and Losses on Sale**
Held-to-Maturity (HTM)	Market value changes are *not* reported in either the balance sheet or income statement	Reported as *other income* in income statement

Changes in market value are not reflected on either the balance sheet or the income statement. The presumption is that these investments are held to maturity, at which time they are settled at their face value. Fluctuations in market value, as a result, are less relevant for this investment classification. Any interest received, and gains and losses on the sale of these investments, are recorded in current income.

MID-CHAPTER REVIEW 1

Part 1: Available-for-sale securities

Prepare the journal entries, post the journal entries to the appropriate t-accounts, and enter the effects (amount and account) relating to the following four transactions involving investments in marketable securities classified as available-for-sale in the financial statement effects template.

1. Purchased 1,000 shares of Pincus common stock for $15 cash per share.
2. Received cash dividend of $2 per share on Pincus common stock.
3. Year-end market price of Pincus common stock is $18 per share.
4. Sold all 1,000 shares of Pincus common stock for $19,000 cash.

Solution for Part 1:

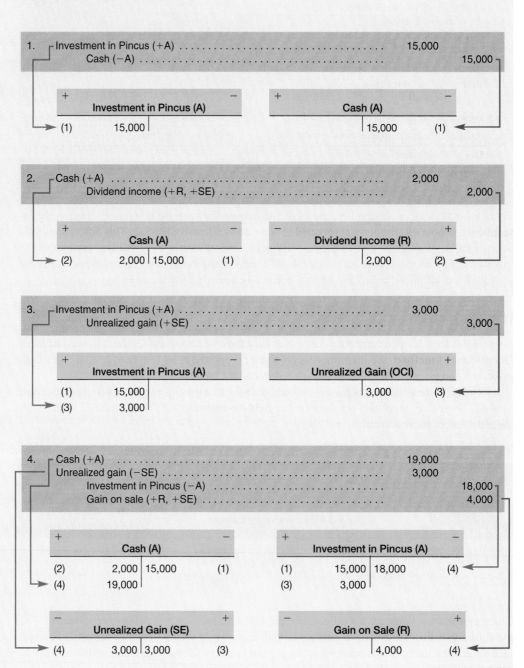

Transaction	Balance Sheet							Income Statement		
	Cash Asset	+ Noncash Assets	= Liabil-ities	+ Contrib. Capital	+ Retained Earnings			Revenues	– Expenses =	Net Income
1. Purchased 1,000 shares of Pincus common stock for $15 cash per share	−15,000 Cash	+15,000 Investments (AFS)	=							=
2. Received cash dividend of $2 per share on Pincus common stock	+2,000 Cash		=		+2,000 Retained Earnings			+2,000 Dividend Income		= +2,000
3. Year-end market price of Pincus common stock is $18 per share		+3,000 Investments (AFS)	=		+3,000 OCI					=
4. Sold all 1,000 shares of Pincus common stock for $19,000 cash	+19,000 Cash	−18,000 Investments (AFS)	=		−3,000 OCI +4,000 Retained Earnings			+4,000 Gain on Sale		= +4,000

Part 2: Trading securities

Using the same transaction information 1 through 4 from part 1, prepare the journal entries, post the journal entries to the related t-accounts, and enter the effects (amount and account) relating to these transactions in the financial statement effects template assuming that the investments are classified as trading securities.

Solution for Part 2

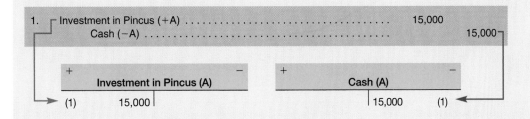

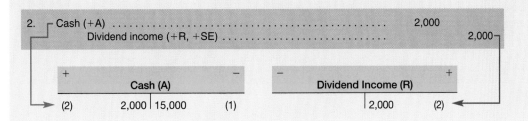

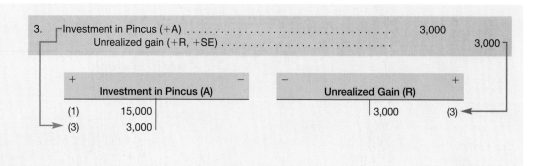

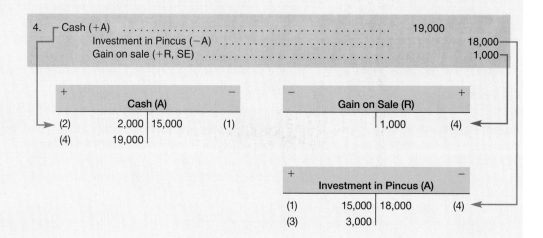

Transaction	Balance Sheet						Income Statement			
	Cash Asset	+ Noncash Assets	=	Liabil-ities	+ Contrib. Capital	+ Retained Earnings	Revenues	− Expenses	=	Net Income
1. Purchased 1,000 shares of Pincus common stock for $15 cash per share	−15,000 Cash	+15,000 Investments	=						=	
2. Received cash dividend of $2 per share on Pincus common stock	+2,000 Cash		=			+2,000 Retained Earnings	+2,000 Dividend Income		=	+2,000
3. Year-end market price of Pincus common stock is $18 per share		+3,000 Investments (Trading)	=			+3,000 Retained Earnings	+3,000 Unrealized Gain		=	+3,000
4. Sold all 1,000 shares of Pincus common stock for $19,000 cash	+19,000 Cash	−18,000 Investments (Trading)	=			+1,000 Retained Earnings	+1,000 Gain on Sale		=	+1,000

INVESTMENTS WITH SIGNIFICANT INFLUENCE

Many companies make investments in other companies that yield them significant influence over those other companies. These intercorporate investments are usually made for strategic reasons such as the following:

LO3 Explain and analyze accounting for investments with significant influence

- **Prelude to acquisition.** Significant ownership can allow the investor company to gain a seat on the board of directors from which it can learn much about the investee company, its products, and its industry.

- **Strategic alliance.** One example of a strategic alliance is an investment in a company that provides inputs for the investor's production process. This relationship is closer than the usual supplier-buyer relationship, often because the investor company provides trade secrets or technical know-how of its production process.

- **Pursuit of research and development.** Many research activities in the pharmaceutical, software, and oil and gas industries are conducted jointly. The common motivation is to reduce risk or the amount of capital invested by the investor. The investor company's equity investment often carries an option to purchase additional shares or the entire company, which it can exercise if the research activities are fruitful.

A crucial feature in each of these investments is that the investor company has ownership sufficient to exert *significant influence* over the investee company. GAAP requires that such investments be accounted for using the *equity method.*

Significant influence is the ability of the investor to affect the financing or operating policies of the investee. Ownership levels of 20% to 50% of the outstanding common stock of the investee presume significant influence. Significant influence can also exist when ownership is less than 20%. Evidence of such influence can be that the investor company is able to gain a seat on the board of directors of the investee by virtue of its equity investment, or the investor controls technical know-how or patents that are used by the investee, or the investor is able to exert significant influence by virtue of legal contracts between it and the investee. (There is growing pressure for determining significant influence by the facts and circumstances of the investment instead of a strict ownership percentage rule.)

Accounting for Investments with Significant Influence

Investments with significant influence must be accounted for using the **equity method**. The equity method of accounting for investments reports the investment on the balance sheet at an amount equal to the percentage of the investee's equity owned by the investor; hence the name equity method. (This accounting assumes acquisition at book value. Acquisition at an amount greater than book value is covered later in this section.) Contrary to passive investments that are reported at market value, equity method investments increase (decrease) with increases (decreases) in the equity of the investee.

Equity method accounting is summarized as follows:

- Investments are initially recorded at their purchase cost.

- Dividends received are treated as a recovery of the investment and, thus, reduce the investment balance (dividends are *not* reported as income as is the case with passive investments).

- The investor reports income equal to its percentage share of the reported income of the investee; the investment account is increased by that income or decreased by its share of any loss.

- The investment is *not* reported at market value as are passive market investments.

To illustrate the accounting for investments using the equity method, consider the following scenario: Assume that **HP** acquires a 30% interest in Mitel Networks, a company seeking to develop a new technology in a strategic alliance with HP. At acquisition, Mitel reports $1,000 of stockholders' equity, and HP purchases its 30% stake for $300. At the first year-end, Mitel reports profits of

$100 and pays $20 in cash dividends to its shareholders ($6 to HP). Following are the financial statement effects for HP (the investor company) for this investment using the equity method:

	Balance Sheet							Income Statement			
Transaction	Cash Asset	+	Noncash Assets	=	Liabil-ities	+	Contrib. Capital	+	Retained Earnings	Revenues − Expenses =		Net Income
1. Purchased 30% invest-ment in Mitel for $300 cash	−300 Cash		+300 Investment in Mitel	=							=	
2. Mitel reports $100 income			+30 Investment in Mitel	=					+30 Retained Earnings	+30 Investment Income	=	+30
3. Mitel pays $20 cash dividends, $6 to HP	+6 Cash		−6 Investment in Mitel	=							=	
4. Ending balance of HP's investment account			324	=							=	

The related journal entries and T-accounts follow.

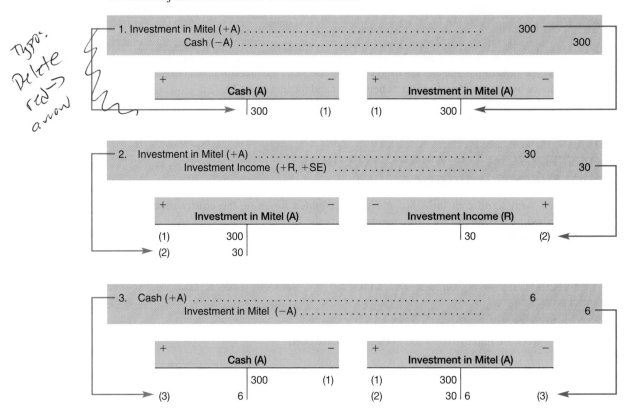

Typo: Delete red → arrow

1. Investment in Mitel (+A) 300
    Cash (−A) 300

+	Cash (A)	−		+	Investment in Mitel (A)	−
		300 (1)		(1)	300	

2. Investment in Mitel (+A) 30
    Investment Income (+R, +SE) 30

+	Investment in Mitel (A)	−		−	Investment Income (R)	+
(1)	300				30	(2)
(2)	30					

3. Cash (+A) 6
    Investment in Mitel (−A) 6

+	Cash (A)	−		+	Investment in Mitel (A)	−
		300 (1)		(1)	300	
(3)	6			(2)	30	6 (3)

The investment is initially reported on HP's balance sheet at its purchase price of $300, representing a 30% interest in Mitel's equity of $1,000. During the year, Mitel's equity increases to $1,080 ($1,000 plus $100 income and less $20 dividends). Likewise, HP's investment increases by $30 to reflect its 30% share of Mitel's $100 income and decreases by $6 from Mitel's $20 of dividends. After these transactions, HP's investment in Mitel is reported on HP's balance sheet at 30% of $1,080, or $324.

Companies sometimes pay more than book value when acquiring equity interest in other companies. For example, if HP paid $400 for its 30% stake in Mitel, HP would initially report its investment at its $400 purchase price. The $400 investment consists of two parts: the $300 equity investment described above and the $100 additional investment. HP is willing to pay the higher purchase price because it believes that Mitel's reported equity is below its current market value (such as when its assets are reported at costs that are below market values or when intangible assets like internally generated goodwill are not recorded on its balance sheet). The $300 portion of the investment is accounted for as described above. The $100 additional investment is accounted for like the purchase of any other asset. That is, if the $100 relates to undervalued depreciable assets, it is depreciated over the estimated useful lives. Or, if it relates to identifiable intangible assets that have a determinable useful life (like patents), it is amortized over the useful lives of the intangible assets. If it relates to goodwill, it is not amortized and remains on the balance sheet at $100 unless and until it is deemed to have become impaired. (See Appendix 12A for an expanded discussion.)

Two final points about equity method accounting: First, just as the equity of a company is different from its market value, so is the balance of the equity investment account different from its market value. Indeed, there can be a substantial difference between the book value of an investment and its market value (as is the case with every asset other than passive market investments that are recorded at market value). (However, if the market value of an investment has permanently declined, the investment is deemed impaired and it is written down to that lower market value.) Second, if the investee company reports income, the investor company also reports income. Recognition of equity income by the investor, however, does not mean that it has received that income in cash. Cash is only received if the investee's directors declare a dividend payment. In the statement of cash flows, investors subtract the difference between reported equity income and dividends received in the operating section of the statement. The net amount is equal to the *cash* income received.

> **NOTE** Investee dividend-paying ability can be (a) restricted by regulatory agencies or foreign governments, (b) prohibited under debt agreements for highly leveraged borrowers, and/or (c) influenced by directors that the investor does not control.

RESEARCH INSIGHT

Equity Income and Stock Prices   The equity method of accounting for investments does not recognize any dividends received from the investee or any market value changes for the investee in the investor's income until the investment is sold. However, research has found a positive relation between investors' and investees' stock prices at the time of investees' earnings and dividend announcements. This relation suggests that the market includes information regarding investees' earnings and dividends when assessing the stock prices of investor companies. This finding implies the market looks beyond the book value of the investment account in determining stock prices of investor companies.

Equity Method Accounting and ROE Effects

The balance sheet amount for equity method investments is equal to the percentage owned of the equity of the investee company when the investment is acquired at book value. To illustrate, consider the case of **SBC Communications Inc**, which owns 60% of **Cingular Wireless**, a nationwide wireless provider formed as a joint venture with BellSouth. SBC accounts for its investment in Cingular using the equity method as described in the following footnote to its 10-K report:

> We account for our 60% economic interest in Cingular under the equity method of accounting in our consolidated financial statements since we share control equally (i.e., 50/50) with our 40% economic partner in the joint venture. We have equal voting rights and representation on the board of directors that controls Cingular.

(SBC's investment is accounted for using the equity method despite its "60% economic interest." Economic interest means that it receives 60% of the income, cash flow, and net asset ownership. Guidelines for use of the equity method versus consolidation are based on whether SBC has the ability to exert "significant influence" or "control" over Cingular. Because voting rights are shared equally, SBC does not have "control" and, as a result, consolidation is inappropriate.)

SBC reports an investment balance at December 31, 2003, of $5,090 million, which is equal to its 60% share of Cingular's equity as reported in the following footnote to the SBC 10-K report:

Cingular Wireless ($ millions)	2003
Income Statements	
Operating revenues	$15,483
Operating income	2,289
Net income	1,022
Balance Sheets	
Current assets	$ 3,300
Noncurrent assets	22,226
Current liabilities	3,187
Noncurrent liabilities	13,855

Specifically, Cingular's equity is equal to $8,484 million ($3,300 + $22,226 − $3,187 − $13,855) and, thus, SBC's 60% economic interest represents an investment balance of $5,090 million (60% × $8,484).

However, the balance sheet of Cingular reports total assets of $25,526 million and total liabilities of $17,042 million. The $5,090 million investment balance on SBC's balance sheet fails to reflect the full asset investment and financial obligations of Cingular—as it reflects only its share of net assets.

SBC also reports equity income of $613 million as reported in the following footnote:

($ millions)	2003	2002
Beginning of year	$10,468	$ 9,441
Contributions	—	299
Equity in net income	613	759
Other adjustments	(78)	(31)
End of year	$11,003	$10,468

The $613 million represents 60% of Cingular's net income of $1,022 million as reported in the Cingular footnote previously presented. Cingular did not pay any cash dividends to SBC in 2003 and, thus, SBC's reported income did not reflect any operating cash inflows for 2003 from the investment in Cingular.

Under equity method accounting, only the net equity owned is reported on the balance sheet (not the assets and liabilities to which the investment relates), and only the net equity in earnings is reported in the income statement (not the investee's sales and expenses). Both the balance sheet and income statements are, therefore, markedly affected. Further, because the assets and liabilities are left off the balance sheet, and because the sales and expenses are omitted from the income statement, the *components* of ROE are also markedly affected as follows:

- **Net operating profit margin (NOPM = NOPAT/Sales).** Most analysts include equity income in NOPAT because it relates to operating investments. The reported NOPM is, thus, *overstated* due to nonrecognition of investee sales and the recognition of investee income.

- **Net operating asset turnover (NOAT = Sales/Average NOA).** The equity investment balance is typically included in operating assets. This means that NOAT is *understated* due to nonrecognition of investee sales and *overstated* by nonrecognition of investee assets in excess of the investment balance. The net effect is, therefore, *indeterminate* (NOAT is overstated provided NOA exceeds sales, and understated otherwise.)

- **Financial leverage (FLEV = Net financial obligations/Average equity).** Financial leverage is *understated* due to nonrecognition of investee liabilities and the recognition of investee equity (the proportionate share of investee earnings is included in SBC's income).

Although ROE components are affected, ROE is unaffected by use of equity method accounting. Still, the evaluation of the *quality* of ROE is affected. Analysis reveals that ROE is impacted from a lower net operating profit margin (actual NOPM is overstated) and higher financial leverage (actual FLEV is understated) than was apparent based on the reported balance sheet and income statement. As we discuss in a later chapter, analysts frequently adjust reported financial statements for these types of items before conducting analysis. One approach would be to consolidate the equity method investee with the investor company.

YOU MAKE THE CALL

You Are the Chief Financial Officer   You are receiving capital expenditure requests for long-term operating asset purchases from various managers. You are concerned that capacity utilization is too low. What potential courses of action can you consider? Explain. [Answer, p. 546]

MID-CHAPTER REVIEW 2

Prepare the journal entries, post the journal entries to the related T-accounts, and enter the effects (amount and account) relating to the following four transactions involving investments in marketable securities accounted for using the equity method in the financial statement effects template.

1. Purchased 5,000 shares of Hribar common stock at $10 cash per share. These shares reflect 30% ownership of Hribar.
2. Received a $2 per share cash dividend on Hribar common stock.
3. Made an adjustment to reflect $100,000 income reported by Hribar.
4. Sold all 5,000 shares of Hribar common stock for $90,000.

Solution

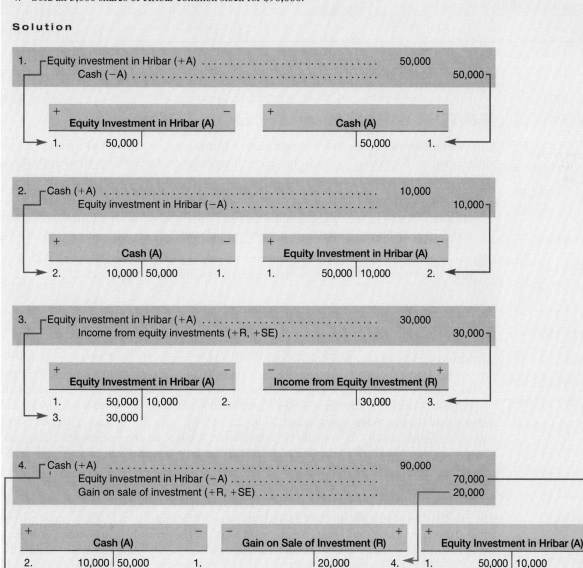

Transaction	Balance Sheet						Income Statement		
	Cash Asset +	Noncash Assets =	Liabil- ities +	Contrib. Capital +	Retained Earnings		Revenues − Expenses =		Net Income
1. Purchased 5,000 Hribar shares at $10 cash per share. These shares reflect 30% ownership of Hribar.	−50,000 Cash	+50,000 Investments =							=
2. Received a $2 per share on cash dividend on Hribar stock	+10,000 Cash	−10,000 Investments =							=
3. Made an adjustment to reflect $100,000 income reported by Hribar		+30,000 Investments =			+30,000 Retained Earnings		+30,000 Equity Income		= +30,000
4. Sold all 5,000 Hribar shares for $90,000	+90,000 Cash	−70,000 =			+20,000 Retained Earnings		+20,000 Gain on Sale		= +20,000

INVESTMENTS WITH CONTROL

LO4 Describe and analyze accounting for investments with control.

This section discusses accounting for investments where the investor company "controls" the investee company. For example, in its footnote describing its accounting policies, Hewlett-Packard reports the following:

> **Principles of Consolidation** The Consolidated Financial Statements include the accounts of HP and its wholly-owned and controlled majority-owned subsidiaries. All significant intercompany accounts and transactions have been eliminated.

This statement means that HP financial statements are an aggregation (an adding up) of those of the parent company and all its subsidiary companies, less any intercompany activities.

Accounting for Investments with Control

Accounting for business combinations (acquisitions) involves one additional step to equity method accounting. Under the equity method, the investment balance represents the proportion of the investee's equity owned by the investor, and the investor company income statement includes its proportionate share of the investee's income. Consolidation accounting (1) replaces the investment balance with the investee's assets and liabilities to which it relates, and (2) replaces the equity income reported by the investor with the investee's sales and expenses to which it relates. Specifically, the consolidated balance sheet includes the gross assets and liabilities of the investee company, and the income statement includes the gross sales and expenses of the investee.

To illustrate, consider the following scenario. Penman Company acquires all of the common stock of Nissim Company by exchanging newly issued shares for all of Nissim's common stock. The purchase price is equal to the $3,000 book value of Nissim's stockholders' equity (contributed capital of $2,000 and retained earnings of $1,000). The investment in Nissim Co. on Penman's balance sheet is accounted for using the equity method (GAAP only requires consolidation for financial statements issued to the public, not for the internal financial records of the separate companies). Penman records an initial balance in the investment account of $3,000, which equals the purchase price. The balance sheets for Penman and Nissim immediately after the acquisition, together with the required consolidating adjustments (or eliminations), and the consolidated balance sheet that the two companies report are shown in Exhibit 12.5.

EXHIBIT 12.5	Mechanics of Consolidation Accounting (Purchased at Book Value)			
	Penman Company	**Nissim Company**	**Consolidating Adjustments***	**Consolidated**
Current assets	$ 5,000	$1,000		$ 6,000
Investment in Nissim	3,000	0	(3,000)	0
PPE, net	10,000	4,000		14,000
Total assets	$18,000	$5,000		$20,000
Liabilities	$ 5,000	$2,000		$ 7,000
Contributed capital	10,000	2,000	(2,000)	10,000
Retained earnings	3,000	1,000	(1,000)	3,000
Total liabilities and equity	$18,000	$5,000		$20,000

*The accounting equation remains in balance with these adjustments.

Because Penman "controls" the activities of Nissim, GAAP requires consolidation of the two balance sheets. This process involves summing the individual lines for each balance sheet less the elimination of any intercompany transactions (investments and loans, or sales and purchases, within the consolidated group). The consolidated balances for current assets, PPE, and liabilities are, for example, the sum of those accounts on each balance sheet. The equity investment, however, represents an intercompany transaction that must be eliminated prior to consolidation. This elimination is accomplished by removing the equity investment of $3,000, and removing Nissim's equity to which that investment relates.[3]

---

[3]In the event that Penman acquires less than 100% of the stock of Nissim, Penman's equity must increase to maintain the accounting equation. This equity account is titled **minority interest**. For example, assume that Penman acquired 80% of Nissim for $2,400 (80% of $3,000).

Mechanics of Consolidation Accounting (Less than 100% Acquisition)				
	Penman Company	**Nissim Company**	**Consolidating Adjustments**	**Consolidated**
Current assets	$ 5,600	$1,000		$ 6,600
Investment in Nissim	2,400	0	(2,400)	0
PPE, net	10,000	4,000		14,000
Total assets	$18,000	$5,000		$20,600
Liabilities	$ 5,000	$2,000		$ 7,000
Minority interest in Nissim	0	0	600	600
Contributed capital	10,000	2,000	(2,000)	10,000
Retained earnings	3,000	1,000	(1,000)	3,000
Total liabilities and equity	$18,000	$5,000		$20,600

The consolidated balance sheet is shown in the far right column of Exhibit 12.5. It shows total assets of $20,000, total liabilities of $7,000 and stockholders' equity of $13,000. Consolidated equity equals that of the parent company—this is always the case.[4]

The illustration above assumes that the purchase price of the acquisition equals book value. What changes, if any, occur when the purchase price and book value are different? To explore this case, consider an acquisition where purchase price exceeds book value (the typical scenario). This situation might arise, for example, if an investor company believes it is acquiring something of value that is not reported on the investee's balance sheet—such as tangible assets whose market values have risen above book value, or unrecorded intangible assets like patents or corporate synergies. If an acquisition is made at a price in excess of book value, all net assets acquired (both tangible and intangible) must be recognized on the consolidated balance sheet.

To illustrate an acquisition where purchase price exceeds book value, assume that Penman Company acquires Nissim Company for $4,000 instead of the $3,000 purchase price we used in the previous illustration. Also assume that in determining its purchase price, Penman feels that the additional $1,000 ($4,000 vs. $3,000) is justified because (1) Nissim's PPE is worth $300 more than its book value, and (2) Penman expects to realize $700 in additional value from corporate synergies.

The $4,000 investment account reflects two components: the book value acquired of $3,000 (as before) and an additional $1,000 of newly acquired assets. The post-acquisition balance sheets of the two companies, together with the consolidating adjustments and the consolidated balance sheet, are shown in Exhibit 12.6.

EXHIBIT 12.6	Mechanics of Consolidation Accounting (Purchased above Book Value)			
	Penman Company	Nissim Company	Consolidating Adjustments	Consolidated
Current assets	$ 5,000	$1,000		$ 6,000
Investment in Nissim	4,000	0	(4,000)	0
PPE, net	10,000	4,000	300	14,300
Goodwill			700	700
Total assets	$19,000	$5,000		$21,000
Liabilities	5,000	$2,000		$ 7,000
Contributed capital	11,000	2,000	(2,000)	11,000
Retained earnings	3,000	1,000	(1,000)	3,000
Total liabilities and equity	$19,000	$5,000		$21,000

The consolidated balances for current assets, PPE, and liabilities are the sum of those accounts on each company's balance sheet. The investment account, however, includes newly acquired assets that must be reported on the consolidated balance sheet. The consolidation process in this case has two steps. First, the $3,000 equity of Nissim Company is eliminated against the investment account as before. Then, the remaining $1,000 of the investment account is eliminated through the adjustments for newly acquired assets ($300 of PPE and $700 of goodwill not reported on Nissim's balance sheet) on the consolidated balance sheet. Thus, the consolidated balance sheet reflects the book value of Penman and the *fair market value* (book value plus the excess of Nissim's market value over book value) for Nissim Company at the acquisition date.

To illustrate consolidation mechanics with an actual case, consider the consolidated balance sheet (parent company, subsidiary and consolidated balance sheet) that General Electric reports in a supplemental schedule to its 10-K report as shown in Exhibit 12.7.

---

[4]Also, consolidated net income always equals the parent company's net income as the subsidiary's net income is already reflected in the parent's income statement as equity income from its investment.

EXHIBIT 12.7	General Electric's Consolidated Balance Sheet		

At December 31, 2003 (In millions)	General Electric Company and Consolidated Affiliates	GE	GECS
ASSETS			
Cash and equivalents	$ 12,664	$ 1,670	$ 11,273
Investment securities	120,724	380	120,344
Current receivables	10,732	10,973	—
Inventories	8,752	8,555	197
Financing receivables (investments in time sales, loans and financing leases)—net	226,029	—	226,029
Insurance receivables—net	27,053	—	27,053
Other GECS receivables	9,545	—	11,901
Property, plant and equipment (including equipment leased to others)—net	53,382	14,566	38,816
Investment in GECS	—	45,308	—
Intangible assets—net	55,025	30,204	24,821
Consolidated, liquidating securitization entities	26,463	—	26,463
All other assets	97,114	30,448	67,629
TOTAL ASSETS	$647,483	$142,104	$554,526
LIABILITIES AND EQUITY			
Short-term borrowings	$134,917	$ 2,555	$132,988
Accounts payable, principally trade accounts	19,824	8,753	13,440
Progress collections and price adjustments accrued	4,433	4,433	—
Dividends payable	2,013	2,013	—
All other current costs and expenses accrued	15,343	15,343	—
Long-term borrowings	170,004	8,388	162,540
Insurance liabilities, reserves and annuity benefits	136,264	—	136,264
Consolidated, liquidating securitization entities	25,721	—	25,721
All other liabilities	41,357	18,449	22,828
Deferred income taxes	12,647	1,911	10,736
Total liabilities	562,523	61,845	504,517
Minority interest in equity of consolidated affiliates	5,780	1,079	4,701
Common stock (10,063,120,000 shares outstanding)	669	669	1
Accumulated gains/(losses)—net			
Investment securities	1,620	1,620	1,823
Currency translation adjustments	2,987	2,987	2,639
Derivatives qualifying as hedges (1,727)	(1,792)	(1,792)	
Other capital	17,497	17,497	12,268
Retained earnings	82,796	82,796	30,304
Less common stock held in treasury	(24,597)	(24,597)	—
Total shareowners' equity	79,180	79,180	45,308
TOTAL LIABILITIES AND EQUITY	$647,483)	$142,104	$554,526

General Electric Company (GE) owns 100% of its financial products' subsidiary, General Electric Capital Services (GECS), whose stockholder's equity is $45,308 million as of 2003. The Investment in GECS account is also reported at $45,308 million on GE's (parent company) balance sheet. This investment account is subsequently removed (eliminated) in the consolidation process, together with the equity of GECS to which it relates. Following this elimination, and the *elimination of all other intercompany sales and advances,* the adjusted balance sheets of the two companies are summed to yield the consolidated balance sheet.

Reporting of Acquired Intangible Assets

Acquisitions are often made at a purchase price in excess of the book value of the investee company's equity. The purchase price is first allocated to the fair market values of tangible assets and liabilities (such as PPE in our example). Then, the remainder is allocated to acquired *intangible* assets.

Hewlett-Packard reported the following allocation of its $24,170 million purchase price for Compaq Computer in the footnotes to its 10-K report ($ millions).

Tangible assets	Cash and cash equivalents	$ 3,615
	Accounts receivable	4,305
	Financing receivables	1,241
	Inventory	1,661
	Current deferred tax assets	1,475
	Other current assets	1,146
	Property, plant and equipment	2,998
	Long-term financing receivables and other assets	1,914
Acquired intangible assets	Amortizable intangible assets	
	Customer contracts and lists, distribution agreements.	1,942
	Developed and core technology, patents	1,501
	Product trademarks	74
	Intangible asset with an indefinite life	1,422
	Goodwill	14,450
Liabilities assumed	Accounts payable	(2,804)
	Short- and long-term debt	(2,704)
	Accrued restructuring	(960)
	Other current liabilities	(5,933)
	Other long-term liabilities	(1,908)
IPR&D →	In-process research and development	735
	Total purchase price	$24,170

Tangible assets acquired and liabilities assumed in the purchase are valued by the purchasing company as of the acquisition date and are recorded on the consolidated balance sheet at fair market value. (In the Exhibit 12.6 example, we sum the $4,000 PPE book value of Nissim with the $300 excess of market over book value to yield the $4,300 PPE fair market value that is included among the assets on the consolidated balance sheet.) Any remaining purchase price above book value is allocated to acquired identifiable *intangible* assets, also valued at the acquisition date. A sampling of the types of intangible assets that are often recognized for such acquisitions follows:

- Marketing-related assets like trademarks and Internet domain names
- Customer-related assets like customer lists and customer contracts
- Artistic-related assets like plays, books, and video
- Contract-based assets like licensing, franchise and royalty agreements, and lease contracts
- Technology-based assets like patents, software, databases, and trade secrets

In its acquisition of Compaq, HP allocated $4.9 billion ($1,942 million + $1,501 million + $74 million + $1,422 million) of its purchase price to identifiable intangible assets (absent goodwill), as described in the following footnote to its 10-K.

Amortizable intangible assets Of the total purchase price, approximately $3.5 billion [$1,942 million + $1,501 million + $74 million] was allocated to amortizable intangible assets including customer contracts and developed and core technology. . . . HP is amortizing the fair value of these assets on a straight-line basis over a weighted average estimated useful life of approximately 9 years. Developed technology, which consists of products that have reached technological feasibility, includes products in most of Compaq's product lines. . . . Core technology and patents represent a combination of Compaq processes, patents and trade secrets. . . . HP is amortizing the developed and core technology and patents on a straight-line basis over a weighted average estimated useful life of approximately 6 years.

Intangible asset with an indefinite life   The estimated fair value of the intangible asset with an indefinite life was $1.4 billion, consisting of the estimated fair value allocated to the Compaq trade name. This intangible asset will not be amortized because it has an indefinite remaining useful life based on many factors and considerations, including the length of time that the Compaq name has been in use, the Compaq brand awareness and market position and the plans for continued use of the Compaq brand.

HP discloses that it allocated a portion of the purchase price to the following identifiable intangible assets:

- Customer contracts
- Customer lists and distribution agreements
- Developed technology
- Core technology and patents
- Compaq trade name

HP deems the first four of these identifiable intangible assets as *amortizable assets,* which are those having a finite useful life. HP, subsequently, amortizes them over their useful lives (similar to depreciation). The last asset (Compaq trade name) is deemed to have an indefinite useful life. It is not amortized, but is tested annually for impairment like goodwill (see Chapter 9).

Once the purchase price has been allocated to identifiable tangible and intangible assets (net of liabilities assumed), any remainder of the purchase price is allocated to goodwill. HP allocated $14.45 billion (60%) of the Compaq purchase price to goodwill. The SEC is scrutinizing companies that assign an excessive proportion of the purchase price to goodwill; companies have been identified as doing this in a desire to avoid the future earnings drag from amortization expense.

Reporting of Goodwill

Goodwill is no longer amortized, as it was prior to 2001. Instead, GAAP requires companies to test it annually for impairment just like any other asset. The impairment test is a two-step process:

1. The market value of the investee company is compared with the book value of the investor's equity investment account.[5]

2. If the market value is less than the investment balance, the investment is deemed impaired. The company must then estimate the goodwill value as if the subsidiary were acquired for its current market value, and the imputed balance for goodwill becomes the amount at which it is recorded. If this imputed amount is less than its book value, goodwill must be written down, resulting in an impairment loss that is reported in the consolidated income statement.

To illustrate the impairment computation, assume that an investment, currently reported at $1 million on the investor's balance sheet, has a current fair market value of $900,000. The consolidated balance sheet reports net assets (absent goodwill) at $700,000 and goodwill at $300,000. Analysis reveals that the current fair market value of the net assets of the investee company (absent goodwill) is $700,000. This indicates goodwill is impaired by $100,000, which is computed as follows.

Fair market value of investee company	$ 900,000
Fair market value of net assets (absent goodwill) ...	(700,000)
Implied goodwill	200,000
Current goodwill balance	(300,000)
Impairment loss	$(100,000)

---

[5]The fair market value of the investee company can be determined using market comparables or another valuation method (such as the discounted cash flow model, residual operating income model, or P/E multiples—see Appendix C at the end of the book).

The related journal entry and T-accounts follow.

Transaction	Balance Sheet						Income Statement		
	Cash Asset	+ Noncash Assets	= Liabil-ities	+ Contrib. Capital	+ Retained Earnings		Revenues	− Expenses =	Net Income
Impairment adjustment to Goodwill		−100,000 Goodwill =			−100,000 Retained Earnings			−100,000 Goodwill Impairment Expense =	−100,000

The financial statements effects follow.

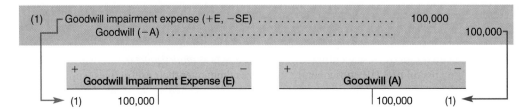

```
(1)  ┌─ Goodwill impairment expense (+E, −SE) . . . . . . . . . . . . . . . . . . . . . . .   100,000
     │        Goodwill (−A) . . . . . . . . . . . . . . . . . . . . . . . . . . . . . . . . . . .          100,000 ┐
     │                                                                                                              │
     │      +                          Goodwill Impairment Expense (E)      −    +          Goodwill (A)          − │
     └─▶  (1)        100,000 │                                                       │  100,000        (1)  ◀───────┘
```

This analysis of investee company implies that goodwill must be written down by $100,000. The impairment loss is reported as a separate line item in the consolidated income statement. The related footnote disclosure describes the reasons for the write-down and the computations involved.

Intel provides an example of a goodwill impairment disclosure in its 10-K report:

> During the fourth quarter of 2003, the company completed its annual impairment review for goodwill and found indicators of impairment for the Wireless Communications and Computing Group (WCCG). . . . The impairment review requires a two-step process. The first step of the review compares the fair value of the reporting units with substantial goodwill against their aggregate carrying values, including goodwill. The company estimated the fair value of the WCCG . . . reporting unit using the income method of valuation, which includes the use of estimated discounted cash flows. Based on the comparison, the carrying value of the WCCG reporting unit exceeded the fair value. Accordingly, the company performed the second step of the test, comparing the implied fair value of the WCCG reporting unit's goodwill with the carrying amount of that goodwill. Based on this assessment, the company recorded a non-cash impairment charge of $611 million, which is included as a component of operating income in the "all other" category.

Nonamortization of goodwill is GAAP policy post-2001. No retroactive adjustment to goodwill is made for years prior to 2001. This means that it is difficult to compare operating results for 2002 and later years to those for earlier years when goodwill amortization was a major item. To alleviate this problem, required footnote disclosures provide pro forma income numbers assuming that nonamortization of goodwill is applied to periods prior to adoption of the new goodwill accounting policy.

BUSINESS INSIGHT

Pitfalls of Acquired Growth   It may be the greatest destruction of shareholder value in history, and it happened in the bull market between 1995 and 2001. That is, the subsequent year's returns of most shareholders of purchasing companies that were hit with merger and acquisition fever fell below those of their peers. The winners were shareholders of target companies who sold their stock within the first week of takeover. What went wrong? The short answer is that companies overpaid as a result of overestimating the cost-cuttings and synergies such takeovers would bring. Then, they failed to quickly integrate operations. The results? Fully 61% of corporate buyers of intercorporate investments decreased their shareholders' wealth.

Reporting of Purchased In-Process R&D

Companies allocate the purchase price to assets acquired in a purchase, including any intangible assets. An intangible asset a company often acquires is *in-process research & development (IPR&D)*. IPR&D is an asset that is purchased just like PPE and other assets. Under GAAP, however, R&D is generally expensed. Thus, the cost of acquired IPR&D assets must be written off immediately upon purchase. This write-off is called *in-process R&D expense,* and is generally reported as a separate item in the income statement if it is material.

An investor company must value the IPR&D assets of an investee company before it can allocate any of the purchase price to them and then write them off. That valuation can use any one of several accepted valuation methods. Hewlett-Packard, for example, in its $24.1 billion acquisition of Compaq Computer, allocated $735 million to IPR&D (see table on page 538), which it immediately expensed in its income statement. HP described its IPR&D valuation process as follows.

In-Process Research & Development

Of the total purchase price, $735 million was allocated to IPR&D and was expensed in the third quarter of fiscal 2002. Projects that qualify as IPR&D represent those that have not yet reached technological feasibility and for which no future alternative uses exist. Technological feasibility is defined as being equivalent to a beta-phase working prototype in which there is no remaining risk relating to the development.

The value assigned to IPR&D was determined by considering the importance of each project to the overall development plan, estimating costs to develop the purchased IPR&D into commercially viable products, estimating the resulting net cash flows from the projects when completed and discounting the net cash flows to their present value. The revenue estimates used to value the purchased IPR&D were based on estimates of the relevant market sizes and growth factors, expected trends in technology and the nature and expected timing of new product introductions by Compaq and its competitors.

The rates utilized to discount the net cash flows to their present values were based on Compaq's weighted average cost of capital. The weighted average cost of capital was adjusted to reflect the difficulties and uncertainties in completing each project and thereby achieving technological feasibility, the percentage-of-completion of each project, anticipated market acceptance and penetration, market growth rates and risks related to the impact of potential changes in future target markets. Based on these factors, discount rates that range from 25%–42% were deemed appropriate for valuing the IPR&D.

IPR&D refers to acquired projects that have not yet reached technological feasibility at the acquisition date, and for which no alternative uses exist. They might have been useful to the acquired company, but are not to the investor, perhaps because they do not fit into the investor's strategic plans.

Excessive allocation of a purchase price to IPR&D artificially reduces current period income and inflates income in successive periods (by the elimination of future depreciation or amortization expense). The SEC monitors purchase allocations closely and challenges those with which it disagrees. As a result of these reviews, a number of companies have subsequently been forced to restate the amounts of their initial IPR&D write-offs. (The FASB recently issued an exposure draft that proposes that IPR&D no longer be expensed at acquisition; instead, the proposal is to record IPR&D as an intangible asset that is subsequently tested for impairment.)

Reporting Subsidiary Stock Issuances

Subsidiaries can issue stock, just like their parent companies do. If issued to outside investors, the result is an infusion of cash into the subsidiary and a reduction in the percentage of the company owned by the parent company. For example, Citigroup Inc. reports the following stock issuance in its 10-K report by one of its subsidiaries.

Travelers Property Casualty Corp. (an indirect wholly owned subsidiary of Citigroup on December 31, 2001) sold 231 million shares of its class A common stock representing approximately 23.1% of its outstanding equity securities in an initial public offering (the IPO) on March 27, 2002. In 2002, Citigroup recognized an after-tax gain of $1.158 billion as a result of the IPO.

Gains on subsidiary stock issuances result from an increase in the investment balance on the parent's balance sheet.

To illustrate, assume that an investor company owns 100% of its investee company and the latter has a book value of stockholders' equity of $500. The investment on the parent's balance sheet, using the equity method, is at $500 (assuming the investment was acquired at book value). Next, assume that the investee company issues previously unissued shares to outsiders for $100 and, in doing so, reduces the investor company's ownership to 90%. The investor company now owns 90% of a subsidiary with a book value of $600 for an investment equivalent of $540 (90% × $600). The value of its investment account has, thus, risen by $40 ($540 vs. $500).

The SEC allows the parent company to report this increase in the book value of the investment as either a gain in the computation of net income (with a consequent increase in retained earnings), as Citigroup did, or as an increase in additional paid-in capital. **Barnes & Noble**'s IPO of its **GameStop** subsidiary provides an example of the latter alternative method as follows.

> GameStop completed an initial public offering of shares of its Class A common stock at a price of $18.00 per share, raising net proceeds of approximately $348,000. The Company recorded an increase in additional paid-in capital of $155,490 ($90,184 after taxes), representing the Company's incremental share in the equity of GameStop.

Although equity of the parent company is the same under both accounting methods, recognition of the gain boosts reported income. We need to be aware of this transitory, nonoperating component of income—most analysts exclude it from the net operating profit (NOPAT) computation for analysis purposes.

Limitations of Consolidation Reporting

Consolidation of financial statements is meant to present a financial picture of the entire set of companies under control of the parent. Because investors typically purchase stock in the parent company and not in the subsidiaries, the view is more relevant than would be one of the parent company's own balance sheet with subsidiaries reported as equity investments. Still, we must be aware of certain limitations that the consolidation process entails:

1. Consolidated income does not imply that cash is received by the parent company and is available for subsidiaries. The parent can only receive cash via dividend payments. It is quite possible, therefore, for an individual subsidiary to experience cash flow problems even though the consolidated group has strong cash flows. Likewise, debts of a subsidiary are not obligations of the consolidated group. Thus, even if the consolidated balance sheet is strong, creditors of a failing subsidiary are often unable to sue the parent or other subsidiaries to recoup losses.

2. Consolidated balance sheets and income statements are a mix of the subsidiaries, often from different industries. Comparisons across companies, even if in similar industries, are often complicated by the different mix of subsidiary companies.

3. Segment disclosures on individual subsidiaries are affected by intercorporate transfer pricing policies that can artificially inflate the profitability of one segment at the expense of another. Companies also have considerable discretion in the allocation of corporate overhead to subsidiaries, which can markedly affect segment and subsidiary profitability.

BUSINESS INSIGHT

HP's Post-Acquisition Accounting under Fire   Post-acquisition accounting can get complicated. Consider the following critique in *The Wall Street Journal's* Heard on the Street column (March 5, 2003) regarding HP's earnings release.

> IT DOESN'T TAKE an H-P 12C calculator to figure out that the fiscal-first-quarter earnings improvement touted by **Hewlett-Packard Co.** for its personal-computing business may not be as impressive as it appears . . . they are just doing some simple math. They are adding back in estimates of certain expenses—such as research-and-development and corporate-governance costs—that H-P moved out of the profit calculation for the business in the quarter ended Jan. 31, in contrast to earlier quarters. H-P executives had held aloft the PC unit's

(Continued on the next page)

profitability—$33 million, the first in-the-black result in about two years—to highlight how its contentious, [$24.2 billion] acquisition of Compaq Computer Corp. last year had paid off.

The upshot: H-P's PC unit, as well as a few other divisions, looked quite a bit healthier. To get a sense of the effect of the changes, consider that, before the recategorizations, H-P's PC business posted a full-year 2002 operating loss of $532 million. But after taking the reclassifications into account, the PC group's fiscal 2002 loss narrowed to $372 million, according to H-P. In other words, the loss shrinks by an average of $40 million a quarter, a pretty hefty sum when compared with the segment's most-recent quarterly profit of $33 million.... Mr. Wayman, H-P's chief financial officer, says of the reclassifications: "This is just what happens when two large companies come together."

Reporting Consolidations under Pooling-of-Interests

Prior to 2001, companies had a choice in their accounting for business combinations. They could use the *purchase method* as described in this chapter (now required for all acquisitions), or they could use the *pooling-of-interests (pooling) method.* A large number of acquisitions were accounted for under pooling-of-interest, and its impact on financial statements will linger for many years.

The main difference between the pooling-of-interest and the purchase method of accounting for acquisitions is this: under the purchase method the investment account is initially recorded at the *fair market value* of the acquired company at acquisition. Under the pooling-of-interest method, the investment account is initially recorded at the *book value* of equity for the acquired company, regardless of the amount of purchase price. As a result, no goodwill is created. Further, because goodwill amortization was required under previous GAAP, subsequent income was larger under pooling in part because no goodwill amortization was recorded. This feature spawned widespread use of the pooling-of-interest, especially for high-tech companies.

Acquisitions previously accounted for under pooling-of-interest remain unaffected under current GAAP. Therefore, we must be aware of at least two points for analysis purposes:

1. Assets were usually understated when using pooling-of-interest because investee companies were recorded at book rather than market value. This implies that consolidated asset turnover ratios are overstated.

2. Incomes of companies using pooling-of-interest were nearly always overstated due to elimination of goodwill amortization. This continues to create difficulties for comparative analysis when looking at companies that previously applied pooling-of-interest accounting.

CHAPTER-END REVIEW

On January 1 of the current year, Bradshaw Company purchased all of the common shares of Dukes Company for $600,000 cash—this is $200,000 in excess of Dukes' book value of its equity. The balance sheets of the two firms immediately after the acquisition follow:

	Bradshaw (Parent)	Dukes (Subsidiary)	Consolidating Adjustments	Consolidated
Current assets	$1,000,000	$100,000		
Investment in Dukes	600,000	—		
PPE, net	3,000,000	400,000		
Goodwill	—	—		
Total assets	$4,600,000	$500,000		
Liabilities	$1,000,000	$100,000		
Contributed capital	2,000,000	200,000		
Retained earnings	1,600,000	200,000		
Total liabilities and equity	$4,600,000	$500,000		

During purchase negotiations, Dukes' PPE was appraised at $500,000, and all of Duke's remaining assets and liabilities were appraised at values approximating their book values. Also, Bradshaw concluded that payment of an additional $100,000 was warranted because of anticipated corporate synergies. Prepare the appropriate journal entry, post the journal entry to the related t-account, record the impact of the transaction in the financial statement effects template, and prepare the consolidated balance sheet at acquisition.

Solution

PPE, net (+A)	100,000	
Goodwill (+A)	100,000	
Dukes common stock (−SE)	200,000	
Retained earnings (−SE)	200,000	
Investment in Dukes (−A)		600,000

+ PPE (A) −	+ Goodwill (A) −	− Dukes Common Stock (SE) +
(1) 100,000	(1) 100,000	(1) 200,000

− Retained Earnings (SE) +	+ Investment Dukes (A) −
(1) 200,000	600,000 (1)

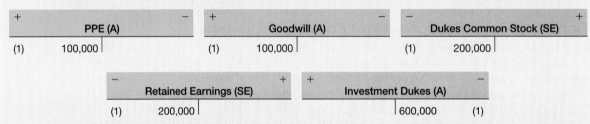

	Balance Sheet					Income Statement		
Transaction	Cash Asset	+ Noncash Assets	= Liabilities	+ Contrib. Capital	+ Retained Earnings	Revenues	− Expenses	= Net Income
Consolidation Adjustment for Bradshaw		+100,000 PPE, net +100,000 Goodwill −600,000 Invest. in Dukes	=	−200,000 Dukes Common Stock	−200,000 Dukes Retained Earnings			=

	Bradshaw (Parent)	Dukes (Subsidiary)	Consolidating Adjustments	Consolidated
Current assets	$1,000,000	$100,000		$1,100,000
Investment in Dukes	600,000	—	$(600,000)	
PPE, net	3,000,000	400,000	100,000	3,500,000
Goodwill	—	—	100,000	100,000
Total assets	$4,600,000	$500,000		$4,700,000
Liabilities	$1,000,000	$100,000		$1,100,000
Contributed capital	2,000,000	200,000	(200,000)	2,000,000
Retained earnings	1,600,000	200,000	(200,000)	1,600,000
Total liabilities and equity	$4,600,000	$500,000		$4,700,000

Notes: The $600,000 investment account is eliminated together with the $400,000 book value of Dukes' equity to which it mainly relates. The remaining $200,000 consists of the additional $100,000 in PPE assets and the $100,000 in goodwill from expected corporate synergies. Following these adjustments, the balance sheet items are summed to yield the consolidated balance sheet.

SUMMARY

LO1   **Explain and interpret the three levels of investor influence over an investee-passive, significant, and controlling. (p. 519)**

■   Ownership of 20% or less in another corporation is treated as a passive investment by the investor.

■ Significance influence is assumed to be available to the investor corporation if it owns more than 20% but not over 50% of the outstanding voting stock of the investee corporation.

■ Control is generally presumed if the investing firm owns more than 50% of the outstanding voting stock of the investee corporation.

Describe and analyze accounting for passive investments. (p. 520)   LO2

■ Ownership of 20% or less in another corporation is treated as a passive investment by the investor. Investing for returns is the objective rather than influencing another corporation's decisions. The investment is reported as a long-term asset only if the intention is to retain the asset for longer that a year. Passive investments are segregated into two types called, trading securities or securities available for sale.

■ Trading securities are securities that will be converted into cash in a very short period of time, typically less than a week. Any trading securities held at the end of an accounting period are marked to their market value. The value change is recognized as an unrealized gain (or loss) in the income statement.

■ Available for sale securities are held for long-tem capital gains or dividends. Any securities held at the end of an accounting period are also marked to their market value. However, the value change bypasses the income statement to become part of retained earnings called other comprehensive income.

■ Gains, losses realized on sale and dividends on passive investments are reported as other income in the income statement.

■ Debt securities that management intends to hold to maturity are carried at cost unless their value is considered impaired in which case the security is written down. Otherwise changes in market value are not recognized on the balance sheet or the income statement.

Explain and analyze accounting for investments with significant influence. (p. 529)   LO3

■ Significance influence is assumed to be available to the investor corporation if it owns more than 20% but not over 50% of the outstanding voting stock of the investee corporation. Typically, the investment is initially recorded as a long-term asset at the purchase price.

■ In the case of significant influence, the equity method of reporting is followed.

■ Under the equity method, the investor corporation reports the investment as a, typically, long-term asset. The investor recognizes its proportionate share of the investee's net income as income and an increase in the investment account. Any dividends received by the investor are treated as a recovery of the investment and reduce the investment balance.

Describe and analyze accounting for investments with control. (p. 534)   LO4

■ If a corporation is considered to have control of another corporation, the financial statements of both firms are consolidated and reported as though they were a single entity.

■ Control is generally presumed if the investing firm owns more than 50% of the outstanding voting stock of the investee corporation.

■ Control can exist in special cases with less than 50% of the outstanding voting stock of the investee. Control means that the investor has the ability to affect the strategic direction of the investee.

Illustrate and analyze accounting mechanics for equity method investments. (p. 546)   LO5

■ Under the equity method of accounting, neither the investee's assets nor its liabilities are reported on the investor's balance sheet. Only the proportionate investment is reported. Further, only the investor's net equity is reported in income; and the investee's sales and expenses are omitted;

■ The result is that revenues and expenses, but not NOPAT, are understated; NOPM (NOPAT/ Sales) is overstated; and net operating assets (NOA) and nonoperating liabilities are understated. Also, net financial obligations (NFO) and financial leverage (FLEV) are understated. ROE remains unaffected.

Apply equity method accounting mechanics to consolidations. (p. 547)   LO6

■ Identifiable intangible assets (such as patents, trademarks, customer lists) often result from the acquisition of one corporation by another. This is a situation in which the acquirer will have control and the consolidation accounting is required.

■ Intangibles are valued at the purchase date and then amortized over their economic life. Any remaining purchase price not allocated to tangible or identifiable intangible assets is treated as goodwill.

■ Goodwill is not amortized but is written down when and if considered impaired. The write-down is an expense of the period.

■ Reports of consolidated corporation are often difficult to understand because they commingle the assets, liabilities, revenues, expenses and cash flows of several businesses that can be very different. General Motors and its finance subsidiary (GMAC) provide an example.

LO7 **Discuss the reporting of derivative securities. (p. 549)**

- Derivatives refer to financial instruments that are utilized by companies to reduce various kinds of risks.

- Derivatives work by offsetting the gain or loss for the asset or liability to which they relate.

- The accounting for derivatives boils down to this: the derivative contract and the asset or liability to which it relates are both reported on the balance sheet at market value. The Asset and liability are offsetting if the hedge is effective. Likewise, the related gains and losses are largely offsetting, leaving income unaffected.

GUIDANCE ANSWERS

YOU MAKE THE CALL

You Are the Chief Financial Officer   Capacity utilization is important. If long-term operating assets are not sufficiently utilized, cost per unit produced is too high. Cost per unit does not relate solely to manufacturing products, but also applies to the cost of providing services and many other operating activities. However, if we purchase assets with little productive slack, our costs of production at peak levels can be excessive. Further, the company may be unable to service peak demand and risk losing customers. In response, many companies have explored alliances. These take many forms. Some require a simple contract to use another company's manufacturing, service, or administrative capability for a fee (note: these executory contracts are not recorded under GAAP). Another type of alliance is that of a joint venture to share ownership of manufacturing or IT facilities. In this case, if demand can be coordinated with that of a partner, perhaps operating assets can be more effectively used. Finally, a variable interest entity (VIE) can be formed to acquire the asset for use by the company and its partner.

APPENDIX 12A   Equity Method Mechanics

LO5 Apply equity method accounting mechanics to consolidations.

The appendix provides a comprehensive example of accounting for an equity method investment. Assume that Petroni Company acquires a 30% interest in the outstanding voting shares of Wahlen Company on January 1, 2005 for $234,000 in cash. On that date, Wahlen's book value of equity is $560,000. Petroni agrees to pay $234,000 for a company with a book value of equity equivalent to $168,000 ($560,000 × 30%) because it feels that (1) Wahlen's balance sheet is undervalued by $140,000 (Petroni estimates PPE is undervalued by $50,000 and that Wahlen has unrecorded patents valued at $90,000) and (2) the investment is expected to yield intangible benefits valued at $24,000. (The $140,000 by which the balance sheet is undervalued translates into an investment equivalent of $42,000 [$140,000 x 30%]. This, plus the intangible benefits valued at $24,000, comprises the $66,000 difference between the purchase price ($234,000) and the book value equivalent [$168,000].)

The effect of the investment on Petroni's books is to reduce cash by $234,000 and to report the investment in Wahlen for $234,000. The investment is reported at its fair market value at acquisition, just like all other asset acquisitions, and it is reported as a noncurrent asset since the expected holding period of equity method investments is in excess of one year. Subsequent to this purchase there are three main aspects of equity method accounting:

1. Dividends received from the investee are treated as a return *of* the investment rather than a return *on* the investment (investor company records an increase in cash received and a decrease in the investment account).

2. When the investee company reports net income for a period, the investor company reports its percentage owner-ship of that income. This is usually reported in the other income section of its income statement. Thus, both equity and the investment account increase from equity method income. If the investee company reports a net *loss* for the period, income of the investor company is reduced as well as its investment account by its proportionate share.

3. The investment balance is not marked-to-market as with passive investments. Instead, it is recorded at its historical cost and is increased (decreased) by the investor company's proportionate share of investee income (loss) and decreased by any cash dividends received. Unrecognized gains (losses) can, therefore, occur if the market value of the investment differs from this adjusted cost.

To illustrate these mechanics, let's return to our illustration and assume that subsequent to acquisition, Wahlen reports net income of $50,000 and pays $10,000 cash dividends. Petroni's balance sheet and income statement are impacted as follows:

Transaction	Change in Investment Account on Petroni's Balance Sheet	Equity Income on Petroni's Income Statement
Acquisition balance	$234,000	
Wahlen reports income of $50,000 (30% for Petroni)	15,000	$15,000
Wahlen pays a $10,000 cash dividend ($3,000 to Petroni)	(3,000)	
Updated balance	$246,000	

Petroni's ending investment balance is $246,000 and its cash balance increased by the $3,000 dividend received (note, the market value of the investment ($234,000) differs from its book value ($168,000). Corresponding to the $15,000 increase in assets from Wahlen's income is a $15,000 increase in retained earnings (following the reporting of income to retained earnings). Petroni reports this $15,000 as investment income. Dividends received are treated as a return of the capital invested in Wahlen and, thus, the investment account is reduced.

There is symmetry between Petroni's investment account and Wahlen's stockholders' equity as follows:

Investment Account on Petroni's Balance Sheet		Wahlen's Stockholders' Equity	
Acquisition balance	$234,000	Acquisition balance	$560,000
Income	15,000	Income	50,000
Dividends	(3,000)	Dividends	(10,000)
Ending balance	$246,000	Ending balance	$600,000

Petroni's ending investment balance of $246,000 is 30% of Wahlen's $600,000 stockholders' equity plus the original $66,000 excess. This explains why the equity investment balance we see reported on a balance sheet does not always equal the percentage owned of the investee company.[6]

A P P E N D I X   12B   Consolidation Accounting Mechanics

This appendix is a continuation of the example we introduced in Appendix 12A, extended to the consolidation of a parent company and one wholly owned subsidiary. Assume that Petroni Company acquires 100 percent (rather than 30% as in Appendix 12A) of the outstanding voting shares of Wahlen Company on January 1, 2005. To obtain these shares, Petroni pays $420,000 cash and issues 20,000 shares of its $10 par value common stock. On this date, Petroni's stock has a fair market value of $18 per share, and Wahlen's book value of equity is $560,000. Petroni is willing to pay $780,000 ($420,000 plus 20,000 shares at $18 per share) for this company with a book value of equity of $560,000 because it believes Wahlen's balance sheet is understated by $140,000 (its PPE is undervalued by $50,000 and it has unrecorded patents valued at $90,000). The remaining $80,000 of the purchase price excess over book value is ascribed to corporate synergies and other unidentifiable intangible assets (goodwill). Thus, the purchase price consists of the following three components:

LO6 Apply equity method accounting mechanics to consolidations.

Investment ($780,000)
{
Book value of Wahlen ($560,000)

Excess fair market value over book ($140,000)

Goodwill ($80,000)
}

The investment in Wahlen on Petroni's books is accounted for using the equity method of accounting.[7] This means that at acquisition, Petroni's assets (investments) increase by $780,000 and its equity (contributed capital) increases by the same amount. The balance sheets of Petroni and Wahlen at acquisition follow, including the adjustments that occur in the consolidation process and the ultimate consolidated balance sheet.

---

[6]To the extent that the excess is attributed to depreciable (amortizable) assets of the subsidiary, the excess is depreciated (amortized) and that amount is reflected in the parent's income statement as expense. Eventually, the excess is entirely depreciated (amortized) and the investment balance equals the percentage owned (30%) of the subsidiary's stockholders' equity with no excess. Any portion of the excess attributed to goodwill is not amortized, resulting in a permanent difference unless and until the goodwill is deemed to be impaired and written down.

[7]The equity method is used for all investments other than passive investments. Once "control" is achieved, the investor company is required to consolidate its financial statements with those of other entities in the control set. The investment account remains unchanged on the parent's books, it is merely replaced with the assets and liabilities of the subsidiaries to which it relates for the consolidation process.

Transaction	Balance Sheet						Income Statement		
	Cash Asset	+ Noncash Assets	= Liabil-ities	+ Contrib. Capital	+ Retained Earnings		Revenues	− Expenses =	Net Income
Entry S		−560,000 = Investment in Wahlen		−80,000 Wahlen Common	−480,000 Wahlen Retained Earnings				=
Entry A		+50,000 = PPE net +80,000 Goodwill +90,000 Patent −220,000 Investment in Wahlen							=

Accounts	Petroni Company	Wahlen Company	Consolidation Adjustments*		Consolidated Balance Sheet
Cash	$ 168,000	$ 80,000			$ 248,000
Receivables, net	320,000	180,000			500,000
Inventory	440,000	260,000			700,000
Investment in Wahlen	780,000	0	[S]	(560,000)	0
			[A]	(220,000)	
Land	200,000	120,000			320,000
PPE, net	1,040,000	320,000	[A]	50,000	1,410,000
Patent	0	0	[A]	90,000	90,000
Goodwill	0	0	[A]	80,000	80,000
Totals	$2,948,000	$960,000			$3,348,000
Accounts payable	$ 320,000	$ 60,000			$ 380,000
Long-term liabilities	760,000	340,000			1,100,000
Contributed capital	1,148,000	80,000	[S]	(80,000)	1,148,000
Retained earnings	720,000	480,000	[S]	(480,000)	720,000
Totals	$2,948,000	$960,000			$3,348,000

*[S] refers to elimination of stockholders' equity and [A] refers to recognition of assets acquired.

The initial balance of the investment account at acquisition ($780,000) reflects the $700,000 market value of Wahlen's net tangible assets ($560,000 book value + $140,000 undervaluation of assets) plus the goodwill ($80,000) acquired. Goodwill is the excess of the purchase price over the fair market of the net assets acquired. It does not appear on Petroni's balance sheet as an explicit asset at this point. It is, however, included in the investment balance and will emerge as a separate asset during consolidation.

The process of completing the initial consolidated balance sheet involves eliminating the investment account and replacing it with the assets and liabilities of Wahlen Company to which it relates. Recall the investment account consists of three items: the book value of Wahlen ($560,000), the excess of market price over book value ($140,000), and goodwill ($80,000). The consolidation process eliminates each item as follows:

[S] Elimination of Wahlen's book value of equity: Investment account is reduced by the $560,000 book value of Wahlen, and each of the components of Wahlen's equity ($80,000 common stock and $480,000 retained earnings) are eliminated.

[A] Elimination of the excess of purchase price over book value: Investment account is reduced by $220,000. The remaining adjustments increase assets (A) by the additional purchase price paid. PPE is written up by $50,000, and a $90,000 patent asset and an $80,000 goodwill asset are reported.

Consolidation is similar in successive periods. To the extent that the excess purchase price has been assigned to depreciable assets, or identifiable intangible assets that are amortized over their useful lives, the new assets recognized initially are depreciated. For example, if the PPE has an estimated life of 20 years with no salvage value, we can depreciate 1/20 of the $50,000 each year. Likewise, the $90,000 patent is amortized over its remaining life. Depreciation and amortization are reflected in Petroni's income statement (depreciation of the book value portion is on Wahlen's income statement). Finally, because goodwill is not amortized under GAAP, it remains at its carrying amount of $80,000 on the consolidated balance sheet unless and until it is impaired and written down.

As the excess of the purchase price over book value acquired is depreciated/amortized, the investment account gradually declines. Assuming goodwill is not impaired, the investment reaches a balance equal to the percentage of the investee's equity owned (100% in this case) plus the balance of goodwill. Generally, the investment account equals the percentage of the equity owned plus any remaining undepreciated/unamortized excess over purchase price.

APPENDIX 12C   Accounting for Derivatives

Derivatives refer to financial instruments that are utilized by companies to reduce various kinds of risks. Some examples follow:

LO7 Discuss the reporting of derivative securities

- A company expects to purchase raw materials for its production process and wants to reduce the risk that the purchase price increases prior to the purchase.
- A company has an accounts receivable on its books that is payable in a foreign currency and wants to reduce the risk that exchange rates move unfavorably prior to collection.
- A company borrows funds on a floating rate of interest (such as linked to the prime rate) and wants to convert the loan to a fixed rate of interest.

Companies are commonly exposed to these and many similar types of risk. Although companies are generally willing to assume the normal market risks that are inherent in their business, many of these financial-type risks can add variability to income and are uncontrollable. Fortunately, commodities, currencies, and interest rates are all traded on various markets and, further, securities have been developed to manage all of these risks. These securities fall under the label of derivatives. They include forward contracts, futures contracts, option contracts, and swap agreements.

Companies use derivatives to manage many of these financial risks. The reduction of risk comes at a price: the fee that another party (called the counterparty) is charging to assume that risk. Most counterparties are financial institutions, and managing financial risk is their business and a source of their profits. Although derivatives can be used effectively to manage financial risk, they can also be used for speculation with potentially disastrous results. It is for this reason that regulators passed standards regarding their disclosure in financial statements.

Reporting of Derivatives

Derivatives work by offsetting the gain or loss for the asset or liability to which they relate. Derivatives thus shelter the company from such fluctuations. For example, if a hedged receivable denominated in a foreign currency declines in value (due to a strengthening of the $US), the derivative security will increase in value by an offsetting amount, at least in theory. As a result, net equity remains unaffected and no gain or loss arises, nor is a loss reported in income.[8]

Although accounting for derivatives is complex, it essentially boils down to this: the derivative contract, and the asset or liability to which it relates, are both reported on the balance sheet at market value. The asset and liability are offsetting *if* the hedge is effective and, thus, net equity is unaffected. Likewise, the related gains and losses are largely offsetting, leaving income unaffected. Income is impacted only to the extent that the hedging activities are ineffective or result from speculative activities. It is this latter activity, in particular, that regulators were concerned about in formulating accounting standards for derivatives.

Disclosure of Derivatives

Companies are required to disclose both qualitative and quantitative information about derivatives in notes to their financial statements and elsewhere (usually in Management's Discussion and Analysis section). The aim of these disclosures is to inform outsiders about potential risks underlying derivative securities.

Following is **Midwest Air**'s disclosures from its 10-K report relating to its use of derivatives.

Derivative Instruments and Hedging Activities
The Company periodically utilizes option contracts to mitigate the exposure to the fluctuation in aircraft fuel prices in accordance with the Company's financial risk management policy. This policy was adopted by the Company to document

---

[8]Unrealized gains and losses on derivatives classified as *cash flow hedges* (such as those relating to planned purchases of commodities) are accumulated in other comprehensive income (OCI) and are not recognized in current income until the transaction is complete (such as when both the purchase and sale of inventory occurs). Unrealized gains and losses on derivatives classified as *fair value hedges* (such as those relating interest rate hedges and swaps, and the hedging of asset values such as relating to securities) as well as the changes in value of the hedged asset (liability) are recorded in current income.

the Company's philosophy toward financial risk and outline acceptable use of derivatives to mitigate that financial risk. The options establish ceiling prices for anticipated jet fuel purchases and serve as hedges of those purchases. The Company does not hold or issue derivative instruments for trading purposes. At December 31, 2002, the Company had options in place to hedge approximately 20% and 15% of its projected fuel purchases in the first quarter and second quarter of 2003, respectively. These contracts expired at various dates through June 30, 2003. At December 31, 2002, the options were valued at $1.0 million and are included in other prepaid expense in the consolidated balance sheet. The value of any options is determined using estimates of fair market value provided by major financial institutions. At December 31, 2003, the Company had no options for current or future periods.

The Company accounts for its fuel hedge derivative instruments as cash flow hedges, as defined in SFAS No. 133, "Accounting for Derivative Instruments and Hedging Activities" and the corresponding amendments under SFAS No. 138, "Accounting for Certain Derivative Instruments and Certain Hedging Activities." Therefore, all changes in the fair value of the derivative instruments that are considered effective are recorded in other comprehensive income until the underlying hedged fuel is consumed, when they are reclassified to the income statement as an offset of fuel expense. The Company reclassified $1.1 million and $1.5 million to the income statement in 2003 and 2002, respectively, as an offset to fuel expense when the hedges expired.

Midwest Air's derivative use is mainly to hedge against fuel cost. Those hedges act to place a ceiling on fuel cost and are used for about 15% to 20% of Midwest Air's fuel purchases.

From a reporting standpoint, unrealized gains and losses on these option contracts are accumulated in the Other Comprehensive Income (OCI) portion of its stockholders' equity until the fuel is purchased. Once that fuel is purchased, those unrealized gains and losses are removed from OCI and the gain (loss) on the option is used to offset the loss (gain) on fuel. In 2003, $1.1 million of hedging gains were used to offset fuel expense for Midwest Air.

Although the market value of derivatives and their related assets or liabilities can be large, the net effect on stockholders' equity is usually minor. This is because companies are mainly using them as hedges and not as speculative securities. SFAS 133, 'Accounting for derivative instruments and hedging activities,' was enacted in response to a concern that speculative activities were not adequately disclosed. However, subsequent to its passage the financial effects have been minimal. Either these companies were not speculating to the extent expected, or they have since reduced their level of speculation in response to increased scrutiny from better disclosures.

KEYTERMS

Available-for-sale (AFS) (p. 522)

Cost method (p. 525)

Equity method (p. 529)

Held-to-maturity (HTM) (p. 525)

In-process research & development (p. 541)

Mark-to-market (p. 522)

Market value (p. 521)

Minority interest (p. 535)

Pooling-of-interests (p. 543)

Purchase method (p. 543)

Significant influence (p. 529)

Trading securities (T) (p. 522)

MULTIPLE CHOICE

1. Corporation A owns 50% of corporation B. This is a case where:
   a. Corporation A controls corporation B.
   b. Corporation A does not control corporation B.
   c. Corporation A has significant influence on corporation B.
   d. Corporation A does not have a significant influence on corporation B.
   e. Both a and c are correct.

2. In accounting for available-for-sale securities, the
   a. Securities are reported at their market value, along with their market adjustment from cost.
   b. Securities are reported at cost.
   c. Increases in market value are reported in income.
   d. Increases in market value are not reported in income.
   e. Both a and d are correct.

3. Which of the following statements is true of investments accounted for under the equity method?
   a. Investor reports its percentage share of the investee's income in its operating income.
   b. Investor reports dividends received from the investee in its operating income.
   c. Investment is reported at its market value.

d. Investment is reported at cost plus any dividends received from the investee.

e. Investment is reported at market value less any dividends received from the investee.

4. Which of the following statements is true about goodwill?

a. Current reporting standards require that goodwill be amortized over its economic life.

b. Goodwill is written down when the market value of the investee implies a goodwill value below the investor's goodwill account.

c. Goodwill can be recognized only when the acquisition price does not exceed the value of the tangible and identifiable intangible assets acquired.

d. The recording of goodwill can be based on the acquisition of assets such as patents and trademarks.

e. Goodwill equals retained earnings.

Superscript ^{A}(^{B,C}) denotes assignments based on Appendix 12A (12B, 12C).

DISCUSSION QUESTIONS

Q12-1. What measure (fair market value or amortized cost) is used for the balance sheet to report (a) trading securities, (b) available-for-sale securities, and (c) held-to-maturity securities?

Q12-2. What is an unrealized holding gain (loss)? Explain.

Q12-3. Where are unrealized holding gains and losses related to trading securities reported in the financial statements? Where are unrealized holding gains and losses related to available-for-sale securities reported in the financial statements?

Q12-4. What does *significant influence* imply regarding intercorporate investments? Describe the accounting procedures used for such investments.

Q12-5. On January 1 of the current year, Yetman Company purchases 40% of the common stock of Livnat Company for $250,000 cash. During the year, Livnat reports $80,000 of net income and pays $60,000 in cash dividends. At year-end, what amount should appear in Yetman's balance sheet for its investment in Livnat?

Q12-6. What accounting method is used when a stock investment represents more than 50% of the investee company's voting stock? Explain.

Q12-7. What is the underlying objective of consolidated financial statements?

Q12-8. Finn Company purchases all of the common stock of Murray Company for $750,000 when Murray Company has $300,000 of common stock and $450,000 of retained earnings. If a consolidated balance sheet is prepared immediately after the acquisition, what amounts are eliminated in preparing it? Explain.

Q12-9.^{B} Bradshaw Company owns 100% of Dee Company. At year-end, Dee owes Bradshaw $75,000. If a consolidated balance sheet is prepared at year-end, how is the $75,000 handled? Explain.

Q12-10. What are some limitations of consolidated financial statements?

MINI EXERCISES

M12-11. Interpreting Disclosures of Available-for-Sale Securities (LO1, 2)

Use the following year-end footnote disclosure from **Pfizer**'s 10-K report to answer parts (a) and (b).　　　　Pfizer (PFE)

(Millions of Dollars)	2003
Cost of available-for-sale equity securities	($234)
Gross unrealized gains	263
Gross unrealized losses	(6)
Fair value of available-for-sale equity securities	$491

a. At what amount is its available-for-sale equity securities reported on Pfizer's 2003 balance sheet? Explain.

b. How is its net unrealized gain of $257 million ($263 million − $6 million) reported by Pfizer in its financial statements?

M12-12. Accounting for Available-for-Sale and Trading Securities   (LO2)

Assume that Wasley Company purchases 6,000 common shares of Pincus Company for $12 cash per share. During the year, Wasley receives a cash dividend of $1.10 per common share from Pincus, and the year-end market price of Pincus common stock is $13 per share. How much income does Wasley report relating to this investment for the year if it accounts for the investment as:

a.   Available-for-sale investment
b.   Trading investment

M12-13. Interpreting Disclosures of Investment Securities   (LO1, 2, 3, 4)

Abbot Laboratories
(ABT)

Abbott Laboratories reports the following disclosure relating to its December 31 after-tax comprehensive income. How is Abbott accounting for its investment in securities? How do you know?

Comprehensive Income, net of tax ($ 000s)	2003
Foreign currency translation adjustments	$1,162,004
Minimum pension liability adjustments, net of taxes of $57,219	(99,155)
Unrealized (losses) gains on marketable equity securities	106,673
Net (losses) gains on derivative instruments designated as cash flow hedges	3,550
Reclassification adjustments for realized (gains)	(20,538)
Other comprehensive income	1,152,534
Net earnings	2,753,233
Comprehensive income	$3,905,767

M12-14. Analyzing and Interpreting Equity Method Investments   (LO1, 3)

Stober Company purchases an investment in Lang Company at a purchase price of $1 million cash, representing 30% of the book value of Lang. During the year, Lang reports net income of $100,000 and pays cash dividends of $40,000. At the end of the year, the market value of Stober's investment is $1.2 million.

a.   At what amount is the investment reported on Stober's balance sheet at year-end?
b.   What amount of income from investments does Stober report? Explain.
c.   Stober's $200,000 unrealized gain in investment market value (choose one and explain):
    (1)   Is not reflected on either its income statement or balance sheet.
    (2)   Is reported in its current income.
    (3)   Is reported on its balance sheet only.
    (4)   Is reported in its other comprehensive income.
d.   Prepare journal entries to record the transactions and events above.
e.   Post the journal entries from *d* to their respective T-accounts.
f.   Record each of the transactions from *d* in the financial statement effects template.

M12-15. Computing Income for Equity Method Investments   (LO1, 3)

Kross Company purchases an equity investment in Penno Company at a purchase price of $5 million, representing 40% of the book value of Penno. During the current year, Penno reports net income of $600,000 and pays cash dividends of $200,000. At the end of the year, the market value of Kross's investment is $5.3 million. What amount of income does Kross report relating to this investment in Penno for the year? Explain.

M12-16. Interpreting Disclosures on Investments in Affiliates   (LO1, 3)

Merck (MRK)

Merck's 10-K report included the following footnote disclosure.

> **Joint Ventures and Other Equity Method Affiliates**   Investments in affiliates accounted for using the equity method . . . totaled $2.2 billion at December 31, 2003 and 2002, respectively. These amounts are reported in Other assets. Dividends and distributions received from these affiliates were $553.4 million in 2003, $488.6 million in 2002 and $572.2 million in 2001.

a.   At what amount are the equity method investments reported on Merck's balance sheet? Does this amount represent Merck's adjusted cost or market value?
b.   How does Merck account for the dividends received on these investments?

M12-17. Computing Consolidating Adjustments and Minority Interest   (LO1, 4)

Philipich Company purchases 80% of Hirst Company's common stock for $600,000 cash when Hirst Company has $300,000 of common stock and $450,000 of retained earnings. If a consolidated balance sheet is prepared immediately after the acquisition, what amounts are eliminated when preparing that statement? What amount of minority interest appears in the consolidated balance sheet?

M12-18. Computing Consolidated Net Income (LO1, 4)

Benartzi Company purchased a 90% interest in Liang Company on January 1 of the current year. Benartzi Company had $600,000 net income for the current year *before* recognizing its share of Liang Company's net income. If Liang Company had net income of $150,000 for the year, what is the consolidated net income for the year?

M12-19. Earnings under Pooling-of-Interest Method (LO1, 4)

DeFond Company acquired 100% of Verduzco Company on September 1 of the current year. Why might the consolidated earnings of the two companies for the current year be higher if the transaction had been treated as a pooling-of-interest (which is no longer accepted under GAAP) rather than as a purchase?

M12-20. Reporting of and Analyzing Financial Effects of Trading (Debt) Securities (LO1, 2)

Hartgraves Company had the following transactions and adjustments related to a bond investment.

2006

Oct. 1   Purchased $500,000 face value of Skyline, Inc.'s 7% bonds at 97 plus a brokerage commission of $1,000. The bonds pay interest on September 30 and March 31 and mature in 20 years. Hartgraves Company expects to sell the bonds in the near future.

Dec. 31   Made the adjusting entry to record interest earned on investment in the Skyline bonds.

31   Made the adjusting entry to record the current fair value of the Skyline bonds. At December 31, 2006, the market value of the Skyline bonds was $490,000.

2007

Mar. 31   Received the semiannual interest payment on investment in the Skyline bonds.

Apr. 1   Sold the Skyline bond investment for $492,300 cash.

a.   Prepare journal entries to record these transactions.
b.   Post the journal entries from *a* to their respective T-accounts.
c.   Record each of the transactions in the financial statement effects template.

M12-21. Reporting of and Analyzing Financial Effects of Trading (Equity) Securities (LO1, 2)

Blouin Company had the following transactions and adjustment related to a stock investment.

2006

Nov. 15   Purchased 6,000 shares of Lane, Inc.'s common stock at $12 per share plus a brokerage commission of $750. Blouin expects to sell the stock in the near future.

Dec. 22   Received a cash dividend of $1.10 per share of common stock from Lane.

31   Made the adjusting entry to reflect year-end fair value of the stock investment in Lane. The year-end market price of the Lane common stock is $11.25 per share.

2007

Jan. 20   Sold all 6,000 shares of the Lane common stock for $66,900.

a.   Prepare journal entries to record these transactions.
b.   Post the journal entries from *a* to their respective T-accounts.
c.   Record each of the transactions in the financial statement effects template.

M12-22. Reporting of and Analyzing Financial Effects of Available-for-Sale (Equity) Securities (LO1, 2)

Refer to the data for Blouin Company in Mini Exercise 12-21. Assume that when the shares were purchased, management did not intend to sell the stock in the near future. Record the transactions and adjustment for Blouin Company under this assumption. In addition, prepare any adjusting entry needed at December 31, 2007.

M12-23. Computing Stockholders' Equity in Consolidation (LO1, 4)

On January 1 of the current year, Halen Company purchased all of the common shares of Jolson Company for $575,000 cash. On this date, the stockholders' equity of Halen Company consisted of $600,000 in common stock and $310,000 in retained earnings. Jolson Company had $350,000 in common stock and $225,000 in retained earnings. What amount of total stockholders' equity appears on the consolidated balance sheet?

EXERCISES

E12-24. Assessing Financial Statement Effects of Trading and Available-for-Sale Securities (LO1, 2)

Four transactions involving investments in marketable securities classified as trading follow.

    (1) Purchased 6,000 common shares of Liu, Inc., for $12 cash per share.
    (2) Received a cash dividend of $1.10 per common share from Liu.
    (3) Year-end market price of Liu common stock is $11.25 per share.
    (4) Sold all 6,000 common shares of Liu for $66,900.

a. Prepare journal entries to record the four transactions,

b. Post the journal entries from *a* to their respective T-accounts, and

c. Record each of the transactions from *a* in the financial statement effects template.

d. Using the same transaction information as above and assuming the investments in marketable securities are classified as available-for-sale, (i) prepare journal entries to record the transactions, (ii) post the journal entries to their respective T-accounts, and (iii) record each of the transactions in the financial statement effects template.

E12-25. **Assessing Financial Statement Effects of Trading and Available-for-Sale Securities** (LO1, 2)

For the following transactions involving investments in marketable securities, assume that:

a. Investments are classified as trading.

    (1) Ohlson Co. purchases 5,000 common shares of Freeman Co. at $16 cash per share.
    (2) Ohlson Co. receives a cash dividend of $1.25 per common share from Freeman.
    (3) Year-end market price of Freeman common stock is $17.50 per share.
    (4) Ohlson Co. sells all 5,000 common shares of Freeman for $86,400 cash.

    (a) Prepare journal entries to record the four transactions, (b) Post the journal entries from *a* to their respective T-accounts, and (c) record each of the transactions from *a* in the financial statement effects template.

b. Investments are classified as available-for-sale (for same four transactions from *a*).

    (i) prepare journal entries to record the transactions, (ii) post the journal entries to their respective T-accounts, and (iii) record each of the transactions in the financial statement effects template.

E12-26. **Interpreting Footnotes on Security Investments** (LO1, 3)

Berkshire Hathaway
(BRKA)

Berkshire Hathaway reports the following footnotes with its 10-K report ($ millions).

Years Ended December 31	2003	2002	2001
Accumulated Other Comprehensive Income			
Unrealized appreciation of investments	$12,049	$ 3,140	$ (5,583)
Applicable income taxes	(4,158)	(1,147)	1,956
Reclassification adjustment for appreciation included in net earnings	(4,129)	(918)	(1,488)
Applicable income taxes	1,379	341	536
Foreign currency translation of adjustments and other	267	272	(114)
Applicable income taxes	(127)	(65)	24
Minimum pension liability adjustment	1	(279)	(35)
Applicable income taxes	(3)	29	12
Other	6	7	40
Other comprehensive income (loss)	5,285	1,380	(4,652)
Accumulated other comprehensive income at beginning of year	14,271	12,891	17,543
Accumulated other comprehensive income at end of year	$19,556	$14,271	$12,891

Investments in equity securities

Data with respect to investments in equity securities are shown below. Amounts are in millions.

American Express
Company (AXP)

The Coca-Cola
Company (KO)

The Gillette
Company (G)

Wells Fargo &
Company (WFC)

December 31, 2003	Cost	Unrealized Gains	Fair Value
Common stock of			
American Express Company	$1,470	$ 5,842	$ 7,312
The Coca-Cola Company	1,299	8,851	10,150
The Gillette Company	600	2,926	3,526
Wells Fargo & Company	463	2,861	3,324
Other equity securities	4,683	6,292	10,975
	$8,515	$26,772	$35,287

a. At what amount is its equity securities investment portfolio reported on its balance sheet? Does that amount include any unrealized gains or losses? Explain.

b. How is Berkshire Hathaway accounting for its equity securities investment portfolio—as an available-for-sale or trading portfolio? How do you know?

c. What does the number $12,049 represent in the Accumulated Other Comprehensive Income footnote? Is this number pretax or after-tax? Explain.

E12-27. Reporting of and Analyzing Financial Effects of Trading (Debt) Securities (LO1, 2)

Barclay, Inc., had the following transactions and adjustments related to a bond investment.

2006

Nov. 1   Purchased $300,000 face value of Joos, Inc.'s 9% bonds at 102 plus a brokerage commission of $900. The bonds pay interest on October 31 and April 30 and mature in 15 years. Barclay expects to sell the bonds in the near future.

Dec. 31   Made the adjusting entry to record interest earned on investment in the Joos bonds.

     31   Made the adjusting entry to record the current fair value of the Joos bonds. At December 31, 2006, the market value of the Joos bonds was $301,500.

2007

Apr. 30   Received the semiannual interest payment on investment in the Joos bonds.

May 1   Sold the Joos bond investment for $300,900 cash.

a. Prepare journal entries to record these transactions.

b. Post the journal entries from a to their respective T-accounts.

c. Record each of the transactions in the financial statement effects template.

E12-28. Reporting of Stockholders' Equity in Consolidation (LO1, 4)

Baylor Company purchased 75% of the common stock of Reed Company for $600,000 in cash when the stockholders' equity of Reed Company consisted of $500,000 in common stock and $300,000 in retained earnings. On the acquisition date, the stockholders' equity of Baylor Company consisted of $900,000 in common stock and $440,000 in retained earnings. Prepare the stockholders' equity section in the consolidated balance sheet as of the acquisition date.

E12-29. Interpreting Footnote Disclosures for Investments (LO1, 2)

CNA Financial Corporation provides the following footnote to its 10-K report:

Valuation of investments: CNA classifies its fixed maturity securities (bonds and redeemable preferred stocks) and its equity securities as available-for-sale, and as such, they are carried at fair value. The amortized cost of fixed maturity securities is adjusted for amortization of premiums and accretion of discounts to maturity, which are included in net investment income. Changes in fair value are reported as a component of other comprehensive income. Investments are written down to fair value and losses are recognized in income when a decline in value is determined to be other-than-temporary.

CNA Financial
Corporation (CNA)

Summary of Fixed Maturity and Equity Securities

December 31, 2003 (In millions)	Cost or Amortized Cost	Gross Unrealized Gains	Gross Unrealized Losses		Estimated Fair Value
			Less than 12 Months	Greater than 12 Months	
Fixed maturity securities					
U.S. Treasury securities and obligations of government agencies .	$ 1,823	$ 91	$ 10	$ 4	$ 1,900
Asset-backed securities	8,634	146	22	1	8,757
States, municipalities and political subdivisions—tax-exempt	7,787	207	22	2	7,970
Corporate securities	6,061	475	40	14	6,482
Other debt securities	2,961	311	4	4	3,264
Redeemable preferred stock	97	7	—	—	104
Options embedded in convertible debt securities	201	—	—	—	201
Total fixed maturity securities	27,564	1,237	98	25	28,678

(Continued on the next page)

(Continued from the previous page)

Summary of Fixed Maturity and Equity Securities *(Continued)*

December 31, 2003 (In millions)	Cost or Amortized Cost	Gross Unrealized Gains	**Gross Unrealized Losses**		Estimated Fair Value
			Less than 12 Months	Greater than 12 Months	
Equity securities					
Common stock	163	222	2	—	383
Nonredeemable preferred stock	130	16	2	—	144
Total equity securities	293	238	4	—	527
Total	$27,857	$1,475	$102	$25	$29,205

    a. At what amount is its investment portfolio reflected on its balance sheet? In your answer identify its market value, cost, and any unrealized gains and losses.

    b. How are its unrealized gains and/or losses reflected in CNA's balance sheet and income statement?

    c. How are any impairment losses and the gains and losses realized from the sale of securities reflected in CNA's balance sheet and income statement?

E12-30. Assessing Financial Statement Effects of Equity Method Securities (LO1, 3)

The following transactions involve investments in marketable securities and are accounted for using the equity method.

    (1) Purchased 12,000 common shares of Barth Co. at $9 cash per share; the shares represent 30% ownership in Barth.

    (2) Received a cash dividend of $1.25 per common share from Barth.

    (3) Recorded income from Barth stock investment when Barth's net income is $80,000.

    (4) Sold all 12,000 common shares of Barth for $120,500.

    a. Prepare journal entries to record these four transactions.

    b. Post the journal entries from *a* to their respective T-accounts.

    c. Record each of the transactions in the financial statement effects template.

E12-31. Assessing Financial Statement Effects of Equity Method Securities (LO1, 3)

The following transactions involve investments in marketable securities and are accounted for using the equity method.

    (1) Healy Co. purchases 15,000 common shares of Palepu Co. at $8 cash per share; the shares represent 25% ownership of Palepu.

    (2) Healy receives a cash dividend of $0.80 per common share from Palepu.

    (3) Palepu reports annual net income of $120,000.

    (4) Healy sells all 15,000 common shares of Palepu for $140,000 cash.

    a. Prepare journal entries to record these four transactions.

    b. Post the journal entries from *a* to their respective T-accounts.

    c. Record each of the transactions in the financial statement effects template.

E12-32. Assessing Financial Statement Effects of Passive and Equity Method Investments (LO1, 2, 3)

On January 1, 2005, Ball Corporation purchased, as a stock investment, 10,000 shares of Leftwich Company common stock for $15 cash per share. On December 31, 2005, Leftwich announced net income of $80,000 for the year and paid a cash dividend of $1.10 per share. At December 31, 2005, the market value of Leftwich's stock was $19 per share.

    a. Assume that the stock acquired by Ball represents 15% of Leftwich's voting stock and that Ball classifies it as available-for-sale. For the following transactions, prepare (1) journal entries, (2) post those journal entries to their respective T-accounts, and (3) record each of the transactions in the financial statement effects template.

        (1) Ball purchased 10,000 common shares of Leftwich at $15 cash per share; the shares represent a 15% ownership in Leftwich.

        (2) Leftwich reported annual net income of $80,000.

        (3) Received a cash dividend of $1.10 per common share from Leftwich.

        (4) Year-end market price of Leftwich common stock is $19 per share.

    b. Assume that the stock acquired by Ball represents 30% of Leftwich's voting stock and that Ball accounts for this investment using the equity method since it is able to exert significant influence. For the following transactions, prepare (1) journal entries, (2) post those journal entries to their respective T-accounts, and (3) record each of the transactions in the financial statement effects template.

(1) Ball purchased 10,000 common shares of Leftwich at $15 cash per share; the shares represent a 30% ownership in Leftwich.

(2) Leftwich reported annual net income of $80,000.

(3) Received a cash dividend of $1.10 per common share from Leftwich.

(4) Year-end market price of Leftwich common stock is $19 per share.

E12-33. Interpreting Equity Method Investment Footnotes (LO1, 3)

DuPont reports the following footnote to its 10-K report relating to its equity method investments ($ millions).   DuPont (DD)

Financial Position at December 31	2003	2002
Current assets	$3,367	$3,463
Noncurrent assets	5,441	5,814
Total assets	$8,808	$9,277
Short-term borrowings[1]	$1,339	$1,178
Other current liabilities	1,814	1,756
Long-term borrowings[1]	915	1,199
Other long-term liabilities	628	730
Total liabilities	4,696	4,863
DuPont's investment in affiliates (includes advances)	$1,304[2]	$2,047

[1]DuPont's pro rata interest in total borrowings was $1,004 in 2003 and $1,098 in 2002, of which $639 in 2003 and $681 in 2002 were guaranteed by the company.

[2]Reflects a $293 reduction in carrying values due to impairment charges recorded in 2003. In addition, $329 is excluded from the 2003 balance and reported as Assets held for sale on the Consolidated Balance Sheet.

a. DuPont reports its investment in equity method affiliates on its balance sheet at $1,304 million. Does this reflect the adjusted cost or market value of its interest in these companies?

b. Approximately what percentage does DuPont own, on average, of these affiliates? Explain.

c. DuPont reports that its equity interest in reported losses of these affiliates is approximately $55 million (46.8% of $118 million in net losses reported by these affiliates) in 2003, and that it received $58 million in dividends from these affiliates in 2003. Use this information, and the above footnote, to explain much of the change in the investment balance from $2,047 million in 2002 to $1,304 million in 2003.

d. How does use of the equity method impact DuPont's ROE and its components (asset turnover and profit margin)?

E12-34. Analyzing and Interpreting Disclosures on Equity Method Investments (LO1, 3)

Caterpillar, Inc. (CAT), owns 50% of Shin Caterpillar Mitsubishi, Ltd. It reports the investment on its balance sheet at $432 million, and provides the following footnote in its 10-K report.   Caterpillar, Inc. (CAT)
Shin Caterpillar Mitsubishi, Ltd.

The company's investment in affiliated companies accounted for by the equity method consists primarily of a 50% interest in Shin Caterpillar Mitsubishi Ltd. (SCM) located in Japan. Combined financial information of the unconsolidated affiliated companies accounted for by the equity method (generally on a three-month lag, e.g., SCM results reflect the periods ending September 30) was as follows:

Years Ended December 31 (Millions of Dollars)	2003	2002	2001
Results of operations			
Sales	$2,946	$2,734	$2,493
Cost of sales	2,283	2,168	1,971
Gross profit	663	566	522
Profit (loss)	$ 48	$ (1)	$ 9
Caterpillar's profit (loss)	$ 20	$ (4)	$ 3

(Continued on the next page)

(Continued from the previous page)

December 31 (Millions of Dollars)	2003	2002	2001
Financial position			
Assets			
Current assets	$1,494	$1,389	$1,451
Property, plant and equipment—net	961	1,209	986
Other assets	202	493	290
	2,657	3,091	2,727
Liabilities			
Current liabilities	$1,247	$1,117	$1,257
Long-term debt due after one year	343	808	414
Other liabilities	257	249	281
	1,847	2,174	1,952
Ownership	$810	$ 917	$ 775
Caterpillar's investment in unconsolidated affiliated companies			
Investment in equity method companies	$ 432	$ 437	$ 437
Plus: Investment in cost method companies	368	310	350
Investment in unconsolidated affiliated companies	$ 800	$ 747	$ 787

a. Did CAT acquire this investment at book value (with no goodwill)? Show computations supporting your response.

b. What assets and liabilities of SCM are omitted from CAT's balance sheet as a result of the equity method of accounting for this investment?

c. Do the liabilities of the investee company affect CAT? Explain.

d. How is use of the equity method impacting CAT's ROE and its components (asset turnover and profit margin)?

E12-35. Reporting of and Analyzing Financial Effects of Trading (Equity) Securities (LO1, 2)

Guay Company had the following transactions and adjustment related to a stock investment.

2006

Nov. 15   Purchased 5,000 shares of Core, Inc.'s common stock at $16 per share plus a brokerage commission of $900. Guay Company expects to sell the stock in the near future.

Dec. 22   Received a cash dividend of $1.25 per share of common stock from Core.

     31   Made the adjusting entry to reflect year-end fair value of the stock investment in Core. The year-end market price of the Core common stock is $17.50 per share.

2007

Jan. 20   Sold all 5,000 shares of the Core common stock for $86,400.

a. Prepare journal entries to record these transactions.

b. Post the journal entries from a to their respective T-accounts.

c. Record each of the transactions in the financial statement effects template.

E12-36. Reporting of and Analyzing Financial Effects of Available-for-Sale (Equity) Securities (LO1, 2)

Refer to the data for Guay Company in Exercise 12-35. Assume that when the shares were purchased, management did not intend to sell the stock in the near future. Record the transactions and adjustment for Guay Company under this assumption. In addition, prepare any adjusting entry needed at December 31, 2007.

E12-37. Reporting and Interpreting Stock Investment Performance (LO1, 2, 3)

Kasznik Company began operations in 2005 and, by year-end (December 31), had made six stock investments. Year-end information on these stock investments follows.

Company	Cost or Equity Basis (as appropriate)	Year-End Market Value	Market Classification
Barth, Inc.	$ 68,000	$ 65,300	Trading
Foster, Inc.	162,500	160,000	Trading
McNichols, Inc.	197,000	192,000	Available-for-sale

(Continued on the next page)

(Continued from the previous page)

Company	Cost or Equity Basis (as appropriate)	Year-End Market Value	Market Classification
Patell, Inc.	157,000	154,700	Available-for-sale
Ertimur, Inc.	100,000	102,400	Equity method
Soliman, Inc.	136,000	133,200	Equity method

a. At what total amount is the trading stock investments reported at in the December 31, 2005, balance sheet?

b. At what total amount is the available-for-sale stock investments reported at in the December 31, 2005, balance sheet?

c. At what total amount is the equity method stock investments reported at in the December 31, 2005, balance sheet?

d. What total amount of unrealized holding gains or unrealized holding losses related to stock investments appear in the 2005 income statement?

e. What total amount of unrealized holding gains or unrealized holding losses related to stock investments appear in the stockholders' equity section of the December 31, 2005, balance sheet?

f. What total amount of market value adjustment to stock investments appears in the December 31, 2005, balance sheet? Which category of stock investments does the market value adjustment relate to? Does the market value adjustment increase or decrease the financial statement presentation of these stock investments?

E12-38. **Interpreting Equity Method Investment Footnotes** (LO1, 3)

Abbott Laboratories reports the following footnote to its 10-K report:

Abbot Laboratories (ABT)

Equity Method Investments *(dollars in millions)* Abbott's 50 percent-owned joint venture, TAP Pharmaceutical Products Inc. (TAP), is accounted for under the equity method of accounting. The investment in TAP was $340, $370, and $392 at December 31, 2003, 2002, and 2001, respectively. Dividends received from TAP were $606, $695, and $433 in 2003, 2002, and 2001, respectively. Abbott's income from the TAP joint venture is recognized net of consolidating adjustments. Abbott performs certain administrative, selling and manufacturing services for TAP at negotiated rates that approximate fair market value for the services performed. Summarized financial information for TAP is as follows:

Year Ended December 31	2003	2002	2001
Net sales	$3,979.6	$4,037.4	$3,787.2
Cost of sales	1,066.8	884.1	938.6
Income before taxes	1,815.5	2,081.4	1,204.1
Net income	1,161.9	1,333.5	669.9

December 31	2003	2002	2001
Current assets	$1,451.6	$1,176.8	$1,191.2
Total assets	1,718.1	1,580.3	1,568.3
Current liabilities	965.8	791.6	713.1
Total liabilities	1,037.2	839.8	804.7

Undistributed earnings of investments accounted for under the equity method amounted to $315 as of December 31, 2003.

a. At what amount is Abbott's equity investment in TAP reported on Abbott's balance sheet? Confirm that this amount is equal to its proportionate share of TAP's equity.

b. How did the receipt of $606 in dividends from TAP affect Abbott's balance sheet and income statement?

c. How much income did Abbott report in 2003 relating to this investment in TAP?

d. Interpret the Abbott statement that "undistributed earnings of investments accounted for under the equity method amounted to $315 as of December 31, 2003."

e. How does use of the equity method impact Abbott's ROE and its components (asset turnover and profit margin)?

E12-39. Constructing the Consolidated Balance Sheet at Acquisition (LO1, 4)

On January 1 of the current year, Healy Company purchased all of the common shares of Miller Company for $500,000 cash. Balance sheets of the two firms at acquisition follow.

	Healy Company	Miller Company	Consolidating Adjustments	Consolidated
Current assets	$1,700,000	$120,000		
Investment in Miller	500,000	—		
Plant assets, net	3,000,000	410,000		
Goodwill	—	—		
Total assets	$5,200,000	$530,000		
Liabilities	$ 700,000	$ 90,000		
Contributed capital	3,500,000	400,000		
Retained earnings	1,000,000	40,000		
Total liabilities and equity	$5,200,000	$530,000		

During purchase negotiations, Miller's plant assets were appraised at $425,000; and, all of its remaining assets and liabilities were appraised at values approximating their book values. Healy also concluded that an additional $45,000 (in goodwill) demanded by Miller's shareholders was warranted because Miller's earning power was better than the industry average. (1) Prepare the consolidating adjustments, (2) Prepare the consolidated balance sheet at acquisition, (3) Prepare journal entries to record the transactions, (4) Post the journal entries to their respective T-accounts, and (5) Record each of the transactions in the financial statement effects template.

E12-40. Constructing the Consolidated Balance Sheet at Acquisition (LO1, 4)

Rayburn Company purchased all of Kanodia Company's common stock for cash on January 1, at which time the separate balance sheets of the two corporations appeared as follows:

	Rayburn Company	Kanodia Company	Consolidating Adjustments	Consolidated
Investment in Kanodia	$ 600,000	—		
Other assets	2,300,000	$700,000		
Goodwill	—	—		
Total assets	$2,900,000	$700,000		
Liabilities	$ 900,000	$160,000		
Contributed capital	1,400,000	300,000		
Retained earnings	600,000	240,000		
Total liabilities and equity	$2,900,000	$700,000		

During purchase negotiations, Rayburn determined that the appraised value of Kanodia's Other Assets was $720,000; and, all of its remaining assets and liabilities were appraised at values approximating their book values. The remaining $40,000 of the purchase price was ascribed to goodwill. (1) Prepare the consolidating adjustments, (2) Prepare the consolidated balance sheet at acquisition, (3) Prepare journal entries to record the transactions, (4) Post the journal entries to their respective T-accounts, and (5) Record each of the transactions in the financial statement effects template.

E12-41. Financial Statement Effects from a Subsidiary Stock Issuance (LO1, 4)

Ryan Company owns 80% of Lev Company. Information reported by Ryan Company and Lev Company as of January 1, 2005, follows:

Ryan Company	
Shares owned of Lev	40,000
Book value of investment in Lev	$320,000

Lev Company

Shares outstanding	50,000
Book value of equity	$400,000
Book value per share	$8

Assume Lev Company issues 30,000 additional shares of previously authorized but unissued common stock solely to outside investors (none to Ryan Company) for $12 cash per share. Indicate the financial statement effects of this stock issuance on Ryan Company using the following template (show computations) for both of the reporting options available under GAAP. Identify and explain both options.

	Balance Sheet						Income Statement		
Transaction	Cash Asset	+ Noncash Assets	= Liabil- ities	+ Contrib. Capital	+ Retained Earnings		Revenues	− Expenses =	Net Income
Lev Co. issues 30,000 shares (Option A)			=						=
Lev Co. issues 30,000 shares (Option B)			=						=

E12-42. Goodwill Impairment (LO1, 4)

On January 1, 2005, Engel Company purchases 100% of Ball Company for $16.8 million. At the time of acquisition, Ball's stockholders' equity is reported at $16.2 million. Engel ascribes the excess of $600,000 to goodwill. Assume that the market value of Ball declines to $12.5 million and that the fair market value of Ball's tangible net assets is estimated at $12.3 million as of December 31, 2005.

Required

a. Provide computations to determine if the goodwill has become impaired and, if so, the amount of the impairment.

b. What impact does the impairment of goodwill have on Engel's financial statements?

E12-43.[B] Constructing the Consolidated Balance Sheet at Acquisition (LO1, 4, 6)

Easton Company acquires 100 percent of the outstanding voting shares of Harris Company on January 1, 2005. To obtain these shares, Easton pays $210,000 in cash and issues 5,000 of its $10 par value common stock. On this date, Easton's stock has a fair market value of $36 per share, and Harris's book value of stockholders' equity is $280,000. Easton is willing to pay $390,000 for a company with a book value for equity of $280,000 because it believes that (1) Harris's buildings are undervalued by $40,000, and (2) Harris has an unrecorded patent that Easton values at $30,000. Easton considers the remaining balance sheet items to be fairly valued (no book-to-market difference). The remaining $40,000 of the purchase price excess over book value is ascribed to corporate synergies and other general unidentifiable intangible assets (goodwill). The January 1, 2005, balance sheets at the acquisition date follow:

	Easton Company	Harris Company	Consolidating Adjustments	Consolidated
Cash	$ 84,000	$ 40,000		
Receivables	160,000	90,000		
Inventory	220,000	130,000		
Investment in Harris	390,000	—		
Land	100,000	60,000		
Buildings, net	400,000	110,000		
Equipment, net	120,000	50,000		
Total assets	$1,474,000	$480,000		
Accounts payable	$ 160,000	$ 30,000		
Long-term liabilities	380,000	170,000		
Common stock	500,000	40,000		
Additional paid-in capital	74,000	—		
Retained earnings	360,000	240,000		
Total liabilities & equity	$1,474,000	$480,000		

Required

a. Show the breakdown of the investment into the book value acquired, the excess of fair value over book value, and the portion of the investment representing goodwill.

b. Prepare the consolidating adjustments and the consolidated balance sheet. Identify the adjustments by whether they relate to the elimination of stockholders' equity [S] or the excess of purchase price over book value [A].

c. How will the excess of the purchase price over book value acquired be treated in years subsequent to the acquisition?

E12-44.[C] **Reporting and Analyzing Derivatives (LO7)**

Hewlett Packard (HP)

Hewlett Packard reports the following schedule of comprehensive income (net income plus other comprehensive income) in its 2003 20-K report:

(In millions)	Accumulated Other Comprehensive Income (Loss)	Total
Net earnings		$2,539
Net unrealized gain on available-for-sale securities	$ 33	33
Net unrealized loss on derivative instruments	(48)	(48)
Reduction of minimum pension liability	211	211
Cumulative translation adjustment	2	2
Comprehensive income		$2,737

Required

a. Identify and describe the usual applications for derivatives.

b. How are derivatives and their related assets (and/or liabilities) reported on the balance sheet?

c. By what amount has the unrealized gain or loss on the HP derivatives affected its current income? What are the analysis implications?

PROBLEMS

P12-45. Analyzing and Interpreting Available-for-Sale Securities Disclosures   Following is a portion of the investments footnote from MetLife's 10-K report. Investment earnings are a crucial component of the financial performance of insurance companies such as MetLife, and investments comprise a large part of its assets. Met Life accounts for its bond investments as available-for-sale securities.

MetLife (MET)

December 31, 2002 ($ millions)	Cost or Amortized Cost	Gross Unrealized Gain	Gross Unrealized Loss	Estimated Fair Value
Fixed maturities—Bonds				
U.S. corporate securities	$ 47,021	$3,193	$ 957	$ 49,257
Mortgage-backed securities	33,256	1,649	22	34,883
Foreign corporate securities	18,001	1,435	207	19,229
U.S. treasuries/agencies	14,373	1,565	4	15,934
Asset-backed securities	9,483	228	208	9,503
Foreign government securities	7,012	636	52	7,596
States and political subdivisions	2,580	182	20	2,742
Other fixed income assets	609	191	103	697
Total bonds	$132,335	$9,079	$1,573	$139,841

December 31, 2001 ($ millions)	Cost or Amortized Cost	Gross Unrealized Gain	Gross Unrealized Loss	Estimated Fair Value
Fixed maturities—Bonds				
U.S. corporate securities	$ 43,141	$1,470	$ 748	$ 43,863
Mortgage-backed securities	25,506	866	192	26,180
Foreign corporate securities	16,836	688	539	16,985
U.S. treasuries/agencies	8,297	1,031	43	9,285
Asset-backed securities	8,115	154	206	8,063
Foreign government securities	5,488	544	37	5,995
States and political subdivisions	2,248	68	21	2,295
Other fixed income assets	1,874	238	142	1,970
Total bonds	$111,505	$5,059	$1,928	$114,636

MetLife also discloses the following for its net investment income and its realized gains (losses) on its fixed-income (bonds) portfolio.

Net Investment Income

The components of net investment income were as follows (dollars in millions):

Years Ended December 31,	2002	2001	2000
Fixed maturities	$8,384	$8,574	$8,538

Sales of fixed maturities and equity securities classified as available-for-sale were as follows

Years Ended December 31, ($ millions)	2002	2001	2000
Proceeds	$37,427	$28,105	$46,205
Gross investment gains	$ 1,661	$ 646	$ 599
Gross investment losses	$ (979)	$ (948)	$ (1,520)

Required

a. At what amount does MetLife's report its bond investments on its balance sheets for 2002 and 2001?

b. What are its net unrealized gains (losses) for 2002 and 2001? By what amount did these unrealized gains (losses) affect its reported income in 2002 and 2001?

c. What is the difference between *realized* and *unrealized* gains and losses? Are realized gains and losses treated differently in the income statement than unrealized gains and losses?

d. Many analysts compute a *mark-to-market investment return* as follows: Net investment income + Realized gains and losses + Change in unrealized gains and losses. Compute this mark-to-market investment return for 2002 and 2001 (note: unrealized gains were $1,677 million in 2000). Do you think that this metric provides insights into the performance of MetLife's investment portfolio beyond that which is included in GAAP income statements? Explain.

P12-46. Preparing the Consolidated Balance Sheet (LO1, 4)

On January 1, 2007, Gem Company purchased for $450,000 cash a 70% stock interest in Alpine, Inc., which then had common stock of $420,000 and retained earnings of $140,000. Balance sheets of the two companies immediately after the acquisition were as follows:

	Gem	Alpine
Current Assets	$200,000	$160,000
Stock Investment-Controlling (Alpine)	450,000	—
Plant and Equipment (net)	265,000	460,000
Total Assets	$915,000	$620,000
Liabilities	$ 50,000	$ 60,000
Common Stock	700,000	420,000
Retained Earnings	165,000	140,000
Total Liabilities and Stockholders' Equity	$915,000	$620,000

Sixty percent of the amount paid by Gem in excess of the equity acquired is attributed to undervalued plant and equipment; the other 40% is based on Alpine's potential for future superior earning power. Prepare the consolidated balance sheet on the acquisition date; include a column for consolidating adjustments (see Exhibits 12.5 and 12.6 for guidance).

E12-47. Purchase Price Allocation including In-Process R&D (LO1, 4)

Amgen Inc. (AMGN)

Amgen Inc., reports the following footnote to its 10-K report.

Immunex acquisition. On July 15, 2002, the Company acquired all of the outstanding common stock of Immunex in a transaction accounted for as a business combination. Immunex was a leading biotechnology company dedicated to developing immune system science to protect human health. The acquisition enhanced Amgen's strategic position within the biotechnology industry by strengthening and diversifying its (1) product base and product pipeline in key therapeutic areas, and (2) discovery research capabilities in proteins and antibodies. The purchase price was allocated to the tangible and identifiable intangible assets acquired and liabilities assumed based on their estimated fair values at the acquisition date. The following table summarizes the estimated fair values of the assets acquired and liabilities assumed as of the acquisition date (in millions):

Current assets, principally cash and marketable securities	$ 1,619.1
Deferred tax assets	200.2
Property, plant, and equipment	571.6
In-process research and development	2,991.8
Identifiable intangible assets, principally developed product technology and core technology	4,803.2
Goodwill	9,774.2
Other assets	26.2
Current liabilities	(579.0)
Deferred tax liabilities	(1,635.5)
Net assets	$17,771.8

The allocation of the purchase price was based, in part, on a third-party valuation of the fair values of in-process research and development, identifiable intangible assets, and certain property, plant, and equipment. The estimated fair value of the in-process R&D projects was determined based on the use of a discounted cash flow model. For each project, the estimated after-tax cash flows were probability weighted to take into account the stage of completion and the risks surrounding the successful development and commercialization. These cash flows were then discounted to a present value using discount rates ranging from 12% to 14%.

Required

a. Of the total assets acquired, what portion is allocated to tangible assets and what portion to intangible assets?

b. Are the assets (both tangible and intangible) of the acquired company reported on the consolidated balance sheet at the book value as reported on the acquired company's balance sheet immediately prior to the acquisition, or at the fair market value on the date of the acquisition? Explain.

c. How are the tangible and intangible assets accounted for subsequent to the acquisition?

d. Comment on the valuation of the in-process R&D and the accounting for this portion of the purchase price.

e. If the amount allocated to in-process R&D was decreased, what effect would this have on the allocation of the purchase price to the remaining acquired assets? What effect would this have on current and future earnings?

12-48. Analyzing and Reporting Debt Investment Performance (LO1, 2, 3)

Columbia Company began operations in 2006 and by year-end (December 31) had made six bond investments. Year-end information on these bond investments follows.

Company	Face Value	Cost or Amortized Cost	Year-End Market Value	Classification
Ling, Inc.	$100,000	$102,400	$105,300	Trading
Wren, Inc.	$250,000	$262,500	$270,000	Trading
Olanamic, Inc.	$200,000	$197,000	$199,000	Available for sale
Fossil, Inc.	$150,000	$154,000	$160,000	Available for sale
Meander, Inc.	$100,000	$101,200	$102,400	Held to maturity
Resin, Inc.	$140,000	$136,000	$137,000	Held to maturity

Required

a. At what total amount will the trading bond investments be reported in the December 31, 2006, balance sheet?

b. At what total amount will the available-for-sale bond investments be reported in the December 31, 2006, balance sheet?

c. At what total amount will the held-to-maturity bond investments be reported in the December 31, 2006, balance sheet?

d. What total amount of unrealized holding gains or unrealized holding losses related to bond investments will appear in the 2006 income statement?

e. What total amount of unrealized holding gains or unrealized holding losses related to bond investments will appear in the stockholders' equity section of the December 31, 2006, balance sheet?

f. What total amount of fair value adjustment to bond investments will appear in the December 31, 2006, balance sheet? Which category of bond investments does the fair value adjustment relate to? Does the fair value adjustment increase or decrease the financial statement presentation of these bond investments?

P12-49. Analyzing and Interpreting Disclosures on Consolidations (LO1, 4)

Caterpillar Inc. consists of two business units: the manufacturing company (parent corporation) and a wholly owned finance subsidiary. These two units are consolidated in Caterpillar's 10-K report. Following is a supplemental disclosure that Caterpillar includes in its 10-K report that shows the separate balance sheets of the parent and its subsidiary, as well as consolidating adjustments and the consolidated balance sheet presented to shareholders. This supplemental disclosure is not mandated under GAAP, but is voluntarily reported by Caterpillar as useful information for investors and creditors. Using this disclosure, answer the following requirements:

Caterpillar Inc. (CAT)

Required

a. Does each individual company (unit) maintain its own financial statements? Explain. Why does GAAP require consolidation instead of providing the financial statements of individual companies (units)?

b. What is the balance of Investments in Financial Products Subsidiaries as of December 31, 2003, on the parent's balance sheet? What is the equity balance of the financial products subsidiary to which this relates as of December 31, 2003? Do you see a relation? Will this relation always exist?

c. Refer to your answer for (a). How does the equity method of accounting for the investment in the subsidiary company obscure the actual financial condition of the parent company that is revealed in the consolidated financial statements?

d. Refer to the Consolidating Adjustments column reported—it is used to prepare the consolidated balance sheet. Generally, what do these adjustments accomplish?

e. Compare the consolidated balance of stockholders' equity with the stockholders' equity of the parent company (Machinery and Engines). Will the relation that is evident always hold? Explain.

f. Recall that the parent company uses the equity method of accounting for its investment in the subsidiary, and that this account is eliminated in the consolidation process. What is the relation between consolidated net income and the net income of the parent company? Explain.

g. What do you believe is the implication for the consolidated balance sheet if the market value of the Financial Products subsidiary is greater than the book value of its stockholders' equity?

December 31, 2003 (Millions of Dollars)	Consolidated	Machinery and Engines	Financial Products	Consolidating Adjustments
Assets				
Current assets				
Cash and short-term investments	$ 342	$ 220	$ 122	$ —
Receivables—trade and other	3,666	2,993	1,642	(969)
Receivables—finance	7,605	—	7,605	—
Deferred and refundable income taxes	707	645	62	—
Prepaid expenses	1,424	1,403	27	(6)
Inventories	3,047	3,047	—	—
Total current assets	16,791	8,308	9,458	(975)
Property, plant and equipment—net	7,290	4,682	2,608	—
Long-term receivables—trade and other	82	81	1	—
Long-term receivables—finance	7,822	—	7,822	—
Investments in unconsolidated affiliated companies	800	426	374	—
Investments in Financial Products subsidiaries	—	2,547	—	(2,547)
Deferred income taxes	616	819	19	(222)
Intangible assets	239	230	9	—
Goodwill	1,398	1,398	—	—
Other assets	1,427	719	708	—
Total assets	$36,465	$19,210	$20,999	$(3,744)
Liabilities				
Current liabilities				
Short-term borrowings	$ 2,757	$ 72	$ 3,160	$ (475)
Accounts payable	3,100	3,078	243	(221)
Accrued expenses	1,638	857	802	(21)
Accrued wages, salaries and employee benefits	1,802	1,788	14	—
Dividends payable	127	127	—	—
Deferred and current income taxes payable	216	166	50	—
Deferred liability	—	—	259	(259)
Long-term debt due within one year	2,981	32	2,949	—
Total current liabilities	12,621	6,120	7,477	(976)
Long-term debt due after one year	14,078	3,367	10,711	—
Liability for postemployment benefits	3,172	3,172	—	—
Deferred income taxes and other liabilities	516	473	264	(221)
Total liabilities	30,387	13,132	18,452	(1,197)
Shareholders' equity				
Common stock	1,059	1,059	890	(890)
Treasury stock	(2,914)	(2,914)	—	—
Profit employed in the business	8,450	8,450	1,495	(1,495)
Accumulated other comprehensive income	(517)	(517)	162	(162)
Total stockholders' equity	6,078	6,078	2,547	(2,547)
Total liabilities and stockholders' equity	$36,465	$19,210	$20,999	$(3,744)

Header note: **Supplemental Consolidating Data**

CASES AND PROJECTS

C12-50. Analyzing and Interpreting Disclosures on Equity Method Investments (LO1, 3, 4)

General Mills (GIS)

General Mills invests in a number of joint ventures to manufacture and distribute its food products as discussed in the following footnote to its fiscal year 2002 10-K report.

INVESTMENTS IN JOINT VENTURES

We have a 50 percent equity interest in Cereal Partners Worldwide (CPW), a joint venture with Nestlé that manufactures and markets ready-to-eat cereals outside the United States and Canada. We have a 40.5 percent equity interest in Snack Ventures Europe (SVE), our joint venture with PepsiCo that manufactures and markets snack foods in continental Europe. We have a 50 percent equity interest in 8th Continent, LLC, a domestic joint venture formed in 2001 with DuPont to develop and market soy foods and beverages. As a result of the Pillsbury acquisition, we have 50 percent interests in . . . joint ventures for the manufacture, distribution and marketing of *Häagen-Dazs* frozen ice cream products and novelties . . . We also have a 50 percent interest in Seretram, a joint venture with Co-op de Pau for the production of *Green Giant* canned corn in France.

The joint ventures are reflected in our financial statements on an equity accounting basis. We record our share of the earnings or losses of these joint ventures. (The table that follows reflects the joint ventures on a 100 percent basis.) We also receive royalty income from certain of these joint ventures, incur various expenses (primarily research and development) and record the tax impact of certain of the joint venture operations that are structured as partnerships.

Our cumulative investment in these joint ventures (including our share of earnings and losses) was $326 million, $218 million and $198 million at the end of 2002, 2001 and 2000, respectively. We made aggregate investments in the joint ventures of $38 million, $25 million and $29 million (net of a $6 million loan repayment) in 2002, 2001 and 2000, respectively. We received aggregate dividends from the joint ventures of $17 million, $3 million and $5 million in 2002, 2001 and 2000, respectively. Summary combined financial information for the joint ventures on a 100 percent basis follows.

Combined Financial Information—Joint Ventures—100% Basis

In Millions, Fiscal Year Ending in May	2002	2001
Net sales	$1,468	$1,429
Gross profit	664	619
Earnings (losses)	61	(4)

In Millions	May 26, 2002	May 27, 2001
Current assets	$587	$476
Noncurrent assets	712	614
Current liabilities	630	585
Noncurrent liabilities	9	2

Required

a. How does General Mills account for its investments in joint ventures? How are these investments reflected on its balance sheet, and how generally is income recognized on these investments?

b. General Mills reports the total of all of these investments on its May 26, 2002, balance sheet at $326 million. Approximately what percent of these joint ventures does it own, on average? Given this percent, approximately how much income would you expect that General Mills reports relating to these investments?

c. Does the $326 million investment reported on General Mills' balance sheet sufficiently reflect the assets and liabilities required to conduct these operations? Explain.

d. Do you believe that the liabilities of these joint venture entities represent actual obligations of General Mills? Explain.

e. What potential problem(s) does equity method accounting present for analysis purposes?

C12-51. Analyzing Financial Statement Effects of Passive and Equity Investments (LO1, 2, 3)
On January 2, 2006, Magee, Inc., purchased, as a stock investment, 20,000 shares of Dye, Inc.'s common stock for $21 per share, including commissions and taxes. On December 31, 2006, Dye announced a net income of $280,000 for the year and a dividend of 80 cents per share, payable January 15, 2007, to stockholders of record on January 5, 2007. At December 31, 2006, the market value of Dye's stock was $18 per share. Magee received its dividend on January 18, 2007.

Required

a. Assume that the stock acquired by Magee represents 10% of Dye's voting stock and is classified in the trading category. Prepare all journal entries appropriate for this investment, beginning with the purchase on January 2, 2006, and ending with the receipt of the dividend on January 18, 2007. (Magee recognizes dividend income when received.)

b. Post the journal entries from part *a* to their respective T-accounts.

    c.   Record each of the transactions from part *a* in the financial statement effects template.

    d.   Assume that the stock acquired by Magee represents 40% of Dye's voting stock. Prepare all journal entries appropriate for this investment, beginning with the purchase on January 2, 2006, and ending with the receipt of the dividend on January 18, 2007.

    e.   Post the journal entries from part *d* to their respective T-accounts.

    f.   Record each of the transactions from part *d* in the financial statement effects template.

C11-52. **Management Interpretation of Consolidated Financial Statements** (LO1, 2, 3, 4)

Demski, Inc., manufactures heating and cooling systems. It has a 75% interest in Asare Company, which manufactures thermostats, switches, and other controls for heating and cooling products. It also has a 100% interest in Demski Finance Company, created by the parent company to finance sales of its products to contractors and other consumers. The parent company's only other investment is a 25% interest in the common stock of Knechel, Inc., which produces certain circuits used by Demski, Inc. A condensed consolidated balance sheet of the entity for the current year follows.

DEMSKI, INC., AND SUBSIDIARIES Consolidated Balance Sheet December 31, 2006		
Assets		
Current Assets		$19,300,000
Stock Investment-Influential (Knechel)		2,600,000
Other Assets		71,400,000
Excess of Cost over Equity Acquired in Net Assets of Asare Company		1,700,000
Total Assets		$95,000,000
Liabilities and Stockholders' Equity		
Current Liabilities		$10,300,000
Long-Term Liabilities		14,200,000
Stockholders' Equity		
Minority Interest	$ 3,800,000	
Common Stock	50,000,000	
Retained Earnings	16,700,000	70,500,000
Total Liabilities and Stockholders' Equity		$95,000,000

This balance sheet, along with other financial statements, was furnished to shareholders before their annual meeting, and all shareholders were invited to submit questions to be answered at the meeting. As chief financial officer of Demski, you have been appointed to respond to the questions at the meeting.

Required

Answer the following stockholder questions.

    a.   What is meant by *consolidated* financial statements?

    b.   Why is the investment in Knechel shown on the consolidated balance sheet, but the investments in Asare and Demski Finance are omitted?

    c.   Explain the meaning of the asset Excess of Cost over Equity Acquired in Net Assets of Asare Company.

    d.   What is meant by *minority interest* and to what company is this account related?

C11-53. **Intercorporate Investments, Accounting Practices, and Managerial Ethics** (LO1, 2, 3)

Doug Stevens, controller of Nexgen, Inc., has asked his assistant, Gayle Sayres, for suggestions as to how the company can improve its financial performance for the year. The company is in the last quarter of the year and projections to the end of the year show the company will have a net loss of about $400,000.

"My suggestion," said Sayres, "is that we sell 1,000 of the 200,000 common shares of Heflin Company that we own. The 200,000 shares gives us a 20% ownership of Heflin, and we have been using the equity method to account for this investment. We have owned this stock a long time and the current market value of the 200,000 shares is about $750,000 above our book value for the stock."

"That sale will only generate a gain of about $3,750," replied Stevens.

"The rest of the story," continued Sayres, "is that once we sell the 1,000 shares, we will own less than 20% of Heflin. We can then reclassify the remaining 199,000 shares from the influential category to the trading category. Once in the trading category, we value the stocks at their current fair value, include the rest of the $750,000 gain in this year's income statement, and finish the year with a healthy net income."

"But," responded Stevens, "we aren't going to sell all the Heflin stock; 1,000 shares maybe, but certainly not any more. We own that stock because they are a long-term supplier of ours. Indeed, we even have representation on their board of directors. The 199,000 shares do not belong in the trading category."

Sayres rolled her eyes and continued, "The classification of an investment as trading or not depends on management's intent. This year-end we claim it was our intent to sell the stock. Next year we change our minds and take the stock out of the trading category. Generally accepted accounting principles can't legislate management intent, nor can our outside auditors read our minds. Besides, why shouldn't we take advantage of the flexibility in GAAP to avoid reporting a net loss for this year?"

Required

a. Should generally accepted accounting principles permit management's intent to influence accounting classifications and measurements?

b. Is it ethical for Doug Stevens to implement the recommendation of Gayle Sayres?

13

Assessing
Off-Balance-Sheet
Financing

LEARNING OBJECTIVES

After completing the chapter, you should be able to:

LO1 Define off-balance-sheet financing and explain its effects on financial ratios. (p. 573)

LO2 Account for leases using the operating lease method or the capital lease method. (p. 573)

LO3 Convert off-balance-sheet operating leases to the capital lease method. (p. 579)

LO4 Explain and interpret the reporting for pension plans. (p. 584)

LO5 Analyze and interpret pension footnote disclosures. (p. 588)

MIDWEST AIRLINES

A Hard Landing

The following headline has become all too familiar for companies in the airline industry: **Midwest Express Holding and its Unions Agree to Concessions in Bid to Avert Reorganization**. This article in *The Wall Street Journal* reports that: "Midwest Air Group's three unions tentatively agreed to concessions meant to help the airline company avoid Chapter 11 bankruptcy reorganization. The company seeks to save $600,000 a month through union workers' wage reductions, work-rule changes or productivity increases and also seeks concessions from aircraft lessors and banks." (*TWSJ* 2003)

Midwest Air Group, Inc. (formerly Midwest Express) is a regional carrier operating out of Milwaukee. Until earnings became losses in the wake of the September 11, 2001, terrorist attack, Midwest Air was a profitable carrier. It had found its niche and was successfully defending its turf against larger and more cumbersome national carriers. It was in an elite group, with Southwest Airlines and JetBlue.

Midwest Air was not, however, a no-frills airline. It was one of the first to offer all leather seating and a wider, less crowded, all-business class. Food service was high quality, served on china with metal utensils, and featured baked on-board chocolate chip cookies. The service was excellent. Passengers willingly paid a premium price for luxury air travel.

By 2000, Midwest Air had amassed nearly $134 million in retained earnings on an initial capital investment of $11.4 million (in 1984). Midwest Air reported 1999 net income of nearly $39 million on revenues of nearly $450 million. Then, the revenue stream sharply declined and the company lost $40 million during 2001–2003. Although technically solvent, with stockholders' equity of $124 million as of 2003, Midwest Air is fighting for its financial survival.

The hard landing endured by Midwest Air's shareholders during the past five years is graphically illustrated in the following stock price chart.

The company, in an effort to stave off bankruptcy, negotiated the following lease, debt, and stock transactions:

- **Lease Restructuring**. In August 2003, the company reached final agreement on renegotiating its contracts with 11 aircraft lessors and lenders. The lessors and lenders, in return for amending its contracts, received warrants to purchase shares of common stock at their option.

(Continued on next page)

(Continued from previous page)

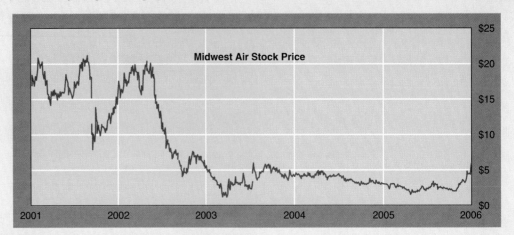

- **Debt Financing**. In September 2003, the company sold convertible senior secured notes to qualified institutional and accredited investors. The notes are generally convertible at any time at the option of the note holders into shares of common stock.

- **Equity Financing**. In November 2003, the company sold 1,882,353 shares of common stock to qualified institutional and accredited investors at a price of $4.25 per share in a private placement for an aggregate purchase price of approximately $8 million.

These transactions have served to effectively convert the standing of its creditors to more like that of equity investors.

This chapter focuses on financing activities, such as those utilized by Midwest Air to fund its operations. As we know, both investors and creditors are vitally concerned with the efficient utilization of assets and the manner in which those assets are financed.

One important financing tool, known as *off-balance-sheet financing,* refers to financing assets where neither the asset nor the liability are reported on the balance sheet. If a company can obtain a revenue stream from an asset without reporting either the asset or the liability on the balance sheet, then all of the usual measures of financial performance appear better than they would with on-balance-sheet financing.

It is often what is *not* reported on the face of the financial statements, particularly the balance sheet, that is of greatest informational value. However, information on these activities is available in the notes to financial statements. We will learn how to read, analyze and interpret such notes in this chapter.

Sources: *Midwest Airlines* 2004 and 2003 Annual Reports; *Midwest Airlines* 2004 10-K; The *Wall Street Journal,* 14 July 2003.

CHAPTER ORGANIZATION

Assessing Off-Balance-Sheet Financing

Leases

- Lessee Reporting of Leases
- Footnote Disclosures of Leases
- Capitalization of Operating Leases

Pensions

- Reporting of Defined Benefit Pension Plans
- Footnote Disclosures
- Other Postretirement Benefits

INTRODUCTION

Investors, creditors, and other users of financial statements assess the composition of a company's balance sheet and its relation to the income statement. Chapter 7 introduced the concept of earnings quality to refer to the extent to which reported income reflects the underlying economic performance of a company. Similarly, the quality of the balance sheet refers to the extent to which the assets and liabilities of a company are reported in a manner that accurately reflects its economic resources and obligations. For example, in previous chapters, we highlighted the reporting of LIFO inventories and noncapitalized intangible assets to illustrate how some assets can be undervalued or even excluded from the balance sheet. This chapter focuses on the reporting of liabilities that often only appear in notes to financial statements.

Financial managers are keenly aware of the importance that financial markets place on the quality of balance sheets. This creates pressure on companies to *window dress* their financial statements to report their financial condition and performance in the best possible light. One means of improving the perceived financial condition of the company is by keeping debt off the balance sheet. **Off-balance-sheet financing** refers to financial obligations of a company that are not reported as liabilities in the balance sheet.

Off-balance-sheet financing reduces the amount of debt reported in the balance sheet, thereby lowering the financial leverage ratio (FLEV). Additionally, many off-balance-sheet financing techniques remove assets from the balance sheet, along with the liabilities, without reducing revenues or markedly affecting net income. Such techniques improve operating ratios, including return on net operating assets (RNOA) and net operating asset turnover (NOAT).

This chapter focuses on two common sources of off-balance-sheet financing—leases and pensions. We will see that GAAP requires detailed footnote disclosures of these obligations. Understanding the information in these disclosures enables us to analyze the impact of off-balance-sheet financing on the financial condition of the company.

LO1 Define off-balance-sheet financing and explain its effects on financial ratios

NOTE
Off-balance-sheet financing usually requires off-balance-sheet assets—this means the off-balance-sheet remains balanced!

BUSINESS INSIGHT

Nike's Off-Balance-Sheet Obligations   Michael Jordan, Tiger Woods, Tom Brady, and Lance Armstrong are just some of the marquee athletes who endorse **Nike** products. These athletes sign long-term, multi-million dollar contracts to use and promote Nike shoes, apparel, and assessories. These long-term endorsement contracts are just one of Nike's off-balance-sheet obligations. Consider the following note from its 10-K report.

Our long-term contractual obligations as of May 31, 2005, follow ($ millions).

Cash Payments Due in the Year Ended May 31	2006	2007	2008	2009	2010	Thereafter	Total
Long-term Debt	$ 6.2	$256.2	$ 31.2	$ 6.2	$ 31.2	$ 353.5	$ 684.5
Operating Leases	186.7	157.6	135.3	112.9	97.8	556.3	1,246.6
Endorsement Contracts	400.3	405.0	276.9	182.3	102.9	317.6	1,685.0
Product Purchase Obligations	1,858.2	2.8	—	—	—	—	1,861.0
Other	250.5	75.9	26.1	25.5	2.1	1.3	381.4
Total	$2,701.9	$897.5	$469.5	$326.9	$234.0	$1,228.7	$5,858.5

Of these obligations disclosed, only its long-term debt is included in the balance sheet. If the other obligations were presented in the balance sheet at their present values, Nike's financial leverage ratio (FLEV) would increase more than 500% from 0.135 to 0.888.

LEASES

We begin the discussion of off-balance-sheet financing with leasing. The following graphic shows that leasing affects both the balance sheet (liabilities and assets) and the income statement.

LO2 Account for leases using the operating lease method or the capital lease method

Income Statement
Sales
Cost of goods sold
Selling, general & administrative
Income taxes
Net income

Balance Sheet	
Cash	Current liabilities
Accounts receivable	**Long-term liabilities**
Inventory	
Long-term operating assets	Shareholders' equity
Investments	

Footnote Disclosures-Off-Balance-Sheet Financing	
Leases	Pensions

A lease is a contract between the owner of an asset (the **lessor**) and the party desiring to use that asset (the **lessee**). Because this is a private contract between two willing parties, it is governed only by applicable commercial law, and can include whatever provisions are negotiated between the parties. The lessor and lessee can be any legal form of organization, including private individuals, corporations, partnerships, and joint ventures.

Leases generally provide for the following terms:

- Lessor allows the lessee the unrestricted right to use the asset during the lease term.

- Lessee agrees to make periodic payments to the lessor and to maintain the asset.

- Asset title remains with the lessor. At the end of the lease, either the lessor takes physical possession of the asset, or the lessee purchases the asset from the lessor at a price specified in the lease contract.

From the lessor's standpoint, lease payments are set at an amount that yields an acceptable return on investment, commensurate with the credit standing of the lessee. The lessor, thus, obtains a quality investment, and the lessee gains use of the asset.

The lease serves as a financing vehicle, similar to an intermediate term secured bank loan. However, there are several advantages to leasing over bank financing:

- Leases often require less equity investment than bank financing. That is, banks often only lend a portion of the asset's cost and require the borrower to make up the difference from its available cash. However, leases usually require the first lease payment be made at the inception of the lease.

- Because leases are contracts between two parties, their terms can be structured in any way to meet their respective needs. For example, a lease can allow variable payments to match seasonal cash inflows of the lessee, or have graduated payments for start-ups.

- The lessee may only require the use of the asset for part of its useful life; thus, leasing avoids the need to sell a used asset.

- Because the lessor retains asset ownership, leases provide the lessor with tax benefits such as accelerated depreciation deductions.

- If the lease is properly structured, neither the leased asset nor the lease liability is reported on the lessee's balance sheet. Accordingly, leasing can be a form of off-balance-sheet financing.

Lessee Reporting of Leases

GAAP identifies two different approaches for the reporting of leases by the lessee:

- **Capital lease method**. This method requires that both the lease asset and the lease liability be reported on the balance sheet. The lease asset is depreciated like any other long-term asset. The lease liability is amortized like debt, where lease payments are separated into interest expense and principal repayment.

- **Operating lease method**. Under this method, neither the lease asset nor the lease liability is on the balance sheet. Lease payments are recorded as rent expense by the lessee when paid.

To illustrate the two approaches to lease accounting, assume that Richardson Electronics agrees to lease retail store space in a shopping center. The lease is a 5-year lease with annual payments of $10,000 due at each year-end. (Most leases require payments at the beginning of each period; we use year-end payments for simplification.) Using a 7% interest rate, the present value of the five annual lease payments equals $41,002, computed as $10,000 × 4.10020. This amount is used for valuing the lease under the capital lease method.

Operating Leases

When the operating lease method is used, lease assets and lease liabilities are not recorded in the balance sheet. No accounting entry is recorded when the lease agreement is signed. At each year-end, Richardson would record the rent payment as rent expense as follows.

```
(1)  Rent expense (+E, −SE) ................................. 10,000
         Cash (−A) ...........................................        10,000
```

Because no asset or liability is reported, the only time an operating lease affects the balance sheet is if rent is prepaid (resulting in prepaid rent in current assets) or if unpaid rent is accrued (resulting in accrued rent payable, a current liability). The income statement reports the lease payment as rent expense and the existence and key details of the lease agreement in a footnote.

Capital Leases

When the capital lease method is applied, the lessee records an asset and a liability at the time that the lease agreement is signed. Both the asset and the liability are valued using the present value of the lease payments. The entry that would be recorded when Richardson Electronics signs its lease follows.

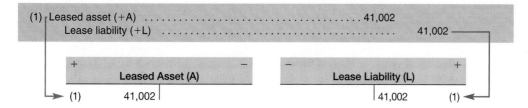

The asset is reported among long-term PPE assets in the balance sheet and the liability is reported in long-term debt.

At the end of the first year, two entries are required, one to account for the asset and the other to account for the lease payment. Like other long-term assets, the lease asset must be depreciated. The entry to depreciate Richardson's lease asset (assuming straight-line depreciation and zero residual value) follows.

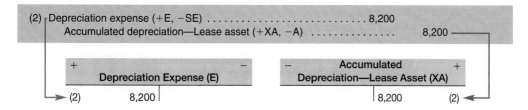

The entry to record the annual lease payment is

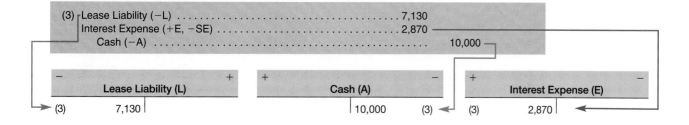

The $10,000 cash payment is split between interest expense and principal repayment. The $2,870 interest expense is computed by multiplying the unpaid balance in the lease liability by the interest rate ($41,002 × 7%). The $7,130 debit to lease liability (principal repayment) is the difference between the lease payment and interest expense ($10,000 − $2,870). The year-end balance in the lease liability account is $33,872 ($41,002 − $2,870). The effects of these entries on the balance sheet and income statement are presented in the following financial statement effects template.

Transaction	Cash Asset	+	Noncash Assets	=	Liabil-ities	+	Contrib. Capital	+	Retained Earnings	Revenues	−	Expenses	=	Net Income
												Income Statement		
(1) Leased store space under capital lease			+41,002 Leased Asset	=	+41,002 Lease Liability								=	
(2) Annual depreciation expense			−8,200 Accumulated Depreciation— Lease Asset	=					−8,200 Retained Earnings			−8,200 Depreciation Expense	=	−8,200
(3) Lease payment	−10,000 Cash			=	−7,130 Lease Liability				−2,870 Retained Earnings			−2,870 Interest Expense	=	−2,870

Exhibit 13.1 presents the amortization table for Richardson's lease liability under the capital lease method.

EXHIBIT 13.1	Amortization Table for a Capital Lease Liability					
A	B	C	D	E	F
Year	Beginning-year Lease Liability	Interest Expense (B × 7%)	Payment	Principal Repayment (D − C)	Ending-year Lease liability (B − E)
1	$41,002	$2,870	$10,000	$7,130	$33,872
2	33,872	2,371	10,000	7,629	26,243
3	26,243	1,837	10,000	8,163	18,080
4	18,080	1,266	10,000	8,734	9,346
5	9,346	654	10,000	9,346	0

Comparing Operating Lease and Capital Lease Methods

In Exhibit 13.1 the interest expense decreases each year as the lease liability decreases. Exhibit 13.2 compares total expenses for the operating lease and the capital lease methods over the 5-year life of the Richardson Electronics lease.

EXHIBIT 13.2	Comparison of Expenses under Alternative Lease Accounting Methods			
		Capital Lease Method		Operating Lease Method
Year	Interest Expense	Depreciation Expense	Total Expense	Rent Expense
1	$2,870	$8,200	$11,070	$10,000
2	2,371	8,200	10,571	10,000
3	1,837	8,200	10,037	10,000
4	1,266	8,201	9,467	10,000
5	654	8,201	8,855	10,000
Total	$8,998	$41,002	$50,000	$50,000

Exhibit 13.2 shows how the capital lease method reports a higher total expense (depreciation plus interest) in the early years of the lease and a lower total expense in the later years. Total expense over the 5-year life of the lease is the same under both methods and is equal to the total of the lease payments ($50,000).

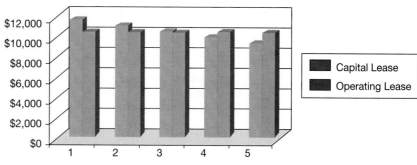

The effects of these two accounting methods on the lessee's financial statements are summarized in Exhibit 13.3.

EXHIBIT 13.3	Financial Statement Effects of Lease Methods for the Lessee			
Lease Type	**Assets**	**Liabilities**	**Expenses**	**Cash Flows**
Capital	Lease asset reported	Lease liability reported	Depreciation and interest expense	Payments per lease contract
Operating	Lease asset not reported	Lease liability not reported	Rent expense	Same as above

GAAP defines four criteria to determine the classification of a lease as capital or operating. The lessee must capitalize the lease if one or more of these criteria are met:

1. The lease automatically transfers ownership of the lease asset to the lessee at the lease-end.
2. The lease agreement allows the lessee to purchase the asset at a discounted price (say $1) at the lease-end; this is called a bargain purchase option.
3. The lease term is at least 75% of the economic useful life of the asset.
4. The present value of the lease payments is at least 90% of the asset's fair market value.

Accounting for leases using the operating lease method offers several benefits to the lessee:

1. The lease asset is not reported on the balance sheet. This reporting means that net operating asset turnover (NOAT) is higher because reported operating assets are lower and revenues are unaffected.
2. The lease liability is not reported on the balance sheet. This means that common balance sheet measures of leverage (such as liabilities divided by equity) are improved. Consequently, many managers believe the company would then command a better debt rating and a lower interest rate on borrowed funds.
3. The portion of ROE derived from operating activities (RNOA) appears higher, and the company's ROE is perceived to be of higher quality.
4. For the early years of the lease term, rent expense reported for an operating lease is less than the depreciation and interest expense reported for a capital lease. This reporting means that net income is higher in those early years with an operating lease. (However, NOPAT is *lower* for an operating lease because rent expense is an operating expense whereas only depreciation expense [not interest expense] is an operating expense for a capital lease.)

The benefits of using the operating method to account for leases are obvious to managers, thus leading them to avoid lease capitalization. Furthermore, the lease accounting standard is structured around rigid requirements relating to capitalization. Whenever accounting standards are rigidly defined, clever managers that are so inclined can structure lease contracts to meet the letter of the standard to achieve a desired accounting result even though the essence of the transaction would suggest a different accounting treatment.

Footnote Disclosures of Leases

Disclosures of expected payments for leases are required under both operating and capital lease methods. **Midwest Air** provides a typical disclosure of its operating leases from its 2003 annual report:

> The Company leases aircraft, terminal space, office space and warehouse space. Future minimum lease payments required under operating leases having initial or remaining noncancellable lease terms in excess of one year as of December 31, 2003 were as follows (in thousands):

Year Ended December 31	
2004	$ 43,248
2005	40,331
2006	38,989
2007	36,931
2008	35,341
2009 and thereafter	413,071

> As of December 31, 2003, Midwest had 19 jet aircraft in service financed by operating leases. These leases have expiration dates ranging from 2004 through 2023 and can generally be renewed, based on the fair market value at the end of the lease term, for one to four years. Most of the leases include purchase options at or near the end of the lease term at fair market value.
>
> As of December 31, 2003, Midwest Connect's 14 turboprop aircraft were financed under operating leases with a lease term of 12 years and an expiration date of 2008. These leases permit renewal for various periods at rates approximating fair market value and purchase options at or near the end of the lease term at fair market value. In the fourth quarter 1999, the Company entered into lease agreements to finance the acquisition of five Fairchild 328JETs. The leases run for a term of 16.5 years, with expiration of all leases occurring in 2016. These leases permit renewal for various periods at rates approximating fair market value and purchase options at or near the end of the lease term at fair market value.
>
> Rent expense for all operating leases, excluding landing fees, was $47,889,000, $40,723,000 and $39,021,000 for 2003, 2002 and 2001, respectively.

The Midwest Air footnote disclosure reports minimum (base) contractual lease payment obligations for each of the next five years and the total lease payment obligations that come due after that five-year period. This is similar to disclosures of future maturities for long-term debt. The company must also provide separate disclosures for operating leases and capital leases. (We know that all of Midwest Air's leases are operating because its footnote does not disclose any payments relating to capital leases.)

As a point of comparison, American Airlines discloses both capital and operating leases in its following December 31, 2004, lease footnote.

> American leases various types of equipment and property, primarily aircraft and airport facilities. The future minimum lease payments required under capital leases, together with the present value of such payments, and future minimum lease payments required under operating leases that have initial or remaining non-cancelable lease terms in excess of one year as of December 31, 2004, were (in millions):

Year Ending December 31	Capital Leases	Operating Leases
2005	$ 211	$ 1,066
2006	233	999
2007	187	982
2008	225	931
2009	174	838
2010 and subsequent	950	7,525
	$ 1,980	$ 12,341
Less amount representing interest	815	
Present value of net minimum lease payments	$ 1,165	

At December 31, 2004, the Company had 231 jet aircraft under operating leases and 94 jet aircraft capital leases. The aircraft leases can generally be renewed at rates based on fair market value at the end of the lease term for one to five years. Some aircraft leases have purchase options at or near the end of the lease term at fair market value, but generally not to exceed a stated percentage of the defined lessor's cost of the aircraft or a predetermined fixed amount.

The purpose of these lease disclosures is to provide information concerning current and future payment obligations. These contractual obligations are similar to debt payments. While the obligations under capital leases are reported in long-term debt, the operating lease obligations are not reported in the balance sheet but yet must be considered in our evaluation of the company's financial condition.

YOU MAKE THE CALL

You Are the Division President   You are the president of an operating division. Your CFO recommends operating lease treatment for asset acquisitions to reduce reported assets and liabilities on your balance sheet. To achieve this classification, you must negotiate leases with terms that you feel are not advantageous to your company. What is your response? [Answer, p. 593]

Capitalization of Operating Leases

Failure to capitalize operating leases excludes a potentially large amount of assets and liabilities from the balance sheet. Most of us would probably agree, however, that these leased properties represent assets as defined under GAAP. That is, the company controls the assets and they provide future benefits. Also, lease liabilities represent real contractual obligations that should be reported in the balance sheet.

LO3 Convert off-balance-sheet operating leases to the capital lease method

Failure to recognize lease assets and lease liabilities when they should be capitalized yields distortions in ROE disaggregation analysis (see Chapter 5)—specifically:

- Net operating asset turnover (NOAT) is overstated due to nonreporting of lease assets.

- Financial leverage is understated by the nonreporting of lease liabilities-recall that lease liabilities are nonoperating.

- Net operating profit margin (NOPM) is understated. Although, over the life of the lease, rent expense under operating leases equals depreciation plus interest expense under capital leases, only depreciation expense is included in net operating profit (NOPAT)-interest is a nonoperating expense.[1]

Failure to capitalize an operating lease results in a balance sheet that neither reflects all of the assets that are used in the business, nor the nonoperating obligations for which the company is liable. Such noncapitalization of leases makes ROE appear to be of higher quality because it results from higher RNOA (due to higher NOA turnover) and not from higher financial leverage (FLEV). This result is, of course, an important reason why managers want to exclude leases from the balance sheet.

Despite structuring leases to achieve off-balance-sheet financing, required lease disclosures allow us to capitalize operating leases for analysis purposes. This capitalization process involves three steps (this is the process that would have been used if the leases had been classified as capital leases):

1. Determine an appropriate discount rate.[2]

2. Compute the present value of operating lease payments provided in the lease footnote.

---

[1]While cash payments are the same whether the lease is classified as operating or capital, *operating cash flow* is higher with capital leases because the reduction of the capital lease obligation is classified as a *financing* outflow rather than operating.

[2]There are at least two means to determine the rate: (1) If the company discloses capital leases, we can infer it to be the rate that yields the present value computed by the company given the projected capital leases payments. (2) Use the rate that corresponds to the company's debt rating or the rate from any recent borrowings involving intermediate term secured obligations.

3. Include the present value from step 2 in the balance sheet as both a lease asset and a lease liability.

To illustrate the capitalization of operating leases, we use **Midwest Air**'s footnote and its long-term secured borrowing rate of 7% as the discount rate to compute the present value of its operating leases in Exhibit 13.4.[3]

EXHIBIT 13.4	Present Value of Operating Lease Payments ($ 000s)		
Year	**Operating Lease Payment**	**Discount Factor (i=0.07)**	**Present Value**
1	$ 43,248	0.93458	$ 40,419
2	40,331	0.87344	35,227
3	38,989	0.81630	31,827
4	36,931	0.76290	28,175
5	35,341	0.71299	25,198
>5	413,071		
	[35,341 for 11.688 years]	7.80743* × 0.71299	196,729[†]
			$357,575

Average life . . . . $413,071/$35,341 = 11.688 years

*We compute the annuity factor for 11.688 years as 7.80743 from the formula $\dfrac{1 - \dfrac{1}{(1 + .07)^{11.688}}}{0.07}$.

[†]$35,341 × 7.80743 × 0.71299 = $196,729.

Specifically, each of the first five lease payments is discounted at the factor for that year. The remaining payments of $413,071 are assumed to reflect an annuity equal to the year 5 payment of $35,341 for a time period necessary to accumulate to the total payments due after year 5, computed as $413,071/$35,341 = 11.688 years. That is, after year 5, we *assume* that the company makes annual lease payments of $35,341 for a period of 11.688 years (sufficient to exhaust the $413,071 disclosed in the lease footnote as the total payments after year 5). The present value of this annuity is computed as $35,341 × 7.80743. Since this present value is at year 5, it must then be discounted to the present (year 0) by multiplying it by the year 5 present value factor of 0.71299. Thus, the present value of this 11.688 year annuity of $35,341, beginning in year 5 and discounted back to year 0, is $196,729. We then add this amount to the earlier years' present values to get Midwest Air's present value of its operating leases of $357,575.

Next, this present value is added to Midwest Air's assets and liabilities to capitalize the operating leases for analysis purposes. These adjustments yield the comparisons in Exhibit 13.5 for Midwest Air at year-end 2003.

EXHIBIT 13.5	Analytical Adjustments from Capitalization of Operating Leases ($ 000s)		
	Reported	**Adjustments**	**Adjusted**
Net operating assets	$291,624	$357,575	$649,199
Net nonoperating liabilities	167,307	357,575	524,882
Equity	124,317		124,317

---

[3]The factors for individual payment amounts for years 1 through 5 are discounted using the present value for a single payment formula $1/(1 + r)^t$. The payment amount for each year is multiplied by this factor with r equal to 7% and t equal to the year number. The payments to be made after year 5 represent an annuity of $35,341 per year for 11.688 years. The present value of this

annuity is computed by the formula $\dfrac{1 - \dfrac{1}{(1 + r)^t}}{r}$ with r equal to 7% and t equal to 11.688.

By adding the present value of the operating lease payments to both the assets and the liabilities in the balance sheet, we are, in effect, treating these leases as capital leases. If these operating leases had been recorded as capital leases all along, the initial entry to record the leases would have been as follows.

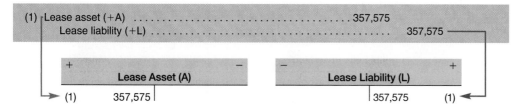

(1) Lease asset (+A) 357,575
    Lease liability (+L) 357,575

+	Lease Asset (A)	−		−	Lease Liability (L)	+
(1)	357,575				357,575	(1)

This entry is summarized in the following financial statement effects template.

	Balance Sheet							Income Statement		
Transaction	Cash Asset	+ Noncash Assets	= Liabil- ities	+ Contrib. Capital	+ Retained Earnings			Revenues	− Expenses =	Net Income
(1) Capitalize operating leases		+357,575 Lease Asset	= +357,575 Lease Liability							=

The capitalization of operating leases has a marked impact on Midwest Air's balance sheet. For the airline and retailing industries, in particular, lease assets (airplanes and real estate) comprise a large portion of net operating assets and these leases are usually classified as operating.

These adjustments can change perception of ROE components. The net operating asset turnover is lower than we would infer from reported financial statements (net operating assets increase and revenues remain constant). Using the year-end data presented in Exhibit 13.5 and given revenues of $383,948 the NOA turnover (using year-end figures) decreases from 1.32 ($383,948/$291,624) to 0.59 ($383,948/ $649,199). Likewise, leverage (liabilities to equity) is higher than we would infer from reported financial statements. Using the same data, liabilities-to-equity ratio is 4.22 times ($524,882/$124,317) versus 1.35 times ($167,307/$124,317) computed from the reported statements. Financial leverage is, therefore, revealed to play a greater role in ROE. The adjusted assets and liabilities arguably present a more realistic picture of the invested capital required to operate Midwest Air and of the amount of leverage represented by the leasing of assets.

BUSINESS INSIGHT

Imputed Discount Rate for Leases   When companies report both operating and capital leases, the average rate used to discount capital leases can be imputed from disclosures in the leasing footnote. Consider the following lease payment schedule reported by Wal-Mart Stores, Inc. in its 10-K report ($ millions):

Fiscal Year	Operating Leases	Capital Leases
2005	$ 665	$ 430
2006	651	427
2007	599	419
2008	553	411
2009	519	397
Thereafter	5,678	3,002
Total minimum rentals	$8,665	5,086
Less estimated executory costs		44
Net minimum lease payments		5,042
Less imputed interest at rates ranging from 4.2% to 14.0%		1,849
Present value of minimum lease payments		$3,193

(Continued on the next page)

(Continued from the previous page)

Wal-Mart reports total undiscounted minimum capital lease payments of $5,042 and a discounted value for those lease payments of $3,193. Using Excel, we can estimate by trial and error the discount rate that yields the present value—which is about 8% (see chart below). The 8% discount rate can then be used to capitalize the operating lease payments ($ millions).

Year	Capital Lease Payment	Discount Factor (i=0.08)	Present Value
1	$ 430	0.92593	$ 398
2	427	0.85734	366
3	419	0.79383	333
4	411	0.73503	302
5	397	0.68058	270
>5	3,002		
	[397 for 7.562 years]	5.51496* × 0.68058	1,490†
			$3,159

Avg. life $3,002/$397 = 7.562 years

*The annuity factor for 7.562 years is 5.51496, from the formula $\dfrac{1 - \dfrac{1}{(1 + 0.08)^{7.562}}}{0.08}$.

†$397 × 5.51496 × 0.68058 = $1,490.

MID-CHAPTER REVIEW 1

PART A

Assume that **Gap Inc.** leased a vacant retail space with the intention of opening another store. The lease calls for annual lease payments of $32,000, due at the end of each of the next ten years. The appropriate discount rate is 7%.

1. If the lease is treated as a capital lease, what journal entry(ies) would Gap make to record the initial signing of the lease agreement?
2. How would Gap record the first lease payment and depreciation expense at the end of the first year of the lease?
3. Post the journal entry(ies) from requirements 1 and 2 to their respective T-accounts.
4. Prepare a financial statement effects template to show how these transactions would affect the balance sheet and income statement.
5. If this lease is accounted for as an operating lease, what entry(ies) would be necessary during the first year?

Solution to Part A

1. The present value of the lease payments is $224,755, computed as $32,000 × 7.02358.

Lease asset (+A)	224,755	
Lease Liability (+L)		224,755

2. At the first year-end, Gap would record depreciation expense of $22,476 ($224,755/10) and interest expense of $15,733 ($224,755 × .07).

Depreciation Expense (+E, −SE)	22,476	
Accumulated Depreciation—Lease Asset (+XA, −A)		22,476
Interest Expense (+E, −SE)	15,733	
Lease Liability* (−L)	16,267	
Cash (−A)		32,000

  * $32,000 − $15,733.

3.

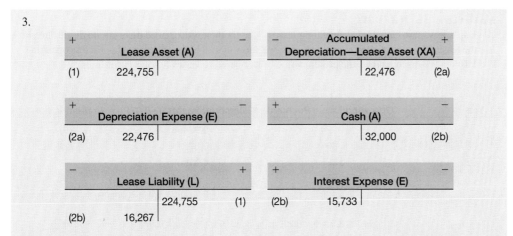

+	Lease Asset (A)	−
(1)	224,755	

−	Accumulated Depreciation—Lease Asset (XA)	+
		22,476 (2a)

+	Depreciation Expense (E)	−
(2a)	22,476	

+	Cash (A)	−
		32,000 (2b)

−	Lease Liability (L)	+
		224,755 (1)
(2b)	16,267	

+	Interest Expense (E)	−
(2b)	15,733	

4.

	Balance Sheet						Income Statement		
Transaction	Cash Asset	+ Noncash Assets	= Liabil- ities	+ Contrib. Capital	+ Retained Earnings		Revenues	− Expenses	= Net Income
(1) Leased store under capital lease		+224,755 Lease Asset	= +224,755 Lease Liability						=
(2) Annual depreciation expense		−22,476 Accumulated Depreciation − Lease Asset	=		−22,476 Retained Earnings			−22,476 Depreciation Expense	= −22,476
(3) Lease payment	−32,000 Cash		= −16,267 Lease Liability		−15,733 Retained Earnings			−15,733 Interest Expense	= −15,733

5. No journal entry is required at lease signing. At the end of the first year, Gap would record the lease payment as rent expense.

```
Rent Expense (+E, −SE) ....................................  32,000
    Cash (−A) ..............................................          32,000
```

PART B

Following is the leasing footnote disclosure from **Gap Inc.**'s 10-K report.

We lease most of our store premises and some of our headquarters facilities and distribution centers. These operating leases expire at various dates through 2033. The aggregate minimum non-cancelable annual lease payments under leases in effect on January 31, 2004, are as follows:

Fiscal Year	(In millions)
2004............................	$ 924
2005............................	835
2006............................	693
2007............................	564
2008............................	484
Thereafter	1,929
Total minimum lease commitment	$5,429

1. Does Gap classify these leases as operating or capital leases? Explain.
2. Assuming its leases are operating leases, compute the adjustments that are necessary for analysis of Gap's balance sheet? (Gap's recent intermediate term borrowing rate is 7%.)
3. Assuming the same facts as in part 2, what income statement adjustments should we consider?

Solution to Part B

1. Gap's leases are classified as operating leases—see footnote. Also, since there are no disclosures in the leasing footnote related to capital leases, we know that all of the leases are classified as operating.
2. Using a 7% discount rate, the present value of its operating leases follows ($ millions):

Year	Operating Lease Payment	Discount Factor (i=0.07)	Present Value
1	$ 924	0.93458	$ 864
2	835	0.87344	729
3	693	0.81630	566
4	564	0.76290	430
5	484	0.71299	345
>5	1,929		
	[484 for 3.9855 years]	3.37654* × 0.71299	1,165†
			$4,099

Average life . . . . . $1,929/$484 = 3.9855 years

*The annuity factor for 3.9855 years is 3.37654, from the formula $\dfrac{1 - \dfrac{1}{(1 + .07)^{3.9855}}}{0.07}$.

†$484 × 3.37654 × 0.71299 = $1,165.

Gap's operating leases represent $4,099 million of unreported operating assets and unreported non-operating liabilities. These amounts should be added to the balance sheet for analysis purposes.

3. Potential income statement adjustments would include elimination of the rent expense currently reported in Gap's SG&A expenses and replacing it with the depreciation of the capitalized lease asset and the interest on the capitalized lease liability. Whereas rent expense is considered as an operating expense, only the depreciation expense is similarly classified. The interest is, of course, a nonoperating expense. NOPAT, as a result, is increased following the financial statement adjustment for operating lease capitalization.

PENSIONS

Companies frequently offer pension plans as a benefit for their employees. There are two general types of pension plans:

1. **Defined contribution plan**. In a defined contribution plan, the company makes periodic contributions to an employee's account (usually with a third party trustee such as a bank). Many plans require an employee matching contribution. Following retirement, the employee makes periodic withdrawals from that account. A tax-advantaged 401(k) account is a typical example. Under a 401(k) plan, the employee makes contributions that are exempt from federal taxes until they are withdrawn after retirement.

2. **Defined benefit plan**. In a defined benefit plan, the company makes periodic payments to an employee after retirement. Payments are usually based on years of service and the employee's retirement age and salary. The company may or may not set aside sufficient funds to make these payments. As a result, defined benefit plans can be *overfunded* or *underfunded*. All pension investments are retained by the pension fund until paid to the employee.

NOTE
The pension fund is a separate entity managed by the company or its designee.

For a defined contribution plan, the company contribution is recorded as an expense in the income statement when the cash is paid or the liability accrued. For a defined benefit plan, it is not so simple. This is because the company holds pension investments, and the pension obligation is not satisfied until paid. How a defined benefit plan affects the financial statements is the focus of this section.

Reporting of Defined Benefit Pension Plans

There are two accounting issues concerning the reporting of defined benefit pension plans.

1. How are these pension plans reported in the balance sheet (if at all)?
2. How are pension costs and returns from the pension plan reported in the income statement?

The following graphic shows that pensions impact both the balance sheet (liabilities and assets) and the income statement (pension expense).

Income Statement
Sales
Cost of goods sold
Selling, general & administrative
Income taxes
Net income

Balance Sheet	
Cash	Current liabilities
Accounts receivable	**Long-term liabilities**
Inventory	
Long-term operating assets	Shareholders' equity
Investments	

Footnote Disclosures-Off-Balance-Sheet Financing	
Leases	Pensions

Balance Sheet Effects

The assets of the pension plan (or **plan assets**) involve investments in stocks and bonds of (mostly) other companies. Pension liabilities (called the **projected benefit obligation** or **PBO**) represent future obligations to current and former employees. The difference between the plan assets and the projected benefit obligation is called the **funded status** of the pension plan. If pension liabilities exceed the pension plan assets, the pension is **underfunded**. Conversely, if plan assets exceed the pension obligation, the pension plan is **overfunded**.

Plan assets are reported at fair market value. A reconciliation of the pension plan asset account from the beginning of the year to year-end takes the following form.

Plan Assets
Beginning balance in plan assets
+ Actual returns on investments (interest, dividends, gains and losses)
+ Company contributions to pension plan
− Benefits paid to retirees
= Ending balance in plan assets

In booming investment markets, like those in the 1990s, the returns on investments in plan assets cause the plan assets to grow rapidly. However, when markets reverse, as in the bear market of the early 2000s, the growth in plan assets slows and the value of the plan assets can sometimes decline.

Pension contributions increase the plan assets account. The amount that the company contributes to the pension plan each year is an investment decision influenced, in part, by market conditions. Minimum required contributions are specified by law. In addition, there are income tax effects and cash flow effects to consider. These cash contributions must come from borrowed funds or operating cash flows.

> NOTE
> The Employee Retirement Income Security Act of 1974 (ERISA) specifies minimum funding requirements.

BUSINESS INSIGHT

How Pensions Confound Income Analysis

Overfunded pension plans and boom markets can balloon income. When the stock market is booming, pension investments realize large gains that flow to income. This is because even though pension assets do not belong to shareholders (as they are the legal entitlement of current and future retirees), the gains and losses from those assets are reported in income. Many analysts consider investment returns and interest expense on the pension obligation as nonoperating activities, so as to highlight the pension impact on profitability.

The pension liability, or PBO, is reported at the present value of the expected future benefit payments owed to employees. This present value is typically estimated by actuaries hired by the company. The estimate depends on several assumptions, not the least of which is the estimated interest rate on the pension liability. (These *actuarial assumptions* include projected retirement ages, projected salaries at retirement, and life expectancy after retirement, among others.) The interest rate (or discount rate) is used to compute the present value of the future benefit payments as well as the accrued interest cost. A reconciliation of the PBO from beginning balance to year-end balance follows.

Pension Obligation
Projected benefit obligation at beginning of year
+ Service cost
+ Interest cost
− Benefits paid to retirees
= Projected benefit obligation at end of year

Normally, increases in PBO are driven by two factors. First, as employees continue to work for the company, they continue to earn additional pension benefits. This annual **service cost** represents the additional pension benefits earned by employees each year. Second, interest accrues on the outstanding pension liability, just as it would with any other long-term liability. Because there are no scheduled interest payments, this **interest cost** is added to the liability each year. As we saw with the plan assets account, pension benefit payments reduce the PBO.

The value of pension liabilities is also affected by *changes in actuarial assumptions*, particularly changes in the assumed interest rate. If the interest rate increases from, say, 8% to 9%, the present value of future benefit payments declines. Conversely, when the interest rate falls to 7%, the present value is increased. During the early 2000s, long-term interest rates were declining, and many companies were forced to lower the assumed interest rate on their pension obligations. This period also witnessed a bear market, causing plan assets to decline in value. The increase in pension liabilities coupled with declining asset values caused many pension funds to become severely underfunded.

GAAP requires that the assets and liabilities of the pension plan be reported *net* on the balance sheet. If assets exceed liabilities (the plan is overfunded) this would result in a net pension asset. The more common circumstance is that liabilities exceed assets (the plan is underfunded). In this case a net pension liability would be reported.

REMEMBER . . .
Only the net pension asset or net pension liability is reported in the balance sheet.

This net liability (or net asset) is modified by two further accounting adjustments. The first, called **unrecognized prior service cost**, represents the portion of the liability that was earned by employees prior to the inception of the plan or prior to a plan amendment. GAAP requires that this portion of the pension liability be recognized ratably (amortized) over the remaining years of service of employees. Unrecognized prior service cost reduces the pension liability that is reported in the balance sheet.

The second adjustment is for deferred (or unrecognized) gains and losses. These arise from two sources: (1) changes in actuarial assumptions causing changes in the value of the pension liability, and (2) differences between the actual return on plan assets and the long-run average (or expected) return. In both cases, GAAP allows companies to defer these gains and losses in value.

The net pension liability (or asset) that is reported in a company's balance sheet is computed as follows.

Actual funded status at year-end, overfunded or (underfunded)
+ Unrecognized prior service cost
+ Deferred or unrecognized losses or *minus* Deferred gains
= Reported pension asset (or liability)

BUSINESS INSIGHT

Johnson & Johnson's Pension Plans   Johnson & Johnson has defined benefit pension plans covering many of its US employees. In 1999, the company reported that its domestic pension plans were overfunded by more than $1 billion. By 2004, the same plans were *underfunded* by more than $1.8 billion. The following chart illustrates its decline in funded status.

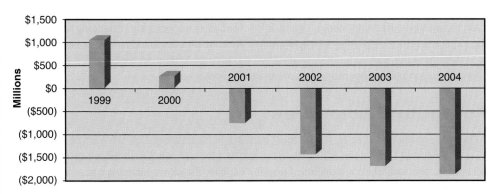

Funded Status of Johnson & Johnson Pension Plans

The following table highlights the huge impact that assumptions have had on the valuation of its pension plans.

($ millions)	1999	2000	2001	2002	2003	2004
Unrecognized actuarial gain (loss)		(186)	(210)	(478)	(714)	(609)
Unexpected return on plan assets		(527)	(689)	(1,058)	468	184
Total unexpected gain (loss)		$(713)	$(899)	$(1,536)	$(246)	$(425)

The decline in the funded status of Johnson and Johnson's pensions is largely due to two factors:

■ The *unrecognized actuarial losses* refer to the increase in the pension obligation due to changes in actuarial assumptions; the largest change has been a steady decline in the assumed discount rate from 7.75% in 1999 to 5.75% in 2004.

■ The *unexpected return on plan assets* is the difference between the actual return earned on the assets in the pension plan and the expected return. Johnson and Johnson assumed a long-run expected return of 9% per year; it exceeded that rate of return in 2003 and 2004, but did much worse in 2000 through 2002.

The sum of these effects its pension plans was a decline in value of $3.8 billion over this 5 year period.

Income Statement Effects

Net pension expense for the year is computed as follows.

	Service cost
+	Interest cost
−	Expected return on plan assets
+	Amortization of prior service cost
+	Amortization of unrecognized losses (gains)
=	Net pension expense

This expense is rarely reported separately on the income statement. Instead, it is usually included along with other forms of compensation expense in selling, general and administrative (SG&A) expenses. However, pension expense is disclosed separately in footnotes.

Computation of pension expense uses the expected return on the plan assets rather than the actual return. The difference between the expected and the actual return is deferred and amortized. Justification for this approach is that market fluctuations would increase the volatility of income unnecessarily if actual returns were used. Company CEOs and CFOs dislike income variability because stockholders react negatively to it.

Most analysts consider the service cost portion of pension expense, as well as amortization of prior service cost, to be a core operating expense, similar to salaries and other benefits. However, the interest cost component is generally viewed as a nonoperating (financing) cost. Similarly, the expected return on plan assets, and amortization of unrecognized losses or gains are considered nonoperating. Consequently, analysis of the income statement requires the parsing of pension expense into these operating and nonoperating components.

Footnote Disclosures

LO5 Analyze and interpret pension footnote disclosures

Although pension reporting is, for the most part, off-balance-sheet, GAAP requires extensive footnote disclosures. These notes allow us to reconstruct the net pension liability reported in the balance sheet, and detail the components of pension expense that are reported as part of SG&A expense in the income statement.

To illustrate, Midwest Air's footnotes (shown below) indicate that it reported $2,083,000 of pension expense in its income statement and a net pension liability of $2,354,000 in its balance sheet.

Midwest Airlines had one qualified defined benefit plan: the Pilot's Supplemental Pension Plan. This plan provides retirement benefits to Midwest Airlines pilots represented by their collective bargaining agreement.

The following table sets forth the funded status of the plan as of December 31 (in thousands):

	2003	2002	2001
Change in Benefit Obligation			
Net benefit obligation at beginning of year	$ 13,665	$ 6,778	
Service cost	924	733	
Interest cost	838	665	
Plan amendments	226	80	
Actuarial loss	2,115	5,425	
Benefits paid	(25)	(16)	
Net benefit obligation at end of year	$ 17,743	$ 13,665	
Change in Plan Assets			
Fair value of assets at beginning of year	$ 1,680	$ 545	
Actual return on plan assets	(15)	(29)	
Employer contributions	1,743	1,180	
Gross benefits paid	(25)	(16)	
Fair value of plan assets at end of year	$ 3,383	$ 1,680	
Funded status at end of year	$(14,360)	$(11,985)	
Unrecognized net actuarial loss	8,707	6,543	
Unrecognized prior service cost	3,299	3,383	
Accrued benefit liability	$ (2,354)	$ (2,059)	
Weighted-average assumptions			
Discount rate	6.00%	6.75%	7.75%
Expected return on plan assets	9.00%	9.00%	9.00%
Rate of compensation increase	5.44%	5.44%	5.44%

The net periodic benefit cost of benefit pension plans for the years ending December 31 . . . includes the following (in thousands):

	2003	2002	2001
Components of Net Periodic Benefit Cost			
Service cost	$ 924	$ 733	$ 539
Interest cost	838	665	443
Expected return on assets	(233)	(95)	(19)
Amortization of			
Prior service cost	310	295	289
Actuarial loss (gain)	199	140	----
Total net periodic benefit cost	$2,038	$1,738	$1,252

By examining the footnote, we learn that Midwest Air contributed $1,743,000 in cash to the pension plan in 2003. However, apart from this contribution, the plan assets lost value, as indicated by the actual loss of $15,000. We can also see that the pension plan is underfunded by $14,360,000. Yet only $2,354,000 is reported as a liability on the balance sheet. This difference is due to the unrecognized prior service cost, and the unrecognized actuarial loss.

In addition to the balance sheet and income statement effects, GAAP requires disclosure of key assumptions used to compute the present value of the pension liability and measure pension expense. These assumptions are typically disclosed for each income statement presented in the annual report or 10-K.

The decrease in Midwest Air's assumed interest rate from 6.75% in 2002 to 6.00% in 2003 caused Midwest Air's pension liability to increase in value. However, this increase in liability, along with the corresponding actuarial loss of $2,115,000, was not recognized immediately. Instead, this change added to the unrecognized actuarial loss reported in the footnote. This increase in the pension liability is, instead, recognized gradually as the unrecognized actuarial loss is amortized.

In sum, Midwest Air is obligated to pay its employees $17,743,000 in future pension benefits at year-end 2003. It has investments of $3,383,000 to cover these obligations. This leaves a net liability of $14,360,000. However, only $2,354,000 of this amount is reported in the balance sheet at year-end 2003. The remainder of $12,006,000 ($8,707,000 + $3,299,000) is unrecognized in accordance with GAAP, but is disclosed in the notes.

How should we treat this information for analysis purposes? One approach is to adjust the balance sheet to include the full unfunded liability of $14,360,000. This would require adding $12,006,000 to long-term liabilities. While this adjustment is not difficult, the offsetting asset adjustments to maintain the accounting equation can be complex and are beyond the scope of this book—simply suffice it to say that assets similarly increase.

Using the information in Midwest Air's footnote, we can parse the pension expense into its operating and nonoperating components. Most analysts treat service cost and amortization of prior service cost as core operating expenses, while the interest cost, expected return on plan assets, and amortization of unrecognized losses or gains are considered nonoperating. Applying this rule to Midwest's pension cost results in the following.

Service cost	$ 924
Amortization of prior service cost	310
Total core operating pension expense	1,234
Interest cost	838
Expected return on plan assets	(233)
Amortization of actuarial losses	199
Total nonoperating pension expense	804
Total pension expense	$2,038

In late 2005, the FASB announced plans to reexamine pension accounting. This project is expected to lead to improved pension disclosures. Possible changes include recognizing pension fund assets and obligations separately on the balance sheet, elimination of some or all of the unrecognized gains and losses, and more scrutiny over assumptions used to value pensions.

RESEARCH INSIGHT

Valuation of Pension Footnote Disclosures   The FASB requires footnote disclosure of the major components of pension cost presumably because it is useful for investors. Pension-related research has examined whether investors assign different valuation multiples to the components of pension cost when assessing company market value. Research finds that pension components differ from one another reflecting differences in information about perceived permanent earnings.

Other Postretirement Benefits

In addition to pension benefits, many companies provide health care and insurance benefits to retired employees. These benefits are referred to as **other postretirement benefits**. These benefits present reporting challenges similar to pension accounting. However, these benefits are often provided on a "pay-as-you-go" basis and we seldom see companies contributing, in advance, to a fund from which these benefits will be paid. As a result, the liability, known as the **accumulated postretirement benefit obligation (APBO)**, is largely, if not totally, unfunded.

GAAP requires that the unfunded liability, net of any unrecognized amounts, be reported in the balance sheet and the annual service costs and interest costs be accrued as expenses each year. This requirement is controversial for two reasons. First, future health care costs are especially difficult to estimate, so the value of the resulting APBO liability (the present value of the future benefits) is fraught with error. Second, these benefits are provided at the discretion of the employer and can be altered or terminated at any time. Consequently, employers argue that without a legal obligation to pay these benefits, the liability should not be reported in the balance sheet.

Midwest Air reports an APBO liability of $10,777,000 in its footnotes. This amount is offset by unrecognized actuarial losses and unrecognized prior service costs totaling $3,521,000. The remaining liability of $7,256,000 is reported in Midwest's balance sheet, along with the reported net pension liability, under the heading "Accrued pension and other postretirement benefits." As this case suggests, these other postretirement benefits can produce large liabilities in the company's financial statements.

CHAPTER-END REVIEW

Following is the pension disclosure footnote from Altria's 10-K report. All required questions relate only to the U.S. plan.

The benefit obligations, plan assets and funded status of Altria Group. Inc.'s pension plans at December 31, 2003 and 2002, were as follows:

(In millions)	2003	2002
Benefit obligation at January 1	$9,002	$ 8,818
Service cost	234	215
Interest cost	579	590
Benefits paid	(604)	(845)
Miller transaction		(650)
Termination, settlement and curtailment	46	126
Actuarial losses	428	756
Other	(2)	(8)
Benefit obligation at December 31	9,683	9,002
Fair value of plan assets at January 1	7,535	9,448
Actual return on plan assets	1,821	(1,304)
Contributions	853	705
Benefits paid	(648)	(858)
Miller transaction		(476)
Actuarial (losses) gains	(6)	20

(Continued on the next page)

(Continued from the previous page)

(In millions)	2003	2002
Fair value of plan assets at December 31	**9,555**	7,535
Funded status (plan assets less than benefit obligations) at December 31	**(128)**	(1,467)
Unrecognized actuarial losses	**3,615**	4,052
Unrecognized prior service cost	**130**	134
Additional minimum liability	**(196)**	(1,096)
Net prepaid pension asset (liability) recognized	**$3,421**	$ 1,623

1. In general, what factors impact a company's pension benefit obligation during a period?
2. In general, what factors impact a company's pension plan investments during a period?
3. What is the funded status (net dollars) of the Altria pension plan at year-end 2003?
4. What amount for funded status is reported on Altria's 2003 balance sheet? Is this an asset or a liability?
5. Identify and explain the difference between the funded status and the pension liability reported for Altria at year-end 2003. What factor is the largest source of this difference for Altria?

Following is Altria's footnote for its pension costs reported in its income statement.

(In millions)	2003	2002
Service cost	**$ 234**	$ 215
Interest cost	**579**	590
Expected return on plan assets	**(936)**	(943)
Amortization		
Net gain on adoption of SFAS No. 87	**—**	(1)
Unrecognized net loss (gain) from experience differences	**46**	23
Prior service cost	**16**	14
Termination settlement and curtailment	**68**	133
Net periodic pension cost (income)	**$ 7**	$ 31

6. What effect does the expected return on plan assets play in determination of pension cost?
7. How does Altria's expected return on plan assets compare with its actual return (in $s) for 2003?
8. How much net pension cost is reflected in Altria's 2003 income statement?

Solution
1. A pension benefit obligation is increased primarily by service cost, interest cost, and actuarial losses (increases in the pension liability as a result of changes in actuarial assumptions). It is decreased by the payment of benefits to retirees.
2. Pension investments are increased by positive investment returns for the period and cash contributions made by the company. Investments are decreased by benefits paid to retirees and by investment losses.
3. The funded status of Altria's pension plan is $128 million underfunded. This amount is determined by subtraction: $9,683 million (obligation) − $9,555 million (assets) = $128 million (an underfunded pension obligation, which is a net liability).
4. Altria reports a net asset of $3,421 million.
5. The difference between Altria's funded amount ($128 million liability) and the reported amount ($3,421 million asset) is due mainly to unrecognized actuarial losses of $3,615 million. As a result, $3,615 million of pension liabilities that contribute to the lower funded status are not recognized on-balance-sheet.
6. Expected return on plan assets acts as an offset to service cost and interest cost in computing net pension cost. As the expected return increases, net pension cost is reduced.
7. Altria's plan assets earned an actual return of $1,821 million in 2003. This amount is greater than its expected return of $936 million. The difference between these two amounts is a deferred unrealized gain. This unrealized gain is neither recognized on the balance sheet nor in the income statement in 2003.
8. Altria reports a net pension cost of $7 million in its 2003 income statement.

SUMMARY

LO1 Define off-balance-sheet financing and explain its effects on financial ratios. (p. 573)

- Off-balance-sheet financing refers to financial obligations of the company that are not recognized as liabilities in the balance sheet. Recognizing these obligations often requires recognizing off-balance-sheet assets.

- Off-balance sheet financing improves financial leverage ratios and its corresponding unrecognized assets improve performance measures such as RNOA.

LO2 Account for leases using the operating lease method and the capital lease method. (p. 573)

- Operating lease payments are treated as ordinary rent expense. No asset or liability is recorded.

- A capital lease records an asset and a liability equal to the present value of the minimum lease payments. The income statement reports interest expense on the liability and depreciation on the asset.

LO3 Convert off-balance-sheet operating leases to the capital lease method. (p. 579)

- Compute the present value of future cash payments required under operating leases. These cash obligations are disclosed in footnotes.

- Add a lease asset and a lease liability to the balance sheet equal to the present value of the future cash payments.

LO4 Explain and interpret the reporting for pension plans. (p. 584)

- Pension and other postretirement obligations represent one of the largest obligations for most companies.

- The projected benefit obligation is the present value of the estimated future benefits that a company expects to pay retired employees. Much of this liability is not reported in the balance sheet.

- The net liability that a company reports on the balance sheet is the projected benefit obligation offset by the plan assets and accounting adjustments.

LO5 Analyze and interpret pension footnote disclosures. (p. 588)

- Pension footnotes provide detailed information about changes in pension obligations, changes in plan assets, and the determinants of pension expense.

- Pension footnotes provide information allowing us to restate financial statements and ratios.

KEY TERMS

Accumulated postretirement benefit obligation (APBO) (p. 590)
Capitalization (p. 579)
Capital lease (p. 574)
Defined benefit plan (p. 584)
Defined contribution plan (p. 584)
Funded status (p. 585)
Interest cost (p. 586)

Lease asset (p. 574)
Lease liability (p. 574)
Lessor (p. 574)
Lessee (p. 574)
Off-balance-sheet financing (p. 573)
Operating lease (p. 574)
Other postretirement benefits (p. 590)

Plan assets (p. 585)
Projected benefit obligation (PBO) (p. 585)
Service cost (p. 586)
Unrecognized prior service cost (p. 586)

MULTIPLE CHOICE

1. GAAP requires that certain leases be accounted for as *capital leases*. The reason for this treatment is that this type of lease
   a. conveys all of the benefits and risks of ownership of the asset.
   b. is an example of form over substance.
   c. provides the use of the lease asset to the lessee for a limited period of time.
   d. is an example of off-balance-sheet financing.

2. For a lease that is accounted for as an operating lease by the lessee, the monthly rental payments should be
   a. allocated between interest expense and depreciation expense.
   b. allocated between a reduction in the liability for lease assets and interest expense.
   c. recorded as a reduction in the liability for lease assets.
   d. recorded as rent expense.

3. The balance sheet liability for a capital lease would be reduced each period by the
   a. lease payment.
   b. lease payment plus the amortization of the related asset.
   c. lease payment less the amortization of the related asset.
   d. lease payment less the periodic interest expense.

4. Which of the following statements characterizes defined benefit pension plans?
   a. The employer's obligation is satisfied by making the necessary periodic contribution.
   b. Retirement benefits are based on the plan's benefit formula.
   c. Retirement benefits depend on how well pension fund assets have been managed.
   d. Contributions are made in equal amounts by employer and employees.

5. When the value of pension plan assets is greater than the projected benefit obligation,
   a. the difference is added to pension expense.
   b. the difference is reported as deferred pension cost.
   c. the difference is reported as a contra equity adjustment.
   d. the pension plan is overfunded.

6. Which of the following is *not* a component of net pension expense?
   a. Interest cost.
   b. Return on plan assets.
   c. Benefits paid to retirees.
   d. Amortization of prior service cost.

GUIDANCE ANSWERS

YOU MAKE THE CALL

You are the Division President   You must take care in accepting lease terms that are not advantageous to your company merely to achieve off-balance-sheet financing. Long-term shareholder value is created by managing your operation well, including negotiating leases with acceptable terms. Lease footnote disclosures also provide sufficient information for skilled analysts to undo the operating lease treatment. This means that you can end up with effective capitalization of a lease with lease terms that are not in the best interests of your company and with few benefits from off-balance-sheet financing. There is also the potential for lost credibility with stakeholders.

DISCUSSION QUESTIONS

Q13-1. What are the financial reporting differences between an operating lease and a capital lease? Explain.

Q13-2. Are footnote disclosures sufficient to overcome nonrecognition on the balance sheet of assets and related liabilities for operating leases? Explain.

Q13-3. Is the expense of a lease over its entire life the same whether or not it is capitalized? Explain.

Q13-4. What are the economic and accounting differences between a defined contribution plan and a defined benefit plan?

Q13-5. Under what circumstances will a company report a net pension asset? A net pension liability?

Q13-6. What are the components of pension expense that is reported in the income statement?

Q13-7. What effect does the use of expected returns on pension investments and the deferral of unexpected gains and losses on those investments have on income?

Q13-8. How is the initial valuation determined for the asset and the liability with a capital lease?

Q13-9. Over what time period should the cost of providing retirement benefits to employees be expensed?

Q13-10. What accounting analysis is required when the accumulated retirement benefits under a firm's pension plan exceed the assets in its pension fund?

MINI EXERCISES

M13-11 Accounting for Leases (LO2)
On January 3, 2006, Hanna Corporation signed a lease on a machine for its manufacturing operation. The lease requires Hanna to make six annual lease payments of $12,000 with the first payment due December 31, 2006. Hanna could have financed the machine by borrowing the purchase price at an interest rate of 7%.
   a. Prepare the journal entries that Hanna Corporation would make on January 3 and December 31, 2006, to record this lease assuming

    i. the lease is reported as an operating lease.

    ii. the lease is reported as a capital lease.

b. Assuming that the lease is treated as a capital lease, post the journal entries of part *a* to the appropriate T-accounts.

c. Show how the entries posted in part *b* would affect the financial statements using the financial statement effects template.

M13-12 Accounting for Leases (LO2)

On July 1, 2006, Stokes Company leased a warehouse building under a 10-year lease agreement. The lease requires quarterly lease payments of $4,500. The first lease payment is due on September 30, 2006. The lease was reported as a capital lease using an 8% annual interest rate.

a. Prepare the journal entry to record the initial signing of the lease on July 1, 2006.

b. Prepare the journal entries that would be necessary on September 30 and December 31, 2006.

c. Post the entries from parts *a* and *b* in their appropriate T-accounts.

d. Prepare a financial statement effects template to show the effects of the entries from parts *a* and *b* on the balance sheet and income statement.

e. Redo parts *a* and *b* assuming that the lease is reported as an operating lease. Is the expense recognized in 2006 under the operating lease method higher or lower than under the capital lease method? Explain.

M13-13. Analysis and Interpretation of Leasing Footnote Disclosures (LO2)

YUM! Brands, Inc., discloses the following footnote to its 2003 10-K report relating to its leasing activities:

> We have non-cancelable commitments under both capital and long-term operating leases, primarily for our restaurants. Capital and operating lease commitments expire at various dates through 2087 and, in many cases, provide for rent escalations and renewal options. Most leases require us to pay related executory costs, which include property taxes, maintenance and insurance.

a. Yum reports the existence of both capital and operating leases. In general, what effects does each of these lease types have on Yum's balance sheet and its income statement?

b. What types of adjustments might you consider to Yum's balance sheet for analysis purposes?

M13-14. Analysis and Capitalization of Operating Lease Payments Disclosed in Footnotes (LO3)

Southwest Airlines Co. discloses the following in the footnotes to its 10-K report relating to its leasing activities:

(In millions)	Capital leases	Operating leases
2004	$ 18	$ 283
2005	24	273
2006	14	219
2007	16	202
2008	13	190
After 2008	39	1,328
Total minimum lease payments	124	$2,495
Less amount representing interest	33	
Present value of minimum lease payments	91	
Less current portion	10	
Long-term portion	$ 81	

Operating leases are not reflected on-balance-sheet. In our analysis of a company, we often desire to capitalize these operating leases, that is, add the present value of these lease payments to both the reported assets and liabilities. (a) Compute the present value of Southwest's operating lease payments assuming a 7% discount rate. (b) What effect does capitalization of Southwest's operating leases have on its total liabilities (it reported total liabilities of $4,826 million for 2003).

M13-15. Analysis and Interpretation of Pension Disclosures-Expenses and Returns (LO4, 5)

American Express discloses the following pension footnote in its 10-K report:

(In millions)	2003
Service cost	$ 115
Interest cost	118
Expected return on plan assets	(146)
Amortization of	
Prior service cost	(8)
Transition obligation	(2)
Recognized net actuarial loss (gain)	18
Settlement/curtailment loss (gain)	10
Net periodic pension benefit cost	$ 105

a. How much pension expense does American Express report in its 2003 income statement?

b. What effect does its 'expected return on plan assets' have on its reported pension expense? Explain.

c. Explain use of the word 'expected' as it relates to results of pension plan investments.

M13-16. Analysis and Interpretation of Pension Disclosures-Expenses and Returns (LO4, 5)

YUM! Brands, Inc., discloses the following pension footnote in its 10-K report:

YUM! Brands, Inc.
(YUM)

	Pension Benefits		
(In millions)	2003	2002	2001
Service cost	$ 26	$ 22	$ 20
Interest cost	34	31	28
Amortization of prior service cost	4	1	1
Expected return on plan assets	(30)	(28)	(29)
Recognized actuarial loss	6	1	1
Net periodic benefit cost	$ 40	$ 27	$ 21

a. How much pension expense does Yum report in its 2003 income statement?

b. What effect does its "expected return on plan assets" have on its reported pension expense? Explain.

c. Explain use of the word *expected* as it relates to results of pension plan investments.

M13-17. Analysis and Interpretation of Retirement Benefit Footnote (LO4, 5)

Abercrombie and Fitch disclose the following footnote relating to its retirement plans in its 2002 10-K report:

Abercrombie and
Fitch (ANF)

RETIREMENT BENEFITS The Company participates in a qualified defined contribution retirement plan and a nonqualified supplemental retirement plan. Participation in the qualified plan is available to all associates who have completed 1,000 or more hours of service with the Company during certain 12-month periods and attained the age of 21. Participation in the nonqualified plan is subject to service and compensation requirements. The Company's contributions to these plans are based on a percentage of associates' eligible annual compensation. The cost of these plans was $5.6 million in 2002, $3.9 million in 2001 and $3.0 million in 2000.

a. Does Abercrombie have a defined contribution or defined benefit pension plan? Explain.

b. How does Abercrombie account for its contributions to its retirement plan?

c. How is Abercrombie's obligation to its retirement plan reported on its balance sheet?

M13-18. Analysis and Interpretation of Pension Plan Benefit Footnote (LO4, 5)

Target Corporation provides the following footnote relating to its retirement plans in its 2003 10-K report:

Target Corporation
(TGT)

Defined Contribution Plans Employees who meet certain eligibility requirements can participate in a defined contribution 401(k) plan by investing up to 80 percent of their compensation. We match 100 percent of each employee's contribution up to 5 percent of respective total compensation. Our contribution to the plan is initially invested in Target Corporation common stock. Benefits expense related to these matching contributions was $117 million. $111 million and $97 million in 2003, 2002 and 2001, respectively.

a. Does Target have a defined contribution or defined benefit pension plan? Explain.
b. How does Target account for its contributions to its retirement plan?
c. How is Target's obligation to its retirement plan reported on its balance sheet?

M13-19. Analysis of Off-Balance-Sheet Financing (LO1)

The 2004 10-K report of **Oakley, Inc.**, provides the following footnote ($ thousands).

Endorsement Contracts The Company has entered into several endorsement contracts with selected athletes and others who endorse the Company's products. The contracts are primarily of short duration. Under the contracts, the Company has agreed to pay certain incentives based on performance and is required to pay minimum annual payments as follows.

Year Ending December 31	
2005	$ 6,735
2006	2,485
2007	1,240
Thereafter	—
	$10,460

a. Compute the present value of Oakley's minimum annual payments under endorsement contracts. Assume a 6% discount rate.
b. In its 2005 balance sheet, Oakley reported average financial liabilities of $29,474 and average stockholders' equity of $346,308. Compute its financial leverage ratio (FLEV). If Oakley reported the present value of endorsement payments in its balance sheet, how would FLEV change?
c. If Oakley reported these endorsement liabilities in its balance sheet, what would be the asset that balances the balance sheet? What is the nature of this asset?

M13-20. Analysis and Interpretation of Footnote on Contract Manufacturers (LO1)

Reebok (RBK)

Reebok reports the following information relating to its manufacturing activities in the footnotes to its 2003 10-K report:

MANUFACTURING Most of our products are produced by independent manufacturers that are principally located outside the United States. We source some of our apparel and some of the component parts used in our footwear, however, from independent manufacturers located in the United States. In addition, we operate facilities in Indianapolis, Indiana and Mattapoisett, Massachusetts that provide apparel and accessory finishing for our sports licensing business.

a. What effect does the use of contract manufacturers have on Reebok's balance sheet?
b. How might Reebok's return on net operating assets (RNOA) and its components be affected by use of contract manufacturers? Explain.
c. Reebok executes purchase contracts with its contract manufacturers to purchase their output. How are executory contracts reported under GAAP? Does your answer suggest a possible motivation for the use of contract manufacturing?

EXERCISES

E13-21. Analysis and Interpretation of Leasing Footnote (LO2)

Fortune Brands, Inc. (FOPRA)

Fortune Brands, Inc., reports the following footnote relating to its leased facilities in its 2002 10-K report. Future minimum rental payments under noncancelable operating leases as of December 31, 2001 are as follows:

(In millions)	
2002	$ 49.0
2003	38.0
2004	31.7
2005	25.5
2006	19.7
Remainder	54.3
Total minimum rental payments	218.2
Less minimum rentals to be received under noncancelable subleases	1.2
	$217.0

a. Assuming that this is the only information available about its leasing activities, does Fortune Brands classify its leases as operating or capital? Explain.

b. What effect has its lease classification had on Fortune Brands' balance sheet? Over the life of the lease, what effect does this classification have on net income?

E13-22. Analysis and Interpretation of Footnote on both Operating and Capital Leases (LO)

Verizon Communications, Inc., provides the following footnote relating to its leasing activities in its 10-K report.

Verizon Communications, Inc. (VZ)

The aggregate minimum rental commitments under noncancelable leases for the periods shown at December 31, 2002, are as follows:

Years (dollars in millions)	Capital Leases	Operating Leases
2003	$ 75	$ 825
2004	89	739
2005	31	643
2006	24	698
2007	19	353
Thereafter	93	1,047
Total minimum rental commitments	331	$4,305
Less interest and executory costs	(90)	
Present value of minimum lease payments	241	
Less current installments	(54)	
Long-term obligation at December 31, 2002	$187	

a. Assuming that this is the only available information relating to its leasing activities, what amount does Verizon report on its balance sheet for its lease obligations? Does this amount represent its total obligation to lessors? How do you know?

b. What effect has its lease classification as capital or operating had on Verizon's balance sheet? Over the life of its leases, what effect does this lease classification have on its net income?

E13-23. Analyzing, Interpreting and Capitalizing Operating Leases (LO3)

Staples, Inc., reports the following footnote relating to its capital and operating leases in its 2003 10-K report ($ thousands).

Staples, Inc. (SPLS)

Other long-term obligations at January 31, 2004 include $90.0 million relating to future rent escalation clauses and lease incentives under certain existing store operating lease arrangements. These rent expenses are recognized on a straight-line basis over the respective terms of the leases. Future minimum lease commitments due for retail and support facilities (including lease commitments for 6 retail stores not yet opened at January 31, 2004) and equipment leases under noncancellable operating leases are as follows (in thousands):

Fiscal Year	Total
2004	$ 504,964
2005	484,560
2006	451,712
2007	421,610
2008	395,472
Thereafter	2,336,640
	$4,594,958

Rent expense approximated $480.0 million, $445.2 million, and $419.8 million for fiscal years 2003, 2002 and 2001, respectively.

a. What dollar adjustment(s) might you consider to Staples' balance sheet given this information and assuming that Staples intermediate-term borrowing rate is 7%? Explain. (Staples reported total liabilities of $2,840,146 ($ 000s) for 2003.)

b. Show how the amount computed in part *a* would be reported in the balance sheet using the financial statement effects template.

c. Prepare journal entries to record the capitalization of these operating leases at the end of 2003. What journal entries would be required to record lease payments and lease related expenses in 2004 if these leases were accounted for as capital leases?

d. Post the journal entries from part *c* to the appropriate T-accounts.

E13-24. Analysis, Interpretation and Capitalization of Operating Leases (LO3)

YUM! Brands, Inc. (YUM)

YUM! Brands, Inc., reports the following footnote relating to its capital and operating leases in its 2003 10-K report ($ millions).

Future minimum commitments and amounts to be received as lessor or sublessor under non-cancelable leases are set forth below:

	Commitments		Lease Receivables	
(In millions)	Capital	Operating	Direct Financing	Operating
2004	$ 15	$ 320	$ 8	$ 22
2005	15	290	8	20
2006	14	250	7	19
2007	13	227	7	18
2008	13	204	6	17
Thereafter	122	1,193	63	102
	$192	$2,484	$99	$198

What adjustment(s), assuming a discount rate of 7%, might you consider making to Yum's balance sheet given this information? Explain. Yum reported total liabilities of $4,500 million for 2003. (Hint: Net the respective operating commitments and lease receivables columns.)

E13-25. Analyzing, Interpreting and Capitalizing Operating Leases (LO3)

Reebok (RBK)

Reebok reports the following footnote relating to its capital and operating leases in its 2003 10-K report.

Minimum annual rentals under operating leases for the five years subsequent to December 31, 2003 and in the aggregate are as follows ($ thousands):

	Total Amount	Less: Amounts Representing Sublease Income	Net Amount
2004	$ 47,102	$1,417	$ 45,685
2005	36,439	1,236	35,203
2006	28,960	1,232	27,728

(Continued on the next page)

(Continued from the previous page)

	Total Amount	Less: Amounts Representing Sublease Income	Net Amount
2007	22,306	1,042	21,264
2008	17,324	433	16,891
2009 and thereafter	12,753	0	12,753
	$164,884	$5,360	$159,524

Total rent expense for all operating leases amounted to $58,919, $58,768 and $55,999 for the years ended December 31, 2003, 2002 and 2001, respectively.

a. What adjustment(s) might you consider to Reebok's balance sheet given this information and assuming that Reebok's discount rate is 7%? Explain.
b. Show how the amount computed in part *a* would be reported in the balance sheet using the financial statement effects template.
c. Prepare journal entries to record the capitalization of these operating leases at the end of 2003. What journal entries would be required to record lease payments and lease related expenses in 2004 if these leases were accounted for as capital leases?
d. Post the journal entries from part *c* to the appropriate T-accounts.

E13-26. Analysis and Interpretation of Pension Footnote-Funded and Reported Amounts (LO)
YUM! Brands, Inc., reports the following pension footnote in its 10-K report.

YUM! Brands, Inc. (YUM)

	Pension Benefits	
September 30 (In millions)	2003	2002
Change in benefit obligation		
Benefit obligation at beginning of year	$501	$420
Service cost	26	22
Interest cost	34	31
Plan amendments	—	14
Curtailment gain	(1)	(3)
Benefits and expenses paid	(21)	(16)
Actuarial loss	90	33
Benefit obligation at end of year	$ 629	$ 501
Change in plan assets		
Fair value of plan assets at beginning of year	$ 251	$ 291
Actual return on plan assets	52	(24)
Employer contributions	157	1
Benefits paid	(21)	(16)
Administrative expenses	(1)	(1)
Fair value of plan assets at end of year	$ 438	$ 251
Funded status	$(191)	$(250)
Employer contributions	—	25
Unrecognized actuarial loss	230	169
Unrecognized prior service cost	12	16
Net amount recognized at year-end	$ 51	$ (40)

a. Describe what is meant by *service cost* and *interest cost*.
b. What is the source of funds to make payments to retirees?
c. Show the computation of the 2003 funded status for Yum.
d. What net pension amount is reported on its 2003 balance sheet? Why is the reported amount different from the funded status?

E13-27. Analysis and Interpretation of Pension Footnote-Funded and Reported Amounts (LO4, 5)
Xerox reports the following pension footnote as part of its 2003 10-K report.

Xerox (XRXPRC)

(In millions)	Pension Benefits	
	2003	2002
Change in Benefit Obligation		
Benefit obligation, January 1	$ 7,931	$ 7,606
Service cost	197	180
Interest cost	934	(210)
Plan participants' contributions	15	18
Plan amendments	1	(31)
Actuarial loss	312	736
Currency exchange rate changes	486	327
Divestitures	(45)	(1)
Curtailments	1	2
Special termination benefits	—	39
Benefits paid/settlements	$(861)	(735)
Benefit obligation, December 31	$ 8,971	$ 7,931
Change in Plan Assets		
Fair value of plan assets, January 1	$ 5,963	$7,040
Actual return on plan assets	1,150	(768)
Employer contribution	672	138
Plan participants' contributions	15	18
Currency exchange rate changes	401	271
Divestitures	(39)	(1)
Benefits paid/settlements	(861)	(735)
Fair value of plan assets, December 31	$ 7,301	$ 5,963
Funded status (including under-funded and non-funded plans)	$(1,670)	$(1,968)
Unamortized transition assets	(2)	—
Unrecognized prior service cost	(24)	(27)
Unrecognized net actuarial loss	1,870	1,843
Net amount recognized	$ 174	$ (152)

(In millions)	Pension Benefits	
	2003	2002
Components of Net Periodic Benefit Cost		
Defined benefit plans		
Service cost	$ 197	$ 180
Interest cost	934	(210)
Expected return on plan assets	(940)	134
Recognized net actuarial loss	53	7
Amortization of prior service cost	—	3
Recognized net transition asset	—	(1)
Recognized curtailment/settlement loss (gain)	120	55
Net periodic benefit cost	364	168
Special termination benefits	—	27
Defined contribution plans	62	10
Total	$ 426	$ 205

a. Describe what is meant by *service cost* and *interest cost* (the service and interest costs appear both in the reconciliation of the PBO and in the computation of pension expense).

b. What is the actual return on pension investments in 2003? Was Xerox's profitability impacted exactly by this amount?

c. Provide an example under which an "actuarial loss," such as the $312 million charge that Xerox reports, might arise.
d. What is the source of funds to make payments to retirees?
e. How much cash did Xerox contribute to its pension plans in 2003?
f. How much cash did the company pay to retirees in 2003?
g. Show the computation of its 2003 funded status.
h. What net pension amount is reported on its 2003 balance sheet? Why is the reported amount different from the funded status?

E13-28. Analysis and Interpretation of Pension Footnote-Funded and Reported Amounts (LO4, 5)

Verizon reports the following pension footnote as part of its 2003 10-K report.

Verizon (VZ)

At December 31 ($ millions)	Pension 2003	2002
Change in Benefit Obligation		
Beginning of year	$37,908	$36,391
Service cost	788	718
Interest cost	2,439	2,488
Plan amendments	854	114
Actuarial loss, net	1,214	2,560
Benefits paid	(3,925)	(3,356)
Termination benefits	2,588	286
Acquisitions and divestitures, net	23	885
Settlements and curtailments	(900)	(2,256)
Other	54	78
End of year	41,043	37,908
Change in Plan Assets		
Beginning of year	38,676	48,558
Actual return on plan assets	8,671	(4,678)
Company contributions	285	157
Benefits paid	(3,925)	(3,356)
Settlements	(900)	(2,536)
Acquisitions and divestitures, net	34	531
End of year	42,841	38,676
Funded Status		
End of year	1,798	768
Unrecognized		
Actuarial loss, net	5,079	8,295
Prior service (benefit) cost	1,512	752
Transition asset	(3)	(44)
Net amount recognized	$ 8,386	$ 9,771

a. Describe what is meant by service cost and interest cost.
b. What is the source of funds to make payments to retirees?
c. Show the computation of Verizon's 2003 funded status.
d. What net pension amount is reported on its 2003 balance sheet? Why is the reported amount different from the funded status?

PROBLEMS

P13-29 Capitalization of Operating Leases (LO2, 3)

The 2004 10-K report of Outback Steakhouse, Inc., included the following footnote.

Outback Steakhouse, Inc. (OSI)

OPERATING LEASES The Company leases restaurant and office facilities and certain equipment under operating leases having initial terms expiring between 2005 and 2021. Certain of these leases require the payment of contingent rentals based on a percentage of gross revenues, as defined by the terms of the applicable lease agreement. Total rental expense for the years ended December 31, 2004, 2003 and 2002 was approximately $77,641,000, $61,991,000, and $49,258,000, respectively, and included contingent rent of approximately $4,695,000, $3,669,000 and $3,392,000, respectively. Future minimum rental payments on operating leases (including leases for restaurants scheduled to open in 2005) are as follows (in thousands):

2005	$ 70,498
2006	67,797
2007	61,492
2008	55,194
2009	48,608
Thereafter	159,677
Total minimum lease payments	$463,266

Required

a. Prepare the journal entry to record Outback's lease expense for 2004. Assume that this expense was paid in cash and none of this expense was prepaid or accrued in other years.

b. Assume that Outback reclassified its operating leases as capital leases and that the appropriate discount rate is 8%. What amount would Outback report as a lease liability in its 2004 balance sheet?

c. If these leases had been treated as capital leases instead of operating leases, what would be the effect on Outback's 2004 income statement? Its 2005 income statement? Show how this change would affect the income statement and balance sheet using the financial statement effects template.

d. If these leases had been treated as capital leases instead of operating leases, what would be the effect on Outback's 2004 statement of cash flows?

P13-30. Analysis, Interpretation and Capitalization of Leasing Disclosures (LO3)

Abercrombie & Fitch (ANF)

The Abercrombie & Fitch 2002 10-K report contains the following footnote relating to its leasing activities. This is the only information it discloses relating to its leasing activity.

At February 1, 2003, the Company was committed to noncancelable leases with remaining terms of one to fourteen years. These commitments include store leases with initial terms ranging primarily from ten to fifteen years. A summary of minimum rent commitments under noncancelable leases follows (thousands):

2003	$120,313	2006	112,899
2004	121,316	2007	99,381
2005	118,695	Thereafter	316,724

Required

a. What is the balance of its lease assets and lease liabilities as reported on Abercrombie's balance sheet? How do you know?

b. Assuming that all of A&F's leases are classified as operating, what effect has this classification had on A&F's balance sheet? Over the life of the lease, what effect does this classification have on its net income?

c. Using a 10% discount rate, estimate the assets and liabilities that A&F fails to report as a result of its off-balance-sheet lease financing.

d. Using the financial statement effects template, show how capitalizing these operating leases would affect the balance sheet and income statement.

e. Prepare journal entries to record the capitalization of these operating leases at the end of fiscal year 2002. What journal entries would be required to record lease payments and lease related expenses in fiscal year 2003 if these leases were accounted for as capital leases?

f. Post the journal entries from part e to the appropriate T-accounts.

g. What financial ratios from ROE disaggregation (such as margins, turnover, and leverage) are affected and in what direction (increased or decreased) by its off-balance-sheet lease financing?

P13-31. Analysis, Interpretation and Capitalization of Leasing Disclosures (LO3)

The Best Buy 10-K report has the following footnote related to its leasing activities. This is the only information it discloses relating to its leasing activity.

Best Buy (BBY)

Future minimum lease obligations by year (not including percentage rentals) for all operating leases at March 2, 2002, were as follows ($ millions):

Fiscal Year	
2003	$ 472
2004	459
2005	417
2006	376
2007	361
Thereafter	2,698

Required

a. What is the balance of its lease assets and lease liabilities as reported on its balance sheet? How do you know?

b. Assuming that all of its leases are classified as operating, what effect has this classification had on its balance sheet? Over the life of the lease, what effect does this classification have on its net income?

c. Using a 10% discount rate, estimate the assets and liabilities that it fails to report as a result of its off-balance-sheet lease financing.

d. Using the financial statement effects template, show how capitalizing these operating leases would affect the balance sheet and income statement.

e. Prepare journal entries to record the capitalization of these operating leases at the end of fiscal year 2002. What journal entries would be required to record lease payments and lease related expenses in fiscal year 2003 if these leases were accounted for as capital leases?

f. Post the journal entries from part e to the appropriate T-accounts.

g. What financial ratios from ROE disaggregation (such as margins, turnover, and leverage) are affected and in what direction (increased or decreased) by its off-balance-sheet lease financing?

P13-32 Accounting for Operating and Capital Leases (LO2, 3)

On January 1, 2006, Springer, Inc., entered into two lease contracts. The first lease contract was a six-year lease for computer equipment with $15,000 annual lease payments due at the end of each year. Springer took possession of the equipment on January 1, 2006. The second lease contract was a six-month lease, beginning January 1, 2006, for warehouse storage space with $1,000 monthly lease payments due the first of each month. Springer made the first month's payment on January 1, 2006. The present value of the lease payments under the first contract is $74,520. The present value of the lease payments under the second contract is $5,853.

a. Assume that the first lease contract is a capital lease. Prepare the appropriate journal entry for this lease on January 1, 2006.

b. Assume the second lease contract is an operating lease. Prepare the proper journal entry for this lease on January 1, 2006.

P13-33. Analysis and Interpretation of Pension Disclosures (LO4, 5)

FedEx's 10-K report has the following disclosures related to its retirement plans.

FedEx (FDX)

In millions	Pension Plans	
	2002	2001
Change in Projected Benefit Obligation		
Projected benefit obligation at beginning of year	$5,384	$4,494
Service cost.	348	325
Interest cost.	409	382
Actuarial loss (gain).	168	211
Benefits paid	(84)	(57)
Amendments, benefit enhancements and other	2	29
Projected benefit obligation at end of year	$6,227	$5,384

(Continued on the next page)

(Continued from the previous page)

In millions	Pension Plans	
	2002	**2001**
Accumulated Benefit Obligation	**$5,097**	$4,104
Change in Plan Assets		
Fair value of plan assets at beginning of year	**$5,622**	$5,727
Actual loss on plan assets	**(191)**	(142)
Company contributions	**161**	97
Benefits paid	**(84)**	(57)
Other	**2**	(3)
Fair value of plan assets at end of year	**$5,510**	$5,622
Funded Status of the Plans	**$ (717)**	$238
Unrecognized actuarial loss (gain)	**823**	(160)
Unamortized prior service cost	**130**	144
Unrecognized transition amount	**(8)**	(9)
Prepaid (accrued) benefit cost	**$ 228**	$213
Amounts Recognized in the Balance Sheet at May 31		
Prepaid benefit cost	**$ 411**	$365
Accrued benefit liability	**(183)**	(152)
Minimum pension liability	**(19)**	(20)
Accumulated other comprehensive income	**5**	—
Intangible asset	**14**	20
Prepaid (accrued) benefit cost	**$ 228**	$213

In millions	Pension Plans		
	2002	**2001**	**2000**
Service cost	**$ 348**	$ 325	$ 338
Interest cost	**409**	382	336
Expected return on plan assets	**(621)**	(624)	(546)
Net amortization and deferral	**13**	(23)	6
	$ 149	$ 60	$ 134
Weighted-Average Actuarial Assumptions			
Discount rate	**7.1%**	7.7%	8.5%
Rate of increase in future compensation levels	**3.3**	4.0	5.0
Expected long-term rate of return on assets	**10.9**	10.9	10.9

Required

a. How much pension expense (revenue) does FedEx report in its 2002 income statement?

b. FedEx reports a $621 million expected return on plan assets as an offset to 2002 pension expense. Approximately, how is this amount computed? What is the actual gain or loss realized on its 2002 plan assets? What is the purpose of using this estimated amount instead of the actual gain or loss?

c. What factors affected its 2002 pension liability? What factors affected its 2002 plan assets?

d. What does the term funded status mean? What is the funded status of the 2002 FedEx retirement plans? What amount of asset or liability does FedEx report on its 2002 balance sheet relating to its retirement plans? What factors account for the difference between these two amounts?

e. FedEx reduced its discount rate from 7.7% to 7.1% in 2002. What effect(s) does this reduction have on its balance sheet and its income statement?

f. FedEx reduced its estimate of expected annual wage increases from 4% to 3.3% in 2002. What effect(s) does this reduction have on its financial statements? In general, does such a reduction increase or decrease income?

P13-34. Accounting for Pension Benefits   (LO4)

Adler Corporation has a defined contribution pension plan for its employees. Each year, Adler contributes to the plan an amount equal to 4% of the employee payroll for the year. Adler's 2007 payroll was $400,000. Adler also provides a life insurance benefit that pays a $50,000 death benefit to the beneficiaries of retired employees. At the end of 2007, Adler estimates that its liability under the life insurance program is $625,000. Adler has assets with a fair value of $175,000 in a trust fund that are available to meet the death benefit payments.

a. Prepare the journal entry at December 31, 2007, to record Adler's 2007 defined contribution to a pension trustee who will manage the pension funds for the firm's employees.

b. What amount of liability for death benefit payments must Adler report in its December 31, 2007, balance sheet? Explain.

CASES AND PROJECTS

C13-35. Analysis, Interpretation and Capitalization of Leasing Disclosures   (LO3)

FedEx reports total assets of $13,812 and total liabilities of $6,545 for 2002 ($ millions). Its 10-K report has the following footnote related to its leasing activities.   FedEx (FDX)

A summary of future minimum lease payments under capital leases and noncancellable operating leases (principally aircraft and facilities) with an initial or remaining term in excess of one year at May 31, 2002 is as follows:

In millions	Capital Leases	Operating Leases
2003	$ 12	$ 1,501
2004	12	1,235
2005	12	1,162
2006	12	1,053
2007	12	1,028
Thereafter	253	8,791
	313	$14,770
Less amount representing interest	(107)	
Present value of net minimum lease payments	$ 206	

Required

a. What is the balance of its lease assets and lease liabilities as reported on its balance sheet? Explain.

b. Impute the discount rate that FedEx is using to compute the present value of its capital leases (see Wal-Mart Business Insight box in the chapter for a description of the mechanics).

c. Using the discount rate imputed in part (b), estimate the amount of assets and liabilities that FedEx fails to report as a result of its off-balance-sheet lease financing. (Hint: If you cannot impute the interest rate in b, use 3.5% for this part.)

d. What financial ratios from ROE disaggregation (such as margins, turnover, and leverage) are affected and in what direction (increased or decreased) by its off-balance-sheet lease financing?

e. What portion of its total lease liabilities is reported on-balance-sheet and what is reported off-balance-sheet?

f. Based on your analysis, do you believe that FedEx's balance sheet adequately reports its aircraft and facilities assets and related obligations? Explain.

C13-36. Analysis and Interpretation of Pension Disclosures   (LO4, 5)

Dow Chemical provides the following footnote disclosures in its 10-K report relating to its pension plans.   Dow Chemical (DOW)

(In million)	Defined Benefit Pension Plans	
	2002	2001
Service cost	$ 219	$ 206
Interest cost	748	708
Expected return on plan assets	(1,105)	(1,072)
Amortization of transition obligation	—	—
Amortization of prior service cost (credit)	20	23
Amortization of unrecognized (gain) loss	(20)	(73)
Special termination/curtailment cost (credit)	(7)	113
Net periodic cost (credit)	$ (145)	$ (95)
Change in projected benefit obligation		
Benefit obligation at beginning of year	$11,341	$ 9,985
Service cost	219	206
Interest cost	748	708
Plan participant's contributions	8	11
Amendments	28	31
Actuarial changes in assumptions and experience	443	629
Acquisition/divestiture activity	5	190
Benefits, paid	(745)	(625)
Currency impact	76	93
Special termination/curtailment cost (credit)	(26)	113
Benefit obligation at end of year	$12,097	$11,341
Change in plan assets		
Market value of plan assets at beginning of year	$11,424	$12,435
Actual return on plan assets	(1,230)	(611)
Employer contributions	112	30
Plan participant's contributions	9	11
Acquisition/divestiture activity	4	158
Benefits paid	(741)	(599)
Special settlement paid	(17)	—
Market value of plan assets at end of year	$ 9,561	$11,424
Funded status and net amounts recognized		
Plan assets in excess of (less than) benefit obligation ...	$ (2,536)	$ 83
Unrecognized net transition obligation	2	5
Unrecognized prior service cost (credit)	132	123
Unrecognized net (gain) loss	2,796	(34)
Net amounts recognized in the consolidated balance sheets	$ 394	$ 177

Assumptions for Pension Plans	2002	2001
Weighted-average discount rate	6.75%	7.00%
Rate of increase in future compensation levels	5.00%	5.00%
Long-term rate of return on assets	9.25%	9.18%

Required

a. How much pension expense (revenue) does Dow Chemical report in its 2002 income statement?

b. Dow reports a $1,105 million expected return on plan assets as an offset to 2002 pension expense. Approximately, how is this amount computed? What is the actual gain or loss realized on its 2002 plan assets? What is the purpose of using this estimated amount instead of the actual gain or loss?

c. What factors affected its 2002 pension liability? What factors affected its 2002 plan assets?

d. What does the term funded status mean? What is the funded status of the 2002 Dow retirement plans? What amount of asset or liability does Dow report on its 2002 balance sheet relating to its retirement plans? What factors account for the difference between these two amounts?

e. Dow reduced its discount rate from 7% to 6.75% in 2002. What effect(s) does this reduction have on its balance sheet and its income statement?

f. Dow increased its estimate of expected returns on plan assets from 9.18% to 9.25% in 2002. What effect(s) does this increase have on its income statement? Explain.

C13-37. Principles Underlying Retirement Benefits (LO4, 5)

An annual report from **Briggs & Stratton Corporation** discloses the following guidelines regarding accrued employee benefits.

Briggs & Stratton Corporation (BGG)

> The Company's life insurance program includes payment of a death benefit to beneficiaries of retired employees. The Company accrues for the estimated cost of these benefits over the estimated working life of the employee. Past service costs for all retired employees have been fully provided for and the Company also accrues for the estimated cost of supplemental retirement and death benefit agreements with executive officers.

a. What is the basic accounting principle that causes Briggs & Stratton to accrue the estimated cost of providing death benefit payments over the estimated working lives of the covered employees? Briefly explain how this principle leads to the accounting treatment Briggs & Stratton uses.

b. The past service costs referred to by Briggs & Stratton relate to the firm's defined benefit pension plan. What are past service costs?

c. Over what time period is Briggs & Stratton recognizing the expense of providing supplemental retirement and death benefit agreements with executive officers?

Constructing and Illustrating a Comprehensive Case

KIMBERLY-CLARK

Reinventing a Consumer Products Company

The past decade has seen a shift in the universe for consumer products companies. Gone are numerous competitors. Many having been gobbled up in the industry's consolidation trend. Also gone is media control. Hundreds of different media outlets and venues compete for promotion space and scarce consumer time.

Fortune (2003) reports that in 1995 it took three TV commercials to reach 80% of 18- to 49-year-old women. Just five years later, it took 97 ads to reach the same group. "Short of being embroiled in a scandal," says ad agency Doremus in a newsletter, "it's almost impossible to get your name in enough channels to build substantial awareness."

Another development is in-store branding. Companies such as Costco with its Kirkland Signature brand on everything from candy to apparel, and Walgreen's with its low cost alternatives, threaten the powerhouse brands from Kimberly-Clark, Procter & Gamble, Colgate-Palmolive, and other consumer products companies. Fortune (2003) declares that the "retail universe has consolidated, and the media universe has shattered. As the mass media have de-massified into 1,000 bits—500 channels . . . In short, brand makers are losing their connection to the consumer."

When Thomas J. Falk assumed the top spot at the nation's largest disposable diaper producer in September 2002, he inherited some extra baggage with it: an identity crisis, a decades-long rivalry with consumer-products behemoth Procter & Gamble, and a group of investors short on patience from a series of earnings misses. (*The Wall Street Journal,* 2002)

On November 30, 2004, in a move aimed at boosting its stock price and its return on equity, Kimberly-Clark announced that it had distributed to its stockholders all the outstanding shares of Neenah Paper Inc. Neenah was formed in 2004 to facilitate the spin-off of the Corporation's fine paper and technical paper business and its Canadian pulp mills. Under CEO Falk's leadership, the company has been moving steadily in improving its focus on its health and hygiene segments. Kimberly-Clark's plan would follow a similar move by rival Procter & Gamble. (*BusinessWeek,* 2004)

Kimberly-Clark has also moved to shore up its brand images across its immense product line. It currently is a $14 billion in sales company that manufactures such well-recognized brands as Huggies and Pull-Ups disposable diapers, Kotex and Lightdays feminine products, Kleenex facial tissue, Viva paper towels, and Scott bathroom tissue.

The rocky ride endured by Kimberly-Clark investors over the past few years is unlikely to subside—see the following stock price chart. Competition is fierce and well-armed. The pending purchase of Gillette by Procter & Gamble further muddies the future of the industry.

(Continued on next page)

(Continued from previous page)

On the positive side, Kimberly-Clark's earnings performance is consistent, and its financial position is solid. Further, Kimberly-Clark's RNOA for 2003 was 18%, and its financial leverage increased its RNOA to yield a robust 24% in return on equity. It also reported $16.8 billion in assets, nearly half of which is concentrated in plant, property, and equipment and another 16% in intangible assets.

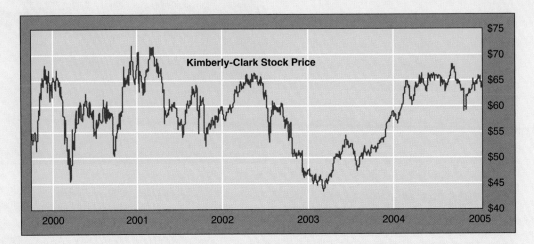

This chapter presents a financial accounting analysis and interpretation of Kimberly-Clark. It is intended to illustrate the key financial reporting topics covered in this book. This analysis is an essential first step in forecasting a company's future financial performance, a topic covered in Appendix B of this book. Forecasting the future financial performance of a company is itself a necessary step in valuing the company and hence in estimating its stock value, a topic covered in Appendix C of this book. The appendix at the end of this chapter applies the forecasting and evaluation methodology to Kimberly-Clark.

Sources: *Kimberly-Clark* 2004 Annual Report; *Kimberly-Clark* 2004 & 2003 10-K Reports; *BusinessWeek,* 2004; *The Wall Street Journal,* 2005; Fortune, 2003.

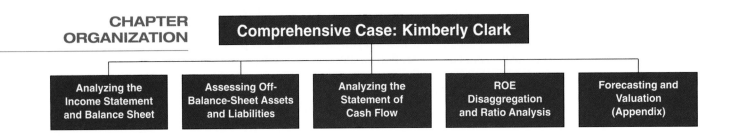

INTRODUCTION

Kimberly-Clark is one of the largest consumer products companies in the world. It is organized into three general business segments (percentages are for 2003):

- **Personal Care (37% of sales)**—manufactures and markets disposable diapers, training and youth pants and swim pants, feminine and incontinence care products, and others.

Products in this segment are primarily for household use and are sold under a variety of brand names, including Huggies, Pull-Ups, Little Swimmers, GoodNites, Kotex, Lightdays, Depend, and Poise.

- **Consumer Tissue (38% of sales)**—manufactures and markets facial and bathroom tissue, paper towels and napkins for household use, wet wipes, and related products. Products in this segment are sold under the Kleenex, Scott, Cottonelle, Viva, Andrex, Scottex, Hakle, Page, Huggies, and other brand names.

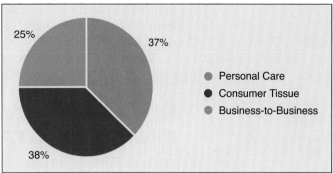

- **Business-to-Business (25% of sales)**—manufactures and markets (1) facial and bathroom tissue, paper towels, wipes and napkins for away-from-home use; (2) health care products such as surgical gowns, drapes, infection control products, sterilization wraps, disposable face masks and exam gloves, respiratory products, and other disposable medical products; (3) printing, premium business and correspondence papers; (4) specialty and technical papers; and other products. Products in this segment are sold under the Kimberly-Clark, Kleenex, Scott, Kimwipes, WypAll, Surpass, Safeskin, Tecnol, Ballard and other brand names.

Approximately 62% of Kimberly-Clark's consolidated sales are in North America, 20% in Europe and 18% in Asia, Latin America, and other areas. Shown below are its U.S. market shares for key categories for each of the years 2001 through 2003:

Product Category	2003	2002	2001
Diapers	38%	40%	39%
Training, youth, and swim pants	68	73	79
Adult incontinence care	56	55	54
Facial tissue	53	54	53
Bathroom tissue	28	27	26
Paper towels	19	19	17

In addition, approximately 13% of Kimberly-Clark's sales are concentrated in **Wal-Mart**, primarily in the personal care and consumer tissue businesses (source: Kimberly-Clark 2003 10-K).

In its MD&A section of its 10-K, Kimberly-Clark describes its competitive environment as follows:

The Corporation experiences intense competition for sales of its principal products in its major markets, both domestically and internationally. The Corporation's products compete with widely advertised, well-known, branded products, as well as private label products, which are typically sold at lower prices. The Corporation has several major competitors in most of its markets, some of which are larger and more diversified than the Corporation. The principal methods and elements of competition include brand recognition and loyalty, product innovation, quality and performance, price, and marketing and distribution capabilities. Inherent risks in the Corporation's competitive strategy include uncertainties concerning trade and consumer acceptance, the effects of recent consolidations of retailers and distribution channels, and competitive reaction. Aggressive competitive reaction may lead to increased advertising and promotional spending by the Corporation in order to maintain market share. Increased competition with respect to pricing would reduce revenue and could have an adverse impact on the Corporation's financial results. In addition, the Corporation relies on the development and introduction of new or improved products as a means of achieving and/or maintaining category leadership. In order to maintain its competitive position, the Corporation must develop technology to support its products.

Beyond the competitive business risks described above, Kimberly-Clark faces fluctuating prices for its principle raw material of cellulose fiber, uncertain energy costs for its manufacturing operations, foreign currency translation risks, and risks resulting from fluctuating interest rates.

Given this background, we now turn to an accounting analysis of Kimberly-Clark with a discussion of its financial statements.

REVIEWING AND ANALYZING FINANCIAL STATEMENTS

This section reviews and analyzes the financial statements of Kimberly-Clark.

Income Statement Reporting and Analysis

LO1 Analyze and interpret Kimberly-Clark's income statement

Kimberly-Clark's 2003 income statement is reproduced in Exhibit 14.1. The remainder of this section provides a brief review and analysis for Kimberly-Clark's income statement line items.

EXHIBIT 14.1	**Kimberly-Clark Income Statement**		

KIMBERLY-CLARK CORPORATION AND SUBSIDIARIES
Consolidated Income Statement

	Year Ended December 31		
(Millions of dollars, except per share amounts)	2003	2002	2001
Net sales	$14,348.0	$13,566.3	$13,287.6
Cost of products sold	9,448.1	8,750.7	8,618.0
Gross profit	4,899.9	4,815.6	4,669.6
Marketing, research and general expenses	2,375.6	2,278.5	2,158.3
Goodwill amortization	—	—	89.4
Other (income) expense, net	111.9	73.3	83.7
Operating profit	2,412.4	2,463.8	2,338.2
Nonoperating expense	(105.5)	—	—
Interest income	18.0	15.7	17.8
Interest expense	(167.9)	(182.1)	(191.6)
Income before income taxes	2,157.0	2,297.4	2,164.4
Provision for income taxes	514.2	666.6	645.7
Income before equity interests	1,642.8	1,630.8	1,518.7
Share of net income of equity companies	107.0	113.3	154.4
Minority owners' share of subsidiaries' net income . .	(55.6)	(58.1)	(63.2)
Income before cumulative effect of accounting change .	1,694.2	1,686.0	1,609.9
Cumulative effect of accounting change, net of income taxes	—	(11.4)	—
Net income	$ 1,694.2	$ 1,674.6	$ 1,609.9
Per share basis			
Basic			
Income before cumulative effect of accounting change	$ 3.34	$ 3.26	$ 3.04
Net income	$ 3.34	$ 3.24	$ 3.04
Diluted			
Income before cumulative effect of accounting change	$ 3.33	$ 3.24	$ 3.02
Net income	$ 3.33	$ 3.22	$ 3.02

Net Sales

Exhibit 14.1 reveals that its sales increased 5.76% in 2003 to $14,348 million ([$14,348.0 / $13,566.3] − 1), following a 2.1% sales increase in the prior year. In its MD&A report, K-C management attributes most of the 2003 increase (4% of the 5.76%) to favorable currency effects resulting from the weak $US as foreign currency denominated sales were translated into a higher $US equivalent. In addition, volume increases amounted to approximately 2% of this 5.76% increase. These two effects more than offset a reduction in Kimberly-Clark's product prices in its highly competitive markets (source: Kimberly-Clark 2003 10-K).

Kimberly-Clark describes its revenue recognition policy as follows:

> Sales revenue for the Corporation and its reportable business segments is recognized at the time of product shipment or delivery, depending on when title passes, to unaffiliated customers, and when all of the following have occurred: a firm sales agreement is in place, pricing is fixed or determinable, and collection is reasonably assured. Sales are reported net of estimated returns, consumer and trade promotions, rebates and freight allowed.

Its revenue recognition conditions are taken directly from GAAP and SEC guidelines, which recognize revenues when "earned and realizable." For Kimberly-Clark, *earned* means when title to the goods passes to the customer, and *realizable* means an account receivable has been recognized whose collection is reasonably assured.

Cost of Products Sold and Gross Profit

Kimberly-Clark's 2003 gross profit margin is 34.2% ($4,899.9/$14,348.0), which is almost a full percentage point below what it was in 2001 (35.1%). As a benchmark, Proctor & Gamble, the company's principle competitor, recently reported sales of $43.4 billion, three times the level of K-C, and a gross profit margin of 49%, up from 43.7% in 2001. This comparison highlights graphically the intense competition that K-C faces from its much larger rival.

Selling, General, and Administrative Costs

Kimberly-Clark's SGA expenses (which include marketing, research, maintenance, and other expenses) have remained steady at about 17.4% of sales. K-C reports 2003 net operating profit after taxes (NOPAT) of $1,945.2 million [$2,412.4 million × {1 − ($514.2 million/$2,157.0 million)} + $107 million] and a net operating profit margin (NOPM) of 13.6% ($1,945.2 million/$14,348 million) of sales.[1] P&G, by contrast, is able to use its higher gross profit margin to fund a higher level of advertising and other SGA expenditures. P&G's NOPM, however, is 12.5%. The difference in NOPM is primarily due to K-C's lower effective tax rate of 23.8% versus 31.1% for P&G.

Pension Costs. The SGA expenses of Kimberly-Clark include $168 million of pension expense. This amount is reported in the following table to its pension footnote disclosures:

Components of Net Periodic Benefit Cost						
	Pension Benefits			Other Benefits		
	Year Ended December 31					
(Millions of dollars)	2003	2002	2001	2003	2002	2001
Service cost	$ 78.5	$ 69.7	$ 65.4	$16.8	$13.0	$12.0
Interest cost	291.4	275.1	266.8	49.9	50.5	48.2
Expected return on plan assets	(290.6)	(335.6)	(368.1)	—	—	—
Amortization of prior service cost	8.7	7.8	8.6	(1.6)	(2.1)	(2.1)
Amortization of transition amount	.1	(2.0)	(4.4)	—	—	—
Recognized net actuarial loss (gain)	74.6	14.5	4.5	2.0	(2.7)	(3.8)
Other	5.3	2.5	7.6	—	—	(.1)
Net periodic benefit cost (credit)	$ 168.0	$ 32.0	$ (19.6)	$67.1	$58.7	$54.2

---

[1] Equity income (labeled as "share of net income of equity companies" in K-C's income statement) is included as operating because it relates to investments in paper-related companies and it, therefore, aligns with K-C's primary operating activities. This amount is reported by K-C net of tax, and therefore, no tax adjustment is necessary when computing NOPAT.

For 2003, the expected return on pension investments ($290.6 million) provides an offset to its pension service and interest costs ($78.5 million and $291.4 million, respectively). Footnotes reveal that its pension investments realized an *actual* return of $498.5 million in 2003 (from the pension footnote in its 10-K report). So, for 2003, use of the expected return results in an unrecognized *gain* that is deferred along with other unrecognized gains and losses that are not reported on the balance sheet.

Kimberly-Clark describes its determination of the expected return in its footnotes. It is instructive to review its rationale:

> Consolidated pension expense for defined benefit pension plans was $168 million in 2003 compared with $32 million for 2002. Pension expense is calculated based upon a number of actuarial assumptions applied to each of the defined benefit plans. The weighted-average expected long-term rate of return on pension fund assets used to calculate pension expense was 8.42 percent in 2003 compared with 9.19 percent in 2002 and will be 8.32 percent in 2004. The expected long-term rate of return on pension fund assets was determined based on several factors, including input from our pension investment consultants and projected long-term returns of broad equity and bond indices. We also considered our U.S. plan's historical 10-year and 15-year compounded annual returns of 10.1 percent and 10.3 percent, respectively, which have been in excess of these broad equity and bond benchmark indices. We anticipate that on average the investment managers for each of the plans comprising the Principal Plans will generate annual long-term rates of return of at least 8.5 percent. Our expected long-term rate of return on the assets in the Principal Plans is based on an asset allocation assumption of about 70 percent with equity managers, with expected long-term rates of return of approximately 10 percent, and 30 percent with fixed income managers, with an expected long-term rate of return of about 6 percent. We regularly review our actual asset allocation and periodically rebalance our investments to our targeted allocation when considered appropriate. Also, when deemed appropriate, we execute hedging strategies using index options and futures to limit the downside exposure of certain investments by trading off upside potential above an acceptable level. We executed such hedging strategies in 2003, 2002 and 2001. No hedging instruments are currently in place beyond January 2004. We will continue to evaluate our long-term rate of return assumptions at least annually and will adjust them as necessary.

Other Income and Expense. Kimberly-Clark's operating profit has benefited from elimination of goodwill amortization expense as mandated under GAAP since 2001 (see discussion below). However, it reports an increased level of $111.9 million for expenses classified as "other." Its footnotes reveal the following composition of this account:

> Other income (expense), net in 2003 included charges of $34 million consisting of $15.6 million for a legal judgment in Europe and $18.4 million for the costs associated with the redemption of $200 million of 7⅞% and $200 million of 7.0% debentures, and nearly $20 million for charges to write-off an investment in an historic restoration project and to record the cost of exiting a nonstrategic facility outside of North America. Also included were $25.1 million of operating losses related to the Corporation's participation in affordable housing and historic renovation projects, an increase of $8.0 million compared with 2002. Included in 2002 were $21 million of charges related to the settlement in December 2002 of securities and shareholder derivative litigation involving Safeskin Corporation ("Safeskin") and a charge of $26.5 million for the write-off of tax credits in Brazil. The litigation predated the Corporation's February 2000 acquisition of Safeskin. In addition, the Corporation recorded currency transaction losses in 2003 compared with gains in 2002.

$18.4 million of this expense relates to the cost of redeeming $200 million of debt. Under GAAP, this cost is treated as a SG&A expense (as opposed to "below the line," that is, after income from continuing operations) unless deemed to be both *unusual* and *infrequent*.

Transitory versus Persistent Classification

When examining operating profit we must look for any transitory items. Analysts typically treat gains and losses on debt redemption as both transitory (if nonrecurring) and nonoperating. In the footnote reproduced above, K-C reports expenses relating to a legal judgment, losses on debt redemption, and the write-off of an investment.[2] Each of these items is transitory, and the losses on debt redemption and the write-off of an investment are arguably nonoperating as well.

Expenses relating to restructuring activities have become increasingly common in the past two decades. Kimberly-Clark pursued its own restructuring activities in 2001 and 2002 and recorded charges of $167 million and $44 million. Classification of these charges as transitory is a judgment call. As a practical matter, the 2001 charge would probably have been viewed as transitory at that time. However, its reoccurrence in 2002 increased the likelihood that the 2002 charge would not be viewed as transitory. Further, its 2003 operating results do not contain restructuring charges. Because the purpose of identifying transitory items is to exclude them when forecasting operating profit and cash flow, and because restructuring charges are absent in 2003, these charges are not an issue when forecasting for 2004 and beyond.

Kimberly-Clark's reported operating profit has improved slightly from $2,338.2 million in 2001 to $2,412.4 million in 2003. However, its relatively flat sales growth is a concern to analysts: Bill Steele, an analyst at **Banc of America Securities** in San Francisco says, "In 10 years of covering this sector, I've never had a company with flat sales growth three years in a row." He adds, "I just hope they give us something to look forward to." (*The Wall Street Journal,* 2002). However, its outlook for improved sales growth is less than certain.

Earnings per Share

Net income for Kimberly-Clark has only slightly increased from $1,609.9 million in 2001 to $1,694.2 million in 2003. Basic (diluted) earnings per share, however, has increased from $3.04 ($3.02) to $3.34 ($3.33). This increase reflects a reduction of the average number of common shares outstanding (the major factor) from 529.6 (533.2) million to 507.0 (508.6) million shares as a result of its share repurchase program (see the financing section in Exhibit 14.5). Following is Kimberly-Clark's computation of earnings per share from its footnotes:

Earnings Per Share A reconciliation of the average number of common shares outstanding used in the basic and diluted EPS computations follows:

(Millions)	Average Common Shares Outstanding		
	2003	**2002**	**2001**
Basic	**507.0**	517.2	529.6
Dilutive effect of stock options	**1.2**	2.5	3.4
Dilutive effect of deferred compensation plan shares	**0.4**	0.3	0.2
Diluted	**508.6**	520.0	533.2

Options outstanding that were not included in the computation of diluted EPS because their exercise price was greater than the average market price of the common shares are summarized below:

Description	2003	2002	2001
Average number of share equivalents (millions) . . .	**20.5**	10.7	5.1
Weighted-average exercise price	**$60.19**	$65.89	$71.36
Expiration date of options	**2006 to 2013**	2006 to 2012	2006 to 2011
Options outstanding at year-end	**20.2**	11.4	5.8

The number of common shares outstanding as of December 31, 2003, 2002 and 2001 was 501.6 million, 510.8 million and 521.0 million, respectively.

---

[2]The losses related to K-C's participation in affordable housing are recurring and, therefore, not transitory, but can be considered nonoperating.

Most of the difference between its basic and diluted earnings per share usually arises from the dilutive effects of employee stock options. For K-C, such effects were minimal in 2003 as most of its stock options were *under water,* meaning that K-C's stock price was lower than the exercise price of the options. The stock options, therefore, are considered *antidilutive,* meaning that including them would increase EPS. Accordingly, they are excluded in the EPS computation, but remain potentially dilutive if K-C's stock price subsequently rises above the exercise price of the options. (Although not present for Kimberly-Clark, convertible debt and preferred shares are also potentially dilutive for many companies.)

Income Taxes

Kimberly-Clark's net income was positively affected by a reduction of its effective tax rate. K-C describes this tax effect in the following footnote:

> The Corporation's effective income tax rate was 23.8 percent in 2003 compared with 29.0 percent in 2002. The lower effective tax rate was primarily due to the benefits from the synthetic fuel partnership.

We discuss this synthetic fuel partnership in our discussion of variable interest entities (VIEs) later in this Chapter. The reduction of K-C's effective tax rate is an important contributor to its after-tax profit and is the primary reason why its NOPAT margin is higher than that for P&G.

Stock Options Expense

Kimberly-Clark's net income is slightly higher as a result of the nonrecognition of stock options expense. K-C accounts for its employee stock options using the intrinsic-value method, as was allowed in 2003 under GAAP. This method does not recognize expense relating to these options as Kimberly-Clark explains in the following footnote:

> ***Stock-Based Employee Compensation*** The Corporation's stock-based employee compensation plan is described in Note 11. The Corporation continues to account for stock-based compensation using the intrinsic-value method permitted by APB Opinion 25, *Accounting for Stock Issued to Employees.* No employee compensation for stock options has been charged to earnings because the exercise prices of all stock options granted under this plan have been equal to the market value of the Corporation's common stock at the date of grant. The following presents information about net income and earnings per share as if the Corporation had applied the fair value expense recognition requirements of Statement of Financial Accounting Standards ("SFAS") 123, *Accounting for Stock-Based Compensation,* to all employee stock options granted under the plan.

	Year Ended December 31		
(Millions of dollars, except per share amounts)	**2003**	**2002**	**2001**
Net income, as reported	**$1,694.2**	$1,674.6	$1,609.9
Less: Stock-based employee compensation determined under the fair value requirements of SFAS 123, net of income tax benefits	55.6	70.2	76.1
Pro forma net income	**$1,638.6**	$1,604.4	$1,533.8

Recognition of its stock options expense would have reduced net income by $55.6 million for 2003 and its earnings per share by 1 cent. Although not material in Kimberly-Clark's case, it is a substantially unrecognized expense for many companies, especially those in high-tech industries. This will no longer be true for firms with reporting periods beginning after June 15, 2005, when this expense must be recognized.

Common-Size Income Statement

It is useful for analysis purposes to compute common-size statements. Kimberly-Clark's common-size income statement covering its recent three years is shown in Exhibit 14.2.

EXHIBIT 14.2	Kimberly-Clark Common-Size Income Statement			
(2003 computations in parentheses)		**2003**	**2002**	**2001**
Net sales		100.0%	100.0%	100.0%
Cost of products sold ($9,448.1 mil./$14,348.0 mil.)		65.8	64.5	64.9
Gross profit ($4,899.9 mil./$14,348.0 mil.)		34.2	35.5	35.1
Marketing, research, and general expense ($2,375.6 mil./$14,348.0 mil.)		16.6	16.8	16.2
Other (income) expense, net ($111.9 mil./$14,348.0 mil.)		0.8	0.5	1.3
Operating profit ($2,412.4 mil./$14,348.0 mil.)		16.8	18.2	17.6
Nonoperating expense ($105.5 mil./$14,348.0 mil.)		0.7	0.0	0.0
Interest expense, net ([$167.9 mil. − $18.0 mil.]/$14,348.0 mil.)		1.0	1.2	1.3
Income before income taxes ($2,157.0 mil./$14,348.0 mil.)		15.0	17.0	16.3
Provision for income taxes ($514.2 mil./$14,348.0 mil.)		3.6	4.9	4.9
Share of income of equity companies ($107.0 mil./$14,348.0 mil.)		0.7	0.8	1.2
Minority owners' share of subsidiaries income ($55.6 mil./$14,348.0 mil.)		0.4	0.4	0.5
Cumulative effect of accounting change, net of tax		0.0	(0.1)	0.0
Net income ($1,694.2 mil./$14,348.0 mil.)		11.8	12.3	12.1

The gross profit margin has declined in 2003 relative to both 2002 and 2001; specifically, from 35.1% in 2001 to 34.2% in 2003. This decline is disappointing and reflects the very competitive environment in which K-C operates. Companies typically offset a declining gross profit margin with reductions in SG&A expense. K-C has been unable to do that, however, as its SG&A expense in 2003 actually exceeds its 2001 level as a percentage of sales. Accordingly, 2003 income before taxes has declined by 1.3 percentage points relative to 2001. Further, income from equity companies (reported net of tax) has declined as a percentage of sales from 1.2% to 0.7% from 2001 to 2003. Yet, despite the 1.3 percentage point reduction in pretax profit, net income has declined by only three-tenths as a percent of sales, from 12.1% in 2001 to 11.8% in 2003. This result is due to reduced tax expense as a percentage of taxable income.

Management Discussion and Analysis

The Management Discussion and Analysis section of a 10-K is usually informative for interpreting company financial statements and for additional insights into company operations. To illustrate, Kimberly-Clark provides the following analysis of its operating results in the MD&A section of its 2003 10-K:

> Consolidated operating profit decreased 2.1 percent due to higher promotional spending, increased fiber, distribution and energy costs, increased pension expense of approximately $140 million and a higher level of expenses in other income (expense), net that more than offset the benefits of cost reduction programs of about $190 million, favorable currency effects and increased sales volumes. Each of the three business segments incurred more than $40 million of the higher pension costs. Operating profit as a percentage of net sales decreased from 18.2 percent in 2002 to 16.8 percent in 2003.

> ■ Operating profit for personal care products increased 6.0 percent primarily because the benefits of cost reduction programs and favorable currency effects more than offset the lower net selling prices, lower sales volumes and higher raw materials and distribution costs. Although the competitive environment remained intense through product pricing and promotional activity, North America achieved strong fourth quarter results compared with the high level of incremental promotional spending in the year-ago quarter associated with diaper and training pant count changes at that time. North American operating profit for the full year increased because the aggressive cost reduction efforts more than offset lower net selling prices and the higher pension costs. Operating profit in Europe advanced as cost savings programs and favorable currency effects more than offset lower sales volumes. In Latin America, operating profit declined due to higher materials and fiber costs and unfavorable currency effects. Operating profit in Asia rose primarily due to higher sales volumes and favorable currency effects in Australia.

■ Operating profit for consumer tissue products decreased 8.4 percent because increased sales volumes and cost reductions were more than offset by higher fiber, distribution and energy costs, the higher pension costs and increased promotional spending. In each of the major regions—North America, Europe, Latin America and Asia—operating profit declined generally due to the same factors that affected the segment overall.

■ Operating profit for the business-to-business segment increased 1.9 percent as the benefits of cost savings programs, higher sales volumes and favorable currency effects more than offset lower net selling prices, higher fiber and other materials costs, higher distribution and energy expenses, and the increased pension costs. Operating profit for professional products rose in both North America and Europe primarily due to cost reductions and favorable currency effects. Operating profit for health care products increased because of higher sales volumes, cost savings and favorable currency effects, tempered by lower net selling prices. Operating profit for other businesses in the segment declined due to lower sales volumes and higher fiber costs.

Business Segments

Companies are required to disclose the composition of their operating profit by business segment. Segments are investment centers (those having both income statement and balance sheet data) that the company routinely evaluates at the chief executive level.

Kimberly-Clark's business segments are those outlined at the beginning of this chapter: personal care, consumer tissue, and business-to-business. The disclosures, per GAAP, for each of its business segments is given in Exhibit 14.3.

EXHIBIT 14.3	Kimberly-Clark Consolidated Operations by Business Segment					
(Millions of dollars)	Personal Care	Consumer Tissue	Business -to- Business	Intersegment Sales	All Other	Consolidated Total
Net Sales						
2003	$5,257.5	$5,441.9	$3,800.8	$(152.2)	$ —	$14,348.0
2002	5,101.7	5,018.6	3,593.0	(147.0)	—	13,566.3
2001	5,156.6	4,747.9	3,544.6	(161.5)	—	13,287.6
Operating Profit						
2003	1,104.9	844.3	683.0	—	(219.8)	2,412.4
2002	1,042.7	921.7	670.0	—	(170.6)	2,463.8
2001	1,042.7	863.7	599.4	—	(167.6)	2,338.2
Depreciation						
2003	245.1	315.3	184.3	—	1.1	745.8
2002	242.7	287.1	176.0	—	0.8	706.6
2001	225.1	259.8	164.2	—	1.1	650.2
Assets						
2003	4,396.1	6,182.3	4,850.1	—	1,351.4	16,779.9
2002	4,065.8	5,281.4	4,768.6	—	1,523.8	15,639.6
2001	3,819.5	5,064.5	4,662.8	—	1,512.3	15,059.1
Capital Spending						
2003	294.2	416.8	145.7	—	20.9	877.6
2002	289.7	340.4	236.5	—	4.1	870.7
2001	381.0	419.6	260.4	—	38.5	1,099.5

Given these data, it is possible for us to perform a rudimentary return disaggregation analysis for each segment (and years 2002 and 2003). This analysis gives us insight into a company's dependence on any one or more segments. A brief summary analysis of K-C's segment return disaggregation for the year 2003 is given in Exhibit 14.4.

EXHIBIT 14.4	Kimberly-Clark Consolidated Operations by Product Line: 2001–2003					
Segment ($ millions)	Net Sales	Operating Profit	Assets	Operating Profit Margin	Asset Turnover	Operating Profit Divided by Assets
Personal care	$5,257.5	$1,104.9	$4,396.1	21.0%	1.20	25.1%
Consumer tissue	5,441.9	844.3	6,182.3	15.5%	0.88	13.7%
Business-to-business	3,800.8	683.0	4,850.1	18.0%	0.78	14.1%

The intensely competitive consumer tissue market is evident in its low profit margin (15.5%) and low return on assets (13.7%). K-C relies to a greater extent on its personal care segment to generate income. Many analysts cite the pricing pressure in the consumer tissue segment as a negative factor in their valuations of K-C.

Balance Sheet Reporting and Analysis

Kimberly-Clark's balance sheet is reproduced in Exhibit 14.5.

LO2 Analyze and interpret Kimberly-Clark's balance sheet.

EXHIBIT 14.5A	Kimberly-Clark Balance Sheet

KIMBERLY-CLARK CORPORATION AND SUBSIDIARIES
Consolidated Balance Sheet

(Millions of dollars)	December 31 2003	2002
Assets		
Current assets		
Cash and cash equivalents	$ 290.6	$ 494.5
Accounts receivable, net	1,955.1	2,005.9
Inventories	1,563.4	1,430.1
Deferred income taxes	281.4	191.3
Other current assets	347.6	205.9
Total current assets	4,438.1	4,327.7
Property		
Land	276.5	266.0
Buildings	2,272.4	2,042.9
Machinery and equipment	12,061.7	10,812.5
Construction in progress	568.9	442.6
	15,179.5	13,564.0
Less accumulated depreciation	6,916.1	5,944.6
Net property	8,263.4	7,619.4
Investments in equity companies	427.7	571.2
Goodwill	2,649.1	2,254.9
Other assets	1,001.6	866.4
	$16,779.9	$15,639.6

EXHIBIT 14.5B	Kimberly-Clark Balance Sheet

KIMBERLY-CLARK CORPORATION AND SUBSIDIARIES
Consolidated Balance Sheet

	December 31	
(Millions of dollars)	**2003**	**2002**
Liabilities and Stockholders' Equity		
Current liabilities		
Debt payable within one year	$ 864.3	$ 1,086.6
Trade accounts payable	857.9	844.5
Other payables	283.5	277.5
Accrued expenses	1,374.7	1,325.2
Accrued income taxes	367.2	404.3
Dividends payable	171.1	154.0
Total current liabilities	3,918.7	4,092.1
Long-term debt	2,733.7	2,844.0
Noncurrent employee benefit and other obligations	1,614.4	1,390.0
Deferred income taxes	880.6	854.2
Minority owners' interests in subsidiaries	298.3	255.5
Preferred securities of subsidiary	567.9	553.5
Stockholders' equity		
Preferred stock—no par value—authorized 20.0 million shares, none issued	—	—
Common stock—$1.25 par value—authorized 1.2 billion shares; issued 568.6 million shares at December 31, 2003 and 2002	710.8	710.8
Additional paid-in capital	406.9	419.0
Common stock held in treasury, at cost—67.0 million and 57.8 million shares at December 31, 2003 and 2002	(3,818.1)	(3,350.6)
Accumulated other comprehensive income (loss)	(1,565.4)	(2,157.7)
Retained earnings	11,059.2	10,054.0
Unearned compensation on restricted stock	(27.1)	(25.2)
Total stockholders' equity	6,766.3	5,650.3
	$16,779.9	$15,639.6

Kimberly-Clark reports total assets of $16,779.9 million in 2003. Its net working capital is relatively illiquid as much of its current assets are tied up in accounts receivable and inventories, and its cash is only 1.7% ($290.6 mil./$16,779.9 mil.) of total assets at year-end 2003, down from 3.2% in 2002. It also reports no marketable securities that can serve as another source of liquidity if needed. The lack of liquidity is usually worrisome, but is not a serious concern in this case given Kimberly-Clark's moderate financial leverage and high free cash flow (see later discussion in this section).

Following is a brief review and analysis for each of Kimberly-Clark's balance sheet line items.

Accounts Receivable

Kimberly-Clark reports $1,955.1 million in net accounts receivable at year-end 2003. This represents 11.7% ($1,955.1 mil./$16,779.9 mil.) of total assets, down from 12.8% in the previous year. Footnotes reveal the following additional information:

	December 31	
Summary of Accounts Receivable, net ($ millions)	**2003**	**2002**
Accounts Receivable		
From customers	$1,815.1	$1,711.3
Other	207.6	362.2
Less allowance for doubtful accounts and sales discounts	(67.6)	(67.6)
Total	$1,955.1	$2,005.9

Most accounts receivables are from customers. This means there are at least two issues we must consider:

1. **Magnitude**—Receivables are generally non-interest-bearing and, therefore, are a nonearning asset. Further, they must be financed at some cost. Accordingly, a company wants to optimize its level of investment in receivables—that is, keep them as low as possible subject to credit policies that meet industry demands.

2. **Collectibility**—Receivables represent unsecured loans to customers. We must, therefore, be cognizant of the creditworthiness of these borrowers. Receivables are reported at net realizable value, that is, net of the allowance for doubtful accounts. Kimberly-Clark reports an allowance of $67.6 million. In addition, the footnotes reveal its following history of its allowance versus its write-offs:

| Description ($ millions) | Balance at Beginning of Period | Additions | | Deductions | Balance at End of Period |
		Charged to Costs and Expenses	Other	Write-Offs and Reclassifications	
December 31, 2003					
Allowances deducted from assets to which they apply					
Allowance for doubtful accounts	$48.4	$ 11.9	$6.5	$ 18.9	$47.9
Allowances for sales discounts	19.2	228.2	1.6	229.3	19.7

The allowance account is broken down into that relating to doubtful accounts and to sales discounts. Concerning the allowance for doubtful accounts, the company reported a balance of $48.4 million at the beginning of 2003, which is 2.3% of receivables [$48.4/($1,711.3 million + $362.2 million)]. During 2003 it increased this allowance account by $11.9 million. This is the amount of bad debt expense that is reported in the income statement. The company also increased the allowance by $6.5 million (see table above) as a result of currency translation effects and acquisitions. Write-offs and reclassifications of uncollectible accounts amounted to $18.9 million during the year, yielding a $47.9 balance at year-end, which is 2.4% of receivables [$47.9 million/($1,815.1 million + $207.6 million)]. It appears, therefore, that the company's receivables were adequately (but not excessively) reserved at year-end relative to the beginning of the year.

Following is Kimberly-Clark's explanation of its allowance policy:

Allowance for Doubtful Accounts We provide an allowance for doubtful accounts that represents our best estimate of the accounts receivable that will ultimately not be collected. We base our estimate on, among other things, historical collection experience, a review of the current aging status of customer receivables, and a review of specific information for those customers that are deemed to be higher risk. When we become aware of a customer whose continued operating success is questionable, we closely monitor collection of their receivable balance and may require the customer to prepay for current shipments. If a customer enters a bankruptcy action, we monitor the progress of that action to determine when and if an additional provision for non-collectibility is warranted. We evaluate the adequacy of the allowance for doubtful accounts on at least a quarterly basis. The allowance for doubtful accounts at December 31, 2003 and 2002 was $47.9 million and $48.4 million, respectively, and our write-off of uncollectible accounts was $15.5 million and $12.0 million in 2003 and 2002, respectively.

The allowance for doubtful accounts should always reflect the company's best estimate of the potential loss in its accounts receivable. This amount should not be overly conservative (which would understate profit), and it should not be inadequate (which would overstate profit). K-C's estimate of its potential losses results from its own (audited) review of the age of its receivables (older receivables are at greater risk of uncollectibility).

Inventories

Kimberly-Clark reports $1,563.4 million in inventories as of 2003. Footnote disclosures reveal the following inventory costing policy:

Inventories and Distribution Costs Most U.S. inventories are valued at the lower of cost, using the Last-In, First-Out (LIFO) method for financial reporting purposes, or market. The balance of the U.S. inventories and inventories of consolidated operations outside the U.S. are valued at the lower of cost. using either the First-In, First-Out (FIFO) or weighted-average cost methods, or market. Distribution costs are classified as cost of products sold.

Most of its U.S. inventories are reported on a LIFO basis. Some of its U.S. inventories, as well as those outside of the U.S., are valued at FIFO or weighted-average. The use of multiple inventory costing methods for different pools of inventories is common and acceptable under GAAP.

We are more interested in the composition of inventories. Kimberly-Clark provides the following footnote disclosure to address this issue:

	December 31	
Summary of Inventories ($ millions)	**2003**	**2002**
Inventories by major class		
At the lower of cost on the FIFO method, weighted-average cost method or market		
Raw materials	$ 353.8	$ 323.2
Work in process	186.8	186.7
Finished goods	935.2	866.9
Supplies and other	238.1	210.7
	1,713.9	1,587.5
Excess of FIFO cost over LIFO cost	(150.5)	(157.4)
Total	$1,563.4	$1,430.1

Companies aim to optimize their investment in inventories as these represent a non-income-producing asset until sold. Inventories must also be financed, stored, moved, and insured at some cost. Kimberly-Clark reports $353.8 million of raw materials, which is 21% of the total $1,713.9 million inventories (see table above). Work-in-process inventories amount to another $186.8 million and supplies and other amount to $238.1 million. The bulk of its inventories, or $935.2 million (55% of total inventories), is in finished goods and shows an 8% increase over 2002.

Kimberly-Clark reports that its total inventory cost *at FIFO* is $1,713.9 million. It then subtracts $150.5 million from this amount (the *LIFO reserve*) to yield its reported inventories of $1,563.4 million at LIFO. This means that Kimberly-Clark has realized a cumulative reduction in gross profit and pretax operating profit of $150.5 million. This amount has also reduced its pretax income, resulting in an approximate tax savings (and consequent increase in cash flow) of $52.675 million—assuming a 35% tax rate, and is computed as $150.5 million × 35%. During 2003, K-C's LIFO reserve actually *decreased* by $6.9 million, resulting in a $6.9 million *increase* in gross profit and pretax operating profit, and a $2.4 million ($6.9 million × 35%) reduction in cash flow from increased taxes, assuming a 35% tax rate.

Deferred Income Taxes

A note to the financial statements indicates that this account is attributable primarily to accrued expenses. These expenses, which were recognized for tax purposes in prior periods, will be paid in the current year thereby yielding tax savings in the current year.

Other Assets

Other assets include prepayments and other items not sufficiently large in magnitude to warrant separate disclosure. The notes indicate that $8.7 million of available-for-sale securities are included in the total. This amount should be added to the numerator of the quick ratio when that calculation is made later in this chapter.

Plant, Property, and Equipment

Net plant, property, and equipment (PPE), titled *net property* by Kimberly-Clark, is reported at $8,263.4 million at year-end 2003; it makes up 49% of total assets and is the largest single asset category. PPE is 46% depreciated assuming straight-line depreciation ($6,916.1 million/ $15,179.5 million) as of 2003. This percentage suggests these assets are about the average age that we would expect assuming a regular replacement policy. Footnotes reveal a useful life range of 7 to 50 years for buildings and 2 to 40 years for machinery as follows:

> For financial reporting purposes, property, plant and equipment are stated at cost and are depreciated on the straight-line or units-of-production method. Buildings are depreciated over their estimated useful lives ranging from 7 to 50 years. Machinery and equipment are depreciated over their estimated useful lives ranging from 2 to 40 years. For income tax purposes, accelerated methods of depreciation are used. Purchases of computer software are capitalized. External costs and certain internal costs (including payroll and payroll-related costs of employees) directly associated with developing significant computer software applications for internal use are capitalized. Training and data conversion costs are expensed as incurred. Computer software costs are amortized on the straight-line method over the estimated useful life of the software but not in excess of five years.

Again assuming straight-line depreciation, Kimberly-Clark's 2003 depreciation expense of $745.8 million (reported in its statement of cash flows, Exhibit 14.5) reveals that its long-term depreciable assets, as a whole, are being depreciated over an average useful life of about 20 years, computed as $15,179.5 million − $276.5 million of nondepreciable land and then divided by $745.8 million depreciation expense.

PPE is tested annually for impairment and written down to its net realizable value if deemed to be impaired. Following is Kimberly-Clark's discussion relating to its impairment testing:

> ***Property and Depreciation*** Estimating the useful lives of property, plant, and equipment requires the exercise of management judgment, and actual lives may differ from these estimates. Changes to these initial useful life estimates are made when appropriate. Property, plant, and equipment are tested for impairment in accordance with SFAS 144, *Accounting for the Impairment or Disposal of Long-Lived Assets,* whenever events or changes in circumstances indicate that the carrying amounts of such long-lived assets may not be recoverable from future net pretax cash flows. Impairment testing requires significant management judgment including estimating the future success of product lines, future sales volumes, growth rates for selling prices and costs, alternative uses for the assets and estimated proceeds from disposal of the assets. Impairment testing is conducted at the lowest level where cash flows can be measured and are independent of cash flows of other assets. An asset impairment would be indicated if the sum of the expected future net pretax cash flows from the use of the asset (undiscounted and without interest charges) is less than the carrying amount of the asset. An impairment loss would be measured based on the difference between the fair value of the asset and its carrying amount. We determine fair value based on an expected present value technique in which multiple cash flow scenarios that reflect a range of possible outcomes and a risk free rate of interest are used to estimate fair value.

The company did not report any impairment losses in the periods covered by its 2004 10-K.

Investments in Equity Companies

K-C's equity investments are reported at $427.7 million at year-end 2003. This amount represents the book value of its investments in affiliated companies over which Kimberly-Clark can exert significant influence, but not control. Footnotes reveal inclusion of investments in the following companies:

> At December 31, 2003, the Corporation's equity companies and ownership interest were as follows: Kimberly-Clark Lever, Ltd. (India) (50%), Kimberly-Clark de Mexico S.A. de C.V. and subsidiaries (47.9%), Olayan Kimberly-Clark Arabia (49%), Olayan Kimberly-Clark (Bahrain) WLL (49%), PT Kimsari Paper Indonesia (50%) and Tecnosur S.A. (34%).

Consolidation is not required unless the affiliate is "controlled." Generally, control is presumed at an ownership level of more than 50%, which none of these companies are. Thus, these investments are accounted for using the equity method. This means that only the net equity owned of these companies is reported on the balance sheet. We further discuss these investments in the section on off-balance-sheet financing.

Goodwill

Kimberly-Clark reports $2,649.1 million of goodwill at year-end 2003. This amount represents the excess of the purchase price for acquired companies over their fair market value of the acquired tangible and identifiable intangible assets (net of liabilities assumed). GAAP dictates that goodwill is not amortized, but is annually tested for impairment.

For periods prior to 2001, GAAP required goodwill amortization. Accordingly, Kimberly-Clark last reported goodwill amortization in 2001 (see Exhibit 14.1). Since that time its annual net income has increased by approximately $89 million as a result of this mandated accounting change that eliminated goodwill amortization.

Other Assets

Kimberly-Clark reports $1,001.6 million as "other assets." There is no table detailing its composition, but footnotes reveal inclusion of the following: $10.5 million of long-term marketable securities, $191.9 million of acquired patents and trademarks that are being amortized, and $230.2 million of noncurrent deferred income tax assets. No information is given on the remaining $569 million of other assets, most likely because this amount represents several assets each of which is not determined to be "material" and, therefore, subject to disclosure.

Concerning the deferred income tax assets, Kimberly-Clark provides the following disclosure relating to its composition ($ millions):

Net noncurrent deferred income tax asset attributable to	
Accumulated depreciation	$ (15.2)
Income tax loss carryforwards	333.7
State tax credits	57.0
Pension and other postretirement benefits	28.5
Other	44.5
Valuation allowances	(218.3)
Net noncurrent deferred income tax asset included in other assets	$ 230.2

Most of this deferred tax asset (benefit) results from tax loss carryforwards. The IRS allows companies to carry forward losses to offset future taxable income, thereby reducing future tax expense. This benefit can only be realized if the company expects taxable income in the specific entity that generated the tax losses before those carryforwards expire. If the company deems it "more likely than not" that the carryforwards will *not* be realized, it is required to establish a valuation allowance for the unrealizable portion (this is similar to establishing an allowance for uncollectible accounts receivable). As of 2003, Kimberly-Clark has set up such a valuation allowance (of $218.3 million), which has reduced net income dollar-for-dollar. Following is K-C's discussion relating to this allowance:

> Valuation allowances increased $7.3 million and $63.4 million in 2003 and 2002, respectively. Valuation allowances at the end of 2003 primarily relate to the potentially unusable portion of income tax loss carryforwards of $1,069.4 million, primarily in jurisdictions outside the United States. If not utilized against taxable income, $483.7 million of the loss carryforwards will expire from 2004 through 2023. The remaining $585.7 million has no expiration date.
>
> Realization of income tax loss carryforwards is dependent on generating sufficient taxable income prior to expiration of these carryforwards. Although realization is not assured, management believes it is more likely than not that all of the deferred tax assets, net of applicable valuation allowances, will be realized. The amount of the deferred tax assets considered realizable could be reduced or increased if estimates of future taxable income change during the carryforward period.

Current Liabilities

Kimberly-Clark reports current liabilities of $3,918.7 million at year-end 2003. Accrued liabilities make up the largest single amount at $1,374.7 million. Footnotes reveal that accrued liabilities constitute the following:

Summary of Accrued Expenses ($ millions)	December 31, 2003
Accrued advertising and promotion	$ 240.6
Accrued salaries and wages	374.1
Other	760.0
Total	$1,374.7

The "other" includes accrued benefit costs from the company's pension plans.

The remaining payables that make up current liabilities commonly arise from external transactions, such as trade accounts payable and taxes payable. These transactions are less prone to any management reporting bias. We must, however, determine any excessive "leaning on the trade" as a means to boost operating cash flow. K-C's trade accounts payable have decreased as a percentage of total liabilities and equity from 5.4% ($844.5 million/ $15,639.6 million) in 2002 to 5.1% ($857.9 million/ $16,779.9 million) in 2003. K-C does not exhibit any increased leaning on the trade as a means to boost its operating cash flow.

The possibility of management reporting bias is typically greater for accrued liabilities as they often are estimated (and difficult to audit), involve no external transaction, and can markedly impact reported balance sheet and income statement amounts. One of Kimberly-Clark's accrued liabilities involves promotions and rebates, which it estimates at $240.6 million as of 2003. Following is the description of its accrual policy in this area:

> **Promotion and Rebate Accruals** Among those factors affecting the accruals for promotions and rebates are estimates of the number of consumer coupons that will be redeemed, the type and number of activities within promotional programs between the Corporation and its trade customers and the quantity of products distributors have sold to specific customers. Generally, we base our estimates for consumer coupon costs on historical patterns of coupon redemption, influenced by judgments about current market conditions such as competitive activity in specific product categories. Estimates of trade promotion liabilities for promotional program costs incurred, but unpaid, are generally based on estimates of the quantity of customer sales, timing of promotional activities and forecasted costs for activities within the promotional programs. Settlement of these liabilities sometimes occurs in periods subsequent to the date of the promotion activity. Trade promotion programs include introductory marketing funds such as slotting fees, cooperative marketing programs, temporary price reductions, favorable end of aisle or in-store product displays and other activities conducted by the customers to promote the Corporation's products. Promotion accruals as of December 31, 2003 and 2002 were $222.0 million and $227.7 million, respectively. Rebate accruals as of December 31, 2003 and 2002 were $136.4 million and $159.5 million, respectively.

The company also reports accruals relating to its insurance risks, obsolete inventories, and environmental risks as described in the following footnote:

> **Retained Insurable Risks** We retain selected insurable risks, primarily related to property damage, workers compensation, and product, automobile and premises liability based upon historical loss patterns and management's judgment of cost effective risk retention. Accrued liabilities for incurred but not reported events, principally related to workers compensation and automobile liability, are based upon loss development factors provided to us by our external insurance brokers.

> **Excess and Obsolete Inventory** We require all excess, obsolete, damaged or off-quality inventories including raw materials, in-process, finished goods, and spare parts to be adequately reserved for or to be disposed of. Our process requires an ongoing tracking of the aging of inventories to be reviewed in conjunction with current marketing plans to ensure that any excess or obsolete inventories are identified on a timely basis. This process requires judgments be made about the salability of existing stock in relation to sales projections. The evaluation of the adequacy of provision for obsolete and excess inventories is performed on at least a quarterly basis. No provisions for future anticipated obsolescence, damage or off-quality inventories are made.

Environmental Expenditures Environmental expenditures related to current operations that qualify as property, plant, and equipment or which substantially increase the economic value or extend the useful life of an asset are capitalized, and all other such expenditures are expensed as incurred. Environmental expenditures that relate to an existing condition caused by past operations are expensed as incurred. Liabilities are recorded when environmental assessments and/or remedial efforts are probable and the costs can be reasonably estimated. Generally, the timing of these accruals coincides with completion of a feasibility study or a commitment to a formal plan of action. At environmental sites in which more than one potentially responsible party has been identified, a liability is recorded for the estimated allocable share of costs related to the Corporation's involvement with the site as well as an estimated allocable share of costs related to the involvement of insolvent or unidentified parties. At environmental sites in which the Corporation is the only responsible party, a liability for the total estimated costs of remediation is recorded. Liabilities for future expenditures for environmental remediation obligations are not discounted and do not reflect any anticipated recoveries from insurers.

K-C's accrued liabilities are 8.2% of total liabilities and equity ($1,374.7/$16,779.9) in 2003, compared with 8.5% ($1,325.2/$15,639.6) in 2002. The company provides a breakdown of these accruals over time in the following disclosure:

Summary of Accrued Expenses ($ millions)	December 31	
	2003	2002
Accrued advertising and promotion	$ 240.6	$ 245.7
Accrued salaries and wages	374.1	385.1
Other	760.0	694.4
Total	$1,374.7	$1,325.2

Neither accrued advertising and promotion nor accrued salaries and wages have changed appreciably from 2002 to 2003. A larger change of $65.6 million occurred in its "other" accrued expenses category. K-C does not provide specific numerical disclosures about this "other" category. Our information is limited to the general descriptions provided in the footnote prior to this numerical summary (for example, retained insurable risks, excess and obsolete inventory, and environmental expenditures). This category is one of the more common ones that management would use to bias the numbers if they were so inclined.

Additional insight can sometimes be gained from a comparison with peer companies. P&G, for example, reports accrued liabilities equal to 11.5% of total liabilities and equity (net of a liability accrual relating to an acquisition). The composition of its accruals is similar to K-C (advertising, promotion, and wages), but P&G's "other" category is markedly greater, which can lessen our concern with the observed increase in K-C's "other" category. Nevertheless, this is the category we must monitor for excessive increases as that would understate current income and provide a "reserve" to increase future income. In some cases, the mere existence of a reserve is a concern. For example, a corporation might wish to establish a reserve for a contingency, say a loss from a fire. The debit would be to an expense account and the credit to a loss reserve treated as a liability. The firm could use the reserve to smooth income over future years. The FASB decided long ago to restrict such reserves to cases where it was probable that the event will occur and the amount of the loss can be reasonably estimated.

Long-Term Debt

Kimberly-Clark reports $2,733.7 million of long-term debt as of 2003. Footnotes reveal the following composition of debt:

Debt Long-term debt is composed of the following:

(Millions of dollars)	Weighted-Average Interest Rate	Maturities	December 31 2003	December 31 2002
Notes and debentures	5.87%	2004–2028	**$2,342.9**	$2,238.4
Industrial development revenue bonds . . .	4.72%	2004–2037	**381.3**	427.1
Bank loans and other financings in various currencies	6.03%	2004–2025	**194.9**	202.8
Total long-term debt			**2,919.1**	2,868.3
Less current portion			**185.4**	24.3
Long-term portion			**$2,733.7**	$2,844.0

Most of its long-term financing is in the form of notes and debentures, $2,342.9 million in 2003, which mature over the next 25 years. GAAP requires disclosure of scheduled maturities for each of the 5 years subsequent to the balance sheet date. Kimberly-Clark's 5-year maturity schedule follows:

> Scheduled maturities of long-term debt for the next five years are $185.4 million in 2004, $584.0 million in 2005, $15.4 million in 2006, $321.6 million in 2007 and $1.4 million in 2008.

Our concern with debt maturity dates is whether or not a company is able to repay it at the time demanded. Alternatively, a company can refinance the debt. If a company is unable or unwilling to repay or refinance its debt, it must approach creditors for a modification of debt terms for those issuances coming due. Creditors are usually willing to oblige with, of course, interest rate increases or imposition of additional debt covenants and restrictions. However, if waivers of default are not forthcoming, the company can ultimately face the prospect of bankruptcy. This prospect highlights the importance of these disclosures.

We have little concern about Kimberly-Clark's debt maturity schedule as the company has strong cash flows. Still, it is worth noting that Standard & Poor's (S&P) recently lowered K-C's debt rating from AA to AA−. This rating is still strong (described as lower "high grade" debt), but lower nonetheless. Following is Kimberly-Clark's explanation of this downgrade disclosed in its 2003 10-K:

> In July 2003, Standard & Poor's ("S&P") revised the Corporation's credit rating for long-term debt from AA to AA−. Moody's Investor Service maintained its short- and long-term ratings but changed the Corporation's outlook to negative from stable, indicating that a ratings downgrade could be possible within the next 12 months. These changes were primarily based on the Corporation's business performance in the heightened competitive environment and because S&P changed the way in which it evaluates liabilities for pensions and other postretirement benefits. Management believes that these actions will not have a material adverse effect on the Corporation's access to credit or its borrowing costs since these credit ratings remain strong and are in the top eight percent of companies listed in S&P's ranking of the 500 largest companies. The Corporation's commercial paper continues to be rated in the top category.

Noncurrent Employee Benefit and Other Obligations

Kimberly-Clark reports $1,614.4 million of employee benefit and other obligations on its balance sheet at year-end 2003. This amount is composed of pension liabilities ($863.6 million), other postretirement benefits ($697.0 million), and other, unspecified liabilities ($53.8 million). The $863.6 million pension liability and the $697.0 million liability for other post-retirement benefits are reported in footnote 10 in K-C's 2004 10-K report. The following schedule from that footnote details K-C's reported pension amounts ($ million):

Funded status

Benefit obligation in excess of plan assets	$(1,205.9)
Unrecognized net actuarial loss	1,634.4
Unrecognized transition amount	0.7
Unrecognized prior service cost (benefit)	51.6
Net amount recognized	$ 480.8

Amounts recognized in the balance sheet

Prepaid benefit cost	$ 19.0
Accrued benefit cost	(863.6)
Intangible asset	56.1
Accumulated other comprehensive income	1,269.3
Net amount recognized	$ 480.8

The reported funded status indicates that K-Cs pension plans are underfunded by $(1,205.9) million. This amount is computed as the difference between the pension benefit obligation (PBO) of $5,233.8 million and the fair market value of the company's pension plan assets of $4,027.9 million. These amounts are also reported in footnote 10, which is not fully reproduced here. The net liability of $1,205.9 million is not reported in the balance sheet, however, because it was offset by unrecognized liabilities totaling $1,686.7 million ($1,634.4 million + $0.7 million + $51.6 million). Most of this offset is due to the unrecognized net actuarial loss of $1,634.4 million.

The unrecognized net actuarial loss is primarily the result of changes in actuarial assumptions used to determine the pension liability and differences between the expected and actual rates of return on plan assets. A significant amount of this unrecognized loss is due to reductions in the assumed interest (discount) rate. K-C reduced its assumed discount rate from 6.62% in 2002 to 5.92% in 2003. Although not reported in the 2003 footnotes, this discount rate has been steadily declining from a high of 8.7% in 1995.

The steady reduction in the assumed discount rate has resulted in increases in the present value of K-Cs pension obligations (PBO) and the unrecognized losses reported in footnote 10. The losses are unrecognized because GAAP allows companies to accumulate these losses off-balance-sheet and recognize them gradually as part of annual pension expense (amortization).

The *bottom line* in K-Cs footnote 10 shows a net pension *asset* of $480.8 million. However, GAAP requires companies to report a minimum pension *liability* whenever the pension plan is severely underfunded. K-C reports that it must recognize a minimum pension liability of $1,325.4 million ($56.1 million + $1,269.3 million).[3] The combination of the $480.8 million asset and the $1,325.4 million liability yields a net pension liability of $844.6 million. This amount is reported in two places on K-Cs balance sheet—other assets ($19 million) and noncurrent employee benefit and other obligations ($863.6 million).

Deferred Income Taxes

Kimberly-Clark reports a deferred tax liability of $880.6 million at year-end 2003. Footnote disclosures reveal this amount consists of the following components ($ millions):

Net noncurrent deferred income tax liability attributable to	
Accumulated depreciation	$(1,318.3)
Pension, postretirement and other employee benefits	531.5
Installment sales	(188.1)
Foreign tax credits and loss carryforwards	59.8
Prepaid royalties	27.2
Other	29.8
Valuation allowances	(22.5)
Net noncurrent deferred income tax liability	$ (880.6)

---

[3]When the minimum pension liability is recorded (credited) the offsetting debit is recorded in intangible assets and other comprehensive loss. K-C reports a debit to accumulated other comprehensive loss of $231.8 million ($146.2 million after tax) resulting from the increase in the minimum pension liability recorded in 2003.

Most of the noncurrent deferred tax liability ($1,318.3 million) arises from use of straight-line depreciation for GAAP reporting and accelerated depreciation for tax reporting. As a result, tax depreciation expense is higher in the early years of the assets' lives. This situation will reverse in later years for individual assets, resulting in higher taxable income and tax liability. It is this expected tax liability that is reflected currently in the deferred tax account.

Although K-C will realize a reduction of depreciation expense for an individual asset, with the consequent increase in taxable income and tax liability, if new assets are added at a sufficient rate, the additional first-year depreciation on those assets will more than offset the reduction of depreciation expense on older assets, resulting in a long-term reduction of tax liability. That is, the deferred tax liability is unlikely to reverse in the aggregate. For this reason, many analysts treat the deferred tax liability as though it were equity.

Still, while deferred taxes can be postponed, they cannot be eliminated. If the company's growth slows markedly, it will realize higher taxable income and tax liability. This is likely to occur when the company can least afford it. That is, when it is declining. We need to be mindful of the potential for a "real" tax liability (requiring cash payment) when companies begin to downsize.

Minority Owner's Interests in Subsidiaries

K-C's reports $298.3 million for the equity interests of minority shareholders in subsidiaries that have been acquired by Kimberly-Clark. Minority interests represent shareholder claims against the net assets and cash flows of the company (after all senior claims are settled). Consequently, we treat minority interest as a component of stockholders' equity; even if not reported in that manner by the company.

Preferred Securities of Subsidiary

The preferred securities represent the sale of preferred stock by a subsidiary of Kimberly-Clark to outside interests. This account is treated like all other contributed capital accounts.

Stockholders' Equity

Kimberly-Clark's statement of stockholders' equity for 2003 is given in Exhibit 14.6.

EXHIBIT 14.6	Kimberly-Clark's Statement of Stockholders' Equity								
(Dollars in millions, shares in thousands)	Common Stock Issued Shares	Amount	Additional Paid-in Capital	Treasury Stock Shares	Amount	Unearned Compensation on Restricted Stock	Retained Earnings	Accumulated Other Comprehensive Income (Loss)	Comprehensive Income
Balance at December 31, 2002	568,597	$710.8	$419.0	57,842	$(3,350.6)	$(25.2)	$10,054.0	$(2,157.7)	
Net income	—	—	—	—	—	—	1,694.2	—	$1,694.2
Other comprehensive income									
Unrealized translation	—	—	—	—	—	—	—	742.8	742.8
Minimum pension liability	—	—	—	—	—	—	—	(146.2)	(146.2)
Other	—	—	—	—	—	—	—	(4.3)	(4.3)
Total comprehensive income									$2,286.5
Options exercised and other awards	—	—	(18.0)	(988)	49.0	—	—	—	
Option and restricted share income tax benefits	—	—	7.4	—	—	—	—	—	
Shares repurchased	—	—	—	10,569	(537.1)	—	—	—	
Net issuance of restricted stock, less amortization	—	—	(1.5)	(415)	20.6	(1.9)	—	—	
Dividends declared	—	—	—	—	—	—	(689.0)	—	
Balance at December 31, 2003	568,597	$710.8	$406.9	67,008	$(3,818.1)	$(27.1)	$11,059.2	$(1,565.4)	

K-C has issued 568.597 million shares of its $1.25 par value common stock. The increase in the dollar value of the common stock account is, therefore, equal to $710.746 million (rounded to $710.8 million), computed as 568,597 million shares × $1.25, the par value (see Exhibit 14.5). The additional paid-in capital (APIC) represents the excess of proceeds from stock issuance over par value. It also includes two additional components for 2003: (1) the difference between the issue price of treasury stock and its original purchase cost is added or deducted from APIC; in this case deducted as the issue price is less than original cost, and (2) the tax benefits received by K-C relating to the value of stock options exercised by employees is reported as an increase in APIC; it is not reflected as a component of net income. Also, APIC is reduced by $1.5 million related to the issuance of restricted stock (see below).

Kimberly-Clark's stockholders' equity is reduced by a cumulative net amount of $3,818.1 million relating to repurchases of its common stock less the reissuance of those securities. These repurchases are the result of a stock purchase plan approved by K-C's board of directors and evidences K-C's conviction that its stock is undervalued by the marketplace. Otherwise, it would issue new shares. The repurchased shares are held in treasury and reduce stockholders' equity by the purchase price until such time they are reissued, perhaps to fund an acquisition or to compensate employees under a stock purchase or stock option plan. They can also be retired.

K-C compensates employees via restricted stock in addition to other forms of compensation. Under its restricted stock plan, eligible employees are issued stock, which is restricted as to sale until fully vested (owned). When issued, the market value of the restricted stock is treated as a reduction of stockholders' equity. As the employees gain ownership of the shares (the shares vest), a portion of this account is transferred to the income statement as compensation expense. The consequent reduction in retained earnings offsets the reduction (and increase in equity) of the restricted stock account. Stockholders' equity is, therefore, unaffected in total, although its components change.

Retained earnings reflect an $1,694.2 million increase relating to net income (Exhibit 14.1) and a $689.0 million decrease from declaration of dividends.[4] Accumulated other comprehensive income (AOCI), which is often aggregated with retained earnings for analysis purposes, began 2003 with a balance of $(2,157.7) million; a reduction of stockholders' equity. During the period, this negative balance was reduced by $742.8 million relating to the increase in net assets of subsidiaries accounted for using currencies other than the $US. This increase in net asset value resulted from a weakened $US vis-à-vis other currencies in 2003. In addition, the AOCI account was reduced by $146.2 million relating to the recognition of a minimum pension liability and $4.3 million designated as "other." Finally, K-C's comprehensive income equals net income plus (minus) the components of other comprehensive income.

Common-Size Balance Sheet

As it was with the analysis of the income statement, it is useful to compute common-size balance sheets. Such statements can reveal changes or relations masked by other analyses. Kimberly-Clark's common-size balance sheet covering its recent two years is shown in Exhibit 14.7.

EXHIBIT 14.7	**Kimberly-Clark Common-Size Balance Sheet**		
	2003 Computations ($ millions)	**2003**	**2002**
Cash and cash equivalents	$290.6/$16,779.9	1.73%	3.16%
Accounts receivable, net	$1,955.1/$16,779.9	11.65	12.83
Inventories	$1,563.4/$16,779.9	9.32	9.14
Deferred income taxes and other current assets	$629.0/$16,779.9	3.75	2.54
Total current assets	$4,438.1/$16,779.9	26.45	27.67
Property, gross	$15,179.5/$16,779.9	90.46	86.73
Less accumulated depreciation	$6,916.1/$16,779.9	41.22	38.01
Net property	$8,263.4/$16,779.9	49.25	48.72

(Continued on the next page)

---

[4]The dividends declared were not all paid in cash during 2003. We can see this is true because dividend cash payments were $671.9 million in 2003 (see Exhibit 14.8).

(Continued from the previous page)

EXHIBIT 14.7	Kimberly-Clark Common-Size Balance Sheet		
	2003 Computations ($ millions)	2003	2002
Investments in equity companies	$427.7/$16,779.9	2.55	3.65
Goodwill	$2,649.1/$16,779.9	15.79	14.42
Other assets	$1,001.6/$16,779.9	5.97	5.54
Total assets		100.00	100.00
Debt payable within one year	$864.3/$16,779.9	5.15	6.95
Trade accounts payable	$857.9/$16,779.9	5.11	5.40
Accrued expenses	$1,374.7/$16,779.9	8.19	8.47
Accrued income taxes	$367.2/$16,779.9	2.19%	2.59%
Dividends payable and other payables	$454.6/$16,779.9	2.71	2.76
Total current liabilities	$3,918.7/$16,779.9	23.35	26.16
Long-term debt	$2,733.7/$16,779.9	16.29	18.18
Noncurrent employee benefit and other	$1,614.4/$16,779.9	9.62	8.89
Deferred income taxes	$880.6/$16,779.9	5.25	5.46
Total long-term liabilities	$5,228.7/$16,779.9	31.16	27.07
Minority owners' interests in subsidiaries . . .	$298.3/$16,779.9	1.78	1.63
Preferred securities of subsidiary	$567.9/$16,779.9	3.38	3.54
Common stock	$710.8/$16,779.9	4.24	4.54
Additional paid-in capital	$406.9/$16,779.9	2.42	2.68
Common stock held in treasury, at cost	$(3,818.1)/$16,779.9	(22.75)	(21.42)
Accumulated other comprehensive income (loss)*	$(1,592.5)/$16,779.9	(9.49)	(13.96)
Retained earnings	$11,059.2/$16,779.9	65.91	64.29
Total stockholders' equity†	$7,632.5/$16,779.9	45.49	36.13
Total liabilities and stockholders' equity		100.00	100.00

*Includes unearned compensation on restricted stock.
†Includes minority owners' interests and preferred securities.

K-C is somewhat less liquid in 2003 than in 2002 as evidenced by the reduction of cash to 1.73% of total assets in 2003 from 3.16% in 2002. (Later in this chapter the statement of cash flows reveals that this is primarily the result of reduced long-term debt.) The remaining assets and liabilities exhibit little variation from the prior year. There is a marked increase in retained earnings, from 64.29% of assets to 72.13%, but it is somewhat offset by the increase in treasury stock as K-C continues to draw on its operating cash flow to repurchase its common stock. At year-end 2003, stockholders provide 45.49% of K-C's total capital, up from 36.13% in 2002.

Off-Balance-Sheet Reporting and Analysis

There are numerous assets and liabilities that do not appear on the balance sheet. Some are excluded because managers and accounting professionals only report what they can reliably measure. Others are excluded because of the rigidity of accounting standards combined with management incentives. Following are some areas we might consider in our evaluation and adjustment of the Kimberly-Clark balance sheet.

LO3 Determine and assess Kimberly-Clark's off-balance-sheet liabilities (and assets)

Internally Developed Intangible Assets

Many brands and their corresponding values are excluded from the balance sheet. For example, consider the brand "Kleenex." Many individuals actually refer to facial tissues as Kleenex—that is successful branding! So, is the Kleenex brand reported and valued on Kimberly-Clark's balance sheet? No. Accountants have concluded that brand value cannot be reliably measured and, hence, it is not reported on K-C's balance sheet.

Likewise, other valuable assets are excluded from the balance sheet. Examples are the value of a competent management team, high employee morale, innovative production know-how, a superior supply chain, customer satisfaction, and a host of other assets.

R&D activities represent another set of internally generated intangible assets that are mostly excluded from the balance sheet. Footnotes reveal that Kimberly-Clark spends over $280 million (nearly 2% of sales) on R&D to remain competitive—and, this is for an admittedly non-high-tech company. Further, K-C reveals that it spends over $408 million (nearly 3% of sales) on advertising. Both R&D and advertising costs are expensed under GAAP. This approach means that they are not capitalized on the balance sheet such as with tangible assets. These unrecognized intangible assets often represent a substantial part of a company's market value.

Equity Method Investments

Kimberly-Clark reports investments in equity companies of $427.7 million at year-end 2003. These are unconsolidated affiliates over which K-C can exert significant influence (but not control) and, hence, are accounted for using the equity method. The amount reported on the balance sheet represents the initial cost of the investment, plus (minus) the percentage share of investee earnings and losses, and minus any cash dividends received. Consequently, the investment balance equals the percentage owned of the affiliates' stockholders' equity (plus any unamortized excess purchase price).

Footnotes reveal that, in sum, these K-C affiliates have total assets of $1,642.4 million, liabilities of $918.3 million, and stockholders' equity of $724.1 million. K-C's reported investment balance of $427.7 in the balance sheet reveals neither the extent of the investment (assets) required to manage these companies, nor the level of potential liability exposure. For instance, in the event of the failure of one of these affiliates, K-C might have to invest cash to support it rather than to let it fail. This is so because failure might affect K-C's ability to finance another such venture in the future.

These investments are reported at cost, not at market as are passive investments. Thus, unrecognized gains and losses can be buried in such investments. For example, K-C footnotes reveal the following:

> Kimberly-Clark de Mexico, S.A. de C.V. is partially owned by the public and its stock is publicly traded in Mexico. At December 31, 2003, the Corporation's investment in this equity company was $374.8 million, and the estimated fair value of the investment was $1.5 billion based on the market price of publicly traded shares.

Thus, for at least one of its investments, there is an unrecognized gain of $1,125.2 million.

Operating Leases

Kimberly-Clark has executed a number of leases that are classified as "operating" for financial reporting purposes. As a result, neither the leased asset nor the lease obligation are reported on its balance sheet. For example, K-C reports the following disclosure relating to its operating leases:

> **Leases** The future minimum obligations under operating leases having a noncancelable term in excess of one year as of December 31, 2003, are as follows (Millions of dollars):

	Amount
Year Ending December 31	
2004	$ 67.5
2005	53.3
2006	37.6
2007	25.0
2008	17.8
Thereafter	47.8
Future minimum obligations	$249.0

These leases represent both an unreported asset and an unreported liability; both amounting to $186.8 million. This amount is computed as follows, assuming a 10% discount rate ($ millions):

Year	Operating Lease Payment	Discount Factor (i = 0.10)	Present Value
1	$67.5	0.90909	$ 61.4
2	53.3	0.82645	44.0
3	37.6	0.75131	28.2
4	25.0	0.68301	17.1
5	17.8	0.62092	11.1
....		2.25816* × 0.62092	25.0†
>5	47.8		$186.8

Average life ....$47.8/$17.8 = 2.6854 years

*The annuity factor for 2.6854 years is 2.25816 computed from the formula $\dfrac{1 - \dfrac{1}{(1 + .10)^{2.6854}}}{0.10}$.

†$17.8 × 2.25816 × 0.62092 = $25.0. Rounding to 3 years and using the compound interest tables in Appendix A yields $17.8 × 2.48685 × 0.62092 = $27.49. The impact of rounding is about 1.3% of the $186.8 value. Given the assumptions required in the analysis, the difference is not material.

The classification of leases as operating for financial reporting purposes is a rigid application of accounting rules, which depends solely on the structure of the lease. A large amount of assets and liabilities is excluded from many companies' balance sheets because the leases are structured as operating leases. For K-C, these excluded assets amount to $186.8 million. The valuation of K-C common stock (shown in the appendix at the end of this chapter) uses net operating assets (NOA) as one of its inputs. Our adjustment to the K-C balance sheet, then, would entail the addition of these assets to NOA and the inclusion of $186.8 million in *non*operating liabilities.

Pensions

Kimberly-Clark pension plan is markedly underfunded as described earlier in the chapter. Total pension obligations amount to $5,233.8 million and pension investments have a market value of $4,027.9 million at year-end 2003. Neither of these amounts appears on the balance sheet, but are reported in the footnotes. In fact, neither does the $1,205.9 million ($5,233.8 million − $4,027.9 million) shortfall appear in the balance sheet because GAAP permits the deferral (nonrecognition) of $1,686.7 million of increased pension liabilities resulting from the reduction in the discount rate in 2003 and the consequent increase in the present value of the pension obligation. However, GAAP requires recognition of additional liabilities if the plans are sufficiently underfunded. For K-C's pension plan, such underfunding resulted in the recognition of an additional $818.1 million of pension liability on its balance sheet. This amount is reflected in long-term liabilities, with an offsetting amount (net of tax) in other comprehensive income (OCI).

BUSINESS INSIGHT

Variable Interest Entities   Footnotes reveal that Kimberly-Clark has two categories of variable interest entities (VIEs). The first relates to two entities that the company established to securitize (sell) $617 million of notes receivable relating to asset sales. K-C sold the notes to these entities, which financed the purchase with debt sold to the capital markets. K-C maintains an equity interest in these entities, but their voting control rests with an independent party (bank) that provided credit guarantees for a fee. The bank is deemed to be the primary beneficiary for financial reporting purposes. As a result, K-C can continue to account for the investment under the equity method and is not required to consolidate the financial statements of the VIE.

The second entity is a synthetic fuel partnership in which it has a 49.5% interest. This entity provides significant tax benefits to K-C, amounting to $131.3 million in 2003 tax credits (from its 10-K footnote 12). Since K-C is the primary beneficiary of the partnership's cash flows, it is required to consolidate its financial statements as of March 2004. K-C asserts that consolidation will not have a material effect on its consolidated financial statements. As a result, it does not provide detailed disclosures of the financial statements of the VIE.

Derivatives

Kimberly-Clark is exposed to a number of market risks as outlined in the following footnote to its 2003 10-K:

> As a multinational enterprise, the Corporation is exposed to risks such as changes in foreign currency exchange rates, interest rates and commodity prices. A variety of practices are employed to manage these risks, including operating and financing activities and, where deemed appropriate, the use of derivative instruments. Derivative instruments are used only for risk management purposes and not for speculation or trading. All foreign currency derivative instruments are either exchange traded or are entered into with major financial institutions. The Corporation's credit exposure under these arrangements is limited to the fair value of the agreements with a positive fair value at the reporting date. Credit risk with respect to the counterparties is considered minimal in view of the financial strength of the counterparties.

The company hedges these risks in a number of ways, including forward, option, and swap contracts. This hedging process results in the transfer of risk from the company to another entity (called the counterparty), which assumes that risk for a fee.

The accounting for derivatives is summarized in an appendix to Chapter 12. In brief, the derivative contracts, and the assets or liabilities to which they relate, are reported on the balance sheet at fair market value. Any unrealized gains and losses are ultimately reflected in net income, although they can be accumulated in OCI for a short time. To the extent that a company's hedging activities are effective, the market values of the contracts and the assets or liabilities to which they relate are largely offsetting, as are the net gains or losses on the hedging activities. As a result, the effect of derivative activities is generally minimal on both income and equity.[5]

Statement of Cash Flows Reporting and Analysis

LO4 Analyze and interpret Kimberly-Clark's statement of cash flows

The statement of cash flows for Kimberly-Clark is shown in Exhibit 14.8.

In 2003, K-C generated $2,613.0 million of operating cash flow, primarily from income (net income plus the depreciation add-back amounts to $2,440 million). This amount is well in excess of K-C's capital expenditures and business acquisitions of $1,136.1 million ($877.6 million + $258.5 million). K-C has used this excess cash to pay dividends to shareholders ($671.9 million), repay debt ($424.2 million − $540.8 million + $481.6 million = $365 million), and repurchase stock ($549.7 million).

Kimberly-Clark offers the following commentary regarding its 2003 operating cash flow:

> ***Cash Flow Commentary*** Cash provided by operations increased $188.8 million or 7.8 percent to a record $2.6 billion. The reported amounts of operating working capital are affected by changes in currency exchange rates. From a cash flow perspective, the Corporation invested less cash in operating working capital in 2003 primarily due to improved cash collections of trade accounts receivable in Europe, income tax refunds of prior year taxes and lower income tax payments.

Beyond the income component of operating cash flows, Kimberly-Clark also realized increased operating cash flows from reduced working capital investment and a lower tax rate.[6] The increased operating cash flows helped K-C pursue several initiatives. Following are three initiatives that K-C highlights in its 10-K:

- Our strong cash flow permitted us to make cash contributions to our defined benefit pension trusts of about $185 million, and we plan to contribute an additional $100 million in 2004.
- We repurchased 10.4 million shares of our common stock under authorized share repurchase programs at a cost of $529 million.
- We increased our annual cash dividend 13 percent in 2003 and will increase it an additional 18 percent in 2004.

---

[5]It is generally only when companies use derivatives for speculative purposes that these investments significantly affect income and equity. The aim of the FASB's derivatives standard was to highlight these speculative activities.

[6]The effective tax rates calculated from data in Exhibit 14.1 are (1) for 2003, $514.2/$2,157 = .24 or 24% and (2) for 2004, $666.7/$2,297.4 = .29 or 29%.

EXHIBIT 14.8	Kimberly-Clark Statement of Cash Flows

KIMBERLY-CLARK CORPORATION AND SUBSIDIARIES
Consolidated Cash Flow Statement

	Year Ended December 31		
(Millions of dollars)	2003	2002	2001
Operations			
Net income	$ 1,694.2	$ 1,674.6	$ 1,609.9
Cumulative effect of accounting change, net of income taxes	—	11.4	—
Depreciation	745.8	706.6	650.2
Goodwill amortization	—	—	89.4
Deferred income tax (benefit) provision	(53.0)	197.6	39.7
Net losses on asset dispositions	35.0	38.4	102.0
Equity companies' earnings in excess of dividends paid	(9.6)	(8.2)	(39.1)
Minority owners' share of subsidiaries' net income	55.6	58.1	63.2
Decrease (increase) in operating working capital	116.4	(197.6)	(232.6)
Postretirement benefits	(58.5)	(118.2)	(54.7)
Other	87.1	61.5	25.8
Cash provided by operations	2,613.0	2,424.2	2,253.8
Investing			
Capital spending	(877.6)	(870.7)	(1,099.5)
Acquisitions of businesses, net of cash acquired	(258.5)	(410.8)	(135.0)
Investments in marketable securities	(10.8)	(9.0)	(19.7)
Proceeds from sales of investments	29.4	44.9	33.1
Net increase in time deposits	(149.0)	(36.8)	(21.3)
Other	2.0	(11.7)	(5.1)
Cash used for investing	(1,264.5)	(1,294.1)	(1,247.5)
Financing			
Cash dividends paid	(671.9)	(612.7)	(590.1)
Net (decrease) increase in short-term debt	(424.2)	(423.9)	288.4
Proceeds from issuance of long-term debt	540.8	823.1	76.5
Repayments of long-term debt	(481.6)	(154.6)	(271.8)
Issuance of preferred securities of subsidiary	—	—	516.5
Proceeds from exercise of stock options	31.0	68.9	101.5
Acquisitions of common stock for the treasury	(549.7)	(680.7)	(891.5)
Other	(18.4)	(34.9)	(33.5)
Cash used for financing	(1,574.0)	(1,014.8)	(804.0)
Effect of exchange rate changes on cash and cash equivalents	18.6	14.7	(24.5)
(Decrease) increase in cash and cash equivalents	(206.9)	130.0	177.8
Cash and cash equivalents, beginning of year	494.5	364.5	186.7
Cash and cash equivalents, end of year	$ 287.6	$ 494.5	$ 364.5

Kimberly-Clark also acknowledged the underfunded status of its pension plan and the need to devote additional cash flows to bolster pension assets. However, K-C cites the repurchase of shares as a priority. This, combined with increased dividend levels, will yield greater cash payments to its shareholders.

Overall, the cash flow picture for Kimberly-Clark is strong: operating cash flows are more than sufficient to cover capital expenditures and acquisitions, leaving excess cash that is being returned to the providers of capital (creditors and shareholders). The strength of its operating cash flows mitigates any concerns we might have regarding its relative lack of liquidity on the balance sheet.

Independent Audit Opinion

Kimberly-Clark is subject to various audit requirements. Its independent auditor is Deloitte & Touche LLP, which issued the following clean opinion on K-C's 2003 financial statements:

INDEPENDENT AUDITORS' REPORT

To the Board of Directors and Stockholders of Kimberly-Clark Corporation:

We have audited the accompanying consolidated balance sheets of Kimberly-Clark Corporation and Subsidiaries as of December 31, 2003 and 2002, and the related consolidated statements of income, stockholders' equity, and cash flows for each of the three years in the period ended December 31, 2003. Our audit also included the financial statement schedule listed in Item 15 (a) 2. These financial statements and the financial statement schedule are the responsibility of the Corporation's management. Our responsibility is to express an opinion on these financial statements and the financial statement schedule based on our audits.

We conducted our audits in accordance with auditing standards generally accepted in the United States of America. Those standards require that we plan and perform the audit to obtain reasonable assurance about whether the financial statements are free of material misstatement. An audit includes examining, on a test basis, evidence supporting the amounts and disclosures in the financial statements. An audit also includes assessing the accounting principles used and significant estimates made by management, as well as evaluating the overall financial statement presentation. We believe that our audits provide a reasonable basis for our opinion.

In our opinion, such consolidated financial statements present fairly, in all material respects, the financial position of Kimberly-Clark Corporation and Subsidiaries at December 31, 2003 and 2002, and the results of their operations and their cash flows for each of the three years in the period ended December 31, 2003, in conformity with accounting principles generally accepted in the United States of America. Also, in our opinion, the financial statement schedule, when considered in relation to the basic consolidated financial statements taken as a whole, presents fairly, in all material respects, the information set forth therein.

As discussed in Note 1 to the consolidated financial statements, effective January 1, 2002, the Corporation changed its method of accounting for customer coupons and its method of accounting for goodwill.

/s/ DELOITTE & TOUCHE LLP
Deloitte & Touche LLP
Dallas, Texas
February 11, 2004

Although this "clean" report is a routine disclosure, it should not be taken for granted (see the appendix to Chapter 1). Exceptions to a clean audit report must be scrutinized. Also, any disagreements between management and the independent auditor must be documented in an SEC filing. If the opinion is not clean, it is a "red flag" that must be investigated. Management activities and reports that cannot meet usual audit standards raise serious concerns about integrity and credibility. At a minimum, the riskiness of investments and relationships with such a company markedly increases.

ASSESSING PROFITABILITY AND CREDITWORTHINESS

LO5 Apply ROE disaggregation to analyze and interpret Kimberly-Clarks profitability

This section reports a profitability analysis of Kimberly-Clark. We begin with computations of several key measures that are used in ROE disaggregation, which is the overriding focus of this section. (These ratios are defined in Chapter 5, and a listing of the ratio acronyms and definitions is in the review section at the end of the book.)

K-C's 2003 net operating profit after-tax (NOPAT) is $1,945.2 million, computed as $2,412.4 million × [1 − ($514.2 million/$2,157.0 million)] + $107 million (see Exhibit 14.1). Its 2003 net operating working capital (NOWC) is $1,383.7 million, computed as its $4,438.1 million in total current assets less $3,054.4 in net current liabilities (equal to its $3,918.7 million in current liabilities less its $864.3 million in current maturities of long-term debt). Its 2003 net operating long-term assets are $9,846.8 million, computed as net PPE plus investments in equity companies, goodwill, and other assets of $16,779.9, and less its long-term operating liabilities such as pension obligations and deferred taxes: $8,263.4 million + $427.7 million + $2,649.1 million + $1,001.6 million − $1,614.4 million − $880.6 million. Thus, K-C's net operating assets (NOA) are $11,230.5 million, computed as $1,383.7 million + $9,846.8 million.

K-C's net financial obligation (NFO) is $3,598.0 million, computed as its current and long-term portion of its interest-bearing debt, or $864.3 million + $2,733.7 million. (K-C does not report any financial assets; if present, they are subtracted from this amount to get NFO.) Its 2003 stockholders' equity is $7,632.5 million, computed as its reported amount of $6,766.3 million plus minority interest ($298.3 million) and preferred securities of subsidiary ($567.9 million). Thus, and as alternatively computed, K-C's net operating assets (NOA) of $11,230.5 million equal its net financial obligations (NFO) plus equity ($3,598.0 million + $7,632.5 million).

Level 1 Analysis—RNOA and Leverage

Our first step in profitability analysis is computation of ROE and, then, its disaggregation into return on net operating assets (RNOA) and leverage. Using the computations in the previous section, the 2003 (Level 1) disaggregation analysis of ROE for Kimberly-Clark follows:[7]

$$\textbf{ROE} = \textbf{RNOA} + (\textbf{FLEV} \times \textbf{Spread})$$
$$\textbf{24.0\%} = \textbf{18.0\%} + (\textbf{53.4\%} \times \textbf{11.3\%})$$

where

ROE = NI/AVG. SE = $1,694.2 mil./[($7,632.5 mil. + $6,459.3 mil.)/2]

RNOA = NOPAT/AVG. NOA = $1,945.2 mil. /[($11,230.5 mil. + $10,389.9 mil.) /2]

FLEV = AVG. NFO/AVG. SE = [($3,598.0 mil. + $3,930.6 mil.)/2]/[($7,632.5 mil. + $6,459.3 mil.)/2]

Spread = RNOA − NFR[8] = 18.0% − 6.7%

RNOA comprises 75% (18%/24%) of K-C's ROE. Its financial leverage is 53.4%, which is slightly higher than the 40% median of all publicly traded companies, but it is not excessive. K-C successfully uses its leverage to increase its 18.0% RNOA to a 24% ROE; this effect is known as a positive borrowing spread. Kimberly-Clark has, therefore, capitalized on its favorable borrowing spread to increase its returns to shareholders.

Level 2 Analysis—Margin and Turnover

The next level analysis of ROE focuses on RNOA disaggregation. Kimberly-Clark's Level 2 analysis uses its net operating profit margin (NOPM) and its net operating asset turnover (NOAT) as follows:

$$\textbf{RNOA} = \textbf{NOPAT/Average Net Operating Assets}$$

$$= \underbrace{\textbf{NOPAT/Sales}}_{\textbf{NOPM}} \times \underbrace{\textbf{Sales/Average Net Operating Assets}}_{\textbf{NOAT}}$$

$$\textbf{18.0\%} = \textbf{13.6\%} \times \textbf{1.33}$$

where

NOPM = $1,945.2 million/$14,348.0 million

NOAT = $14,348.0 million/([$11,230.5 million + $10,389.9 million]/2)

---

[7]Many of these ratios require computation of averages, such as average assets. If we wanted to compute ratios for years prior to 2003, then we need to obtain information from prior 10-Ks to compute the necessary averages for these ratios.

[8]NFR is 6.7%, computed as ($1,945.2 mil. − $1,694.2 mil.)/([$3,598.0 mil. + $3,930.6 mil.]/2).

Kimberly-Clark's RNOA of 18% is comprised of a net operating profit margin of 13.6% and a net operating asset turnover of 1.33 times. In comparison, Procter and Gamble's 2003 RNOA is 18.7% with a NOPM of 12.5% and a NOAT of 1.50. K-C's reliance on NOPM for its RNOA is a potential risk factor given the intense competition in this industry and the consequent pressure on profit margins. To be competitive, K-C must increase its NOAT of 1.33 to at least be competitive with P&G's NOAT of 1.50.

Level 3 Analysis—Disaggregation of Margin and Turnover

This section focuses on Level 3 analysis, which is the disaggregation of profit margin and asset turnover to better understand the drivers of RNOA. The drivers of financial performance (RNOA) are key to predicting future company performance. Level 3 analysis of the drivers of operating profit margin and asset turnover for Kimberly-Clark follows:

Disaggregation of NOPM

Gross profit margin (GPM) ($4,899.9 mil./$14,348.0 mil.) 34.2%

Operating expense margin (OEM) [($2,375.6 mil. + $111.9 mil)/$14,348.0 mil] 17.3%

Disaggregation of NOAT

Accounts receivable turnover (ART) {$14,348.0 mil./[($1,955.1 mil. + $2,005.9 mil.)/2]} 7.24

Inventory turnover (INVT) {$9,448.1 mil./[($1,563.4 mil. + $1,430.1 mil.)/2]} 6.31

Long-term operating asset turnover (LTOAT) {$14,348.0 mil./[($8,263.4 mil. +
    $7,619.4 mil.)/2]} 1.81

Accounts payable turnover (APT) {$9,448.1 mil./[($857.9 mil. + $844.5 mil.)/2]} 11.10

Net operating working capital turnover (NOWCT) {$14,348.0 mil./[($1,383.7 mil. +
    $1,322.2 mil.)/2]} 10.60

Related turnover measures

Average collection period [$1,955.1 mil./($14,348.0 mil./365)] . . . . 49.7 days

Average inventory days outstanding [$1,563.1 mil./($9,448.1 mil./365)] . . . . 60.4 days

Average payable days outstanding [$857.9 mil./($9,448.1 mil./365)] . . . . 33.1 days

First, let's look at the disaggregation of NOPM. K-C reports a gross profit margin of 34.2%. A schedule to its 2003 10-K indicates that this important measure has declined by 2 percentage points in the past four years—which is a significant decline. K-C provides the following explanation of this decline in its MD&A:

> *Competitive Environment* The Corporation experiences intense competition for sales of its principal products in its major markets, both domestically and internationally. The Corporation's products compete with widely advertised, well-known, branded products, as well as private label products, which are typically sold at lower prices. The Corporation has several major competitors in most of its markets, some of which are larger and more diversified than the Corporation.

Declines in gross profit margin are usually countered with reductions in operating expenses to maintain a company's operating profit margin. However, for K-C, it has not decreased its operating expenses to offset the decline in gross profit margin. Our analysis above showed that the stability in K-C's NOPM was driven primarily by K-C's decline in its effective tax rate from 29% in 2002 to 23.8% in 2003. This tax rate decline is mainly due to its synthetic fuel partnership. Although a laudable activity, we prefer to see cost reductions from improvements in operating activities; further, tax benefits are often transitory.

Next, let's look at the disaggregation of NOAT. K-C's receivables turnover rate of 7.24 times corresponds to an average collection period of 49.7 days, which is reasonable for normal credit terms. However, the more important issue here is asset productivity (turnover) instead of credit quality. This is because most of K-C's sales are to large retailers; for example, 13% of Kimberly-Clark's sales are to Wal-Mart.

Inventories turn over 6.31 times a year, resulting in an average inventory days outstanding of 60.4 days in 2003. Inventories are an important (and large) asset for companies like Kimberly-Clark.

Improved turnover is always a goal so long as the company maintains sufficient inventories to meet market demand. For comparison, Procter and Gamble's average inventory days outstanding is 60.0 for the comparable period.

K-C's long-term operating assets are turning over 1.81 times a year, which is about average for publicly traded companies. However, K-C's LTOAT of 1.81 does not favorably compare with P&G's LTOAT of 3.28. P&G's level of goodwill is much greater than that for K-C. Thus, it is possible that P&G has acquired substantial manufacturing capacity via acquisition and that considerable PPE cost is in goodwill. In any case, the issue with respect to LTOAT is throughput, and K-C does not discuss this aspect of its business in its financial filings.

K-C's trade accounts payable turnover is 11.1, resulting in an average payable days outstanding of 33.1 days. Since payables represent a low cost source of financing, we would prefer to see its days payable lengthened so long as K-C is not endangering its relationships with suppliers. In comparison, P&G is able to use its bargaining power vis-à-vis suppliers to keep payables outstanding for over 41 days, on average.

Credit Analysis

Credit analysis is an important part of a complete company analysis. Following is a selected set of measures for 2003 that can help us gauge the relative credit standing of Kimberly-Clark:

LO6   Apply ratio analysis to determine Kimberly-Clark's creditworthiness.

Current ratio[a]	1.13
Quick ratio[b]	0.57
Total liabilities/Equity[c]	1.20
Long-term debt/Equity[d]	0.40
Earnings before interest and taxes/Interest expense[e]	14.15
Net operating cash flows/Total liabilities[f]	0.67
Net operating cash flows/Total current liabilities[g]	0.29

[a]($4,438.1/$3,918.7)

[b]($290.6 + $1,955.1)/$3,918.7

[c]($3,918.7 + $2,733.7 + $1,614.7 + $880.6)/($298.3 + $567.9 + $6,766.3)

[d]($2,733.7/$6,766.3)

[e]($1,694.2 + $167.9 + $514.2)/167.9

[f]($2,613/$3,918.7)

[g]$2,613/($16,779.9 − $6,766.3 − $567.9 − $298.3)

K-C's current and quick ratios are not particularly high, but both have increased over the past three years (not shown here). Further, these ratios do not imply any excess liquidity, and probably do not suggest any room for a further decrease in liquidity.

K-C's financial leverage, as reflected in both the total liability-to-equity and long-term-debt-to-equity ratios, is slightly above the median for all publicly traded companies. Normally, this is cause for some concern. However, Kimberly-Clark has strong operating and free cash flows that mitigate this concern.

K-C's times interest earned ratio of 14.15 is quite healthy, indicating a sufficient buffer to protect creditors if a downturn in earnings occurs. It also has relatively little off-balance-sheet exposure. Thus, we do not have any serious concerns about K-C's ability to repay its maturing debt obligations.

Analysis Summary of Profitability and Creditworthiness

An increasingly competitive environment has resulted in a decreasing gross profit margin for Kimberly-Clark. It has not reduced its operating expenses sufficiently to offset this decline. However, it has been able to maintain its NOPAT as a result of a decline in its effective tax rate (which is less than persistent). Its operating working capital and long-term operating assets yield acceptable, although not stellar, turnover levels. K-C does not provide sufficient discussion to further assess the throughput performance of its operating assets. Finally, its financial leverage, although higher than average, is not of great concern given K-C's strong cash flows.

APPENDIX 14A: Adjusting and Forecasting Financial Performance

LO7 Adjust and forecast Kimberly-Clark's financial performance.

Kimberly-Clark

The valuation of a share of K-C common stock requires forecasts of NOPAT and NOA over a forecast horizon period and a forecast terminal period. We can, of course, project individual income statement and balance sheet items using the methodology we discuss in Appendix B. However, in this section, we employ the parsimonious method of forecasting NOPAT and NOA using only sales forecasts, profit margins, and asset turnover rates—described in a latter section of Appendix B. We first discuss some possible adjustments to the financial statements that we can consider before commencing the forecasting process.

The two main targets of our parsimonious forecasting process are NOPAT and NOA. This means that we are primarily concerned with income statement and balance sheet adjustments that affect these two financial statements. Some adjustments we might consider for this purpose are shown in Exhibit 14A.1 for **Kimberly-Clark**.

EXHIBIT 14A.1	Kimberly-Clark Adjustments for NOPAT and NOA	
Adj.	**($ millions)**	
	Reported NOPAT	$ 1,945.2
1	Interest cost, expected return, and actuarial loss from pension plan	75.4
2	Legal judgment	15.6
3	Redemption of debentures	18.4
4	Write-off of investment	20.0
5	Affordable housing and historic renovation project	25.1
6	Unrecognized stock option expense	(55.6)
7	Rent expense on operating leases, net of depreciation	43.7
	Total adjustments, pretax	142.6
8	Effect of adjustments on tax expense (23.8% rate)	(33.9)
	Total adjustments, after-tax	108.7
	Adjusted NOPAT	$ 2,053.9
	Reported NOA	$11,230.5
9	Capitalization of operating leases	186.8
	Adjusted NOA	$11,417.3

Following is an explanation of the adjustments we make to NOPAT and NOA, which are coded by the number shown in the left column of Exhibit 14A.1:

1. Pension expense is included in operating profit under GAAP. Many analysts consider the pension plan investment returns and the interest expense portion of the pension cost to be nonoperating. For K-C, the net pension investment cost is $75.4 million, computed as $291.4 million − $290.6 million + $74.6 million (which reflects interest cost less the expected return on plan assets less a net actuarial loss).

2. K-C experienced a $15.6 million legal judgment. This is reported as an operating expense, but it is excluded from NOPAT because it is transitory.

3. Its loss from redemption of debentures (debt) is a financial (nonoperating) expense.

4. The write-off of an investment is a financial (nonoperating) expense.

5. K-C's costs for its investment in affordable housing are not transitory, but they are not operating either.

6. K-C reports its stock options under GAAP (*APB* 25), and as a result, no options expense is reported in its income statement. Footnotes report that this stock option expense is $55.6 million for 2003 and it is included for adjusting NOPAT.

7. K-C reports operating leases that are capitalized and used in the NOA adjustment below. Thus, the related expense of $68 million is added back, net of depreciation on the capitalized leased assets of $24.3 million ($186.8 million/7.6854 years), for a total of $43.7 million in adjusting NOPAT.

8. Total additional pretax operating profit is $142.6 million. Using K-C's effective tax rate of 23.8%, the net after-tax add-back to NOPAT is $108.7 million, resulting in an adjusted NOPAT of $2,053.9 million.

9. The lone NOA adjustment is for the present value of K-C's operating leases, $186.8 million. The adjusted NOA is $11,417.3 million. K-C's net financial obligations are, likewise, increased by the $186.8 million lease obligation from $3,598.0 million to $3,784.8 million.

These adjusted NOPAT and NOA amounts become the starting point for our forecasts that are used to estimate the value of K-C common stock. The simplified forecast process uses three inputs: sales growth, NOPAT margin, and NOA turnover. Our adjusted net operating profit margin (NOPM) is 14.31% ($2,053.9 million/$14,348 million) and the adjusted net operating asset turnover (NOAT) is 1.26 ($14,348 million/$11,417.3 million). (Note: For forecasting, turnover metrics use year-end figures; see Chapter 10.)

The sales growth forecast is complicated by the foreign currency exchange effects that we discussed earlier. K-C's sales increased by 5.76% in 2003, but 4% of this increase resulted from the weaker $US. The "real" increase was only about 1.76% in 2003. Also, our forecasts would be prepared around March 2004, after the 10-K was published. By then, K-C estimated that first quarter sales for 2004 increased approximately 10% year-over-year, with EPS increases in the 14% range (reflecting cost cutting and efficiency programs put in place in the prior two years). It is unknown how much of the 10% revenue increase in the first quarter of 2004 was due to a continued weakening of the $US. Accordingly, for our forecasts, we use a more conservative 5% sales increase—this forecast is somewhat conservative as it leans to the lower end of the range. We also use a NOPM of 14.31% and a NOAT of 1.26, both from 2003.

Exhibit 14A.2 shows forecasts of **Kimberly-Clark**'s sales, net operating profit after tax (NOPAT), and net operating assets (NOA)—these follow from our forecasting process explained in Chapter 10 and include the terminal year forecast assuming a terminal growth rate of 2%.

Kimberly-Clark

EXHIBIT 14A.2	Kimberly-Clark Forecasts of Sales, NOPAT, and NOA					
		Horizon Period				
(In millions)	Reported 2003	2004	2005	2006	2007	Terminal Period
Sales	$14,348	$15,065	$15,819	$16,610	$17,440	$17,789
NOPAT	2,054	2,157	2,264	2,378	2,497	2,547
NOA	11,418	11,988	12,588	13,217	13,878	14,156

Valuing Firm Equity and Stock Value

This section estimates the values of Kimberly-Clark's equity and common stock per share (refer to Appendix C). Exhibit 14A.3 shows the discounted cash flow (DCF) model results for this purpose. In addition to the forecast assumptions from the prior section, these results assume a discount (WACC) rate of 7.5%, a terminal growth rate of 2%, shares outstanding of 508 million, and net financial obligations (NFO) of $3,785 million.

LO8 Apply DCF and ROPI valuation models to estimate equity value for Kimberly-Clark

EXHIBIT 14A.3	Kimberly-Clark Discounted Cash Flow (DCF) Valuation					
			Horizon Period			
(In millions, except per share values and discount factors)	2003	2004	2005	2006	2007	Terminal Period
Increase in NOA		$ 571	$ 599	$ 629	$ 661	$ 278
FCFF (NOPAT − Increase in NOA)		1,586	1,665	1,748	1,836	2,269
Discount factor [$1/(1+ r_w)^t$]		0.93023	0.86533	0.80496	0.74880	
Present value of horizon FCFF		1,475	1,441	1,407	1,375	
Cum. present value of horizon FCFF . .	$ 5,698					
Present value of terminal FCFF	30,890[a]					
Total firm value	36,588					
Less (plus) NFO	3,785					
Firm equity value	$32,803					
Stock outstanding	508					
Stock value per share	$64.57					

[a]Computed as $\dfrac{\left(\dfrac{\$2{,}269 \text{ million}}{0.075 - 0.02}\right)}{(1.075)^4}$

Exhibit 14A.4 reports estimates of the values of Kimberly-Clark's equity and common stock per share using the residual operating income (ROPI) model.

EXHIBIT 14A.4	**Kimberly-Clark Residual Operating Income (ROPI) Valuation**					
		Horizon Period				**Terminal Period**
(In millions, except per share values and discount factors)	2003	2004	2005	2006	2007	
ROPI [NOPAT − (NOA$_{Beg}$ × r_w)]		$1,300	$1,365	$1,434	$1,505	$1,506
Discount factor [1/(1+ r_w)^t]		0.93023	0.86533	0.80496	0.74880	
Present value of horizon ROPI		1,210	1,181	1,154	1,127	
Cum. present value of horizon ROPI . . .	$ 4,672					
Present value of terminal ROPI[a]	20,498					
NOA	11,418					
Total firm value	36,588					
Less (plus) NFO	3,785					
Firm equity value	$32,803					
Stock outstanding	508					
Stock value per share	$64.57					

$$^a\text{Computed as } \frac{\left(\dfrac{\$1,506 \text{ million}}{0.075 - 0.02}\right)}{(1.075)^4}.$$

Kimberly-Clark's equity value is estimated at $32,803 million as of December 2003, which is equivalent to a per share value estimate of $64.57. As expected, equity value estimates are identical for both models (because K-C is assumed to be in a steady state, that is, NOPAT and NOA growing at the same rate and, therefore, RNOA is constant).

The closing stock price on December 31, 2003, for Kimberly-Clark (KMB) was $59.09 per share. Our model's estimates, therefore, suggest that K-C stock is undervalued as of that date. As it turns out, this valuation proved prophetic as its stock price increased to the mid- to upper-$60s subsequent to that date as shown in the following graph:

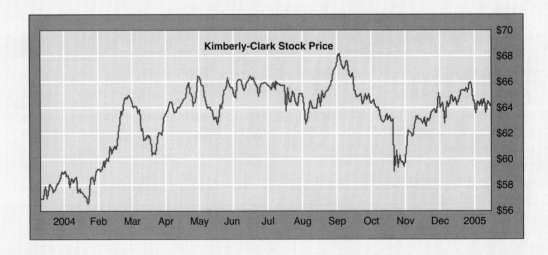

Overall, this chapter presented a financial accounting analysis and interpretation of Kimberly-Clark. It illustrated many of the key financial reporting topics covered in the book. We began with a detailed review of its financial statements and notes, followed by the forecasting of key accounts, and concluded with estimates of K-C's equity value.

Although no two companies are identical, the Kimberly-Clark case provided an opportunity for us to apply many of the procedures conveyed in the book (and course) in a comprehensive manner. With analyses of additional companies, we become more comfortable with and knowledgeable of variations in financial reporting, which enhances our analysis and business decision-making skills. As we discuss in Chapter 1, our analysis of a company must go beyond the accounting numbers to include competitor and economic factors, and we must appreciate that estimation and judgment are key ingredients in financial accounting. This comprehensive case, textbook, and course provide us with skills necessary to effectively use financial accounting and to advance our business and career opportunities.

SUMMARY

Analyze and interpret Kimberly-Clark's income statement. (p. 612) **LO1**

- Kimberly Clark is one of the largest consumer products companies in the world. Understanding the consumer products industry is necessary in order to understand whether the various operating and financial measures place the company in a strong or weak competitive position.
  - Approximately 60% of KC's sales are in North America, 20% in Europe.
  - About 15% of KC's sales are made to one customer, Wall-Mart.
  - The company faces intense competition in its markets, the risks of operating beyond North America, increasing (under-funded) pension liabilities and fluctuating prices for both its raw materials and energy needs.
- KC's sales are increasing but its profit margins are declining while Proctor and Gamble, its main competitor is experiencing increase in both sale and profit margins. Operating profits are at best flat.
- A rudimentary breakdown of KC's business segments indicates that two out of three of their main businesses are showing low profit margins and returns on assets even though operating profits increased slightly.

Analyze and interpret Kimberly-Clark's balance sheet. (p. 619) **LO2**

- No obvious transitory items, with the possible exception of restructuring costs, need to be considered in forecasting future operating profit levels.
- KC uses LIFO accounting for its inventories resulting in significant tax savings and the avoidance of "phantom inventory profits." Operating equipment is approximately 50% depreciated. Equity investments and operating leases are not significant.

Determine and assess Kimberly-Clark's off-balance-sheet liabilities (and assets). (p. 631) **LO3**

- Assets and liabilities are misstated due to the failure to recognize the under-funded pension liability of $1.2 billion. In addition, valuable assets including brand names such as Kleenex are excluded because no objective means of measuring their value is accepted.

Analyze and interpret Kimberly-Clark's statement of cash flows. (p. 634) **LO4**

Apply ROE disaggregation to analyze and interpret Kimberly-Clarks profitability. (p. 636) **LO5**

A ratio analysis shows the following relevant facts:

- KC's ROE of 24% is made supported by a 75% contribution from its return of 18% on net operating assets.
- Financially leverage is a reasonable 53% and increases ROE by 65.
- However, NOPM is only 13.6% and NOAT is at 1.3 times compared to P&G with a NOPM of 12.5 and NOAT of 1.5. The low NOPM represents a risk to KC.
- KC's gross profit margin of 34% has declined by 2 percentage points over the last 4 years.
- An anemic LTOAT indicates a problem with throughput.

Apply ratio analysis to determine Kimberly-Clark's creditworthiness. (p. 639) **LO6**

- The competitive environment has resulted in a measurable decline in KC's GPM, which the firm has not been able to lower its operating costs sufficiently to counter this decline. It has been able to maintain NOPAT in large part through reducing its effective tax rate, a tactic that is not likely to be sustainable. Otherwise the firm appears to be in a reasonable if not stellar condition.

LO7 **Adjust and forecast Kimberly-Clark's financial performance. (p. 640)**

- Reported NOPAT was adjusted to remove the effects of nonoperating expenses and transitory items, and to deduct unrecognized expenses, such as unrecognized employee option expense.

- Reported NOA was adjusted to reflect off-balance sheet financing (operating leases).

- The parsimonious forecasting method was used to forecast NOPAT and NOA assuming a 5% growth rate during the forecast horizon period, and a 2% growth rate thereafter.

LO8 **Apply DCF and ROPI valuation models to estimate equity value for Kimberly-Clark. (p. 641)**

- Kimberly-Clark's equity value was estimated at $64.57 per share using both the discounted free cash flow (DCF) model and the residual operating profit (ROPI) model.

- Estimate values are based on forecasts of NOPAT and NOA and a WACC discount rate of 7.5%.

APPENDIX

A

Compound Interest Tables

TABLE 1	Present Value of Single Amount										$p = 1/(1 + i)^t$	

						Interest Rate						
Period	0.01	0.02	0.03	0.04	0.05	0.06	0.07	0.08	0.09	0.10	0.11	0.12
1	0.99010	0.98039	0.97087	0.96154	0.95238	0.94340	0.93458	0.92593	0.91743	0.90909	0.90090	0.89286
2	0.98030	0.96117	0.94260	0.92456	0.90703	0.89000	0.87344	0.85734	0.84168	0.82645	0.81162	0.79719
3	0.97059	0.94232	0.91514	0.88900	0.86384	0.83962	0.81630	0.79383	0.77218	0.75131	0.73119	0.71178
4	0.96098	0.92385	0.88849	0.85480	0.82270	0.79209	0.76290	0.73503	0.70843	0.68301	0.65873	0.63552
5	0.95147	0.90573	0.86261	0.82193	0.78353	0.74726	0.71299	0.68058	0.64993	0.62092	0.59345	0.56743
6	0.94205	0.88797	0.83748	0.79031	0.74622	0.70496	0.66634	0.63017	0.59627	0.56447	0.53464	0.50663
7	0.93272	0.87056	0.81309	0.75992	0.71068	0.66506	0.62275	0.58349	0.54703	0.51316	0.48166	0.45235
8	0.92348	0.85349	0.78941	0.73069	0.67684	0.62741	0.58201	0.54027	0.50187	0.46651	0.43393	0.40388
9	0.91434	0.83676	0.76642	0.70259	0.64461	0.59190	0.54393	0.50025	0.46043	0.42410	0.39092	0.36061
10	0.90529	0.82035	0.74409	0.67556	0.61391	0.55839	0.50835	0.46319	0.42241	0.38554	0.35218	0.32197
11	0.89632	0.80426	0.72242	0.64958	0.58468	0.52679	0.47509	0.42888	0.38753	0.35049	0.31728	0.28748
12	0.88745	0.78849	0.70138	0.62460	0.55684	0.49697	0.44401	0.39711	0.35553	0.31863	0.28584	0.25668
13	0.87866	0.77303	0.68095	0.60057	0.53032	0.46884	0.41496	0.36770	0.32618	0.28966	0.25751	0.22917
14	0.86996	0.75788	0.66112	0.57748	0.50507	0.44230	0.38782	0.34046	0.29925	0.26333	0.23199	0.20462
15	0.86135	0.74301	0.64186	0.55526	0.48102	0.41727	0.36245	0.31524	0.27454	0.23939	0.20900	0.18270
16	0.85282	0.72845	0.62317	0.53391	0.45811	0.39365	0.33873	0.29189	0.25187	0.21763	0.18829	0.16312
17	0.84438	0.71416	0.60502	0.51337	0.43630	0.37136	0.31657	0.27027	0.23107	0.19784	0.16963	0.14564
18	0.83602	0.70016	0.58739	0.49363	0.41552	0.35034	0.29586	0.25025	0.21199	0.17986	0.15282	0.13004
19	0.82774	0.68643	0.57029	0.47464	0.39573	0.33051	0.27651	0.23171	0.19449	0.16351	0.13768	0.11611
20	0.81954	0.67297	0.55368	0.45639	0.37689	0.31180	0.25842	0.21455	0.17843	0.14864	0.12403	0.10367
21	0.81143	0.65978	0.53755	0.43883	0.35894	0.29416	0.24151	0.19866	0.16370	0.13513	0.11174	0.09256
22	0.80340	0.64684	0.52189	0.42196	0.34185	0.27751	0.22571	0.18394	0.15018	0.12285	0.10067	0.08264
23	0.79544	0.63416	0.50669	0.40573	0.32557	0.26180	0.21095	0.17032	0.13778	0.11168	0.09069	0.07379
24	0.78757	0.62172	0.49193	0.39012	0.31007	0.24698	0.19715	0.15770	0.12640	0.10153	0.08170	0.06588
25	0.77977	0.60953	0.47761	0.37512	0.29530	0.23300	0.18425	0.14602	0.11597	0.09230	0.07361	0.05882
30	0.74192	0.55207	0.41199	0.30832	0.23138	0.17411	0.13137	0.09938	0.07537	0.05731	0.04368	0.03338
35	0.70591	0.50003	0.35538	0.25342	0.18129	0.13011	0.09366	0.06763	0.04899	0.03558	0.02592	0.01894
40	0.67165	0.45289	0.30656	0.20829	0.14205	0.09722	0.06678	0.04603	0.03184	0.02209	0.01538	0.01075

TABLE 2	Present Value of Ordinary Annuity										$p = \{1 - [1/(1 + i)^t]\}/i$	

						Interest Rate						
Period	0.01	0.02	0.03	0.04	0.05	0.06	0.07	0.08	0.09	0.10	0.11	0.12
1	0.99010	0.98039	0.97087	0.96154	0.95238	0.94340	0.93458	0.92593	0.91743	0.90909	0.90090	0.89286
2	1.97040	1.94156	1.91347	1.88609	1.85941	1.83339	1.80802	1.78326	1.75911	1.73554	1.71252	1.69005
3	2.94099	2.88388	2.82861	2.77509	2.72325	2.67301	2.62432	2.57710	2.53129	2.48685	2.44371	2.40183
4	3.90197	3.80773	3.71710	3.62990	3.54595	3.46511	3.38721	3.31213	3.23972	3.16987	3.10245	3.03735
5	4.85343	4.71346	4.57971	4.45182	4.32948	4.21236	4.10020	3.99271	3.88965	3.79079	3.69590	3.60478
6	5.79548	5.60143	5.41719	5.24214	5.07569	4.91732	4.76654	4.62288	4.48592	4.35526	4.23054	4.11141
7	6.72819	6.47199	6.23028	6.00205	5.78637	5.58238	5.38929	5.20637	5.03295	4.86842	4.71220	4.56376
8	7.65168	7.32548	7.01969	6.73274	6.46321	6.20979	5.97130	5.74664	5.53482	5.33493	5.14612	4.96764
9	8.56602	8.16224	7.78611	7.43533	7.10782	6.80169	6.51523	6.24689	5.99525	5.75902	5.53705	5.32825
10	9.47130	8.98259	8.53020	8.11090	7.72173	7.36009	7.02358	6.71008	6.41766	6.14457	5.88923	5.65022
11	10.36763	9.78685	9.25262	8.76048	8.30641	7.88687	7.49867	7.13896	6.80519	6.49506	6.20652	5.93770
12	11.25508	10.57534	9.95400	9.38507	8.86325	8.38384	7.94269	7.53608	7.16073	6.81369	6.49236	6.19437
13	12.13374	11.34837	10.63496	9.98565	9.39357	8.85268	8.35765	7.90378	7.48690	7.10336	6.74987	6.42355
14	13.00370	12.10625	11.29607	10.56312	9.89864	9.29498	8.74547	8.24424	7.78615	7.36669	6.98187	6.62817
15	13.86505	12.84926	11.93794	11.11839	10.37966	9.71225	9.10791	8.55948	8.06069	7.60608	7.19087	6.81086
16	14.71787	13.57771	12.56110	11.65230	10.83777	10.10590	9.44665	8.85137	8.31256	7.82371	7.37916	6.97399
17	15.56225	14.29187	13.16612	12.16567	11.27407	10.47726	9.76322	9.12164	8.54363	8.02155	7.54879	7.11963
18	16.39827	14.99203	13.75351	12.65930	11.68959	10.82760	10.05909	9.37189	8.75563	8.20141	7.70162	7.24967
19	17.22601	15.67846	14.32380	13.13394	12.08532	11.15812	10.33560	9.60360	8.95011	8.36492	7.83929	7.36578
20	18.04555	16.35143	14.87747	13.59033	12.46221	11.46992	10.59401	9.81815	9.12855	8.51356	7.96333	7.46944
21	18.85698	17.01121	15.41502	14.02916	12.82115	11.76408	10.83553	10.01680	9.29224	8.64869	8.07507	7.56200
22	19.66038	17.65805	15.93692	14.45112	13.16300	12.04158	11.06124	10.20074	9.44243	8.77154	8.17574	7.64465
23	20.45582	18.29220	16.44361	14.85684	13.48857	12.30338	11.27219	10.37106	9.58021	8.88322	8.26643	7.71843
24	21.24339	18.91393	16.93554	15.24696	13.79864	12.55036	11.46933	10.52876	9.70661	8.98474	8.34814	7.78432
25	22.02316	19.52346	17.41315	15.62208	14.09394	12.78336	11.65358	10.67478	9.82258	9.07704	8.42174	7.84314
30	25.80771	22.39646	19.60044	17.29203	15.37245	13.76483	12.40904	11.25778	10.27365	9.42691	8.69379	8.05518
35	29.40858	24.99862	21.48722	18.66461	16.37419	14.49825	12.94767	11.65457	10.56682	9.64416	8.85524	8.17550
40	32.83469	27.35548	23.11477	19.79277	17.15909	15.04630	13.33171	11.92461	10.75736	9.77905	8.95105	8.24378

TABLE 3	Future Value of Single Amount											$f = (1 + i)^t$
						Interest Rate						
Period	0.01	0.02	0.03	0.04	0.05	0.06	0.07	0.08	0.09	0.10	0.11	0.12
1	1.01000	1.02000	1.03000	1.04000	1.05000	1.06000	1.07000	1.08000	1.09000	1.10000	1.11000	1.12000
2	1.02010	1.04040	1.06090	1.08160	1.10250	1.12360	1.14490	1.16640	1.18810	1.21000	1.23210	1.25440
3	1.03030	1.06121	1.09273	1.12486	1.15763	1.19102	1.22504	1.25971	1.29503	1.33100	1.36763	1.40493
4	1.04060	1.08243	1.12551	1.16986	1.21551	1.26248	1.31080	1.36049	1.41158	1.46410	1.51807	1.57352
5	1.05101	1.10408	1.15927	1.21665	1.27628	1.33823	1.40255	1.46933	1.53862	1.61051	1.68506	1.76234
6	1.06152	1.12616	1.19405	1.26532	1.34010	1.41852	1.50073	1.58687	1.67710	1.77156	1.87041	1.97382
7	1.07214	1.14869	1.22987	1.31593	1.40710	1.50363	1.60578	1.71382	1.82804	1.94872	2.07616	2.21068
8	1.08286	1.17166	1.26677	1.36857	1.47746	1.59385	1.71819	1.85093	1.99256	2.14359	2.30454	2.47596
9	1.09369	1.19509	1.30477	1.42331	1.55133	1.68948	1.83846	1.99900	2.17189	2.35795	2.55804	2.77308
10	1.10462	1.21899	1.34392	1.48024	1.62889	1.79085	1.96715	2.15892	2.36736	2.59374	2.83942	3.10585
11	1.11567	1.24337	1.38423	1.53945	1.71034	1.89830	2.10485	2.33164	2.58043	2.85312	3.15176	3.47855
12	1.12683	1.26824	1.42576	1.60103	1.79586	2.01220	2.25219	2.51817	2.81266	3.13843	3.49845	3.89598
13	1.13809	1.29361	1.46853	1.66507	1.88565	2.13293	2.40985	2.71962	3.06580	3.45227	3.88328	4.36349
14	1.14947	1.31948	1.51259	1.73168	1.97993	2.26090	2.57853	2.93719	3.34173	3.79750	4.31044	4.88711
15	1.16097	1.34587	1.55797	1.80094	2.07893	2.39656	2.75903	3.17217	3.64248	4.17725	4.78459	5.47357
16	1.17258	1.37279	1.60471	1.87298	2.18287	2.54035	2.95216	3.42594	3.97031	4.59497	5.31089	6.13039
17	1.18430	1.40024	1.65285	1.94790	2.29202	2.69277	3.15882	3.70002	4.32763	5.05447	5.89509	6.86604
18	1.19615	1.42825	1.70243	2.02582	2.40662	2.85434	3.37993	3.99602	4.71712	5.55992	6.54355	7.68997
19	1.20811	1.45681	1.75351	2.10685	2.52695	3.02560	3.61653	4.31570	5.14166	6.11591	7.26334	8.61276
20	1.22019	1.48595	1.80611	2.19112	2.65330	3.20714	3.86968	4.66096	5.60441	6.72750	8.06231	9.64629
21	1.23239	1.51567	1.86029	2.27877	2.78596	3.39956	4.14056	5.03383	6.10881	7.40025	8.94917	10.80385
22	1.24472	1.54598	1.91610	2.36992	2.92526	3.60354	4.43040	5.43654	6.65860	8.14027	9.93357	12.10031
23	1.25716	1.57690	1.97359	2.46472	3.07152	3.81975	4.74053	5.87146	7.25787	8.95430	11.02627	13.55235
24	1.26973	1.60844	2.03279	2.56330	3.22510	4.04893	5.07237	6.34118	7.91108	9.84973	12.23916	15.17863
25	1.28243	1.64061	2.09378	2.66584	3.38635	4.29187	5.42743	6.84848	8.62308	10.83471	13.58546	17.00006
30	1.34785	1.81136	2.42726	3.24340	4.32194	5.74349	7.61226	10.06266	13.26768	17.44940	22.89230	29.95992
35	1.41660	1.99989	2.81386	3.94609	5.51602	7.68609	10.67658	14.78534	20.41397	28.10244	38.57485	52.79962
40	1.48886	2.20804	3.26204	4.80102	7.03999	10.28572	14.97446	21.72452	31.40942	45.25926	65.00087	93.05097

TABLE 4	Future Value of an Ordinary Annuity											$f = [(1 + i)^t - 1]/i$
						Interest Rate						
Period	0.01	0.02	0.03	0.04	0.05	0.06	0.07	0.08	0.09	0.10	0.11	0.12
1	1.00000	1.00000	1.00000	1.00000	1.00000	1.00000	1.00000	1.00000	1.00000	1.00000	1.00000	1.00000
2	2.01000	2.02000	2.03000	2.04000	2.05000	2.06000	2.07000	2.08000	2.09000	2.10000	2.11000	2.12000
3	3.03010	3.06040	3.09090	3.12160	3.15250	3.18360	3.21490	3.24640	3.27810	3.31000	3.34210	3.37440
4	4.06040	4.12161	4.18363	4.24646	4.31013	4.37462	4.43994	4.50611	4.57313	4.64100	4.70973	4.77933
5	5.10101	5.20404	5.30914	5.41632	5.52563	5.63709	5.75074	5.86660	5.98471	6.10510	6.22780	6.35285
6	6.15202	6.30812	6.46841	6.63298	6.80191	6.97532	7.15329	7.33593	7.52333	7.71561	7.91286	8.11519
7	7.21354	7.43428	7.66246	7.89829	8.14201	8.39384	8.65402	8.92280	9.20043	9.48717	9.78327	10.08901
8	8.28567	8.58297	8.89234	9.21423	9.54911	9.89747	10.25980	10.63663	11.02847	11.43589	11.85943	12.29969
9	9.36853	9.75463	10.15911	10.58280	11.02656	11.49132	11.97799	12.48756	13.02104	13.57948	14.16397	14.77566
10	10.46221	10.94972	11.46388	12.00611	12.57789	13.18079	13.81645	14.48656	15.19293	15.93742	16.72201	17.54874
11	11.56683	12.16872	12.80780	13.48635	14.20679	14.97164	15.78360	16.64549	17.56029	18.53117	19.56143	20.65458
12	12.68250	13.41209	14.19203	15.02581	15.91713	16.86994	17.88845	18.97713	20.14072	21.38428	22.71319	24.13313
13	13.80933	14.68033	15.61779	16.62684	17.71298	18.88214	20.14064	21.49530	22.95338	24.52271	26.21164	28.02911
14	14.94742	15.97394	17.08632	18.29191	19.59863	21.01507	22.55049	24.21492	26.01919	27.97498	30.09492	32.39260
15	16.09690	17.29342	18.59891	20.02359	21.57856	23.27597	25.12902	27.15211	29.36092	31.77248	34.40536	37.27971
16	17.25786	18.63929	20.15688	21.82453	23.65749	25.67253	27.88805	30.32428	33.00340	35.94973	39.18995	42.75328
17	18.43044	20.01207	21.76159	23.69751	25.84037	28.21288	30.84022	33.75023	36.97370	40.54470	44.50084	48.88367
18	19.61475	21.41231	23.41444	25.64541	28.13238	30.90565	33.99903	37.45024	41.30134	45.59917	50.39594	55.74971
19	20.81090	22.84056	25.11687	27.67123	30.53900	33.75999	37.37896	41.44626	46.01846	51.15909	56.93949	63.43968
20	22.01900	24.29737	26.87037	29.77808	33.06595	36.78559	40.99549	45.76196	51.16012	57.27500	64.20283	72.05244
21	23.23919	25.78332	28.67649	31.96920	35.71925	39.99273	44.86518	50.42292	56.76453	64.00250	72.26514	81.69874
22	24.47159	27.29898	30.53678	34.24797	38.50521	43.39229	49.00574	55.45676	62.87334	71.40275	81.21431	92.50258
23	25.71630	28.84496	32.45288	36.61789	41.43048	46.99583	53.43614	60.89330	69.53194	79.54302	91.14788	104.60289
24	26.97346	30.42186	34.42647	39.08260	44.50200	50.81558	58.17667	66.76476	76.78981	88.49733	102.17415	118.15524
25	28.24320	32.03030	36.45926	41.64591	47.72710	54.86451	63.24904	73.10594	84.70090	98.34706	114.41331	133.33387
30	34.78489	40.56808	47.57542	56.08494	66.43885	79.05819	94.46079	113.28321	136.30754	164.49402	199.02088	241.33268
35	41.66028	49.99448	60.46208	73.65222	90.32031	111.43478	138.23688	172.31680	215.71075	271.02437	341.58955	431.66350
40	48.88637	60.40198	75.40126	95.02552	120.79977	154.76197	199.63511	259.05652	337.88245	442.59256	581.82607	767.09142

B

Adjusting and Forecasting Financial Statements

INTRODUCTION

Forecasting financial performance is integral to a variety of business decisions ranging from investing to managing a company effectively. We might, for example, wish to value a company's common stock before purchasing its shares. To that end, we forecast free cash flows or residual operating income as inputs into one of the valuation models we discuss in Appendix C. Or, we might be interested in evaluating the creditworthiness of a prospective borrower. In that case, we forecast cash flows to estimate the ability of the borrowing firm to repay its obligations. We might also be interested in evaluating alternative strategic plans for management decisions. In this case, our forecasts can be evaluated with respect to the creation of shareholder value.

The forecasting process begins with a retrospective analysis. That is, we analyze current and prior years' statements to be sure that they reflect our analysis of the financial condition and performance of the company. If we believe that they do not, we adjust those statements to better reflect our analysis inferences. Once we've adjusted the historical results, we are ready to forecast future results.

Why would we need to adjust historical results? The answer resides in the fact that financial statements prepared in conformity with GAAP do not always accurately reflect the "true" financial condition and performance of the company. This situation can arise for several reasons including the following:

- The income statement might include transitory items, such as an asset write-down or the accrual of expected restructuring costs.

- The balance sheet might include nonoperating assets and liabilities such as those from discontinued operations. Conversely, the balance sheet might exclude operating assets and liabilities such as those from operating leases or from investments accounted for using the equity method.

- The statement of cash flows might include operating cash inflows from excessive inventory reductions, from securitization of accounts receivable, or from tax benefits on the exercise of employee stock options.

These are just a few examples of how financial statements can be prepared in conformity with GAAP, but do not accurately reflect core operating activities of the company. Consequently, we want to adjust such financial statements before forecasting financial statements.

ADJUSTING FINANCIAL STATEMENTS

We begin with a discussion of the process by which financial statements are adjusted for purposes of forecasting—the **adjusting process** is also referred to as **recasting** or **reformulating**. To be sure, the adjusting process is not "black and white." It requires judgment and estimation. Our discussion of adjusting (and forecasting) financial statements is meant to introduce a reasonable and reliable, but not the only, process for these tasks.[1]

Adjusting the Income Statement

This section describes adjustments that are often made to the income statement for forecasting purposes. These adjustments generally fall into one of three categories:

1. **Separate core (persistent) and transitory items**—The aim of forecasting is to project financial results. Since transitory items are, by definition, nonrecurring, they are generally excluded from current operating results. Common transitory items include gains and losses from asset sales, the results of discontinued operations, and costs related to restructuring activities.

2. **Separate operating and nonoperating items**—Core operating activities have the most long-lasting (persistent) effects on future profitability and cash flows and, thus, are the primary value drivers for company stakeholders. It is important to separate core operating items from nonoperating items for effective profitability analysis.

3. **Include expenses that net income excludes**—We review the composition and level of operating expenses to determine their reasonableness. To the extent a company fails to recognize expenses, whether due to underaccrual of reserves or liabilities or due to reduced expenditures for key operating activities, reported income is overstated. Such unrecognized expenses are included in the adjusting process.

Exhibit B.1 lists some typical adjustments. Exhibit B.1 is not meant to be an exhaustive list, only an indication of the types of adjustments that are commonly made.

The first category in Exhibit B.1 includes gains and losses from asset sales and asset write-downs, and the financial gains and losses from debt retirements and subsidiary stock sales. These items are transitory and should not be included when forecasting operating results. GAAP also help by identifying two items that it specifically highlights as transitory and then reports (net of tax) below income from continuing operations—those are discontinued operations and extraordinary items. These should likewise be excluded from the forecasting process. Finally, any other transitory items in current income are excluded. Common items include restructuring expenses, merger and acquisition costs, LIFO liquidation gains and losses, excessive liability accruals, and increases and decreases in tax expense (and, thus, net income) from changes in the deferred tax asset valuation account.

---

[1] It is important to separate the purposes of GAAP-based financial statements and the adjusting process of this appendix for purposes of forecasting. Specifically, GAAP-based statements serve more than just information for forecasting. For example, financial statements are key inputs in contracting between business parties. This means that historical results, including any transitory activities, must be reported to meet management's fiduciary responsibilities. On the other hand, forecasting wishes to purge itself of transitory activities and focus on those items that persist, with a special emphasis on persistent operating activities.

EXHIBIT B.1	Common Income Statement Adjustments

1. Separate core (persistent) and transitory items—examples of items to exclude:
   a. Gains and losses relating to
      (1) Asset sales on long-term assets and investments
      (2) Asset write-downs of long-term assets and inventories
      (3) Stock issuances by subsidiaries
      (4) Debt retirements
   b. Transitory items reported after income from continued operations
      (1) Discontinued operations
      (2) Extraordinary items
   c. Restructuring expenses
   d. Merger costs
   e. LIFO liquidation gains
   f. Liability accruals deemed excessive
   g. Gains and losses from changes in deferred tax valuation allowance

2. Separate operating and nonoperating items—examples:
   a. Treating interest revenue and expense, and investment gains and losses, as nonoperating
   b. Treating pension service cost as operating, and pension interest costs and expected returns as nonoperating
   c. Treating debt retirement gains and losses as nonoperating
   d. Treating income and losses from discontinued operations as nonoperating
   e. Treating short-term fluctuations in tax expense as nonoperating

3. Include expenses not reflected in net income—examples:
   a. Employee stock option expense
   b. Inadequate reserves for bad debts or asset impairment
   c. Reductions in R&D, advertising, and other discretionary expenses that were made to achieve short-term income targets

The second category focuses on separating operating and nonoperating components. The financial (nonoperating) income items commonly excluded are interest revenue and expense, the gains and losses from sales of investments, and pension interest costs and expected returns. Nonoperating components also include gains and losses on debt retirements and income or losses related to discontinued operations. Short-term gains and losses from temporary swings in the tax position are also commonly treated as nonoperating.

The third category of adjustments involves inclusion of expenses not included in current income per GAAP. These commonly include expenses relating to employee stock option plans, the inadequate reserve for uncollectible accounts receivable, and unrecognized asset impairment costs. Adjustments might also involve additional amounts for R&D, advertising, and other operating expenses that reflect discretionary reductions of operating activities to achieve short-term income targets.

BUSINESS INSIGHT

What Is eBay's Income? How much income did eBay earn over the past five years? Albert Meyer, an accounting sleuth who runs 2nd Opinion Research says, "For the life of me, I wouldn't be able to tell." The main culprit is its stock options. eBay's reported income from 1999 through 2003 is $840 million. Under GAAP, this doesn't include its stock option costs of $827 million. If we subtract that cost, eBay has earned just $13 million in total for the past five years. Even that cost estimate only measures the value of options when granted. Alternatively, Meyer estimates that eBay employees pocketed $1.6 billion in option-based compensation over this five-year period. So, did the options cost $827 million or $1.6 billion? Consider that $1.6 billion is the cumulative figure eBay claimed as expense on its tax return. At $1.6 billion, eBay has *lost* $760 million for this five-year period. (*Fortune* May 31, 2004)

Adjusting the Balance Sheet

The primary focus of balance sheet adjustments is to separate (exclude) nonoperating assets and liabilities that are reported on the balance sheet and to include operating assets and liabilities that are *not* reported on the balance sheet. These adjustments typically require use of footnote disclosures, including information for capitalizing assets and liabilities that are excluded by the company per GAAP.

Exhibit B.2 lists several common balance sheet adjustments, but this listing is not meant to be exhaustive.

EXHIBIT B.2	**Common Balance Sheet Adjustments**

1. Separate nonoperating assets and liabilities—examples of items to exclude:
    a. Eliminate assets and liabilities from discontinued operations
    b. Write-downs on any assets, including goodwill, that is judged to be impaired

2. Include operating assets and liabilities not reflected in balance sheet—examples:
    a. Capitalize assets and liabilities from operating leases
    b. Consolidate off-balance-sheet investments
        (1) Equity method investments
        (2) Variable interest entities (VIEs)
    c. Accrue understated liabilities and assets

The first category in Exhibit B.2 involves separating (excluding) nonoperating assets and liabilities on the balance sheet. Discontinued operations are segregated in the income statement (see Exhibit B.1), and their assets and liabilities are commonly segregated, as well, in the balance sheet. Those assets and liabilities are excluded in the adjusting process since, by definition, neither those assets and liabilities, nor the sales and expenses of discontinued operations, remain in continuing operations. Other adjustments to the balance sheet include the write-down of impaired assets. Adjustments to reduce assets are difficult judgment calls, which benefit from information outside of the financial statements such as financial reports of competitors and analyst reports of the state of the industry so as to form an opinion about such potential asset impairments.

The second category focuses on including operating assets and liabilities not reported in the balance sheet per GAAP. One example is operating leases that are prevalent in several industries, including the retailing, franchising, and airline industries. Lease disclosures mandated under GAAP provide sufficient information for us to effectively capitalize these lease assets and liabilities for forecasting purposes (see Chapter 13). Investments that confer significant influence, but not control, and are reported using the equity method of accounting are another example of assets and liabilities not reported in the balance sheet per GAAP.[2] The equity method reports an investment balance equal to the percentage of the equity in the investee company that is owned, rather than the assets and liabilities of the investee company that would be recognized on-balance-sheet if the entity were consolidated. This means that many assets and liabilities are unreported. Unfortunately, usual footnote disclosures by companies with equity method investments are poor and insufficient to estimate the assets and liabilities (and risk) of the investee companies. To the extent that summary balance sheets and income statements are provided in the footnotes, the adjustment process replaces the investment account with the assets and liabilities to which they relate using the consolidation mechanics discussed in Chapter 12.

---

[2]The equity method of accounting is used for investments in partnerships, joint ventures, and trusts in addition to minority interest in corporations.

Other adjustments to the balance sheet include the accrual of understated liabilities. Common accruals such as those relating to operating activities like warranties, premiums, and coupons are somewhat easier to assess and estimate from prior balance sheet data. Accruals for contingent liabilities such as environmental and litigation exposure are more difficult and require use of information outside of the financial statements.

RESEARCH INSIGHT

Earnings Quality and Accounting Conservatism Accounting researchers commonly measure *earnings quality* in terms of sustainability, meaning that the income items persist in future periods. This is consistent with the definition of *core* income described in Chapter 7. Sustainability is important because core income items are better indicators of future earnings than are transitory items. One factor that affects earnings quality is accounting conservatism. Research finds that conservative accounting leads to transitory earnings changes when the levels of investment within the firm changes. Researchers have constructed a conservatism index to study the effect conservatism and growth have on earnings changes. The index is defined as the level of estimated reserves created by conservative accounting (such as LIFO versus FIFO, and expensing of R&D and advertising) divided by the level of net operating assets. Earnings quality is then a function of changes in the conservatism index for each firm, and it is a function of the difference between the firm-specific and industry-specific conservatism index. Poor earnings quality occurs when the firm grows its estimated reserves at a different rate than the growth of its net operating assets. A firm-specific conservatism index that substantially differs from that of the firm's industry is one sign of poor earnings quality. This is because profitability trends toward the industry mean. While the index is one indicator of firms with unsustainable earnings, market participants do not appear to fully consider the information contained in this index when determining stock prices.

Adjusting the Statement of Cash Flows

The focus of cash flow adjustments is threefold: (1) to adjust operating cash flows for any nonoperating (abnormal) items, (2) to adjust (exclude) transitory items from cash flows, and (3) to review the assignment of cash flows into their proper sections—investing, investing, and financing. These adjustments typically require use of the other financial statements, including footnote disclosures, and sometimes information from outside the financial statements.

Exhibit B.3 lists several common statement of cash flow adjustments, but this listing is not meant to be exhaustive.

EXHIBIT B.3   Common Statement of Cash Flow Adjustments

1. Adjust operating cash flows for nonoperating items—examples:
   a. Adjust discretionary costs (advertising, R&D, maintenance) to normal, expected levels
   b. Adjust current operating assets (receivables, inventory) to normal, expected levels
   c. Adjust current operating liabilities (payables, accruals) to normal, expected levels

2. Adjust cash flows for transitory items—examples:
   a. Separate (exclude) operating cash flows from tax benefits due to exercise of employee stock options

3. Review cash flows and reassign them, if necessary, to operating, investing, or financing sections—examples:
   a. Separate and reassign operating cash inflows from asset securitization to financing section
   b. Separate and reassign operating cash flows from discontinued operations to investing section

The first category in Exhibit B.3 involves adjusting operating cash flows for nonoperating items. These nonoperating items commonly involve discretionary activities whose amounts are determined by management and are not in line with reasonable norms. To better understand, recall that operating cash flows increase with an increase in operating income and/or a decrease in net operating working capital (the latter occurs from either or both a decrease in current assets or an increase in current liabilities). Although higher operating cash flows are generally viewed favorably, it is necessary to understand the drivers of that increase to discern whether or not future cash flows are expected to exhibit similar behavior. Following are several common adjustments to operating cash flows for nonoperating items:

■ **Cost decreases.** Transitory, abnormal reductions of necessary, expected operating costs related to discretionary expenditures on advertising, promotion, R&D, and maintenance. Such reductions increase income and operating cash flows, which usually yield short-term benefits at long-term costs.

■ **Current asset decreases.** Transitory, abnormal reductions in current operating assets such as accounts receivable and inventory increase net cash flows from operations. Such reductions are generally desirable. However, if such reductions are the result of overly restrictive credit policies or result in inventories below what is necessary to conduct operations, then increased (short-term) operating cash flows likely arise from long-term costs as customers leave or face stock-outs causing the company's image to deteriorate.

■ **Current liability increases.** Transitory, abnormal increases in current operating liabilities such as accounts payable and other accrued liabilities increase operating cash flows. After some point, however, the cash inflows from extending the payment of accounts payable or other liabilities come at the cost of supplier and creditor relations.

The second category involves adjusting cash flows for transitory items. One example is tax benefits from exercise of employee stock options, which are typically transitory. The IRS considers the cost of employee stock options a tax-deductible expense, even if unrecognized as an expense under GAAP. The persistence of this tax benefit, however, is predicated on increased stock prices. When the stock price falls below the option's exercise (strike) price, options are no longer exercised and the tax benefit ceases.

BUSINESS INSIGHT

What is eBay's Operating Cash Flow? Steve Milunovich of Merrill Lynch believes that operating cash flow should exclude what companies spend to buy back stock to offset option-related dilution. This gets tricky in eBay's case because it, unlike many others, hasn't bought back any stock. This means that, even if you're a stockholder who never sold a share, you own less of eBay now than you did five years ago. It is estimated that had eBay bought back shares to enable stockholders to maintain their ownership stake rather than seeing it decline, the cash outflow would have been $1.2 billion—which is huge relative to eBay's five-year cumulative operating cash flow of $1.8 billion. (*Fortune* May 31, 2004)

The third category involves the proper categorization of cash flows into operating, investing, and financing sections. One example is cash inflows from asset securitizations, which are reported as operating cash flows per GAAP. However, companies commonly sell accounts receivable to a variable interest entity, which is categorized as an operating cash inflow in the year of sale, but is better viewed as a financing cash inflow (similar to borrowing against the receivables). Another example is cash flows from discontinued operations that should be reclassified from operating to investing.

BUSINESS INSIGHT

Tyco Buys Operating Cash Flow Corporate management is aware of the market's focus on operating cash flow, which is a main driver of free cash flow and is used in many stock valuation models (see Appendix C). In 2001, Tyco touted its free cash flows in a press release: *Free Cash Flow Reaches $1.7 Billion for the Fourth Quarter and $4.75 Billion for the Fiscal Year.* Said L. Dennis Kozlowski, chairman and CEO of Tyco, "Strong cash flow generation throughout all of our businesses funds further investment in these businesses and provides the means to opportunistically expand them as circumstances allow." Tyco eventually admitted to spending $830 million in 2001 to purchase roughly 800,000 individual customer contracts for its security-alarm business from a network of independent dealers. Cash outflows relating to this purchase were reported in the *investing* section of the statement of cash flows. However, fees paid by these new customers were reported in net income and immediately added to its *operating* cash flow. *The Wall Street Journal* (March 5, 2002) declared that Tyco effectively bought earnings and operating cash flow with its contract purchases.

MID-APPENDIX REVIEW

Following is the income statement ($ millions) of **Time Warner, Inc.**:

	2003	2002	2001
Revenues			
Subscriptions	$ 20,448	$ 18,959	$ 15,657
Advertising	6,182	6,299	6,869
Content	11,446	10,216	8,654
Other	1,489	1,840	2,327
Total revenues	39,565	37,314	33,507
Costs of revenues	(23,285)	(22,116)	(18,789)
Selling, general and administrative	(9,862)	(8,835)	(7,486)
Merger and restructuring costs	(109)	(327)	(214)
Amortization of intangible assets	(640)	(557)	(6,366)
Impairment of goodwill and other intangible assets ...	(318)	(44,039)	—
Net gain on disposal of assets	14	6	—
Operating income (loss)	5,365	(38,554)	652
Interest expense, net	(1,844)	(1,758)	(1,316)
Other income (expense), net	1,210	(2,447)	(3,458)
Minority interest income (expense)	(214)	(278)	46
Income (loss) before income taxes, discontinued operations and cumulative effect of accounting change	4,517	(43,037)	(4,076)
Income tax provision	(1,371)	(412)	(145)
Income (loss) before discontinued operations and cumulative effect of accounting change	3,146	(43,449)	(4,221)
Discontinued operations, net of tax	(495)	(1,012)	(713)
Income (loss) before cumulative effect of accounting change	2,651	(44,461)	(4,934)
Cumulative effect of accounting change	(12)	(54,235)	—
Net income (loss)	$ 2,639	$(98,696)	$ (4,934)

Identify and discuss any items that you believe should be considered in the adjusting process as we prepare to forecast Time Warner's earnings performance based on results for this three-year period.

Solution
Several items from its income statement should be considered when adjusting Time Warner's earnings for this period in anticipation of generating forecasts. Consider the following three categories of common income statement adjustments and potential Time Warner adjustments:

1. *Separate core (persistent) and transitory items*
   a. Its cost of revenues increases from 54.5% to 59% of sales over this period. We want more information regarding the causes of this trend. For example, has the cost of revenues been impacted by transitory items, like the write-off of inventory?
   b. Merger and restructuring costs, while they have recurred over this period, are usually transitory. Further, Time Warner is not a typical *roll-up company* (achieving growth via acquisitions). Thus, we treat these costs as nonrecurring and we want to know more about the details of these costs.
   c. Its impairment of goodwill and other intangibles is mainly related to its write-off of goodwill from the merger of Time Warner and AOL. This amount is now written off and is not recurring.
   d. Its net gain on disposal of assets, although a minor amount in this case, warrants attention. We must watch for recognition of gains and losses on asset sales, especially when the gain

allows a company to achieve earnings targets or the loss is taken in a year of excessive income (or losses).

    e. Its income (loss) from discontinued operations is, by definition, eliminated from the income statement once the operations are disposed of.

    f. Its cumulative effect of accounting change is the cumulative adjustment following adoption of a new accounting rule. It is treated as nonrecurring.

2. *Separate operating and nonoperating items*

    a. Its SGA expenses increase from 22.3% to 24.9% of sales. Aside from the potential for out-of-control overhead, we are interested in knowing whether SG&A includes transitory and/or nonoperating items that would distort the underlying economic picture. Footnote disclosures are one source of information.

3. *Include expenses not reflected in net income*

    a. Its other income and expense item has fluctuated over the past three years, from a loss of $3,458 million to a gain of $1,210 million. The composition of this account is of great interest and we would search the footnotes for any insights. (This also fits under adjustment no. 1.)

FORECASTING FINANCIAL STATEMENTS

Common stock valuation models use forecasted financial information to compute estimates of stock price. Creditors also utilize forecasted financial information to evaluate the cash flows available to repay indebtedness. Knowledge of the forecasting process is, therefore, an important skill to master. In this section, we introduce the most common method to forecast the income statement, balance sheet, and statement of cash flows. It is important to forecast the income statement first, then the balance sheet, and then the statement of cash flows in that order since each succeeding statement uses forecast information from the previous forecasted statement(s). Our description, therefore, proceeds in that same order.

    We use **Procter & Gamble**'s fiscal 2004 financial statements for illustration. In practice, the forecasting process uses adjusted financial statements resulting from the adjusting process explained in the prior section. However, for ease in learning, we deliberately select P&G because it is generally free from needed adjustments. This allows us to focus on the forecasting mechanics.

Forecasting the Income Statement

Procter & Gamble's fiscal year income statement is shown in Exhibit B.4.

EXHIBIT B.4	Procter & Gamble Income Statement		
		Years Ended June 30	
Amounts in millions	**2004**	**2003**	**2002**
Net sales	$51,407	$43,377	$40,238
Cost of products sold	25,076	22,141	20,989
Selling, general and administrative expense	16,504	13,383	12,571
Operating income	9,827	7,853	6,678
Interest expense	629	561	603
Other nonoperating income, net	152	238	308
Earnings before income taxes	9,350	7,530	6,383
Income taxes	2,869	2,344	2,031
Net earnings	$ 6,481	$ 5,186	$ 4,352

Assuming that we have made all necessary adjustments (see prior section), we identify several important financial relations from the income statement information in Exhibit B.4. These relations are identified and reported in Exhibit B.5.[3]

EXHIBIT B.5	Key Procter & Gamble Income Statement Relations
($ millions)	**2004**
Sales growth ([$51,407/$43,377] − 1)	18.5%
Cost of goods sold percentage ($25,076/$51,407)	48.8%
Gross profit margin (1 − 48.8%)	51.2%
Selling, general and administrative expense margin ($16,504/$51,407)	32.1%
Depreciation expense (per statement of cash flow)	$1,733
Net nonoperating expense ($629 − $152)	$ 477
Tax expense/Pretax income ($2,869/$9,350)	30.7%

We use these key income statement relations and measures to forecast future performance. In practice, we also review the MD&A section, footnotes, and nonfinancial information to assess whether these historical income statement relations are representative of core operating performance and, if not, adjust these income statement relations accordingly. Following are examples of how we can use nonfinancial information to enhance our income statement relations and measures:

Company Scenario	Forecasting Implications
McDonalds reports an 11% increase in 2003 sales; its MD&A reports that sales increased by 5% from a weakened $US	We might forecast a less than 11% sales growth if we do not expect the $US to further weaken or strengthen
Altria reports a $2.6 billion gain on sale of its Miller Brewing subsidiary	This is a transitory item and we do not want to forecast its recurrence; we also do not want to include any operating results from this discontinued subsidiary in our forecasting process
Hewlett-Packard reports a 28% increase in 2003 revenues, from $57 billion in 2002 to $73 billion in 2003; note that in May 2002 it acquired Compaq	Compaq's revenues impact HP's consolidated totals from the date of acquisition onward; footnotes reveal that 2002 revenues would have been $72 billion had Compaq been included for an entire year, meaning that we do not want to assume continuation of a 28% growth
Target reports a 2003 sales increase of 12%; most of this is from new store openings as comparable store growth is 4.4%	Growth via acquisition or construction requires capital outlays, and is different from *organic growth;* if we forecast continuation of a 12% growth, we also must forecast the required capital outlays
Boeing reports a 2003 goodwill impairment charge of $913 million	This is a transitory item that we should not forecast as it is nonrecurring (assuming remaining goodwill is not further impaired)

This chapter aims to illustrate forecasting mechanics given key financial statement relations as assumptions. In practice, these relations must be carefully reviewed and modified from reported levels if needed. This is the *art* of forecasting.

Using the income statement relations from Exhibit B.5, the P&G forecasted income statement is shown in Exhibit B.6. Net nonoperating expense is assumed constant as we do not forecast any changes to the investing and financing activities of the company (at this point).

---

[3] A key to financial statement forecasting is the sales forecast. Although there is no perfect method, the more information we can gather and assimilate, the more accurate the forecast will be. Use of the current sales growth rate is a simple, but often reasonable, sales forecast and is applied in this appendix and its assignments. Many other forecasting methods are available, with varying claims of success. For example, we could use a time series of sales and fit a trend line. We also could use other company, industry, and economic variables in a so-called multivariate forecast model in a desire to better predict sales. However, there is no guarantee that the costs of such forecasts are worth the benefits. Forecasting is an uncertain setting.

EXHIBIT B.6	Procter & Gamble Forecasted Income Statement	
($ millions)		**2005 Est.**
Net sales ($51,407 × 1.185)		**$60,917**
Cost of goods sold ($51,407 × 1.185 × 48.8%)		**29,727**
Gross profit ($60,917 × 51.2%)		**31,190**
Selling, general and administrative expense ($60,917 × 32.1%)		**19,554**
Operating income (subtotal)		**11,636**
Net nonoperating expense (unchanged)		**477**
Income before income taxes (subtotal)		**11,159**
Income taxes ($11,158 × 30.7%)		**3,426**
Net income (total)		**$ 7,733**

Forecasting the Balance Sheet

Forecasting the balance sheet requires information from our forecasted income statement as well as historical financial and nonfinancial information. It, therefore, is prepared *after* forecasting the income statement. P&G's historical balance sheet is reproduced in Exhibit B.7.

EXHIBIT B.7	Procter & Gamble Balance Sheet	
	June 30	
Amounts in millions	**2004**	**2003**
Assets		
Current Assets		
Cash and cash equivalents	$ 5,469	$ 5,912
Investment securities	423	300
Accounts receivable	4,062	3,038
Inventories		
Materials and supplies	1,191	1,095
Work in process	340	291
Finished goods	2,869	2,254
Total inventories	4,400	3,640
Deferred income taxes	958	843
Prepaid expenses and other receivables	1,803	1,487
Total current assets	17,115	15,220
Property, Plant, and Equipment		
Buildings	5,206	4,729
Machinery and equipment	19,456	18,222
Land	642	591
	25,304	23,542
Accumulated depreciation	(11,196)	(10,438)
Net property, plant, and equipment	14,108	13,104
Goodwill and Other Intangible Assets		
Goodwill	19,610	11,132
Trademarks and other intangible assets, net	4,290	2,375
Net Goodwill and Other Intangible Assets	23,900	13,507
Other Noncurrent Assets	1,925	1,875
Total Assets	$ 57,048	$ 43,706

(Continued on the next page)

(Continued from the previous page)

EXHIBIT B.7	Procter & Gamble Balance Sheet		
		June 30	
Amounts in millions		**2004**	**2003**
Liabilities and Shareholders' Equity			
Current Liabilities			
Accounts payable		$ 3,617	$ 2,795
Accrued and other liabilities		7,689	5,512
Taxes payable		2,554	1,879
Debt due within one year		8,287	2,172
Total current liabilities		22,147	12,358
Long-Term Debt		12,554	11,475
Deferred income taxes		2,261	1,396
Other noncurrent liabilities		2,808	2,291
Total Liabilities		39,770	27,520
Shareholders' Equity			
Convertible Class A preferred stock, stated value $1 per share (600 shares authorized)		1,526	1,580
Common stock, stated value $1 per share (5,000 shares authorized; shares outstanding: 2004—2,543.8, 2003—2,594.4)		2,544	2,594
Additional paid-in capital		$ 2,425	$ 1,634
Reserve for ESOP debt retirement		(1,283)	(1,308)
Accumulated other comprehensive income		(1,545)	(2,006)
Retained earnings		13,611	13,692
Total shareholders' equity		17,278	16,186
Total liabilities and shareholders' equity		$ 57,048	$ 43,706

Forecasting of the balance sheet follows two general steps:

1. Forecast each asset account (*other than cash*) and each liability and equity account
2. Compute the cash amount needed to balance the forecasted accounting equation (Assets = Liabilities + Equity)

To obtain forecasts of specific asset, liability, and equity accounts, several methods can be used such as:

■ Assume no change in balance sheet amounts.

■ Use detailed relations and predicted events; such as capital expenditures to sales and the depreciation expense to prior year gross PPE, and identify events such as scheduled payments of long-term debt and dividend policies drawn from information gleaned from MD&A and footnote disclosures.

■ Use turnover rates and simple assumptions to forecast balance sheet amounts.

The first method is straightforward. The second method requires estimates and assumptions beyond the scope of this book. The third method is the one we use and, thus, requires some explanation. Recall the definition of a generic turnover rate *based on year-end account balances:*

Turnover Rate = Sales (or Cost of Goods Sold)/Account Balance at Year-End

Rearranging terms, we get the forecasted year-end balance as

$$\textbf{Forecasted Year-End Account Balance} = \frac{\textbf{Forecasted Sales (or Cost of Goods Sold)}}{\textbf{Estimated Turnover Rate}}$$

The reason for the use of year-end amounts in the denominator of the turnover rate estimate, while inconsistent with the turnover definition in Chapter 5, is because of the year-end forecast target.

Namely, since we are estimating year-end account balances (and not the average balance), we must compute the turnover rate using year-end balances. The forecasted year-end balance is, thus, forecasted sales (or forecasted cost of goods sold, COGS) divided by the turnover rate estimated from prior year-end balances.

Assuming that we have made all necessary adjustments (see adjusting section), we identify and estimate several important turnover relations and other measures from information in the balance sheet and income statement. These relations and measures are identified and reported in Exhibit B.8, and are used to forecast the balance sheet.

EXHIBIT B.8	Key P&G Relations using Income Statement and Balance Sheet Information	
($ millions)		2004
Sales/Year-end accounts receivable ($51,407/$4,062)		12.66
Cost of goods sold/Year-end inventories ($25,076/$4,400)		5.70
Cost of goods sold/Year-end accounts payable ($25,076/$3,617)		6.93
Sales/Year-end accrued and tax liabilities ($51,407/[$7,689 + $2,554])		5.02
Capital expenditures/Sales ($2,024/$51,407)		3.9%
Cash dividends (per statement of cash flows in Exhibit B.10)		$2,539
Current maturities of long-term debt (per footnotes)		$1,519

There is support for the relations and amounts in Exhibit B.8. For example, accounts receivable and accrued liabilities are typically related to sales levels (because receivables are at selling prices and accruals typically include operating costs that relate to sales volume). Also, inventories and accounts payable are logically related to cost of goods sold (because inventories are at costs and payables typically relate to inventory volume). The amounts for capital expenditures and dividends are taken from the statement of cash flows (see Exhibit B.10), and the current maturities of long-term debt is provided in the long-term debt footnote (not reproduced here).

Using the income statement and balance sheet relations from Exhibit B.8, the P&G forecasted balance sheet is shown in Exhibit B.9—detailed computations are shown in parentheses.

EXHIBIT B.9	Procter & Gamble Forecasted Balance Sheet	
($ millions)		2005 Est.
Cash (total equity and liabilities less all other assets)		$ 9,501
Investment securities (no change assumed)		423
Accounts receivable ($60,917/12.66)		4,812
Inventories ($29,727/5.7)		5,215
Other current assets ($958 + $1,803, no change assumed)		2,761
Total current assets		22,712
Net property, plant, and equipment ($14,108 + [$60,917 × 3.9%] − $1,733)		14,751
Other noncurrent assets ($23,900 + $1,925, no change assumed)		25,825
Total assets (set equal to total liabilities and equity)		$63,288
Accounts payable ($29,727/6.93)		$ 4,290
Accrued and tax liabilities ($60,917/5.02)		12,135
Debt due within one year (no change assumed)		8,287
Total current liabilities		24,712
Long-term debt ($12,554 − $1,519; 2004 debt less current maturities)		11,035
Other long-term liabilities ($2,261 + $2,808, no change assumed)		5,069
Stock and additional paid-in capital ($1,526 + $2,544 + $2,425, no change assumed)		6,495
Retained earnings, AOCI, and ESOP reserve ([$13,611 + $(1,283) + $(1,545)] + $7,733 − $2,539)		15,977
Shareholders' equity		22,472
Total liabilities and equity		$63,288

The final step in forecasting the balance sheet is computing the cash balance, which equals total assets less all noncash assets. Since this is a residual amount, it can be unusually high, low, or even negative. The residual cash balance is an indicator of whether the company is accumulating too much or too little cash from its operating activities less its capital expenditures (note that we are holding financing activities constant at this point). The following table presents two alternative levels of cash and possible adjustments that we would consider at this point in the forecasting process:

Residual Cash	Possible Adjustments to Forecasted Balance Sheet and Income Statement
Too low	• Liquidate marketable securities (then adjust forecasted investment income) • Raise cash by increasing long-term debt and/or equity (then adjust forecasted interest expense and/or expected dividends)
Too high	• Invest excess in marketable securities (then adjust investment income) • Repay debt or pay out to shareholders as treasury stock or dividends (then adjust forecasted interest expense and/or expected dividends)

What benchmark should we use to determine whether the resulting cash balance is too high or too low? This is a judgment call. Many use the historical cash balance as a percentage of total assets (for our company or the industry in general) as the benchmark. When determining the proper cash balance, we must take care to not inadvertently change the financial leverage of the company in this cash adjustment process. Financial leverage is an important consideration in both the analysis and forecasting of company financials (see Chapter 5 for a discussion). Accordingly, we must adjust the proportion of debt and equity affected to ensure that financial leverage is not inadvertently shifted.

To illustrate, the projected cash balance for P&G of $9,501 million is 15% of total assets. In 2004, PG's cash level was 10% of total assets. This suggests that P&G will accumulate excess cash in 2005 and will not require additional financing. We can take its excess cash, say $3,172 ($9,501 − [$63,288 × 10%]) and (1) invest it in securities, in which case we must adjust the forecast of investment returns, or (2) assume the P&G repays some of its debt and repurchases some of its stock in the proportion to maintain P&G's existing financial leverage ratio (which stood at 3.30, computed as $57,048/$17,278, at December 31, 2003).

Forecasting the Statement of Cash Flows

Procter & Gamble's fiscal year statement of cash flows is shown in Exhibit B.10.

EXHIBIT B.10	Procter & Gamble Statement of Cash Flows		
	Years Ended June 30		
Amounts in millions	**2004**	**2003**	**2002**
Operating Activities			
Net earnings	$ 6,481	$ 5,186	$ 4,352
Depreciation and amortization	1,733	1,703	1,693
Deferred income taxes	415	63	389
Change in accounts receivable	(159)	163	96
Change in inventories	56	(56)	159
Change in accounts payable, accrued and other liabilities	625	936	684
Change in other operating assets and liabilities	(88)	178	(98)
Other	299	527	467
Total operating activities	9,362	8,700	7,742
Investing Activities			
Capital expenditures	(2,024)	(1,482)	(1,679)
Proceeds from asset sales	230	143	227
Acquisitions	(7,476)	(61)	(5,471)
Change in investment securities	(121)	(107)	88
Total investing activities	(9,391)	(1,507)	(6,835)

(Continued on the next page)

(Continued from the previous page)

EXHIBIT B.10	Procter & Gamble Statement of Cash Flows		
	Years Ended June 30		
Amounts in millions	**2004**	**2003**	**2002**
Financing Activities			
Dividends to shareholders	**(2,539)**	(2,246)	(2,095)
Change in short-term debt	**4,911**	(2,052)	1,394
Additions to long-term debt	**1,963**	1,230	1,690
Reductions of long-term debt	**(1,188)**	(1,060)	(461)
Proceeds from the exercise of stock options	**555**	269	237
Treasury purchases	**(4,070)**	(1,236)	(568)
Total financing activities	**(368)**	(5,095)	197
Effect of Exchange Rate Changes on Cash and Cash Equivalents	**(46)**	387	17
Change in cash and cash equivalents	**(443)**	2,485	1,121
Cash and cash equivalents, beginning of year	**$ 5,912**	$ 3,427	$ 2,306
Cash and cash equivalents, end of year	**$ 5,469**	$ 5,912	$ 3,427

The forecasted statement of cash flows is prepared using the forecasted income statement and forecasted balance sheet, the historical statement of cash flows is primarily used for reasonableness checks (outside of the information that was already used to forecast the income statement and balance sheet). We draw on the mechanics from preparation of the statement of cash flows, which are discussed in Chapter 4. Specifically, once we have forecasts of the balance sheet and income statement, we can compute the forecasted statement of cash flows just as we would its historical statement. The forecasted statement of cash flows for P&G, and its related computations, is in Exhibit B.11.

EXHIBIT B.11	Procter & Gamble Forecasted Statement of Cash Flows
($ millions)	**2005 Est.**
Operating activities	
Net income	$ 7,733
Depreciation expense (per Exhibit B.5)	1,733
Change in accounts receivable ($4,062 − $4,812)	(750)
Change in inventories ($4,400 − $5,215)	(815)
Change in other current assets (assume no change)	0
Change in accounts payable ($4,290 − $3,617)	673
Change in accrued and tax liabilities ($12,135 − [$7,689 + $2,554])	1,892
Net cash flow from operating activities (subtotal)	10,466
Investing activities	
Capital expenditures ($60,917 × 3.9%, per Exhibit B.8)	(2,376)
Change in other noncurrent assets (assume no change)	0
Net cash flow from investing activities (subtotal)	(2,376)
Financing activities	
Change in current and long-term debt (per Exhibit B.8)	(1,519)
Cash dividends to shareholders (per Exhibit B.8)	(2,539)
Net cash flow from financing activities (subtotal)	(4,058)
Net change in cash (subtotal)	4,032
Cash, beginning of year (per Exhibit B.10)	5,469
Cash, end of year (total)	$ 9,501

Reassessing the Forecasts

It is useful to reassess the set of forecasted financial statements for reasonableness in light of current economic and company conditions. This task is subjective and benefits from your knowledge of company, industry, and economic factors.

Many prepare "what-if" forecasted financial statements. Specifically, key assumptions are changed, such as the forecasted sales growth, and then forecasted financial statements are recomputed. These alternative forecasting scenarios give management a set of predicted outcomes under different assumptions of future economic conditions. Such forecasts can be useful for setting contingency plans and in identifying areas of vulnerability for future company performance and condition.

Forecasting Multiple Years

Many business decisions require forecasted financial statements for more than one year ahead. For example, managerial and capital budgeting, security valuation, and strategic analyses all benefit from reliable multiyear forecasts. Appendix C uses multiyear forecasts of financial results to estimate current stock price for investment purposes.

Although there are different methods to achieve multiyear forecasts, we apply a straightforward approach. To illustrate, using the forecasting assumptions underlying Exhibit B.6, we can forecast P&G's 2006 sales as $72,187 million, computed as $60,917 million $\times$ 1.185. The remainder of the income statement can be forecasted from this sales level using the methodology discussed above for one-year-ahead forecasts. Similarly for the balance sheet, assuming a continuation of the current asset (and liability) turnover rates, we can forecast current assets and liabilities using the same methodology for one-year-ahead forecast. For example, 2006 accounts receivable are forecasted as $5,702 million, computed as $72,187/12.66.

Exhibit B.12 illustrates two-year-ahead (2006) forecasting for P&G's income statement, balance sheet, and statement of cash flows—the 2005 forecasts are shown in the first column for reference purposes. The two-year-ahead forecast is prepared using the same forecast assumptions we employed previously. Any forecast assumptions (such as cost percentages and turnover rates) can be changed in future years if we feel it necessary. An example might be a reduction in expected sales growth if we feel that the market is becoming saturated or a reduction in the accounts receivable turnover rate if the economy is expected to slow. The process can then be replicated for any desired forecast horizon.

EXHIBIT B.12	Procter & Gamble Two-Year-Ahead Forecasted Income Statement	
2005 Est.	**($ millions)**	**2006 Est.**
$60,917	Net sales ($60,917 $\times$ 1.185)	$72,187
29,727	Cost of goods sold ($72,187 $\times$ 48.8%)	35,227
31,190	Gross profit ($72,187 $\times$ 51.2%)	36,960
19,554	Selling, general and administrative expense ($72,187 $\times$ 32.1%)	23,172
11,636	Operating income (subtotal)	13,788
477	Net nonoperating expense (unchanged)	477
11,159	Income before income taxes (subtotal)	13,311
3,426	Income taxes ($13,311 $\times$ 30.7%)	4,087
$7,733	Net income (total)	$ 9,224

(Continued on the next page)

(Continued from the previous page)

EXHIBIT B.12	Procter & Gamble Two-Year-Ahead Forecasted Balance Sheet	

2005 Est.	($ millions)	2006 Est.
$ 9,501	Cash (total equity and liabilities less all other assets)	$14,768
423	Investment securities (no change assumed)	423
4,812	Accounts receivable ($72,187/12.66)	5,702
5,215	Inventories ($35,227/5.7)	6,180
2,761	Other current assets (no change assumed)	2,761
22,712	Total current assets	29,834
14,751	Net property, plant, and equipment ($14,751 + [$72,187 × 3.9%] − $1,733)	15,833
25,825	Other noncurrent assets (no change assumed)	25,825
$63,288	Total assets (equal to total liabilities and equity)	$71,492
$ 4,290	Accounts payable ($35,227/6.93)	$ 5,083
12,135	Accrued and tax liabilities ($72,187/5.02)	14,380
8,287	Debt due within one year (no change assumed)	8,287
24,712	Total current liabilities	27,750
11,035	Long-term debt ($11,035 − $1,518)	9,516
5,069	Other long-term liabilities (no change assumed)	5,069
6,495	Stock and additional paid-in capital (no change assumed)	6,495
15,977	Retained earnings, AOCI, and ESOP reserve ($15,977 + $9,224 − $2,539)	22,662
22,472	Shareholders' equity	29,157
$63,288	Total liabilities and equity	$71,492

	Procter & Gamble Two-Year-Ahead Forecasted Statement of Cash Flows	

2005 Est.	($ millions)	2006 Est.
	Operating activities	
$ 7,733	Net income	$ 9,224
1,733	Depreciation expense (same level assumed)	1,733
(750)	Change in accounts receivable ($4,812 − $5,702)	(890)
(815)	Change in inventories ($5,215 − $6,180)	(965)
0	Change in other current assets (assume no change)	0
673	Change in accounts payable ($5,083 − $4,290)	$ 793
1,892	Change in accrued and tax liabilities ($14,380 − 12,135)	2,245
10,466	Net cash flow from operating activities (subtotal)	12,140
	Investing activities	
(2,376)	Capital expenditures ($72,187 × 3.9%)	(2,815)
0	Change in other noncurrent assets (assume no change)	0
(2,376)	Net cash flow from investing activities (subtotal)	(2,815)
	Financing activities	
(1,519)	Change in current and long-term debt (assume same scheduled payment)	(1,519)
(2,539)	Cash dividends to shareholders (assume no change in level)	(2,539)
(4,058)	Net cash flow from financing activities (subtotal)	(4,058)
4,032	Net change in cash (subtotal)	5,267
5,469	Cash, beginning of year	9,501
$ 9,501	Cash, end of year (total)	$14,768

The two-year-ahead forecasts in Exhibit B.12 illustrate the technique used to forecast an additional year. To simplify exposition, we have not altered any of the forecast assumptions, and focus solely on the forecasting mechanics. However, we often do modify these assumptions. For example, we might wish to increase the forecasted depreciation expense due to the forecasted acquisition of $2,376 million of depreciable long-term operating assets in 2005, and to reduce the forecasted interest expense for 2006 in consideration of the repayment of $1,519 million of long-term debt. Also, we might want to forecast investment returns on the $3,172 million of excess cash generated in 2005. Alternatively, if the excess cash is forecasted to be used for debt repayment, we would want to incorporate that payment into our forecast of 2006 interest expense.

Parsimonious Method to Multiyear Forecasting

The forecasting process described in this appendix uses a considerable amount of available information to, presumably, increase forecast accuracy. We can simplify the process considerably using less information. Stock valuation models commonly use more parsimonious methods to compute multiyear forecasts. For example, in Appendix C we introduce two stock valuation models that use parsimonious methods. One model utilizes forecasted free cash flows and the other uses forecasted net operating profits after tax (NOPAT) and net operating assets (NOA)—see Chapter 5 for descriptions of the variables. Since free cash flows are equal to net operating profits after tax (NOPAT) less the change in net operating assets (NOA), we can accommodate both models with forecasts of NOPAT and NOA.

One approach is to forecast NOPAT and NOA using the methodology outlined in this appendix. Alternatively, we can use a more parsimonious method that requires three crucial inputs:

1. Sales growth

2. Net operating profit margin (NOPM)—defined in Chapter 5 as NOPAT as a percent of sales

3. Net operating asset turnover (NOAT)—defined in Chapter 5 as sales divided by average NOA

To illustrate, we compute P&G's 2004 NOPAT as $6,812, from $9,827 × (1 − [$2,869/$9,350])[4], and its 2004 NOA as $37,696, from $57,048 − $423 − [$22,147 − $8,287] − $2,261 − $2,808. Assuming a sales growth of 18.5% per year, a NOPM of 13.25% ($6,812/$51,407), and a NOAT of 1.36 ($51,407/$37,696), we generate 2005 through 2008 forecasts of NOPAT and NOA in Exhibit B.13—supporting computations are in parentheses.

EXHIBIT B.13	Procter & Gamble Multiyear Forecasts of NOPAT and NOA ($ millions)				
	2004	**2005 Est.**	**2006 Est.**	**2007 Est.**	**2008 Est.**
Sales	$51,407	**$60,917**	**$72,187**	**$85,542**	**$101,367**
		($51,407 × 1.185)	($60,917 × 1.185)	($72,187 × 1.185)	($85,542 × 1.185)
NOPAT	$ 6,812	**$ 8,072**	**$ 9,566**	**$11,335**	**$ 13,432**
	($51,407 × 0.1325)	($60,917 × 0.1325)	($72,187 × 0.1325)	($85,542 × 0.1325)	($101,367 × 0.1325)
NOA	$37,696	**$44,792**	**$53,079**	**$62,898**	**$ 74,534**
		($60,917/1.36)	($72,187/1.36)	($85,542/1.36)	($101,367/1.36)

This forecasting process can be continued for any desired forecast horizon. Also, the forecast assumptions such as sales growth, NOPM, and NOAT can be varied by year, if desired. This alternative, parsimonious method is much simpler than the primary method illustrated in this chapter. However, its simplicity does forgo information that can impact forecast accuracy.

---

[4]$2,869/$9,350 is the estimated average tax rate and, thus, [1 − $2,869/$9,350] is the after-tax rate.

APPENDIX-END REVIEW

Following is financial statement information from Kraft Foods, Inc.

Income Statements

($ 000s)	2003	2002
Net sales	$31,010	$29,723
Cost of goods sold	18,828	17,720
Gross profit	12,182	12,003
Marketing, administrative, research and amortization	6,209	5,716
Other expense (revenue)	(38)	173
Interest expense	665	847
Income before taxes	5,346	5,267
Income taxes	1,870	1,873
Net income	$ 3,476	$ 3,394

Balance Sheets

($ 000s)	2003	2002
Cash	$ 514	$ 215
Receivables	3,369	3,116
Inventories	3,343	3,382
Other current assets	898	743
Total current assets	8,124	7,456
Property, plant, and equipment, gross	15,805	14,450
Less accumulated depreciation	5,650	4,891
Property, plant, and equipment, net	10,155	9,559
Prepaid pension assets	3,243	2,814
Intangible assets	36,879	36,420
Other assets	884	851
Total assets	$59,285	$57,100
Notes payable	553	220
Accounts payable	2,005	1,939
Current maturities of long-term debt	$ 775	$ 352
Accrued liabilities	3,534	3,400
Income taxes payable	451	363
Other current liabilities	543	895
Total current liabilities	7,861	7,169
Deferred income	7,750	7,317
Long-term debt	11,591	10,416
Other long-term liabilities	3,553	6,366
Total liabilities	30,755	31,268
Common stock and paid-in capital	23,704	23,655
Retained earnings	7,020	4,814
Treasury stock	402	170
Other equities	(1,792)	(2,467)
Shareholders' equity	28,530	25,832
Total liabilities and equity	$59,285	$57,100

Forecast the Kraft balance sheet and income statement for 2004 using the following additional information:

Key Financial Relations and Measures ($000s)	2003
Sales growth ($31,010/$29,723 − 1)	4.33%
Gross profit margin ($12,182/$31,010)	39.28%
Marketing, administrative and R&D expense incl. depreciation/Sales ($6,209/$31,010)	20.0%
Other expense/Sales ($38/$31,010)	0.124%
Interest expense	$ 665
Tax rate ($1,870/$5,346)	34.9%
Cash dividends (per statement of cash flows)	$1,089
Sales/Year-end accounts receivable ($31,010/$3,369)	9.205
COGS/Year-end inventories ($18,828/$3,343)	5.632
Depreciation expense	$ 813
COGS/Year-end accounts payable	9.391
Sales/Year-end accrued liabilities	8.775
Capital expenditures/Sales	0.035
Income taxes payable/Income taxes	0.242

Solution

Forecasted 2004 financial statements for Kraft Foods follow:

Forecasted Income Statement	
($ 000s)	2004 Est.
Net sales ($31,010 × 1.0433)	$32,353
Cost of goods sold ($31,010 × [1 − 39.28%])	19,643
Gross profit ($32,353 × 39.28%)	12,709
Marketing, administrative and R&D expense ($32,353 × 20.0%)	6,471
Other expense (revenue) ($32,353 × 0.124%)	40
Interest expense	665
Income before taxes	5,534
Income taxes ($5,534 × 34.9%)	1,932
Net income	$ 3,603

Forecasted Balance Sheet	
($ 000s)	2004 Est.
Cash (amount needed to yield total assets)	$ 1,898
Receivables ($32,353/9.205)	3,515
Inventories ($19,645/5.632)	3,488
Other current assets (assumed level unchanged)	898
Total current assets (subtotal)	9,799
Property, plant, and equipment ($15,805 + $32,353 × 0.035)	16,937
Less accumulated depreciation ($5,650 + $813)	6,463
Property, plant, and equipment, net (subtotal)	10,474
Deferred charges (assumed level unchanged)	3,243
Intangible assets (assumed level unchanged)	36,879
Deposits and other asset (assumed level unchanged)	884
Total assets (equals liabilities plus equity)	$61,279
Notes payable (assumed level unchanged)	$ 553
Accounts payable ($19,645/9.391)	2,092
Current maturities of long-term debt (assumed level unchanged)	775

(Continued on the next page)

(Continued from the previous page)

Forecasted Balance Sheet	
($ 000s)	2004 Est.
Accrued liabilities ($32,353/8.775)	3,687
Income taxes payable ($1,932 × 0.242)	467
Other current liabilities (assumed level unchanged)	543
Total current liabilities (subtotal)	8,117
Deferred income (assumed level unchanged)	7,750
Long-term debt ($11,591 − $775)	10,816
Other long-term liabilities (assumed level unchanged)	3,553
Total liabilities (subtotal)	30,236
Common stock and paid-in capital (assumed level unchanged)	23,704
Retained earnings ($7,020 + $3,603 − $1,089)	9,534
Treasury stock (assumed level unchanged)	(402)
Other equities (assumed level unchanged)	(1,792)
Shareholders' equity (subtotal)	31,044
Total liabilities and equity (total)	$61,279

Note: To compute the residual cash balance, we initially assume no change in the capital accounts and the level of debt (other than repayment of $775 in current maturities of long-term debt). This yields a forecasted cash balance of $1,898, which is 3.10% of projected total assets. In 2003, Kraft reported cash at 0.87% of total assets. It appears, therefore, that the forecasting process suggests an accumulation of excess cash—that is, more cash than necessary to efficiently operate. One forecasting adjustment would be to assume either the investment of the excess cash in securities or the use of it to retire long-term debt and equity (in a manner to maintain the present leverage ratio).

GUIDANCE ANSWERS

YOU MAKE THE CALL

You are a Corporate Analyst GAAP allows considerable flexibility in the format of the income statement, as long as all of the required elements are present. Although combining operating and nonoperating items and subtotaling to pretax profit is common in practice, many companies subtotal to pretax operating profit, which segregates nonoperating items. The argument to break with tradition and subtotal to pretax operating profit rests on the concept of *transparency.* Transparency in financial reporting means that the financial statements are clearer to the reader. Many feel that greater transparency results in more trust and credibility by users of financial information. Since analysts are concerned with operating profits, your company might reap intangible benefits by being up-front in its presentation. Conversely, seeking to mask operating results, especially if misleading to outsiders, can damage management credibility.

KEY TERMS

Adjusting process (p. 649)

Core (persistent) item (p. 649)

Forecasting (p. 648)

Forecast Year-End Account
  Balance (p. 658)

Recasting (reformulating) (p. 649)

Transitory item (p. 649)

Turnover rate (p. 658)

DISCUSSION QUESTIONS

QB-1. Describe the process of *adjusting* financial statements in preparation for forecasting them.

QB-2. Identify three types of adjustments (for forecasting purposes) that relate to the income statement and provide two examples of each.

QB-3. What is the objective of the adjusting process as it relates to forecasting of the balance sheet?

QB-4. What are the main types of adjustments (for forecasting purposes) that relate to the statement of cash flows? Provide two examples of each.

QB-5. Identify at least two applications that benefit from use of forecasted financial statements.

QB-6. What procedures must normally take place before the forecasting process begins?

QB-7. In addition to recent trends, what other types and sources of information can be brought to bear in the forecasting of sales?

QB-8. Describe the rationale for use of year-end balances in the computation of turnover rates that are used to forecast selected balance sheet accounts.

QB-9. Identify and describe the steps in forecasting the income statement.

QB-10. Describe the two-step process of forecasting and adjusting the residual cash balance when forecasting the balance sheet.

MINI EXERCISES

MB-11. Forecasting an Income Statement

Abercrombie & Fitch (ANF)

Abercrombie & Fitch reports the following income statement:

(Thousands)	2003	2002
Net sales	$1,707,810	$1,595,757
Cost of goods sold, occupancy and buying costs	990,412	939,708
Gross income	717,398	656,049
General, administrative, and store operating expenses	385,764	343,432
Operating income	331,634	312,617
Net interest income	3,708	3,768
Income before income taxes	335,342	316,385
Provision for income taxes	130,240	121,450
Net Income	$ 205,102	$ 194,935

Forecast its 2004 income statement assuming the following income statement relations ($ 000s):

Net sales growth	7.02%
Gross income margin	42.0%
General, administrative and store operating expenses/Net sales	22.6%
Net interest income	$4,000
Provision for income taxes/Income before income taxes	38.8%

Best Buy (BBY)

MB-12. Forecasting an Income Statement

Best Buy reports the following income statement:

For the Fiscal Years Ended ($ in millions)	February 28, 2004	March 1, 2003	March 2, 2002
Revenue	$24,547	$20,946	$17,711
Cost of goods sold	18,350	15,710	13,941
Gross profit	6,197	5,236	3,770
Selling, general and administrative expenses	4,893	4,226	2,862
Operating income	1,304	1,010	908
Net interest (expense) income	(8)	4	18
Earnings from continuing operations before income tax expense	1,296	1,014	926
Income tax expense	496	392	356
Earnings from continuing operations	800	622	570
Loss from discontinued operations, net of $17 and $119 tax	$ (29)	$ (441)	$ —
Loss on disposal of discontinued operations, net of $0 tax	(66)	—	—
Cumulative effect of change in accounting principle for goodwill, net of $24 tax	—	(40)	—
Cumulative effect of change in accounting principle for vendor allowances, net of $26 tax	—	(42)	—
Net earnings	$ 705	$ 99	$ 570

Forecast its fiscal year 2005 income statement assuming the following income statement relations (*Hint:* Do not project discontinued operations for 2005 as they are sold in 2004):

Revenue growth	17.19%
Gross profit margin	25.2%
Selling, general, and administrative expenses/Revenue	19.9%
Net interest (expense) income	$(8) mil.
Income tax expense/Earnings before income tax expense	38.3%

MB-13. Forecasting an Income Statement

General Mills reports the following income statement:

General Mills (GIS)

In millions	May 30, 2004	May 25, 2003
Net sales	$11,070	$10,506
Costs and expenses		
Cost of sales	6,584	6,109
Selling, general and administrative	2,443	2,472
Net interest expense	508	547
Restructuring and other exit costs	26	62
Total costs and expenses	9,561	9,190
Earnings before taxes and earnings from joint ventures	1,509	1,316
Income taxes	528	460
Earnings from joint ventures, net of tax	74	61
Net earnings	$ 1,055	$ 917

Forecast its fiscal year 2005 income statement assuming the following income statement relations (*Note:* combine restructuring and exit costs with selling, general, and administrative for forecasting:

Net sales growth	5.4%
Gross profit margin	40.5%
Selling, general and administrative (incl. restructuring and exit costs)/Net sales	22.3%
Net interest expense	$508 mil.
Income taxes/Earnings before taxes and earnings from joint ventures	35.0%
Earnings from joint ventures, net of tax (assume no change)	$ 74 mil.

MB-14. Analyzing, Forecasting, and Interpreting Working Capital

Harley-Davidson reports 2003 net operating working capital of $1,587 million and 2003 long-term operating assets of $1,854 million.

Harley-Davidson (HDI)

a. Forecast its 2004 net operating working capital assuming forecasted sales of $5,227 million, net operating working capital turnover of 2.91 times, and long-term operating asset turnover of 2.49 times. (Both turnover rates use year-end balances.)

b. Does it seem reasonable that its net operating working capital turnover is higher than its long-term operating asset turnover? Explain.

MB-15. Analyzing, Forecasting, and Interpreting Working Capital

Nike reports 2003 net operating working capital of $3,255 million and 2003 long-term operating assets of $1,961 million.

Nike (NKE)

a. Forecast its 2004 net operating working capital assuming forecasted sales of $14,036 million, net operating working capital turnover of 3.76 times, and long-term operating asset turnover of 6.25 times. (Both turnover rates use year-end balances.)

b. Does it seem reasonable that its operating working capital turnover is less than its long-term operating asset turnover? Explain.

MB-16. Interpreting and Adjusting Balance Sheet Forecasts for a Negative Cash Balance

Assume that your initial forecast of a balance sheet yields a negative cash balance.

a. What does a forecasted negative cash balance imply?

b. Given a negative cash balance, what would be your next step in forecasting the balance sheet? Explain.

MB-17. Forecasting the Balance Sheet and Operating Cash Flows

Refer to the General Mills information in MB-13. General Mills reports the following current assets and current liabilities from its 2004 balance sheet:

General Mills (GIS)

In millions	May 30, 2004
Cash	$ 751
Accounts receivable	1,010
Inventories	1,063
Other current assets	391
Total current assets	$3,215
Accounts payable	$1,145
Accrued liabilities	796
Notes payable	816
Total current liabilities	$2,757

Using your forecasted income statement from MB-13, and the following information on General Mills' financial statement relations, forecast its:

a. Current asset and current liability sections of its balance sheet.
b. Net cash flow from operating activities section of its statement of cash flows.

Key Financial Relations ($ millions)	2004
Net sales/Year-end accounts receivable	10.96
Cost of sales/Year-end inventories	6.19
Cost of sales/Year-end accounts payable	5.75
Net sales/Year-end accrued liabilities	13.93
Depreciation expense (included in forecasted SGA expense in MB-13)	$399
Other current assets (including cash)	no change
Notes payable	no change

Black & Decker
Corporation (BDK)

MB-18. Adjusting the Balance Sheet

Black & Decker Corporation (BDK) reports the following footnote to its 2003 10-K:

DISCONTINUED OPERATIONS As of December 31, 2003, the Corporation met the requirements to classify its European security hardware business as discontinued operations. The European security hardware business, consisted of the NEMEF, Corbin, and DOM businesses. . . . In January 2004, the Corporation completed the sale of the NEMEF and Corbin businesses to Assa Abloy for an aggregate sales price of $80.0 million, subject to post-closing adjustments. Also, in January 2004, the Corporation signed an agreement with Assa Abloy to sell . . . DOM for $28.0 million. The Corporation's sale of its European security hardware business in 2004 is expected to result in a net gain.

Assets of the European hardware business are reported on Black & Decker's balance sheet in separate asset categories titled "current assets of discontinued operations" and "long-term assets of discontinued operations." What balance sheet adjustment(s) might you consider in anticipation of your forecasting of its balance sheet?

EXERCISES

EB-19. Analyzing, Forecasting, and Interpreting both Income Statement and Balance Sheet

Wal-Mart (WMT)

Following are the fiscal year income statement and balance sheet of Wal-Mart:

Income Statement ($ millions)	2004	2003
Net sales	$258,681	$231,577
Cost of goods sold	198,747	178,299
Gross profit	59,934	53,278
Operating, selling, general, and administrative expense	44,909	39,983
Operating profit	15,025	13,295
Interest expense	832	927
Income before taxes	14,193	12,368

(Continued on the next page)

(Continued from the previous page)

Income Statement ($ millions)	2004	2003
Tax expense	5,118	4,357
Income from continuing operations	9,075	8,011
Minority interest expense	214	193
Discontinued operations	193	137
Net income	$ 9,054	$ 7,955

Balance Sheet ($ millions)	1/31/2004	1/31/2003
Cash	$ 5,199	$ 2,736
Receivables	1,254	1,569
Inventories	26,612	24,401
Other current assets	1,356	2,016
Total current assets	34,421	30,722
Property, plant, and equipment, gross	75,887	66,100
Accumulated depreciation	17,357	14,726
Property, plant, and equipment, net	58,530	51,374
Other noncurrent assets	11,961	12,712
Total assets	$104,912	$ 94,808
Accounts payable	$ 19,332	$ 16,829
Accrued liabilities	11,719	9,605
Short-term debt and current maturities of long-term debt	6,367	6,085
Total current liabilities	37,418	32,519
Long-term debt	20,099	19,597
Other long-term liabilities	2,288	1,869
Minority interest	1,484	1,362
Common stock and additional paid-in capital	2,566	2,394
Retained earnings and other comprehensive income	41,057	37,067
Shareholders' equity	43,623	39,461
Total liabilities and equity	$104,912	$ 94,808

a. Forecast its fiscal 2005 income statement and fiscal 2005 year-end balance sheet using the following
    relations (assume all other accounts remain constant at January 2004 levels). Apply the same
    forecasting procedures illustrated in the appendix ($ millions).

Net sales growth	11.70%
Gross profit margin	23.2%
Operating and SGA expense (includes depreciation)/Net sales	17.4%
Depreciation expense/Prior year gross PPE*	5.8%
Interest expense/Short- and long-term debt and current maturities	3.2%
Tax expense/Pretax income	36.1%
Cash dividends	$1,569
Net sales/Year-end receivables	206.28
Cost of goods sold/Year-end inventories	7.47
Cost of goods sold/Year-end accounts payable	10.28
Net sales/Year-end accrued liabilities	22.07
Capital expenditures/Net sales	3.8%
Current maturities of long-term debt	$2,904

*Depreciation expense is included in SGA expense. This relation is provided as it is required to
compute accumulated depreciation on the balance sheet.

(*Note:* Its discontinued operations were sold in 2004 and those assets do not appear in the January
2004 balance sheet; thus, do not forecast 2005 income for the discontinued.)

b. What does your forecasted cash balance from part *a* reveal to you about the forecasted financing needs of the company? Explain.

EB-20. Analyzing, Forecasting, and Interpreting both Income Statement and Balance Sheet

Abercrombie & Fitch (ANF)

Following are the fiscal year income statement and balance sheet of Abercrombie & Fitch:

Income statement ($ millions)	2003	2002
Net sales	$1,708	$1,596
Cost of goods sold	991	940
Gross profit	717	656
General, administrative, and store operating expense	386	343
Operating profit	331	313
Net interest revenue	4	4
Income before taxes	335	317
Income taxes	130	122
Net income	$ 205	$ 195

Balance sheet ($ millions)	2003	2002
Cash	$ 511	$ 420
Marketable securities	10	10
Receivables	7	11
Inventories	171	143
Other current assets	54	45
Total current assets	753	629
Property, plant, and equipment, net	445	393
Other noncurrent assets	1	1
Total assets	$1,199	$1,023
Accounts payable	$ 91	$ 79
Accrued and other liabilities	189	166
Total current liabilities	280	245
Other long-term liabilities	48	28
Common stock and additional paid-in capital	140	144
Retained earnings	920	715
Treasury stock	(189)	(109)
Shareholders' equity	871	750
Total liabilities and equity	$1,199	$1,023

a. Forecast its fiscal 2004 income statement and balance sheet using the following relations (assume all other accounts remain constant at 2003 levels). Apply the same forecasting procedures illustrated in the appendix.

Net sales growth	7.02%
Gross profit margin	42.0%
GA and store expense (includes depreciation expense)/Net sales*	22.6%
Depreciation expense/Prior year net PPE*	17.0%
Tax expense/Pretax income	38.8%
Net sales/Year-end receivables	244.00
Cost of goods sold/Year-end inventories	5.80
Cost of goods sold/Year-end accounts payable	10.89
Net sales/Year-end accrued and other liabilities	9.04
Capital expenditures/Net sales	5.8%
Cash dividends	$0 mil.
Net interest revenue	$4 mil.

*Depreciation expense is included in GA and store expense. This relation is provided as it is required to compute accumulated depreciation on the balance sheet.

b.   What does your forecasted cash balance from part *a* reveal to you about the forecasted financing needs of the company? Explain.

EB-21.   Analyzing, Forecasting, and Interpreting both Income Statement and Balance Sheet

Following are the fiscal year income statement and balance sheet of Merck & Company:

Merck & Company
(MRK)

Income Statement ($ millions)	2003	2002
Sales	$ 22,486	$ 21,446
Cost of goods sold	4,315	3,907
Gross profit	18,171	17,539
Marketing and administrative expense	6,395	5,652
Research and development expense	3,280	2,677
Other income	474	644
Operating profit	8,970	9,854
Interest expense (revenue)	(82)	202
Income before taxes	9,052	9,652
Income taxes expense	2,462	2,857
Income from continuing operations	6,590	6,795
Discontinued operations	241	355
Net income	$ 6,831	$ 7,150

Balance Sheet ($ millions)	2003	2002
Cash	$ 1,201	$ 2,243
Short-term investments	2,972	2,728
Accounts receivable	4,024	5,423
Inventories	2,555	2,964
Other current assets	776	1,028
Total current assets	11,528	14,386
Property, plant, and equipment, gross	21,294	20,984
Accumulated depreciation	7,125	6,788
Property, plant, and equipment, net	14,169	14,196
Long-term investments	7,941	7,255
Other long-term assets	6,950	11,724
Total assets	$ 40,588	$ 47,561
Trade accounts payable	$ 735	$ 2,413
Accrued and other current liabilities	7,134	6,292
Notes payable	1,700	3,670
Total current liabilities	9,569	12,375
Long-term debt	5,096	4,879
Other long-term liabilities	6,430	7,178
Minority interest	3,915	4,928
Common stock and additional paid-in capital	6,987	6,974
Retained earnings and other comprehensive income	34,208	35,336
Treasury stock	(25,617)	(24,109)
Shareholders' equity	15,578	18,201
Total liabilities and equity	$ 40,588	$ 47,561

a.   Forecast its fiscal 2004 income statement and balance sheet using the following relations (assume all other accounts remain constant at 2003 levels). Apply the same forecasting procedures illustrated in the appendix ($ millions).

Sales growth	4.80%
Gross profit margin	80.8%
Marketing & admin. expense (includes depreciation expense)/Sales	28.4%
R&D expense/Sales	14.6%
Depreciation expense/Prior year gross PPE*	6.3%
Income taxes expense/Pretax income	27.2%
Cash dividends	$3,250
Current maturities of long-term debt	$310
Sales/Year-end accounts receivable	5.59
Cost of goods sold/Year-end inventories	1.69
Cost of goods sold/Year-end trade accounts payable	5.87
Sales/Year-end accrued and other liabilities	3.15
Capital expenditures/Sales	8.5%
Interest revenue	$ 82

*Depreciation expense is included in marketing and admin. expense. This relation is provided as it is required to compute accumulated depreciation on the balance sheet.

(*Note:* Its discontinued operations were sold in the past year and those assets do not appear in the fiscal year 2003 balance sheet; thus, do not forecast 2004 income for the discontinued operations.)

b. What does your forecasted cash balance from part *a* reveal to you about the forecasted financing needs of the company? Explain.

EB-22. **Analyzing, Forecasting, and Interpreting Both Income Statement and Balance Sheet**

Nike, Inc. (NKE)

Following are the fiscal year income statement and balance sheet of Nike, Inc.:

Income Statement ($ millions)	2004	2003
Sales	$12,253	$10,697
Cost of goods sold	7,001	6,314
Gross profit	5,252	4,383
Selling, general, and administrative expense	3,777	3,232
Operating profit	1,475	1,151
Interest expense	25	29
Income before taxes	1,450	1,122
Income taxes expense	504	382
Net income	$ 946	$ 740
Cash	$ 828	$ 634
Marketable securities	401	—
Accounts receivable	2,120	2,084
Inventories	1,634	1,515
Other current assets	529	554
Total current assets	5,512	4,787
Property, plant, and equipment, net	1,587	1,621
Other noncurrent assets	792	413
Total assets	$ 7,891	$ 6,821
Accounts payable	$ 764	$ 573
Accrued liabilities	1,092	1,167
Notes payable	153	281
Total current liabilities	2,009	2,021
Long-term debt	682	552
Other long-term liabilities	418	258
Common stock and paid-in capital	891	592
Retained earnings and other comprehensive income	3,891	3,398
Shareholders' equity	4,782	3,990
Total liabilities and equity	$ 7,891	$ 6,821

a. Forecast its fiscal year 2005 income statement and balance sheet using the following relations (assume all other accounts remain constant at 2004 levels). Apply the same forecasting procedures illustrated in the appendix.

Sales growth	14.55%
Gross profit margin	42.9%
SGA expense (includes depreciation expense)/Sales	30.8%
Depreciation expense/Prior year PPE, net*	15.5%
Income taxes expense/Pretax income	34.8%
Sales/Year-end accounts receivable	5.78
Cost of goods sold/Year-end inventories	4.28
Cost of goods sold/Year-end accounts payable	9.16
Sales/Year-end accrued liabilities	11.22
Capital expenditures/Sales	1.7%
Current maturities of long-term debt	$ 6 mil.
Interest expense	$25 mil.

*Depreciation expense is included in SGA expense. This relation is provided as it is required to compute accumulated depreciation on the balance sheet.

b. What does your forecasted cash balance from part *a* reveal to you about the forecasted financing needs of the company? Explain.

EB-23. Analyzing, Forecasting, and Interpreting both Income Statement and Balance Sheet

Following are the fiscal year income statement and balance sheet of **Toys 'R' US, Inc.**:

Toys 'R' US,
Inc. (TOY)

Balance Sheet ($ millions)	2004	2003
Cash	$ 2,003	$ 1,083
Accounts receivable	146	202
Inventories	2,123	2,190
Other current assets	412	111
Total current assets	4,684	3,586
Property, plant, and equipment, net	4,572	4,743
Other noncurrent assets	962	1,068
Total assets	$10,218	$ 9,397
Accounts payable	$ 991	$ 896
Accrued and other liabilities	1,124	1,103
Debt due within one year	657	379
Total current liabilities	2,772	2,378
Long-term debt	2,349	2,139
Other long-term liabilities	866	837
Common stock and paid-in capital	446	457
Retained earnings and other comprehensive income	5,492	5,308
Treasury stock	(1,707)	(1,722)
Stockholders' equity	4,231	5,765
Total liabilities and equity	$10,218	$11,119

Income Statement ($ millions)	2004	2003
Sales	$11,566	$11,305
Cost of goods sold	7,849	7,799
Gross profit	3,717	3,506
SG&A, depreciation, and other expenses	3,455	3,035
Operating income	262	471
Interest expense	124	110
Income before taxes	138	361
Taxes expense	50	132
Net income	$ 88	$ 229

a. Forecast its fiscal year 2005 income statement and balance sheet using the following relations (assume all other accounts remain constant at 2004 levels). Apply the same forecasting procedures illustrated in the appendix ($ millions).

Sales growth	2.30%
Gross profit margin	32.1%
SGA, depreciation, and other expenses/Sales	29.9%
Depreciation expense*	$348
Interest expense	$142
Taxes expense/Pretax income	36.2%
Sales/Year-end accounts receivable	79.22
Cost of goods sold/Year-end inventories	3.70
Cost of goods sold/Year-end accounts payable	7.92
Sales/Year-end accrued and other liabilities	10.29
Capital expenditures/Sales	12.8%
Cash dividends	$ 0
Debt due within one year	$657

*Amount is required to compute accumulated depreciation on the balance sheet.

b. What does your forecasted cash balance from part *a* reveal to you about the forecasted financing needs of the company? Explain.

EB-24. **Forecasting the Statement of Cash Flows**

Toys 'R' US, Inc. (TOY)

Refer to the Toys 'R' Us, Inc., financial information from Exercise B-23. Prepare a forecast of its fiscal year 2005 statement of cash flows.

Walgreen Co. (WAG) **EB-25.** **Analyzing, Forecasting and Interpreting both Income Statement and Balance Sheet**

Following are the fiscal year income statement and balance sheet of Walgreen Co.:

Balance Sheet ($ millions)	2003	2002
Cash	$ 1,017	$ 450
Accounts receivable	1,018	955
Inventories	4,202	3,645
Other current assets	121	116
Total current assets	6,358	5,166
Property, plant, and equipment, net	4,940	4,591
Other noncurrent assets	108	121
Total assets	$11,406	$ 9,878
Accounts payable	$ 2,077	$ 1,836
Accrued and other liabilities	1,344	1,119
Total current liabilities	3,421	2,955
Other long-term liabilities	790	694
Common stock and paid-in capital	778	828
Retained earnings and other comprehensive income	6,418	5,402
Stockholders' equity	7,196	6,230
Total liabilities and equity	$11,407	$ 9,879

Income Statement ($ millions)	2003	2002
Sales	$32,505	$28,681
Cost of goods sold	23,706	21,076
Gross profit	8,799	7,605
SGA, depreciation, and other expenses	6,951	5,981
Operating income	1,848	1,624
Net interest revenue	40	13
Income before taxes	1,888	1,637
Taxes expense	713	618
Net income	$ 1,175	$ 1,019

a. Forecast its fiscal year 2004 income statement and balance sheet using the following relations (assume all other accounts remain constant at 2003 levels). Apply the same forecasting procedures illustrated in the appendix ($ millions).

Sales growth	13.30%
Gross profit margin	27.1%
SGA, depreciation, and other expenses/Sales	21.4%
Depreciation expense*	$346
Net interest revenue	$ 40
Taxes expense/Pretax income	37.8%
Sales/Year-end accounts receivable	31.93
Cost of goods sold/Year-end inventories	5.64
Cost of goods sold/Year-end accounts payable	11.41
Sales/Year-end accrued and other liabilities	24.19
Capital expenditures / sales	2.4%
Cash dividends	$152

*Amount is required to compute accumulated depreciation on the balance sheet.

b. What does your forecasted cash balance from part *a* reveal to you about the forecasted financing needs of the company? Explain.

EB-26. Forecasting the Statement of Cash flows

Refer to the Walgreen Co. financial information from Exercise B-25. Prepare a forecast of its fiscal year 2004 statement of cash flows.

Walgreen Co. (WAG)

EB-27. Adjusting the Balance Sheet for Operating Leases

Midwest Air reports total net operating assets of $291.6 million, liabilities of $167.3 million, and equity of $124.3 in its 2003 10-K. Footnotes reveal the existence of operating leases that carry a present value of $357.5 million (see Chapter 9 for computations). (a) What balance sheet adjustment(s) might you consider relating to these operating leases in anticipation of forecasting its financial statements? (*Hint:* Consider the distinction between operating and nonoperating assets and liabilities.) (b) What income statement adjustment(s) might you consider? (*Hint:* Reflect on the operating and nonoperating distinction for lease-related expenses.)

Midwest Air (MEH)

EB-28. Adjusting the Balance Sheet for Equity Method Investments

SBC Communications Inc., reports its 60% investment in Cingular Wireless under the equity method of accounting (footnotes reveal that Cingular Wireless is a joint venture between SBC and Southwest Bell where SBC has significant influence, but not control), and it reports an investment balance of $5.1 billion on its 2003 balance sheet. Cingular has total assets of $25.5 billion, liabilities of $17 billion, and equity of $8.5 billion. SBC's investment balance is, thus, equal to its 60% interest in Cingular's equity ($8.5 billion × 60% = $5.1 billion). What adjustment(s) might you consider to SBC's balance sheet in anticipation of forecasting its financial statements? (*Hint:* Consider the distinction between operating and nonoperating assets and liabilities.) What risks might SBC face that are not revealed on the face of its balance sheet?

SBC Communications Inc. (SBC)

Cingular Wireless

PROBLEMS

PB-29. **Forecasting the Income Statement, Balance Sheet, and Statement of Cash Flows**

Gap Inc. (GPS)

Following are fiscal year financial statements of Gap Inc.:

($ In millions)	52 Weeks Ended Jan. 31, 2004	Percentage to Net Sales	52 Weeks Ended Feb. 1, 2003	Percentage to Net Sales
Net sales	$15,854	100.0%	$14,455	100.0%
Cost and expenses				
Cost of goods sold and occupancy expenses	9,886	62.4	9,542	66.0
Operating expenses	4,089	25.8	3,901	27.0
Interest expense	234	1.5	249	1.7
Interest income	(38)	(0.2)	(37)	(0.3)
Earnings before income taxes	1,683	10.6	800	5.5
Income taxes	653	4.1	323	2.2
Net earnings (loss)	$ 1,030	6.5%	$ 477	3.3%

($ In millions except par value)	Jan. 31, 2004	Feb. 1, 2003
Assets		
Current Assets		
Cash and equivalents	$ 2,261	$ 3,027
Short-term investments	1,073	313
Restricted cash	1,351	49
Cash and equivalents, short-term investments and restricted cash	4,685	3,389
Merchandise inventory	1,704	2,048
Other current assets	300	303
Total current assets	6,689	5,740
Property and Equipment		
Leasehold improvements	2,224	2,242
Furniture and equipment	3,591	3,439
Land and buildings	$ 1,033	$ 943
Construction-in-progress	131	202
	6,979	6,826
Accumulated depreciation and amortization	(3,611)	(3,049)
Property and equipment, net	3,368	3,777
Other assets	286	385
Total assets	$10,343	$ 9,902
Liabilities and Shareholders' Equity		
Current Liabilities		
Current maturities of long-term debt	$ 283	$ 500
Accounts payable	1,178	1,159
Accrued expenses and other current liabilities	872	874
Income taxes payable	159	193
Total current liabilities	2,492	2,726
Long-Term Liabilities		
Long-term debt	1,107	1,516
Senior convertible notes	1,380	1,380
Lease incentives and other liabilities	581	621
Total long-term liabilities	3,068	3,517

(Continued on the next page)

(Continued from the previous page)

($ In millions except par value)	Jan. 31, 2004	Feb. 1, 2003
Shareholders' Equity		
Common stock $.05 par value; Authorized 2,300,000,000 shares; issued 976,154,229 and 968,010,453 shares; outstanding 897,202,485 and 887,322,707 shares	49	48
Additional paid-in capital	732	638
Retained earnings	6,241	5,290
Accumulated other comprehensive earnings (loss)	31	(16)
Deferred compensation	(9)	(13)
Treasury stock, at cost	(2,261)	(2,288)
Total shareholders' equity	4,783	3,659
Total liabilities and shareholders' equity	$10,343	$ 9,902

($ In millions)	52 Weeks Ended Jan. 31, 2004	52 Weeks Ended Feb. 1, 2003	52 Weeks Ended Feb. 2, 2002
Cash Flows from Operating Activities			
Net earnings (loss)	$ 1,030	$ 477	$ (8)
Adjustments to reconcile net earnings (loss) to net cash provided by operating activities:			
Depreciation and amortization	664	693	732
Tax benefit from exercise of stock options and vesting of restricted stock	7	44	58
Deferred income taxes	103	6	(29)
Loss on disposal and other non-cash items affecting net earnings	70	117	64
Change in operating assets and liabilities:			
Merchandise inventory	385	(258)	122
Prepaid expenses and other	5	33	(13)
Accounts payable	(10)	(47)	134
Accrued expenses	$ (79)	$ 129	$ 176
Deferred lease credits and other long-term liabilities	(4)	44	99
Net cash provided by operating activities	2,171	1,238	1,335
Cash Flows from Investing Activities			
Purchase of property and equipment	(272)	(303)	(957)
Proceeds from sale of property and equipment	1	9	—
Purchase of short-term investments	(1,202)	(472)	—
Maturities and sales of short-term investments	442	159	—
Acquisition of lease rights, net increase (decrease) of other assets	5	3	(11)
Net cash used for investing activities	(1,026)	(604)	(968)
Cash Flows from Financing Activities			
Net decrease in notes payable	—	(42)	(735)
Net issuance of long-term debt	—	—	1,194
Net issuance of senior convertible notes	—	1,346	—
Payments of long-term debt	(668)	—	(250)
Restricted cash	(1,303)	(20)	(15)
Issuance of common stock	111	153	139
Net purchase of treasury stock	—	—	(1)
Cash dividends paid	(79)	(78)	(76)

(Continued on the next page)

(Continued from the previous page)

($ In millions)	52 Weeks Ended Jan. 31, 2004	52 Weeks Ended Feb. 1, 2003	52 Weeks Ended Feb. 2, 2002
Net cash (used for) provided by financing activities	(1,939)	1,359	256
Effect of exchange rate fluctuations on cash	28	27	(11)
Net (decrease) increase in cash and equivalents	(766)	2,020	612
Cash and equivalents at beginning of year	3,027	1,007	395
Cash and equivalents at end of year	$ 2,261	$3,027	$1,007

Required

Forecast its fiscal year 2005 income statement, balance sheet, and statement of cash flows applying the same forecasting procedures illustrated in the chapter ($ millions). Clearly identify all relations you estimate and assumptions made. What do your forecasts imply about the financing needs of Gap?

PB-30. **Forecasting the Income Statement, Balance Sheet, and Statement of Cash Flows**

Target Corporation
(TGT)

Following are the fiscal year financial statements of Target Corporation:

	Year Ended		
(millions)	Jan. 31, 2004	Feb. 1, 2003	Feb. 2, 2002
Sales	$46,781	$42,722	$39,114
Net credit card revenues	1,382	1,195	712
Total revenues	48,163	43,917	39,826
Cost of sales	31,790	29,260	27,143
Selling, general and administrative expense	$10,696	$ 9,416	$ 8,461
Credit card expense	838	765	463
Depreciation and amortization	1,320	1,212	1,079
Interest expense	559	588	473
Earnings before income taxes	2,960	2,676	2,207
Provision for income taxes	1,119	1,022	839
Net earnings	$ 1,841	$ 1,654	$ 1,368

(millions)	January 31, 2004	February 1, 2003
Assets		
Cash and cash equivalents	$ 716	$ 758
Accounts receivable, net	5,776	5,565
Inventory	5,343	4,760
Other	1,093	852
Total current assets	12,928	11,935
Property and equipment		
Land	3,629	3,236
Buildings and improvements	13,091	11,527
Fixtures and equipment	5,432	4,983
Construction-in-progress	995	1,190
Accumulated depreciation	(6,178)	(5,629)
Property and equipment, net	16,969	15,307
Other	1,495	1,361
Total assets	$31,392	$28,603

(Continued on the next page)

(Continued from the previous page)

(millions)	January 31, 2004	February 1, 2003
Liabilities and shareholders' investment		
Accounts payable	$ 5,448	$ 4,684
Accrued liabilities	1,618	1,545
Income taxes payable	382	319
Current portion of long-term debt and notes payable	866	975
Total current liabilities	8,314	7,523
Long-term debt	10,217	10,186
Deferred income taxes and other	1,796	1,451
Shareholders' investment		
Common stock*	76	76
Additional paid-in-capital	1,341	1,256
Retained earnings	9,645	8,107
Accumulated other comprehensive income	3	4
Total shareholders' investment	11,065	9,443
Total liabilities and shareholders' investment	$31,392	$28,603

*Common Stock Authorized 6,000,000,000 shares, $.0833 pare value; 911,808,051 shares issued and outstanding at January 31, 2004; 909,801,560 shares issued and outstanding at February 1, 2003.

Preferred Stock Authorized 5,000,000 shares, $.01 par value; no shares were issued or outstanding at January 31, 2004 or February 1, 2003.

	Year Ended		
(millions)	Jan. 31, 2004	Feb. 1, 2003	Feb. 2, 2002
Operating activities			
Net earnings	$ 1,841	$ 1,654	$ 1,368
Reconciliation to cash flow			
Depreciation and amortization	1,320	1,212	1,079
Bad debt provision	532	460	230
Deferred tax provision	249	248	49
Loss on disposal of fixed assets, net	54	67	52
Other non-cash items affecting earnings	11	159	160
Changes in operating accounts providing (requiring) cash			
Accounts receivable	(744)	(2,194)	(1,193)
Inventory	(583)	(311)	(201)
Other current assets	(255)	15	(91)
Other assets	(196)	(174)	(178)
Accounts payable	764	524	584
Accrued liabilities	57	(21)	29
Income taxes payable	91	(79)	124
Other	19	30	—
Cash flow provided by operations	3,160	1,590	2,012
Investing activities			
Expenditures for property and equipment	(3,004)	(3,221)	(3,163)
Increase in receivable-backed securities	—	—	(174)
Proceeds from disposals of property and equipment	85	32	32
Other	—	—	(5)
Cash flow required for investing activities	(2,919)	(3,189)	(3,310)

(Continued on the next page)

(Continued from the previous page)

(millions)	Year Ended		
	Jan. 31, 2004	Feb. 1, 2003	Feb. 2, 2002
Financing activities			
Decrease in notes payable, net	**(100)**	—	(808)
Additions to long-term debt	**1,200**	3,153	3,250
Reductions of long-term debt	**(1,172)**	(1,071)	(793)
Dividends paid	**(237)**	(218)	(203)
Repurchase of stock	**—**	(14)	(20)
Other	**26**	8	15
Cash flow (required for) provided by financing activities	**(283)**	1,858	1,441
Net (decrease) increase in cash and cash equivalents	**(42)**	259	143
Cash and cash equivalents at beginning of year	**758**	499	356
Cash and cash equivalents at end of year	**$ 716**	$ 758	$ 499

Required

Forecast its fiscal year 2005 income statement, balance sheet, and statement of cash flows applying the same forecasting procedures illustrated in the chapter. Clearly identify all relations you estimate and assumptions made. (*Note:* Target's long-term debt footnote reveals that its current maturities of long-term debt for fiscal 2005 are $857 million.) What do your forecasts imply about Target's financing needs for the upcoming year?

Tyco International, Ltd. (TYC)

PB-31.   **Adjusting the Income Statement Prior to Forecasting**

Following is the income statement of Tyco International, Ltd.:

Year Ended September 30 (in millions)	2003	2002	2001
Revenue from product sales	**$29,427.7**	$28,741.8	$28,953.1
Service revenue	**7,373.6**	6,848.0	5,049.0
Net Revenues	**36,801.3**	35,589.8	34,002.1
Cost of product sales	**19,740.2**	19,495.1	18,319.7
Cost of services	**4,151.7**	3,570.2	2,615.9
Selling, general and administrative expenses	**8,813.4**	8,181.6	6,745.3
Restructuring and other (credits) charges, net	**(74.3)**	1,124.3	400.4
Charges for the impairment of long-lived assets	**824.9**	3,309.5	120.1
Goodwill impairment	**278.4**	1,343.7	—
Write off of purchased in-process research and development	**—**	17.8	184.3
Operating Income (Loss)	**3,067.0**	(1,452.4)	5,616.4
Interest income	**107.2**	117.3	128.3
Interest expense	**(1,148.0)**	(1,077.0)	(904.8)
Other (expense) income, net	**(223.4)**	(216.6)	250.3
Net gain on sale of common shares of a subsidiary	**—**	—	24.5
Income (Loss) from Continuing Operations before Income Taxes and Minority Interest	**1,802.8**	(2,628.7)	5,114.7
Income taxes	**(764.5)**	(208.1)	(1,172.3)
Minority interest	**(3.6)**	(1.4)	(47.5)
Income (Loss) from Continuing Operations	**1,034.7**	(2,838.2)	3,894.9
Income (loss) from discontinued operations of Tyco Capital (net of tax expense of $0, $316.1 million and $195.0 million for the years ended September 30, 2003, 2002 and 2001, respectively)	**20.0**	(6,282.5)	252.5
Loss on sale of Tyco Capital, net of $0 tax	**—**	(58.8)	—

(Continued on the next page)

(Continued from the previous page)

Year Ended September 30 (in millions)	2003	2002	2001
Income (loss) before cumulative effect of accounting changes	**1,054.7**	(9,179.5)	4,147.4
Cumulative effect of accounting changes, net of tax benefit of $40.4 million and $351.9 million for the year ended September 30, 2003 and 2001, respectively	**(75.1)**	—	(683.4)
Net Income (Loss)	**$ 979.6**	$ (9,179.5)	$ 3,464.0

Required

Identify and explain any income statement line items over the past three years that you believe should be considered for potential adjustment in preparation for forecasting the income statement of Tyco.

PB-32. **Adjusting the Income Statement Prior to Forecasting**

Following is the 2003 income statement of Xerox Corporation:

Xerox Corporation
(XRX)

Year ended December 31, (in millions, except per-share data)	2003	2002	2001
Revenues			
Sales	$ 6,970	$ 6,752	$ 7,443
Service, outsourcing and rentals	7,734	8,097	8,436
Finance income	997	1,000	1,129
Total revenues	15,701	15,849	17,008
Costs and Expenses			
Cost of sales	4,436	4,233	5,170
Cost of service, outsourcing and rentals	4,311	4,494	4,880
Equipment financing interest	362	401	457
Research and development expenses	868	917	997
Selling, administrative, and general expenses	4,249	4,437	4,728
Restructuring and asset impairment charges	$ 176	$ 670	$ 715
Gain on sale of half of interest in Fuji Xerox	—	—	(773)
Gain on affiliate's sale of stock	(13)	—	(4)
Provision for litigation	239	—	—
Other expenses, net	637	593	510
Total costs and expenses	15,265	15,745	16,680
Income before Income Taxes, Equity Income, and Cumulative Effect of Change in Accounting Principle	436	104	328
Income taxes	134	4	473
Income (Loss) before Equity Income and Cumulative Effect of Change in Accounting Principle	302	100	(145)
Equity in net income of unconsolidated affiliates	58	54	53
Income (Loss) before Cumulative Effect of Change in Accounting Principle	360	154	(92)
Cumulative effect of change in accounting principle	—	(63)	(2)
Net Income (Loss)	360	91	(94)

Required

Identify and explain any income statement line items over the past 3 years that you believe should be considered for potential adjustment in preparation for forecasting the income statement of Xerox.

PB-33. **Adjusting the Income Statement and Forecasting the Income Statement, Balance Sheet, and Statement of Cash Flows**

Following is the income statement and balance sheet of Bristol-Myers Squibb:

Bristol-Myers Squibb
(BMY)

Dollars in Millions	Year Ended December 31,		
	2003	Restated 2002	Restated 2001
Net Sales	$20,894	$18,106	$18,044
Cost of products sold	7,592	6,532	5,515
Marketing, selling and administrative	4,660	4,124	4,058
Advertising and product promotion	1,416	1,143	1,201
Research and development	2,279	2,206	2,157
Acquired in-process research and development	—	169	2,772
Provision for restructuring and other items	26	14	456
Litigation charges, net	199	659	77
Gain on sales of businesses/product lines	—	(30)	(475)
Asset impairment charge for investment in ImClone	—	379	—
Equity in net income from affiliates	(151)	(80)	(78)
Other expense, net	179	229	98
Total Expenses	16,200	15,345	15,781
Earnings from Continuing Operations Before Minority Interest and Income Taxes	4,694	2,761	2,263
Provision for income taxes	1,215	391	213
Minority interest, net of taxes	373	303	179
Earnings from Continuing Operations	3,106	2,067	1,871
Discontinued Operations			
Net earnings	—	32	226
Net gain on disposal	—	38	2,565
	—	70	2,791
Net Earnings	$ 3,106	$ 2,137	$ 4,662

Dollars in Millions	December 31,	
	2003	Restated 2002
Assets		
Current Assets		
Cash and cash equivalents	$ 2,444	$ 2,367
Marketable securities	3,013	1,622
Receivables, net of allowances of $154 and $129	3,646	2,968
Inventories, including consignment inventory	1,601	1,608
Deferred income taxes, net of valuation allowances	864	1,013
Prepaid expenses	350	482
Total Current Assets	11,918	10,060
Property, plant and equipment, net	5,712	5,334
Goodwill	4,836	4,836
Other intangible assets, net	1,732	1,904
Deferred income taxes, net of valuation allowances	1,234	1,097
Other assets	2,039	1,791
Total Assets	$27,471	$25,022
Liabilities		
Current Liabilities		
Short-term borrowings	$ 127	$ 1,379
Accounts payable	1,893	1,551
Accrued expenses	2,967	2,537

(Continued on the next page)

(Continued from the previous page)

Dollars in Millions	December 31, 2003	Restated 2002
Current Liabilities *(continued)*		
Accrued rebates and returns	950	883
U.S. and foreign income taxes payable	707	525
Dividends payable	543	542
Accrued litigation liabilities	267	600
Deferred revenue on consigned inventory	76	470
Total Current Liabilities	7,530	8,487
Other liabilities	1,633	1,518
Long-term debt	8,522	6,261
Total Liabilities	17,685	16,266
Stockholders' Equity		
Preferred stock, $2 convertible series: Authorized 10 million shares; issued and outstanding 8,039 in 2003 and 8,308 in 2002, liquidation value of $50 per share	—	—
Common stock, par value of $.10 per share: Authorized 4.5 billion shares; 2,201,012,432 issued in 2003 and 2,200,823,544 in 2002	220	220
Capital in excess of par value of stock	2,477	2,491
Restricted stock	(55)	(52)
Other accumulated comprehensive loss	(855)	(904)
Retained earnings	19,439	18,503
	21,226	20,258
Less cost of treasury stock—261,029,539 common shares in 2003 and 263,994,580 in 2002	11,440	11,502
Total Stockholders' Equity	9,786	8,756
Total Liabilities and Stockholders' Equity	$27,471	$25,022

Required

a. Identify and explain any income statement line items over the past three years that you believe should be considered for potential adjustment in preparation for forecasting the income statement of Bristol-Myers Squibb.

b. Prepare an adjusted income statement for 2003 (for forecasting purposes).

c. Forecast its 2004 income statement, balance sheet, and statement of cash flows applying the same forecasting procedures illustrated in the chapter. Clearly identify all assumptions you make.
   (*Note:* Its long-term debt footnote reveals that its current maturities of long-term debt for 2004 are $13 million and is included in short-term borrowings; 2003 depreciation expense is $491 million; 2003 capital expenditures are $937 million; 2003 interest expense, included in other expense, is $212 million; and cash dividends are $2,169 million).

d. What do your forecasts imply about BMS's financing needs for 2004?

C

Analyzing and Valuing Equity Securities

INTRODUCTION TO SECURITY VALUATION

This appendix focuses on determining the value of equity securities (we explain the valuation of debt securities in Chapter 10). We describe two approaches to valuing equity securities: the discounted free cash flow (DCF) and residual operating income (ROPI) models. We then conclude with a discussion of the management implications from an increased understanding of the factors that impact values of equity securities. It is important that we understand the determinants of equity value to make informed decisions from financial reports. Further, employees at all levels of an organization, whether public or private, should understand the factors that create shareholder value so that they can work effectively toward that objective. For many senior managers, stock value serves as a scorecard. Successful managers are those that better understand the factors determining that scorecard.

Equity Valuation Models

Chapter 10 explains that the value of a debt security is the present value of the interest and principal payments that the investor *expects* to receive from it. The valuation of equity securities is similar, and is also based on expectations. The main difference is the increased uncertainty surrounding the payments from equity securities.

There are several equity valuation models in use today. Each of them defines the value of an equity security in terms of the present value of future forecasted amounts. They differ primarily in terms of what is forecasted.

The basis of equity valuation is the premise that the value of an equity security is determined by the payments that the investor can expect to receive from an investment in that security. There are two types of payoffs from an equity investment: (1) dividends received during the holding period and (2) capital gains when the security is sold.[1] The value of an equity security is, then, based

---

[1] The future stock price is, itself, also assumed to be related to the expected dividends that the new investor expects to receive. As a result, the expected receipt of dividends is the sole driver of stock price under this type of valuation model.

on the present value of expected dividend receipts plus the value of the security at the end of the forecasted holding period. This valuation mechanism is called the **dividend discount model,** and is appealing in its simplicity and its intuitive focus on dividend distribution. As a practical matter, however, it is not useful in valuation as many companies that have a positive stock price have never paid a dividend and are not expected to pay a dividend in the foreseeable future.

A more practical approach to valuing equity securities focuses, instead, on the company's operating and investing activities—that is, the *generation* (and use) of cash rather than the *distribution* of cash. This approach is called the **discounted cash flow (DCF)** model. The focus of the forecasting process for this model is the expected *free cash flows* of the company, which are defined as operating cash flows net of the expected new investment in long-term operating assets that are required to support the business.

A second practical approach to equity valuation also focuses on operating and investing activities. It is known as the **residual operating income (ROPI)** model. This model uses both net operating profits after tax (NOPAT) and the net operating assets (NOA) to determine equity value—see Chapter 5 for complete descriptions of these measures. This approach highlights the importance of return on net operating assets (RNOA), and the disaggregation of RNOA into NOPAT margin and NOA turnover, for equity valuation. We discuss the implications of this insight for managers later in this chapter.

DISCOUNTED CASH FLOW (DCF) MODEL

The discounted cash flow (DCF) model defines company value as follows:

> **Firm Value = Present Value of Expected Free Cash Flows to Firm**

The expected free cash flows to the firm do not include the cash flows from financing activities. Instead, the **free cash flows to the firm (FCFF)** are typically defined as net cash flows from operations ± net cash flows from investing activities. That is, FCFF reflects increases and decreases in net operating working capital and in long-term operating assets.[2] Using the terminology of Chapter 5

> **FCFF = NOPAT − Increase in NOA**

where
    NOPAT = Net operating profit after tax
    NOA   = Net operating assets

Stated differently, free cash flows to the firm equal net operating profit that is not used to grow net operating assets.

Net operating profit after tax is normally positive and net cash flows from investments (increases) in net operating assets are normally negative. The sum of the two (positive or negative) represents the net cash flows available to financiers of the firm, both creditors and shareholders. Positive FCFF imply funds available for distribution to creditors and shareholders either in the form of debt repayments, dividends, or stock repurchases (treasury stock). Negative FCFF imply funds are required from creditors and shareholders in the form of new loans or equity investments to support its business activities.

The DCF valuation model requires forecasts of *all* future free cash flows; that is, free cash flows for the remainder of the company's life. Generating such forecasts is not realistic. Consequently, practicing analysts typically estimate FCFF over a horizon period, often 4 to 10 years, and then make simplifying assumptions about the behavior of those FCFFs subsequent to that horizon period.

Application of the DCF model to equity valuation involves five steps:

1.   Forecast and discount FCFF for the **horizon period**.[3]

---

[2]FCFF is sometimes approximated by net cash flows from operating activities less capital expenditures.

[3]When discounting FCFF, the appropriate discount rate (r) is the **weighted average cost of capital (WACC)**, where the weights are the relative percentages of debt (d) and equity (e) in the capital structure that are applied to the expected returns on debt (r_d) and equity (r_e), respectively: $\text{WACC} = r_w = (r_d \times \% \text{ of debt}) + (r_e \times \% \text{ of equity})$.

2. Forecast and discount FCFF for the post-horizon period, called **terminal period**.[4]

3. Sum the present values of the horizon and terminal periods to yield firm (enterprise) value.

4. Subtract net financial obligations (NFO) from firm value to yield firm equity value.

5. Divide firm equity value by the number of shares outstanding to yield stock value per share.

To illustrate, we apply DCF to our focus company, Johnson & Johnson. J&J's recent financial statements are reproduced in Appendix C-1. Forecasted financials for J&J (forecast horizon 2004–2007 and terminal period 2008) are in Exhibit C.1. These forecasts are based on analysts' expectations regarding J&J's future operating results and balance sheet for the next four years.[5] The forecasts (in bold) are for sales, NOPAT, and NOA. These forecasts assume an annual 8% (analysts' consensus) sales growth during the horizon period, a terminal period sales growth of 2%, and a continuation of the current period's 17.24% net operating profit margin (NOPM) and its 1.57 net operating asset turnover (NOAT).[6,7]

EXHIBIT C.1	Application of Discounted Cash Flow Model					
(In millions, except per share values and discount factors)	**2003**	**Horizon Period**				**Terminal Period**
		2004	**2005**	**2006**	**2007**	
Sales	$ 41,862	**$45,211**	**$48,828**	**$52,734**	**$56,953**	**$58,092**
NOPAT*	7,216	**7,793**	**8,417**	**9,090**	**9,817**	**10,014**
NOA*	26,733	**28,872**	**31,181**	**33,676**	**36,370**	**37,097**
Increase in NOA		2,139	2,309	2,495	2,694	727
FCFF (NOPAT − Increase in NOA)		5,654	6,108	6,595	7,123	9,287
Discount factor [$1/(1 + r_w)^t$]		0.94127	0.88598	0.83394	0.78496	
Present value of horizon FCFF		5,322	5,412	5,500	5,591	
Cum present value of horizon FCFF . . .	21,825					
Present value of terminal FCFF	171,932					
Total firm value	193,757					
Less (plus) NFO†	(136)					
Firm equity value	$193,893					
Stock outstanding	2,968					
Stock value per share	$ 65.33					

*2003 computations: NOPAT = ($41,862 − $12,176 − $14,131 − $4,684 − $918 + $385) × (1-[$3,111/$10,308]) = $7,216; NOA = $48,263 − $4,146 − $84 − ($13,448 − $1,139) − $780 − $2,262 − $1,949 = $26,733

†NFO is negative when investments exceed borrowings (such as for J&J); in this case NFO is added, not subtracted (see footnote 10 for the NFO computation).

---

[4]For an assumed growth, g, the terminal period (T) present value of FCFF in perpetuity (beyond the horizon period) is given by, $\dfrac{FCFF_T}{r_w - g}$, where $FCFF_T$ is the free cash flow to the firm for the terminal period, r_w is WACC, and g is the assumed growth rate of those cash flows. The resulting amount is then discounted back to the present using the horizon period discount factor.

[5]We use a four-period horizon in the text and assignments to simplify the exposition and to reduce the computational burden. In practice, we perform the forecasting and valuation process using a spreadsheet, and the number of periods in the forecast horizon is increased to typically 7 to 9 periods.

[6]**NOPAT** equals revenues less operating expenses such as cost of goods sold, selling, general, and administrative expenses, and taxes; it excludes any interest revenue and interest expense and any gains or losses from financial investments. NOPAT reflects the operating side of the firm as opposed to nonoperating activities such as borrowing and security investment activities. **NOA** equals operating assets less operating liabilities. (See Chapter 5.)

[7]NOPAT and NOA are typically forecasted using the detailed forecasting procedures discussed in Appendix B. This chapter uses the parsimonious method to multiyear forecasting (see Appendix B) to focus attention on the valuation process.

The bottom line of Exhibit C.1 is the estimated J&J equity value of $193,893 million, or a per share stock value of $65.33. Present value computations use a 6.24% WACC(r_w) as the discount rate.[8] Specifically, we obtain this stock valuation as follows:

1. **Compute present value of horizon period FCFF.** The forecasted 2004 FCFF of $5,654 million is computed from the forecasted 2004 NOPAT less the forecasted increase in 2004 NOA. The present value of this $5,654 million as of 2003 is $5,322 million, computed as $5,654 million $\times$ 0.94127 (the present value factor for one year discounted at 6.24%).[9] Similarly, the present value of 2005 FCFF (2 years from the current date) is $5,412 million, computed as $6,108 million $\times$ 0.88598, and so on through 2007. The sum of these present values (*cumulative present value*) is $21,825 million.

2. **Compute present value of terminal period FCFF.** The present value of the terminal period FCFF is $171,932 million, computed as $\dfrac{\left(\dfrac{\$9,287 \text{ million}}{0.0624 - 0.02}\right)}{(1.0624)^4}$

3. **Compute firm equity value.** Sum present values from the horizon and terminal period FCFF to get firm (enterprise) value of $193,757 million. Subtract (add) the value of its net financial obligations (investments) of $(136) million to get firm equity value of $193,893.[10] Dividing firm equity value by the 2,968 million shares outstanding yields the estimated per share valuation of $65.33.

This valuation would be performed in early 2004 (when J&J's 10-K is released in mid-March 2004). J&J's stock closed at $51.66 at year-end 2003. Our valuation estimate of $65.33 indicates that its stock is undervalued. In January 2005 (roughly one year later) J&J stock traded at near $63 and analysts continued to recommend it as a BUY with a price target in the high $60s to low $70s per share.

BUSINESS INSIGHT

Analysts' Earnings Forecasts Estimates of earnings and cash flows are key to security valuation. Following are earnings estimates, as of January 2005, for Johnson & Johnson by the forecasting firm I/B/E/S, a division of Thomson Financial™:

Period	Ending	Mean EPS	High EPS	Low EPS
Fiscal Year	Dec. 2005	3.40	3.43	3.30
Fiscal Year	Dec. 2006	3.72	3.81	3.57
Long-term growth (%)	—	11.0*	15.0	9.40

*Median instead of mean.

The mean (consensus) EPS estimate for 2005 (one year ahead) is $3.40 per share, with a high of $3.43 and a low of $3.30. For 2006, the mean (consensus) EPS estimate is $3.72, with a high

(*Continued on the next page*)

---

[8]The weighted average cost of capital (WACC) for J&J is computed as follows:

  a. The cost of equity capital is given by the capital asset pricing model (CAPM): $r_e = r_f + \beta \, (r_m - r_f)$, where β is the beta of the stock (an estimate of its variability that is reported by several services such as Standard and Poors), r_f is the risk free rate (commonly assumed as the 10-year government bond rate), and r_m is the expected return to the entire market. The expression $(r_m - r_f)$ is the "spread" of equities over the risk free rate, often assumed to be around 5%. For J&J, given its beta of 0.476 and a 10-year treasury bond rate of 4.15% (r_f) as of January 2004, r_e is estimated as 6.53%, computed as 4.15% + (0.476 $\times$ 5%).

  b. The cost of debt capital is the 3.66% after-tax weighted average rate on J&J borrowings as disclosed in its footnotes (5.23% pretax rate $\times$ [1 − 30% effective tax rate of J&J]).

  c. WACC is the weighted average of the two returns. For J&J, 90% is weighted on equity and 10% on debt, which reflects the relative proportions of the two financing sources in J&J's capital structure: (90% $\times$ 6.53%) + (10% $\times$ 3.66%) = 6.24%.

[9]Horizon period discount factors follow: $1/(1.0624)^1 = 0.94127$; $1/(1.0624)^2 = 0.88598$; $1/(1.0624)^3 = 0.83394$; $1/(1.0624)^4 = 0.78496$.

[10]J&J's net financial obligation (NFO) is equal to $(136), computed as its debt ($1,139 + $2,955) less its investments ($4,146 − $84). J&J is in a net investment position (more investments than debt) rather than a net debt position.

(Continued from the previous page)

of $3.81 and a low of $3.57. The estimated long-term growth rate for EPS (similar to our terminal year growth rate) ranges from 9.4% to 15%, with a mean (consensus) estimate of 11%. Since the terminal year valuation is such a large proportion of total firm valuation, especially for the DCF model, the variability in stock price estimates across analysts covering JNJ is due more to variation in estimates for long-term growth rates than to 1- and 2-year-ahead earnings forecasts.

YOU MAKE THE CALL

You are the Division Manager   Assume that you are managing a division of a company that has a large investment in plant assets and sells its products on credit. Identify steps you can take to increase its cash flow. [Answers on page 698]

MID-APPENDIX REVIEW

Following are forecasts of **Procter & Gamble**'s sales, net operating profit after tax (NOPAT), and net operating assets (NOA)—these are taken from our forecasting process in Appendix B and now include a terminal year forecast:

| (In millions) | 2004 | Horizon Period | | | | Terminal Period |
		2005	2006	2007	2008	
Sales	$51,407	$60,917	$72,187	$85,542	$101,367	$103,394
NOPAT	6,812	8,072	9,566	11,335	13,432	13,701
NOA	37,696	44,792	53,079	62,898	74,534	76,025

Drawing on these forecasts, compute P&G's free cash flows to the firm (FCFF) and an estimate of its stock value using the DCF model and assuming the following: discount rate (WACC) of 7.5%, shares outstanding of 2,543 million, and net financial obligations (NFO) of $20,841 million.

Solution

The following DCF results yield a P&G stock value estimate of $58.98 as of December 31, 2003. P&G's stock closed at a split-adjusted price of $49.94 on that date. This estimate suggests that P&G's stock is undervalued on that date. P&G stock traded at $55.08 one year later.

| (In millions, except per share values and discount factors) | 2004 | Horizon Period | | | | Terminal Period |
		2005	2006	2007	2008	
Increase in NOA[a]		$ 7,096	$ 8,287	$ 9,819	$11,636	$ 1,491
FCFF (NOPAT − Increase in NOA)		976	1,279	1,516	1,796	12,210
Discount factor [1/(1 + r_w)^t]		0.93023	0.86533	0.80496	0.74880	
Present value of horizon FCFF		908	1,107	1,220	1,345	
Cum present value of horizon FCFF ...	$ 4,580					
Present value of terminal FCFF	166,236[b]					
Total firm value	170,816					
Less (plus) NFO	20,841					
Firm equity value	$149,975					
Stock outstanding	2,543					
Stock value per share	$ 58.98					

[a]NOA increases are viewed as a cash outflow.

[b]Computed as $\dfrac{\left(\dfrac{\$12{,}210 \text{ million}}{0.075 - 0.02}\right)}{(1.075)^4}$, where 7.5% is WACC and 2% is the long-term growth rate subsequent to the horizon period (used to estimate terminal period FCFF).

RESIDUAL OPERATING INCOME (ROPI) MODEL

The residual operating income (ROPI) model focuses on net operating profit after tax (NOPAT) and net operating assets (NOA). This means it uses key measures from both the income statement and balance sheet in determining firm value. The ROPI model defines firm value as the sum of two components:

$$\text{Firm Value} = \text{NOA} + \text{Present Value of Expected ROPI}$$

where
  NOA = Net operating assets
  ROPI = Residual operating income

Net operating assets (NOA) are the foundation of firm value under the ROPI model. The measure of NOA using the balance sheet is the outcome of accounting procedures, which are unlikely to fully and contemporaneously capture the true (or intrinsic) value of these assets.[11] However, the ROPI model adds an adjustment that corrects for the usual undervaluation (but sometimes overvaluation) of NOA. This amount is the present value of expected residual operating income and is defined as follows:

$$\text{ROPI} = \text{NOPAT} - \underbrace{(\text{NOA}_{\text{Beg}} \times r_w)}_{\text{Expected NOPAT}}$$

where
  NOA_{Beg} = Net operating assets at beginning (*Beg*) of period
  r_w = Weighted average cost of capital (WACC)

The ROPI model's use of the balance sheet (NOA_{Beg}), in addition to the income statement (NOPAT), is informative because book values of net operating assets incorporate estimates (of varying relevance) of their future cash flows. Understanding this model also helps us reap the benefits from disaggregation of return on net operating assets (DuPont analysis) in Chapter 5. Finally, the ROPI model is the foundation for many internal and external performance evaluation and compensation systems marketed by management consulting and accounting services firms.[12]

Application of the ROPI model to equity valuation involves five steps:

1. Forecast and discount ROPI for the horizon period.[13]

2. Forecast and discount ROPI for the terminal period.[14]

3. Sum the present values of the horizon and terminal periods; then add this sum to current NOA to get firm (enterprise) value.

4. Subtract net financial obligations (NFO) from firm value to yield firm equity value.

5. Divide firm equity value by the number of shares outstanding to yield stock value per share.

---

[11]For example, R&D and advertising are not fully and contemporaneously reflected on the balance sheet as assets though they likely produce future cash inflows. Likewise, internally generated goodwill is not fully reflected on the balance sheet as an asset. Also, companies can delay or accelerate the write-down of impaired assets and, thus, overstate their book values. Similarly, assets are generally not written up to reflect unrealized gains. These examples, and a host of others, can yield reported book values of NOA that differs from its market value.

[12]Examples are economic value added (EVA™) from Stern Stewart & Company, the economic profit model from McKinsey & Co., the cash flow return on investment (CFROI) from Holt Value Associates, the economic value management from KPMG, and the value builder from PricewaterhouseCoopers (PwC).

[13]The present value of expected ROPI uses the weighted average cost of capital (WACC) as its discount rate—same as with the DCF model.

[14]As with the DCF model, for an assumed growth, g, the present value of the perpetuity of ROPI beyond the horizon period is given by $\dfrac{\text{ROPI}_T}{r_w - g}$, where ROPI_T is the residual operating income for the terminal period, r_w is WACC for the firm, and g is the assumed growth rate of ROPI following the horizon period. The resulting amount is then discounted back to the present at the horizon period discount factor.

To illustrate application of the ROPI model, we again use Johnson & Johnson. Forecasted financials for J&J (forecast horizon 2004–2007 and terminal period 2008) are in Exhibit C.2. The forecasts (in bold) are for sales, NOPAT, and NOA, and are the same forecasts from the illustration of the DCF model.

EXHIBIT C.2 Application of Residual Operating Income Model						
(In millions, except per share values and discount factors)	2003	Horizon Period				Terminal Period
		2004	2005	2006	2007	
Sales	$ 41,862	**$45,211**	**$48,828**	**$52,734**	**$56,953**	**$58,092**
NOPAT........................	7,216	**7,793**	**8,417**	**9,090**	**9,817**	**10,014**
NOA	26,733	**28,872**	**31,181**	**33,676**	**36,370**	**37,097**
ROPI (NOPAT − [NOA$_{Beg}$ × r_w])		6,125	6,615	7,144	7,716	7,745
Discount factor [1/(1 + r_w)^t]		0.94127	0.88598	0.83394	0.78496	
Present value of horizon ROPI		5,765	5,861	5,958	6,056	
Cum present value of horizon ROPI ...	23,641					
Present value of terminal ROPI	143,385					
NOA	26,733					
Total firm value	193,759					
Less (plus) NFO*	(136)					
Firm equity value	$193,895					
Stock outstanding	2,968					
Stock value per share	$ 65.33					

*NFO is negative when investments exceed borrowings (such as for J&J); in this case NFO is added, not subtracted.

The bottom line of Exhibit C.2 is the estimated J&J equity value of $193,895 million, or a per share stock value of $65.33. As before, present value computations use a 6.24% WACC as the discount rate. Specifically, we obtain this stock valuation as follows:

1. **Compute present value of horizon period ROPI.** The forecasted 2004 ROPI of $6,125 million is computed from the forecasted 2004 NOPAT less the product of beginning period NOA and WACC. The present value of this ROPI as of 2003 is $5,765 million, computed as $6,125 million × 0.94127 (the present value 1 year hence discounted at 6.24%). Similarly, the present value of 2005 ROPI (2 years hence) is $5,861 million, computed as $6,615 million × 0.88598, and so on through 2007. The sum of these present values (cumulative present value) is $23,641 million.

2. **Compute present value of terminal period ROPI.** The present value of the terminal period ROPI is $143,385 million, computed as $\dfrac{\left(\dfrac{\$7,745 \text{ million}}{0.0624 - 0.02}\right)}{(1.0624)^4}$

3. **Compute firm equity value.** We must sum the present values from the horizon period ($23,641 million) and terminal period ($143,385 million), plus NOA ($26,733 million), to get firm (enterprise) value of $193,758 million. Subtract (add) the value of its net financial obligations (investments) of $(136) million to get firm equity value of $193,894 (the $1 difference from the DCF value of $193,893 is from rounding). Dividing firm equity value by the 2,968 million shares outstanding yields the estimated per share valuation of $65.33.

J&J's stock closed at $51.66 at year-end 2003. The ROPI model estimate of $65.33 indicates that its stock is undervalued. In January 2005 (roughly one year later) J&J stock traded at near $63.

The ROPI model estimate is equal to that computed using the DCF model. This is the case so long as the firm is in a steady state, that is, NOPAT and NOA are growing at the same rate (for example, when RNOA is constant).

Power of NOPAT Forecasts   Discounted cash flow (DCF) and residual operating income (ROPI) models yield identical estimates when the expected payoffs are forecasted for an infinite horizon. For practical reasons, we must use horizon period forecasts and a terminal period forecast. This truncation of the forecast horizon is a main cause of any difference in value estimates for these models. Importantly, research finds that forecasting (GAAP-based) NOPAT, rather than FCFF, yields more accurate estimates of firm value given a finite horizon.

MANAGERIAL INSIGHTS FROM THE ROPI MODEL

The ROPI model defines firm value as the sum of NOA and the present value of expected residual operating income as follows:

$$\text{Firm Value} = \text{NOA} + \text{Present Value of } [\underbrace{\text{NOPAT} - (\text{NOA}_{\text{Beg}} \times r_w)}_{\text{ROPI}}]$$

Increasing ROPI, therefore, increases firm value. This can be accomplished in two ways:

1.   Decrease the NOA required to generate a given level of NOPAT

2.   Increase NOPAT with the same level of NOA investment (improve profitability)

These are two very important observations. It means that achieving better performance requires effective management of *both* the income statement and balance sheet. Most operating managers are accustomed to working with income statements. Further, they are often evaluated on profitability measures, such as achieving desired levels of gross profit or efficiently managing operating expenses. The ROPI model focuses management attention on the balance sheet as well.

The two points above highlight two paths to increase ROPI and, accordingly, firm value. First, let's consider how management can reduce the level of NOA while maintaining a given level of NOPAT. Many managers begin by implementing procedures that reduce net operating working capital, such as:

- Reducing receivables through:
    - Better underwriting of credit quality
    - Better controls to identify delinquencies and automated payment notices

- Reducing inventories through:
    - Use of less costly components (of equal quality) and production with lower wage rates
    - Elimination of product features not valued by customers
    - Outsourcing to reduce product cost
    - Just-in-time deliveries of raw materials
    - Elimination of manufacturing bottlenecks to reduce work-in-process inventories
    - Producing to order rather than to estimated demand

- Increasing payables through:
    - Extending the payment of low or no-cost payables—so long as the relationship is not harmed

Managment would next look at its net operating long-term assets for opportunities to reduce unnecessary net operating assets, such as the:

- Sale of unused and unnecessary assets

- Acquisition of production and administrative assets in partnership with other entities for greater throughput

- Acquisition of finished or semifinished goods from suppliers to reduce manufacturing assets

The second path to increase ROPI and, accordingly, firm value is to increase NOPAT with the same level of NOA investment. Management would look to strategies that maximize NOPAT, such as:

- Increasing gross profit dollars through:
  - Better pricing and mix of products sold
  - Reduction of raw material and labor cost without sacrificing product quality, perhaps by outsourcing, better design, or better manufacturing
  - Increase of throughput to minimize overhead costs per unit, provided inventory does not build up
- Reducing selling, general, and administrative expenses through:
  - Better management of personnel
  - Reduction of overhead
  - Use of derivatives to reduce commodity and interest costs
  - Minimization of tax burden

Management must pursue these actions with consideration of both short- and long-run implications for the company. The ROPI model helps managers assess company performance (income statement) relative to the net operating assets committed (balance sheet).

YOU MAKE THE CALL

You are the Operations Manager The residual operating income (ROPI) model highlights the importance of increasing NOPAT and reducing net operating assets, which are the two major components of the return on net operating assets (RNOA). What specific steps can you take to improve RNOA through improvement of its components: net operating profit margin and turnover of net operating assets? [Answers on page 699]

ASSESSMENT OF VALUATION MODELS

Exhibit C.3 provides a brief summary of the advantages and disadvantages of the DCF and ROPI models. No model dominates the other—and both are theoretically equivalent. Instead, professionals must pick and choose the model that performs best under the practical circumstances confronted.

EXHIBIT C.3	Advantages and Disadvantages of DCF and ROPI Valuation Models		
Model	**Advantages**	**Disadvantages**	**Performs Best**

DCF	• Popular and widely accepted model
	
	• Cash flows are unaffected by accrual accounting
	
	• FCFF is intuitive
		• Cash investments in plant assets are treated as cash outflows, even when creating shareholder value
		• No recognition of value unless evidenced by cash flows
		• Computing FCFF can be difficult as operating cash flows are affected by
		    —Cutbacks on investments (receivables, inventories, plant assets); can yield short-run benefits at long-run costs
		    —Tax benefits of stock option exercise; but likely are transitory as they depend on maintenance of current stock price
		    —GAAP treats securitization as an operating cash flow when many view it as a financing activity
			• When the firm reports positive FCFF
			
			• When FCFF grows at a relatively constant rate

ROPI	• Focuses on value drivers such as profit margins and asset turnovers • Uses both balance sheet and income statement, including accrual accounting information • Reduces weight placed on terminal period value	• Financial statements do not reflect all company assets, especially for knowledge-based industries (for example, R&D assets and goodwill) • Requires some knowledge of accrual accounting	• When financial statements reflect all assets and liabilities; including items often reported off-balance-sheet

There are numerous other equity valuation models in practice. Many require forecasting, but several others do not. A quick review of selected models follows:

The **method of comparables** (often called *multiples*) **model** predicts equity valuation or stock value using price multiples. Price multiples are defined as stock price divided by some key financial statement number. That financial number varies across investors but is usually one of the following: net income, net sales, book value of equity, total assets, or cash flow. Companies are then compared with competitors on their price multiples to assign value.

The **net asset valuation model** draws on the financial reporting system to assign value. That is, equity is valued as reported assets less reported liabilities. Some investors adjust reported assets and liabilities for several perceived shortcomings in GAAP prior to computing net asset value. This method is also commonly applied by privately held companies.

The **dividend discount model** predicts that equity valuation or stock values equal the present value of expected cash dividends. This model is founded on the dividend discount formula and depends on the reliability of forecasted cash dividends.

There are additional models applied in practice that involve dividends, cash flows, research and development outlays, accounting rates of return, cash recovery rates, and real option models. Further, some practitioners, called *chartists* and *technicians,* chart price behavior over time and use it to predict equity value.

RESEARCH INSIGHT

Using Models to Identify Mispriced Stocks   Implementation of the ROPI model can include parameters to capture differences in growth opportunities, persistence of ROPI, and the conservatism in accounting measures. Research finds differences in how such factors, across firms and over time, affect ROPI and changes in NOA. This research also hints that investors do not understand the properties underlying these factors and, consequently, individual stocks are mispriced for short periods of time. Other research contends that the apparent mispricing is due to an omitted valuation variable related to riskiness of the firm.

APPENDIX-END REVIEW

Following are forecasts of **Procter & Gamble**'s sales, net operating profit after tax (NOPAT), and net operating assets (NOA). These are taken from our forecasting process in Appendix B and now include a terminal year forecast:

(In millions)	2004	Horizon Period 2005	2006	2007	2008	Terminal Period
Sales	$51,407	$60,917	$72,187	$85,542	$101,367	$103,394
NOPAT	6,812	8,072	9,566	11,335	13,432	13,701
NOA	37,696	44,792	53,079	62,898	74,534	76,025

Drawing on these forecasts, compute P&G's residual operating income (ROPI) and an estimate of its stock value using the ROPI model. Assume the following: discount rate (WACC) of 7.5%, shares outstanding of 2,543 million, and net financial obligations (NFO) of $20,841 million.

Solution
Results from the ROPI model below yield a P&G stock value estimate of $58.98 as of December 31, 2003. P&G's stock closed at a split-adjusted price of $49.94 on that date. This estimate suggests that P&G's stock is undervalued on that date. P&G stock traded at $55.08 one year later as shown in the stock price chart below.

(In millions, except per share values and discount factors)	2004	Horizon Period 2005	2006	2007	2008	Terminal Period
ROPI (NOPAT − [NOA_Beg × r_w])		$5,245	$6,206	$7,354	$8,715	$8,111
Discount factor [$1/(1 + r_w)^t$]		0.93023	0.86533	0.80496	0.74880	
Present value of horizon ROPI		4,879	5,370	5,920	6,526	

(Continued on the next page)

(Continued from the previous page)

(In millions, except per share values and discount factors)	Horizon Period					Terminal Period
	2004	2005	2006	2007	2008	
Cum present value of horizon ROPI ...	$ 22,695					
Present value of terminal ROPI	110,425[a]					
NOA	37,696					
Total firm value	170,816					
Less (plus) NFO	20,841					
Firm equity value	$149,975					
Stock outstanding	2,543					
Stock value per share	$ 58.98					

[a]Computed as $\dfrac{\left(\dfrac{\$8{,}111 \text{ million}}{0.075 - 0.02}\right)}{(1.075)^4}$.

The P&G stock price chart, extending from year-end 2003 through early 2005, follows:

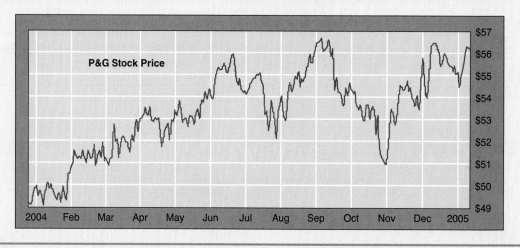

APPENDIX C-1: Johnson & Johnson Financial Statements

Income Statement

(Dollars in Millions)	2003	2002	2001
Sales to customers	$41,862	$36,298	$32,317
Cost of products sold	12,176	10,447	9,581
Gross profit	29,686	25,851	22,736
Selling, marketing and administrative expenses	14,131	12,216	11,260
Research expense	4,684	3,957	3,591
Purchased in-process research and development	918	189	105
Interest income	(177)	(256)	(456)
Interest expense, net of portion capitalized	207	160	153
Other (income) expense, net	(385)	294	185
	19,378	16,560	14,838
Earnings before provision for taxes on income	10,308	9,291	7,898
Provision for taxes on income	3,111	2,694	2,230
Net earnings	$ 7,197	$ 6,597	$ 5,668

Balance Sheet

At December 28, 2003 and December 29, 2002 (Dollars in Millions Except Share and Per Share Data)	2003	2002
Assets		
Current assets		
Cash and cash equivalents	$ 5,377	$ 2,894
Marketable securities	4,146	4,581
Accounts receivable trade, less allowances for doubtful accounts $192 (2002, $191)	6,574	5,399
Inventories	3,588	3,303
Deferred taxes on income	1,526	1,419
Prepaid expenses and other receivables	1,784	1,670
Total current assets	22,995	19,266
Marketable securities, non-current	84	121
Property, plant and equipment, net	9,846	8,710
Intangible assets, net	11,539	9,246
Deferred taxes on income	692	236
Other assets	3,107	2,977
Total assets	$48,263	$40,556
Liabilities and Shareholders' Equity		
Current liabilities		
Loans and notes payable	$ 1,139	$ 2,117
Accounts payable	4,966	3,621
Accrued liabilities	2,639	2,059
Accrued rebates, returns and promotions	2,308	1,761
Accrued salaries, wages and commissions	1,452	1,181
Accrued taxes on income	944	710
Total current liabilities	13,448	11,449
Long-term debt	$ 2,955	$ 2,022
Deferred tax liability	780	643
Employee related obligations	2,262	1,967
Other liabilities	1,949	1,778
Shareholders' equity		
Preferred stock—without par value (authorized and unissued 2,000,000 shares)	—	—
Common stock—par value $1.00 per share (authorized 4,320,000,000 shares; issued 3,119,842,000 shares)	3,120	3,120
Note receivable from employee stock ownership plan	(18)	(25)
Accumulated other comprehensive income	(590)	(842)
Retained earnings	30,503	26,571
	33,015	28,824
Less: common stock held in treasury, at cost (151,869,000 and 151,547,000)	6,146	6,127
Total shareholders' equity	26,869	22,697
Total liabilities and shareholders' equity	$48,263	$40,556

Statement of Cash Flows

(Dollars in Millions)	2003	2002	2001
Cash flows from operating activities			
Net earnings	$ 7,197	$ 6,597	$ 5,668
Adjustments to reconcile net earnings to cash flows			
Depreciation and amortization of property and intangibles	1,869	1,662	1,605
Purchased in-process research and development	918	189	105
Deferred tax provision	(720)	(74)	(106)
Accounts receivable reserves	6	(6)	99
Changes in assets and liabilities, net of effects from acquisition of businesses			
Increase in accounts receivable	(691)	(510)	(258)
Decrease (increase) in inventories	39	(109)	(167)
Increase in accounts payable and accrued liabilities	2,192	1,420	1,401
Increase in other current and non-current assets	(746)	(1,429)	(270)
Increase in other current and non-current liabilities	531	436	787
Net cash flows from operating activities	10,595	8,176	8,864
Cash flows from investing activities			
Additions to property, plant and equipment	(2,262)	(2,099)	(1,731)
Proceeds from the disposal of assets	335	156	163
Acquisition of businesses, net of cash acquired	(2,812)	(478)	(225)
Purchases of investments	(7,590)	(6,923)	(8,188)
Sales of investments	8,062	7,353	5,967
Other	(259)	(206)	(79)
Net cash used by investing activities	(4,526)	(2,197)	(4,093)
Cash flows from financing activities			
Dividends to shareholders	(2,746)	(2,381)	(2,047)
Repurchase of common stock	(1,183)	(6,538)	(2,570)
Proceeds from short-term debt	3,062	2,359	338
Retirement of short-term debt	$ (4,134)	$ (560)	$(1,109)
Proceeds from long-term debt	1,023	22	14
Retirement of long-term debt	(196)	(245)	(391)
Proceeds from the exercise of stock options	311	390	514
Net cash used by financing activities	(3,863)	(6,953)	(5,251)
Effect of exchange rate changes on cash and cash equivalents	277	110	(40)
Increase/(decrease) in cash and cash equivalents	2,483	(864)	(520)
Cash and cash equivalents, beginning of year	2,894	3,758	4,278
Cash and cash equivalents, end of year	$ 5,377	$ 2,894	$ 3,758

GUIDANCE ANSWERS

YOU MAKE THE CALL

You are the Division Manager   Cash flow is increased with asset reductions. For example, receivables are reduced by the following:

■ Encouraging up-front payments or progress billings on long-term contracts
■ Increasing credit standards to remove slow-paying accounts before sales are made
■ Monitoring account age and sending reminders to past due customers
■ Selling accounts receivable to a financial institution or special purpose entity

As another example, plant assets are reduced by the following:

■ Selling unused or excess plant assets
■ Forming alliances with other companies for special purpose plant asset requirements
■ Owning assets in a special purpose entity with other companies
■ Selling production facilities to a contract manufacturer and purchasing the output

YOU MAKE THE CALL

You are the Operations Manager   RNOA can be disaggregated into its two key drivers: NOPAT margin and net operating asset turnover. NOPAT margin can be increased by improving gross profit margins (better product pricing, lower cost manufacturing, etc.) and closely monitoring and controlling operating expenses. Net operating asset turnover can be increased by reducing net operating working capital (better monitoring of receivables, better management of inventories, extending payables, etc.) and making more effective use of plant assets (disposing of unused assets, forming corporate alliances to increase plant asset capacity, selling productive assets to contract producers and purchasing the output, etc). The ROPI model effectively focuses managers on the balance sheet *and* income statement.

DISCUSSION QUESTIONS

QC-1.   Explain how information contained in financial statements is useful in pricing securities. Are there some components of earnings that are more useful than others in this regard? What nonfinancial information might also be useful?

QC-2.   In general, what role do expectations play in pricing equity securities? What is the relation between security prices and expected returns (the discount rate, or WACC, in this case)?

QC-3.   What are free cash flows to the firm (FCFF) and how are they used in the pricing of equity securities?

QC-4.   Define the weighted average cost of capital.

QC-5.   Define net operating profit after tax (NOPAT).

QC-6.   Define net operating assets (NOA).

QC-7.   Define the concept of residual operating income. How is the concept of residual operating income used in pricing equity securities?

QC-8.   What insight does disaggregation of RNOA into profit margin and asset turnover provide for managing a company?

KEY TERMS

Discounted Cash Flow Model (DCF) (p. 687)

Dividend Discount Model (p. 687)

Economic Value Added (EVA) (p. 695)

Firm Value (p. 687)

Free Cash Flow to the Firm (FCFF) (p. 687)

Horizon Period (p. 687)

Method of Comparables Model (multiples) (p. 695)

Net Asset Valuation Model (p. 695)

Residual Operating Income Model (ROPI) (p. 687)

Terminal Period (p. 688)

Weighted Average Cost of Capital (WACC) (p. 687)

MINI EXERCISES

MC-9.   Interpreting Earnings Announcement Effects on Stock Prices   In a recent quarterly earnings announcement, Starbucks announced that its earnings had markedly increased (up 7 cents per share over the prior year) and were 1 cent higher than analyst expectations. Starbucks' stock "edged higher," according to *The Wall Street Journal,* but did not markedly increase. Why do you believe that Starbucks stock price did not markedly increase given the good news?

Starbucks (SBUX)

MC-10.   Computing Residual Operating Income (ROPI)   3M Company reports net operating profit after tax (NOPAT) of $2,491 million in 2003. Its net operating assets at the beginning of 2003 are $9,370 million. Assuming a 6.25% weighted average cost of capital (WACC), what is 3M's residual operating income for 2003? Show computations.

3M Company (MMM)

MC-11.   Computing Free Cash Flows to the Firm (FCFF)   3M Company reports net operating profit after tax (NOPAT) of $2,491 million in 2003. Its net operating assets at the beginning of 2003 are $9,370 million and are $10,822 million at the end of 2003. What are 3M's free cash flows to the firm (FCFF) for 2003? Show computations.

3M Company (MMM)

MC-12.   Computing, Analyzing and Interpreting Residual Operating Income (ROPI)   In its 2003 fiscal year annual report, PepsiCo reports 2003 net operating income after tax (NOPAT) of $3,649.4 million. As of the beginning of fiscal year 2003 it reports net operating working capital of $716 million and net operating long-term assets of $11,349 million.

PepsiCo (PEP)

a. Did PepsiCo earn positive residual operating income (ROPI) in 2003 if its weighted average cost of capital (WACC) is 8.7%? Explain.

b. At what level of WACC would PepsiCo not report positive residual operating income for 2003? Explain.

EXERCISES

Target Corporation
(TGT)

EC-13. **Estimating Share Value using the DCF and ROPI Models** Following are forecasts of Target Corporation's sales, net operating profit after tax (NOPAT), and net operating assets (NOA) as of January 31, 2004:

(In millions)	Reported 2004	Horizon Period				Terminal Period
		2005	2006	2007	2008	
Sales	$48,163	$52,979	$58,277	$64,105	$70,516	$72,631
NOPAT	2,189	2,408	2,649	2,914	3,205	3,301
NOA	22,148	24,363	26,799	29,479	32,427	33,400

Answer the following requirements assuming a discount rate (WACC) of 6.2%, shares outstanding of 911.8 million, and net financial obligations (NFO) of $11,083 million.

a. Estimate the value of a share of Target common stock using the (1) discounted cash flow (DCF) model and (2) residual operating income (ROPI) model as of January 31, 2004.

b. Target Corporation (TGT) stock closed at $37.96 on January 31, 2004. How does your valuation estimate compare with this closing price? What do you believe are some reasons for the difference? What investment position does it suggest you pursue?

Abercrombie & Fitch
(ANF)

EC-14. **Estimating Share Value using the DCF and ROPI Models** Following are forecasts of Abercrombie & Fitch's sales, net operating profit after tax (NOPAT), and net operating assets (NOA) as of January 31, 2003:

(In millions)	Reported 2003	Horizon Period				Terminal Period
		2004	2005	2006	2007	
Sales	$1,708	$1,879	$2,067	$2,274	$2,501	$2,551
NOPAT	203	223	246	270	297	303
NOA	861	947	1,042	1,146	1,261	1,286

Answer the following requirements assuming a discount rate (WACC) of 10.0%, common shares outstanding of 94.6 million, and net financial obligations (NFO) of $(10) million (negative NFO reflects net investments rather than net obligations).

a. Estimate the value of a share of Abercrombie & Fitch common stock using the (1) discounted cash flow (DCF) model and (2) residual operating income (ROPI) model as of January 31, 2003.

b. Abercrombie & Fitch (ANF) stock closed at $26.80 on January 31, 2003. How does your valuation estimate compare with this closing price? What do you believe are some reasons for the difference?

Albertson (ABS)

EC-15. **Estimating Share Value using the DCF and ROPI Models** Following are forecasts of Albertson's sales, net operating profit after tax (NOPAT), and net operating assets (NOA) as of January 29, 2004:

(In millions)	Reported 2004	Horizon Period				Terminal Period
		2005	2006	2007	2008	
Sales	$35,436	$36,499	$37,594	$38,722	$39,884	$40,682
NOPAT	809	833	858	884	911	929
NOA	10,705	11,026	11,357	11,698	12,049	12,290

Answer the following requirements assuming a discount rate (WACC) of 6.5%, common shares outstanding of 368.0 million, and net financial obligations (NFO) of $5,324 million.

a. Estimate the value of a share of Albertson's common stock using the (1) discounted cash flow (DCF) model and (2) residual operating income (ROPI) model as of January 29, 2004.

b. Albertson (ABS) stock closed at $24.14 on January 29, 2004. How does your valuation estimate compare with this closing price? What do you believe are some reasons for the difference?

EC-16. Identifying and Computing Net Operating Assets (NOA) and Net Financial Obligations (NFO)
Following is the balance sheet for **3M Company**:

3M Company (MMM)

At December 31 (Dollars in millions)	2003	2002
Assets		
Current assets		
Cash and cash equivalents	$ 1,836	$ 618
Accounts receivable—net	2,714	2,527
Inventories	1,816	1,931
Other current assets	1,354	983
Total current assets	7,720	6,059
Investments	218	238
Property, plant and equipment—net	5,609	5,621
Goodwill	2,419	1,898
Intangible assets	274	269
Other assets	1,360	1,244
Total assets	$17,600	$15,329
Liabilities and Stockholders' Equity		
Current liabilities		
Short-term borrowings and current portion of long-term debt	$ 1,202	$ 1,237
Accounts payable	1,087	945
Accrued payroll	436	411
Accrued income taxes	880	518
Other current liabilities	1,477	1,346
Total current liabilities	5,082	4,457
Long-term debt	1,735	2,140
Other liabilities	2,898	2,739
Total liabilities	9,715	9,336
Stockholders' equity		
Common stock, par value $.01 per share	9	5
Shares outstanding—2003: 784,117,360		
Shares outstanding—2002: 780,391,362		
Capital in excess of par value	287	291
Retained earnings	14,010	12,748
Treasury stock	(4,641)	(4,767)
Unearned compensation	(226)	(258)
Accumulated other comprehensive income (loss)	(1,554)	(2,026)
Stockholders' equity—net	7,885	5,993
Total liabilities and stockholders' equity	$17,600	$15,329

a. Compute net operating assets (NOA) and net financial obligations (NFO) for 2003.

b. For 2003, show that: NOA = NFO + Stockholders' equity.

EC-17. Identifying and Computing Net Operating Profit after Tax (NOPAT) and Net Financial Expense (NFE) Following is the income statement for **3M Company**:

3M Company (MMM)

Year Ended December 31 (Millions)	2003	2002	2001
Net sales	$18,232	$16,332	$16,054
Operating expenses			
Cost of sales	9,285	8,496	8,749
Selling, general and administrative expenses	4,039	3,720	4,036
Research, development and related expenses	1,102	1,070	1,084
Other expense (income)	93	—	(88)
Total operating expenses	14,519	13,286	13,781
Operating income	3,713	3,046	2,273
Interest expense and income			
Interest expense	84	80	124
Interest income	(28)	(39)	(37)
Total	56	41	87
Income before income taxes and minority interest	3,657	3,005	2,186
Provision for income taxes	1,202	966	702
Minority interest	52	65	54
Net income	$ 2,403	$ 1,974	$ 1,430

a. Compute net operating profit after tax (NOPAT) and net financial expense (NFE) for 2003. (*Hint:* Other expense is an operating item for 3M.)

b. For 2003, show that: Net income = NOPAT − NFE.

3M Company (MMM) **EC-18.** **Estimating Share Value Using the DCF and ROPI Models** Following are forecasts of **3M Company**'s sales, net operating profit after tax (NOPAT), and net operating assets (NOA) as of December 31, 2003:

	Reported	Horizon Period				Terminal
(In millions)	2003	2004	2005	2006	2007	Period
Sales	$18,232	$19,691	$21,266	$22,967	$24,804	$25,300
NOPAT	2,493	2,693	2,908	3,140	3,392	3,459
NOA	10,604	11,453	12,369	13,358	14,426	14,715

Answer the following requirements assuming a discount rate (WACC) of 5.75%, common shares outstanding of 784 million, and net financial obligations (NFO) of $2,719 million.

a. Estimate the value of a share of 3M's common stock using the (1) discounted cash flow (DCF) model and (2) residual operating income (ROPI) model as of December 31, 2003.

b. 3M (MMM) stock closed at $85.03 on December 31, 2003. How does your valuation estimate compare with this closing price? What do you believe are some reasons for the difference?

EC-19. **Equivalence of Valuation Models and the Relevance of Earnings** This appendix focused on two different valuation models: the discounted cash flow (DCF) model and the residual operating income (ROPI) model. We stressed that these two models are theoretically equivalent.

a. What is the *intuition* for why these models—which focus on either free cash flows to the firm or on residual operating income and net operating assets—are equivalent?

b. Some analysts focus on cash flows as they feel that companies manage earnings, which presumably makes earnings less relevant. Are earnings relevant? Explain.

EC-20. **Applying and Interpreting Value Driver Components of RNOA** The net operating profit margin and the asset turnover components of net operating assets are often termed *value drivers,* which refers to their positive influence on stock value by virtue of their role as components of return on net operating assets (RNOA).

a. Why are profit margins and asset turnover ratios viewed as influencing stock values?

b. Assuming that profit margins and asset turnover ratios are value drivers, what insight does this give us about managing companies if the goal is to create shareholder value?

PROBLEMS

PC-21. **Forecasting and Valuation Using Discounted Cash Flow (DCF) and Residual Operating Income (ROPI) Models** Following are the income statement and balance sheet for FedEx Corporation:

FedEx Corporation (FDX)

Income Statement

Years Ended May 31, (In millions)	2004	2003	2002
Revenues	$24,710	$22,487	$20,607
Operating Expenses			
Salaries and employee benefits	10,728	9,778	9,099
Purchased transportation	2,407	2,155	1,825
Rentals and landing fees	1,918	1,803	1,780
Depreciation and amortization	1,375	1,351	1,364
Fuel	1,481	1,349	1,100
Maintenance and repairs	1,523	1,398	1,240
Business realignment costs	435	—	—
Airline stabilization compensation	—	—	(119)
Other	3,403	3,182	2,997
	23,270	21,016	19,286
Operating Income	$ 1,440	$ 1,471	$ 1,321
Other Income (Expense)			
Interest expense	(136)	(124)	(144)
Interest income	20	6	5
Other, net	(5)	(15)	(22)
	(121)	(133)	(161)
Income Before Income Taxes	1,319	1,338	1,160
Provision for Income Taxes	481	508	435
Income Before Cumulative Effect of Change in Accounting Principle	838	830	725
Cumulative Effect of Change in Accounting for Goodwill, Net of Tax Benefit of $10	—	—	(15)
Net income	$ 838	$ 830	$ 710

Balance Sheet

May 31, (In millions)	2004	2003
Assets		
Current Assets		
Cash and cash equivalents	$ 1,046	$ 538
Receivables, less allowances of $151 and $149	3,027	2,627
Spare parts, supplies and fuel, less allowances of $124 and $101	249	228
Deferred income taxes	489	416
Prepaid expenses and other	159	132
Total current assets	4,970	3,941
Property and Equipment, at Cost		
Aircraft and related equipment	7,001	6,624
Package handling and ground support equipment and vehicles	5,296	5,013
Computer and electronic equipment	3,537	3,180
Other	4,477	4,200
	20,311	19,017
Less accumulated depreciation and amortization	11,274	10,317
Net property and equipment	9,037	8,700

(Continued on the next page)

(Continued from the previous page)

May 31, (In millions)	2004	2003
Other Long-Term Assets		
Goodwill	2,802	1,063
Prepaid pension cost	1,127	1,269
Intangible and other assets	1,198	412
Total other long-term assets	5,127	2,744
Total Assets	$19,134	$15,385
Liabilities and Stockholders' Investment		
Current liabilities		
Current portion of long-term debt	$ 750	$ 308
Accrued salaries and employee benefits	1,062	724
Accounts payable	1,615	1,168
Accrued expenses	1,305	1,135
Total current liabilities	4,732	3,335
Long-Term Debt, Less Current Portion	2,837	1,709
Other Long-Term Liabilities		
Deferred income taxes	1,181	882
Pension, postretirement healthcare and other benefit obligations	$ 768	$ 657
Self-insurance accruals	591	536
Deferred lease obligations	503	466
Deferred gains, principally related to aircraft transactions	426	455
Other liabilities	60	57
Total other long-term liabilities	3,529	3,053
Common Stockholders' Investment		
Common stock, $0.10 par value; 800 million shares authorized; 300 million shares issued for 2004 and 299 million shares issued for 2003	30	30
Additional paid in capital	1,079	1,088
Retained earnings	7,001	6,250
Accumulated other comprehensive loss	(46)	(30)
	8,064	7,338
Less deferred compensation and treasury stock, at cost	28	50
Total common stockholders investment	8,036	7,288
Total liabilities and shareholders' investment	$19,134	$15,385

Required

a. Compute net operating assets (NOA) and net financial obligations (NFO) for fiscal year-end 2004. Show that: NOA = NFO + Stockholders' equity.

b. Compute net operating profit after tax (NOPAT) and net financial expense (NFE) for fiscal year 2004. Show that: Net income = NOPAT − NFE.

c. Forecast FedEx' sales, NOPAT, and NOA for fiscal years 2005 through 2008 using the following assumptions:

Sales growth	10%
Net operating profit margin (NOPM)	7%
Net operating asset turnover (NOAT)	2.13

Forecast the terminal period (2009) values assuming a 2% terminal year growth and using the NOPM and NOAT assumptions above.

d. Estimate the value of a share of FedEx common stock using the (1) discounted cash flow (DCF) model, and (2) residual operating income (ROPI) model as of May 31, 2004; assume a discount rate (WACC) of 6.9%, common shares outstanding of 300 million, and net financial obligations (NFO) of $3,587 million.

e. FedEx (FDX) stock closed at $73.58 on May 28, 2004 (the last closing price prior to May 31, 2004). How does your valuation estimate compare with this closing price? What do you believe are some reasons for the difference? What investment position is suggested from your results?

PC-22. **Forecasting and Valuation Using Discounted Cash Flow (DCF) and Residual Operating Income (ROPI) Models** Following are the income statement and balance sheet for Harley-Davidson:

Harley-Davidson (HDI)

Income Statement

Years Ended December 31 (In thousands)	2003	2002	2001
Net revenue	$4,624,274	$4,090,970	$3,406,786
Cost of goods sold	2,958,708	2,673,129	2,253,815
Gross profit	1,665,566	1,417,841	1,152,971
Financial services income	279,459	211,500	181,545
Financial services expense	111,586	107,273	120,272
Operating income from financial services	167,873	104,227	61,273
Selling, administrative and engineering expense	684,175	639,366	551,743
Income from operations	$1,149,264	$ 882,702	$ 662,501
Interest income, net	23,088	16,541	17,478
Other, net	(6,317)	(13,416)	(6,524)
Income before provision for income taxes	1,166,035	885,827	673,455
Provision for income taxes	405,107	305,610	235,709
Net income	$ 760,928	$ 580,217	$ 437,746

Balance Sheet

December 31 (In thousands)	2003	2002
Assets		
Current assets		
Cash and cash equivalents	$ 812,449	$ 280,928
Marketable securities	510,211	514,800
Accounts receivable, net	112,406	108,694
Current portion of finance receivables, net	1,001,990	855,771
Inventories	207,726	218,156
Deferred income taxes	51,156	41,430
Prepaid expenses & other current assets	33,189	46,807
Total current assets	2,729,127	2,066,586
Finance receivables, net	735,859	589,809
Property, plant, and equipment, net	1,046,310	1,032,596
Goodwill	53,678	49,930
Other assets	358,114	122,296
	$4,923,088	$3,861,217
Liabilities and Shareholders' Equity		
Current liabilities		
Accounts payable	$ 223,902	$ 226,977
Accrued expenses and other liabilities	407,566	380,496
Current portion of finance debt	324,305	382,579
Total current liabilities	955,773	990,052
Finance debt	670,000	380,000
Other long-term liabilities	86,337	123,353
Postretirement health care benefits	127,444	105,419
Deferred income taxes	125,842	29,478

(Continued on the next page)

(Continued from the previous page)

December 31 (In thousands)	2003	2002
Shareholders' equity		
Series A Junior participating preferred stock, none issued	—	—
Common stock, 326,489,291 and 325,298,404 shares issued in 2003 and 2002, respectively	3,266	3,254
Additional paid-in capital	419,455	386,284
Retained earnings	3,074,037	2,372,095
Accumulated other comprehensive income (loss)	47,174	(46,266)
	3,543,932	2,715,367
Less		
Treasury stock (24,978,798 and 22,636,295 shares in 2003 and 2002, respectively), at cost	(586,240)	(482,360)
Unearned compensation	—	(92)
Total shareholders' equity	2,957,692	2,232,915
	$4,923,088	$3,861,217

Required

a. Compute net operating assets (NOA) and net financial obligations (NFO) for year-end 2003. Show that: NOA = NFO + Shareholders' equity. (*Hint:* Treat HDI's financial receivables as an operating item and finance debt as a nonoperating item.)

b. Compute net operating profit after tax (NOPAT) and net financial expense (NFE) for 2003. Show that: Net income = NOPAT − NFE.

c. Forecast Harley-Davidson's sales, NOPAT, and NOA for 2004 through 2007 using the following assumptions:

Sales growth	13%
Net operating profit margin (NOPM)	18%
Net operating asset turnover (NOAT)	1.34

Forecast the terminal period (2008) values assuming a 2% terminal year growth and using the NOPM and NOAT assumptions above.

d. Estimate the value of a share of Harley-Davidson common stock using the (1) discounted cash flow (DCF) model and (2) residual operating income (ROPI) model as of December 31, 2003; assume a discount rate (WACC) of 8%, common shares outstanding of 301.5 million, and net financial obligations (NFO) of $484 million.

e. Harley-Davidson (HDI) stock closed at $47.53 on December 31, 2003. How does your valuation estimate compare with this closing price? What do you believe are some reasons for the difference?

PC-23. **Forecasting and Valuation using Discounted Cash Flow (DCF) and Residual Operating Income (ROPI) Models** Following are the income statement and balance sheet for Abbott Laboratories (ABT):

Abbott Laboratories (ABT)

Income Statement

Year Ended December 31, (In thousands)	2003
Net sales	$19,680,561
Cost of products sold	9,473,416
Research and development	1,733,472
Acquired in-process research and development	100,240
Selling, general, and administrative	5,050,901
Total operating cost and expenses	16,358,029
Operating earnings	3,322,532

(Continued on the next page)

(Continued from the previous page)

Year Ended December 31, (In thousands)	2003
Net interest expense	146,123
(Income) from TAP Pharmaceutical Products Inc. joint venture	(580,950)
Net foreign exchange (gain) loss	55,298
Other (income) expense, net	(32,356)
Earnings before taxes	3,734,417
Taxes on earnings	981,184
Net earnings	$ 2,753,233

Balance Sheet

December 31, (In thousands)	2003
Assets	
Current assets	
Cash and cash equivalents	$ 995,124
Investment securities	291,297
Trade receivables, less allowances of $259,514	3,313,377
Inventories	
Finished products	1,467,441
Work in process	545,977
Materials	725,021
Total inventories	2,738,439
Deferred income taxes	$ 1,165,259
Other prepaid expenses and receivables	1,786,919
Total Current Assets	10,290,415
Investment securities	406,357
Property and equipment, at cost	
Land	356,757
Buildings	2,662,023
Equipment	9,479,044
Construction in progress	792,923
	13,290,747
Less: accumulated depreciation and amortization	7,008,941
Net property and equipment	6,281,806
Intangible assets, net of amortization	4,089,882
Goodwill	4,449,408
Deferred income taxes, investments in joint ventures and other assets	1,197,474
Total assets	$26,715,342
Liabilities and Shareholders' Investment	
Current Liabilities	
Short-term borrowings	$ 828,092
Trade accounts payable	1,754,367
Salaries, wages and commissions	625,525
Other accrued liabilities	2,180,098
Dividends payable	383,352
Income taxes payable	158,836
Current portion of long-term debt	1,709,265
Total Current Liabilities	7,639,535
Long-term debt	3,452,329
Post-employment obligations and other long-term liabilities	2,551,220

(Continued on the next page)

(Continued from the previous page)

December 31, (In thousands)	2003
Shareholders' investment:	
Preferred shares, one dollar par, Authorized—1,000,000 shares, none issued	—
Common shares, without par value, Authorized—2,400,000,000 shares; Issued at stated capital amount—Shares: 1,580,247,227	3,034,054
Common shares held in treasury, at cost—Shares: 15,729,296	$ (229,696)
Unearned compensation—restricted stock awards	(56,336)
Earnings employed in the business	9,691,484
Accumulated other comprehensive income (loss)	632,752
Total shareholders' investment	13,072,258
Total liabilities and shareholders' investment	$26,715,342

Required

a. Compute net operating assets (NOA) and net financial obligations (NFO) for year-end 2003. Show that: NOA = NFO + Shareholders' Investment.

b. Compute net operating profit after tax (NOPAT) and net financial expense (NFE) for 2003. (*Hint:* Treat equity income from TAP Pharmaceutical Products, foreign exchange loss, and other income as operating items.) Show that: Net income = NOPAT − NFE.

c. Forecast Abbott Laboratories' sales, NOPAT, and NOA for 2004 through 2007 using the following assumptions:

Sales growth	11.30%
Net operating profit margin (NOPM)	14.53%
Net operating asset turnover (NOAT)	1.07

Forecast the terminal period (2008) values assuming a 2% terminal year growth and using the NOPM and NOAT assumptions above.

d. Estimate the value of a share of Abbott Laboratories' common stock using the (1) discounted cash flow (DCF) model, and (2) residual operating income (ROPI) model as of December 31, 2003; assume a discount rate (WACC) of 6%, common shares outstanding of 1,564.5 million, and net financial obligations (NFO) of $5,293 million.

e. Abbott Laboratories (ABT) stock closed at a split-adjusted price of $43.59 on December 31, 2003. How does your valuation estimate compare with this closing price? What do you believe are some reasons for the difference? What investment position is suggested from your results?

PC-24. Forecasting and Valuation using Discounted Cash Flow (DCF) and Residual Operating Income (ROPI) Models Following are the 2003 income statement and balance sheet for PepsiCo (PEP):

PepsiCo (PEP)

Income Statement

(in millions)	2003	2002	2001
Net revenue	$26,971	$25,112	$23,512
Cost of sales	12,379	11,497	10,750
Selling, general and administrative expenses	9,460	8,958	8,574
Amortization of intangible assets	145	138	165
Merger-related costs	59	224	356
Impairment and restructuring charges	147	—	31
Operating profit	4,781	4,295	3,636
Bottling equity income	323	280	160
Interest expense	(163)	(178)	(219)
Interest income	51	36	67
Income before income taxes	4,992	4,433	3,644
Provision for income taxes	1,424	1,433	1,244
Net income	$ 3,568	$ 3,000	$ 2,400

Balance Sheet

(in millions except per share amounts)	2003	2002
Assets		
Current assets		
Cash and cash equivalents	$ 820	$ 1,638
Short-term investments, at cost	1,181	207
	2,001	1,845
Accounts and notes receivable, net	2,830	2,531
Inventories	1,412	1,342
Prepaid expenses and other current assets	687	695
Total current assets	6,930	6,413
Property, plant, and equipment, net	7,828	7,390
Amortizable intangible assets, net	718	801
Goodwill	3,796	3,631
Other nonamortizable intangible assets	869	787
Nonamortizable intangible assets	4,665	4,418
Investments in noncontrolled affiliates	2,920	2,611
Other assets	2,266	1,841
Total assets	$25,327	$23,474
Liabilities and Shareholders' Equity		
Current liabilities		
Short-term obligations	$ 591	$ 562
Accounts payable and other current liabilities	5,213	4,998
Income taxes payable	611	492
Total current liabilities	6,415	6,052
Long-term debt obligations	1,702	2,187
Other liabilities	4,075	4,226
Deferred income taxes	1,261	1,486
Total liabilities	13,453	13,951
Preferred stock, no par value	41	41
Repurchased preferred stock	(63)	(48)
Common shareholders' equity		
Common stock, par value 1⅔¢ per share (issued 1,782 shares)	30	30
Capital in excess of par value	548	207
Retained earnings	15,961	13,489
Accumulated other comprehensive loss	(1,267)	(1,672)
	15,250	12,057
Less: repurchased common stock, at cost (77 and 60 shares, respectively)	(3,376)	(2,524)
Total common shareholders' equity	11,874	9,533
Total liabilities and shareholders' equity	$25,327	$23,474

Required

a. Compute net operating assets (NOA) and net financial obligations (NFO) for year-end 2003. Show that: NOA = NFO + Stockholders' Equity.

b. Compute net operating profit after tax (NOPAT) and net financial expense (NFE) for 2003. (*Hint:* Treat bottling equity income as an operating item.) Show that: Net Income = NOPAT − NFE.

c. Forecast PepsiCo's sales, NOPAT, and NOA for 2004 through 2007 using the following assumptions:

Sales growth	7.40%
Net operating profit margin (NOPM)	13.53%
Net operating asset turnover (NOAT)	2.08

Forecast the terminal period (2008) values assuming a 2% terminal year growth and using the NOPM and NOAT assumptions above.

d.   Estimate the value of a share of PepsiCo common stock using the (1) discounted cash flow (DCF) model, and (2) residual operating income (ROPI) model; assume a discount rate (WACC) of 6%, common shares outstanding of 1,705 million, and net financial obligations (NFO) of $1,112 million.

e.   PepsiCo (PEP) stock closed at $46.62 on December 31, 2003. How does your valuation estimate compare with this closing price? What do you believe are some reasons for the difference?

GLOSSARY

A

accelerated depreciation Depreciation method in which more depreciation expense is recorded early in an asset's useful life and less in its later life

account An individual record of increases and decreases for an item in the accounting system

accounting cycle The sequence of activities used to accumulate and report financial statements during a fiscal year

accounting equation The basic financial relationship that investing equals financing, commonly expressed as assets = liabilities + equity

accounts payable turnover Ratio defined as cost of goods sold divided by average accounts payable

accounts receivable Amounts due to a company from customers arising from the sale of products on credit

accounts receivable turnover (ART) Annual net sales divided by average accounts receivable (net)

accrual accounting The recognition of revenue when earned and the matching of expenses when incurred

accruals Adjustments that reflect revenues earned but not received or recorded and expenses incurred but not paid or recorded

accrued expense An expense incurred before payment is made, such as wages, utilities, and taxes; recognized with an adjusting entry

accrued revenue The value of services provided that have not as yet been billed or paid for by a client

accumulated other comprehensive income or loss Accumulated changes in equity that are not reported in the income statement

accumulated postretirement obligation (APBO) A pay-as-you-go liability that is rarely contributed to by a company

additional paid-in capital Amounts received from the primary owners of a company in addition to the par or stated value of common stock

adjusted trial balance A listing of all general ledger account balances prepared after adjustments are recorded and posted

adjusting process The method by which financial statements are adjusted for purposes of forecasting; also called *recasting* or *reformulating*

aging analysis Estimate of expected uncollectible accounts based on the number of days past invoices are outstanding

allowance for uncollectible accounts An estimate of the receivables that a company will be unable to collect; used in financial statements

Altman's Z-score A well-known model of financial distress that uses multiple ratios to predict the likelihood of bankruptcy or nonbankruptcy

amortization The systematic allocation of an account balance to expense; usually refers to the periodic writing off of an intangible asset

annuity A pattern of cash flows in which equal amounts are spaced equally over a number of periods

articulation The linkage of financial statements within and across accounting periods

asset a resource owned by the company that is expected to provide the company future economic benefits

asset turnover The sales to average assets ratio, which reflects effectiveness in generating sales from assets; also called *total asset turnover*

asset utilization The efficiency a company has in turning over assets

asset write-downs Restructuring activity where long-term assets or unsalable inventory is reduced in value in the company financial reports; also called *write-offs* or *charge-offs*

available-for-sale (AFS) Investments in securities that management intends to hold for capital gains and dividend revenue

average inventory days outstanding (AIDO) An indication of how long, on average, inventories are on the shelves, computed as inventory divided by average daily cost of goods sold

average cash cycle (ACC) The average period of time from when cash is invested in inventories until they are sold; the addition of the average collection period and modified average inventory days outstanding less the modified average payable days outstanding

average collection period (ACP) A measure related to accounts receivable turnover, which is defined as accounts receivable divided by average daily sales

average cost (AC) Inventory costing method that views cost of goods sold as an average of the cost to purchase all inventories available for sale during a particular period

average inventory days outstanding (AIDO) A companion measure to inventory computed as inventory divided by average daily cost of goods sold; also called *days inventory outstanding*

average payable days outstanding A ratio defined as accounts payable divided by average daily cost of goods sold

B

bad debt expense The cost of uncollectible accounts; also called *provision for uncollectible accounts*

balance sheet A financial report based on the accounting equation that lists a company's assets, liabilities, and equity at a certain point in time

bank reconciliation A schedule that accounts for all differences between the ending balance on the bank statement and the ending balance of the general ledger's cash account, as well as determining the reconciled cash balance at the end of the month

basic EPS Earnings per share, defined as net income less dividends on preferred stock divided by weighted average of common shares outstanding for the year

big bath Situation where a company recognizes its restructuring costs in a period of already depressed income

book value The dollar amount carried in the accounts of a particular item; the value of an item less its accumulated depreciation; also called *net book value* or *carrying value*

book value per share The net book value of a company available to common shareholders, defined as stockholders' equity less preferred stock divided by the number of common shares outstanding

bundled sales Two or more products sold together under one lump-sum price

C

calendar year A fiscal year that runs from January 1 to December 31

call provision A company's right to repurchase its own bond

capital The assets that provide value to the company

capital asset pricing model (CAPM) Method of determining the cost of equity capital

capital expenditures Financial outlays to acquire property, plant, and equipment

capital lease method Method of reporting leases that requires both the lease asset and lease liability to be reported on the balance sheet

capital markets Financing sources that often involve a company's issuance of securities (stocks, bonds, and notes)

capitalization The recording of an asset's cost as an asset on the balance sheet rather than as an expense on the income statement; these costs are transferred to expense as the asset is used up

capitalized To include a portion of an asset's cost on the balance sheet

cash Currency, bank deposits, certificates of deposit, and other cash equivalents

cash accounting Accounting method where revenues are only recognized when received in cash and expenses are only recognized when paid in cash

cash and cash equivalents A balance sheet account that combines cash with certain short-term, highly liquid investments

cash equivalents Short-term, highly liquid investments that are easily convertible into a known cash amount and are relatively unaffected by interest rate changes

cash flow from operations divided by net income An objective performance measure; the higher this ratio, the higher the quality of income

change in accounting estimate Adjustment in a generally accepted accounting principle, such as varying the time period an item is depreciated, that is applied prospectively from the date of change

change in accounting principle Adoption of a generally accepted accounting principle that differs from one previously used for reporting purposes

chart of accounts Form that facilitates transaction analysis and the preparation of general ledger entries

check A written order directing a particular bank to pay a specified amount of money to a person named on the check

closing procedures Part of the accounting cycle in which the balances of temporary accounts are transferred into permanent accounts

collateral Mortgages on assets a company owns as security for debt financing

collectibility risk The chance that items sold on credit will not be paid in full

common-size comparative financial statement A financial statement in which each item is presented as a percentage of a key figure such as sales or total assets

common stock The basic ownership class of corporate capital stock, carrying the rights to vote, share in earnings, participate in future stock issues, and share in any liquidation proceeds after prior claims have been settled

comparative balance sheet Financial statement that compares the assets, liabilities, and equity of a company over several distinct periods

comparative financial statements A frequently encountered form of horizontal analysis that compares dollar and percentage changes for important items and classification totals

comparative income statement Financial statement that compares the revenues and expenses of a company over several distinct periods

compensating balance A minimum amount that a bank requires a firm to maintain in a bank account as part of a borrowing arrangement

completed contract method Revenue recognition method in which revenue is deferred until the contract is complete

compound journal entry A journal entry that involves more than two accounts

contingent liability A potential obligation, the eventual occurrence of which usually depends on some future event beyond the control of the firm; contingent liabilities may originate with such events as lawsuits, credit guarantees, and environmental damages

contra accounts Accounts used to record reductions in or offsets to a related account

contra-asset account A means to offset an asset account without directly reducing that account

contributed capital The net funding that a company receives from issuing and reacquiring its equity shares; the difference between what the company receives from issuing shares and the cost it takes to buy them back

conversion feature Contract provision that allows preferred shareholders to convert their shares into common stock at a predetermined conversion ratio

convertible securities Debt and equity securities that provide the holder with an option to convert those securities into other securities

cookie jar reserve Accounting method in which income is shifted from the current period to a future period

core (persistent) components Elements of income that are most likely to persist and are most relevant for projecting future financial performance

cost method Accounting method in which investment is continually reported at its historical cost, and cash dividends and interest are recognized in current income

coupon (contract or stated) rate The interest rate stated in the bond contract; used to compute interest payments during the bond's life

covenants Contractual requirements that the loan recipient maintain minimum levels of capital to safeguard lenders

credit Purchasing an item with financing other than cash

credit sales A business transaction between companies where no cash immediately changes hands; also called *sales on account*

currency translation adjustment The unrecognized gain on assets and liabilities denominated in foreign currencies

current assets The most liquid assets, which can be quickly converted into cash

current liabilities Obligations such as accounts payable, accrued liabilities, unearned revenues, short-term notes payable, and current maturities of long-term debt that are due within one year

current maturities of long-term debt Long-term borrowings that are scheduled to mature in whole or in part during the upcoming year, including accrued interest

current rate method Method of translating foreign currency transactions under which balance sheet amounts are translated using exchange rates in effect at the period-end consolidation date and income statements using the period's average exchange rate

current ratio Measure of liquidity defined as current assets divided by current liabilities; a ratio greater than 1.0 implies positive net working capital

D

days sales outstanding (DSO) The average collection period for a receivable, defined as accounts receivable divided by average daily sales

debt-to-equity (DE) A common measure of financial leverage, defined as total liabilities divided by stockholder's equity

default The nonpayment of interest and principal or the failure to adhere to various terms and conditions of an investment

deferral An accounting adjustment in which assets and revenues received in advance of a certain accounting period are allocated as expenses and revenues during that period

deferred income taxes Money stored in a temporary account for future payment of taxes

deferred revenue See *unearned revenue*

deferred tax asset Situation when tax reporting income is less than financial reporting income; the deferred tax asset expires when the temporary difference reverses

deferred tax liability Taxes to be paid in the future when taxable income is higher than financial reporting income; also called *deferred taxes*

defined benefit plan Pension plan in which the company makes periodic payments to an employee after retirement, generally based on years of service and employee's age

defined contribution plan Pension plan in which a company makes periodic contributions to a current employee's account, which the employee may drawn upon following retirement; many plans require an employee matching contribution

definite life A determinable period of time that an asset, such as a patent or franchise right, exists

depletion The process of transferring costs from the resource account into inventory as resources are used up

deposits in transit Deposits not yet recorded by the bank

depreciation The decline in value of equipment and assets due to wear, deterioration, and obsolescence; process of allocating costs of equipment, vehicles, and buildings to the periods benefiting from their use

depreciation and amortization expenses Write-offs of previously recorded assets added to net income as it is converted to net operating cash flow

depreciation base The capitalized cost of an asset less the estimated residual value

depreciation method Means of calculating the reduction in an asset's value over its useful life

depreciation rate Method of depreciation equal to one divided by the item's useful life

derivatives Financial instruments that are utilized by companies to reduce various kinds of risk

detection control An internal control a company adopts to discover problems soon after they arise

diluted EPS Earnings per share that includes all stock options and convertible securities in the calculations

direct association Recognizing a cost directly associated with a specific source of revenue at the same time the related revenue is recognized

direct method Accounting method that presents net cash flow from operating activities by showing the major categories of operating cash receipts and payments

discount Situation where a bond's coupon rate is less than market rate

discounted cash flow (DCF) model An approach to valuing equity securities that focuses on the generation of cash rather than its distribution

dividend discount model Valuation mechanism for equity based on the present value of expected dividend receipts plus the value of the security at the end of the forecasted holding period

dividend preference The order in which shareholders receive dividends; preferred shareholders take precedence over common shareholders

dollar change Financial statement adjustment computed as analysis period amount minus base period amount

double entry accounting system The dual effects where, in order to maintain the equality of the accounting equation, each transaction must affect at least two accounts

E

earned capital The cumulative net income (losses) retained by the company; income not paid to shareholders as dividends

earned income Income in which the seller has executed its duties under the terms of the sales agreement and the title has passed to the buyer

earnings management Discretionary choices management makes that mask the underlying economic performance of a company

earnings quality A measure of earnings in terms of sustainability, the ability for income to persist in future periods

economic consequences Issues resulting from accounting changes

economic value added (EVA) Net operating profits after tax less a charge for the use of capital equal to beginning capital utilized in the business multiplied by the weighted average cost of capital

EDGAR Database maintained by the SEC where financial statements are available for download

effective cost The cost to a bond's issuing company for offering the bond, generally as cash interest paid plus the discount or premium incurred

employee severance costs Accrued (estimated) costs for termination of employees as part of a restructuring program

equity Capital provided by the company's owners, including stock, retained earnings, and additional paid-in capital; the owners' claim in the company

equity carve outs Corporate divestitures that are generally motivated by the belief that consolidated financial statements obscure the performance of individual business units

equity method Accounting method that reports investment on the balance sheet at an amount equal to the percentage of the investee's equity owned by the investor

equity valuation model A means of defining the value of an equity security in terms of the present value of future forecasted amounts

executory contract Situation such as a purchase order where a future sacrifice is probable and the amount of the sacrifice can be reasonably estimated, but the transaction that caused the obligation has not yet occurred

expense Outflow or use of assets, including costs of products and services sold, operating costs, and interest on debt, to generate revenue

expensed Situation when a cost is recorded in the income statement and labeled as an expense

F

face amount The principal amount of a bond, which is repaid at maturity

fair market value The value of an asset based on current rates in the general public

Financial Accounting Standards Board (FASB) Standard-setting organization which publishes accounting standards governing the preparation of financial reports

financial leverage (FLEV) The proportionate use of borrowed funds in the capital structure, computed as net financial obligations (NFO) divided by average equity

financial statement effects template Form that captures each transaction and its financial statement effects on the balance sheet and income statement

financing activities Methods companies use to fund investment resources

finished goods Inventory account that records completed manufactured items waiting to be sold

firm value The present value of expected free cash flows to the firm

first-in first-out (FIFO) Inventory costing method that transfers costs from inventory in the order they were initially recorded

fiscal year The annual (one year) accounting period adopted by a company for its financial activities

fixed costs Expenses that do not change with changes in sales volume (over a reasonable range)

forecast horizon See *horizon period*

forecasted year-end account balance Projection defined as forecasted sales (or cost of goods sold) divided by estimated turnover rate

forecasting The projection of financial results over the forecast horizon and terminal periods

foreign currency translation The amount needed to convert foreign currencies in order to balance the accounting equation

franchise A contractual agreement that gives a company the right to operate a particular business in an area for a particular period of time

free cash flows to the firm (FCFF) The net cash flows from operations plus or minus net cash flows from investing activities

fundamental analysis Method of using a company's financial information to estimate its value, which is used in buy-sell strategies

funded status The difference between a company's pension plan assets and the projected benefit obligation

future benefits Revenues or some other compensation a company expects to receive in a later period

future value The amount that a specific investment is worth at a future date if invested at a given rate of compound interest

G

gain on bond retirement Situation where the repurchase price of a bond is less than the net bonds payable

general journal A flexible journal that allows any type of business transaction to be included

generally accepted accounting principles (GAAP) An overall set of standards and procedures accountants have developed that apply to the preparation of financial statements

goodwill An intangible asset recorded when a company acquires another company, consisting of the value of a company above and beyond its specific physical assets

gross profit The difference between revenues (at selling prices) and cost of goods sold (at purchasing price or manufacturing cost)

gross profit margin (GPM) A measure that reflects the net impact on profitability if there are changes in a company's pricing structure, sales mix, and merchandise costs, defined as gross profit divided by net sales

H

held-to-maturity (HTM) Debt securities that management holds on to for their full term

historical cost The original acquisition cost, less the portion that that has expired or been transferred to the income statement

horizon period The forecast period for which detailed estimates are made, typically 5-10 years

horizontal analysis An examination of data across two or more consecutive time periods, which assists in analyzing company performance and predicting future performance

I

immediate recognition Costs recognized as expenses in a period when they were incurred, even though they cannot be directly linked to specific revenues

impact of conglomerates Impairment of comparisons between different companies as some may have subsidiaries that place them on a different playing field

impairment Loss of property, plant, and equipment value determined by comparing the sum of expected future cash flows from the asset's net book value

income smoothing Timing transitory gains and losses so that the company maintains a steady improvement in income each year

income statement A financial report on operating activities that lists revenues less expenses over a period of time, yielding a company's net income

indefinite lives Situation where an asset's expected useful life extends far enough into the future that it is practically impossible to accurately determine

indirect method Accounting method for preparing the statement of cash flows in which the operating section begins with net income and converts it to cash flows from operations

in-process research and development An intangible asset whose cost must be written off immediately upon purchase

installment method Revenue recognition method which recognizes revenue when cash is collected, and records costs and gross profit in proportion to the amount of cash collected

insufficient write-down Impairment of assets to a larger degree than is recognized

intangible assets Assets such as trademarks and patents that supply the owner rights rather than physical objects

interest cost Interest accrued on outstanding pension liability, which is added to the liability each year

internal auditing A company function that provides independent appraisals of the company's financial statements, its internal controls, and its operations

internal controls Policies and procedures used to protect assets, ensure reliable accounting, promote efficient operations, and urge adherence to company policies

inventory Goods purchased or produced for sale to customers

inventory quality The rate at which inventory is turned over; the faster the turnover, the higher the quality

inventory turnover (INVT) Measure of inventory management computed as cost of goods sold divided by average inventory

investing activities Methods companies use to acquire and dispose of assets in the course of production and sales

J

journal A tabular record in which business activities are analyzed in terms of debits and credits and recorded in chronological order before they are entered in the general ledger; also called *book of original entry*

journal entries An accounting entry in a company's financial records that accountants use to represent individual transactions

L

last-in, first-out (LIFO) Inventory costing method that transfers the most recent costs from inventory first

leaning on the trade An increase in accounts payable, which results in an increase in net cash flows from operating activities

lease asset The value of a leased item

lease liability The payments required to lease an item

lessee A party to a lease who wishes to use the asset

lessor The owner of an asset

liability A probable future economic sacrifice resulting from a past or current event

licenses See *operating rights*

LIFO layer New layer added to inventory at an updated price each time inventory is purchased in companies using LIFO inventory costing; the most recent costs are transferred to cost of goods sold

LIFO liquidation Situation when, in companies using LIFO inventory costing, quantity of inventory sold exceeds that purchased, in which case the costs of older inventory is transferred to cost of good sold

LIFO reserve The difference between the cost of inventories using FIFO and the cost using LIFO

liquidation preference In the event of a company's failure, preferred shareholders are reimbursed in full before common shareholders are paid

liquidity The ease of converting noncash assets into cash

long-term debt Amounts borrowed from creditors that are scheduled to be repaid more than one year into the future

long-term debt-to-equity A common measure of leverage that focuses on long-term financing, defined as long-term debt divided by stockholders' equity

long-term investments Investments that the company does not intend to sell in the near future

long-term operating asset turnover The rate that reflects capital intensity relative to sales, defined as net sales divided by average long-term operating assets

loss on bond retirement Situation if a bond's issuer pays more to retire the bonds than the amount carried on its balance sheet

lower of cost or market (LCM) Process of reporting inventories at the lower of its cost or its current market value

M

maker Owner of a checking account

manufacturing costs Expenses associated with product production, including materials, labor, and overhead

mark-to-market Method of valuing assets that results in an adjustment of an asset's carrying amount to its market value

market rate The interest rate that investors expect to earn on their debt security investment; used to price the bond; also called *yield rate*

market value Company value computed by multiplying the number of outstanding shares of common stock by the market price per share

marketable securities Short-term investments that can be quickly sold to raise cash

markup The difference between an item's selling price and the cost incurred to produce it

method of comparables model An equity valuation model that uses price multiples, defined as stock price divided by some key financial number; also called *multiples model*

minimum pension liability The additional pension liability that must be recorded under GAAP if pension plans are underfunded

minority interest An ownership in a company that is less than a majority or controlling interest

N

Net asset valuation model An equity valuation model that draws on the financial reporting system to assign value; equity is valued as reported assets les reported liabilities

net financial expense Net operating profit after tax less net income

net financial obligations (NFO) The difference between financial (nonoperating) obligations and financial (nonoperating) assets; positive if obligations exceed assets

net financial rate Net financial expense divided by average net financial obligations

net income The difference between revenues and expenses when revenues exceed expenses

net loss The difference between revenues and expenses when expenses exceed revenues

net operating assets (NOA) Current and long-term operating assets less current and long-term operating liabilities

net operating assets turnover (NOAT) A measure of turnover defined as sales divided by average net operating assets

net operating profit after tax (NOPAT) Sales less operating expenses (including taxes)

net operating working capital (NOWC) Operating current assets less operating current liabilities

net operating working capital turnover (NOWCT) Management's effectiveness in using operating working capital, defined as net sales divided by average net operating working capital

net profit margin The income to sales ratio, which reflects the profitability of sales; also called simply *profit margin*

net realizable value The value of a company's receivables, less an allowance for uncollectible accounts

net working capital The difference between current assets and current liabilities; also called *working capital*

nominal cost Cash interest paid on a debt

non pro rata distribution A case where stockholders can accept or reject the distribution of shares

noncash investing and financing activities Significant financial events that do not affect current cash flows, such as issuance of stocks and bonds in exchange for property, plant, and equipment

noncurrent liabilities Obligations such as long-term debt and other long-term liabilities that are to be paid after one year

non-operating revenues and expenses Costs related to the company's financing and investing activities, including interest revenue and interest expense

notes payable Account assigned to a company's financial borrowings

O

off-balance-sheet financing A company's financial obligations that are not reported as liabilities in the balance sheet

on-balance-sheet financing The reporting of financing effects, namely current and noncurrent liabilities, on the balance sheet

operating activities Methods companies use to produce, promote, and sell its products and services

operating cash flow to capital expenditures ratio A measure that helps assess a firm's ability to replace its property, plant, and equipment, or expand as needed; calculated as operating cash flows from operating activities divided by annual capital expenditures

operating cash flow to current liabilities ratio A measure of the ability to liquidate current liabilities, calculated as net cash flow from operating activities divided by average current liabilities

operating cash flow to liabilities (OCFL) A method to compare operating flows to liabilities, defined as net cash flow from operations divided by total liabilities

operating cycle The time between paying cash for goods or employee services and receiving cash from customers

operating expense The usual and customary costs a company incurs to support its main business activities, including cost of goods sold, selling expenses, depreciation expenses, amortization expenses, and research and development expenses

operating expense margin (OEM) The ratio obtained by dividing any operating expense category by sales

operating lease method Method of reporting leases where neither the lease asset nor the lease liability is on the balance sheet

operating rights A contractual agreement similar to franchise rights, but typically granted by government agencies

options Variations allowed within debt contracts, such as the right to convert debt into stock

ordinary annuity A series of fixed payments made at the end of each period over a specified time period

other long-term liabilities Various obligations, such as pension liabilities and long-term tax liabilities, that will be satisfied at least one year in the future

other postretirement benefits Items such as health care and insurance benefits offered to retired employees

outstanding checks Checks not yet recorded by the bank

overfunded Situation where pension plan assets exceed pension liabilities

P

par value Face value of a bond; in stocks, an arbitrary amount set by company organizers at the time of formation

participation feature Contract provision that allows preferred shareholders to share ratably with common shareholders in dividends

patent An exclusive right to produce a product or use a technology

payee The person named on a check who will receive compensation

payer The bank that will compensate the recipient of a check

percent change Financial statement adjustment computed by dollar change (analysis period amount less base period amount) divided by base period amount, with the result multiplied by 100

percentage-of-completion method Revenue recognition method which recognizes revenue by determining the costs incurred under the contract relative to its total expected costs

percentage of sales A means to estimate uncollectible accounts that computes bad debts expense as a percentage of total sales

periodic interest payment Interest payments made in the form of equal cash flows at periodic intervals

permanent account An account used to prepare the balance sheet; that is, asset, liability, and equity capital (capital stock and retained earnings) accounts; any balance in a permanent account at the end of an accounting period is carried forward to the next period

permanent difference A difference in amount between two financial statements that does not reverse in time

plan assets The assets of a pension plan that involve investments in stocks and bonds

pooling of interests method A method of accounting for business combinations under which the acquired company is recorded on the acquirer's balance sheet at its book value, rather than market value; this method is no longer acceptable under GAAP for acquisitions occurring after 2001

post-closing trial balance Accounting balance prepared after closing entries are recorded and posted to verify the equality between debits and credits in the general ledger after the adjusting and closing process

posting The transfer of debit and credit entries from the journal to their related general ledger accounts

preferred stock Stock that possesses priority over common stock, such as first right to dividends or liquidation payout

premium When a bond's coupon rate is greater than the market rate

prepaid expenses Costs paid in advance for rent, insurance, or other services

present value The amount of money a stock or bond is worth at the current time

prevention control An internal control companies adopt to deter problems before they arise

pro forma income GAAP income from continuing operations (excluding discontinued operations and extraordinary items), less transitory items

pro rata distribution Shares distributed to stockholders on a pro rata basis

projected benefit obligation (PBO) Pension liabilities that represent future obligations to current and former employees

property, plant, and equipment (PPE) Tangible assets recorded on a balance sheet, including land, factory buildings, warehouses, office buildings, office equipment, and other items used in the operation of a business

purchase method The prescribed method of accounting for business combinations; under the purchase method, assets and liabilities of the acquired company are recorded at fair market value, together with identifiable intangible assets; the balance is ascribed to goodwill

Q

quality of earnings The extent to which reported income reflects the underlying economic performance of a company

quick ratio (QR) A ratio that reflects a company's ability to meet its current liabilities without liquidating inventories

R

raw materials and supplies Inventory account that records items used in production processes

realized or realizable income Income in which the company's net assets increase

recasting See *adjusting process*

receivables quality The likelihood of collecting on a receivables account, which a company can change by extending credit terms, taking on longer-paying customers, and increasing the allowance provision

reconciled cash balance A company's cash balance after accounting for deposits in transit and outstanding checks

redeem Company repurchasing their bonds prior to maturity

relevance The usefulness of information to those who use financial statements in decision making

reliability The ability to objectively determine and accurately measure a value, such as historical cost

residual operating income (ROPI) model An approach to equity valuation that focuses on operating and investing activities

residual (or salvage) value The expected realizable value of an asset at the end of its useful life

restructuring costs Expenses typically associated with activities such as consolidating production facilities, reorganizing sales operations, outsourcing activities, or discontinuing product lines

retained earnings Earned capital, the cumulative net income and loss, of the company (from its inception) that has not been paid to shareholders as dividends

return The amount of money earned on an investment, often expressed as investment income divided by the amount invested; also called *yield*

return on assets (ROA) A computation of net income divided by average total assets; also called *return on invested capital*

return on equity (ROE) The ultimate measure of performance from the shareholders' perspective, computed as net income divided by average equity

return on sales An overall test of operating efficiency defined as net income divided by net sales **revenue** Increase in net assets (assets less liabilities) as a result of business activities

revenue recognition The timing and amount of revenue reported by a company

revenue recognition criteria Requirements that must be met for income to be recognized on the income statement; according to GAAP, revenue must be realized/realizable and earned

revenue recognition principle Accounting rule that requires revenue to be recognized (recorded) only when earned

right of return The allowance for a customer to return a product within a specified period of time

risk The uncertainty of expected return, which is an intrinsic part of each investment

risk-free rate The market rate of interest defined as the yield on U.S. Government borrowings, computed as yield rate less spread

S

Sarbanes-Oxley Act Act passed in 2002 which requires a company's CEO and CFO to personally sign a statement attesting to the accuracy and completeness of financial statements

Securities and Exchange Commision (SEC) Commision created by the 1934 Securities Act to regulate the issuance and trading of securities

security valuation A determination of the value of equity securities

sell-off The outright sale of a business unit

service cost The additional pension benefits earned by employees each year

shareholders' equity See *equity*

short-term interest-bearing debt Short-term bank borrowings and notes expected to mature in whole or in part during the upcoming year

short-term notes payable Short-term debt payable to banks or other creditors

significant influence The ability of an investor to affect an investee's financing or operating policies

solvency A company's ability to meet its obligations, mainly to creditors

solvency analysis A review of a company's ability to meet its financial obligations, which is aided by financial leverage ratios

spin-off A form of equity carve out in which a company distributes subsidiary shares it owns as dividends to its shareholders, making shareholders owners of the subsidiary

split-off Form of equity carve out where the parent company exchanges stock in an owned subsidiary for shares of the parent company, making the subsidiary an independent publicly traded company

spread The difference between the net financial return (NFR) and the return on net operating activities (RNOA); also called *risk premium*

statement of cash flows A financial report that identifies net cash flows into and out of a company from operating, investing, and financing activities over a period of time

statement of responsibility Form included with each financial statement of a publicly traded company assuring management is responsible for the statements, they have been prepared using GAAP, and they are audited by an outside organization

statement of stockholder's equity A financial statement that reports on changes in key equity accounts over a period of time; also called a *statement of equity*

stock option Right to compensate officers and other employees of a corporation with stock

stock rights A stockholder's option to acquire a specified number of shares of capital stock under prescribed conditions and within a stated period

stock warrant A certificate that provides the holder with stock rights

stockholders' equity See *equity*

straight-line depreciation Determination of annual depreciation expense by dividing the asset's cost by its estimated useful life

systematic allocation Costs that benefit more than one accounting period and cannot be associated with specific revenues

T

T-account A graphic representation of an account, shaped like a large T, which uses one side to record increases to the account and the other side to record decreases

tangible assets Assets that have physical substance, such as property, plant, and equipment

temporary account An account used to gather information for an accounting period; at the end of the period, the balance is transferred to a permanent owners' equity account; revenue, expense, and dividends accounts are temporary accounts

temporary difference A difference in amount between two financial statements that reverses in time

terminal period The post-horizon period

times interest earned (TIE) A determination of how much income is available to service debt, defined as earnings before interest and taxes divided by interest expense

tombstone An announcement of debt offered to the public

total debits equal total credits for each entry The basic rule of accounting

trade credit The financing used to purchase inventories on credit from other companies

trademark A registered name, logo, package design, image, jingle, or slogan associated with a product

trading securities Investments in securities that management intends to actively buy and sell for trading profits as market prices fluctuate

transitory components Elements of income that are not recurring; financial projections are improved if these are excluded from them

treasury stock Shares of outstanding stock that have been acquired by the issuing corporation; a contra equity account

trend analysis A type of horizontal analysis in which a base period is chosen and all subsequent period amounts are defined relative to the base

trend percentages A comparison of the same financial item over two or more years, stated as a percentage of a base-year amount

turnover rate In forecasting, it is defined as sales (or cost of goods sold) divided by account balance at year-end

U

unadjusted trial balance Account balances before any adjustments are made

underfunded Situation where pension liabilities exceed pension plan assets

unearned revenue Cash received for products or services to be provided at a later time

unrecognized prior service cost An accounting adjustment to a pension that represents the portion of the liability earned by employees prior to the plan's inception or a plan amendment

useful life The period of time over which the asset in expected to provide economic benefits to the company

V

variable costs Expenses that change in proportion to changes in sales volume

vertical analysis A means of overcoming size differences among companies by expressing income statement items as a percentage of net sales and all balance sheet items as a percentage of total assets

W

wasting assets Assets consumed as they are used, including natural resources such as oil reserves, mineral deposits, or timberland

weighted average cost of capital (WACC) The discount rate where the weights are the relative percentages of debt and equity in the capital structure and are applied to the expected returns on debt and equity, respectively

work in process Inventory account that tracks the value of items currently being produced

SUBJECT INDEX

COMPANY INDEX

CITATIONS AND REFERENCES

CHAPTER 1

Berkshire Hathaway 2005, 2004, 2003, and 2002 Annual Reports and 10-K Reports

CHAPTER 2

The Walt Disney Company 2005, 2004, and 2001 Annual Reports and 10-K Reports
Mark Albright, "Mutiny at the Mouse," St. Petersburg Times, March 1, 2004
Laura M. Holson, "Disney Performance to Get Tough Scrutiny Quarterly Results under A Microscope," The New York Times, March 26, 2004
Frank Ahrens, "Disney's New Drama: Dissension; Angry Shareholders Turn Harsh Spotlight on CEO Eisner," The Washington Post, March 1, 2004
Bruce Orwall and Peter Grant, "Mouse Trap: Disney, Struggling to Regain Glory, Gets $48.7 Billion Bid from Comcast—Already on Defense, Eisner Faces Biggest Challenge of Nearly 20-Year Reign—Cable Giant's Huge Ambitions," The Wall Street Journal, February 12, 2004
"ABC, Inc.," Hoover's, Inc., Hoover's Company Profiles, May 12, 2004
Bruce Orwall, "Disney to Close Go.Com `Portal,' Absorb Internet Tracking Stock," The Wall Street Journal, January 30, 2001
Jacqueline Doherty, "Wishing on a Star: There's Lots of Magic Left at Disney—With or without Its Chief Mouseketeer," Barron's, November 4, 2002

CHAPTER 3

FedEx 10-K Report, 2006; FedEx Annual Report, 2005; FedEx.com Website, January 2006; BusinessWeek, November 28, 2005, pp. 42–43.

CHAPTER 4

Ball and Leung, "Latte Versus Latte—Starbucks, Dunkin' Donuts Seek Growth by Capturing Each Other's Customers." The Wall Street Journal 9 September 2005, Fortune 18 April 2005; Starbucks 2005, 2004, and 2003 Annual Reports and 10-K Reports.

CHAPTERS 5 AND 6

3M Company 2005, 2004, and 2003 Annual Reports and 10-K Reports
Michael Arndt with Diane Brady, "3M's Rising Star; Jim McNerney Is Racking Up Quite a Record at 3M. Now, Can He Rev Up Its Innovation Machine?" BusinessWeek, April 12, 2004, 62, Number 3878
Jerry Useem, "[3M] + [General Electric] = ? ; Jim Mcnerney Thinks He Can Turn 3M from a Good Company into a Great One—With a Little Help from His Former Employer, General Electric," Fortune, August 12, 2002, 127, Vol. 146, Issue: 3
Simon London, "When Quality Is Not Quite Enough," Financial Times (FT.Com), July 14. 2002.

CHAPTER 7

Cisco Systems, Inc. 2005, 2004, 2003, and 2001 10-K Reports and Annual Reports
John Chambers: "We Never Lost Track," BusinessWeek online, November 24, 2003.
"Chambers: Stock Options Inspire Innovation," BusinessWeek online, December 22, 2003.

CHAPTER 8

The Gillette Company 2005, 2004, and 200310-K Reports and Annual Reports
Charles Forelle, "Gillette's Profit and Sales Jump; Restructuring Starts To Pay Off," The Wall Street Journal, April 30, 2004.
Charles Forelle, "Gillette Earnings Are Squeezed by Cost-Reduction Expenses," The Wall Street Journal, January 31, 2003.

CHAPTER 9

The Procter & Gamble Company 2005, 2004, and 2003 10-K Reports and Annual Reports
Robert Berner, Nanette Byrnes, and Wendy Zellner, "P&G Has Rivals in a Wringer; Colgate and Unilever Are Hurting As It Rolls Out Creative Products and Marketing," BusinessWeek, October 4, 2004, 74, Volume 3902.

CHAPTER 10

Verizon Communications, Inc. 2005, 2004, and 2003 Annual Reports and 10-K Reports
Julie Creswell, "Ivan Seidenberg, CEO of Verizon, Vows to Overpower the Cable Guys by Plowing Billions into a '90s-Style Broadband Buildout. But Will He Really? Or Is the Most Powerful Man in Telecom Pulling a Megabluff?" Fortune, May 31, 2004.
Steve Rosenbush, Tom Lowry, Roger O. Crockett, and Brian Grow, "Verizon: Take That, Cable; It Seeks to Reclaim Lost Ground with a Gutsy Plunge into Pay-TV Services," BusinessWeek, May 24, 2004, 81, Number 3884.
Steve Rosenbush, "Verizon's Mega-Makeover Its Network Upgrade May Create a New Industry Standard," BusinessWeek, March 31, 2003, 68, Number 3826
"Verizon's Daring Vision," BusinessWeek, August 4, 2003, 112, Number 3844.
Almar Latour, "Verizon Revenue Increases 3.9%—Wireless Business Surges, But Profit Plunges on Costs of Huge Employee Buyout," The Wall Street Journal, April 28, 2004, B5
Scott Moritz, "'Tough Spot for Verizon on Debt Front," Thestreet.Com, 10/25/2002 02:55 PM EDT

CHAPTER 11

Pfizer, Inc. 2005, 2004, and 2003 Annual Reports and 10-K Reports
Bill Alpert, "Drug War: Who Wins and Loses in the Brawl over Cholesterol-Lowering Medications," Barron's, June 14, 2004, 21
Andrew Bary, "Buying Time Again: Corporate Earnings Are Running Ahead of Stocks; How High Can the S&P 500 Go This Year?," Barron's, May 31, 2004, 17
Allison Fass, "Make War, Not Love; Pfizer's Shrinking Viagra Sales," Forbes, May 10, 2004, 56, Volume 173, Issue 10
John Carey and Michael Arndt, "Making Pills the Smart Way; Drugmakers Are Revamping Factories to Save Money and Avoid Production Mishaps," BusinessWeek, May 3, 2004, 102, Number 3881
Matthew Herper and Robert Langreth, "The Immortal Pill; Pfizer's Plans for Lipitor's Successor," Forbes, April 26, 2004, 50, Volume 173, Issue 9
Jeffrey E. Garten, "The Right Remedy for Pricey Drugs," BusinessWeek, April 12, 2004, 28, Number 3878
Scott Hensley, "Pfizer's Earnings Dropped by Half in First Quarter," The Wall Street Journal, April 21, 2004

CHAPTER 12

Hewlett-Packard Company 2005, 2004, 2003, and 2002 Annual Reports and 10-K Reports
Pui-Wing Tam, "H-P Posts Big Loss Due to Compaq Purchase," The Wall Street Journal, August 28,2002.
Quentin Hardy, "We Did It; Carly Fiorina's Boast: HP Pulled Off a Complex Merger and Saved $3.5 Billion. Her Sales Pitch: We Can Work This Magic on Your Company," Forbes, August 11, 2003, 76, Volume 171 Issue 16
Stephen Manning, "Fiorina: Compaq Merger Was Critical for HP," Associated Press Newswires, October 10, 2003, 17:49
"Carly Fiorina, Up Close—How Shrewd Strategic Moves in Grueling Proxy Battle Let H-P Chief Take Control," The Wall Street Journal, January 13, 2003.
San Jose Mercury News, Calif.," Hewlett-Packard's Compaq Purchase Proves Beneficial," KRTBN Knight-Ridder Tribune Business News: San Jose Mercury News, April 13, 2003

CHAPTER 13

Midwest Air Group, Inc. 2005, 2004, and 2003 10-K Reports and 2004 Annual Reports
"Business Brief—Midwest Express Holding Inc.: Unions Agree to Concessions in Bid to Avert Reorganization," The Wall Street Journal, July 14, 2003, B2

CHAPTER 14

Kimberly-Clark 2005, 2004, and 2003 Annual Reports and 10-K Reports
Allison Fass, "Diaper Rash; Kimberly-Clark," Forbes, April 26, 2004, Volume 173, Issue 9
Edited By Monica Roman, "Paper Cuts at Kimberly?" BusinessWeek, March 8, 2004, 41, Number 3873.
Matthew Boyle, "Brand Killers ; Store Brands Aren't for Losers Anymore. In Fact, They're Downright Sizzling. and That Scares the Soap Out of the Folks Who Bring Us Tide and Minute Maid and Alpo and. . . ," Fortune, August 11, 2003, 88
Aliya Sternstein, "Paper Chase; Procter & Gamble," Forbes, March 17, 2003, 40, Volume 171, Issue 06
Matthew Boyle, "Dueling Diapers; Think Big Companies Can't Innovate? Look How Kimberly-Clark and P&G Are Fighting Over Disposable Training Pants," Fortune, February 17, 2003, 115, Vol. 147, Issue: 3
Robert Levering, Milton Moskowitz, Ann Harrington and Christopher Tkaczyk, "100 Best Companies to Work For," Fortune, January 20, 2003, 127, Vol. 147, Issue: 1
"Business Brief—Kimberly-Clark Corp.: Net Climbs 8.9%, As Cost Cuts Offset Rising Materials Prices," The Wall Street Journal, July 23, 2004.
"Consumer Products Brief—Kimberly-Clark Corp.: First-Quarter Profit Rose 15% on Weak Dollar, U.S. Sales," The Wall Street Journal, April 23, 2004, A10
Sarah Ellison, "Kimberly-Clark Raises Profit Target," The Wall Street Journal, April 13, 2004, B3
Sarah Ellison, "Kimberly-Clark To Reorganize; High-Ranking Official To Retire—Split between Developing and Developed Markets Is Planned for Businesses," The Wall Street Journal, January 20, 2004, A3
"Consumer Products Brief—Kimberly-Clark Corp.: Argentine Plant to Get Upgrade with Investment of $12 Million," The Wall Street Journal, December 29, 2003, C3
Sarah Ellison, "Kimberly-Clark Slashes Outlook for Second Time," The Wall Street Journal, December 12, 2002, B7
Sarah Ellison," Kimberly-Clark: Paper Tiger?—CEO Falk to Give Forecast Amid Multiple Challenges, Rivalries," The Wall Street Journal, December 11, 2002, B3

APPENDIX B

The Procter & Gamble Company 2005, 2004, and 2003 10-K Reports and Annual Reports
Robert Berner, Nanette Byrnes, and Wendy Zellner, "P&G Has Rivals in a Wringer; Colgate and Unilever Are Hurting As It Rolls Out Creative Products and Marketing," BusinessWeek, October 4, 2004, 74, Volume 3902.

APPENDIX C

Johnson & Johnson 2005, 2004, and 2003 Annual Reports and 10-K Reports
Gregory Zuckerman and Scott Hensley, "Drug-Stock Ills Are Hard to Cure," The Wall Street Journal, December 21, 2004, C1
Scott Hensley and Thomas M. Burton, "Johnson & Johnson-Guidant Deal Constructs a Cardiac Powerhouse," The Wall Street Journal, December 17, 2004, B5
Scott Hensley, "A Takeover of Guidant Won't Fix Pharmaceutical Problems at J&J," The Wall Street Journal, December 13, 2004, A3